	Chapter Title	Focus Company	Managerial Focus	Contrast Companies	Key Ratios
9	Reporting and Interpreting Liabilities	**STARBUCKS** Retailer and roaster of specialty coffee	Capital structure	Panera Bread Krispy Kreme General Mills Toyota Toys "R" Us Ford Harley-Davidson	**Current Ratio** **Accounts Payable Turnover**
10	Reporting and Interpreting Bonds	**Harrah's** ENTERTAINMENT, INC. Operator of gambling casinos and hotels	Long-term debt financing	Mirage Resorts Trump Casinos Home Depot Outback Steakhouse General Mills	**Debt-to-Equity** **Times Interest Earned**
11	Reporting and Interpreting Owners' Equity	**OUTBACK** STEAKHOUSE® NO RULES. JUST RIGHT.® Restaurant chain	Corporate ownership	Ruby Tuesday Wendy's Lone Star Ind. May Department Stores General Mills Home Depot	**Dividend Yield** **Earnings per Share**
12	Reporting and Interpreting Investments in Other Corporations	**DOW JONES & CO.** Publisher of business and financial news and information	Strategic investment in other companies	Wal-Mart New York Times Knight-Ridder	**Return on Assets**
13	Statement of Cash Flows	**SAMUEL ADAMS** Beer brewing company	Management of cash	Big Rock Brewery Foster's Brewing Anheuser Busch Coors Redhook Ale Pacific Aerospace & Electronics	**Quality of Income** **Capital Acquisitions**
14	Analyzing Financial Statements	**THE HOME DEPOT**® Home improvement retailer	Financial statement analysis	Hechinger Lowe's	**Ratio Summary**

McGraw-Hill's
HOMEWORK MANAGER PLUS™

THE COMPLETE SOLUTION

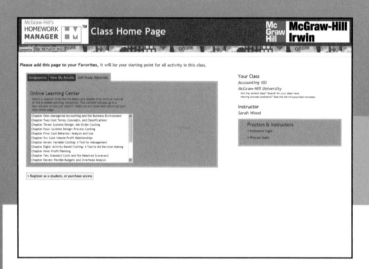

McGraw-Hill's
Homework Manager

 ™ This online homework management solution contains the textbook's end-of-chapter material. Now you have the option to build assignments from static and algorithmic versions of the text problems and exercises or to build self-graded quizzes from the additional questions provided in the online test bank.

Features:

- Assigns book-specific problems/exercises to students
- Provides integrated test bank questions for quizzes and tests
- Automatically grades assignments and quizzes, storing results in one grade book
- Dispenses immediate feedback to students regarding their work

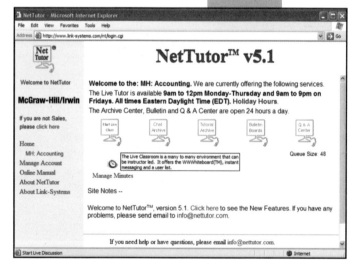

NetTutor

NetTutor™   Only available through Homework Manager Plus, NetTutor connects students with qualified tutors online. Students can submit questions online for a response within 24 hours, explore archived questions, or engage in a real-time tutoring session online.

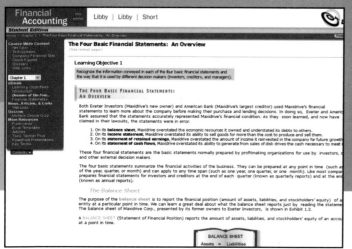

Interactive Online Version
of the Textbook

In addition to the textbook, students can rely on this online version of the text for a convenient way to study. The interactive content is fully integrated with Homework Manager to give students quick access to relevant content as they work through problems, exercises, and practice quizzes.

Features:

- Online version of the text integrated with Homework Manager

- Students referred to appropriate sections of the online book as they complete an assignment or take a practice quiz

- Direct link to related material that corresponds with the learning objective within the text

McGraw-Hill's Homework Manager Plus combines the power of Homework Manager with the latest interactive learning technology to create a comprehensive, fully integrated online study package. Students working on assignments in Homework Manager can click a simple hotlink and instantly review the appropriate material in the Interactive Online Textbook. NetTutor rounds out the package by offering live tutoring with a qualified expert in the course material.

By including Homework Manager Plus with your textbook adoption, you're giving your students a vital edge as they progress through the course and ensuring that the help they need is never more than a mouse click away. Contact your McGraw-Hill representative or visit the book's website to learn how to add Homework Manager Plus to your adoption.

HOMEWORK **MANAGER**
HELPS YOU EFFICIENTLY

McGraw-Hill's

HOMEWORK
MANAGER ™

Problems and exercises from the book, as well as questions from the test bank, have been integrated into Homework Manager to give you a variety of options as you deliver assignments and quizzes to students via the web. You can choose from static or algorithmic questions and have the graded results automatically stored in your grade book online.

Have you ever wished that you could assign a different set of problems to each of your students, individualizing their educational experience? The algorithmic question capabilities of Homework Manager give you the opportunity to do so. The problem-making function inserts new numbers and data from an endless supply into the set question structure. Each student will have a different answer while learning the same principles from the text. This also enables the students to master concepts by revisiting the same questions with different data.

Assign coursework online.

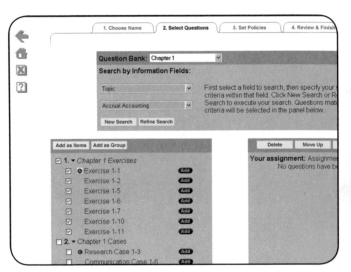

MANAGE YOUR CLASS.

Control how content is presented.

Homework Manager gives you a flexible and easy way to present course work to students. You determine which questions to ask and how much help students will receive as they work through assignments. You can determine the number of attempts a student can make with each problem or provide hints and feedback with each question. The questions can also be linked to an online version of the text for quick and simple reference while students complete an assignment.

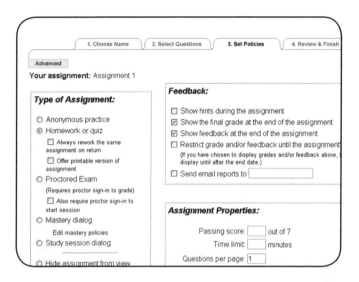

Track student progress.

Assignments are graded automatically, with the results stored in your private grade book. Detailed results let you see at a glance how each student does on an assignment or an individual problem. You can even see how many attempts it took them to solve it. You can monitor how the whole class does on each problem and even determine where individual students might need extra help.

PROFESSORS CAN ALLOW HOMEWORK **MANAGER** TO GIVE STUDENTS HELPFUL FEEDBACK

Auto-grading and feedback.

Question 1: *Score 6.5/8*

Your response	Correct response

Exercise 2-1: Using Cost Terms [LO2, LO5, LO7]

Following are a number of cost terms introduced in the chapter:

Period cost	Fixed cost
Variable cost	Prime cost
Opportunity cost	Conversion cost
Product cost	Sunk cost

Choose the cost term or terms above that most appropriately describe the costs identified in each of the following situations. A cost term can be used more than once.

1. Crestline Books, Inc., prints a small book titled *The Pocket Speller* . The paper going into the manufacture of the book would be called direct materials and classified as a Product cost (6%). In terms of cost behavior, the paper could also be described as a Product cost (0%) with respect to the number of books printed.
2. Instead of compiling the words in the book, the author hired by the company could have earned considerable fees consulting with business organizations. The consulting fees forgone by the author would be called Opportunity cost (6%).
3. The paper and other materials used in the manufacture of the book, combined with the direct labor cost involved, would be called Prime cost (6%).
4. The salary of Crestline Books' president would be classified as a Product cost (0%), and the salary will appear on the income statement as an expense in the time period in which it is incurred.
5. Depreciation on the equipment used to print the book would be classified by Crestline Books as a Product cost (6%). However, depreciation on any equipment used by the company in selling and administrative activities would be classified as a Period cost (6%). In terms of cost behavior, depreciation would probably be classified as a Fixed cost (6%) with respect to the number of books printed.
6. A Product cost (6%) is also known as an inventoriable cost,

Exercise 2-1: Using Cost Terms [LO2, LO5, LO7]

Following are a number of cost terms introduced in the chapter:

Period cost	Fixed cost
Variable cost	Prime cost
Opportunity cost	Conversion cost
Product cost	Sunk cost

Choose the cost term or terms above that most appropriately describe the costs identified in each of the following situations. A cost term can be used more than once.

1. Crestline Books, Inc., prints a small book titled *The Pocket Speller* . The paper going into the manufacture of the book would be called direct materials and classified as a Product cost. In terms of cost behavior, the paper could also be described as a variable cost with respect to the number of books printed.
2. Instead of compiling the words in the book, the author hired by the company could have earned considerable fees consulting with business organizations. The consulting fees forgone by the author would be called Opportunity cost.
3. The paper and other materials used in the manufacture of the book, combined with the direct labor cost involved, would be called Prime cost.
4. The salary of Crestline Books' president would be classified as a Period cost, and the salary will appear on the income statement as an expense in the time period in which it is incurred.
5. Depreciation on the equipment used to print the book would be classified by Crestline Books as a Product cost. However, depreciation on any equipment used by the company in selling and administrative activities would be classified as a Period cost. In terms of cost behavior, depreciation would probably be classified as a Fixed cost with respect to the number of books printed.
6. A Product cost is also known as an inventoriable cost, since

Immediately after finishing an assignment, students can compare their answers side-by-side with the detailed solutions. Students can try again with new numbers to see if they have mastered the concept.

Financial Accounting

Robert Libby
Cornell University

Patricia A. Libby
Ithaca College

Daniel G. Short
Texas Christian University

McGraw-Hill
Irwin

Boston   Burr Ridge, IL   Dubuque, IA   Madison, WI   New York   San Francisco   St. Louis
Bangkok   Bogotá   Caracas   Kuala Lumpur   Lisbon   London   Madrid   Mexico City
Milan   Montreal   New Delhi   Santiago   Seoul   Singapore   Sydney   Taipei   Toronto

To:

Jenni, Jon, Emma, and Sophia Drago

Herman and Doris Hargenrater

Laura Libby, Oscar, and Selma Libby

Bob and Mary Ann Short, Heather Short,

and Maryrose Short

FINANCIAL ACCOUNTING

Published by McGraw-Hill/Irwin, a business unit of The McGraw-Hill Companies, Inc., 1221 Avenue of the Americas, New York, NY, 10020. Copyright © 2007 by The McGraw-Hill Companies, Inc. All rights reserved. No part of this publication may be reproduced or distributed in any form or by any means, or stored in a database or retrieval system, without the prior written consent of The McGraw-Hill Companies, Inc., including, but not limited to, in any network or other electronic storage or transmission, or broadcast for distance learning.

Some ancillaries, including electronic and print components, may not be available to customers outside the United States.

This book is printed on acid-free paper.

1 2 3 4 5 6 7 8 9 0 WCK/WCK 0 9 8 7 6 5

ISBN-13: 978-0-07-293117-4
ISBN-10: 0-07-293117-5

Editorial director: *Stewart Mattson*
Senior sponsoring editor: *Steve DeLancey*
Senior developmental editor: *Kimberly D. Hooker*
Marketing manager: *Melissa Larmon*
Media producer: *Elizabeth Mavetz*
Lead project manager: *Mary Conzachi*
Senior production supervisor: *Sesha Bolisetty*
Senior designer: *Adam Rooke*
Senior photo research coordinator: *Jeremy Cheshareck*
Photo researcher: *Emily Tietz*
Media project manager: *Matthew Perry*
Senior supplement producer: *Carol Loreth*
Cover design: *Asylum Studios*
Typeface: *10.5/12 Times Roman*
Compositor: *Cenveo*
Printer: *Quebecor World Versailles Inc.*

Library of Congress Cataloging-in-Publication Data

Libby, Robert.
 Financial accounting / Robert Libby, Patricia A. Libby, Danial G. Short—5th ed.
  p. cm.
 Includes index.
 ISBN-13: 978-0-07-293117-4
 ISBN-10: 0-07-293117-5 (alk. paper)
 1. Accounting. 2. Corporations—Accounting. 3. Financial statements. I. Libby, Patricia
A. II. Short, Daniel G. III. Title
HF5635.L684 2007
657—dc22   2005053414

www.mhhe.com

Robert Libby

Robert Libby is the David A. Thomas Professor of Management at the Johnson Graduate School of Management at Cornell University, where he teaches the introductory financial accounting course. He previously taught at the University of Illinois, Pennsylvania State University, University of Texas at Austin, University of Chicago, and University of Michigan. He received his B.S. from Pennsylvania State University and his M.A.S. and Ph.D. from the University of Illinois; he is also a CPA.

Bob is a widely published author specializing in behavioral accounting. He was selected as the AAA Outstanding Educator in 2000. His prior text, *Accounting and Human Information Processing* (Prentice Hall, 1981), was awarded the AICPA/AAA Notable Contributions to the Accounting Literature Award. He received this award again in 1996 for a paper. He has published numerous articles in the *Journal of Accounting Research; Accounting, Organizations, and Society*; and other accounting journals. He is past Vice President-Publications of the American Accounting Association and is a member of the American Institute of CPAs and the editorial boards of *The Accounting Review; Accounting, Organizations, and Society; Journal of Accounting Literature; and Journal of Behavioral Decision Making.*

Patricia A. Libby

Patricia Libby is Chair of the Department of Accounting and Associate Professor of Accounting at Ithaca College, where she teaches the undergraduate financial accounting course. She previously taught graduate and undergraduate financial accounting at Eastern Michigan University and the University of Texas. Before entering academe, she was an auditor with Price Waterhouse (now PricewaterhouseCoopers) and a financial administrator at the University of Chicago. She received her B.S. from Pennsylvania State University, her M.B.A. from DePaul University, and her Ph.D. from the University of Michigan; she is also a CPA.

Pat conducts research on using cases in the introductory course and other parts of the accounting curriculum. She has published articles in *The Accounting Review, Issues in Accounting Education,* and *The Michigan CPA*. She has also conducted seminars nationwide on active learning strategies, including cooperative learning methods.

Daniel G. Short

Daniel Short is Professor of Accounting and Dean of the M.J. Neeley School of Business at Texas Christian University in Fort Worth, Texas. Formerly he was Dean at the Richard T. Farmer School of Business at Miami University (Ohio) and the College of Business at Kansas State University. Prior to that, he was Associate Dean at the University of Texas at Austin, where he taught the undergraduate and graduate financial accounting courses. He also taught at the University of Michigan and the University of Chicago. He received his undergraduate degree from Boston University and his M.B.A. and Ph.D. from the University of Michigan.

Dan has won numerous awards for his outstanding teaching abilities and has published articles in *The Wall Street Journal, The Accounting Review,* the *Journal of Accounting Research,* and other business journals. He has worked with a number of Fortune 500 companies, commercial banks, and investment banks to develop and teach executive education courses on the effective use of accounting information. Dan has also served on boards of directors in several industries, including manufacturing, commercial banking, and medical services. He is currently on the economic development committee of the Fort Worth Chamber of Commerce.

The proven favorite

O ver four editions, authors Bob Libby, Pat Libby, and Dan Short have made *Financial Accounting* into the best-selling book on the market.* How? By helping the instructor and student to become partners in learning, using a remarkable learning approach that keeps students engaged and involved in the material from the first day of class.

* Monument Information Resource, 2003 Report

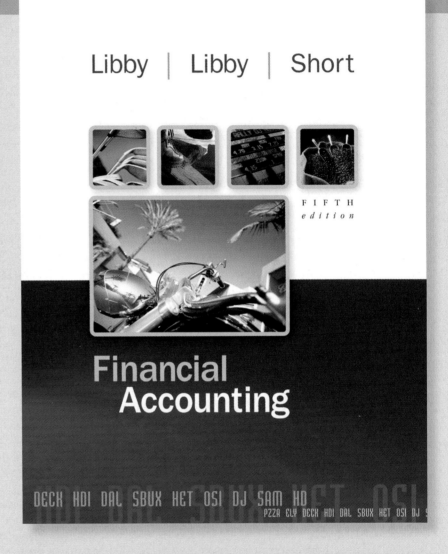

Libby | Libby | Short

FIFTH
edition

Financial
Accounting

Financial Accounting's distinctive focus company method motivates students by involving them in the business decisions of a real company, demonstrating how financial accounting makes a difference in the success of a firm. That, combined with pedagogical features and technology assets that serve a variety of learning styles, makes Libby/Libby/Short the textbook that both students and instructors agree is the best of its kind on the market today.

# of students and instructors alike.

Financial Accounting maintains its leadership by focusing on three key attributes:

REVELANCE. Libby/Libby/Short's trademark focus company approach is your best tool for demonstrating the relevance of financial accounting topics. Ethics continues to be a crucial topic within accounting, and *Financial Accounting* integrates coverage of ethical issues throughout the book. Furthering its real-world applicability, the end-of-chapter cases tie into the bundled annual report from Pacific Sunwear of California and the contrasting report from American Eagle Outfitters. This gives students valuable practice in reading and interpreting real financial data. Finally, Real-World Excerpts expand important chapter topics with insight into how real firms use financial accounting to their competitive advantage.

CLARITY. Do students complain that their textbook is hard to read? They don't if they're reading *Financial Accounting*. Libby/Libby/Short's clean, engaging writing is cited as a consistent strength by both instructors and students. In addition, the organization of the material is constantly refined to ensure maximum readability for students and flexibility for teachers.

TECHNOLOGY AIDES. Today's students have divergent learning styles and numerous time commitments, and they want technology supplements that help them study more efficiently and effectively. McGraw-Hill's Homework Manager and Homework Manager Plus, Topic Tackler, and ALEKS for Financial Accounting provide students with three powerful tools tied directly to *Financial Accounting*, fifth edition, that will help them maximize their study time and make their learning experience more enjoyable. In addition, a **new** Algorithmic Test Bank allows instructors to create an infinite number of algorithm-generated quizzes and test assignments.

Libby/Libby/Short's *Financial Accounting* is the proven choice for presenting financial accounting in a clear, relevant approach that keeps students engaged throughout your course. Read on for more insight into what has made this textbook such a success with faculty and students.

The Financial Accounting

Libby/Libby/Short's Digital Learning System complements the textbook every step of the way, giving students the extra help they need while providing instructors with tools for teaching a stimulating and rewarding class.

TOPIC TACKLER PLUS DVD

For today's technologically savvy students, **Topic Tackler Plus** is a DVD tutorial that offers a virtual helping hand in understanding the most challenging topics of the financial accounting course. Through a step-by-step sequence of video clips, audio-narrated slides, interactive practice exercises, and self-tests, Topic Tackler offers help on two key topics for every chapter, keeping your students engaged and learning as they read.

Topic Tackler Plus content is also accessible from the textbook's Online Learning Center, allowing students to access these powerful resources anywhere, at any time.

Video clips provide real-world perspectives from a variety of accounting experts.

Fun, interactive exercises help students remember key terminology.

VIDEO CLIPS

EXERCISES

Audio-narrated slide shows offer step-by-step coverage of challenging topics and make a great resource for review. Many also feature animations.

Self-grading quizzes cover all of the main topics, providing an ideal way to brush up before a test.

NARRATED SLIDES

SELF-TESTS

Concepts appearing in the text that receive additional treatment in Topic Tackler are marked with a unique icon.

Digital Learning System

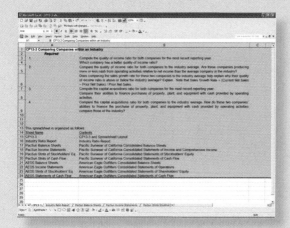

Excel Templates for Use with the Annual Report Cases

If you're going to work in accounting (or business in general), you have to know Microsoft Excel. Students use the real annual reports of American Eagle Outfitters and Pacific Sunwear of California with accompanying Excel Templates to manipulate real-world data and solve problems. These assignments allow students to experience problem solving as it truly happens in real companies. (The annual reports are found in the textbook appendixes and on this DVD. Prepared by Beth Kern at Indiana University–South Bend, the Excel Templates are found on the DVD and on the book's website.)

Algorithmic Test Bank

If you've ever thought that no test bank, however well made, could have all of the problems you could possibly need, think again. The Algorithmic Test Bank available with Libby/Libby/Short includes a problem generator that replicates the structure of text problems while populating them with fresh numbers. Create unique versions of every homework assignment, every quiz, every test—or use it to provide dozens of similar but distinct problems for students to practice on.

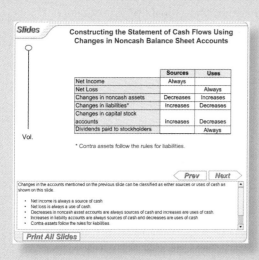

Narrated Slides

The next best thing to a private lecture, Libby/Libby/Short's narrated slides combine spoken narration, animation, and easy navigability to provide a comprehensive, easy-to-follow study aid for students brushing up for a quiz or a test. Every chapter has its own presentation that closely follows that chapter's organization, even reproducing key chapter figures and exhibits.

Proven Learning Solutions

Financial Accounting offers a host of pedagogical tools that complement the ways you like to teach and the ways your students like to learn. Some offer information and tips that help you present a complex subject; others highlight issues relevant to what your students read online or see on television. Either way, *Financial Accounting's* pedagogical support will make a real difference in your course and in your students' learning.

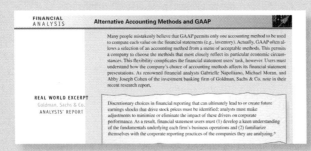

Financial Analysis

These features tie important chapter concepts to real-world decision-making examples. They also highlight alternative viewpoints and add to the critical thinking and decision-making focus of the text.

Self-Study Quizzes

This active learning feature engages the student, provides interactivity, and promotes efficient learning. Research shows that students learn best when they are actively engaged in the learning process. These quizzes ask students to pause at strategic points throughout each chapter to ensure that they understand key points before moving ahead.

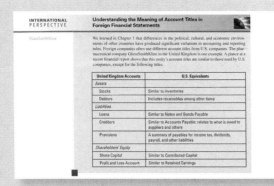

International Perspective

These sections highlight the emergence of global competition and resulting business issues throughout the text as well as the end-of-chapter material.

Real-World Excerpts

These insightful excerpts appear throughout the text and include annual report information from the focus companies, as well as numerous other companies, news articles from various publications, analysts' reports, 10-K forms, press releases, and First Call notes.

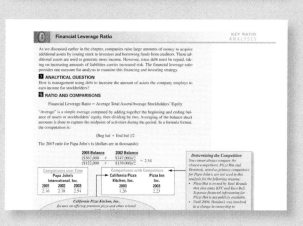

Key Ratio Analysis

Students will be better prepared to use financial information if they learn to evaluate elements of financial performance as they learn how to measure and report them. For this reason, we include relevant key ratios in each chapter in Key Ratio Analysis sections. Each Key Ratio Analysis box presents ratio analysis for the focus company in the chapter as well as for comparative companies. Cautions are also provided to help students understand the limitations of certain ratios.

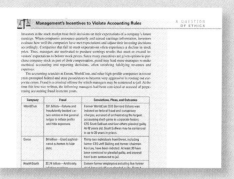

A Question of Ethics

These boxes appear throughout the text, conveying the importance of acting responsibly in business practice.

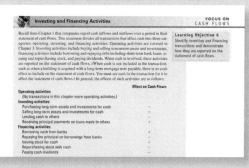

Focus on Cash Flows

Each of the first 12 chapters includes a discussion and analysis of changes in the cash flow of the focus company and explores the decisions that caused those changes. The early and consistent coverage of cash flows encourages students to think more critically about the decisions they will face as managers and the impact those decisions will have on the company's cash flow.

Proven **Learning Solutions**

ORGANIZATION OF THE CHAPTER SCHEMATIC

A unique feature of Libby/Libby/Short, this visual framework provides a powerful visual schematic of each chapter's content, easily enabling students to find exactly the chapter topic or concept they're looking for.

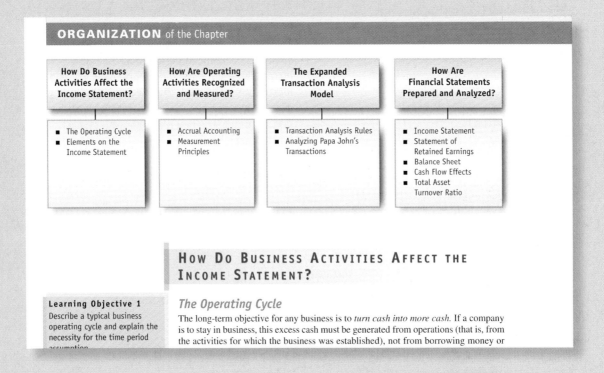

ALL JOURNAL ENTRIES TIED TO THE ACCOUNTING EQUATION

Journal entries marked with (A), (L), (SE), (R), (E), or (X, if a contra-account) and plus and minus signs in early chapters assist students in transaction analysis. In addition, following each journal entry is a summary of the effects of the transaction on the fundamental accounting equation.

Flexible End-of-Chapter Content and Organization

Each chapter is followed by an extensive selection of end-of-chapter assignments that examine single concepts or integrate multiple concepts presented in the chapter, arranged by level of difficulty and in learning objective order. To maintain the real-world flavor of the chapter material, they are often based on other real domestic and international companies and require analysis, conceptual thought, calculation, and written communication. Assignments suitable for individual or group written projects and oral presentations are included in strategic locations.

- Chapter Take-Aways: bulleted end-of-chapter summaries that compliment the learning objectives outlined at the beginning of the chapter.
- Key Ratios: summary of the key ratios presented in the chapter.
- Key Terms: page referenced to the chapter text.
- Finding Financial Information: highlights the chapter's key concepts, numbers, and totals in an easy-to-review graphic. The graphic includes Balance Sheet, Income Statement, Statement of Cash Flows, and Note Information.
- Questions
- Multiple-Choice Questions
- Mini-Exercises
- Exercises
- Problems: cross-referenced in blue to the Alternative Problems.
- Alternative Problems: similar in level and content to the end-of-chapter problems
- Cases and Projects: include Annual Report Cases, Financial Reporting and Analysis Cases, Critical Thinking Cases, and Financial Reporting and Analysis Projects

What's New in the Fifth Edition?

The primary goals of the fifth edition revisions are to provide instructors with more flexibility in key topical coverage, to simplify explanations of complex topics; to make the end-of-chapter material match instructor needs better, and to accurately reflect the exciting changes taking place in the accounting environment. As a result, the authors have revised at least 50 percent of the end-of-chapter material in each chapter, as well as making the detailed revisions noted in the following sections.

Chapter 1
- Updated coverage of recent accounting scandals
- New exhibit (Exhibit 1.7) summarizing the four basic financial statements
- New International Perspective feature discussing International Accounting Standards Board
- Substantially revised end-of-chapter exercises and problems using new real-world companies and numbers
- New annual report cases and new financial reporting cases

Chapter 2
- Updated opening discussion for Papa John's International
- Moved financial leverage ratio later in the chapter
- Enhanced discussion and visuals within Key Ratio Analysis feature
- Updated articles and ratio comparisons
- Substantially revised end-of-chapter exercises and problems using new real-world companies and numbers
- Upgraded Team Project to follow concept of a continuous project from prior and subsequent chapters
- New annual report cases

Chapter 3
- Updated opening discussion for Papa John's International
- New International Perspective discussing foreign financial statements
- Updated articles and ratio comparisons
- Added summary chart to enhance understanding of how statements are linked
- Clarified requirement and transactions
- Upgraded Team Project to follow concept of a continuous project from prior and subsequent chapters
- Substantially revised end-of-chapter exercises and problems using new real-world companies and numbers
- New annual report cases

Chapter 4
- Updated opening discussion for Papa John's International
- Added new section on Analysis of Adjusting Entries
- New art integrated into discussion of deferrals and accruals
- Realigned discussion by Revenues (deferred and accrued) and Expenses (deferred and accrued) in fifth edition versus Deferrals (revenues and expenses) and Accruals (revenues and expenses) in fourth edition.
- Added summary exhibits— Exhibits 4.3 and 4.4—for deferrals and accruals to highlight the differences in the earning of revenue (or incurring of expense) versus cash receipts (or payments)
- Expanded introductory summary of accounts to be adjusted in the Papa John's illustration to emphasize the identification of deferrals and accruals and the timing of cash receipts and payments
- Rearranged illustrations to follow revisions made to text
- Simplified account titles to follow more closely with end-of-chapter account titles (e.g., Supplies Expense instead of General and Administrative Expense)
- Updated articles and ratio comparisons
- Substantially revised end-of-chapter exercises and problems using new real-world companies and numbers
- Upgraded Team Project to follow concept of a continuous project from prior and subsequent chapters
- New annual report cases

Chapter 5
- Added coverage of recent accounting scandals and new Sarbanes-Oxley requirements
- Added new exhibits explaining the corporate governance and accounting communication process
- Introduced new discussion of common-size income statements
- Included new discussion of International Accounting Standards Board
- Added new self-study quizzes
- Simplified financial statement presentations
- Substantially revised end of chapter using new real companies and numbers
- Added new financial reporting and ethics cases
- New annual report cases

Chapter 6
- New focus company (Deckers Outdoors, maker of Teva sandals)
- New self-study quiz on accounting for doubtful accounts
- New self-study quiz on aging of accounts receivable
- Introduced new, simpler presentation of aging method for estimation of doubtful accounts
- Substantially revised end-of-chapter exercises and problems using new real-world companies and numbers
- New annual report cases

Chapter 7
- Reorganized discussion of effects of inventory methods on financial statement analysis moved to follow ratio discussions.
- Simplified presentation of cost of goods sold calculations
- Introduced new contrast company Ducati Motorcycles
- New step-by-step self-study quizzes

- Added new basic exercises on the effects of cost-flow assumptions on cost of goods sold and ending inventory added to end of chapter material
- Substantially revised end-of-chapter exercises and problems using new real-world company data (Ford, Kodak, Dell, American Eagle Outfitters, etc.)
- Upgraded Team Project to follow concept of a continuous project from prior and subsequent chapters
- New annual report cases

Chapter 8
- Updated all articles and real-world information
- Clarified discussions/illustrations on revenue and capital expenditures, depreciation concepts, depreciation methods, and amortization
- Substantially revised end-of-chapter exercises and problems using new real-world companies and numbers
- Upgraded Team Project to follow concept of a continuous project from prior and subsequent chapters
- New annual report cases

Chapter 9
- New focus company (Starbucks)
- Introdcued new chapter supplements—using Excel and Future Value Concepts to compute present values
- Integrated Excel commands in discussion of present

value computations
- Revised payroll accounting discussion
- Provided new discussion showing relationship between operating activities and the creation of current liabilities
- Expanded discussion of lease liabilities
- Substantially revised end-of-chapter exercises and problems using new real-world companies and numbers and expanded number of present value problems
- Upgraded Team Project to follow concept of a continuous project from prior and subsequent chapters
- New annual report cases

Chapter 10
- Moved discussion of bond basics into new section
- Focused discussion of types of bonds on only the most commonly used bonds
- New chapter supplement—using Excel to determine the present value of bonds
- Integrated Excel commands into discussion of computing the value of bonds
- Expanded amortization schedules to include full life of bonds
- Updated discussion of early retirement of bonds to include rule change
- Reorganized discussion of straight-line and effective-interest amortization to permit users to easily cover either or both methods
- Changed all interest

payments to an annual basis to reduce repetitive computations
- Expanded discussion of how interest expense is reported
- Substantially revised end-of-chapter exercises and problems
- Upgraded Team Project to follow concept of a continuous project from prior and subsequent chapters
- New annual report cases

Chapter 11
- Updated real-world excerpts
- Removed coverage of stock issued for noncash assets so focus is now on the most common transactions
- Substantially revised end-of-chapter exercises and problems using new real-world companies and numbers
- Upgraded Team Project to follow concept of a continuous project from prior and subsequent chapters
- New annual report cases

Chapter 12
- Significantly updated all real world excerpts and articles
- Added a marginal visual
- Substantially revised end-of-chapter exercises and problems using new real-world companies and numbers
- Upgraded Team Project to follow concept of a continuous project from prior and subsequent chapters
- New annual report cases

Chapter 13
- Revised chapter to be used any time after Chapter 4
- Revised chapter to be used to cover direct, indirect, or both methods for presenting the Operating section
- Simplified presentation of the steps involved in preparing the operating section using the indirect method
- Expanded use of T-accounts to explain indirect method
- Added new problems with data that can be assigned for direct and/or indirect method
- Added Enron-based ethics case
- Substantially revised end-of-chapter exercises and problems using new real-world companies and numbers
- Upgraded Team Project to follow concept of a continuous project from prior and subsequent chapters
- New annual report cases

Chapter 14
- Updated focus and comparison companies
- Revised financial analysis of focus and comparison companies
- Substantially revised end-of-chapter exercises and problems using new real-world companies and numbers
- Upgraded Team Project to follow concept of a continuous project from prior and subsequent chapters
- New annual report cases

Teaching With Technology

ONLINE LEARNING CENTER
www.mhhe.com/libby5e

For instructors, Libby's Online Learning Center contains the Instructor's Resource Manual, PowerPoint slides, Solutions Manual, Excel Templates tied to the end-of-chapter material, and the Annual Report Cases Templates, all organized by chapter. There are also links to professional resources.

In addition, for students and instructors, there are two appendixes linked to the text material, check figures, articles tied to end-of-chapter material, Web links to the focus company financial statements, and McGraw-Hill's Homework Manager (see the next item). Instructors can pull all of this material into their PageOut course syllabus or use it as part of another online course management system.

The student section of the site includes (in addition to the preceding elements) Topic Tackler Plus content (see page VI), self-quizzes, learning objectives, PowerPoint slides, chapter outlines, chapter take-aways, and digital flashcards.

MCGRAW-HILL'S HOMEWORK MANAGER

ISBN 978-007322614-9 (ISBN 0073226149)
McGraw-Hill's Homework Manager is a Web-based supplement that duplicates problem structures directly from the end-of-chapter material in *Financial Accounting,* fifth edition, using algorithms to provide a limitless supply of online self-graded practice for students or assignments and tests with unique versions of every problem. Say goodbye to cheating in your classroom; say hello to the power and flexibility you've been waiting for in creating assignments.

McGraw-Hill's Homework Manager is also a useful grading tool. All assignments can be delivered over the Web and graded automatically, with the results stored in your private gradebook. Detailed results let you see at a glance how each student does on an assignment or an individual problem—you can even see how many tries it took the student to solve it.

Learn more about McGraw-Hill's Homework Manager by referring to the front cover insert.

MCGRAW-HILL'S HOMEWORK MANAGER PLUS

ISBN 978-007322587-6 (ISBN 0073225878)
McGraw-Hill's Homework Manager Plus gathers all of *Financial Accounting's* online student resources under one convenient access point. Combining the power and flexibility of McGraw-Hill's Homework Manager with other proven technology tools, McGraw-Hill's Homework Manager Plus provides the best value available for the student eager to embrace the full benefits of online study and review.

In addition to McGraw-Hill's Homework Manager, students may also access:

NetTutor
Only available through McGraw-Hill's Homework Manager Plus, NetTutor connects students with qualified tutors online. Students can work with an online tutor in real time, or post a question to be answered within 24 hours. Homework Manager Plus adopters receive unlimited tutoring time on NetTutor.

Interactive Online Version of the Textbook
In addition to the textbook, students can rely on this online version of the text for a convenient way to study. This interactive Web-based textbook contains hotlinks to key definitions and real company websites and is integrated with Homework Manager to give students quick access to relevant content as they work through problems, exercises, and practice quizzes.

Technology

CAROL YACHT'S GENERAL LEDGER AND PEACHTREE COMPLETE 2007 CD-ROM

Carol Yacht's General Ledger Software is McGraw-Hill/Irwin's custom-built general ledger package. Carol Yacht's General Ledger can help your students master every aspect of the general ledger, from inputting sales and cash receipts to calculating ratios for analysis or inventory valuations.

Carol Yacht's General Ledger allows students to review an entire report and then double-click any single transaction to review or edit it. The report will then be updated on the fly to include the revised figures. When it comes to learning how an individual transaction affects the outcome of an entire report, no other approach matches that of Carol Yacht's General Ledger.

Also on Carol Yacht's General Ledger CD, students receive the educational version of Peachtree Complete 2007, along with templates containing data for many of the text exercises and problems. Familiarity with Peachtree Complete will be essential for students entering the job market, and Carol Yacht's Peachtree templates for use with Libby/Libby/Short's Financial Accounting, fifth edition, ensures that they get plenty of practice.

 Students can use Carol Yacht's General Ledger to solve numerous problems from the textbook; the data for these problems are already included on Carol Yacht's General Ledger CD-ROM. You can even populate Carol Yacht's General Ledger with your own custom data.

ALEKS®

ALEKS (Assessment and LEarning in Knowledge Spaces) delivers precise, qualitative diagnostic assessments of students' knowledge, guides them in the selection of appropriate new study material, and records their progress toward mastery of curricular goals in a robust classroom management system.

ALEKS interacts with the student much as a skilled human tutor would, moving between explanation and practice as needed, correcting and analyzing errors, defining terms and changing topics on request. By sophisticated modeling of

a student's knowledge state for a given subject, ALEKS can focus clearly on what the student is most ready to learn next. When students focus on exactly what they are ready to learn, they build confidence and a learning momentum that fuels success.

ALEKS Math Prep for Accounting provides coverage of the basic math skills needed to succeed in introductory financial accounting while ALEKS for the Accounting Cycle provides a detailed, guided overview through every stage of the accounting cycle.

For more information, visit the ALEKS website at **www.business.aleks.com.**

PAGEOUT

PageOut is McGraw-Hill's unique point-and-click course website tool. With PageOut, you can post your syllabus online, assign McGraw-Hill Online Learning Center or eBook content, add links to important off-site resources, and maintain student results in the online grade book. PageOut is free for every McGraw-Hill/Irwin user and, if you're short on time, we even have a team ready to build your site from scratch!

You can also use PageOut content with WebCT, eCollege.com, or Blackboard. To learn more about these digital solutions, visit **www.mhhe.com/solutions.**

KNOWLEDGE GATEWAY

Developed with the help of our partner Eduprise, the McGraw-Hill Knowledge Gateway is an all-purpose service and resource center for instructors teaching online. While training programs from WebCT and Blackboard will help teach you their software, only McGraw-Hill has services to help you actually *manage and teach* your online course, as well as run and maintain the software. To see how these platforms can assist your online course, visit www.mhhe.com/solutions. And remember: All Libby digital content is easily incorporated into any online course management system.

Supplements for the Instructor

Instructor CD-ROM
ISBN 978-007293130-3 (ISBN 0072931302)
This integrated CD-ROM allows you to access most of the text's ancillary materials. You no longer need to worry about the various supplements that accompany your text. Instead, almost everything is available on one convenient CD-ROM: PowerPoint slides, Solutions Manual, Instructor's Resource Manual, Test Bank and Computerized Test Bank, Annual Report Cases Templates, Excel Templates for the end-of-chapter material (along with a guide), text exhibits, video, and links to the Web.

Online Learning Center
www.mhhe.com/libby5e
See page (XIV) for details.

Instructor's Resource Manual
ISBN 978-007293126-6 (ISBN 0072931264)
Prepared by Kathryn Yarbrough at the University of North Carolina–Charlotte. All supplements, including the Test Bank, Videos, Study Guide, and PowerPoint slides, are topically cross-referenced in the IRM to help instructors direct students to specific ancillaries to reinforce key concepts. Transparency masters of text exhibits are included. Electronic files are available on the website.

Solutions Manual
ISBN 978-007293120-4 (ISBN 0072931205)
Prepared by Robert Libby, Patricia Libby, and Daniel Short. Provides solutions for end-of-chapter questions, mini-exercises, exercises, problems, and cases. Electronic files are available on the website.

PowerPoint Slides
Prepared by Jon Booker and Charles Caldwell at Tennessee Technological University and Susan Galbreath at David Lipscomb University. Completely customized PowerPoint presentations for use in your classroom. They are available on the Instructor CD-ROM and the website.

Solutions Acetates
ISBN 978-007293124-2 (ISBN 0072931248)
These overhead transparencies provide both in-class visuals as well as solutions to most of the end-of-chapter material.

Test Bank (Print version)
ISBN 978-007293119-8 (ISBN 0072931191)
Prepared by Anne Clem at Iowa State University. This comprehensive Test Bank includes more than 3,000 true/false, multiple-choice, essay, and matching questions, including questions on ratios and ethics which meet requirements of AACSB Standards on Assurance Learning.

Algorithmic-Diploma Testbank (from Brownstone)
ISBN 978-007321661-4 (ISBN 0073216615)
Add and edit questions; create up to 99 versions of each test; attach graphic files to questions; import and export ASCII files; and select questions based on type, level of difficulty, or learning objective. This software provides password protection for saved tests and question databases and is able to run on a network.

EZ Test
McGraw-Hill's EZ Test is a flexible and easy-to-use electronic testing program that allows instructors to create tests from book-specific items. EZ Test accommodates a wide range of question types and allows instructors to add their own questions. Multiple versions of the test can be created, and any test can be exported for use with course management systems such as WebCT, BlackBoard, or PageOut. EZ Test Online is a new service that gives instructors a place to easily administer EZ Test-created exams and quizzes online. The program is available for Windows and Macintosh environments.

 ## Instructor Excel Templates
These Excel Templates allow students to develop important spreadsheet skills by using them to solve selected end-of-chapter assignments. They are available on the Instructor CD-ROM and on the website.

Carol Yacht's General Ledger and Peachtree Complete CD-ROM
See page (XV).

Check Figures
Prepared by Paula Miller at Collin County Community College. Provides answers to selected problems and cases. These figures are available on the book's website.

Instructor's Manual to Accompany the MBA Companion Supplement
ISBN 978-007293132-7 (ISBN 0072931329)
Prepared by Peggy Bishop Lane and Catherine Schrand, both of The Wharton School at the University of Pennsylvania. The MBA Companion includes expanded material on leases and deferred taxes.

Instructor's Manual to Accompany *Understanding Corporate Annual Reports* by William R. Pasewark
ISBN 978-007310182-8 (ISBN 0073101826)

Financial Accounting Video Library
ISBN 978-007237616-6 (ISBN 0072376163)
Created to stimulate classroom discussion, illustrate key concepts, and review important material. Selected videos were produced by Dallas TeleLearning of the Dallas County Community Colleges © 1999. To acquire Accounting in Action as a Comprehensive Telecourse package, call Dallas TeleLearning at 1-866-347-8576 or visit its website at
http://telelearning.dcccd.edu.

Supplements for the Student

Topic Tackler Plus DVD
ISBN 978-007293129-7 (ISBN 0072931299)
See page (VI) for details.

Online Learning Center
www.mhhe.com/libby5e
See page (XIV) for details.

MBA Companion
ISBN 978-007-293131-0 (ISBN 0072931310)
Prepared by Peggy Bishop Lane and Catherine Schrand, both of The Wharton School at the University of Pennsylvania. This supplement includes expanded material on topics prominent in MBA-level programs, including leases and deferred taxes.

Working Papers
ISBN 978-007293122-8 (ISBN 0072931221)
Prepared by Robert Libby, Patricia Libby and Daniel Short. Contains all the forms necessary for completing end-of-chapter assignments.

Study Guide
ISBN 978-007293121-1 (ISBN 0072931213)
Prepared by Jeannie Folk of the College of DuPage. An outstanding learning tool, this guide gives students a deeper understanding of the course material and reinforces, step by step, what they are learning in the main text.

PowerPoint Notes
ISBN 978-007326269-7 (ISBN 0073262692)
Selected PowerPoint slides are reproduced for students in a handy booklet, allowing them to focus on the lecture and selectively annotate the slide rather than scramble to recreate it themselves.

eXcel Student Excel Templates
These templates are tied to selected end-of-chapter material and are available on the website.

Telecourse Guide
ISBN 978-007293118-1 (ISBN 0072931183)
This guide accompanies the instructional videos produced by Dallas County Community Colleges and has been revised for the fifth edition.

Understanding Corporate Annual Reports by William R. Pasewark
ISBN 978-007310181-1 (ISBN 0073101818)
This financial analysis project emphasizes the interpretation and analysis of financial statements. It contains extensive instructions for obtaining an annual report from a publicly traded corporation. Students gain hands-on experience working with annual reports and are then better prepared to understand financial accounting concepts and their use in the business world.

Computerized Accounting Practice Sets
Business simulations and practice sets using Windows by Leland Mansuetti and Keith Weidkamp of Sierra College include:
Granite Bay Jet Ski, Level 1 ISBN 978-007296762-5 (ISBN 0072947624)
Granite Bay Jet Ski, Level 2 ISBN 978-007308016-1 (ISBN 0073080160)
Wheels Exquisite, Inc. ISBN 978-007242845-2 (ISBN 0072428457)
Thunder Mountain Snowmobile ISBN 978-007293188-4 (ISBN 0072931884)
Gold Run Snowmobile, Inc. ISBN 978-007295788-4 (ISBN 0072957883)

Acknowledgments

Over the years many dedicated instructors have devoted their time and effort to help us make each edition better. We would like to acknowledge and thank all of our colleagues who have helped guide our development decisions for this edition and all previous editions. This text would not be the success it is without the help of all of you.

Fifth Edition Reviewers

Nas Ahadiat, *California Polytechnic University*
Vern Allen, *Central Florida Community College*
Bridget Anakwe, *Plattsburgh State University of New York*
Brenda Anderson, *Boston University*
Joseph Antenucci, *Youngstown State University*
Laurel Barfitt, *Delta State University*
Daisy Beck, *Louisiana State University*
John Bedient, *Albion College*
Eric Blazer, *Millersville University*
Mark Bradshaw, *Harvard Business School*
Christopher Brandon, *Indiana University—Purdue University Columbus*
Nina Brown, *Tarrant County College*
Helen Brubeck, *San Jose State University*
Terri Brunsdon, *The University of Akron*
Kay Carnes, *Gonzaga University*
Kam Chan, *Pace University*
Chiaho Chang, *Montclair State University*
Gretchen Charrier, *University of Texas—Austin*
Agnes Cheng, *University of Houston*
Antoinette Clegg, *Palm Beach Community College*
Anne Clem, *Iowa State University*
Judy Colwell, *Northern Oklahoma College*
Teresa Conover, *University of North Texas*
Marcia Croteau, *University of Maryland—Baltimore*
Elizabeth Demers, *University of Rochester*
Allan Drebin, *Northwestern University*
Virginia Fullwood, *Texas A&M University—Commerce*
Joseph Galante, *Millersville University of Pennsylvania*
Jeffrey Haber, *Iona College*
Leon Hanouille, *Syracuse University*
Russell Hardin, *Pittsburgh State University*
Shelia Hardy, *Lafayette College*
Betty Harper, *Middle Tennessee State*
Ann Ownby Hicks, *North Park University*
Marc Hyman, *University of California at Berkeley*
Courtland Huber, *University of Texas—Austin*
Norma Jacobs, *Austin Community College*
Scott Jerris, *San Francisco State University*
Carol Johnson, *Oklahoma State University*
Shondra Johnson, *Bradley University*
Christopher Jones, *George Washington University*
John Karayan, *Cal Poly Pomona*
Beth Kern, *Indiana University—South Bend*
Dennis Lee Kovach, *Community College of Allegheny*
Tammy Kowalczyk, *Western Washington University*
Janet Kimbrell, *Oklahoma State University*
Charles Ladd, *University of St. Thomas*

Terry Lease, *Sonoma State*
Marc Lebow, *Christopher Newport University*
Elliott Levy, *Bentley*
Daniel Litt, *UCLA*
Patricia Lopez, *Valencia Community College*
Chao-Shin Liu, *University of Notre Dame*
Joshua Livnat, *New York University*
Lawrence Logan, *University of Massachusetts—Dartmouth*
Nick McGaughey, *San Jose State University*
Florence McGovern, *Bergen Community College*
Noel McKeon, *Florida Community College—Jacksonville*
Paulette Miller, *Collin County Community College*
Haim Mozes, *Fordham University*
Ramesh Narasimhan, *Montclair State University*
Presha Neidermeyer, *Union College*
Lori Mason-Olson, *University of Northern Iowa*
Sharon Parrish, *Kentucky State University*
Donald Pagach, *North Carolina State—Raleigh*
Catherine Plante, *University of New Hampshire*
Grace Pownall, *Emory University*
Charles Ransom, *Oklahoma State University*
Laura Rickett, *Kent State University*
Brandi Roberts, *Southeastern Louisiana University*
Lawrence Roman, *Cuyahoga Community College*
John Rossi III, *Moravian College*
John Rude, *Bloomsburg University*
Angela Sandberg, *Jacksonville State University*
Cindy Seipel, *New Mexico State*
Ann Selk, *University of Wisconsin—Green Bay*
Howard Shapiro, *Eastern Washington University*
Sri Sridhanen, *Northwestern University*
David Stein, *Metropolitan State University*
Gina Sturgill, *Concord College*
Joel Strong, *St. Cloud State University*
Susan Sullivan, *University of Massachusetts—Dartmouth*
Martin Taylor, *University of Texas—Arlington*
Mack Tennyson, *College of Charleston*
Theodore Tully, *DeVry University*
Ingrid Ulstad, *University of Wisconsin—Eau Claire*
Marcia Veit, *University of Central Florida*
Charles Wasley, *University of Rochester*
Lori Holder-Webb, *University of Wisconsin*
Cheryl Westen, *Western Illinois University*
David Weiner, *University of San Francisco*
Patrick Wilkie, *University of Virginia*
Jefferson Williams, *University of Michigan*
Peter Woodlock, *Youngstown State University*
Kathryn Yarbrough, *University of North Carolina—Charlotte*
Xiao-Jun Zhang, *University of California at Berkeley*

Previous Edition Reviewers

Dawn Addington, *University of New Mexico*
Anwer Ahmed, *Syracuse University*
Matthew Anderson, *Michigan State University*
Richard Anderson, *Stonehill College*
William Appleyard, *Salem State College*
Susan Armstrong, *Inver Hills Community College*
Stephen Kwaku Asare, *University of Florida*
Holly Ashbaugh, *University of Wisconsin*
Wendy Bailey, *University of Pittsburgh*
Roderick Barclay, *University of Texas—Dallas*
Cecil Battiste, *El Paso Community College*
Paul Bayes, *East Tennessee State University*
D'Arcy Becker, *University of New Mexico*
Linda Bell, *William Jewell College*
Martin Birr, *Indiana University at Indianapolis*
Eric Blazer, *Millersville University*
Robert Bloom, *John Carroll University*
Charles Bokemeier, *Michigan State University*
Wayne Boutell, *University of California at Berkeley*
Ken Boze, *University of Alaska—Anchorage*
Daniel Brickner, *Eastern Michigan University*
Russell Briner, *University of Texas—San Antonio*
Kevin Brown, *Drexel University*
David Byrd, *Southwest Missouri State University*
Matthew Calderisi, *Farleigh Dickinson University*
Thomas Calderon, *University of Akron*
Michael Capsuto, *Cypress College*
Barbara Cassidy, *St. Edward's University*
Nancy Cassidy, *Texas A&M University*
Ted Christensen, *Case Western University*
Virginia Clark, *University of Cincinnati*
Anne Clem, *Iowa State University*
Paul Clikeman, *University of Richmond*
Mark Coffey, *Western New England College*
Sue Cook, *Tulsa Community College*
Michael Cornick, *University of North Carolina—Charlotte*
Rosalind Cranor, *Virginia Polytechnic Institute and State University*
Barbara Croteau, *Santa Rosa Junior College*
Gary Cunningham, *University of Minnesota*
Charles Davis, *California State University—Sacramento*
Bruce Dehning, *University of New Hampshire*
Carol Dicino, *University of Southern Colorado*
Manuel Dieguez, *Florida International University*
Patricia Doherty, *Boston University*
Patricia Douglas, *Loyola Marymount University*
Tim Doupnik, *University of South Carolina*
Allan Drebin, *Northwestern University*
Marie Dubke, *University of Memphis*
David Durkee, *Weber State University*
Robert Egenolf, *University of Texas—Austin*
Jim Emig, *Villanova University*
Tom English, *Boise State University*
Taylor Ernst, *Lehigh University*
Jack Ethridge, *Stephen Austin State University*
Thomas Evans, *University of Central Florida*
Kel-Ann Eyler, *Brenau University*
Alan Falcon, *Loyola Marymount University*
Larry Farmer, *Middle Tennessee State University*
Gary Fish, *Illinois State University*
Al Frakes, *Washington State University*
Kimberly Frank, *University of Nevada—Las Vegas*
Joseph Galanate, *Millersville University*
Alan Glazer, *Franklin and Marshall College*
Arthur Goldman, *University of Kentucky*
Tim Griffin, *University of Missouri—Kansas City*
Flora Guidry, *University of New Hampshire*
Marcia Halvorsen, *University of Cincinnati*
Leon Hanouille, *Syracuse University*
Bill Harden, *University of North Carolina—Greensboro*

Russell Hardin, *Pittsburg State University*
John Hatcher, *Purdue University*
Paul Healy, *Harvard University*
Robin Hegedus, *Franklin University*
Roger Hehman, *University of Cincinnati*
Kurt Heisinger, *Sierra College*
Donna Hetzel, *Western Michigan University*
Ken Hiltebeitel, *Villanova University*
Peggy Hite, *Indiana University*
David Hoffman, *University of North Carolina at Chapel Hill*
Jim Hood, *Mt. Hood Community College*
Kathy Horton, *University of Illinois at Chicago*
Marge Hubbert, *Cornell University*
Richard Hulme, *California State University—Pomona*
Afshad Irani, *University of New Hampshire*
Sharon Jackson, *Samford University*
Christopher Jones, *George Washington University*
Jefferson Jones, *Auburn University*
Naida Kaen, *University of New Hampshire*
Susan Kattelus, *Eastern Michigan University*
Howard Keller, *Indiana University at Indianapolis*
Cindi Khanlarian, *University of North Carolina—Greensboro*
Sungsoo Kim, *Rutgers University*
Charles Klemstine, *University of Michigan*
John Koeplin, *University of San Francisco*
Michael Knapp, *University of Oklahoma*
Frank Korman, *Mountain View College*
Linda Kropp, *Modesto Junior College*
Jim Kurtenbach, *Iowa State University*
David Lavin, *Florida International University*
Donald Leonard, *Nichols College*
Cynthia Levick, *Austin Community College*
Seth Levine, *University of Miami*
Elliott Levy, *Bentley College*
Lawrence Logan, *University of Massachusetts—Dartmouth*
Gina Lord, *Santa Rosa Junior College*
Joan Luft, *Michigan State University*
George Machlan, *Susquehanna University*
Ron Mannino, *University of Massachusetts—Amherst*
David Marcinko, *University at Albany—SUNY*
Bobbie Martindale, *Dallas Baptist College*
Dawn Massey, *Fairfield University*
Alan Mayer-Sommer, *Georgetown University*
Paul McGee, *Salem State College*
Noel McKeon, *Florida Community College*
Betty McMechen, *Mesa State College*
Bharat Merchant, *Baruch College*
Greg Merrill, *California State University at Fullerton*
Alfred Michenzi, *Loyola College*
Paul Mikalek, *University of Hartford*
Ronald Milne, *University of Nevada—Las Vegas*
Richard Muchow, *Palomar College*
Dennis Murphy, *California State University—Los Angeles*
Muroki Mwaura, *William Patterson University*
Brian Nagle, *Duquesne University*
Sarah Nutter, *George Mason University*
Kanalis Ockree, *Washburn University*
Emeka Ofobike, *University of Akron*
Marge O'Reily-Allen, *Rider University*
John Osborn, *California State University—Fresno*
John O'Shaughnessy, *San Francisco State University*
Ron Pawliczek, *Boston College*
Kathy Petroni, *Michigan State University*
Rosemarie Pilcher, *Richland College*
Elizabeth Plummer, *Southern Methodist University*
Margaret Pollard, *American River College*
Peter Poznanski, *Cleveland State University*
Don Putnam, *California State University Polytechnic at Pomona*

Jeffrey Quirin, *University of Wichita*
Mawdudur Rahman, *Suffolk University*
Keith Richardson, *Indiana State University*
Shirley Rockel, *Iowa Wesleyan College*
Glenn Rechtshaffen, *University of Auckland*
Anne Rich, *Quinnipiac University*
Thomas Robinson, *University of Alaska—Fairbanks*
Michael Ruble, *Western Washington University*
Clayton Sager, *University of Wisconsin—Whitewater*
Bruce Samuelson, *Pepperdine University*
Shahrokh Saudagaran, *Santa Clara University*
Gene Sauls, *California State University—Sacramento*
Kenneth Schwartz, *Boston College*
Richard Scott, *University of Virginia*
Wayne Shaw, *Southern Methodist University*
Franklin Shuman, *Utah State University*
Mike Slaubaugh, *Indiana University—Purdue University*
Ken Smith, *Idaho State University*
Virginia Smith, *St. Mary's College*
William Smith, *Xavier University*
Beverly Soriano, *Framingham State College*
Ralph Spanswick, *California State University—Los Angeles*
Kevin Stocks, *Brigham Young University*
Iris Stuart, *California State University—Fullerton*
Pamela Stuerke, *Case Western Reserve University*
Kathryn Sullivan, *George Washington University*
John Surdick, *Xavier University*
Bill Svihla, *Indiana State University*
Diane Tanner, *University of North Florida*
Karen Taylor, *Butte Community College*
Martin Taylor, *University of Texas—Arlington*
Blair Terry, *Fresno City College*
Laverne Thompson, *St. Louis Community College at Meramec*
Ben Trotter, *Texas Tech University*
Theodore Tully, *DeVry Institute—Fremont*
Joan VanHise, *Fairfield University*
Marilyn Vito, *Richard Stockton College*
James Wallace, *University of California—Irvine*
Nancy Weatherholt, *University of Missouri—Kansas City*
Michael Welker, *Drexel University*
Paul Wertheim, *Pepperdine University*
T. Sterling Wetzel, *Oklahoma State University*
L.K. Williams, *Morehead State University*
Patricia Williams, *Friends University*
Steven Wong, *San Jose City College*
Gail Wright, *Bryant College*
Suzanne Wright, *Penn State University*
William Zorr, *University of Wisconsin—Oshkosh*
Linda Zucca, *Kent State University*

We are grateful to the following individuals who helped develop, critique, and shape the extensive ancillary package: Anne Clem, Iowa State University; Jeannie Folk, College of DuPage; Beth Kern, University of Indiana—South Bend; Barbara Schnathorst, The Write Solution, Inc.; Ann Selk, University of Wisconsin—Green Bay; Kimberly Temme, Maryville University; Katherine Yarbrough, University of North Carolina—Charlotte; Peggy Bishop Lane, The Wharton School at the University of Pennsylvania; Cathy Schrand, The Wharton School at the University of Pennsylvania; Jon Booker, Tennessee Technological University; Charles Caldwell, Tennessee Technological University; Susan Galbreath, David Lipscomb University; Jack Terry, ComSource Associates, Inc.; Deborah Jackson-Jones, Boardwork, Inc.

We also received invaluable input and support through the years from present and former colleagues and students. We also appreciate the additional comments, suggestions, and support of our students and our colleagues at Cornell University, Ithaca College, and Texas Christian University.

Last, we thank the extraordinary efforts of a talented group of individuals at McGraw-Hill/Irwin who made all of this come together. We would especially like to thank our Editorial Director, Stewart Mattson; our senior sponsoring editor, Steve DeLancey; Kimberly Hooker, our senior developmental editor; Melissa Larmon, our marketing manager; Adam Rooke, our designer; Mary Conzachi, our lead project manager; Dan Wiencek, our copywriter; Sesha Bolisetty, our production supervisor; Elizabeth Mavetz, our media producer; Matthew Perry, our media project manager; Carol Loreth, our supplements coordinator; Jeremy Cheshareck, our photo research coordinator; and Emily Tietz, our photo researcher.

Robert Libby
Patricia A. Libby
Daniel G. Short

To Our Student Readers

This book is aimed at two groups of readers:
1. *Future managers,* who will need to interpret and use financial statement information in business decisions.
2. *Future accountants,* who will prepare financial statements for those managers.

Future managers need a firm basis for using financial statement information in their careers in marketing, finance, banking, manufacturing, human resources, sales, information systems, or other areas of management. Future accountants need a solid foundation for further professional study.

Both managers and accountants must understand how to *use financial statements in making real business decisions* to perform their duties successfully. The best way to learn to do this is to study accounting in real business contexts. This is the key idea behind our *focus company approach,* which we introduce in the first chapter and which integrates each chapter's material around a focus company, its decisions, and its financial statements. The focus companies are drawn from 12 different industries, providing you with a broad range of experience with realistic business and financial accounting practices. In each chapter, *you will actually work with these real companies' statements* and those of additional contrast companies.

When you complete this book, you will be able to read and understand financial statements of real companies. We help you achieve this goal by:
1. Selecting learning objectives and content based on the way that seasoned managers use financial statements in modern businesses. *We emphasize the topics that count.*
2. Recognizing that students using this book have no previous exposure to accounting and financial statements and often little exposure to the business world. We take you through the financial statements three times at increasing levels of detail (in Chapter 1, Chapters 2 through 5, and Chapters 6 through 14). This is the secret to our *"building block approach."*

3. Helping you *"learn how to learn"* by teaching efficient and effective approaches for learning the material. Keep these learning hints in mind as you work your way through each chapter.
4. Providing regular feedback in *Self-Study Quizzes,* which occur throughout each chapter. *Complete the quizzes before you move on.* Then check your answers against the solution provided in the footnote. If you are still unclear about any of the answers, you should refer back to the chapter material preceding the quiz before moving on.
5. Highlighting the *Key Terms* in **bold, print** and repeating their definitions in the margins. You should pay special attention to the definitions of these terms and review them at the end of the chapter. A handy glossary is provided at the end of the book; consult it if you forget the meaning of an important term.
6. Introducing the *Key Financial Ratios* used to assess different elements of financial performance at the same time you are learning how to measure and report those elements. These will show you what kinds of accounting information managers use and how they interpret it.

At the end of each chapter, you can test what you have learned by working the Demonstration Cases. *Working problems is one of the keys* to learning accounting. Good luck in your first accounting course.

Bob Libby

Pat Libby

Daniel G. Short

CONTENTS IN BRIEF

CONTENTS

Chapter Three

Operating Decisions and the Income Statement   104

Chapter Six

Reporting and Interpreting Sales Revenue, Receivables, and Cash 282

Chapter Seven

Reporting and Interpreting Cost of Goods Sold and Inventory 336

Chapter Eight

Reporting and Interpreting Property, Plant, and Equipment: Natural Resources and Intangibles 396

Chapter Nine

Reporting and Interpreting Liabilities 460

Chapter Ten

Reporting and Interpreting Bonds   514

Harrah's Entertainment, Inc.   515

Understanding the Business   515
Characteristics of Bonds Payable   517

FINANCIAL ANALYSIS:

Bond Information from the Business Press   519

Reporting Bond Transactions   520

■ Self-Study Quiz   521

Bonds Issued at Par   522

■ Self Study Quiz   524

KEY RATIO ANALYSIS:

Times Interest Earned   524

Bonds Issued at a Discount   525

■ Self-Study Quiz   526

■ Self-Study Quiz   528

FINANCIAL ANALYSIS:

Zero Coupon Bonds   529

Bonds Issued at a Premium   529

■ Self-Study Quiz   531

■ Self-Study Quiz   532

KEY RATIO ANALYSIS:

Debt-to-Equity Ratio   533

Early Retirement of Debt   533

■ Self-Study Quiz   534

FOCUS ON CASH FLOWS:

Bonds Payable   535

Demonstration Case   536

Chapter Eleven

Reporting and Interpreting Owners' Equity   558

Outback Steakhouse   559

Understanding the Business   559
Ownership of a Corporation   562
Benefits of Stock Ownership   562
Authorized, Issued, and Outstanding Shares   563

KEY RATIO ANALYSIS:

Earnings per Share (EPS)   564

Common Stock Transactions   565
Initial Sale of Stock   566
Sale of Stock in Secondary Markets   566
Stock Issued for Employee Compensation   566
Repurchase of Stock   567

■ Self-Study Quiz   568

Dividends on Common Stock   569

KEY RATIO ANALYSIS:

Dividend Yield   569

FINANCIAL ANALYSIS:

Impact of Dividends on Stock Price   571

■ Self-Study Quiz   571

Stock Dividends and Stock Splits   572
Stock Dividends   572
Stock Splits   573

■ Self-Study Quiz   574

Preferred Stock   574
Dividends on Preferred Stock   574

FINANCIAL ANALYSIS:

Impact of Dividends in Arrears   575

Restrictions on Retained Earnings   576

FIFTH EDITION

Financial Accounting

After studying this chapter, you should be able to:

1. Recognize the information conveyed in each of the four basic financial statements and the way that it is used by different decision makers (investors, creditors, and managers). p. 5

2. Identify the role of generally accepted accounting principles (GAAP) in determining the content of financial statements. p. 21

3. Distinguish the roles of managers and auditors in the accounting communication process. p. 23

4. Appreciate the importance of ethics, reputation, and legal liability in accounting. p. 24

Financial Statements and Business Decisions

I n January, Exeter Investors purchased Maxidrive Corp., a fast-growing manufacturer of personal computer disk drives, for $33 million. The price Exeter paid was determined by considering the value of Maxidrive's assets, its debts to others, its ability to sell goods for more than the cost to produce them, and its ability to generate the cash necessary to pay its current bills. Much of this assessment was based on financial information that Maxidrive provided to Exeter in the form of financial statements. By July, Exeter had discovered a variety of problems in the company's operations and its financial statements. Maxidrive appeared to be worth only about half of what Exeter had paid for the company.

Furthermore, Maxidrive did not have enough cash to pay its debt to American Bank. Exeter Investors filed a lawsuit against the previous owners and others responsible for Maxidrive's financial statements to recover its losses.

FOCUS COMPANY:

Maxidrive Corporation

VALUING AN ACQUISITION USING FINANCIAL STATEMENT INFORMATION*

UNDERSTANDING THE BUSINESS

The Players

Maxidrive was founded by two engineers who had formerly worked for General Data, then a manufacturer of large computers. Predicting the rise in demand for personal computers with a hard disk drive, they started a company to manufacture this component. The founders invested a major portion of their savings, becoming the sole owners of Maxidrive. As is common in new businesses, the founders also functioned as managers of the business (they were **owner-managers**).

The founders soon discovered that they needed additional money to develop the business. Based on the recommendation of a close friend, they asked American Bank for a loan. American Bank continued to lend to Maxidrive as the need arose, becoming its largest lender, or **creditor**. Early last year, one of the founders of the business became gravely ill. This event, plus the stresses of operating in their highly competitive industry, led the founders to search for a buyer for their company. In January of this year, they struck a deal for the sale of the company to Exeter Investors, a small group of wealthy

*The Maxidrive case is a realistic representation of an actual case of fraud. No names in the case are real. The actual fraud is discussed in the epilogue to the chapter.

private **investors**. Both founders retired and a new manager was hired to run Maxidrive for the new owners. The new **manager** worked on behalf of Exeter Investors, but was not an owner of the company.

Whether investors are groups such as Exeter who recently bought all of Maxidrive Corp. or individuals who buy small percentages of large corporations, they make their purchases hoping to gain in two ways. They hope to receive a portion of what the company earns in the form of cash payments called **dividends** and eventually sell their share of the company at a higher price than they paid. As the Maxidrive case suggests, not all companies increase in value or have sufficient cash to pay dividends. Creditors lend money to a company for a specific length of time. They hope to gain by charging interest on the money they lend. As American Bank, Maxidrive's major creditor, has learned, some borrowers cannot repay their debts. When Maxidrive exchanges money with its lenders and owners, these are called *financing activities*. When Maxidrive buys or sells items such as plant and equipment used in producing disk drives, these are called *investing activities*.

The Business Operations

To understand any company's financial statements, you must first understand its *operating activities*. As noted, Maxidrive designs and manufactures hard disk drives for personal computers. The major parts that go into the drive include the disks on which information is stored, the motors that spin the disks, the heads that read and write to the disks, and the computer chips that control the operations of the drive. Maxidrive purchases the disks and motors from other companies, called **suppliers**. It designs and manufactures the heads and chips and then assembles the drives. Maxidrive does not sell disk drives directly to the public. Instead, its **customers** are computer manufacturers such as Dell Computer and Apple Computer, which install the drives in machines they sell to retailers such as CompUSA and to consumers. Thus, Maxidrive is a supplier to Dell and Apple.

The Accounting System

Like all businesses, Maxidrive has an accounting system that collects and processes financial information about an organization and reports that information to decision makers. Maxidrive's managers (often called **internal decision makers**) and parties outside the firm such as Exeter Investors and American Bank (often called **external decision makers**) use the reports produced by this system. Exhibit 1.1 outlines the two parts of the accounting system. Internal managers typically require continuous, detailed information because they must plan and manage the day-to-day operations of the organization. Developing accounting information for internal decision makers, called **managerial** or **management accounting,** is the subject of a separate accounting course. The focus of this text is accounting for external decision makers, called **financial accounting,** and the four basic financial statements and related disclosures that are the output of that system.

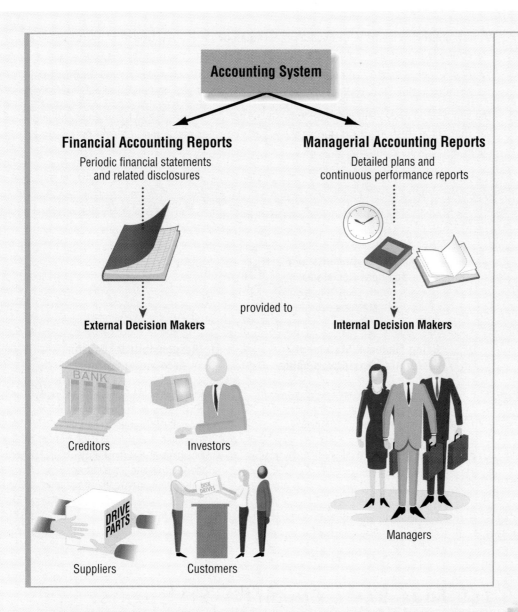

EXHIBIT 1.1

The Accounting System
and Decision Makers

We begin with a brief but comprehensive overview of the information reported in four basic financial statements and the people and organizations involved in their preparation and use. This overview provides you a context in which you can learn the more detailed material presented in the following chapters. In particular, we focus on how two primary users of the statements, investors (owners) and creditors (lenders), relied on each of Maxidrive's four basic financial statements in their ill-fated decisions to buy and lend money to Maxidrive. Then we test what you have learned by trying to correct the errors in the statements and discuss the implications of the errors for Maxidrive's value. Finally, we discuss the ethical and legal responsibilities of various parties for those errors.

To understand the way in which Exeter Investors used Maxidrive's financial statements in its decision and the way it was misled, we must first understand what specific information is presented in the four basic financial statements for a company such as Maxidrive. **Rather than trying to memorize the definitions of every term used in this chapter, try to focus your attention on learning the general structure and content of the statements. Specifically:**

1. What categories of items (often called **elements**) are reported on each of the four statements? (What type of information does a statement convey, and where can you find it?)

Learning Objective 1
Recognize the information conveyed in each of the four basic financial statements and the way that it is used by different decision makers (investors, creditors, and managers).

2. How are the elements within a statement related? (These **relationships** are usually described by an equation that tells you how the elements fit together.)

3. Why is each element important to owners' or creditors' decisions? (How **important** is the information to decision makers?)

The self-study quizzes will help you assess whether you have reached these goals. Remember that since this chapter is an overview, each concept discussed here will be discussed again in Chapters 2 through 5.

ORGANIZATION of the Chapter

```
        ┌───────────────────────────┐
        │ Financial Statements and   │
        │    Business Decisions      │
        └───────────────────────────┘
```

The Four Basic Financial Statements	Using Financial Statements to Determine Maxidrive's Value	Responsibilities for the Accounting Process
■ Balance Sheet ■ Income Statement ■ Statement of Retained Earnings ■ Statement of Cash Flows ■ Relationships Among the Statements ■ Notes	■ Correcting Maxidrive's Income Statement ■ Determining Maxidrive's Purchase Price	■ Generally Accepted Accounting Principles ■ Management Responsibility and the Demand for Auditing ■ Ethics, Reputation, and Legal Liability

THE FOUR BASIC FINANCIAL STATEMENTS: AN OVERVIEW

Topic Tackler

PLUS

Topic Tackler 1–1

Both Exeter Investors (Maxidrive's new owner) and American Bank (Maxidrive's largest creditor) used Maxidrive's financial statements to learn more about the company before making their purchase and lending decisions. In doing so, Exeter and American Bank assumed that the statements accurately represented Maxidrive's financial condition. As they soon learned, and now have claimed in their lawsuits, the statements were in error.

1. On its **balance sheet,** Maxidrive overstated the economic resources it owned and understated its debts to others,

2. On its **income statement,** Maxidrive overstated its ability to sell goods for more than the cost to produce and sell them,

3. On its **statement of retained earnings,** Maxidrive overstated the amount of income it reinvested in the company for future growth, and

4. On its **statement of cash flows,** Maxidrive overstated its ability to generate from sales of disk drives the cash necessary to meet its current debts.

These four financial statements are the basic statements normally prepared by profit-making organizations for use by investors, creditors, and other external decision makers.

The four basic statements summarize the financial activities of the business. They can be prepared at any point in time (such as the end of the year, quarter, or month) and can apply to any time span (such as one year, one quarter, or one month). Like most companies, Maxidrive prepares financial statements for investors and creditors at the end of each quarter (known as **quarterly reports**) and at the end of the year (known as **annual reports**).

The Balance Sheet

The purpose of the balance sheet is to report the financial position (amount of assets, liabilities, and stockholders' equity) of an accounting entity at a particular point in time. We can learn a great deal about what the balance sheet reports just by reading the statement from the top. The balance sheet of Maxidrive Corp., presented by its former owners to Exeter Investors, is shown in Exhibit 1.2.

A **BALANCE SHEET** (Statement of Financial Position) reports the amount of assets, liabilities, and stockholders' equity of an accounting entity at a point in time.

Structure

Notice that the **heading** specifically identifies four significant items related to the statement:

1. **name of the entity,** Maxidrive Corp.
2. **title of the statement,** Balance Sheet.
3. **specific date of the statement,** At December 31, 2006.
4. **unit of measure** (in thousands of dollars).

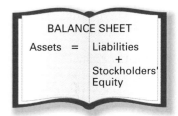

The organization for which financial data are to be collected, called an accounting entity, must be precisely defined. On the balance sheet, the business entity itself, not the business owners, is viewed as owning the resources it uses and as owing its debts. The heading of each statement indicates the time dimension of the report. The balance

An **ACCOUNTING ENTITY** is the organization for which financial data are to be collected.

EXHIBIT 1.2

Balance Sheet

MAXIDRIVE CORP. Balance Sheet At December 31, 2006 (in thousands of dollars)		
		name of the entity
		title of the statement
		specific date of the statement
		unit of measure
Assets		
Cash	$ 4,895	the amount of cash in the company's bank accounts
Accounts receivable	5,714	amounts owed by customers from prior sales
Inventories	8,517	parts and completed but unsold disk drives
Plant and equipment	7,154	factories and production machinery
Land	981	land on which the factories are built
Total assets	$27,261	
Liabilities		
Accounts payable	$ 7,156	amounts owed to suppliers for prior purchases
Notes payable	9,000	amounts owed on written debt contracts
Total liabilities	16,156	
Stockholders' Equity		
Contributed capital	2,000	amounts invested in the business by stockholders
Retained earnings	9,105	past earnings not distributed to stockholders
Total stockholders' equity	11,105	
Total liabilities and stockholders' equity	$27,261	

The notes are an integral part of these financial statements.

sheet is like a financial snapshot indicating the entity's financial position at a specific point in time—in this case, December 31, 2006—which is stated clearly on the balance sheet. Financial reports are normally denominated in the currency of the country in which they are located. U.S. companies report in U.S. dollars, Canadian companies in Canadian dollars, and Mexican companies in Mexican pesos. Medium-sized companies such as Maxidrive often report in thousands of dollars; that is, they round the last three digits to the nearest thousand. The listing of Cash $4,895 on Maxidrive's balance sheet actually means $4,895,000.

Maxidrive's balance sheet first lists the company's assets. Assets are economic resources owned by the entity. It next lists its liabilities and stockholders' equity. They are the sources of financing or claims against the company's economic resources. Financing provided by creditors creates a liability. Financing provided by owners creates owners' equity. Since Maxidrive is a corporation, its owners' equity is designated as stockholders' equity.[1] Since each asset must have a source of financing, a company's assets must, by definition, equal the combined total of its liabilities and stockholders' equity. This **basic accounting equation,** often called the balance sheet equation, is written:

BASIC ACCOUNTING EQUATION (balance sheet equation): Assets = Liabilities + Stockholders' Equity.

Assets	=	**Liabilities + Stockholders' Equity**
Economic resources		Sources of financing for the economic resources
(e.g., cash, inventory)		Liabilities: From creditors
		Stockholders' Equity: From stockholders

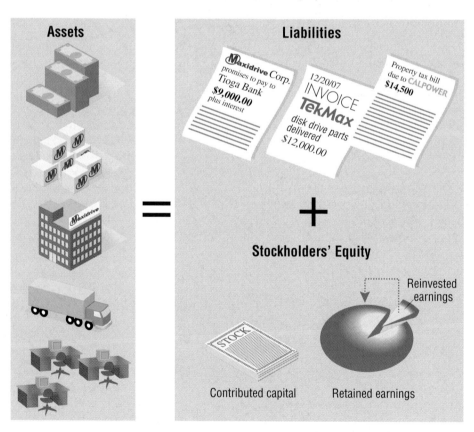

----

[1] A corporation is a business that is incorporated under the laws of a particular state. The owners are called **stockholders** or **shareholders.** Ownership is represented by shares of capital stock that usually can be bought and sold freely. The corporation operates as a separate legal entity, separate and apart from its owners. The stockholders enjoy limited liability; they are liable for the debts of the corporation only to the extent of their investments. Chapter Supplement A discusses forms of ownership in more detail.

The basic accounting equation shows what we mean when we refer to a company's **financial position:** the economic resources that the company owns and the sources of financing for those resources.

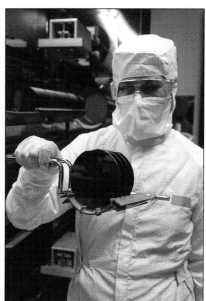

Elements

Assets are the economic resources owned by the company. Maxidrive lists five items under the category Assets. The exact items listed as assets on a company's balance sheet depend on the nature of its operations. But these are common names used by many companies. The five items listed by Maxidrive are the economic resources needed to manufacture and sell disk drives to companies such as Dell. Each of these economic resources is expected to provide future benefits to the firm. To prepare to manufacture the drives, Maxidrive first needed cash to purchase land on which to build factories and install production machinery (buildings and equipment). Maxidrive then began purchasing parts and producing disk drives, which led to the balance assigned to inventories. When Maxidrive sells its disk drives to Dell and others, it sells them on credit and receives promises to pay called accounts receivable, which are collected in cash later.

Every asset on the balance sheet is initially measured at the total cost incurred to acquire it. For example, the balance sheet for Maxidrive reports Land, $981; this is the amount paid (in thousands) for the land when it was acquired. Balance sheets do not generally show the amounts for which the assets could currently be sold.

Liabilities are the company's debts or obligations. Under the category Liabilities, Maxidrive lists two items. The accounts payable arise from the purchase of goods or services from suppliers on credit without a formal written contract (or a note). The notes payable result from cash borrowings based on a formal written debt contract with lending institutions such as banks.

Stockholders' equity indicates the amount of financing provided by owners of the business and earnings. The investment of cash and other assets in the business by the owners is called contributed capital. The amount of earnings (profits) reinvested in the business (and thus not distributed to stockholders in the form of dividends) is called retained earnings.

In Exhibit 1.2, the Stockholders' Equity section reports two items. The two founding stockholders' investment of $2,000,000 is reported as contributed capital. Maxidrive's total earnings (or losses incurred) less all dividends paid to the stockholders since formation of the corporation equaled $9,105,000 and is reported as retained earnings. Total stockholders' equity is the sum of the contributed capital plus the retained earnings.

Interpreting Assets, Liabilities, and Stockholders' Equity on the Balance Sheet

FINANCIAL ANALYSIS

Assessment of Maxidrive's assets was important to its creditor, American Bank, and its prospective investor, Exeter, because assets provide a basis for judging whether the company has sufficient resources available to operate. Assets were also important because they could be sold for cash in the event that Maxidrive went out of business.

Exeter Investors was interested in Maxidrive's debts because of its concern about whether the company has sufficient sources of cash to pay its debts. Maxidrive's debts were also relevant to American Bank's decision to lend money to the company because existing creditors share American Bank's claim against Maxidrive's assets. If a business does not pay its creditors, the creditors may force the sale of assets sufficient to meet their claims. The sale of assets often fails to cover all of a company's debts, and some creditors may take a loss.

continued

Maxidrive's stockholders' equity or net worth is important to American Bank because creditors' claims legally come before those of owners. If Maxidrive goes out of business and its assets are sold, the proceeds of that sale must be used to pay back creditors such as American Bank before the owners receive any money. Thus, creditors consider stockholders' equity a protective "cushion."

SELF-STUDY **QUIZ**

1. Maxidrive's *assets* are listed in one section and *liabilities* and *stockholders' equity* in another. Notice that the two sections balance in conformity with the basic accounting equation. In the following chapters, you will learn that the basic accounting equation is the basic building block for the entire accounting process. Your task here is to verify that the amount of assets of $27,261,000 is correct using the numbers for liabilities and stockholders' equity presented in Exhibit 1.2. Recall the basic accounting equation:

$$\text{Assets} = \text{Liabilities} + \text{Stockholders' Equity}$$

2. Learning which items belong in each of the balance sheet categories is an important first step in understanding their meaning. Without referring to Exhibit 1.2, mark each balance sheet item in the following list as an asset (A), liability (L), or stockholders' equity (SE).

_____ Accounts payable	_____ Inventories
_____ Accounts receivable	_____ Land
_____ Cash	_____ Notes payable
_____ Contributed capital	_____ Retained earnings
_____ Buildings and equipment	

After you have completed your answers, check them with the solutions at the bottom of the page.

The Income Statement

Structure

The **income statement** (statement of income, statement of earnings, or statement of operations) reports the accountant's primary measure of performance of a business, revenues less expenses during the accounting period. The term profit is used widely for this measure of performance, but accountants prefer to use the technical terms **net income** or net earnings. Maxidrive's net income measures its success in selling disk drives for more than the cost to generate those sales.

A quick reading of Maxidrive's income statement (Exhibit 1.3) indicates a great deal about its purpose and content. The heading identifies the name of the entity, the title of the report, and the unit of measure used in the statement. Unlike the balance sheet, however, which reports as of a certain date, the income statement reports for a specified period of time (for the year ended December 31, 2006). The time period covered by the financial statements (one year in this case) is called an **accounting period**. Notice that Maxidrive's income statement has three major captions, revenues, expenses, and net income. The income statement equation that describes their relationship is

Revenues − Expenses = Net Income

The **INCOME STATEMENT** (Statement of Income, Statement of Earnings, Statement of Operations) reports the revenues less the expenses of the accounting period.

Income
Statement

Revenues
− Expenses
Net Income

The **ACCOUNTING PERIOD** is the time period covered by the financial statements.

Self-Study Quiz
Solutions

1. Assets ($27,261,000) = Liabilities ($16,156,000) + Stockholders' Equity ($11,105,000).
2. L, A, A, SE, A, A, A, L, SE (reading down the columns).

Revenues   −   Expenses   =   Net Income

Elements

Companies earn **revenues** from the sale of goods or services to customers (in Maxidrive's case, from the sale of disk drives). Revenues normally are reported for goods or services that have been sold to a customer **whether or not they have yet been paid for.** Retail stores such as Wal-Mart and McDonald's often receive cash at the time of sale. However, when Maxidrive sells its disk drives to Dell and Apple Computer, it receives a promise of future payment called an account receivable, which later is collected in cash. In either case, the business recognizes total sales (cash and credit) as revenue for the period. Various terms are used in income statements to describe different sources of revenue (e.g., provision of services, sale of goods, rental of property). Maxidrive lists only one, sales revenue, in its income statement.

Expenses represent the dollar amount of resources the entity used to earn revenues during the period. Expenses reported in one accounting period may actually be paid for in another accounting period. Some expenses require the payment of cash immediately while some require payment at a later date. Some may also require the use of another

EXHIBIT 1.3

Income Statement

MAXIDRIVE CORP. Income Statement For the Year Ended December 31, 2006 (in thousands of dollars)		*name of the entity* *title of the statement* *accounting period* *unit of measure*
Revenues		
Sales revenue	$37,436	*cash and promises received from sale of disk drives*
Total revenues	37,436	
Expenses		
Cost of goods sold expense	26,980	*cost to produce disk drives sold*
Selling, general, and administrative expense	3,624	*operating expenses not directly related to production*
Research and development expense	1,982	*expenses incurred to develop new products*
Interest expense	450	*cost of using borrowed funds*
Total expenses	33,036	
Pretax income	4,400	
Income tax expense	1,100	*income taxes on period's pretax income ($4,400 × 25%)*
Net income	$ 3,300	

The notes are an integral part of these financial statements.

resource, such as an inventory item, which may have been paid for in a prior period. Maxidrive lists five types of expenses on its income statement, which are described in Exhibit 1.3. These expenses include income tax expense, which, as a corporation, Maxidrive must pay on pretax income.[2]

Net income or net earnings (often called "the bottom line") is the excess of total revenues over total expenses. If total expenses exceed total revenues, a net loss is reported.[3] When revenues and expenses are equal for the period, the business has operated at breakeven.

We noted earlier that revenues are not necessarily the same as collections from customers and expenses are not necessarily the same as payments to suppliers. As a result, net income normally **does not equal** the net cash generated by operations. This latter amount is reported on the cash flow statement discussed later in this chapter.

SELF-STUDY QUIZ

1. Learning which items belong in each of the income statement categories is an important first step in understanding their meaning. Without referring to Exhibit 1.3, mark each income statement item in the following list as a revenue (R) or an expense (E).

   _____ Cost of goods sold   _____ Sales

   _____ Income tax   _____ Selling, general, and administrative

2. During the period 2006, Maxidrive delivered disk drives for which customers paid or promised to pay amounts totaling $37,436,000. During the same period, it collected $33,563,000 in cash from its customers. Without referring to Exhibit 1.3, indicate which of these two amounts will be shown on Maxidrive's income statement as **sales revenue** for 2006. Why did you select your answer?

3. During the period 2006, Maxidrive **produced** disk drives with a total cost of production of $27,130,000. During the same period, it **delivered** to customers disk drives that had cost a total of $26,980,000 to produce. Without referring to Exhibit 1.3, indicate which of the two numbers will be shown on Maxidrive's income statement as **cost of goods sold expense** for 2006. Why did you select your answer?

After you have completed your answers, check them with the solutions at the bottom of the page.

---

[2]This example uses a 25 percent rate. Federal tax rates for corporations actually ranged from 15 percent to 35 percent at the time this book was written. State and local governments may levy additional taxes on corporate income, resulting in a higher total income tax rate.

[3]Net losses are normally noted by parentheses around the income figure.

Self-Study Quiz
Solutions

1. E, E, R, E (reading down the columns).

2. Sales revenue in the amount of $37,436,000 is recognized. Sales revenue is normally reported on the income statement when goods or services have been delivered to customers who have either paid or promised to pay for them in the future.

3. Cost of goods sold expense is $26,980,000. Expenses are the dollar amount of resources used up to earn revenues during the period. Only those disk drives that have been delivered to customers have been used up. Those disk drives that are still on hand are part of the asset inventory.

Analyzing the Income Statement: Beyond the Bottom Line

FINANCIAL
ANALYSIS

Investors such as Exeter and creditors such as American Bank closely monitor a firm's net income because it indicates the firm's ability to sell goods and services for more than they cost to produce and deliver. Investors buy stock when they believe that future earnings will improve and lead to a higher stock price. Lenders also rely on future earnings to provide the resources to repay loans. The details of the statement also are important. For example, Maxidrive had to sell more than $37 million worth of disk drives to make just over $3 million. If a competitor were to lower prices just 10 percent, forcing Maxidrive to do the same, or if Maxidrive had to triple research and development expense to catch up to a competitor, its net income could easily turn into a net loss. These factors and others help investors and creditors estimate the company's future earnings.

Statement of Retained Earnings

Structure

Maxidrive prepares a separate statement of retained earnings, shown in Exhibit 1.4. The heading identifies the name of the entity, the title of the report, and the unit of measure used in the statement. Like the income statement, the statement of retained earnings covers a specified period of time (the accounting period), which in this case is one year. The statement reports the way that net income and the distribution of dividends affected the company's financial position during the accounting period.[4] Net income earned during the year increases the balance of retained earnings, showing the relationship of the income statement to the balance sheet. The declaration of dividends to the stockholders decreases retained earnings.[5]

The retained earnings equation that describes these relationships is

Beginning Retained Earnings + Net Income − Dividends = Ending Retained Earnings

Elements

The statement begins with Maxidrive's **beginning-of-the-year retained earnings.** The current year's **net income** reported on the income statement is added and the current year's **dividends** are subtracted from this amount. During 2006, Maxidrive earned

The **STATEMENT OF RETAINED EARNINGS** reports the way that net income and the distribution of dividends affected the financial position of the company during the accounting period.

MAXIDRIVE CORP. Statement of Retained Earnings For the Year Ended December 31, 2006 (in thousands of dollars)		
Retained earnings, January 1, 2006	$6,805	last period's ending retained earnings
Net income for 2006	3,300	net income reported on the income statement
Dividends for 2006	(1,000)	dividends declared during the period
Retained earnings, December 31, 2006	$9,105	ending retained earnings on the balance sheet

name of the entity
title of the statement
accounting period
unit of measure

EXHIBIT 1.4

Statement of Retained Earnings

The notes are an integral part of these financial statements.

[4]Other corporations report these changes at the end of the income statement or in a more general statement of stockholders' equity, which we discuss in Chapter 4.
[5]Net losses are subtracted.

$3,300,000, as shown on the income statement (Exhibit 1.3). This amount was added to the beginning-of-the-year retained earnings. Also, during 2006, Maxidrive declared and paid a total of $1,000,000 in dividends to its two original stockholders. This amount was subtracted in computing **end-of-the-year retained earnings** on the balance sheet. Note that retained earnings increased by the portion of income reinvested in the business ($3,300,000 − 1,000,000 = $2,300,000). The ending retained earnings amount of $9,105,000 is the same as that reported in Exhibit 1.2 on Maxidrive's balance sheet. Thus, the retained earnings statement indicates the relationship of the income statement to the balance sheet.

FINANCIAL
ANALYSIS   **Interpreting Retained Earnings**

Reinvestment of earnings, or retained earnings, is an important source of financing for Maxidrive, representing more than one-third of its financing. Creditors such as American Bank closely monitor a firm's retained earnings statement because the firm's policy on dividend payments to the stockholders affects its ability to repay its debts. Every dollar Maxidrive pays to stockholders as a dividend is not available for use in paying back its debt to American Bank. Investors examine retained earnings to determine whether the company is reinvesting a sufficient portion of earnings to support future growth.

SELF-STUDY QUIZ

Maxidrive's statement of retained earnings reports the way that net income and the distribution of dividends affected the financial position of the company during the accounting period. In a prior period, Maxidrive's financial statements reported the following amounts: beginning retained earnings $5,510, total assets, $20,450, dividends $900, cost of goods sold expense $19,475, net income $1,780. Without referring to Exhibit 1.4, compute ending retained earnings.

After you have completed your answer, check it with the solution at the bottom of the page.

Statement of Cash Flows

Structure

The **STATEMENT OF CASH FLOWS** (Cash Flow Statement) reports inflows and outflows of cash during the accounting period in the categories of operating, investing, and financing.

Maxidrive's statement of cash flows is presented in Exhibit 1.5. The statement of cash flows (cash flow statement) divides Maxidrive's cash inflows and outflows (receipts and payments) into the three primary categories of cash flows in a typical business: cash flows from operating, investing, and financing activities. The heading identifies the name of the entity, the title of the report, and the unit of measure used in the statement. Like the income statement, the cash flow statement covers a specified period of time (the accounting period), which in this case is one year.

As discussed earlier in this chapter, reported revenues do not always equal cash collected from customers because some sales may be on credit. Also, expenses reported on the income statement may not be equal to the cash paid out during the period be-

---

Self-Study Quiz
Solution

Beginning Retained Earnings ($5,510) + Net Income ($1,780) − Dividends ($900) = Ending Retained Earnings ($6,390).

cause expenses may be incurred in one period and paid for in another. Because the income statement does not provide information concerning cash flows, accountants prepare the statement of cash flows to report inflows and outflows of cash. The cash flow statement equation describes the causes of the change in cash reported on the balance sheet from the end of last period to the end of the current period:

+/− Cash Flows from Operating Activities (CFO)

+/− Cash Flows from Investing Activities (CFI)

+/− Cash Flows from Financing Activities (CFF)

Change in Cash

Note that each of the three cash flow sources can be positive or negative.

Elements

Cash flows from operating activities are cash flows that are directly related to earning income. For example, when Dell, Apple Computer, and other customers pay Maxidrive for the disk drives it has delivered to them, it lists the amounts collected as cash collected from customers. When Maxidrive pays salaries to its employees in research and development or pays bills received from its parts suppliers, it includes the amounts in cash paid to suppliers and employees.[6]

   Cash flows from investing activities include cash flows related to the acquisition or sale of the company's productive assets. This year, Maxidrive had only one cash outflow

---

EXHIBIT 1.5

Statement of Cash Flows

MAXIDRIVE CORP.
Statement of Cash Flows
For the Year Ended December 31, 2006
(in thousands of dollars)

		name of the entity
		title of the statement
		accounting period
		unit of measure
Cash flows from operating activities		*directly related to earning income*
Cash collected from customers	$33,563	
Cash paid to suppliers and employees	(30,854)	
Cash paid for interest	(450)	
Cash paid for taxes	(1,190)	
Net cash flow from operating activities	1,069	
Cash flows from investing activities		*purchase/sale of productive assets*
Cash paid to purchase manufacturing equipment	(1,625)	
Net cash flow from investing activities	(1,625)	
Cash flows from financing activities		*from investors and creditors*
Cash received from bank loan	1,400	
Cash paid for dividends	(1,000)	
Net cash flow from financing activities	400	
Net decrease in cash during the year	(156)	*change in cash during the period ($1,069 − 1,625 + 400)*
Cash at beginning of year	5,051	*last period's ending cash balance*
Cash at end of year	$ 4,895	*ending cash on the balance sheet*

The notes are an integral part of these financial statements.

---

[6]Alternative ways to present cash flows from operations are discussed in Chapter 5.

from investing activities, the purchase of additional manufacturing equipment to meet growing demand for its products. **Cash flows from financing activities** are directly related to the financing of the enterprise itself. They involve the receipt or payment of money to investors and creditors (except for suppliers). This year, Maxidrive borrowed an additional $1,400,000 from the bank to purchase most of the new manufacturing equipment. It also paid out $1,000,000 in dividends to the founding stockholders.

FINANCIAL ANALYSIS

Interpreting the Cash Flow Statement

Many analysts believe that the statement of cash flows is particularly useful in predicting future cash flows that may be available for payment of debt to creditors and dividends to investors. Bankers often consider the Operating Activities section to be most important because it indicates the company's ability to generate cash from sales to meet its current cash needs. Any amount left over can be used to pay back the bank debt or expand the company.

Stockholders will invest in a company only if they believe that it will eventually generate more cash from operations than it uses so that cash will become available to pay dividends and expand. The Investing Activities section shows that Maxidrive is making heavy investments in new manufacturing capacity, a good sign if demand continues to increase. But, as the Financing Activities section indicates, if Maxidrive is not able to sell more drives, it may have trouble meeting the payments on the new bank debt.

SELF-STUDY QUIZ

1. During the period 2006, Maxidrive delivered disk drives to customers who paid or promised to pay a total of $37,436,000. During the same period, it collected $33,563,000 in cash from customers. Without referring to Exhibit 1.5, indicate which of the two amounts will be shown on Maxidrive's cash flow statement for 2006.

2. Learning which items belong in each cash flow statement category is an important first step in understanding their meaning. Without referring to Exhibit 1.5, mark each item in the following list as a cash flow from operating activities (O), investing activities (I), or financing activities (F). Place **parentheses** around the letter only if it is a cash **outflow.**

    _____ Cash paid for dividends

    _____ Cash received from bank loan

    _____ Cash paid for taxes

    _____ Cash paid to purchase manufacturing equipment

    _____ Cash paid to suppliers and employees

    _____ Cash collected from customers

After you have completed your answers, check them with the solutions at the bottom of the page.

Self-Study Quiz
Solutions

1. The firm recognizes $33,563,000 on the cash flow statement because this number represents the actual cash collected from customers related to current and prior years' sales.
2.   (F), F, (O), (I), (O), O.

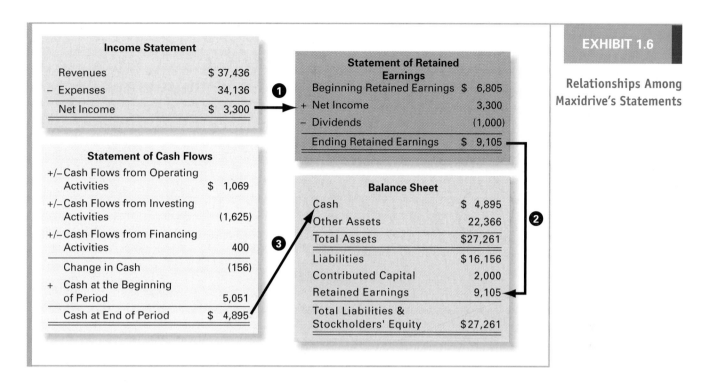

EXHIBIT 1.6

Relationships Among Maxidrive's Statements

Relationships among the Statements

Our discussion of the four basic financial statements focused on what elements are reported in each statement, how the elements are related by the equation for each statement, and how the elements are important to the decisions of investors, creditors, and others. We have also discovered how the statements, all of which are outputs from the same system, are related to one another. In particular, we learned:

1. Net income from the income statement results in an increase in ending retained earnings on the statement of retained earnings.

2. Ending retained earnings from the statement of retained earnings is one of the two components of stockholders' equity on the balance sheet.

3. The change in cash on the cash flow statement added to the beginning-of-the-year balance in cash equals the end-of-year balance in cash on the balance sheet.

Thus, we can think of the income statement as explaining, through the statement of retained earnings, how the operations of the company improved or harmed the financial position of the company during the year. The cash flow statement explains how the operating, investing, and financing activities of the company affected the cash balance on the balance sheet during the year. These relationships are illustrated in Exhibit 1.6 for Maxidrive's financial statements.

Notes

At the bottom of each of Maxidrive's four basic financial statements is this statement: **"The notes are an integral part of these financial statements."** This is the accounting equivalent of the Surgeon General's warning on a package of cigarettes. It warns users that failure to read the notes (or footnotes) to the financial statements will result in an incomplete picture of the company's financial health. Notes provide supplemental information about the financial condition of a company without which the financial statements cannot be fully understood.

There are three basic types of notes. The first type provides descriptions of the accounting rules applied in the company's statements. The second presents additional

NOTES (footnotes) provide supplemental information about the financial condition of a company without which the financial statements cannot be fully understood.

Notes to Financial Statements

detail about a line on the financial statements. For example, Maxidrive's inventory note indicates the amount of parts, drives under construction, and finished disk drives included in the total inventory amount listed on the balance sheet. The third type of note provides additional financial disclosures about items not listed on the statements themselves. For example, Maxidrive leases one of its production facilities; terms of the lease are disclosed in a note. Throughout this book, we will discuss many note disclosures because understanding their content is critical to understanding the company.

A few additional formatting conventions are worth noting here. Assets are listed on the balance sheet by ease of conversion to cash. Liabilities are listed by their maturity (due date). Most financial statements include the monetary unit sign (in the United States, the $) beside the first dollar amount in a group of items (e.g., the cash amount in the assets). Also, it is common to place a single underline below the last item in a group before a total or subtotal (e.g., land). A dollar sign is also placed beside group totals (e.g., total assets) and a double underline below. The same conventions are followed in all four basic financial statements.

FINANCIAL
ANALYSIS

Management Uses of Financial Statements

In our discussion of financial analysis thus far, we have focused on the perspectives of investors and creditors. Managers within the firm also make direct use of financial statements. For example, Maxidrive's **marketing managers** and **credit managers** use customers' financial statements to decide whether to extend credit for purchases of disk drives. Maxidrive's **purchasing managers** analyze parts suppliers' financial statements to see whether the suppliers have the resources to meet Maxidrive's demand and invest in the development of new parts. Both the **employees' union** and Maxidrive's **human resource managers** use Maxidrive's financial statements as a basis for contract negotiations over pay rates. The net income figure even serves as a basis for calculating **employee bonuses.** Regardless of the functional area of management in which you are employed, you will use financial statement data. You also will be evaluated based on the impact of your decisions on your company's financial statement data.

Summary of the Four Basic Financial Statements

We have learned a great deal about the content of the four basic statements. Exhibit 1.7 summarizes this information. Take a few minutes to review the information in the exhibit before you move on to the next section of the chapter.

USING FINANCIAL STATEMENTS TO DETERMINE MAXIDRIVE'S VALUE

Correcting Maxidrive's Income Statement

Let's look at the errors that Exeter Investors later found in Maxidrive's statements to see whether we have learned enough to make the necessary corrections.

Among Exeter's claims are that

1. Disk drives inventory included $1,000,000 of obsolete drives that could not be sold and must be scrapped.

2. Reported sales to customers and accounts receivable for last year included $1,200,000 of overstatements. Maxidrive had cut the price of a certain type of disk drive by 40 percent, but employees had created fake customer bills (called invoices) at the old higher prices to inflate reported sales.

Together, these two items significantly overstated Maxidrive's assets and its net income.

EXHIBIT 1.7

Summary of
Four Basic
Financial
Statements

Financial Statement	Purpose	Structure	Examples of Content
Balance Sheet (Statement of Financial Position)	Reports the financial position (economic resources and sources of financing) of an accounting entity *at a point in time*.	BALANCE SHEET Assets = Liabilities + Stockholders' Equity	Cash, accounts receivable, plant and equipment, notes payable, contributed capital
Income Statement (Statement of Income, Statement of Earnings, Statement of Operations)	Reports the accountant's primary measure of economic performance *during the accounting period*.	Income Statement Revenues − Expenses Net Income	Sales revenue, cost of goods sold, selling expense, interest expense
Statement of Retained Earnings	Reports the way that net income and the distribution of dividends affected the financial position of the company *during the accounting period*.	Statement of Retained Earnings Beginning RE + Net Income − Dividends Ending RE	Net income is taken from the income statement; Dividends are distributions to stockholders
Statement of Cash Flows (Cash Flow Statement)	Reports inflows (receipts) and outflows (payments) of cash *during the accounting period* in the categories operating, investing, and financing.	Statement of Cash Flows +/− CFO +/− CFI +/− CFF Change in Cash	Cash collected from customers, cash paid to suppliers, cash paid to purchase equipment, cash borrowed from banks

For purposes of our discussion, we focus on the effects on the income statement because they were most relevant to Exeter Investors' evaluation of Maxidrive. The simplest way to determine the effects of these two errors on the income statement is to use the income statement equation as we have in Exhibit 1.8. Correcting the two errors reduces pretax income to $2,200,000. After we subtract 25 percent for income tax expense, we are left with a corrected net income equal to $1,650,000, just half of the $3,300,000 amount Maxidrive initially reported.

Determining the Purchase Price for Maxidrive

Even at this early stage in your study of accounting, we can illustrate part of the process Exeter Investors went through in determining the price it was willing to pay for Maxidrive Corp. The price Exeter paid was decided by considering a variety of factors including the value of Maxidrive's assets, its debts to others, its ability to sell goods for more than their production cost, and its ability to generate the cash necessary to pay its current bills. These factors are the subject matter of the balance sheet, income statement, and cash flow statement.

Maxidrive's current and prior years' income statements played a particularly important part in Exeter's evaluation. Prior years' income statements (which were not presented here) indicated that the company had earned income every year since its

EXHIBIT 1.8

Correction of the Income
Statement Amounts (in
thousands of dollars)

	Computations	Corrected Income Statement
Revenues (as reported)	$37,436	
Error 1: Employees created fake invoices for $1,200,000 in sales revenue. Accordingly revenues should decrease by $1,200,000.	(1,200)	
Revenues (corrected)		$36,236
Expenses (as reported)	33,036	
Error 2: The cost of obsolete inventory items should be added to this year's expenses. Accordingly, expenses should increase by $1,000,000.	1,000	
Expenses (corrected)		34,036
Pretax income (corrected)		2,200
Income tax expense (corrected) 25% × $2,200		550
Net Income (corrected)		$ 1,650

founding except for the first year. Furthermore, both sales revenue and net income had risen every year.

In general, investors use prior years' financial performance to make projections about future performance. They will be willing to pay more for a firm that reports higher net income in the past if they believe it will produce greater income in the future. One method for estimating the value of a company that follows this logic is the **price/earnings ratio** (P/E ratio, or P/E multiple). The P/E ratio measures how many times current year's earnings investors are willing to pay for a company's stock. A higher P/E ratio means that investors have more confidence in the company's ability to produce higher profits in future years.

Competitors' P/E ratios often serve as a starting point in analyzing the price that should be paid for a company or its stock. Other companies in the same industry with similar performance and past growth were selling for 12 times their current earnings. Accordingly, the opportunity to buy Maxidrive for 10 times its current earnings seemed to be an excellent one, particularly since economic forecasts suggested that the next five years would see continuing growth and profitability for disk drive manufacturers. The key calculation that determined the price Exeter paid was based on the following manipulation of the P/E ratio:

$$\text{Price/Earnings Ratio} = \frac{\text{Market Price}}{\text{Net Income}}$$

$$\text{Market (Purchase) Price} = \text{P/E Ratio} \times \text{Net Income}$$

$$\text{Market (Purchase) Price} = 10 \times \text{Net Income}$$

$$\$33,000,000 = 10 \times \$3,300,000$$

Using the same formula, the corrected net income figure suggests a much lower price for Maxidrive:

$$\$16,500,000 = 10 \times \$1,650,000$$

The P/E ratio provides a good approximation of Exeter's loss—a $16.5 million overpayment ($33 million paid minus $16.5 million estimated value based on corrected earnings). This is the amount that Exeter hopes to recover from those responsible for the fraudulent financial statements it relied on in its analysis. (The role of net income in determining the value of a company will be discussed in more detail in your corporate finance course and more advanced courses in financial statement analysis.[7])

RESPONSIBILITIES FOR THE ACCOUNTING COMMUNICATION PROCESS

For the decision makers at Exeter to use the information in Maxidrive's financial statements effectively, they had to understand what information each of the statements conveyed. Yet the fraud perpetrated by Maxidrive employees suggests that this understanding is not sufficient. Exeter clearly needed to know that the numbers in the statements represented what they claimed. Numbers that do not represent what they claim to are meaningless. For example, if the balance sheet lists $2,000,000 for a factory that does not exist, that part of the statement does not convey useful information.

Decision makers also need to understand the **measurement rules** applied in computing the numbers on the statements. A swim coach would never try to evaluate a swimmer's time in the 100 freestyle without first asking if the time was for a race in meters or in yards. Likewise, a decision maker should never attempt to use accounting information without first understanding the measurement rules that were used to develop the information. These measurement rules are called generally accepted accounting principles, or GAAP.

Generally Accepted Accounting Principles

How Are Generally Accepted Accounting Principles Determined?

The accounting system in use today has a long history. Its foundations are normally traced back to the works of an Italian monk and mathematician, Fr. Luca Pacioli, published in 1494. However, prior to 1933, each company's management largely determined its financial reporting practices. Thus, little uniformity in practice existed among companies.

Following the dramatic stock market decline of 1929, the Securities Act of 1933 and the Securities Exchange Act of 1934 were passed into law by the U.S. Congress. These acts created the Securities and Exchange Commission (SEC) and gave it broad powers to determine the measurement rules for financial statements that companies issuing stock to the public (publicly traded companies) must provide to stockholders.[8] The SEC has worked with organizations of professional accountants to establish groups that are given the primary responsibilities to work out the detailed rules that become generally accepted accounting principles. Today, the Financial Accounting Standards Board (FASB) has this responsibility. The Board has seven full-time voting members and a permanent staff who consider the appropriate financial reporting responses to ever-changing business practices. As of the date of publication of this book, the official pronouncements of the FASB (**Financial Accounting Standards**) and its predecessors totaled more than 5,000 pages of very fine print. Such detail is made necessary by the enormous diversity and complexity of current business practices.

Most managers do not need to learn all the details included in these standards. Our approach is to focus on those details that have the greatest impact on the numbers presented in financial statements and are appropriate for an introductory course.

Why Is GAAP Important to Managers and External Users?

Generally accepted accounting principles (GAAP) are of great interest to the companies that must prepare financial statements, their auditors, and the readers of the statements.

Learning Objective 2
Identify the role of generally accepted accounting principles (GAAP) in determining the content of financial statements.

Topic Tackler
PLUS
Topic Tackler 1–2

GENERALLY ACCEPTED ACCOUNTING PRINCIPLES (GAAP) are the measurement rules used to develop the information in financial statements.

The **SECURITIES AND EXCHANGE COMMISSION** (SEC) is the U.S. government agency that determines the financial statements that public companies must provide to stockholders and the measurement rules that they must use in producing those statements.

The **FINANCIAL ACCOUNTING STANDARDS BOARD** (FASB) is the private sector body given the primary responsibility to work out the detailed rules that become generally accepted accounting principles.

---

[7]See for example, K.R. Palepu, P.M. Healy, and V.B. Bernard, *Business Analysis and Valuation* (Cincinnati, OH: South-Western, 2004), chapter 11.

[8]Contrary to popular belief, these rules are different from those that companies follow when filing their income tax returns. We discuss these differences further in later chapters.

Companies and their managers and owners are most directly affected by the information presented in financial statements. Companies incur the cost of preparing the statements and bear the major economic consequences of their publication, which include, among others,

1. Effects on the selling price of a company's stock.
2. Effects on the amount of bonuses received by management and employees.
3. Loss of competitive information to other companies.

Recall that the amount that Exeter was willing to pay to purchase Maxidrive was determined in part by net income computed under GAAP. This presents the possibility that changes in GAAP can affect the price buyers are willing to pay for companies. Employees who receive part of their pay based on reaching stated targets for net income are directly concerned with any changes in how net income is computed under GAAP. Managers and owners also often are concerned that publishing certain information in financial statements will give away trade secrets to other companies that compete with them. As a consequence of these and other concerns, changes in GAAP are actively debated, political lobbying often takes place, and final rules are often a compromise among the wishes of interested parties.

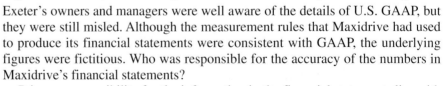

INTERNATIONAL
PERSPECTIVE

The International Accounting Standards Board and Global Convergence of Accounting Standards

Financial accounting standards and disclosure requirements are set by national regulatory agencies and standard setting bodies. However, since 2002, there has been substantial movement to develop international financial reporting standards (IFRS) by the International Accounting Standards Board (IASB). The current status of these standards in different countries is indicated in the following excerpt from the IASB's website.

REAL WORLD EXCERPT

International Accounting Standards Board website

In many countries, stock exchange listing requirements or national securities legislation permits foreign companies that issue securities in those countries to prepare their consolidated financial statements using IFRSs. The principal capital markets in this category are Australia, Germany and the United Kingdom. From 1 January 2005, all publicly listed companies in the European Union will be required to prepare their financial statements in conformity with IFRSs. From the same date, Australia will adopt IFRSs as its national accounting standards. New Zealand will require IFRSs from 2007.

Certain countries do not permit companies to use IFRSs without a reconciliation to domestic generally accepted accounting principles (GAAP). Most notable among these countries are Canada, Japan and the United States. In the US the Securities and Exchange Commission has indicated . . . strong support for moves to achieve convergence between US GAAP and IFRSs.

Management Responsibility and the Demand for Auditing

Exeter's owners and managers were well aware of the details of U.S. GAAP, but they were still misled. Although the measurement rules that Maxidrive had used to produce its financial statements were consistent with GAAP, the underlying figures were fictitious. Who was responsible for the accuracy of the numbers in Maxidrive's financial statements?

Primary responsibility for the information in the financial statements lies with management, represented by the highest officer of the company and the highest financial officer. Companys take three important steps to assure investors that the company's records are accurate: (1) they maintain a system of controls over both the records and the assets of the company, (2) they hire outside independent auditors to verify the fairness of the financial statements, and (3) they form a committee of the board of directors to oversee the integrity of these other two safeguards. These responsibilities are often reiterated in a formal **report of management** or **management certification** in the annual report. These three safeguards and a management certification are required for companies with publicly traded stock. These safeguards failed in Maxidrive's case. Managers of companies that prepare fraudulent financial statements are subject to criminal and civil penalties.

Learning Objective 3
Distinguish the roles of managers and auditors in the accounting communication process.

Three steps to ensure the accuracy of records:

System of Controls   External Auditors   Board of Directors

The role of the independent auditor is described in more detail in the **audit report** in Exhibit 1.9 (report of independent accountants or independent registered public acounting firm). The audit report describes the auditor's opinion of the fairness of the financial statements and the evidence gathered to support that opinion. An accountant may be licensed as a **certified public accountant,** or **CPA,** only on completion of requirements specified by each state. Only a licensed CPA can issue an audit report. In this role, accountants are known as independent CPAs (or independent accountants) because they have certain responsibilities that extend to the general public as well as to the specific business that pays for this service.

EXHIBIT 1.9

Report of Independent Accountants

Report of Independent Accountants to the Stockholders and Board of Directors of Maxidrive Corp.

We have audited the accompanying balance sheet of Maxidrive Corp. as of December 31, 2006, and the related statements of income, retained earnings, and cash flows for the period ended December 31, 2006. These financial statements are the responsibility of the Company's management. Our responsibility is to express an opinion on these financial statements based on our audits.

We conducted our audits in accordance with generally accepted auditing standards in the United States of America. Those standards require that we plan and perform the audit to obtain reasonable assurance about whether the financial statements are free of material misstatement. An audit includes examining, on a test basis, evidence supporting the amounts and disclosures in the financial statements. An audit also includes assessing the accounting principles used and significant estimates made by management, as well as evaluating the overall financial statement presentation. We believe that our audits provide a reasonable basis for our opinion.

In our opinion, the financial statements referred to above present fairly, in all material respects, the financial position of Maxidrive Corp. at December 31, 2006, and the results of its operations and its cash flows for the year ended December 31, 2006, in conformity with generally accepted accounting principles in the United States of America.

Smith and Walker, CPAs

Smith and Walker, CPAs

An **AUDIT** is an examination of the financial reports to ensure that they represent what they claim and conform with GAAP.

The **PUBLIC COMPANY ACCOUNTING OVERSIGHT BOARD** (PCAOB) is the private sector body given the primary responsibility to issue detailed auditing standards.

Learning Objective 4
Appreciate the importance of ethics, reputation, and legal liability in accounting.

An audit involves the examination of the financial reports (prepared by the management of the entity) to ensure that they represent what they claim to and conform with generally accepted accounting principles (GAAP). In performing an audit, the independent CPA examines the underlying transactions and the accounting methods used to account for these transactions. Because of the enormous number of transactions involving a major enterprise such as General Motors, the CPA does not examine each of these transactions. Rather, professional approaches are used to ascertain beyond reasonable doubt that transactions were measured and reported properly. The Public Company Accounting Oversight Board (PCAOB), in consultation with the SEC, sets standards for these tests for the audits of public companies.[9]

Ethics, Reputation, and Legal Liability

If financial statements are to be of any value to decision makers, users must have confidence in the fairness of the information they present. Users will have greater confidence in the information if they know that the people who audited the statements were required to meet professional standards of ethics and competence.

The American Institute of Certified Public Accountants (AICPA) requires all of its members to adhere to a professional code of ethics and professional auditing standards, and auditors of public companies must register with and comply with standards set by the PCAOB. Failure to comply with the rules of conduct can result in serious professional penalties. CPAs' reputations for honesty and competence are their most important assets. The potential economic effects of damage to reputation, malpractice liability, and potential fines provide even stronger incentives to abide by professional standards.

In case of malpractice, the independent CPA may be held liable for losses suffered by those who relied on the statements the CPA examined. As a result of the fraud, Maxidrive filed for bankruptcy and will likely be sold in an attempt to pay off creditors. In a civil lawsuit, Exeter Investors and American Bank claimed losses of $16.5 million and $9 million, respectively, charging that the officers of Maxidrive had "perpetrated a massive fraud" and the auditors had "overlooked the errors" in the audit. Exeter and American Bank also have asked for punitive damages for gross negligence. In addition, the president and the chief financial officer of Maxidrive were convicted by a federal jury on three counts of criminal securities fraud for which they were fined and imprisoned.

EPILOGUE

Although financial statement fraud is a fairly rare event, the misrepresentations in Maxidrive's statements aptly illustrate the importance of fairly presented financial statements to investors and creditors. They also indicate the crucial importance of the public accounting profession in ensuring the integrity of the financial reporting system. The recent Enron and WorldCom debacles have brought the importance of these issues to the attention of the general public.

As noted at the beginning of this chapter, Maxidrive is not a real company but is based on a real company that perpetrated a similar fraud. (The focus companies and contrasting examples in the remaining chapters are *real* companies.) Maxidrive is loosely based on the infamous fraud at MiniScribe, a real disk drive manufacturer. The size of the real fraud, however, was more than 10 times as great as that in the fictional case, as were the losses incurred and the damages claimed in the lawsuits that followed. (Many of the numbers in Maxidrive's financial statements are simply one-tenth the amounts presented in MiniScribe's fraudulent statements.) The nature of the fraud also was quite similar. At MiniScribe, sales revenue was overstated by transferring nonexistent inventory between two facilities and creating phony documents to make it look as though the inventory was transferred to customers. MiniScribe even packaged

---

[9]For a detailed description of the auditor's role, see, for example, William R. Kinney, *Information Quality Assurance and Internal Control for Management Decision Making* (New York: McGraw-Hill/Irwin, 2000).

bricks as finished products, shipped them to distributors, and counted them as sold. Cost of goods sold was understated by activities such as counting scrap parts and damaged drives as usable inventory. MiniScribe managers even broke into the auditors' locked trunks to change numbers on their audit papers.

As a consequence, MiniScribe reported net income of $31 million, which was subsequently shown to be $9 million. MiniScribe's investors and creditors filed lawsuits claiming more than $1 billion in damages. Actual damages in the hundreds of millions were paid. Both the chairman and the chief financial officer of MiniScribe were convicted of federal securities and wire fraud charges and sentenced to jail. Although most managers and owners act in an honest and responsible fashion, this incident, and the much larger frauds at Enron and WorldCom, are stark reminders of the economic consequences of lack of fair presentation in financial reports. Both companies were forced into bankruptcy when their fraudulent financial reporting practices were brought to light. Penalties against their audit firm, Arthur Andersen, also led to its bankruptcy and dissolution. A sampling of firms that have recently been involved in financial statement misrepresentations follows:

Enron	Zerox	Homestore.com
WorldCom	Rite-Aid	Dynegy
Adelphia	Aurora Foods	Fannie Mae
Global Crossing	Halliburton	Freddie Mac
Computer Associates	Parmalat	Qwest Communications
Tyco	Nortel	Gerber Scientific
HealthSouth	Goodyear	Stanley Works
McKesson	Cardinal Health	AIG

DEMONSTRATION **CASE**

At the end of most chapters, one or more demonstration cases are presented. These cases provide an overview of the primary issues discussed in the chapter. Each demonstration case is followed by a recommended solution. You should read the case carefully and then prepare your own solution before you study the recommended solution. This self-evaluation is highly recommended. The introductory case presented here reviews the elements reported on the income statement and balance sheet and how the elements within the statements are related.

The stores owned and franchised by Krispy Kreme Donuts can each make between 4,000 and 10,000 donuts per day. This capacity and the fanatical loyalty of its customers have made this expanding company a great success. Following is a list of the financial statement items and amounts adapted from a recent Krispy Kreme Donuts Inc. income statement and balance sheet. The numbers are presented in thousands of dollars for the year ended February 1, 2004.

Krispy Kreme Donuts

Accounts payable	$ 19,107	Other liabilities	141,294
Accounts receivable	45,363	Pretax income	94,677
Cash	21,029	Property and equipment	284,716
Contributed capital	294,477	Retained earnings	157,730
General and administrative		Sales revenues	665,592
expenses	36,912	Total assets	660,664
Income tax expense	37,590	Total expenses	570,915
Inventories	28,864	Total liabilities	208,457
Net income	57,087	Total liabilities and	
Notes payable	48,056	stockholders' equity	660,664
Operating expenses	507,396	Total revenues	665,592
Other assets	280,692	Total stockholders' equity	452,207
Other expenses	26,607		

Required:

1. Prepare a balance sheet and an income statement for the year following the formats in Exhibits 1.2 and 1.3.

2. Specify what information these two statements provide.

3. Indicate the other two statements that would be included in its annual report.

4. Suggest why Krispy Kreme would voluntarily subject its statements to an independent audit.

SUGGESTED SOLUTION

1.

KRISPY KREME DONUTS INC. Balance Sheet At February 1, 2004 (in thousands of dollars)	
Assets	
Cash	$ 21,029
Accounts receivable	45,363
Inventories	28,864
Property and equipment	284,716
Other assets	280,692
Total assets	$660,664
Liabilities	
Accounts payable	$ 19,107
Notes payable	48,056
Other liabilities	141,294
Total liabilities	208,457
Stockholders' Equity	
Contributed capital	294,477
Retained earnings	157,730
Total stockholders' equity	452,207
Total liabilities and stockholders' equity	$660,664

KRISPY KREME DONUTS INC. Income Statement For the Year Ended February 1, 2004 (in thousands of dollars)	
Revenues	
Sales revenues	$665,592
Total revenues	$665,592
Expenses	
Operating expenses	507,396
General and administrative expenses	36,912
Other expenses	26,607
Total expenses	570,915
Pretax income	94,677
Income tax expense	37,590
Net income	$ 57,087

2. The balance sheet reports the amount of assets, liabilities, and stockholders' equity of an accounting entity at a point in time. The income statement reports the accountant's primary measure of performance of a business, revenues less expenses, during the accounting period.

3. Krispy Kreme would also present a statement of retained earnings and a statement of cash flows.

4. Users will have greater confidence in the accuracy of financial statement information if they know that the people who audited the statements were required to meet professional standards of ethics and competence.

Chapter Supplement A

Types of Business Entities

This textbook emphasizes **accounting for profit-making business entities.** The three main types of business entities are sole proprietorship, partnership, and corporation. A **sole proprietorship** is an unincorporated business owned by one person; it usually is small in size and is common in the service, retailing, and farming industries. Often the owner is the manager. Legally, the business and the owner are not separate entities. Accounting views the business as a separate entity, however, that must be accounted for separately from its owner.

A **partnership** is an unincorporated business owned by two or more persons known as **partners.** Some partnerships are large in size (e.g., international public accounting firms and law firms). The agreements between the owners are specified in a partnership contract. This contract deals with matters such as division of income each reporting period and distribution of resources of the business on termination of its operations. A partnership is not legally separate from its owners. Legally, each partner in a general partnership is responsible for the debts of the business (each general partner has **unlimited liability**). The partnership, however, is a separate business entity to be accounted for separately from its several owners.

A **corporation** is a business incorporated under the laws of a particular state. The owners are called **stockholders** or **shareholders.** Ownership is represented by shares of capital stock that usually can be bought and sold freely. When the organizers file an approved application for incorporation, the state issues a charter. This charter gives the corporation the right to operate as a separate legal entity, separate and apart from its owners. The stockholders enjoy **limited liability.** Stockholders are liable for the corporation's debts only to the extent of their investments. The corporate charter specifies the types and amounts of capital stock that can be issued. Most states require a minimum of two or three stockholders and a minimum amount of resources to be contributed at the time of organization. The stockholders elect a governing board of directors, which in turn employs managers and exercises general supervision of the corporation. Accounting also views the corporation as a separate business entity that must be accounted for separately from its owners.

In terms of economic importance, the corporation is the dominant form of business organization in the United States. This dominance is caused by the many advantages of the corporate form: (1) limited liability for the stockholders, (2) continuity of life, (3) ease in transferring ownership (stock), and (4) opportunities to raise large amounts of money by selling shares to a large number of people. The primary disadvantage of a corporation is that its income may be subject to double taxation (it is taxed when it is earned and again when it is distributed to stockholders as dividends). In this textbook, we emphasize the corporate form of business. Nevertheless, the accounting concepts and procedures that we discuss also apply to other types of businesses.

Chapter Supplement B

Employment in the Accounting Profession Today

Since 1900, accounting has attained the stature of professions such as law, medicine, engineering, and architecture. As with all recognized professions, accounting is subject to professional competence requirements, is dedicated to service to the public, requires a high level of academic study, and rests on a common body of knowledge. An accountant may be licensed as a certified public accountant, or CPA. This designation is granted only on completion of requirements specified by the state that issues the license. Although CPA requirements vary among states, they include a college degree with a specified number of accounting courses, good character, one to five years of professional experience, and successful completion of a professional examination. The CPA examination is prepared by the American Institute of Certified Public Accountants.

Accountants (including CPAs) commonly are engaged in professional practice or are employed by businesses, government entities, nonprofit organizations, and so on. Accountants employed in these activities may take and pass a professional examination to become a certified management accountant, or CMA (the CMA examination is administered by the Institute of Management Accountants) or a certified internal auditor, or CIA (the CIA examination is administered by the Institute of Internal Auditors).

Practice of Public Accounting

Although an individual may practice public accounting, usually two or more individuals organize an accounting firm in the form of a partnership (in many cases, a limited liability partnership, or LLP). Accounting firms vary in size from a one-person office, to regional firms, to the Big Four firms (Deloitte & Touche, Ernst & Young, KPMG, and PricewaterhouseCoopers), which have hundreds of offices located worldwide. Accounting firms usually render three types of services: audit or assurance services, management consulting services, and tax services.

Audit or Assurance Services

Audit or assurance services are independent professional services that improve the quality of information, or its context, for decision makers. The most important assurance service performed by the CPA in public practice is financial statement auditing. The purpose of an audit is to lend credibility to the financial reports, that is, to ensure that they fairly represent what they claim. An audit involves an examination of the financial reports (prepared by the management of the entity) to ensure that they conform with GAAP. Other areas of assurance services include electronic commerce integrity and security and information systems reliability.

Management Consulting Services

Many independent CPA firms offer management consulting services. These services usually are accounting based and encompass such activities as the design and installation of accounting, data processing, and profit-planning and control (budget) systems; financial advice; forecasting; inventory controls; cost-effectiveness studies; and operational analysis. To maintain their independence, CPAs are prohibited from performing certain consulting services for the public companies that they audit.

Tax Services

CPAs in public practice usually provide income tax services to their clients. These services include both tax planning as a part of the decision-making process and the determination of the income tax liability (reported on the annual income tax return). Because of the increasing complexity of state and federal tax laws, a high level of competence is required, which CPAs specializing in taxation can provide. The CPA's involvement in tax planning often is quite significant. Most major business decisions have significant tax impacts; in fact, tax-planning considerations often govern certain business decisions.

Employment by Organizations

Many accountants, including CPAs, CMAs, and CIAs, are employed by profit-making and nonprofit organizations. An organization, depending on its size and complexity, may employ from a few to hundreds of accountants. In a business enterprise, the chief financial officer (usually a vice president or controller) is a member of the management team. This responsibility usually entails a wide range of management, financial, and accounting duties.

In a business entity, accountants typically are engaged in a wide variety of activities, such as general management, general accounting, cost accounting, profit planning and control (budgeting), internal auditing, and computerized data processing. A primary function of the accountants in organizations is to provide data that are useful for internal managerial decision making and for controlling operations. The functions of external reporting, tax planning, control of assets, and a host of related responsibilities normally are also performed by accountants in industry.

Employment in the Public and Not-for-Profit Sector

The vast and complex operations of governmental units, from the local to the international level, create a need for accountants. The same holds true for other not-for-profit organizations such as hospitals and universities. Accountants employed in the public and not-for-profit sector perform functions similar to those performed by their counterparts in private organizations. The Government Accountability Office (GAO) and the regulatory agencies, such as the SEC and Federal Communications Commission (FCC), also use the services of accountants in carrying out their regulatory duties.

CHAPTER **TAKE-AWAYS**

1. **Recognize the information conveyed in each of the four basic financial statements and the way that it is used by different decision makers (investors, creditors, and managers).   p. 5**

   The **balance sheet** is a statement of financial position that reports dollar amounts for the assets, liabilities, and stockholders' equity at a specific point in time.

   The **income statement** is a statement of operations that reports revenues, expenses, and net income for a stated period of time.

   The **statement of retained earnings** explains changes to the retained earnings balance that occurred during the reporting period.

   The **statement of cash flows** reports inflows and outflows of cash for a stated period of time.

   The statements are used by investors and creditors to evaluate different aspects of the firm's financial position and performance.

2. **Identify the role of generally accepted accounting principles (GAAP) in determining the content of financial statements.   p. 21**

   GAAP are the measurement rules used to develop the information in financial statements. Knowledge of GAAP is necessary for accurate interpretation of the numbers in financial statements.

3. **Distinguish the roles of managers and auditors in the accounting communication process p. 23**

   Management has primary responsibility for the accuracy of a company's financial information. Auditors are responsible for expressing an opinion on the fairness of the financial statement presentations based on their examination of the reports and records of the company.

4. **Appreciate the importance of ethics, reputation, and legal liability in accounting.   p. 24**

   Users will have confidence in the accuracy of financial statement numbers only if the people associated with their preparation and audit have reputations for ethical behavior and competence. Management and auditors can also be held legally liable for fraudulent financial statements and malpractice.

   In this chapter, we studied the basic financial statements that communicate financial information to external users. Chapters 2, 3, and 4 provide a more detailed look at financial statements and examine how to translate data about business transactions into these statements. Learning how to translate back and forth between business transactions and financial statements is the key to using financial statements in planning and decision making. Chapter 2 begins our discussion of the way that the accounting function collects data about business transactions and processes the data to provide periodic financial statements, with emphasis on the balance sheet. To accomplish this purpose, Chapter 2 discusses key accounting concepts, the accounting model, transaction analysis, and analytical tools. We examine typical business activities of an actual service-oriented company to demonstrate the concepts in Chapters 2, 3, and 4.

FINDING **FINANCIAL INFORMATION**

Balance Sheet
Assets = Liabilities + Stockholders' Equity

Income Statement
  Revenues
− Expenses
  ─────────
  Net Income

Statement of Retained Earnings
  Retained Earnings, beginning of the period
+ Net Income
− Dividends
  ─────────────────────────────────
  Retained Earnings, end of the period

Statement of Cash Flows
+/−   Cash Flow from Operating Activities
+/−   Cash Flow from Investing Activities
+/−   Cash Flow from Financing Activities
  ─────────────────────────────────
      Net Change in Cash

KEY TERMS

Accounting p. 4
Accounting Entity p. 7
Accounting Period p. 10
Audit p. 24
Balance Sheet (Statement of
    Financial Position) p. 7
Basic Accounting Equation
    (Balance Sheet Equation) p. 8

Financial Accounting Standards
    Board (FASB) p. 21
Generally Accepted Accounting
    Principles (GAAP) p. 21
Income Statement (Statement of
    Income, Statement of Earnings, or
    Statement of Operations) p. 10
Notes (Footnotes) p. 17

Public Company Accounting
    Oversight Board (PCAOB)
    p. 24
Securities and Exchange
    Commission (SEC) p. 21
Statement of Cash Flows p. 14
Statement of Retained
    Earnings p. 13

QUESTIONS

1. Define *accounting*.
2. Briefly distinguish financial accounting from managerial accounting.
3. The accounting process generates financial reports for both internal and external users. Identify some of the groups of users.
4. Briefly distinguish investors from creditors.
5. What is an accounting entity? Why is a business treated as a separate entity for accounting purposes?
6. Complete the following:

Name of Statement	Alternative Title
a. Income statement	*a.* _____
b. Balance sheet	*b.* _____
c. Audit report	*c.* _____

7. What information should be included in the heading of each of the four primary financial statements?
8. What are the purposes of (*a*) the income statement, (*b*) the balance sheet, (*c*) the statement of cash flows, and (*d*) the statement of retained earnings?
9. Explain why the income statement and the statement of cash flows are dated "For the Year Ended December 31, 2008," whereas the balance sheet is dated "At December 31, 2008."
10. Briefly explain the importance of assets and liabilities to the decisions of investors and creditors.
11. Briefly define the following: *net income, net loss,* and *breakeven.*
12. Explain the accounting equation for the income statement. What are the three major items reported on the income statement?
13. Explain the accounting equation for the balance sheet. Define the three major components reported on the balance sheet.
14. Explain the accounting equation for the statement of cash flows. Explain the three major components reported on the statement.
15. Explain the accounting equation for the statement of retained earnings. Explain the four major items reported on the statement of retained earnings.
16. Financial statements discussed in this chapter are aimed at *external* users. Briefly explain how a company's *internal* managers in different functional areas (e.g., marketing, purchasing, human resources) might use financial statement information from their own and other companies.
17. Briefly describe the way that accounting measurement rules (generally accepted accounting principles) are determined in the United States.
18. Briefly explain the responsibility of company management and the independent auditors in the accounting communication process.
19. (Supplement A) Briefly differentiate between a sole proprietorship, a partnership, and a corporation.
20. (Supplement B) List and briefly explain the three primary services that CPAs in public practice provide.

MULTIPLE-**CHOICE QUESTIONS**

1. Which of the following is *not* one of the four basic financial statements?
   - a. balance sheet
   - b. audit report
   - c. income statement
   - d. statement of cash flows
2. As stated in the audit report, or *Report of Independent Accountants*, the primary responsibility for a company's financial statements lies with
   - a. the owners of the company
   - b. independent financial analysts
   - c. the auditors
   - d. the company's management
3. Which of the following is true?
   - a. FASB creates SEC.
   - b. GAAP creates FASB.
   - c. SEC creates AICPA.
   - d. FASB creates GAAP.
4. Which of the following regarding retained earnings is false?
   - a. Retained earnings is increased by net income and decreased by a net loss.
   - b. Retained earnings is a component of stockholders' equity on the balance sheet.
   - c. Retained earnings is an asset on the balance sheet.
   - d. Retained earnings represents earnings not distributed to stockholders in the form of dividends.
5. Which of the following is *not* one of the four items required to be shown in the heading of a financial statement?
   - a. the financial statement preparer's name
   - b. the title of the financial statement
   - c. the unit of measure in the financial statement
   - d. the name of the business entity
6. How many of the following statements regarding the statement of cash flows is true?
   - ■ The statement of cash flows separates cash inflows and outflows into three major categories: operations, investing, and financing.
   - ■ The ending cash balance shown on the statement of cash flows must agree with the amount shown on the balance sheet for the same fiscal period.
   - ■ The total increase or decrease in cash shown on the statement of cash flows must agree with the "bottom line" (net income or net loss) reported on the income statement.
   - a. none
   - b. one
   - c. two
   - d. three
7. Which of the following is *not* a typical footnote included in an annual report?
   - a. A note describing the auditor's opinion of the management's past and future financial planning for the business
   - b. A note providing more detail about a specific item shown in the financial statements
   - c. A note describing the accounting rules applied in the financial statements
   - d. A note describing financial disclosures about items not appearing in the financial statements
8. Which of the following is true regarding the income statement?
   - a. The income statement is sometimes called the *statement of operations*.
   - b. The income statement reports revenues, expenses, and liabilities.
   - c. The income statement reports only revenue for which cash was received at the point of sale.
   - d. The income statement reports the financial position of a business at a particular point in time.
9. Which of the following is false regarding the balance sheet?
   - a. The accounts shown on a balance sheet represent the basic accounting equation for a particular business entity.
   - b. The retained earnings balance shown on the balance sheet must agree with the ending retained earnings balance shown on the statement of retained earnings.
   - c. The balance sheet reports the changes in specific account balances over a period of time.
   - d. The balance sheet reports the amount of assets, liabilities, and stockholders' equity of an accounting entity at a point in time.
10. Which of the following regarding GAAP is true?
    - a. U.S. GAAP is the body of accounting knowledge followed by all countries in the world.
    - b. Changes in GAAP can affect the interests of managers and stockholders.
    - c. GAAP is the abbreviation for generally accepted auditing procedures.
    - d. Changes to GAAP must be approved by the Senate Finance Committee.

To practice with more multiple choice questions, go to the text website **www.mhhe.com/libby5e** or the Topic Tackler DVD for use with this text.

MINI-**EXERCISES**

Available with McGraw-Hill's Homework Manager

M1-1
LO1

Matching Elements with Financial Statements

Match each element with its financial statement by entering the appropriate letter in the space provided.

Element	Financial Statement
___ (1) Expenses	A. Balance sheet
___ (2) Cash flow from investing activities	B. Income statement
___ (3) Assets	C. Statement of retained earnings
___ (4) Dividends	D. Statement of cash flows
___ (5) Revenues	
___ (6) Cash flow from operating activities	
___ (7) Liabilities	
___ (8) Cash flow from financing activities	

M1-2
LO1

Matching Financial Statement Items to Financial Statement Categories

Mark each item in the following list as an asset (A), liability (L), or stockholders' equity (SE) that would appear on the balance sheet or a revenue (R) or expense (E) that would appear on the income statement.

___ (1) Retained earnings	___ (6) Inventories
___ (2) Accounts receivable	___ (7) Interest expense
___ (3) Sales revenue	___ (8) Accounts payable
___ (4) Property, plant, and equipment	___ (9) Land
___ (5) Cost of goods sold expense	

M1-3
LO2, 3

Identifying Important Accounting Abbreviations

The following is a list of important abbreviations used in the chapter. These abbreviations also are used widely in business. For each abbreviation, give the full designation. The first one is an example.

Abbreviation	Full Designation
(1) CPA	Certified Public Accountant
(2) GAAP	_____
(3) CMA	_____
(4) AICPA	_____
(5) SEC	_____
(6) FASB	_____

EXERCISES

Matching Definitions with Terms or Abbreviations

E1-1
LO1, 2, 3

Match each definition with its related term or abbreviation by entering the appropriate letter in the space provided.

Term or Abbreviation	Definition
___ (1) SEC	A. A system that collects and processes financial information about an organization and reports that information to decision makers.
___ (2) Audit	
___ (3) Sole proprietorship	
___ (4) Corporation	B. Measurement of information about an entity in the monetary unit—dollars or other national currency.
___ (5) Accounting	
___ (6) Accounting entity	C. An unincorporated business owned by two or more persons.
___ (7) Audit report	D. The organization for which financial data are to be collected (separate and distinct from its owners).
___ (8) Cost principle	
___ (9) Partnership	E. An incorporated entity that issues shares of stock as evidence of ownership.
___ (10) FASB	
___ (11) CPA	F. Initial recording of financial statement elements at acquisition cost.
___ (12) Unit of measure	
___ (13) GAAP	G. An examination of the financial reports to ensure that they represent what they claim and conform with generally accepted accounting principles.
___ (14) Publicly traded	
	H. Certified public accountant.
	I. An unincorporated business owned by one person.
	J. A report that describes the auditor's opinion of the fairness of the financial statement presentations and the evidence gathered to support that opinion.
	K. Securities and Exchange Commission.
	L. Financial Accounting Standards Board.
	M. A company with stock that can be bought and sold by investors on established stock exchanges.
	N. Generally accepted accounting principles.

Matching Financial Statement Items to Financial Statement Categories

E1-2
LO1
Procter & Gamble

According to its annual report, "P&G's more than 250 brands include Pampers, Tide, Ariel, Always, Whisper, Pantene, Bounty, Pringles, Folgers, Charmin, Downy, Lenor, Iams, Olay, Crest, Vicks and Actonel." The following are items taken from its recent balance sheet and income statement. Note that different companies use slightly different titles for the same item. Mark each item in the following list as an asset (A), liability (L), or stockholders' equity (SE) that would appear on the balance sheet or a revenue (R) or expense (E) that would appear on the income statement.

___ (1)	Accounts payable	___ (9)	Land
___ (2)	Accounts receivable	___ (10)	Marketing, administrative, and other operating expenses
___ (3)	Cash and cash equivalents		
___ (4)	Cost of products sold	___ (11)	Long-term debt
___ (5)	Property, plant, and equipment	___ (12)	Net sales
___ (6)	Income taxes	___ (13)	Notes payable
___ (7)	Interest expense	___ (14)	Retained earnings
___ (8)	Inventories	___ (15)	Taxes payable

E1-3
LO1
Tootsie Roll

Matching Financial Statement Items to Financial Statement Categories

Tootsie Roll Industries is engaged in the manufacture and sale of candy. Major products include Tootsie Roll, Tootsie Roll Pops, Tootsie Pop Drops, Tootsie Flavor Rolls, Charms, and Blow-Pop lollipops. The following items were listed on Tootsie Roll's recent income statement and balance sheet. Mark each item from the balance sheet as an asset (A), liability (L), or shareholders' equity (SE) and each item from the income statement as a revenue (R) or expense (E).

___	(1) Accounts payable	___	(10) Buildings
___	(2) Accounts receivable	___	(11) Cash and cash equivalents
___	(3) Cost of goods sold	___	(12) Land
___	(4) Distribution and warehousing costs	___	(13) Machinery and equipment
___	(5) Dividends payable	___	(14) Marketing, selling, and advertising
___	(6) General and administrative	___	(15) Net sales
___	(7) Income taxes payable	___	(16) Notes payable to banks
___	(8) Inventories	___	(17) Provision for income taxes*
___	(9) Investments (in other companies)	___	(18) Retained earnings

E1-4
LO1
Toyota Motor Co.

Preparing a Balance Sheet

Toyota Motor Corporation of Japan is a leading international manufacturer of automobiles and a pioneer in developing hybrid and fuel cell vehicles. As a Japanese company, it follows Japanese GAAP and reports its financial statements in billions of yen (the sign for yen is ¥). Its recent balance sheet contained the following items (in billions). Prepare a balance sheet as of March 31, 2004, solving for the missing amount. (*Hint*: Exhibit 1.2 in the chapter provides a good model for completing this exercise.)

Cash and cash equivalents	¥ 1,592
Contributed capital	891
Accounts payable and other current liabilities	7,054
Inventories	1,026
Investments	1,652
Long-term debt	4,138
Net property, plant, and equipment	5,204
Other assets	9,203
Other liabilities	1,525
Retained earnings	6,545
Total assets	20,153
Total liabilities and stockholders' equity	?
Trade accounts, notes, and other receivables	1,476

E1-5
LO1

Completing a Balance Sheet and Inferring Net Income

Terry Lloyd and Joan Lopez organized Read More Store as a corporation; each contributed $50,000 cash to start the business and received 4,000 shares of common stock. The store completed its first year of operations on December 31, 2006. On that date, the following financial items for the year were determined: December 31, 2006, cash on hand and in the bank, $48,900; December 31, 2006, amounts due from customers from sales of books, $25,000; unused portion of store and office equipment, $49,000; December 31, 2006, amounts owed to publishers for books purchased, $7,000; one-year note payable to a local bank for $3,000. No dividends were declared or paid to the stockholders during the year.

Required:
1. Complete the following balance sheet as of the end of 2006.
2. What was the amount of net income for the year? (*Hint*: Use the retained earnings equation [Beginning Retained Earnings + Net Income − Dividends = Ending Retained Earnings] to solve for net income.)

_____

_____

_____

(continued on next page)

---

*In the United States, "provision for income taxes" is most often used as a synonym for "income tax expense."

Assets		Liabilities	
Cash	$ ____	Accounts payable	$ ____
Accounts receivable	____	Note payable	____
Store and office equipment	____	Interest payable	120
		Total liabilities	$ ____
		Stockholders' Equity	
		Contributed capital	$ ____
		Retained earnings	12,780
		Total stockholders' equity	____
		Total liabilities and	
Total assets	$ ____	stockholders' equity	$ ____

Analyzing Revenues and Expenses and Preparing an Income Statement

Assume that you are the owner of The University Shop, which specializes in items that interest students. At the end of January 2006, you find (for January only) this information:

a. Sales, per the cash register tapes, of $119,000, plus one sale on credit (a special situation) of $1,000.
b. With the help of a friend (who majored in accounting), you determined that all of the goods sold during January had cost $40,000 to purchase.
c. During the month, according to the checkbook, you paid $38,000 for salaries, rent, supplies, advertising, and other expenses; however, you have not yet paid the $600 monthly utilities for January on the store and fixtures.

Required:
On the basis of the data given (disregard income taxes), what was the amount of net income for January? Show computations. (*Hint:* A convenient form to use has the following major side captions: Revenue from Sales, Expenses, and the difference—Net Income.)

E1-6
LO1

Preparing an Income Statement and Inferring Missing Values

Wal-Mart Stores, Inc., is the largest retail chain in the United States, operating more than 3,000 stores. Its recent quarterly income statement contained the following items (in millions). Solve for the missing amounts and prepare an income statement for the quarter ended October 31, 2004. (*Hint:* First order the items as they would appear on the income statement and then solve for the missing values. Exhibit 1.3 in the chapter provides a good model for completing this exercise.)

E1-7
LO1
Wal-Mart

Cost of sales	$ 52,567
Interest costs	241
Net income	?
Net sales	68,520
Operating, selling, and general and administrative expenses	12,910
Provision for income taxes*	1,207
Rental and other income	741
Total costs and expenses	?
Total revenues	?
Pretax income	?

Analyzing Revenues and Expenses and Completing an Income Statement

Home Realty, Incorporated, has been operating for three years and is owned by three investors. J. Doe owns 60 percent of the total outstanding stock of 9,000 shares and is the managing executive in

E1-8
LO1

---

*In the United States, "provision for income taxes" is a common synonym for "income tax expense."

charge. On December 31, 2008, the following financial items for the entire year were determined: commissions earned and collected in cash, $150,000, plus $16,000 uncollected; rental service fees earned and collected, $20,000; salaries expense paid, $62,000; commissions expense paid, $35,000; payroll taxes paid, $2,500; rent paid, $2,200 (not including December rent yet to be paid); utilities expense paid, $1,600; promotion and advertising paid, $8,000; income taxes paid, $18,500; and miscellaneous expenses paid, $500. There were no other unpaid expenses at December 31. Also during the year, the company paid the owners "out-of-profit" cash dividends amounting to $12,000. Complete the following income statement:

Revenues		
Commissions earned	$ ____	
Rental service fees	____	
Total revenues		$ ____
Expenses		
Salaries expense	$ ____	
Commission expense	____	
Payroll tax expense	____	
Rent expense	____	
Utilities expense	____	
Promotion and advertising expense	____	
Miscellaneous expenses	____	
Total expenses (excluding income taxes)	____	
Pretax income		$ ____
Income tax expense		____
Net income		$55,500

E1-9
LO1

Inferring Values Using the Income Statement and Balance Sheet Equations

Review the chapter explanations of the income statement and the balance sheet equations. Apply these equations in each independent case to compute the two missing amounts for each case. Assume that it is the end of 2006, the first full year of operations for the company. (*Hint:* Organize the listed items as they are presented in the balance sheet and income statement equations and then compute the missing amounts.)

Independent Cases	Total Revenues	Total Expenses	Net Income (Loss)	Total Assets	Total Liabilities	Stockholders' Equity
A	$100,000	$75,000	$	$150,000	$70,000	$
B		80,000	12,000	112,000		60,000
C	80,000	85,000		104,000	26,000	
D	50,000		13,000		22,000	77,000
E	81,000	6,000			73,000	28,000

E1-10
LO1

Preparing an Income Statement and Balance Sheet

Clay Corporation was organized by five individuals on January 1, 2006. At the end of January 2006, the following monthly financial data are available:

Total revenues	$150,000
Total expenses (excluding income taxes)	100,000
Income tax expense (all unpaid as of January 31)	15,000
Cash balance, January 31, 2006	20,000
Receivables from customers (all considered collectible)	25,000
Merchandise inventory (by inventory count at cost)	42,000

Payables to suppliers for merchandise purchased from them
(will be paid during February 2006)   11,000
Contributed capital (2,600 shares)   26,000
No dividends were declared or paid during 2006.

Required:
Complete the following two statements:

CLAY CORPORATION
Income Statement
For the Month of January 2006

Total revenues	$ ____
Less: Total expenses (excluding income tax)	____
Pretax income	____
Less: Income tax expense	____
Net income	$ ____

CLAY CORPORATION
Balance Sheet
At January 31, 2006

Assets	
Cash	$ ____
Receivables from customers	____
Merchandise inventory	____
Total assets	$ ____
Liabilities	
Payables to suppliers	$ ____
Income taxes payable	____
Total liabilities	____
Stockholders' equity	
Contributed capital	____
Retained earnings	____
Total stockholders' equity	____
Total liabilities and stockholders' equity	$ ____

Preparing a Statement of Retained Earnings

E1-11
LO1

Stone Culture Corporation was organized on January 1, 2005. For its first two years of operations, it reported the following:

Net income for 2005	$ 36,000
Net income for 2006	45,000
Dividends for 2005	15,000
Dividends for 2006	20,000
Total assets at the end of 2005	125,000
Total assets at the end of 2006	242,000

Required:
On the basis of the data given, prepare a statement of retained earnings for 2006. Show computations.

E1-12   **Analyzing and Interpreting an Income Statement and Price/Earnings Ratio**

LO1

Pest Away Corporation was organized by three individuals on January 1, 2006, to provide insect extermination services. At the end of 2006, the following income statement was prepared:

PEST AWAY CORPORATION
Income Statement
For the Year Ended December 31, 2006

Revenues		
Service revenue (cash)	$192,000	
Service revenue (credit)	24,000	
Total revenues		$216,000
Expenses		
Salaries expense	$ 76,000	
Rent expense	21,000	
Utilities expense	12,000	
Advertising expense	14,000	
Supplies expense	25,000	
Interest expense	8,000	
Total expenses		156,000
Pretax income		$ 60,000
Income tax expense		21,000
Net income		$ 39,000

Required:

1. What was the average monthly revenue amount?
2. What was the monthly rent amount?
3. Explain why supplies are reported as an expense.
4. Explain why interest is reported as an expense.
5. Can you determine how much cash the company had on December 31, 2006? Explain.
6. If the company had a market value of $468,000, what is its price/earnings ratio?

E1-13   **Focus on Cash Flows: Matching Cash Flow Statement Items to Categories**

LO1

The following items were taken from a recent cash flow statement. Note that different companies use slightly different titles for the same item. Without referring to Exhibit 1.5, mark each item in the list as a cash flow from operating activities (O), investing activities (I), or financing activities (F). Also place parentheses around the letter only if it is a cash outflow.

____ (1) Cash paid to suppliers
____ (2) Cash received from customers
____ (3) Income taxes paid
____ (4) Cash paid to employees
____ (5) Cash paid for dividends to stockholders
____ (6) Cash proceeds received from sale of investment in another company
____ (7) Purchases of property, plant, and equipment
____ (8) Repayment of borrowings

E1-14   **Preparing a Statement of Cash Flows**

LO1

NITSU Manufacturing Corporation is preparing the annual financial statements for the stockholders. A statement of cash flows must be prepared. The following data on cash flows were developed for the entire year ended December 31, 2009: cash collections from sales, $270,000; cash expended for operating expenses, $180,000; sale of unissued NITSU stock for cash, $30,000; cash dividends declared and paid to stockholders during the year, $22,000; and payments on long-term notes payable, $80,000. During the year, a tract of land held as an investment was sold for $15,000 cash (which was the same price that NITSU had paid for the land in 2008), and $38,000 cash was expended for two new machines. The machines were used in the factory. The beginning-of-the-year cash balance was $63,000.

Required:

Prepare the statement of cash flows for 2009. Follow the format illustrated in the chapter.

Comparing Income and Cash Flows from Operations (A Challenging Exercise)

Paul's Painters, a service organization, prepared the following special report for the month of January 2006:

Service Revenue, Expenses, and Income		
Service revenue		
Cash services (per cash register tape)	$105,000	
Credit services (per charge bills; not yet		
collected by end of January)	30,500	
		$135,500
Expenses		
Salaries and wages expense (paid by check)	$ 50,000	
Salary for January not yet paid	3,000	
Supplies used (taken from stock, purchased		
for cash during December)	2,000	
Other expenses (paid by check)	26,000	81,000
Pretax income		$ 54,500
Income tax expense (not yet paid)		13,500
Income for January		$ 41,000

Required:

1. The owner (who knows little about the financial part of the business) asked you to compute the amount by which cash had increased in January 2006 from the operations of the company. You decided to prepare a detailed report for the owner with the following major side captions: Cash Inflows (collections), Cash Outflows (payments), and the difference—Net Increase (or decrease) in Cash.

2. See if you can reconcile the difference—net increase (or decrease) in cash—you computed in requirement (1) with the income for January 2006 by filling in the following chart.

Reconciliation with income:	
Income	$41,000
Noncash services	(?)
Noncash expenses (? + ? + ?)	?
Net increase (decrease) in cash	$29,000

 Available with McGraw-Hill's Homework Manager

PROBLEMS

Preparing an Income Statement, Statement of Retained Earnings, and Balance Sheet (AP1-1)

Assume that you are the president of Propane Company. At the end of the first year (December 31, 2006) of operations, the following financial data for the company are available:

Cash	$20,000
Receivables from customers (all considered collectible)	12,000
Inventory of merchandise (based on physical count and priced at cost)	90,000
Equipment owned, at cost less used portion	45,000
Accounts payable owed to suppliers	52,370
Salary payable for 2006 (on December 31, 2006, this was	
owed to an employee who was away because of an emergency;	
will return around January 10, 2007, at which time the payment	
will be made)	2,000
Total sales revenue	155,000

Expenses, including the cost of the merchandise sold (excluding income taxes)	104,100
Income taxes expense at 30% × pretax income; all paid during 2006	?
Contributed capital, 7,000 shares outstanding	87,000
Dividends declared and paid during 2006	10,000

Required (show computations):

Using the financial statement exhibits in the chapter as models:

1. Prepare a summarized income statement for the year 2006.
2. Prepare a statement of retained earnings for the year 2006.
3. Prepare a balance sheet at December 31, 2006.

P1-2

LO1

Analyzing a Student's Business and Preparing an Income Statement (AP1-2)

During the summer between her junior and senior years, Susan Irwin needed to earn sufficient money for the coming academic year. Unable to obtain a job with a reasonable salary, she decided to try the lawn care business for three months. After a survey of the market potential, Susan bought a used pickup truck on June 1 for $1,500. On each door she painted "Susan's Lawn Service, Phone 471-4487." She also spent $900 for mowers, trimmers, and tools. To acquire these items, she borrowed $2,500 cash by signing a note payable promising to pay the $2,500 plus interest of $75 at the end of the three months (ending August 31).

At the end of the summer, Susan realized that she had done a lot of work, and her bank account looked good. This fact prompted her to become concerned about how much profit the business had earned.

A review of the check stubs showed the following: Bank deposits of collections from customers totaled $12,600. The following checks had been written: gas, oil, and lubrication, $920; pickup repairs, $210; mower repair, $75; miscellaneous supplies used, $80; helpers, $4,500; payroll taxes, $175; payment for assistance in preparing payroll tax forms, $25; insurance, $125; telephone, $110; and $2,575 to pay off the note including interest (on August 31). A notebook kept in the pickup, plus some unpaid bills, reflected that customers still owed her $800 for lawn services rendered and that she owed $200 for gas and oil (credit card charges). She estimated that the cost for use of the truck and the other equipment (called *depreciation*) for three months amounted to $500.

Required:

1. Prepare a quarterly income statement for Susan's Lawn Service for the months June, July, and August 2006. Use the following main captions: Revenues from Services, Expenses, and Net Income. Because this is a sole proprietorship, the company will not be subject to income tax.
2. Do you see a need for one or more additional financial reports for this company for 2006 and thereafter? Explain.

P1-3

LO1

Comparing Income with Cash Flow (A Challenging Problem)

Ace Trucking Company was organized on January 1, 2006. At the end of the first quarter (three months) of operations, the owner prepared a summary of its activities as shown in the first row of the following tabulation:

	Computation of	
Summary of Transactions	**Income**	**Cash**
a. Services performed for customers, $66,000, of which $11,000 remained uncollected at the end of the quarter.	+$66,000	+$55,000
b. Cash borrowed from the local bank, $30,000 (one-year note).		
c. Small service truck purchased at the end of the quarter to be used in the business for two years starting the next quarter: cost, $9,000 cash.		
d. Wages earned by employees, $26,500, of which one-half remained unpaid at the end of the quarter.		

e. Service supplies purchased for use in the business, $3,000 cash, of which $600 were unused (still on hand) at the end of the quarter.		
f. Other operating expenses, $36,000, of which $6,000 remained unpaid at the end of the quarter.		

Based only on these transactions, compute the following for the quarter:
     Income (or loss)
     Cash inflow (or outflow)		

Required:

1. For each of the six transactions given in this tabulation, enter what you consider the correct amounts. Enter a zero when appropriate. The first transaction is illustrated.
2. For each transaction, explain the basis for your dollar responses.

Evaluating Data to Support a Loan Application (A Challenging Problem)

P1-4
LO1

On January 1, 2006, three individuals organized West Company as a corporation. Each individual invested $10,000 cash in the business. On December 31, 2006, they prepared a list of resources owned (assets) and a list of the debts (liabilities) to support a company loan request for $70,000 submitted to a local bank. None of the three investors had studied accounting. The two lists prepared were as follows:

Company resources	
Cash	$ 12,000
Service supplies inventory (on hand)	7,000
Service trucks (four practically new)	68,000
Personal residences of organizers (three houses)	190,000
Service equipment used in the business (practically new)	30,000
Bills due from customers (for services already completed)	15,000
Total	$322,000

Company obligations	
Unpaid wages to employees	$19,000
Unpaid taxes	8,000
Owed to suppliers	10,000
Owed on service trucks and equipment (to a finance company)	50,000
Loan from organizer	10,000
Total	$97,000

Required:

Prepare a short memo indicating:

1. Which of these items do not belong on the balance sheet? (Bear in mind that the company is considered to be separate from the owners.)
2. What additional questions would you raise about the measurement of items on the list? Explain the basis for each question.
3. If you were advising the local bank on its loan decision, which amounts on the list would create special concerns? Explain the basis for each concern and include any recommendations that you have.
4. In view of your response to (1) and (2), what do you think the amount of stockholders' equity (i.e., assets minus liabilities) of the company would be? Show your computations.

ALTERNATE **PROBLEMS**

AP1-1   Preparing an Income Statement, Statement of Retained Earnings, and Balance Sheet
LO1   (P1-1)

Assume that you are the president of McClaren Corporation. At the end of the first year (June 30, 2008) of operations, the following financial data for the company are available:

Cash	$13,150
Receivables from customers (all considered collectible)	9,500
Inventory of merchandise (based on physical count and priced at cost)	27,000
Equipment owned, at cost less used portion	66,000
Accounts payable owed to suppliers	31,500
Salary payable for 2008 (on June 30, 2008, this was owed to an employee who was away because of an emergency; will return around July 7, 2008, at which time the payment will be made)	1,500
Total sales revenue	100,000
Expenses, including the cost of the merchandise sold (excluding income taxes)	70,500
Income taxes expense at 30% × pretax income; all paid during 2008	?
Contributed capital, 5,000 shares outstanding	62,000
No dividends were declared or paid during 2008.	

Required (show computations):

Using the financial statement exhibits in the chapter as models:

1. Prepare a summarized income statement for the year ended June 30, 2008.
2. Prepare a statement of retained earnings for the year ended June 30, 2008.
3. Prepare a balance sheet at June 30, 2008.

AP1-2   Analyzing a Student's Business and Preparing an Income Statement (P1-2)
LO1

Upon graduation from high school, John Abel immediately accepted a job as an electrician's assistant for a large local electrical repair company. After three years of hard work, John received an electrician's license and decided to start his own business. He had saved $12,000, which he invested in the business. First, he transferred this amount from his savings account to a business bank account for Abel Electric Repair Company, Incorporated. His lawyer had advised him to start as a corporation. He then purchased a used panel truck for $9,000 cash and secondhand tools for $1,500; rented space in a small building; inserted an ad in the local paper; and opened the doors on October 1, 2006. Immediately, John was very busy; after one month, he employed an assistant.

Although John knew practically nothing about the financial side of the business, he realized that a number of reports were required and that costs and collections had to be controlled carefully. At the end of the year, prompted in part by concern about his income tax situation (previously he had to report only salary), John recognized the need for financial statements. His wife Jane developed some financial statements for the business. On December 31, 2006, with the help of a friend, she gathered the following data for the three months just ended. Bank account deposits of collections for electric repair services totaled $32,000. The following checks had been written: electrician's assistant, $8,500; payroll taxes, $175; supplies purchased and used on jobs, $9,500; oil, gas, and maintenance on truck, $1,200; insurance, $700; rent, $500; utilities and telephone, $825; and miscellaneous expenses (including advertising), $600. Also, uncollected bills to customers for electric repair services amounted to $3,000. The $200 rent for December had not been paid. John estimated the cost of using the truck and tools (depreciation) during the three months to be $1,200. Income taxes for the three-month period were $3,480.

Required:

1. Prepare a quarterly income statement for Abel Electric Repair for the three months October through December 2006. Use the following main captions: Revenues from Services, Expenses, Pretax Income, and Net Income.
2. Do you think that John may need one or more additional financial reports for 2006 and thereafter? Explain.

Annual Report Cases

Finding Financial Information

Refer to the financial statements of Pacific Sunwear of California (PacSun) in Appendix B at the end of this book, or open file PSUN.pdf in the Annual Report Cases directory on the student DVD.

CP1-1
LO1, 3

PACIFIC SUNWEAR
OF CALIFORNIA, INC.

Required:
Read the annual report. Look at the income statement, balance sheet, and cash flow statement closely and attempt to infer what kinds of information they report. Then answer the following questions based on the report.

1. What types of products does it sell?
2. Did the Chief Executive Officer (CEO) and Executive Chairman of the Board believe that the company had a good year? What do they cite as indicators of their company's recent performance?
3. On what date does PacSun's most recent reporting year end?
4. For how many years does it present complete
   a. Balance sheets?
   b. Income statements?
   c. Cash flow statements?
5. Are its financial statements audited by independent CPAs? How do you know?
6. Did its total assets increase or decrease over the last year?
7. How much inventory (in dollars) did PacSun have as of January 29, 2005 (accountants would call this the ending balance)?
8. Write out its basic accounting (balance sheet) equation and provide the values in dollars reported by the company as of January 29, 2005.

Finding Financial Information

Refer to the financial statements of American Eagle Outfitters in Appendix C at the end of this book, or open file AEOS.pdf in the Annual Report Cases directory on the student DVD.

CP1-2
LO1, 3

AMERICAN EAGLE
OUTFITTERS
ae.com

Required:
1. What is the amount of net income for the most recent year?
2. What amount of revenue was earned in the most recent year?
3. How much inventory (in dollars) does the company have as of January 29, 2005?
4. By what amount did cash and cash equivalents* change during the most recent year?
5. Who is the auditor for the company?

Comparing Companies Within an Industry

Refer to the financial statements of Pacific Sunwear of California (PacSun) given in Appendix B and American Eagle Outfitters given in Appendix C and the Industry Ratio Report given in Appendix D at the end of this book, or open file CP1-3.xls in the Annual Report Cases directory on the student DVD.

CP1-3
LO1, 3

PACIFIC SUNWEAR
OF CALIFORNIA, INC.

AMERICAN EAGLE
OUTFITTERS
ae.com

eXcel

Required:
1. Both companies report "basic" earnings per share on their income statements and the market price per share of their stock in Item 5 of the 10-K disclosed with the annual report. Using the most recent year's earnings per share and the highest stock price per share reported for the last quarter of the most recent year, compute the price/earnings ratio. Which company provided the highest price/earnings ratio for the most recent year? *(Note: Some companies will label a year that has a January year end as having a fiscal year end dated one year earlier. For example, a January 2005 year end may be labeled as Fiscal 2004 since the year actually has more months that fall in the 2004 calendar year than in the 2005 calendar year.)*

Cash equivalents are short-term investments readily convertible to cash whose value is unlikely to change.

2. Which company do investors believe will have the higher growth in earnings in the future?
3. Examine the Annual Report Cases Industry Ratio Report. Compare the price/earnings ratio for each company to the industry average. Did you expect these two companies, which are relative newcomers to the industry, to have price/earnings ratios above or below the industry average? Why?

Financial Reporting and Analysis Cases

CP1-4

LO1

Using Financial Reports: Identifying and Correcting Deficiencies in an Income Statement and Balance Sheet

Performance Corporation was organized on January 1, 2006. At the end of 2006, the company had not yet employed an accountant; however, an employee who was "good with numbers" prepared the following statements at that date:

PERFORMANCE CORPORATION
December 31, 2006

Income from sales of merchandise	$175,000
Total amount paid for goods sold during 2006	(90,000)
Selling costs	(25,000)
Depreciation (on service vehicles used)	(10,000)
Income from services rendered	52,000
Salaries and wages paid	(62,000)

PERFORMANCE CORPORATION
December 31, 2006

Resources		
Cash		$ 32,000
Merchandise inventory (held for resale)		42,000
Service vehicles		50,000
Retained earnings (profit earned in 2006)		30,000
Grand total		$154,000
Debts		
Payables to suppliers		$ 22,000
Note owed to bank		25,000
Due from customers		13,000
Total		$ 60,000
Supplies on hand (to be used in rendering services)	$15,000	
Accumulated depreciation* (on service vehicles)	10,000	
Contributed capital, 6,500 shares	65,000	
Total		90,000
Grand total		$150,000

Required:
1. List all deficiencies that you can identify in these statements. Give a brief explanation of each one.
2. Prepare a proper income statement (correct net income is $30,000 and income tax expense is $10,000) and balance sheet (correct total assets are $142,000).

Accumulated depreciation represents the used portion of the asset and should be subtracted from the asset balance.

Using Financial Reports: Applying the Balance Sheet Equation to Liquidate a Company

CP1-5
LO1

On June 1, 2008, Bland Corporation prepared a balance sheet just prior to going out of business. The balance sheet totals showed the following:

Assets (no cash)	$90,000
Liabilities	50,000
Stockholders' equity	40,000

Shortly thereafter, all of the assets were sold for cash.

Required:

1. How would the balance sheet appear immediately after the sale of the assets for cash for each of the following cases? Use the format given here.

		BALANCES IMMEDIATELY AFTER SALE				
	Cash Received for the Assets	Assets	=	Liabilities	+	Stockholders' Equity
Case A	$ 90,000	$ _____		$ _____		$ _____
Case B	80,000	$ _____		$ _____		$ _____
Case C	100,000	$ _____		$ _____		$ _____

2. How should the cash be distributed in each separate case? (*Hint:* Creditors must be paid in full before owners receive any payment.) Use the format given here:

	To Creditors	To Stockholders	Total
Case A	$ _____	$ _____	$ _____
Case B	$ _____	$ _____	$ _____
Case C	$ _____	$ _____	$ _____

Critical Thinking Cases

Making Decisions as an Owner: Deciding about a Proposed Audit

CP1-6
LO3

You are one of three partners who own and operate Mary's Maid Service. The company has been operating for seven years. One of the other partners has always prepared the company's annual financial statements. Recently you proposed that the statements be audited each year because it would benefit the partners and preclude possible disagreements about the division of profits. The partner who prepares the statements proposed that his Uncle Ray, who has a lot of financial experience, can do the job and at little cost. Your other partner remained silent.

Required:

1. What position would you take on the proposal? Justify your response.
2. What would you strongly recommend? Give the basis for your recommendation.

Evaluating an Ethical Dilemma: Ethics and Auditor Responsibilities

CP1-7
LO3, 4

A key factor that an auditor provides is independence. The *AICPA Code of Professional Conduct* states that "a member in public practice should be independent in fact and appearance when providing auditing and other attestation services."

Required:

Do you consider the following circumstances to suggest a lack of independence? Justify your position. (Use your imagination. Specific answers are not provided in the chapter.)

1. Jack Jones is a partner with a large audit firm and is assigned to the Ford audit. Jack owns 10 shares of Ford.
2. Jane Winkler has invested in a mutual fund company that owns 500,000 shares of Sears stock. She is the auditor of Sears.

3. Bob Franklin is a clerk/typist who works on the audit of AT&T. He has just inherited 50,000 shares of AT&T stock. (Bob enjoys his work and plans to continue despite his new wealth.)

4. Nancy Sodoma worked on weekends as the controller for a small business that a friend started. Nancy quit the job in midyear and now has no association with the company. She works full-time for a large CPA firm and has been assigned to do the audit of her friend's business.

5. Mark Jacobs borrowed $100,000 for a home mortgage from First City National Bank. The mortgage was granted on normal credit terms. Mark is the partner in charge of the First City audit.

Financial Reporting and Analysis Project

CP1-8   **Team Project: Examining an Annual Report**

As a team, select an industry to analyze. *Reuters* provides lists of industries and their makeup at **www.investor.reuters.com/Industries.aspx**. Each team member should acquire the annual report or 10-K for one publicly traded company in the industry, with each member selecting a different company. (Library files, the SEC EDGAR service at **www.sec.gov**, or the company itself are good sources.)

Required:

On an individual basis, each team member should write a short report answering the following questions about the selected company. Discuss any patterns across the companies that you as a team observe. Then, as a team, write a short report comparing and contrasting your companies.

1. What types of products or services does it sell?
2. On what day of the year does its fiscal year end?
3. For how many years does it present complete
   a. Balance sheets?
   b. Income statements?
   c. Cash flow statements?
4. Are its financial statements audited by independent CPAs? If so, by whom?
5. Did its total assets increase or decrease over last year? By what percentage? [Percentage change is calculated as (current year − last year) ÷ last year. Show supporting computations.]
6. Did its net income increase or decrease over last year? By what percentage?

LEARNING OBJECTIVES

After studying this chapter, you should be able to:

1. Define the objective of financial reporting, the elements of the balance sheet, and the related key accounting assumptions and principles. p. 51

2. Identify what constitutes a business transaction and recognize common balance sheet account titles used in business. p. 56

3. Apply transaction analysis to simple business transactions in terms of the accounting model: Assets = Liabilities + Stockholders' Equity. p. 57

4. Determine the impact of business transactions on the balance sheet using two basic tools, journal entries and T-accounts. p. 62

5. Prepare and analyze a simple balance sheet using the financial leverage ratio. p. 69

6. Identify investing and financing transactions and demonstrate how they are reported on the statement of cash flows. p. 73

Investing and Financing Decisions and the Balance Sheet

In the pizza segment of the highly competitive restaurant business, Papa John's continues to fight the battle to become the No. 1 pizza brand in the world, taking on industry leader Pizza Hut as its primary target. In 2000, through aggressive expansion, Papa John's moved ahead of Little Caesar's to rank third in sales behind giants Pizza Hut and Domino's.

With more than 2,800 restaurants in the United States and abroad, the company has grown tremendously since its beginnings in 1983 when John Schnatter, founder and chief executive officer, knocked down closet walls at a bar he was tending to install a pizza oven. Ten years later, Papa John's became a public company with stock trading on the NASDAQ exchange (under the symbol PZZA). The company's balance sheets at the end of 2003 compared to the end of 1994 (in thousands of dollars*) highlight its growth:

FOCUS COMPANY:

Papa John's International

EXPANSION STRATEGY IN THE "PIZZA WARS"

www.papajohns.com

	Assets	= Liabilities	+ Stockholders' Equity
End of 2003	$347,214	$187,942	$159,272
End of 1994	76,173	13,564	62,609
Change	+$271,041	+$174,378	+$ 96,663

In recent years, competition has stiffened not only from traditional pizza chains but also from niche dwellers—take-and-bake pizza chains, frozen pizza companies, carry-out initiatives from restaurants such as Applebee's and Chili's, and restaurants meeting the shift in consumer interests to low-carb menu options. While addressing the competition, Papa John's continues to expand, with plans to add approximately 200 new restaurants in 2004 in the United States and abroad. The Pizza Wars continue.

UNDERSTANDING THE BUSINESS

Pizza is a global commodity, generating more than $32 billion in sales annually. While the business depends heavily on human capital, companies can compete through product quality and marketing. Papa John's strategy is to offer "Better Ingredients. Better Pizza."

These totals are rounded amounts from the actual financial statements for the respective years. Amounts used in illustrations throughout Chapters 2, 3, and 4 are realistic estimates of actual monthly amounts.

To do so requires an almost fanatical focus on testing ingredients and checking product quality, right down to the size of the black olives and the fat content of the mozzarella and meat. The company keeps operations simple, sticking to a focused menu of pizza, breadsticks, cheesesticks, chicken strips, and soft drinks for pick-up or delivery. To control quality and increase efficiency, the company builds regional commissaries (called *quality control centers*) that make the dough and sell it to the stores. The commissaries plus new company-owned stores and the sale of franchises† explain most of the change in Papa John's assets and liabilities from year to year.

To understand how the results of Papa John's growth strategy are communicated in the balance sheet, we must answer the following questions:

- What business activities cause changes in the balance sheet amounts from one period to the next?
- How do specific business activities affect each of the balance sheet amounts?
- How do companies keep track of the balance sheet amounts?

Once we have answered these questions, we will be able to perform two key analytical tasks:

1. Analyze and predict the effects of business decisions on a company's financial statements.
2. Use the financial statements of other companies to identify and evaluate the activities managers engaged in during a past period. This is a key task in **financial statement analysis.**

In this chapter, we focus on some typical asset acquisition activities (often called **investing activities**), along with related **financing activities,** such as borrowing funds from creditors or selling stock to investors to acquire the assets. We examine only those activities that affect balance sheet amounts. Operating activities that affect both the income statement and the balance sheet are covered in Chapters 3 and 4. To begin, let's return to the basic concepts introduced in Chapter 1.

---

†*Franchises are contracts in which a franchisor (such as Papa John's International) provides rights to franchisees (in this case, local restaurant operators) to sell or distribute a specific line of products or provide a particular service. In return, franchisees usually pay an initial fee to obtain the franchise, along with annual payments for ongoing services such as accounting, advertising, and training. Approximately 80 percent of Papa John's restaurants worldwide are franchises.*

ORGANIZATION of the Chapter

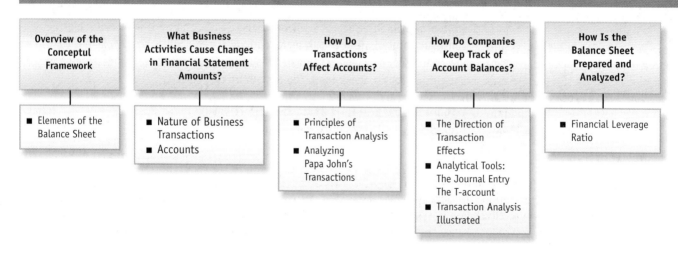

Overview of the Conceptul Framework	What Business Activities Cause Changes in Financial Statement Amounts?	How Do Transactions Affect Accounts?	How Do Companies Keep Track of Account Balances?	How Is the Balance Sheet Prepared and Analyzed?
■ Elements of the Balance Sheet	■ Nature of Business Transactions ■ Accounts	■ Principles of Transaction Analysis ■ Analyzing Papa John's Transactions	■ The Direction of Transaction Effects ■ Analytical Tools: The Journal Entry The T-account ■ Transaction Analysis Illustrated	■ Financial Leverage Ratio

OVERVIEW OF THE CONCEPTUAL FRAMEWORK

The key accounting terms and concepts defined in Chapter 1 are part of a theoretical framework developed over many years and synthesized by the Financial Accounting Standards Board (FASB). This conceptual framework is presented in Exhibit 2.1 as an overview with key concepts discussed in each of the next four chapters. An understanding of these accounting concepts will be helpful as you study because learning and remembering **how** the accounting process works is much easier if you know **why** it works a certain way. A clear understanding of these concepts will also help you in future chapters as we examine more complex business activities.

Learning Objective 1
Define the objective of financial reporting, the elements of the balance sheet, and the related key accounting assumptions and principles.

Concepts Emphasized in Chapter 2

Objective of Financial Reporting

The top of the pyramid in Exhibit 2.1 indicates the primary objective of external financial reporting that guides the remaining sections of the conceptual framework. The primary objective of financial accounting is to provide useful economic information about a business to help external parties, primarily investors and creditors, make sound financial decisions. The users of accounting information are identified as **decision makers.** These decision makers include average investors, creditors, and experts who provide financial advice. They are all expected to have a reasonable understanding of accounting concepts and procedures (this may be one of the reasons you are studying accounting). Of course, as we discussed in Chapter 1, many other groups, such as suppliers and customers, also use external financial statements.

Users usually are interested in information to assist them in projecting a business's future cash inflows and outflows. For example, creditors and potential creditors need to assess an entity's ability to pay interest on a loan over time and pay back the principal on the loan. Investors and potential investors want to assess the entity's ability to pay dividends in the future. They also want to judge how successful the company might be so that the stock price rises and investors can then sell the stock for more than was paid.

The **PRIMARY OBJECTIVE OF EXTERNAL FINANCIAL REPORTING** is to provide useful economic information about a business to help external parties make sound financial decisions.

Underlying Assumptions of Accounting

Three of the four basic assumptions that underlie accounting measurement and reporting were discussed briefly in Chapter 1. Under the separate-entity assumption, each business must be accounted for as an individual organization, separate and apart from its owners, all other persons, and other entities. Under the unit-of-measure assumption, each business entity accounts for and reports its financial results in terms primarily of the national monetary unit (dollars in the United States, yen in Japan, euros in Germany). Under the continuity assumption (sometimes called the **going-concern assumption**), a business normally is assumed to continue operating long enough to meet its contractual commitments and plans. If a company was not expected to continue, for example, due to the likelihood of bankruptcy, then its assets and liabilities should be valued and reported on the balance sheet as if the company were to be liquidated (that is, discontinued, with all of its assets sold and all debts paid). In future chapters, unless otherwise indicated, we assume that businesses meet the continuity assumption.

Assets, liabilities, and shareholders' equity are the key elements of a corporation's balance sheet, as we learned in Chapter 1. Let's examine the definitions in more detail.

SEPARATE-ENTITY ASSUMPTION states that business transactions are separate from the transactions of the owners.

UNIT-OF-MEASURE ASSUMPTION states that accounting information should be measured and reported in the national monetary unit.

CONTINUITY (GOING-CONCERN) ASSUMPTION states that businesses are assumed to continue to operate into the foreseeable future.

Elements of the Balance Sheet

Assets are resources with probable future economic benefits owned or controlled by an entity as a result of past transactions. In other words, they are the resources the entity can use to operate in the future. So as not to mislead users when reporting information to them, managers use judgment (and past experience) to determine an asset's most

ASSETS are resources with probable future economic benefits owned by the entity as a result of past transactions.

EXHIBIT 2.1

Financial Accounting and
Reporting Conceptual
Framework

PRIMARY OBJECTIVE OF EXTERNAL FINANCIAL REPORTING [Ch. 2]

To provide useful economic information to external users for decision making (for assessing future cash flows)

QUALITATIVE CHARACTERISTICS OF FINANCIAL INFORMATION [Ch. 5]

To be useful, information should possess:

Relevancy—be capable of making a difference in decisions
- Predictive value (extrapolate into the future)
- Feedback value (assess prior expectations)
- Timeliness (available to help with decisions)

Reliability—can be relied upon
- Verifiability (can be verified independently)
- Representational faithfulness (represents reality)
- Neutrality (unbiased)

Information should also be
  Comparable across companies
  Consistent over time

ELEMENTS OF FINANCIAL STATEMENTS

Asset—economic resource with probable future benefits. [Ch. 2]

Liability—probable future sacrifices of economic resources. [Ch. 2]

Stockholders' Equity—financing provided by owners and operations (residual interest to owners). [Ch. 2]

Revenue—increase in assets or settlement of liabilities from ongoing operations. [Ch. 3]

Expense—decrease in assets or increase in liabilities from ongoing operations. [Ch. 3]

Gain—increase in assets or settlement of liabilities from peripheral activities. [Ch. 3]

Loss—decrease in assets or increase in liabilities from peripheral activities. [Ch. 3]

ASSUMPTIONS

- **Separate entity**—activities of the business are separate from activities of the owners. [Ch. 2]

- **Unit of measure**—accounting measurements will be in the national monetary unit. [Ch. 2]

- **Continuity** (going concern)—entity will not go out of business in the near future. [Ch. 2]

- **Time period**—the long life of a company can be reported over a series of shorter time periods. [Ch. 3]

PRINCIPLES

- **Historical cost**—cash equivalent price on the transaction date is used initially to measure elements. [Ch. 2]

- **Revenue recognition**—record when *measurable, realizable,* and *earned* (i.e., company performs, evidence of customer payment arrangement exists, price is determinable, and collection is reasonably assured). [Ch. 3]

- **Matching**—record when expenses are incurred to generate revenues. [Ch. 3]

- **Full disclosure**—provide information sufficiently important to influence a decision (e.g., notes). [Ch. 5]

CONSTRAINTS [Ch. 5]

- **Cost benefit**—benefits to users should outweigh costs of providing information.

- **Materiality**—relatively small amounts not likely to influence decisions are to be recorded in the most cost-beneficial way.

- **Industry practices**—industry-specific measurements and reporting deviations may be acceptable.

- **Conservatism**—exercise care not to overstate assets and revenues or understate liabilities and expenses.

likely future benefit. For example, a company may have a list of customers who owe $10,000. History suggests, however, that only $9,800 is likely to be collected. The lower, more probable and more conservative figure is reported to users for purposes of projecting future cash flows.

As shown in Papa John's balance sheet presented in Exhibit 2.2, most companies list assets **in order of liquidity,** or how soon an asset is expected to be turned into cash or used. Notice that several of Papa John's assets are categorized as current assets. Current assets are those resources that Papa John's will use or turn into cash within one year. Note that inventory is always considered a current asset, regardless of how long it takes to produce and sell the inventory. As indicated in Exhibit 2.2, Papa John's current assets include Cash, Accounts Receivable, Supplies, Prepaid Expenses, and Other Current Assets.

All other assets are considered long term, to be used or turned into cash beyond the coming year. For Papa John's, that includes Long-Term Investments, Property and Equipment (net of amounts used in the past), Long-Term Notes Receivable, Intangi-

CURRENT ASSETS are assets that will be used or turned into cash within one year. Inventory is always considered a current asset regardless of the time needed to produce and sell it.

PAPA JOHN'S INTERNATIONAL, INC. AND SUBSIDIARIES Consolidated Balance Sheet December 28, 2003 (dollars in thousands)		
Assets		
Current assets		
Cash	$ 7,000	
Accounts receivable	20,000	payments due from franchisees and others on account
Supplies	17,000	food, beverages, and paper supplies on hand
Prepaid expenses	11,000	rent and insurance paid in advance
Other current assets	7,000	a summary of several current assets with smaller balances
Total current assets	62,000	
Long-term investments	8,000	another company's stocks and bonds purchased with excess cash
Property and equipment (net of accumulated depreciation of $149,000)	204,000	the remaining cost of long-lived assets to be used in future operations (original cost minus the estimated portion of cost already used in the past)
Long-term notes receivable	11,000	from franchisees
Intangibles	49,000	patents, trademarks, and goodwill
Other assets	13,000	a summary of several long-term assets with smaller balances
Total assets	$347,000	
Liabilities and Stockholders' Equity		
Current liabilities		
Accounts payable	$ 28,000	payments due to suppliers
Accrued expenses payable	53,000	a summary of payroll, rent, and other obligations
Total current liabilities	81,000	
Unearned franchise fees	6,000	amounts paid by franchisees for services they will receive
Long-term notes payable	61,000	loans from creditors
Other long-term liabilities	40,000	
Stockholders' equity*		
Contributed capital	1,000	
Retained earnings	158,000	
Total stockholders' equity	159,000	
Total liabilities and stockholders' equity	$347,000	

the last Sunday in December of each year

EXHIBIT 2.2

Papa John's Balance Sheet

*Contributed capital and retained earnings totals have been simplified. In actuality, contributed capital is approximately $220 million and retained earnings is approximately $290 million. However, the Company has spent approximately $351 million repurchasing shares of its stock, a concept discussed in Chapter 11.

bles, and Other Assets. The Papa John's balance sheet includes assets of its company-owned restaurants, about 20 percent of all Papa John's restaurants. The assets of the remaining 80 percent belong to franchisees and are appropriately reported in their own financial statements.

Basic Accounting Principle

The **historical cost principle** states that the cash-equivalent cost needed to acquire the asset on the date of the acquisition (the historical cost) should be used initially for recording all financial statement elements. Under the cost principle, cost is measured on the date of the transaction as the cash paid plus the current dollar value of all non-cash considerations (any assets, privileges, or rights) also given in the exchange. For

The **HISTORICAL COST PRINCIPLE** requires assets to be recorded at the historical cash-equivalent cost, which on the date of the transaction is cash paid plus the current dollar value of all noncash considerations also given in the exchange.

example, if you trade your computer plus cash for a new car, the cost of the new car is equal to the cash paid plus the market value of the computer. Thus, in most cases, cost is relatively easy to determine and can be verified. A disadvantage of this approach is that, subsequent to the date of acquisition, the continued reporting of historical cost on the balance sheet does not reflect any changes in market value, usually because market value is a less verifiable and objective measure.

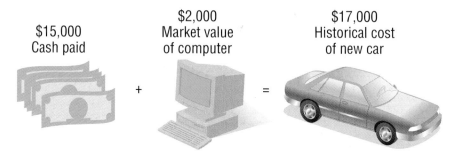

$15,000
Cash paid

+

$2,000
Market value
of computer

=

$17,000
Historical cost
of new car

FINANCIAL ANALYSIS   Unrecorded but Valuable Assets

Many very valuable intangible assets, such as trademarks, patents, and copyrights developed inside a company, have no value reported on the balance sheet. For example, General Electric's balance sheet reveals no listing for the GE trademark because it was developed internally over time, created through research, development, and advertising (it was not purchased). Likewise, the Coca Cola Company does not report any asset for its patented Coke formulae, although it does report more than $2 billion in various trademarks that it has purchased.

LIABILITIES are probable debts or obligations of the entity that result from past transactions, which will be paid with assets or services.

Liabilities are probable debts or obligations (claims to a company's resources) that result from an entity's past transactions and will be paid for with assets or services. Those entities that a company owes money to are called **creditors.** Creditors usually receive payment of the amounts owed and sometimes interest on those amounts. Papa John's balance sheet includes five liabilities: Accounts Payable, Accrued Expenses Payable, Unearned Franchise Fees, Long-Term Notes Payable, and Other Long-Term Liabilities. These and other liabilities will be discussed in subsequent chapters.

CURRENT LIABILITIES are obligations that will be paid in cash (or other current assets) or satisfied by providing cash, goods, or services within the coming year.

Just as assets are reported in order of liquidity, liabilities are usually listed on the balance sheet **in order of maturity** (how soon an obligation is to be paid). Those liabilities that Papa John's will need to pay within the coming year (with cash, services, or other current assets) are classified as current liabilities. Distinguishing current assets and current liabilities assists external users of the financial statements in assessing the amounts and timing of future cash flows. Most corporations report current assets and liabilities separately, even though classifying them as such is not required.

A QUESTION OF ETHICS   Environmental Liabilities: The "Greening of GAAP"

For many years, companies have faced growing pressure to estimate and disclose environmental liabilities, such as the cleanup of hazardous waste sites. Since 1982, the Securities and Exchange Commission (SEC) requires disclosure of material information on environmental liabilities. Generally Accepted Accounting Principles (GAAP) require companies to report their best estimate of probable liabilities, including environmental liabilities, and to note other reasonably possible liabilities. It is estimated, however, that more than 70 percent of companies underreport or fail to report such liabilities, often due to the way disclosure rules are applied.

A recent report* suggests that aggressive corporate accounting and asset management tactics can lead companies to engage in environmental accounting fraud. Among these tactics are idling (also known as **mothballing**) facilities to avoid resolving potential environmental liabilities, hiding information reported to insurance companies on the extent of environmental liabilities, and denying or deferring emerging hazards until after lawsuits are in progress.

Recently, numerous environmental and corporate social responsibility groups have called for improved transparency in financial reporting. The SEC is now working more closely with the Environmental Protection Agency, has created a searchable database of comment letters and company responses, and is investigating a proposal to close reporting loopholes—all to improve information available to investors and creditors for decision making.

*Sanford Lewis and Tim Little, "Fooling Investors & Fooling Themselves," The Rose Foundation for Communities and the Environment, July 2004.

Stockholders' equity (also called **owners' equity** or **shareholders' equity**) is the financing provided by the owners and by business operations. Owner-provided cash (and sometimes other assets) is referred to as contributed capital. Owners invest in the business and receive shares of stock as evidence of ownership. The major investor in Papa John's International, Inc., is John Schnatter, founder and CEO, who owns approximately 30 percent of the stock. FMR Corporation of Boston owns another 14 percent of the stock; corporate employees, directors, and the general public own the rest.

Owners invest (or buy stock) in a company in the hope of receiving two types of cash flows: **dividends,** which are a distribution of a company's earnings (a return on the shareholders' investment), and gains from selling the stock for more than they paid (known as **capital gains**). Earnings that are not distributed to the owners but instead are reinvested in the business by management are called retained earnings.[1] A look at Papa John's balance sheet (Exhibit 2.2) indicates that its growth has been financed by substantial reinvestment of retained earnings. Ninety-nine percent of Papa John's stockholders' equity is retained earnings ($158 million Retained Earnings ÷ $159 million total stockholders' equity).

STOCKHOLDERS' EQUITY (also called owners' equity or shareholders' equity) is the financing provided by the owners and by business operations.

CONTRIBUTED CAPITAL results from owners providing cash (and sometimes other assets) to the business.

RETAINED EARNINGS refers to the cumulative earnings of a company that are not distributed to the owners and are reinvested in the business.

SELF-STUDY **QUIZ**

The following is a list of items from a recent Wendy's International, Inc., balance sheet. Indicate on the line provided whether each of the following is categorized on the balance sheet as a current asset (CA), noncurrent asset (NCA), current liability (CL), noncurrent liability (NCL), or stockholders' equity (SE).

_____ Accrued Expenses Payable   _____ Retained Earnings

_____ Property and Equipment   _____ Inventories

_____ Accounts Receivable   _____ Notes Receivable (due in five years)

_____ Long-term Obligations   _____ Accounts Payable

After you have completed your answers, check them with the solutions at the bottom of the page.

Now that we have reviewed the basic elements of the balance sheet, let's see what economic activities cause changes in the amounts reported on this financial statement.

[1]Retained earnings can increase only from profitable operations. Retained earnings decrease when a firm has a loss. In addition, as we discuss in Chapter 3, a company's annual income from operations is usually not equal to the net cash flows for the year.

Column 1: CL; NCA; CA; NCL. Column 2: SE; CA; NCA; CL.   Self-Study Quiz Solutions

WHAT BUSINESS ACTIVITIES CAUSE CHANGES IN FINANCIAL STATEMENT AMOUNTS?

Nature of Business Transactions

Accounting focuses on certain events that have an economic impact on the entity. Those events that are recorded as part of the accounting process are called transactions. The first step in translating the results of business events to financial statement numbers is determining which events to include. As the definitions of assets and liabilities indicate, only economic resources and debts **resulting from past transactions** are recorded on the balance sheet. Transactions include two types of events:

1. **External events:** These are **exchanges** of assets and liabilities between the business and one or more other parties. Examples include the purchase of a machine, the sale of merchandise, the borrowing of cash, and investment in the business by the owners.

2. **Internal events:** These include certain events that are not exchanges between the business and other parties but nevertheless have a direct and measurable effect on the entity. Examples include losses due to fire or other natural disasters and the use of property, plant, and equipment.

Throughout this textbook, the word *transaction* is used in the broad sense to include both types of events.

Some important events that have a future economic impact on a company are *not* reflected in the financial statements. In most cases, signing a contract is not considered to be a transaction because it involves only the exchange of promises, not of assets such as cash, goods, services, or property. For example, assume that Papa John's signs an employment contract with a new regional manager. From an accounting perspective, no transaction has occurred because no exchange of assets or liabilities has been made. Each party to the contract has exchanged promises (the manager agrees to work; Papa John's agrees to pay the manager for work rendered). For each day the new manager works, however, the exchange of services for pay results in a transaction that Papa John's must record. Because of their importance, long-term employment contracts, leases, and other commitments may need to be disclosed in notes to the financial statements.

Accounts

To accumulate the dollar effect of transactions on each financial statement item, organizations use a standardized format called an account. The resulting balances are kept separate for financial statement purposes. To facilitate the recording of transactions, each company establishes a **chart of accounts,** a list of all account titles and their unique numbers. The accounts are usually organized by financial statement element, with asset accounts listed first, followed by liability, stockholders' equity, revenue, and expense accounts in that order. Exhibit 2.3 lists account titles that are quite common and are used by most companies. When you are completing assignments and are unsure of an account title, refer to this listing for help.

Notice that

1. Accounts with "receivable" in the title are always assets; they represent amounts owed by (receivable from) customers and others to the business.

2. Accounts with "payable" in the title are always liabilities and represent amounts owed by the company to be paid to others in the future.

3. The account Prepaid Expenses is an asset since it represents amounts paid to others for future benefits, such as future insurance coverage or rental of property.

4. Accounts with "unearned" in the title are always liabilities representing amounts paid in the past to the company by others expecting future goods or services from the company.

Learning Objective 2
Identify what constitutes a business transaction and recognize common balance sheet account titles used in business.

A TRANSACTION is (1) an exchange between a business and one or more external parties to a business or (2) a measurable internal event such as the use of assets in operations.

Topic Tackler
PLUS

Topic Tackler 2–1

An ACCOUNT is a standardized format that organizations use to accumulate the dollar effect of transactions on each financial statement item.

Assets	Liabilities	Stockholders' Equity	Revenues	Expenses
Cash	Accounts Payable	Contributed Capital	Sales Revenue	Cost of Goods Sold
Short-Term Investments	Accrued Expenses	Retained Earnings	Fee Revenue	Wages Expense
Accounts Receivable	Payable		Interest Revenue	Rent Expense
Notes Receivable	Notes Payable		Rent Revenue	Interest Expense
Inventory (to be sold)	Taxes Payable			Depreciation Expense
Supplies	Unearned Revenue			Advertising Expense
Prepaid Expenses	Bonds Payable			Insurance Expense
Long-Term Investments				Repair Expense
Equipment				Income Tax Expense
Buildings				
Land				
Intangibles				

EXHIBIT 2.3

Typical Account Titles

Every company has a variation on this chart of accounts, depending on the nature of its business activities. For example, a small lawn care service may have an asset account Lawn Mowing Equipment, but a large corporation such as General Motors is unlikely to need such an account. These differences in accounts will become more apparent as we examine the balance sheets of various companies. Because each company has its own chart of accounts, you should **not** try to memorize a typical chart of accounts. In homework problems, you will either be given the account names or be expected to select appropriate names, similar to the ones in the preceding lists. Once you select a name for an account, you must use the exact name in all transactions affecting that account.

The accounts you see in the financial statements of most large corporations are actually summations (or aggregations) of a number of specific accounts. For example, Papa John's keeps separate accounts for paper supplies, food supplies, and beverage supplies, but combines them under *Supplies* on the balance sheet. Equipment, buildings, and land are also combined into an account called *Property and Equipment*. Since our aim is to understand financial statements of actual entities, we will focus on aggregated accounts.

HOW DO TRANSACTIONS AFFECT ACCOUNTS?

Managers' business decisions often result in transactions that affect the financial statements. For example, the decisions to expand the number of stores, advertise a new product, change an employee benefit package, and invest excess cash would all affect the financial statements. Sometimes these decisions have unintended consequences as well. The decision to purchase additional inventory for cash in anticipation of a major sales initiative, for example, will increase inventory and decrease cash. But if there is no demand for the additional inventory, the lower cash balance will also reduce the company's ability to pay its other obligations.

Because business decisions often involve an element of risk, managers should understand exactly how transactions impact the financial statements. The process for determining the effects of transactions is called **transaction analysis.**

Principles of Transaction Analysis

Transaction analysis is the process of studying a transaction to determine its economic effect on the entity in terms of the accounting equation (also known as the *accounting model*). We outline the process in this section of the chapter and create a visual tool representing the process (the transaction analysis model). The basic accounting equation

Learning Objective 3
Apply transaction analysis to simple business transactions in terms of the accounting model: Assets = Liabilities + Stockholders' Equity.

TRANSACTION ANALYSIS is the process of studying a transaction to determine its economic effect on the business in terms of the accounting equation.

Understanding the Meaning of Account Titles in Foreign Financial Statements

GlaxoSmithKline

We learned in Chapter 1 that differences in the political, cultural, and economic environments of other countries have produced significant variations in accounting and reporting rules. Foreign companies often use different account titles from U.S. companies. The pharmaceutical company GlaxoSmithKline in the United Kingdom is one example. A glance at a recent financial report shows that this entity's account titles are similar to those used by U.S. companies, except for the following titles:

United Kingdom Accounts	U.S. Equivalents
Assets	
Stocks	Similar to inventories
Debtors	Includes receivables among other items
Liabilities	
Loans	Similar to Notes and Bonds Payable
Creditors	Similar to Accounts Payable; relates to what is owed to suppliers and others
Provisions	A summary of payables for income tax, dividends, payroll, and other liabilities
Shareholders' Equity	
Share Capital	Similar to Contributed Capital
Profit and Loss Account	Similar to Retained Earnings

and two principles are the foundation for this model. Recall from Chapter 1 that the basic accounting equation for a business that is organized as a corporation is as follows:

$$\text{Assets (A)} = \text{Liabilities (L)} + \text{Stockholders' Equity (SE)}$$

The two principles underlying the transaction analysis process follow:

1. Every transaction affects at least two accounts; correctly identifying those accounts and the direction of the effect (whether an increase or a decrease) is critical.

2. The accounting equation must remain in balance after each transaction.

Success in performing transaction analysis depends on a clear understanding of these principles. Study the following material well.

The Duality of Effects

The idea that every transaction has **at least two effects** on the basic accounting equation is known as the **duality of effects.**[2] Most transactions with external parties involve an **exchange** by which the business entity both receives something and gives up something in return. For example, suppose Papa John's purchased some paper napkins for cash. In this exchange, Papa John's would receive supplies (an increase in an asset) and in return would give up cash (a decrease in an asset).

---

[2]From the duality concept, accountants have developed what is known as the *double-entry system* of recordkeeping.

Transaction	Papa John's Received	Papa John's Gave
Purchased paper napkins for cash	Supplies (increased)	Cash (decreased)

In analyzing this transaction, we determined that the accounts affected were Supplies and Cash. As we discussed in Chapter 1, however, most supplies are purchased on credit (that is, money is owed to suppliers). In that case, Papa John's would engage in *two* transactions: (1) the purchase of an asset on credit and (2) the eventual payment. In the first transaction, Papa John's would receive supplies (an increase in an asset) and would give in return a promise to pay later called *accounts payable* (an increase in a liability). In the second transaction, Papa John's would eliminate or receive back its promise to pay (a decrease in the accounts payable liability) and would give up cash (a decrease in an asset).

Transactions	Papa John's Received	Papa John's Gave
(1) Purchased paper napkins on credit	Supplies (increased)	Accounts Payable (increased) [a promise to pay]
(2) Paid on its accounts payable	Accounts Payable (decreased) [a promise was eliminated]	Cash (decreased)

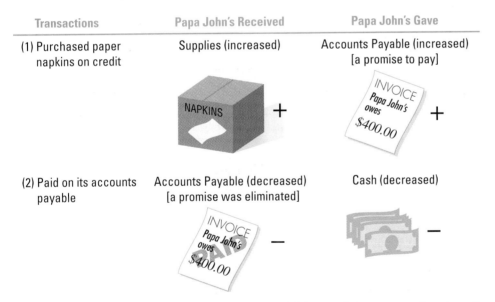

As noted earlier, not all important business activities result in a transaction that affects the financial statements. Most importantly, signing a contract involving the exchange of two promises to perform does *not* result in an accounting transaction that is recorded. For example, if Papa John's sent an order for more napkins to its paper supplier and the supplier accepted the order but did not fill it immediately, no transaction took place. As soon as the goods are shipped to Papa John's, however, the supplier has given up its inventory in exchange for a promise from Papa John's to pay for the items in the near future, and Papa John's has exchanged its promise to pay for the supplies it receives. Because a *promise* has been exchanged for *goods,* a transaction has taken place. Both Papa John's and the supplier's statements will be affected.

Maintaining the Accounting Equation Balance

The accounting equation must remain in balance after each transaction. That is, total assets (resources) must equal total liabilities and stockholders' equity (claims to resources). If all correct accounts have been identified and the appropriate direction of the effect on each account has been determined, the equation should remain in balance. A systematic transaction analysis includes the following steps, in this order:

1. *Accounts and effects*
   a. **Identify the accounts (by title) affected and classify them by type of account,** making sure that at least two accounts change. Ask yourself what is received and what is given. Classifications are an asset (A), a liability (L), or a stockholders' equity account (SE).
   b. **Determine the direction of the effect** (an increase [+] or decrease [−] on each account).
2. *Balancing*
   c. **Verify that the accounting equation (A = L + SE) remains in balance.**

Analyzing Papa John's Transactions

To illustrate the use of the transaction analysis process, let's consider some typical transactions of Papa John's that are also common to most businesses. Remember that this chapter presents transactions that affect only the balance sheet accounts. Assume that Papa John's engages in the following events during January 2004, the month following the balance sheet in Exhibit 2.2. Account titles are from that balance sheet, and remember that, for simplicity, all amounts are in **thousands of dollars:**

(a) **Papa John's issues $2,000 of additional common stock, receiving cash from investors.**

1. *Identify and classify accounts and effects:*
   Cash (A) is received + $2,000. Additional stock certificates are given, Contributed Capital (SE) + $2,000.

2. *Is the accounting equation in balance?*
   Yes. There is a $2,000 increase on the left side and a $2,000 increase on the right side of the equation.

Assets	=	Liabilities	+	Stockholders' Equity
Cash				**Contributed Capital**
(a) + 2,000	=			+2,000

(b) **Papa John's borrows $6,000 from its local bank, signing a note to be paid in three years.**

1. *Identify and classify accounts and effects:*
   Cash (A) is received + $6,000. A written promise to pay is given to the bank, Long-Term Notes Payable (L) + $6,000.

2. *Is the accounting equation in balance?*
   Yes. There is a $6,000 increase on the left side and a $6,000 increase on the right side of the equation.

Assets	=	Liabilities	+	Stockholders' Equity
Cash		**Long-Term Notes Payable**		**Contributed Capital**
(a) + 2,000	=			+2,000
(b) + 6,000	=	+ 6,000		

Events (*a*) and (*b*) are *financing* transactions. Companies that need cash for *investing* purposes (to buy or build additional facilities) often seek funds by selling stock to investors as in Event (*a*) or by borrowing from creditors as in Event (*b*).

(c) Papa John's purchases $10,000 of new ovens, counters, refrigerators, and other equipment, paying $2,000 in cash and signing a two-year note payable to the equipment manufacturer for the rest.

1. *Identify and classify accounts and effects:*

   Property and Equipment (A) is received + $10,000. Cash (A) − $2,000 and a written promise to pay, Long-Term Notes Payable (L) + $8,000, are given to the manufacturer.

2. *Is the accounting equation in balance?*

   Yes. There is an $8,000 increase on the left side and an $8,000 increase on the right side of the equation.

	Assets		=	Liabilities	+	Stockholders' Equity
	Cash	Property and Equipment		Long-Term Notes Payable		Contributed Capital
(a)	+ 2,000		=			+2,000
(b)	+ 6,000		=	+ 6,000		
(c)	− 2,000	+10,000	=	+ 8,000		

Notice that more than two accounts were affected by this transaction.

The effects of Events (*a*), (*b*), and (*c*) are listed in the chart at the bottom of the next page following the Self-Study Quiz. Space is left on the chart for your analysis of Events (*d*), (*e*), and (*f*).

SELF-STUDY QUIZ

Practice is the most effective way to develop your transaction analysis skills. Review the analysis in Events (*a*) through (*c*) and complete the analysis of Events (*d*) through (*f*) in the following chart. Repeat the steps until they become a natural part of your thought process. After you have completed the chart, check your answers with the solutions at the bottom of the following page.

(d) Papa John's lends $3,000 to new franchisees who sign notes agreeing to repay the loans in five years.

1. *Identify and classify accounts and effects:*

   Written promises from the franchisees are received, Long-Term Notes Receivable (A) +$3,000. What and how much is given? _____

2. *Is the accounting equation in balance?*

   Yes. The equation remains the same because assets increase and decrease by the same amount.

(e) Papa John's purchases the stock of other companies as a long-term investment, paying $1,000 in cash.

1. *Identify and classify accounts and effects:*

   Stock certificates from the other companies are received, Long-Term Investments (A) +$1,000. Cash (A) is given −$1,000.

2. *Is the accounting equation in balance?*

   _____ Why? _____

(f) Papa John's board of directors declares that the Company will pay $3,000 in cash dividends to shareholders next month.* When a company's board of directors declares a cash dividend, a legal obligation is created.

1. Identify and classify accounts and effects:

In this transaction, earnings retained in the business are distributed to investors, Retained Earnings (SE) — $3,000. What and how much is given? _____

2. Is the accounting equation in balance?

_____ Why? _____

	Assets				=	Liabilities	+	Stockholders' Equity	
	Cash	Long-Term Notes Receivable	Property and Equipment	Long-Term Investments		Long-Term Notes Payable	Dividends Payable	Contributed Capital	Retained Earnings
(a)	+2,000				=			+2,000	
(b)	+6,000				=	+6,000			
(c)	−2,000		+10,000		=	+8,000			
(d)	_____	+3,000			=				
(e)	−1,000			+1,000	=				
(f)					=		_____		−3,000

After you have completed your answers, check them with the solutions at the bottom of the page.

Learning Objective 4
Determine the impact of business transactions on the balance sheet using two basic tools, journal entries and T-accounts.

HOW DO COMPANIES KEEP TRACK OF ACCOUNT BALANCES?

For most organizations, recording transaction effects and keeping track of account balances in the manner just presented is impractical. To handle the multitude of daily transactions that business generates, companies establish accounting systems, usually computerized, that follow a cycle. The accounting cycle, illustrated in Exhibit 2.4, highlights the primary activities during the accounting period to analyze, record, and post transactions. In Chapters 2 and 3, we will illustrate these activities during the period. In Chapter 4, we will complete the accounting cycle by discussing and illustrating activities at the end of the period to adjust the records, prepare financial statements, and prepare the records for the next cycle.

During the accounting period, transactions that result in exchanges between the company and other external parties are analyzed and recorded in the **general journal** in chronological order, and the related accounts are updated in the **general ledger.** In place of these formal records, accountants rely on two very important tools: journal entries and T-accounts. From the standpoint of accounting systems design, these analytical tools are a more efficient way to reflect the effects of transactions, determine account balances, and prepare financial statements. As future business managers, you

---

*At the time this chapter is being written, Papa John's has not declared dividends; this transaction is included for purposes of illustration only.

Self-Study Quiz
Solutions

(*d*) Cash (A) is given −$3,000.

(*e*) Yes. The equation remains the same because assets increase and decrease by the same amount.

(*f*) Dividends Payable (L) is given +$3,000. Yes, there is a $3,000 increase and a $3,000 decrease on the right side.

If your answers did not agree with ours, we recommend that you go back to each event to make sure that you have completed each of the steps of transaction analysis.

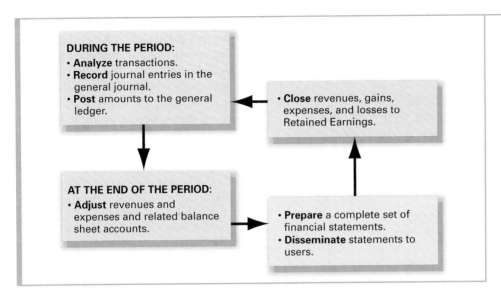

EXHIBIT 2.4

The Accounting Cycle

should develop your understanding and use of these tools in financial analysis. For those studying accounting, this knowledge is the foundation for an understanding of the accounting system and future accounting coursework. After we explain how to perform transaction analysis using these tools, we illustrate their use in financial analysis.

The Direction of Transaction Effects

As we saw earlier, transactions increase and decrease assets, liabilities, and stockholders' equity. To reflect these effects efficiently, we need to structure the transaction analysis model in a manner that shows the **direction** of the effects. In Exhibit 2.5, notice that:

- The increase symbol + is located on the left side of the T for accounts on the left side of the accounting equation and on the right side of the T for accounts on the right side of the equation.

- The symbols **dr** for **debit** and **cr** for **credit** are always written on the left and the right of each account, respectively. Debit means the left side of an account, and credit means the right.

DEBIT means the left side of an account.

CREDIT means the right side of an account.

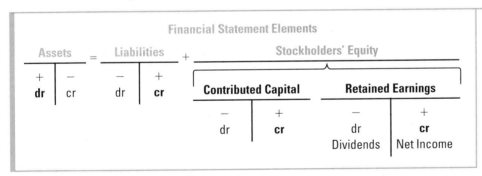

EXHIBIT 2.5

Transaction Analysis Model

From this transaction analysis model, we can observe the following:

- Asset accounts increase on the left (debit) side; they have debit balances. It would be highly unusual for an asset account, such as Inventory, to have a negative (credit) balance.

- Liability and stockholders' equity accounts increase on the right (credit) side, creating credit balances.

As you are learning to perform transaction analysis, you should refer to this model often until you can construct it on your own without assistance.

Many students have trouble with accounting because they forget that the meaning of *debit* is simply the left side of an account and the meaning of *credit* is simply the right side of an account. Perhaps someone once told you that you were a credit to your school or your family. As a result, you may think that credits are good and debits are bad. Such is not the case. Just remember that **debit means left** and **credit means right.**

To remember which accounts debits increase and which accounts credits increase, recall that a debit (left) increases asset accounts because assets are on the left side of the accounting equation (A = L + SE). Similarly, a credit (right) increases liability and stockholders' equity accounts because they are on the right side of the accounting equation.

If you have identified the correct accounts and effects through transaction analysis, the accounting equation will remain in balance. Moreover, **the total dollar value of all debits will equal the total dollar value of all credits** in a transaction. For an extra measure of assurance, add this equality check (Debits = Credits) to the transaction analysis process.

Analytical Tool: The Journal Entry

In a bookkeeping system, transactions are recorded in chronological order in a **journal.** (See **www.mhhe.com/libby5e** Appendix E for an illustration of formal recordkeeping procedures.) After analyzing the business documents that describe a transaction, the bookkeeper enters the effects on the accounts in the journal using debits and credits. The **journal entry,** then, is an accounting method for expressing the effects of a transaction on accounts. It is written in a debits-equal-credits format.

The journal entry for Event (*c*) in the Papa John's illustration is as follows:

A JOURNAL ENTRY is an accounting method for expressing the effects of a transaction on accounts in a debits-equal-credits format.

(date or reference)	Property and equipment (+A)	10,000	
	Cash (−A)		2,000
	Long-term notes payable (+L)		8,000

Notice the following:

■ It is useful to include a date or some form of reference for each transaction.

■ The debits are written first (on top); the credits are written below the debits and are indented to the right (both the words and the amounts). The order of the debited accounts or credited accounts does not matter, as long as the debits are on top and the credits are on the bottom and indented.

■ Total debits ($10,000) equal total credits ($2,000 + $8,000).

■ Three accounts are affected by this transaction. Any journal entry that affects more than two accounts is called a **compound entry.** Although this is the only transaction in the Papa John's illustration that affects more than two accounts, many transactions in subsequent chapters require a compound journal entry.

While you are learning to perform transaction analysis, use the symbols A, L, and SE next to each account title, as in the preceding journal entry. Specifically identifying accounts as assets (A), liabilities (L), or stockholders' equity (SE) clarifies the transaction analysis and makes journal entries easier to write. For example, if Cash is to be increased, we write Cash (+A). Throughout subsequent chapters, we include the direction of the effect along with the symbol to help you understand the effects of each transaction on the financial statements.

Many students try to memorize journal entries without understanding or using the transaction analysis model. As more detailed transactions are presented in subsequent chapters, the task becomes increasingly more difficult. In the long run, **memorizing, understanding, and using the transaction analysis model** presented here will save you time and prevent confusion.

Analytical Tool: The T-Account

By themselves, journal entries do not provide the balances in accounts. After the journal entries have been recorded, the bookkeeper posts (transfers) the dollar amounts to

EXHIBIT 2.6

GENERAL JOURNAL				
				Page 1

Date	Account Titles and Explanations	Posted Ref.	Debit	Credit
4/1/2007	Cash	101	9,000	
	Contributed capital	301		9,000
	Issued 1,500 shares of stock to investors (names).			
4/3/2007	Equipment	110	600	
	Cash	101		200
	Short-term notes payable	201		400
	Purchased hand tools (supplier and invoice data			
	indicated), paying part in cash (check number			
	indicated) and part on account.			

GENERAL LEDGER					
Account Title Cash				Account Number 101	

Date	Explanation	Posted Ref.	Debit	Credit	Balance
4/1/2007	Investments by owners	1	9,000		9,000
4/3/2007	Hand tools purchased	1		200	8,800
4/4/2007	Land purchased	1		5,000	3,800
4/5/2007	Fuel purchased	1		90	3,710
4/6/2007	Revenue in advance	2	1,600		5,310
4/8/2007	Insurance purchased	2		300	5,010
4/10/2007	Collection from customers	2	3,500		8,510
4/14/2007	Wages paid	3		3,900	4,610
4/18/2007	Note and interest paid	3		740	3,870
4/21/2007	Suppliers paid	3		100	3,770
4/29/2007	Collection from city	4	1,262		5,032

each account affected by the transaction to determine the new account balances. (In most computerized accounting systems, this happens automatically.)

As a group, the accounts are called a **ledger.** In the manual accounting system used by some small organizations, the ledger is often a three-ring binder with a separate page for each account. In a computerized system, accounts are stored on a disk. See Exhibit 2.6 for an illustration of a journal page and the related Cash ledger page. Note that the cash effects from the journal entries have been posted to the Cash ledger page.

One very useful tool for summarizing the transaction effects and determining the balances for individual accounts is a T-account, a simplified representation of a ledger account. Exhibit 2.7 shows the T-accounts for Papa John's Cash and Long-Term Notes Payable accounts based on Events (*a*) through (*f*). Notice that, for Cash, which is classified as an asset, increases are shown on the left and decreases on the right side of the T-account. For Long-Term Notes Payable, however, increases are shown on the right and decreases on the left since notes payable is a liability. Many small businesses still use handwritten or manually maintained accounts in this T-account format. Computerized systems retain the concept but not the format of the T-account.

The T-ACCOUNT is a tool for summarizing transaction effects for each account, determining balances, and drawing inferences about a company's activities.

EXHIBIT 2.7

T-Accounts Illustrated

+ Cash (A) −			
Beg. balance	7,000		
(*a*)	2,000	(*c*)	2,000
(*b*)	6,000	(*d*)	3,000
		(*e*)	1,000
End. balance	9,000		

− Long-Term Notes Payable (L) +		
	Beg. balance	61,000
	(*b*)	6,000
	(*c*)	8,000
	End. balance	75,000

In Exhibit 2.7, notice that the ending balance is indicated on the positive side with a double underline. To find the account balances, we can express the T-accounts as equations:

	Cash	Long-Term Notes Payable
Beginning balance	$ 7,000	$ 61,000
+ "+" side	+8,000	+14,000
− "−" side	−6,000	− 0
Ending balance	$ 9,000	$ 75,000

A word on terminology: The words *debit* and *credit* may be used as verbs, nouns, and adjectives. For example, we can say that Papa John's Cash account was debited (verb) when stock was issued to investors, meaning that the amount was entered on the left side of the T-account. Or we can say that a credit (noun) was entered on the right side of an account. Notes Payable may be described as a credit account (adjective). These terms will be used instead of *left* and *right* throughout the rest of this textbook. The next section illustrates the steps to follow in analyzing the effects of transactions, recording the effects in journal entries, and determining account balances using T-accounts.

Transaction Analysis Illustrated

In this section, we will use the monthly transactions for Papa John's that were presented earlier to demonstrate transaction analysis and the use of journal entries and T-accounts. We analyze each transaction, checking to make sure that the accounting equation remains in balance and that debits equal credits. In the T-accounts, located together at the end of the illustration, the amounts from Papa John's December 31, 2003, balance sheet have been inserted as the beginning balances. After reviewing or preparing each journal entry, trace the effects to the appropriate T-accounts using the transaction letters (*a*) to (*f*) as a reference. The first transaction has been highlighted for you.

Study this illustration carefully, including the explanations of transaction analysis. Careful study is **essential** to an understanding of (1) the accounting model, (2) transaction analysis, (3) the dual effects of each transaction, and (4) the dual-balancing system. The most effective way to learn these critical concepts, which are basic to material throughout the rest of the text, is to practice, practice, practice.

(a) Papa John's issues $2,000 of additional common stock, receiving cash from investors.

Cash (+A) 2,000
    Contributed capital (+SE) 2,000

Assets	=	Liabilities	+	Stockholders' Equity	
Cash	+2,000			Contributed capital	+2,000

Equality checks: (1) Debits $2,000 = Credits $2,000; (2) the accounting equation is in balance.

These effects have been posted to the appropriate T-accounts at the end of the illustration. To post the amounts, transfer or copy the debit or credit amount on each line to the appropriate T-account. For example, the $2,000 debit is listed in the debit (increase) column of the Cash T-account.

(b) Papa John's borrows $6,000 from its local bank, signing a note to be paid in three years.

Cash (+A) 6,000
    Long-term notes payable (+L) 6,000

Assets	=	Liabilities	+	Stockholders' Equity
Cash	+6,000	Long-term notes payable	+6,000	

Equality checks: (1) Debits $6,000 = Credits $6,000; (2) the accounting equation is in balance.

(c) Papa John's purchases $10,000 of new ovens, counters, refrigerators, and other equipment, paying $2,000 in cash and signing a two-year note payable to the equipment manufacturer for $8,000.

Property and equipment (+A) 10,000
    Cash (−A) 2,000
    Long-term notes payable (+L) 8,000

Assets	=	Liabilities	+	Stockholders' Equity
Property and equipment +10,000		Long-term notes payable +8,000		
Cash −2,000				

Equality checks: (1) Debits $10,000 = Credits $10,000; (2) the accounting equation is in balance.

SELF-STUDY QUIZ

For Events (d), (e), and (f), fill in the missing information indicated; then post the entries to the T-accounts.

(d) Papa John's lends $3,000 to new franchisees who sign notes agreeing to repay the loans in five years. Write the journal entry, post it to the T-accounts, and complete the equality checks.

_____ (   ) .... _____

_____ (   ) .... _____

Assets	=	Liabilities	+	Stockholders' Equity
Cash −3,000				
Long-term notes receivable +3,000				

Equality checks: (1) Debits $_____ = Credits $_____; (2) the accounting equation is in balance.

(e) Papa John's purchases the stock of other companies as a long-term investment, paying $1,000 in cash. Complete the effects on the accounting equation by indicating the accounts, amounts, and direction of the effect.

Long-term investments (+A) 1,000

Cash (−A) 1,000

Assets	=	Liabilities	+	Stockholders' Equity
_____ _____				
_____ _____				

Equality checks: (1) Debits $1,000 = Credits $1,000; (2) the accounting equation is in balance? _____

After you have completed your answers, check them with the solutions at the bottom of the page.

Self-Study Quiz Solutions

(d) Journal entry:

Long-term notes receivable (+A) 3,000

   Cash (−A) 3,000

Debits $3,000 = Credits $3,000

(e) Effect on the Accounting Equation:

Assets	=	Liabilities	+	Stockholders' Equity
Cash − 1,000				
Long-term investments +1,000				

The accounting equation is in balance.

(f) Papa John's board of directors declares that the Company will pay $3,000 in cash dividends to shareholders next month.* When a company's board of directors declares a cash dividend, a legal obligation is created. Write the journal entry, post it to the T-accounts, and complete the effects on the accounting equation.

_____ ( )	....	3,000
_____ ( )	....	3,000

Assets	=	Liabilities	+	Stockholders' Equity
		+3,000		−3,000

Equality checks: (1) Debits $3,000 = Credits $3,000; (2) the accounting equation is in balance.

After you have completed your answers, check them with the solutions at the bottom of the page.

Following are the T-accounts that *changed* during the period because of these transactions. The beginning balances are the amounts from the December 31, 2003, Papa John's balance sheet. The balances of all other accounts remained the same.

+ Cash (A) −

12/28/03 bal.	7,000		
(a)	2,000	2,000	(c)
(b)	6,000	_____	(d)
	_____		(e)
1/31/04 bal.	9,000		

+ Long-Term Investments (A) −

12/28/03 bal.	8,000	
(e)	_____	
1/31/04 bal.	9,000	

+ Property and Equipment, Net (A) −

12/28/03 bal.	204,000	
(c)	10,000	
1/31/04 bal.	214,000	

+ Long-Term Notes Receivable (A) −

12/28/03 bal.	11,000	
(d)	_____	
1/31/04 bal.	14,000	

− Long-Term Notes Payable (L) +

		61,000	12/28/03 bal.
		6,000	(b)
		8,000	(c)
		75,000	1/31/04 bal.

− Dividends Payable (L) +

		0	12/28/03 bal.
		_____	(f)
		3,000	1/31/04 bal.

− Contributed Capital (SE) +

		1,000	12/28/03 bal.
		2,000	(a)
		3,000	1/31/04 bal.

− Retained Earnings (SE) +

		158,000	12/28/03 bal.
(f)	_____		
		155,000	1/31/04 bal.

*At the time this chapter is being written, Papa John's has not declared dividends; this transaction is included for purposes of illustration only.

Self-Study Quiz
Solutions

(f) Journal entry:

Retained earnings (−SE)	....	3,000	
Dividends payable (+L)	....		3,000

Effect on the Accounting Equation:

Assets	=	Liabilities		+	Stockholders' Equity	
		Dividends payable	+3,000		Retained earnings	−3,000

You can verify that you posted the entries properly by adding the increase side and subtracting the decrease side of each T-account and comparing your answer with the ending balance for each T-account.

Inferring Business Activities from T-Accounts

T-accounts are useful primarily for instructional and analytical purposes. In many cases, we will use T-accounts to determine what transactions a company engaged in during a period. For example, the primary transactions affecting Accounts Payable for a period are purchases of assets on account and cash payments to suppliers. If we know the beginning and ending balances of Accounts Payable and all the amounts that were purchased on credit during a period, we can determine the amount of cash paid. A T-account analysis would include the following:

− Accounts Payable (L) +			
Cash payments to suppliers	?	600	Beg. bal.
		1,500	Purchases on account
		300	End. bal.

Solution:

Beginning Balance	+	Purchases on Account	−	Cash Payments to Suppliers	=	Ending Balance
$600	+	$1,500	−	?	=	$ 300
		$2,100	−	?	=	$ 300
				?	=	$1,800

HOW IS THE BALANCE SHEET PREPARED?

It is possible to prepare a balance sheet at any point in time using the balances in the accounts. The balance sheet in Exhibit 2.8 was prepared using the new balances shown in the T-accounts in the preceding Papa John's illustration (shaded lines in the exhibit) plus the original balances in the accounts that did not change. It compares the account balances at January 31, 2004, with those at December 28, 2003. Note that when multiple periods are presented, the most recent balance sheet amounts are usually listed on the left.

At the beginning of the chapter, we presented the changes in Papa John's balance sheets from the years 1994 to 2003. We questioned what made the accounts change and what the process was for reflecting the changes. Now we can see that the accounts have changed again in one month due to the transactions illustrated in this chapter:

	Assets	=	Liabilities	+	Stockholders' Equity
End of January 2004	$363,000		$205,000		$158,000
End of 2003	347,000		188,000		159,000
Change	+$ 16,000		+$ 17,000		−$ 1,000

Learning Objective 5
Prepare and analyze a simple balance sheet using the financial leverage ratio.

Topic Tackler

PLUS

Topic Tackler 2–2

EXHIBIT 2.8

Papa John's Balance Sheet

PAPA JOHN'S INTERNATIONAL, INC. AND SUBSIDIARIES
Consolidated Balance Sheets
(dollars in thousands)

	January 31, 2004	December 28, 2003
Assets		
Current assets		
Cash	$ 9,000	$ 7,000
Accounts receivable	20,000	20,000
Supplies	17,000	17,000
Prepaid expenses	11,000	11,000
Other current assets	7,000	7,000
Total current assets	64,000	62,000
Long-term investments	9,000	8,000
Property and equipment (net of accumulated depreciation of $149,000)	214,000	204,000
Long-term notes receivable	14,000	11,000
Intangibles	49,000	49,000
Other assets	13,000	13,000
Total assets	$363,000	$347,000
Liabilities and Stockholders' Equity		
Current liabilities		
Accounts payable	$ 28,000	$ 28,000
Dividends payable	3,000	0
Accrued expenses payable	53,000	53,000
Total current liabilities	84,000	81,000
Unearned franchise fees	6,000	6,000
Long-term notes payable	75,000	61,000
Other long-term liabilities	40,000	40,000
Stockholders' equity		
Contributed capital	3,000	1,000
Retained earnings	155,000	158,000
Total stockholders' equity	158,000	159,000
Total liabilities and stockholders' equity	$363,000	$347,000

Total Liabilities = $205,000 on January 31, 2004 and $188,000 on December 28, 2003

KEY RATIO ANALYSIS

Financial Leverage Ratio

Users of financial information compute a number of ratios in analyzing a company's past performance and financial condition as input in predicting its future potential. How ratios change over time and how they compare to the ratios of the company's competitors or industry averages provide valuable information about a company's strategies for its operating, investing, and financing activities.

We introduce here the first of many ratios that will be presented throughout the rest of this textbook, with a final summary of ratio analysis in Chapter 14. In Chapters 2, 3, and 4, we present three ratios that provide information about management's effectiveness at managing debt and equity financing (financial leverage ratio), utilizing assets (total asset turnover ratio), and controlling revenues and costs (net profit margin), all for the purpose of enhancing returns to shareholders. In Chapter 5, we discuss the powerful effects of combining these three general ratios. The remaining chapters discuss the specific ratios affecting each of the general ratios for a more precise assessment of a company's strategies, strengths, and areas for concern.

As we discussed earlier in the chapter, companies raise large amounts of money to acquire additional assets by issuing stock to investors and borrowing funds from creditors. These additional assets are used to generate more income. However, since debt must be repaid, taking on increasing amounts of liabilities carries increased risk. The financial leverage ratio provides one measure for analysts to examine this financing and investing strategy.

? ANALYTICAL QUESTION

How is management using debt to increase the amount of assets the company employs to earn income for stockholders?

% RATIO AND COMPARISONS

Financial Leverage Ratio = Average Total Assets/Average Stockholders' Equity

"Average" is a simple average computed by adding together the beginning and ending balance of assets or stockholders' equity, then dividing by two. Averaging of the balance sheet amounts is done to capture the midpoint of activities during the period. In a formula format, the computation is:

$$(\text{Beg bal} + \text{End bal})/2$$

The 2003 ratio for Papa John's is (dollars are in thousands):

$$\frac{\text{2003 Balance} \quad \text{2002 Balance}}{(\$367{,}000 \quad + \quad \$347{,}000)/2} = 2.54$$
$$\overline{(\$122{,}000 \quad + \quad \$159{,}000)/2}$$

Comparisons over Time		
Papa John's International, Inc.		
2001	2002	2003
2.16	2.38	2.54

Comparisons with Competitors	
California Pizza Kitchen, Inc.	Pizza Inn Inc.
2003	2003
1.26	2.23

California Pizza Kitchen, Inc., focuses on offering premium pizza and other related menu items, operates over 160 casual dining restaurants (82 percent company owned) located in 27 states and five foreign countries. *Pizza Inn, Inc.,* has over 410 restaurants, mostly franchised, in 20 states, primarily in the southern half of the United States and 10 foreign countries.

Determining the Competition
You cannot always compare the closest competitors. Pizza Hut and Domino's, noted as primary competitors for Papa John's, are not used in this analysis for the following reasons:
- *Pizza Hut is owned by Yum! Brands that also owns KFC and Taco Bell. Separate financial information for Pizza Hut is not publicly available.*
- *Until 2004, Domino's was involved in a change in ownership in previous years, causing a negative amount in stockholders' equity. The results would be unusual and, therefore, not useful as a basis for comparison.*

💡 INTERPRETATIONS

In General → The financial leverage ratio measures the relationship between total assets and the stockholders' equity that finances the assets. As noted, companies finance their assets with stockholders' equity and debt. The higher the proportion of assets financed by debt, the higher the financial leverage ratio. Conversely, the higher the proportion of assets financed with stockholders' equity, the lower the ratio. A ratio of 1.00 indicates the company has no liabilities. A ratio of 2.00 means the company uses debt and equity financing equally to acquire assets. A ratio above 2.00 suggests a heavier reliance on debt than equity. Let's illustrate this:

Selected Focus Companies' Financial Leverage Ratios

Harrah's   4.03

Harley-Davidson   1.69

Home Depot   1.53

	Assets	=	Liabilities	+	Stockholders' Equity	
If a company has no debt,	10		0		10	then the ratio = 1.00
If a company adds equal debt,	20		10		10	then the ratio = 2.00

In this case, twice as many assets are now available to generate revenues for shareholders.

If a company adds more debt,	30		20		10	then the ratio = 3.00

In this case, even more revenues can be generated with the additional assets, but the company has twice as much debt as stockholders' equity, and creditors will charge higher interest rates as a company's debt burden increases. The company is seen as riskier.

Increasing debt (and the leverage ratio) increases the amount of assets the company employs to earn income for stockholders, which increases the chances of earning higher income. However, it also increases *risk*. Debt financing is riskier than financing with stockholders' equity because the interest payments on debt must be made every period (they are legal obligations), whereas dividends on stock can be postponed. An increasing ratio over time signals more reliance on debt financing and more risk.

Creditors and security analysts use this ratio to assess a company's risk level, while managers use the ratio in deciding whether to expand by adding debt. As long as the interest on borrowing is less than the additional earnings generated, utilizing debt will enhance the stockholders' earnings.

Focus Company Analysis → Papa John's financial leverage increased each year. In 2003, the company financed its assets over one-and-one-half times more with debt than with stockholders' equity. Since December 1999, Papa John's has undertaken a major effort to repurchase its issued stock from shareholders. The money to buy back the shares is financed primarily by borrowing. This results in decreasing stockholders' equity while increasing liabilities without increasing assets. Thus, the financial leverage ratio increases. Papa John's has assumed more risk over time.

When compared against two other pizza restaurants, Papa John's 2003 financial leverage ratio is the largest. The two competitors listed are eat-in restaurants that must invest more in facilities than Papa John's, which primarily rents space instead of constructing buildings. However, Papa John's share repurchase program causes its ratio to exceed the two competitors. Reuters reports that the restaurant industry has an average leverage ratio of 1.58 (approximately half as much debt as equity financing). This suggests that Papa John's at 2.54 is following a much riskier (more aggressive) financing strategy than are other companies in the restaurant industry.

A Few Cautions: A financial leverage ratio near 1.00 indicates a company that is choosing not to utilize debt to expand. This suggests the company has lower risk but is not enhancing the return to stockholders. When comparing competitors, the ratio may be influenced by differences in business strategies, such as whether the company rents or buys facilities.

SELF-STUDY QUIZ

Wendy's International

Wendy's International, Inc., had the following balances on its recent balance sheets (in thousands):

Beginning of year: Assets—$2,723,427; Liabilities—$1,274,822; Stockholders' equity—$1,448,605

End of year: Assets—$3,164,013; Liabilities—$1,405,407; Stockholders' equity—$1,758,606

Compute Wendy's financial leverage ratio. What does this ratio suggest about Wendy's level of financial risk and financing strategy?

After you have completed your answers, check them with the solutions at the bottom of the page.

Self-Study Quiz
Solutions

($3,164,013 + $2,723,427)/2 ÷ ($1,758,606 + $1,448,605)/2 = 1.84, so Wendy's is following a slightly riskier financing strategy than other companies in the industry. This ratio is higher than the industry average but lower than Papa John's.

Investing and Financing Activities

Recall from Chapter 1 that companies report cash inflows and outflows over a period in their statement of cash flows. This statement divides all transactions that affect cash into three categories: operating, investing, and financing activities. Operating activities are covered in Chapter 3. Investing activities include buying and selling noncurrent assets and investments; financing activities include borrowing and repaying debt including short-term bank loans, issuing and repurchasing stock, and paying dividends. When cash is involved, these activities are reported on the statement of cash flows. (When cash is not included in the transaction, such as when a building is acquired with a long-term mortgage note payable, there is no cash effect to include on the statement of cash flows. You must see cash in the transaction for it to affect the statement of cash flows.) In general, the effects of such activities are as follows:

> **Learning Objective 6**
> Identify investing and financing transactions and demonstrate how they are reported on the statement of cash flows.

	Effect on Cash Flows
Operating activities	
(No transactions in this chapter were operating activities.)	
Investing activities	
Purchasing long-term assets and investments for cash	−
Selling long-term assets and investments for cash	+
Lending cash to others	−
Receiving principal payments on loans made to others	+
Financing activities	
Borrowing cash from banks	+
Repaying the principal on borrowings from banks	−
Issuing stock for cash	+
Repurchasing stock with cash	−
Paying cash dividends	−

Focus Company Analysis   Exhibit 2.9 shows a statement of cash flows for Papa John's based on the activities listed in this chapter. It reports the sources and uses of cash that created the $2,000 increase in cash (from $7,000 to $9,000) in January 2004. Remember that only transactions that affect cash are reported on the cash flow statement.

The pattern of cash flows shown in Exhibit 2.9 (net cash outflows for investing activities and net cash inflows from financing activities) is typical of Papa John's past several annual statements of cash flows. Companies seeking to expand usually report cash outflows for investing activities.

SELF-STUDY **QUIZ**

Lance, Inc., manufactures and sells snack products. Indicate whether these transactions from a recent annual statement of cash flows were investing (I) or financing (F) activities and the direction of their effects on cash (+ = increases cash; − = decreases cash):

Lance, Inc.

TRANSACTIONS	TYPE OF ACTIVITY (I OR F)	EFFECT ON CASH FLOWS (+ OR −)
1. Paid dividends.	_____	_____
2. Sold property.	_____	_____
3. Sold marketable securities (investments).	_____	_____
4. Purchased vending machines.	_____	_____
5. Repurchased its own common stock.	_____	_____

After you have completed the schedule, check it with the solutions at the bottom of the page.

1. F −   2. I +   3. I +   4. I −   5. F −

EXHIBIT 2.9

Papa John's Statement
of Cash Flows

Items are referenced to Events (a) *through* (f)
illustrated in this chapter.

PAPA JOHN'S INTERNATIONAL, INC.
Consolidated Statement of Cash Flows
For the month ended January 31, 2004
(in thousands)

Operating Activities	
(None in this chapter.)	
Investing Activities	
Purchased property and equipment (c)	$(2,000)
Purchased investments (e)	(1,000)
Lent funds to franchisees (d)	(3,000)
Net cash used in investing activities	**(6,000)**
Financing Activities	
Issued common stock (a)	2,000
Borrowed from banks (b)	6,000
Net cash provided by financing activities	**8,000**
Net increase in cash	**2,000**
Cash at beginning of month	7,000
Cash at end of month	**$ 9,000**

Agrees with the amount on the balance sheet. ──▶

DEMONSTRATION CASE

On April 1, 2007, three ambitious college students started Terrific Lawn Maintenance Corporation. A summary of transactions completed through April 30, 2007, for Terrific Lawn Maintenance Corporation follows:

(a)   Issued 500 shares of stock (1,500 shares in total) to each of the three investors in exchange for $9,000 cash.

(b)   Acquired rakes and other hand tools (equipment) with a list price of $690 for $600; paid the hardware store $200 cash and signed a three-month note for the balance.

(c)   Ordered three lawn mowers and two edgers from XYZ Lawn Supply, Inc., for $4,000.

(d)   Purchased 4 acres of land for the future site of a storage garage; paid cash, $5,000.

(e)   Received the mowers and edgers that had been ordered, signing a note to pay XYZ Lawn Supply in full in 30 days.

(f)   Sold for $1,250 one acre of land to the city for a park. Accepted a note from the city for payment by the end of the month.

(g)   One of the owners borrowed $3,000 from a local bank for personal use.

Required:

1. Set up T-accounts for Cash, Short-Term Notes Receivable (from the city), Equipment (hand tools and mowing equipment), Land, Short-Term Notes Payable (to equipment supply companies), and Contributed Capital. Beginning balances are $0; indicate these beginning balances in the T-accounts. Analyze each transaction using the process outlined in the chapter. Prepare journal entries in chronological order. Enter the effects of the transactions in the appropriate T-accounts; identify each amount with its letter in the preceding list.

2. Use the amounts in the T-accounts developed in requirement (1) to prepare a classified balance sheet for Terrific Lawn Maintenance Corporation at April 30, 2007. Show the account balances for all assets, liabilities, and stockholders' equity. Use the following transaction analysis model.

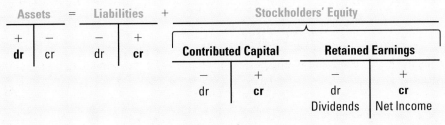

3. Prepare the investing and financing sections of the statement of cash flows. Check your answers with the solution in the following section.

SUGGESTED SOLUTION

1. Transaction analysis, journal entries, and T-accounts:

| (a) | Cash (+A) .... | 9,000 | |
| | Contributed capital (+SE) .... | | 9,000 |

	Assets	=	Liabilities	+	Stockholders' Equity	
Cash	+ 9,000				Contributed capital	+ 9,000

Equality checks: (1) Debits $9,000 = Credits $9,000; (2) the accounting equation is in balance.

(b)	Equipment (+A)	600	
	Cash (−A)		200
	Short-term notes payable (+L)		400

	Assets	=	Liabilities	+	Stockholders' Equity
Equipment	+ 600	Short-term notes			
Cash	− 200	payable	+ 400		

Equality checks: (1) Debits $600 = Credits $600; (2) the accounting equation is in balance.

The **historical cost principle** states that assets should be recorded at the amount paid on the date of the transaction, or $600, rather than at the $690 list price.

| (c) | This is not an accounting transaction; no exchange has taken place. No accounts are affected. |

| (d) | Land (+A) .... | 5,000 | |
| | Cash (−A) .... | | 5,000 |

	Assets	=	Liabilities	+	Stockholders' Equity
Land	+ 5,000				
Cash	− 5,000				

Equality checks: (1) Debits $5,000 = Credits $5,000; (2) the accounting equation is in balance.

| (e)   Equipment (+A) .... | 4,000 | |
| Short-term notes payable (+L) .... | | 4,000 |

Assets	=	Liabilities	+	Stockholders' Equity
Equipment + 4,000		Short-term notes payable + 4,000		

Equality checks: (1) Debits $4,000 = Credits $4,000; (2) the accounting equation is in balance.

| (f)   Short-term notes receivable (+A) .... | 1,250 | |
| Land (−A) .... | | 1,250 |

Assets	=	Liabilities	+	Stockholders' Equity
Short-term notes receivable + 1,250				
Land − 1,250				

Equality checks: (1) Debits $1,250 = Credits $1,250; (2) the accounting equation is in balance.

| (g)   There is no transaction for the company. The separate-entity assumption states that transactions of the owners are separate from transactions of the business. |

Cash (A)			
+(dr)		**−(cr)**	
Beg. bal.	0		
(a)	9,000	(b)	200
		(d)	5,000
End. bal.	3,800		

Short-Term Notes Receivable (A)			
+(dr)		**−(cr)**	
Beg. bal.	0		
(f)	1,250		
End. bal.	1,250		

Equipment (A)			
+(dr)		**−(cr)**	
Beg. bal.	0		
(b)	600		
(e)	4,000		
End. bal.	4,600		

Land (A)			
+(dr)		**−(cr)**	
Beg. bal.	0		
(d)	5,000		
		(f)	1,250
End. bal.	3,750		

Short-Term Notes Payable (L)			
−(dr)		**+(cr)**	
		Beg. bal.	0
		(b)	400
		(e)	4,000
		End. bal.	4,400

Contributed Capital (SE)			
−(dr)		**+(cr)**	
		Beg. bal.	0
		(a)	9,000
		End. bal.	9,000

2. Balance sheet:

TERRIFIC LAWN MAINTENANCE CORPORATION
Balance Sheet
At April 30, 2007

Assets		Liabilities	
Current Assets		*Current Liability*	
Cash	$ 3,800	Short-term notes payable	$4,400
Short-term notes receivable	1,250		
Total current assets	5,050		
Equipment	4,600	**Stockholders' Equity**	
Land	3,750	Contributed capital	9,000
Total assets	$13,400	Total liabilities and stockholders' equity	$13,400

Notice that the balance sheets presented earlier in the text listed assets on the top and liabilities and stockholders' equity on the bottom. It is also acceptable practice to prepare a balance sheet with assets on the left side and liabilities and stockholders' equity on the right side, as in the preceding example.

3. Investing and financing effects of the statement of cash flows:

TERRIFIC LAWN MAINTENANCE CORPORATION
Statement of Cash Flows
For the Month Ended April 30, 2007

Operating Activities	
(none in this case)	
Investing Activities	
Purchased land (*d*)	$(5,000)
Purchased equipment (*b*)	(200)
Net cash used in investing activities	**(5,200)**
Financing Activities	
Issued common stock (*a*)	9,000
Net cash provided by financing activities	**9,000**
Change in cash	3,800
Beginning cash balance	0
Ending cash balance	**$ 3,800**

CHAPTER TAKE-AWAYS

1. **Define the objective of financial reporting, the elements of the balance sheet, and the related key accounting assumptions and principles.   p. 51**

    • The primary objective of external financial reporting is to provide useful economic information about a business to help external parties, primarily investors and creditors, make sound financial decisions.

    • Elements of the balance sheet:
      a. Assets—probable future economic benefits owned by the entity as a result of past transactions.
      b. Liabilities—probable debts or obligations acquired by the entity as a result of past transactions, to be paid with assets or services.
      c. Stockholders' equity—the financing provided by the owners and by business operations.

    • Key accounting assumptions and principles:
      a. Separate-entity assumption—transactions of the business are accounted for separately from transactions of the owner.
      b. Unit-of-measure assumption—financial information is reported in the national monetary unit.
      c. Continuity (going-concern) assumption—a business is expected to continue to operate into the foreseeable future.
      d. Historical cost principle—financial statement elements should be recorded at the cash-equivalent cost on the date of the transaction.

2. **Identify what constitutes a business transaction and recognize common balance sheet account titles used in business.   p. 56**

    A transaction includes:

    • An exchange between a business and one or more external parties to a business.

    or

    • A measurable internal event, such as adjustments for the use of assets in operations.

    An account is a standardized format that organizations use to accumulate the dollar effects of transactions related to each financial statement item. Typical balance sheet account titles include the following:

    • Assets: Cash, Accounts Receivable, Inventory, Prepaid Expenses, and Buildings and Equipment.

    • Liabilities: Accounts Payable, Notes Payable, Accrued Expenses Payable, Unearned Revenues, and Taxes Payable.

    • Stockholders' equity: Contributed Capital and Retained Earnings.

3. **Apply transaction analysis to simple business transactions in terms of the accounting model: Assets = Liabilities + Stockholders' Equity.   p. 57**

    To determine the economic effect of a transaction on an entity in terms of the accounting equation, each transaction must be analyzed to determine the accounts (at least two) that are affected. In an exchange, the company receives something and gives up something. If the accounts, direction of the effects, and amounts are correctly analyzed, the accounting equation must stay in balance. The transaction analysis model is

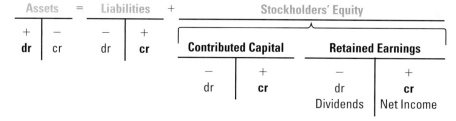

4. **Determine the impact of business transactions on the balance sheet using two basic tools, journal entries and T-accounts. p. 62**

   • Journal entries express the effects of a transaction on accounts in a debits-equal-credits format. The accounts and amounts to be debited are listed first. Then the accounts and amounts to be credited are listed below the debits and indented, resulting in debits on the left and credits on the right.

   (date or reference) Account xxx
                   Account   xxx

   • T-accounts summarize the transaction effects for each account. These tools can be used to determine balances and draw inferences about a company's activities.

+ Assets −		− Liabilities and Stockholders' Equity +	
Beginning balance Increases	Decreases	Decreases	Beginning balance Increases
Ending Balance			Ending Balance

5. **Prepare and analyze a simple balance sheet using the financial leverage ratio. p. 69**

   Classified balance sheets are structured with

   • Assets categorized as "current assets" (those to be used or turned into cash within the year, with inventory always considered a current asset) and noncurrent assets, such as long-term investments, property and equipment, and intangible assets.

   • Liabilities categorized as "current liabilities" (those that will be paid with current assets) and long-term liabilities.

   • Stockholders' equity accounts are listed as Contributed Capital first followed by Retained Earnings.

   The financial leverage ratio (Average Total Assets ÷ Average Stockholders' Equity) measures the relationship between total assets and the stockholders' capital that finances the assets. The higher the ratio, the more debt is used to finance the assets. As the ratio (and thus debt) increases, risk increases.

6. **Identify investing and financing transactions and demonstrate how they are reported on the statement of cash flows. p. 73**

   A statement of cash flows reports the sources and uses of cash for the period by the type of activity that generated the cash flow: operating, investing, and financing. Investing activities are purchasing and selling long-term assets and making loans and receiving principal repayments from others. Financing activities are borrowing and repaying to banks the principal on loans, issuing and repurchasing stock, and paying dividends.

   In this chapter, we discussed the fundamental accounting model and transaction analysis. Journal entries and T-accounts were used to record the results of transaction analysis for investing and financing decisions that affect balance sheet accounts. In Chapter 3, we continue our detailed look at the financial statements, in particular the income statement. The purpose of Chapter 3 is to build on your knowledge by discussing the measurement of revenues and expenses and illustrating the transaction analysis of operating decisions.

KEY **RATIO**

Financial leverage ratio measures the relationship between total assets and the stockholders' capital that finances them. The higher the ratio, the more debt is assumed by the company to finance assets. It is computed as follows (p. 71):

$$\text{Financial Leverage Ratio} = \frac{\text{Average Total Assets}}{\text{Average Stockholders' Equity}}$$

"Average" is (Last Year's Amount + This Year's Amount) ÷ 2

FINDING **FINANCIAL INFORMATION**

Balance Sheet

Current Assets
Cash
Accounts and notes
   receivable
Inventory
Prepaid expenses

Noncurrent Assets
Long-term investments
Property and equipment
Intangibles

Current Liabilities
Accounts payable
Notes payable
Accrued expenses payable
Unearned revenue

Noncurrent Liabilities
Long-term debt

Stockholders' Equity
Contributed capital
Retained earnings

Income Statement
To be presented in Chapter 3

Statement of Cash Flows

Under Operating Activities
To be presented in Chapter 3

Under Investing Activities
+ Sales of noncurrent assets for cash
− Purchases of noncurrent assets for cash
− Loans to others
+ Receipt of loan principal payments from others

Under Financing Activities
+ Borrowing from banks
− Repayment of loan principal to banks
+ Issuance of stock
− Repurchasing stock
− Payment of dividends

Notes
To be discussed in future chapters

KEY **TERMS**

Account p. 56
Assets p. 51
Continuity (Going-Concern)
   Assumption p. 51
Contributed Capital p. 55
Credit p. 63
Current Assets p. 52
Current Liabilities p. 54

Debit p. 63
Historical Cost Principle p. 53
Journal Entry p. 64
Liabilities p. 54
Primary Objective of External
   Financial Reporting p. 51
Retained Earnings p. 55
Separate-Entity Assumption p. 51

Stockholders' Equity (Owners' or
   Shareholders' Equity) p. 55
T-account p. 65
Transaction p. 56
Transaction Analysis p. 57
Unit-of-Measure Assumption p. 51

QUESTIONS

1. What is the primary objective of financial reporting for external users?
2. Define the following:
   a. Asset.
   b. Current asset.
   c. Liability.
   d. Current liability.
   e. Contributed capital.
   f. Retained earnings.
3. Explain what the following accounting terms mean:
   a. Separate-entity assumption.
   b. Unit-of-measure assumption.
   c. Continuity assumption.
   d. Historical cost principle.
4. Why are accounting assumptions necessary?
5. For accounting purposes, what is an account? Explain why accounts are used in an accounting system.
6. What is the fundamental accounting model?
7. Define a business transaction in the broad sense, and give an example of two different kinds of transactions.
8. Explain what *debit* and *credit* mean.
9. Briefly explain what is meant by *transaction analysis*. What are the two steps in transaction analysis?
10. What two accounting equalities must be maintained in transaction analysis?
11. What is a *journal entry?*
12. What is a *T-account?* What is its purpose?
13. How is the financial leverage ratio computed and interpreted?
14. What transactions are classified as investing activities in a statement of cash flows? What transactions are classified as financing activities?

MULTIPLE-CHOICE QUESTIONS

1. If a publicly traded company is trying to maximize its perceived value to decision makers external to the corporation, the company is most likely to *understate* which of the following on its balance sheet?
   a. Assets
   b. Liabilities
   c. Retained Earnings
   d. Contributed Capital
2. Which of the following is not an asset?
   a. Short-Term Investments
   b. Land
   c. Prepaid Expense
   d. Contributed Capital
3. Which of the following is false if a company's financial leverage ratio is increasing over time?
   a. The amount of average stockholders' equity is decreasing relative to average total assets.
   b. The amount of average total liabilities is increasing relative to average total assets.
   c. The company is decreasing its risk related to required interest payments associated with debt.
   d. The company is increasing its risk related to required interest payments associated with debt.
4. Total assets on a balance sheet prepared on any date must agree with which of the following?
   a. the sum of total liabilities and net income as shown on the income statement
   b. the sum of total liabilities and contributed capital
   c. the sum of total liabilities and retained earnings
   d. the sum of total liabilities and contributed capital and retained earnings
5. The "duality of effects" can best be described as follows:
   a. When one records a transaction in the accounting system, at least two effects on the basic accounting equation will result.
   b. When an exchange takes place between two parties, both parties must record the transaction.
   c. When a transaction is recorded, both the balance sheet and the income statement must be impacted.
   d. When a transaction is recorded, one account will always increase and one account will always decrease.

6. The T-account is a tool commonly used for analyzing which of the following?
   a. increases and decreases to a single account in the accounting system
   b. debits and credits to a single account in the accounting system
   c. changes in specific account balances over a time period
   d. all of the above describe how T-accounts are used by accountants

7. Which of the following describes how assets are listed on the balance sheet?
   a. in alphabetical order
   b. in order of magnitude, lowest value to highest value
   c. from most liquid to least liquid
   d. from least liquid to most liquid

8. Which of the following is *not* a financing activity on the statement of cash flows?
   a. when the company lends money
   b. when the company borrows money
   c. when the company pays dividends
   d. when the company issues stock to shareholders

9. How many of the following are true regarding *debits* and *credits?*
   ■ In any given transaction, the total amount of the debits and the total amount of the credits must be equal.
   ■ Debits decrease certain accounts and credits decrease certain accounts.
   ■ Liabilities and stockholders' equity accounts usually end in credit balances, while assets usually end in debit balances.
   a. none   b. one   c. two   d. three

10. How many of the following statements are true regarding the balance sheet?
    ■ One cannot determine the true "fair market value" of a company by reviewing its balance sheet.
    ■ Certain internally generated assets, such as a trademark, are not reported on a company's balance sheet.
    ■ A balance sheet shows only the ending balances, in a summarized format, of all "balance sheet accounts" in the accounting system as of a particular date.
    a. none   b. one   c. two   d. three

For more practice with multiple-choice questions, go to the text website at www.mhhe.com/ libby5e or the Topic Tackler DVD for use with the text.

MINI-**EXERCISES**   **Available with McGraw-Hill's Homework Manager**

M2-1
LO1, 4

Matching Definitions with Terms

Match each definition with its related term by entering the appropriate letter in the space provided. There should be only one definition per term (that is, there are more definitions than terms).

Term	Definition
___ (1) Separate-entity assumption	A. = Liabilities + Stockholders' Equity.
___ (2) Historical cost principle	B. Reports assets, liabilities, and stockholders' equity.
___ (3) Credits	C. Accounts for a business separate from its owners.
___ (4) Assets	D. Increase assets; decrease liabilities and stockholders' equity.
___ (5) T-account	E. An exchange between an entity and other parties.
	F. The concept that businesses will operate into the foreseeable future.
	G. Decrease assets; increase liabilities and stockholders' equity.
	H. The concept that assets should be recorded at cash-equivalent cost.
	I. A standardized format used to accumulate data about each item reported on financial statements.

Matching Definitions with Terms

Match each definition with its related term by entering the appropriate letter in the space provided. There should be only one definition per term (that is, there are more definitions than terms).

Term	Definition
___ (1) Journal entry	A. Accounting model.
___ (2) A = L + SE, and Debits = Credits	B. Four periodic financial statements.
	C. The two equalities in accounting that aid in providing accuracy.
___ (3) Assets = Liabilities + Stockholders' Equity	D. The results of transaction analysis in accounting format.
___ (4) Liabilities	E. The account that is debited when money is borrowed from a bank.
___ (5) Income statement, balance sheet, statement of retained earnings, and statement of cash flows	F. Probable future economic benefits owned by an entity.
	G. Cumulative earnings of a company that are not distributed to the owners.
	H. Every transaction has a least two effects.
	I. Probable debts or obligations to be paid with assets or services.

Identifying Events as Accounting Transactions

For each of the following events, which events result in an exchange transaction for Dittman Company (Y for yes and N for no)?

___ (1) Dittman purchased a machine that it paid for by signing a note payable.
___ (2) Six investors in Dittman Company sold their stock to another investor.
___ (3) The company lent $150,000 to a member of the board of directors.
___ (4) Dittman Company ordered supplies from Staples to be delivered next week.
___ (5) The founding owner, Megan Dittman, purchased additional stock in another company.
___ (6) The company borrowed $1,000,000 from a local bank.

Classifying Accounts on a Balance Sheet

The following are several of the accounts of Gomez-Sanchez Company:

___ (1) Accounts Payable
___ (2) Accounts Receivable
___ (3) Buildings
___ (4) Cash
___ (5) Contributed Capital
___ (6) Land
___ (7) Merchandise Inventory
___ (8) Income Taxes Payable
___ (9) Long-Term Investments
___ (10) Notes Payable (due in three years)
___ (11) Notes Receivable (due in six months)
___ (12) Prepaid Rent
___ (13) Retained Earnings
___ (14) Supplies
___ (15) Utilities Payable
___ (16) Wages Payable

In the space provided, classify each as it would be reported on a balance sheet. Use:

CA for current asset   CL for current liability   SE for stockholders' equity
NCA for noncurrent asset   NCL for noncurrent liability

Determining Financial Statement Effects of Several Transactions

For each of the following transactions of Burress Inc. for the month of January 2008, indicate the accounts, amounts, and direction of the effects on the accounting equation. A sample is provided.

a. (Sample) Borrowed $1,000 from a local bank.
b. Sold $3,000 additional stock to investors.
c. Purchased $500 in equipment, paying $100 cash and the rest on a note due in one year.
d. Declared and paid $100 in dividends to stockholders.
e. Lent $200 to an affiliate; accepted a note due in one year.

Assets	=	Liabilities	+	Stockholders' Equity
a. Sample: Cash +1,000		Notes Payable +1,000		

M2-6
L04

Identifying Increase and Decrease Effects on Balance Sheet Elements

Complete the following table by entering either the word *increases* or *decreases* in each column.

	Debit	Credit
Assets	_____	_____
Liabilities	_____	_____
Stockholders' equity	_____	_____

M2-7
L04

Identifying Debit and Credit Effects on Balance Sheet Elements

Complete the following table by entering either the word *debit* or *credit* in each column.

	Increase	Decrease
Assets	_____	_____
Liabilities	_____	_____
Stockholders' equity	_____	_____

M2-8
L04

Recording Simple Transactions

For each transaction in M2-5 (including the sample), write the journal entry in good form.

M2-9
L04

Completing T-Accounts

For each transaction in M2-5 (including the sample), post the effects to the appropriate T-accounts and determine ending account balances. Beginning balances are provided.

Cash	
Beg. bal. 1,000	
═══	

Notes Receivable	
Beg. bal. 1,000	
═══	

Equipment	
Beg. bal. 16,300	
═══	

Notes Payable	
	Beg. bal. 3,000
	═══

Contributed Capital	
	Beg. bal. 5,500
	═══

Retained Earnings	
	Beg. bal. 9,800
	═══

M2-10
L05

Reporting a Simple Balance Sheet

Starting with the beginning balances in M2-9 and given the transactions in M2-5 (including the sample), prepare a balance sheet for Burress Inc. as of January 31, 2008, classified into current and noncurrent assets and liabilities.

M2-11
L05

Computing and Interpreting the Financial Leverage Ratio

Calculate the financial leverage ratio for Fullem Company based on the following data:

	Assets	Liabilities	Stockholders' Equity
End of 2002	$245,600	$ 90,300	$155,300
End of 2003	278,100	110,200	167,900

What does the result suggest about the company? What can you say about Fullem's ratio when compared to Papa John's 2003 ratio?

M2-12
L06

Identifying Transactions as Investing or Financing Activities on the Statement of Cash Flows

For the transactions in M2-5, identify each as an investing (I) activity or financing (F) activity on the statement of cash flows.

Available with McGraw-Hill's Homework Manager

EXERCISES

Matching Definitions with Terms

E2-1
LO1, 2, 3, 4

Match each definition with its related term by entering the appropriate letter in the space provided. There should be only one definition per term (that is, there are more definitions than terms).

Term	Definition
____ (1) Transaction	A. Economic resources to be used or turned into cash within one year.
____ (2) Continuity assumption	
____ (3) Balance sheet	B. Reports assets, liabilities, and stockholders' equity.
____ (4) Liabilities	C. Accounts for a business separate from its owners.
____ (5) Assets = Liabilities + Stockholders' Equity	D. Increase assets; decrease liabilities and stockholders' equity.
____ (6) Current assets	E. An exchange between an entity and other parties.
____ (7) Note payable	F. The concept that businesses will operate into the foreseeable future.
____ (8) Duality	G. Decrease assets; increase liabilities and stockholders' equity.
____ (9) Retained earnings	
____ (10) Debits	H. The concept that assets should be recorded at cash-equivalent cost.
	I. A standardized format used to accumulate data about each item reported on financial statements.
	J. The accounting model.
	K. The two equalities in accounting that aid in providing accuracy.
	L. The account that is credited when money is borrowed from a bank.
	M. Cumulative earnings of a company that are not distributed to the owners.
	N. Every transaction has at least two effects.
	O. Probable debts or obligations to be paid with assets or services.

Identifying Account Titles

E2-2
LO2

The following are independent situations.

a. A company orders and receives 10 personal computers for office use for which it signs a note promising to pay $25,000 within three months.

b. A company purchases for $21,000 cash a new delivery truck that has a list, or sticker, price of $24,000.

c. A women's clothing retailer orders 30 new display stands for $300 each for future delivery.

d. A new company is formed and sells 100 shares of stock for $12 per share to investors.

e. A manufacturing company signs a contract for the construction of a new warehouse for $500,000. At the signing, the company writes a check for $50,000 to the construction company as the initial payment for the construction (receiving construction in progress). Answer from the standpoint of the manufacturing company.

f. A publishing firm purchases for $40,000 cash the copyright (an intangible asset) to a manuscript for an introductory accounting text.

g. A manufacturing firm pays stockholders a $100,000 cash dividend.

h. A company purchases 100 shares of Apple Computer common stock for $5,000 cash.

i. A company purchases a piece of land for $50,000 cash. An appraiser for the buyer valued the land at $52,500.

j. A manufacturing company acquires the patent (an intangible asset) on a new digital satellite system for television reception, paying $500,000 cash and signing a $400,000 note payable due in one year.

k. A local company is a sole proprietorship (one owner); its owner buys a car for $10,000 for personal use. Answer from the company's point of view.

l. A company borrows $1,000 from a local bank and signs a six-month note for the loan.

m. A company pays $1,500 principal on its note payable (ignore interest).

Required:

1. Indicate the appropriate account titles, if any, affected in each of the preceding events. Consider what is received and what is given.

2. At what amount would you record the truck in (*b*)? The land in (*i*)? What measurement principle are you applying?

3. For (*c*), what accounting concept did you apply? For (*k*), what accounting concept did you apply?

E2-3
L02, 4
Polaroid
Corporation

Classifying Accounts and Their Usual Balances

As described in a recent annual report, Polaroid Corporation designs, manufactures, and markets worldwide a variety of products primarily in instant image-recording fields, including instant photographic cameras and films, electronic imaging recording devices, conventional films, and light-polarizing filters and lenses. The following are accounts from a recent balance sheet for Polaroid.

(1) Land	(6) Long-Term Investments
(2) Retained Earnings	(7) Machinery and Equipment
(3) Taxes Payable	(8) Accounts Payable
(4) Prepaid Expenses	(9) Short-Term Investments
(5) Contributed Capital	(10) Notes Payable (due in 3 years)

Required:

For each account, indicate whether the account is classified as a current asset (CA), noncurrent asset (NCA), current liability (CL), noncurrent liability (NCL), or stockholders' equity (SE), and whether the account usually has a debit or credit balance.

E2-4
L03

Determining Financial Statement Effects of Several Transactions

The following events occurred for Syrena Company:

a. Received investment of $200,000 cash by organizers and distributed stock to them.

b. Borrowed $60,000 cash from a bank.

c. Purchased $120,000 in land; paid $10,000 in cash and signed a mortgage note for the balance.

d. Loaned $3,000 to an employee who signed a note.

e. Purchased $80,000 of equipment, paying $10,000 in cash and signing a note for the rest.

Required:

For each of the events (*a*) through (*e*), perform transaction analysis and indicate the account, amount, and direction of the effect (+ for increase and − for decrease) on the accounting equation. Check that the accounting equation remains in balance after each transaction. Use the following headings:

Event	Assets	=	Liabilities	+	Stockholders' Equity

E2-5
L03
Nike, Inc.

Determining Financial Statement Effects of Several Transactions

Nike, Inc., with headquarters in Beaverton, Oregon, is one of the world's leading manufacturers of athletic shoes and sports apparel. The following activities occurred during a recent year. The amounts are rounded to millions of dollars.

a. Purchased additional buildings for $182.0 and equipment for $21.9; paid $48.1 in cash and signed a long-term note for the rest.

b. Issued $253.6 in additional stock for cash.

c. Declared $179.2 in dividends to be paid in the following year.

d. Purchased additional short-term investments for $400.8 cash.

e. Several Nike investors sold their own stock to other investors on the stock exchange for $36.

f. Sold $1.4 in short-term investments in other companies for $1.4 cash.

Required:

1. For each of these events, perform transaction analysis and indicate the account, amount, and direction of the effect on the accounting equation. Check that the accounting equation remains in balance after each transaction. Use the following headings:

Event	Assets	=	Liabilities	+	Stockholders' Equity

2. Explain your response to Event (*e*).

Recording Investing and Financing Activities

Refer to E2-4.

Required:

For each of the events in E2-4, prepare journal entries, checking that debits equal credits.

E2-6
L04

Recording Investing and Financing Activities

Refer to E2-5.

Required:

1. For each of the events in E2-5, prepare journal entries, checking that debits equal credits.
2. Explain your response to Event (*e*).

E2-7
L04
Nike, Inc.

Analyzing the Effects of Transactions in T-Accounts

Parillo Service Company, Inc., was organized by James Parillo and five other investors. The following activities occurred during the year:

a. Received $60,000 cash from the investors; each was issued 1,000 shares of capital stock.
b. Purchased equipment for use in the business at a cost of $12,000; one-fourth was paid in cash and the company signed a note for the balance (due in six months).
c. Signed an agreement with a cleaning service to pay it $120 per week for cleaning the corporate offices.
d. Lent $2,000 to one of the investors who signed a note due in six months.
e. Received an additional contribution from investors who provided $4,000 in cash and land valued at $10,000 in exchange for stock in the company.
f. James Parillo borrowed $10,000 for personal use from a local bank, signing a one-year note.

E2-8
L04

Required:

1. Create T-accounts for the following accounts: Cash, Note Receivable, Equipment, Land, Note Payable, and Contributed Capital. Beginning balances are zero. For each of the preceding transactions, record the effects of the transaction in the appropriate T-accounts. Include good referencing and totals for each T-account.
2. Using the balances in the T-accounts, fill in the following amounts for the accounting equation:
   Assets $_____ = Liabilities $_____ + Stockholders' Equity $_____
3. Explain your response to Events (*c*) and (*f*).

Inferring Investing and Financing Transactions and Preparing a Balance Sheet

During its first week of operations, January 1–7, 2008, Faith's Fine Furniture Company completed six transactions with the dollar effects indicated in the following schedule:

E2-9
L04, 5

Accounts	DOLLAR EFFECT OF EACH OF THE SIX TRANSACTIONS						Ending Balance
	1	2	3	4	5	6	
Cash	$12,000	$(4,000)	$50,000		$(7,000)	$(3,000)	
Short-term note receivable						3,000	
Store fixtures					7,000		
Land		12,000		$3,000			
Short-term note payable		8,000	50,000	3,000			
Contributed capital	12,000						

Required:

1. Write a brief explanation of each transaction. Explain any assumptions that you made.
2. Compute the ending balance in each account and prepare a classified balance sheet for Faith's Fine Furniture Company on January 7, 2008.

E2-10
LO4, 5

Inferring Investing and Financing Transactions and Preparing a Balance Sheet

During its first month of operations, March 2007, Candee's Candies, Inc., completed six transactions with the dollar effects indicated in the following schedule:

Accounts	DOLLAR EFFECT OF EACH OF THE SIX TRANSACTIONS						Ending Balance
	1	2	3	4	5	6	
Cash	$50,000	$(4,000)	$(4,000)	$(6,000)	$2,000		
Short-term investments				6,000	(2,000)		
Short-term note receivable			4,000				
Computer equipment						$4,000	
Delivery truck		25,000					
Long-term note payable		21,000					
Contributed capital	50,000					4,000	

Required:

1. Write a brief explanation of Transactions 1 through 6. Explain any assumptions that you made.
2. Compute the ending balance in each account and prepare a classified balance sheet for Candee's Candies, Inc., at the end of March 2007.

E2-11
LO4

Recording Journal Entries

Evans Corporation was organized on May 1, 2008. The following events occurred during the first month.

a. Received $160,000 cash from the three investors who organized Evans Corporation.
b. Borrowed $80,000 cash and signed a note due in two years.
c. Purchased $40,000 in equipment, paying $10,000 in cash and signing a six-month note for the balance.
d. Ordered store fixtures costing $26,000.
e. Lent $4,000 to an employee who signed a note to repay the loan in three months.
f. Received and paid for the store fixtures ordered in (d).

Required:

Prepare journal entries for each transaction. (Remember that debits go on top and credits go on the bottom, indented.) Be sure to use good referencing and categorize each account as an asset (A), liability (L), or stockholders' equity (SE). If a transaction does not require a journal entry, explain the reason.

Recording Journal Entries

E2-12
LO4
DaimlerChrysler AG

DaimlerChrysler, headquartered in Stuttgart, Germany, manufactures several automotive brands including Mercedes-Benz, Chrysler, Jeep, and Dodge and has alliances with Mitsubishi Motors and Hyundai. Financial information is reported in the euro (€) monetary unit. The following transactions were adapted from the annual report; amounts are in millions of euros.

a. Declared €2,358 in dividends to be paid next month.
b. Ordered €22,100 in equipment.
c. Paid €2,379 in dividends declared in prior months.
d. Issued additional stock for €112 in cash.
e. Sold equipment at its cost of €809 for cash.
f. Received the equipment ordered in Event (b), paying €19,117 in cash and signing a note for the balance.
g. Purchased short-term investments for €4,883 cash.

Required:
Prepare journal entries for each transaction. (Remember that debits go on top and credits go on the bottom, indented.) Be sure to use good referencing and categorize each account as an asset (A), liability (L), or stockholders' equity (SE). If a transaction does not require a journal entry, explain the reason.

Analyzing the Effects of Transactions Using T-Accounts and Interpreting the Financial Leverage Ratio as a Manager of the Company

E2-13
LO4, 5

Masaya Company has been operating for one year (2008). You are a member of the management team investigating expansion ideas that will require borrowing funds from banks. At the start of 2009, Masaya's T-account balances were as follows:

Assets:

Cash	Short-Term Investments	Property and Equipment
5,000	2,000	4,000

Liabilities:

Short-Term Notes Payable	Long-Term Notes Payable
300	600

Stockholders' Equity:

Contributed Capital	Retained Earnings
8,100	2,000

Required:

1. Using the data from these T-accounts, determine the amounts for the following on January 1, 2009:

   Assets $_____ = Liabilities $_____ + Stockholders' Equity $_____.

2. Enter the following 2009 transactions in the T-accounts:
   (a) Sold $1,500 of the investments for $1,500 cash.
   (b) Sold one-fourth of the property and equipment for $1,000 in cash.
   (c) Borrowed $2,600 at 10 percent interest from a local bank, signing a note with principal and interest due in three years.
   (d) Paid $600 cash dividends to stockholders.

3. Compute ending balances in the T-accounts to determine amounts for the following on December 31, 2009:

   Assets $_____ = Liabilities $_____ + Stockholders' Equity $_____.

4. Calculate the financial leverage ratio at December 31, 2009. If the industry average for the financial leverage ratio is 2.00, what does your computation suggest to you about Masaya Company? Would you support expansion by borrowing? Why or why not?

E2-14

L05

Preparing a Balance Sheet

Refer to E2-13.

Required:

From the ending balances in the T-accounts in E2-13, prepare a classified balance sheet at December 31, 2009, in good form.

E2-15

L04, 5

Analyzing the Effects of Transactions Using T-Accounts, Preparing a Balance Sheet, and Evaluating the Financial Leverage Ratio over Time as a Bank Loan Officer

Li Delivery Company, Inc., was organized in 2007. The following transactions occurred during year 2007:

(*a*) Received $40,000 cash from organizers in exchange for stock in the new company.

(*b*) Purchased land for $12,000, signing a one-year note (ignore interest).

(*c*) Bought two used delivery trucks for operating purposes at the start of the year at a cost of $10,000 each; paid $2,000 cash and signed a note due in three years for the rest (ignore interest).

(*d*) Sold one-fourth of the land for $3,000 to Critton Moving, which signed a six-month note.

(*e*) Paid $2,000 cash to a truck repair shop for a new motor for one of the trucks. (*Hint:* Increase the account you used to record the purchase of the trucks since the productive life of the truck has been improved.)

(*f*) Stockholder Chu Li paid $22,000 cash for a vacant lot (land) for his personal use.

Required:

1. Set up appropriate T-accounts with beginning balances of zero for Cash, Short-Term Note Receivable, Land, Equipment, Short-Term Notes Payable, Long-Term Notes Payable, and Contributed Capital. Using the T-accounts, record the effects of these transactions by Li Delivery Company.

2. Prepare a classified balance sheet for Li Delivery Company at December 31, 2007.

3. At the end of the next two years, Li Delivery Company reported the following amounts on its balance sheets:

	December 31, 2008	December 31, 2009
Assets	$90,000	$120,000
Liabilities	40,000	70,000
Stockholders' Equity	50,000	50,000

Compute the company's financial leverage ratio for 2008 and 2009. What is the trend, and what does this suggest about the company?

4. At the beginning of year 2010, Li Delivery Company applied to your bank for a $100,000 loan to expand the business. The vice president of the bank asked you to review the information and make a recommendation on lending the funds based solely on the results of the financial leverage ratio. What recommendation would you make to the bank's vice president about lending the money to Li Delivery Company?

E2-16

L04

Explaining the Effects of Transactions on Balance Sheet Accounts Using T-Accounts

Staub and Gever Furniture Repair Service, a company with two stockholders, began operations on June 1, 2008. The following T-accounts indicate the activities for the month of June.

Cash (A)			
6/1/08	0		
a.	17,000	b.	10,000
d.	800	c.	1,500

Notes Receivable (A)			
6/1/08	0		
c.	1,500		

Tools and Equipment (A)			
6/1/08	0		
a.	3,000	d.	800

Building (A)			
6/1/08	0		
b.	50,000		

Notes Payable (L)			
		6/1/08	0
		b.	40,000

Contributed Capital (SE)			
		6/1/08	0
		a.	20,000

Required:

Explain Events (*a*) through (*d*) that resulted in the entries in the T-accounts. That is, for each account, what transactions made it increase and/or decrease?

Inferring Typical Investing and Financing Activities in Accounts

E2-17
LO4

The following T-accounts indicate the effects of normal business transactions:

Equipment				Note Receivable				Notes Payable		
1/1	400			1/1	75				130	1/1
	250	?			?	190		?	270	
12/31	450			12/31	50				180	12/31

Required:

1. Describe the typical investing and financing transactions that affect each T-account. That is, what economic events occur to make each of these accounts increase and decrease?
2. For each T-account, compute the missing amounts.

Identifying Investing and Financing Activities Affecting Cash Flows

E2-18
LO6
Foot Locker, Inc.

Foot Locker, Inc., (formally Woolworth Corporation) is a large global retailer of athletic footwear and apparel selling directly to customers and through the Internet, including the Foot Locker family of stores, Champs Sports, and Eastbay. The following are several of Foot Locker's investing and financing activities as reflected in a recent annual statement of cash flows.

a. Reduction of long-term debt.
b. Sale of land.
c. Issuance of common stock.
d. Capital expenditures (for property, plant, and equipment).
e. Issuance of short-term debt.

Required:

For each of these, indicate whether the activity is investing (I) or financing (F) and the direction of the effect on cash flows (+ = increases cash; − = decreases cash).

Preparing the Investing and Financing Sections of the Statement of Cash Flows

E2-19
LO6
Hilton Hotels

Hilton Hotels Corporation constructs, operates, and franchises domestic and international hotel and hotel-casino properties. Information from the company's recent annual statement of cash flows indicates the following investing and financing activities during that year (simplified, in millions of dollars):

Additional borrowing from banks	$992
Purchase of investments	139
Sale of property (assume sold at cost)	230
Issuance of stock	6
Purchase and renovation of properties	370
Payment of debt principal	24
Receipt of principal payment on a note receivable	125

Required:

Prepare the investing and financing sections of the statement of cash flows for Hilton Hotels. Assume that year-end is December 31, 2008.

Finding Financial Information as a Potential Investor

E2-20
LO2, 5, 6

You are considering investing the cash you inherited from your grandfather in various stocks. You have received the annual reports of several major companies.

Required:

For each of the following, indicate where you would locate the information in an annual report. The information may be in more than one location.

1. Total current assets.

2. Amount of debt principal repaid during the year.
3. Summary of significant accounting policies.
4. Cash received from sales of noncurrent assets.
5. Amount of dividends paid during the year.
6. Short-term obligations.
7. Date of the statement of financial position.

PROBLEMS

 Available with McGraw-Hill's Homework Manager

P2-1
LO1, 2
ChevronTexaco
Corporation

Identifying Accounts on a Classified Balance Sheet and Their Normal Debit or Credit Balances (AP2-1)

ChevronTexaco Corporation explores, produces, refines, markets, and supplies crude oil, natural gas, and petroleum products in the United States and 24 other countries. The following are accounts from a recent balance sheet of ChevronTexaco Corporation:

(1) Cash and Cash Equivalents
(2) Long-Term Capital Lease Obligations
(3) Contributed Capital
(4) Long-Term Debt
(5) Prepaid Expenses
(6) Patents (an intangible asset)
(7) Federal and Other Taxes Payable
(8) Material, Supplies, and Other Inventories
(9) Accounts Payable
(10) Marketable Securities (short-term)
(11) Accounts and Notes Receivable (short-term)
(12) Retained Earnings
(13) Property, Plant, and Equipment
(14) Long-Term Investments
(15) Crude Oil and Petroleum Products

Required:

For each account, indicate how it normally should be categorized on a classified balance sheet. Use CA for current asset, NCA for noncurrent asset, CL for current liability, NCL for noncurrent liability, and SE for stockholders' equity. Also indicate whether the account normally has a debit or credit balance.

P2-2
LO2, 3, 5
e**X**cel

Determining Financial Statement Effects of Various Transactions (AP2-2)

Goodmore's Home Healthcare Services was organized on January 1, 2006, by four friends. Each organizer invested $10,000 in the company and, in turn, was issued 8,000 shares of stock. To date, they are the only stockholders. At the end of the most recent year, the accounting records reflected total assets of $400,000 ($30,000 cash; $80,000 land; $90,000 equipment; and $200,000 buildings), total liabilities of $210,000 (notes payable), and stockholders' equity of $190,000 ($120,000 contributed capital; $70,000 retained earnings). During the current year, 2008, the following summarized events occurred:

a. Sold 10,000 additional shares of stock to the original organizers for a total of $100,000 cash.
b. Purchased a building for $65,000, equipment for $16,000, and three acres of land for $12,000; paid $10,000 in cash and signed a note for the balance (the mortgage is due in 15 years). (*Hint:* Five different accounts are affected.)
c. One stockholder reported to the company that 500 shares of his Goodmore stock had been sold and transferred to another stockholder for $5,000 cash.
d. Purchased short-term investments for $20,000 cash.
e. Sold one acre of land for $4,000 cash to another company.
f. Lent one of the shareholders $5,000 for moving costs, receiving a signed six-month note from the shareholder.

Required:

1. Was Goodmore's Home Healthcare Services organized as a sole proprietorship, a partnership, or a corporation? Explain the basis for your answer.
2. During 2008, the records of the company were inadequate. You were asked to prepare the summary of the preceding transactions. To develop a quick assessment of their economic effects on Goodmore's Home Healthcare Services, you have decided to complete the tabulation that follows and to use plus (+) for increases and minus (−) for decreases for each account. The first event is used as an example.

	ASSETS					=	LIABILITIES	+	STOCKHOLDERS' EQUITY	
Cash	Short-term Investments	Notes Receivable	Land	Building	Equipment		Notes Payable		Contributed Capital	Retained Earnings
Beg. 30,000			80,000	200,000	90,000	=	210,000		120,000	70,000
(a) +100,000						=			+100,000	

3. Did you include the transaction between the two stockholders—Event (*c*)—in the tabulation? Why?
4. Based only on the completed tabulation, provide the following amounts (show computations):
   a. Total assets at the end of the month.
   b. Total liabilities at the end of the month.
   c. Total stockholders' equity at the end of the month.
   d. Cash balance at the end of the month.
   e. Total current assets at the end of the month.
5. Compute the financial leverage ratio for 2008. What does this suggest about the company?

Recording Transactions in T-Accounts, Preparing the Balance Sheet, and Evaluating the Financial Leverage Ratio (AP2-3)

P2-3
LO2, 4, 5

Peters Plastics Company has been operating for three years. At December 31, 2007, the accounting records reflected the following:

Cash	$ 35,000	Intangibles	$ 5,000
Short-term investments	3,000	Accounts payable	25,000
Accounts receivable	5,000	Accrued liabilities payable	3,000
Inventory	40,000	Short-term note payable	12,000
Long-term note receivable	2,000	Long-term note payable	80,000
Equipment	80,000	Contributed capital	150,000
Factory building	150,000	Retained earnings	50,000

During the year 2008, the company had the following summarized activities:

a. Purchased equipment that cost $30,000; paid $10,000 cash and signed a one-year note for the balance.
b. Issued an additional 2,000 shares of capital stock for $20,000 cash.
c. Lent $10,000 to a supplier who signed a two-year note.
d. Purchased short-term investments for $15,000 cash.
e. Borrowed $20,000 cash from a local bank, payable June 30, 2009.
f. Purchased a patent (an intangible asset) for $6,000 cash.
g. Built an addition to the factory for $42,000; paid $15,000 in cash and signed a three-year note for the balance.
h. Hired a new president at the end of the year. The contract was for $85,000 per year plus options to purchase company stock at a set price based on company performance.
i. Returned defective equipment to the manufacturer, receiving a cash refund of $2,000.

Required:
1. Create T-accounts for each of the accounts on the balance sheet and enter the balances at the end of 2007 as beginning balances for 2008.
2. Record each of the events for 2008 in T-accounts (including referencing) and determine the ending balances.
3. Explain your response to Event (*h*).
4. Prepare a classified balance sheet at December 31, 2008.
5. Compute the financial leverage ratio for 2008. What does this suggest about Peters Plastics?

Identifying Effects of Transactions on the Statement of Cash Flows (AP2-4)

P2-4
LO6

Refer to P2-3.

Required:

Using the events (*a*) through (*i*) in P2-3, indicate whether each is an investing (I) or financing (F) activity for the year and the direction of the effect on cash flows (+ for increase and − for decrease). If there is no effect on cash flows, write NE.

P2-5
LO2, 4, 5
Dell, Inc.

Recording Transactions, Preparing Journal Entries, Posting to T-Accounts, Preparing the Balance Sheet, and Evaluating the Financial Leverage Ratio

Dell, Inc., headquartered in Austin, Texas, is the global leader in selling computer products and services. The following is Dell's (simplified) balance sheet from a recent year.

DELL, INC.
Balance Sheet
at January 30, 2004
(dollars in millions)

Assets
Current Assets

Cash	$ 4,317
Short-term investments	835
Receivables and other assets	3,635
Inventories	327
Other	1,519
	10,633

Noncurrent Assets

Property, plant, and equipment	1,517
Long-term investments	6,770
Other noncurrent assets	391
Total assets	**$19,311**

Liabilities and Stockholders' Equity
Current Liabilities

Accounts payable	$ 7,316
Other short-term obligations	3,580
	10,896
Long-Term Liabilities	**2,135**

Stockholders' Equity

Contributed capital	284
Retained earnings	5,996
Total stockholders' equity and liabilities	**$19,311**

Assume that the following transactions (in millions of dollars) occurred during the remainder of 2004 (ending on January 28, 2005):

a. Issued additional shares of stock for $200 in cash.

b. Borrowed $30 from banks due in two years.

c. Purchased additional investments for $13,000 cash; one-fifth were long term and the rest were short term.

d. Purchased property, plant, and equipment; paid $875 in cash and $1,410 with additional long-term bank loans.

e. Lent $250 to affiliates, who signed a six-month note.

f. Sold short-term investments costing $10,000 for $10,000 cash.

g. Dell does not actually pay dividends; it reinvests its earnings into the company for growth purposes. Assume instead for this problem that Dell declared and paid $52 in dividends during 2004.

Required:

1. Prepare a journal entry for each transaction.
2. Create T-accounts for each balance sheet account and include the January 30, 2004, balances. Post each journal entry to the appropriate T-accounts.
3. Prepare a balance sheet from the T-account ending balances for Dell at January 28, 2005, based on these transactions.
4. Compute Dell's financial leverage ratio for 2004 (year ending on January 28, 2005). What does this suggest about the company?

Preparing the Investing and Financing Sections of a Statement of Cash Flows

P2-6
LO6
Dell, Inc.

Refer to P2-5.

Required:

Based on the activities for the year ended January 28, 2005, prepare the Investing and Financing sections of a statement of cash flows.

ALTERNATE **PROBLEMS**

Identifying Accounts on a Classified Balance Sheet and Their Normal Debit or Credit Balances (P2-1)

AP2-1
LO1, 2, 4
Hasbro, Inc.

According to a recent Form 10-K report of Hasbro, Inc., the company is "a worldwide leader in children's and family leisure time and entertainment products and services, including the design, manufacture and marketing of games and toys, ranging from traditional to high-tech." Hasbro produces products under several brands including Tonka, Milton Bradley, Playskool, and Parker Brothers. The following are several of the accounts from a recent balance sheet:

(1) Accounts Receivable
(2) Short-Term Borrowings
(3) Contributed Capital
(4) Long-Term Debt
(5) Prepaid Expenses
(6) Intangibles
(7) Property, Plant, and Equipment

(8) Retained Earnings
(9) Accounts Payable
(10) Cash and Cash Equivalents
(11) Accrued Liabilities Payable
(12) Deferred Long-Term Liabilities
(13) Inventories
(14) Income Taxes Payable

Required:

Indicate how each account normally should be categorized on a classified balance sheet. Use CA for current asset, NCA for noncurrent asset, CL for current liability, NCL for noncurrent liability, and SE for stockholders' equity. Also indicate whether the account normally has a debit or credit balance.

Determining Financial Statement Effects of Various Transactions (P2-2)

AP2-2
LO2, 3, 5

Russeck Incorporated is a small manufacturing company that makes model trains to sell to toy stores. It has a small service department that repairs customers' trains for a fee. The company has been in business for five years. At December 31, 2007 (the company's fiscal year-end), the accounting records reflected total assets of $500,000 (cash, $130,000; buildings, $300,000; equipment, $70,000), total liabilities of $200,000 (short-term notes payable, $150,000; long-term notes payable, $50,000), and total stockholders' equity of $300,000 (contributed capital, $200,000; retained earnings, $100,000). During the current year, 2008, the following summarized events occurred:

a. Issued an additional 10,000 shares of capital stock for $100,000 cash.
b. Borrowed $120,000 cash from the bank and signed a 10-year note.
c. Built an addition on the factory for $200,000 and paid cash to the contractor.
d. Purchased equipment for the new addition for $30,000, paying $3,000 in cash and signing a note due in six months for the balance.
e. Purchased $85,000 in long-term investments.
f. Returned a $3,000 piece of equipment purchased in (*d*) because it proved to be defective; received a reduction of its short-term note payable.

g. Purchased a delivery truck (equipment) for $10,000; paid $5,000 cash and signed a short-term note payable for the remainder.

h. Lent $2,000 cash to the company president, Kalman Russeck, who signed a note with terms showing the principal plus interest due in one year.

i. A stockholder sold $5,000 of his capital stock in Russeck Incorporated to his neighbor.

Required:

1. Was Russeck Incorporated organized as a sole proprietorship, a partnership, or a corporation? Explain the basis for your answer.

2. During 2008, the records of the company were inadequate. You were asked to prepare the summary of the preceding transactions. To develop a quick assessment of their economic effects on Russeck Incorporated, you have decided to complete the tabulation that follows and to use plus (+) for increases and minus (−) for decreases for each account. The first transaction is used as an example.

										STOCKHOLDERS' EQUITY	
	ASSETS				=	LIABILITIES		+			
		Notes	Long-Term				Short-Term	Long-Term		Contributed	Retained
Cash	Receivable	Investments	Equipment	Building			Notes Payable	Notes Payable		Capital	Earnings
Beg. 130,000			70,000	300,000	=		150,000	50,000		200,000	100,000
(a) +100,000					=					+100,000	

3. Did you include Event (*i*) in the tabulation? Why?

4. Based on beginning balances plus the completed tabulation, provide the following amounts (show computations):

   a. Total assets at the end of the year.

   b. Total liabilities at the end of the year.

   c. Total stockholders' equity at the end of the year.

   d. Cash balance at the end of the year.

   e. Total current assets at the end of the year.

5. Compute the financial leverage ratio for 2008. What does this suggest about the company?

AP2-3
LO2, 4, 5
Ethan Allen
Interiors, Inc.

Recording Transactions in T-Accounts, Preparing the Balance Sheet, and Evaluating the Financial Leverage Ratio (P2-3)

Ethan Allen Interiors, Inc., is a leading manufacturer and retailer of home furnishings in the United States and abroad. The following is adapted from Ethan Allen's June 30, 2003, annual financial report. Dollars are in thousands.

Cash and cash equivalents	$ 81,856	Other assets	$ 2,944
Short-term investments	0	Accounts payable	81,314
Accounts receivable	26,439	Accrued expenses payable	52,116
Inventories	198,212	Long-term debt (includes the	
Prepaid expenses and		current portion of $996)	10,218
other current assets	53,755	Other long-term liabilities	50,221
Property, plant, and equipment	289,423	Contributed capital	76,663
Intangibles	78,939	Retained earnings	461,036

Assume that the following events occurred in the first quarter ended September 30, 2003:

a. Purchased $3,400 in additional intangibles for cash.

b. Sold equipment at its cost for $4,020 cash.

c. Purchased $2,980 in short-term investments for cash.

d. Issued additional shares of stock for $1,020 in cash.

e. Ordered $43,500 in wood and other raw materials for the manufacturing plants.

f. Purchased property, plant, and equipment; paid $1,830 in cash and signed additional long-term notes for $9,400.

g. Sold at cost other assets for $310 cash.

h. Declared and paid $300 in dividends.

Required:

1. Create T-accounts for each of the accounts on the balance sheet; enter the balances at June 30, 2003.
2. Record each of the transactions for the first quarter ended September 30, 2003, in the T-accounts (including referencing) and determine the ending balances.
3. Explain your response to Event (*e*).
4. Prepare a classified balance sheet at September 30, 2003.
5. Compute the financial leverage ratio for the quarter ended September 30, 2003. What does this suggest about Ethan Allen Interiors, Inc.?

Identifying Effects of Transactions on the Statement of Cash Flows (P2-4)

Refer to AP2-3.

Required:

Using the events (*a*) through (*h*) in AP2-3, indicate whether each transaction is an investing (I) or financing (F) activity for the quarter and the direction of the effect on cash flows (+ for increase and − for decrease). If there is no effect on cash flows, write NE.

AP2-4
LO6
Ethan Allen
Interiors, Inc.

CASES **AND PROJECTS**

Annual Report Cases

Finding Financial Information

Refer to the financial statements and accompanying notes of Pacific Sunwear of California given in Appendix B at the end of this book or open file PSUN.pdf in the Annual Report Cases directory on the student DVD.

Required:

1. Is the company a corporation, a partnership, or a sole proprietorship? How do you know?
2. Use the company's balance sheet to determine the amounts in the accounting equation (A = L + SE) as of the end of the most recent reporting year.
3. The company shows on the balance sheet that inventories are worth $175,081,000. Does this amount represent the expected selling price? Why or why not?
4. What is the company's fiscal year-end? Where did you find the exact date?
5. List the types of current obligations this company has. You need not provide the amounts.
6. Compute the company's financial leverage ratio and explain its meaning.
7. How much cash did the company spend on purchasing property and equipment each year (capital expenditures)? Where did you find the information?

CP2-1
LO1, 2, 5, 6

OF CALIFORNIA, INC.

Finding Financial Information

Refer to the financial statements and accompanying notes of American Eagle Outfitters given in Appendix C at the end of this book or open file AEOS.pdf in the Annual Report Cases directory on the student DVD.

Required:

1. Use the company's balance sheet to determine the amounts in the accounting equation (A = L + SE) as of January 29, 2005.
2. If the company was liquidated at the end of the current year (January 29, 2005), are the shareholders guaranteed to receive $963,486,000?
3. What are the company's noncurrent liabilities?
4. What is the company's financial leverage ratio?
5. Did the company have a cash inflow or outflow from financing activities? Of how much?

CP2-2
LO1, 2, 5, 6
AMERICAN EAGLE
OUTFITTERS
ae.com

CP2-3

LO2, 5, 6

PACIFIC SUNWEAR
OF CALIFORNIA, INC.

AMERICAN EAGLE
OUTFITTERS
ae.com

Comparing Companies within an Industry

Refer to the financial statements and accompanying notes of Pacific Sunwear of California given in Appendix B, American Eagle Outfitters given in Appendix C, and the Ratio Report given in Appendix D at the end of this book or open file CP2-3.xls in the Annual Report Cases directory on the student DVD.

Required:

1. Which company is larger in terms of total assets?
2. Compute the financial leverage ratio for both companies. Which company is assuming more risk? Why do you think that this is so?
3. Compare the financial leverage ratio for both companies to the industry average from the Ratio Report. Are these two companies financing assets with debt more or less than the industry average? How is the financial leverage ratio influenced by these companies' choice to rent space instead of buying it?
4. In the most recent year, how much cash, if any, was spent buying back (repurchasing) the company's own common stock?
5. How much, if any, did each company pay in dividends for the most recent year?
6. What account title or titles does each company use to report any land, buildings, and equipment it may have?

Financial Reporting and Analysis Cases

CP2-4

LO2, 5, 6

Broadening Financial Research Skills: Locating Financial Information on the SEC's Database

The Securities and Exchange Commission (SEC) regulates companies that issue stock on the stock market. It receives financial reports from public companies electronically under a system called *EDGAR* (Electronic Data Gathering and Retrieval Service). Using the Internet, anyone may search the database for the reports that have been filed.

Using your Web browser, access the EDGAR database at www.sec.gov. To search the database, click on "Search for Company Filings," click on "Companies and Other Filers," type in "Papa Johns," and then click on "View Filings" when Papa John's International appears.

Required:

To look at SEC filings, skim down the left side until you locate the Form 10Q (quarterly report) dated August 4, 2004. Click on the 10-Q and skim down to "Document 1" and click on it. Skim to the Table of Contents to Item 1.

1. Click on "Balance Sheet."
   a. What was the amount of Papa John's total assets for the most recent quarter reported?
   b. Did long-term debt increase or decrease for the quarter?
   c. Compute the financial leverage ratio. How does it compare to the ratio indicated for Papa John's in the chapter? What does this suggest about the company?
2. Click on "Cash Flow Statement."
   a. What amount did Papa John's spend on property and equipment for the period?
   b. What was the total amount of cash flows from financing activities?

CP2-5

Business Week

Interpreting the Financial Press

The December 22, 2003, edition of *BusinessWeek* magazine includes the article "Is Wilbur Ross Crazy?" You can access the article on the Libby/Libby/Short website at www.mhhe.com/libby5e.

Required:

Read the article and then answer the following questions:

1. What is *distressed investing* according to the article?
2. Mr. Ross usually becomes a bondholder but often swaps the debt for equity. Why is this riskier?
3. According to the article, what makes Mr. Ross successful (i.e., what is his approach and attitude toward investing)?

Using Financial Reports: Evaluating the Reliability of a Balance Sheet

CP2-6
LO1

Frances Sabatier asked a local bank for a $50,000 loan to expand her small company. The bank asked Frances to submit a financial statement of the business to supplement the loan application. Frances prepared the following balance sheet.

Balance Sheet June 30, 2009	
Assets	
Cash and CDs (investments)	$ 9,000
Inventory	30,000
Equipment	46,000
Personal residence (monthly payments, $2,800)	300,000
Remaining assets	20,000
Total assets	**$405,000**
Liabilities	
Short-term debt to suppliers	$ 62,000
Long-term debt on equipment	38,000
Total debt	100,000
Stockholders' Equity	**305,000**
Total liabilities and stockholders' equity	**$405,000**

Required:

The balance sheet has several flaws. However, there is at least one major deficiency. Identify it and explain its significance.

Using Financial Reports: Analyzing the Balance Sheet

CP2-7
LO2, 4, 5
Gateway, Inc.

Recent balance sheets of Gateway, Inc., producer and marketer of a broad range of personal computers, consumer electronic products, and related tools and services, are provided.

Required:

1. Is Gateway a corporation, sole proprietorship, or partnership? Explain the basis of your answer.
2. Use the company's balance sheet to determine the amounts in the accounting equation (A = L + SE) for 2003.
3. Calculate the company's financial leverage ratio for 2003. Interpret the ratio that you calculated. What other information would make your interpretation more useful?
4. Give the journal entry the company will make in 2004 when it pays its 2003 accrued liabilities.
5. Does the company appear to have been profitable over its years in business? On what account are you basing your answer? Assuming no dividends were paid, how much was net income (or net loss) in 2003? If it is impossible to determine without an income statement, state so.

GATEWAY INC.
Consolidated Balance Sheets
December 31, 2003 and 2002
(dollars in millions)

	2003	2002
Assets		
Current assets		
Cash and cash equivalents	$ 349	$ 465
Marketable securities	740	601
Accounts receivable	210	198
Inventory	114	89
Other	250	602
Total current assets	1,663	1,955
Property, plant and equipment, net	331	481
Intangibles	14	23
Other assets	20	50
	$2,028	$2,509
Liabilities and Stockholders' Equity		
Current liabilities		
Accounts payable	$ 416	$ 278
Accrued liabilities	277	365
Accrued royalties	49	57
Other current liabilities	257	240
Total current liabilities	999	940
Other long-term obligations	307	323
Total liabilities	1,306	1,263
Stockholders' equity		
Contributed capital	938	936
Retained earnings (accumulated deficit)	(216)	310
Total stockholders' equity	722	1,246
	$2,028	$2,509

CP2-8 **Using Financial Reports: Preparing a Classified Balance Sheet and Analyzing the Financial**
L05 **Leverage Ratio**

McDonald's
Corporation

The following accounts, in alphabetical order, are adapted from a recent McDonald's Corporation's balance sheet (amounts are in millions of dollars):

	Current Year	Prior Year
Accounts and Notes Receivable	$ 609.4	$ 483.5
Accounts Payable	621.3	650.6
Accrued Liabilities	783.3	503.5
Cash and Equivalents	299.2	341.4
Contributed Capital	1,065.3	787.8
Current Maturities of Long-Term Debt	168.0	335.6
Intangible Assets	973.1	827.5
Inventories	77.3	70.5
Investments in and Advances to Affiliates (long-term)	854.1	634.8
Long-Term Debt	6,188.6	4,834.1
Notes Payable (short-term)	686.8	1,293.8

	Current Year	Prior Year
Notes Receivable due after One Year	$ 67.9	$ 67.0
Other Long-Term Liabilities	1,574.5	1,491.0
Other Noncurrent Assets	538.3	608.5
Prepaid Expenses and Other Current Assets	323.5	246.9
Property and Equipment, Net	16,041.6	14,961.4
Retained Earnings	8,458.9	8,144.1
Taxes Payable	237.7	201.0

Required:

1. Construct a classified balance sheet (with two years reported) for McDonald's Corporation in good form (assume that the current year ends on December 31, 2008).
2. Compute the company's financial leverage ratio for the current year.
3. In comparison to the ratio for the companies in the restaurant industry (as indicated in the chapter for Papa John's and others), how do you interpret this ratio for McDonald's?

Critical Thinking Cases

Making a Decision as a Financial Analyst: Preparing and Analyzing a Balance Sheet

CP2-9
LO1, 5

Your best friend from home writes you a letter about an investment opportunity that has come her way. A company is raising money by issuing shares of stock and wants her to invest $20,000 (her recent inheritance from her great-aunt's estate). Your friend has never invested in a company before and, knowing that you are a financial analyst, asks that you look over the balance sheet and send her some advice. An *unaudited* balance sheet, in only moderately good form, is enclosed with the letter:

DEWEY, CHEETUM, AND HOWE, INC.
Balance Sheet
For the Year Ending December 31, 2009

Accounts receivable	$ 8,000
Cash	1,000
Inventory	8,000
Furniture and fixtures	52,000
Delivery truck	12,000
Buildings (estimated market value)	98,000
Total assets	**$179,000**
Accounts payable	$ 16,000
Payroll taxes payable	13,000
Notes payable (due in three years)	15,000
Mortgage payable	50,000
Total liabilities	**$ 94,000**
Contributed capital	$ 80,000
Retained earnings	5,000
Total stockholders' equity	**$ 85,000**

There is only one footnote, and it states that the building was purchased for $65,000, has been depreciated by $5,000 on the books, and still carries a mortgage (shown in the liability section). The footnote also states that, in the opinion of the company president, the building is "easily worth $98,000."

Required:

1. Draft a new balance sheet for your friend, correcting any errors you note. (If any of the account balances need to be corrected, you may need to adjust the retained earnings balance correspondingly.) If no errors or omissions exist, state so.

2. Write a letter to your friend explaining the changes you made to the balance sheet, if any, and offer your comments on the company's apparent financial condition based only on this information. Suggest other information your friend might want to review before coming to a final decision on whether to invest.

CP2-10

U.S. Foodservice, Inc.

Evaluating an Ethical Dilemma: Analyzing Management Incentives

In July 2004, the U.S. government filed civil and criminal charges against four former executives of Netherlands-based Ahold's subsidiary U. S. Foodservice Inc., an operator of supermarkets such as Bi-Lo and Giant food stores. Two of the four executives have pleaded guilty, and the other two were indicted. The alleged widespread fraud included recording completely fictitious revenues for false promotions and persuading vendors to confirm to auditors the false promotional payments. U.S. Attorney David Kelley suggested the fraud was motivated by the greed of the executives to reap fat bonuses if the company met certain financial goals. The auditors were unable to catch the fraud.

Required:

1. Describe the parties who were harmed or helped by this fraud.
2. Explain how greed may have contributed to the fraud.
3. Why do you think the independent auditors failed to catch the fraud?

Financial Reporting and Analysis Team Project

CP2-11
LO2, 5, 6

Team Project: Analysis of Balance Sheets and Ratios

As a team, select an industry to analyze. *Reuters* provides lists of industries and their makeup at **www.investor.reuters.com/Industries.aspx**. Each team member should acquire the annual report or 10-K for one publicly traded company in the industry, with each member selecting a different company. (Library files, the SEC EDGAR service at **www.sec.gov**, or the company itself are good sources.)

Required:

On an individual basis, each team member should write a short report answering the following questions about the selected company. Discuss any patterns across the companies that you as a team observe. Then, as a team, write a short report comparing and contrasting your companies.

1. For the most recent year, what are the top three asset accounts by size? What percentage is each of total assets? [Calculated as Asset A ÷ Total Assets]
2. What are the major investing and financing activities (by dollar size) for the most recent year? [Look at the Statement of Cash Flows.]
3. Ratio Analysis:
   a. What does the financial leverage ratio measure in general?
   b. Compute the financial leverage ratio for the last three years. [You may find prior years' information in the section of the annual report or 10-K called "Selected Financial Information," or you may search for prior years' annual reports.]
   c. What do your results suggest about the company?
   d. If available, find the industry ratio for the most recent year, compare it to your results, and discuss why you believe your company differs or is similar to the industry ratio.

After studying this chapter, you should be able to:

1. Describe a typical business operating cycle and explain the necessity for the time period assumption. p. 106

2. Explain how business activities affect the elements of the income statement. p. 108

3. Explain the accrual basis of accounting and apply the revenue and matching principles to measure income. p. 111

4. Apply transaction analysis to examine and record the effects of operating activities on the financial statements. p. 118

5. Prepare financial statements. p. 123

6. Compute and interpret the total asset turnover ratio. p. 129

Operating Decisions and the Income Statement

P apa John's and Pizza Hut follow different operating strategies:

- Number-one Pizza Hut regularly creates new pizza varieties (such as the Big New Yorker, the Twisted Crust, the Stuffed Crust pizza you can eat backwards, and the "4forAll" with four individually topped pizzas in one) to attract customers to its eat-in, take-out, and delivery services. The company releases a new variety, advertises like crazy, waits for the customers to rush in, and hopes they will return.

- Papa John's focuses on producing a limited variety of pizzas for pick up or delivery. The company believes it can build strong customer loyalty and repeat business by advertising the simple slogan "Better Ingredients. Better Pizza."

FOCUS COMPANY:

Papa John's International

IT'S MORE THAN DOUGH, CHEESE, AND TOMATOES

www.papajohns.com

Despite these different strategies, Papa John's, ranked number three through aggressive expansion, aims to become the number-one pizza brand in the world by building the strongest brand loyalty. Papa John's believes this requires extensive local marketing efforts supplemented with radio and television advertising. In 2003, for instance, Papa John's aired six national television campaigns to compete against its rivals. To reach new markets, the company continues to expand its company-owned and franchising operations. Adding new restaurants increases efficiencies in the operation of its quality control centers by taking advantage of volume purchasing of food and supplies, thus lowering operating costs. At the same time, Papa John's spends additional resources in developing and motivating its team members, including hefty raises to restaurant managers.

However, one of the most significant effects on a pizza restaurant's financial performance for a period is the cost of cheese. When cheese prices are low, the pizza chains compete by offering low-price deals. When cheese prices are high, they use other gimmicks. In 2004, for example, Papa John's developed a twist on a concept first embraced by Starbucks, a promotional offer called "4 to Go." Aimed at the teen market, any customer purchasing at least four 20-ounce Coca-Cola beverages received codes for free digital music downloads.

UNDERSTANDING THE BUSINESS

To become the number-one pizza brand globally, Papa John's executives develop strategies, plans, and measurable indicators of progress toward their goals. For example, their growth plan in 2004 was to add 200 new restaurants and continue to tell customers about their fresh dough, tomato sauce, and high-quality cheese in various promotional advertising programs. In developing their growth strategies, companies such as Papa John's plan their companywide operations in terms of the elements of the income statement (specific revenues and expenses).

Financial analysts develop their own set of expectations about Papa John's future performance. Its published income statement provides the primary basis for comparing analysts' projections to the actual results of operations. We will discuss these comparisons and the stock market's reactions to Papa John's results throughout this chapter as we learn about income recognition and measurement. To understand how business plans and the results of operations are reflected on the income statement, we need to answer the following questions:

1. How do business activities affect the income statement?
2. How are business activities measured?
3. How are business activities reported on the income statement?

In this chapter we focus on Papa John's operating activities that involve the sale of food to the public and the sale of ingredients and services to franchisees. The results of these activities are reported on the income statement.

ORGANIZATION of the Chapter

How Do Business Activities Affect the Income Statement?	**How Are Operating Activities Recognized and Measured?**	**The Expanded Transaction Analysis Model**	**How Are Financial Statements Prepared and Analyzed?**
■ The Operating Cycle ■ Elements on the Income Statement	■ Accrual Accounting ■ Measurement Principles	■ Transaction Analysis Rules ■ Analyzing Papa John's Transactions	■ Income Statement ■ Statement of Retained Earnings ■ Balance Sheet ■ Cash Flow Effects ■ Total Asset Turnover Ratio

HOW DO BUSINESS ACTIVITIES AFFECT THE INCOME STATEMENT?

Learning Objective 1
Describe a typical business operating cycle and explain the necessity for the time period assumption.

The Operating Cycle

The long-term objective for any business is to **turn cash into more cash.** If a company is to stay in business, this excess cash must be generated from operations (that is, from the activities for which the business was established), not from borrowing money or selling long-lived assets.

Companies (1) acquire inventory and the services of employees and (2) sell inventory or services to customers. The length of time between when the company pays for the inventory and employee services and when customers pay cash to the company (known as the operating (cash-to-cash) cycle) depends on the nature of the business.

The **OPERATING (CASH-TO-CASH) CYCLE** is the time it takes for a company to pay cash to suppliers, sell goods and services to customers, and collect cash from customers.

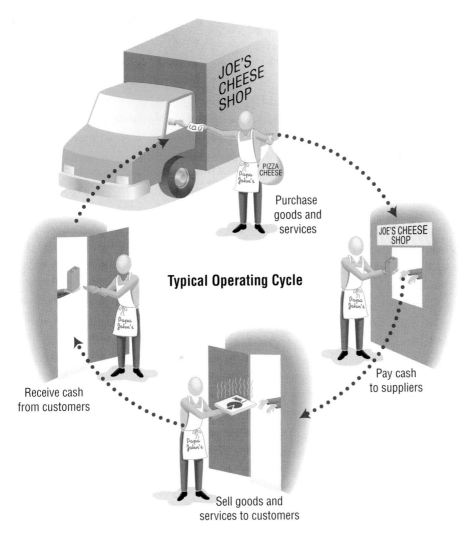

Typical Operating Cycle

Purchase goods and services

Pay cash to suppliers

Sell goods and services to customers

Receive cash from customers

The operating cycle for Papa John's is relatively short. It spends cash to purchase ingredients, makes pizzas, and sells them to customers for cash. In some companies, inventory is paid for well before it is sold. Toys R Us, for example, builds its inventory for months preceding the year-end holiday season. It borrows funds from banks to pay for the inventory and repays the loans with interest when it receives cash from customers. In other companies, cash is received from customers well after a sale takes place. For example, car dealerships often sell cars over time with monthly payments from customers due over several years. Shortening the operating cycle by creating incentives that encourage customers to buy sooner and/or pay faster improves a company's cash flows.

Managers know that reducing the time needed to turn cash into more cash (that is, shortening the operating cycle) means higher profit and faster growth. With the excess cash, managers may purchase additional inventory or other assets for growth, repay debt, or distribute it to owners as dividends.

Until a company ceases its activities, the operating cycle is repeated continuously. However, decision makers require information periodically about the company's financial condition and performance. To measure income for a specific period of time,

The **TIME PERIOD ASSUMPTION** indicates that the long life of a company can be reported in shorter time periods.

accountants follow the time period assumption, which assumes that the long life of a company can be reported in shorter time periods, such as months, quarters, and years.[1] Two types of issues arise in reporting periodic income to users:

1. Recognition issues: **When** should the effects of operating activities be recognized (recorded)?

2. Measurement issues: **What amounts** should be recognized?

Before we examine the rules accountants follow in resolving these issues, however, let's examine the elements of financial statements that are affected by operating activities.

Elements on the Income Statement

Learning Objective 2
Explain how business activities affect the elements of the income statement.

Exhibit 3.1 shows a recent income statement for Papa John's, simplified for purposes of this chapter.[2] It has multiple subtotals, such as **operating income** and **income before income taxes.** This format is known as **multiple-step** and is very common.[3] As we discuss the elements of the income statement, also refer to the conceptual framework outlined in Exhibit 2.1.

REVENUES are increases in assets or settlements of liabilities from ongoing operations.

Revenues

Revenues are defined as increases in assets or settlements of liabilities from ongoing operations of the business (that is, an increase in net assets [A − L]). Operating revenues result from the sale of goods or services. When Papa John's sells pizza to consumers or supplies to franchisees, it has earned revenue. When revenue is earned, assets, usually cash or receivables, often increase. Sometimes if a customer pays for goods or services in advance, a liability account, usually deferred or unearned revenue, is created. At this point, no revenue has been earned. There is simply a receipt of cash in exchange for a promise to provide a good or service in the future. When the company provides the promised goods or services to the customer, the revenue is recognized and the liability settled.

Like most companies, Papa John's generates revenues from a variety of sources. Exhibit 3.1 shows revenues from two primary sources:

Revenues earned

Papa John's Primary Operating Revenues

Sell pizza to customers in company-owned restaurants

and

dough, supplies, and equipment to franchised restaurants

Sell franchises

1. **Restaurant and Commissary Sales.** Approximately 20 percent of Papa John's stores are owned by the company, while 80 percent are owned by others through franchise agreements. In addition, to reduce costs and control quality and consistency, Papa John's builds regional commissaries (centralized kitchens and supply facilities) that provide all of the chain's pizza supplies. The largest revenue on Papa

---

[1]In addition to the audited annual statements, most businesses prepare quarterly financial statements (also known as **interim reports** covering a three-month period) for external users. The Securities and Exchange Commission requires public companies to do so.

[2]For simplification, dollar amounts have been rounded and several accounts in the original statement have been combined with other accounts and/or shown in a different section of the statement in the exhibit. In addition, only one year's income statement is presented. Publicly traded companies such as Papa John's are actually required to present income information for three years to help users assess trends over time.

[3]Another common format, **single step,** reorganizes all accounts on the multiple-step format. All revenues and gains are listed together and all expenses and losses except taxes are listed together. The two subtotals are then subtracted to arrive at income before income taxes, the same subtotal as on the multiple-step statement.

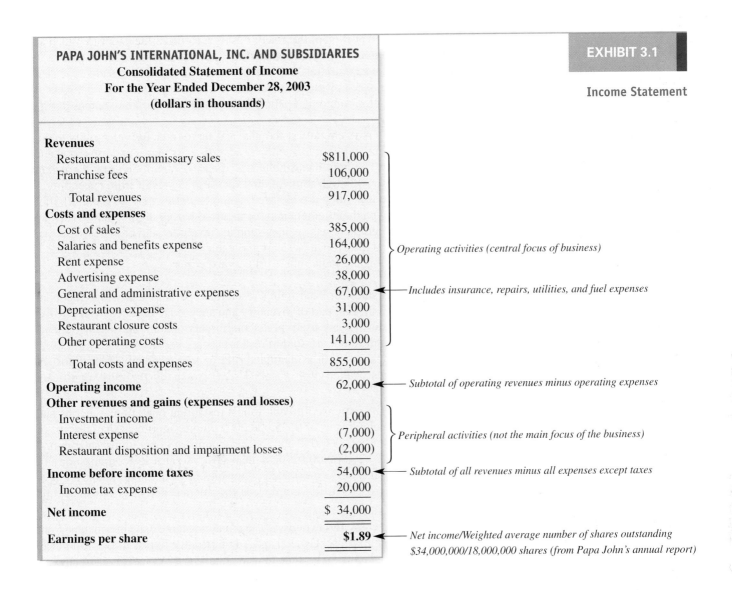

EXHIBIT 3.1

Income Statement

PAPA JOHN'S INTERNATIONAL, INC. AND SUBSIDIARIES
Consolidated Statement of Income
For the Year Ended December 28, 2003
(dollars in thousands)

Revenues		
Restaurant and commissary sales	$811,000	
Franchise fees	106,000	
Total revenues	917,000	
Costs and expenses		
Cost of sales	385,000	
Salaries and benefits expense	164,000	*Operating activities (central focus of business)*
Rent expense	26,000	
Advertising expense	38,000	
General and administrative expenses	67,000	← *Includes insurance, repairs, utilities, and fuel expenses*
Depreciation expense	31,000	
Restaurant closure costs	3,000	
Other operating costs	141,000	
Total costs and expenses	855,000	
Operating income	62,000	← *Subtotal of operating revenues minus operating expenses*
Other revenues and gains (expenses and losses)		
Investment income	1,000	
Interest expense	(7,000)	*Peripheral activities (not the main focus of the business)*
Restaurant disposition and impairment losses	(2,000)	
Income before income taxes	54,000	← *Subtotal of all revenues minus all expenses except taxes*
Income tax expense	20,000	
Net income	$ 34,000	
Earnings per share	**$1.89**	← *Net income/Weighted average number of shares outstanding*
		$34,000,000/18,000,000 shares (from Papa John's annual report)

John's income statement, Restaurant and Commissary Sales, results from pizza sales in company-owned stores and sales by the commissaries. Pizza sales for the franchised restaurants are reported in the franchisees' financial statements, not Papa John's.

2. **Franchise Fees.** Approximately 6 percent of all Papa John's revenues in 2003 came from selling franchises. Franchisees pay initial fees of at least $25,000 for the right to open and operate a specified number of restaurants in a specific geographic area. Papa John's records these fees as a liability (Unearned Franchise Fees) until it provides management training, site selection, restaurant design, and other promised services. As part of the franchise agreement, franchisees also pay Papa John's a fixed percentage (between 4 and 5 percent) of their store sales as franchise royalties. Both the initial fees and annual royalty payments are reported on Papa John's income statement as Franchise Fees.

Costs and Expenses

Some students confuse the terms **expenditures** and **expenses.** An expenditure is any outflow of money for any purpose, whether to buy equipment or pay off a bank loan. An expense is more narrowly defined. When an asset is **used to generate revenues**

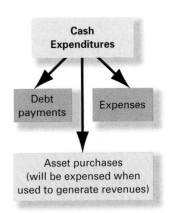

EXPENSES are decreases in assets or increases in liabilities from ongoing operations incurred to generate revenues during the period.

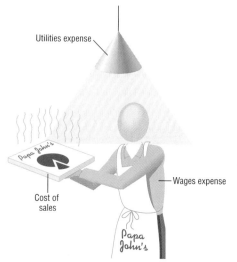

Expenses incurred to generate revenues

Papa John's Primary Operating Expenses

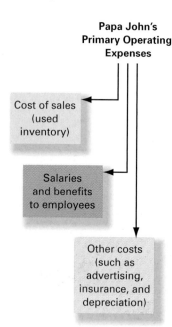

GAINS are increases in assets or decreases in liabilities from peripheral transactions.

LOSSES are decreases in assets or increases in liabilities from peripheral transactions.

during a period, all or a portion of the asset's cost is recorded as an expense. When an amount is **incurred to generate revenues during a period,** whether already paid or to be paid in the future, an expense results. Therefore, not all expenditures are expenses, and expenses are necessary to generate revenues. Expenses are decreases in assets or increases in liabilities from ongoing operations incurred to generate revenues during the period.

Papa John's pays employees to make and serve food, uses electricity to operate equipment and light its facilities, advertises its pizza, and uses food and paper supplies. Without incurring these expenses, Papa John's could not generate revenues. Although some of the expenses may result from expenditures of cash at the time they are incurred, some expenses may be incurred after cash has been paid and others may be incurred before cash is paid. When an expense is incurred, assets such as supplies inventory and cash decrease (are used up) **or** liabilities such as salaries payable or utilities payable increase.

The following are Papa John's primary expenses:

1. **Cost of sales.** In Papa John's restaurant operations, any ingredients or supplies that are part of inventory and are used to produce meals are expensed as they are used. In its commissary operations, any ingredients and supplies that are sold to restaurants are expensed as they are used. In companies with a manufacturing or merchandising focus, cost of sales (also called *cost of goods sold*) is usually the most significant expense.

2. **Salaries and benefits expense.** In Papa John's restaurant operations, salaries and benefits expense to employees of $135,000,000 is more significant than its cost of sales by restaurants of $93,000,000 but, for the commissary operations, salaries and benefits expense of $29,000,000 is less than cost of sales by commissaries of $292,000,000. In purely service-oriented companies in which no products are produced or sold, the cost of using employees to generate revenues is usually the largest expense.

3. **All other operating costs and expenses.** The remaining large expenses include Rent Expense, Advertising Expense, General and Administrative Expenses (for insurance, executive salaries, and rental of headquarters facilities), and Depreciation Expense reflecting the use of a part of long-lived assets such as buildings and equipment.

Other Revenues, Gains, Expenses, and Losses

Not all activities affecting an income statement are central to ongoing operations. Using excess cash to purchase stocks in other companies is an investing activity for Papa John's. However, any interest or dividends earned on the investment is called **investment income** or **revenue.** Likewise, borrowing money is a financing activity. However, the cost of then using that money is called **interest expense.** Except for financial institutions, incurring interest expense or earning investment income are not the central operations of most businesses including Papa John's. We say these are peripheral (normal but not central) transactions.

In similar fashion, companies sell property, plant, and equipment from time to time to maintain modern facilities. Selling land for more than the original purchase price does not result in a revenue because the transaction is not the central operating focus for the business. The gain results in an increase in assets or decrease in liabilities from a peripheral transaction. Papa John's did not report any gains in its 2003 income statement. However, it did report losses due to disposing of restaurants. Losses are decreases in assets or increases in liabilities from peripheral transactions. If land with a recorded cost of $2,800 were sold for $2,500, Papa John's would recognize a loss of $300 on the sale. Items such as "Restaurant disposition and impairment losses" shown in Exhibit 3.1 will be discussed in Chapter 8.

Income Tax Expense

Income Tax Expense is the last expense listed on the income statement. All profit-making corporations are required to compute income taxes owed to federal, state, and foreign governments. Income tax expense is calculated as a percentage of the difference between revenues and expenses determined by applying the tax rates of the federal, state, local, and foreign taxing authorities. Papa John's effective tax rate in 2003 was 37 percent (income tax expense, $20,000,000, divided by income before income taxes, $54,000,000). This indicates that for every dollar of income before taxes that Papa John's made in 2003, the company paid $0.37 to taxing authorities.

Earnings per Share

Corporations are required to disclose earnings per share on the income statement or in the notes to the financial statements. This ratio is widely used in evaluating the operating performance and profitability of a company. To compute earnings per share, net income is divided by the weighted average number of shares of stock outstanding. The calculation of the denominator is complex and is presented in other accounting courses. We used the actual number reported by Papa John's. For 2003, Papa John's reported $1.89 in earnings for each share of stock owned by investors.

Understanding the Meaning of Account Titles in Foreign Financial Statements

INTERNATIONAL PERSPECTIVE

GlaxoSmithKline plc
Diageo plc
Fosters Group Limited

We learned in Chapters 1 and 2 that foreign companies often use different account titles from U.S. companies. For example, the U.K. companies of GlaxoSmithKline (pharmaceutical industry) and Diageo (alcoholic beverage industry) use the term "Turnover" to refer to sales revenue. The Australian beer manufacturer Foster's Group Limited, on the other hand, uses "Sales Revenue."

Foreign companies also may use different statement titles. Diageo titles the income statement "Consolidated Profit and Loss Account." Similarly, GlaxoSmithKline uses "Consolidated Statement of Profit and Loss." The Australian beer manufacturer Foster's Group Limited titles its income statement "Statement of Financial Performance."

HOW ARE OPERATING ACTIVITIES RECOGNIZED AND MEASURED?

You probably determine your personal financial position by the cash balance in your bank account. Your financial performance is measured as the difference between your cash balance at the beginning of the period and the cash balance at the end of the period (that is, whether you end up with more or less cash). If you have a higher cash balance, cash receipts exceeded cash disbursements for the period. Many local retailers, medical offices, and other small businesses use **cash basis accounting** in which revenues are recorded when cash is received, and expenses are recorded when cash is paid, regardless of when the revenues were earned or the expenses incurred. This basis is often quite adequate for organizations that do not need to report to external users.

Accrual Accounting

Financial statements created under cash basis accounting normally postpone or accelerate recognition of revenues and expenses long before or after goods and services are produced and delivered (when cash is received or paid). They also do not necessarily reflect all assets or liabilities of a company on a particular date. For these reasons, cash basis financial statements are not very useful to external decision makers. Therefore,

Learning Objective 3
Explain the accrual basis of accounting and apply the revenue and matching principles to measure income.

CASH BASIS ACCOUNTING records revenues when cash is received and expenses when cash is paid.

CASH BASIS
Income Measurement
Revenues (= cash receipts)
− Expenses (= cash payments)
Net Income (cash basis)

ACCRUAL BASIS ACCOUNTING records revenues when earned and expenses when incurred, regardless of the timing of cash receipts or payments.

ACCRUAL BASIS
Income Measurement
Revenues (= when earned)
− Expenses (= when incurred)
Net Income (accrual basis)

The **REVENUE PRINCIPLE** states that revenues are recognized when goods or services are delivered, there is persuasive evidence of an arrangement for customer payment, the price is fixed or determinable, and collection is reasonably assured.

Topic Tackler
PLUS

Topic Tackler 3–1

generally accepted accounting principles require accrual basis accounting for financial reporting purposes.

In accrual basis accounting, revenues and expenses are recognized when the transaction that causes them occurs, not necessarily when cash is received or paid. That is, **revenues are recognized when they are earned and expenses when they are incurred.** The two basic accounting principles that determine when revenues and expenses are recorded under accrual basis accounting are the **revenue principle** and the **matching principle.**

Revenue Principle

Under the revenue principle, four criteria or conditions must normally be met for revenue to be recognized. If *any* of the following criteria is *not* met, revenue normally is *not* recognized and cannot be recorded.

1. **Delivery has occurred or services have been rendered.** The company has performed or substantially performed the acts promised to the customer by providing goods or services.
2. **There is persuasive evidence of an arrangement for customer payment.** In exchange for the company's performance, the customer has provided cash or a promise to pay cash (a receivable).
3. **The price is fixed or determinable.** There are no uncertainties as to the amount to be collected.
4. **Collection is reasonably assured.** For cash sales, collection is not an issue since it is received on the date of the exchange. For sales on credit, the company reviews the customer's ability to pay. If the customer is considered creditworthy, collecting cash from the customer is reasonably likely.

These conditions normally occur when the title, risks, and rewards of ownership have transferred to the customers. For most businesses, these conditions are met at the point of delivery of goods or services. As is typical in the fast-food industry, Papa John's receives most of its revenues from restaurant sales at the time pizza is delivered to customers (criterion 1). Because a determinable amount of cash (criterion 3) is paid by customers in exchange for food service from Papa John's (criterion 2), there is no uncertainty as to the probability of collecting cash (criterion 4).

Papa John's also sells franchises from which the company receives cash from new franchisees **before** providing start-up services to them (criteria 2, 3, and 4 are met). Until the company provides the services, it records no revenue. It records monies received from franchisees in the liability account Unearned Franchise Fees. This deferred or unearned revenue account represents the amount of goods or services owed to the franchisees. Later, when Papa John's provides the services (criterion 1), it earns and records the revenue by reducing the liability account.

Revenue is recorded according to the revenue principle when the four conditions are met, **regardless of when cash is received.** Cash may be received before, during, or after revenue is earned. An entry will be made on the date the revenue is earned and another on the date the cash is received, if at different times.

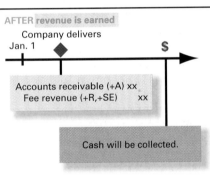

Cash is received:

• If cash is received before the company delivers goods or services, the liability account Unearned Revenue is recorded because the company still owes goods or services. Examples include companies that sell magazine subscriptions and companies that sell insurance. Although not corporations, colleges and universities also receive tuition revenue and sell season tickets to sporting events and plays before any revenue is earned.	**BEFORE** revenue is earned — Company delivers Jan. 1 — $ Cash (+A) xx Unearned revenue (+L) xx Revenue will be recorded when earned
• If cash is received at the same time of delivery of the goods or services, revenue is recorded.	**ON the date** revenue is earned $ Company delivers Jan. 1 Cash (+A) xx Fee revenue (+R,+SE) xx
• If cash will be received after goods or services are delivered, a receivable account is created to reflect what customers owe the company. Gas and electric utility companies provide service before customers pay bills.	**AFTER** revenue is earned Company delivers Jan. 1 — $ Accounts receivable (+A) xx Fee revenue (+R,+SE) xx Cash will be collected.

Companies usually disclose their revenue recognition practices in a note to the financial statements. The following excerpt from Papa John's note describes how it recognizes its two forms of franchise-related income and pizza sales at restaurants:

2. SIGNIFICANT ACCOUNTING POLICIES

Revenue Recognition

Franchise fees are recognized when a franchised restaurant begins operations, at which time we have performed our obligations related to such fees. Fees received pursuant to development agreements which grant the right to develop franchised restaurants in future periods in specific geographic areas are deferred and recognized on a pro rata basis as the franchised restaurants subject to the development agreements begin operations. Both franchise and development fees are nonrefundable. Retail sales from Company-owned restaurants and franchise royalties, which are based on a percentage of franchised restaurants' sales, are recognized as revenue when the products are delivered to or carried out by customers.

SELF-STUDY **QUIZ**

This self-study quiz allows you to practice applying the revenue principle under accrual accounting. We recommend that you refer back to the four *revenue recognition criteria* presented earlier as you answer each question. Complete this quiz now to make sure you can apply the principle. The following transactions are samples of typical monthly operating activities of Papa John's (dollars in thousands). If revenue is to be recognized in *January,* indicate the title of the revenue account and the amount of revenue to be recognized.

ACTIVITY	REVENUE ACCOUNT TITLE	AMOUNT OF REVENUE RECOGNIZED IN JANUARY
(*a*) In January, Papa John's company-owned restaurants sold food to customers for $32,000 cash.		
(*b*) In January, Papa John's sold new franchises for $625 cash, providing $400 in services to these new franchisees during January; the remainder of services will be provided over the next three months.		
(*c*) In January, franchisees paid Papa John's $2,750 in cash for royalties based on the franchisees' weekly sales; $750 related to December sales and the rest to Janaury sales.		
(*d*) In January, Papa John's commissaries sold sauce and dough to restaurants for $30,000 of which $20,000 was in cash and the rest was on account.		
(*e*) In January, franchisees paid $1,200 on account to Papa John's from December purchases of dough and sauce.		

After you have completed your answers, check them with the solutions at the bottom of the page.

A QUESTION OF ETHICS
Management's Incentives to Violate Accounting Rules

Investors in the stock market base their decisions on their expectations of a company's future earnings. When companies announce quarterly and annual earnings information, investors evaluate how well the companies have met expectations and adjust their investing decisions accordingly. Companies that fail to meet expectations often experience a decline in stock price. Thus, managers are motivated to produce earnings results that meet or exceed investors' expectations to bolster stock prices. Since many executives are given options to purchase com-

Self-Study Quiz Solutions

Revenue Account Title	Amount of Revenue Recognized in January
(a) Restaurant and Commissary Sales Revenue	$32,000
(b) Franchise Fees Revenue	$400
(c) Franchise Fees Revenue	$2,000
(d) Restaurant and Commissary Sales Revenue	$30,000
(e) No revenue earned in January.	—

pany stock as part of their compensation, greed may lead some managers to make unethical accounting and reporting decisions, often involving falsifying revenues and expenses.

The accounting scandals at Enron, WorldCom, and other high-profile companies in recent years prompted federal and state prosecutors to become very aggressive in rooting out corporate crime. Fraud is a criminal offense for which managers may be sentenced to jail. At the time this text was written, the following managers had been convicted or accused of perpetrating accounting fraud in recent years.

Company	Fraud	Convictions, Pleas, and Outcomes
WorldCom	$11 billion—Falsely and fraudulently booked certain entries in the general ledger to inflate profits and hide expenses.	Sixty-three-year-old former WorldCom CEO Bernard Ebbers was found guilty of federal fraud and conspiracy and sentenced to 25 years in prison for orchestrating the largest accounting shell-game in corporate history. CFO Scott Sullivan and four others pleaded guilty. At 42 years old, Scott Sullivan may be sentenced to up to 25 years in prison.
Enron	$4 billion—Used sophisticated schemes to hide debt.	Thirty-two individuals from Enron, including former CEO Jeff Skilling and former chairman Ken Lay, have been indicted. At least 30 have been convicted or pleaded guilty, and several have been sentenced to jail.
HealthSouth	$2.74 billion—Artificially inflating earnings matched by a false increase in assets.	Sixteen former employees, including five former chief financial officers, pleaded guilty. Ousted CEO Richard Scrushy pleaded not guilty.
Rite Aid	$1.6 billion—Created a scheme to manipulate earnings; also charged with destroying evidence and fabricating documents.	Former officers of Rite Aid pleaded guilty and former vice chairman Franklin Brown was convicted.

Besides the people who end up in jail, many others are affected by fraud. Stockholders lose stock value, employees may lose their jobs (and pension funds, as in the case of Enron), and customers and suppliers may become wary of dealing with a company operating under the cloud of fraud. As a manager, you may face an ethical dilemma in the workplace. The ethical decision is the one you will be proud of 20 years later.

The Matching Principle

The matching principle requires that costs incurred to generate revenues be recognized in the same period—a matching of costs with benefits. For example, when Papa John's restaurants provide food service to customers, revenue is earned. The costs of generating the revenue include expenses incurred such as these:

The MATCHING PRINCIPLE requires that expenses be recorded when incurred in earning revenue.

- Wages to employees who worked **during the period** (Wages Expense)
- Utilities for the electricity used **during the period** (Utilities Expense)
- Food and paper products used **during the period** (Cost of Sales)
- Facilities rental **during the period** (Rent Expense)
- The use of ovens and other equipment **during the period** (Depreciation Expense)

As with revenues and cash receipts, expenses are recorded as incurred, **regardless of when cash is paid.** Cash may be paid before, during, or after an expense is incurred. An entry will be made on the date the expense is incurred and another on the date the cash is paid, if at different times.

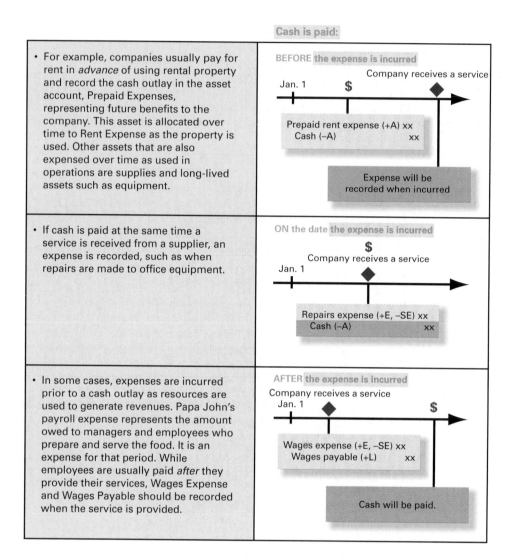

For example, companies usually pay for rent in *advance* of using rental property and record the cash outlay in the asset account, Prepaid Expenses, representing future benefits to the company. This asset is allocated over time to Rent Expense as the property is used. Other assets that are also expensed over time as used in operations are supplies and long-lived assets such as equipment.

If cash is paid at the same time a service is received from a supplier, an expense is recorded, such as when repairs are made to office equipment.

In some cases, expenses are incurred prior to a cash outlay as resources are used to generate revenues. Papa John's payroll expense represents the amount owed to managers and employees who prepare and serve the food. It is an expense for that period. While employees are usually paid *after* they provide their services, Wages Expense and Wages Payable should be recorded when the service is provided.

SELF-STUDY QUIZ

This self-study quiz allows you to practice applying the **matching principle** under accrual accounting. Complete this quiz now to make sure you can apply this principle. The following transactions are samples of typical monthly operating activities of Papa John's (dollars in thousands). If expense is to be recognized in **January,** indicate the title of the expense account and the amount of the expense to be recognized. You should refer to the Papa John's income statement presented in Exhibit 3.1 for account titles.

ACTIVITY	EXPENSE ACCOUNT TITLE	AMOUNT OF EXPENSE RECOGNIZED IN JANUARY
(a) At the beginning of January, Papa John's restaurants paid $3,000 in rent for the months of January, February, and March.		
(b) In January, Papa John's paid suppliers $10,000 on account for supplies received in December.		

(c) In January, the food and paper products inventory used in selling pizza products to customers was $9,500.		
(d) In late January, Papa John's received a $500 utility bill for electricity used in January. The bill will be paid in February.		

After you have completed your answers, check them with the solutions at the bottom of the page.

The Feedback Value of Accounting Information and Stock Market Reaction

Stock market analysts and investors use accounting information to make their investment decisions. Thus, the stock market, which is based on investors' expectations about a company's future performance, often reacts negatively when a company does not meet previously specified operating targets.

A net loss does not have to occur for a company to recognize that it is experiencing difficulty. Any unexpected variance in actual performance from the operating plan, such as lower than expected quarterly earnings, needs to be explained. On December 12, 2000, Papa John's announced that it anticipated it would report lower than expected earnings due to lower than expected franchisee sales, "fewer and later than expected restaurant openings," and "higher than expected labor and energy related costs."* On the day of the announcement, its stock had been selling at $26.81 per share. On the day following the announcement, the price dropped by $4.93 to $21.88 per share, an 18.4 percent decrease in one day.†

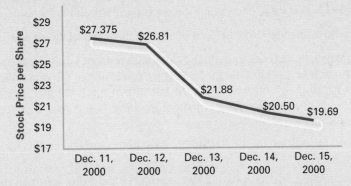

This is a clear example of how corporate decisions affect financial data and how internal and external users use the information. Accounting information has a pervasive effect on all forms of corporate decision making, as well as on the economic decisions that investors and creditors make.

*"Papa John's Announces November Comparable Sales and Revised Earnings Estimates and Restaurant Openings for 4Q, Full-Year 2000 and 2001," Business Wire, December 12, 2000.
†Bigcharts.com

Expense Account Title	Amount of Expense Recognized in January
(a) Rent Expense	$1,000 ($3,000 ÷ 3 months)
(b) No expense in January	Supplies will be expensed when used.
(c) Cost of Sales	$9,500
(d) Utilities Expense (General and Administrative Expenses)	$ 500

THE EXPANDED TRANSACTION ANALYSIS MODEL

We discussed the variety of business activities affecting the income statement and how they are measured. Now we need to determine how these business activities are recorded in the accounting system and reflected in the financial statements. Chapter 2 covered investing and financing activities that affect assets, liabilities, and contributed capital. We now expand the transaction analysis model presented in that chapter to include operating activities.

Transaction Analysis Rules

The complete transaction model presented in Exhibit 3.2 includes all five elements: Assets, Liabilities, Stockholders' Equity, Revenues, and Expenses. Recall that the Retained Earnings account is the accumulation of all past revenues and expenses minus any income distributed to stockholders as dividends[4] (that is, earnings not retained in the business). When net income is positive, Retained Earnings increases; a net loss decreases Retained Earnings.

Before illustrating the use of the expanded transaction analysis model, we want to emphasize the following:

- Revenues increase stockholders' equity through Retained Earnings and therefore have **credit** balances.

- Expenses decrease net income, thus decreasing Retained Earnings and stockholders' equity. Therefore they have **debit** balances (opposite of the balance in Retained Earnings). That is, to increase an expense, you debit it, which decreases net income and Retained Earnings. You are adding up the expenses when you debit the account.

- When revenues exceed expenses, the company reports net income, increasing Retained Earnings and stockholders' equity. However, when expenses exceed revenues, a net loss results, decreasing Retained Earnings and stockholders' equity.

When constructing and using the transactions analysis model, as we saw in Chapter 2:

- All accounts can increase or decrease, although revenues and expenses tend to increase throughout a period. For accounts on the left side of the accounting equation, the increase symbol + is written on the left side of the T-account. For accounts on the right side of the accounting equation, the increase symbol + is written on the right side of the T-account.

- Debits (dr) are written on the left side of each T-account and credits (cr) are written on the right.

- Every transaction affects at least two accounts. In analyzing transactions:

  a. **Identify the accounts affected by title and classify them by type of account,** making sure that at least two accounts change. Ask yourself what is received and what is given. Classifications are an asset (A), a liability (L), a stockholders' equity (SE), a revenue (R), and an expense account (E).

  b. **Determine the direction of the effect** (an increase [+] or decrease [−] on each account).

  c. **Verify that the accounting equation (A = L + SE) remains in balance.**

  d. The total dollar value of the **debits** in the transaction **should equal** the total dollar value of the **credits.**

Since revenues are defined as inflows of net assets, then by definition, recording a revenue results in either increasing an asset or decreasing a liability. In like manner, when recording an expense, an asset is decreased or a liability is increased.

---

[4]Instead of reducing Retained Earnings directly when dividends are declared, companies may use the account Dividends Declared, which has a debit balance.

Sidebar

Learning Objective 4

Apply transaction analysis to examine and record the effects of operating activities on the financial statements.

Topic Tackler 3–2

Assets	
DR +	

Liabilities	
	CR +

Stockholders' Equity Accounts	
	CR +

Revenues and Gains	
	CR +

Expenses and Losses	
DR +	

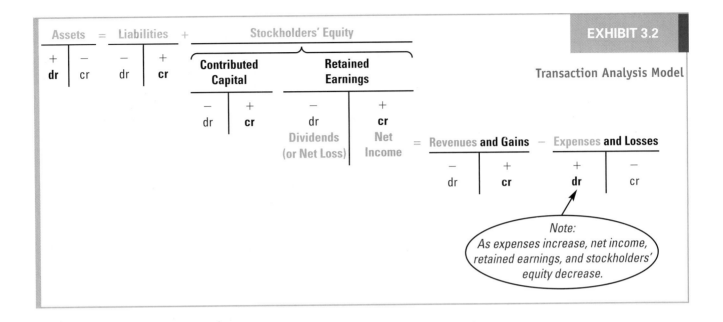

EXHIBIT 3.2

Transaction Analysis Model

Note:
As expenses increase, net income, retained earnings, and stockholders' equity decrease.

You should refer to the expanded transaction analysis model until you can construct it on your own without assistance. Study the illustration above carefully to make sure you understand the impact of operating activities on both the balance sheet and income statement.

Analyzing Papa John's Transactions

Now we build on the Papa John's balance sheet presented at the end of Chapter 2 that included investing and financing transactions occurring during the accounting cycle. We analyze, record, and post to the T-accounts the effects of this chapter's operating activities that also occurred during the accounting cycle (the month of January). In Chapter 4, we complete the accounting cycle with the activities at the end of the period (on January 31). All amounts are in thousands of dollars and the effects are posted to the appropriate T-accounts at the end of the illustration.

(*a*) **Papa John's restaurants sold pizza to customers for $36,000 cash. In addition, Papa John's commissaries sold $30,000 in supplies to restaurants, receiving $21,000 cash with the rest due on account.**

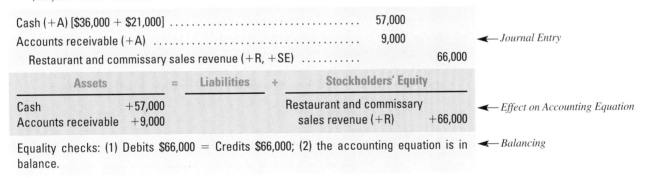

Cash (+A) [$36,000 + $21,000] 57,000
Accounts receivable (+A) 9,000
   Restaurant and commissary sales revenue (+R, +SE) 66,000   ◄— *Journal Entry*

Assets	=	Liabilities	+	Stockholders' Equity	
Cash +57,000				Restaurant and commissary	
Accounts receivable +9,000				sales revenue (+R) +66,000	◄— *Effect on Accounting Equation*

Equality checks: (1) Debits $66,000 = Credits $66,000; (2) the accounting equation is in   ◄— *Balancing*
balance.

(*b*) **The cost of the dough, sauce, cheese, and other ingredients for the restaurant sales in (*a*) was $10,000. The cost of the supplies for the commissary sales in (*a*) was $20,000.**

Cost of sales (+E, −SE) 30,000
   Supplies (−A) 30,000

Assets		=	Liabilities	+	Stockholders' Equity	
Supplies	−30,000				Cost of sales (+E)	−30,000

Equality checks: (1) Debits $30,000 = Credits $30,000; (2) the accounting equation is in balance.

(c) **Papa John's sold new franchises for $400 cash. The company earned $100 immediately by performing services for franchisees; the rest will be earned over the next several months.**

Cash (+A)	400	
Franchise fees revenue (+R, +SE)		100
Unearned franchise fees (+L)		300

Assets		=	Liabilities		+	Stockholders' Equity	
Cash	+400		Unearned franchise fees	+300		Franchise fees revenue (+R)	+100

Equality checks: (1) Debits $400 = Credits $400; (2) the accounting equation is in balance.

(d) **In January, Papa John's paid $7,000 for utilities, repairs, and fuel for delivery vehicles, all considered general and administrative expenses.**

| General and administrative expenses (+E, −SE) . . . . | 7,000 | |
| Cash (−A) . . . . | | 7,000 |

Assets		=	Liabilities	+	Stockholders' Equity	
Cash	−7,000				General and administrative expenses (+E)	−7,000

Equality checks: (1) Debits $7,000 = Credits $7,000; (2) the accounting equation is in balance.

(e) **Papa John's commissaries ordered and received $29,000 in supplies, paying $9,000 in cash and owing the rest on account to suppliers.**

Supplies (+A)	29,000	
Cash (−A)		9,000
Accounts payable (+L)		20,000

Assets		=	Liabilities		+	Stockholders' Equity
Cash	−9,000		Accounts payable	+20,000		
Supplies	+29,000					

Equality checks: (1) Debits $29,000 = Credits $29,000; (2) the accounting equation is in balance.

(f) **Papa John's paid $14,000 cash to employees for their work in January.**

| Salaries and benefits expense (+E, −SE) . . . . | 14,000 | |
| Cash (−A) . . . . | | 14,000 |

Assets		=	Liabilities	+	Stockholders' Equity	
Cash	−14,000				Salaries and benefits expense (+E)	−14,000

Equality checks: (1) Debits $14,000 = Credits $14,000; (2) the accounting equation is in balance.

(g) **At the beginning of January, Papa John's paid the following, all of which are considered prepaid expenses when paid:**
   • **$2,000 for insurance (covering the next four months beginning January 1),**

- **$6,000 for renting space in shopping centers (over the next three months beginning January 1), and**
- **$1,000 for advertising (to be run in February).**

Prepaid expenses (+A) 9,000
   Cash (−A) 9,000

Assets		=	Liabilities	+	Stockholders' Equity
Cash	−9,000				
Prepaid expenses	+9,000				

Equality checks: (1) Debits $9,000 = Credits $9,000; (2) the accounting equation is in balance.

(h) Papa John's sold land with an historical cost of $1,000 for $4,000 cash.*

Cash (+A) 4,000
   Property and equipment (−A) 1,000
   Gain on sale of land (+Gain, +SE) 3,000

Assets		=	Liabilities	+	Stockholders' Equity	
Property and equipment	−1,000				Gain on sale of land (+R)	+3,000
Cash	+4,000					

Equality checks: (1) Debits $4,000 = Credits $4,000; (2) the accounting equation is in balance.

*This is an example of a peripheral activity; it will be covered in more depth in Chapter 8.

SELF-STUDY **QUIZ**

For transactions (i) through (k), fill in the missing information. Be sure to transfer (post) the effects of the journal entries to the T-accounts at the end of the illustration. After you have completed your answers, check them with the solution at the bottom of the page.

(i) Papa John's received $3,500 in franchisee fees based on their weekly sales; $800 of the amount was due from franchisees' sales recorded as accounts receivable in December and the rest from January sales.

Write the journal entry; post the effects to the T-accounts.

Assets		=	Liabilities	+	Stockholders' Equity	
Cash	+3,500				Franchise fees revenue (+R)	+ 2,700
Accounts receivable	−800					

Equality checks: (1) Debits $3,500 = Credits $3,500; (2) the accounting equation is in balance.

(j) Papa John's paid $10,000 on accounts owed to suppliers.

Write the journal entry; post the effects to the T-accounts.

Assets	=	Liabilities	+	Stockholders' Equity

Show the effects on the accounting equation.

Equality checks: (1) Debits $10,000 = Credits $10,000; (2) the accounting equation is in balance.

(k) Papa John's received $13,000 in cash: $1,000 in interest earned on invest-ments and $12,000 in payments made by franchisees on their accounts.

Cash (+A) 13,000
   Investment income (+R, +SE) 1,000
   Accounts receivable (−A) 12,000

Assets	=	Liabilities	+	Stockholders' Equity

Show the effects on the →
accounting equation.

Verify equalities → Equality checks: (1) Debits $_____ = Credits $_____ (2) Is the accounting equation in balance? _____

Exhibit 3.3 shows the T-accounts that changed during the period because of transactions (*a*) through (*k*). The balances of all other accounts remained the same. Note that the amounts from Papa John's balance sheet at the end of Chapter 2 have been included as the beginning balances in Exhibit 3.3. At the beginning of every period, income statement accounts have a zero beginning balance; therefore, there is no balance in the revenue and expense accounts at the beginning of the month.

EXHIBIT 3.3

T-Accounts

Balance Sheet Accounts (beginning balances are taken from Exhibit 2.8)

Cash			
Bal.	9,000		
(a)	57,000	7,000	(d)
(c)	400	9,000	(e)
(h)	4,000	14,000	(f)
(i)	_____	9,000	(g)
(k)	13,000	_____	(j)
Bal.	37,900		

Accounts Receivable			
Bal.	20,000	_____	(i)
(a)	9,000	12,000	(k)
Bal.	16,200		

Property and Equipment			
Bal.	214,000	1,000	(h)
Bal.	213,000		

Supplies			
Bal.	17,000	30,000	(b)
(e)	29,000		
Bal.	16,000		

Prepaid Expenses			
Bal.	11,000		
(g)	9,000		
Bal.	20,000		

Self-Study Quiz
Solutions

(i) Cash (+A) 3,500
    Accounts receivable (−A) 800
    Franchise fees revenue (+R, +SE) 2,700

(j) Accounts Payable (−L) 10,000
    Cash (−A) 10,000

Assets		=	Liabilities		+	Stockholders' Equity
Cash	−10,000		Accounts payable	−10,000		

(k)

Assets		=	Liabilities	+	Stockholders' Equity
Cash	+13,000				Investment income (+R) +1,000
Accounts receivable	−12,000				

Debits $13,000 = Credits $13,000; the equation is in balance.

EXHIBIT 3.3

continued

Accounts Payable			
(j)	____	28,000	Bal.
		20,000	(e)
		38,000	Bal.

Unearned Franchise Fees			
		6,000	Bal.
		300	(c)
		6,300	Bal.

Income Statement Accounts

Restaurant and Commissary Sales Revenue			
		66,000	(a)
		66,000	Bal.

Franchise Fees Revenue			
		100	(c)
		____	(i)
		2,800	Bal.

Cost of Sales			
(b)	30,000		
Bal.	30,000		

Salaries and Benefits Expense			
(f)	14,000		
Bal.	14,000		

General and Administrative Expense			
(d)	7,000		
Bal.	7,000		

Gain on Sale of Land			
		3,000	(h)
		3,000	Bal.

Investment Income			
		1,000	(k)
		1,000	Bal.

You can verify that you posted the entries for transactions (i) through (k) properly by adding the increase side and subtracting the decrease side and then comparing your answer to the ending balance in each of the T-accounts.

HOW ARE FINANCIAL STATEMENTS PREPARED?

Based on the January transactions that have just been posted in the T-accounts, we can now prepare financial statements reflecting the operating activities for January. Recall from prior chapters what the four statements are and how they relate to each other.

Learning Objective 5
Prepare financial statements.

Statement	Formula
Income statement	Revenues − Expenses = Net Income
Statement of retained earnings	Beginning Retained Earnings + Net Income − Dividends Declared = Ending Retained Earnings
Balance sheet	Assets = Liabilities + Stockholders' Equity (Contributed Capital and Retained Earnings) (includes Cash)
Statement of cash flows	Change in Cash = Cash provided by or used in Operating Activities + Cash provided by or used in Investing Activities + Cash provided by or used in Financing Activities

These statements are not yet adjusted for all revenues earned or expenses incurred in January. For example, the account Prepaid Expenses includes rent and insurance used in January, but the expenses are not yet recorded. This is true of the equipment used during the month as well. Also notice that we have not calculated income taxes. Because in Chapter 4 adjustments will be discussed and added to the information from Chapters 2 and 3, the amount of tax expense is not yet determinable. These statements do not at this point reflect generally accepted accounting principles based on accrual accounting until we adjust the accounts and financial statements as illustrated in Chapter 4.

Income Statement

PAPA JOHN'S INTERNATIONAL, INC. AND SUBSIDIARIES
Consolidated Statement of Income
For the Month Ended January 31, 2004
(dollars in thousands)

Revenues	
Restaurant and commissary sales	$66,000
Franchise fees	2,800
Total revenues	68,800
Costs and expenses	
Cost of sales	30,000
Salaries and benefits expense	14,000
General and administrative expenses	7,000
Supplies expense	0
Rent expense	0
Insurance expense	0
Utilities expense	0
Depreciation expense	0
Interest expense	0
Other operating costs	0
Total costs and expenses	51,000
Operating income	17,800
Other revenues and gains (expenses and losses)	
Investment income	1,000
Interest expense	(0)
Gain on sale of land	3,000
Income before income taxes	21,800
Income tax expense	0
Net income	$21,800
Earnings per share (for the month)	$1.21

$21,800,000 net income divided by average number of shares outstanding (approximately 18,000,000 shares from Papa John's annual report) ⟶ Earnings per share (for the month)

In our illustration for Papa John's, the company earned positive net income of $21,800,000, nearly 32 percent of operating revenues ($21,800,000 net income ÷ $68,800,000 total revenues) before adjustments. Net income is a component of the statement of retained earnings.

FINANCIAL
ANALYSIS

Reporting Financial Information by Geographic and Operating Segments

Many companies, especially very large ones, operate in more than one geographic area. These companies are often called **multinationals.** A consolidated income statement that is based on aggregated data may not prove useful to investors seeking to assess possible risks and returns from companies operating in foreign markets. The same may be true if a company operates more than a single business. Therefore, many companies provide additional information about geographic and business segments in notes to the financial statements. An excerpt from Papa John's 2003 annual report provides information on geographic segments:

NOTES TO CONSOLIDATED FINANCIAL STATEMENTS

19. Segment Information

We have defined four reportable segments: domestic restaurants, domestic commissaries, domestic franchising and international operations....

(dollars in thousands)	2003	2002	2001
Revenues from external customers:			
Domestic restaurants	$416,049	$429,813	$445,849
Domestic commissaries	369,825	381,217	390,889
Domestic franchising	51,326	53,120	53,695
International	31,637	32,014	31,909
All others	48,541	50,055	52,730
Total revenues from external customers	$917,378	$946,219	$975,072

Statement of Retained Earnings

The statement of retained earnings ties the information on Papa John's income statement to the balance sheet. Any transactions affecting Retained Earnings, such as generating net income and declaring dividends, are summarized in this statement.

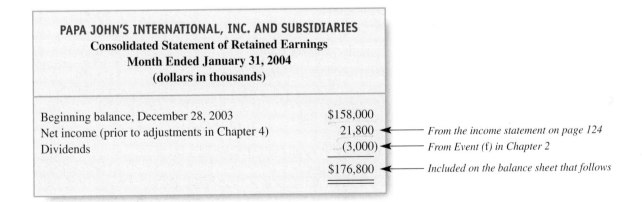

PAPA JOHN'S INTERNATIONAL, INC. AND SUBSIDIARIES
Consolidated Statement of Retained Earnings
Month Ended January 31, 2004
(dollars in thousands)

Beginning balance, December 28, 2003	$158,000
Net income (prior to adjustments in Chapter 4)	21,800	◀— *From the income statement on page 124*
Dividends	(3,000)	◀— *From Event (f) in Chapter 2*
	$176,800	◀— *Included on the balance sheet that follows*

Balance Sheet

Finally, we can revise the balance sheet from Chapter 2 to reflect the effects of the operating activities discussed in this chapter. Notice that the ending balance in the statement of retained earnings flows into the Stockholders' Equity section of the balance sheet. Revenues, expenses, and dividends are not listed separately on the balance sheet but are summarized in Retained Earnings. We explore the relationships among the financial statements further in the next chapter.

PAPA JOHN'S INTERNATIONAL, INC. AND SUBSIDIARIES
Consolidated Balance Sheet
January 31, 2004
(dollars in thousands)

Assets	
Current assets	
Cash	$ 37,900
Accounts receivable	16,200
Supplies	16,000
Prepaid expenses	20,000
Other current assets	7,000
Total current assets	97,100
Long-term investments	9,000
Property and equipment (net of accumulated depreciation of $149,000)	213,000
Long-term notes receivable	14,000
Intangibles	49,000
Other assets	13,000
Total assets	$395,100
Liabilities and Stockholders' Equity	
Current liabilities	
Accounts payable	$ 38,000
Dividends payable	3,000
Accrued expenses payable	53,000
Total current liabilities	94,000
Unearned franchise fees	6,300
Long-term notes payable	75,000
Other long-term liabilities	40,000
Stockholders' equity	
Contributed capital	3,000
Retained earnings	176,800
Total stockholders' equity	179,800
Total liabilities and stockholders' equity	$395,100

From the Statement of Retained Earnings ⟶ (Retained earnings)

FOCUS ON
CASH FLOWS

Operating Activities

Chapter 2 presented a statement of cash flows for Papa John's investing and financing activities. Recall that investing activities relate primarily to transactions affecting long-term assets; financing activities are those from bank borrowings, stock issuances, and dividend payments to stockholders.

In this chapter, we focus on cash flows from operating activities. This section of the statement of cash flows reports **cash from** operating sources and **cash to** suppliers and others involved in operations. When operating cash inflows and outflows are presented in this manner, the company is using the **direct method** of reporting cash flows from operations. However, most companies report cash from operations using the **indirect method** that will be discussed in later chapters. The accounts most often associated with operating activities are current assets, such as Accounts Receivable, Inventories, and Prepaid Expenses, and current liabilities, such as Accounts Payable, Wages Payable, and Unearned Revenue.

When a transaction affects cash, it is included on the statement of cash flows. When a transaction does not affect cash, such as acquiring a building with a long-term mortgage note payable or selling goods on account to customers, there is no cash effect to include on the statement.

		Effect on Cash Flows
Operating activities		
Cash received:	Customers	+
	Interest and dividends on investments	+
Cash paid:	Suppliers	−
	Employees	−
	Interest on debt obligations	−
	Income taxes	−
Investing activities (see Chapter 2)		
Financing activities (see Chapter 2)		

Focus Company Analysis   The operating activities section of the following statement of cash flows for Papa John's is based on the transactions illustrated in this chapter; the investing and financing activities relate primarily to transactions from Chapter 2. The statement reports the sources and uses of cash that created the overall $30,900 cash increase (from $7,000 to $37,900) in our Papa John's example. Remember that only the transactions that affect cash are reported.

In the long run, to remain in business, companies must generate positive cash flows from operations. Cash is needed to pay suppliers and employees. If the cash flow from operations is negative for a sustained period of time, the only other ways to obtain the necessary funds are to (1) sell long-lived assets (which reduces future productivity), (2) borrow from creditors (at increasing rates of interest as the risk of default rises), or (3) issue additional shares of stock (at a time when investors' expectations of poor future performance tends to drive the stock price down). Clearly, there are limits on how many of these activities companies can undertake.

Papa John's not only has realized positive cash flows from operations over the years, but also has reported growth in the cash generated from operations in comparison to net income earned, from 2.04 times more cash than reported net income in 2001 to 2.53 times in 2003. This represents a conservative approach to reporting revenues and expenses that builds analysts' confidence about the reliability of the income information reported.

PAPA JOHN'S INTERNATIONAL, INC. Consolidated Statement of Cash Flows For the month ended January 31, 2004 (dollars in thousands)			*Each operating activity is referenced to the event illustrated in the chapter.*
Operating Activities			
Cash from:	Customers	$57,000	*[(a) $57,000]*
	Franchisees	15,900	*[(c) $400 + (i) 3,500 + (k) 12,000]*
	Interest on investments	1,000	*[(k) $1,000]*
Cash to:	Suppliers	(35,000)	*[(d) $7,000 + (e) 9,000 + (g) 9,000 + (j) 10,000]*
	Employees	(14,000)	*[(f) $14,000]*
Net cash provided by operating activities		**24,900**	
		continued	

	Investing Activities	
[(h) $4,000]	Sold land	4,000
	Purchased property and equipment	(2,000)
Except for the sale of land,	Purchased investments	(1,000)
investing and financing	Lent funds to franchisees	(3,000)
activities are illustrated	Net cash used in investing activities	**(2,000)**
in Chapter 2.	**Financing Activities**	
	Issued common stock	2,000
	Borrowed from banks	6,000
	Net cash provided by financing activities	**8,000**
	Net increase in cash	**30,900**
	Cash at beginning of month	7,000
Agrees with the amount on ➡	**Cash at end of month**	**$37,900**
the balance sheet.		

Note that Papa John's had net income of $21,800 before adjustments in January, yet the balance in the Cash account increased by $30,900. This is a very clear example of the difference between the accrual basis of accounting and the cash basis. **On an accrual basis, net income is rarely equivalent to the change in cash for the period.**

SELF-STUDY QUIZ

PETCO Animal
Supplies, Inc.

PETCO Animal Supplies, Inc., is a leading specialty retailer of premium pet food and supplies, with over 650 stores across the United States. Indicate whether the following transactions from a recent statement of cash flows affected cash flow as an operating (O), investing (I), or financing (F) activity, and show the direction of the effect (+ = an increase in cash; − = a decrease in cash):

TRANSACTIONS	TYPE OF ACTIVITY (O, I, OR F)	EFFECT ON CASH FLOWS (+ OR −)
1. Distribution to shareholders	_____	_____
2. Receipt of cash from customers	_____	_____
3. Additions to property	_____	_____
4. Payment of income taxes	_____	_____
5. Payment of cash to suppliers	_____	_____
6. Repayment of long-term debt principal	_____	_____
7. Receipt of interest on investments	_____	_____
8. Borrowings of long-term debt	_____	_____
9. Issuance of common stock	_____	_____
10. Payment of interest on debt	_____	_____
11. Payment of cash to employees	_____	_____
12. Sale of property	_____	_____

After you have completed your answers, check them with the solutions at the bottom of the page.

Self-Study Quiz
Solutions

1. F −   2. O +   3. I −   4. O −   5. O −   6. F −   7. O +   8. F +   9. F +   10. O −
11. O −   12. I +

The Total Asset Turnover Ratio

In Chapter 2, we discussed the financial leverage ratio, a tool to evaluate management's use of debt to improve earnings. We now introduce a ratio to assess managers' use of assets in total to improve earnings. As we will see in other chapters, similar analysis on the use of each specific type of asset provides additional information for decision makers.

> **Learning Objective 6**
> Compute and interpret the total asset turnover ratio.

ANALYTICAL QUESTION
How effective is management in generating sales from assets (resources)?

% RATIO AND COMPARISONS

$$\text{Total Asset Turnover Ratio} = \frac{\text{Sales (or Operating) Revenues}}{\text{Average Total Assets}}$$

The 2003 ratio for Papa John's is:

$$\frac{\$917,000}{(\$347,000 + \$367,000)/2} = 2.57$$

COMPARISONS OVER TIME		
Papa John's		
2001	**2002**	**2003**
2.49	2.51	2.57

COMPARISONS WITH COMPETITORS	
Domino's Inc.	**Yum! Brands***
2003	**2003**
2.89	1.52

INTERPRETATIONS

In General → The total asset turnover ratio measures the sales generated per dollar of assets. A high asset turnover ratio signifies efficient management of assets; a low asset turnover ratio signifies less efficient management. A company's products and business strategy contribute significantly to its asset turnover ratio. However, when competitors are similar, management's ability to control the firm's assets is vital in determining its success. Stronger financial performance improves the asset turnover ratio.

Creditors and security analysts use this ratio to assess a company's effectiveness at controlling both current and noncurrent assets. In a well-run business, creditors expect the ratio to fluctuate due to seasonal upswings and downturns. For example, as inventory is built up prior to a heavy sales season, companies need to borrow funds. The asset turnover ratio declines with this increase in assets. Eventually, the season's high sales provide the cash needed to repay the loans. The asset turnover ratio then rises with the increased sales.

Focus Company Analysis → Papa John's asset turnover ratio has increased slightly since 2001, suggesting an increase in management effectiveness in using assets to generate sales. In fact, Papa John's reported that as the number of stores in a geographic area increased, regional commissaries showed higher sales, allowing management to use the commissary assets more efficiently.

Compared to its main competitors, Papa John's 2003 total asset turnover ratio falls in the middle. The difference in ratios is due in part to differences in operating strategy: Pizza Hut (and KFC and Taco Bell) operate primarily eat-in restaurants, so they must invest more in their facilities (that is, they are more asset intensive). Domino's, the leading pizza delivery company, operates primarily from rented facilities (that is, it is less asset intensive).

A Few Cautions: While the total asset turnover ratio may decrease due to seasonal fluctuations, a declining ratio may also be caused by changes in corporate policies leading to a rising level of assets. Examples include relaxing credit policies for new customers or reducing collection efforts in accounts receivable. A detailed analysis of the changes in the key components of assets is needed to determine the causes of a change in the asset turnover ratio and thus management's decisions.

**Selected Focus
Companies' Total Asset
Turnover Ratios for
2003**

Delta Air Lines	0.52
Harley-Davidson	1.05
Boston Beer	2.14

*Yum! Brands is the parent company of Pizza Hut, KFC, and Taco Bell.

DEMONSTRATION **CASE**

This case is a continuation of the Terrific Lawn Maintenance Corporation case introduced in Chapter 2. The company was established and supplies, property, and equipment were purchased. Terrific Lawn is ready for business. The balance sheet at April 30, 2007, based on investing and financing activities (from Chapter 2) is as follows:

TERRIFIC LAWN MAINTENANCE CORPORATION Balance Sheet At April 30, 2007				
Assets		**Liabilities**		
Current Assets		*Current Liability*		
Cash	$ 3,800	Short-term notes payable		$4,400
Short-term notes receivable	1,250			
Total current assets	5,050			
Equipment	4,600	**Stockholders' Equity**		
Land	3,750	Contributed capital		9,000
Total assets	$13,400	Total liabilities and stockholders' equity		$13,400

The following completed activities occurred during April 2007:

a. Purchased and used gasoline for mowers and edgers, paying $90 in cash at a local gas station.

b. In early April, received from the city $1,600 cash in advance for lawn maintenance service for April through July ($400 each month). The entire amount was recorded as Unearned Revenue.

c. In early April, purchased $300 of insurance covering six months, April through September. The entire payment was recorded as Prepaid Expenses.

d. Mowed lawns for residential customers who are billed every two weeks. A total of $5,200 of service was billed in April.

e. Residential customers paid $3,500 on their accounts.

f. Paid wages every two weeks. Total cash paid in April was $3,900.

g. Received a bill for $320 from the local gas station for additional gasoline purchased on account and used in April.

h. Paid $700 principal and $40 interest on notes owed to XYZ Lawn Supply and the hardware store.

i. Paid $100 on accounts payable.

j. Collected $1,250 principal and $12 interest on the note owed by the city to Terrific Lawn Maintenance Corporation.

Required:

1. a. On a separate sheet of paper, set up T-accounts for Cash, Accounts Receivable, Short-Term Notes Receivable, Prepaid Expenses, Equipment, Land, Accounts Payable, Unearned Revenue (same as deferred revenue), Short-Term Notes Payable, Contributed Capital, Retained Earnings, Mowing Revenue, Interest Revenue, Wages Expense, Fuel Expense, and Interest Expense. Beginning balances for the balance sheet accounts should be taken from the preceding balance sheet. Beginning balances for the operating accounts are $0. Indicate these balances on the T-accounts.

   b. Analyze each transaction referring to the expanded transaction analysis model presented in this chapter.

  c. On a separate sheet of paper, prepare journal entries in chronological order and indicate their effects on the accounting model (Assets = Liabilities + Stockholders' Equity). Include the equality checks: (1) Debits = Credits and (2) the accounting equation is in balance.

  d. Enter the effects of each transaction in the appropriate T-accounts. Identify each amount with its letter in the preceding list of activities.

  e. Compute balances in each of the T-accounts.

2. Use the amounts in the T-accounts to prepare a full set of financial statements—income statement, statement of retained earnings, balance sheet, and statement of cash flows— for Terrific Lawn Maintenance Corporation at April 30, 2007. Refer to the cash flow statement presented in Chapter 2 for the investing and financing activities. (Adjustments to accounts will be presented in Chapter 4.)

Now check your answers with the following suggested solution.

SUGGESTED SOLUTION

1. Transaction analysis, journal entries, and T-accounts:

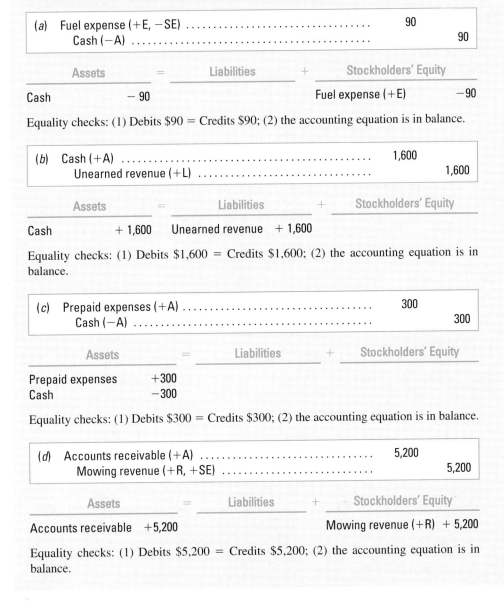

(a)	Fuel expense (+E, −SE)	90	
	Cash (−A)		90

Assets	=	Liabilities	+	Stockholders' Equity
Cash − 90				Fuel expense (+E) − 90

Equality checks: (1) Debits $90 = Credits $90; (2) the accounting equation is in balance.

(b)	Cash (+A)	1,600	
	Unearned revenue (+L)		1,600

Assets	=	Liabilities	+	Stockholders' Equity
Cash + 1,600		Unearned revenue + 1,600		

Equality checks: (1) Debits $1,600 = Credits $1,600; (2) the accounting equation is in balance.

(c)	Prepaid expenses (+A)	300	
	Cash (−A)		300

Assets	=	Liabilities	+	Stockholders' Equity
Prepaid expenses +300				
Cash −300				

Equality checks: (1) Debits $300 = Credits $300; (2) the accounting equation is in balance.

(d)	Accounts receivable (+A)	5,200	
	Mowing revenue (+R, +SE)		5,200

Assets	=	Liabilities	+	Stockholders' Equity
Accounts receivable +5,200				Mowing revenue (+R) + 5,200

Equality checks: (1) Debits $5,200 = Credits $5,200; (2) the accounting equation is in balance.

(e) Cash (+A) 3,500
         Accounts receivable (−A) 3,500

Assets	=	Liabilities	+	Stockholders' Equity

Cash   + 3,500
Accounts receivable   − 3,500

Equality checks: (1) Debits $3,500 = Credits $3,500; (2) the accounting equation is in balance.

(f) Wages expense (+E, −SE) 3,900
         Cash (−A) 3,900

Assets	=	Liabilities	+	Stockholders' Equity

Cash   − 3,900   Wages expense (+E) − 3,900

Equality checks: (1) Debits $3,900 = Credits $3,900; (2) the accounting equation is in balance.

(g) Fuel expense (+E, −SE) 320
         Accounts payable (+L) 320

Assets	=	Liabilities	+	Stockholders' Equity

                                         Accounts payable   +320   Fuel expense (+E)   −320

Equality checks: (1) Debits $320 = Credits $320; (2) the accounting equation is in balance.

(h) Interest expense (+E, −SE) 40
         Short-term notes payable (−L) 700
         Cash (−A) 740

Assets	=	Liabilities	+	Stockholders' Equity

Cash   − 740   Notes payable   − 700   Interest expense (+E)   − 40

Equality checks: (1) Debits $740 = Credits $740; (2) the accounting equation is in balance.

(i) Accounts payable (−L) 100
         Cash (−A) 100

Assets	=	Liabilities	+	Stockholders' Equity

Cash   −100   Accounts payable   − 100

Equality checks: (1) Debits $100 = Credits $100; (2) the accounting equation is in balance.

(j) Cash (+A) 1,262
         Short-term notes receivable (−A) 1,250
         Interest revenue (+R, +SE) 12

Assets	=	Liabilities	+	Stockholders' Equity

Cash   +1,262   Interest revenue (+R) +12
Short-term notes receivable   − 1,250

Equality checks: (1) Debits $1,262 = Credits $1,262; (2) the accounting equation is in balance.

T-Accounts

Assets

	Cash		
Beg.	3,800		
(b)	1,600	90	(a)
(e)	3,500	300	(c)
(j)	1,262	3,900	(f)
		740	(h)
		100	(i)
Bal.	5,032		

	Accounts Receivable		
Beg.	0		
(d)	5,200	3,500	(e)
Bal.	1,700		

	Short-Term Notes Receivable		
Beg.	1,250	1,250	(j)
Bal.	0		

	Equipment	
Beg.	4,600	
Bal.	4,600	

	Prepaid Expenses	
Beg.	0	
(c)	300	
Bal.	300	

	Land	
Beg.	3,750	
Bal.	3,750	

Liabilities

	Accounts Payable		
		0	Beg.
(i)	100	320	(g)
		220	Bal.

	Short-Term Notes Payable		
		4,400	Beg.
(h)	700		
		3,700	Bal.

	Unearned Revenue		
		0	Beg.
		1,600	(b)
		1,600	Bal.

Stockholders' Equity

	Contributed Capital	
	9,000	Beg.
	9,000	Bal.

	Retained Earnings	
	0	Beg.
	0	Bal.

Revenues

	Mowing Revenue	
	0	Beg.
	5,200	(d)
	5,200	Bal.

	Interest Revenue	
	0	Beg.
	12	(j)
	12	Bal.

Expenses

	Wages Expense	
Beg.	0	
(f)	3,900	
Bal.	3,900	

	Fuel Expense	
Beg.	0	
(a)	90	
(g)	320	
Bal.	410	

	Interest Expense	
Beg.	0	
(h)	40	
Bal.	40	

2. Financial statements:

TERRIFIC LAWN MAINTENANCE CORPORATION
Income Statement
For the Month Ended April 30, 2007

Operating Revenues		
Mowing revenue		$5,200
Operating Expenses		
Fuel expense	410	
Wages expense	3,900	
		4,310
Operating income		890
Other items		
Interest revenue		12
Interest expense		(40)
Pretax income		862
Income tax expense		0
Net Income		**$ 862**
Earnings per share for the month		**$.57**

($862 net income divided by 1,500 shares outstanding)

TERRIFIC LAWN MAINTENANCE CORPORATION
Statement of Retained Earnings
For the Month Ended April 30, 2007

Balance, April 1, 2007	$ 0
Net income	862
Dividends	0
Balance, April 30, 2007	$862

TERRIFIC LAWN MAINTENANCE CORPORATION
Statement of Cash Flows
For the Month Ended April 30, 2007

Cash Flows from Operating Activities		
Cash received: Customers (*b, e*)		$5,100
Interest on notes receivable (*j*)		12
Cash paid: Suppliers (*a, c, i*)		(490)
Employees (*f*)		(3,900)
Interest on notes payable (*h*)		(40)
Cash flows provided by operations		**682**
Cash Flows from Investing Activities		
Purchased land		(5,000)
Purchased equipment		(200)
Received principal payment on note receivable (*j*)		1,250
Cash flows used in investing activities		**(3,950)**
Cash Flows from Financing Activities		
Issued common stock		9,000
Payments on principal of notes payable (*h*)		(700)
Cash flows provided by financing activities		**8,300**
Change in cash		5,032
Beginning cash balance		0
Ending cash balance		**$5,032**

TERRIFIC LAWN MAINTENANCE CORPORATION
Balance Sheet
April 30, 2007

ASSETS			LIABILITIES		
Current Assets			Current Liabilities		
Cash	$ 5,032		Accounts payable	$	220
Accounts receivable	1,700		Short-term notes payable		3,700
Prepaid expenses	300		Unearned revenue		1,600
Total current assets	7,032		Total current liabilities		5,520
Equipment	4,600		**STOCKHOLDERS' EQUITY**		
Land	3,750		Contributed capital		9,000
			Retained earnings		862
Total assets	**$15,382**		**Total liabilities and stockholders' equity**		**$15,382**

1. **Describe a typical business operating cycle and explain the necessity for the time period assumption. p. 106**

   - The operating cycle, or cash-to-cash cycle, is the time needed to purchase goods or services from suppliers, sell the goods or services to customers, and collect cash from customers.
   - Time period assumption—to measure and report financial information periodically, we assume the long life of a company can be cut into shorter periods.

2. **Explain how business activities affect the elements of the income statement. p. 108**

   - Elements on the income statement:
     - *a.* Revenues—increases in assets or settlements of liabilities from ongoing operations.
     - *b.* Expenses—decreases in assets or increases in liabilities from ongoing operations.
     - *c.* Gains—increases in assets or settlements of liabilities from peripheral activities.
     - *d.* Losses—decreases in assets or increases in liabilities from peripheral activities.

3. **Explain the accrual basis of accounting and apply the revenue and matching principles to measure income. p. 111**

   In accrual basis accounting, revenues are recognized when earned and expenses are recognized when incurred.

   - Revenue principle—recognize revenues when (1) delivery has occurred, (2) there is persuasive evidence of an arrangement for customer payment, (3) the price is fixed or determinable, and (4) collection is reasonably assured.
   - Matching principle—recognize expenses when they are incurred in generating revenue.

4. **Apply transaction analysis to examine and record the effects of operating activities on the financial statements. p. 118**

   The expanded transaction analysis model includes revenues and expenses:

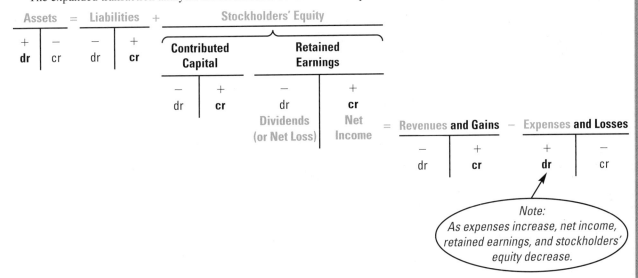

5. **Prepare financial statements. p. 123**

   Until the accounts have been updated to include all revenues earned and expenses incurred in the period (due to a difference in the time when cash is received or paid), the financial statements are unadjusted:

   - Income statement.
   - Statement of retained earnings.
   - Balance sheet.
   - Statement of cash flows.

6. Compute and interpret the total asset turnover ratio. p. 129

The total asset turnover ratio (Sales ÷ Average Total Assets) measures the sales generated per dollar of assets. The higher the ratio, the more efficient the company is at managing assets.

In this chapter, we discussed the operating cycle and accounting concepts relevant to income determination: the time period assumption, definitions of the income statement elements (revenues, expenses, gains, and losses), the revenue principle, and the matching principle. The accounting principles are defined in accordance with the accrual basis of accounting, which requires revenues to be recorded when earned and expenses to be recorded when incurred in the process of generating revenues. We expanded the transaction analysis model introduced in Chapter 2 by adding revenues and expenses and prepared unadjusted financial statements. In Chapter 4, we discuss the activities that occur at the end of the accounting period: the adjustment process, the preparation of adjusted financial statements, and the closing process.

KEY **RATIO**

Total asset turnover ratio measures the sales generated per dollar of assets. A high ratio suggests that a company is managing its assets (the resources used to generate revenues) efficiently. The ratio is computed as follows (p. 129):

$$\text{Total Asset Turnover Ratio} = \frac{\text{Sales (or Operating) Revenues}}{\text{Average Total Assets}}$$

"Average" is (Last Year's Value + This Year's Value) ÷ 2.

FINDING **FINANCIAL INFORMATION**

Balance Sheet

Current Assets
Cash
Accounts and notes receivable
Inventory
Prepaid expenses

Noncurrent Assets
Long-term investments
Property and equipment
Intangibles

Current Liabilities
Accounts payable
Notes payable
Accrued liabilities payable

Noncurrent Liabilities
Long-term debt

Stockholders' Equity
Contributed capital
Retained earnings

Income Statement

Revenues
Sales (from various operating activities)

Expenses
Cost of sales (used inventory)
Rent, wages, depreciation, insurance, etc.

Operating Income

Other Items
Interest expense
Investment income
Gains on sale of assets
Losses on sale of assets

Pretax Income
Income tax expense

Net Income

Earnings per share

Statement of Cash Flows

Under Operating Activities
+ Cash from customers
+ Cash from interest and dividends
− Cash to suppliers
− Cash to employees
− Interest paid
− Income taxes paid

Notes

Under Summary of Significant Accounting Policies
Description of the company's revenue recognition policy.

Accrual Basis Accounting   p. 112
Cash Basis Accounting   p. 111
Expenses   p. 110
Gains   p. 110

Losses   p. 110
Matching Principle   p. 115
Operating (Cash-to-Cash)
  Cycle   p. 107

Revenues   p. 108
Revenue Principle   p. 112
Time Period Assumption   p. 108

QUESTIONS

1. Describe a typical business operating cycle.
2. Explain what the time period assumption means.
3. Write the income statement equation and define each element.
4. Explain the difference between
   a. Revenues and gains.
   b. Expenses and losses.
5. Define *accrual accounting* and contrast it with cash basis accounting.
6. What four conditions must normally be met for revenue to be recognized under accrual basis accounting?
7. Explain the matching principle.
8. Explain why stockholders' equity is increased by revenues and decreased by expenses.
9. Explain why revenues are recorded as credits and expenses as debits.
10. Complete the following matrix by entering either *debit* or *credit* in each cell:

Item	Increase	Decrease
Revenues		
Losses		
Gains		
Expenses		

11. Complete the following matrix by entering either *increase* or *decrease* in each cell:

Item	Debit	Credit
Revenues		
Losses		
Gains		
Expenses		

12. Identify whether the following transactions affect cash flow from operating, investing, or financing activities, and indicate the effect of each on cash (+ for increase and − for decrease). If there is no cash flow effect, write "None":

Transaction	Operating, Investing, or Financing Effect on Cash	Direction of the Effect on Cash
Cash paid to suppliers		
Sale of goods on account		
Cash received from customers		
Purchase of investments		
Cash paid for interest		
Issuance of stock for cash		

13. State the equation for the asset turnover ratio and explain how it is interpreted.

MULTIPLE-CHOICE QUESTIONS

1. Which of the following is not a specific account in a company's chart of accounts?
   a. Gains
   b. Net Income
   c. Revenue
   d. Unearned Revenue

2. Which of the following is *not* one of the four conditions that normally must be met for revenue to be recognized according to the revenue principle for accrual basis accounting?
   a. The price is determinable.
   b. Services have been performed.
   c. Cash has been collected.
   d. Evidence of an arrangement exists.

3. The matching principle controls
   a. where on the income statement expenses should be presented.
   b. how costs are allocated between Cost of Sales (sometimes called *Cost of Goods Sold*) and general and administrative expenses.
   c. the ordering of current assets and current liabilities on the balance sheet.
   d. when costs are recognized as expenses on the income statement.

4. You have observed that the asset turnover ratio for a retail chain has increased steadily over the last three years. The *most* likely explanation is which of the following?
   a. A successful advertising campaign increased sales companywide, but no new store locations were added over the last three years.
   b. Salaries for upper management as a percentage of total expenses have decreased over the last three years.
   c. New stores were added throughout the last three years, and sales increased as a result of the additional new locations.
   d. The company began construction of a new, larger main office location three years ago that was put into use at the end of the second year.

5. Cash payments for salaries are reported in what section of the Statement of Cash Flows?
   a. Financing
   b. Operating
   c. Investing
   d. None of the above

6. A company collects this period $100 cash on an account receivable from a customer for a sale last period. How would the receipt of cash impact the following two financial statements this period?

	INCOME STATEMENT	STATEMENT OF CASH FLOWS
a.	Revenue + $100	Inflow from investing
b.	No impact	Inflow from financing
c.	Revenue − $100	Inflow from operations
d.	No impact	Inflow from operations

7. When expenses exceed revenues in a given period,
   a. retained earnings is not impacted.
   b. retained earnings is increased.
   c. retained earnings is decreased.
   d. one cannot determine the impact on retained earnings without additional information.

8. Which account is least likely to be debited when revenue is recorded?
   a. Accounts Payable
   b. Accounts Receivable
   c. Cash
   d. Unearned Revenue

9. Which is the most likely goal of a business with regard to its operating cycle?
   a. To sustain its current operating cycle
   b. To expand its current operating cycle
   c. To shorten its current operating cycle
   d. To ignore its current operating cycle

10. Which of the following is the entry to be recorded by a law firm when it receives a retainer from a new client at the initial client meeting?
    a. debit to Accounts Receivable; credit to Sales Revenue
    b. debit to Unearned Revenue; credit to Sales Revenue
    c. debit to Cash; credit to Unearned Revenue
    d. debit to Unearned Revenue; credit to Cash

For more practice on multiple-choice questions, go to the text website at www.mhhe.com/libby5e or the Topic Tackler DVD for use with this text.

Matching Definitions with Terms

M3-1
LO1, 2, 3

Match each definition with its related term by entering the appropriate letter in the space provided. There should be only one definition per term (that is, there are more definitions than terms).

Term	Definition
___ (1) Losses	A. Decreases in assets or increases in liabilities from on-going operations.
___ (2) Matching principle	B. Record revenues when earned and measurable (delivery of goods or services has been performed, there is persuasive evidence of an arrangement, the price is fixed or determinable, and collection is reasonably assured).
___ (3) Revenues	
___ (4) Time period assumption	
___ (5) Operating cycle	
	C. Report the long life of a company in shorter time periods.
	D. Record expenses when incurred in earning revenue.
	E. The time it takes to purchase goods or services from suppliers, sell goods or services to customers, and collect cash from customers.
	F. Decreases in assets or increases in liabilities from peripheral transactions.
	G. Increases in assets or decreases in liabilities from ongoing operations.

Reporting Cash Basis versus Accrual Basis Income

M3-2
LO3

McNamara Music Company had the following transactions in March:

a. Sold instruments to customers for $10,000; received $6,000 in cash and the rest on account. The cost of the instruments was $7,000.
b. Purchased $4,000 of new instruments inventory; paid $1,000 in cash and owed the rest on account.
c. Paid $600 in wages for the month.
d. Received a $200 bill for March utilities that will be paid in April.
e. Received $1,000 from customers as deposits on orders of new instruments to be sold to the customers in April.

Complete the following statements:

Cash Basis Income Statement		Accrual Basis Income Statement	
Revenues		Revenues	
Cash sales		Sales to customers	
Customer deposits			
Expenses		Expenses	
Inventory purchases		Cost of sales	
Wages paid		Wages expense	
		Utilities expense	___
	___		
Net income	===	Net income	===

Identifying Revenues

M3-3
LO2, 3

The following transactions are July 2008 activities of Bob's Bowling, Inc., which operates several bowling centers (for games and equipment sales). If revenue is to be recognized in July, indicate the revenue account title and amount. If revenue is not to be recognized in July, explain why.

Activity	Revenue Account Title and Amount
a. Bob's collected $10,000 from customers for games played in July.	
b. Bob's sold bowling equipment inventory for $5,000; received $3,000 in cash and the rest on account. [The cost of goods sold (expense) related to these sales is in M3-4e.]	
c. Bob's received $1,000 from customers on account who purchased merchandise in June.	
d. The men's and ladies' bowling leagues gave Bob's a deposit of $1,500 for the upcoming fall season.	

M3-4 Identifying Expenses

LO2, 3

The following transactions are July 2008 activities of Bob's Bowling, Inc., which operates several bowling centers (for games and equipment sales). If expense is to be recognized in July, indicate the expense account title and amount. If expense is not to be recognized in July, explain why.

Activity	Expense Account Title and Amount
e. Bob's sold bowling merchandise costing $2,000.	
f. Bob's paid $2,000 on the electricity bill for June.	
g. Bob's paid $4,000 to employees for work in July.	
h. Bob's purchased $1,200 in insurance for coverage from July 1 to October 1.	
i. Bob's paid $1,000 to plumbers for repairing a broken pipe in the restrooms.	
j. Bob's received the July electricity bill for $2,200 to be paid in August.	

M3-5 Recording Revenues

LO4

For each of the transactions in M3-3, write the journal entry in good form.

M3-6 Recording Expenses

LO4

For each of the transactions in M3-4, write the journal entry in good form.

M3-7 Determining the Financial Statement Effects of Operating Activities Involving Revenues

LO4

The following transactions are July 2008 activities of Bob's Bowling, Inc., which operates several bowling centers (for games and equipment sales). For each of the following transactions, complete the tabulation, indicating the amount and effect (+ for increase and − for decrease) of each transaction. (Remember that A = L + SE, R − E = NI, and NI affects SE through Retained Earnings.) Write NE if there is no effect. The first transaction is provided as an example.

| | BALANCE SHEET | | | INCOME STATEMENT | | |
Transaction	Assets	Liabil-ities	Stock-holders' Equity	Revenues	Expenses	Net Income
a. Bob's collected $10,000 from customers for games played in July.	+10,000	NE	+10,000	+10,000	NE	+10,000
b. Bob's sold $5,000 in bowling equipment inventory; received $3,000 in cash and the rest on account. [The cost of goods sold (expense) related to these sales is in M3-8e.]	+5,000		+5,000	+5,000		+5,000
c. Bob's received $1,000 from customers on account who purchased merchandise in June.						
d. The men's and ladies' bowling leagues gave Bob's a deposit of $1,500 for the upcoming fall season.						

Determining the Financial Statement Effects of Operating Activities Involving Expenses

M3-8
L04

The following transactions are July 2008 activities of Bob's Bowling, Inc., which operates several bowling centers (for games and equipment sales). For each of the following transactions, complete the tabulation, indicating the amount and effect (+ for increase and − for decrease) of each transaction. (Remember that A = L + SE, R − E = NI, and NI affects SE through retained earnings.) Write NE if there is no effect. The first transaction is provided as an example.

| | BALANCE SHEET | | | INCOME STATEMENT | | |
Transaction	Assets	Liabil-ities	Stock-holders' Equity	Revenues	Expenses	Net Income
e. Bob's sold bowling merchandise costing $2,000.	−2,000	NE	−2,000	NE	+2,000	−2,000
f. Bob's paid $2,000 on the electricity bill for June.						
g. Bob's paid $4,000 to employees for work in July.						
h. Bob's purchased $1,200 in insurance for coverage from July 1 to October 1.						
i. Bob's paid $1,000 to plumbers for repairing a broken pipe in the restrooms.						
j. Bob's received the July electricity bill for $2,200 to be paid in August.						

Preparing a Simple Income Statement

M3-9
L05

Given the transactions in M3-7 and M3-8 (including the examples), prepare an income statement for Bob's Bowling, Inc., for the month of July 2008.

Preparing the Operating Activities Section of a Statement of Cash Flows

M3-10
L05

Given the transactions in M3-8 and M3-9 (including the examples), prepare the Operating Activities section of the statement of cash flows for Bob's Bowling, Inc., for the month of July 2008.

M3-11
LO6

Computing and Explaining the Total Asset Turnover Ratio

The following data are from annual reports of Julian's Jewelry Company:

	2009	2008	2007
Total assets	$ 60,000	$ 50,000	$ 40,000
Total liabilities	12,000	10,000	5,000
Total stockholders' equity	48,000	40,000	35,000
Sales	154,000	144,000	130,000
Net income	50,000	38,000	25,000

Compute Julian's total asset turnover ratio for 2009 and 2008. What do these results suggest to you about Julian's Jewelry Company?

EXERCISES

Available with McGraw-Hill's Homework Manager

E3-1
LO1, 2, 3

Matching Definitions with Terms

Match each definition with its related term by entering the appropriate letter in the space provided. There should be only one definition per term (that is, there are more definitions than terms).

Term	Definition
(1) Expenses	A. Report the long life of a company in shorter periods.
(2) Gains	B. Record expenses when incurred in earning revenue.
(3) Revenue principle	C. The time it takes to purchase goods or services from suppliers, sell goods or services to customers, and collect cash from customers.
(4) Cash basis accounting	
(5) Unearned revenue	
(6) Operating cycle	D. A liability account used to record cash received before revenues have been earned.
(7) Accrual basis accounting	
(8) Prepaid expenses	E. Increases in assets or decreases in liabilities from peripheral transactions.
(9) Revenues − Expenses = Net Income	
(10) Ending Retained Earnings = Beginning Retained Earnings + Net Income − Dividends Declared	F. Decreases in assets or increases in liabilities from on-going operations.
	G. Record revenues when earned and measurable (delivery of goods or services has occurred, there is persuasive evidence of an arrangement for customer payment, the price is fixed or determinable, and collection is reasonably assured).
	H. Decreases in assets or increases in liabilities from peripheral transactions.
	I. Record revenues when received and expenses when paid.
	J. The income statement equation.
	K. An asset account used to record cash paid before expenses have been incurred.
	L. The retained earnings equation.
	M. Record revenues when earned and expenses when incurred.

E3-2
LO3

Reporting Cash Basis versus Accrual Basis Income

Ru's Sports, Inc., sells sports equipment to customers. Its fiscal year ends on December 31. The following transactions occurred in 2008:

a. Paid employees $54,200 in wages for the year; an additional $4,800 for 2008 wages will be paid in January 2009.

b. Purchased $334,000 of new sports equipment inventory; paid $90,000 in cash and owed the rest on account.

c. Sold sports equipment to customers for $410,000; received $340,000 in cash and the rest on account. The cost of the equipment was $287,000.

d. Paid $7,200 cash for utilities for the year.

e. Received $21,000 from customers as deposits on orders of new winter sports equipment to be sold to the customers in January 2009.

f. Received a $680 bill for December 2008 utilities that will be paid in January 2009.

Required:

1. Complete the following statements:

Cash Basis Income Statement		Accrual Basis Income Statement	
Revenues		Revenues	
Cash sales		Sales to customers	
Customer deposits			
Expenses		Expenses	
Inventory purchases		Cost of sales	
Wages paid		Wages expense	
Utilities paid	___	Utilities expense	___
Net income	═══	Net income	═══

2. Which basis of accounting (cash or accrual) provides more useful information to investors, creditors, and other users? Why?

Identifying Revenues

E3-3
LO2, 3

Revenues are normally recognized when the delivery of goods or services has occurred, there is persuasive evidence of an arrangement for customer payment, the price is fixed or determinable, and collection is reasonably assured. The amount recorded is the cash-equivalent sales price. The following transactions occurred in September 2009:

a. A customer orders and receives 10 personal computers from Dell; the customer promises to pay $25,000 within three months. Answer from Dell's standpoint.

b. Fucillo Hyundai, Inc., sells a truck with a list, or "sticker," price of $24,000 for $21,000 cash.

c. Bon-Ton Department Store orders 1,000 men's shirts from Arrow Shirt Company for $18 each for future delivery. The terms require payment in full within 30 days of delivery. Answer from Arrow's standpoint.

d. Arrow Shirt Company completes production of the shirts described in (c) and delivers the order. Answer from Arrow's standpoint.

e. Arrow receives payment from Bon-Ton for the order described in (c). Answer from Arrow's standpoint.

f. A customer purchases a ticket from American Airlines for $500 cash to travel the following January. Answer from American Airlines' standpoint.

g. General Motors issues $26 million in new common stock.

h. Penn State University receives $20,000,000 cash for 80,000 five-game season football tickets.

i. Penn State plays the first football game referred to in (h).

j. McPherson Construction Company signs a contract with a customer for the construction of a new $500,000 warehouse. At the signing, McPherson receives a check for $50,000 as a deposit on the future construction. Answer from McPherson's standpoint.

k. On September 1, 2009, a bank lends $100,000 to a company; the note principal and 12 percent annual interest are due in one year. Answer from the bank's standpoint.

l. A popular ski magazine company receives a total of $12,800 today from subscribers. The subscriptions begin in the next fiscal year. Answer from the magazine company's standpoint.

m. Sears, a retail store, sells a $100 lamp to a customer who charges the sale on his store credit card. Answer from Sears' standpoint.

Required:

For each of the transactions, if revenue is to be recognized in September, indicate the revenue account title and amount. If revenue is not to be recognized in September, explain why.

E3-4

LO2, 3

Identifying Expenses

Revenues are normally recognized when goods or services have been provided and payment or promise of payment has been received. Expense recognition is guided by an attempt to match the costs associated with the generation of those revenues to the same time period. The following transactions occurred in January 2009:

a. Dell pays its computer service technicians $90,000 in salaries for the two weeks ended January 7. Answer from Dell's standpoint.

b. At the beginning of January, Turner Construction Company pays $4,500 in worker's compensation insurance for the first three months of the year.

c. McGraw-Hill Publishing Company uses $6,000 worth of electricity and natural gas in its headquarters building for which it has not yet been billed.

d. Arrow Shirt Company completes production of 500 men's shirts ordered by Bon-Ton's Department Store at a cost of $9 each and delivers the order. Answer from Arrow's standpoint.

e. The campus bookstore receives 500 accounting texts at a cost of $100 each. The terms indicate that payment is due within 30 days of delivery.

f. During the last week of January, the campus bookstore sold 450 accounting texts received in (e) at a sales price of $120 each.

g. Fucillo Hyndai, Inc., pays its salespersons $13,500 in commissions related to December automobile sales. Answer from Fucillo's standpoint.

h. On January 31, Fucillo Hyndai, Inc., determines that it will pay its salespersons $14,200 in commissions related to January sales. The payment will be made in early February. Answer from Fucillo's standpoint.

i. A new grill is purchased and installed at a Wendy's restaurant at the end of the day on January 31; a $32,000 cash payment is made on that day.

j. The University of Florida orders 60,000 season football tickets from its printer and pays $6,000 in advance for the custom printing. The first game will be played in September. Answer from the university's standpoint.

k. Carousel Mall had janitorial supplies costing $4,000 in storage. An additional $2,600 worth of supplies was purchased during January. At the end of January, $1,800 worth of janitorial supplies remained in storage.

l. An Iowa State University employee works eight hours, at $15 per hour, on January 31; however, payday is not until February 3. Answer from the university's point of view.

m. Wang Company paid $3,600 for a fire insurance policy on January 1. The policy covers 12 months beginning on January 1. Answer from Wang's point of view.

n. Darrius Incorporated has its delivery van repaired in January for $280 and charges the amount on account.

o. Haas Company, a farm equipment company, receives its phone bill at the end of January for $230 for January calls. The bill has not been paid to date.

p. Martin Company receives and pays in January a $11,500 invoice (bill) from a consulting firm for services received in January.

q. Parillo's Taxi Company pays a $600 invoice from a consulting firm for services received and recorded in December.

Required:

For each of the transactions, if an expense is to be recognized in January, indicate the expense account title and the amount. If an expense is not to be recognized in January, indicate why.

E3-5

LO4

Determining Financial Statement Effects of Various Transactions

The following transactions occurred during a recent year:

a. Issued stock to organizers for cash (example).

b. Purchased equipment on credit.

c. Borrowed cash from local bank.

d. Earned revenue, collected cash.

e. Incurred expenses, on credit.

f. Earned revenue, on credit.

g. Paid cash on account.

h. Incurred expenses; paid cash.
i. Earned revenue; collected three-fourths in cash, balance on credit.
j. Declared and paid cash dividends.
k. Collected cash from customers on account.
l. Experienced theft of $100 cash.
m. Incurred expenses; paid four-fifths in cash, balance on credit.
n. Paid income tax expense for the period.

Required:
For each of the transactions, complete the tabulation, indicating the effect (+ for increase and − for decrease) of each transaction. (Remember that A = L + SE, R − E = NI, and NI affects SE through Retained Earnings.) Write NE if there is no effect. The first transaction is provided as an example.

	BALANCE SHEET			INCOME STATEMENT		
Transaction	Assets	Liabil-ities	Stock-holders' Equity	Revenues	Expenses	Net Income
(a) (example)	+	NE	+	NE	NE	NE

Determining Financial Statement Effects of Various Transactions

E3-6
LO4
Wolverine World Wide, Inc.

Wolverine World Wide, Inc., manufactures military, work, sport, and casual footwear and leather accessories under a variety of brand names, such as Hush Puppies, Wolverine, and Bates, to a global market. The following transactions occurred during a recent year. Dollars are in thousands.

a. Issued common stock to investors for $7,570 cash (example).
b. Purchased $561,346 of additional raw materials inventory on account.
c. Borrowed $66,194 on long-term notes.
d. Sold $888,926 of products to customers on account; cost of the products sold was $562,338.
e. Paid cash dividends of $8,588.
f. Purchased $16,015 in additional property, plant, and equipment.
g. Incurred $246,652 in selling expenses, paying three-fourths in cash and owing the rest on account.
h. Earned $422 interest on investments, receiving 90 percent in cash.
i. Incurred $5,896 in interest expense to be paid at the beginning of next year.

Required:
For each of the transactions, complete the tabulation, indicating the effect (+ for increase and − for decrease) of each transaction. (Remember that A = L + SE, R − E = NI, and NI affects SE through Retained Earnings.) Write NE if there is no effect. The first transaction is provided as an example.

	BALANCE SHEET			INCOME STATEMENT		
Transaction	Assets	Liabil-ities	Stock-holders' Equity	Revenues	Expenses	Net Income
(a) (example)	+7,570	NE	+7,570	NE	NE	NE

Recording Journal Entries

E3-7
LO4
Sysco

Sysco, formed in 1969, is North America's largest marketer and distributor of food service products, serving nearly 400,000 restaurants, hotels, schools, hospitals, and other institutions. The following summarized transactions are typical of those that occurred in a recent year.

a. Borrowed $185,000,000 from a bank, signing a short-term note.
b. Provided $29,335,000 in service to customers during the year, with $21,300,000 on account and the rest received in cash.
c. Purchased plant and equipment for $530,000,000 in cash.
d. Purchased $23,836,000 inventory on account.
e. Paid payroll, $3,102,000 during the year.

f. Received $21,120,000 on account paid by customers.
g. Purchased and used fuel of $730,000,000 in delivery vehicles during the year (paid for in cash).
h. Declared and paid $310,000,000 in dividends for the year.
i. Paid $4,035,000 cash on accounts payable.
j. Incurred $61,000,000 in utility usage during the year; paid $53,000,000 in cash and owed the rest on account.

Required:

For each of the transactions, prepare journal entries. Determine whether the accounting equation remains in balance and debits equal credits after each entry.

E3-8
L04
Vail Resorts, Inc.

Recording Journal Entries

Vail Resorts, Inc., owns and operates five premier year-round ski resort properties (Vail Mountain, Beaver Creek Resort, Breckenridge Mountain, and Keystone Resort, all located in the Colorado Rocky Mountains, and Heavenly Valley Mountain Resort, located in the Lake Tahoe area of California/Nevada). The company also owns a collection of luxury hotels, resorts, and lodging properties. The company sells lift tickets, ski lessons, and ski equipment. The following hypothetical December transactions are typical of those that occur at the resorts.

a. Borrowed $2,500,000 from the bank on December 1, signing a note payable due in six months.
b. Purchased a new snow plow for $90,000 cash on December 31.
c. Purchased ski equipment inventory for $40,000 on account to sell in the ski shops.
d. Incurred $62,000 in routine maintenance expenses for the chair lifts; paid cash.
e. Sold $372,000 of January through March season passes and received cash.
f. Sold daily lift passes in December for a total of $270,000 in cash.
g. Sold a pair of skis from a ski shop to a customer for $750 on account. (The cost of the skis was $450.)
h. Received a $3,200 deposit on a townhouse to be rented for five days in January.
i. Paid half the charges incurred on account in (c).
j. Received $200 on account from the customer in (g).
k. Paid $258,000 in wages to employees for the month of December.

Required:

1. Prepare journal entries for each transaction. (Remember to check that debits equal credits and that the accounting equation is in balance after each transaction.)
2. Assume that Vail Resorts had a $1,200 balance in Accounts Receivable at the beginning of December. Determine the ending balance in the Accounts Receivable account at the end of December based on transactions (a) through (k). Show your work in T-account format.

E3-9
L04

Recording Journal Entries

Rowland & Sons Air Transport Service, Inc., has been in operation for three years. The following transactions occurred in February:

February 1	Paid $200 for rent of hangar space in February.
February 2	Purchased fuel costing $450 on account for the next flight to Dallas.
February 4	Received customer payment of $800 to ship several items to Philadelphia next month.
February 7	Flew cargo from Denver to Dallas; the customer paid $900 for the air transport.
February 10	Paid pilot $1,200 in wages for flying in January.
February 14	Paid $60 for an advertisement in the local paper to run on February 19.
February 18	Flew cargo for two customers from Dallas to Albuquerque for $1,700; one customer paid $500 cash and the other asked to be billed.
February 25	Purchased on account $1,350 in spare parts for the planes.
February 27	Declared a $200 cash dividend to be paid in March.

Required:

Prepare journal entries for each transaction. Be sure to categorize each account as an asset (A), liability (L), stockholders' equity (SE), revenue (R), or expense (E).

Analyzing the Effects of Transactions in T-Accounts and Computing Cash Basis versus Accrual Basis Net Income

E3-10
LO3, 4

Eddy's Piano Rebuilding Company has been operating for one year (2007). At the start of 2008, its income statement accounts had zero balances and its balance sheet account balances were as follows:

Cash	$ 6,000	Accounts payable	8,000
Accounts receivable	25,000	Unearned fee revenue (deposits)	3,200
Supplies	1,200	Note payable (long-term)	40,000
Equipment	8,000	Contributed capital	8,000
Land	6,000	Retained earnings	9,000
Building	22,000		

Required:

1. Create T-accounts for the balance sheet accounts and for these additional accounts: Rebuilding Fees Revenue, Rent Revenue, Wages Expense, and Utilities Expense. Enter the beginning balances.

2. Enter the following January 2008 transactions in the T-accounts, using the letter of each transaction as the reference:
   a. Received a $500 deposit from a customer who wanted her piano rebuilt.
   b. Rented a part of the building to a bicycle repair shop; received $300 for rent in January.
   c. Rebuilt and delivered five pianos in January to customers who paid $14,500 in cash.
   d. Received $6,000 from customers as payment on their accounts.
   e. Received an electric and gas utility bill for $350 to be paid in February.
   f. Ordered $800 in supplies.
   g. Paid $1,700 on account in January.
   h. Received from the home of Ms. Eddy, the major shareholder, a $600 tool (equipment) to use in the business.
   i. Paid $10,000 in wages to employees who worked in January.
   j. Declared and paid a $3,000 dividend.
   k. Received and paid cash for the supplies in (f).

3. Using the data from the T-accounts, amounts for the following on January 31, 2008, were

   Revenues $_____ – Expenses $_____ = Net Income $_____
   Assets $_____ = Liabilities $_____ + Stockholders' Equity $_____

4. What is net income if Eddy's used the cash basis of accounting? Why does this differ from accrual basis net income (in requirement 3)?

Preparing an Income Statement, Statement of Retained Earnings, and Classified Balance Sheet

E3-11
LO5

Refer to E3-10.

Required:
Use the ending balances in the T-accounts in E3-10 to prepare the following:
1. An income statement for January 2008 in good form.
2. A statement of retained earnings for January 2008.
3. A classified balance sheet as of January 31, 2008, in good form.

Preparing a Statement of Cash Flows

E3-12
LO5

Refer to E3-10.

Required:
Use the transactions in E3-10 to prepare a statement of cash flows in good form.

E3-13 Analyzing the Effects of Transactions in T-Accounts

LO4

Wendy Fonder and Susan Engelkemeyer had been operating a catering business, Traveling Gourmet, for several years. In March 2008, the partners were planning to expand by opening a retail sales shop and decided to form the business as a corporation called Traveling Gourmet, Inc. The following transactions occurred in March 2008:

a. Received $20,000 cash from each of the two shareholders to form the corporation, in addition to $2,000 in accounts receivable, $5,300 in equipment, a van (equipment) appraised at a fair market value of $13,000, and $1,200 in supplies.

b. Purchased a vacant store for sale in a good location for $160,000 with a $20,000 cash down payment and a mortgage from a local bank for the rest.

c. Borrowed $75,000 from the local bank on a 10 percent, one-year note.

d. Purchased and used food and paper supplies costing $8,830 in March; paid cash.

e. Made and sold food at the retail store for $10,900 cash.

f. Catered four parties in March for $3,200; $1,500 was billed, and the rest was received in cash.

g. Received a $320 telephone bill for March to be paid in April.

h. Paid $63 in gas for the van in March.

i. Paid $5,080 in wages to employees who worked in March.

j. Paid a $300 dividend from the corporation to each owner.

k. Purchased $35,000 of equipment (refrigerated display cases, cabinets, tables, and chairs) and renovated and decorated the new store for $20,000 (added to the cost of the building); paid cash.

Required:

1. Set up appropriate T-accounts for Cash, Accounts Receivable, Supplies, Equipment, Building, Accounts Payable, Note Payable, Mortgage Payable, Contributed Capital, Retained Earnings, Food Sales Revenue, Catering Sales Revenue, Cost of Food and Paper Products, Utilities Expense, Wages Expense, and Fuel Expense.

2. Record in the T-accounts the effects of each transaction for Traveling Gourmet, Inc., in March. Identify the amounts with the letters starting with (*a*). Compute ending balances.

E3-14 Preparing an Income Statement, Statement of Retained Earnings, and Classified Balance

LO5 Sheet

Refer to E3-13.

Required:

Use the balances in the completed T-accounts in E3-13 to respond to the following:

1. Prepare an income statement in good form for the month of March 2008.

2. Prepare a statement of retained earnings for the month of March 2008.

3. Prepare a classified balance sheet in good form as of March 2008.

4. What do you think about the success of this company based on the results of the first month of operation?

E3-15 Preparing a Statement of Cash Flows

LO5

Refer to E3-13.

Required:

Use the transactions in E3-13 to prepare a statement of cash flows in good form.

E3-16 Inferring Operating Transactions and Preparing an Income Statement and Balance Sheet

LO2, 3, 4, 5

Katie's Kite Company (a corporation) sells and repairs kites from manufacturers around the world. Its stores are located in rented space in malls and shopping centers. During its first month of operations ended April 30, 2007, Katie's Kite Company completed eight transactions with the dollar effects indicated in the following schedule:

Accounts	DOLLAR EFFECT OF EACH OF THE EIGHT TRANSACTIONS								Ending Balance
	(a)	(b)	(c)	(d)	(e)	(f)	(g)	(h)	
Cash	$50,000	$(10,000)	$(5,000)	$ 7,000	$(2,000)	$(1,000)		$3,000	
Accounts Receivable				3,000					
Inventory			20,000	(3,000)					
Prepaid Expenses					1,500				
Store Fixtures		10,000							
Accounts Payable			15,000				$1,200		
Unearned Revenue								2,000	
Contributed Capital	50,000								
Sales Revenue				10,000				1,000	
Cost of Sales				3,000					
Wages Expense						1,000			
Rent Expense					500				
Utilities Expense							1,200		

Required:

1. Write a brief explanation of Transactions (a) through (h). Include any assumptions that you made.
2. Compute the ending balance in each account and prepare an income statement and a classified balance sheet for Katie's Kite Company on April 30, 2007.

Analyzing the Effects of Transactions Using T-Accounts and Interpreting the Total Asset Turnover Ratio as a Financial Analyst

E3-17
LO4, 6

DeVita Company, which has been operating for three years, provides marketing consulting services worldwide for dot-com companies. You are a financial analyst assigned to report on the DeVita management team's effectiveness at managing its assets efficiently. At the start of 2009 (its fourth year), DeVita's T-account balances were as follows. Dollars are in thousands.

Assets

Cash		Accounts Receivable		Long-Term Investments	
4,000		10,000		8,000	

Liabilities

Accounts Payable		Unearned Revenue		Long-Term Notes Payable	
	3,000		7,000		2,000

Stockholders' Equity

Contributed Capital		Retained Earnings	
	6,000		4,000

Revenues

Consulting Fee Revenue		Investment Income	

Expenses

Wages Expense		Travel Expense		Utilities Expense		Rent Expense	

Required:

1. Using the data from these T-accounts, amounts for the following on January 1, 2009, were

    Assets $_____ = Liabilities $_____ + Stockholders' Equity $_____.

2. Enter the following 2009 transactions in the T-accounts:

    a. Received $7,000 cash from clients on account.

    b. Provided $70,000 in services to clients who paid $60,000 in cash and owed the rest on account.

    c. Received $500 in cash as income on investments.

    d. Paid $20,000 in wages, $20,000 in travel, $12,000 rent, and $2,000 on accounts payable.

    e. Received a utility bill for $1,000 for 2009 services.

    f. Paid $600 in dividends to stockholders.

    g. Received $2,000 in cash from clients in advance of services DeVita will provide next year.

3. Compute ending balances in the T-accounts to determine amounts for the following on December 31, 2009:

    Revenues $_____ − Expenses $_____ = Net Income $_____.

    Assets $_____ = Liabilities $_____ + Stockholders' Equity $_____.

4. Calculate the total asset turnover ratio for 2009. If the company had an asset turnover ratio in 2008 of 2.00 and in 2007 of 1.80, what does your computation suggest to you about DeVita Company? What would you say in your report?

E3-18
LO4
Dow Jones &
Company

Inferring Transactions and Computing Effects Using T-Accounts

A recent annual report of Dow Jones & Company, the world leader in business and financial news and information (and publisher of *The Wall Street Journal*), included the following accounts. Dollars are in millions:

Accounts Receivable				Prepaid Expenses				Unearned Revenue			
1/1	313			1/1	25					240	1/1
	2,573	?			43	?		?		328	
12/31	295			12/31	26					253	12/31

Required:

1. For each T-account, describe the typical transactions that affect each account (that is, the economic events that occur to make these accounts increase and decrease).
2. For each T-account, compute the missing amounts.

E3-19

Finding Financial Information as an Investor

You are evaluating your current portfolio of investments to determine those that are not performing to your expectations. You have all of the companies' most recent annual reports.

Required:

For each of the following, indicate where you would locate the information in an annual report. (*Hint:* The information may be in more than one location.)

1. Description of a company's primary business(es).
2. Income taxes paid.
3. Accounts receivable.
4. Cash flow from operating activities.
5. Description of a company's revenue recognition policy.
6. The inventory sold during the year.
7. The data needed to compute the total asset turnover ratio.

PROBLEMS

Recording Nonquantitative Journal Entries (AP3-1)

The following list includes a series of accounts for Choudhury Corporation that has been operating for three years. These accounts are listed and numbered for identification. Following the accounts is a series of transactions. For each transaction, indicate the account(s) that should be debited and credited by entering the appropriate account number(s) to the right of each transaction. If no journal entry is needed, use number 16. The first transaction is used as an example.

P3-1
LO4

Account No.	Account Title	Account No.	Account Title
1	Cash	9	Wages Payable
2	Accounts Receivable	10	Income Taxes Payable
3	Supplies on Hand	11	Contributed Capital
4	Prepaid Expenses	12	Retained Earnings
5	Equipment	13	Service Revenue
6	Patents	14	Operating Expenses (wages, supplies)
7	Accounts Payable	15	Income Tax Expense
8	Note Payable	16	Interest expense

Transactions	Debit	Credit
a. Example: Purchased equipment for use in the business; paid one-third cash and signed a note payable for the balance.	5	1, 8
b. Issued stock to new investors.	——	——
c. Paid cash for salaries and wages.	——	——
d. Collected cash for services performed this period.	——	——
e. Collected cash on accounts receivable for services performed last period.	——	——
f. Performed services this period on credit.	——	——
g. Paid operating expenses incurred this period.	——	——
h. Paid cash on accounts payable for expenses incurred last period.	——	——
i. Incurred operating expenses this period to be paid next period.	——	——
j. Purchased supplies to be used later; paid cash.	——	——
k. Used some of the supplies on hand for operations.	——	——
l. Purchased a patent (an intangible asset); paid cash.	——	——
m. Made a payment on the equipment note in (*a*); the payment was part principal and part interest expense.	——	——
n. Paid three-fourths of the income tax expense for the year; the balance will be paid next year.	——	——
o. On the last day of the current period, paid cash for an insurance policy covering the next two years.	——	——

Recording Journal Entries (AP3-2)

Chris Chudkosky organized a new company, CollegeCaps, Inc. The company operates a small store in an area mall and specializes in baseball-type caps with logos printed on them. Chris, who is never without a cap, believes that his target market is college and high school students. You have been hired to record the transactions occurring in the first two weeks of operations.

P3-2
LO4

a. Issued 1,000 shares of stock to investors for $30 per share.
b. Borrowed $50,000 from the bank to provide additional funding to begin operations; the note is due in two years.
c. Paid $2,200 for the current month's rent and another $2,200 for next month's rent.
d. Paid $2,400 for a one-year fire insurance policy (recorded as a prepaid expense).
e. Purchased furniture and fixtures for the store for $25,000 on account. The amount is due within 30 days.
f. Purchased a supply of The University of Texas, Texas Christian University, and Michigan State University baseball caps for the store for $2,800 cash.

g. Placed advertisements in local college newspapers for a total of $450 cash.

h. Sold caps totaling $1,400, half of which was charged on account. The cost of the caps sold was $400.

i. Made full payment for the furniture and fixtures purchased on account in (e).

j. Received $250 from a customer on account.

Required:

For each of the transactions, prepare journal entries. Be sure to categorize each account as an asset (A), liability (L), stockholders' equity (SE), revenue (R), or expense (E). Note that transaction (h) will require two entries, one for revenue and one for the related expense.

P3-3
LO4

Wendy's
International,
Inc.

Determining Financial Statement Effects of Various Transactions and Identifying Cash Flow Effects (AP3-3)

According to its annual report, Wendy's International serves "the best hamburgers in the business" and other fresh food including salads, chicken sandwiches, and baked potatoes in more than 6,400 restaurants worldwide. The company operates its own restaurants and sells franchises to others. The following activities were inferred from a recent annual report.

a. Purchased additional investments.

b. Served food to customers for cash.

c. Used food and paper products.

d. Paid cash dividends.

e. Incurred restaurant operating costs in company-owned facilities; paid part in cash and the rest on account.

f. Sold franchises, receiving part in cash and the rest in notes due from franchisees.

g. Paid interest on debt.

h. Purchased food and paper products; paid part in cash and the rest on account.

Required:

1. For each of the transactions, complete the tabulation, indicating the effect (+ for increase and − for decrease) of each transaction. (Remember that A = L + SE, R − E = NI, and NI affects SE through Retained Earnings.) Write NE if there is no effect. The first transaction is provided as an example.

	BALANCE SHEET			INCOME STATEMENT		
Transaction	Assets	Liabil-ities	Stock-holders' Equity	Revenues	Expenses	Net Income
(a) (example)	+/−	NE	NE	NE	NE	NE

2. Where, if at all, would each transaction be reported on the statement of cash flows? Use O for operating activities, I for investing activities, F for financing activities, and NE if the transaction would not be included on the statement.

P3-4
LO4, 5, 6

Analyzing the Effects of Transactions Using T-Accounts, Preparing Financial Statements, and Evaluating the Total Asset Turnover Ratio as a Manager (AP3-4)

Syrena Shirley, a connoisseur of fine chocolate, opened Syrena's Sweets in Collegetown on February 1, 2008. The shop specializes in a selection of gourmet chocolate candies and a line of gourmet ice cream. You have been hired as manager. Your duties include maintaining the store's financial records. The following transactions occurred in February 2008, the first month of operations.

a. Received four shareholders' contributions totaling $16,000 cash to form the corporation; issued stock.

b. Paid three months' rent for the store at $1,800 per month (recorded as prepaid expenses).

c. Purchased supplies for $900 cash.

d. Purchased and received candy for $5,000 on account, due in 60 days.

e. Negotiated and signed a two-year $20,000 loan at the bank.

f. Used the money from (*e*) to purchase a computer for $3,500 (for recordkeeping and inventory tracking) and the balance for furniture and fixtures for the store.

g. Placed a grand opening advertisement in the local paper for $625 cash.

h. Made sales on Valentine's Day totaling $5,800; $4,925 was in cash and the rest on accounts receivable. The cost of the candy sold was $3,000.

i. Made a $500 payment on accounts payable.

j. Incurred and paid employee wages of $1,420.

k. Collected accounts receivable of $250 from customers.

l. Made a repair to one of the display cases for $315 cash.

m. Made cash sales of $3,000 during the rest of the month. The cost of the candy sold was $1,700.

Required:

1. Set up appropriate T-accounts for Cash, Accounts Receivable, Supplies, Merchandise Inventory, Prepaid Expenses, Equipment, Furniture and Fixtures, Accounts Payable, Notes Payable, Contributed Capital, Sales Revenue, Cost of Goods Sold (Expense), Advertising Expense, Wage Expense, and Repair Expense. All accounts begin with zero balances.

2. Record in the T-accounts the effects of each transaction for Syrena's Sweets in February, referencing each transaction in the accounts with the transaction letter. Show the ending balances in the T-accounts. Note that transactions (*h*) and (*m*) require two types of entries, one for revenue recognition and one for the expense.

3. Prepare financial statements at the end of the month ended February 29, 2008 (a leap year) (income statement, statement of retained earnings, and balance sheet).

4. Write a short memo to Syrena offering your opinion on the results of operations during the first month of business.

5. After three years in business, you are being evaluated for a promotion. One measure is how efficiently you managed the assets of the business. The following data are available:

	2010*	2009	2008
Total assets	$80,000	$45,000	$35,000
Total liabilities	45,000	20,000	15,000
Total stockholders' equity	35,000	25,000	20,000
Total sales	85,000	75,000	50,000
Net income	20,000	10,000	4,000

*At the end of 2010, Syrena decided to open a second store, requiring loans and inventory purchases prior to the opening in early 2011.

Compute the total asset turnover ratio for 2009 and 2010 and evaluate the results. Do you think you should be promoted? Why?

Preparing a Statement of Cash Flows (AP3-5)

Refer to P3-4.

Required:

For the transactions listed in P3-4, prepare a statement of cash flows for the month.

Analyzing the Effects of Transactions Using T-Accounts, Preparing Financial Statements, and Evaluating the Total Asset Turnover Ratio (AP3-6)

The following are several account balances (in millions of dollars) from a recent annual report of Federal Express Corporation, followed by several typical transactions. Assume that the following account balances are on June 30, 2006:

Account	Balance	Account	Balance
Flight and ground equipment	$3,476	Contributed capital	$ 702
Retained earnings	970	Receivables	923
Accounts payable	554	Other assets	1,011
Prepaid expenses	64	Cash	155
Accrued expenses payable	761	Spare parts, supplies, and fuel	164
Long-term notes payable	2,016	Other noncurrent liabilities	790

P3-5
L05

P3-6
L04, 5, 6
Federal Express

These accounts are not necessarily in good order and have normal debit or credit balances. The following transactions (in millions of dollars) occurred the next year ending June 30, 2007:

   a. Provided delivery service to customers, receiving $7,200 in accounts receivable and $600 in cash.

   b. Purchased new equipment costing $816; signed a long-term note.

   c. Paid $744 cash to rent equipment and aircraft, with $648 for rental this year and the rest for rent next year.

   d. Spent $396 cash to maintain and repair facilities and equipment during the year.

   e. Collected $6,524 from customers on account.

   f. Borrowed $900 by signing a long-term note.

   g. Issued additional stock for $240.

   h. Paid employees $3,804 during the year.

   i. Purchased for cash and used $492 in fuel for the aircraft and equipment during the year.

   j. Paid $384 on accounts payable.

   k. Ordered $72 in spare parts and supplies.

Required:

   1. Prepare T-accounts for June 30, 2006, from the preceding list; enter the respective beginning balances. You will need additional T-accounts for income statement accounts; enter zero balances.

   2. For each transaction, record the 2007 effects in the T-accounts. Label each using the letter of the transaction. Compute ending balances.

   3. Prepare an income statement, statement of retained earnings, balance sheet, and statement of cash flows in good form for June 30, 2007.

   4. Compute the company's total asset turnover ratio for the year ended June 30, 2007. What does it suggest to you about Federal Express?

P3-7
LO4
Cedar Fair

Recording Journal Entries and Identifying Cash Flow Effects

Cedar Fair, L. P. (Limited Partnership), owns and operates four seasonal amusement parks: Cedar Point in Ohio, Valleyfair near Minneapolis/St. Paul, Dorney Park and Wildwater Kingdom near Allentown, Pennsylvania, and Worlds of Fun/Oceans of Fun in Kansas City. The following are summarized transactions similar to those that occurred in a recent year (assume 2008):

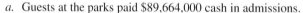

   a. Guests at the parks paid $89,664,000 cash in admissions.

   b. The primary operating expenses (such as employee wages, utilities, and repairs and maintenance) for the year were $66,347,000 with $60,200,000 paid in cash and the rest on account.

   c. Interest paid on long-term debt was $6,601,000.

   d. The parks sell food and merchandise and operate games. The cash received during the year for these combined activities was $77,934,000. The cost of merchandise sold during the year was $19,525,000.

   e. Cedar Fair purchased and built additional buildings, rides, and equipment during the year, paying $23,813,000 in cash.

   f. The most significant assets for the company are land, buildings, rides, and equipment. Therefore, a large expense for Cedar Fair is depreciation expense (related to using these assets to generate revenues during the year). For the year, the amount was $14,473,000 (credit Accumulated Depreciation).

   g. Guests may stay in the parks at accommodations owned by the company. During the year, Accommodations Revenue was $11,345,000; $11,010,000 was paid by the guests in cash and the rest was owed on account.

   h. Cedar Fair paid $2,900,000 principal on notes payable.

   i. The company purchased $19,100,000 in food and merchandise inventory for the year, paying $18,000,000 in cash and owing the rest on account.

   j. The selling, general, and administrative expenses such as the president's salary and advertising for the parks, classified as operating expenses, for the year were $21,118,000; $19,500,000 was paid in cash, and the rest was owed on account.

   k. Cedar Fair paid $8,600,000 on accounts payable during the year.

Required:

   1. For each of these transactions, record journal entries. Use the letter of each transaction as its reference. Note that transaction (*d*) will require two entries, one for revenue recognition and one for the related expense.

2. Use the following chart to identify whether each transaction results in a cash flow effect from operating (O), investing (I), or financing (F) activities, and indicate the direction and amount of the effect on cash (+ for increase and − for decrease). If there is no cash flow effect, write *none*. The first transaction is provided as an example.

Transaction	Operating, Investing, or Financing Effect	Direction and Amount of the Effect
(a)	O	+89,664,000

Recording Nonquantitative Journal Entries (P3-1)

AP3-1
LO4

The following is a series of accounts for Martin & Parillo, Incorporated, that has been operating for two years. The accounts are listed and numbered for identification. Following the accounts is a series of transactions. For each transaction, indicate the account(s) that should be debited and credited by entering the appropriate account number(s) to the right of each transaction. If no journal entry is needed, write *none* after the transaction. The first transaction is given as an example.

Account No.	Account Title	Account No.	Account Title
1	Cash	9	Wages Payable
2	Accounts Receivable	10	Income Taxes Payable
3	Supplies	11	Contributed Capital
4	Prepaid Expenses	12	Retained Earnings
5	Buildings	13	Service Revenue
6	Land	14	Other Expenses (wages, supplies, interest)
7	Accounts Payable	15	Income Tax Expense
8	Mortgage Payable		

Transactions	Debit	Credit
a. Example: Issued stock to new investors.	1	11
b. Performed services for customers this period on credit.	___	___
c. Purchased on credit but did not use supplies this period.	___	___
d. Prepaid a fire insurance policy this period to cover the next 12 months.	___	___
e. Purchased a building this period by making a 20 percent cash down payment and signed a mortgage loan for the balance.	___	___
f. Collected cash this year for services rendered and recorded in the prior year.	___	___
g. Paid cash this period for wages earned and recorded last period.	___	___
h. Paid cash for operating expenses charged on accounts payable in the prior period.	___	___
i. Paid cash for operating expenses incurred in the current period.	___	___
j. Incurred and recorded operating expenses on credit to be paid next period.	___	___
k. Collected cash for services rendered this period.	___	___
l. Used supplies on hand to clean the offices.	___	___
m. Recorded income taxes for this period to be paid at the beginning of the next period.	___	___
n. Declared and paid a cash dividend this period.	___	___
o. Made a payment on the building, which was part principal repayment and part interest.	___	___
p. This period a shareholder sold some shares of her stock to another person for an amount above the original issuance price.	___	___

AP3-2 **Recording Journal Entries** (P3-2)
L04

Tom Masaya is the president of ServicePro, Inc., a company that provides temporary employees for not-for-profit companies. ServicePro has been operating for five years; its revenues are increasing with each passing year. You have been hired to help Tom analyze the following transactions for the first two weeks of April:

a. Purchased office supplies for $1,500 on account.
b. Billed the local United Way office $13,950 for temporary services provided.
c. Paid $1,250 for supplies purchased and recorded on account last period.
d. Placed an advertisement in the local paper for $600 cash.
e. Purchased a new computer for the office costing $4,300 cash.
f. Paid employee wages of $8,200. Of this amount, $1,200 had been earned and recorded in the Wages Payable account in the prior period.
g. Received $10,000 on account from the local United Way office from the services provided in (b).
h. Purchased land as the site of a future office for $10,000. Paid $2,000 down and signed a note payable for the balance.
i. Issued 2,000 additional shares of capital stock for $40 per share in anticipation of building a new office.
j. Billed Family & Children's Service $12,000 for services rendered.
k. Received the April telephone bill for $1,245 to be paid next month.

Required:
For each of the transactions, prepare journal entries. Be sure to categorize each account as an asset (A), liability (L), stockholders' equity (SE), revenue (R), or expense (E).

AP3-3 **Determining Financial Statement Effects of Various Transactions and Identifying Cash**
L04 **Flow Effects** (P3-3)

Big Dog
Holdings, Inc.

Big Dog Holdings, Inc., is the parent company of Big Dog USA, a company that develops, markets and retails a collection of consumer products centered around the signature BIG DOGS® name, logo, and "Big Dog" characters. The following activities were inferred from a recent annual report.

a. Example: Incurred expenses, paid part cash and part on credit.
b. Sold merchandise to customers on account. (*Hint:* Indicate the effects for the sale; then reduce inventory for the amount sold—two transactions.)
c. Sold investments for cash for more than their cost.
d. Collected cash on account.
e. Used supplies.
f. Repaid long-term debt principal.
g. Paid interest on long-term debt.
h. Purchased equipment; paid part cash and part on credit.
i. Paid cash on account.
j. Issued additional stock.
k. Paid rent to discount mall owners.
l. Received dividends and interest on investments.

Required:
1. For each of the transactions, complete the tabulation, indicating the effect (+ for increase and − for decrease) of each transaction. (Remember that A = L + SE, R − E = NI, and NI affects SE through Retained Earnings.) Write NE if there is no effect. The first transaction is provided as an example.

	BALANCE SHEET			INCOME STATEMENT		
Transaction	Assets	Liabil-ities	Stock-holders' Equity	Revenues	Expenses	Net Income
(*a*) (example)	−	+	−	NE	+	−

2. For each transaction, indicate where, if at all, it would be reported on the statement of cash flows. Use O for operating activities, I for investing activities, F for financing activities, and NE if the transaction would not be included on the statement.

Analyzing the Effects of Transactions Using T-Accounts, Preparing Financial Statements, and Evaluating the Total Asset Turnover Ratio as a Manager (P3-4)

AP3-4
LO4, 5, 6

Spicewood Stables, Inc., was established in Austin, Texas, on April 1, 2007. The company provides stables, care for animals, and grounds for riding and showing horses. You have been hired as the new assistant controller. The following transactions for April 2007 are provided for your review.

a. Received contributions from five investors of $50,000 in cash ($10,000 each), a barn valued at $100,000, land valued at $60,000, and supplies valued at $2,000. Each investor received 3,000 shares of stock.

b. Built a small barn for $42,000. The company paid half the amount in cash on April 1, 2007, and signed a three-year note payable for the balance.

c. Provided $15,260 in animal care services for customers, all on credit.

d. Rented stables to customers who cared for their own animals; received cash of $13,200.

e. Received from a customer $1,500 to board her horse in May, June, and July (record as unearned revenue).

f. Purchased hay and feed supplies on account for $3,210 to be used in the summer.

g. Paid $840 in cash for water utilities incurred in the month.

h. Paid $1,700 on accounts payable for previous purchases.

i. Received $1,000 from customers on accounts receivable.

j. Paid $4,000 in wages to employees who worked during the month.

k. At the end of the month, purchased a two-year insurance policy for $3,600.

l. Received an electric utility bill for $1,200 for usage in April; the bill will be paid next month.

m. Paid $100 cash dividend to each of the investors at the end of the month.

Required:

1. Set up appropriate T-accounts. All accounts begin with zero balances.

2. Record in the T-accounts the effects of each transaction for Spicewood Stables in April, referencing each transaction in the accounts with the transaction letter. Show the ending balances in the T-accounts.

3. Prepare financial statements at the end of April (income statement, statement of retained earnings, and balance sheet).

4. Write a short memo to the five owners offering your opinion on the results of operations during the first month of business.

5. After three years in business, you are being evaluated for a promotion to chief financial officer. One measure is how efficiently you managed the assets of the business. The following annual data are available:

	2009*	2008	2007
Total assets	$480,000	$320,000	$300,000
Total liabilities	125,000	28,000	30,000
Total stockholders' equity	355,000	292,000	270,000
Total sales	450,000	400,000	360,000
Net income	50,000	30,000	(10,000)

*At the end of 2009, Spicewood Stables decided to build an indoor riding arena for giving lessons year-round. The company borrowed construction funds from a local bank, and the arena was opened in early 2010.

Compute the total asset turnover ratio for 2008 and 2009 and evaluate the results. Do you think you should be promoted? Why?

Preparing a Statement of Cash Flows (P3-5)

AP3-5
LO5

Refer to AP3-4.

Required:
For the transactions listed in AP3-4, prepare a statement of cash flows for the month.

AP3-6
LO4, 5, 6
Exxon Mobil
Corporation

Analyzing the Effects of Transactions Using T-Accounts, Preparing Financial Statements, and Evaluating the Total Asset Turnover Ratio (P3-6)

The following are the summary account balances from a recent balance sheet of Exxon Mobil Corporation. The accounts have normal debit or credit balances, but they are not necessarily listed in good order. The amounts are shown in millions of dollars. Assume the year-end is December 31, 2007.

Cash	$ 1,157	Marketable securities	$ 618
Notes payable (long-term)	3,858	Accounts payable	13,391
Accounts receivable	8,073	Income tax payable	2,244
Inventories	5,541	Prepaid expenses	1,071
Other debt	30,954	Investments	5,394
Property & equipment, net	63,425	Intangibles, net	2,583
Shareholders' equity*	37,415		

*This account is a combination of Contributed Capital and Retained Earnings.

The following is a list of hypothetical transactions for January 2008.

a. Purchased on account $150,000,000 of new equipment.
b. Received $500,000,000 on accounts receivable.
c. Received and paid $1,000,000 for utility bills.
d. Earned $5,000,000 in sales on account with customers; cost of sales was $1,000,000.
e. Paid employees $1,000,000 for wages earned during the month.
f. Paid half of the income taxes payable.
g. Purchased $23,000,000 in supplies on account (include in Inventories).
h. Prepaid $12,000,000 to rent a warehouse next month.
i. Paid $10,000,000 of other debt and $1,000,000 in interest on the debt.
j. Purchased a patent (an intangible asset) for $8,000,000 cash.

Required:

1. Prepare T-accounts for December 31, 2007, from the preceding list; enter the beginning balances. You will need additional T-accounts for income statement accounts; enter zero balances.
2. For each transaction, record the effects in the T-accounts. Label each using the letter of the transaction. Compute ending balances. (*Note:* Record two transactions in (*d*), one for revenue recognition and one for the expense.)
3. Prepare an income statement, statement of stockholders' equity (since contributed capital and retained earnings are not separately reported), balance sheet, and statement of cash flows in good form.
4. Compute the company's total asset turnover ratio for the month ended January 31, 2008. What does it suggest to you about Exxon Mobil?

CASES **AND PROJECTS**

Annual Report Cases

CP3-1
LO2, 4, 6

Finding Financial Information

Refer to the financial statements and accompanying notes of Pacific Sunwear of California given in Appendix B at the end of the book, or open file PSUN.pdf in the Annual Report Cases directory on the student DVD.

Required:

1. State the amount of the largest expense on the income statement for the year ended January 29, 2005 and describe the transaction represented by the expense.
2. Give the journal entry for interest income for the year ended January 29, 2005 (for this question, assume that the amount has not yet been received).

3. Assuming that all net sales are on credit, how much cash did Pacific Sunwear of California collect from customers?* (*Hint:* Use a T-account of accounts receivable to infer collection.)

4. A shareholder has complained that "more dividends should be paid because the company had net earnings of $106.9 million. Since this amount is all cash, more of it should go to the owners." Explain why the shareholder's assumption that earnings equal net cash inflow is valid. If you believe that the assumption is not valid, state so and support your position concisely.

5. Describe and contrast the purpose of an income statement versus a balance sheet.

6. Compute the company's total asset turnover for the year ended January 29, 2005. Explain its meaning.

Finding Financial Information

Refer to the financial statements and accompanying notes of American Eagle Outfitters given in Appendix C at the end of the book, or open file AEOS.pdf in the Annual Report Cases directory on the student DVD.

Required:

1. What is the company's revenue recognition policy? (*Hint:* Look in notes to the financial statements.)

2. Assuming that $50 million of cost of sales was due to noninventory purchase expenses (occupancy and warehousing costs), how much inventory did the company buy during the year? (*Hint:* Use a T-account of inventory to infer how much was purchased.)

3. Calculate general, administrative, and selling expenses as a percent of sales for the years ended January 29, 2005, and January 31, 2004 (fiscal years 2004, and 2003 respectively). By what percent did it increase or decrease from fiscal year 2003 to 2004? (*Hint:* Percentage Change = Current Year Amount − Prior Year Amount]/Prior Year.)

4. Compute the company's total asset turnover for the year ended January 29, 2005, and explain its meaning.

Comparing Companies within an Industry

Refer to the financial statements of Pacific Sunwear of California given in Appendix B, American Eagle Outfitters given in Appendix C, and the Industry Ratio Report given in Appendix D at the end of this book or open file CP3-3.xls in the Annual Report Cases directory on the student DVD.

Required:

1. What title does each company call its income statement? Explain what "Consolidated" means.

2. Which company had higher net income for the year ended January 29, 2005?

3. Compute the total asset turnover ratio for both companies for the year ended January 29, 2005. Which company is utilizing assets more effectively to generate sales? Why do you think that?

4. Compare the total asset turnover ratio for both companies to the industry average. On average, are these two companies utilizing assets to generate sales better or worse than their competitors?

5. How much cash was provided by operating activities for the year ended January 29, 2005 by each company? What was the percentage change in operating cash flows (1) from the year ended January 31, 2004 to the year ended January 29, 2005 and (2) from the year ended February 1, 2003 to the year ended January 31, 2004 for each company? (*Hint:* [Current Year Amount − Prior Year Amount]/Prior Year Amount.)

Financial Reporting and Analysis Cases

Comparing a Company over Time

Refer to the annual report for American Eagle Outfitters in Appendix C, or open file AEOS.pdf in the Annual Report Cases directory on the student DVD.

CP3-2
LO2, 4, 6
AMERICAN EAGLE
OUTFITTERS
ae.com

CP3-3
LO2, 3, 5
PACIFIC SUNWEAR
OF CALIFORNIA, INC.
AMERICAN EAGLE
OUTFITTERS
ae.com

CP3-4
LO6
AMERICAN EAGLE
OUTFITTERS
ae.com

---

*Note that most retailers settle sales in cash at the register and would not have accounts receivable related to sales unless they had layaway or private credit. For PacSun, the accounts receivable on the balance sheet primarily relates to amounts owed from landlords for their construction allowances for building new PacSun stores in malls.

Required:

1. The annual report or 10-K report for American Eagle Outfitters provides selected financial data for the last five years. Compute the total asset turnover ratio for each of the most recent four years (*Hint:* See Item 6 from the 10-K, which is disclosed within the annual report for the data. *Note:* some companies will label a year that has a January year-end as having a fiscal year-end dated one year earlier. For example, a January 2005 year-end may be labeled as Fiscal 2004 since the year actually has more months that fall in the 2004 calendar year than in the 2005 calendar year.)

2. In Chapter 2, we discussed the financial leverage ratio. Compute this ratio for the most recent four years.

3. What do your results from the trends in the two ratios suggest to you about American Eagle Outfitters?

CP3-5
LO3

Interpreting the Financial Press

The October 4, 2004, edition of *BusinessWeek* presented an article titled "Fuzzy Numbers" on issues related to accrual accounting and its weaknesses that have lead some corporate executives to manipulate estimates in their favor, sometimes fraudulently. You can access the article on the Libby/Libby/Short website at **www.mhhe.com/libby5e**.

Required:
Read the article and then answer the following questions:
1. What is accrual accounting?
2. What does the article's title "Fuzzy Numbers" mean?
3. What does the article suggest about the reforms adopted by Congress and the SEC?

CP3-6
LO4, 5

Using Financial Reports: Analyzing Changes in Accounts and Preparing Financial Statements

Lippitt Painting Service Company was organized on January 20, 2008, by three individuals, each receiving 5,000 shares of stock from the new company. The following is a schedule of the *cumulative* account balances immediately after each of the first 10 transactions ending on January 31, 2008.

Accounts	CUMULATIVE BALANCES									
	(a)	(b)	(c)	(d)	(e)	(f)	(g)	(h)	(i)	(j)
Cash	$75,000	$70,000	$85,000	$71,000	$61,000	$61,000	$57,000	$46,000	$41,000	$57,000
Accounts Receivable			12,000	12,000	12,000	26,000	26,000	26,000	26,000	10,000
Office Fixtures		20,000	20,000	20,000	20,000	20,000	20,000	20,000	20,000	20,000
Land				18,000	18,000	18,000	18,000	18,000	18,000	18,000
Accounts Payable					3,000	3,000	3,000	10,000	5,000	5,000
Note Payable (long-term)		15,000	15,000	19,000	19,000	19,000	19,000	19,000	19,000	19,000
Contributed Capital	75,000	75,000	75,000	75,000	75,000	75,000	75,000	75,000	75,000	75,000
Retained Earnings							(4,000)	(4,000)	(4,000)	(4,000)
Paint Revenue			27,000	27,000	27,000	41,000	41,000	41,000	41,000	41,000
Supplies Expense					5,000	5,000	5,000	8,000	8,000	8,000
Wages Expense					8,000	8,000	8,000	23,000	23,000	23,000

Required:
1. Analyze the changes in this schedule for each transaction; then explain the transaction. Transactions (*a*) and (*b*) are examples:
   (*a*) Cash increased $75,000, and Contributed Capital (stockholders' equity) increased $75,000. Therefore, transaction (*a*) was an issuance of the capital stock of the corporation for $75,000 cash.
   (*b*) Cash decreased $5,000, office fixtures (an asset) increased $20,000, and note payable (a liability) increased $15,000. Therefore, transaction (*b*) was a purchase of office fixtures that cost $20,000. Payment was made as follows: cash, $5,000; note payable, $15,000.
2. Based only on the preceding schedule after transaction (*j*), prepare an income statement, a statement of retained earnings, and a balance sheet.

3. For each of the transactions, indicate the type of effect on cash flows (O for operating, I for investing, or F for financing) and the direction (+ for increase and − for decrease) and amount of the effect. If there is no effect, write none. The first transaction is provided as an example.

Transaction	Operating, Investing, or Financing Effect	Direction and Amount of the Effect
(a)	F	+75,000

Critical Thinking Cases

Making a Decision as a Bank Loan Officer: Analyzing and Restating Financial Statements That Have Major Deficiencies: A Challenging Case

CP3-7
LO3, 4, 5

Julio Estela started and operated a small boat repair service company during 2009. He is interested in obtaining a $100,000 loan from your bank to build a dry dock to store boats for customers in the winter months. At the end of the year, he prepared the following statements based on information stored in a large filing cabinet:

ESTELA COMPANY

Profit for 2009

Service fees collected during 2009		$ 55,000
Cash dividends received		10,000
Total		65,000
Expense for operations paid during 2009	$22,000	
Cash stolen	500	
New tools purchased during 2009 (cash paid)	1,000	
Supplies purchased for use on service jobs (cash paid)	3,200	
Total		26,700
Profit		$ 38,300

Assets Owned at the End of 2009

Cash in checking account	$ 29,300
Building (at current market value)	32,000
Tools and equipment	18,000
Land (at current market value)	30,000
Stock in ABC Industrial	130,000
Total	$239,300

The following is a summary of completed transactions:

(a) Received the following contributions (at fair market value) to the business from the owner when it was started in exchange for 1,000 shares of stock in the new company:

Building	$21,000	Land	$20,000
Tools and equipment	17,000	Cash	1,000

(b) Earned service fees during 2009 of $87,000; of the cash collected, $20,000 was for deposits from customers on work to be done by Julio in the next year.

(c) Received the cash dividends on shares of ABC Industrial stock purchased by Julio Estela six years earlier (not owned by the company).

(d) Incurred expenses during 2009 of $61,000.

(e) Determined amount of supplies on hand (unused) at the end of 2009 as $700.

Required:

1. Did Julio prepare the income statement on a cash basis or an accrual basis? Explain how you can tell. Which basis should be used? Explain why.

2. Reconstruct the correct entries under accrual accounting principles and post the effects to T-accounts.

3. Prepare an accrual-based income statement, balance sheet, and statement of cash flows. Explain (using footnotes) the reason for each change that you make to the income statement.

4. What additional information would assist you in formulating your decision regarding the loan to Julio?

5. Based on the revised statements and additional information needed, write a letter to Julio explaining your decision at this time regarding the loan.

CP3-8 Evaluating an Ethical Dilemma

L03

Mike Lynch is the manager of an upstate New York regional office for an insurance company. As the regional manager, his compensation package comprises a base salary, commissions, and a bonus when the region sells new policies in excess of its quota. Mike has been under enormous pressure lately, stemming largely from two factors. First, he is experiencing a mounting personal debt due to a family member's illness. Second, compounding his worries, the region's sales of new policies have dipped below the normal quota for the first time in years.

You have been working for Mike for two years, and like everyone else in the office, you consider yourself lucky to work for such a supportive boss. You also feel great sympathy for his personal problems over the last few months. In your position as accountant for the regional office, you are only too aware of the drop in new policy sales and the impact this will have on the manager's bonus. While you are working late at year-end, Mike stops by your office.

Mike asks you to change the manner in which you have accounted for a new property insurance policy for a large local business. A substantial check for the premium came in the mail on December 31, the last day of the reporting year. The premium covers a period beginning on January 5. You deposited the check and correctly debited cash and credited an *unearned revenue* account. Mike says, "Hey, we have the money this year, so why not count the revenue this year? I never did understand why you accountants are so picky about these things anyway. I'd like you to change the way you have recorded the transaction. I want you to credit a *revenue* account. And anyway, I've done favors for you in the past, and I am asking for such a small thing in return." With that, he leaves for the day.

Required:

1. How should you handle this situation?
2. What are the ethical implications of Mike's request?
3. Who are the parties who would be helped or harmed if you complied with the request?
4. If you fail to comply with his request, how will you explain your position to him in the morning?

Financial Reporting and Analysis Team Project

CP3-9 Team Project: Analysis of Income Statements and Ratios

L02, 3, 6

As a team, select an industry to analyze. *Reuters* provides lists of industries and their makeup at www.investor.reuters.com/Industries.aspx. Each team member should acquire the annual report or 10-K for one publicly traded company in the industry, with each member selecting a different company. (Library files, the SEC EDGAR service at www.sec.gov, or the company itself are good sources.)

Required:

On an individual basis, each team member should write a short report answering the following questions about the selected company. Discuss any patterns across the companies that you as a team observe. Then, as a team, write a short report comparing and contrasting your companies.

1. For the most recent year, what is/are the major revenue account/s? What percentage is each to total operating revenues? [Calculated as Revenue A ÷ Total revenues.]

2. For the most recent year, what is/are the major expense account/s? What percentage is each to total operating expenses? [Calculated as Expense A ÷ Total expenses.]

3. Ratio Analysis:
   a. What does the total asset turnover ratio measure in general?
   b. Compute the ratio for the last three years.
   c. What do your results suggest about the company?
   d. If available, find the industry ratio for the most recent year, compare it to your results, and discuss why you believe your company differs or is similar to the industry ratio.
4. Describe the company's revenue recognition policy, if reported. [Usually in the Significant Accounting Policies footnote.]
5. The percentage of cash from operating activities to net income measures how liberal (that is, speeding up revenue recognition or delaying expense recognition) or conservative (that is, taking care not to record revenues too early or expenses too late) a management is in choosing among various revenue and expense recognition policies. A ratio above 1.0 suggests more conservative policies and below 1.0, more liberal policies. Compute the percentage for each of the last three years. What do your results suggest about the company's choice in accounting policies?

After studying this chapter, you should be able to:

1. Explain the purpose of a trial balance. p. 167

2. Analyze the adjustments necessary at the end of the period to update balance sheet and income statement accounts. p. 169

3. Present an income statement with earnings per share, statement of stockholders' equity, balance sheet, and supplemental cash flow information. p. 178

4. Compute and interpret the net profit margin. p. 183

5. Explain the closing process. p. 184

LEARNING OBJECTIVES

Adjustments, Financial Statements, and the Quality of Earnings

The end of the accounting period is a very busy time for Papa John's. Although the last day of the fiscal year for Papa John's falls on the last Sunday of December each year, the financial statements are not distributed to users until management and the external auditors (independent CPAs) make many critical evaluations.

- Management must ensure that the correct amounts are reported on the balance sheet and income statement. This often requires estimations, assumptions, and judgments about the timing of revenue and expense recognition and values for assets and liabilities.

- The auditors have to (1) assess the strength of the controls established by management to safeguard the company's assets and ensure the accuracy of the financial records, and (2) evaluate the appropriateness of estimates and accounting principles used by management in determining revenues and expenses.

FOCUS COMPANY:

Papa John's International
ESTIMATING REVENUES AND EXPENSES

AT YEAR END

www.papajohns.com

Managers of most companies understand the need to present financial information fairly so as not to mislead users. However, since end-of-period adjustments are the most complex portion of the annual recordkeeping process, they are prone to error. External auditors examine the company's records on a test, or sample, basis. To maximize the chance of detecting any errors significant enough to affect users' decisions, CPAs allocate more of their testing to transactions most likely to be in error.

Several accounting research studies have documented the most error-prone transactions for medium-size manufacturing companies. End-of-period adjustment errors such as failure to provide adequate product warranty liability, failure to include items that should be expensed, and end-of-period transactions recorded in the wrong period (called **cut-off errors**) are in the top category and thus receive a great deal of attention from the auditors.

For 2003, Papa John's year-end estimation and auditing process took until March 1, 2004, the date on which the auditor Ernst & Young LLP completed the audit work and signed its audit opinion. At that point, the financial statements were made available to the public.

UNDERSTANDING THE BUSINESS

Managers are responsible for preparing financial statements that are useful to investors, creditors, and others. Financial information is most useful for analyzing the past and predicting the future when it is considered by users to be of **high quality.** High-quality information should be relevant (that is, important in the analysis and available in a timely manner) and reliable (that is, verifiable and unbiased in portraying economic reality).

Users expect revenues and expenses to be reported in the proper period based on the revenue and matching principles discussed in Chapter 3. Revenues are to be recorded when earned, and expenses are to be recorded when incurred regardless of when cash receipts or payments occur. Many operating activities take place over a period of time or over several periods, such as using insurance that has been prepaid or owing wages to employees for past work. Because recording these and similar activities daily is often very costly, most companies wait until the end of the period to make **adjustments** to record related revenues and expenses in the correct period. These entries update the records and are the focus of this chapter.

Analysts assess the quality of financial information by determining how **conservative** the managers' estimates and judgments are. Choices that managers make that do not overstate assets and revenues or understate liabilities and expenses are considered more conservative. By applying conservative estimates and judgments, the resulting financial information is of higher quality for use by analysts. The information should not mislead the users into expecting the company to have a stronger financial position or higher earnings potential than exists. The effects of management's choices among alternative accounting methods and the use of estimates are presented throughout the rest of the text.

In this chapter, we emphasize the use of the same analytical tools illustrated in Chapters 2 and 3 (T-accounts and journal entries) to understand how the necessary adjustments are analyzed and recorded at the end of the accounting period. Then we prepare financial statements using adjusted accounts. Finally, we illustrate how to prepare the accounting records for the next period by "closing the books."

ORGANIZATION of the Chapter

Adjusting Revenues and Expenses	Preparing Financial Statements	Closing the Books
■ Accounting Cycle ■ Unadjusted Trial Balance ■ Analysis of Adjusting Entries ■ Papa John's Illustration	■ Income Statement ■ Statement of Stockholders' Equity ■ Balance Sheet ■ Supplemental Cash Flows Information ■ Net Profit Margin Ratio	■ End of the Accounting Cycle ■ Post-Closing Trial Balance

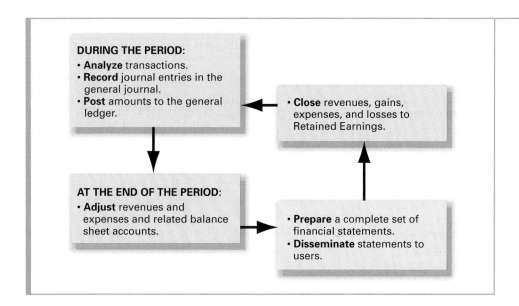

EXHIBIT 4.1

The Accounting Cycle

ADJUSTING REVENUES AND EXPENSES

Accounting Cycle

Exhibit 4.1 presents the basic steps in the accounting cycle. As discussed initially in Chapter 2, the accounting cycle is the process followed by entities to analyze and record transactions, adjust the records at the end of the period, prepare financial statements, and prepare the records for the next cycle. **During** the accounting period, transactions that result in exchanges between the company and other external parties are analyzed and recorded in the general journal in chronological order (journal entries), and the related accounts are updated in the general ledger (T-accounts), similar to our Papa John's illustrations in Chapters 2 and 3. In this chapter, we examine the **end-of-period** steps that focus primarily on adjustments to record revenues and expenses in the proper period and to update the balance sheet accounts for reporting purposes.

The **ACCOUNTING CYCLE** is the process followed by entities to analyze and record transactions, adjust the records at the end of the period, prepare financial statements, and prepare the records for the next cycle.

Unadjusted Trial Balance

Before adjusting the accounting records, managers normally review an unadjusted trial balance produced either manually or, more often, generated by computerized software. A trial balance is a list of individual accounts in one column, usually in financial statement order, with their ending debit or credit balances in the next two columns. Debit balances are indicated in the left column and credit balances are indicated in the right column. Then the two columns are totaled to provide a check on the equality of the debits and credits. In fact, that is all that the trial balance reflects. Errors in a computer-generated trial balance may still exist even though debits equal credits when wrong accounts and/or amounts are used in the journal entries.[1]

Based on the T-accounts from the Papa John's illustration in Chapter 3, an unadjusted trial balance is presented in Exhibit 4.2. Notice that the Property and Equipment

Learning Objective 1
Explain the purpose of a trial balance.

A **TRIAL BALANCE** is a list of all accounts with their balances to provide a check on the equality of the debits and credits.

---

[1]Errors in a manually created trial balance also may occur in a manual recordkeeping system when wrong accounts and/or amounts are posted from correct journal entries. If the two columns are not equal, errors have occurred in one or more of the following:

- In preparing journal entries when debits do not equal credits.
- In posting the correct dollar effects of transactions from the journal entry to the ledger.
- In computing ending balances in accounts.
- In copying ending balances in the ledger to the trial balance.

These errors can be traced and should be corrected before adjusting the records.

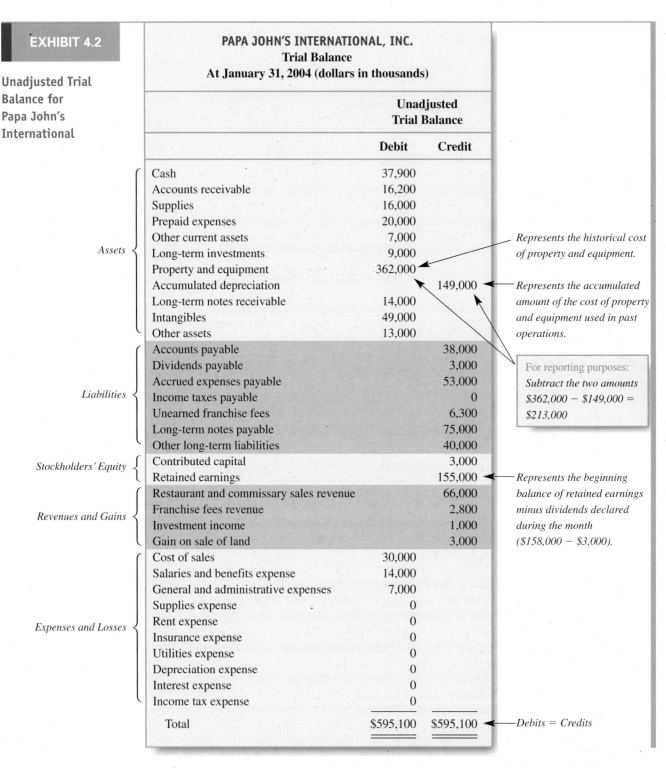

EXHIBIT 4.2

Unadjusted Trial
Balance for
Papa John's
International

PAPA JOHN'S INTERNATIONAL, INC.
Trial Balance
At January 31, 2004 (dollars in thousands)

	Unadjusted Trial Balance	
	Debit	**Credit**
Assets		
Cash	37,900	
Accounts receivable	16,200	
Supplies	16,000	
Prepaid expenses	20,000	
Other current assets	7,000	
Long-term investments	9,000	
Property and equipment	362,000	
Accumulated depreciation		149,000
Long-term notes receivable	14,000	
Intangibles	49,000	
Other assets	13,000	
Liabilities		
Accounts payable		38,000
Dividends payable		3,000
Accrued expenses payable		53,000
Income taxes payable		0
Unearned franchise fees		6,300
Long-term notes payable		75,000
Other long-term liabilities		40,000
Stockholders' Equity		
Contributed capital		3,000
Retained earnings		155,000
Revenues and Gains		
Restaurant and commissary sales revenue		66,000
Franchise fees revenue		2,800
Investment income		1,000
Gain on sale of land		3,000
Expenses and Losses		
Cost of sales	30,000	
Salaries and benefits expense	14,000	
General and administrative expenses	7,000	
Supplies expense	0	
Rent expense	0	
Insurance expense	0	
Utilities expense	0	
Depreciation expense	0	
Interest expense	0	
Income tax expense	0	
Total	$595,100	$595,100

Represents the historical cost of property and equipment.

Represents the accumulated amount of the cost of property and equipment used in past operations.

For reporting purposes:
Subtract the two amounts $362,000 − $149,000 = $213,000

Represents the beginning balance of retained earnings minus dividends declared during the month ($158,000 − $3,000).

Debits = Credits

account is stated at original cost of $362,000 in the trial balance but was stated at $213,000 (original cost minus the portion allocated to past operations) in previous chapters.

Long-lived asset accounts such as Property and Equipment increase when assets are purchased and decrease when assets are sold. These assets are also used in operations. To reflect the used-up portion of the long-lived assets' cost, a contra-account is created. **Any contra-account is directly related to another account but has the opposite balance.**

A CONTRA-ACCOUNT is an account that is an offset to, or reduction of, the primary account.

Property and Equipment (A)		Accumulated Depreciation (XA)	
+	−	−	+
Beginning bal.			Beginning bal.
Purchases	Sales		Use of assets
Ending Balance			Ending Balance

= **Net book value**
  (reported on the balance sheet)

As a contra-account increases, the net book value (also called **book value** or **carrying value**) reported on the balance sheet decreases. Net book value is the historical cost balance less the contra-account balance. For property and equipment, the contra-account is called **Accumulated Depreciation.** For Papa John's, Accumulated Depreciation has a credit balance of $149,000.

On the Balance Sheet:

Property and equipment (net of accumulated depreciation of $149,000) $213,000

We will discuss many contra-accounts in other chapters and will designate contra-accounts with an X in front of the type of account to which it is related (e.g., Accumulated Depreciation [XA]).

Analysis of Adjusting Entries

Recall that, under accrual accounting concepts,

- Revenues are recorded when earned (the revenue principle) and
- Expenses are recorded when incurred to generate revenues during the same period (the matching principle).

As you learned in Chapter 3, revenues and expenses are easy to measure when cash is received or paid at the same time that the company performs services, delivers goods, or incurs expenses. However, sometimes cash is received before the company performs and earns the revenues; sometimes cash is received after the company performs and earns revenues. The same is true for expenses.

This difference in the timing of recording cash receipts and payments versus revenues and expenses requires adjustments. Since recording revenues and expenses daily as they are earned or incurred would be too costly in terms of the time and labor needed to make the numerous entries, companies wait until the end of the accounting period to adjust certain accounts. Adjusting entries are necessary to report appropriate amounts of revenues, expenses, assets, liabilities, and stockholders' equity. A good tool to help you visualize the impact of the timing difference is a timeline as illustrated in the following discussion.

Recognizing Revenues in the Proper Period

When cash is received **prior** to earning a revenue by delivering goods or performing services, the company records a journal entry (❶ on the timeline to the left), debiting Cash and crediting the liability account Unearned Revenue to recognize the obligation to perform services or deliver goods in the future. Unearned Revenue is considered a deferred revenue account, since recording revenue is postponed until the company

NET BOOK VALUE (BOOK VALUE, CARRYING VALUE) of an asset is the difference between its acquisition cost and accumulated depreciation, its related contra-account.

> **Learning Objective 2**
> Analyze the adjustments necessary at the end of the period to update balance sheet and income statement accounts.

Topic Tackler 4–1

ADJUSTING ENTRIES are entries necessary at the end of the accounting period to measure all revenues and expenses of that period.

DEFERRED REVENUES are previously recorded liabilities that need to be adjusted at the end of the accounting period to reflect the amount of revenue earned.

EXAMPLES:
- Unearned Ticket Revenue
- Deferred Subscription Revenue

ADJUSTING ENTRY:
↓ Liability and ↑ Revenue

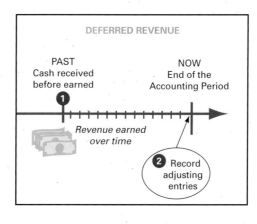

meets its obligation. At the end of the accounting period, Unearned Revenue needs to be reduced and a revenue account needs to be increased by the amount of the revenue earned over time during the period (**2** adjusting entry on the timeline).

When revenues are earned but not yet recorded at the end of the accounting period because cash changes hands **after** the service is performed or goods delivered, we call

ACCRUED REVENUES are previously unrecorded revenues that need to be adjusted at the end of the accounting period to reflect the amount earned and the related receivable account.

EXAMPLES:
• Interest Receivable
• Rent Receivable

ADJUSTING ENTRY:
↑Asset and ↑ Revenue

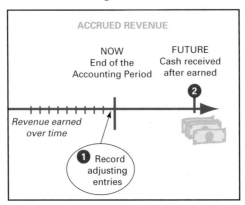

them accrued revenues. They result when services have been provided but not billed or collected. Examples include earning interest on loans made to others and earning fees that have not yet been billed. Since no entry was made during the accounting period, an adjusting entry (**1** on the timeline to the right) is necessary to increase a receivable account and its related revenue account to record revenue in the proper period. When the cash is received in the future, the receivable account is reduced (**2** on the timeline).

Exhibit 4.3 summarizes the process involved in adjusting deferred revenues and accrued revenues using unearned fees and interest revenue as examples. AJE in the exhibit refers to **adjusting journal entry.** Note that in both cases, the goal is the same—to record revenues in the proper period. Also note that adjusting entries affect one balance sheet and one income statement account, but cash is never adjusted. Cash was recorded when received prior to the end of the period, or will be collected in a future period.

EXHIBIT 4.3

Illustration of Adjusting Deferred and Accrued Revenues

Revenues recorded in the proper period!

		Deferred Revenues	Accrued Revenues
During the period	Entry when **cash is received before** company performs (earns revenue)	Cash (+A) Unearned fee revenue (+L)	

End of period	**AJE** needed because company has performed (earned a revenue) during period	Unearned fee revenue (−L)
		    Fee revenue (+R, +SE)
			Interest receivable (+A)
			    Interest revenue (+R, +SE)

Next period	Entry when **cash is received after** company performs (earns revenue)		Cash (+A) Interest receivable (−A)

DEFERRED EXPENSES are previously acquired assets that need to be adjusted at the end of the accounting period to reflect the amount of expense incurred in using the asset to generate revenue.

EXAMPLES:
• Supplies
• Prepaid Expenses (e.g., rent, advertising, insurance)
• Buildings and Equipment

ADJUSTING ENTRY:
↑ Expense and ↓ Asset

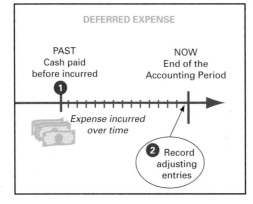

Recording Expenses in the Proper Period

When cash is paid prior to incurring an expense, the company records a journal entry to debit an asset account and credit Cash (**1** on the timeline to the left). Common examples of deferred expenses include Supplies; Prepaid Expenses such as rent, advertising, and insurance; Buildings, Equipment, and Intangible Assets such as patents and copyrights. When the assets are used during the period to generate revenues, an adjusting entry is necessary that decreases the asset and increases the related expense account (❷ adjusting entry on the timeline).

Numerous expenses are incurred in the current period but not billed or paid for until the next period. Common examples are Interest Expense incurred on debt; Wages Expense owed to employees; and Utilities Expense for water, gas, and electricity used during the period for which the company has not yet received a bill. These unrecorded expenses are called accrued expenses that require an adjusting entry (❶ on the timeline to the right) to create a payable account along with the related expense account. When cash is paid in the future for these expenses, the payable account is reduced (❷ on the timeline).

ACCRUED EXPENSES are previously unrecorded expenses that need to be adjusted at the end of the accounting period to reflect the amount incurred and the related payable account.

EXAMPLES:
- Interest Payable
- Wages Payable
- Property Taxes Payable

ADJUSTING ENTRY:
↑ Expense and ↑ Liability

Exhibit 4.4 summarizes the process involved in adjusting deferred expenses and accrued expenses using prepaid insurance and wages expense as examples. AJE refers again to **adjusting journal entry.** Note that in both cases, the goal is to record expenses in the proper period. In addition, note that the adjusting journal entry involves one balance sheet and one income statement account, and cash is never affected. Cash was recorded when paid prior to the end of the period or will be recorded in a future period.

		Deferred Expenses	Accrued Expenses
During the period	Entry when **cash is paid before** company incurs expense	Prepaid insurance (+A) Cash (−A)	
End of period	**AJE** needed because company has incurred an expense during period	Insurance expense (+E, −SE) Prepaid insurance (−A)	Wages expense (+E, −SE) Wages payable (+L)
Next period	Entry when **cash is paid after** company incurs an expense		Wages payable (−L) Cash (−A)

EXHIBIT 4.4

Illustration of Adjusting Deferred and Accrued Expenses

Expenses recorded in the proper period!

The Adjustment Process

Throughout the rest of the text, you will discover that nearly every account on a company's balance sheet except cash will need to be adjusted, often requiring management to make judgments and estimates. In this chapter, we will illustrate common adjusting entries. To assist you in identifying and calculating adjusting entries,

- Think about the kinds of transactions that make balance sheet accounts increase and decrease. For example:

Supplies (A)	
+	−
Beginning bal.	
Purchase	*Use*
Ending Balance	

Accrued Expenses Payable (L)	
−	+
	Beginning bal.
Pay cash	*Accrue expense*
	Ending Balance

such as wages, interest, and taxes

■ Then follow three steps:

Step 1: Identify whether the adjustment is to an existing deferred revenue or expense or an unrecorded accrued revenue or expense. (Ask, "Was cash already received or paid prior to the end of the period—or—will cash be received or paid in the future?") If a deferred account is to be adjusted, show the T-account for the deferred revenue or expense account and its unadjusted balance.

Step 2: Compute the revenue earned or expense incurred in the accounting period.

Step 3: Record the adjusting journal entry. If you have difficulty determining the accounts to use, usually name the revenue or expense account for what it is, such as Interest Expense or Fee Revenue. The related asset or liability should be similar, such as Interest Payable or Unearned Fee Revenue.

Papa John's Illustration

Papa John's trial balance in Exhibit 4.2 lists several accounts that suggest adjusting entries are necessary. Note that you can identify them as deferrals or accruals by whether cash is received or paid in the past or future.

Account	Cash Received or Paid in the Past		Revenue Earned or Expense Incurred (during the month)		Cash to Be Received or Paid in the Future
Supplies	Deferred expense (*d*)	→	A portion of food and paper products purchased in the past has been used during the month.		
Prepaid Expenses	Deferred expense (*e*) (*f*)	→	All or a portion of the (1) prepaid insurance and (2) prepaid rent has been used by month-end.		
Accounts Receivable			Franchisees owe royalties to Papa John's from weekly sales at the franchises.	→	Accrued revenue (*b*)
Long-Term Notes Receivable			Franchisees owe interest on loans from Papa John's for purchasing and equipping new franchises, but no revenue has yet been recorded.	→	Accrued revenue (*c*)
Property and Equipment	Deferred expense (*g*)	→	The long-lived assets have been used during the month to generate revenues. A portion of their historical cost is recorded as an expense.		
Accrued Expenses Payable			Papa John's owes (1) wages to employees for work during the last week of January and (2) amounts due for utilities used during the month but not yet billed. Neither has yet been recorded as an expense.	→	Accrued expense (*h*) (*i*)
Unearned Franchise Fees	Deferred revenue (*a*)	→	All or a portion has been earned by month-end.		
Long-Term Notes Payable			Papa John's owes interest on borrowed funds.	→	Accrued expense (*j*)
Income Taxes Payable			Income tax expense needs to be recorded for the period.	→	Accrued expense (*k*)

We will now use the adjustment process to record adjusting entries for Papa John's at the end of January. The reference for each adjustment is noted in the preceding chart. Refer to Exhibits 4.3 and 4.4 for the examples of deferred revenues, accrued revenues, deferred expenses, and accrued expenses.

Deferred Revenues

(a) **Unearned Franchise Fees:** Papa John's performed $100 in additional services in January for new franchisees who had previously paid Papa John's.

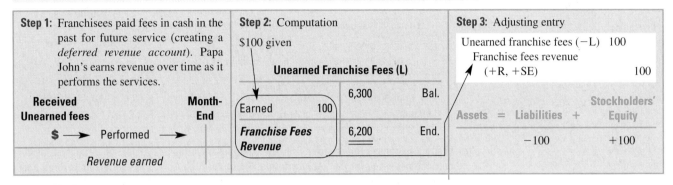

Accrued Revenues

(b) **Accounts Receivable:** Papa John's franchisees reported that they will pay Papa John's in February $830 in royalties for sales the franchisees made in the last week of January.

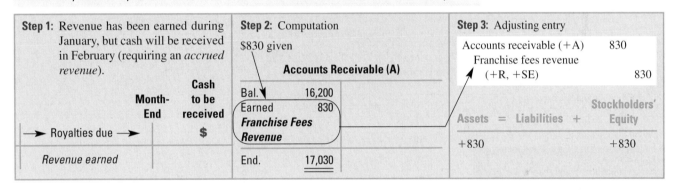

(c) **Notes Receivable (Interest):** Papa John's loaned $14,000 to franchisees in the past at 6 percent interest per year with interest to be paid at the end of each year. There are two components when lending money: **principal** and **interest**. Note principal was recorded properly when the money was loaned. However, interest revenue is earned over time as the money is used by the franchisees. It is important to note that **the interest rate is always given as an annual percentage.** To compute interest revenue for less than a full year, the number of months needed in the calculation is divided by 12.

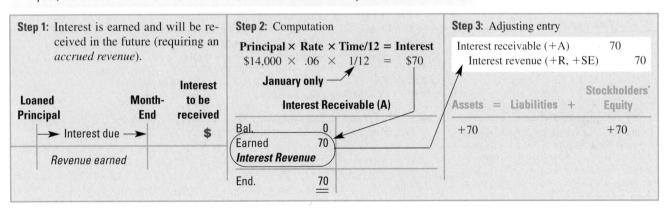

Deferred Expenses

(d) **Supplies:** Supplies include food and paper products. At the end of the month, Papa John's counted $12,000 in supplies on hand, but the Supplies account indicated a balance of $16,000 (from Exhibit 4.2). The difference is the supplies used during the month.

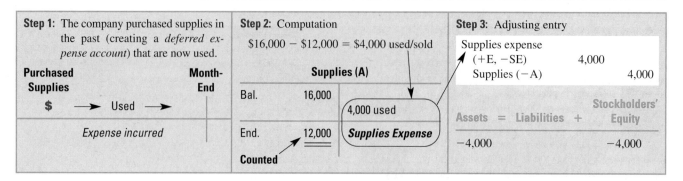

(e) **Prepaid Expenses (Insurance):** Prepaid Expenses includes $2,000 paid on January 1 for insurance coverage for four months from January through April. One month has expired and there remains three months of future insurance benefits. Used insurance is called Insurance Expense.

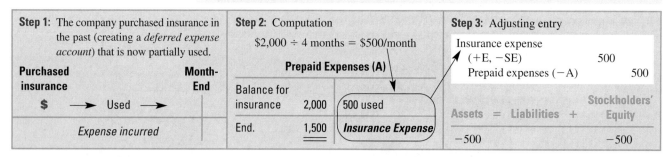

For (f), fill in the missing information. After you have completed your answers, check them with the solutions at the bottom of the page.

(f) **Prepaid Expenses (Rent):** Prepaid Expenses also includes $6,000 for rental of space at shopping centers over the next three months from January through March. One month has expired and two months of future rental benefits remain.

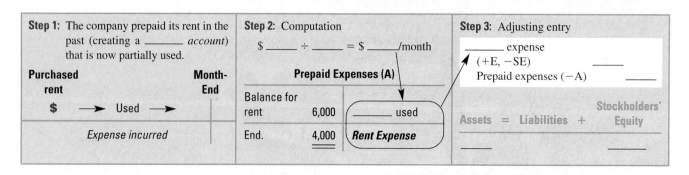

Self-Study Quiz Solutions

(f) **Step 1:** A deferred expense **Step 2:** Computation $6,000 ÷ 3 months = $2,000 used

Step 3: Adjusting entry
Rent expense (+E, −SE) 2,000
    Prepaid expenses (−A) 2,000

Assets	= Liabilities +	Stockholders' Equity
− 2,000		− 2,000

(g) Property and Equipment:

When buildings and equipment are used over time to generate revenues, a part of their cost should be expensed in the same period (the matching principle). Accountants say that buildings and equipment are **depreciated** over time as used. Depreciation expense is computed as an allocation of an asset's cost over its useful life to the company.

A common misconception held by students and others unfamiliar with accounting terminology is that depreciation reflects the asset's decline in market value. You may have heard the statement that a new car "depreciates" when it is driven off the dealer's lot. The car's market value has declined; it is now a "used" car. However, until the car is actually used to generate revenues, it has not depreciated from an accounting standpoint. **In accounting, depreciation is simply a cost allocation concept, not a way of reporting a reduction in market value.** Depreciation describes the portion of the asset's historical cost estimated to have been used during the period.

As previously discussed, a contra-account, Accumulated Depreciation, is used to accumulate the amount of the historical cost allocated to prior periods. It is directly related to the Property and Equipment account but has the opposite balance (a credit balance). Depreciation is discussed in more detail in Chapter 8. Now we illustrate depreciation for Papa John's.

Property and equipment have an historical cost of $362,000 at the end of the month. The accumulated depreciation of $149,000 is the used-up portion of the historical cost prior to this month. The depreciation is estimated to be $30,000 per year or $2,500 per month.

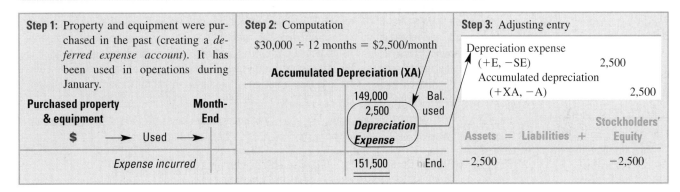

Accrued Expenses

(h) **Accrued Expenses Payable (Salaries):** Papa John's owed its employees salaries and benefits for working four days at the end of January at $500 per day. The employees will be paid during the first week in February.

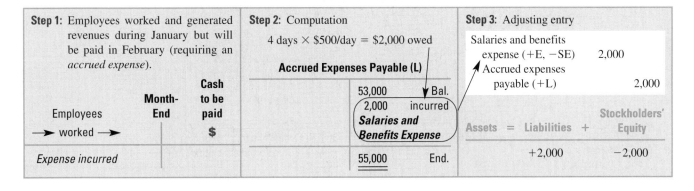

SELF-STUDY **QUIZ**

For (*i*), fill in the missing information. After you have completed your answers, check them with the solutions at the bottom of the page.

(*i*) **Accrued Expenses Payable (Utilities):** Papa John's estimated it owed $600 for gas and electricity used in January. The bill will be received and paid in February.

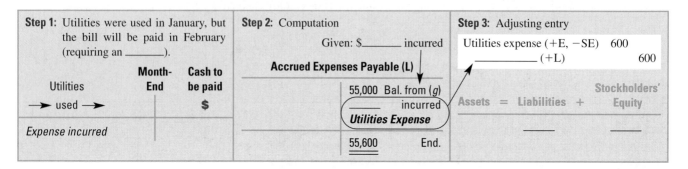

(*j*) **Notes Payable (Interest):** Papa John's borrowed $6,000 at the beginning of January, signing a note payable due in three years at 12 percent interest per year with interest to be paid at the end of each year. There are two components when borrowing money: **principal** and **interest**. Note that principal was recorded properly when the money was borrowed. However, interest expense is incurred over time as the bank's money is used. It is important to note that **the interest rate is always given as an annual percentage.** To compute interest expense for less than a full year, the number of months needed in the calculation is divided by 12.

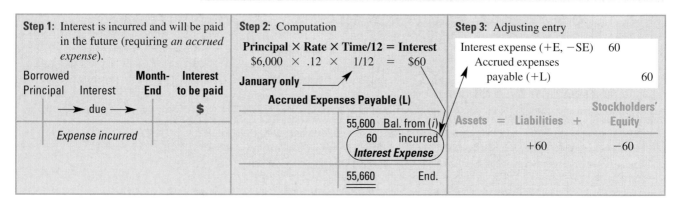

(*k*) **Income Taxes Payable:** The final adjusting journal entry is to record the accrual of income taxes that will be paid in the next quarter. This requires computing adjusted pretax income:

	Revenues and Gains	Expenses and Losses	
Unadjusted totals	$72,800	$51,000	From Exhibit 4.2
Adjustments (*a*)	100		
(*b*)	830		
(*c*)	70		
(*d*)		4,000	
(*e*)		500	
(*f*)		2,000	
(*g*)		2,500	
(*h*)		2,000	
(*i*)		600	
(*j*)		60	
	$73,800 −	$62,660	= **$11,140** Adjusted pretax income

Papa John's average income tax rate is 35 percent.

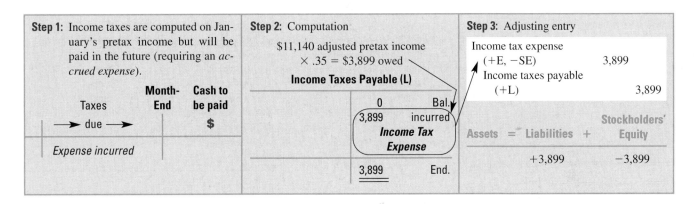

Step 1: Income taxes are computed on January's pretax income but will be paid in the future (requiring an *accrued expense*).

Taxes	Month-End	Cash to be paid
→ due →		$
Expense incurred		

Step 2: Computation

$11,140 adjusted pretax income
× .35 = $3,899 owed

Income Taxes Payable (L)

	0	Bal.
	3,899	incurred
	Income Tax Expense	
	3,899	End.

Step 3: Adjusting entry

Income tax expense		
(+E, −SE)	3,899	
Income taxes payable		
(+L)		3,899

Assets	=	Liabilities	+	Stockholders' Equity
		+3,899		−3,899

Adjustments and Incentives

A QUESTION OF ETHICS

Owners and managers of companies are most directly affected by the information presented in financial statements. If the financial performance and condition of the company appear strong, the company's stock price rises. Shareholders usually receive dividends and increase their investment value. Managers often receive bonuses based on the strength of a company's financial performance, and many in top management are compensated with options to buy their company's stock at prices below market.* The higher the market value, the more compensation they earn. When actual performance lags behind expectations, managers and owners may be tempted to manipulate accruals and deferrals to make up part of the difference. For example, managers may record cash received in advance of being earned as revenue in the current period or may fail to accrue certain expenses at year-end.

Evidence from studies of large samples of companies indicates that some managers do engage in such behavior. This research is borne out by enforcement actions of the Securities and Exchange Commission against companies and sometimes against their auditors. In January 2003, an SEC study reported that, in a five-year period, there were 227 enforcement investigations. Of these, "126 involved improper revenue recognition and 101 involved

continued

improper expense recognition. . . . Of the 227 enforcement matters during the Study period, 157 resulted in charges against at least one senior manager. . . . Furthermore, the Study found that 57 enforcement matters resulted in charges for auditing violations. . . ." (p. 47).[†]

In many of these cases, the firms involved, their managers, and their auditors are penalized for such actions. Furthermore, owners suffer because news of an SEC investigation negatively affects the company's stock price.

*M. Nelson, J. Elliott, and R. Tarpley, "How Are Earnings Managed? Examples from Auditors," Accounting Horizons, Supplement 2003, pp. 17–35.
[†]These statistics are reported in the Securities and Exchange Commission's study, "Report Pursuant to Section 704 of the Sarbanes-Oxley Act of 2002," January 27, 2003.

PREPARING FINANCIAL STATEMENTS

Learning Objective 3
Present an income statement with earnings per share, statement of stockholders' equity, balance sheet, and supplemental cash flow information.

Before we prepare a complete set of financial statements, let's update the trial balance to reflect the adjustments and provide us with adjusted balances for the statements.[2] In Exhibit 4.5, four new columns are added. Two are used to reflect the adjustments to each of the accounts. The other two are the updated balances, determined by adding (or subtracting) across each row. Again, we note that the total debits equal the total credits in each of the columns. It is from these adjusted balances that we will prepare an income statement, statement of stockholders' equity, and a balance sheet, with supplemental cash flow information to accompany the statement of cash flows.

Income Statement

The financial statements are interrelated. That is, the numbers in one statement flow into the next statement. Exhibit 4.6 presents the transaction analysis model from Chapter 3 simplified for illustrating the connections between the statements. Starting on the right, we see that net income is a component of Retained Earnings, Retained Earnings is a component of Stockholders' Equity, and Stockholders' Equity is a component on the balance sheet.

EXHIBIT 4.6

Relationships of the Financial Statements Using the Transaction Analysis Model

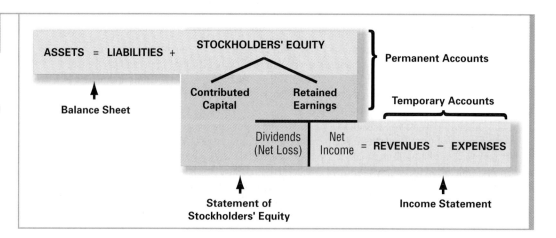

---

[2]For a discussion and illustration of the use of a worksheet for end-of-period adjustments, refer to Appendix E located on the website at www.mhhe.com/libby5e.

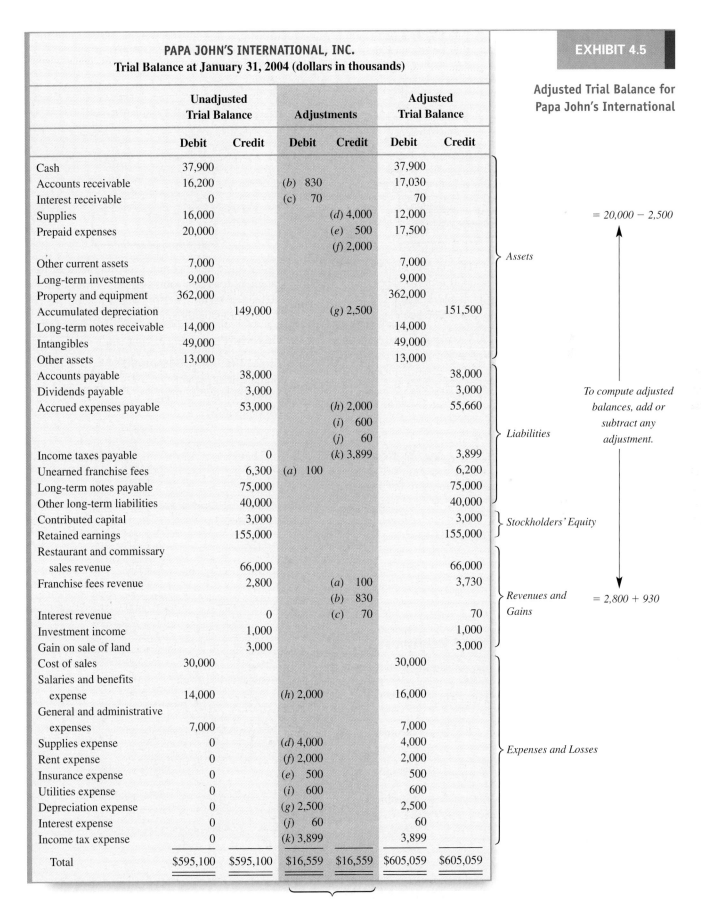

EXHIBIT 4.5

Adjusted Trial Balance for Papa John's International

PAPA JOHN'S INTERNATIONAL, INC.
Trial Balance at January 31, 2004 (dollars in thousands)

	Unadjusted Trial Balance		Adjustments		Adjusted Trial Balance	
	Debit	Credit	Debit	Credit	Debit	Credit
Cash	37,900				37,900	
Accounts receivable	16,200		(b) 830		17,030	
Interest receivable	0		(c) 70		70	
Supplies	16,000			(d) 4,000	12,000	
Prepaid expenses	20,000			(e) 500	17,500	
				(f) 2,000		
Other current assets	7,000				7,000	
Long-term investments	9,000				9,000	
Property and equipment	362,000				362,000	
Accumulated depreciation		149,000		(g) 2,500		151,500
Long-term notes receivable	14,000				14,000	
Intangibles	49,000				49,000	
Other assets	13,000				13,000	
Accounts payable		38,000				38,000
Dividends payable		3,000				3,000
Accrued expenses payable		53,000		(h) 2,000		55,660
				(i) 600		
				(j) 60		
Income taxes payable		0		(k) 3,899		3,899
Unearned franchise fees		6,300	(a) 100			6,200
Long-term notes payable		75,000				75,000
Other long-term liabilities		40,000				40,000
Contributed capital		3,000				3,000
Retained earnings		155,000				155,000
Restaurant and commissary sales revenue		66,000				66,000
Franchise fees revenue		2,800		(a) 100		3,730
				(b) 830		
Interest revenue		0		(c) 70		70
Investment income		1,000				1,000
Gain on sale of land		3,000				3,000
Cost of sales	30,000				30,000	
Salaries and benefits expense	14,000		(h) 2,000		16,000	
General and administrative expenses	7,000				7,000	
Supplies expense	0		(d) 4,000		4,000	
Rent expense	0		(f) 2,000		2,000	
Insurance expense	0		(e) 500		500	
Utilities expense	0		(i) 600		600	
Depreciation expense	0		(g) 2,500		2,500	
Interest expense	0		(j) 60		60	
Income tax expense	0		(k) 3,899		3,899	
Total	$595,100	$595,100	$16,559	$16,559	$605,059	$605,059

Assets

$= 20{,}000 - 2{,}500$

To compute adjusted balances, add or subtract any adjustment.

Liabilities

Stockholders' Equity

Revenues and Gains

$= 2{,}800 + 930$

Expenses and Losses

Effects of the adjusting entries

Another way of presenting the relationships among the statements follows. If a number on the income statement changes, it will impact the other statements.

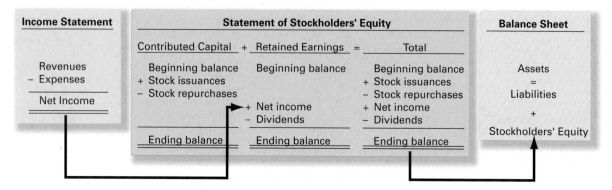

The income statement is prepared first because net income is a component of Retained Earnings. The January income statement for Papa John's based on transactions in Chapters 2 and 3 and adjustments in Chapter 4 follows. Note that a few of the expenses have been collapsed into specific categories on the income statement.

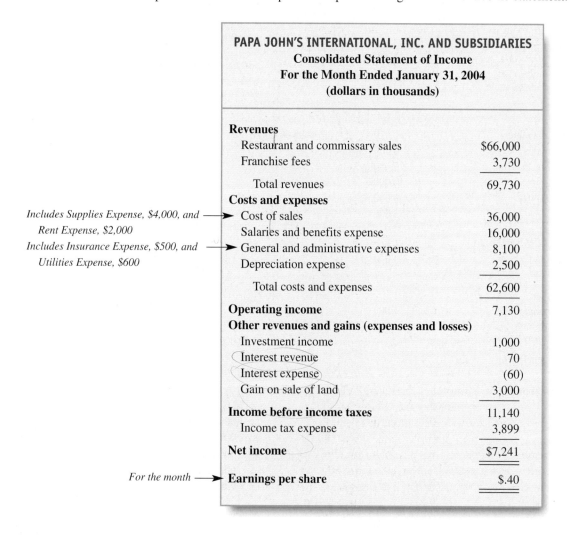

PAPA JOHN'S INTERNATIONAL, INC. AND SUBSIDIARIES	
Consolidated Statement of Income	
For the Month Ended January 31, 2004	
(dollars in thousands)	
Revenues	
Restaurant and commissary sales	$66,000
Franchise fees	3,730
Total revenues	69,730
Costs and expenses	
Cost of sales	36,000
Salaries and benefits expense	16,000
General and administrative expenses	8,100
Depreciation expense	2,500
Total costs and expenses	62,600
Operating income	7,130
Other revenues and gains (expenses and losses)	
Investment income	1,000
Interest revenue	70
Interest expense	(60)
Gain on sale of land	3,000
Income before income taxes	11,140
Income tax expense	3,899
Net income	$7,241
Earnings per share	$.40

Includes Supplies Expense, $4,000, and Rent Expense, $2,000

Includes Insurance Expense, $500, and Utilities Expense, $600

For the month

You will note that the earnings per share (EPS) ratio is reported on the income statement. It is widely used in evaluating the operating performance and profitability of a company, and it is the only ratio required to be disclosed on the statement or in the notes to the statements. Earnings per share is computed as:

$$\text{Earnings per Share} = \frac{\text{Net Income Available to the Common Stockholders}}{\text{Weighted Average Number of Shares of Common Stock Outstanding during the Period}}$$

Since the computation of the denominator is complex and appropriate for more advanced accounting courses, we will use the information provided by Papa John's actual annual report for 2003. The weighted average number of shares of stock outstanding was approximately 17,938,000. For simplicity, we use this same denominator in the computations of the earnings per share shown on the income statement.

$$\frac{\$7,241,000 \text{ Net Income}}{17,938,000 \text{ Shares}} = \$.40 \text{ earnings per share for the month}$$

Statement of Stockholders' Equity

The final total from the income statement, net income, is carried forward to the Retained Earnings column of the statement of stockholders' equity. To this, the additional elements of the statement are added. Dividends declared and an additional stock issuance from prior chapters are also included in the statement:

PAPA JOHN'S INTERNATIONAL, INC. AND SUBSIDIARIES
Consolidated Statement of Stockholders' Equity
For the Month Ended January 31, 2004
(dollars in thousands)

	Contributed Capital	Retained Earnings	Stockholders' Equity
Beginning balance	$1,000	$158,000	$159,000
Stock issuance	2,000		2,000
Net income		7,241	7,241 ← *From the income statement*
Dividends		(3,000)	(3,000)
Ending balance	$3,000	$162,241	$165,241

Balance Sheet

The ending balances for contributed capital and retained earnings from the statement of stockholders' equity are included on the balance sheet. You will notice that the contra-asset account, Accumulated Depreciation, has been subtracted from the Property and Equipment account to reflect net book value (or carrying value) at month-end for balance sheet purposes. Also recall that assets are listed in order of liquidity, and liabilities are listed in order of due dates. Current assets are those used or turned into cash within one year (as well as inventory). Current liabilities are obligations to be paid with current assets within one year.

PAPA JOHN'S INTERNATIONAL, INC. AND SUBSIDIARIES
Consolidated Balance Sheet
January 31, 2004
(dollars in thousands)

Assets

Current assets

Cash	$ 37,900
Accounts receivable	17,030
Interest receivable	70
Supplies	12,000
Prepaid expenses	17,500
Other current assets	7,000
Total current assets	91,500
Long-term investments	9,000
Property and equipment (net of accumulated depreciation of $151,500)	210,500
Long-term notes receivable	14,000
Intangibles	49,000
Other assets	13,000
Total assets	$387,000

Liabilities and Stockholders' Equity

Current liabilities

Accounts payable	$38,000
Dividends payable	3,000
Accrued expenses payable	55,660
Income taxes payable	3,899
Total current liabilities	100,559
Unearned franchise fees	6,200
Long-term notes payable	75,000
Other long-term liabilities	40,000
Total liabilities	221,759

Stockholders' equity

Contributed capital	3,000
Retained earnings	162,241
Total stockholders' equity	165,241
Total liabilities and stockholders' equity	$387,000

From the Statement of Stockholders' Equity → **Total stockholders' equity**

**FOCUS ON
CASH FLOWS**

Disclosure

As presented in the previous chapters, the statement of cash flows explains the difference between the ending and beginning balances in the Cash account on the balance sheet during the accounting period. Put simply, the cash flow statement is a categorized list of all transactions of the period that affected the Cash account. The three categories are operating, investing, and financing activities. Since no adjustments made in this chapter affected cash, the statement of cash flows presented for Papa John's at the end of Chapter 3 has not changed.

For complete disclosure, however, companies are required to provide additional information on the statement itself or in the notes to the statements.

In General → Disclosure (on the statement or in the notes): (1) interest paid, (2) income taxes paid, and (3) a schedule of the nature and amounts of significant noncash transactions (e.g., land exchanged for stock, acquisition of a building by signing a long-term mortgage payable).

Focus Company Analysis → For meeting the disclosure requirement using our Papa John's illustration, no significant noncash transactions and no income taxes or interest were paid during January. In the notes to its actual 2003 annual report, Papa John's disclosed $6.9 million in interest paid and $23.2 million in income taxes paid. No significant noncash transactions were disclosed.

Cash Flows from Operations, Net Income, and the Quality of Earnings

FINANCIAL
ANALYSIS

Many standard financial analysis texts warn analysts to look for unusual deferrals and accruals when they attempt to predict future periods' earnings. They often suggest that wide disparities between net income and cash flow from operations is a useful warning sign. For example, Wild et. al. suggest that

> Cash flows are often less subject to distortion than is net income. Accounting accruals determining net income rely on estimates, deferrals, allocations, and valuations. These considerations typically admit more subjectivity than factors determining cash flows. For this reason we often relate cash flows from operations to net income in assessing its quality. *Certain users consider earnings of higher quality when the ratio of cash flows from operations divided by net income is greater.* This derives from a concern with revenue recognition or expense accrual criteria yielding high net income but low cash flows. (emphasis added)[*]

The cash flows from operations to net income ratio is illustrated and discussed in more depth in Chapter 13.

[*]*J. Wild, K. Subramanyan, and R. Halsey,* Financial Statement Analysis *(New York, McGraw-Hill/Irwin, 2004), p. 394.*

Net Profit Margin

KEY RATIO
ANALYSIS

In Chapter 2, we introduced the financial leverage ratio to examine managers' use of debt as a tool to increase resources that would generate more profit for the shareholders. In Chapter 3, we introduced the total asset turnover ratio to examine managers' effectiveness at utilizing assets efficiently to generate more revenues for the shareholders. Now let's examine the third ratio, net profit margin, to examine managers' effectiveness at controlling revenues and expenses to generate more profit for the shareholders. These three ratios are the primary components of Return on Equity to shareholders to be discussed in Chapter 5.

Learning Objective 4
Compute and interpret the net profit margin.

? ANALYTICAL QUESTION:
How effective is management in generating profit on every dollar of sales?

% RATIO AND COMPARISONS:

$$\text{Net Profit Margin} = \frac{\text{Net Income}}{\text{Net Sales (or Operating Revenues)}^*}$$

The 2003 ratio for Papa John's using actual reported amounts:

$$\frac{\$33,563,000}{\$917,378,000} = .0366 \ (3.66\%)$$

Selected Focus Companies' Net Profit Margin Ratios for 2003

Dow Jones	11.0%
Harley-Davidson	16.5%
Wal-Mart Stores	3.5%

COMPARISONS OVER TIME		
Papa John's		
2001	**2002**	**2003**
4.85%	4.95%	3.66%

COMPARISONS WITH COMPETITORS	
Domino's Inc.	**Yum! Brands[†]**
2003	**2003**
2.92%	7.36

💡 INTERPRETATIONS:

In General → Net profit margin measures how much of every sales dollar generated during the period is profit. A rising net profit margin signals more efficient management of sales and expenses. Differences among industries result from the nature of the products or services provided and the intensity of competition. Differences among competitors in the same industry reflect how each company responds to changes in competition (and demand for the product or service) and changes in managing sales volume, sales price, and costs. Financial analysts expect well-run businesses to maintain or improve their net profit margin over time.

Focus Company Analysis → Papa John's net profit margin decreased in 2003, suggesting difficulties in the control of sales and costs. While operating revenues steadily declined over the period, salaries and benefits, advertising, and restaurant closure losses increased in 2003, causing higher expenses. In the Management's Discussion and Analysis section of the annual report, Papa John's noted, among other factors, increases in salaries and benefits resulting from base pay increases for managers.

Domino's is Papa John's main competitor in the delivery segment of the pizza business. Domino's has a 20 percent lower net profit margin at 2.92%. This may suggest reduced efficiency in commissary activities by Domino's. On the other hand, Yum! Brands has a 7.36 percent net profit margin, double Papa John's. Yum! Brands operates dine-in, take-out, and delivery restaurants that rely more heavily on facilities. Differences in business strategies explain some of the variation in the ratio analysis.

A Few Cautions: The decisions that management makes to maintain the company's net profit margin in the current period may have negative long-run implications. Analysts should perform additional analysis of the ratio to identify trends in each component of revenues and expenses. This involves dividing each line on the income statement by net sales. Statements presented with these percentages are called **common-sized income statements.** Changes in the percentages of the individual components of net income provide information on shifts in management's strategies.

*Net sales is sales revenue less any returns from customers and other reductions. For companies in the service industry, total operating revenues is equivalent to net sales.
†Yum! Brands is the parent company of Pizza Hut, KFC, and Taco Bell.

PERMANENT (REAL) ACCOUNTS are the balance sheet accounts that carry their ending balances into the next accounting period.

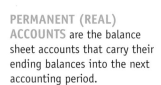

Learning Objective 5
Explain the closing process.

Topic Tackler 4–2

TEMPORARY (NOMINAL) ACCOUNTS are income statement accounts that are closed to Retained Earnings at the end of the accounting period.

CLOSING ENTRY transfers balances in temporary accounts to Retained Earnings and establishes zero balances in temporary accounts.

CLOSING THE BOOKS

End of the Accounting Cycle

The ending balance in each of the asset, liability, and stockholders' equity accounts becomes the beginning account balance for the next period. These accounts, called **permanent** or **real accounts** (shown in Exhibit 4.6), are not reduced to a zero balance at the end of the accounting period. For example, the ending Cash balance of the prior accounting period is the beginning Cash balance of the next accounting period. The only time a permanent account has a zero balance is when the item it represents is no longer owned or owed.

On the other hand, revenue, expense, gain, and loss accounts are used to accumulate data for the **current accounting period only;** they are called **temporary** or **nominal accounts** (see Exhibit 4.6). The final step in the accounting cycle, closing the books, is done to prepare income statement accounts for the next accounting cycle. Therefore, at the end of each period, the balances in the temporary accounts are transferred, or **closed,** to the Retained Earnings account by recording a closing entry.

The **closing entry** has two purposes:

1. To transfer net income or loss to Retained Earnings.[3]

2. To establish a zero balance in each of the temporary accounts to start the accumulation in the next accounting period.

---

[3]Companies may close income statement accounts to a special temporary summary account, called *Income Summary,* that is then closed to Retained Earnings.

In this way, the income statement accounts are again ready for their temporary accumulation function for the next period. The closing entry is dated the last day of the accounting period, entered in the usual debits-equal-credits format (in the journal), and immediately posted to the ledger (or T-accounts). Temporary accounts with debit balances are credited and accounts with credit balances are debited. The net amount, equal to net income, affects Retained Earnings.

To illustrate the process, we create an example using just a few accounts. The journal entry amounts are taken from the pre-closing balances in the T-accounts:

Sales revenue (−R)	100	
Gain on sale of assets (−R)	30	
Wages expense (−E)		40
Loss on sale of assets (−E)		10
Retained earnings (+SE)		80

Wages Expense			
Bal.	40	40	CE
Closed balance	0		

Retained Earnings			
		6,000	Bal.
		80	CE
		6,080	Bal.

Sales Revenue			
CE	100	100	Bal.
		0	Closed balance

Loss on Sale of Assets			
Bal.	10	10	CE
Closed balance	0		

130 debits − 50 credits = 80 credit

Gain on Sale of Assets			
CE	30	30	Bal.
		0	Closed balance

We will now illustrate closing the books by preparing the closing entry for Papa John's at January 31, 2004, although companies close their records only at the end of the fiscal year.[4] These amounts are taken from the adjusted trial balance in Exhibit 4.5.

Restaurant and commissary sales revenue (−R)	66,000	
Franchise fees revenue (−R)	3,730	
Interest revenue (−R)	70	
Investment income (−R)	1,000	
Gain on sale of land (−R)	3,000	
Cost of sales (−E)		30,000
Salaries and benefits expense (−E)		16,000
General and administrative expenses (−E)		7,000
Supplies expense (−E)		4,000
Rent expense (−E)		2,000
Insurance expense (−E)		500
Utilities expense (−E)		600
Depreciation expense (−E)		2,500
Interest expense (−E)		60
Income tax expense (−E)		3,899
Retained earnings (+SE)		7,241

[4]Most companies use computerized accounting software to record journal entries, produce trial balances and financial statements, and close the books.

SELF-STUDY **QUIZ**

The following is an adjusted trial balance from a recent year for Toys "R" Us. Dollars are in millions. Record the closing journal entry at the end of the accounting cycle to close the books. You can check your answer with the solution at the bottom of the page.

	DEBIT	CREDIT
Cash	2,003	
Accounts receivable	146	
Buildings	6,719	
Accumulated depreciation		1,984
Other assets	3,334	
Accounts payable		991
Notes payable		2,349
Other liabilities		2,656
Contributed capital		437
Retained earnings		3,698
Sales revenue		11,565
Interest income		15
Gain on sale of business		3
Cost of sales	7,849	
Selling, general, and administrative expenses	3,022	
Depreciation expense	348	
Other operating expenses	85	
Interest expense	142	
Income tax expense	50	
Totals	**23,698**	**23,698**

Closing entry:

Post-Closing Trial Balance

A **POST-CLOSING TRIAL BALANCE** should be prepared as the last step of the accounting cycle to check that debits equal credits and all temporary accounts have been closed.

After the closing process is complete, all income statement accounts have a zero balance. These accounts are then ready for recording revenues and expenses in the new accounting period. The ending balance in Retained Earnings now is up-to-date (matches the amount on the balance sheet) and is carried forward as the beginning balance for the next period. As the last step of the accounting information processing cycle, a **post-closing trial balance** (Exhibit 4.7) should be prepared as a check that debits still equal credits and that all temporary accounts have been closed.

Self-Study Quiz
Solutions

Sales revenue (−R)	11,565	
Interest income (−R)	15	
Gain on sale of business (−R)	3	
Cost of sales (−E)		7,849
Selling, general, and administrative expenses (−E)		3,022
Depreciation expense (−E)		348
Other operating expenses (−E)		85
Interest expense (−E)		142
Income tax expense (−E)		50
Retained earnings (+SE)		87

EXHIBIT 4.7

Post-Closing Trial Balance for
Papa John's International

PAPA JOHN'S INTERNATIONAL, INC.
Trial Balance
At January 31, 2004 (dollars in thousands)

	Adjusted Trial Balance		Post-Closing Trial Balance	
	Debit	**Credit**	**Debit**	**Credit**
Cash	37,900		37,900	
Accounts receivable	17,030		17,030	
Interest receivable	70		70	
Supplies	12,000		12,000	
Prepaid expenses	17,500		17,500	
Other current assets	7,000		7,000	
Long-term investments	9,000		9,000	
Property and equipment	362,000		362,000	
Accumulated depreciation		151,500		151,500
Long-term notes receivable	14,000		14,000	
Intangibles	49,000		49,000	
Other assets	13,000		13,000	
Accounts payable		38,000		38,000
Dividends payable		3,000		3,000
Accrued expenses payable		55,660		55,660
Income taxes payable		3,899		3,899
Unearned franchise fees		6,200		6,200
Long-term notes payable		75,000		75,000
Other long-term liabilities		40,000		40,000
Contributed capital		3,000		3,000
Retained earnings		155,000		162,241
Restaurant and commissary sales revenue		66,000		0
Franchise fees revenue		3,730		0
Interest revenue		70		0
Investment income		1,000		0
Gain on sale of land		3,000		0
Cost of sales	30,000		0	
Salaries and benefits expense	16,000		0	
General and administrative expenses	7,000		0	
Supplies expense	4,000		0	
Rent expense	2,000		0	
Insurance expense	500		0	
Utilities expense	600		0	
Depreciation expense	2,500		0	
Interest expense	60		0	
Income tax expense	3,899		0	
Total	$605,059	$605,059	$538,500	$538,500

Assets

Liabilities

Stockholders' Equity

Revenues and Gains

Expenses and Losses

*Net income of $7,241 is closed to Retained Earnings:
$155,000 + $7,241 = $162,241*

FINANCIAL
ANALYSIS

Accruals and Deferrals: Judging Earnings Quality

Most of the adjustments discussed in this chapter, such as the allocation of prepaid insurance or the determination of accrued interest expense, involve direct calculations and require little judgment on the part of the company's management. In later chapters, we discuss many other adjustments that involve difficult and complex estimates about the future. These include, for example, estimates of customers' ability to make payments to the company for purchases on account, the useful lives of new machines, and future amounts that a company may owe on warranties of products sold in the past. Each of these estimates and many others can have significant effects on the stream of net earnings that companies report over time.

When attempting to value firms based on their balance sheet and income statement data, analysts also evaluate the estimates that form the basis for the adjustments. Those firms that make relatively pessimistic estimates that reduce current income are judged to follow *conservative* financial reporting strategies, and experienced analysts give these reports more credence. The earnings numbers reported by these companies are often said to be of "higher quality" because they are less influenced by management's natural optimism. Firms that consistently make optimistic estimates that result in reporting higher net income, however, are judged to be *aggressive*. Analysts judge these companies' operating performance to be of lower quality.

DEMONSTRATION CASE

We take our final look at the accounting activities of Terrific Lawn Maintenance Corporation by illustrating the activities at the end of the accounting cycle: the adjustment process, financial statement preparation, and the closing process. No adjustments had been made to the accounts to reflect all revenues earned and expenses incurred in April. The trial balance for Terrific Lawn on April 30, 2007, based on the unadjusted balances in Chapter 3, is as follows:

TERRIFIC LAWN MAINTENANCE CORPORATION		
Unadjusted Trial Balance		
At April 30, 2007		
	Debit	**Credit**
Cash	5,032	
Accounts receivable	1,700	
Notes receivable	0	
Prepaid expenses	300	
Land	3,750	
Equipment	4,600	
Accumulated depreciation		0
Accounts payable		220
Accrued expenses payable		0
Notes payable		3,700
Income taxes payable		0
Unearned revenues		1,600
		continued

Contributed capital		9,000
Retained earnings		0
Mowing revenue		5,200
Interest revenue		12
Wages expense	3,900	
Fuel expense	410	
Insurance expense	0	
Utilities expense	0	
Depreciation expense	0	
Interest expense	40	
Income tax expense	0	
Total	$19,732	$19,732

Additional Information

a. One-fourth of the $1,600 cash received from the city at the beginning of April for future mowing service has been earned in April. The $1,600 in Unearned Revenues represents four months of service (April through July).

b. Insurance costing $300 providing coverage for six months (April through September) paid by Terrific Lawn at the beginning of April has been partially used in April.

c. Mowers, edgers, rakes, and hand tools (equipment) have been used in April to generate revenues. The company estimates $300 in depreciation each year.

d. Wages have been paid through April 28. Employees worked the last two days of April and will be paid in May. Wages accrue at $200 per day.

e. An extra telephone line was installed in April at an estimated cost of $52, including hookup and usage charges. The bill will be received and paid in May.

f. Interest accrues on the outstanding notes payable at an annual rate of 12 percent. The $3,700 in principal has been outstanding all month.

g. The estimated income tax rate for Terrific Lawn is 35 percent.

Required:

1. Identify deferred revenue, accrued revenue, deferred expense, and accrued expense accounts for items (*a*) through (*g*).

2. Using the process outlined in this chapter, analyze and record adjusting journal entries for April.

3. Prepare an adjusted trial balance.

4. Prepare an income statement, statement of stockholders' equity, and balance sheet from the amounts in the adjusted trial balance. Include earnings per share on the income statement. The company issued 1,500 shares. Also prepare a schedule of supplemental disclosure for the statement of cash flows. If none is necessary, so indicate.

5. Prepare the closing entry for April 30, 2007.

6. Compute the company's net profit margin for the month.

Now you can check your answers with the following solution to these requirements.

SUGGESTED SOLUTION

1.

Item	Account to be Adjusted	Type of Adjustment	Explanation
a.	Unearned Revenues	Deferred revenue	Cash was received prior to being earned.
b.	Prepaid Expenses	Deferred expense	Cash was paid for insurance prior to being used.
c.	Accumulated Depreciation	Deferred expense	Long-lived assets were purchased and used.
d.	Accrued Expenses Payable (Wages)	Accrued expense	Cash will be paid to employees in the future.
e.	Accrued Expenses Payable (Utilities)	Accrued expense	Cash will be paid for utilities in the future.
f.	Accrued Expenses Payable (Interest)	Accrued expense	Cash will be paid for interest in the future.
g.	Income Taxes Payable	Accrued expense	Taxes will be paid in the future.

2. Analysis of deferrals and accruals and related adjusting entries:

Deferred Revenue

a. One-fourth of the $1,600 cash received from the city at the beginning of April for future mowing service has been earned in April. The $1,600 in Unearned Revenues represents four months of service (April through July).

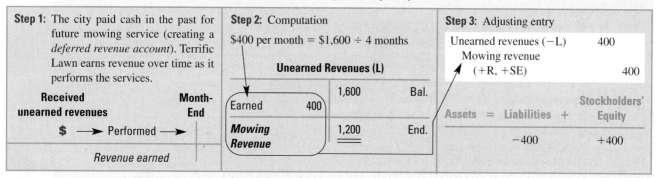

Deferred Expenses

b. Insurance costing $300 providing coverage for six months (April through September) paid by Terrific Lawn at the beginning of April has been partially used in April.

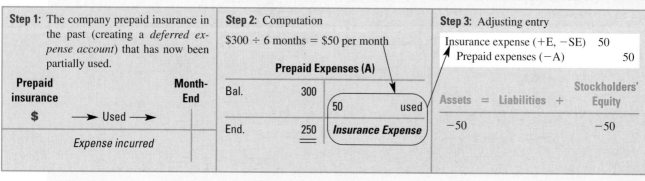

c. Mowers, edgers, rakes, and hand tools (equipment) have been used in April to generate revenues. The company estimates $300 in depreciation each year.

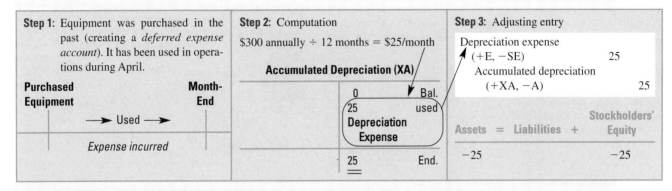

Accrued Expenses

d. Wages have been paid through April 28. Employees worked the last two days of April and will be paid in May. Wages accrue at $200 per day.

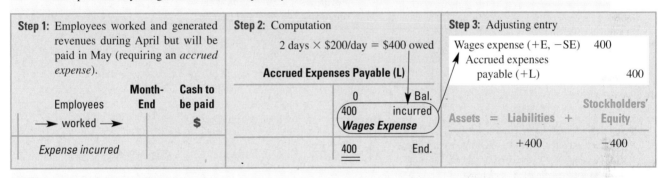

e. An extra telephone line was installed in April at an estimated cost of $52, including hookup and usage charges. The bill will be received and paid in May.

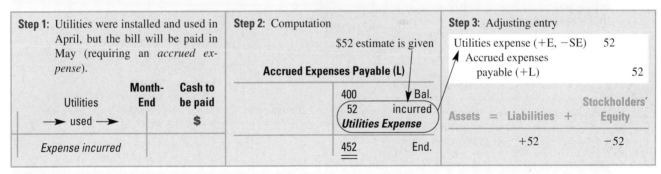

f. Interest accrues on the outstanding notes payable at an annual rate of 12 percent. The $3,700 in principal has been outstanding all month.

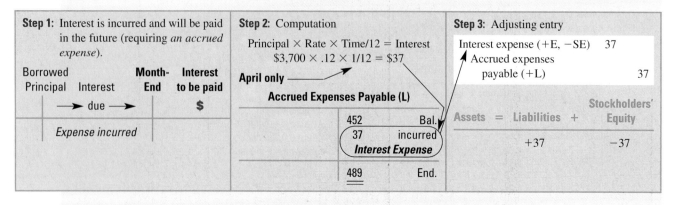

g. The estimated income tax rate for Terrific Lawn is 35 percent.

Computation of adjusted pretax income:

	Revenues and Gains	Expenses and Losses	
Unadjusted totals	$5,212	$4,350	From Chapter 3
Adjustments: (*a*)	400		
(*b*)		50	
(*c*)		25	
(*d*)		400	
(*e*)		52	
(*f*)		37	
	$5,612 −	$4,914	= **$698** Adjusted pretax income

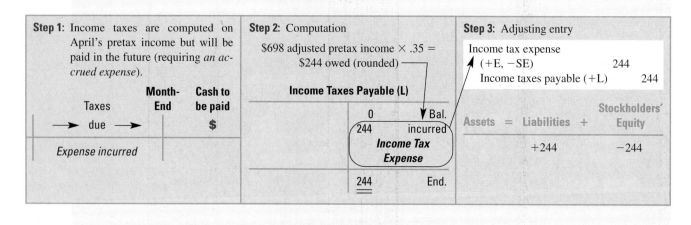

3. Adjusted trial balance:

TERRIFIC LAWN MAINTENANCE CORPORATION
Adjusted Trial Balance
At April 30, 2007

	Unadjusted Trial Balance		Adjustments		Adjusted Trial Balance	
	Debit	**Credit**	**Debit**	**Credit**	**Debit**	**Credit**
Cash	5,032				5,032	
Accounts receivable	1,700				1,700	
Notes receivable	0				0	
Prepaid expenses	300			(b) 50	250	
Land	3,750				3,750	
Equipment	4,600				4,600	
Accumulated depreciation		0		(c) 25		25
Accounts payable		220				220
Accrued expenses payable		0		(d) 400		489
				(e) 52		
				(f) 37		
Notes payable		3,700				3,700
Income taxes payable		0		(g) 244		244
Unearned revenues		1,600	(a) 400			1,200
Contributed capital		9,000				9,000
Retained earnings		0				0
Mowing revenue		5,200		(a) 400		5,600
Interest revenue		12				12
Wages expense	3,900		(d) 400		4,300	
Fuel expense	410				410	
Insurance expense	0		(b) 50		50	
Utilities expense	0		(e) 52		52	
Depreciation expense	0		(c) 25		25	
Interest expense	40		(f) 37		77	
Income tax expense	0		(g) 244		244	
Total	$19,732	$19,732	$1,208	$1,208	$20,490	$20,490

4. Financial statements

TERRIFIC LAWN MAINTENANCE CORPORATION
Income Statement
For the Month Ended April 30, 2007

Operating Revenues	
Mowing revenue	$5,600
Operating Expenses	
Fuel expense	410
Wages expense	4,300
Insurance expense	50
Utilities expense	52
Depreciation expense	25
	4,837
Operating income	763
Other items	
Interest revenue	12
Interest expense	(77)
Pretax income	698
Income tax expense	244
Net Income	**$ 454**
Earnings per share ($454 ÷ 1,500 shares)	**$.30**

TERRIFIC LAWN MAINTENANCE CORPORATION
Statement of Stockholders' Equity
For the Month Ended April 30, 2007

	Contributed Capital	Retained Earnings	Total
Balance, April 1, 2007	$ 0	$ 0	$ 0
Stock issuance	9,000		9,000
Net income		454	454
Dividends		0	0
Balance, April 30, 2007	**$9,000**	**$454**	**$9,454**

TERRIFIC LAWN MAINTENANCE CORPORATION
Balance Sheet
April 30, 2007

Assets		**Liabilities**	
Current Assets		Current Liabilities	
Cash	$ 5,032	Accounts payable	$ 220
Accounts receivable	1,700	Accrued expenses payable	489
Prepaid expenses	250	Notes payable	3,700
Total current assets	6,982	Income taxes payable	244
		Unearned revenues	1,200
		Total current liabilities	5,853
Equipment (net of $25			
accumulated depreciation)	4,575		
Land	3,750	**Stockholders' Equity**	
		Contributed capital	9,000
		Retained earnings	454
		Total liabilities and	
Total assets	**$15,307**	**stockholders' equity**	**$15,307**

Statement of Cash Flows—Disclosure
Interest paid—$40.
No income taxes were paid.
There were no significant noncash transactions.

5. Closing entry:

Mowing revenue (−R)	5,600	
Interest revenue (−R)	12	
Wages expense (−E)		4,300
Fuel expense (−E)		410
Insurance expense (−E)		50
Utilities expense (−E)		52
Depreciation expense (−E)		25
Interest expense (−E)		77
Income tax expense (−E)		244
Retained earnings (+SE)		454

6. Net Profit Margin for April:

$$\frac{\text{Net Income}}{\text{Net Sales}} = \$454 \div \$5,600 = 8.1\% \text{ for the month of April.}$$

CHAPTER TAKE-AWAYS

1. Explain the purpose of a trial balance. p. 167

A trial balance is a list of all accounts with their debit or credit balances indicated in the appropriate column to provide a check on the equality of the debits and credits. The trial balance may be

- Unadjusted—before adjustments are made.
- Adjusted—after adjustments are made.
- Post-closing—after revenues and expenses are closed to Retained Earnings.

2. Analyze the adjustments necessary at the end of the period to update balance sheet and income statements accounts. p. 169

- Adjusting entries are necessary at the end of the accounting period to measure income properly, correct errors, and provide for adequate valuation of balance sheet accounts. The analysis involves
  a. Identifying deferred accounts (created in the past when cash was received or paid before being earned or incurred) and accrued accounts (revenues earned and expenses incurred before cash is received or paid; cash will be received or paid in the future).
  b. Drawing a timeline and setting up T-accounts with any computations.
  c. Recording the adjusting entry needed to obtain the appropriate ending balances in the accounts.
- Recording adjusting entries has no effect on the Cash account.

3. Present an income statement with earnings per share, statement of stockholders' equity, balance sheet, and supplemental cash flow information. p. 178

Adjusted account balances are used in preparing the following financial statements:

- Income Statement: Revenues − Expenses = Net Income (including earnings per share computed as net income available to the common stockholders divided by the weighted average number of shares of common stock outstanding during the period).
- Statement of Stockholders' Equity: (Beginning Contributed Capital + Stock Issuances − Stock Repurchases) + (Beginning Retained Earnings + Net Income − Dividends) = Ending Total Stockholders' Equity.
- Balance Sheet: Assets = Liabilities + Stockholders' Equity.
- Supplemental cash flow information: Interest paid, income taxes paid, and significant noncash transactions.

4. Compute and interpret the net profit margin. p. 183

Net profit margin (Net Income ÷ Net Sales) measures how much of every dollar of sales generated during the period is profit. A rising net profit margin signals more efficient management of sales and expenses.

FOR DEFERRED ACCOUNTS— Adjusting Entry:
↓ Liability and ↑ Revenue
or
↑ Expense and ↓ Asset

FOR ACCRUED ACCOUNTS— Adjusting Entry:
↑ Expense and ↑ Liability
or
↑ Asset and ↑ Revenue

Closing Entry:

Each revenue	xx
Each gain	xx
Each expense	xx
Each loss	xx
Retained earnings	xx

(assumes net income is positive)

5. Explain the closing process.   p. 184

Temporary accounts (revenues, expenses, gains, and losses) are closed to a zero balance at the end of the accounting period to allow for the accumulation of income items in the following period. To close these accounts, debit each revenue and gain account, credit each expense and loss account, and record the difference (equal to net income) to Retained Earnings.

This chapter discussed the important steps in the accounting process that take place at year-end. These include the adjustment process, the preparation of the basic financial statements, and the closing process that prepares the records for the next accounting period. This end to the internal portions of the accounting process, however, is just the beginning of the process of communicating accounting information to external users.

In the next chapter we take a closer look at more sophisticated financial statements and related disclosures. We also examine the process by which financial information is disseminated to professional analysts, investors, the Securities and Exchange Commission, and the public, and the role each plays in analyzing and interpreting the information. These discussions will help you consolidate much of what you have learned about the financial reporting process from previous chapters. It will also preview many of the important issues we address later in the book.

KEY **RATIO**

Net profit margin measures how much of every sales dollar generated during the period is profit. A high or rising ratio suggests that the company is managing its sales and expenses efficiently. It is computed as follows (p. 183):

$$\text{Net Profit Margin} = \frac{\text{Net Income}}{\text{Net Sales (or Operating Revenues)}}$$

FINDING **FINANCIAL INFORMATION**

Balance Sheet

Current Assets
Accruals include:
   Interest receivable
   Rent receivable
Deferrals include:
   Supplies
   Prepaid expenses

Noncurrent Assets
Deferrals include:
   Property and equipment
   Intangibles

Current Liabilities
Accruals include:
   Interest payable
   Wages payable
   Utilities payable
   Income tax payable
Deferrals include:
   Unearned revenue

Income Statement

Revenues
   Increased by adjusting entries

Expenses
   Increased by adjusting entries

Pretax Income
   Income tax expense

Net Income

Statement of Cash Flows

Adjusting Entries Do Not Affect Cash
Supplemental Disclosure:
   Interest paid
   Income taxes paid
   Significant noncash transactions

Notes

In Various Notes if Not on the Balance Sheet
Details of accrued expenses payable
Interest paid, income taxes paid,
   significant noncash transactions
   (if not reported on the statement of
   cash flows)

KEY TERMS

Accounting Cycle p. 167
Accrued Expenses p. 171
Accrued Revenues p. 170
Adjusting Entries p. 169
Closing Entries p. 184
Contra-Account p. 168

Deferred Expenses p. 170
Deferred Revenues p. 169
Net Book Value (Book Value,
  Carrying Value) p. 169
Permanent (Real)
  Accounts p. 184

Post-Closing Trial Balance p. 186
Temporary (Nominal)
  Accounts p. 184
Trial Balance p. 167

QUESTIONS

1. What is a trial balance? What is its purpose?
2. Briefly explain adjusting entries. List the four types of adjusting entries, and give an example of each type.
3. What is a contra-asset? Give an example of one.
4. Explain how the financial statements relate to each other.
5. What is the equation for each of the following statements: (a) income statement, (b) balance sheet, (c) statement of cash flows, and (d) statement of stockholders' equity?
6. Explain the effect of adjusting entries on cash.
7. How is earnings per share computed and interpreted?
8. How is net profit margin computed and interpreted?
9. Contrast an unadjusted trial balance with an adjusted trial balance. What is the purpose of each?
10. What is the purpose of closing entries?
11. Differentiate among (a) permanent, (b) temporary, (c) real, and (d) nominal accounts.
12. Why are the income statement accounts closed but the balance sheet accounts are not?
13. What is a post-closing trial balance? Is it a useful part of the accounting information processing cycle? Explain.

MULTIPLE-CHOICE QUESTIONS

1. Which of the following accounts would not appear in a closing entry?
   a. Interest Income
   b. Accumulated Depreciation
   c. Retained Earnings
   d. Salary Expense
2. Which account is least likely to appear in an adjusting journal entry?
   a. Cash
   b. Interest Receivable
   c. Property Tax Expense
   d. Salaries Payable
3. When a concert promoting company collects cash for ticket sales two months in advance of the show date, which of the following accounts is recorded?
   a. Accrued Expense
   b. Accrued Revenue
   c. Deferred Expense
   d. Deferred Revenue
4. On December 31 (fiscal year-end), an adjustment is made to reclassify a portion of unearned revenue as earned revenue. How many accounts will be affected on the year-end balance sheet by this entry?
   a. None
   b. One
   c. Two
   d. Three
5. Failure to make an adjusting entry to recognize accrued salaries payable would cause which of the following?
   a. an overstatement of assets and stockholders' equity
   b. an overstatement of assets and liabilities
   c. an understatement of expenses, liabilities, and stockholders' equity
   d. an understatement of expenses and liabilities and an overstatement of stockholders' equity

6. An adjusted trial balance
   a. shows the ending account balances in a "debit" and "credit" format before posting the adjusting journal entries.
   b. is prepared after closing entries have been posted.
   c. is a tool used by financial analysts to review the performance of publicly traded companies.
   d. shows the ending account balances resulting from the adjusting journal entries in a "debit" and "credit" format.
7. Company A owns a building. Which of the following statements regarding depreciation as used by accountants is false?
   a. As the value of the building decreases over time, it "depreciates."
   b. Depreciation is an estimated expense to be recorded over the building's estimated useful life.
   c. As depreciation is recorded, stockholders' equity is reduced.
   d. As depreciation is recorded, the net book value of the asset is reduced.
8. Which of the following columns in a trial balance is used as a source for preparing the income statement?
   a. Unadjusted Trial Balance
   b. Adjustments
   c. Adjusted Trial Balance
   d. Post-Closing Trial Balance
9. What ratio is required by GAAP to be reported on the financial statements or in the notes to the statements?
   a. Return on equity ratio
   b. Net profit margin ratio
   c. Current ratio
   d. Earnings per share ratio
10. If a company is successful in reducing selling and administrative costs while maintaining sales volume and the sales price of its product, what is the effect on the net profit margin ratio?
   a. The ratio will not change.
   b. The ratio will increase.
   c. The ratio will decrease.
   d. Either (a) or (c).

For more practice on multiple-choice questions, go to the text website at www.mhhe.com/ libby5e or the Topic Tackler DVD for use with this text.

MINI-**EXERCISES**

 Available with McGraw-Hill's Homework Manager

M4-1
L01
Preparing a Trial Balance

Puglisi Company has the following adjusted accounts and balances at year-end (June 30, 2007):

Accounts Payable	200	Interest Expense	80
Accounts Receivable	350	Interest Income	50
Accrued Expenses Payable	150	Inventories	610
Accumulated Depreciation	250	Land	200
Buildings and Equipment	1,400	Long-Term Debt	1,300
Cash	120	Prepaid Expenses	40
Contributed Capital	300	Salaries Expense	660
Cost of Sales	820	Sales Revenue	2,400
Depreciation Expense	110	Rent Expense	400
Income Taxes Expense	110	Retained Earnings	120
Income Taxes Payable	30	Unearned Fees	100

Required:
Prepare an adjusted trial balance in good form for the Puglisi Company at June 30, 2007.

M4-2
L02
Matching Definitions with Terms

Match each definition with its related term by entering the appropriate letter in the space provided.

Definition	Term
____ (1) A revenue not yet earned; collected in advance.	A. Accrued expense
____ (2) Office supplies on hand to be used next accounting period.	B. Deferred expense
____ (3) Rent revenue collected; not yet earned.	C. Accrued revenue
____ (4) Rent not yet collected; already earned.	D. Deferred revenue
____ (5) An expense incurred; not yet paid or recorded.	
____ (6) A revenue earned; not yet collected.	
____ (7) An expense not yet incurred; paid in advance.	
____ (8) Property taxes incurred; not yet paid.	

Matching Definitions with Terms

M4-3
LO2

Match each definition with its related term by entering the appropriate letter in the space provided.

Definition	Term
____ (1) At year-end, wages payable of $3,600 had not been recorded or paid.	A. Accrued expense
	B. Deferred expense
____ (2) Office supplies were purchased during the year for $500, and $100 of them remained on hand (unused) at year-end.	C. Accrued revenue
	D. Deferred revenue
____ (3) Interest of $250 on a note receivable was earned at year-end, although collection of the interest is not due until the following year.	
____ (4) At year-end, service revenue of $2,000 was collected in cash but was not yet earned.	

Recording Adjusting Entries (Deferred Accounts)

M4-4
LO2

For each of the following transactions (*a*) through (*c*) for Morgan Company,
1. Identify if the adjustment is to a deferred revenue or deferred expense account.
2. Give the adjusting entry required for the year ended December 31, 2007, using the process illustrated in the chapter:
   a. Collected $800 rent for the period December 1, 2007, to April 1, 2008, which was credited to Unearned Rent Revenue on December 1, 2007.
   b. Paid $3,600 for a two-year insurance premium on July 1, 2007; debited Prepaid Insurance for that amount.
   c. Purchased a machine for $32,000 cash on January 1, 2004. The company estimates annual depreciation of $3,000.

Determining Financial Statement Effects of Adjusting Entries (Deferred Accounts)

M4-5
LO2

For each of the transactions in M4-4, indicate the amounts and direction of effects of the adjusting entry on the elements of the balance sheet and income statement. Using the following format, indicate + for increase, − for decrease, and NE for no effect.

	BALANCE SHEET			INCOME STATEMENT		
Transaction	Assets	Liabilities	Stockholders' Equity	Revenues	Expenses	Net Income
a.						
b.						
c.						

Recording Adjusting Entries (Accrued Accounts)

M4-6
LO2

For each of the following transactions for Morgan Company,
1. Identify if the adjustment is to an accrued revenue or accrued expense account.
2. Give the adjusting entry required for the year ended December 31, 2007, using the process illustrated in the chapter:
   a. Estimated electricity usage at $320 for December to be paid in January 2008.

b. Owed wages to 10 employees who worked three days at $150 each per day at the end of December. The company will pay employees at the end of the first week of January 2008.

c. On September 1, 2007, loaned $5,000 to an officer who will repay the loan principal and interest in one year at an annual interest rate of 12 percent.

M4-7
LO2

Determining Financial Statement Effects of Adjusting Entries (Accrued Accounts)

For each of the transactions in M4-6, indicate the amounts and direction of effects of the adjusting entry on the elements of the balance sheet and income statement. Using the following format, indicate + for increase, − for decrease, and NE for no effect.

	BALANCE SHEET			INCOME STATEMENT		
Transaction	Assets	Liabilities	Stockholders' Equity	Revenues	Expenses	Net Income
a.						
b.						
c.						

M4-8
LO3

Reporting an Income Statement with Earnings per Share

Morgan Company has the following adjusted trial balance at December 31, 2007. No dividends were declared. However, 400 shares issued at the end of the year for $2,000 are included below:

	Debit	Credit
Cash	$ 1,500	
Accounts receivable	2,000	
Interest receivable	120	
Prepaid insurance	1,800	
Long-term notes receivable	3,000	
Equipment	12,000	
Accumulated depreciation		$ 2,000
Accounts payable		1,600
Accrued expenses payable		3,820
Income taxes payable		2,900
Unearned rent revenue		600
Contributed capital (500 shares)		2,400
Retained earnings		1,000
Sales revenue		42,000
Interest revenue		120
Rent revenue		300
Wages expense	21,600	
Depreciation expense	2,000	
Utilities expense	220	
Insurance expense	600	
Rent expense	9,000	
Income tax expense	2,900	
Total	$56,740	$56,740

Prepare an income statement in good form for 2007. Include earnings per share.

M4-9
LO3

Reporting a Statement of Stockholders' Equity

Refer to M4-8. Prepare a statement of stockholders' equity in good form for 2007.

Reporting a Balance Sheet and Explaining the Effects of Adjustments on the Statement of Cash Flows

M4-10
LO3

Refer to M4-8.
1. Prepare a classified balance sheet in good form at December 31, 2007.
2. Explain how the adjustments in M4-4 and M4-6 affected the operating, investing, and financing activities on the statement of cash flows.

Analyzing Net Profit Margin

M4-11
LO4

Compute net income based on the trial balance in M4-8. Then compute Morgan Company's net profit margin for 2007.

Recording Closing Entry

M4-12
LO5

Refer to the adjusted trial balance in M4-8. Prepare the closing entry on December 31, 2007.

Available with McGraw-Hill's Homework Manager

EXERCISES

Preparing a Trial Balance

E4-1
LO1

Darrius Consultants, Inc., provides marketing research for clients in the retail industry. The company had the following unadjusted balances at September 30, 2008:

Accumulated Depreciation	
	18,100

Accrued Expenses Payable	
	25,650

Cash	
163,000	

General and Administrative Expenses	
320,050	

Supplies	
12,200	

Wages and Benefits Expense	
1,590,000	

Prepaid Expenses	
10,200	

Interest Expense	
17,200	

Accounts Receivable	
225,400	

Consulting Fees Revenue	
	2,564,200

Retained Earnings	
	?

Income Taxes Payable	
	2,030

Travel Expense	
23,990	

Building and Equipment	
323,040	

Utilities Expense	
25,230	

Gain on Sale of Land	
	5,000

Unearned Consulting Fees	
	32,500

Investment Income	
	10,800

Accounts Payable	
	86,830

Land	
60,000	

Other Operating Expenses	
188,000	

Contributed Capital	
	223,370

Professional Development Expense	
18,600	

Notes Payable	
	160,000

Rent Expense (on leased computers)	
152,080	

Investments	
145,000	

Required:

Prepare in good form an unadjusted trial balance for Darrius Consultants, Inc., at September 30, 2008.

E4-2
LO1, 2, 5
Hewlett Packard Company

Identifying Adjusting Entries from Unadjusted Trial Balance

In its annual report, Hewlett-Packard Company states, "We are a leading global provider of products, technologies, solutions and services to consumers and businesses. Our offerings span information technology ('IT') infrastructure, personal computing and other access devices, global services and imaging and printing. Our products and services are available worldwide." Following is a trial balance listing accounts that Hewlett-Packard uses. Assume that the balances are unadjusted at the end of a recent fiscal year ended October 31.

HEWLETT-PACKARD COMPANY
Unadjusted Trial Balance
(dollars in millions)

	Debit	Credit
Cash	$14,200	
Short-term investments	400	
Accounts receivable	11,900	
Inventory	6,000	
Other current assets	8,500	
Property, plant, and equipment	13,300	
Accumulated depreciation		$ 6,800
Intangible assets	16,300	
Other assets	10,900	
Short-term note payable		1,000
Accounts payable		9,300
Accrued liabilities		11,000
Deferred revenue		3,700
Income tax payable		1,600
Long-term debt		6,500
Other liabilities		3,800
Contributed capital		24,600
Retained earnings		10,700
Product revenue		58,900
Service revenue		13,700
Interest revenue		500
Cost of products	43,700	
Cost of services	10,000	
Interest expense	200	
Research and development expense	3,700	
Selling, general, and administrative expense	11,000	
Other expenses	1,600	
Loss on investments	100	
Income tax expense	300	
Total	$152,100	$152,100

Required:

1. Based on the information in the unadjusted trial balance, list the deferred revenues and deferred expenses on the balance sheet that may need to be adjusted at October 31 and the related income statement account for each (no computations are necessary).
2. Based on the information in the unadjusted trial balance, list the accrued revenues and accrued expenses that may need to be adjusted at October 31 and the related income statement account for each (no computations are necessary).
3. Which accounts should be closed at the end of the year? Why?

Recording Adjusting Entries

E4-3
LO2

Gonzalez Company completed its first year of operations on December 31, 2008. All of the 2008 entries have been recorded except for the following:

a. At year-end, employees earned wages of $6,000, which will be paid on the next payroll date, January 6, 2009.
b. At year-end, the company had earned interest revenue of $3,000. The cash will be collected March 1, 2009.

Required:
1. What is the annual reporting period for this company?
2. Identify whether each transaction results in adjusting a deferred account or recording an accrued account. Using the process illustrated in the chapter, give the required adjusting entry for transactions (a) and (b). Include appropriate dates and write a brief explanation of each entry.
3. Why are these adjustments made?

Recording Adjusting Entries and Reporting Balances in Financial Statements

E4-4
LO2

Latta Company is making adjusting entries for the year ended December 31, 2007. In developing information for the adjusting entries, the accountant learned the following:

a. A two-year insurance premium of $7,800 was paid on September 1, 2007, for coverage beginning on that date.
b. At December 31, 2007, the following data relating to shipping supplies were obtained from the records and supporting documents.

Shipping supplies on hand, January 1, 2007	$14,000
Purchases of shipping supplies during 2007	72,000
Shipping supplies on hand, counted on December 31, 2007	11,000

Required:
1. What amount should be reported on the 2007 income statement for Insurance Expense? For Shipping Supplies Expense?
2. What amount should be reported on the December 31, 2007, balance sheet for Prepaid Insurance? For Shipping Supplies?
3. Using the process illustrated in the chapter, record the adjusting entry for insurance at December 31, 2007, assuming that the premium was paid on September 1, 2007, and the bookkeeper debited the full amount to Prepaid Insurance.
4. Using the process illustrated in the chapter, record the adjusting entry for supplies at December 31, 2007, assuming that the purchases of shipping supplies were debited in full to Shipping Supplies.

Determining Financial Statement Effects of Adjusting Entries

E4-5
LO2

Refer to E4-3 and E4-4.

Required:
For each of the transactions in E4-3 and E4-4, indicate the amount and direction of effects of the adjusting entry on the elements of the balance sheet and income statement. Using the following format, indicate + for increase, − for decrease, and NE for no effect.

	BALANCE SHEET			INCOME STATEMENT		
Transaction	Assets	Liabilities	Stockholders' Equity	Revenues	Expenses	Net Income
E4-3 (a)						
E4-3 (b)						
E4-4 (a)						
E4-3 (b)						

E4-6

LO2

Recording Seven Typical Adjusting Entries

Heald's Variety Store is completing the accounting process for the year just ended, December 31, 2007. The transactions during 2007 have been journalized and posted. The following data with respect to adjusting entries are available:

a. Office supplies on hand at January 1, 2007, totaled $350. Office supplies purchased and debited to Office Supplies during the year amounted to $800. The year-end count showed $300 of supplies on hand.

b. Wages earned by employees during December 2007, unpaid and unrecorded at December 31, 2007, amounted to $3,700. The last payroll was December 28; the next payroll will be January 6, 2008.

c. Three-fourths of the basement of the store is rented for $1,500 per month to another merchant, M. Dittman Inc. Dittman sells compatible, but not competitive, merchandise. On November 1, 2007, the store collected six months' rent in the amount of $9,000 in advance from Dittman; it was credited in full to Unearned Rent Revenue when collected.

d. The remaining basement space is rented to Kathy's Specialty Shop for $820 per month, payable monthly. On December 31, 2007, the rent for November and December 2007 had not been collected or recorded. Collection is expected January 10, 2008.

e. The store used delivery equipment that cost $30,000; $5,000 was the estimated depreciation for 2007.

f. On July 1, 2007, a two-year insurance premium amounting to $4,200 was paid in cash and debited in full to Prepaid Insurance. Coverage began on July 1, 2007.

g. Heald's operates a repair shop to meet its own needs. The shop also does repairs for M. Dittman. At the end of December 31, 2007, Dittman had not paid $750 for completed repairs. This amount has not yet been recorded as Repair Shop Revenue. Collection is expected during January 2008.

Required:

1. Identify each of these transactions as a deferred revenue, deferred expense, accrued revenue, or accrued expense.
2. Using the process illustrated in the chapter, for each situation record the adjusting entry that should be recorded for Heald's at December 31, 2007.

E4-7

LO2

Recording Seven Typical Adjusting Entries

Johnson's Boat Yard, Inc., is completing the accounting process for the year just ended, November 30, 2006. The transactions during 2006 have been journalized and posted. The following data with respect to adjusting entries are available:

a. Johnson's winterized (cleaned and covered) three boats for customers at the end of November, but did not bill the customers $2,100 for the service until December.

b. The Carter family paid Johnson's $2,400 on November 1, 2006, to store their sailboat for the winter until May 1, 2007. Johnson's credited the full amount to Unearned Storage Revenue on November 1.

c. Wages earned by employees during November 2006, unpaid and unrecorded at November 30, 2006, amounted to $2,900. The next payroll date will be December 5, 2006.

d. On October 1, 2006, Johnson's paid $600 to the local newspaper for an advertisement to run every Thursday for 12 weeks. All ads have been run except for three Thursdays in December to complete the 12-week contract.

e. Johnson's used boat-lifting equipment that cost $230,000; $23,000 was the estimated depreciation for 2006.

f. Boat repair supplies on hand at December 1, 2005, totaled $15,600. Repair supplies purchased and debited to Supplies during the year amounted to $47,500. The year-end count showed $12,200 of the supplies on hand.

g. Johnson's borrowed $150,000 at a 10 percent annual interest rate on April 1, 2006, to expand its boat storage facility. The loan requires Johnson's to pay the interest quarterly until the note is repaid in three years. Johnson's paid quarterly interest on July 1 and October 1.

Required:

1. Identify each of these transactions as a deferred revenue, deferred expense, accrued revenue, or accrued expense.

2. Using the process illustrated in the chapter, for each situation record the adjusting entry that should be recorded for Johnson's at November 30, 2006.

Determining Financial Statement Effects of Seven Typical Adjusting Entries

E4-8
LO2

Refer to E4-6.

Required:

For each of the transactions in E4-6, indicate the amount and direction of effects of the adjusting entry on the elements of the balance sheet and income statement. Using the following format, indicate + for increase, − for decrease, and NE for no effect.

	BALANCE SHEET			INCOME STATEMENT		
Transaction	Assets	Liabilities	Stockholders' Equity	Revenues	Expenses	Net Income
a.						
b.						
c.						
etc.						

Determining Financial Statement Effects of Seven Typical Adjusting Entries

E4-9
LO2

Refer to E4-7.

Required:

For each of the transactions in E4-7, indicate the amount and direction of effects of the adjusting entry on the elements of the balance sheet and income statement. Using the following format, indicate + for increase, − for decrease, and NE for no effect.

	BALANCE SHEET			INCOME STATEMENT		
Transaction	Assets	Liabilities	Stockholders' Equity	Revenues	Expenses	Net Income
a.						
b.						
c.						
etc.						

Recording Transactions Including Adjusting and Closing Entries (Nonquantitative)

E4-10
LO2, 5

The following accounts are used by Britt's Knits, Inc.

Codes	Accounts	Codes	Accounts
A	Cash	J	Contributed capital
B	Office supplies	K	Retained earnings
C	Accounts receivable	L	Service revenue
D	Office equipment	M	Interest revenue
E	Accumulated depreciation	N	Wage expense
F	Note payable	O	Depreciation expense
G	Wages payable	P	Interest expense
H	Interest payable	Q	Supplies expense
I	Unearned service revenue	R	None of the above

Required:

For each of the following nine independent situations, give the journal entry by entering the appropriate code(s) and amount(s).

Independent Situations	DEBIT Code	DEBIT Amount	CREDIT Code	CREDIT Amount
a. Accrued wages, unrecorded and unpaid at year-end, $400 (example).	N	400	G	400
b. Service revenue collected in advance, $800.				
c. Dividends declared and paid during the year, $900.				
d. Depreciation expense for the year, $1,000.				
e. Service revenue earned but not yet collected at year-end, $600.				
f. Office Supplies on hand during the year, $400; supplies on hand at year-end, $150.				
g. At year-end, interest on note payable not yet recorded or paid, $220.				
h. Balance at year-end in Service Revenue account, $62,000. Give the closing entry at year-end.				
i. Balance at year-end in Interest Expense account, $420. Give the closing entry at year-end.				

E4-11 Determining Financial Statement Effects of Three Adjusting Entries

LO2

DuPage Company started operations on January 1, 2007. It is now December 31, 2007, the end of the annual accounting period. The part-time bookkeeper needs your help to analyze the following three transactions:

a. On January 1, 2007, the company purchased a special machine for cash at a cost of $12,000. The machine's cost is estimated to depreciate at $1,200 per year.

b. During 2007, the company purchased office supplies that cost $1,400. At the end of 2007, office supplies of $400 remained on hand.

c. On July 1, 2007, the company paid cash of $400 for a two-year premium on an insurance policy on the machine; coverage begins on July 1, 2007.

Required:
Complete the following schedule with the amounts that should be reported for 2007:

Selected Balance Sheet Amounts at December 31, 2007	Amount to Be Reported
Assets	
Equipment	$_____
Accumulated depreciation	_____
Carrying value of equipment	_____
Office supplies	_____
Prepaid insurance	_____

Selected Income Statement Amounts for the Year Ended December 31, 2007	
Expenses	
Depreciation expense	$_____
Office supplies expense	_____
Insurance expense	_____

E4-12 Determining Financial Statement Effects of Adjustments for Interest on Two Notes

LO2

Note 1: On April 1, 2008, Seaquist Corporation received a $20,000, 10 percent note from a customer in settlement of a $20,000 open account receivable. According to the terms, the principal of the note and interest are payable at the end of 12 months. The annual accounting period for Seaquist ends on December 31, 2008.

Note 2: On August 1, 2008, to meet a cash shortage, Seaquist Corporation obtained a $20,000, 12 percent loan from a local bank. The principal of the note and interest expense are payable at the end of six months.

Required:

For the relevant transaction dates of each note, indicate the amounts and direction of effects on the elements of the balance sheet and income statement. Using the following format, indicate + for increase, − for decrease, and NE for no effect. (*Reminder:* Assets = Liabilities + Stockholders' Equity; Revenues − Expenses = Net Income; and Net Income accounts are closed to Retained Earnings, a part of Stockholders' Equity.)

	BALANCE SHEET			INCOME STATEMENT		
Date	Assets	Liabilities	Stockholders' Equity	Revenues	Expenses	Net Income
Note 1 April 1, 2008						
December 31, 2008						
March 31, 2009						
Note 2 August 1, 2008						
December 31, 2008						
January 31, 2009						

Inferring Transactions

Deere & Company is the world's leading producer of agricultural equipment; a leading supplier of a broad range of industrial equipment for construction, forestry, and public works; a producer and marketer of a broad line of lawn and grounds care equipment; and a provider of credit, managed health care plans, and insurance products for businesses and the general public. The following information is from a recent annual report (in millions of dollars):

E4-13
LO2
Deere & Company

Income Taxes Payable			Dividends Payable			Interest Payable		
		Beg. bal. 71			Beg. bal. 43			Beg. bal. 45
(a)	?	(b) 332	(c)	?	(d) 176	(e)	297	(f) ?
		End. bal. 80			End. bal. 48			End. bal. 51

Required:

1. Identify the nature of each of the transactions (*a*) through (*f*). Specifically, what activities cause the accounts to increase and decrease?
2. For transactions (*a*), (*c*), and (*f*), compute the amount.

Analyzing the Effects of Errors on Financial Statement Items

Goldberg & Broverman, Inc., publishers of movie and song trivia books, made the following errors in adjusting the accounts at year-end (December 31):

E4-14
LO2

a. Did not record $12,000 depreciation on the equipment costing $130,000.
b. Failed to adjust the Unearned Fee Revenue account to reflect that $2,000 was earned by the end of the year.
c. Recorded a full year of accrued interest expense on a $15,000, 12 percent note payable that has been outstanding only since November 1.
d. Failed to adjust Prepaid Insurance to reflect that $600 of insurance coverage has been used.
e. Did not accrue $850 owed to the company by another company renting part of the building as a storage facility.

Required:

1. For each error, prepare the adjusting journal entry (a) that was made, if any, and (b) that should have been made at year-end.
2. Using the following headings, indicate the effect of each error and the amount of the effect (that is, the difference between the entry that was or was not made and the entry that should have been made). Use O if the effect overstates the item, U if the effect understates the item, and NE if there is no effect. (*Reminder:* Assets = Liabilities + Stockholders' Equity; Revenues − Expenses = Net Income; and Net Income accounts are closed to Retained Earnings, a part of Stockholders' Equity.)

	BALANCE SHEET			INCOME STATEMENT		
Transaction	Assets	Liabilities	Stockholders' Equity	Revenues	Expenses	Net Income
a.						
b.						
c.						
etc.						

E4-15
LO2

Analyzing the Effects of Adjusting Entries on the Income Statement and Balance Sheet

On December 31, 2007, Quinlan-Cohen Company prepared an income statement and balance sheet and failed to take into account four adjusting entries. The income statement, prepared on this incorrect basis, reflected pretax income of $40,000. The balance sheet (before the effect of income taxes) reflected total assets, $80,000; total liabilities, $30,000; and stockholders' equity, $50,000. The data for the four adjusting entries follow:

a. Depreciation of $9,000 for the year on equipment that cost $95,000 was not recorded.
b. Wages amounting to $17,000 for the last three days of December 2007 were not paid and not recorded (the next payroll will be on January 10, 2008).
c. Rent revenue of $4,800 was collected on December 1, 2007, for office space for the period December 1, 2007, to February 28, 2008. The $4,800 was credited in full to Unearned Rent Revenue when collected.
d. Income taxes were not recorded. The income tax rate for the company is 30 percent.

Required:

Complete the following tabulation to correct the financial statements for the effects of the four errors (indicate deductions with parentheses):

Items	Net Income	Total Assets	Total Liabilities	Stockholders' Equity
Balances reported	$40,000	$80,000	$30,000	$50,000
Effect of depreciation	————	————	————	————
Effect of wages	————	————	————	————
Effect of rent revenue	————	————	————	————
Adjusted balances	————	————	————	————
Effect of income taxes	————	————	————	————
Correct balances	————	————	————	————

E4-16
LO2, 3

Recording the Effects of Adjusting Entries and Reporting a Corrected Income Statement and Balance Sheet

On December 31, 2006, the bookkeeper for Joseph Company prepared the following income statement and balance sheet summarized here but neglected to consider three adjusting entries.

	As Prepared	Effects of Adjusting Entries	Corrected Amounts
Income Statement			
Revenues	$98,000	_____	_____
Expenses	(72,000)	_____	_____
Income tax expense	_____	_____	_____
Net income	$26,000	_____	_____
Balance Sheet			
Assets			
Cash	$20,000	_____	_____
Accounts receivable	22,000	_____	_____
Rent receivable		_____	_____
Equipment	50,000	_____	_____
Accumulated depreciation	(10,000)	_____	_____
	$82,000		
Liabilities			
Accounts payable	$10,000	_____	_____
Income taxes payable		_____	_____
Stockholders' Equity			
Contributed capital	40,000	_____	_____
Retained earnings	32,000	_____	_____
	$82,000		

Data on the three adjusting entries follow:

a. Depreciation of $5,000 on the equipment for 2006 was not recorded.
b. Rent revenue of $2,000 earned for December 2006 was neither collected nor recorded.
c. Income tax expense of $6,900 for 2006 was neither paid nor recorded.

Required:
  1. Prepare the three adjusting entries that were omitted. Use the account titles shown in the income statement and balance sheet data.
  2. Complete the two columns to the right in the preceding tabulation to show the correct amounts on the income statement and balance sheet.

Reporting a Correct Income Statement with Earnings per Share to Include the Effects of Adjusting Entries and Evaluating the Net Profit Margin as an Auditor

E4-17
LO2, 3, 4

Derek, Inc., a party rental business, completed its first year of operations on December 31, 2007. Because this is the end of the annual accounting period, the company bookkeeper prepared the following tentative income statement:

Income Statement, 2007	
Rental revenue	$114,000
Expenses	
Salaries and wages expense	28,500
Maintenance expense	12,000
Rent expense	9,000
Utilities expense	4,000
Gas and oil expense	3,000
Miscellaneous expenses (items not listed elsewhere)	1,000
Total expenses	57,500
Income	$ 56,500

You are an independent CPA hired by the company to audit the company's accounting systems and review the financial statements. In your audit, you developed additional data as follows:

a. Wages for the last three days of December amounting to $310 were not recorded or paid.
b. Derek estimated telephone usage at $400 for December 2007, but nothing has been recorded or paid.
c. Depreciation on rental autos, amounting to $23,000 for 2007, was not recorded.
d. Interest on a $20,000, one-year, 10 percent note payable dated October 1, 2007, was not recorded. The 10 percent interest is payable on the maturity date of the note.
e. The Unearned Rental Revenue account includes $4,000 of revenue to be earned in January 2008.
f. Maintenance expense excludes $1,000 that is the cost of maintenance supplies used during 2007.
g. The income tax expense is $7,000. Payment of income tax will be made in 2008.

Required:
1. What adjusting entry for each item (*a*) through (*g*) do you recommend Derek should record at December 31, 2007? If none is required, explain why.
2. Prepare a corrected income statement for 2007 in good form, including earnings per share, assuming that 7,000 shares of stock are outstanding. Show computations.
3. Compute the net profit margin based on the corrected information. What does this ratio suggest? If the average net profit margin for the industry is 18 percent, what might you infer about Derek?

E4-18
L01, 2

Recording Four Adjusting Entries and Completing the Trial Balance Worksheet

Seneca Company prepared the following trial balance at the end of its first year of operations ending December 31, 2007. To simplify the case, the amounts given are in thousands of dollars.

	UNADJUSTED		ADJUSTMENTS		ADJUSTED	
Account Titles	Debit	Credit	Debit	Credit	Debit	Credit
Cash	38					
Accounts receivable	9					
Prepaid insurance	6					
Machinery	80					
Accumulated depreciation						
Accounts payable		9				
Wages payable						
Income taxes payable						
Contributed capital (4,000 shares)		76				
Retained earnings	4					
Revenues (not detailed)		84				
Expenses (not detailed)	32					
Totals	169	169				

Other data not yet recorded at December 31, 2007:

a. Insurance expired during 2007, $5.
b. Depreciation expense for 2007, $7.
c. Wages payable, $5.
d. Income tax expense, $9.

Required:
1. Prepare the adjusting entries for 2007.
2. Complete the trial balance Adjustments and Adjusted columns.

E4-19
L03

Reporting an Income Statement, Statement of Stockholders' Equity, and Balance Sheet

Refer to E4-18.

Required:

Using the adjusted balances in E4-18, prepare an income statement, statement of stockholders' equity, and balance sheet for 2007.

Recording Closing Entries and Preparing a Post-Closing Trial Balance

E4-20
LO5

Refer to E4-18.

Required:

1. What is the purpose of "closing the books" at the end of the accounting period?
2. Using the adjusted balances in E4-18, give the closing entry for 2007.
3. Prepare a post-closing trial balance for 2007.

 Available with McGraw-Hill's Homework Manager

PROBLEMS

Preparing a Trial Balance (AP4-1)

P4-1
LO1
Dell Inc.

Dell Inc. is the world's largest computer systems company selling directly to customers. Products include desktop computer systems, notebook computers, workstations, network server and storage products, and peripheral hardware and software. The following is a list of accounts and amounts reported in a recent year. The accounts have normal debit or credit balances and the dollars are rounded to the nearest million. Assume the company's year ended on January 31, 2006.

Accounts payable	$ 2,397	Marketable securities	$2,661
Accounts receivable	2,094	Other assets	806
Accrued expenses payable	1,298	Other expenses	38
Accumulated depreciation	252	Other liabilities	349
Cash	520	Property, plant, and equipment	775
Contributed capital	1,781	Research and development expense	272
Cost of sales	14,137	Retained earnings	?
Income tax expense	624	Sales revenue	18,243
Inventories	273	Selling, general, and	
Long-term debt	512	administrative expenses	1,788

Required:

1. Prepare an adjusted trial balance at January 31, 2006.
2. How did you determine the amount for retained earnings?

Recording Adjusting Entries (AP4-2)

P4-2
LO2

Burress Company's annual accounting year ends on December 31. It is December 31, 2007, and all of the 2007 entries except the following adjusting entries have been made:

a. On September 1, 2007, Burress collected six months' rent of $7,200 on storage space. At that date, Burress debited Cash and credited Unearned Rent Revenue for $7,200.
b. At December 31, 2007, wages earned by employees totaled $14,300. The employees will be paid on the next payroll date, January 15, 2008.
c. The company earned service revenue of $2,000 on a special job that was completed December 29, 2007. Collection will be made during January 2008. No entry has been recorded.
d. On October 1, 2007, the company borrowed $20,000 from a local bank and signed a 12 percent note for that amount. The principal and interest are payable on the maturity date, September 30, 2008.
e. On November 1, 2007, Burress paid a one-year premium for property insurance, $6,000, for coverage starting on that date. Cash was credited and Prepaid Insurance was debited for this amount.
f. Depreciation of $1,500 must be recognized on a service truck purchased on July 1, 2007, at a cost of $12,000.
g. Cash of $2,400 was collected on November 1, 2007, for services to be rendered evenly over the next year beginning on November 1. Unearned Service Revenue was credited when the cash was received.

h. On December 31, 2007, the company estimated it owed $400 for 2007 property taxes on land. The tax will be paid when the bill is received in January 2008.

Required:

1. Indicate whether each transaction relates to a deferred revenue, deferred expense, accrued revenue, or accrued expense.
2. Give the adjusting entry required for each transaction at December 31, 2007.

P4-3   **Recording Adjusting Entries** (AP4-3)

LO2

Totka Towing Company is at the end of its accounting year, December 31, 2008. The following data that must be considered were developed from the company's records and related documents:

a. On July 1, 2008, a three-year insurance premium on equipment in the amount of $1,200 was paid and debited in full to Prepaid Insurance on that date. Coverage began on July 1.

b. During 2008, office supplies amounting to $800 were purchased for cash and debited in full to Supplies. At the end of 2007, the count of supplies remaining on hand was $200. The inventory of supplies counted on hand at December 31, 2008, was $300.

c. On December 31, 2008, HH's Garage completed repairs on one of the company's trucks at a cost of $800; the amount is not yet recorded and by agreement will be paid during January 2009.

d. On December 31, 2008, property taxes on land owned during 2008 were estimated at $1,600. The taxes have not been recorded, and will be paid in 2009 when billed.

e. On December 31, 2008, the company completed a contract for an out-of-state company for $8,000 payable by the customer within 30 days. No cash has been collected, and no journal entry has been made for this transaction.

f. On January 1, 2008, the company purchased a new hauling van at a cash cost of $23,600. Depreciation estimated at $1,100 for the year has not been recorded for 2008.

g. On October 1, 2008, the company borrowed $10,000 from the local bank on a one-year, 12 percent note payable. The principal plus interest is payable at the end of 12 months.

h. The income before any of the adjustments or income taxes was $30,000. The company's federal income tax rate is 30 percent. (*Hint:* Compute adjusted income based on (*a*) through (*g*) to determine income tax expense.)

Required:

1. Indicate whether each transaction relates to a deferred revenue, deferred expense, accrued revenue, or accrued expense.
2. Give the adjusting entry required for each transaction at December 31, 2008.

P4-4   **Determining Financial Statement Effects of Adjusting Entries** (AP4-4)

LO2

Refer to P4-2.

e**X**cel

Required:

1. Indicate whether each transaction relates to a deferred revenue, deferred expense, accrued revenue, or accrued expense.
2. Using the following headings, indicate the effect of each adjusting entry and the amount of the effect. Use + for increase, − for decrease, and NE for no effect. (*Reminder:* Assets = Liabilities + Stockholders' Equity; Revenues − Expenses = Net Income; and Net Income accounts are closed to Retained Earnings, a part of Stockholders' Equity.)

	BALANCE SHEET			INCOME STATEMENT		
Transaction	Assets	Liabilities	Stockholders' Equity	Revenues	Expenses	Net Income
a.						
b.						
c.						
etc.						

Determining Financial Statement Effects of Adjusting Entries (AP4-5)

P4-5
LO2

Refer to P4-3.

Required:

1. Indicate whether each transaction relates to a deferred revenue, deferred expense, accrued revenue, or accrued expense.
2. Using the following headings, indicate the effect of each adjusting entry and the amount of each. Use + for increase, − for decrease, and NE for no effect. (*Reminder:* Assets = Liabilities + Stockholders' Equity; Revenues − Expenses = Net Income; and Net Income accounts are closed to Retained Earnings, a part of Stockholders' Equity.)

	BALANCE SHEET			INCOME STATEMENT		
Transaction	Assets	Liabilities	Stockholders' Equity	Revenues	Expenses	Net Income
a.						
b.						
c.						
etc.						

Computing Amounts on Financial Statements and Finding Financial Information

P4-6
LO2

The following information was provided by the records of Collegetown Apartments (a corporation) at the end of the annual fiscal period, December 31, 2007:

Rent

a.	Rent revenue collected in cash during 2007 for occupancy in 2007	$512,000
b.	Rent revenue earned for occupancy in December 2007; not collected until 2008	16,000
c.	In December 2007, collected rent revenue in advance for January 2008	12,000

Salaries

d.	Cash payment in January 2007 to employees for work in December 2006 (accrued in 2006)	4,000
e.	Salaries incurred and paid during 2007	62,000
f.	Salaries earned by employees during December 2007 that will be paid in January 2008	3,000
g.	Cash advances to employees in December 2007 for salaries that will be earned in January 2008	1,500

Supplies

h.	Maintenance supplies on January 1, 2007 (balance on hand)	3,000
i.	Maintenance supplies purchased for cash during 2007	8,000
j.	Maintenance supplies counted on December 31, 2007	1,700

Required:

For each of the following accounts, compute the balance to be reported in 2007, the statement the account will be reported on, and the effect (direction and amount) on cash flows (+ for increases cash and − for decreases cash). (*Hint:* Create T-accounts to determine balances.)

Account	2007 Balance	Financial Statement	Effect on Cash Flows
1. Rent revenue			
2. Salary expense			
3. Maintenance supplies expense			
4. Rent receivable			
5. Receivables from employees			
6. Maintenance supplies			
7. Unearned rent revenue			
8. Salaries payable			

P4-7
LO1, 2, 4, 5

Inferring Year-End Adjustments, Computing Earnings per Share and Net Profit Margin, and Recording Closing Entries (AP4-6)

Wagonblatt Company is completing the information processing cycle at its fiscal year-end, December 31, 2006. Following are the correct balances at December 31, 2006, for the accounts both before and after the adjusting entries for 2006.

	Trial Balance, December 31, 2006						
	Before Adjusting Entries		Adjustments		After Adjusting Entries		
Items	Debit	Credit	Debit	Credit	Debit	Credit	
a. Cash	$ 9,000				$ 9,000		
b. Accounts receivable					400		
c. Prepaid insurance	600				400		
d. Equipment	120,200				120,200		
e. Accumulated depreciation, equipment		$31,500				$40,000	
f. Income taxes payable						4,700	
g. Contributed capital		80,000				80,000	
h. Retained earnings, January 1, 2006		14,000				14,000	
i. Service revenue		46,000				46,400	
j. Salary expense	41,700				41,700		
k. Depreciation expense					8,500		
l. Insurance expense					200		
m. Income tax expense					4,700		
	$171,500	$171,500			$185,100	$185,100	

Required:

1. Compare the amounts in the columns before and after the adjusting entries to reconstruct the adjusting entries made in 2006. Provide an explanation of each.
2. Compute the amount of income assuming that it is based on the amounts (a) before adjusting entries and (b) after adjusting entries. Which income amount is correct? Explain why.
3. Compute earnings per share, assuming that 3,000 shares of stock are outstanding all year.
4. Compute the net profit margin. What does this suggest to you about the company?
5. Record the closing entry at December 31, 2006.
6. Prepare a post-closing trial balance at December 31, 2006.

P4-8
LO1, 2, 3, 5

Recording Adjusting and Closing Entries and Preparing a Balance Sheet and Income Statement Including Earnings per Share (AP4-7)

St. Denis, Inc., a small service company, keeps its records without the help of an accountant. After much effort, an outside accountant prepared the following unadjusted trial balance as of the end of the annual accounting period, December 31, 2007:

Account Titles	Debit	Credit
Cash	$60,000	
Accounts receivable	13,000	
Supplies	800	
Prepaid insurance	1,000	
Service trucks	20,000	
Accumulated depreciation, service trucks		$12,000
Other assets	11,200	
Accounts payable		3,000
Wages payable		
		continued

Income taxes payable		
Note payable (3 years; 10% interest due each December 31)		20,000
Contributed capital (5,000 shares outstanding)		28,200
Retained earnings		7,500
Service revenue		77,000
Remaining expenses (not detailed; excludes income tax)	41,700	
Income tax expense		
Totals	$147,700	$147,700

Data not yet recorded at December 31, 2007:

a. The supplies counted on December 31, 2007, reflected $300 remaining on hand to be used in 2008.

b. Insurance expired during 2007, $500.

c. Depreciation expense for 2007, $4,000.

d. Wages earned by employees not yet paid on December 31, 2007, $900.

e. Income tax expense was $7,350.

Required:

1. Record the 2007 adjusting entries.

2. Prepare an income statement and a classified balance sheet that include the effects of the preceding five transactions.

3. Record the 2007 closing entry.

Comprehensive Review Problem: From Recording Transactions (including Adjusting and Closing Entries) to Preparing a Complete Set of Financial Statements and Performing Ratio Analysis (see Chapters 2, 3, and 4) (AP4-8)

P4-9

L01, 2, 3, 4, 5

Brothers Steve and Herman Hargenrater began operations of their tool and die shop (H & H Tool, Inc.) on January 1, 2007. The annual reporting period ends December 31. The trial balance on January 1, 2008, follows:

Account Titles	Debit	Credit
Cash	$ 3,000	
Accounts receivable	5,000	
Supplies	12,000	
Land		
Equipment	60,000	
Accumulated depreciation (on equipment)		$ 6,000
Other assets (not detailed to simplify)	4,000	
Accounts payable		$ 5,000
Wages payable		
Interest payable		
Income taxes payable		
Long-term notes payable		
Contributed capital (65,000 shares)		65,000
Retained earnings		8,000
Service revenue		
Depreciation expense		
Income tax expense		
Interest expense		
Supplies expense		
Wages expense		
Remaining expenses (not detailed to simplify)		
Totals	$84,000	$84,000

Transactions during 2008 follow:

a. Borrowed $10,000 cash on a five-year, 12 percent note payable, dated March 1, 2008.
b. Purchased land for a future building site; paid cash, $9,000.
c. Earned revenues for 2008, $160,000, including $40,000 on credit.
d. Sold 3,000 additional shares of capital stock for cash at $1 market value per share on January 1, 2008.
e. Recognized $85,000 in remaining expenses for 2008, including $15,000 on credit.
f. Collected accounts receivable, $24,000.
g. Purchased other assets, $10,000 cash.
h. Paid accounts payable, $13,000.
i. Purchased supplies on account for future use, $18,000.
j. Signed a three-year $24,000 service contract to start February 1, 2009.
k. Declared and paid cash dividends, $17,000.

Data for adjusting entries:

l. Supplies counted on December 31, 2008, $14,000.
m. Depreciation for the year on the equipment, $6,000.
n. Interest accrued on notes payable (to be computed).
o. Wages earned by employees since the December 24 payroll but are not yet paid, $12,000.
p. Income tax expense was $8,000, payable in 2009.

Required:

1. Set up T-accounts for the accounts on the trial balance and enter beginning balances.
2. Prepare journal entries for transactions (*a*) through (*k*) and post them to the T-accounts.
3. Journalize and post the adjusting entries (*l*) through (*p*).
4. Prepare an income statement (including earnings per share), statement of stockholders' equity, balance sheet, and statement of cash flows.
5. Journalize and post the closing entry.
6. Prepare a post-closing trial balance.
7. Compute the following ratios for 2008 and explain what the results suggest about the company:
   a. Financial leverage
   b. Total asset turnover
   c. Net profit margin

ALTERNATE **PROBLEMS**

AP4-1
LO1
Starbucks
Corporation

Preparing a Trial Balance (P4-1)

Starbucks Corporation purchases and roasts high-quality whole bean coffees and sells them along with fresh-brewed coffees, Italian-style espresso beverages, a variety of pastries and confections, coffee-related accessories and equipment, and a line of premium teas. In addition to sales through its company-operated retail stores, Starbucks also sells coffee and tea products through other channels of distribution. The following is a simplified list of accounts and amounts reported in recent financial statements. The accounts have normal debit or credit balances, and the dollars are rounded to the nearest million. Assume that the year ended on September 30, 2006.

Accounts payable	$ 56	Inventories	$ 181
Accounts receivable	48	Long-term investments	68
Accrued liabilities	131	Long-term liabilities	40
Accumulated depreciation	321	Net revenues	1,680
Cash	66	Other current assets	21
Contributed capital	647	Other long-lived assets	38
Cost of sales	741	Other operating expenses	51
Depreciation expense	98	Prepaid expenses	19
General and administrative		Property, plant, and equipment	1,081
expenses	90	Retained earnings	?
Income tax expense	62	Short-term bank debt	64
Interest expense	1	Short-term investments	51
Interest income	9	Store operating expenses	544

Required:
1. Prepare an adjusted trial balance at September 30, 2006.
2. How did you determine the amount for retained earnings?

Recording Adjusting Entries (P4-2)

AP4-2
LO2

Brandon Company's annual accounting year ends on June 30. It is June 30, 2007, and all of the 2007 entries except the following adjusting entries have been made:

a. On March 30, 2007, Brandon paid a six-month premium for property insurance, $3,200, for coverage starting on that date. Cash was credited and Prepaid Insurance was debited for this amount.
b. At June 30, 2007, wages of $900 were earned by employees but not yet paid. The employees will be paid on the next payroll date, July 15, 2007.
c. On June 1, 2007, Brandon collected two months' maintenance revenue of $450. At that date, Brandon debited Cash and credited Unearned Maintenance Revenue for $450.
d. Depreciation of $3,000 must be recognized on a service truck that cost $15,000 when purchased on July 1, 2006.
e. Cash of $4,200 was collected on May 1, 2007, for services to be rendered evenly over the next year beginning on May 1. Unearned Service Revenue was credited when the cash was received.
f. On February 1, 2007, the company borrowed $16,000 from a local bank and signed a 9 percent note for that amount. The principal and interest are payable on maturity date, January 31, 2008.
g. On June 30, 2007, the company estimated that it owed $500 in property taxes on land it owned in the first half of 2007. The taxes will be paid when billed in August 2007.
h. The company earned service revenue of $2,000 on a special job that was completed June 29, 2007. Collection will be made during July 2007; no entry has been recorded.

Required:
1. Indicate whether each transaction relates to a deferred revenue, deferred expense, accrued revenue, or accrued expense.
2. Give the adjusting entry required for each transaction at June 30, 2007.

Recording Adjusting Entries (P4-3)

AP4-3
LO2

Wendy's Catering Company is at its accounting year-end, December 31, 2008. The following data that must be considered were developed from the company's records and related documents:

a. During 2008, office supplies amounting to $1,200 were purchased for cash and debited in full to Supplies. At the beginning of 2008, the count of supplies on hand was $350 and, at December 31, 2008, was $400.
b. On December 31, 2008, the company catered an evening gala for a local celebrity. The $7,500 bill was payable by the end of January 2009. No cash has been collected, and no journal entry has been made for this transaction.
c. On December 31, 2008, repairs on one of the company's delivery vans were completed at a cost estimate of $600; the amount is not yet paid or recorded. The repair shop will bill Wendy's Catering at the beginning of January 2009.
d. On October 1, 2008, a one-year insurance premium on equipment in the amount of $1,200 was paid and debited in full to Prepaid Insurance on that date. Coverage began on November 1.
e. In November 2008, Wendy's signed a lease for a new retail location, providing a down payment of $2,100 for the first three months' rent that was debited in full to Prepaid Rent. The lease began on December 1, 2008.
f. On July 1, 2008, the company purchased new refrigerated display counters at a cash cost of $18,000. Depreciation of $1,600 has not been recorded for 2008.
g. On November 1, 2008, the company loaned $4,000 to one of its employees on a one-year, 12 percent note. The principal plus interest is payable by the employee at the end of 12 months.
h. The income before any of the adjustments or income taxes was $22,400. The company's federal income tax rate is 30 percent. Compute adjusted income based on (*a*) through (*g*) to determine income tax expense.

Required:
1. Indicate whether each transaction relates to a deferred revenue, deferred expense, accrued revenue, or accrued expense.
2. Give the adjusting entry required for each transaction at December 31, 2008.

AP4-4   **Determining Financial Statement Effects of Adjusting Entries** (P4-4)

LO2   Refer to AP4-2.

Required:
1. Indicate whether each transaction relates to a deferred revenue, deferred expense, accrued revenue, or accrued expense.
2. Using the following headings, indicate the effect of each adjusting entry and the amount of the effect. Use + for increase, − for decrease, and NE for no effect. (*Reminder:* Assets = Liabilities + Stockholders' Equity; Revenues − Expenses = Net Income; and Net Income accounts are closed to Retained Earnings, a part of Stockholders' Equity.)

	BALANCE SHEET			INCOME STATEMENT		
Transaction	Assets	Liabilities	Stockholders' Equity	Revenues	Expenses	Net Income
a.						
b.						
c.						
etc.						

AP4-5   **Determining Financial Statement Effects of Adjusting Entries** (P4-5)

LO2   Refer to AP4-3.

Required:
1. Indicate whether each transaction relates to a deferred revenue, deferred expense, accrued revenue, or accrued expense.
2. Using the following headings, indicate the effect of each adjusting entry and the amount of each. Use + for increase, − for decrease, and NE for no effect. (*Reminder:* Assets = Liabilities + Stockholders' Equity; Revenues − Expenses = Net Income; and Net Income accounts are closed to Retained Earnings, a part of Stockholders' Equity.)

	BALANCE SHEET			INCOME STATEMENT		
Transaction	Assets	Liabilities	Stockholders' Equity	Revenues	Expenses	Net Income
a.						
b.						
c.						
etc.						

AP4-6   **Inferring Year-End Adjustments, Computing Earnings per Share and Net Profit Margin,**

LO1, 2, 4, 5   **and Recording Closing Entries** (P4-7)

Abraham Company is completing the information processing cycle at the end of its fiscal year, December 31, 2006. Following are the correct balances at December 31, 2006, for the accounts both before and after the adjusting entries for 2006.

Trial Balance, December 31, 2006						
	Before Adjusting Entries		Adjustments		After Adjusting Entries	
Items	Debit	Credit	Debit	Credit	Debit	Credit
a. Cash	$ 18,000				$ 18,000	
b. Accounts receivable					1,500	
c. Prepaid rent	1,200				800	
d. Property, plant, and equipment	210,000				210,000	
e. Accumulated depreciation		$ 52,500				$ 70,000
f. Income taxes payable						6,500
g. Deferred revenue		16,000				8,000
h. Contributed capital		110,000				110,000
i. Retained earnings, January 1, 2006		21,700				21,700
j. Service revenue		83,000				92,500
k. Salary expense	54,000				54,000	
l. Depreciation expense					17,500	
m. Rent expense					400	
n. Income tax expense					6,500	
	$283,200	$283,200			$308,700	$308,700

Required:
1. Compare the amounts in the columns before and after the adjusting entries to reconstruct the adjusting entries made in 2006. Provide an explanation of each.
2. Compute the amount of income, assuming that it is based on the amount (a) before adjusting entries and (b) after adjusting entries. Which income amount is correct? Explain why.
3. Compute earnings per share, assuming that 5,000 shares of stock are outstanding.
4. Compute the net profit margin. What does this suggest to you about the company?
5. Record the closing entries at December 31, 2006.
6. Prepare a post-closing trial balance at December 31, 2006.

Recording Adjusting and Closing Entries and Preparing a Balance Sheet and Income Statement Including Earnings per Share (P4-8)

AP4-7
LO1, 2, 3, 5

Austin Co., a small service repair company, keeps its records without the help of an accountant. After much effort, an outside accountant prepared the following unadjusted trial balance as of the end of the annual accounting period, December 31, 2007:

Account Titles	Debit	Credit
Cash	$19,600	
Accounts receivable	7,000	
Supplies	1,300	
Prepaid insurance	900	
Equipment	27,000	
Accumulated depreciation, equipment		$12,000
Other assets	5,100	
Accounts payable		2,500
Wages payable		
Income taxes payable		
Note payable (2 years; 12% interest due each December 31)		5,000
Contributed capital (4,000 shares outstanding)		16,000
Retained earnings		10,300
Service revenue		48,000
Remaining expenses (not detailed; excludes income tax)	32,900	
Income tax expense		
Totals	$93,800	$93,800

Data not yet recorded at December 31, 2007:

a. Depreciation expense for 2007, $3,000.

b. Insurance expired during 2007, $450.

c. Wages earned by employees but not yet paid on December 31, 2007, $1,100.

d. The supplies count on December 31, 2007, reflected $600 remaining on hand to be used in 2008.

e. Income tax expense was $2,950.

Required:

1. Record the 2007 adjusting entries.
2. Prepare an income statement and a classified balance sheet for 2007 to include the effects of the preceding five transactions.
3. Record the 2007 closing entry.

AP4-8

LO1, 2, 3, 4, 5

Comprehensive Review Problem: From Recording Transactions (including Adjusting and Closing Entries) to Preparing a Complete Set of Financial Statements and Performing Ratio Analysis (see Chapters 2, 3, and 4) (P4-9)

Joe Gaskins and Matthew Perry began operations of their furniture repair shop (New Again Furniture, Inc.) on January 1, 2007. The annual reporting period ends December 31. The trial balance on January 1, 2008, was as follows:

Account Titles	Debit	Credit
Cash	$ 5,000	
Accounts receivable	4,000	
Supplies	2,000	
Small tools	6,000	
Equipment		
Accumulated depreciation (equipment)		
Other assets (not detailed to simplify)	9,000	
Accounts payable		$ 7,000
Notes payable		
Wages payable		
Interest payable		
Income taxes payable		
Unearned revenue		
Contributed capital (15,000 shares)		15,000
Retained earnings		4,000
Service revenue		
Depreciation expense		
Wages expense		
Income tax expense		
Interest expense		
Remaining expenses (not detailed to simplify)		
Totals	$26,000	$26,000

Transactions during 2008 follow:

a. Borrowed $20,000 cash on July 1, 2008, signing a one-year 10 percent note payable.

b. Purchased equipment for $18,000 cash on July 1, 2008.

c. Sold 5,000 additional shares of capital stock for cash at $1 market value per share.

d. Earned revenues for 2008, $65,000, including $9,000 on credit.

e. Recognized remaining expenses for 2008, $35,000, including $7,000 on credit.

f. Purchased additional small tools, $3,000 cash.

g. Collected accounts receivable, $8,000.

h. Paid accounts payable, $11,000.

i. Purchased $10,000 of supplies on account.

j. Received a $3,000 deposit on work to start January 15, 2009.

k. Declared and paid a cash dividend, $10,000.

Data for adjusting entries:
l. Supplies of $4,000 and small tools of $8,000 were counted on December 31, 2008 (debit Remaining Expenses).
m. Depreciation for 2008, $2,000.
n. Interest accrued on notes payable (to be computed).
o. Wages earned since the December 24 payroll but not yet paid, $3,000.
p. Income tax expense was $4,000, payable in 2009.

Required:
1. Set up T-accounts for the accounts on the trial balance and enter beginning balances.
2. Prepare journal entires for transactions (*a*) through (*k*) and post them to the T-accounts.
3. Journalize and post the adjusting entries (*l*) through (*p*).
4. Prepare an income statement (including earnings per share), statement of stockholders' equity, balance sheet, and the statement of cash flows.
5. Journalize and post the closing entry.
6. Prepare a post-closing trial balance.
7. Compute the following ratios for 2008 and explain what the results suggest about the company:
   a. Financial leverage
   b. Total asset turnover
   c. Net profit margin

CASES AND PROJECTS

Annual Report Cases

Finding Financial Information

Refer to the financial statements and accompanying notes of Pacific Sunwear of California given in Appendix B at the end of this book, or open file PSUN.pdf in the Annual Report Cases directory on the student DVD.

CP4-1
LO2, 3, 4, 5

Required:
1. How much is in the prepaid expenses account at the end of the 2004 fiscal year (for the year ended January 29, 2005)? Of that amount, how much was prepaid rent? Where did you find this information?
2. What did the company report for deferred rent at January 29, 2005? Where did you find this information?
3. What is the difference between prepaid rent and deferred rent?
4. Describe in general terms what Accrued Liabilities are.
5. How much did the company owe in currently payable sales taxes at the end of the 2004 fiscal year? Where did you find this information? (*Note:* The notes to the financial statements may be helpful for this question.)
6. What would generate the Interest Income that is reported on the income statement?
7. What company accounts would not have balances on a post-closing trial balance?
8. Give the closing entry, if any, for Prepaid Expenses.
9. What is the company's earnings per share (basic only) for the three years reported?
10. Compute the company's net profit margin for the three years reported. What does the trend suggest to you about Pacific Sunwear of California?

Finding Financial Information

Refer to the financial statements and accompanying notes of American Eagle Outfitters given in Appendix C at the end of this book, or open the AEOS.pdf in the Annual Report Cases directory on the student DVD.

CP4-2
LO2, 3, 4, 5
AMERICAN EAGLE
OUTFITTERS
ae.com

Required:
(Hint: the notes to the financial statements may be helpful for many of these questions.)

1. How much cash did the company pay for income taxes in its 2004 fiscal year (for the year ended January 29, 2005)?
2. What was the company's best quarter in terms of sales in its 2004 fiscal year? Where did you find this information?
3. Give the closing entry for the Other Income (net) account.
4. What does Accounts and Note Receivable consist of? Provide the names of the accounts and their balances as of January 29, 2005. Where did you find this information?
5. Compute the company's net profit margin for the three years reported. What does the trend suggest to you about American Eagle Outfitters?

CP4-3
LO2, 4

PACIFIC SUNWEAR
OF CALIFORNIA, INC.

AMERICAN EAGLE
OUTFITTERS
ae.com

Comparing Companies within an Industry and over Time

Refer to the financial statement of Pacific Sunwear of California given in Appendix B, American Eagle Outfitters in Appendix C, and the Industry Ratio Report given in Appendix D at the end of this book or open file CP4-3.xls in the Annual Report Cases directory on the student DVD.

Required:
1. What was Advertising Expense for each company for fiscal 2004 (for the year ending on January 29, 2005)? Where did you find the information?
2. Compute the percentage of Advertising Expense to Net Sales for fiscal year 2004 for both companies. Which company incurred the higher percentage? Show computations. Are you able to perform the same comparison for fiscal years 2003 and 2002? If so, show the computations. If not, explain why not.
3. Compare the Advertising Expense to Net Sales ratio for fiscal year 2004 computed in requirement (2) to the industry average found in the Industry Ratio Report. Were these two companies spending more or less than their average competitor on advertising (on a relative basis)? What does this ratio tell you about the general effectiveness of each company's advertising strategy?
4. Both companies have a note to the financial statements explaining the accounting policy for advertising. How do the policies differ, if at all?
5. Compute each company's net profit margin for the three years reported. What do your results suggest to you about each company over time and in comparison to each other?
6. Compare each company's net profit margin for fiscal 2004 to the industry average net profit margin in the Industry Ratio Report. Were these two companies performing better or worse than the average company in the industry?

CP4-4

Interpreting the Financial Press

A March 8, 2004, article in *The Wall Street Journal* discusses the underlying cause of accounting scandals and offers a suggestion for improved reporting.* You can access the article on the Libby/Libby/Short Web site at **www.mhhe.com/libby5e**.

Required:
Read the brief article and answer the following questions:
1. What did the author suggest as the root cause of accounting scandals?
2. What are the uncertainties referred to in the article and why does the author believe these are problems in current financial reporting?

CP4-5
LO1, 2, 5

Using Financial Reports: Inferring Adjusting Entries and Information Used in Computations and Recording Closing Entries

The pre-closing balances in the T-accounts of Hook M Horns Company at the end of the third year of operations, December 31, 2007, follow. The 2007 adjusting entries are identified by letters.

Cash		Note Payable (8%)		Contributed Capital (8,000 shares)	
Bal. 20,000			Bal. 10,000		Bal. 56,000

*Alfred Rappaport, "Shareholder Scoreboard (A Special Report): The Best & Worst Performers of the WSJ 1000—Beyond Quarterly Earnings: How to Improve Financial Reporting," *The Wall Street Journal*, March 8, 2004.

Maintenance Supplies		
Bal. 500	(a)	300

Interest Payable	
(b)	800

Retained Earnings	
Bal.	9,000

Service Equipment	
Bal. 90,000	

Income Taxes Payable	
(f)	13,020

Service Revenue	
(c) 6,000	Bal. 220,000

Accumulated Depreciation, Service Equipment		
	Bal.	18,000
	(d)	9,000

Wages Payable	
(e)	500

Expenses	
Bal. 160,000	
(a) 300	
(b) 800	
(d) 9,000	
(e) 500	
(f) 13,020	

Remaining Assets	
Bal. 42,500	

Unearned Revenue	
(c)	6,000

Required:

1. Develop three 2007 trial balances for Hook M Horns Company using the following format:

Account	Unadjusted Trial Balance		Adjusted Trial Balance		Post-Closing Trial Balance	
	Debit	Credit	Debit	Credit	Debit	Credit

2. Write an explanation for each adjusting entry for 2007.
3. Record the closing journal entry.
4. What was the average income tax rate for 2007?
5. What was the average issue (sale) price per share of the capital stock?

Using Financial Reports: Analyzing the Effects of Adjustments

CP4-6
LO2

S. Shirley Land Company, a closely held corporation, invests in commercial rental properties. Shirley's annual accounting period ends on December 31. At the end of each year, numerous adjusting entries must be made because many transactions completed during current and prior years have economic effects on the financial statements of the current and future years. Assume that the current year is 2008.

Required:
This case concerns four transactions that have been selected for your analysis. Answer the questions for each.

TRANSACTION (*a*): On January 1, 2006, the company purchased office equipment costing $14,000 for use in the business. The company estimates that the equipment's cost should be allocated at $1,400 annually.

1. Over how many accounting periods will this transaction directly affect Shirley's financial statements? Explain.
2. How much depreciation expense was reported on the 2006 and 2007 income statements?
3. How should the office equipment be reported on the 2008 balance sheet?
4. Would Shirley make an adjusting entry at the end of each year during the life of the equipment? Explain your answer.

TRANSACTION (*b*): On September 1, 2008, Shirley collected $24,000 rent on office space. This amount represented the monthly rent in advance for the six-month period, September 1, 2008, through February 28, 2009. Unearned Rent Revenue was increased (credited) and Cash was increased (debited) for $24,000.

1. Over how many accounting periods will this transaction affect Shirley's financial statements? Explain.

2. How much rent revenue on this office space should Shirley report on the 2008 income statement? Explain.

3. Did this transaction create a liability for Shirley as of the end of 2008? Explain. If yes, how much?

4. Should Shirley make an adjusting entry on December 31, 2008? Explain why. If your answer is yes, give the adjusting entry.

TRANSACTION (c): On December 31, 2008, Shirley owed employees unpaid and unrecorded wages of $7,500 because the employees worked the last three days in December 2008. The next payroll date is January 5, 2009.

1. Over how many accounting periods does this transaction affect Shirley's financial statements? Explain.

2. How would this $7,500 affect Shirley's 2008 income statement and balance sheet?

3. Should Shirley make an adjusting entry on December 31, 2008? Explain why. If your answer is yes, give the adjusting entry.

TRANSACTION (d): On January 1, 2008, Shirley agreed to supervise the planning and subdivision of a large tract of land for a customer, V. Vulchkov. This service job that Shirley will perform involves four separate phases. By December 31, 2008, three phases had been completed to Vulchkov's satisfaction. The remaining phase will be performed during 2009. The total price for the four phases (agreed on in advance by both parties) was $60,000. Each phase involves about the same amount of services. On December 31, 2008, Shirley had collected no cash for the services already performed.

1. Should Shirley record any service revenue on this job for 2008? Explain why. If yes, how much?

2. If your answer to part (1) is yes, should Shirley make an adjusting entry on December 31, 2008? If yes, give the entry. Explain.

3. What entry will Shirley make when it completes the last phase, assuming that the full contract price is collected on the completion date, February 15, 2009?

CP4-7
LO1, 2, 4, 5

Using Financial Reports: Inferring Adjusting and Closing Entries and Answering Analytical Questions

Erickson Company was organized on January 1, 2006. At the end of the first year of operations, December 31, 2006, the bookkeeper prepared the following trial balances (amounts in thousands of dollars):

Account Titles	Unadjusted Trial Balance		Adjustments		Adjusted Trial Balance	
	Debit	Credit	Debit	Credit	Debit	Credit
Cash	40				40	
Accounts receivable	17				17	
Prepaid insurance	2				1	
Rent receivable					2	
Property, plant, and equipment	46				46	
Accumulated depreciation						11
Other assets	6				6	
Accounts payable		27				27
Wages payable						3
Income taxes payable						5
Unearned rent revenue		7				4
Note payable (10% interest; dated January 1, 2006)		20				20
Contributed capital (1,000 shares)		30				30
Retained earnings	3				3	
Revenues (total)		98				103
Expenses (total including interest)	68				83	
Income tax expense					5	
Totals	182	182			203	203

Required:

1. Based on inspection of the two trial balances, give the 2006 adjusting entries developed by the bookkeeper (provide brief explanations).
2. Based on these data, give the 2006 closing entry with a brief explanation.
3. Answer the following questions (show computations):
   a. How many shares of stock were outstanding at year-end?
   b. What was the amount of interest expense included in the total expenses?
   c. What was the balance of Retained Earnings on December 31, 2006 after closing the books?
   d. What was the average income tax rate?
   e. How would the two accounts Rent Receivable and Unearned Rent Revenue be reported on the balance sheet?
   f. Explain why cash increased by $40,000 during the year even though net income was comparatively very low.
   g. What was the amount of earnings per share for 2006?
   h. What was the average selling price of the shares?
   i. When was the insurance premium paid and over what period of time did the coverage extend?
   j. What was the net profit margin for the year?

Using Financial Reports: Analyzing Financial Information in a Sale of a Business: A Challenging Case

CP4-8
LO2, 3

Crystal Mullinex owns and operates Crystal's Day Spa and Salon, Inc. She has decided to sell the business and retire. She has had discussions with a representative from a regional chain of day spas. The discussions are at the complex stage of agreeing on a price. Among the important factors have been the financial statements of the business. Crystal's secretary, Tiana, under Crystal's direction, maintained the records. Each year they developed a statement of profits on a cash basis; no balance sheet was prepared. Upon request, Crystal provided the other company with the following statement for 2008 prepared by Tiana:

CRYSTAL'S DAY SPA AND SALON, INC. Statement of Profits 2008		
Spa fees collected		$1,115,000
Expenses paid:		
Rent for office space	$130,000	
Utilities expense	43,600	
Telephone expense	12,200	
Salaries expense	522,000	
Supplies expense	31,900	
Miscellaneous expenses	12,400	
Total expenses		752,100
Profit for the year		$ 362,900

Upon agreement of the parties, you have been asked to examine the financial figures for 2008. The other company's representative said, "I question the figures because, among other things, they appear to be on a 100 percent cash basis." Your investigations revealed the following additional data at December 31, 2008:

a. Of the $1,115,000 in spa fees collected in 2008, $132,000 was for services performed prior to 2008.
b. At the end of 2008, spa fees of $29,000 for services performed during the year were uncollected.
c. Office equipment owned and used by Crystal cost $205,000. Depreciation was estimated at $20,500 annually.

d. A count of supplies at December 31, 2008, reflected $5,200 worth of items purchased during the year that were still on hand. Also, the records for 2007 indicate that the supplies on hand at the end of that year were about $3,125.

e. At the end of 2008, the secretary whose salary is $18,000 per year had not been paid for December because of a long trip that extended to January 15, 2009.

f. Telephone bills average $1,400 per month. The December 2008 bill has not been received or paid. The $12,200 amount on the statement does not include any December 2007 bill payments.

g. The $130,000 office rent paid was for 13 months (it included the rent for January 2009).

Required:

1. On the basis of this information, prepare a corrected income statement for 2008 (ignore income taxes). Show your computations for any amounts changed from those in the statement prepared by Crystal's secretary. (Suggested solution format with four-column headings: Items; Cash Basis per Crystal's Statement, $; Explanation of Changes; and Corrected Basis, $.)

2. Write a memo to support your schedule prepared in requirement (1). The purpose should be to explain the reasons for your changes and to suggest other important items that should be considered in the pricing decision.

Critical Thinking Cases

CP4-9
LO2, 3, 4

Using Financial Reports: Evaluating Financial Information as a Bank Loan Officer

Magliochetti Moving Corporation has been in operation since January 1, 2007. It is now December 31, 2007, the end of the annual accounting period. The company has not done well financially during the first year, although revenue has been fairly good. The three stockholders manage the company, but they have not given much attention to recordkeeping. In view of a serious cash shortage, they have applied to your bank for a $20,000 loan. You requested a complete set of financial statements. The following 2007 annual financial statements were prepared by a clerk and then were given to the bank.

MAGLIOCHETTI MOVING CORP. Income Statement For the Period Ended December 31, 2007		
Transportation revenue		$85,000
Expenses:		
Salaries expense	17,000	
Supplies expense	12,000	
Other expenses	18,000	
Total expenses		47,000
Net income		$38,000

MAGLIOCHETTI MOVING CORP. Balance Sheet At December 31, 2007	
Assets	
Cash	$ 2,000
Receivables	3,000
Supplies	6,000
Equipment	40,000
Prepaid insurance	4,000
Remaining assets	27,000
Total assets	$82,000
Liabilities	
Accounts payable	$ 9,000
Stockholders' Equity	
Contributed capital (10,000 shares outstanding)	35,000
Retained earnings	38,000
Total liabilities and stockholders' equity	$82,000

After briefly reviewing the statements and "looking into the situation," you requested that the statements be redone (with some expert help) to "incorporate depreciation, accruals, inventory counts, income taxes, and so on." As a result of a review of the records and supporting documents, the following additional information was developed:

a. The Supplies of $6,000 shown on the balance sheet has not been adjusted for supplies used during 2007. A count of the supplies on hand on December 31, 2007, showed $1,800.

b. The insurance premium paid in 2007 was for years 2007 and 2008. The total insurance premium was debited in full to Prepaid Insurance when paid in 2007 and no adjustment has been made.

c. The equipment cost $40,000 when purchased January 1, 2007. It had an estimated annual depreciation of $8,000. No depreciation has been recorded for 2007.

d. Unpaid (and unrecorded) salaries at December 31, 2007, amounted to $2,200.

e. At December 31, 2007, transportation revenue collected in advance amounted to $7,000. This amount was credited in full to Transportation Revenue when the cash was collected earlier during 2007.

f. Income tax expense was $3,650 (the tax rate is 25 percent).

Required:

1. Record the six adjusting entries required on December 31, 2007, based on the preceding additional information.

2. Recast the preceding statements after taking into account the adjusting entries. You do not need to use classifications on the statements. Suggested form for the solution:

| | Amounts | CHANGES | | Corrected |
Items	Reported	Plus	Minus	Amounts
(List here each item from the two statements)				

3. Omission of the adjusting entries caused:
   a. Net income to be overstated or understated (select one) by $_____.
   b. Total assets on the balance sheet to be overstated or understated (select one) by $_____.

4. For both of the unadjusted and adjusted balances, calculate these ratios for the company: (a) earnings per share and (b) net profit margin. Explain the causes of the differences and the impact of the changes on financial analysis.

5. Write a letter to the company explaining the results of the adjustments, your analysis, and your decision regarding the loan.

Evaluating the Effect of Adjusting Unearned Subscriptions on Cash Flows and Performance as a Manager

CP4-10
LO2

You are the regional sales manager for Bruzzese News Company. Bruzzese is making adjusting entries for the year ended March 31, 2008. On September 1, 2007, customers in your region paid $18,000 cash for three-year magazine subscriptions beginning on that date. The magazines are published and mailed to customers monthly. These were the only subscription sales in your region during the year.

Required:

1. What amount should be reported as cash from operations on the statement of cash flows?

2. What amount should be reported on the income statement for subscriptions revenue for the year ended March 31, 2008?

3. What amount should be reported on the March 31, 2008, balance sheet for unearned subscriptions revenue?

4. Give the adjusting entry at March 31, 2008, assuming that the subscriptions received on September 1, 2007, were recorded for the full amount in Unearned Subscriptions Revenue.

5. The company expects your region's annual revenue target to be $4,000.
   a. Evaluate your region's performance, assuming that the revenue target is based on cash sales.
   b. Evaluate your region's performance, assuming that the revenue target is based on accrual accounting.

Financial Reporting and Analysis Project

CP4-11
LO2, 3, 4

Team Project: Analysis of Accruals, Earnings per Share, and Net Profit Margin

As a team, select an industry to analyze. *Reuters* provides lists of industries and their makeup at www.investor.reuters.com/Industries.aspx. Each team member should acquire the annual report or 10-K for one publicly traded company in the industry, with each member selecting a different company. (Library files, the SEC EDGAR service at www.sec.gov, or the company itself are good sources.)

Required:

On an individual basis, each team member should write a short report answering the following questions about the selected company. Discuss any patterns across the companies that you as a team observe. Then, as a team, write a short report comparing and contrasting your companies.

1. From the Income Statement, what is the company's earnings per share for each of the last three years?
2. Ratio Analysis:
   a. What does the Net Profit Margin ratio measure in general?
   b. Compute the ratio for the last three years.
   c. What do your results suggest about the company? [You may refer to the Management Discussion and Analysis section of the 10-K or annual report to read what the company says about the reasons for any change over time.]
   d. If available, find the industry ratio for the most recent year, compare it to your results, and discuss why you believe your company differs or is similar to the industry ratio.
3. List the accounts and amounts of accrued expenses payable on the most recent balance sheet. [You may find the detail in the notes to the statements.] What is the ratio of the total accrued expenses payable to total liabilities?

After studying this chapter, you should be able to:

1. Recognize the people involved in the accounting communication process (regulators, managers, directors, auditors, information intermediaries, and users), their roles in the process, and the guidance they receive from legal and professional standards. p. 233

2. Identify the steps in the accounting communication process, including the issuance of press releases, annual reports, quarterly reports, and SEC filings as well as the role of electronic information services in this process. p. 240

3. Recognize and apply the different financial statement and disclosure formats used by companies in practice. p. 243

4. Analyze a company's performance based on return on equity and its components. p. 252

Communicating and Interpreting Accounting Information

Founded by heralded entrepreneur Ely Callaway, the company that bears his name is the number one manufacturer of premium golf clubs. In just 20 years, Mr. Callaway took a small manufacturer of specialty golf clubs with $500,000 in annual sales and built it into the industry leader with sales of more than $800 million. Callaway Golf's growth was based on its laserlike focus on product innovations that make the game easier to learn and play. Both touring pros like Masters champion Phil Mickelson and average golfers, including former presidents Bill Clinton and George Bush, use Callaway clubs.

Financing this type of growth requires an equal commitment to satisfying the highest standards of integrity in corporate governance and communication with the financial markets. In 1989, Callaway and then chief financial officer (CFO) Carol Kerley applied that commitment to integrity in communication when they persuaded managers of the General Electric Pension Fund to invest $10 million in the company, and during the company's initial public offering (first stock issuance to the public, or IPO) in 1992. The CFO and her accounting staff worked tirelessly with the company's outside auditor, PricewaterhouseCoopers, and its investment bankers at Merrill Lynch to prepare the financial information necessary for the IPO.

As a publicly traded company, Callaway Golf is required to provide detailed information in regular filings with the Securities and Exchange Commission. As the certifying officers of the company, current Chairman and CEO William C. Baker and Bradley J. Holiday, Senior Executive Vice President and Chief Financial Officer, are responsible for the accuracy of the filings. The board of directors and auditors monitor the integrity of the system that produces the disclosures. Integrity in communication with investors and other users of financial statements is a key to maintaining relationships with suppliers of capital.

FOCUS COMPANY

Callaway Golf

COMMUNICATING FINANCIAL INFORMATION

AND CORPORATE STRATEGY

www.callawaygolf.com

UNDERSTANDING THE BUSINESS

Callaway Golf Company designs, manufactures, and markets high-quality innovative golf clubs that sell at premium prices. Its ERC Fusion and Big Bertha oversized titanium woods and titanium, tungsten, and steel irons and putters account for most of its sales. The company manufactures most of its clubs in its new Carlsbad, California, factories using clubheads, shafts, and grips supplied by independent vendors. The clubs are sold at pro shops and sporting goods stores. Callaway Golf invests considerable sums in research and development and is known for introducing new and innovative products long before the end of existing products' life cycles.

CORPORATE GOVERNANCE is the procedures designed to ensure that the company is managed in the interests of the shareholders.

Callaway Golf also invests in **corporate governance**, the procedures designed to ensure that the company is managed in the interests of the shareholders. Much of its corporate governance system is aimed at ensuring integrity in the financial reporting process. Good corporate governance eases the company's access to capital, lowering both the costs of borrowing (interest rates) and the perceived riskiness of Callaway Golf's stock.[1]

Callaway Golf knows that when investors lose faith in the truthfulness of a firm's accounting numbers, they also normally punish the company's stock. The accounting scandals at Enron and WorldCom are the best recent examples. In an attempt to restore investor confidence, Congress passed the Public Accounting Reform and Investor Protection Act (the Sarbanes-Oxley Act), which strengthens financial reporting and corporate governance for public companies. Even with these added safeguards, the wisdom of famed analyst Jack Ciesielski's warning to financial statement users is still evident:

REAL WORLD EXCERPT

Analyst's Accounting Observer

One usual answer to the question "why does accounting matter?" is that it helps to avoid "blow-ups": the unpleasant outcome when a stock crashes because the firm's management engaged in accounting chicanery that subsequently becomes visible. . . . the analyst who understands accounting matters will know . . . where the "soft spots" are in financial reporting, the ones that can be manipulated in order to meet an expected earnings target or avoid breaking a loan covenant.

Source: Analyst's Accounting Observer, www.aaopub.com, August 2000.

While even the savviest analysts can still be surprised by fraudulent reports in some cases, accounting knowledge and healthy skepticism are the best protection from such surprises.

Chapters 2 through 4 focused on the mechanics of preparing the income statement, balance sheet, statement of stockholders' equity, and cash flow statement. Based on our better understanding of financial statements, we will next take a more detailed look at the people involved and the regulations that govern the process that conveys accounting information to statement users in the Internet age. We will also take a more detailed look at statement formats and additional disclosures provided in financial reports to help you learn how to find relevant information. Finally, we will examine a general framework for assessing a company's performance based on these reports.

---

[1]Examples of accounting research that examine this relationship are R. C. Anderson, S. A. Mansi, D. M. Reeb, "Board Characteristics, Accounting Report Integrity, and the Cost of Debt," *Journal of Accounting and Economics* (September 2004), pp. 315–342; and C. A. Botosan and M. A. Plumlee, A Re-Examination of Disclosure Level and the Expected Cost of Equity Capital," *Journal of Accounting Research* (March 2002), pp. 21–40.

ORGANIZATION of the Chapter

Players in the Accounting Communication Process	**The Disclosure Process**	**A Closer Look at Financial Statements Formats and Notes**	**ROE Analysis: A Framework for Evaluating Company Performance**

- Regulators (SEC, FASB, PCAOB, Stock Exchanges)
- Managers (CEO, CFO, and Accounting Staff)
- Boards of Directors (Audit Committee)
- Auditors
- Information Intermediaries: Analysts and Information Services
- Users: Institutional and Private Investors, Creditors, and Others
- Guiding Principles for Communicating Useful Information

- Press Releases
- Annual Reports
- Quarterly Reports
- SEC Reports—10-K, 10-Q, 8-K

- Classified Balance Sheet
- Classified Income Statement
- Statement of Stockholders' Equity
- Statement of Cash Flows
- Notes to Financial Statements
- Voluntary Disclosures

- Return on Equity
- ROE Profit Driver Analysis
- Profit Drivers and Business Strategy

PLAYERS IN THE ACCOUNTING COMMUNICATION PROCESS

Exhibit 5.1 summarizes the major actors involved in ensuring the integrity of the financial reporting process.

Regulators (SEC, FASB, PCAOB, Stock Exchanges)

The mission of the **U.S. Securities and Exchange Commission** (SEC) is to protect investors and maintain the integrity of the securities markets. As part of this mission, the SEC oversees the work of the Financial Accounting Standards Board (FASB) in setting generally accepted accounting principles (GAAP), the Public Company Accounting Oversight Board (PCAOB) that sets auditing standards for independent auditors (CPAs) of public companies, and the Stock Exchanges (e.g., New York Stock Exchange) that, along with state governments, set overall corporate governance standards.

The SEC staff also reviews the reports filed with it for compliance with its standards, investigates irregularities, and punishes violators. During the period July 31, 1997, though July 30, 2002, the SEC brought 515 enforcement actions against 164 companies and 705 individuals.[2] As a consequence, a number of high-profile company officers have recently been fined and sentenced to jail. Consequences to the company can include enormous financial penalties as well as bankruptcy as in the cases of Enron and WorldCom. You can read about recent SEC enforcement actions at

www.sec.gov/divisions/enforce/friactions.shtml

Learning Objective 1
Recognize the people involved in the accounting communication process (regulators, managers, directors, auditors, information intermediaries, and users), their roles in the process, and the guidance they receive from legal and professional standards.

---

[2]These statistics are reported in the Securities and Exchange Commission, "Report Pursuant to Section 704 of the Sarbanes-Oxley Act of 2002," 2004. Statistics for earlier periods are reported in M. S. Beasley, J. V. Carcello, and D. R. Hermanson, "Fraudulent Financial Reporting: 1987–1997: An Analysis of U.S. Public Companies," *The Auditor's Report* (Summer 1999), pp. 15–17.

EXHIBIT 5.1

Ensuring the
Integrity of
Financial
Information

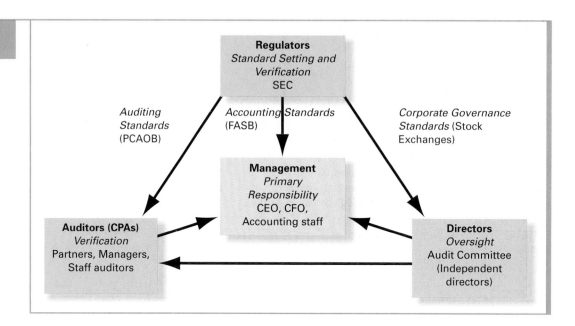

Managers (CEO, CFO, and Accounting Staff)

The primary responsibility for the information in Callaway Golf's financial statements and related disclosures lies with management, specifically the highest officer in the company, often called the **chairman and chief executive officer** (CEO), and the highest officer associated with the financial and accounting side of the business, often called the **chief financial officer** (CFO). At Callaway Golf and all public companies, these two officers must personally certify that:

- Each report filed with the Securities and Exchange Commission does not contain any untrue material statement or omit a material fact and fairly presents in all material respects the financial condition, results of operations, and cash flows of the company.

- There are no significant deficiencies and material weaknesses in the internal controls over financial reporting.

- They have disclosed to the auditors and audit committee of the board any weaknesses in internal controls or any fraud involving management or other employees who have a significant role in financial reporting.

Executives who knowingly certify false financial reports are subject to a fine of $5 million and a 20-year prison term.[3] The members of the **accounting staff,** who actually prepare the details of the reports, also bear professional responsibility for the accuracy of this information, although their legal responsibility is smaller. Their future professional success depends heavily on their reputation for honesty and competence.

Board of Directors (Audit Committee)

The **BOARD OF DIRECTORS,** elected by the shareholders to represent their interests, is responsible for maintaining the integrity of the company's financial reports.

As Callaway Golf's statement on corporate governance indicates, the board of directors (elected by the stockholders) is responsible for ensuring that processes are in place for maintaining the integrity of the company's accounting, financial statement preparation, and financial reporting. The audit committee of the board, which must be composed of

---

[3]For further discussion of new corporate governance regulations see A. Klein, "Likely Effects of Stock Exchange Governance Proposals and Sarbanes-Oxley on Corporate Boards and Financial Reporting," *Accounting Horizons* (2003), pp. 343–355.

nonmanagement (independent) directors with financial knowledge, is responsible for hiring the company's independent auditors. They also meet separately with the auditors to discuss management's compliance with their financial reporting responsibilities.

Auditors

The SEC requires publicly traded companies to have their statements and their control systems over the financial reporting process audited by an independent registered public accounting firm (independent auditor) following auditing standards established by the PCAOB. Many privately owned companies also have their statements audited. By signing an **unqualified** (or **clean**) **audit opinion,** a CPA firm assumes part of the financial responsibility for the fairness of the financial statements and related presentations. This opinion, which adds credibility to the statements, is also often required by agreements with lenders and private investors. Subjecting the company's statements to independent verification reduces the risk that the company's financial condition is misrepresented in the statements. As a result, rational investors and lenders should lower the rate of return (interest) they charge for providing capital.

Deloitte & Touche is currently Callaway Golf's auditor. This firm, along with KPMG, PricewaterhouseCoopers, and Ernst & Young, make up what are referred to as the "Big 4" CPA firms. Each of these firms employs thousands of CPAs in offices scattered throughout the world. They audit the great majority of publicly traded companies as well as many that are privately held. Some public companies and most private companies are audited by smaller CPA firms. A list of the auditors for selected focus companies follows.

UNQUALIFIED (CLEAN) AUDIT OPINION Auditors' statement that the financial statements are fair presentations in all material respects in conformity with GAAP.

Focus Company	Industry	Auditor
Harrah's	Casinos and hotels	Deloitte & Touche
Deckers' Outdoor	Footwear	KPMG
Papa John's	Fast food	Ernst & Young
Outback Steakhouse	Restaurants	PricewaterhouseCoopers

Information Intermediaries: Financial Analysts and Information Services

Students often view the communication process between companies and financial statement users as a simple process of mailing the report to individual shareholders who read the report and then make investment decisions based on what they have learned. This simple picture is far from today's reality. Now most investors rely on sophisticated financial analysts and information services to gather and analyze information. Exhibit 5.2 summarizes this process.

EXHIBIT 5.2

Using Financial Reports

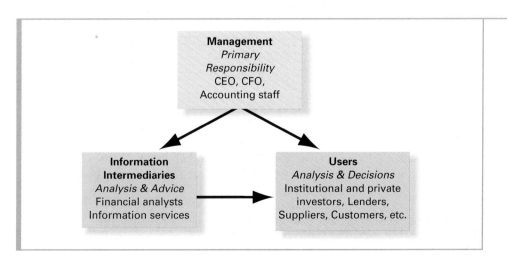

EARNINGS FORECASTS are predictions of earnings for future accounting periods.

REAL WORLD EXCERPT

Analysts' Reports

Financial analysts receive accounting reports and other information about the company from electronic information services. They also gather information through conversations with company executives and visits to company facilities and competitors. The results of their analyses are combined into analysts' reports. Analysts' reports normally include forecasts of future quarterly and annual earnings per share and share price; a buy, hold, or sell recommendation for the company's shares; and explanations for these judgments. In making their earnings forecasts, the analysts rely heavily on their knowledge of the way the accounting system translates business events into the numbers on a company's financial statements, which is the subject matter of this text. Individual analysts often specialize in particular industries (such as sporting goods or energy companies). Analysts are regularly evaluated based on the accuracy of their forecasts, as well as the profitability of their stock picks.[4] At the time this chapter was written, three major firms provided the following forecasts and recommendations for Callaway Golf:

COMPANY: CALLAWAY GOLF

Firm	Stock Recommendation	Earnings Forecast for 2004	Earnings Forecast for 2005
A.G. Edwards	Hold	0.33	0.64
Barrington Research	Market Perform	0.19	0.80
J.P. Morgan	Neutral	0.13	0.48

The large differences among the analysts' forecasts indicate a good deal of uncertainty about the company's future.

Analysts often work in the research departments of brokerage and investment banking houses such as Merrill Lynch, mutual fund companies such as Fidelity Investments, and investment advisory services such as Value Line that sell their advice to others. Through their reports and recommendations, analysts are transferring their knowledge of accounting, the company, and the industry to their customers who lack this expertise. Many believe that decisions made based on analysts' advice cause stock market prices to react quickly to information in financial statements. A quick, unbiased reaction to information is called **market efficiency** in finance. It is highly unlikely that unsophisticated investors can glean more information from financial statements than the sophisticated analysts have already learned. The **information services** discussed next allow investors to gather their own information about the company and monitor the recommendations of a variety of analysts.

Companies actually file their SEC forms electronically through the EDGAR (Electronic Data Gathering and Retrieval) Service, which is sponsored by the SEC. Users can retrieve information from EDGAR within 24 hours of its submission, long before it is available through the mail. EDGAR is a free service available on the Web at

www.sec.gov

Many companies also provide direct access to their financial statements and other information over the web. You can contact Callaway Golf by clicking on "investor relations" at

www.callawaygolf.com

---

[4]See M. B. Mikhail, B. R. Walther, and R. H. Willis, "Does Forecast Accuracy Matter to Security Analysts?" *The Accounting Review,* April 1999, pp. 185–200; and R. A. McEwen and J. E. Hunton, "Is Analyst Forecast Accuracy Associated with Accounting Information Use?" *Accounting Horizons,* March 1999, pp. 1–16.

Financial analysts and other sophisticated users obtain much of the information they use from the wide variety of commercial online information services. Services such as Compustat and Thompson Research provide broad access to financial statements and news information. They also allow users to search the database by key words, including various financial statement terms. Their websites describe their services in more detail:

www.compustat.com

research.thomsonib.com

Readers should be aware that the definitions used to compute key ratios often differ across these sources.

More general information services include Factiva and Bloomberg. Factiva provides access to news stories about companies and company press releases, including the initial announcements of annual and quarterly financial results. The Bloomberg service also provides the ability to combine these sources of information in sophisticated analyses. The graph presented in Exhibit 5.3 plots Callaway Golf's quarterly price per share and earnings per share over nine years. Their websites describe their services in more detail:

www.factiva.com

www.bloomberg.com

An increasing number of other resources offering a mixture of free and fee-based information exist on the Web. These include

www.investor.reuters.com

www.hoovers.com

finance.yahoo.com

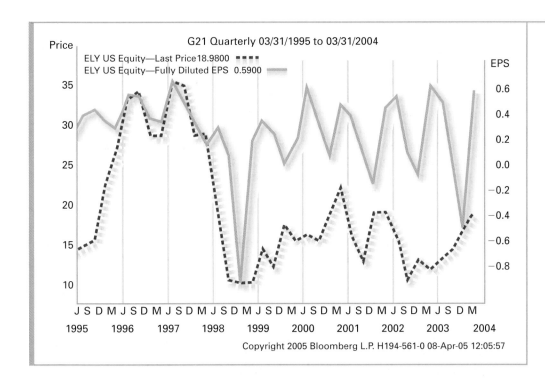

EXHIBIT 5.3

Price and Earnings per Share Graph from the Bloomberg Terminal

Information services have become the primary tool for professional analysts and marketing strategists who use them to analyze competing firms. Sales representatives also use these services to analyze potential customers' needs for their products and creditworthiness. Growing, creditworthy companies are the most profitable targets for the sales representatives' efforts.

Information services are also an important source of information for term papers and job searches. Potential employers expect job applicants to demonstrate knowledge of their companies during an interview, and electronic information services are an excellent source of company information. To learn more about electronic information services, contact the business or reference librarian at your college or university or explore the preceding websites.

Users: Institutional and Private Investors, Creditors, and Others

INSTITUTIONAL INVESTORS are managers of pension, mutual, endowment, and other funds that invest on the behalf of others.

Institutional investors include pension funds (associated with unions and employees of specific companies or government agencies); mutual funds; and endowment, charitable foundation, and trust funds (such as the endowment of your college or university). These institutional stockholders usually employ their own analysts who also rely on the information intermediaries just discussed. Institutional shareholders control the majority of publicly traded shares of U.S. companies. For example, at the end of the current fiscal year, institutional investors owned 97 percent of Callaway Golf stock. Callaway Golf's three largest institutional investors follow:

Institution	Approximate Ownership
Royce & Associates	7,423,300
Kaplan Associates LLC	4,272,505
Barclays Global Investors Intl.	4,111,598

Most small investors own stock in companies such as Callaway Golf indirectly through mutual and pension funds.

PRIVATE INVESTORS include individuals who purchase shares in companies.

Private investors include large individual investors such as Ely Callaway and his friends who originally invested directly in Callaway Golf, as well as small retail investors who buy shares of publicly traded companies through brokers such as Merrill Lynch. Retail investors normally lack the expertise to understand financial statements and the resources to gather data efficiently. They often rely on the advice of information intermediaries or turn their money over to the management of mutual and pension funds (institutional investors).

LENDERS (CREDITORS) include suppliers and financial institutions that lend money to companies.

Lenders, or **creditors,** include suppliers, banks, commercial credit companies, and other financial institutions that lend money to companies. Lending officers and financial analysts in these organizations use the same public sources of information. They also use additional financial information (e.g., monthly statements) that companies often agree to provide as part of the lending contract. Lenders are the primary external user group for financial statements of private companies. Institutional and private investors also become creditors when they buy a company's publicly traded bonds.

Financial statements also play an important role in the relationships between suppliers and customers. Customers evaluate the financial health of suppliers to determine whether they will be reliable, up-to-date sources of supply. Suppliers evaluate their customers to estimate their future needs and ability to pay debts. Competitors also attempt to learn useful information about a company from its statements. The potential loss of competitive advantage is one of the costs of public financial disclosures. Accounting regulators consider these costs as well as the direct costs of preparation when they consider requiring new disclosures. They apply what is called the cost-benefit constraint, which suggests that the benefits of accounting for and reporting information should outweigh the costs.

Guiding Principles for Communicating Useful Information

For accounting information to be useful, it must be relevant and reliable. Relevant information is capable of influencing decisions by allowing users to assess past activities and/or predict future activities. Reliable information is accurate, unbiased, and verifiable (independent parties can agree on the nature of the transaction and amount). Our discussions of ratio analysis have emphasized the importance of comparing ratios for the same company over time, as well as with those of competitors. Such comparisons are valid only if the information is prepared on a consistent and comparable basis. Consistent information means that within a company, similar accounting methods have been applied over time. Comparable information means that similar accounting methods have been applied across companies. These characteristics of useful information, along with the full-disclosure principle, guide the FASB in deciding what financial information should be reported.

Accurate interpretation of financial statements requires that the statement reader be aware of important constraints of accounting measurement. First, small amounts do not have to be reported separately or accounted for precisely according to GAAP if they would not influence users' decisions. Accountants usually designate such items and amounts as **immaterial.** Determining material amounts is often very subjective.

Second, conservatism requires that special care be taken to avoid (1) overstating assets and revenues and (2) understating liabilities and expenses. This guideline attempts to offset managers' natural optimism about their operations, which sometimes creeps into the financial reports they prepare. This constraint produces more conservative income statement and balance sheet amounts. Finally, in certain industries such as public utilities, special industry reporting practices are followed to better reflect the economics of those industries.

The **COST-BENEFIT CONSTRAINT** suggests that the benefits of accounting for and reporting information should outweigh the costs.

RELEVANT INFORMATION can influence a decision; it is timely and has predictive and/or feedback value.

RELIABLE INFORMATION is accurate, unbiased, and verifiable.

CONSISTENT INFORMATION can be compared over time because similar accounting methods have been applied.

COMPARABLE INFORMATION allows comparisons across businesses because similar accounting methods have been applied.

MATERIAL AMOUNTS are amounts that are large enough to influence a user's decision.

CONSERVATISM suggests that care should be taken not to overstate assets and revenues or understate liabilities and expenses.

International Accounting Standards Board and Global Differences in Accounting Standards

INTERNATIONAL PERSPECTIVE

Financial accounting standards and disclosure requirements are set by national regulatory agencies and standard-setting bodies. Many countries, including the members of the European Union, are committed to adopting international financial reporting standards (IFRS) issued by the International Accounting Standards Board (IASB). IFRS are similar to U.S. GAAP, but there are several important differences. A partial list of the differences* at the time this chapter is being written is presented below, along with the chapter in which these issues will be addressed:

Difference	U.S. GAAP	IFRS	Chapter
Extraordinary items	Permitted	Prohibited	5
Last-in, first-out method for inventory	Permitted	Prohibited	7
Reversal of inventory write-downs	Prohibited	Required	7
Basis for property, plant, and equipment	Historical cost	Fair value or historical cost	8

The FASB and IASB are working together to eliminate these and other differences.

*Source: *Deloitte IAS Plus,* June 2004.

SELF-STUDY QUIZ

Match the key terms in the left column with their definitions in the right column.

1. Relevant information
2. CEO and CFO
3. Financial analyst
4. Auditor
5. Cost-benefit constraint

a. Management primarily responsible for accounting information.

b. An independent party who verifies financial statements.

c. Information that influences users' decisions.

d. Reporting only information that provides benefits in excess of costs.

e. An individual who analyzes financial information and provides advice.

After you have completed your answers, check them with the solutions at the bottom of the page.

THE DISCLOSURE PROCESS

Learning Objective 2
Identify the steps in the accounting communication process, including the issuance of press releases, annual reports, quarterly reports, and SEC filings as well as the role of electronic information services in this process.

As noted in our discussion of information services and information intermediaries, the accounting communication process includes more steps and participants than one would envision in a world in which annual and quarterly reports are simply mailed to shareholders. SEC regulation FD, for "Fair Disclosure," requires that companies provide all investors equal access to all important company news. Managers and other insiders are also prohibited from trading their company's shares based on nonpublic (insider) information so that no party benefits from early access.

Press Releases

A **PRESS RELEASE** is a written public news announcement normally distributed to major news services.

To provide timely information to external users and to limit the possibility of selective leakage of information, Callaway Golf and other public companies announce quarterly and annual earnings through a press release as soon as the verified figures (audited for annual and reviewed for quarterly earnings) are available. Callaway Golf normally issues its earnings press releases within four weeks of the end of the accounting period. The announcements are sent electronically to the major print and electronic news services including *DowJones, Reuters,* and *Bloomberg,* which make them immediately available to subscribers. Exhibit 5.4 shows an excerpt from a typical earnings press release for Callaway Golf that includes key financial figures. This excerpt is followed by management's discussion of the results and condensed income statements and balance sheets, which will be included in the formal report to shareholders, distributed after the press release.

Many companies, including Callaway Golf, follow these press releases with a conference call during which senior managers answer questions about the quarterly results from analysts. These calls are open to the investing public. Listening to these recordings is a good way to learn about a company's business strategy and its expectations for the future, as well as key factors that analysts consider when they evaluate a company.

For actively traded stocks such as Callaway Golf, most of the stock market reaction (stock price increases and decreases from investor trading) to the news in the press release usually occurs quickly. Recall that a number of analysts follow Callaway Golf and regularly predict the company's earnings. When the actual earnings are published, the market reacts *not* to the amount of earnings but to the difference between expected

EXHIBIT 5.4

Earnings Press Release
Excerpt for Callaway
Golf Company

GOLF

Callaway Golf Announces 2003 Results and Reiterates 2004 Guidance

CARLSBAD, Calif.–(BUSINESS WIRE)–Jan. 22, 2004–Callaway Golf Company (NYSE:ELY) today released its consolidated financial results for the fourth quarter and full year ended December 31, 2003, announcing net sales for the full year of $814 million compared with $793 million for the prior year. Net income for the full year was $46 million versus $69 million for the prior year. Fully diluted earnings per share for the period were $0.68 compared with $1.03 for the prior year. Currency fluctuations had a favorable impact on 2003 net sales of $28 million.

Net sales for the fourth quarter ended December 31, 2003 were $147 million versus $123 million in the comparable period during the prior year. Net loss for the quarter was $33 million versus $6 million for the prior period. Loss per share was $0.50 compared with $0.08 for the comparable period in the prior year. Currency fluctuations had a favorable impact on net sales of $6 million.

Source: For more information about Callaway Golf Company, please visit our website on the Internet at www.callawaygolf.com.

2285 Rutherford Road • Carlsbad, CA 92008-8815
Telephone: (619) 931-1771 • Outside California (800) 228-2767
FAX: (619) 931-9539

earnings and actual earnings. This amount is called **unexpected earnings.** For example, *The San Diego Union-Tribune* recently reported the following:

Callaway Bogeyed in Quarter, Say Analysts
Net Income Fell Short of Wall Street Expectations

Callaway Golf yesterday reported sales of $363.8 million for the three months that ended March 31, but analysts said the Carlsbad golf company took too many strokes to reach the green.
Callaway posted first-quarter net income of $40.5 million, or 64 cents a share, excluding one-time charges, but that fell short of Wall Street's expectations. The consensus estimate of analysts polled by Thomson First Call was 70 cents a share.

Source: *The San Diego Union-Tribune,* April 23, 2004, p. C-1.

Unexpected earnings (actual–expected) were −6 cents per share (64–70 cents), and, as a result, the share price dropped around $2. The following excerpt from a recent article in *Harvard Business Review* points out the growing importance of meeting or beating the average or consensus analysts' estimate:

The Earnings Game: Everyone Plays, Nobody Wins

Quarterly earnings numbers dominate the decisions of executives, analysts, investors, and auditors . . . meeting analysts' expectations that earnings will rise in a smooth, steady, unbroken line has become, at many corporations, a game whose imperatives override even the imperative to deliver the highest possible return to shareholders.

Source: *Harvard Business Review,* June 2001, p. 65.

Companies such as Callaway Golf also issue press releases concerning other important events including new product announcements and new endorsement contracts with professional golfers. Press releases related to annual earnings and quarterly earnings often precede the issuance of the quarterly or annual report by 15 to 45 days. This time is necessary to prepare the additional detail and to print and distribute those reports.

Annual Reports

For privately held companies, **annual reports** are relatively simple documents photocopied on white bond paper. They normally include only the following:

1. Four basic financial statements: income statement, balance sheet, stockholders' equity or retained earnings statement, and cash flow statement.
2. Related notes (footnotes).
3. Report of Independent Accountants (Auditor's Opinion) if the statements are audited.

The annual reports of public companies are significantly more elaborate, both because of additional SEC reporting requirements and because many companies use their annual reports as public relations tools.

The annual reports of public companies are normally split into two sections. The first, "nonfinancial," section usually includes a letter to stockholders from the chairman and CEO; descriptions of the company's management philosophy, products, successes (and occasionally failures); and exciting prospects and challenges for the future. Beautiful photographs of products, facilities, and personnel often are included. The second, "financial," section includes the core of the report. The SEC sets minimum disclosure standards for the financial section of the annual reports of public companies. The principal components of the financial section include these:

1. Summarized financial data for a 5- or 10-year period.
2. Management's Discussion and Analysis of Financial Condition and Results of Operations and Disclosures about Market Risk.
3. The four basic financial statements.
4. Notes (footnotes).
5. Report of Independent Accountants (Auditor's Opinion) and the Management Certification.
6. Recent stock price information.
7. Summaries of the unaudited quarterly financial data (described later).
8. Lists of directors and officers of the company and relevant addresses.

The order of these components varies.

Except for the Management's Discussion and Analysis and Disclosures about Market Risks, most of these elements have been covered in earlier chapters. This element includes an explanation of key figures on the financial statements and the risks the company faces in the future.

Quarterly Reports

Quarterly reports normally begin with a short letter to shareholders. This is followed by a condensed income statement for the quarter, which often shows less detail than the annual income statement, and a condensed balance sheet dated at the end of the quarter (e.g., March 31 for the first quarter). These condensed financial statements are not audited and so are marked **unaudited.** Often the cash flow statement, statement of stockholders' equity (or retained earnings statement), and some notes to the financial statements are omitted. Private companies also normally prepare quarterly reports for their lenders.

SEC Reports—10-K, 10-Q, 8-K

Public companies must file periodic reports with the SEC. They include the annual report on Form 10-K, quarterly reports on Form 10-Q, and current event reports on Form 8-K. These reports are normally referred to by number (for example, the "10-K"). In general, the 10-K and 10-Q present all information in the annual and quarterly reports, respectively, along with additional management discussion and several required schedules.

For example, the Form 10-K provides a more detailed description of the business including its products, product development, sales and marketing, manufacturing, and competitors. It also lists properties owned or leased, any legal proceedings it is involved in, and significant contracts it has signed. The 10-K also provides more detailed schedules concerning various figures on the income statement and balance sheet including bad debts, warranties, inventories, and advertising. There has been a recent trend to combine the information in the 10-K into the company annual reports.

The **FORM 10-K** is the annual report that publicly traded companies must file with the SEC.

FORM 10-Q is the quarterly report that publicly traded companies must file with the SEC.

FORM 8-K is used by publicly traded companies to disclose any material event not previously reported that is important to investors (e.g., auditor changes, mergers).

A CLOSER LOOK AT FINANCIAL STATEMENT FORMATS AND NOTES

To make financial statements more useful to investors, creditors, and analysts, specific **classifications** of information are included on the statements. Various classifications are used in practice. You should not be confused when you notice slightly different formats used by different companies. In this section, we will focus on similarities and differences in the classifications and line items presented on Callaway Golf's and Papa John's balance sheet, income statement, and cash flow statement. We also discuss some of Callaway Golf's note disclosures in more detail.

Learning Objective 3
Recognize and apply the different financial statement and disclosure formats used by companies in practice.

Topic Tackler 5–1

Classified Balance Sheet

Exhibit 5.5 shows the December 31, 2003, balance sheet for Callaway Golf. Its balance sheet looks very similar in structure to Papa John's presented in Chapter 4. Its balance sheet is classified as follows:

Assets (by order of liquidity)
   Current assets (short term)
   Noncurrent assets
     Total assets
Liabilities (by order of time to maturity)
   Current liabilities (short-term)
   Long-term liabilities
     Total liabilities
Stockholders' equity (by source)
   Contributed capital (by owners)
   Retained earnings (accumulated earnings minus accumulated dividends declared)
     Total stockholders' equity
     Total liabilities and stockholders' equity

These classifications will play a major role in our discussions of ratio analysis in later chapters.

Callaway Golf's balance sheet contains two items, not included in Papa John's, that are worthy of additional discussion. **Intangible Assets** have no physical existence and a long life. Examples are patents, trademarks, copyrights, franchises, and goodwill from purchasing other companies. Most intangibles except goodwill are amortized as

CALLAWAY GOLF COMPANY
Consolidated Balance Sheets*
At December 31, 2003 and 2002

(dollars in thousands, except share and per share data)	December 31, 2003	December 31, 2002
ASSETS		
Current assets:		
Cash and cash equivalents	$ 47,340	$108,452
Accounts receivable, net	100,664	63,867
Inventories, net	185,389	151,760
Other current assets	50,069	44,948
Total current assets	$383,462	$369,027
Property, plant and equipment, net	164,763	167,340
Intangible assets, net	169,851	121,317
Other assets	30,490	22,161
	$748,566	$679,845
LIABILITIES AND SHAREHOLDERS' EQUITY		
Current liabilities:		
Accounts payable and accrued expenses	$117,958	$ 98,352
Note payable, current portion	240	3,160
Income taxes payable	11,962	7,649
Total current liabilities	$130,160	$109,161
Long-term liabilities:		
Other liabilities	29,023	27,297
Commitment and contingencies (Note 13)		
Shareholders' equity:		
Common Stock, $.01 par value, 83,710,094 shares and 83,577,427 shares issued at December 31, 2003 and 2002, respectively	837	836
Additional paid-in capital	122,105	103,097
Retained earnings	466,441	439,454
Total shareholders' equity	$589,383	$543,387
	$748,566	$679,845

The accompanying notes are an integral part of these financial statements.

Callaway's statements have been simplified for purposes of our discussion.

they are used, in a manner similar to the depreciation of tangible assets. They are reported net of accumulated amortization on the balance sheet.

Until this chapter, we have identified the financing by investors as **Contributed Capital.** In practice, however, this account often is shown as two accounts: Common Stock and Additional Paid-in Capital.[5] Each share of common stock usually has a nominal (low) **par value** printed on the face of the certificate. Par value is a legal amount

PAR VALUE is a legal amount per share established by the board of directors; it establishes the minimum amount a stockholder must contribute and has no relationship to the market price of the stock.

[5]The face of Callaway's balance sheet (as is common for most companies) discloses information on the number of shares that the company is authorized to issue (240 million) and the number of shares issued (83,710,094). Callaway's actual statement lists an amount as treasury stock that is the shares that have been repurchased by the company from shareholders. Chapter 11 discusses these terms in more detail.

per share established by the board of directors; it has no relationship to the market price of the stock. Its significance is that it establishes the minimum amount that a stockholder must contribute. Callaway Golf's common stock has a par value of $.01 per share, but the 1,000,000 shares were sold in its 1992 initial public offering at a market price of $16 per share.[6] When a corporation issues capital stock, the amount received is recorded in part as Common Stock (Number of Shares × Par Value per Share) and the excess above par as Additional Paid-in Capital (also called Paid-in Capital or Contributed Capital in Excess of Par). The journal entry to record Callaway Golf's 1992 initial public offering follows:

ADDITIONAL PAID-IN CAPITAL (Paid-in Capital, Contributed Capital in Excess of Par) is the amount of contributed capital less the par value of the stock.

Cash (+A) ($16 × 1,000,000 shares) 16,000,000
      Common stock (+SE) ($.01 per share × 1,000,000 shares)   10,000
      Additional paid-in capital (+SE) ($16,000,000 − 10,000) 15,990,000

Assets		=	Liabilities	+	Stockholders' Equity	
Cash	+16,000,000				Common Stock	+ 10,000
					Additional Paid-in Capital	+ 15,990,000

Topic Tackler 5–2

Classified Income Statement

Callaway Golf's 2003 consolidated income statement is reprinted for you in Exhibit 5.6. Income statements have two major sections. The first presents the income statement as we have in prior chapters. The second presents net income on a per share basis or earnings per share.

Continuing Operations

Callaway Golf's income statements are prepared using the following basic structure.

	Net sales
−	Cost of goods sold
	Gross profit
−	Operating expenses
	Income from operations
+/−	Nonoperating revenues/expenses and gains/losses
	Income before income taxes
−	Income tax expense
	Net income

Callaway Golf is a manufacturing company, whereas Papa John's is a service firm. Consequently, Callaway Golf's income statement includes one subtotal not included in Papa John's. Like most manufacturing and merchandising companies,[7] Callaway Golf reports the subtotal Gross Profit (Gross Margin), which is the difference between Net Sales and Cost of Goods Sold. Another subtotal—Income from Operations (also called Operating Income)—is computed by subtracting operating expenses from gross profit.

    Nonoperating (other) Items are income, expenses, gains, and losses that do not relate to the company's primary operations. Examples include interest income, interest expense, and gains and losses on the sale of fixed assets and investments. These non-

GROSS PROFIT (GROSS MARGIN) is net sales less cost of goods sold.

INCOME FROM OPERATIONS (OPERATING INCOME) equals net sales less cost of goods sold and other operating expenses.

---

[6]These numbers are rounded.

[7]A merchandiser buys products from manufacturers for resale, and a manufacturer produces goods for sale to wholesalers or retail merchandisers.

CALLAWAY GOLF COMPANY
Consolidated Statement of Operations
For the Years Ended December 31, 2001–2003

(dollars in thousands, except per share data)	Years Ended December 31,					
	2003		2002		2001	
Net sales	$814,032	100%	$793,219	100%	$818,072	100%
Cost of sales	445,417	55%	393,068	50%	411,585	50%
Gross profit	368,615	45%	400,151	50%	406,487	50%
Selling expenses	207,783	26%	200,329	25%	188,415	23%
General and administrative expenses	65,448	8%	56,580	7%	71,058	9%
Research and development expenses	29,529	4%	32,182	4%	32,697	4%
Total operating expenses	302,760	37%	289,091	36%	292,170	36%
Income from operations	65,855	8%	111,060	14%	114,317	14%
Interest and other income, net	3,550		2,271		5,349	
Interest expense	(1,522)		(1,660)		(1,552)	
Other gains/losses	—		—		(19,922)	
Income before income taxes	67,883	8%	111,671	14%	98,192	12%
Provision for income taxes	22,360		42,225		39,817	
Net income	$ 45,523	6%	$ 69,446	9%	$ 58,375	7%
Earnings per common share:	$0.69		$1.04		$0.84	
Common equivalent shares:	66,027		66,517		69,809	

The accompanying notes are an integral part of these financial statements.

INCOME BEFORE INCOME TAXES (PRETAX EARNINGS) is revenues minus all expenses except income tax expense.

operating items are added to or subtracted from income from operations to obtain **Income before Income Taxes**, also called **Pretax Earnings**. At this point, Income Tax Provision (Income Tax Expense) is normally subtracted to obtain Net Income. Some companies show fewer subtotals on their income statements. No difference exists in the revenue, expense, gain, and loss items reported using the different formats. Only the categories and subtotals differ.

Nonrecurring Items

Companies may also report one or more of three nonrecurring items on their income statements:

1. Discontinued operations.

2. Extraordinary items.

3. Cumulative effect of changes in accounting methods.

If any one of these three items exists, an additional subtotal is presented for Income from Continuing Operations (or Income before Nonrecurring Items), after which the nonrecurring items are presented. These three items are presented separately because they are not useful in predicting the future income of the company given their nonrecurring nature.

When a major component of a business is sold or abandoned, income or loss from that component, as well as any gain or loss on disposal, are included as discontinued operations. Extraordinary Items are gains or losses incurred that are both unusual and infrequent in occurrence. The cumulative effect of changes in accounting methods presents the effects on the balance sheet of changing from one acceptable accounting method to another. The cumulative effect of that change on assets and liabilities on the balance sheet is reflected on the income statement, which flows through to retained earnings on the balance sheet. The Chapter Supplement explains these three nonrecurring items in more detail.

Earnings per Share

As we discussed in Chapter 4, simple computations for earnings per share (EPS) are as follows:

$$\text{EPS} = \frac{\text{Net Income Available to Common Shareholders}}{\text{Weighted Average Number of Shares Outstanding During the Reporting Period}}$$

Common-Size Income Statement

Notice that Callaway Golf also reports income statement line items as a percentage of net sales, which are often called **common-size income statements.** Many analysts compute these common-size statements as a first step in analysis because they ease year-to-year comparisons.

Interpreting the Common-Size Income Statement

FINANCIAL ANALYSIS

The common-size income statement reports line items as a percentage of net sales (divide each line item by net sales and multiply by 100). Callaway Golf's common-size statement presented in Exhibit 5.6 dramatically displays the cause of its declining income. Even though Net sales have risen between 2002 and 2003, Cost of sales has risen at a much faster rate, increasing from 50% to 55% of net sales. This resulted from declines in sales of higher gross margin products as well as price pressure from competitors. At the same time, Total operating expenses have also risen from 36% to 37%. Taken together, these factors produced the decrease in net profit margin from 9% to 6%.

SELF-STUDY **QUIZ**

1. Prepare a journal entry for the following transaction: Issued 1,000 shares of $1 par value stock for $12 per share.

2. Complete the following tabulation, indicating the direction (+ for increase, − for decrease, and NE for no effect) and amount of the effect of each transaction. Consider each item independently.

   a. Recorded and paid rent expense of $200.

   b. Recorded the sale of goods on account for $400 and cost of goods sold of $300.

TRANSACTION	CURRENT ASSETS	GROSS PROFIT	INCOME FROM OPERATIONS
a.			
b.			

After you have completed your answers, check them with the solutions at the bottom of the page.

Statement of Stockholders' Equity

The statement of stockholders' (shareholders') equity reports the changes in each of the company's stockholders' equity accounts during the accounting period. We will discuss this statement in more detail in Chapter 11.

Statement of Cash Flows

We introduced the three cash flow statement classifications in prior chapters:

Cash Flows from Operating Activities. This section reports cash flows associated with earning income.

Cash Flows from Investing Activities. Cash flows in this section are associated with purchase and sale of (1) productive assets (other than inventory) and (2) investments in other companies.

Cash Flows from Financing Activities. These cash flows are related to financing the business through debt issuances and repayments, stock (equity) issuances and repurchases, and dividend payments.

Exhibit 5.7 presents Callaway Golf's 2003 consolidated statement of cash flows. The first section (Cash Flows from Operating Activities) can be reported using either the **direct** or **indirect** method. For Callaway, this first section is reported using the indirect method, which presents a reconciliation of net income on an accrual basis to cash flows from operations. This more common format differs from the format in the statement prepared for Papa John's, which was constructed using the direct method.

FOCUS ON
CASH FLOWS

Operating Activities (Indirect Method)

The Operating Activities section prepared using the indirect method helps the analyst understand the **causes of differences** between a company's net income and its cash flows. Net income and cash flows from operating activities can be quite different. Remember that the income statement is prepared under the accrual concept. Revenues are recorded when earned without regard to when the related cash flows occur. Likewise, expenses are matched with revenues and recorded in the same period without regard to when the related cash flows occur.

In the indirect method, the Operating Activities section starts with net income computed under the accrual concept and then eliminates noncash items leaving cash flow from operating activities:

Net income
$+/-$ Adjustments for noncash items
———————————————————
Cash provided by operating activities

The items listed between these two amounts explain the reasons they differ. For example, since no cash is paid during the current period for Callaway Golf's depreciation expense reported on the income statement, this amount is added back in the conversion process. Similarly, increases and decreases in current assets and liabilities also account for some of the difference between net income and cash flow from operations. For example, sales on account increase net income as well as the current asset accounts receivable, but do not increase cash. As we cover different portions of the income statement and balance sheet in more detail in Chapters 6 through 12, we will also discuss the relevant sections of the cash flow statement. Then the complete cash flow statement will be discussed in detail in Chapter 13.

Notes to Financial Statements

While the numbers reported on the various financial statements provide important information, users require additional details to facilitate their analysis. All financial

CALLAWAY GOLF COMPANY Consolidated Statement of Cash Flows For the Years Ended December 31			
(dollars in thousands)	**2003**	**2002**	**2001**
Cash flows from operating activities:			
Net income	$ 45,523	$ 69,446	$ 58,375
Adjustments to reconcile net income to net cash provided by operating activities:			
Depreciation and amortization	44,496	37,640	37,467
Other noncash items	17,593	16,361	33,592
Changes in assets and liabilities, net of effects from acquisitions:			
Accounts receivable, net	12,698	(9,279)	3,182
Inventories, net	4,897	21,785	(37,147)
Other assets	(4,743)	10,202	5,630
Accounts payable and accrued expenses	(7,297)	(12,204)	2,285
Income taxes payable	4,004	6,185	(1,644)
Other liabilities	1,572	(922)	(1,587)
Net cash provided by operating activities	$118,743	$139,214	$100,153
Cash flows from investing activities:			
Capital expenditures	(7,810)	(73,502)	(35,274)
Acquisitions, net of cash acquired	(160,321)	—	(5,758)
Investment in marketable securities	—	(2,000)	(6,422)
Proceeds from sale of marketable securities	24	6,998	—
Proceeds from sale of capital assets	178	871	4,629
Net cash used in investing activities	($167,929)	($67,633)	($42,825)
Cash flows from financing activities:			
Payments on financing arrangements	(8,117)	(2,374)	(1,168)
Issuance of Common Stock	17,994	18,305	50,651
Acquisition of Common Stock	(4,755)	(46,457)	(104,049)
Dividends paid, net	(18,536)	(18,601)	(19,447)
Net cash used in financing activities	($13,414)	($49,127)	($74,013)
Effect of exchange rate changes on cash and cash equivalents	1,488	1,735	(1,648)
Net increase (decrease) in cash and cash equivalents	(61,112)	24,189	(18,333)
Cash and cash equivalents at beginning of year	108,452	84,263	102,596
Cash and cash equivalents at end of year	$ 47,340	$108,452	$ 84,263

EXHIBIT 5.7

Cash Flows Statement of Callaway Golf

REAL WORLD EXCERPT

ANNUAL REPORT

The accompanying notes are an integral part of these financial statements.

reports include additional information in notes that follow the statements. Callaway Golf's 2003 notes include three types of information:

1. Descriptions of the key accounting rules applied to the company's statements.
2. Additional detail supporting reported numbers.
3. Relevant financial information not disclosed on the statements.

Accounting Rules Applied in the Company's Statements

One of the first notes is typically a summary of significant accounting policies. As you will see in your study of subsequent chapters, generally accepted accounting principles (GAAP) permit companies to select from alternative methods for measuring the effects of transactions. The summary of significant accounting policies tells the user which accounting methods the company has adopted. Callaway Golf's accounting policy for property, plant, and equipment is as follows:

REAL WORLD EXCERPT

Callaway
G O L F

ANNUAL REPORT

> *Note 2*
>
> **Significant Accounting Policies**
>
> *Property, Plant, and Equipment*
>
> Property, plant and equipment are stated at cost less accumulated depreciation. Depreciation is computed using the straight-line method over estimated useful lives as follows:
>
> | | |
> |---|---|
> | Buildings and improvements | 10–30 years |
> | Machinery and equipment | 5–15 years |
> | Furniture, computers, and equipment | 3–5 years |
> | Production molds | 2 years |

Without an understanding of the various accounting methods used, it is impossible to analyze a company's financial results effectively.

FINANCIAL ANALYSIS

Alternative Accounting Methods and GAAP

Many people mistakenly believe that GAAP permits only one accounting method to be used to compute each value on the financial statements (e.g., inventory). Actually, GAAP often allows a selection of an accounting method from a menu of acceptable methods. This permits a company to choose the methods that most closely reflect its particular economic circumstances. This flexibility complicates the financial statement users' task, however. Users must understand how the company's choice of accounting methods affects its financial statement presentations. As renowned financial analysts Gabrielle Napolitano, Michael Moran, and Abby Joseph Cohen of the investment banking firm of Goldman, Sachs & Co. note in their recent research report,

REAL WORLD EXCERPT

Goldman, Sachs & Co.
ANALYSTS' REPORTS

> Discretionary choices in financial reporting that can ultimately lead to or create future earnings shocks that drive stock prices must be identified; analysts must make adjustments to minimize or eliminate the impact of these drivers on corporate performance. As a result, financial statement users must (1) develop a keen understanding of the fundamentals underlying each firm's business operations and (2) familiarize themselves with the corporate reporting practices of the companies they are analyzing.*

For example, before analyzing two companies' statements prepared using different accounting methods, one company's statements must be converted to the other's methods to make them comparable. Otherwise, the reader is in a situation analogous to comparing distances in kilometers and miles without converting to a common scale. In later chapters, we will focus on developing the ability to make these conversions.

*Gabrielle Napolitano, Michael A. Moran, and Abby Joseph Cohen, "Demand for Forensic Accounting Intensifies," *Global Strategy Research* (New York: Goldman, Sachs & Co., February 11, 2002).

Additional Detail Supporting Reported Numbers

The second category of notes provides supplemental information concerning the data shown on the financial statements. Among other information, these notes may show revenues broken out by geographic region or business segment, describe unusual transactions, and/or offer expanded detail on a specific classification. For example, in Note 5, Callaway Golf indicates the makeup of accounts receivable; inventory; property, plant, and equipment; and other items presented on the balance sheet. Note 16, which follows, shows sales reported on the income statement and long-lived assets from the balance sheet divided by geographic region:

Note 16

Segment Information

(dollars in thousands)	Sales	Long-Lived Assets
2003		
United States	$449,424	$305,176
Europe	145,148	16,995
Japan	101,259	3,590
Rest of Asia	58,327	846
Other foreign countries	59,874	8,007
	$814,032	$334,614

Relevant Financial Information Not Disclosed on the Statements

The final category includes information that impacts the company financially but is not shown on the statements. Examples include information on legal matters, and any material event that occurred subsequent to year-end but before the financial statements are published. In Note 13, Callaway Golf disclosed the details of its lease commitments:

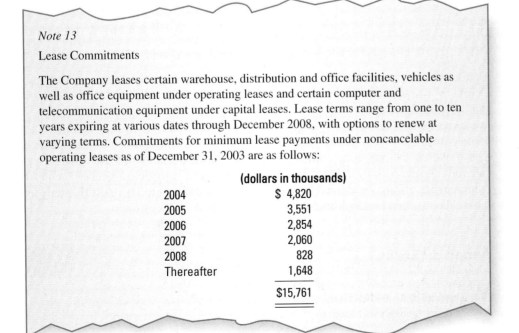

Note 13

Lease Commitments

The Company leases certain warehouse, distribution and office facilities, vehicles as well as office equipment under operating leases and certain computer and telecommunication equipment under capital leases. Lease terms range from one to ten years expiring at various dates through December 2008, with options to renew at varying terms. Commitments for minimum lease payments under noncancelable operating leases as of December 31, 2003 are as follows:

	(dollars in thousands)
2004	$ 4,820
2005	3,551
2006	2,854
2007	2,060
2008	828
Thereafter	1,648
	$15,761

Voluntary Disclosures

GAAP and SEC regulations set only the minimum level of required financial disclosures. Many companies provide important disclosures beyond those required. For example, in its annual report, 10-K, and recent earnings press release, Callaway Golf discloses sales by major product category, which helps investors track the success of new products.

Accounting and Sustainable Development

REAL WORLD EXCERPT
CFO Magazine

A growing area of voluntary disclosure in the United States is sustainability reporting, as described by *CFO Magazine:*

> The idea that a company should conduct its business in ways that benefit not just shareholders but the environment and society, too, is called sustainability, or sustainable development. It's an idea championed by a small but growing number of companies around the globe. One business group, the World Business Council for Sustainable Development, lists some 170 international members, including more than 30 Fortune 500 companies. According to the council's website, these companies share the belief that "the pursuit of sustainable development is good for business and business is good for sustainable development."
>
> To tell their stakeholders about that pursuit, companies are issuing sustainability reports. Many, like Suncor, are doing so following the strict guidelines of the Global Reporting Initiative (GRI), an independent institution founded in 1997, to develop a common framework for sustainability reporting. Enter the words "sustainability reporting" into your favorite search engine and you'll find such well-known company names as Alcoa, Alcan, Bristol-Myers Squibb, General Motors, Baxter International, and FedEx Kinko's. In all, some 500 organizations publish sustainability reports according to GRI guidelines. Some countries, such as France, South Africa, and the Netherlands, now mandate environmental or social sustainability reporting as a condition to being listed on their stock exchanges.

Such reports are voluntary disclosures in the United States. However, many believe that managing a company in the interests of a wider group of stakeholders and reporting on these efforts is an ethical imperative.

Source: *CFO Magazine,* November 2004, pp. 97–100.

RETURN ON EQUITY ANALYSIS: A FRAMEWORK FOR EVALUATING COMPANY PERFORMANCE

Learning Objective 4
Analyze a company's performance based on return on equity and its components.

Evaluating company performance is the primary goal of financial statement analysis. Company managers, as well as competitors, use financial statements to better understand and evaluate a company's business strategy. Analysts, investors, and creditors use these same statements to judge company performance when they estimate the value of the company's stock and its creditworthiness. Our discussion of the financial data contained in accounting reports has now reached the point where we can develop an overall framework for using that data to evaluate company performance. The most comprehensive framework of this type is called **return on equity** or **ROE analysis** (also called **return on stockholders' equity** or **return on investment**).

Return on Equity

▶ ANALYTICAL QUESTION:

How well has management used the stockholders' investment during the period?

RATIO AND COMPARISONS:

$$\text{Return on Equity} = \frac{\text{Net Income}}{\text{Average Stockholders' Equity}^{*}}$$

The 2003 ratio for Callaway Golf:

$$\frac{\$45{,}523}{(\$589{,}383 + 543{,}387) \div 2} = 0.080\ (8.0\%)$$

COMPARISONS OVER TIME		
Callaway Golf		
2001	2002	2003
11.4%	13.1%	8.0%

COMPARISONS WITH COMPETITORS	
Adams Golf	Recreational Products Industry
2003	2003
9.6%	23.8%

INTERPRETATIONS:

In General → ROE measures how much the firm earned for each dollar of stockholders' investment. In the long run, firms with higher ROE are expected to have higher stock prices than firms with lower ROE, all other things equal. Managers, analysts, and creditors use this ratio to assess the effectiveness of the company's overall business strategy (its operating, investing, and financing strategies).

Focus Company Analysis → Callaway Golf's ROEs from 1995 to 1997 were 47.5 percent, 41.7 percent, and 31.5 percent. Such high levels of ROE tend to be driven down over time by additional competition from new and existing competitors. Financial analysts sometimes call this **economic gravity.** Callaway Golf is facing just such a situation as large companies such as Adidas-owned Taylor-Made invest millions in marketing to unseat Callaway Golf from the top of its market. At the same time, new entrants such as Adams Golf chip away at Callaway Golf from below. Callaway Golf's ROE dropped dramatically in 1998, which coincided with a decline in its share price from $28 per share in January 1998 to $10 by September 1998. Its stock price returned to the $28 level when its improved 2000 ROE was announced. It has subsequently fallen to the $10 level again in response to the slide in ROE during 2003 and 2004. The relationship between ROE and share price is well established in the stock valuation literature.†

A Few Cautions: An increasing ROE can also indicate that a company is failing to invest in research and development or modernization of plant and equipment. While such a strategy will decrease expenses and thus increase ROE in the short run, it normally results in future declines in ROE as the company's products or plant and equipment reach the end of their life cycles. As a consequence, experienced decision makers evaluate ROE in the context of a company's business strategy.

*Average Stockholders' Equity = (Beginning Stockholders' Equity + Ending Stockholders' Equity) ÷ 2
†See Robert F. Halsey, "Using the Residual-Income Stock Price Valuation Model to Teach and Learn Ratio Analysis," *Issues in Accounting Education,* May 2001.

ROE Profit Driver Analysis

Effective analysis of Callaway Golf's performance also requires understanding **why** its ROE differs both from prior levels and from those of its competitors. ROE profit driver analysis (also called **ROE decomposition** or **DuPont analysis**) breaks down ROE into the three factors shown in Exhibit 5.8. These factors are often called **profit drivers** or **profit levers** because they describe the three ways that management can improve ROE. They are measured by the key ratios you learned in Chapters 2 through 4.

A. Net profit margin. Net profit margin is Net Income/Net Sales. It measures how much of every sales dollar is profit. It can be increased by

1. Increasing sales volume.

EXHIBIT 5.8

ROE Profit Driver Analysis

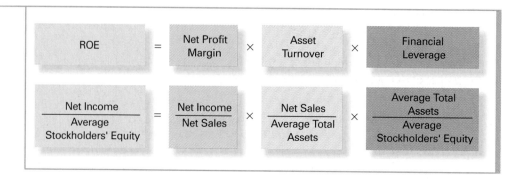

2. Increasing sales price.
3. Decreasing expenses.

B. Asset turnover (efficiency). Asset turnover is Net Sales/Average Total Assets. It measures how many sales dollars the company generates with each dollar of assets. It can be increased by
1. Increasing sales volume.
2. Disposing of (decreasing) less productive assets.

C. Financial leverage. Financial leverage is Average Total Assets/Average Stockholders' Equity. It measures how many dollars of assets are employed for each dollar of stockholder investment. It can be increased by
1. Increased borrowing.
2. Repurchasing (decreasing) outstanding stock.

These three ratios report on the effectiveness of the company's operating, investing, and financing activities, respectively.

Profit Drivers and Business Strategy

Successful manufacturers often follow one of two business strategies. The first is a **high-value** or **product-differentiation** strategy. Companies following this strategy rely on research and development and product promotion to convince customers of the superiority or distinctiveness of their products. This allows the company to charge higher prices and earn a higher net profit margin. The second is a **low-cost strategy,** which relies on efficient management of accounts receivable, inventory, and productive assets to produce high asset turnover.

Callaway Golf follows a classic high-value strategy. The ROE profit driver analysis presented in Exhibit 5.9 indicates the sources of its ROE, as well as reasons for its recent decline. The analysis indicates a large drop in net profit margin during 2003, as well as a slow but steady decline in asset turnover. This indicates that Callaway Golf is generating fewer sales dollars for each dollar of assets and lower profits on each dollar of sales. These changes result mainly from competitive pressures on sales prices discussed earlier, as well as slow growth in the industry as a whole. Callaway Golf's low financial leverage means less risk to shareholders if it should face another bad year in the future.

Companies often consider a variety of changes to increase ROE. These include

■ Reducing promotional activities and fees paid to distributors to increase profit margin.

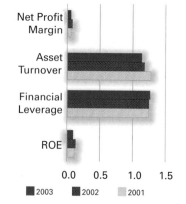

EXHIBIT 5.9

Callaway Golf ROE Profit Driver Analysis

Fiscal Year Ending	12/31/2001	12/31/2002	12/31/2003
Net Income / Net Sales	0.07	0.09	0.06
× Net Sales / Avg. Total Assets	1.28	1.19	1.14
× Avg. Total Assets / Avg. Stockholders' Equity	1.25	1.25	1.26
= Net Income / Avg. Stockholders' Equity	0.11	0.13	0.08

■ Collecting accounts receivable more quickly, centralizing distribution to reduce inventory kept on hand, and consolidating production facilities in fewer factories to reduce the amount of assets necessary to generate each dollar of sales.

■ Using more borrowed funds (financial leverage) so that more assets can be employed per dollar of stockholder investment.

If Callaway Golf follows the same strategy it has in the past, the secret to increasing ROE must be improved product development to support premium selling prices.

Companies that follow a low-cost strategy, such as Gateway and Dell Computer, usually produce high ROE with higher asset turnover and higher leverage to make up for their lower net profit margin. This strategy is illustrated in the self-study quiz that follows this section.

As the preceding discussion indicates, a company can take many different actions to try to affect its profit drivers. To understand the impact of these actions, financial analysts disaggregate each of the profit drivers into more detailed ratios. For example, the asset turnover ratio is further disaggregated into turnover ratios for specific assets such as accounts receivable, inventory, and fixed assets. We will develop our understanding of these more specific ratios in the next eight chapters of the book. Then, in Chapter 14, we will combine the ratios in a comprehensive review.

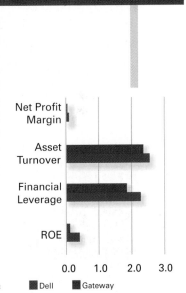

SELF-STUDY QUIZ

We used ROE analysis in Exhibit 5.9 to understand how Callaway Golf's ROE had changed over the last three years. This type of analysis is often called **time-series analysis.** ROE analysis can also be used to explain why a company has an ROE different from its competitors at a single point in time. This type of analysis is called **cross-sectional analysis.** The following is the recent year's ROE analysis for Dell Computer and Gateway, the largest computer manufacturers employing phone/Internet distribution. Both of these companies have followed a low-cost strategy, developing reputations for good products and service at low prices. Dell has produced a higher ROE than Gateway, and its stock price has held up much better in the face of the general decline in technology stock prices. Using ROE analysis, explain how Dell has produced its higher ROE.

ROE PROFIT DRIVERS	DELL	GATEWAY
Net Income / Net Sales	.068	.025
× Net Sales / Average Total Assets	2.56	2.37
× Avg. Total Assets / Average Stockholders' Equity	2.28	1.84
= Net Income / Average Stockholders' Equity	0.40	0.11

After you have completed your answers, check them with the solutions at the bottom of the page.

Both Dell and Gateway are well known for the efficiency of their operations, which is reflected in their high asset turnover ratios. Dell has the edge in asset efficiency, but the edge is small. Dell's major strength is its 170 percent higher net profit margin. This reflects Dell's success with its primary market segment, business customers. Dell purchases in higher quantity, which decreases order-processing and production costs. Its customers also often purchase higher-end, higher-net profit margin machines than customers in Gateway's primary market segment, individuals. The effect of this edge in net profit margin is multiplied further by Dell's greater reliance on leverage (debt financing). However, this greater leverage could come back to haunt Dell if there is a downturn in the personal computer market.

Self-Study Quiz
Solutions

EPILOGUE

In the second quarter of 2004, citing slow sales of titanium drivers, slow sales in Japan, continuing losses from operations at golf-ball maker Top-Flite Golf Co., and fierce price competition from TaylorMade, Callaway Golf warned that earnings would be sharply lower than forecasted by analysts for the second quarter and year. In response to that earnings warning and continuing bad news, investors drove its stock price down to $10 per share. You can evaluate Callaway Golf's responses to these challenges by going to the Web at www.callawaygolf.com to check its latest annual and quarterly reports

DEMONSTRATION **CASE**

MICROSOFT CORPORATION

Complete the following requirements before proceeding to the suggested solution. Microsoft Corporation, developer of a broad line of computer software including the Windows operating systems, Word (word processing), and Excel (spreadsheet) programs, is now the largest computer-related company in the world. Following is a list of the financial statement items and amounts adapted from a recent Microsoft income statement and balance sheet. These items have normal debit and credit balances and are reported in millions of dollars. For that year, 5,341 million (weighted average) shares of stock were outstanding. The company closes its books on June 30, 2001.

Accounts payable	$ 1,188	Other current liabilities	$ 2,120
Accounts receivable	3,671	Other investments	14,141
Accrued compensation	742	Other revenues and expenses	
Cash and short-term		(debit balance)	(534)
investments	31,600	Other noncurrent assets	3,170
Common stock and		Property, plant, and	
paid-in capital	28,390	equipment (net)	2,309
Cost of goods sold	3,455	Provision for income taxes	3,804
General and administrative	857	Research and development	4,379
Income taxes payable	1,468	Retained earnings	18,899
Investment income (loss)	(36)	Sales and marketing	4,885
Net revenues	25,296	Unearned revenue	5,614
Other current assets	3,530		

Required:

1. Prepare in good form a multiple-step income statement (showing gross profit, operating income, and income before income taxes) and a classified balance sheet for the year.

2. Prepare an ROE profit driver analysis. Briefly explain its meaning and compare the result with that of Dell Computer as shown in the Self-Study Quiz. (Microsoft's total assets and total shareholders' equity at the beginning of the year were $52,150 million and $41,368 million, respectively.)

SUGGESTED SOLUTION

1.

MICROSOFT CORPORATION
Income Statement
For the Year Ended June 30, 2001
(dollars in millions)

Net revenues	$25,296
Cost of goods sold	3,455
Gross profit	21,841
Operating expenses:	
Research and development	4,379
Sales and marketing	4,885
General and administrative	857
Total operating expenses	10,121
Operating income	**11,720**
Nonoperating income and expenses:	
Investment income (loss)	(36)
Other revenues and expenses	(534)
Income before income taxes	11,150
Provision for income taxes	3,804
Net income	**$ 7,346**
Earnings per share	**$1.38**

MICROSOFT CORPORATION
Balance Sheet
June 30, 2001
(dollars in millions)

Assets	
Current assets	
Cash and short-term investments	$31,600
Accounts receivable	3,671
Other current assets	3,530
Total current assets	38,801
Noncurrent assets	
Property, plant, and equipment (net)	2,309
Other investments	14,141
Other noncurrent assets	3,170
Total assets	$58,421
Liabilities	
Current liabilities	
Accounts payable	$ 1,188
Accrued compensation	742
Income taxes payable	1,468
Unearned revenue	5,614
Other current liabilities	2,120
Total current liabilities	11,132
Stockholders' equity	
Common stock and paid-in-capital	28,390
Retained earnings	18,899
Total stockholders' equity	47,289
Total liabilities and stockholders' equity	$58,421

2.

Fiscal Year Ending	June 30, 2001
Net Income/Net Sales	0.29
× Net Sales/Average Total Assets	0.46
× Avg. Total Assets/Average Stockholders' Equity	1.25
= Net Income/Average Stockholders' Equity	0.17

For the year ended June 30, Microsoft's shareholders earned an ROE of 17 percent. This is much lower than Dell's recent results presented in the Self-Study Quiz, as the detailed analysis shows. In contrast to Dell's results (see the Self-Study Quiz), Microsoft maintains high profit margins, earning $0.29 of net income for every $1 of net sales but a lower asset efficiency with only $0.46 in sales generated for each $1 of assets. The analysis also indicates Microsoft's dominance of the computer software business, which allows the company to charge premium prices for its products. However, the financial leverage ratio indicates that Microsoft's capital is primarily equity (not debt) based. With $1.25 in assets for each $1.00 of shareholders' equity, Microsoft has chosen not to leverage (or borrow) as much, for example, as Dell Computer, which faces stiff competition in the computer hardware industry.

Chapter Supplement

Nonrecurring Items

As noted in the chapter, companies may report any of three nonrecurring items: discontinued operations, extraordinary items, and cumulative effects of accounting method changes. The income statement of Dura Automotive Systems, Inc., a global manufacturer of automotive parts, contains two of the three items, and is presented in Exhibit 5.10.

EXHIBIT 5.10

Income Statements for Dura Automotive Systems, Inc.

REAL WORLD EXCERPT

Dura Automotive Systems, Inc.

ANNUAL REPORT

DURA AUTOMOTIVE SYSTEMS, INC. AND SUBSIDIARIES
Consolidated Statements of Operations
For the Years Ended December 31

(dollars in thousands, except per share amounts)	2003	2002	2001
Revenues	$2,380,794	$2,360,323	$2,333,705
Cost of sales	2,089,243	2,035,021	2,013,585
Gross profit	291,551	325,302	320,120
Selling, general, and administrative expenses	154,935	135,571	134,380
Facility consolidation and other charges	9,252	16,121	24,119
Amortization expense	370	989	26,725
Operating income	126,994	172,621	134,896
Interest expense, net	81,921	83,908	100,514
Loss on early extinguishment of debt, net	2,852	5,520	—
Income from continuing operations before provision for income taxes and minority interest	42,221	83,193	34,382
Provision for income taxes	14,355	37,605	10,589
Minority interest—dividends on trust preferred securities, net	2,735	2,486	2,569
Income from continuing operations	25,131	43,102	21,224
Loss from discontinued operations, including loss on disposal of $916 in 2003 and $68,322 in 2002	(2,793)	(126,581)	(10,005)
Income (loss) before accounting change	22,338	(83,479)	11,219
Cumulative effect of change in accounting	—	(205,192)	—
Net income (loss)	$ 22,338	$ (288,671)	$ 11,219

See notes to consolidated financial statements.

Discontinued Operations

Discontinued operations result from abandoning or selling a major business component. Operating income generated by the discontinued component and any gain or loss on the disposal (the difference between the book value of the net assets being disposed of and the sale price or the abandonment costs) are included. These amounts may be separately disclosed in a note or on the face of the income statement. Each amount is reported net of the income tax effects. Separate reporting of discontinued operations informs users that these results are not predictive of the company's future.

During 2002 and 2003, Dura sold its European Mechanical Assemblies business. The results of the operations of that business and the loss on sale of the business are listed as discontinued operations,

DISCONTINUED OPERATIONS result from the disposal of a major component of the business and are reported net of income tax effects.

nct of tax, on the income statement shown in Exhibit 5.10. The income statement reports the separate amounts of the operating loss and loss on sale.

Extraordinary Items

Extraordinary items are gains or losses that are considered both unusual in nature and infrequent in occurrence. Examples include losses suffered from natural disasters such as floods and hurricanes in geographic areas where such disasters are rare. These items must be reported separately on the income statement net of income tax effects. Separate reporting again informs decision makers that these items are not likely to recur, and so are not predictive of the company's future. Note disclosure is needed to explain the nature of the extraordinary item. Such items are now reported very rarely.[8]

Cumulative Effects of Changes in Accounting Methods

The final nonrecurring item reflects the income statement effects of any adjustment made to balance sheet accounts because of a change to a different acceptable accounting method. These amounts are called **cumulative effects of changes in accounting methods.** The goal is to determine what the balance sheet amount would be if the new accounting method had always been applied, net of any tax effects. Often these changes are required by new FASB pronouncements. At other times, corporate management determines that a change to an alternative accounting method is necessary because of changes in business activities. Note disclosure to explain the nature and effects of the change also is necessary. In 2002, Dura made one accounting method change related to implementation of a new accounting standard for goodwill. Again, the effects of accounting method changes are separated because they are normally not relevant to predicting the company's future.

---

[8]As can be seen on Dura's income statement, gains and losses on early retirement of debt are separately disclosed (if material) as part of income from continuing operations. They are no longer treated as extraordinary items.

CHAPTER **TAKE-AWAYS**

1. **Recognize the people involved in the accounting communication process (regulators, managers, directors, auditors, information intermediaries, and users), their roles in the process, and the guidance they receive from legal and professional standards.   p. 233**
   Management of the reporting company must decide on the appropriate format (categories) and level of detail to present in its financial reports. Independent audits increase the credibility of the information. Directors monitor managers' compliance with reporting standards and hire the auditor. Financial statement announcements from public companies usually are first transmitted to users through electronic information services. The SEC staff reviews public financial reports for compliance with legal and professional standards, investigates irregularities, and punishes violators. Analysts play a major role in making financial statement and other information available to average investors through their stock recommendations and earnings forecasts.

2. **Identify the steps in the accounting communication process, including the issuance of press releases, annual reports, quarterly reports, and SEC filings as well as the role of electronic information services in this process.   p. 240**
   Earnings are first made public in press releases. Companies follow these announcements with annual and quarterly reports containing statements, notes, and additional information. Public companies must file additional reports with the SEC, including the 10-K, 10-Q, and 8-K, which contain more details about the company. Electronic information services are the key source of dissemination of this information to sophisticated users.

3. **Recognize and apply the different financial statement and disclosure formats used by companies in practice.   p. 243**
   Most statements are classified and include subtotals that are relevant to analysis. On the balance sheet, the most important distinctions are between current and noncurrent assets and liabilities. On the income and cash flow statements, the distinction between operating and nonoperating items are

most important. The notes to the statements provide descriptions of the accounting rules applied, add more information about items disclosed on the statements, and present information about economic events not included in the statements.

4. **Analyze a company's performance based on return on equity and its components.**   p. 252
ROE measures how well management used the stockholders' investment during the period. Its three determinants, net profit margin, asset turnover, and financial leverage, indicate why ROE differs from prior levels or the ROEs of competitors. They also suggest strategies to improve ROE in future periods.

In Chapter 6, we will begin our in-depth discussion of individual items presented in financial statements. We will start with two of the most liquid assets, cash and accounts receivable, and transactions that involve revenues and certain selling expenses. Accuracy in revenue recognition and the related recognition of cost of goods sold (discussed in Chapter 7) are the most important determinants of the accuracy—and, thus, the usefulness—of financial statements. We will also introduce concepts related to the management and control of cash and receivables, a critical business function. A detailed understanding of these topics is crucial to future managers, accountants, and financial analysts.

KEY **RATIO**

Return on equity (ROE) measures how much the firm earned for each dollar of stockholders' investment. It is computed as follows (p. 253):

$$\text{Return on Equity} = \frac{\text{Net Income}}{\text{Average Stockholders' Equity}}$$

FINDING **FINANCIAL INFORMATION**

Balance Sheet
Key Classifications:
Current and noncurrent assets and liabilities
Contributed capital and retained earnings

Income Statement
Key Subtotals:
Gross profit
Income from operations
Income before income taxes
Net income
Earnings per share

Statement of Cash Flows
Under Operating Activities
   (indirect method):
Net income
± Adjustments for noncash items
Cash provided by operating activities

Notes
Key Classifications:
Descriptions of accounting rules applied in the
   statements
Additional detail supporting reported numbers
Relevant financial information not disclosed
   on the statements

KEY **TERMS**

QUESTIONS

1. Describe the roles and responsibilities of management and independent auditors in the financial reporting process.
2. Define the following three users of financial accounting disclosures and the relationships among them: *financial analysts, private investors,* and *institutional investors.*
3. Briefly describe the role of information services in the communication of financial information.
4. Explain why information must be relevant and reliable to be useful.
5. What basis of accounting does GAAP require on the (a) income statement, (b) balance sheet, and (c) statement of cash flows?
6. Briefly explain the normal sequence and form of financial reports produced by private companies in a typical year.
7. Briefly explain the normal sequence and form of financial reports produced by public companies in a typical year.
8. What are the four major subtotals or totals on the income statement?
9. Define *extraordinary items.* Why should they be reported separately on the income statement?
10. List the six major classifications reported on a balance sheet.
11. For property, plant, and equipment, as reported on the balance sheet, explain (a) cost, (b) accumulated depreciation, and (c) net book value.
12. Briefly explain the major classifications of stockholders' equity for a corporation.
13. What are the three major classifications on a statement of cash flows?
14. What are the three major categories of notes or footnotes presented in annual reports? Cite an example of each.
15. Briefly define *return on equity* and what it measures.

MULTIPLE-**CHOICE QUESTIONS**

1. If average total assets increase, but net income, net sales, and average stockholders' equity remain the same, what is the impact on the return on equity ratio?
   a. Increases
   b. Decreases
   c. Remains the same
   d. Cannot be determined without additional information
2. If a company plans to differentiate its products by offering low prices and discounts for items packaged in bulk (like a discount retailer that requires memberships for its customers), which component in the ROE profit driver analysis is the company attempting to boost?
   a. Net profit margin
   b. Asset turnover
   c. Financial leverage
   d. All of the above
3. If a company reported the following items on its income statement (cost of goods sold $5,000, income tax expense $2,000, interest expense $500, operating expenses $3,500, sales revenue $14,000), what amount would be reported for the subtotal "income from operations"?
   a. $9,000
   b. $3,000
   c. $5,000
   d. $5,500

4. Which of the following is not one of the possible nonrecurring items that must be shown in a separate line item *below* the Income from Continuing Operations subtotal in the income statement?
   a. Gains and losses from the sale of fixed assets
   b. Discontinued operations
   c. Cumulative effect of changes in accounting methods
   d. Extraordinary items

5. Which of the following reports is filed annually with the SEC?
   a. Form 10-Q
   b. Form 10-K
   c. Form 8-K
   d. Press release

6. Common-size income statements are used for which of the following?
   a. Comparing the performance of different companies in the same industry
   b. Comparing the performance of a single company over time
   c. Both a and b
   d. None of the above

7. Which of the following is *not* a normal function of a financial analyst?
   a. Issue earnings forecasts
   b. Examine the records underlying the financial statements to certify their conformance with GAAP
   c. Make buy, hold, and sell recommendations on companies' stock
   d. Advise institutional investors on their securities holdings

8. The classified balance sheet format allows one to ascertain quickly which of the following?
   a. The most valuable asset of the company
   b. The specific due date for all liabilities of the company
   c. What liabilities must be paid within the upcoming year
   d. None of the above

9. When companies issue par value stock for cash, which accounts are normally affected?
   a. Common Stock; Additional Paid-in Capital; and Property, Plant, and Equipment, Net
   b. Cash and Property, Plant, and Equipment, Net
   c. Common Stock, Additional Paid-in Capital, and Retained Earnings
   d. Common Stock, Additional Paid-in Capital, and Cash

10. What type of audit report does a client hope to include with its annual report?
    a. Conservative
    b. Qualified
    c. Comparable
    d. Unqualified

To practice on more multiple-choice questions, go to the text website at www.mhhe.com/libby5e or the Topic Tackler DVD for use with this text.

MINI-EXERCISES

 Available with McGraw-Hill's Homework Manager

M5-1
LO1

Matching Players in the Accounting Communication Process with Their Definitions

Match each player with the related definition by entering the appropriate letter in the space provided.

Players	Definitions
___ (1) CEO and CFO	A. Adviser who analyzes financial and other economic information to form forecasts and stock recommendations.
___ (2) Independent auditor	B. Institutional and private investors and creditors (among others).
___ (3) Users	C. Chief executive officer and chief financial officer who have primary responsibility for the information presented in financial statements.
___ (4) Financial analyst	D. Independent CPA who examines financial statements and attests to their fairness.

Identifying the Disclosure Sequence

Indicate the order in which the following disclosures or reports are normally issued by public companies.

No.	Title
_____	Annual report
_____	Form 10-K
_____	Earnings press release

Finding Financial Information: Matching Financial Statements with the Elements of Financial Statements

Match each financial statement with the items presented on it by entering the appropriate letter in the space provided.

Elements of Financial Statements	Financial Statements
____ (1) Liabilities	A. Income statement
____ (2) Cash from operating activities	B. Balance sheet
____ (3) Losses	C. Cash flow statement
____ (4) Assets	D. None of the above
____ (5) Revenues	
____ (6) Cash from financing activities	
____ (7) Gains	
____ (8) Owners' equity	
____ (9) Expenses	
____ (10) Assets personally owned by a stockholder	

Determining the Effects of Transactions on Balance Sheet and Income Statement Categories

Complete the following tabulation, indicating the sign of the effect (+ for increase, − for decrease, and NE for no effect) of each transaction. Consider each item independently.

a. Recorded sales on account of $100 and related cost of goods sold of $60.
b. Recorded advertising expense of $10 incurred but not paid for.

Transaction	Current Assets	Gross Profit	Current Liabilities
(a)			
(b)			

Determining Financial Statement Effects of Sales and Cost of Goods Sold and Issuance of Par Value Stock

Using the following categories, indicate the effects of the following transactions. Use + for increase and − for decrease and indicate the accounts affected and the amounts.

a. Sales on account were $500 and related cost of goods sold was $360.
b. Issued 10,000 shares of $1 par value stock for $90,000 cash.

Event	Assets	=	Liabilities	+	Stockholders' Equity

Recording Sales and Cost of Goods Sold and Issuance of Par Value Stock

Prepare journal entries for each transaction listed in M5-5.

M5-7 **Computing and Interpreting Return on Equity**

LO4

Chen, Inc., recently reported the following December 31 amounts in its financial statements (dollars in thousands):

	Current Year	Prior Year
Gross profit	$ 170	$140
Net income	85	70
Total assets	1,000	900
Total shareholders' equity	800	750

Compute return on equity for the current year. What does this ratio measure?

EXERCISES

 Available with McGraw-Hill's Homework Manager

E5-1 **Matching Players in the Accounting Communication Process with Their Definitions**

LO1

Match each player with the related definition by entering the appropriate letter in the space provided.

Players	Definitions
___ (1) SEC	A. Adviser who analyzes financial and other economic information to form forecasts and stock recommendations.
___ (2) Independent auditor	
___ (3) Institutional investor	B. Financial institution or supplier that lends money to the company.
___ (4) CEO and CFO	
___ (5) Creditor	C. Chief executive officer and chief financial officer who have primary responsibility for the information presented in financial statements.
___ (6) Financial analyst	
___ (7) Private investor	
___ (8) Information service	D. Independent CPA who examines financial statements and attests to their fairness.
	E. Securities and Exchange Commission, which regulates financial disclosure requirements.
	F. A company that gathers, combines, and transmits (paper and electronic) financial and related information from various sources.
	G. Individual who purchases shares in companies.
	H. Manager of pension, mutual, and endowment funds that invest on the behalf of others.

E5-2 **Matching Definitions with Information Releases Made by Public Companies**

LO2

Following are the titles of various information releases. Match each definition with the related release by entering the appropriate letter in the space provided.

Information Release	Definitions
___ (1) Annual report	A. Written public news announcement that is normally distributed to major news services.
___ (2) Form 8-K	
___ (3) Press release	B. Report containing the four basic financial statements for the year, related notes, and often statements by management and auditors.
___ (4) Form 10-Q	
___ (5) Quarterly report	
___ (6) Form 10-K	C. Brief unaudited report for quarter normally containing summary income statement and balance sheet (unaudited).
	D. Annual report filed by public companies with the SEC that contains additional detailed financial information.
	E. Quarterly report filed by public companies with the SEC that contains additional unaudited financial information.
	F. Report of special events (e.g., auditor changes, mergers) filed by public companies with the SEC.

Finding Financial Information: Matching Information Items to Financial Reports

E5-3
LO2

Following are information items included in various financial reports. Match each information item with the report(s) in which it would most likely be found by entering the appropriate letter(s) in the space provided.

Information Item	Report
____ (1) Summarized financial data for 5- or 10-year period.	A. Annual report
(2) Initial announcement of quarterly earnings.	B. Form 8-K
(3) Announcement of a change in auditors.	C. Press release
____ (4) Complete quarterly income statement, balance sheet, and cash flow statement.	D. Form 10-Q
	E. Quarterly report
(5) The four basic financial statements for the year.	F. Form 10-K
(6) Summarized income statement information for the quarter.	G. None of the above
(7) Detailed discussion of the company's competition.	
____ (8) Notes to financial statements.	
____ (9) Description of those responsible for the financial statements.	
____ (10) Initial announcement of hiring of new vice president for sales.	

Ordering the Classifications on a Typical Balance Sheet

E5-4
LO3

Following is a list of classifications on the balance sheet. Number them in the order in which they normally appear on a balance sheet.

No.	Title
_____	Current liabilities
_____	Long-term liabilities
_____	Long-term investments
_____	Intangible assets
_____	Property, plant, and equipment
_____	Current assets
_____	Retained earnings
_____	Contributed capital
_____	Other noncurrent assets

Preparing a Classified Balance Sheet

E5-5
LO3
Apple Computer

Apple Computer, Inc., manufactures the Macintosh® line of desktop and notebook computers and iPod™ digital music players. Presented here are the items listed on its recent balance sheet (dollars in millions) presented in alphabetical order:

Accounts payable	1,154	Cash and cash equivalents	3,396
Accrued expenses	899	Common stock, no par value	1,864
Intangible assets	109	Inventories	56
Other assets	150	Other current assets	499
Other current debt	304	Other noncurrent liabilities	235
Property, plant, and equipment, net	669	Retained earnings	2,359
Accounts receivable	766	Short-term investments	1,170

Required:
Prepare a classified consolidated balance sheet for Apple for the current year (ended September 27) using the categories presented in the chapter.

Preparing and Interpreting a Classified Balance Sheet with Discussion of Terminology (Challenging)

E5-6
LO3
Lance, Inc.

Lance, Inc., manufactures, markets, and distributes a variety of snack foods. Product categories include sandwich crackers, cookies, restaurant crackers and bread basket items, candy, chips, meat snacks, nuts, and cake items. These items are sold under tradenames including Lance, Toastchee, Toasty, Choc-O-Lunch, Captain's Wafers, and Cape Cod. Presented here are the items listed on its recent balance sheet (dollars in millions) in alphabetical order:

Accounts payable	$14,718	Inventories	23,205
Accounts receivable, net	47,188	Long-term debt	63,536
Accrued compensation	8,844	Other assets (noncurrent)	3,216
Accrued postretirement health		Other current assets	4,161
care costs	11,317	Other intangible assets, net	10,177
Additional paid-in capital	1,229	Other long-term liabilities	28,231
Cash and cash equivalents	1,224	Other payables and accrued	
Common stock, 28,947,222 shares		liabilities	15,439
outstanding	24,123	Prepaid expenses and other	6,550
Current portion of long-term debt	395	Property, plant, and equipment, net	179,283
Goodwill, net	42,069	Retained earnings	149,241

Required:
1. Prepare a classified consolidated balance sheet for Lance, Inc., for the current year (ended December 31) using the categories presented in the chapter.
2. Four of the items end in the term *net*. Explain what this term means in each case.

E5-7   Recording Stock Issuances with Par Value

LO3

GAP, Inc.

In a recent year, GAP, Inc., owner of GAP, Banana Republic, and Old Navy stores, issued 13,000,000 shares of its $0.05 par value stock for $111,000,000 (these numbers are rounded). These additional shares were issued under an employee stock option plan. Prepare the journal entry required to record the stock issuance.

E5-8   Inferring Stock Issuances and Cash Dividends from Changes in Stockholders' Equity

LO3

Oakley

Oakley, designer and manufacturer of high-performance eyewear, reported the following December 31 balances in its stockholders' equity accounts (dollars in thousands):

	Current Year	Prior Year
Common stock	$ 688	$ 686
Paid-in capital	40,805	36,484
Retained earnings	227,648	177,277

During the current year, Oakley reported net income of $50,371.

Required:
1. How much did Oakley pay in dividends for the year?
2. Assume that the only other transaction that affected stockholders' equity during the current year was a single stock issuance. Recreate the journal entry reflecting the stock issuance.

E5-9   Matching Definitions with Income Statement–Related Terms

LO3

Following are terms related to the income statement. Match each definition with its related term by entering the appropriate letter in the space provided.

Terms	Definitions
___ (1) Cost of goods sold	A. Sales Revenue − Cost of Goods Sold.
___ (2) Interest expense	B. Item that is both unusual and infrequent.
___ (3) Extraordinary item	C. Sales of services for cash or on credit.
___ (4) Service revenue	D. Revenues + Gains − Expenses − Losses including effects
___ (5) Income tax expense	of discontinued operations, extraordinary items, and cumu-
on operations	lative effects of accounting changes (if any).
___ (6) Income before	E. Amount of resources used to purchase or produce the
extraordinary items	goods that were sold during the reporting period.
___ (7) Net income	F. Income Tax on Revenues − Operating Expenses.
___ (8) Gross margin on sales	G. Cost of money (borrowing) over time.
___ (9) EPS	H. Net income divided by average shares outstanding.

(*continued on next page*)

___ (10) Operating expenses

___ (11) Pretax income from operations

I. Income before unusual and infrequent items and the related income tax.

J. Total expenses directly related to operations.

K. Income before all income tax and before discontinued operations, extraordinary items, and cumulative effects of accounting changes (if any).

L. None of the above.

Inferring Income Statement Values

E5-10
LO3

Supply the missing dollar amounts for the 2007 income statement of Ultimate Style Company for each of the following independent cases (*Hint:* Organize each case in the format of the classified or multiple-step income statement discussed in the chapter. Rely on the amounts given to infer the missing values.):

	Case A	Case B	Case C	Case D	Case E
Sales revenue	$900	$700	$410	$?	$?
Selling expense	?	150	80	400	250
Cost of goods sold	?	370	?	500	310
Income tax expense	?	30	20	40	30
Gross margin	500	?	?	?	440
Pretax income	200	90	?	190	?
Administrative expense	100	?	60	100	80
Net income	170	?	50	?	80

Preparing a Multiple-Step Income Statement

E5-11
LO3

The following data were taken from the records of Village Corporation at December 31, 2007:

Sales revenue	$70,000
Gross profit	24,500
Selling (distribution) expense	8,000
Administrative expense	?
Pretax income	12,000
Income tax rate	30%
Shares of stock outstanding	3,000

Required:

Prepare a complete multiple-step income statement for the company (showing both gross profit and income from operations). Show all computations. (*Hint:* Set up the side captions or rows starting with sales revenue and ending with earnings per share; rely on the amounts and percentages given to infer missing values.)

Preparing a Multiple-Step Income Statement

E5-12
LO3

The following data were taken from the records of Thayer Appliances, Incorporated, at December 31, 2009:

Sales revenue	$130,000
Administrative expense	10,000
Selling (distribution) expense	18,000
Income tax rate	25%
Gross profit	58,000
Shares of stock outstanding	2,000

Required:

Prepare a complete multiple-step income statement for the company (showing both gross profit and income from operations). Show all computations. (*Hint:* Set up the side captions or rows starting with sales revenue and ending with earnings per share; rely on the amounts and percentages given to infer missing values.)

E5-13
LO3

Fruit of the Loom

Determining the Effects of Transactions on Balance Sheet and Income Statement Categories

Fruit of the Loom, Inc., is one of the largest domestic producers of underwear and activewear, selling products under the FRUIT OF THE LOOM®, BVD®, MUNSINGWEAR®, WILSON®, and other brand names. Listed here are selected aggregate transactions from the first quarter of a recent year (dollars in millions). Complete the following tabulation, indicating the sign (+ for increase, − for decrease, and NE for no effect) and amount of the effect of each transaction. Consider each item independently.

a. Recorded sales on account of $501.1 and related cost of goods sold of $370.4.
b. Borrowed $306.4 on line of credit with a bank with principal payable within one year.
c. Incurred research and development expense of $10, which was paid in cash.

Transaction	Current Assets	Gross Profit	Current Liabilities
a.			
b.			
c.			

E5-14
LO3

Rowe Furniture

Determining the Effects of Transactions on Balance Sheet, Income Statement, and Statement of Cash Flows Categories

Rowe Furniture Corporation is a Virginia-based manufacturer of furniture. Listed here are selected aggregate transactions from the first quarter of a recent year (dollars in millions). Complete the following tabulation, indicating the sign (+ for increase, − for decrease, and NE for no effect) and amount of the effect of each additional transaction. Consider each item independently.

a. Recorded collections of cash from customers owed on open account of $32.2.
b. Repaid $2.1 in principal on line of credit with a bank with principal payable within one year.

Transaction	Current Assets	Gross Profit	Current Liabilities	Cash Flow from Operating Activities
a.				
b.				

E5-15
LO3

Preparing a Simple Statement of Cash Flows Using the Indirect Method

Blackwell Corporation is preparing its annual financial statements at December 31, 2006. Listed here are the items on its statement of cash flows presented in alphabetical order. Parentheses indicate that a listed amount should be subtracted on the cash flow statement. The beginning balance in cash was $36,000 and the ending balance was $41,000.

Cash borrowed on three-year note	$25,000
Decrease in inventory	2,000
Decrease in accounts payable	(4,000)
Increase in accounts receivable	(10,000)
Net income	18,000
Stock issued for cash	22,000
New delivery truck purchased for cash	(12,000)
Land purchased	(36,000)

Required:
Prepare the 2006 statement of cash flows for Blackwell Corporation. The section reporting cash flows from operating activities should be prepared using the indirect method discussed in the chapter.

E5-16
LO4

GAP, Inc.

Analyzing and Interpreting Return on Equity

Gap, Inc., is a leading international specialty retailer offering clothing, accessories and personal care products for men, women, children, and babies under the Gap, Banana Republic, and Old Navy brand names. Presented here are selected income statement and balance sheet amounts (dollars in millions).

	Current Year	Prior Year
Net sales	$15,854	$14,455
Net income	1,030	477
Average shareholders' equity	4,221	3,334
Average total assets	10,123	8,793

Required:
1. Compute ROE for the current and prior years and explain the meaning of the change.
2. Explain the major cause(s) of the change in ROE using ROE profit driver analysis.

Analyzing and Evaluating Return on Equity from a Security Analyst's Perspective

Papa John's is one of the fastest-growing pizza delivery and carry-out restaurant chains in the country. Presented here are selected income statement and balance sheet amounts (dollars in thousands).

E5-17
LO4
Papa John's

	Current Year	Prior Year
Net sales	$917,378	$946,219
Net income	33,563	46,797
Average shareholders' equity	140,610	148,790
Average total assets	357,023	377,136

Required:
1. Compute ROE for the current and prior years and explain the meaning of the change.
2. Explain the major cause(s) of the change in ROE using ROE profit driver analysis.
3. Would security analysts more likely increase or decrease their estimates of share value on the basis of this change? Explain.

Available with McGraw-Hill's Homework Manager

PROBLEMS

Matching Transactions with Concepts

P5-1
LO1, 2

Following are the concepts of accounting covered in Chapters 2 through 5. Match each transaction with its related concept by entering the appropriate letter in the space provided. Use one letter for each blank.

Concepts	Transactions
____ (1) Users of financial statements	A. Recorded a $1,000 sale of merchandise on credit.
____ (2) Objective of financial statements	B. Counted (inventoried) the unsold items at the end of the period and valued them in dollars.
	C. Acquired a vehicle for use in operating the business.
Qualitative Characteristics	D. Reported the amount of depreciation expense because it likely will affect important decisions of statement users.
____ (3) Relevance	E. Identified as the investors, creditors, and others interested in the business.
____ (4) Reliability	F. Used special accounting approaches because of the uniqueness of the industry.
Assumptions	
____ (5) Separate entity	G. Sold and issued bonds payable of $1 million.
____ (6) Continuity	H. Paid a contractor for an addition to the building with $10,000 cash and $20,000 market value of the stock of the company ($30,000 was deemed to be the cash-equivalent price).
____ (7) Unit of measure	
____ (8) Time period	I. Engaged an outside independent CPA to audit the financial statements.
Elements of Financial Statements	J. Sold merchandise and services for cash and on credit during the year; then determined the cost of those goods sold and the cost of rendering those services.
____ (9) Revenues	
____ (10) Expenses	K. Established an accounting policy that sales revenue shall be recognized only when ownership to the goods sold passes to the customer.
____ (11) Gains	
____ (12) Losses	
____ (13) Assets	

(*continued on next page*)

___ (14) Liabilities	✓L. To design and prepare the financial statements to assist the
___ (15) Stockholders' equity	users in making decisions.

Principles

___ (16) Cost

___ (17) Revenue

___ (18) Matching

___ (19) Full disclosure

Constraints of Accounting

___ (20) Materiality threshold

___ (21) Cost-benefit constraint

___ (22) Conservatism constraint

___ (23) Special industry practices

✓M. Established a policy not to include in the financial statements the personal financial affairs of the owners of the business.

✓N. Sold an asset at a loss that was a peripheral or incidental transaction.

✓O. The user value of a special financial report exceeds the cost of preparing it.

✓P. Valued an asset, such as inventory, at less than its purchase cost because the replacement cost is less.

✓Q. Dated the income statement "For the Year Ended December 31, 2007."

✓R. Used services from outsiders—paid cash for some and put the remainder on credit.

✓S. Acquired an asset (a pencil sharpener that will have a useful life of five years) and recorded it as an expense when purchased for $1.99.

✓T. Disclosed in the financial statements all relevant financial information about the business; necessitated the use of notes to the financial statements.

✓U. Sold an asset at a gain that was a peripheral or incidental transaction.

✓V. Assets of $500,000 − Liabilities of $300,000 = Stockholders' Equity of $200,000.

✓W. Accounting and reporting assume a "going concern."

P5-2 Matching Definitions with Balance Sheet–Related Terms

L03

Following are terms related to the balance sheet, which were discussed in Chapters 2 through 5. Match each definition with its related term by entering the appropriate letter in the space provided.

Terms

___ (1) Retained earnings

___ (2) Current liabilities

___ (3) Liquidity

___ (4) Contra-asset account

___ (5) Accumulated depreciation

___ (6) Intangible assets

___ (7) Other assets

___ (8) Shares outstanding

___ (9) Normal operating cycle

___ (10) Book value

___ (11) Capital in excess of par

___ (12) Liabilities

___ (13) Fixed assets

___ (14) Shareholders' equity

___ (15) Current assets

___ (16) Assets

___ (17) Long-term liabilities

Definitions

A. A miscellaneous category of assets.

B. Amount of contributed capital less the par value of the stock.

C. Total assets minus total liabilities.

D. Nearness of assets to cash (in time).

E. Assets expected to be collected in cash within one year or operating cycle, if longer.

F. Same as carrying value; cost less accumulated depreciation to date.

G. Accumulated earnings minus accumulated dividends.

H. Asset offset account (subtracted from asset).

I. Balance of the Common Stock account divided by the par value per share.

J. Assets that do not have physical substance.

K. Probable future economic benefits owned by the entity from past transactions.

L. Liabilities expected to be paid out of current assets normally within the next year.

M. The average cash-to-cash time involved in the operations of the business.

N. Sum of the annual depreciation expense on an asset from its acquisition to the current date.

O. All liabilities not classified as current liabilities.

P. Property, plant, and equipment.

Q. Debts or obligations from past transactions to be paid with assets or services.

R. None of the above.

Preparing a Balance Sheet and Analyzing Some of Its Parts (AP5-1)

Gold Jewelers is developing its annual financial statements for 2008. The following amounts were correct at December 31, 2008: cash, $42,000; accounts receivable, $51,300; merchandise inventory, $110,000; prepaid insurance, $800; investment in stock of Z corporation (long-term), $26,000; store equipment, $48,000; used store equipment held for disposal, $7,000; accumulated depreciation, store equipment, $9,600; accounts payable, $42,000; long-term note payable, $29,000; income taxes payable, $8,000; retained earnings, $86,500; and common stock, 100,000 shares outstanding, par $1.00 per share (originally sold and issued at $1.10 per share).

P5-3
LO3

Required:

1. Based on these data, prepare a December 31, 2008 balance sheet. Use the following major captions (list the individual items under these captions):
    a. Assets: Current Assets, Long-Term Investments, Fixed Assets, and Other Assets.
    b. Liabilities: Current Liabilities and Long-Term Liabilities.
    c. Stockholders' Equity: Contributed Capital and Retained Earnings.
2. What is the net book value of the store equipment? Explain what this value means.

Reporting Stockholders' Equity on a Balance Sheet and Recording the Issuance of Stock (AP5-2)

At the end of the 2006 annual reporting period, El Paso Corporation's balance sheet showed the following:

P5-4
LO3

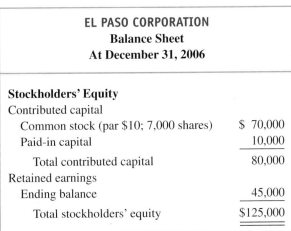

EL PASO CORPORATION	
Balance Sheet	
At December 31, 2006	
Stockholders' Equity	
Contributed capital	
Common stock (par $10; 7,000 shares)	$ 70,000
Paid-in capital	10,000
Total contributed capital	80,000
Retained earnings	
Ending balance	45,000
Total stockholders' equity	$125,000

During 2007, the following selected transactions (summarized) were completed:
a. Sold and issued 1,000 shares of common stock at $15 cash per share (at year-end).
b. Determined net income, $40,000.
c. Declared and paid a cash dividend of $3 per share on the beginning shares outstanding.

Required:

1. Prepare the stockholders' equity section of the balance sheet at December 31, 2007.
2. Give the journal entry to record the sale and issuance of the 1,000 shares of common stock.

Preparing a Multiple-Step Income Statement

Tommy Hilfiger Corporation designs, sources, and markets men's and women's sportswear, jeanswear, and childrenswear under the Tommy Hilfiger trademarks. The company prides itself in producing distinctive designs that recognize tradition while adding a fresh, youthful perspective. The items reported on its income statement for a recent year (ended March 31) are presented here (dollars in thousands) in alphabetical order:

P5-5
LO3
Tommy Hilfiger

Cost of goods sold	1,012,156	Other selling, general, and	
Depreciation and amortization	76,307	administrative expenses	583,502
Interest expense	31,756	Provision for income taxes	37,445
Interest income	3,577	Weighted average shares outstanding	90,692
Net revenue	1,875,797		

Required:

Prepare a multiple-step consolidated income statement (showing gross profit, operating income, and income before income taxes). Include a presentation of basic earnings per share.

P5-6
LO3
eXcel

Preparing Both an Income Statement and Balance Sheet from a Trial Balance (AP5-3)

Thomas Sales Company (organized as a corporation on April 1, 2006) has completed the accounting cycle for the second year, ended March 31, 2008. Thomas also has completed a correct trial balance as follows:

THOMAS SALES COMPANY **Trial Balance** **At March 31, 2008**		
Account Titles	**Debit**	**Credit**
Cash	53,000	
Accounts receivable	44,800	
Office supplies inventory	300	
Automobiles (company cars)	30,000	
Accumulated depreciation, automobiles		10,000
Office equipment	3,000	
Accumulated depreciation, office equipment		1,000
Accounts payable		20,250
Income taxes payable		0
Salaries and commissions payable		1,500
Note payable, long term		30,000
Capital stock (par $1; 30,000 shares)		30,000
Paid-in capital		5,000
Retained earnings (on April 1, 2007)		7,350
Dividends declared and paid during the current year	8,000	
Sales revenue		90,000
Cost of goods sold	30,000	
Operating expenses (detail omitted to conserve your time)	18,000	
Depreciation expense (on autos and including $500 on office equipment)	5,500	
Interest expense	2,500	
Income tax expense (not yet computed)		
Totals	195,100	195,100

Required:

Complete the financial statements, as follows:

a. Classified (multiple-step) income statement for the reporting year ended March 31, 2008. Include income tax expense, assuming a 30 percent tax rate. Use the following subtotals: Gross Profit, Total Operating Expenses, Income from Operations, Income before Income Taxes, and Net Income, and show EPS.

b. Classified balance sheet at the end of the reporting year, March 31, 2008. Include (1) income taxes for the current year in Income Taxes Payable and (2) dividends in Retained Earnings. Use the following captions (list each item under these captions).

Assets	**Stockholders' Equity**
Current Assets	Contributed Capital
Noncurrent Assets	Retained Earnings
Liabilities	
Current Liabilities	
Long-Term Liabilities	

Determining and Interpreting the Effects of Transactions on Income Statement Categories and Return on Equity (AP5-4)

Creative Technology, a computer hardware company based in Singapore, developed the modern standard for computer sound cards in the early 1990s. Recently, Creative has released a line of portable audio products to directly compete with Apple's popular iPod mp3 player. Presented here is a recent income statement (dollars in millions).

P5-7
LO3, 4
Creative Technology

Net sales	$815
Costs and expenses	
Cost of sales	534
Research and development	70
Selling, general and administrative	168
Operating income (loss)	43
Interest and other income (expenses), net	82
Income (loss) before provision (benefit) for income taxes	125
Provision (benefit) for income taxes	(9)
Net income (loss)	$134

Its beginning and ending stockholders' equity was $429 and $691, respectively.

Required:

1. Listed here are hypothetical *additional* transactions. Assuming that they had *also* occurred during the fiscal year, complete the following tabulation, indicating the sign of the effect of each *additional* transaction (+ for increase, − for decrease, and NE for no effect). Consider each item independently and ignore taxes.
   a. Recorded sales on account of $500 and related cost of goods sold of $475.
   b. Incurred additional research and development expense of $100, which was paid in cash.
   c. Issued additional shares of common stock for $200 cash.
   d. Declared and paid dividends of $90.

Transaction	Gross Profit	Operating Income (Loss)	Return on Equity
a.			
b.			
c.			
d.			

2. Assume that next period, Creative does not pay any dividends, does not issue or retire stock, and earns the same income as during the current period. Will Creative's ROE next period be higher, lower, or the same as the current period? Why?

(Supplement A) Preparing a Multiple-Step Income Statement with Discontinued Operations and Cumulative Effects of Accounting Changes

Adolph Coors Company, established in 1873, is the third-largest brewer of beer in the United States. Its products include Coors, Coors Light, ZIMA, and many other malt beverages. Recently, Coors discontinued its ceramics, aluminum, packaging, and technology-based developmental businesses. In the same year, it reported two changes in accounting methods mandated by the FASB. The items reported on its income statement for that year (ended December 26) are presented here (dollars in thousands) in alphabetical order:

P5-8
Adolph Coors
Company

Cost of goods sold	$1,035,544
Cumulative effect of change in accounting for income taxes	30,500
Cumulative effect of change in accounting for postretirement benefits (net of tax)	(38,800)

Income tax expense	22,900
Interest expense	16,014
Interest income	255
Marketing, general and administrative	429,573
Miscellaneous income—net	1,087
Net loss from discontinued operations	29,415
Net sales	1,550,788
Research and project development	12,370

Required:

Using appropriate headings and subtotals, prepare a multiple-step consolidated income statement (showing gross profit, operating income, and any other subheadings you deem appropriate).

ALTERNATE PROBLEMS

AP5-1

LO3

Preparing a Balance Sheet and Analyzing Some of Its Parts (P5-3)

Carpet Bazaar is developing its annual financial statements for 2008. The following amounts were correct at December 31, 2008: cash, $35,000; investment in stock of ABC corporation (long term), $32,000; store equipment, $51,000; accounts receivable, $47,500; carpet inventory, $118,000; prepaid insurance, $1,300; used store equipment held for disposal, $3,500; accumulated depreciation, store equipment, $10,200; income taxes payable, $6,000; long-term note payable, $26,000; accounts payable, $45,000; retained earnings, $76,100; and common stock, 100,000 shares outstanding, par $1 per share (originally sold and issued at $1.25 per share).

Required:

1. Based on these data, prepare a 2008 balance sheet. Use the following major captions (list the individual items under these captions):
   a. Assets: Current Assets, Long-Term Investments, Fixed Assets, and Other Assets.
   b. Liabilities: Current Liabilities and Long-Term Liabilities.
   c. Stockholders' Equity: Contributed Capital and Retained Earnings.
2. What is the net book value of the store equipment? Explain what this value means.

AP5-2

LO3

Reporting Stockholders' Equity on a Balance Sheet and Recording the Issuance of Stock (P5-4)

At the end of the 2006 annual reporting period, Potamia Corporation's balance sheet showed the following:

POTAMIA CORPORATION Balance Sheet At December 31, 2006	
Stockholders' Equity	
Common stock (par $10; 9,500 shares)	$ 95,000
Additional paid-in capital	28,500
Retained earnings—Ending balance	70,000
Total stockholders' equity	$193,500

During 2007, the following selected transactions (summarized) were completed:

a. Sold and issued 1,500 shares of common stock at $17 cash per share (at year-end).
b. Determined net income, $50,000.
c. Declared and paid a cash dividend of $2 per share on the beginning shares outstanding.

Required:

1. Prepare the stockholders' equity section of the balance sheet at December 31, 2007.
2. Give the journal entry to record the sale and issuance of the 1,500 shares of common stock.

Preparing Both an Income Statement and Balance Sheet from a Trial Balance (P5-6)

AP5-3
LO3

ACME Sales (organized as a corporation on September 1, 2006) has completed the accounting cycle for the second year, ended August 31, 2008. ACME also has completed a correct trial balance as follows:

ACME SALES Trial Balance At August 31, 2008		
Account Titles	**Debit**	**Credit**
Cash	26,000	
Accounts receivable	30,800	
Supplies inventory	1,300	
Service vehicles (company vans)	60,000	
Accumulated depreciation, service vehicles		20,000
Equipment	14,000	
Accumulated depreciation, equipment		4,000
Accounts payable		16,700
Income taxes payable		0
Salaries payable		1,100
Note payable, long term		34,000
Capital stock (par $1; 10,000 shares)		10,000
Paid-in capital		30,000
Retained earnings (on September 1, 2007)		4,300
Dividends declared and paid during the current year	2,000	
Sales revenue		55,000
Cost of goods sold	17,000	
Operating expenses (detail omitted to conserve your time)	10,000	
Depreciation expense (on vehicles and including $2,000 on equipment)	12,000	
Interest expense	2,000	
Income tax expense (not yet computed)		
Totals	175,100	175,100

Required:

Complete the financial statements, as follows:

a. Classified (multiple-step) income statement for the reporting year ended August 31, 2008. Include income tax expense, assuming a 30 percent tax rate. Use the following subtotals: Gross Profit, Total Operating Expenses, Income from Operations, Income before Income Taxes, and Net Income, and show EPS.

b. Classified balance sheet at the end of the reporting year, August 31, 2008. Include (1) income taxes for the current year in Income Taxes Payable and (2) dividends in Retained Earnings. Use the following captions (list each item under these captions).

Assets	Stockholders' Equity
Current Assets	Contributed Capital
Noncurrent Assets	Retained Earnings
Liabilities	
Current Liabilities	
Long-Term Liabilities	

AP5-4
LO3, 4
Barnes & Noble

Determining and Interpreting the Effects of Transactions on Income Statement Categories and Return on Equity (P5-7)

Barnes & Noble, Inc., revolutionized bookselling by making its stores public spaces and community institutions where customers may browse, find a book, relax over a cup of coffee, talk with authors, and join discussion groups. Today it is fighting increasing competition not only from traditional sources but also from online booksellers. Presented here is a recent income statement (dollars in millions).

Net sales	$5,951
Costs and expenses	
Cost of sales	4,324
Selling, general and administrative	1,125
Depreciation and amortization	164
Preopening expenses	9
Operating income (loss)	329
Interest and other income (expenses), net	(34)
Income (loss) before provision (benefit) for income taxes	295
Provision (benefit) for income taxes	121
Net income (loss)	$ 174

Its beginning and ending stockholders' equity was $1,028 and $1,260, respectively.

Required:

1. Listed here are hypothetical *additional* transactions. Assuming that they had *also* occurred during the fiscal year, complete the following tabulation, indicating the sign of the effect of each *additional* transaction (+ for increase, − for decrease, and NE for no effect).

    Consider each item independently and ignore taxes.
    a. Recorded and received additional interest income of $4.
    b. Purchased $25 of additional inventory on open account.
    c. Recorded and paid additional advertising expense of $9.
    d. Additional shares of common stock are issued for $50 cash.

Transaction	Operating Income (Loss)	Net Income	Return on Equity
a.			
b.			
c.			
d.			

2. Assume that next period, Barnes & Noble does not pay any dividends, does not issue or retire stock, and earns 20 percent more than during the current period. Will Barnes & Noble's ROE next period be higher, lower, or the same as in the current period? Why?

CASES AND PROJECTS

Annual Report Cases

CP5-1
LO2, 3, 4

Finding Financial Information

Refer to the financial statements of Pacific Sunwear of California given in Appendix B at the end of this book, or open file PSUN.pdf in the Annual Report Cases directory on the student DVD. At the bottom of each statement, the company warns readers to "see accompanying notes." The following questions illustrate the types of information that you can find in the financial statements and accompanying notes. (*Hint:* Use the notes.)

Required:

1. What items were included as "Other Assets" on the balance sheet?
2. How much land did the company own at the end of the most recent reporting year?
3. What portion of accrued liabilities were "Accrued gift cards and store merchandise credits" during the current year?
4. At what point were website sales recognized as revenue?
5. The company reported cash flows from operating activities of $143,012,000. However, its cash and cash equivalents decreased for the year. Explain how that happened.
6. What was the highest stock price for the company during fiscal 2004? (*Note:* Some companies will label a year that has a January year-end as having a fiscal year-end dated one year earlier. For example, a January 2005 year-end may be labeled as Fiscal 2004 since the year actually has more months that fall in the 2004 calendar year than in the 2005 calendar year.)
7. Calculate the company's ROE for fiscal 2004 and 2003. Did it increase or decrease? (Pacific Sunwear of California's shareholders' equity balance was $302,373,000 at the end of the 2002 fiscal year.) How would you expect the change in ROE to be reflected in the company's share price?

Finding Financial Information

Refer to the financial statements of American Eagle Outfitters given in Appendix C at the end of this book, or open file AEOS.pdf in the Annual Report Cases directory on the student DVD. At the bottom of each statement, the company warns readers to "See notes to consolidated financial statements." The following questions illustrate the types of information that you can find in the financial statements and accompanying notes. (*Hint:* Use the notes.)

CP5-2
LO2, 3
AMERICAN EAGLE
OUTFITTERS
ae.com

Required:

1. What subtotals does it report on its income statement?
2. The company spent $97,288,000 on capital expenditures (property, plant, and equipment) and $483,083,000 purchasing investments during the most recent year. Were operating activities or financing activities the major source of cash for these expenditures?
3. What was the company's largest asset (net) at the end of the most recent year?
4. Was women's apparel an increasing or decreasing percentage of its sales over the last three years?
5. Over what useful lives are buildings depreciated?
6. What portion of "Property and Equipment" is composed of "Buildings"?

Comparing Companies within an Industry

Refer to the financial statements of Pacific Sunwear of California given in Appendix B, American Eagle Outfitters given in Appendix C, and Industry Ratio Report given in Appendix D at the end of this book or open file CP5-3.xls in the Annual Report Cases directory on the student DVD.

CP5-3
LO4
PACIFIC SUNWEAR
OF CALIFORNIA, INC.

AMERICAN EAGLE
OUTFITTERS
ae.com

Required:

1. Compute return on equity for the most recent year. Which company provided the highest return to shareholders during the current year?
2. Use ROE profit driver analysis to determine the cause(s) of any differences. How might the ownership versus the rental of property, plant, and equipment affect the total asset turnover ratio?
3. Compare the ROE profit driver analysis for American Eagle Outfitters and Pacific Sunwear of California to the ROE profit driver analysis for their industry. Where does American Eagle Outfitters outperform or underperform the industry? Where does Pacific Sunwear of California outperform or underperform the industry?

Financial Reporting and Analysis Cases

Interpreting the Financial Press

The Committee of Sponsoring Organizations (COSO) published a research study that examined financial statement fraud occurrences between 1987 and 1997. A summary of the findings by M. S. Beasley, J. V. Carcello, and D. R. Hermanson, "Fraudulent Financial Reporting: 1987–1997: An Analysis of U.S. Public Companies," *The Auditor's Report,* Summer 1999, pp. 15–17, is available on the

CP5-4
LO1
The Auditor's Report

Libby/Libby/Short website at **www.mhhe.com/libby5e**.* You should read the article and then write a short memo outlining the following:

1. The size of the companies involved.
2. The extent of top management involvement.
3. The specific accounting fraud techniques involved.
4. What might lead managers to introduce misstatements into the income statement near the end of the accounting period.

CP5-5
LO3

Using Financial Reports: Financial Statement Inferences

The following amounts were selected from the annual financial statements for Genesis Corporation at December 31, 2008 (end of the third year of operations):

From the 2008 income statement:	
Sales revenue	$275,000
Cost of goods sold	(170,000)
All other expenses (including income tax)	(95,000)
Net income	$ 10,000
From the December 31, 2008, balance sheet:	
Current assets	$ 90,000
All other assets	212,000
Total assets	302,000
Current liabilities	40,000
Long-term liabilities	66,000
Capital stock (par $10)	100,000
Paid-in capital	16,000
Retained earnings	80,000
Total liabilities and stockholders' equity	$302,000

Required:

Analyze the data on the 2008 financial statements of Genesis by answering the questions that follow. Show computations.

1. What was the gross margin on sales?
2. What was the amount of EPS?
3. If the income tax rate was 25 percent, what was the amount of pretax income?
4. What was the average sales price per share of the capital stock?
5. Assuming that no dividends were declared or paid during 2008, what was the beginning balance (January 1, 2008) of retained earnings?

Critical Thinking Cases

CP5-6
LO4
Sony

Making Decisions as a Manager: Evaluating the Effects of Business Strategy on Return on Equity

Sony is a world leader in the manufacture of consumer and commercial electronics as well as the entertainment and insurance industries. Its ROE has increased from 9 percent to 14 percent over the last three years.

Required:

Indicate the most likely effect of each of the changes in business strategy on Sony's ROE for the next period and future periods (+ for increase, − for decrease, and NE for no effect), assuming all other things are unchanged. Explain your answer for each. Treat each item independently.

a. Sony decreases its investment in research and development aimed at products to be brought to market in more than one year.
b. Sony begins a new advertising campaign for a movie to be released during the next year.

---

*Copyright © 1999 by American Institute of Certified Public Accountants, Inc. Reprinted with permission.

c. Sony issues additional stock for cash, the proceeds to be used to acquire other high-technology companies in future periods.

Strategy Change	Current Period ROE	Future Periods' ROE
a.		
b.		
c.		

Making a Decision as an Auditor: Effects of Errors on Income, Assets, and Liabilities

CP5-7
LO1, 3

Megan Company (not a corporation) was careless about its financial records during its first year of operations, 2006. It is December 31, 2006, the end of the annual accounting period. An outside CPA examined the records and discovered numerous errors, all of which are described here. Assume that each error is independent of the others.

Required:

Analyze each error and indicate its effect on 2006 and 2007 income, assets, and liabilities if not corrected. Do not assume any other errors. Use these codes to indicate the effect of each dollar amount: O = overstated, U = understated, and NE = no effect. Write an explanation of your analysis of each transaction to support your response.

	Net Income 2006	Net Income 2007	Assets 2006	Assets 2007	Liabilities 2006	Liabilities 2007
Independent Errors — Effect On						
1. Depreciation expense for 2006, not recorded in 2006, $950.	O $950	NE	O $950	O $950	NE	NE
2. Wages earned by employees during 2006 not recorded or paid in 2006 but recorded and paid in 2007, $500.						
3. Revenue earned during 2006 but not collected or recorded until 2007, $600.						
4. Amount paid in 2006 and recorded as expense in 2006 but not an expense until 2007, $200.						
5. Revenue collected in 2006 and recorded as revenue in 2006 but not earned until 2007, $900.						
6. Sale of services and cash collected in 2006. Recorded as a debit to Cash and as a credit to Accounts Receivable, $300.						
7. On December 31, 2006, bought land on credit for $8,000, not recorded until payment was made on February 1, 2007.						

Following is a sample explanation of analysis of errors if not corrected, using the first error as an example:

1. Failure to record depreciation in 2006 caused depreciation expense to be too low; therefore, income was overstated by $950. Accumulated depreciation also is too low by $950, which causes assets to be overstated by $950 until the error is corrected.

CP5-8
LO1, 3
Royal Ahold

Evaluating an Ethical Dilemma: Management Incentives and Fraudulent Financial Statements

Netherlands-based Royal Ahold ranks among the world's three largest food retailers. In the United States it operates the Stop & Shop and Giant supermarket chains. Dutch and U.S. regulators and prosecutors have brought criminal and civil charges against the company and its executives for overstating earnings by more than $1 billion. The nature of the fraud is described in the following excerpt:

> *Two Former Execs of Ahold Subsidiary Plead Not Guilty to Fraud*
>
> 28 July 2004 Associated Press Newswires
>
> © 2004. The Associated Press.
>
> NEW YORK (AP)—Two former executives pleaded not guilty Wednesday to devising a scheme to inflate the earnings of U.S. Foodservice Inc., a subsidiary of Dutch supermarket giant Royal Ahold NV.
>
> Former chief financial officer Michael Resnick and former chief marketing officer Mark Kaiser entered their pleas in a Manhattan federal court, a day after prosecutors announced fraud and conspiracy charges against them.
>
> The government contends they worked together to boost the company's earnings by $800 million from 2000 to 2003 by reporting fake rebates from suppliers—and sweetened their own bonuses in the process. Two other defendants have already pleaded guilty in the alleged scheme: Timothy Lee, a former executive vice president, and William Carter, a former vice president. Both are set for sentencing in January. Netherlands-based Ahold's U.S. properties include the Stop & Shop and Giant supermarket chains. U.S. Foodservice is one of the largest distributors of food products in the country, providing to restaurants and cafeterias.
>
> Ahold said last year it had overstated its earnings by more than $1 billion, mostly because of the fraud at U.S. Foodservice. Its stock lost 60 percent of its value, and about $6 billion in market value evaporated.

Required:

Using more recent new reports (*Wall Street Journal Index, Factiva,* and *Bloomberg Business News* are good sources), answer the following questions.

1. Whom did the courts and regulatory authorities hold responsible for the misstated financial statements?
2. Did the company cooperate with investigations into the fraud? How did this affect the penalties imposed against the company?
3. How might executive compensation plans that tied bonuses to accounting earnings motivate unethical conduct in this case?

Financial Reporting and Analysis Team Project

CP5-9
LO2, 3

Analyzing the Accounting Communication Process

As a team, select an industry to analyze. Reuters provides lists of industries and their makeup at www.investor.reuters.com/Industries.aspx. Each team member should acquire the annual report or 10-K for one publicly traded company in the industry, with each member selecting a different company. (Library files, the SEC EDGAR service at www.sec.gov, Compustat CD, or the company itself are good sources.)

Required:

On an individual basis, each team member should write a short report answering the following questions about the selected company. Discuss any patterns across the companies that you as a team observe. Then, as a team, write a short report comparing and contrasting your companies.

1. What formats are used to present the
   a. Balance Sheets?
   b. Income Statements?
   c. Operating Activities section of the Statement of Cash Flows?
2. Find one footnote for each of the following and describe its contents in brief:
   a. An accounting rule applied in the company's statements.
   b. Additional detail about a reported financial statement number.
   c. Relevant financial information but with no number reported in the financial statements.
3. Using electronic sources, find one article reporting the company's annual earnings announcement. When is it dated and how does that date compare to the balance sheet date?
4. Using electronic sources, find two analysts' reports for your company.
   a. Give the date, name of the analyst, and his or her recommendation from each report.
   b. Discuss why the recommendations are similar or different. Look at the analysts' reasoning for their respective recommendation.
5. Using the SEC EDGAR website (www.sec.gov), what is the most recent document filed by your company with the SEC (e.g., 8K, S1) and what did it say in brief?
6. Ratio analysis:
   a. What does the return on equity ratio measure in general?
   b. Compute the ratio for the last three years.
   c. What do your results suggest about the company?
   d. If available, find the industry ratio for the most recent year, compare it to your results, and discuss why you believe your company differs from or is similar to the industry ratio.
7. Use the ROE profit driver analysis to determine the cause(s) of any differences in the ROE ratio over the last three years. [Remember that you computed the three profit driver ratios in the last three chapters.]

After studying this chapter, you should be able to:

1. Apply the revenue principle to determine the accepted time to record sales revenue for typical retailers, wholesalers, manufacturers, and service companies. p. 284

2. Analyze the impact of credit card sales, sales discounts, and sales returns on the amounts reported as net sales. p. 285

3. Analyze and interpret the gross profit percentage. p. 288

4. Estimate, report, and evaluate the effects of uncollectible accounts receivable (bad debts) on financial statements. p. 290

5. Analyze and interpret the accounts receivable turnover ratio and the effects of accounts receivable on cash flows. p. 297

6. Report, control, and safeguard cash. p. 299

Reporting and Interpreting Sales Revenue, Receivables, and Cash

6

F ounded by current CEO (then UCSB student), Doug Otto, Deckers Outdoor is best known for its Teva sports sandals and UGG sheepskin boots. Deckers has become a major player in the casual, outdoor, and athletic footwear market by building on its commitment to the needs of hikers, trail runners, kayakers, surfers, and whitewater rafters for comfort, function, and performance. Its growth strategy requires building brand recognition by developing and introducing additional innovative footwear that satisfies the company's high standards of comfort, performance, and quality. "Building the brands" allows Deckers to maintain a loyal consumer following and penetrate new markets.

There is a second key component to Deckers' successful growth strategy. Success in the ultracompetitive footwear market requires careful matching of production schedules to customers' needs and careful management of customer receivables. Deckers' successful focus on brand development, product innovation, and working capital management has allowed the company to report the highest gross profit and net income in its history.

UNDERSTANDING THE BUSINESS

The success of each element of Deckers' strategy can be seen in the information presented in the income statement excerpt in Exhibit 6.1. Net Sales (Revenue) is reported first, and Cost of Sales (Cost of Goods Sold Expense, Cost of Products Sold) is set out separately from the remaining expenses. Next, the income statement shows **gross profit** (**gross margin, gross profit margin**), which is net sales revenue minus cost of sales.

Planning Deckers' growth strategy requires careful coordination of sales and production activities, as well as cash collections from customers. Much of this coordination revolves around the use of credit card and sales discounts, and managing sales returns and bad debts. These activities affect **net sales revenue** on the income statement and **cash** and **accounts receivable** on the balance sheet, which are the focus of this chapter. We will also introduce the gross profit percentage ratio as a basis for evaluating changes in gross profit, as well as the receivables turnover ratio as a measure of the efficiency of credit-granting and collection activities. Finally, since the cash collected from customers is also a tempting target for fraud and embezzlement, we will discuss how accounting systems commonly include controls to prevent and detect such misdeeds.

DECKERS OUTDOOR CORPORATION AND SUBSIDIARIES
CONSOLIDATED STATEMENTS OF OPERATIONS
Three Years Ended December 31, 2001, 2002, and 2003
(amounts in dollars in thousands except share data)

	2001	2002	2003
Net sales	$91,461	$99,107	$121,055
Cost of sales	52,903	57,577	69,710
Gross profit	38,558	41,530	51,345

ORGANIZATION of the Chapter

Accounting for Sales Revenue	Measuring and Reporting Receivables	Reporting and Safeguarding Cash
■ Credit Card Sales to Consumers ■ Sales Discounts to Businesses ■ Sales Returns and Allowances ■ Reporting Net Sales ■ Gross Profit Percentage	■ Classifying Receivables ■ Accounting for Bad Debts ■ Reporting Accounts Receivable and Bad Debts ■ Estimating Bad Debts ■ Receivables Turnover Ratio ■ Control over Accounts Receivable	■ Cash and Cash Equivalents Defined ■ Cash Management ■ Internal Control of Cash ■ Reconciliation of Cash Accounts and the Bank Statements

ACCOUNTING FOR SALES REVENUE

Learning Objective 1

Apply the revenue principle to determine the accepted time to record sales revenue for typical retailers, wholesalers, manufacturers, and service companies.

As indicated in Chapter 3, the **revenue principle** requires that revenues be recorded when they are earned (delivery has occurred or services have been rendered, there is persuasive evidence of an arrangement for customer payment, the price is fixed or determinable, and collection is reasonably assured). For sellers of goods, these criteria are most often met and sales revenue is recorded when title and risks of ownership transfer to the buyer.[1] The point at which title (ownership) changes hands is determined by the shipping terms in the sales contract. When goods are shipped **FOB (free on board) shipping point,** title changes hands at shipment, and the buyer normally pays for shipping. When they are shipped **FOB destination,** title changes hands on delivery, and the seller normally pays for shipping. Revenues from goods shipped FOB shipping point are normally recognized at shipment. Revenues from goods shipped FOB delivery are normally recognized at delivery.

Service companies most often record sales revenue when they have provided services to the buyer. Companies disclose the revenue recognition rule they follow in the

[1]See SEC Staff Accounting Bulletin 101, *Revenue Recognition in Financial Statements,* 2000.

footnote to the financial statements entitled Summary of Significant Accounting Policies. In that note, Deckers reports the following:

NOTES TO CONSOLIDATED FINANCIAL STATEMENTS

1. Summary of Significant Accounting Policies

Recognition of Revenue

The Company recognizes revenue when products are shipped and the customer takes title and assumes risk of loss, collection of relevant receivable is probable, persuasive evidence of an arrangement exists, and the sales price is fixed or determinable.

Like Deckers, many manufacturers, wholesalers, and retailers recognize revenue at shipment. This is when title and risks of ownership pass for Deckers' sales. Auditors expend a great deal of effort ensuring that revenues are recognized in the proper period.

The appropriate **amount** of revenue to record is the **cash equivalent sales price.** Some sales practices differ depending on whether sales are made to businesses or consumers. Deckers sells footwear and apparel to other **businesses** (retailers), including Athletes Foot and Eastern Mountain Sports, which then sell the goods to consumers. It also operates its own Internet and catalog retailing business that sells footwear directly to **consumers.**

Deckers uses a variety of methods to motivate both groups of customers to buy its products and make payment for their purchases. The principal methods include (1) allowing consumers to use credit cards to pay for purchases, (2) providing business customers direct credit and discounts for early payment, and (3) allowing returns from all customers under certain circumstances. These methods, in turn, affect the way we compute **net sales revenue.**

Credit Card Sales to Consumers

Deckers accepts cash or credit card payment for its catalogue and Internet sales. Deckers' managers decided to accept credit cards (mainly Visa, Mastercard, and American Express) for a variety of reasons:

Learning Objective 2
Analyze the impact of credit card sales, sales discounts, and sales returns on the amounts reported as net sales.

1. Increasing customer traffic.
2. Avoiding the costs of providing credit directly to consumers, including recordkeeping and bad debts (discussed later).
3. Lowering losses due to bad checks.
4. Avoiding losses from fraudulent credit card sales. (As long as Deckers follows the credit card company's verification procedure, the credit card company [e.g., Visa] absorbs any losses.)
5. Faster receipt of its money. (Since credit card receipts can be directly deposited in its bank account, Deckers receives its money faster than it would if it provided credit directly to consumers.)

The credit card company charges a fee for the service it provides. When Deckers deposits its credit card receipts in the bank, it might receive credit for only 97 percent of the sales price. The credit card company is charging a 3 percent fee (the credit card discount) for its service. If daily credit card sales were $3,000, Deckers would report the following:

A CREDIT CARD DISCOUNT is the fee charged by the credit card company for services.

Sales revenue	$3,000
Less: Credit card discounts (0.03 × 3,000)	90
Net sales (reported on the income statement)	$2,910

Sales Discounts to Businesses

Most of Deckers' sales to businesses are credit sales on open account; that is, there is no formal written promissory note or credit card. When Deckers sells footwear to retailers on credit, credit terms are printed on the sales document and invoice (bill) sent to the customer. Often credit terms are abbreviated using symbols. For example, if the full price is due within 30 days of the invoice date, the credit terms would be noted as **n/30.** Here, the **n** means the sales amount **net** of, or less, any sales returns.

A SALES DISCOUNT (cash discount) is a cash discount offered to encourage prompt payment of an account receivable.

In some cases, a sales discount (often called a cash discount) is granted to the purchaser to encourage early payment.[2] For example, Deckers may offer standard credit terms of 2/10, n/30, which means that the customer may deduct 2 percent from the invoice price if cash payment is made within 10 days from the date of sale. If cash payment is not made within the 10-day discount period, the full sales price (less any returns) is due within a maximum of 30 days.

Early Payment Incentive

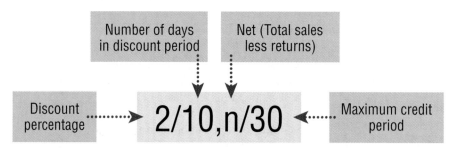

Number of days in discount period	Net (Total sales less returns)

Discount percentage ········▶ **2/10,n/30** ◀········ Maximum credit period

Deckers offers this sales discount to encourage customers to pay more quickly. This provides two benefits to Deckers.

1. Prompt receipt of cash from customers reduces the necessity to borrow money to meet operating needs.

2. Since customers tend to pay bills providing discounts first, a sales discount also decreases the chances that the customer will run out of funds before Deckers' bill is paid.

Companies commonly record sales discounts taken by subtracting the discount from sales if payment is made **within** the discount period (the usual case).[3] For example, if credit sales of $1,000 are recorded with terms 2/10, n/30 and payment of $980 ($1,000 × 0.98 = $980) is made within the discount period, net sales of the following amount would be reported:

Sales revenue	$1,000
Less: Sales discounts (0.02 × $1,000)	20
Net sales (reported on the income statement)	$ 980

If payment is made after the discount period, the full $1,000 would be reported as net sales.

---

[2]It is important not to confuse a cash discount with a trade discount. Vendors sometimes use a **trade discount** for quoting sales prices; the sales price is the list or printed catalog price **less** the trade discount. For example, an item may be quoted at $10 per unit subject to a 20 percent trade discount on orders of 100 units or more; thus, the price for the large order is $8 per unit. Sales revenue should always be recorded net of trade discounts. Deckers also offers discounts for early order and shipment to help manage production flows.

[3]We use the gross method in all examples in this text. Some companies use the alternative net method, which records sales revenue after deducting the amount of the cash discount. Since the choice of method has little effect on the financial statements, discussion of this method is left for an advanced course.

Note that both the purpose of and accounting for sales discounts are very similar to the purpose of and the accounting for credit card discounts. Both sales discounts and credit card discounts provide an attractive service to customers while promoting faster receipt of cash, reducing recordkeeping costs, and minimizing bad debts. Accounting for sales discounts is discussed in more detail in Supplement A.

To Take or Not to Take the Discount, That Is the Question

FINANCIAL ANALYSIS

Customers usually pay within the discount period because the savings are substantial. With terms 2/10, n/30, customers save 2 percent by paying 20 days early (on the 10th day instead of the 30th). This translates into a 37 percent annual interest rate. To calculate the annual interest rate, first compute the interest rate for the discount period. When the 2 percent discount is taken, the customer pays only 98 percent of the gross sales price. For example, on a $100 sale with terms 2/10, n/30, $2 would be saved and $98 would be paid 20 days early.

The interest rate for the 20-day discount period is computed as follows:

$$\frac{\text{Amount Saved}}{\text{Amount Paid}} = \text{Interest Rate for 20 Days}$$

$$\frac{\$2}{\$98} = 2.04\% \text{ for 20 Days}$$

The annual interest rate is:

$$\text{Interest Rate for 20 Days} \times \frac{365 \text{ Days}}{20 \text{ Days}} = \text{Annual Interest Rate}$$

$$2.04\% \times \frac{365 \text{ Days}}{20 \text{ Days}} = 37.23\% \text{ Annual Interest Rate}$$

As long as the bank's interest rate is less than the interest rate associated with failing to take cash discounts, the customer will save by taking the cash discount. For example, even if credit customers had to borrow from that bank at a high rate such as 15 percent, they would save a great deal.

Sales Returns and Allowances

Retailers and consumers have a right to return unsatisfactory or damaged merchandise and receive a refund or an adjustment to their bill. Such returns are often accumulated in a separate account called Sales Returns and Allowances and must be deducted from gross sales revenue in determining net sales. This account informs Deckers' managers of the volume of returns and allowances providing an important measure of the quality of customer service. Assume that Fontana Shoes of Ithaca, New York, buys 40 pairs of sandals from Deckers for $2,000 on account. Before paying for the sandals, Fontana discovers that 10 pairs of sandals are not the color ordered and returns them to Deckers.[4] Deckers computes net sales as follows:

SALES RETURNS AND ALLOWANCES is a reduction of sales revenues for return of or allowances for unsatisfactory goods.

Sales revenue	$2,000
Less: Sales returns and allowances (0.25 × $2,000)	500
Net sales (reported on the income statement)	$1,500

Cost of goods sold related to the 10 pairs of sandals would also be reduced.

[4]Alternatively, Deckers might offer Fontana a $200 allowance to keep the wrong-color sandals. If Fontana accepts the offer, Deckers reports $200 as sales returns and allowances.

Reporting Net Sales

On the company's books, credit card discounts, sales discounts, and sales returns and allowances are accounted for separately to allow managers to monitor the costs of credit card use, sales discounts, and returns. Using the numbers in the preceding examples, the amount of net sales reported on the income statement is computed in the following manner:

Sales revenue	$6,000
Less: Credit card discounts (a contra-revenue)	90
Sales discounts (a contra-revenue)	20
Sales returns and allowances (a contra-revenue)	500
Net sales (reported on the income statement)	$5,390

Deckers indicates in its revenue recognition footnote that the appropriate subtractions are made.

REAL WORLD EXCERPT

DECKERS
outdoor corporation

ANNUAL REPORT

> **NOTES TO CONSOLIDATED FINANCIAL STATEMENTS**
>
> **1. The Company and Summary of Significant Accounting Policies**
>
> *Revenue Recognition*
>
> . . . Allowances for estimated returns, discounts . . . are provided for when related revenue is recorded.

In 2003, Deckers disclosed that it provided its customers with $741,000 in sales discounts based on meeting certain order, shipment, and payment timelines.

As we noted earlier, net sales less cost of goods sold equals the subtotal **gross profit** or **gross margin.** Analysts often examine gross profit as a percentage of sales (the gross profit or gross margin percentage).

**KEY RATIO
ANALYSIS**

Gross Profit Percentage

Learning Objective 3

Analyze and interpret the gross profit percentage.

❓ ANALYTICAL QUESTION:

How effective is management in selling goods and services for more than the costs to purchase or produce them?

% RATIO AND COMPARISONS:

The gross profit percentage ratio is computed as follows:

$$\text{Gross Profit Percentage} = \frac{\text{Gross Profit}}{\text{Net Sales}}$$

The 2003 ratio for Deckers (see Exhibit 6.1):

$$\frac{\$51,345}{\$121,055} = 0.424 \ (42.4\%)$$

Selected Focus Company Comparisons

Papa John's	41.9%
Harley-Davidson	36.0%
General Mills	41.8%

COMPARISONS OVER TIME			COMPARISONS WITH COMPETITORS	
Deckers			**Skechers U.S.A.**	**Timberland**
2001	**2002**	**2003**	**2003**	**2003**
42.2%	41.9%	42.4%	38.0%	46.5%

💡 INTERPRETATIONS:

In General → The gross profit percentage measures how much of every sales dollar is gross profit. It reflects a company's ability to charge premium prices and produce goods and services at low cost. All other things equal, a higher gross profit results in higher net income.

Business strategy, as well as competition, affects the gross profit percentage. Companies pursuing a product-differentiation strategy use research and development and product promotion activities to convince customers of the superiority or distinctiveness of the company's products. This allows them to charge premium prices, producing a higher gross profit percentage. Companies following a low-cost strategy rely on more efficient management of production to reduce costs and increase the gross profit percentage. Managers, analysts, and creditors use this ratio to assess the effectiveness of the company's product development, marketing, and production strategy.

Focus Company Analysis → Deckers' gross profit percentage has remained steady over the past three years at around the industry average of 42 percent,* and between its competitors Skechers and Timberland. At the beginning of the chapter, we discussed key elements of Deckers' business strategy that focused on introducing new technologies, product lines, and styles, as well as managing production and inventory costs. Each of these elements can have a large effect on gross margin.

A Few Cautions: To assess the company's ability to sustain its gross margins, you must understand the sources of any change in the gross profit percentage. For example, an increase in margin resulting from increased sales of high-margin boots during a hard winter would be less sustainable than an increase resulting from introducing new products. Also, higher prices must often be sustained with higher R&D and advertising costs, which can eat up any increase in gross margin. Finally, be aware that a small change in the gross profit percentage can lead to a large change in net income.

*www.investor.reuters.com

SELF-STUDY QUIZ

1. Assume that Deckers sold $30,000 worth of footwear to various retailers with terms 1/10, n/30 and half of that amount was paid within the discount period. Gross catalogue and Internet sales were $5,000 for the same period, 80 percent being paid with credit cards with a 3 percent discount and the rest in cash. Compute net sales for the period.

   _____

   _____

2. During the first quarter of 2004, Deckers' net sales totaled $44,272, and cost of sales was $23,866. Verify that its gross profit percentage was 46.09 percent.

   _____

   _____

After you have completed your answers, check them with the solutions at the bottom of the page.

Self-Study Quiz
Solutions

1. Gross Sales $35,000
   Less: Sales discounts (0.01 × 1/2 × $30,000) 150
        Credit card discounts (0.03 × 0.80 × $5,000) ... 120
   Net Sales $34,730

2. Net Sales $44,272
   Cost of Sales   23,866
   Gross Profit $20,406

   $20,406 / 44,272 = 46.09% Gross profit percentage

MEASURING AND REPORTING RECEIVABLES

Classifying Receivables

Receivables may be classified in three common ways. First, they may be classified as either an account receivable or a note receivable. An account receivable is created by a credit sale on an open account. For example, an account receivable is created when Deckers sells shoes on open account to Fontana Shoes in Ithaca, New York. A note receivable is a promise in writing (a formal document) to pay (1) a specified amount of money, called the **principal,** at a definite future date known as the **maturity date** and (2) a specified amount of **interest** at one or more future dates. The interest is the amount charged for use of the principal. We discuss the computation of interest when we discuss notes payable in a later chapter.

Second, receivables may be classified as trade or nontrade receivables. A **trade receivable** is created in the normal course of business when a sale of merchandise or services on credit occurs. A **nontrade receivable** arises from transactions other than the normal sale of merchandise or services. For example, if Deckers loaned money to a new vice president to help finance a home at the new job location, the loan would be classified as a nontrade receivable. Third, in a classified balance sheet, receivables also are classified as either **current or noncurrent** (short term or long term), depending on when the cash is expected to be collected. Like many companies, Deckers reports only one type of receivable account, Trade Accounts Receivable, from customers and classifies the asset as a current asset because the accounts receivable are all due to be paid within one year.

INTERNATIONAL
PERSPECTIVE

Foreign Currency Receivables

Selected Foreign Currency Exchange Rates (in US$)	
Mexican Peso	$0.09
Singapore Dollar	$0.59
Euro	$1.26

Export (international) sales are a growing part of the U.S. economy. For example, international sales amounted to 18.5 percent of Deckers' revenues in 2003. As is the case with domestic sales to other businesses, most export sales to businesses are on credit. When the buyer has agreed to pay in its local currency instead of U.S. dollars, Deckers cannot add the resulting accounts receivable, which are denominated in foreign currency, directly to its U.S. dollar accounts receivable. Deckers' accountants must first convert them to U.S. dollars using the end-of-period exchange rate between the two currencies. For example, if a French department store owed Deckers €20,000 (euros, the common currency of the European Monetary Union) on December 31, 2003, and each euro was worth US$1.26 on that date, it would add US$25,200 to its accounts receivable on the balance sheet.

Accounting for Bad Debts

For billing and collection purposes, Deckers keeps a separate accounts receivable account (called a **subsidiary account**) for each of the retail stores that resell its footwear and apparel. The accounts receivable amount on the balance sheet represents the total of these individual customer accounts.

When Deckers extends credit to its commercial customers, it knows that some of these customers will not pay their debts. The matching principle requires recording of bad debt expense in the **same** accounting period in which the related sales are made.

This presents an important accounting problem. Deckers may not learn which particular customers will not pay until the **next** accounting period. So, at the end of the period of sale, it normally does not know which customers' accounts receivable are bad debts.

Deckers resolves this problem and satisfies the matching principle by using the allowance method to measure bad debt expense. The allowance method is based on **estimates** of the expected amount of bad debts. Two primary steps in employing the allowance method are:

The ALLOWANCE METHOD bases bad debt expense on an estimate of uncollectible accounts.

1. Making the end-of-period adjusting entry to record estimated bad debt expense.

2. Writing off specific accounts determined to be uncollectible during the period.

Recording Bad Debt Expense Estimates

Bad debt expense (also called doubtful accounts expense, uncollectible accounts expense, provision for uncollectible accounts) is the expense associated with estimated uncollectible accounts receivable. An **adjusting journal entry** at the **end of the accounting period** records the bad debt estimate. For the year ended December 31, 2003, Deckers estimated bad debt expense to be $504 (all numbers in thousands of dollars) and made the following adjusting entry:

BAD DEBT EXPENSE (doubtful accounts expense, uncollectible accounts expense, provision for uncollectible accounts) is the expense associated with estimated uncollectible accounts receivable.

```
Bad debt expense (+E, −SE) .....................................   504
     Allowance for doubtful accounts (+XA, −A) ...................          504
```

Assets	=	Liabilities	+	Stockholders' Equity	
Allowance for doubtful accounts −504				Bad debt expense −504

The Bad Debt Expense is included in the category "Selling" expenses on the income statement. It decreases net income and stockholder's equity. Accounts Receivable could not be credited in the journal entry because there is no way to know which customers' accounts receivable are involved. So the credit is made, instead, to a contra-asset account called Allowance for Doubtful Accounts (Allowance for Bad Debts or Allowance for Uncollectible Accounts). As a contra-asset, the balance in Allowance for Doubtful Accounts is always subtracted from the balance of the asset Accounts Receivable. Thus, the entry decreases the net book value of Accounts Receivable and total assets.

ALLOWANCE FOR DOUBTFUL ACCOUNTS (allowance for bad debts, allowance for uncollectible accounts) is a contra-asset account containing the estimated uncollectible accounts receivable.

Writing Off Specific Uncollectible Accounts

Throughout the year, when it is determined that a customer will not pay its debts (e.g., due to bankruptcy), the write-off of that individual bad debt is recorded through a journal entry. Now that the specific uncollectible customer account receivable has been identified, it can be removed with a credit. At the same time, we no longer need the related estimate in the contra-asset Allowance for Doubtful Accounts, which is removed by a debit. The journal entry summarizing Deckers' total write-offs of $876 during 2003 follows:

```
Allowance for doubtful accounts (−XA, +A) ......................   876
     Accounts Receivable (−A) ....................................          876
```

Assets	=	Liabilities	+	Stockholders' Equity
Allowance for doubtful accounts +876				
Accounts receivable −876				

Notice that this journal entry did **not affect any income statement accounts.** It did not record a bad debt expense because the estimated expense was recorded with an adjusting entry in the period of sale. Also, the entry did **not change the net book value**

of accounts receivable, since the decrease in the asset account (Accounts Receivable) was offset by the decrease in the contra-asset account (Allowance for Doubtful Accounts). Thus, it also did not affect total assets.

When a customer makes a payment on an account that has already been written off, the journal entry to write off the account is reversed to put the receivable back on the books, and the collection of cash is recorded.

Summary of the Accounting Process

It is important to remember that accounting for bad debts is a two-step process:

Step	Timing	Accounts Affected	Financial Statement Effects
1. Record estimated bad debts adjustment	End of period in which sales are made	Bad Debt Expense (E) ↑	Net Income ↓
		Allowance for Doubtful Accounts (XA) ↑	Assets (Accounts Receivable, Net) ↓
2. Identify and write off actual bad debts	Throughout period as bad debts become known	Accounts Receivable (A) ↓	Net Income
		Allowance for Doubtful Accounts (XA) ↓	Assets (Accounts Receivable, Net)

(No Effect)

Deckers' complete 2003 accounting process for bad debts can now be summarized in terms of the changes in Accounts Receivable (Gross) and the Allowance for Doubtful Accounts:[5]

Accounts Receivable Dec. 31, 2003

Accounts Receivable (Gross) (A)	$20,326
− Allowance for Doubtful Accounts (XA)	1,581
Accounts Receivable (Net) (A)	$18,745

Accounts Receivable (Gross) (A)			
Beginning balance	22,804	Collections on account	122,657
Sales on account	121,055	Write-offs	876
Ending balance	20,326		

Allowance for Doubtful Accounts (XA)			
		Beginning balance	1,953
Write-offs	876	Bad debt expense adjustment	504
		Ending balance	1,581

Accounts Receivable (Gross) includes the total accounts receivable, both collectible and uncollectible. The balance in the Allowance for Doubtful Accounts is the portion of the accounts receivable balance the company estimates to be uncollectible. Accounts Receivable (Net) reported on the balance sheet is the portion of the accounts the company expects to collect (or its estimated net realizable value).

Reporting Accounts Receivable and Bad Debts

Analysts who want information on Deckers' receivables will find Accounts Receivable, net of allowance for doubtful accounts (the **net book value**), of $20,851 and $18,745 for 2002 and 2003, respectively, reported on the balance sheet (Exhibit 6.2). The balance in the Allowance for Doubtful Accounts ($1,953 in 2002 and $1,581 in

---

[5]This assumes that all sales are on account.

EXHIBIT 6.2

Accounts Receivable on
the Balance Sheet

REAL WORLD EXCERPT

DECKERS
outdoor corporation

ANNUAL REPORT

DECKERS OUTDOOR CORPORATION AND SUBSIDIARIES
CONSOLIDATED BALANCE SHEETS
December 31, 2002 and 2003
(amounts in dollars in thousands except share data)

	2002	2003
Assets		
Current assets:		
Cash and cash equivalents	$ 3,941	$ 6,662
Trade accounts receivable, less allowance for doubtful accounts of $1,953 and $1,581 as of December 31, 2002 and 2003, respectively	20,851	18,745
Inventories	17,067	18,004
Prepaid expenses and other current assets	783	694
Deferred tax assets	1,919	2,137
Total current assets	$44,561	$46,242

2003) is also reported. Accounts Receivable (Gross), the total accounts receivable, can be computed by adding the allowance back to the net book value.

The amounts of bad debt expense and accounts receivable written off for the period normally are not disclosed in the annual report. If they are material, these amounts are reported on a schedule that publicly traded companies include in their Annual Report Form 10-K filed with the SEC. Exhibit 6.3 presents this schedule from Deckers' 2003 filing.[6]

EXHIBIT 6.3

Accounts Receivable
Valuation Schedule
(Form 10-K)

REAL WORLD EXCERPT

DECKERS
outdoor corporation

FORM 10-K

DECKERS OUTDOOR CORPORATION AND SUBSIDIARIES
Valuation and Qualifying Accounts
Three Years Ended December 31, 2001, 2002, and 2003

Description	Balance at Beginning of Year	Additions	Deductions	Balance at End of Year
Allowance for doubtful accounts Year ended				
December 31, 2001	$2,144	$1,658	$1,788	$2,014
December 31, 2002	2,014	1,785	1,846	1,953
December 31, 2003	1,953	504	876	1,581

---

[6]Deckers' balance sheet and accompanying note also disclose the reserve for sales discounts, which is also subtracted in computing accounts receivable (net).

SELF-STUDY **QUIZ**

In a recent year, Timberland, a major Deckers competitor, had a beginning credit balance in the Allowance for Doubtful Accounts of $4,910 (all numbers in dollars in thousands). It wrote off accounts receivable totaling $1,480 during the year and made a bad debt expense adjustment for the year of $2,395.

1. What adjusting journal entry did Timberland make for bad debts at the end of a year?
2. Make the journal entry summarizing Timberland's total write-offs of bad debts during the year.
3. Compute the balance in the Allowance for Doubtful Accounts at the end of the year.

After you have completed your answers, check them with the solutions at the bottom of the page.

Estimating Bad Debts

The bad debt expense amount recorded in the end-of-period adjusting entry often is estimated based on either (1) a percentage of total credit sales for the period or (2) an aging of accounts receivable. Both methods are acceptable under GAAP and are widely used in practice. The percentage of credit sales method is simpler to apply, but the aging method is generally more accurate. Many companies use the simpler method on a weekly or monthly basis and use the more accurate method on a monthly or quarterly basis to check the accuracy of the earlier estimates. In our example, both methods produce exactly the same estimate, which rarely occurs in practice.

Percentage of Credit Sales Method

PERCENTAGE OF CREDIT SALES METHOD bases bad debt expense on the historical percentage of credit sales that result in bad debts.

Many companies make their estimates using the percentage of credit sales method, which bases bad debt expense on the historical percentage of credit sales that result in bad debts. The average percentage of credit sales that result in bad debts can be computed by dividing total bad debt losses by total **credit** sales. A company that has been operating for some years has sufficient experience to project probable future bad debt losses. For example, if we assume that, during the next year, 2004, Deckers expected bad debt losses of 0.5 percent of credit sales and its credit sales were $150,000, it would estimate current year's bad debts as:

Credit sales	$150,000
× Bad debt loss rate (.5%)	× .005
Bad debt expense	$ 750

This amount would be directly recorded as Bad Debt Expense (and an increase in Allowance for Doubtful Accounts) for 2004. Our beginning balance in the Allowance for Doubtful Accounts for 2004 would be the ending balance for 2003. Assuming write-offs during 2004 of $931, the ending balance is computed as follows:

Self-Study Quiz
Solutions

1. Bad debt expense (+E, −SE) 2,395
     Allowance for doubtful accounts (+XA, −A) 2,395
2. Allowance for doubtful accounts (−XA, +A) 1,480
     Accounts receivable (−A) 1,480
3. Beginning Balance + Bad Debt Expense Estimate − Write-Offs = Ending Balance
     $4,910 + 2,395 − 1,480 = $5,825

Allowance for Doubtful Accounts (XA)			
		2004 Beginning balance	1,581
		2004 Bad debt expense	
2004 Write-offs	931	adjustment	750
		2004 Ending balance	?

percent of credit
sales estimate

= 1,400 ◄

Beginning balance	$1,581
+ Bad debt expense	750
− Write-offs	931
Ending balance	$1,400

Aging of Accounts Receivable

As an alternative to the percentage of credit sales method, many companies use the aging of accounts receivable method. This method relies on the fact that, as accounts receivable become older and more overdue, it is less likely that they will prove to be collectible. For example, a receivable that was due in 30 days but has not been paid after 45 days is more likely to be collected, on average, than a similar receivable that remains unpaid after 120 days. Based on prior experience, the company can estimate what portion of receivables of different ages will not be paid.

Suppose that Deckers split its 2004 ending balance in accounts receivables (gross) of $25,000 into three age categories. Management would first examine the individual customer accounts receivable and sort them into the three age categories. Management would then **estimate** the probable bad debt loss rates for each category: for example, not yet due, 2 percent; 1 to 90 days past due, 8 percent; over 90 days, 20 percent.

As illustrated in the aging schedule below, this results in an estimate of total uncollectible amounts of $1,400. This amount computed using the aging method is the ending balance that **should be** in the Allowance for Doubtful Accounts. This is called the **estimated ending balance.** From this, the adjustment to record Bad Debt Expense (and an increase in Allowance for Doubtful Accounts) for 2004 would be computed.

AGING OF ACCOUNTS RECEIVABLE METHOD estimates uncollectible accounts based on the age of each account receivable.

Aging Schedule 2004

Aged Accounts Receivable			Estimated Percentage Uncollectible		Estimated Amount Uncollectible
Not yet due	$16,000	×	2%	=	$ 320
Up to 90 days past due	6,000	×	8%	=	480
Over 90 days past due	3,000	×	20%	=	600
Estimated ending balance in Allowance for Doubtful Accounts					1,400
Less: Balance in Allowance for Doubtful Accounts before adjustment ($1,581 − 931)					650
Bad Debt Expense for the year					$ 750

Allowance for Doubtful Accounts (XA)			
		2004 Beginning balance	1,581
		2004 Bad debt expense	
2004 Write-offs	931	adjustment	?
		2004 Ending balance	1,400

= 750 ◄

total estimated uncollectible accounts

Comparison of the Two Methods

Students often fail to recognize that the approach to recording bad debt expense using the percentage of credit sales method is different from that for the aging method:

- **Percentage of credit sales.** Directly compute the amount to be recorded as **Bad Debt Expense** on the **income statement** for the period in the adjusting journal entry.

■ **Aging.** Compute the **final ending balance** we would like to have in the **Allowance for Doubtful Accounts** on the **balance sheet** after we make the necessary adjusting entry. The **difference** between the current balance in the account before the adjustment is made and the estimated balance is recorded as the adjusting entry for Bad Debt Expense for the period.

In either case, the balance sheet presentation for 2004 would show:

Accounts Receivable (gross)	$25,000
Less: Allowance for Doubtful Accounts	1,400
Accounts Receivable, Net of Allowance for Doubtful Accounts	$23,600

Actual Write-Offs Compared with Estimates

Deckers' Form 10-K provides particularly clear information on its approach to estimating uncollectible accounts and the potential effect of any errors in those estimates:

Critical Accounting Policies

Allowance for Doubtful Accounts. We provide a reserve against trade accounts receivable for estimated losses that may result from customers' inability to pay. We determine the amount of the reserve by analyzing known uncollectible accounts, aged trade accounts receivables, economic conditions, historical experience and the customers' credit-worthiness. . . . Our use of different estimates and assumptions could produce different financial results. For example, a 1.0% change in the rate used to estimate the reserve for the accounts not specifically identified as uncollectible would change the allowance for doubtful accounts by $174.

If uncollectible accounts actually written off differ from the estimated amount previously recorded, a higher or lower amount is recorded in the next period to make up for the previous period's error in estimate. **When estimates are found to be incorrect, financial statement values for prior annual accounting periods are not corrected.**

Control over Accounts Receivable

Many managers forget that extending credit will increase sales volume, but unless the related receivables are collected, they do not add to the bottom line. These companies that emphasize sales without monitoring the collection of credit sales will soon find much of their current assets tied up in accounts receivable. The following practices can help minimize bad debts:

1. Require approval of customers' credit history by a person independent of the sales and collections functions.
2. Age accounts receivable periodically and contact customers with overdue payments.
3. Reward both sales and collections personnel for speedy collections so that they work as a team.

To assess the effectiveness of overall credit-granting and collection activities, managers and analysts often compute the receivables turnover ratio.

Receivables Turnover

❓ ANALYTICAL QUESTION:

How effective are credit-granting and collection activities?

% RATIO AND COMPARISONS:

The receivables turnover ratio is computed as follows (see Exhibits 6.1 and 6.2):

$$\text{Receivables Turnover} = \frac{\text{Net Sales*}}{\text{Average Net Trade Accounts Receivable†}}$$

The 2003 receivables turnover ratio for Deckers:

$$\frac{\$121,055}{(\$18,745 + 20,851) \div 2} = 6.1$$

> **Learning Objective 5**
> Analyze and interpret the accounts receivable turnover ratio and the effects of accounts receivable on cash flows.

COMPARISONS OVER TIME		
Deckers		
2001	**2002**	**2003**
4.2	4.8	6.1

COMPARISONS WITH COMPETITORS	
Skechers U.S.A.	**Timberland**
2003	**2003**
8.5	10.4

💡 INTERPRETATIONS:

In General → The receivables turnover ratio reflects how many times average trade receivables are recorded and collected during the period. The higher the ratio, the faster the collection of receivables. A higher ratio benefits the company because it can invest the money collected to earn interest income or reduce borrowings to reduce interest expense. Overly generous payment schedules and ineffective collection methods keep the receivables turnover ratio low. Analysts and creditors watch this ratio because a sudden decline may mean that a company is extending payment deadlines in an attempt to prop up lagging sales or is even recording sales that will later be returned by customers. Many managers and analysts compute the related number **average collection period** or **average days sales in receivables,** which is equal to 365 ÷ Receivables Turnover Ratio. It indicates the average time it takes a customer to pay its accounts. For Deckers, the amount would be computed as follows for 2003:

$$\text{Average Collection Period} = \frac{365}{\text{Receivables Turnover}} = \frac{365}{6.1} = 59.8 \text{ days}$$

Selected Industry Comparisons: Receivables Turnover Ratio

Variety stores	98.6
Malt beverages	14.9
Lumber and building materials	12.7

Focus Company Analysis → Deckers' receivables turnover rose significantly from a 2001 low of 4.2 to 6.1 in 2003. This indicates significant improvement in Deckers' receivables management strategy. However, the ratio is still below the industry average of 7.8,‡ and its competitors Skechers and Timberland.

A Few Cautions: Since differences across industries and between firms in the manner in which customer purchases are financed can cause dramatic differences in the ratio, a particular firm's ratio should be compared only with its prior years' figures or with other firms in the same industry following the same financing practices.

*Since the amount of net credit sales is normally not reported separately, most analysts use net sales in this equation.
†Average Net Trade Accounts Receivable = (Beginning Net Trade Accounts Receivable + Ending Net Trade Accounts Receivable) ÷ 2.
‡Dun and Bradstreet, Industry Norms and Key Business Ratios (2002).

FOCUS ON
CASH FLOWS

Accounts Receivable

The change in accounts receivable can be a major determinant of a company's cash flow from operations. While the income statement reflects the revenues of the period, the cash flow from operating activities reflects cash collections from customers. Since sales on account increase the balance in accounts receivable and cash collections from customers decrease the balance in accounts receivable, the change in accounts receivable from the beginning to the end of the period is the difference between sales and collections.

EFFECT ON STATEMENT OF CASH FLOWS

In General When there is a net **decrease in accounts receivable** for the period, cash collected from customers is more than revenue; thus, the decrease must be **added** in computing cash flows from operations. When a net **increase in accounts receivable** occurs, cash collected from customers is less than revenue; thus, the increase must be **subtracted** in computing cash flows from operations.*

	Effect on Cash Flows
Operating activities (indirect method)	
Net income	$xxx
Adjusted for	
Add accounts receivable decrease	+
or	
Subtract accounts receivable increase	−

Focus Company Analysis Exhibit 6.4 shows the Operating Activities section of Deckers' statement of cash flows. Due to improvements in receivables management in 2003, Deckers has been able to reduce the balance in receivables. This decrease is added in reconciling net income to cash flow from operating activities because cash collected from customers is higher than revenues for 2003. When receivables rise, the amount of the additional receivables is subtracted in reconciling net income to cash flow from operating activities because cash collected from customers is lower than revenues.

For companies with receivables in foreign currency or business acquisitions/dispositions, the change reported on the cash flow statement will not equal the change in the accounts receivable reported on the balance sheet.

SELF-STUDY **QUIZ**

1. In an earlier year, Deckers' competitor Timberland reported a beginning balance in the Allowance for Doubtful Accounts of $723. It also wrote off bad debts amounting to $648 during the year. At the end of the year, it computed total estimated uncollectible accounts using the aging method to be $904 (all numbers in dollars in thousands). What amount did Deckers record as bad debt expense for the period? (**Solution approach:** Use the Allowance for Doubtful Accounts T-account to solve for the missing value.)

Allowance for Doubtful Accounts (XA)

2. Indicate whether **granting later payment deadlines** (e.g., 60 days instead of 30 days) will most likely **increase** or **decrease** the accounts receivable turnover ratio. Explain.

After you have completed your answers, check them with the solutions at the bottom of the next page.

DECKERS OUTDOOR CORPORATION AND SUBSIDIARIES Consolidated Statements of Cash Flows Three Years Ended December 31, 2001, 2002, and 2003			
	2001	**2002**	**2003**
Cash flows from operating activities:			
Net income (loss)	$ 1,626	$(7,353)	$ 9,154
Adjustments to reconcile net income (loss) to net cash provided by operating activities:			
. . . .	. . .	. . .	. . .
Changes in assets and liabilities:			
(Increase) decrease in:			
Trade accounts receivable, net of provision for doubtful accounts	2,442	(439)	2,106
Inventories	(3,373)	650	(2,266)
Prepaid expenses and other current assets	(594)	943	89
Refundable income taxes	(961)	995	—
Other assets	275	286	543
Increase (decrease) in:			
Trade accounts payable	5,951	(844)	(1,696)
Accrued expenses	1,137	(1,056)	669
Income taxes payable	—	732	2,736
Net cash provided by operating activities	$11,049	$7,441	$16,781

EXHIBIT 6.4

Accounts Receivable on the Cash Flow Statement

REAL WORLD EXCERPT

DECKERS outdoor corporation

ANNUAL REPORT

REPORTING AND SAFEGUARDING CASH

Cash and Cash Equivalents Defined

Cash is defined as money or any instrument that banks will accept for deposit and immediate credit to a company's account, such as a check, money order, or bank draft. Cash equivalents are investments with original maturities of three months or less that are readily convertible to cash and whose value is unlikely to change (that is, are not sensitive to interest rate changes). Typical instruments included as cash equivalents are bank certificates of deposit and treasury bills that the U.S. government issues to finance its activities.

Even though a company may have several bank accounts and several types of cash equivalents, all cash accounts and cash equivalents are usually combined in one amount

Learning Objective 6
Report, control, and safeguard cash.

CASH is money or any instrument that banks will accept for deposit and immediate credit to a company's account, such as a check, money order, or bank draft.

CASH EQUIVALENTS are short-term investments with original maturities of three months or less that are readily convertible to cash and whose value is unlikely to change.

Self-Study Quiz Solutions

1.

Allowance for Doubtful Accounts (XA)		
	Beginning balance	723
Write-offs 648	Bad debt expense (*solve*)	829
	Ending balance	904

Estimated ending balance in Allowance for Doubtful Accounts	904
Less: Current balance in Allowance for Doubtful Accounts ($723 − 648)	75
Bad Debt Expense for the year	$829

2. Granting later payment deadlines will most likely **decrease** the accounts receivable turnover ratio because later collections from customers will increase the average accounts receivable balance (the denominator of the ratio), decreasing the ratio.

for financial reporting purposes. Deckers reports a single account, Cash and Equivalents. It also reports that the book values of cash equivalents on the balance sheet equal their fair market values—which we should expect given the nature of the instruments (investments whose value is unlikely to change).

Cash Management

Many businesses receive a large amount of cash, checks, and credit card receipts from their customers each day. Anyone can spend cash, so management must develop procedures to safeguard the cash it uses in the business. Effective cash management involves more than protecting cash from theft, fraud, or loss through carelessness. Other cash management responsibilities include:

1. Accurate accounting so that reports of cash flows and balances may be prepared.
2. Controls to ensure that enough cash is available to meet (a) current operating needs, (b) maturing liabilities, and (c) unexpected emergencies.
3. Prevention of the accumulation of excess amounts of idle cash. Idle cash earns no revenue. Therefore, it is often invested in securities to earn a return until it is needed for operations.

Internal Control of Cash

INTERNAL CONTROLS are the processes by which a company safeguards its assets and provides reasonable assurance regarding the reliability of the company's financial reporting, the effectiveness and efficiency of its operations, and its compliance with applicable laws and regulations.

The term **internal controls** refers to the process by which a company safeguards its assets and provides reasonable assurance regarding the reliability of the company's financial reporting, the effectiveness and efficiency of its operations, and its compliance with applicable laws and regulations. Internal control procedures should extend to all assets: cash, receivables, investments, plant and equipment, and so on. Controls that ensure the accuracy of the financial records are designed to prevent inadvertent errors and outright fraud such as occurred in the Maxidrive case discussed in Chapter 1. Because internal control increases the reliability of the financial statements, it is reviewed by the outside independent auditor.

Because cash is the asset most vulnerable to theft and fraud, a significant number of internal control procedures should focus on cash. You have already observed internal control procedures for cash, although you may not have known it at the time. At most movie theaters, one employee sells tickets and another employee collects them. Having one employee do both jobs would be less expensive, but that single employee could easily steal cash and admit a patron without issuing a ticket. If different employees perform the tasks, a successful theft requires participation of both.

Effective internal control of cash should include the following:

1. Separation of duties.
   a. Complete separation of the jobs of receiving cash and disbursing cash.
   b. Complete separation of the procedures of accounting for cash receipts and cash disbursements.
   c. Complete separation of the physical handling of cash and all phases of the accounting function.
2. Prescribed policies and procedures.
   a. Require that all cash receipts be deposited in a bank daily. Keep any cash on hand under strict control.
   b. Require separate approval of the purchases and the actual cash payments. Prenumbered checks should be used. Special care must be taken with payments by electronic funds transfers since they involve no controlled documents (checks).

   c. Assign the responsibilities for cash payment approval and check-signing or electronic funds transfer transmittal to different individuals.

   d. Require monthly reconciliation of bank accounts with the cash accounts on the company's books (discussed in detail in the next section).

The separation of duties and the use of prescribed policies and procedures are important elements of the control of cash. Separation of duties deters theft because it requires the collusion of two or more persons to steal cash and then conceal the theft in the accounting records. Prescribed procedures are designed so that work done by one individual is checked against the results reported by other individuals. For example, the amount of cash collected at the cash register by the sales clerk can be compared with the amount of cash deposited at the bank by another employee. Reconciliation of the cash accounts to the bank statements provides a further control on deposits.

 Ethics and the Need for Internal Control

Some people are bothered by the recommendation that all well-run companies should have strong internal control procedures. These people believe that control procedures suggest that management does not trust the company's employees. Although the vast majority of employees are trustworthy, employee theft does cost businesses billions of dollars each year. Interviews with convicted felons indicate that in many cases they stole from their employers because they thought that it was easy and that no one cared (there were no internal control procedures).

   Many companies have a formal code of ethics that requires high standards of behavior in dealing with customers, suppliers, fellow employees, and the company's assets. Although each employee is ultimately responsible for his or her own ethical behavior, internal control procedures can be thought of as important value statements from management.

Reconciliation of the Cash Accounts and the Bank Statements

Content of a Bank Statement

Proper use of the bank accounts can be an important internal cash control procedure. Each month, the bank provides the company (the depositor) with a bank statement that lists (1) each deposit recorded by the bank during the period, (2) each check cleared by the bank during the period, and (3) the balance in the company's account. The bank statement also shows the bank charges or deductions (such as service charges) made directly to the company's account by the bank. A typical bank statement for ROW.COM, Inc., is shown in Exhibit 6.5.

   Exhibit 6.5 lists three items that need explanation. Notice that listed under Checks and Debits, there is a deduction for $18 coded *NSF.*[7] This entry refers to a check for $18 received from a customer and deposited by ROW.COM with its bank. The bank processed the check through banking channels to the customer's bank, but the account did not have sufficient funds to cover the check. The customer's bank therefore returned it to ROW.COM's bank, which then charged it back to ROW.COM's account. This type of check often is called an **NSF check** (not sufficient funds). The NSF check is now a receivable; consequently, ROW.COM must make an entry to debit Receivables and credit Cash for the $18.

   Notice the $6 listed on June 30 under Checks and Debits and coded **SC.** This is the code for bank service charges. The bank statement included a memo by the bank explaining this service charge (which was not documented by a check). ROW.COM must

A **BANK STATEMENT** is a monthly report from a bank that shows deposits recorded, checks cleared, other debits and credits, and a running bank balance.

Topic Tackler 6–2

---

[7]These codes vary among banks.

Example of a
Bank Statement

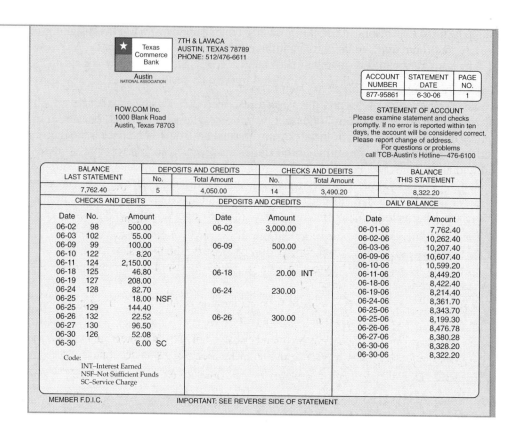

make an entry to reflect this $6 decrease in the bank balance as a debit to a relevant expense account, such as Bank Service Expense, and a credit to Cash.

Notice the $20 listed on June 18 under Deposits and Credits and the code *INT* for interest earned. The bank pays interest on checking account balances, and increased ROW.COM's account for interest earned during the period. ROW.COM must record the interest by making an entry to debit Cash and credit Interest Income for the $20.

Need for Reconciliation

A BANK RECONCILIATION is the process of verifying the accuracy of both the bank statement and the cash accounts of a business.

A **bank reconciliation** is the process of comparing (reconciling) the ending cash balance in the company's records and the ending cash balance reported by the bank on the monthly bank statement. A bank reconciliation should be completed at the end of each month. Usually, the ending cash balance as shown on the bank statement does not agree with the ending cash balance shown by the related Cash ledger account on the books of the company. For example, the Cash ledger account of ROW.COM showed the following at the end of June (ROW.COM has only one checking account):

Cash (A)			
June 1 balance	7,090.00	June checks written	3,800.00
June deposits	5,750.00		
Ending balance	9,040.00		

The $8,322.20 ending cash balance shown on the bank statement (Exhibit 6.5) differs from the $9,040.00 ending balance of cash shown on the books of ROW.COM. Most of this difference exists because of timing differences in the recording of transactions:

1. Some transactions affecting cash were recorded in the books of ROW.COM but were not shown on the bank statement.

2. Some transactions were shown on the bank statement but had not been recorded in the books of ROW.COM.

Some of the difference may also be caused by errors in recording transactions.

The most common causes of differences between the ending bank balance and the ending book balance of cash are as follows:

1. **Outstanding checks.** These are checks written by the company and recorded in the company's ledger as credits to the Cash account that have not cleared the bank (they are not shown on the bank statement as a deduction from the bank balance). The outstanding checks are identified by comparing the list of canceled checks on the bank statement with the record of checks (such as check stubs or a journal) maintained by the company.

2. **Deposits in transit.** These are deposits sent to the bank by the company and recorded in the company's ledger as debits to the Cash account. The bank has not recorded these deposits (they are not shown on the bank statement as an increase in the bank balance). Deposits in transit usually happen when deposits are made one or two days before the close of the period covered by the bank statement. Deposits in transit are determined by comparing the deposits listed on the bank statement with the company deposit records.

3. **Bank service charges.** An expense for bank services that is listed on the bank statement but is not recorded on the company's books.

4. **NSF checks.** A "bad check" or "bounced check" that was deposited but must be deducted from the company's cash account and rerecorded as an account receivable.

5. **Interest.** The interest paid by the bank to the company on its bank balance.

6. **Errors.** Both the bank and the company may make errors, especially when the volume of cash transactions is large.

Bank Reconciliation Illustrated

The company should make a bank reconciliation immediately after receiving each bank statement. The general format for the bank reconciliation follows:

Ending cash balance per books	$xxx	Ending cash balance per bank statement	$xxx
+ Interest paid by bank	xx	+ Deposits in transit	xx
− NSF checks/Service charges	xx	− Outstanding checks	xx
± Company errors	xx	± Bank errors	xx
Ending correct cash balance	$xxx	Ending correct cash balance	$xxx

Exhibit 6.6 shows the bank reconciliation prepared by ROW.COM for the month of June to reconcile the ending bank balance ($8,322.20) with the ending book balance ($9,040.00). On the completed reconciliation, the correct cash balance is $9,045.00. This correct balance is the amount that should be shown in the Cash account after the reconciliation. Since ROW.COM has only one checking account and no cash on hand, it is also the correct amount of cash that should be reported on the balance sheet.

ROW.COM followed these steps in preparing the bank reconciliation:

1. **Identify the outstanding checks.** A comparison of the checks listed on the bank statement with the company's record of all checks drawn showed the following checks were still outstanding (had not cleared the bank) at the end of June:

Check No.	Amount
101	$ 145.00
123	815.00
131	117.20
Total	$1,077.20

This total was entered on the reconciliation as a deduction from the bank account. These checks will be deducted by the bank when they clear the bank.

EXHIBIT 6.6

Bank Reconciliation
Illustrated

ROW.COM INC.
Bank Reconciliation
For the Month Ending June 30, 2006

Company's Books		Bank Statement	
Ending cash balance per books	$9,040.00	Ending cash balance per bank statement	$ 8,322.20
Additions		Additions	
Interest paid by the bank	20.00	Deposit in transit	1,800.00
Error in recording check No. 99	9.00		
	9,069.00		10,122.20
Deductions		Deductions	
NSF check of R. Smith	18.00	Outstanding checks	1,077.20
Bank service charges	6.00		
Ending correct cash balance	$9,045.00	Ending correct cash balance	$ 9,045.00

2. **Identify the deposits in transit.** A comparison of the deposit slips on hand with those listed on the bank statement revealed that a deposit of $1,800 made on June 30 was not listed on the bank statement. This amount was entered on the reconciliation as an addition to the bank account. It will be added by the bank when it records the deposit.

3. **Record bank charges and credits:**
   a. Interest received from the bank, $20—entered on the bank reconciliation as an addition to the book balance; it already has been included in the bank balance.
   b. NSF check of R. Smith, $18—entered on the bank reconciliation as a deduction from the book balance; it has been deducted from the bank statement balance.
   c. Bank service charges, $6—entered on the bank reconciliation as a deduction from the book balance; it has been deducted from the bank balance.

4. **Determine the impact of errors.** At this point, ROW.COM found that the reconciliation did not balance by $9. Upon checking the journal entries made during the month, check No. 99 written for $100 to pay an account payable was found. The check was recorded in the company's accounts as $109. Therefore, $9 (i.e., $109 − $100) must be added to the book cash balance on the reconciliation; the bank cleared the check for the correct amount, $100.

Note that in Exhibit 6.6 the two sections of the bank reconciliation now agree at a correct cash balance of $9,045.00.

A bank reconciliation as shown in Exhibit 6.6 accomplishes two major objectives:

1. Checks the accuracy of the bank balance and the company cash records, which involves developing the correct cash balance. The correct cash balance (plus cash on hand, if any) is the amount of cash that is reported on the balance sheet.

2. Identifies any previously unrecorded transactions or changes that are necessary to cause the company's Cash account(s) to show the correct cash balance. Any transactions or changes on the **Company's Books side** of the bank reconciliation need journal entries. Therefore, the following journal entries based on the Company's Books side of the bank reconciliation (Exhibit 6.6) must be entered into the company's records.

Accounts of ROW.COM

(a)	Cash (+A)	20	
	Interest income (+R, +SE)		20
	To record interest by bank.		
(b)	Accounts receivable (+A)	18	
	Cash (−A)		18
	To record NSF check.		
(c)	Bank service expense (+E, −SE)	6	
	Cash (−A)		6
	To record service fees charged by bank.		
(d)	Cash (+A)	9	
	Accounts payable (+L)		9
	To correct error made in recording a check payable to a creditor.		

Assets	=	Liabilities	+	Stockholders' Equity
Cash (+20, −18, −6, +9) +5		Accounts payable +9		Interest income +20
Accounts receivable +18				Bank service expense −6

Notice again that all of the additions and deductions on the Company's Books side of the reconciliation need journal entries to update the Cash account. The additions and deductions on the Bank Statement side do not need journal entries because they will work out automatically when they clear the bank.

SELF-STUDY QUIZ

Indicate which of the following items discovered while preparing a company's bank reconciliation will result in adjustment of the cash balance on the balance sheet.

1. Outstanding checks.

2. Deposits in transit.

3. Bank service charges.

4. NSF checks that were deposited.

After you have completed your answer, check it with the solution at the bottom of the page.

EPILOGUE

As we noted at the beginning of the chapter, Deckers recognized that to turn growth into profits, it had to (1) continually refresh its product lines by introducing new technologies, new styles, and new product categories, (2) become a leaner and more nimble manufacturer, taking advantage of lower-cost, more flexible production locations, and (3) focus attention on inventory management and collections of accounts receivable since an uncollected account is of no value to the company. Each of these efforts is aimed at increasing net sales and/or decreasing cost of goods sold, thereby increasing gross profit.

3. Bank service charges are deducted from the company's account; thus, cash must be reduced and an expense must be recorded. 4. NSF checks that were deposited were recorded on the books as increases in the cash account; thus, cash must be decreased and the related accounts receivable increased if payment is still expected.

Self-Study Quiz
Solution

The first half of 2004 has sent positive signals about the continued success of Deckers' strategy. Both net sales and gross profit have increased 40 percent over 2003. You can evaluate the further success of Deckers' strategy by going to the Web at www.deckers.com to check Deckers' latest annual and quarterly reports.

DEMONSTRATION CASE A

(Complete the requirements before proceeding to the suggested solutions.) Wholesale Warehouse Stores sold $950,000 in merchandise during 2005, $400,000 of which was on credit with terms 2/10, n/30 (75 percent of these amounts were paid within the discount period), $500,000 was paid with credit cards (there was a 3 percent credit card discount), and the rest was paid in cash. On December 31, 2005, the Accounts Receivable balance was $80,000. The beginning balance in the Allowance for Doubtful Accounts was $9,000 and $6,000 of bad debts was written off during the year.

Required:

1. Compute net sales for 2005, assuming that sales and credit card discounts are treated as contra-revenues.

2. Assume that Wholesale uses the percentage of sales method for estimating bad debt expense and that it estimates that 2 percent of credit sales will produce bad debts. Record bad debt expense for 2005.

3. Assume instead that Wholesale uses the aging of accounts receivable method and that it estimates that $10,000 worth of current accounts is uncollectible. Record bad debt expense for 2005.

SUGGESTED SOLUTION

1. Both sales discounts and credit card discounts should be subtracted from sales revenues in the computation of net sales.

Sales revenue	$950,000
Less: Sales discounts (0.02 × 0.75 × $400,000)	6,000
Credit card discounts (0.03 × $500,000)	15,000
Net sales	$929,000

2. The percentage estimate of bad debts should be applied to credit sales. Cash sales never produce bad debts.

Bad debt expense (+E, −SE) (0.02 × $400,000)	8,000	
Allowance for doubtful accounts (+XA, −A)		8,000

Assets	=	Liabilities	+	Stockholders' Equity
Allowance for doubtful accounts −8,000				Bad debt expense −8,000

3. The entry made when using the aging of accounts receivable method is the estimated balance minus the current balance.

Estimated ending balance in Allowance for Doubtful Accounts	$10,000
Less: Current balance in Allowance for Doubtful Accounts ($9,000 − 6,000)	3,000
Bad Debt Expense for the year	$ 7,000

Bad debt expense (+E, −SE)	7,000	
Allowance for doubtful accounts (+XA, −A)....................		7,000

Assets	=	Liabilities	+	Stockholders' Equity
Allowance for doubtful accounts −7,000				Bad debt expense −7,000

DEMONSTRATION CASE B

(Complete the requirements before proceeding to the suggested solution that follows.)
Heather Ann Long, a freshman at a large state university, has just received her first checking
account statement. This was her first chance to attempt a bank reconciliation. She had the
following information to work with:

Bank balance, September 1	$1,150
Deposits during September	650
Checks cleared during September	900
Bank service charge	25
Bank balance, October 1	875

Heather was surprised that the deposit of $50 she made on September 29 had not been
posted to her account and was pleased that her rent check of $200 had not cleared her ac-
count. Her checkbook balance was $750.

Required:

1. Complete Heather's bank reconciliation.

2. Why is it important for individuals such as Heather and businesses to do a bank reconciliation each month?

SUGGESTED SOLUTION

1. Heather's bank reconciliation:

Heather's Books		Bank Statement	
October 1 cash balance	$750	October 1 cash balance	$875
Additions		Additions	
None		Deposit in transit	50
Deductions		Deductions	
Bank service charge	(25)	Outstanding check	(200)
Correct cash balance	$725	Correct cash balance	$725

2. Bank statements, whether personal or business, should be reconciled each month. This
   process helps ensure that a correct balance is reflected in the customer's books. Failure to
   reconcile a bank statement increases the chance that an error will not be discovered and
   may result in bad checks being written. Businesses must reconcile their bank statements
   for an additional reason: The correct balance that is calculated during reconciliation is
   recorded on the balance sheet.

Chapter Supplement A

Recording Discounts and Returns

In this chapter, both **credit card discounts** and **cash discounts** have been recorded as contra-revenues. For example, if the credit card company is charging a 3 percent fee for its service and Internet credit card sales were $3,000 for January 2, Deckers records the following:

Cash (+A) 2,910
Credit card discount (+XR, −R, −SE) 90
   Sales revenue (+R, +SE) 3,000

Assets		=	Liabilities	+	Stockholders' Equity	
Cash	+2,910				Sales revenue	+3,000
					Credit card discount	−90

Similarly, if credit sales of $1,000 are recorded with terms 2/10, n/30 ($1,000 × 0.98 = $980), and payment is made within the discount period, Deckers would record the following:

Accounts receivable (+A) 1,000
   Sales revenue (+R, +SE) 1,000

Assets		=	Liabilities	+	Stockholders' Equity	
Accounts receivable	+1,000				Sales revenue	+1,000

Cash (+A) 980
Sales discount (+XR, −R, −SE) 20
   Accounts receivable (−A) 1,000

Assets		=	Liabilities	+	Stockholders' Equity	
Cash	+980				Sales discount	−20
Accounts receivable	−1,000					

   Sales returns and allowances should always be treated as a contra-revenue. Assume that Fontana Shoes of Ithaca, New York, bought 40 pairs of sandals from Deckers for $2,000 on account. On the date of sale, Deckers makes the following journal entry:

Accounts receivable (+A) 2,000
   Sales revenue (+R, +SE) 2,000

Assets		=	Liabilities	+	Stockholders' Equity	
Accounts receivable	+2,000				Sales revenue	+2,000

Before paying for the sandals, Fontana discovered that 10 pairs of sandals were not the color ordered and returned them to Deckers. On that date Deckers records:

Sales returns and allowances (+XR, −R, −SE) 500
   Accounts receivable (−A) 500

Assets		=	Liabilities	+	Stockholders' Equity	
Accounts receivable	−500				Sales returns and allowances	−500

In addition, the related cost of goods sold entry for the 10 pairs of sandals would be reversed.

Chapter Supplement B

Applying the Revenue Principle in Special Circumstances
(This supplement can be found on our website www.mhhe.com/libby5e.)

1. **Apply the revenue principle to determine the accepted time to record sales revenue for typical retailers, wholesalers, manufacturers, and service companies.   p. 284**
   Revenue recognition policies are widely recognized as one of the most important determinants of the fair presentation of financial statements. For most merchandisers and manufacturers, the required revenue recognition point is the time that title changes to the buyer (shipment or delivery of goods). For service companies, it is the time that services are provided.

2. **Analyze the impact of credit card sales, sales discounts, and sales returns on the amounts reported as net sales.   p. 285**
   Both *credit card discounts* and *sales* or *cash discounts* can be recorded either as contra-revenues or as expenses. When recorded as contra-revenues, they reduce net sales. *Sales returns and allowances,* which should always be treated as a contra-revenue, also reduce net sales.

3. **Analyze and interpret the gross profit percentage.   p. 288**
   Gross profit percentage measures the ability to sell goods or services for more than the cost to produce or purchase. It reflects the ability to charge premium prices and produce goods and services at lower cost. Managers, analysts, and creditors use this ratio to assess the effectiveness of the company's product development, marketing, and production strategy.

4. **Estimate, report, and evaluate the effects of uncollectible accounts receivable (bad debts) on financial statements.   p. 290**
   When receivables are material, companies must employ the allowance method to account for uncollectibles. These are the steps in the process:

   a. The end-of-period adjusting entry to record bad debt expense estimates.
   b. Writing off specific accounts determined to be uncollectible during the period.

   The adjusting entry reduces net income as well as net accounts receivable. The write-off affects neither.

5. **Analyze and interpret the accounts receivable turnover ratio and the effects of accounts receivable on cash flows.   p. 297**
   a. *Accounts receivable turnover ratio*—Measures the effectiveness of credit-granting and collection activities. It reflects how many times average trade receivables were recorded and collected during the period. Analysts and creditors watch this ratio because a sudden decline in it may mean that a company is extending payment deadlines in an attempt to prop up lagging sales or even is recording sales that later will be returned by customers.
   b. *Effects on cash flows*—When a net decrease in accounts receivable for the period occurs, cash collected from customers is always more than revenue, and cash flows from operations increases. When a net increase in accounts receivable occurs, cash collected from customers is always less than revenue. Thus, cash flows from operations declines.

6. **Report, control, and safeguard cash.   p. 299**
   Cash is the most liquid of all assets, flowing continually into and out of a business. As a result, a number of critical control procedures, including the reconciliation of bank accounts, should be applied. Also, management of cash may be critically important to decision makers who must have cash available to meet current needs yet must avoid excess amounts of idle cash that produce no revenue.

   Closely related to recording revenue is recording the cost of what was sold. Chapter 7 will focus on transactions related to inventory and cost of goods sold. This topic is important because cost of goods sold has a major impact on a company's gross profit and net income, which are watched closely by investors, analysts, and other users of financial statements. Increasing emphasis on quality, productivity, and costs have further focused production managers' attention on cost of goods sold and inventory. Since inventory cost figures play a major role in product introduction and pricing decisions, they also are important to marketing and general managers. Finally, since inventory accounting has a major effect on many companies' tax liabilities, this is an important place to introduce the effect of taxation on management decision making and financial reporting.

KEY **RATIOS**

Gross profit percentage measures the excess of sales prices over the costs to purchase or produce the goods or services sold as a percentage. It is computed as follows (p. 288):

$$\text{Gross Profit Percentage} = \frac{\text{Gross Profit}}{\text{Net Sales}}$$

Receivables turnover ratio measures the effectiveness of credit-granting and collection activities. It is computed as follows (p. 297):

$$\text{Receivables Turnover} = \frac{\text{Net Sales}}{\text{Average Net Trade Accounts Receivable}}$$

FINDING **FINANCIAL INFORMATION**

Balance Sheet

Under Current Assets
Accounts receivable (net of allowance for doubtful accounts)

Income statement

Revenues
Net sales (sales revenue less discounts and sales returns and allowances)

Expenses
Selling expenses (including bad debt expense)

Statement of Cash Flows

Under Operating Activities (indirect method)
Net income
+ decreases in accounts receivable (net)
− increases in accounts receivable (net)

Notes

Under Summary of Significant Accounting Policies
Revenue recognition policy

Under a Separate Note on Form 10-K
Bad debt expense and write-offs of bad debts

KEY **TERMS**

Accounts Receivable (trade receivables or receivables) p. 290
Aging of Accounts Receivable Method p. 295

Allowance for Doubtful Accounts (Allowance for Bad Debts or Allowance for Uncollectible Accounts) p. 291
Allowance Method p. 291

Bad Debt Expense (Doubtful Accounts Expense, Uncollectible Accounts Expense, or Provision for Uncollectible Accounts) p. 291

QUESTIONS

1. Explain the difference between sales revenue and net sales.
2. What is gross profit or gross margin on sales? How is the gross profit ratio computed? In your explanation, assume that net sales revenue was $100,000 and cost of goods sold was $60,000.
3. What is a credit card discount? How does it affect amounts reported on the income statement?
4. What is a sales discount? Use 1/10, n/30 in your explanation.
5. What is the distinction between *sales allowances* and *sales discounts?*
6. Differentiate accounts receivable from notes receivable.
7. Which basic accounting principle is the allowance method of accounting for bad debts designed to satisfy?
8. Using the allowance method, is bad debt expense recognized in (a) the period in which sales related to the uncollectible account were made or (b) the period in which the seller learns that the customer is unable to pay?
9. What is the effect of the write-off of bad debts (using the allowance method) on (a) net income and (b) accounts receivable, net?
10. Does an increase in the receivables turnover ratio generally indicate faster or slower collection of receivables? Explain.
11. Define *cash* and *cash equivalents* in the context of accounting. Indicate the types of items that should be included and excluded.
12. Summarize the primary characteristics of an effective internal control system for cash.
13. Why should cash-handling and cash-recording activities be separated? How is this separation accomplished?
14. What are the purposes of a bank reconciliation? What balances are reconciled?
15. Briefly explain how the total amount of cash reported on the balance sheet is computed.
16. (Chapter Supplement A) Under the gross method of recording sales discounts discussed in this chapter, is the amount of sales discount taken recorded (a) at the time the sale is recorded or (b) at the time the collection of the account is recorded?

MULTIPLE-CHOICE QUESTIONS

1. What is the best description of a *credit card discount?*
   a. The discount offered by a seller to a consumer for using a national credit card such as VISA
   b. The fee charged by a seller to a consumer for the right to use a credit card, calculated as a percentage of total revenue for the sale
   c. The discount offered by a seller to a customer for early payment of an account receivable
   d. The percentage fee charged by a credit card company to a seller
2. Sales discounts with terms 2/10, n/30 mean:
   a. 10 percent discount for payment within 30 days
   b. 2 percent discount for payment within 10 days or the full amount (less returns) is due within 30 days
   c. Two-tenths of a percent discount for payment within 30 days
   d. None of the above
3. A company has been successful in reducing the costs of its manufactured inventory by relocating the factory to another locale. What effect will this factor have on the company's gross profit percentage ratio, all other things equal?
   a. The ratio will not change.
   b. The ratio will increase.
   c. The ratio will decrease.
   d. Either (b) or (c).

4. When a company using the allowance method writes off a specific customer's account receivable from the accounting system, which of the following statements are true?
   1. Total stockholders' equity remains the same.
   2. Total assets remain the same.
   3. Total expenses remain the same.
   a. 2
   b. 1 and 3
   c. 1 and 2
   d. 1, 2, and 3

5. You have determined that Company X estimates bad debt expense with an aging of accounts receivable schedule. Company X's estimate of uncollectible receivables resulting from the aging analysis equals
   a. bad debt expense for the current period.
   b. the ending balance in the Allowance for Doubtful Accounts for the period.
   c. the change in the Allowance for Doubtful Accounts for the period.
   d. both (a) and (c).

6. Upon review of the most recent bank statement, you discover that you recently received an "insufficient funds check" from a customer. Which of the following describes the actions to be taken when preparing your bank reconciliation?

	Balance per Books	*Balance per Bank*
a.	No change	Decrease
b.	Decrease	Increase
c.	Decrease	No change
d.	Increase	Decrease

7. Which of the following is *not* a step toward effective internal control over cash?
   a. Require signatures from a manager and one financial officer on all checks.
   b. Require that cash be deposited daily at the bank.
   c. Require that the person responsible for removing the cash from the register have no access to the accounting records.
   d. All of the above are steps toward effective internal control.

8. When using the allowance method, as bad debt expense is recorded,
   a. total assets remain the same and stockholders' equity remains the same.
   b. total assets decrease and stockholders' equity decreases.
   c. total assets increase and stockholders' equity decreases.
   d. total liabilities increase and stockholders' equity decreases.

9. Which of the following best describes the proper presentation of accounts receivable in the financial statements?
   a. gross accounts receivable plus the allowance for doubtful accounts in the asset section of the balance sheet
   b. gross accounts receivable in the asset section of the balance sheet and the allowance for doubtful accounts in the expense section of the income statement
   c. gross accounts receivable less bad debt expense in the asset section of the balance sheet
   d. gross accounts receivable less the allowance for doubtful accounts in the asset section of the balance sheet

10. Which of the following is not a component of net sales?
    a. sales returns and allowances
    b. sales discounts
    c. cost of goods sold
    d. credit card discounts

To practice on more multiple-choice questions, go to the text website www.mhhe.com/libby5e or the Topic Tackler DVD for use with this text.

MINI-**EXERCISES**

 Available with McGraw-Hill's Homework Manager

M6-1 Interpreting the Revenue Principle
L01

Indicate the *most likely* time you expect sales revenue to be recorded for each of the listed transactions.

Transaction	Point A	Point B
a. Airline tickets sold by an airline on a credit card	_____ Point of sale	_____ Completion of flight
b. Computer sold by mail order company on a credit card	_____ Shipment	_____ Delivery
c. Sale of inventory to a business customer on open account	_____ Shipment	_____ Collection of account

Reporting Net Sales with Sales Discounts

M6-2
LO2

Merchandise invoiced at $2,000 is sold on terms 2/10, n/30. If the buyer pays within the discount period, what amount will be reported on the income statement as net sales?

Reporting Net Sales with Sales Discounts, Credit Card Discounts, and Sales Returns

M6-3
LO2

Total gross sales for the period include the following:

Credit card sales (discount 3%)	$8,000
Sales on account (2/15, n/60)	$9,500

Sales returns related to sales on account were $500. All returns were made before payment. One-half of the remaining sales on account was paid within the discount period. The company treats all discounts and returns as contra-revenues. What amount will be reported on the income statement as net sales?

Computing and Interpreting the Gross Profit Percentage

M6-4
LO3

Net sales for the period was $56,000 and cost of sales was $48,000. Compute gross profit percentage for the current year. What does this ratio measure?

Recording Bad Debts

M6-5
LO4

Prepare journal entries for each transaction listed.

a. During the period, bad debts are written off in the amount of $17,000.
b. At the end of the period, bad debt expense is estimated to be $14,000.

Determining Financial Statement Effects of Bad Debts

M6-6
LO4

Using the following categories, indicate the effects of the following transactions. Use + for increase and − for decrease and indicate the accounts affected and the amounts.

a. At the end of the period, bad debt expense is estimated to be $10,000.
b. During the period, bad debts are written off in the amount of $8,000.

Assets	=	Liabilities	+	Stockholders' Equity

Determining the Effects of Credit Policy Changes on Receivables Turnover Ratio

M6-7
LO5

Indicate the most likely effect of the following changes in credit policy on the receivables turnover ratio (+ for increase, − for decrease, and NE for no effect).

_____ *a.* Granted credit with shorter payment deadlines.
_____ *b.* Increased effectiveness of collection methods.
_____ *c.* Granted credit to less creditworthy customers.

Matching Reconciling Items to the Bank Reconciliation

M6-8
LO6

Indicate whether the following items would be added (+) or subtracted (−) from the company's books or the bank statement during the construction of a bank reconciliation.

Reconciling Item	Company's Books	Bank Statement
a. Outstanding checks		
b. Bank service charge		
c. Deposit in transit		

M6-9   (Chapter Supplement A) Recording Sales Discounts

A sale is made for $700; terms are 2/10, n/30. At what amount should the sale be recorded under the gross method of recording sales discounts? Give the required entry. Also give the collection entry, assuming that it is during the discount period.

EXERCISES

 Available with McGraw-Hill's Homework Manager

E6-1 **Reporting Net Sales with Credit Sales and Sales Discounts**
LO2

During the months of January and February, Gold Corporation sold goods to three customers. The sequence of events was as follows:

Jan. 6 Sold goods for $1,000 to S. Green and billed that amount subject to terms 2/10, n/30.
      6 Sold goods to M. Munoz for $900 and billed that amount subject to terms 2/10, n/30.
     14 Collected cash due from S. Green.
Feb. 2 Collected cash due from M. Munoz.
     28 Sold goods for $500 to R. Reynolds and billed that amount subject to terms 2/10, n/45.

Required:
Assuming that Sales Discounts is treated as a contra-revenue, compute net sales for the two months ended February 28.

E6-2 **Reporting Net Sales with Credit Sales, Sales Discounts, Sales Returns, and**
LO2 **Credit Card Sales**

The following transactions were selected from the records of Evergreen Company:

July 12 Sold merchandise to Customer R, who charged the $1,000 purchase on his Visa credit card. Visa charges Evergreen a 2 percent credit card fee.
July 15 Sold merchandise to Customer S at an invoice price of $5,000; terms 3/10, n/30.
     20 Sold merchandise to Customer T at an invoice price of $3,000; terms 3/10, n/30.
     22 Customer T returned items purchased on July 20 with an invoice price of $1,000; the items were not the proper color, and credit was given to the customer.
     23 Collected payment from Customer S from July 15 sale.
Aug. 25 Collected payment from Customer T from July 20 sale.

Required:
Assuming that Sales Returns and Allowances, Sales Discounts, and Credit Card Discounts are treated as contra-revenues, compute net sales for the two months ended August 31 by filling in the following schedule.

Sales revenue	$_____
Less: Sales returns and allowances	_____
Less: Sales discounts	_____
Less: Credit card discounts	_____
Net sales	$_____

E6-3 **Reporting Net Sales with Credit Sales, Sales Discounts, Sales Returns, and**
LO2 **Credit Card Sales**

The following transactions were selected from among those completed by Clem Wholesalers in 2007:

Nov. 20   Sold two items of merchandise to Customer B, who charged the $400 sales price on her Visa credit card. Visa charges Clem Wholesalers a 2 percent credit card fee.

25   Sold 20 items of merchandise to Customer C at an invoice price of $5,000 (total); terms 3/10, n/30.

28   Sold 10 identical items of merchandise to Customer D at an invoice price of $6,000 (total); terms 3/10, n/30.

29   Customer D returned one of the items purchased on the 28th; the item was defective, and credit was given to the customer.

Dec. 6   Customer D paid the account balance in full.

30   Customer C paid in full for the invoice of November 25, 2007.

Required:
Assuming that Sales Returns and Allowances, Sales Discounts, and Credit Card Discounts are treated as contra-revenues, compute net sales for the two months ended December 31, 2007.

Determining the Effects of Credit Sales, Sales Discounts, Credit Card Sales, and Sales Returns and Allowances on Income Statement Categories

E6-4
LO2

Rockland Shoe Company records Sales Returns and Allowances, Sales Discounts, and Credit Card Discounts as contra-revenues. Complete the following tabulation, indicating the sign (+ for increase, − for decrease, and NE for no effect) and amount of the effects of each transaction, including related cost of goods sold.

July 12   Sold merchandise to customer at factory store who charged the $300 purchase on her American Express card. American Express charges a 1 percent credit card fee. Cost of goods sold was $200.

July 15   Sold merchandise to Customer T at an invoice price of $5,000; terms 3/10, n/30. Cost of goods sold was $3,000.

July 20   Collected cash due from Customer T.

July 21   Before paying for the order, a customer returned shoes with an invoice price of $1,000 and cost of goods sold of $600.

Transaction	Net Sales	Cost of Goods Sold	Gross Profit
July 12			
July 15			
July 20			
July 21			

Evaluating the Annual Interest Rate Implicit in a Sales Discount with Discussion of Management Choice of Financing Strategy

E6-5
LO2

Laura's Landscaping bills customers subject to terms 3/10, n/60.

Required:
1. Compute the annual interest rate implicit in the sales discount.
2. If his bank charges 15 percent interest, should the customer borrow from the bank so that he can take advantage of the discount? Explain your recommendation.

Analyzing Gross Profit Percentage on the Basis of an Income Statement and Within-Industry Comparison

E6-6
LO3

Wolverine World Wide Inc. prides itself as being the "world's leading marketer of U.S. branded non-athletic footwear." It competes in many markets with Deckers, often offering products at a lower price point. Its brands include Wolverine, Bates, Sebago, and Hush Puppies. The following data were taken from its recent annual report (dollars in thousands):

Sales of merchandise	$888,926
Income taxes	23,262
Cash dividends declared	8,588
Selling and administrative expense	246,652
Cost of products sold	562,338
Interest expense	5,474
Other income	686
Items not included in above amounts:	
Number of shares of common stock outstanding 40,721	

Required:

1. Based on these data, prepare an income statement (showing gross profit, income from operations, and pretax income as subtotals). Include a "percentage" column reporting each line item as a percentage of sales (see Chapter 5 for a discussion of common-size income statements and percentage analysis).
2. How much was the gross profit margin? What was the gross profit percentage ratio? Explain what these two amounts mean. Compare the gross profit percentage with that of Deckers. What do you believe accounts for the difference?

E6-7

LO2, 3, 4

Analyzing Gross Profit Percentage on the Basis of an Income Statement

The following summarized data were provided by the records of Slate, Incorporated, for the year ended December 31, 2007:

Sales of merchandise for cash	$220,000
Sales of merchandise on credit	32,000
Cost of goods sold	147,000
Selling expense	40,200
Administrative expense	19,000
Sales returns and allowances	7,000
Items not included in above amounts:	
Estimated bad debt loss, 2.5% of credit sales	
Average income tax rate, 30%	
Number of shares of common stock outstanding 5,000	

Required:

1. Based on these data, prepare an income statement (showing both gross profit and income from operations). Include a "percentage" column reporting each line item as a percentage of sales (see Chapter 5 for a discussion of common-size income statements and percentage analysis).
2. What was the amount of gross profit margin? What was the gross profit percentage ratio? Explain what these two amounts mean.

E6-8

LO4

Recording Bad Debt Expense Estimates and Write-Offs Using the Percentage of Credit Sales Method

During 2006, Chun Productions, Inc., recorded credit sales of $650,000. Based on prior experience, it estimates a 2 percent bad debt rate on credit sales.

Required:

Prepare journal entries for each transaction:

a. The appropriate bad debt expense adjustment was recorded for the year 2006.
b. On December 31, 2006, an account receivable for $1,000 from March of the current year was determined to be uncollectible and was written off.

E6-9

LO4

Recording Bad Debt Expense Estimates and Write-Offs Using the Percentage of Credit Sales Method

During 2006, Gonzales Electronics, Incorporated, recorded credit sales of $720,000. Based on prior experience, it estimates a 0.5 percent bad debt rate on credit sales.

Required:

Prepare journal entries for each transaction:

a. The appropriate bad debt expense adjustment was recorded for the year 2006.

b. On December 31, 2006, an account receivable for $300 from a prior year was determined to be uncollectible and was written off.

Determining Financial Statement Effects of Bad Debts Using the Percentage of Credit Sales Method

E6-10
LO4

Using the following categories, indicate the effects of the transactions listed in E6-9. Use + for increase and − for decrease and indicate the accounts affected and the amounts.

Assets	=	Liabilities	+	Stockholders' Equity

Recording and Determining the Effects of Bad Debt Transactions on Income Statement Categories Using the Percentage of Credit Sales Method

E6-11
LO4

During 2006, Kim and Silverman Electronics recorded credit sales of $600,000. Based on prior experience, it estimates a 3 percent bad debt rate on credit sales.

Required:

1. Prepare journal entries for each of the following transactions.
   a. The appropriate bad debt expense adjustment was recorded for the year 2006.
   b. On December 31, 2006, an account receivable for $1,600 from a prior year was determined to be uncollectible and was written off.
2. Complete the following tabulation, indicating the amount and effect (+ for increase, − for decrease, and NE for no effect) of each transaction.

Transaction	Net Sales	Gross Profit	Income from Operations
a.			
b.			

Computing Bad Debt Expense Using Aging Analysis

E6-12
LO4

Brown Cow Dairy uses the aging approach to estimate bad debt expense. The balance of each account receivable is aged on the basis of three time periods as follows: (1) not yet due $12,000, (2) up to 120 days past due $5,000, and (3) more than 120 days past due $3,000. Experience has shown that for each age group, the average loss rate on the amount of the receivables at year-end due to uncollectability is (1) 2 percent, (2) 10 percent, and (3) 30 percent, respectively. At December 31, 2008 (end of the current year), the Allowance for Doubtful Accounts balance was $300 (credit) before the end-of-period adjusting entry is made.

Required:

What amount should be recorded as Bad Debt Expense for the current year?

Recording and Reporting a Bad Debt Estimate Using Aging Analysis

E6-13
LO4

Arias Company uses the aging approach to estimate bad debt expense. The balance of each account receivable is aged on the basis of three time periods as follows: (1) not yet due $65,000, (2) up to 180 days past due $10,000, and (3) more than 180 days past due $4,000. Experience has shown that for each age group, the average loss rate on the amount of the receivables at year-end due to uncollectability is (1) 1 percent, (2) 15 percent, and (3) 40 percent, respectively. At December 31, 2008 (end of the current year), the Allowance for Doubtful Accounts balance was $100 (credit) before the end-of-period adjusting entry is made.

Required:

1. Prepare the appropriate bad debt expense adjusting entry for the year 2008.
2. Show how the various accounts related to accounts receivable should be shown on the December 31, 2008 balance sheet.

E6-14
LO4

Recording and Reporting a Bad Debt Estimate Using Aging Analysis

Bhojraj Company uses the aging approach to estimate bad debt expense. The balance of each account receivable is aged on the basis of three time periods as follows: (1) not yet due $300,000, (2) up to 120 days past due $50,000, and (3) more than 120 days past due $26,000. Experience has shown that for each age group, the average loss rate on the amount of the receivables at year-end due to uncollectability is (1) .5 percent, (2) 10 percent, and (3) 30 percent, respectively. At December 31, 2008 (end of the current year), the Allowance for Doubtful Accounts balance was $200 (credit) before the end-of-period adjusting entry is made.

Required:

1. Prepare the appropriate bad debt expense adjusting entry for the year 2008.
2. Show how the various accounts related to accounts receivable should be shown on the December 31, 2008 balance sheet.

E6-15
LO4
DaimlerChrysler AG

Interpreting Bad Debt Disclosures

DaimlerChrysler is the largest industrial group headquartered in Germany. Best known as the manufacturer of Mercedes-Benz and Chrysler cars and trucks, it also manufactures products in the fields of rail systems, aerospace, propulsion, defense, and information technology. In a recent filing pursuant to its listing on the New York Stock Exchange, it disclosed the following information concerning its allowance for doubtful accounts (Euros in millions denoted as €):

Balance at Beginning of Period	Charged to Costs and Expenses	Amounts Written Off	Balance at End of Period
629	23	(48)	604

Required:

1. Record summary journal entries related to the allowance for doubtful accounts for the current year.
2. If DaimlerChrysler had written off an additional €10 million of accounts receivable during the period, how would receivables, net, and net income have been affected? Explain why.

E6-16
LO4
Microsoft

Inferring Bad Debt Write-Offs and Cash Collections from Customers

Microsoft develops, produces, and markets a wide range of computer software including the Windows operating system. On a recent balance sheet, Microsoft reported the following information about net sales revenue and accounts receivable.

	Current Year	Prior Year
Accounts receivable, net of allowances of $166 and $242	$ 5,196	$ 5,129
Net revenues	36,835	32,187

According to its Form 10-K, Microsoft recorded bad debt expense of $44 and did not reinstate any previously written-off accounts during the current year. (*Hint:* Refer to the summary of the effects of accounting for bad debts on the Accounts Receivable (Gross) and the Allowance for Doubtful Accounts T-accounts. Use the T-accounts to solve for the missing values.)

Required:

1. What amount of bad debts was written off during the current year?
2. Based on your answer to requirement (1), solve for cash collected from customers for the current year assuming that all of Microsoft's sales during the period were on open account.

E6-17
LO4
Target

Inferring Bad Debt Expense and Determining the Impact of Uncollectible Accounts on Income and Working Capital

A recent annual report for Target contained the following information (dollars in thousands) at the end of its fiscal year:

	Year 1	Year 2
Accounts receivable	$5,992,000	$5,964,000
Allowance for doubtful accounts	(399,000)	(419,000)
	$5,593,000	$5,545,000

A footnote to the financial statements disclosed that uncollectible accounts amounting to $322,000 were written off as bad debts during year 1 and $512,000 during year 2. Assume that the tax rate for Target was 30 percent.

Required:

1. Determine the bad debt expense for year 2 based on the preceding facts. (*Hint:* Use the allowance for doubtful accounts T-account to solve for the missing value.)
2. *Working capital* is defined as current assets minus current liabilities. How was Target's working capital affected by the write-off of $512,000 in uncollectible accounts during year 2? What impact did the recording of bad debt expense have on working capital in year 2?
3. How was net income affected by the $512,000 write-off during year 2? What impact did recording bad debt expense have on net income for year 2?

Recording, Reporting, and Evaluating a Bad Debt Estimate

During 2009, Martin's Camera Shop had sales revenue of $170,000, of which $85,000 was on credit. At the start of 2009, Accounts Receivable showed a $10,000 debit balance, and the Allowance for Doubtful Accounts showed an $800 credit balance. Collections of accounts receivable during 2009 amounted to $68,000.

Data during 2009 follows:

a. On December 31, 2009, an Account Receivable (J. Doe) of $1,500 from a prior year was determined to be uncollectible; therefore, it was written off immediately as a bad debt.
b. On December 31, 2009, on the basis of experience, a decision was made to continue the accounting policy of basing estimated bad debt losses on 2 percent of credit sales for the year.

Required:

1. Give the required journal entries for the two items on December 31, 2009 (end of the accounting period).
2. Show how the amounts related to Accounts Receivable and Bad Debt Expense would be reported on the income statement and balance sheet for 2009. Disregard income tax considerations.
3. On the basis of the data available, does the 2 percent rate appear to be reasonable? Explain.

E6-18
LO4

Computing and Interpreting the Receivables Turnover Ratio

A recent annual report for FedEx contained the following data:

E6-19
LO5
FedEx

| | (dollars in thousands) ||
	Current Year	Previous Year
Accounts receivable	$ 3,178,000	$2,776,000
Less: Allowance for doubtful accounts	151,000	149,000
Net accounts receivable	$ 3,027,000	$2,627,000
Net sales (assume all on credit)	$24,710,000	

Required:

1. Determine the accounts receivable turnover ratio and average days sales in receivables for the current year.
2. Explain the meaning of each number.

E6-20
LO5
Dell

Computing and Interpreting the Receivables Turnover Ratio

A recent annual report for Dell, Inc., contained the following data:

	(dollars in thousands)	
	Current Year	Previous Year
Accounts receivable	$ 3,719,000	$2,657,000
Less: Allowance for doubtful accounts	84,000	71,000
Net accounts receivable	$ 3,635,000	$2,586,000
Net sales (assume all on credit)	$41,444,000	

Required:

1. Determine the accounts receivable turnover ratio and average days sales in receivables for the current year.
2. Explain the meaning of each number.

E6-21
LO5
Stride Rite

Interpreting the Effects of Sales Declines and Changes in Receivables on Cash Flow from Operations

Stride Rite Corporation manufactures and markets shoes under the brand names Stride Rite®, Keds®, and Sperry Top-Sider®. Three recent years produced a combination of declining sales revenue and net income culminating in a net loss of $8,430,000. Each year, however, Stride Rite was able to report positive cash flows from operations. Contributing to that positive cash flow was the change in accounts receivable. The current and prior year balance sheets reported the following:

	(dollars in thousands)	
	Current Year	Previous Year
Accounts and notes receivable, less allowances	$48,066	$63,403

Required:

1. On the current year's cash flow statement (indirect method), how would the change in accounts receivable affect cash flow from operations? Explain why it would have this effect.
2. Explain how declining sales revenue often leads to (a) declining accounts receivable and (b) cash collections from customers being higher than sales revenue.

E6-22
LO5
Apple

Interpreting the Effects of Sales Growth and Changes in Receivables on Cash Flow from Operations

Apple Computer, Inc., is best known for its iMac and iPod product lines. Three recent years produced a pattern of strong increases in sales revenue and net income. Cash flows from operations declined in the middle of the period, however. Contributing to that declining cash flow was the change in accounts receivable. The current and prior year balance sheets reported the following:

	(dollars in thousands)	
	Current Year	Previous Year
Accounts receivable, less allowance for doubtful accounts	$707,000	$534,000

Required:

1. On the current year's cash flow statement (indirect method), how would the change in accounts receivable affect cash flow from operations? Explain why it would have this effect.

2. Explain how increasing sales revenue often leads to (a) increasing accounts receivable and thus (b) cash collections from customers being lower than sales revenue.

Preparing Bank Reconciliation, Entries, and Reporting Cash

E6-23
LO6

Jones Company has the June 30, 2007, bank statement and the June ledger accounts for cash, which are summarized here:

BANK STATEMENT			
	Checks	Deposits	Balance
Balance, June 1, 2007			$ 6,800
Deposits during June		$17,000	23,800
Checks cleared during June	$17,700		6,100
Bank service charges	50		6,050
Balance, June 30, 2007			6,050

Cash (A)					
June 1	Balance	6,800	June	Checks written	18,400
June	Deposits	19,000			

Required:
1. Reconcile the bank account. A comparison of the checks written with the checks that have cleared the bank shows outstanding checks of $700. A deposit of $2,000 is in transit at the end of June.
2. Give any journal entries that should be made as a result of the bank reconciliation.
3. What is the balance in the Cash account after the reconciliation entries?
4. What is the total amount of cash that should be reported on the balance sheet at June 30?

Preparing Bank Reconciliation, Entries, and Reporting Cash

E6-24
LO6

The September 30, 2006, bank statement for Russell Company and the September ledger accounts for cash are summarized here:

BANK STATEMENT			
	Checks	Deposits	Balance
Balance, September 1, 2006			$ 6,300
Deposits recorded during September		$27,000	33,300
Checks cleared during September	$28,500		4,800
NSF checks—Betty Brown	250		4,550
Bank service charges	50		4,500
Balance, September 30, 2006			4,500

Cash (A)					
Sept. 1	Balance	6,300	Sept.	Checks written	28,600
Sept.	Deposits	28,000			

No outstanding checks and no deposits in transit were carried over from August; however, there are deposits in transit and checks outstanding at the end of September.

Required:
1. Reconcile the bank account.
2. Give any journal entries that should be made as the result of the bank reconciliation.
3. What should the balance in the Cash account be after the reconciliation entries?
4. What total amount of cash should the company report on the September 30 balance sheet?

E6-25 **(Chapter Supplement A) Recording Credit Sales, Sales Discounts, Sales Returns, and Credit Card Sales**

The following transactions were selected from among those completed by Hailey Retailers in 2007:

Nov. 20 Sold two items of merchandise to Customer B, who charged the $400 sales price on her Visa credit card. Visa charges Hailey a 2 percent credit card fee.

25 Sold 20 items of merchandise to Customer C at an invoice price of $4,000 (total); terms 3/10, n/30.

28 Sold 10 identical items of merchandise to Customer D at an invoice price of $6,000 (total); terms 3/10, n/30.

30 Customer D returned one of the items purchased on the 28th; the item was defective, and credit was given to the customer.

Dec. 6 Customer D paid the account balance in full.

30 Customer C paid in full for the invoice of November 25, 2007.

Required:

Give the appropriate journal entry for each of these transactions, assuming the company records sales revenue under the gross method. Do not record cost of goods sold.

PROBLEMS

 Available with McGraw-Hill's Homework Manager

P6-1
LO1
Applying the Revenue Principle

At what point should revenue be recognized in each of the following independent cases?

Case A. For Christmas presents, a McDonald's restaurant sells coupon books for $10. Each of the $1 coupons may be used in the restaurant any time during the following 12 months. The customer must pay cash when purchasing the coupon book.

Case B. Howard Land Development Corporation sold a lot to Quality Builders to construct a new home. The price of the lot was $50,000. Quality made a down payment of $100 and agreed to pay the balance in six months. After making the sale, Howard learned that Quality Builders often entered into these agreements but refused to pay the balance if it did not find a customer who wanted a house built on the lot.

Case C. Driscoll Corporation has always recorded revenue at the point of sale of its refrigerators. Recently, it has extended its warranties to cover all repairs for a period of seven years. One young accountant with the company now questions whether Driscoll has completed its earning process when it sells the refrigerators. She suggests that the warranty obligation for seven years means that a significant amount of additional work must be performed in the future.

P6-2
LO2, 4
Reporting Net Sales and Expenses with Discounts, Returns, and Bad Debts (AP6-1)

The following data were selected from the records of Larker Company for the year ended December 31, 2005.

Balances January 1, 2005	
Accounts receivable (various customers)	$120,000
Allowance for doubtful accounts	6,000

In the following order, except for cash sales, the company sold merchandise and made collections on credit terms 2/10, n/30 (assume a unit sales price of $500 in all transactions and use the gross method to record sales revenue).

Transactions during 2005

a. Sold merchandise for cash, $226,000.

b. Sold merchandise to R. Jones; invoice price, $12,000.

c. Sold merchandise to K. Black; invoice price, $26,000.

d. Two days after purchase date, R. Jones returned one of the units purchased in (b) and received account credit.

e. Sold merchandise to B. Sears; invoice price, $24,000.

f. R. Jones paid his account in full within the discount period.

g. Collected $98,000 cash from customer sales on credit in prior year, all within the discount periods.

h. K. Black paid the invoice in (c) within the discount period.

i. Sold merchandise to R. Roy; invoice price, $17,000.

j. Three days after paying the account in full, K. Black returned seven defective units and received a cash refund.

k. After the discount period, collected $6,000 cash on an account receivable on sales in a prior year.

l. Wrote off a 2003 account of $2,900 after deciding that the amount would never be collected.

m. The estimated bad debt rate used by the company was 2 percent of credit sales net of returns.

Required:

1. Using the following categories, indicate the effect of each listed transaction, including the write-off of the uncollectible account and the adjusting entry for estimated bad debts (ignore cost of goods sold). Indicate the sign and amount of the effect or "NE" for "no effect."

	Sales Revenue	Sales Discounts (taken)	Sales Returns and Allowances	Bad Debt Expense
(a)	+226,000	NE	NE	NE

2. Show how the accounts related to the preceding sale and collection activities should be reported on the 2005 income statement. (Treat sales discounts as a contra-revenue.)

Understanding the Income Statement Based on the Gross Profit Percentage

P6-3
LO3
eXcel

The following data presented in income statement order were taken from the year-end records of Nomura Export Company. You are to fill in all of the missing amounts. Show computations. (*Hint:* In Case B, start from the bottom.)

	Independent Cases	
Income Statement Items	Case A	Case B
Gross sales revenue	$232,000	$160,000
Sales returns and allowances	18,000	16,250?
Net sales revenue	214,000?	143,750
Cost of goods sold	149,800?	97,750(68%)?
Gross profit	64,200 (30%)?	46,000?
Operating expenses	44,200?	18,500
Pretax income	20,000	27,500?
Income tax expense (20%)	4000?	5,500?
Net income	16,000?	22,000?
EPS (10,000 shares)	1.60 ?	$2.20

46,000 = .32 X

P x .80 = 22,000

Interpreting Disclosure of Allowance for Doubtful Accounts (AP6-2)

P6-4
LO4
Peet's Coffee & Tea

Peet's Coffee & Tea, Inc. is a specialty coffee roaster and marketer of branded fresh roasted whole bean coffee. It recently disclosed the following information concerning the Allowance for Doubtful Accounts on its Form 10-K Annual Report submitted to the Securities and Exchange Commission.

A summary of the Allowance for Doubtful Accounts is as follows (dollars in thousands):

Allowance for Doubtful Accounts	Balance at Beginning of Period	Additions Charges to Expense	Write-offs	Balance at End of Period
Year 1	$61	$?	$ 15	$69
Year 2	69	30	?	58
Year 3	58	162	145	75

Required:

1. Record summary journal entries related to bad debts for year 3.
2. Supply the missing dollar amounts noted by (?) for year 1 and year 2.

P6-5
LO4

Determining Bad Debt Expense Based on Aging Analysis (AP6-3)

Blue Skies Equipment Company uses the aging approach to estimate bad debt expense at the end of each accounting year. Credit sales occur frequently on terms n/60. The balance of each account receivable is aged on the basis of three time periods as follows: (1) not yet due, (2) up to one year past due, and (3) more than one year past due. Experience has shown that for each age group, the average loss rate on the amount of the receivable at year-end due to uncollectability is (a) 1 percent, (b) 5 percent, and (c) 30 percent, respectively.

At December 31, 2008 (end of the current accounting year), the Accounts Receivable balance was $42,000, and the Allowance for Doubtful Accounts balance was $1,020 (credit). In determining which accounts have been paid, the company applies collections to the oldest sales first. To simplify, only five customer accounts are used; the details of each on December 31, 2008, follow:

Date	Explanation	Debit	Credit	Balance
		B. Brown—Account Receivable		
3/11/2007	Sale	14,000		14,000
6/30/2007	Collection		5,000	9,000
1/31/2008	Collection		4,000	5,000
		D. Donalds—Account Receivable		
2/28/2008	Sale	22,000		22,000
4/15/2008	Collection		10,000	12,000
11/30/2008	Collection		8,000	4,000
		N. Napier—Account Receivable		
11/30/2008	Sale	9,000		9,000
12/15/2008	Collection		2,000	7,000
		S. Strothers—Account Receivable		
3/2/2006	Sale	5,000		5,000
4/15/2006	Collection		5,000	–0–
9/1/2007	Sale	10,000		10,000
10/15/2007	Collection		8,000	2,000
2/1/2008	Sale	19,000		21,000
3/1/2008	Collection		5,000	16,000
12/31/2008	Sale	3,000		19,000
		T. Thomas—Account Receivable		
12/30/2008	Sale	7,000		7,000

Required:

1. Compute the total accounts receivable in each age category.
2. Compute the estimated uncollectible amount for each age category and prepare an aging schedule as presented in the chapter.
3. Give the adjusting entry for bad debt expense at December 31, 2008.
4. Show how the amounts related to accounts receivable should be presented on the 2008 income statement and balance sheet.

Preparing an Income Statement and Computing the Gross Profit Percentage and Receivables Turnover Ratio with Discounts, Returns, and Bad Debts (AP6-4)

P6-6

LO2, 3, 4, 5

Builders Company, Inc., sells heavy construction equipment. There are 10,000 shares of capital stock outstanding. The annual fiscal period ends on December 31. The following condensed trial balance was taken from the general ledger on December 31, 2006:

Account Titles	Debit	Credit
Cash	$ 42,000	
Accounts receivable (net)	18,000	
Inventory, ending	65,000	
Operational assets	50,000	
Accumulated depreciation		$ 21,000
Liabilities		30,000
Capital stock		90,000
Retained earnings, January 1, 2006		11,600
Sales revenue		182,000
Sales returns and allowances	7,000	
Cost of goods sold	98,000	
Selling expense	17,000	
Administrative expense	18,000	
Bad debt expense	2,000	
Sales discounts	8,000	
Income tax expense	9,600	
Totals	$334,600	$334,600

Required:

1. Beginning with the amount for net sales, prepare an income statement (showing both gross profit and income from operations). Treat sales discounts and sales returns and allowances as a contra-revenue.

2. The beginning balance in Accounts Receivable (net) was $16,000. Compute the gross profit percentage and receivables turnover ratio and explain their meaning.

Preparing a Bank Reconciliation and Related Journal Entries

P6-7

LO6

The bookkeeper at Hopkins Company has not reconciled the bank statement with the Cash account, saying, "I don't have time." You have been asked to prepare a reconciliation and review the procedures with the bookkeeper.

The April 30, 2006, bank statement and the April ledger accounts for cash showed the following (summarized):

BANK STATEMENT			
	Checks	Deposits	Balance
Balance, April 1, 2006			$25,850
Deposits during April		$36,000	61,850
Interest collected		1,070	62,920
Checks cleared during April	$44,200		18,720
NSF check—A. B. Wright	140		18,580
Bank service charges	50		18,530
Balance, April 30, 2006			18,530

Cash (A)					
Apr. 1	Balance	23,250	Apr.	Checks written	43,800
Apr.	Deposits	42,000			

A comparison of checks written before and during April with the checks cleared through the bank showed outstanding checks at the end of April of $2,200. No deposits in transit were carried over from March, but a deposit was in transit at the end of April.

Required:

1. Prepare a detailed bank reconciliation for April.
2. Give any required journal entries as a result of the reconciliation. Why are they necessary?
3. What was the balance in the cash account in the ledger on May 1, 2006?
4. What total amount of cash should be reported on the balance sheet at the end of April?

P6-8
LO6

Computing Outstanding Checks and Deposits in Transit and Preparing a Bank Reconciliation and Journal Entries (AP6-5)

The August 2007 bank statement for Hirst Company and the August 2007 ledger account for cash follow:

BANK STATEMENT			
Date	Checks	Deposits	Balance
Aug. 1			$17,470
2	$ 300		17,170
3		$12,000	29,170
4	400		28,770
5	250		28,520
9	900		27,620
10	300		27,320
15		4,000	31,320
21	400		30,920
24	21,000		9,920
25		7,000	16,920
30	800		16,120
30		2,180*	18,300
31	100†		18,200

*$2,180 interest collected.
†Bank service charge.

Cash (A)				
Aug. 1 Balance	16,520	Checks written		
Deposits		Aug. 2		300
Aug. 2	12,000	4		900
12	4,000	15		290
24	7,000	17		550
31	5,000	18		800
		20		400
		23		21,000

Outstanding checks at the end of July were for $250, $400, and $300. No deposits were in transit at the end of July.

Required:

1. Compute the deposits in transit at the end of August by comparing the deposits on the bank statement to the deposits listed on the cash ledger account.
2. Compute the outstanding checks at the end of August by comparing the checks listed on the bank statement with those on the cash ledger account and list of outstanding checks at the end of July.
3. Prepare a bank reconciliation for August.
4. Give any journal entries that the company should make as a result of the bank reconciliation. Why are they necessary?
5. What total amount of cash should be reported on the August 31, 2007, balance sheet?

(Chapter Supplement A) Recording Sales, Returns, and Bad Debts

P6-9

Use the data presented in P6-2, which was selected from the records of Larker Company for the year ended December 31, 2005.

Required:
  1. Give the journal entries for these transactions, including the write-off of the uncollectible account and the adjusting entry for estimated bad debts. Do not record cost of goods sold. Show computations for each entry.
  2. Show how the accounts related to the preceding sale and collection activities should be reported on the 2005 income statement. (Treat sales discounts as a contra-revenue.)

ALTERNATE **PROBLEMS**

Reporting Net Sales and Expenses with Discounts, Returns, and Bad Debts (P6-2)

AP6-1
LO2, 4

The following data were selected from the records of Fluwars Company for the year ended December 31, 2007.

Balances January 1, 2007:	
Accounts receivable (various customers)	$97,000
Allowance for doubtful accounts	5,000

In the following order, except for cash sales, the company sold merchandise and made collections on credit terms 3/10, n/30 (assume a unit sales price of $400 in all transactions and use the gross method to record sales revenue).

Transactions during 2007
  a. Sold merchandise for cash, $122,000.
  b. Sold merchandise to Abbey Corp; invoice price, $6,800.
  c. Sold merchandise to Brown Company; invoice price, $14,000.
  d. Abbey paid the invoice in (b) within the discount period.
  e. Sold merchandise to Cavendish Inc; invoice price, $12,400.
  f. Two days after paying the account in full, Abbey returned four defective units and received a cash refund.
  g. Collected $78,000 cash from customer sales on credit in prior year, all within the discount periods.
  h. Three days after purchase date, Brown returned two of the units purchased in (c) and received account credit.
  i. Brown paid its account in full within the discount period.
  j. Sold merchandise to Decca Corporation; invoice price, $9,000.
  k. Cavendish paid its account in full after the discount period.
  l. Wrote off a 2005 account of $1,600 after deciding that the amount would never be collected.
  m. The estimated bad debt rate used by the company was 2 percent of credit sales net of returns.

Required:
  1. Using the following categories, indicate the effect of each listed transaction, including the write-off of the uncollectible account and the adjusting entry for estimated bad debts (ignore cost of goods sold). Indicate the sign and amount of the effect or "NE" for "no effect."

	Sales Revenue	Sales Discounts (taken)	Sales Returns and Allowances	Bad Debt Expense
(a)	+122,000	NE	NE	NE

  2. Show how the accounts related to the preceding sale and collection activities should be reported on the 2007 income statement. (Treat sales discounts as a contra-revenue.)

AP6-2
LO4
Saucony, Inc.

Interpreting Disclosure of Allowance for Doubtful Accounts (P6-4)

Under various registered brand names, Saucony, Inc., and its subsidiaries develop, manufacture, and market bicycles and component parts, athletic apparel, and athletic shoes. It recently disclosed the following information concerning the allowance for doubtful accounts on its Form 10-K Annual Report submitted to the Securities and Exchange Commission.

		SCHEDULE II		
		VALUATION AND QUALIFYING ACCOUNTS		
		(DOLLARS IN THOUSANDS)		
Allowances for Doubtful Accounts	Balance at Beginning of Year	Additions Charged to Costs and Expenses	Deductions from Reserve	Balance at End of Year
Year 3	$2,032	$4,908	$5,060	(?)
Year 2	1,234	(?)	4,677	$2,032
Year 1	940	5,269	(?)	1,234

Required:
1. Record summary journal entries related to bad debts for year 3.
2. Supply the missing dollar amounts noted by (?) for year 1, year 2, and year 3.

AP6-3
LO4

Determining Bad Debt Expense Based on Aging Analysis (P6-5)

Briggs & Stratton Engines Inc. uses the aging approach to estimate bad debt expense at the end of each accounting year. Credit sales occur frequently on terms n/45. The balance of each account receivable is aged on the basis of four time periods as follows: (1) not yet due, (2) up to 6 months past due, (3) 6 to 12 months past due, and (4) more than one year past due. Experience has shown that for each age group, the average loss rate on the amount of the receivable at year-end due to uncollectability is (a) 1 percent, (b) 5 percent, (c) 20 percent, and (d) 50 percent, respectively.

At December 31, 2006 (end of the current accounting year), the Accounts Receivable balance was $39,500, and the Allowance for Doubtful Accounts balance was $1,550 (credit). In determining which accounts have been paid, the company applies collections to the oldest sales first. To simplify, only five customer accounts are used; the details of each on December 31, 2006, follow:

Date	Explanation	Debit	Credit	Balance
	R. Devens—Account Receivable			
3/13/2006	Sale	19,000		19,000
5/12/2006	Collection		10,000	9,000
9/30/2006	Collection		7,000	2,000
	C. Howard—Account Receivable			
11/01/2005	Sale	31,000		31,000
06/01/2006	Collection		20,000	11,000
12/01/2006	Collection		5,000	6,000
	D. McClain—Account Receivable			
10/31/2006	Sale	12,000		12,000
12/10/2006	Collection		8,000	4,000
	T. Skibinski—Account Receivable			
05/02/2006	Sale	15,000		15,000
06/01/2006	Sale	10,000		25,000
06/15/2006	Collection		15,000	10,000
07/15/2006	Collection		10,000	0
10/01/2006	Sale	26,000		26,000
11/15/2006	Collection		16,000	10,000
12/15/2006	Sale	4,500		14,500

Date	Explanation	Debit	Credit	Balance
	H. Wu—Account Receivable			
12/30/2006	Sale	13,000		13,000

Required:
1. Compute the total accounts receivable in each age category.
2. Compute the estimated uncollectible amount for each age category and in total.
3. Give the adjusting entry for bad debt expense at December 31, 2006.
4. Show how the amounts related to accounts receivable should be presented on the 2006 income statement and balance sheet.

Preparing an Income Statement and Computing the Gross Profit Percentage and Receivables Turnover Ratio with Discounts, Returns, and Bad Debts (P6-6)

AP6-4
LO2, 3, 4, 5

Big Tommy Corporation is a local grocery store organized seven years ago as a corporation. At that time, 6,000 shares of common stock were issued to the three organizers. The store is in an excellent location, and sales have increased each year. At the end of 2009, the bookkeeper prepared the following statement (assume that all amounts are correct; note the incorrect terminology and format):

BIG TOMMY CORPORATION
Profit and Loss
December 31, 2009

	Debit	Credit
Sales		$420,000
Cost of goods sold	$279,000	
Sales returns and allowances	10,000	
Selling expense	58,000	
Administrative and general expense	16,000	
Bad debt expense	1,000	
Sales discounts	6,000	
Income tax expense	15,000	
Net profit	35,000	
Totals	$420,000	$420,000

Required:
1. Beginning with the amount of net sales, prepare an income statement (showing both gross profit and income from operations). Treat sales discounts as an expense.
2. The beginning and ending balances in accounts receivable were $38,000 and $42,000, respectively. Compute the gross profit percentage and receivables turnover ratio and explain their meaning.

Computing Outstanding Checks and Deposits in Transit and Preparing a Bank Reconciliation and Journal Entries (P6-8)

AP6-5
LO6

The December 31, 2007, bank statement for Packer Company and the December 2007 ledger account for cash follow.

BANK STATEMENT			
Date	Checks	Deposits	Balance
Dec. 1			$48,000
2	$400; 300	$17,000	64,300
4	7,000; 90		57,210
6	120; 180; 1,600		55,310
11	500; 1,200; 70	28,000	81,540
13	480; 700; 1,900		78,460
17	12,000; 8,000		58,460
23	60; 23,500	36,000	70,900
26	900; 2,650		67,350
28	2,200; 5,200		59,950
30	17,000; 1,890; 300*	19,000	59,760
31	1,650; 1,350; 150†	5,250‡	61,860

*NSF check, J. Left, a customer.

†Bank service charge.

‡Interest collected.

Cash (A)					
Dec. 1	Balance	64,100	Checks written during December:		
Deposits			60	5,000	2,650
Dec. 11		28,000	17,000	5,200	1,650
23		36,000	700	1,890	2,200
30		19,000	3,300	1,600	7,000
31		13,000	1,350	120	300
			180	90	480
			12,000	23,500	8,000
			70	500	1,900
			900	1,200	

The November 2007 bank reconciliation showed the following: correct cash balance at November 30, $64,100; deposits in transit on November 30, $17,000; and outstanding checks on November 30, $400 + $500 = $900.

Required:

1. Compute the deposits in transit December 31, 2007, by comparing the deposits on the bank statement to the deposits listed on the cash ledger account and the list of deposits in transit at the end of November.
2. Compute the outstanding checks at December 31, 2007, by comparing the checks listed on the bank statement with those on the cash ledger account and list of outstanding checks at the end of November.
3. Prepare a bank reconciliation at December 31, 2007.
4. Give any journal entries that should be made as a result of the bank reconciliation made by the company. Why are they necessary?
5. What total amount of cash should be reported on the December 31, 2007, balance sheet?

Annual Report Cases

Finding Financial Information

CP6-1
LO3, 5, 6

Refer to the financial statements of Pacific Sunwear of California given in Appendix B at the end of this book or open file PSUN.pdf in the Annual Report Cases directory on the student DVD.

Required:
1. What does the company include in its category of cash and cash equivalents? How close do you think the disclosed amount is to actual fair market value? (Hint: The notes may be helpful in answering this question.)
2. What expenses does Pacific Sunwear of California subtract from net sales in the computation of gross profit? How does this differ from Deckers' practice and how might it affect the manner in which you interpret the gross profit percentage?
3. Compute Pacific Sunwear of California's receivables turnover ratio for the year ended January 29, 2005. What characteristics of its business might cause it to be so high?
4. What was the change in accounts receivable and how did it affect net cash provided by operating activities for the current year?

Finding Financial Information

CP6-2
LO1, 3, 4, 6

Refer to the financial statements of American Eagle Outfitters given in Appendix C at the end of this book or open file AEOS.pdf in the Annual Report Cases directory on the student DVD.

Required:
1. How much cash and cash equivalents does the company report at the end of the most recent year?
2. Does the company report an allowance for doubtful accounts on the balance sheet or in the notes? Explain why it does or does not. (*Hint:* Consider the makeup of its receivables.)
3. Compute the company's gross profit percentage for the most recent two years. Has it risen or fallen? Explain the meaning of the change.
4. Where does the company disclose its revenue recognition policy? When does the company record revenues for the "sale" of gift cards?

Comparing Companies within an Industry

CP6-3
LO3, 5

Refer to the financial statements of Pacific Sunwear of California given in Appendix B, American Eagle Outfitters given in Appendix C, and the Industry Ratio Report given in Appendix D at the end of this book or open file CP6-3.xls in the Annual Report Cases directory on the student DVD.

Required:
1. Compute gross profit percentage for both companies for the current and previous years. What do these changes suggest?
2. Knowing that these two companies are specialty or niche retailers compared to some others in their industry (see the list of companies used in the Industry Ratio Report), do you expect their gross profit percentage to be higher or lower than the industry average? Why?
3. Compare the gross profit percentage for each company for the most recent reporting year to the industry average. Are these two companies doing better or worse than the industry average? Does this match your expectations from requirement (2)?

Financial Reporting and Analysis Cases

CP6-4
LO4, 5
Foster's Brewing

Using Financial Reports: International Bad Debt Disclosure

Foster's Brewing controls more than 50 percent of the beer market in Australia and owns 40 percent of Molson Breweries of Canada and 100 percent of Courage Limited of the United Kingdom. As an Australian company, it follows Australian GAAP and uses Australian accounting terminology. In the footnotes to its recent annual report, it discloses the information on receivables (all numbers are reported in thousands of Australian dollars).

Note 3: Receivables	Year 2	Year 1
Current		
Trade debtors	792,193	999,159
Provision for doubtful debts	(121,449)	(238,110)
Other debtors	192,330	130,288
Provision for doubtful debts	(384)	(2,464)
Non-current		
Trade debtors	164,808	200,893
Other debtors	15,094	16,068
Provision for doubtful debts	(7,920)	(7,400)
Note 15: Operation Profit	Year 2	Year 1
Amounts set aside to provisions for		
Doubtful debts—trade debtors	(21,143)	(53,492)
Doubtful debts—other debtors	(228)	(2,570)

Required:

1. The account titles used by Foster's are different from those normally used by U.S. companies. What account titles does it use in place of Allowance for Doubtful Accounts and Bad Debt Expense?

2. Sales on account for year 2 were $9,978,875. Compute the accounts receivable (trade debtors) turnover ratio for year 2 (ignore uncollectible accounts).

3. Compute the provision for doubtful debts as a percentage of current receivables separately for receivables from trade debtors and receivables from others. Explain why these percentages might be different.

4. What was the total amount of receivables written off in year 2?

Critical Thinking Cases

CP6-5
LO1
UPS,
Federal Express,
and Airborne

Making a Decision as a Manager: Choosing among Alternative Recognition Points

UPS, Federal Express, and Airborne are three of the major players in the highly competitive package delivery industry. Comparability is a key qualitative characteristic of accounting numbers that allows analysts to compare similar companies. The revenue recognition footnotes of the three competitors reveal three different revenue recognition points for package delivery revenue: package delivery, percentage of service completed, and package pickup. These points correspond to the end, continuous recognition, and the beginning of the earnings process.

United Parcel Service of America, Inc.

Revenue is recognized upon delivery of a package.

Federal Express Corporation

Revenue is generally recognized upon delivery of shipments. For shipments in transit, revenue is recorded based on the percentage of service completed.

Airborne Freight Corp.

Domestic revenues and most domestic operating expenses are recognized when shipments are picked up from the customer. . . .

The Airborne footnote goes on to say, however: "The net revenue resulting from existing recognition policies does not materially differ from that which would be recognized on a delivery date basis."

Required:
1. Do you believe that the difference between Airborne's and UPS's revenue recognition policies materially affects their reported earnings? Why or why not?
2. Assume that all three companies pick up packages from customers and receive payment of $1 million for services each day of the year and that each package is delivered the next day. What would each company's service revenue for a year be given its stated revenue recognition policy?
3. Given your answers to requirement (2), under what conditions would that answer change?
4. Which revenue recognition rule would you prefer as a manager? Why?

Evaluating an Ethical Dilemma: Management Incentives, Revenue Recognition, and Sales with the Right of Return

CP6-6
LO1
Symbol
Technologies

Symbol Technologies, Inc., was a fast-growing maker of bar-code scanners. According to the federal charges, Tomo Razmilovic, the CEO at Symbol, was obsessed with meeting the stock market's expectation for continued growth. His executive team responded by improperly recording revenue and allowances for returns, as well as a variety of other tricks, to overstate revenues by $230 million and pretax earnings by $530 million. What makes this fraud nearly unique is that virtually the whole senior management team is charged with participating in the six-year fraud. At the time this case is being written, five have pleaded guilty, another eight are under indictment, and the former CEO has fled the country to avoid prosecution. The exact nature of the fraud is described in the following excerpt dealing with the guilty plea by the former vice president for finance:

Ex-Official At Symbol Pleads Guilty

By Kara Scannell
26 March 2003
The Wall Street Journal
(Copyright (c) 2003, Dow Jones & Company, Inc.)

continued

A former finance executive at Symbol Technologies Inc. pleaded guilty to participating in a vast accounting fraud that inflated revenue at the maker of bar-code scanners by roughly 10%, or $100 million a year, from 1999 through 2001.

The criminal information and civil complaint filed yesterday accused Mr. Asti and other high-level executives of stuffing the firm's distribution channel with phony orders at the end of each quarter to meet revenue and earnings targets. Under generally accepted accounting practices, revenue can be booked only when the products are shipped to a customer. Symbol's customers include delivery services and grocery stores.

Investigators alleged that Mr. Asti and others engaged in "candy" deals, where Symbol bribed resellers with a 1% fee to "buy" products from a distributor at the end of a quarter, which Symbol would later buy back. Symbol then allegedly would convince the distributor to order more products from the company to satisfy the newly created inventory void.

The SEC said the inflated revenue figures helped boost Symbol's stock price, as well as enriching Mr. Asti. He allegedly sold thousands of shares of Symbol stock, which he received from exercising stock options, when the stock was trading at inflated levels.

Required:
1. What facts, if any, presented in the article suggest that Symbol violated the revenue principle?
2. Assuming that Symbol did recognize revenue when goods were shipped, how could it have properly accounted for the fact that customers had a right to cancel the contracts (make an analogy with accounting for bad debts)?
3. What do you think may have motivated management to falsify the statements? Why was management concerned with reporting continued growth in net income?
4. Explain who was hurt by management's unethical conduct.
5. Assume that you are the auditor for other firms. After reading about the fraud, what types of transactions would you pay special attention to in the audit of your clients in this industry? What ratio might provide warnings about possible channel stuffing?

CP6-7
LO6

Evaluating Internal Control

Cripple Creek Company has one trusted employee who, as the owner said, "handles all of the bookkeeping and paperwork for the company." This employee is responsible for counting, verifying, and recording cash receipts and payments, making the weekly bank deposit, preparing checks for major expenditures (signed by the owner), making small expenditures from the cash register for daily expenses, and collecting accounts receivable. The owners asked the local bank for a $20,000 loan. The bank asked that an audit be performed covering the year just ended. The independent auditor (a local CPA), in a private conference with the owner, presented some evidence of the following activities of the trusted employee during the past year:

a. Cash sales sometimes were not entered in the cash register, and the trusted employee pocketed approximately $50 per month.
b. Cash taken from the cash register (and pocketed by the trusted employee) was replaced with expense memos with fictitious signatures (approximately $12 per day).
c. A $300 collection on an account receivable of a valued out-of-town customer was pocketed by the trusted employee and was covered by making a $300 entry as a debit to Sales Returns and a credit to Accounts Receivable.
d. An $800 collection on an account receivable from a local customer was pocketed by the trusted employee and was covered by making an $800 entry as a debit to Allowance for Doubtful Accounts and a credit to Accounts Receivable.

Required:
1. What was the approximate amount stolen during the past year?
2. What would be your recommendations to the owner?

Financial Reporting and Analysis Team Project

Team Project: Analyzing Revenues and Receivables

CP6-8

As a team, select an industry to analyze. Reuters provides lists of industries and their makeup at www.investor.reuters.com/Industries.aspx. Each team member should acquire the annual report or 10-K for one publicly traded company in the industry, with each member selecting a different company. (Library files, the SEC EDGAR service at www.sec.gov, or the company itself are good sources.)

Required:

On an individual basis, each team member should write a short report answering the following questions about the selected company. Discuss any patterns across the companies that you as a team observe. Then, as a team, write a short report comparing and contrasting your companies.

1. If your company lists receivables in its balance sheet, what percentage is it of total assets for each of the last three years? If your company does not list receivables, discuss why this is so.

2. Ratio analysis:
   a. What does the accounts receivable turnover ratio measure in general?
   b. If your company lists receivables, compute the ratio for the last three years.
   c. What do your results suggest about the company?
   d. If available, find the industry ratio for the most recent year, compare it to your results, and discuss why you believe your company differs or is similar to the industry ratio.

3. If your company lists receivables, use the 10-K to determine what additional disclosure is available concerning the allowance for doubtful accounts. (Usually the information is in a separate schedule, Item 15.)
   a. What is bad debt expense as a percentage of sales for the last three years?

4. What is the effect of the change in receivables on cash flows from operating activities for the most recent year (that is, did the change increase or decrease operating cash flows)? Explain your answer.

Reporting and Interpreting Cost of Goods Sold and Inventory

The Harley-Davidson eagle trademark was once known best as a popular request in tattoo parlors. Now, following 18 years of unparalleled growth in sales and profits, Harley-Davidson still faces a problem that most other companies envy. Though the Milwaukee-based company increased annual motorcycle production from 37,000 to 291,000 in that period, meeting customer demand is still difficult. Many of its motorcycle models still sell for more than the manufacturer's suggested retail price. To close the gap between supply and demand for its products, Harley-Davidson spent $1.2 billion over the last five years to expand and improve its production facilities in Wisconsin, Missouri, and Pennsylvania.

However, increasing production numbers is only part of Harley's strategy. It is introducing new and improved products to stay ahead of major competitors Honda, Yamaha, and BMW. It also focuses on controlling inventory quality and cost to maintain gross profit margin. Empowering, educating, and training both salaried and unionized employees; establishing long-term, mutually beneficial relationships with its suppliers; and developing accounting information systems that provide real-time inventory and order information are keys to many of these efforts. Furthermore, selection of appropriate accounting methods for inventory can have a dramatic effect on the amount Harley-Davidson pays in income taxes. Continuous improvement in product development, manufacturing, inventory management, and information system design will be necessary for the Harley-Davidson eagle to continue its rise.

FOCUS COMPANY

Harley-Davidson, Inc.

BUILDING A LEGEND INTO A

WORLD-CLASS MANUFACTURER

www.harley-davidson.com

UNDERSTANDING THE BUSINESS

Concerns about the cost and quality of inventory face all modern manufacturers and merchandisers and turn our attention to **cost of goods sold** (cost of sales, cost of products sold) on the income statement and **inventory** on the balance sheet. Exhibit 7.1 presents the relevant excerpts from Harley-Davidson's financial statements that include these accounts. Note that Cost of Goods Sold is subtracted from Net Sales to produce gross profit on its income statement. On the balance sheet, Inventory is a current asset; it is reported

HARLEY-DAVIDSON, INC.
CONSOLIDATED STATEMENTS OF INCOME
(dollars in thousands, except per share amounts)

Years Ended December 31,	2003	2002	2001
Net sales	$4,624,274	$4,090,970	$3,406,786
Cost of goods sold	2,958,708	2,673,129	2,253,815
Gross profit	1,665,566	1,417,841	1,152,971

HARLEY-DAVIDSON, INC.
CONSOLIDATED BALANCE SHEETS
(dollars in thousands, except share amounts)

December 31,	2003	2002
ASSETS		
Current Assets		
Cash and cash equivalents	$ 812,449	$ 280,928
Marketable securities	510,211	514,800
Accounts receivable, net	112,406	108,694
Finance receivables, net	1,001,990	855,771
Inventories	207,726	218,156
Deferred income taxes	51,156	41,430
Prepaid expenses	33,189	46,807
Total current assets	2,729,127	2,066,586

below Cash, Marketable Securities, and Accounts and Finance Receivables because it is less liquid than those assets.

The primary goals of inventory management are to have sufficient quantities of high-quality inventory available to serve customers' needs while minimizing the costs of carrying inventory (production, storage, obsolescence, and financing). Low quality leads to customer dissatisfaction, returns, and a decline in future sales. Also, purchasing or producing too few units of a hot-selling item causes stock-outs that mean lost sales revenue and decreases in customer satisfaction. Conversely, purchasing too many units of a slow-selling item increases storage costs as well as interest costs on short-term borrowings that finance the purchases. It may even lead to losses if the merchandise cannot be sold at normal prices.

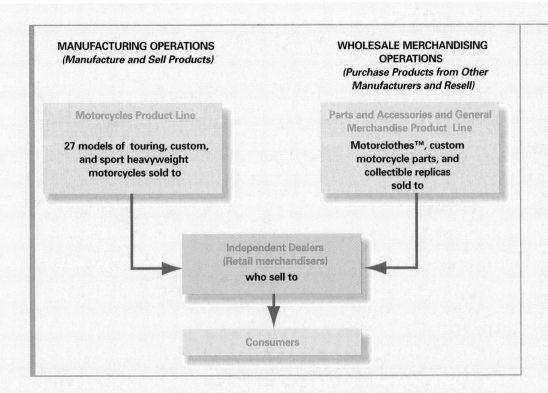

EXHIBIT 7.2

Harley-Davidson
Motorcycle Division
Product Lines

The accounting system plays three roles in the inventory management process. First, the system must provide accurate information for preparation of periodic financial statements and tax returns. Second, it must provide up-to-date information on inventory quantities and costs to facilitate ordering and manufacturing decisions. Third, since inventories are subject to theft and other forms of misuse, the system must also provide the information needed to help protect these important assets.

Harley's successful production and inventory management strategy and its mix of product lines (see Exhibit 7.2) make it a particularly good example for this chapter. Although best known as a **manufacturer** of motorcycles, Harley also purchases and resells completed products such as its popular line of Motorclothes™ apparel. In the second case, it acts as a **wholesaler.** Both the motorcycle and Motorclothes™ product lines are sold to their network of independent dealers. From an accounting standpoint, these independent dealers are Harley-Davidson's customers. The independent dealers are the **retailers** who sell the products to the public.

First we discuss the makeup of inventory, the important choices management must make in the financial and tax reporting process, and how these choices affect taxes paid. Then we will discuss how managers and analysts evaluate the efficiency of inventory management. Finally, we will briefly discuss how accounting systems are organized to keep track of inventory quantities and costs for decision making and control. This topic will be the principal subject matter of your managerial accounting course.

ORGANIZATION of the Chapter

Nature of Inventory and Cost of Goods Sold	Inventory Costing Methods	Valuation at Lower of Cost or Market	Evaluating Inventory Management	Control of Inventory
■ Items Included in Inventory ■ Costs Included in Inventory Purchases ■ Flow of Inventory Costs ■ Nature of Costs of Goods Sold	■ Specific Identification Method ■ Cost Flow Assumptions (FIFO, LIFO, Weighted Average) ■ Financial Statement Effects of Inventory Methods ■ Managers' Choice of Inventory Methods		■ Measuring Efficiency in Inventory Management ■ Inventory Turnover Ratio ■ Inventory and Cash Flows ■ Inventory Methods and Financial Statement Analysis	■ Internal Control of Inventory ■ Perpetual and Periodic Inventory Systems ■ Errors in Measuring Ending Inventory

NATURE OF INVENTORY AND COST OF GOODS SOLD

Items Included in Inventory

Learning Objective 1
Apply the cost principle to identify the amounts that should be included in inventory and the matching principle to determine cost of goods sold for typical retailers, wholesalers, and manufacturers.

INVENTORY is tangible property held for sale in the normal course of business or used in producing goods or services for sale.

MERCHANDISE INVENTORY includes goods held for resale in the ordinary course of business.

RAW MATERIALS INVENTORY includes items acquired for the purpose of processing into finished goods.

WORK IN PROCESS INVENTORY includes goods in the process of being manufactured.

FINISHED GOODS INVENTORY includes manufactured goods that are complete and ready for sale.

Inventory is tangible property that is (1) held for sale in the normal course of business or (2) used to produce goods or services for sale. Inventory is reported on the balance sheet as a current asset, because it normally is used or converted into cash within one year or the next operating cycle. The types of inventory normally held depend on the characteristics of the business.

Merchandisers (wholesale or retail businesses) hold the following:

Merchandise inventory Goods (or merchandise) held for resale in the normal course of business. The goods usually are acquired in a finished condition and are ready for sale without further processing.

For Harley-Davidson, merchandise inventory includes the Motorclothes™ line and the parts and accessories it purchases for sale to its independent dealers.

Manufacturing businesses hold three types of inventory:

Raw materials inventory Items acquired for processing into finished goods. These items are included in raw materials inventory until they are used, at which point they become part of work in process inventory.

Work in process inventory Goods in the process of being manufactured but not yet complete. When completed, work in process inventory becomes finished goods inventory.

Finished goods inventory Manufactured goods that are complete and ready for sale.

Inventories related to Harley-Davidson's motorcycle manufacturing operations are recorded in these accounts.

Harley-Davidson's recent inventory note reports the following:

HARLEY-DAVIDSON, INC.

NOTES TO CONSOLIDATED FINANCIAL STATEMENTS

2. ADDITIONAL BALANCE SHEET AND CASH FLOWS INFORMATION
(dollars in thousands)

	December 31,	
	2003	**2002**
Inventories:		
Components at the lower of FIFO cost or market:		
Raw materials and work in process	$89,823	$82,209
Motorcycle finished goods	57,778	57,076
Parts and accessories and general merchandise	77,417	95,888

Note that Harley-Davidson combines the raw materials and work in process into one number. Other companies separate the two components. The parts and accessories and general merchandise category includes purchased parts and Motorclothes™ and other accessories that make up merchandise inventory.[1]

Costs Included in Inventory Purchases

Goods in inventory are initially recorded at cost. Inventory cost includes the sum of the costs incurred in bringing an article to usable or salable condition and location. When Harley-Davidson purchases raw materials and merchandise inventory, the amount recorded should include the invoice price to be paid plus other expenditures related to the purchase, such as freight charges to deliver the items to its warehouses (freight-in) and inspection and preparation costs. In general, the company should cease accumulating purchase costs when the raw materials are **ready for use** or when the merchandise inventory is **ready for shipment.** Any additional costs related to selling the inventory to the dealers, such as marketing department salaries and dealer training sessions, are incurred after the inventory is ready for use. So they should be included in selling, general, and administrative expenses in the period they are incurred.

Applying the Materiality Constraint in Practice

FINANCIAL
ANALYSIS

Incidental costs such as inspection and preparation costs often are not material in amount (see the discussion of the materiality constraint in Chapter 5) and do not have to be assigned to the inventory cost. Thus, for practical reasons, many companies use the invoice price, less returns and discounts, to assign a unit cost to raw materials or merchandise and record other indirect expenditures as a separate cost that is reported as an expense.

Flow of Inventory Costs

The flow of inventory costs for merchandisers (wholesalers and retailers) is relatively simple, as Exhibit 7.3A shows. When merchandise is purchased, the merchandise inventory account is increased. When the goods are sold, cost of goods sold is increased and merchandise inventory is decreased.

---

[1]These do not add up to the balance reported in Exhibit 7.1 because they do not include the LIFO adjustment discussed later.

EXHIBIT 7.3

Flow of
Inventory Costs

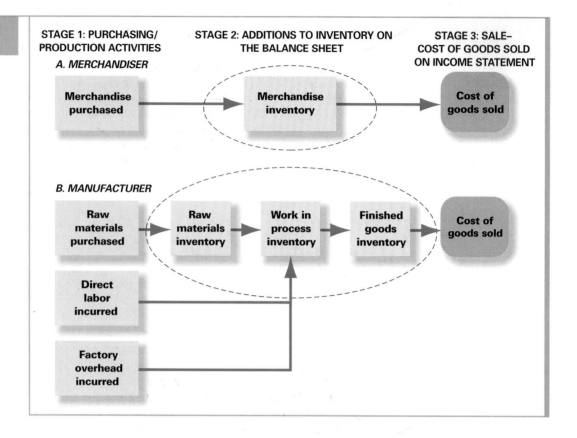

The flow of inventory costs in a manufacturing environment is more complex, as diagrammed in Exhibit 7.3B. First, **raw materials** (also called **direct materials**) must be purchased. For Harley-Davidson, these raw materials include steel and aluminum castings, forgings, sheet, and bars, as well as certain motorcycle component parts produced by its small network of suppliers, including carburetors, batteries, and tires. When they are used, the cost of these materials is removed from the raw materials inventory and added to the work in process inventory.

Two other components of manufacturing cost, direct labor and factory overhead, are also added to the work in process inventory when they are used. Direct labor cost represents the earnings of employees who work directly on the products being manufactured. Factory overhead costs include all other manufacturing costs. For example, the factory supervisor's salary and the cost of heat, light, and power to operate the factory are included in factory overhead. When the motorcycles are completed and ready for sale, the related amounts in work in process inventory are transferred to finished goods inventory. When the finished goods are sold, cost of goods sold increases, and finished goods inventory decreases.

As Exhibit 7.3 indicates, there are three stages to inventory cost flows for both merchandisers and manufacturers. The first involves purchasing and/or production activities. In the second, these activities result in additions to inventory accounts on the balance sheet. In the third stage, the inventory items are sold and the amounts become cost of goods sold expense on the income statement. Since the flow of inventory costs from merchandise inventory and finished goods to cost of goods sold are very similar, we will focus the rest of our discussion on merchandise inventory.

DIRECT LABOR refers to the earnings of employees who work directly on the products being manufactured.

FACTORY OVERHEAD are manufacturing costs that are not raw material or direct labor costs.

FINANCIAL
ANALYSIS

Modern Manufacturing Techniques and Inventory Costs

The flows of inventory costs diagrammed in Exhibit 7.3B represent the keys to manufacturing cost and quality control. Since the company must pay to finance and store raw materials and purchased parts, minimizing the size of these inventories in keeping with projected manufacturing demand is the first key to the process. To do so, Harley-Davidson must work closely with suppliers in design, production, and delivery of manufactured parts and the delivery of raw materials. (This approach to inventory management is called **just in time.**) Review and redesign of manufacturing operations and worker training and involvement programs are the keys to minimizing direct labor and factory overhead costs. New products are often designed to be simpler to manufacture, which improves product quality and reduces scrap and rework costs.

Harley-Davidson's management accounting system is designed to monitor the success of these changes and promote continuous improvements in manufacturing. The design of such systems is the subject matter of management accounting and cost accounting courses.

Nature of Cost of Goods Sold

Cost of goods sold (CGS) expense is directly related to sales revenue. Sales revenue during an accounting period is the number of units sold multiplied by the sales price. Cost of goods sold is the same number of units multiplied by their unit costs.

Let's examine the relationship between cost of goods sold on the income statement and inventory on the balance sheet. Harley-Davidson starts each accounting period with a stock of inventory called **beginning inventory** (BI). During the accounting period, new **purchases** (P) are added to inventory. The sum of the two amounts is the goods available for sale during that period. What remains unsold at the end of the period becomes **ending inventory** (EI) on the balance sheet. The portion of goods available for sale that is sold becomes **cost of goods sold** on the income statement. The ending inventory for one accounting period then becomes the beginning inventory for the next period. The relationships between these various inventory amounts are brought together in the cost of goods sold equation.

To illustrate, assume that Harley-Davidson began the period with $40,000 worth of Motorclothes™ in beginning inventory, purchased additional merchandise during the period for $55,000, and had $35,000 left in inventory at the end of the period. These amounts are combined as follows to compute cost of goods sold of $60,000:

GOODS AVAILABLE FOR SALE refers to the sum of beginning inventory and purchases (or transfers to finished goods) for the period.

COST OF GOODS SOLD EQUATION: $BI + P - EI = CGS$

Beginning inventory	$40,000
+ Purchases of merchandise during the year	55,000
Goods available for sale	95,000
− Ending inventory	35,000
Cost of goods sold	$60,000

These same relationships are illustrated in Exhibit 7.4 and can be represented in the merchandise inventory T-account as follows:

Merchandise Inventory (A)			
Beginning inventory	40,000		
Add: Purchases of inventory	55,000	Deduct: Cost of goods sold	60,000
Ending balance	35,000		

If three of these four values are known, either the cost of goods sold equation or the inventory T-account can be used to solve for the fourth value.

EXHIBIT 7.4

Cost of Goods Sold for
Merchandise Inventory

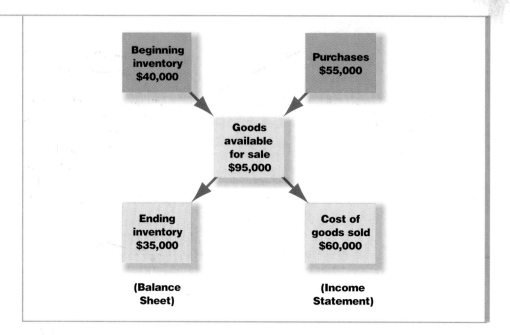

SELF-STUDY QUIZ

1. Assume the following facts for Harley-Davidson's Motorclothes™ leather baseball jacket
   product line for the year 2007:

   Beginning inventory 400 units at unit cost of $75.

   Purchases 600 units at unit cost of $75.

   Sales 700 units at a sales price of $100 (cost per unit $75).

   Using the cost of goods sold equation, compute the dollar amount of *goods available for
   sale, ending inventory*, and *cost of goods sold* of leather baseball jackets for the period.

   > Beginning inventory
   > + Purchases of merchandise during the year
   >
   > Goods available for sale
   > − Ending inventory
   >
   > Cost of goods sold

2. Assume the following facts for Harley-Davidson's Motorclothes™ leather baseball jacket
   product line for the year 2008:

   Beginning inventory 300 units at unit cost of $75.

   Ending inventory 600 units at unit cost of $75.

   Sales 1,100 units at a sales price of $100 (cost per unit $75).

   Using the cost of goods sold equation, compute the dollar amount of *purchases* of leather
   baseball jackets for the period. Remember that if three of these four values are known, the
   cost of goods sold equation can be used to solve for the fourth value.

   > Beginning inventory
   > + Purchases of merchandise during the year
   > − Ending inventory
   >
   > Cost of goods sold

   After you have completed your answers, check them with the solutions at the bottom of the
   next page.

INVENTORY COSTING METHODS

Learning Objective 2
Report inventory and cost of goods sold using the four inventory costing methods.

In the Motorclothes™ example presented in the Self-Study Quiz, the cost of all units of the leather baseball jackets was the same—$75. If inventory costs normally did not change, this would be the end of our discussion. As we are all aware, the prices of most goods do change. In recent years, the costs of many manufactured items such as automobiles and motorcycles have risen gradually. In some industries such as computers, costs of production have dropped dramatically along with retail prices.

When inventory costs have changed, which inventory items are treated as sold or remaining in inventory can turn profits into losses and cause companies to pay or save millions in taxes. A simple example will illustrate these dramatic effects. Do not let the simplicity of our example mislead you. It applies broadly to actual company practices.

Assume that a Harley-Davidson dealer made the following purchases:

Jan.	1	Had beginning inventory of two units of a Model A leather jacket at $70 each.
March 12		Purchased four units of Model A leather jacket at $80 each.
June	9	Purchased one unit of Model A leather jacket at $100 each.
Nov.	5	Sold four units for $120 each.

Note that **cost of the leather jackets rose** rapidly between January and June! On November 5, four units are sold for $120 each and revenues of $480 are recorded. What amount is recorded as cost of goods sold? The answer depends on which specific goods we assume are sold. Four generally accepted inventory costing methods are available for doing so:

1. Specific identification.

2. First-in, first-out (FIFO).

3. Last-in, first-out (LIFO).

4. Weighted average.

The four inventory costing methods are alternative ways to assign the total dollar amount of goods available for sale between (1) ending inventory and (2) cost of goods sold. The first method identifies individual items that remain in inventory or are sold. The remaining three methods assume that the inventory costs follow a certain flow.

Specific Identification Method

When the specific identification method is used, the cost of each item sold is individually identified and recorded as cost of goods sold. This method requires keeping track of the purchase cost of each item. This is done by either (1) coding the purchase cost on each unit before placing it in stock or (2) keeping a separate record of the unit and identifying it with a serial number. In the leather jacket example, any four of the items could have been sold. If we assume that one of the $70 items, two of the $80 items, and

The SPECIFIC IDENTIFICATION METHOD identifies the cost of the specific item that was sold.

Self-Study Quiz
Solutions

1. Beginning inventory (400 × $75)		$30,000
+ Purchases of merchandise during the year (600 × $75)		45,000
Goods available for sale (1,000 × $75)		75,000
− Ending inventory (300 × $75)		22,500
Cost of goods sold (700 × $75)		52,500

2. BI = 300 × $75 = $22,500   BI + P − EI = CGS

   EI = 600 × $75 = $45,000   22,500 + P − 45,000 = 82,500

   CGS = 1,100 × $75 = $82,500   P = 105,000

the one $100 item have been sold, the cost of those items ($70 + $80 + $80 + $100) would become cost of goods sold ($330). The cost of the remaining items would be ending inventory.

The specific identification method is impractical when large quantities of similar items are stocked. On the other hand, when dealing with expensive unique items such as houses or fine jewelry, this method is appropriate. This method may also be manipulated when the units are identical because one can affect the cost of goods sold and the ending inventory accounts by picking and choosing from among the several available unit costs. As a consequence, most inventory items are accounted for using one of three cost flow assumptions.

Cost Flow Assumptions

The **choice of an inventory costing method is NOT based on the physical flow of goods** on and off the shelves. That is why they are called **cost flow assumptions.** A useful tool for representing inventory cost flow assumptions is a bin, or container. Try visualizing these inventory costing methods as flows of inventory in and out of the bin. **Following practice, we will apply the methods as if all purchases during the period take place before any sales and cost of goods sold are recorded.**

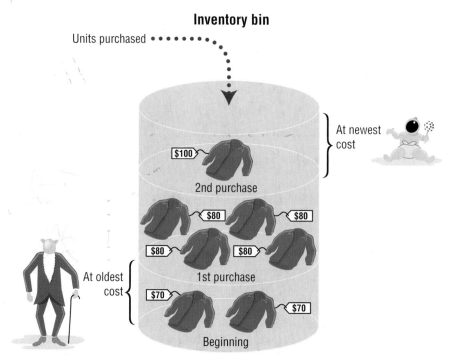

First-In, First-Out Method

The FIRST-IN, FIRST-OUT (FIFO) METHOD assumes that the first goods purchased (the first in) are the first goods sold.

Topic Tackler 7–1

The **first-in, first-out method,** frequently called FIFO, assumes that the earliest goods purchased (the first ones in) are the first goods sold, and the last goods purchased are left in ending inventory. Under FIFO, cost of goods sold and ending inventory are computed as if the flows in and out of the FIFO inventory bin in Exhibit 7.5 had taken place. First, each purchase is treated as if it were deposited in the bin from the top in sequence (two units of beginning inventory at $70 followed by purchases of four units at $80 and one unit at $100) producing goods available for sale of $560. Each good sold is then removed from the **bottom** in sequence (two units at $70 and two at $80); **first in is first out.** These goods totaling $300 become cost of goods sold (CGS). The remaining units (two units at $80 and one at $100 = $260) become ending inventory. FIFO allocates the **oldest** unit costs **to cost of goods sold** and the **newest** unit costs **to ending inventory.**

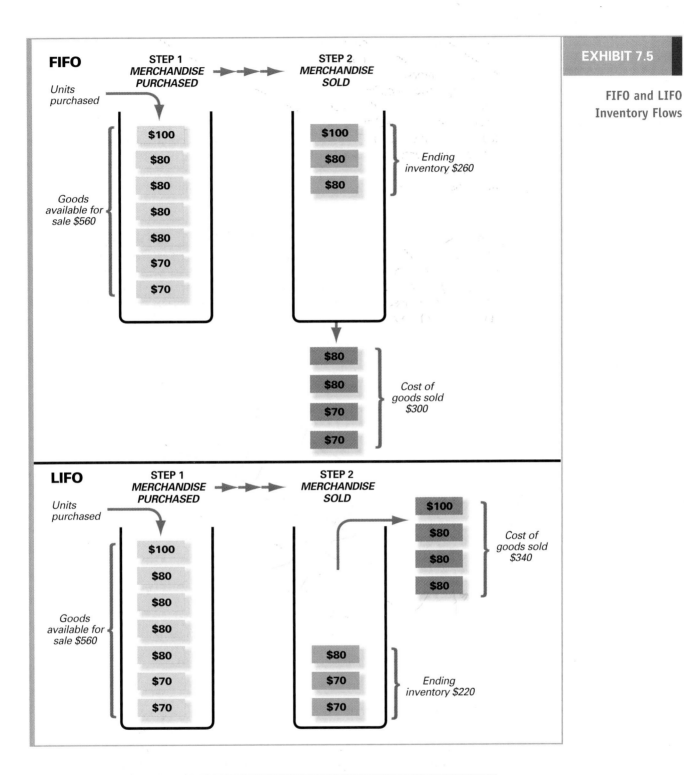

EXHIBIT 7.5

FIFO and LIFO
Inventory Flows

Cost of Goods Sold Calculation (FIFO)		
Beginning inventory	(2 units at $70 each)	$140
+ Purchases	(4 units at $80 each)	320
	(1 unit at $100 each)	100
Goods available for sale		560
− Ending inventory	(2 units at $80 each and 1 unit at $100 each)	260
Cost of goods sold	(2 units at $70 and 2 units at $80 each)	$300

Last-In, First-Out Method

The **LAST-IN, FIRST-OUT (LIFO) METHOD** assumes that the most recently purchased units (the last in) are sold first.

The last-in, first-out method, often called LIFO, assumes that the most recently purchased goods (the last ones in) are sold first and the oldest units are left in ending inventory. It is illustrated by the LIFO inventory bin in Exhibit 7.5. As in FIFO, each purchase is treated as if it were deposited in the bin from the top (two units of beginning inventory at $70 followed by purchases of four units at $80 and one unit at $100) resulting in the goods available for sale of $560. Unlike FIFO, however, each good sold is treated as if it were removed from the top in sequence (one unit at $100 followed by three units at $80). These goods totaling $340 become cost of goods sold (CGS). The remaining units (one at $80 and two at $70) become ending inventory. LIFO allocates the **newest** unit costs **to cost of goods sold** and the **oldest** unit costs **to ending inventory.**

Cost of Goods Sold Calculation (LIFO)		
Beginning inventory	(2 units at $70 each)	$140
+ Purchases	(4 units at $80 each)	320
	(1 unit at $100 each)	100
Goods available for sale		560
− Ending inventory	(2 units at $70 each and 1 unit at $80 each)	220
Cost of goods sold	(3 units at $80 and 1 unit at $100 each)	$340

The LIFO flow assumption is the exact opposite of the FIFO flow assumption:

	FIFO	LIFO
Cost of goods sold on income statement	Oldest unit costs	Newest unit costs
Inventory on balance sheet	Newest unit costs	Oldest unit costs

Average Cost Method

The **AVERAGE COST METHOD** uses the weighted average unit cost of the goods available for sale for both cost of goods sold and ending inventory.

The average cost method uses the weighted average unit cost of the goods available for sale for both cost of goods sold and ending inventory. The weighted average unit cost of the goods available for sale is computed as follows.

Number of Units	×	Unit Cost	=	Total Cost
2	×	$70	=	$140
4	×	$80	=	320
1	×	$100	=	100
7				$560

$$\text{Average Cost} = \frac{\text{Cost of Goods Available for Sale}}{\text{Number of Units Available for Sale}}$$

$$\text{Average Cost} = \frac{\$560}{7 \text{ Units}} = \$80 \text{ per Unit}$$

Cost of goods sold and ending inventory are assigned the same weighted average cost per unit of $80.

Cost of Goods Sold Calculation (Average Cost)		
Beginning inventory	(2 units at $70 each)	$140
+ Purchases	(4 units at $80 each)	320
	(1 unit at $100 each)	100
Goods available for sale	(7 units at $80 average cost each)	560
− Ending inventory	(3 units at $80 average cost each)	240
Cost of goods sold	(4 units at $80 average cost each)	$320

These flows are illustrated in Exhibit 7.6.

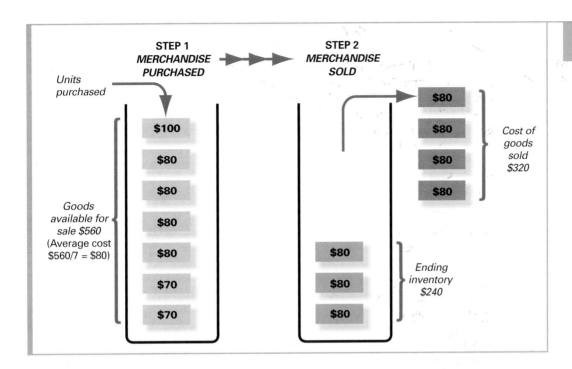

EXHIBIT 7.6

Average Cost Inventory Flows

Financial Statement Effects of Inventory Methods

Each of the four alternative inventory costing methods is in conformity with GAAP and the tax law. To understand why managers choose different methods in different circumstances, we must first understand their effects on the income statement and balance sheet. Exhibit 7.7 summarizes the financial statement effects of FIFO, LIFO, and weighted average methods in our example. Remember that the methods differ only in the portion of goods available for sale allocated to cost of goods sold versus ending inventory. For that reason, the method that gives the highest ending inventory amount also gives the lowest cost of goods sold and the highest gross profit, income tax expense, and income amounts, and vice versa. The weighted average cost method generally gives income and inventory amounts that are between the FIFO and LIFO extremes.

EXHIBIT 7.7

Financial Statement Effects of Inventory Costing Methods

	FIFO	LIFO	Weighted Average
Effect on the Income Statement			
Sales	$480	$480	$480
Cost of Goods Sold:			
Beginning inventory	$140	$140	$140
Add: Purchases	420	420	420
Goods available for sale	560	560	560
Subtract: Ending inventory (to balance sheet)	260	220	240
Cost of goods sold	300	340	320
Gross profit	180	140	160
Other expenses	80	80	80
Income before income taxes	100	60	80
Income tax expense (25%)	25	15	20
Net income	$ 75	$ 45	$ 60
Effect on the Balance Sheet			
Inventory	$260	$220	$240

In the comparison in Exhibit 7.7, unit costs were increasing. **When unit costs are rising, LIFO produces lower income and a lower inventory valuation than FIFO.** Even in inflationary times, some companies' costs decline. **When unit costs are declining, LIFO produces higher income and higher inventory valuation than FIFO.** These effects, which hold as long as inventory quantities are constant or rising,[2] are summarized in the following table:

Increasing Costs: Normal Financial Statement Effects

	FIFO	LIFO
Cost of goods sold on income statement	Lower	Higher
Net income	Higher	Lower
Income taxes	Higher	Lower
Inventory on balance sheet	Higher	Lower

Decreasing Costs: Normal Financial Statement Effects

	FIFO	LIFO
Cost of goods sold on income statement	Higher	Lower
Net income	Lower	Higher
Income taxes	Lower	Higher
Inventory on balance sheet	Lower	Higher

Managers' Choice of Inventory Methods

What motivates companies to choose different inventory costing methods? Most managers choose accounting methods based on two factors:

1. Net income effects (managers prefer to report higher earnings for their companies).

2. Income tax effects (managers prefer to pay the least amount of taxes allowed by law as late as possible—the **least-latest rule**).

Any conflict between the two motives is normally resolved by choosing one accounting method for external financial statements and a different method for preparing its tax return. The choice of inventory costing methods is a special case, however, because of what is called the *LIFO* **conformity rule:** If LIFO is used on the income tax return, it must also be used to calculate inventory and cost of goods sold for the financial statements.

FIFO **LIFO**

Income statement:
Costs of goods sold

Oldest unit cost   Newest unit cost

Balance sheet:
Inventory

Newest unit cost   Oldest unit cost

Increasing Cost Inventories

■ **For inventory with increasing costs, LIFO is used on the tax return because it normally results in lower income taxes.**

This is illustrated in Exhibit 7.7, where income before income taxes was lowered from $100 under FIFO to $60 under LIFO. On the income tax expense line, this lowers income taxes from $25 under FIFO to $15 under LIFO, generating cash tax savings of $10 under LIFO.[3] The LIFO con-

---

[2]The impact of a decline in inventory **quantity** on LIFO amounts is discussed in Supplement A to this chapter.

[3]In theory, LIFO cannot provide permanent tax savings because (1) when inventory levels drop or (2) costs drop, the income effect reverses and the income taxes deferred must be paid. The economic advantage of deferring income taxes in such situations is due to the fact that interest can be earned on the money that otherwise would be paid as taxes for the current year.

formity rule leads companies to adopt LIFO for **both** tax and financial reporting purposes for increasing cost inventories located in the United States. Harley-Davidson is a fairly typical company facing increasing costs. It has saved approximately $6 million in taxes from the date it adopted the LIFO method through 2003.

For inventory located in countries that do not allow LIFO for tax purposes or that do not have a LIFO conformity rule, companies with increasing costs most often use FIFO or weighted average to report higher income on the income statement.

Decreasing Cost Inventories

■ **For inventory with decreasing costs, FIFO is most often used for both the tax return and financial statements.**

Using this method (along with lower of cost or market valuation, discussed later) produces the lowest tax payments for companies with decreasing cost inventories. Many high-technology companies are facing declining costs. In such circumstances, the FIFO method, in which the oldest, most expensive goods become cost of goods sold, produces the highest cost of goods sold, the lowest pretax earnings, and thus the lowest income tax liability. For example, Apple Computer and Dell Computer account for inventories using FIFO.

Since most companies in the same industry face similar cost structures, clusters of companies in the same industries often choose the same accounting method.

Consistency in Use of Inventory Methods

It is important to remember that regardless of the physical flow of goods, a company can use any of the inventory costing methods. Also, a company is not required to use the same inventory costing method for all inventory items, and no particular justification is needed for the selection of one or more of the acceptable methods. Harley-Davidson, and most large companies, use different inventory methods for different inventory items.[4] However, accounting rules require companies to apply their accounting methods on a consistent basis over time. A company is not permitted to use LIFO one period, FIFO the next, and then go back to LIFO. A change in method is allowed only if the change will improve the measurement of financial results and financial position.

 LIFO and Conflicts between Managers' and Owners' Interests

We have seen that the selection of an inventory method can have significant effects on the financial statements. Company managers may have an incentive to select a method that is not consistent with the owners' objectives. For example, during a period of rising prices, using LIFO may be in the best interests of the owners, because LIFO often reduces a company's tax liability. If managers' compensation is tied to reported profits, they may prefer FIFO, which typically results in higher profits.

While a well-designed compensation plan should reward managers for acting in the best interests of the owners, that is not always the case. Clearly, a manager who selects an accounting method that is not optimal for the company solely to increase his or her compensation is engaging in questionable ethical behavior.

[4]*Accounting Trends & Techniques* (New York: AICPA, 2003) reported that, although 255 (42.5 percent) of the 600 companies surveyed reported using LIFO for some portion of inventories, only 17 (2.8 percent) use LIFO for all inventories.

SELF-STUDY **QUIZ**

1. Compute cost of goods sold and pretax income for **2007** under the FIFO and LIFO accounting methods. Assume that a company's beginning inventory and purchases for 2007 included:

Beginning inventory	10 units @ $6 each
Purchases January	5 units @ $10 each
Purchases May	5 units @ $12 each

During 2007, 15 units were sold for $20 each, and other operating expenses totaled $100.

2. Compute cost of goods sold and pretax income for **2008** under the FIFO and LIFO accounting methods. (*Hint:* The 2007 ending inventory amount becomes the 2008 beginning inventory amount.) Assume that the company's purchases for 2008 included:

Purchases March	6 units @ $13 each
Purchases November	5 units @ $14 each

During 2008, 10 units were sold for $24 each, and other operating expenses totaled $70.

3. Which method would you recommend that the company adopt? Why?

After you have completed your answers, check them with the solutions at the bottom of the page.

Self-Study Quiz
Solutions

1.

2007	FIFO	LIFO		FIFO	LIFO
Beginning inventory	$ 60	$ 60	Sales revenue (15 × $20)	$300	$300
Purchases (5 × $10) + (5 × $12)	110	110	Cost of goods sold	110	140
Goods available for sale	170	170	Gross profit	190	160
Ending inventory*	60	30	Other expenses	100	100
Cost of goods sold	$110	$140	Pretax income	$ 90	$ 60

*FIFO ending inventory = (5 × $12) = $60
   cost of goods sold = (10 × $6) + (5 × $10) = $110
LIFO ending inventory = (5 × $6) = $30
   cost of goods sold = (5 × $12) + (5 × $10) + (5 × $6) = $140

2.

2008	FIFO	LIFO		FIFO	LIFO
Beginning inventory	$ 60	$ 30	Sales revenue (10 × $24)	$240	$240
Purchases (6 × $13) + (5 × $14)	148	148	Cost of goods sold	125	135
Goods available for sale	208	178	Gross profit	115	105
Ending inventory*	83	43	Other expenses	70	70
Cost of goods sold	$125	$135	Pretax income	$ 45	$ 35

*FIFO ending inventory = (5 × $14) + (1 × $13) = $83
   cost of goods sold = (5 × $12) + (5 × $13) = $125
LIFO ending inventory = (5 × $6) + (1 × $13) = $43
   cost of goods sold = (5 × $14) + (5 × $13) = $135

3. LIFO would be recommended because it produces lower pretax income and lower taxes when inventory costs are rising.

VALUATION AT LOWER OF COST OR MARKET

Inventories should be measured initially at their purchase cost in conformity with the cost principle. When the goods remaining in ending inventory can be replaced with identical goods at a lower cost, however, the lower cost should be used as the inventory valuation. Damaged, obsolete, and deteriorated items in inventory should also be assigned a unit cost that represents their current estimated net realizable value (sales price less costs to sell) if that is below cost. This rule is known as measuring inventories at the lower of cost or market (LCM).

This departure from the cost principle is based on the **conservatism** constraint, which requires special care to avoid overstating assets and income. It is particularly important for two types of companies: (1) high-technology companies such as Dell Computer that manufacture goods for which costs of production and selling price are declining and (2) companies such as American Eagle Outfitters that sell seasonal goods such as clothing, the value of which drops dramatically at the end of each selling season (fall or spring).

Under LCM, companies recognize a "holding" loss in the period in which the replacement cost of an item drops, rather than the period in which the item is sold. The holding loss is the difference between the purchase cost and the lower replacement cost. It is added to the cost of goods sold for the period. To illustrate, assume that Dell Computer had the following in the current period ending inventory:

Item	Quantity	Cost per Item	Replacement Cost (Market) per Item	Lower of Cost or Market per Item	Total Lower of Cost or Market
Pentium chips	1,000	$250	$200	$200	1,000 × $200 = $200,000
Disk drives	400	100	110	100	400 × $100 = 40,000

The 1,000 Pentium chips should be recorded in the ending inventory at the current market value ($200) because it is **lower** than the cost ($250). Dell makes the following journal entry to record the write-down:

Cost of goods sold (+E, −SE) (1,000 × $50) 50,000
    Inventory (−A) 50,000

Assets	=	Liabilities	+	Stockholders' Equity	
Inventory	−50,000			Cost of Goods Sold	−50,000

Since the market price of the disk drives ($110) is higher than the original cost ($100), no write-down is necessary. The drives remain on the books at their cost of $100 per unit ($40,000 in total). Recognition of holding gains on inventory is not permitted by GAAP.

The write-down of the Pentium chips to market produces the following effects on the income statement and balance sheet:

Effects of LCM Write-Down	Current Period	Next Period (if sold)
Cost of goods sold	Increase $50,000	Decrease $50,000
Pretax income	Decrease $50,000	Increase $50,000
Ending inventory on balance sheet	Decrease $50,000	Unaffected

Note that the effects in the period of sale are the opposite of those in the period of the write-down. Lower of cost or market changes only the timing of cost of goods sold. It transfers cost of goods sold from the period of sale to the period of write-down.

In the case of seasonal goods such as clothing, obsolete goods, or damaged goods, if the sales price less selling costs (or net realizable value) drops below cost, this

Learning Objective 4
Report inventory at the lower of cost or market (LCM).

LOWER OF COST OR MARKET (LCM) is a valuation method departing from the cost principle; it serves to recognize a loss when replacement cost or net realizable value drops below cost.

REPLACEMENT COST is the current purchase price for identical goods.

NET REALIZABLE VALUE is the expected sales price less selling costs (e.g., repair and disposal costs).

difference is subtracted from ending inventory and added to cost of goods sold for the period. This has the same effect on current and future periods' financial statements as the write-down to replacement cost.

Note that in the two examples that follow, both Harley-Davidson, which is a mixed LIFO company, and Dell Computer, which is a FIFO company, report the use of lower of cost or market for financial statement purposes.[5]

HARLEY-DAVIDSON, INC.

NOTES TO CONSOLIDATED FINANCIAL STATEMENTS

1. SUMMARY OF SIGNIFICANT ACCOUNTING POLICIES

INVENTORIES—Inventories are valued at the lower of cost or market. Substantially all inventories located in the United States are valued using the last-in, first-out (LIFO) method. Other inventories totaling $74.9 million in 2003 and $76.4 million in 2002 are valued at the lower of cost or market using the first-in, first-out (FIFO) method.

DELL COMPUTER

Notes to Consolidated Financial Statements

NOTE 1—Description of Business and Summary of Significant Accounting Policies

Inventories—Inventories are stated at the lower of cost or market with cost being determined on a first-in, first-out basis.

EVALUATING INVENTORY MANAGEMENT

Measuring Efficiency in Inventory Management

As noted at the beginning of the chapter, the primary goals of inventory management are to have sufficient quantities of high-quality inventory available to serve customers' needs while minimizing the costs of carrying inventory (production, storage, obsolescence, and financing). The inventory turnover ratio is an important measure of the company's success in balancing these conflicting goals:

KEY RATIO
ANALYSIS

Inventory Turnover

❓ ANALYTICAL QUESTION:
How efficient are inventory management activities?

％ RATIO AND COMPARISONS:

$$\text{Inventory Turnover} = \frac{\text{Cost of Goods Sold}}{\text{Average Inventory}}$$

---

[5]For tax purposes, lower of cost or market may be applied with all inventory costing methods except LIFO.

The 2003 ratio for Harley-Davidson (see Exhibit 7.1 for the inputs to the equation):

$$\frac{\$2,958,708}{(\$207,726 + 218,156) \div 2} = 13.9$$

COMPARISONS OVER TIME		
Harley-Davidson		
2001	**2002**	**2003**
12.1	13.4	13.9

COMPARISONS WITH COMPETITORS	
Ducati Motor	**Honda Motor**
2003	**2003**
2.2	8.1

INTERPRETATIONS:

In General → The inventory turnover ratio reflects how many times average inventory was produced and sold during the period. A higher ratio indicates that inventory moves more quickly through the production process to the ultimate customer, reducing storage and obsolescence costs. Because less money is tied up in inventory, the excess can be invested to earn interest income or reduce borrowing, which reduces interest expense. More efficient purchasing and production techniques such as just-in-time inventory, as well as high product demand cause this ratio to be high. Analysts and creditors also watch the inventory turnover ratio because a sudden decline may mean that a company is facing an unexpected drop in demand for its products or is becoming sloppy in its production management. Many managers and analysts compute the related number of average days to sell inventory, which, for Harley-Davidson, is equal to:

$$\text{Average Days to Sell Inventory} = \frac{365}{\text{Inventory Turnover}} = \frac{365}{13.9} = 26.3 \text{ days.}$$

It indicates the average time it takes the company to produce and deliver inventory to customers.

Focus Company Analysis → Harley-Davidson's inventory turnover has increased from 12.1 in 2001 to 13.9 in 2003. This increase in inventory turnover resulted from increases in production volume at each of Harley's plants as well as use of just-in-time inventory principles. Harley's ratio is much higher than its smaller European rival, Ducati, whose operations are much less efficient. Harley-Davidson benefits from what economists call "economies of scale." Harley's turnover is even higher than the ratio for the giant Japanese auto and motorcycle manufacturer Honda.

A Few Cautions: Differences across industries in purchasing, production, and sales processes cause dramatic differences in this ratio. For example, restaurants such as Outback Steakhouse, which must turn over their perishable inventory very quickly, tend to have much higher inventory turnover. A particular firm's ratio should be compared only with its figures from prior years or with figures for other firms in the same industry.

Selected Focus Company Inventory Turnover

Outback Steakhouse	20.87
General Mills	5.72
Boston Beer	9.41
HomeDepot	5.08

Inventory and Cash Flows

When companies expand production to meet increases in demand, this increases the amount of inventory reported on the balance sheet. However, when companies overestimate demand for a product, they usually produce too many units of the slow-selling item. This increases storage costs as well as the interest costs on short-term borrowings that finance the inventory. It may even lead to losses if the excess inventory cannot be sold at normal prices. The cash flow statement often provides the first sign of such problems.

FOCUS ON
CASH FLOWS   **Inventory**

As with a change in accounts receivable, a change in inventories can have a major effect on a company's cash flow from operations. Cost of goods sold on the income statement may be more or less than the amount of cash paid to suppliers during the period. Since most inventory is purchased on open credit (borrowing from suppliers is normally called accounts payable), reconciling cost of goods sold with cash paid to suppliers requires consideration of the changes in both the Inventory and Accounts Payable accounts.

The simplest way to think about the effects of changes in inventory is that buying (increasing) inventory eventually decreases cash, while selling (decreasing) inventory eventually increases cash. Similarly, borrowing from suppliers, which increases accounts payable, increases cash. Paying suppliers, which decreases accounts payable, decreases cash.

EFFECT ON STATEMENT OF CASH FLOWS

In General → When a net **decrease in inventory** for the period occurs, sales are greater than purchases; thus, the decrease must be **added** in computing cash flows from operations.

When a net **increase in inventory** for the period occurs, sales are less than purchases; thus, the increase must be **subtracted** in computing cash flows from operations.

When a net **decrease in accounts payable** for the period occurs, payments to suppliers are greater than new purchases; thus, the decrease must be **subtracted** in computing cash flows from operations.

When a net **increase in accounts payable** for the period occurs, payments to suppliers are less than new purchases; thus, the increase must be **added** in computing cash flows from operations.

	Effect on Cash Flows
Operating activities (indirect method)	
Net income	$xxx
Adjusted for	
Add inventory **decrease**	+
or	
Subtract inventory **increase**	−
Add accounts payable **increase**	+
or	
Subtract accounts payable **decrease**	−

Focus Company Analysis → Exhibit 7.8 is the Operating Activities section of Harley-Davidson's statement of cash flows. When the inventory balance decreases during the period, as was the case at Harley-Davidson in 2003, the company has sold more inventory than it has purchased or produced. Thus, the decrease is added in the computation of cash flow from operations. Conversely, when the inventory balance increases during the period, as was the case at Harley-Davidson in 2002, the company has purchased or produced more inventory than it sold. Thus, the increase is subtracted in the computation of cash flow from operations. When the accounts payable balance increases during the period, the company has borrowed more from suppliers than it has paid them (or postponed payments). Thus, the increase is added in the computation of cash flow from operations.*

*For companies with foreign currency or business acquisitions/dispositions, the amount of the change reported on the cash flow statement will not equal the change in the accounts reported on the balance sheet.

CONSOLIDATED STATEMENTS OF CASH FLOWS Years Ended December 31, 2003 and 2002 (dollars in thousands)		
	2003	**2002**
Cash flows from operating activities:		
Net Income	$760,928	$580,217
Adjustments to reconcile net income to		
net cash provided by operating activities:		
Depreciation and amortization	196,918	175,778
Provision for long-term employee benefits	76,422	57,124
Provision for finance credit losses	4,076	6,167
Current year gain on securitizations	(82,221)	(56,139)
Collection of retained securitization interests	118,113	89,970
Contributions to pension plan	(192,000)	(153,636)
Tax benefit from the exercise of stock options	13,805	14,452
Deferred income taxes	42,105	38,560
Other	16,051	7,057
Net changes in current assets and current liabilities:		
Accounts receivable	(3,712)	10,149
Inventories	10,430	(37,041)
Prepaid expenses & other current assets	13,889	(13,067)
Finance receivables—accrued interest and other	(54,796)	(36,382)
Accounts payable and accrued liabilities	15,545	92,430
Total adjustments	174,625	195,422
Net cash provided by operating activities	935,553	775,639

EXHIBIT 7.8

Inventories on the
Cash Flow Statement

REAL WORLD EXCERPT

HARLEY-
DAVIDSON,
INC.

ANNUAL REPORT

SELF-STUDY QUIZ

1. Refer to the Key Ratio Analysis for Harley-Davidson's inventory turnover. Based on the computations for 2003, answer the following question. If Harley-Davidson had been able to manage its inventory more efficiently and decrease purchases and ending inventory by $10,000 for 2003, would its inventory turnover ratio have increased or decreased? Explain.

2. Based on the Focus on Cash Flows section, answer the following question. If Harley-Davidson had managed its inventory less efficiently and **increased** ending inventory, would its cash flow from operations have increased or decreased?

After you have completed your answers, check them with the solutions at the bottom of the page.

1. Inventory turnover would have increased because the denominator of the ratio (average inventory) would have decreased by $5,000.

$$\frac{\$2,958,708}{(\$197,226 + \$218,156)/2} = 14.2$$

2. An increase in inventory would have decreased cash flow from operations. (See the Focus on Cash Flows section.)

Inventory Methods and Financial Statement Analysis

Learning Objective 6
Compare companies that use different inventory costing methods.

What would analysts do if they wanted to compare two companies that prepared their statements using different inventory accounting methods? Before meaningful comparisons could be made, one company's statements would have to be converted to a comparable basis. Making such a conversion is eased by the requirement that U.S. public companies using LIFO also report beginning and ending inventory on a FIFO basis in the notes if the FIFO values are materially different. We can use this information along with the cost of goods sold equation to convert the balance sheet and income statement to the FIFO basis.

Converting the Income Statement to FIFO

Recall that the choice of a cost flow assumption affects how goods available for sale are allocated to ending inventory and cost of goods sold. It does not affect the recording of purchases. Ending inventory will be different under the alternative methods, and, since last year's ending inventory is this year's beginning inventory, beginning inventory will also be different:

Beginning inventory	*Different*
+ Purchases of merchandise during the year	*Same*
− Ending inventory	*Different*
Cost of goods sold	*Different*

This equation suggests that if we know the differences between a company's inventory valued at LIFO and FIFO for both beginning and ending inventory, we can compute the difference in cost of goods sold. Exhibit 7.9 shows Harley-Davidson's 2003 disclosure of the differences between LIFO and FIFO values for beginning and ending inventory. These amounts, referred to as the LIFO reserve or "Excess of FIFO over LIFO inventory," are disclosed by LIFO users in their inventory footnotes.

Using Harley-Davidson's LIFO reserve values reported in the footnote in Exhibit 7.9, we see that, cost of goods sold would have been $275 **lower** had it used FIFO.

LIFO RESERVE is a contra-asset for the excess of FIFO over LIFO inventory.

Beginning LIFO Reserve (Excess of FIFO over LIFO)	$17,017
− Less: Ending LIFO Reserve (Excess of FIFO over LIFO)	− 17,292
Difference in Cost of Goods Sold under FIFO	($ 275)

Since FIFO cost of goods sold expense is **lower,** income before income taxes would have been $275 **higher.** As a result, income taxes would be that amount times its tax rate of 35 percent **higher** had it used FIFO.

EXHIBIT 7.9

Financial Statement Effects of Inventory Costing Methods

REAL WORLD EXCERPT

HARLEY-DAVIDSON, INC.

ANNUAL REPORT

LIFO Reserve

HARLEY-DAVIDSON, INC.
NOTES TO CONSOLIDATED FINANCIAL STATEMENTS
2. ADDITIONAL BALANCE SHEET AND CASH FLOW INFORMATION
(dollars in thousands)

	December 31,	
	2003	**2002**
Inventories:		
. . .		
Components at FIFO:	225,018	235,173
Excess of FIFO over LIFO inventories	17,292	17,017
Components at LIFO:	$207,726	$218,156

Difference in pretax income under FIFO	$275
Tax rate	× .35
Difference in taxes under FIFO	$96

Combining the two effects, net income would be increased by the change in cost of goods sold of $275 and decreased by the change in income tax expense of $96, resulting in an overall increase in net income of $179.

Decrease in Cost of Goods Sold Expense (*Income increases*)	$275
Increase in Income Tax Expense (*Income decreases*)	(96)
Increase in Net Income	$179

These Harley-Davidson computations are for 2003. It is important to note that even companies that usually face increasing costs occasionally face decreasing costs. For example, during 2000, Harley-Davidson's costs of new inventory declined due to manufacturing efficiencies. Consequently, when we convert from LIFO to FIFO, cost of goods sold for 2000 actually **increases** by $1,851, and the conversion's effect on pretax income is the opposite—a **decrease** of $1,851. As a result, even though LIFO usually **saves** it taxes, Harley paid **extra** taxes in 2000.

Converting Inventory on the Balance Sheet to FIFO

You can adjust the inventory amounts on the balance sheet to FIFO by substituting the FIFO values in the note ($225,018 and $235,173 for 2003 and 2002, respectively) for the LIFO values (see Exhibit 7.9). Alternatively, you can add the LIFO reserve to the FIFO value on the balance sheet to arrive at the same numbers.

LIFO and Inventory Turnover Ratio

FINANCIAL
ANALYSIS

For many LIFO companies, the inventory turnover ratio can be deceptive. Remember that, for these companies, the beginning and ending inventory numbers that make up the denominator of the ratio will be artificially small because they reflect old lower costs. Consider Deere & Co., manufacturer of John Deere farm, lawn, and construction equipment. Its inventory note lists the following values:

REAL WORLD EXCERPT
Deere & Company
ANNUAL REPORT

DEERE & COMPANY
NOTES TO CONSOLIDATED FINANCIAL STATEMENTS
INVENTORIES
(dollars in millions)

	2003	2002
Total FIFO value	$2,316	$2,320
Adjustment to LIFO basis	950	948
Inventories	$1,366	$1,372

John Deere's cost of goods sold for 2003 was $10,752.7 million. If the ratio is computed using the reported LIFO inventory values for the ratio, it would be

$$\text{Inventory Turnover Ratio} = \frac{\$10,752.7}{(\$1,366 + \$1,372)/2} = 7.9$$

Converting cost of goods sold (the numerator) to a FIFO basis and using the more current FIFO inventory values in the denominator, it would be

$$\text{Inventory Turnover Ratio} = \frac{\$10,752.7 - 2.0}{(\$2,316 + \$2,320)/2} = 4.6$$

Note that the major difference between the two ratios is in the denominator. FIFO inventory values are nearly two times the LIFO values. So the FIFO ratio is just over half the LIFO amount. The LIFO beginning and ending inventory numbers are artificially small because they reflect older lower costs. Thus, the numerator in the first calculation does not relate in a meaningful way to the denominator.*

*Since the LIFO values for cost of goods sold on the income statement and the FIFO inventory numbers on the balance sheet are closer to current prices, they are often thought to be the most appropriate numerator and denominator, respectively, for use in this ratio.

INTERNATIONAL PERSPECTIVE

LIFO and International Comparisons

The methods of accounting for inventories discussed in this chapter are used in most major industrialized countries. In several countries, however, the LIFO method is not generally used. In England and Canada, for example, LIFO is not acceptable for tax purposes, nor is it widely used in financial reporting. LIFO is not used in Australia and Singapore, but it may be used in China for both financial reporting and tax purposes. These differences can create comparability problems when one attempts to compare companies across international borders. For example, General Motors and Ford use LIFO to value U.S. inventories and average cost or FIFO for non-U.S. inventories, while Honda (of Japan) uses FIFO for all inventories.

SELF-STUDY QUIZ

1. In a recent year, Caterpillar Inc., a major manufacturer of farm and construction equipment, reported pretax earnings of $1,615 million. Its inventory note indicated "if the FIFO (first-in, first-out) method had been in use, inventories would have been $2,103 and $2,035 higher than reported at the end of the current and prior year, respectively." (The amounts noted are for the LIFO reserve.) Convert pretax earnings for the current year from a LIFO to a FIFO basis.

Caterpillar Inc.

Beginning LIFO Reserve (Excess of FIFO over LIFO)	_____
Less: Ending LIFO Reserve (Excess of FIFO over LIFO)	_____
Difference in cost of goods sold under FIFO	_____
Pretax income (LIFO)	_____
Difference in pretax income under FIFO	_____
Pretax income (FIFO)	_____

After you have completed your answers, check them with the solutions at the bottom of the page.

Self-Study Quiz Solution

1.				
Beginning LIFO Reserve	$2,035	Pretax income (LIFO)	$1,615
Less: Ending LIFO Reserve	2,103	Difference in pretax income	68
Difference in cost of goods sold	($ 68)	Pretax income (FIFO)	$1,683

CONTROL OF INVENTORY

Internal Control of Inventory

After cash, inventory is the asset second most vulnerable to theft. Efficient management of inventory to avoid cost of stock-outs and overstock situations is also crucial to the profitability of most companies. As a consequence, a number of control features focus on safeguarding inventories and providing up-to-date information for management decisions. Key among these are:

1. Separation of responsibilities for inventory accounting and physical handling of inventory.
2. Storage of inventory in a manner that protects it from theft and damage.
3. Limiting access to inventory to authorized employees.
4. Maintaining perpetual inventory records (described below).
5. Comparing perpetual records to periodic physical counts of inventory.

Learning Objective 7
Understand methods for controlling and keeping track of inventory and analyze the effects of inventory errors on financial statements.

Topic Tackler 7–2

Perpetual and Periodic Inventory Systems

The amount of purchases for the period is always accumulated in the accounting system. The amount of cost of goods sold and ending inventory can be determined by using one of two different inventory systems: perpetual or periodic.

Perpetual Inventory System

In a **perpetual inventory system,** a detailed record is maintained for each type of merchandise stocked, showing (1) units and cost of the beginning inventory, (2) units and cost of each purchase, (3) units and cost of the goods for each sale, and (4) units and cost of the goods on hand at any point in time. This up-to-date record is maintained on a transaction-by-transaction basis. In a complete perpetual inventory system, the inventory record gives the amount of both ending inventory and cost of goods sold at any point in time. Under this system, a physical count should also be performed from time to time to ensure that records are accurate in case of errors or theft.

To this point in the text, all journal entries for purchase and sale transactions have been recorded using a perpetual inventory system. In a perpetual inventory system, purchase transactions are recorded directly in an inventory account. When each sale is recorded, a companion cost of goods sold entry is made, decreasing inventory and recording cost of goods sold. As a result, information on cost of goods sold and ending inventory is available on a continuous (perpetual) basis.

Periodic Inventory System

Under the **periodic inventory system,** no up-to-date record of inventory is maintained during the year. An actual physical count of the goods remaining on hand is required at the **end of each period.** The number of units of each type of merchandise on hand is multiplied by their unit cost to compute the dollar amount of the ending inventory. Cost of goods sold is calculated using the cost of goods sold equation.

Because the amount of inventory is not known until the end of the period when the inventory count is taken, the amount of cost of goods sold cannot be reliably determined until the inventory count is complete. Inventory purchases are debited to an account called **Purchases,** which is part of the asset inventory. Revenues are recorded at the time of each sale. However, cost of goods sold is not recorded until after the inventory count is completed. At other times, companies using a periodic system must estimate the amount of inventory on hand. Estimation methods are discussed in intermediate accounting courses.

In a **PERPETUAL INVENTORY SYSTEM,** a detailed inventory record is maintained, recording each purchase and sale during the accounting period.

In a **PERIODIC INVENTORY SYSTEM,** ending inventory and cost of goods sold are determined at the end of the accounting period based on a physical count.

Before affordable computers and bar code readers were available, the primary reason for using a periodic inventory system was its low cost. The primary disadvantage of a periodic inventory system is the lack of inventory information. Managers are not informed about low stock or overstocked situations. Most modern companies could not survive without this information. As noted at the beginning of the chapter, cost and quality pressures brought on by increasing competition, combined with dramatic declines in the cost of computers, have made sophisticated perpetual inventory systems a requirement at all but the smallest companies. The entries made when using both systems are compared in Supplement C at the end of this chapter.

Perpetual Inventory Records and Cost Flow Assumptions in Practice

Systems that do keep track of the costs of individual items or lots normally do so on a FIFO or estimated average (or standard) cost basis. For distinguishable high-value items, specific identification may be used. Perpetual records are rarely kept on a LIFO basis for two reasons: (1) doing so is more complex and costly and (2) it can increase tax payments. LIFO companies convert the outputs of their perpetual inventory system to LIFO with an adjusting entry.

Errors in Measuring Ending Inventory

As the cost of goods sold equation indicates, a direct relationship exists between ending inventory and cost of goods sold because items not in the ending inventory are assumed to have been sold. Thus, the measurement of ending inventory quantities and costs affects both the balance sheet (assets) and the income statement (cost of goods sold, gross profit, and net income). The measurement of ending inventory affects not only the net income for that period but also the net income for the next accounting period. This two-period effect occurs because the ending inventory for one period is the beginning inventory for the next accounting period.

Greeting card maker Gibson Greetings had overstated its net income by 20 percent because one division had overstated ending inventory for the year. You can compute the effects of the error on both the current year's and the next year's income before taxes using the cost of goods sold equation. Assume that ending inventory was overstated by $10,000 due to a clerical error that was not discovered. This would have the following effects in the current year and next year:

	Current Year
Beginning inventory	
+ Purchases of merchandise during the year	
− Ending inventory	**Overstated $10,000**
Cost of goods sold	**Understated $10,000**

	Next Year
Beginning inventory	**Overstated $10,000**
+ Purchases of merchandise during the year	
− Ending inventory	
Cost of goods sold	**Overstated $10,000**

Because cost of goods sold was understated, **income before taxes would be overstated** by $10,000 in the **current year.** And, since the current year's ending inventory becomes next year's beginning inventory, it would have the following effects: Because cost of goods sold was overstated, **income before taxes would be understated** by the same amount in the **next year.**

Each of these errors would flow into retained earnings so that at the end of the current year, retained earnings would be overstated by $10,000 (less the related income tax expense). This error would be offset in the next year, and retained earnings and inventory at the end of next year would be correct.

In this example, we assumed that the overstatement of ending inventory was inadvertent, the result of a clerical error. However, inventory fraud is a common form of financial statement fraud. It occurred in the Maxidrive case discussed in Chapter 1 as well as in the real MiniScribe fraud.

SELF-STUDY QUIZ

Assume that it is now the end of 2008, and for the first time, the company will undergo an audit by an independent CPA. The annual income statement prepared by the company is presented here. Assume further that the independent CPA discovered that the ending inventory for 2008 was understated by $15,000. Correct and reconstruct the income statement in the space provided.

FOR THE YEAR ENDED DECEMBER 31

	2008 UNCORRECTED	2008 CORRECTED
Sales revenue	$750,000	
Cost of goods sold		
Beginning inventory	$ 45,000	
Add purchases	460,000	_____
Goods available for sale	505,000	
Less ending inventory	40,000	_____
Cost of goods sold	465,000	_____
Gross margin on sales	285,000	
Operating expenses	275,000	_____
Pretax income	10,000	
Income tax expense (20%)	2,000	_____
Net income	$ 8,000	_____

After you have completed your answer, check it with the solution at the bottom of the page.

Sales revenue		$750,000
Cost of goods sold		
Beginning inventory	45,000	
Add purchases	460,000	
Goods available for sale	505,000	
Less ending inventory	55,000	
Cost of goods sold		450,000
Gross margin on sales		300,000
Operating expenses		275,000
Pretax income		25,000
Income tax expense (20%)		5,000
Net income		$ 20,000

Self-Study Quiz Solution

Note: An ending inventory error in one year affects pretax income by the amount of the error and in the next year affects pretax income again by the same amount, but in the opposite direction.

DEMONSTRATION **CASE**

(Complete the requirements before proceeding to the suggested solution that follows.) This case reviews the application of the FIFO and LIFO inventory costing methods and the inventory turnover ratio.

Balent Appliances distributes a number of household appliances. One product, microwave ovens, has been selected for case purposes. Assume that the following summarized transactions were completed during the year ended December 31, 2008 in the order given (assume that all transactions are cash):

	Units	Unit Cost
a. Beginning inventory	11	$200
b. New inventory purchases	9	220
c. Sales (selling price, $420)	8	?

Required:

1. Compute the following amounts, assuming the application of the FIFO and LIFO inventory costing methods:

	Ending Inventory		Cost of Goods Sold	
	Units	Dollars	Units	Dollars
FIFO				
LIFO				

2. Assuming that inventory cost was expected to follow current trends, which method would you suggest that Balent select to account for these inventory items? Explain your answer.

3. Assuming that other operating expenses were $500 and the income tax rate is 25 percent, prepare the income statement for the period using your selected method.

4. Compute the inventory turnover ratio for the current period using your selected method. What does it indicate?

SUGGESTED SOLUTION

1.

	Ending Inventory		Cost of Goods Sold	
	Units	Dollars	Units	Dollars
FIFO	12	$2,580	8	$1,600
LIFO	12	$2,420	8	$1,760

Computations

Beginning inventory (11 units × $200)	$2,200
+ Purchases (9 units × $220)	1,980
Goods available for sale	$4,180

FIFO inventory (costed at end of period)

Goods available for sale (from above)	$4,180
− Ending inventory (9 units × $220) + (3 units × $200) =	2,580
Cost of goods sold (8 units × $200)	$1,600

LIFO inventory (costed at end of period)

Goods available for sale (from above)	$4,180
− Ending inventory (11 units × $200) + (1 unit × $220) =	2,420
Cost of goods sold (8 units × $220)	$1,760

2. LIFO should be selected. Because costs are rising, LIFO produces higher cost of goods sold, lower pretax income, and lower income tax payments. It is used on the tax return and income statement because of the LIFO conformity rule.

3.

BALENT APPLIANCES
Statement of Income
Year Ended December 31, 2008

Sales	$3,360
Cost of goods sold	1,760
Gross profit	1,600
Other expenses	500
Income before income taxes	1,100
Income tax expense (25%)	275
Net income	$ 825

Computations
Sales = 8 × $420 = $3,360.

4. Inventory turnover ratio = Cost of Goods Sold ÷ Average Inventory

   = $1,760 ÷ [($2,200 + $2,420) ÷ 2 = $2,310]

   = 0.76

The inventory turnover ratio reflects how many times average inventory was produced and sold during the period. Thus, Balent Appliances produced and sold its average inventory less than one time during the year.

Chapter Supplement A

LIFO Liquidations

When a LIFO company sells more inventory than it purchases or manufactures, items from beginning inventory become part of cost of goods sold. This is called a LIFO liquidation. When inventory costs are rising, these lower cost items in beginning inventory produce a higher gross profit, higher taxable income, and higher taxes when they are sold. We illustrate this process by continuing our Harley-Davidson store Model A leather jacket example into its second year.

A **LIFO LIQUIDATION** is a sale of a lower-cost inventory item from beginning LIFO inventory.

Financial Statement Effects of LIFO Liquidations

Recall that, in its first year of operation, the store purchased units for $70, $80, and $100 in sequence. Then, the $100 unit and three of the $80 units were sold under LIFO, leaving one $80 unit and two $70 units in ending inventory. These events were represented using the LIFO inventory bin in Exhibit 7.5. Exhibit 7.10 on page 367 continues this illustration into a second year. The ending inventory from year

1 becomes the beginning inventory for year 2. In part (a) of Exhibit 7.10, we assume that in year 2, the Harley-Davidson store purchased a total of **three** inventory units at the current $120 price, the sales price has been raised to $140, and three units are sold. Using LIFO, the three recently purchased $120 inventory items become part of cost of goods sold of $360, and the old $80 and $70 items from beginning inventory become ending inventory. Given that revenue is $140 per unit, the gross profit on the three newly purchased units is 3 units × $20 = $60.

Now assume instead, as we do in part (b) of Exhibit 7.10, that the store purchased only *two* additional units at $120 each. Using LIFO, these two new $120 units and the old $80 unit would become cost of goods sold. Given that revenue is $140 per unit, the gross profit on the newly purchased units is 2 units × $20 = $40. Since the cost of the old unit is only $80, the gross profit on this one unit is $60 ($140 − $80) instead of $20, raising total gross profit to $100.

Compared to part (a), cost of goods sold has decreased by $40, and gross profit and income before taxes have increased by $40. This $40 change is the **pretax effect of the LIFO liquidation.** Given the assumed tax rate of 25 percent, taxes paid are $10 (0.25 × $40) higher than in part (a).

In practice, LIFO liquidations and extra tax payments can be avoided even if purchases of additional inventory take place **after** the sale of the item it replaces. Tax law allows LIFO to be applied **as if** all purchases during an accounting period took place before any sales and cost of goods sold were recorded. Thus, temporary LIFO liquidations can be eliminated by purchasing additional inventory before year-end. Most companies apply LIFO in this manner.

LIFO Liquidations and Financial Statement Analysis

During the decade prior to 1993, Deere & Company and other companies in its industry faced declining demand and increasing competition in most major segments of their businesses. These economic changes reduced the inventory quantities necessary to meet customers' needs. Deere had also instituted modern manufacturing techniques that further decreased inventory levels. Deere, a long-time LIFO user, experienced continuing LIFO liquidations over this period. Companies must disclose the effects of LIFO liquidations in the notes when they are material, as Deere did in the note that follows. The second paragraph of the note explains the effect. The last sentence lists the pretax (after-tax) effects of the liquidations.

REAL WORLD EXCERPT

Deere & Company

ANNUAL REPORT

DEERE & COMPANY

NOTES TO CONSOLIDATED FINANCIAL STATEMENTS

INVENTORIES

Substantially all inventories owned by Deere & Company and its United States equipment subsidiaries are valued at cost on the "last-in, first-out" (LIFO) method. . . .

Under the LIFO inventory method, cost of goods sold ordinarily reflects current production costs thus providing a matching of current costs and current revenues in the income statement. However when LIFO-valued inventories decline, as they did in 1993 and 1992, lower costs that prevailed in prior years are matched against current year revenues, resulting in higher reported net income. Benefits from the reduction of LIFO inventories totaled $51 million ($33 million or $0.43 per share after income taxes) in 1993, $65 million ($43 million or $0.56 per share after income taxes) in 1992 and $128 million ($84 million or $1.11 per share after income taxes) in 1991.

According to this note, over the prior three years, LIFO liquidations increased Deere's reported income before taxes by a total of $244 million ($51 + $65 + $128). (These numbers are the equivalent of the $40 effect of the liquidation computed in the Harley-Davidson store example.) To compute pretax income as if the liquidations had not taken place (as if current year's production were large enough so that no items from beginning inventory were sold), simply subtract the LIFO liquidation effect from pretax income.

Pretax income on LIFO for 3 years (reported on the income statements)	$290
Less: Pretax effect of LIFO liquidations (from note)	244
Pretax income on LIFO for 3 years as if no liquidations	$ 46

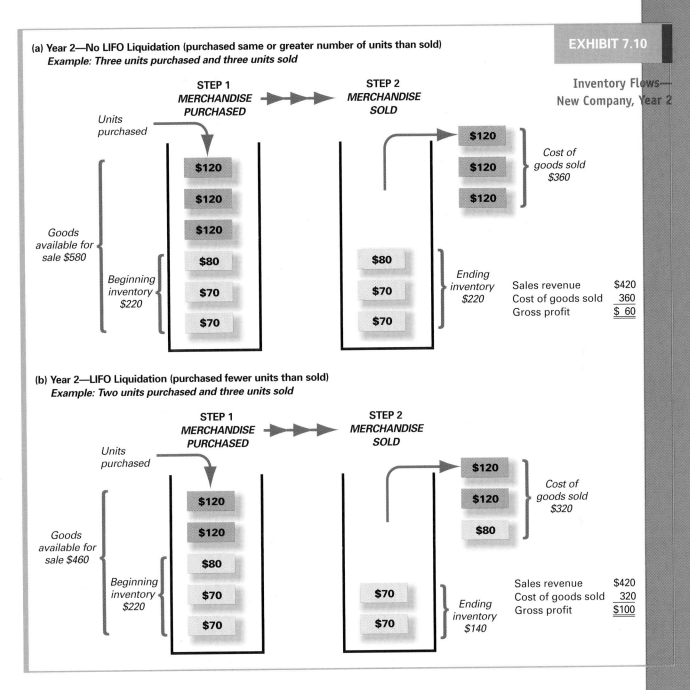

(a) Year 2—No LIFO Liquidation (purchased same or greater number of units than sold)
Example: Three units purchased and three units sold

EXHIBIT 7.10

Inventory Flows—
New Company, Year 2

(b) Year 2—LIFO Liquidation (purchased fewer units than sold)
Example: Two units purchased and three units sold

Fully 84 percent ($244 ÷ $290) of Deere's reported pretax profit over the three years resulted from LIFO liquidations. Since the $46 million pretax profit figure reflected Deere's current costs of production, educated analysts used it when comparing Deere's performance to that of other LIFO companies. It is important to emphasize that these numbers still are on a **LIFO** basis but are computed **as if no liquidation had taken place.**

Inventory Management and LIFO Liquidations

FINANCIAL
ANALYSIS

Several research studies* have documented the year-end inventory purchasing decisions of firms that use LIFO. Many firms avoid LIFO liquidations and the accompanying increase in tax expense by purchasing sufficient quantities of inventory at year-end to ensure that ending inventory quantities are greater than or equal to beginning inventory quantities. While this practice increases the costs of carrying inventory (storage, financing, etc.), for these firms, the taxes saved exceed these amounts.

As noted earlier in the chapter, Harley-Davidson and many other firms have moved to more efficient just-in-time inventory techniques that greatly reduce the amount of inventory manufacturers keep on hand. When managers compare the savings in carrying costs against the costs of implementing the new system (new computers, training, etc.), they must also consider the added taxes they may pay if they account for the inventory using the LIFO method. When the company switches to the new just-in-time system, ending inventory quantity will normally decline below beginning inventory quantity, causing a LIFO liquidation and a one-time increase in taxes. This cost should be considered when deciding whether to adopt the new system. In this case, the tax law provides an incentive for U.S. companies not to become more efficient.

*See, for example, R. Jennings, P.J. Simko, and R.B.I. Thompson. 1996. "Does LIFO Inventory Accounting Improve the Income Statement at the Expense of the Balance Sheet?" *Journal of Accounting Research* 34 (1): 85–110.

Chapter Supplement B

Additional Issues in Measuring Purchases

Purchase Returns and Allowances

PURCHASE RETURNS AND ALLOWANCES are a reduction in the cost of purchases associated with unsatisfactory goods.

Purchased goods may be returned to the vendor if they do not meet specifications, arrive in damaged condition, or are otherwise unsatisfactory. Purchase returns and allowances require a reduction in the cost of inventory purchases and the recording of a cash refund or a reduction in the liability to the vendor. For example, assume that Harley-Davidson returned to a supplier damaged harness boots that cost $1,000. The return would be recorded as follows:

Accounts payable (−L) (or Cash +A)	1,000	
Inventory (−A)		1,000

Assets	=	Liabilities	+	Stockholders' Equity
Inventory −1,000		Accounts Payable −1,000		

Purchase Discounts

A **PURCHASE DISCOUNT** is a cash discount received for prompt payment of an account.

Cash discounts must be accounted for by both the seller and the buyer (accounting by the seller was discussed in Chapter 6). When merchandise is bought on credit, terms such as 2/10, n/30 are sometimes specified. That is, if payment is made within 10 days from the date of purchase, a 2 percent cash discount known as the purchase discount is granted. If payment is not made within the discount period, the full invoice cost is due 30 days after the purchase.

Assume that on January 17, Harley-Davidson bought goods that had a $1,000 invoice price with terms 2/10, n/30. The purchase should be recorded as follows (using what is called the **gross method**):

Date of Purchase

Jan. 17 Inventory (+A)	1,000	
Accounts payable (+L)		1,000

Assets	=	Liabilities	+	Stockholders' Equity
Inventory +1,000		Accounts Payable +1,000		

Date of Payment, within the Discount Period

Jan. 26 Accounts payable (−L)	1,000	
Inventory (−A)		20
Cash (−A)		980

Assets		=	Liabilities		+	Stockholders' Equity
Inventory	−20		Accounts Payable	−1,000		
Cash	−980					

If for any reason Harley-Davidson did not pay within the 10-day discount period, the following entry would be needed:

Date of Payment, after the Discount Period

Feb. 1 Accounts payable (−L) 1,000

Cash (−A) 1,000

Assets		=	Liabilities		+	Stockholders' Equity
Cash	−1,000		Accounts Payable	−1,000		

Chapter Supplement C

Comparison of Perpetual and Periodic Inventory Systems

To simplify the discussion of how accounting systems keep track of these amounts, we will focus this discussion on the Motorclothes™ line for which Harley-Davidson is a wholesaler. Assume, for this illustration only, that Harley-Davidson stocks and sells only one item, its Eagle Harness Boots, and that only the following events occurred in 2008:

Jan. 1 Had beginning inventory: 800 units, at unit cost of $50.

April 14 Purchased: 1,100 additional units, at unit cost of $50.

Nov. 30 Sold: 1,300 units, at unit sales price of $83.

In the two types of inventory systems, the following sequential steps would take place:

Perpetual Records	**Periodic Records**
1. Record all purchases in the Inventory account and in a detailed perpetual inventory record.	1. Record all purchases in an account called Purchases.

April 14, 2008
 	
Inventory (+A) (1,100 units at $50)* 55,000
 	
  Accounts payable (+L) (or Cash−A).... 55,000
 	
*Also entered in the detailed perpetual inventory record as 1,100 harness boots at $50 each.
	April 14, 2008
	
	Purchases (+A) (1,100 units at $50) 55,000
	
	  Accounts payable (+L) (or Cash−A).... 55,000

2. Record all sales in the Sales Revenue account and record the cost of goods sold.	2. Record all sales in a Sales Revenue account.

November 30, 2008
 	
Accounts receivable (+A) (or Cash+A) ... 107,900
 	
  Sales revenue (+R, +SE)
  (1,300 units at $83) 107,900
 	
Cost of goods sold (+E, −SE)........... 65,000
 	
  Inventory (−A) (1,300 units at $50)*..... 65,000
 	
*Also entered in the perpetual inventory record as a reduction of 1,300 units at $50 each.
	November 30, 2008
	
	Accounts receivable (+A) (or Cash+A) ... 107,900
	
	  Sales revenue (+R, +SE)
	  (1,300 units at $83) 107,900

Perpetual Records	Periodic Records

3. Use cost of goods sold and inventory amounts. At the end of the accounting period, the balance in the Cost of Goods Sold account is reported on the income statement. It is not necessary to compute cost of goods sold because the Cost of Goods Sold account is up-to-date. Also, the Inventory account shows the ending inventory amount reported on the balance sheet. A physical inventory count is still necessary to assess the accuracy of the perpetual records and identify theft and other forms of misuse (called *shrinkage*).	3. At end of period:
	  a. Count the number of units on hand.
	  b. Compute the dollar valuation of the ending inventory.
	  c. Compute and record the cost of goods sold.

Periodic Records

Beginning inventory (last period's ending)	$40,000
Add purchases (balance in the Purchases account)	55,000
Goods available for sale	95,000
Deduct ending inventory (physical count—600 units at $50)	30,000
Cost of goods sold	$65,000

December 31, 2008

Transfer beginning inventory and purchases to cost of goods sold:

Cost of goods sold (+E, −SE)	95,000	
Inventory (−A) (beginning)		40,000
Purchases (−A).....................		55,000

Subtract the ending inventory amount from the cost of goods sold to complete its computation and establish the ending inventory balance:

Inventory (+A) (ending)	30,000	
Cost of goods sold (−E, +SE)..........		30,000

Perpetual Records — No entry

Assets		=	Liabilities		+	Stockholders' Equity	
Inventory	+55,000		Accounts Payable	+55,000		Sales Revenue	+107,900
Accts. Rec.	+107,900					Cost of Goods Sold	−65,000
Inventory	−65,000						

Assets		=	Liabilities		+	Stockholders' Equity	
Purchases	+55,000		Accounts Payable	+55,000		Sales Revenue	+107,900
Accts. Rec.	+107,900					Cost of Goods Sold	−95,000
Inventory	−40,000					Cost of Goods Sold	+30,000
Purchases	−55,000						
Inventory	+30,000						

Note that the effects of the entries on the accounting equation are the same under both systems. Only the timing of the recording of amounts changes.

CHAPTER TAKE-AWAYS

1. **Apply the cost principle to identify the amounts that should be included in inventory and the matching principle to determine cost of goods sold for typical retailers, wholesalers, and manufacturers.   p. 340**

   Inventory should include all items owned that are held for resale. Costs flow into inventory when goods are purchased or manufactured. They flow out (as an expense) when they are sold or disposed of. In conformity with the matching principle, the total cost of the goods sold during the period must be matched with the sales revenue earned during the period.

2. **Report inventory and cost of goods sold using the four inventory costing methods.   p. 345**

   The chapter discussed four different inventory costing methods used to allocate costs between the units remaining in inventory and the units sold, and their applications in different economic circumstances. The methods discussed were FIFO, LIFO, weighted average cost, and specific identification. Each of the inventory costing methods conforms with GAAP. Public companies using LIFO must provide note disclosures that allow conversion of inventory and cost of goods sold to FIFO amounts. Remember that the cost flow assumption need not match the physical flow of inventory.

3. **Decide when the use of different inventory costing methods is beneficial to a company.** p. 350

The selection of an inventory costing method is important because it will affect reported income, income tax expense (and hence cash flow), and the inventory valuation reported on the balance sheet. In a period of rising prices, FIFO normally results in a higher income and higher taxes than LIFO; in a period of falling prices, the opposite occurs. The choice of methods is normally made to minimize taxes.

4. **Report inventory at the lower of cost or market (LCM).** p. 353

Ending inventory should be measured based on the lower of actual cost or replacement cost (LCM basis). This practice can have a major effect on the statements of companies facing declining costs. Damaged, obsolete, and out-of-season inventory should also be written down to their current estimated net realizable value if below cost. The LCM adjustment increases cost of goods sold, decreases income, and decreases reported inventory in the year of the write-down.

5. **Evaluate inventory management using the inventory turnover ratio and the effects of inventory on cash flows.** p. 354

The inventory turnover ratio measures the efficiency of inventory management. It reflects how many times average inventory was produced and sold during the period. Analysts and creditors watch this ratio because a sudden decline may mean that a company is facing an unexpected drop in demand for its products or is becoming sloppy in its production management. When a net *decrease in inventory* for the period occurs, sales are more than purchases; thus, the decrease must be *added* in computing cash flows from operations. When a net *increase in inventory* for the period occurs, sales are less than purchases; thus, the increase must be *subtracted* in computing cash flows from operations.

6. **Compare companies that use different inventory costing methods.** p. 358

These comparisons can be made by converting the LIFO company's statements to FIFO. Public companies using LIFO must disclose the differences between LIFO and FIFO values for beginning and ending inventory. These amounts are often called the LIFO reserve. The beginning LIFO reserve minus the ending LIFO reserve equals the difference in cost of goods sold under FIFO. Pretax income is affected by the same amount in the opposite direction. This amount times the tax rate is the tax effect.

7. **Understand methods for controlling and keeping track of inventory and analyze the effects of inventory errors on financial statements.** p. 361

Various control procedures can limit inventory theft or mismanagement. A company can keep track of the ending inventory and cost of goods sold for the period using (1) the perpetual inventory system, which is based on the maintenance of detailed and continuous inventory records, and (2) the periodic inventory system, which is based on a physical count of ending inventory and use of the inventory equation to determine cost of goods sold. An error in the measurement of ending inventory affects cost of goods sold on the current period's income statement and ending inventory on the balance sheet. Because this year's ending inventory becomes next year's beginning inventory, it also affects cost of goods sold in the following period by the same amount but in the opposite direction. These relationships can be seen through the cost of goods sold equation (BI + P − EI = CGS).

In this and previous chapters, we discussed the current assets of a business. These assets are critical to operations, but many of them do not directly produce value. In Chapter 8, we will discuss the noncurrent assets property, plant, and equipment; natural resources; and intangibles that are the elements of productive capacity. Many of the noncurrent assets produce value, such as a factory that manufactures cars. These assets present some interesting accounting problems because they benefit a number of accounting periods.

KEY **RATIO**

Inventory turnover ratio measures the efficiency of inventory management. It reflects how many times average inventory was produced and sold during the period. (p. 354):

$$\text{Inventory Turnover} = \frac{\text{Cost of Goods Sold}}{\text{Average Inventory}}$$

FINDING **FINANCIAL INFORMATION**

Balance Sheet

Under Current Assets
Inventories

Income Statement

Expenses
Cost of goods sold

Statement of Cash Flows

*Under Operating Activities
(indirect method):*
Net income
− increases in inventory
+ decreases in inventory
+ increases in accounts payable
− decreases in accounts payable

Notes

*Under Summary of Significant Accounting
   Policies:*
Description of management's choice of
   inventory accounting policy (FIFO, LIFO,
   LCM, etc.)

In Separate Note
If not listed on balance sheet, components of
   inventory (merchandise, raw materials,
   work in progress, finished goods)
If using LIFO, LIFO reserve (excess of FIFO
   over LIFO)

KEY **TERMS**

Average Cost Method   p. 348
Cost of Goods Sold
   Equation   p. 343
Direct Labor   p. 342
Factory Overhead   p. 342
Finished Goods Inventory   p. 340
First-In, First-Out (FIFO)
   Method   p. 346
Goods Available for Sale   p. 343
Inventory   p. 340

Last-In, First-Out (LIFO) Method
   p. 348
LIFO Liquidation   p. 365
LIFO Reserve   p. 358
Lower of Cost or Market
   (LCM)   p. 353
Merchandise Inventory   p. 340
Net Realizable Value   p. 353
Periodic Inventory System   p. 361
Perpetual Inventory System   p. 361

Purchase Discount   p. 368
Purchase Returns and
   Allowances   p. 368
Raw Materials Inventory   p. 340
Replacement Cost   p. 353
Specific Identification
   Method   p. 345
Work in Process Inventory   p. 340

QUESTIONS

1. Why is inventory an important item to both internal (management) and external users of financial statements?
2. What are the general guidelines for deciding which items should be included in inventory?
3. Explain the application of the cost principle to an item in the ending inventory.

4. Define *goods available for sale.* How does it differ from cost of goods sold?
5. Define *beginning inventory* and *ending inventory.*
6. The chapter discussed four inventory costing methods. List the four methods and briefly explain each.
7. Explain how income can be manipulated when the specific identification inventory costing method is used.
8. Contrast the effects of LIFO versus FIFO on reported assets (i.e., the ending inventory) when (a) prices are rising and (b) prices are falling.
9. Contrast the income statement effect of LIFO versus FIFO (i.e., on pretax income) when (a) prices are rising and (b) prices are falling.
10. Contrast the effects of LIFO versus FIFO on cash outflow and inflow.
11. Explain briefly the application of the LCM concept to the ending inventory and its effect on the income statement and balance sheet when market is lower than cost.
12. When a perpetual inventory system is used, unit costs of the items sold are known at the date of each sale. In contrast, when a periodic inventory system is used, unit costs are known only at the end of the accounting period. Why are these statements correct?

MULTIPLE-**CHOICE QUESTIONS**

1. Which of the following statements are true regarding *Cost of Goods Sold?*
   1. Cost of goods sold represents the cost that a company incurred to purchase or produce inventory in the current period.
   2. Cost of goods sold is an expense on the income statement.
   3. Cost of goods sold is affected by the inventory method selected by a company (FIFO, LIFO, etc.).

   a. 2   c. 2 and 3
   b. 3   d. all three

2. The inventory costing method selected by a company will affect
   a. the balance sheet.   c. the statement of retained earnings.
   b. the income statement.   d. all of the above.

3. Which of the following is *not* a component of the cost of inventory?
   a. administrative overhead   c. raw materials
   b. direct labor   d. factory overhead

4. Each period, the cost of goods available for sale is allocated between
   a. assets and liabilities.   c. assets and revenues.
   b. assets and expenses.   d. expenses and liabilities.

5. A New York bridal dress designer who makes high-end custom wedding dresses most likely uses which inventory costing method?
   a. FIFO   c. Weighted average
   b. LIFO   d. Specific identification

6. An increasing inventory turnover ratio
   a. indicates a longer time span between the ordering and receiving of inventory.
   b. indicates a shorter time span between the ordering and receiving of inventory.
   c. indicates a shorter time span between the purchase and sale of inventory.
   d. indicates a longer time span between the purchase and sale of inventory.

7. If the ending balance in accounts payable decreases from one period to the next, which of the following is true?
   a. Cash payments to suppliers exceeded current period purchases.
   b. Cash payments to suppliers were less than current period purchases.
   c. Cash receipts from customers exceeded cash payments to suppliers.
   d. Cash receipts from customers exceeded current period purchases.

8. Which of the following regarding the *lower of cost or market rule* for inventory are true?
   1. The lower of cost or market rule is an example of the historical cost principle.
   2. When the replacement cost of inventory drops below the cost shown in the financial records, net income is reduced.

3. When the replacement cost of inventory drops below the cost shown in the financial records, total assets are reduced.
   a. 1
   b. 2
   c. 2 and 3
   d. all three

9. Which inventory method provides a better matching of current costs with sales revenue on the income statement and outdated values for inventory on the balance sheet?
   a. FIFO
   b. weighted average
   c. LIFO
   d. specific identification

10. Which of the following is false regarding a perpetual inventory system?
    a. Physical counts are not needed since records are maintained on a transaction-by-transaction basis.
    b. The balance in the inventory account is updated with each inventory purchase and sale transaction.
    c. Cost of goods sold is increased as sales are recorded
    d. The account Purchases is not used as inventory is acquired.

For more practice on multiple-choice questions, go to the text website www.mhhe.com/libby5e or the Topic Tackler DVD for use with this text.

MINI-EXERCISES

 Available with McGraw-Hill's Homework Manager

M7-1
L01

Matching Inventory Items to Type of Business

Match the type of inventory with the type of business in the following matrix:

	TYPE OF BUSINESS	
Type of Inventory	Merchandising	Manufacturing
Merchandise		
Finished goods		
Work in process		
Raw materials		

M7-2
L01

Recording the Cost of Purchases for a Merchandiser

Elite Apparel purchased 80 new shirts and recorded a total cost of $3,140 determined as follows:

Invoice cost	$2,600
Shipping charges	165
Import taxes and duties	115
Interest (10%) on $2,600 borrowed to finance the purchase	260
	$3,140

Required:
Make the needed corrections in this calculation. Give the journal entry(ies) to record this purchase in the correct amount, assuming a perpetual inventory system. Show computations.

M7-3
L01

Identifying the Cost of Inventories for a Manufacturer

Operating costs incurred by a manufacturing company become either (*a*) part of the cost of inventory to be expensed as cost of goods sold at the time the finished goods are sold or (*b*) expenses at the time they are incurred. Indicate whether each of the following costs belongs in category *a.* or *b.*

	a. Part of Inventory	b. Expense as Incurred
1. Wages of factory workers		
2. Sales salaries		
3. Costs of raw materials purchased		
4. Heat, light, and power for the factory building		
5. Heat, light, and power for the headquarters office building		

Inferring Purchases Using the Cost of Goods Sold Equation

M7-4
LO1
JCPenney

JCPenney Company, Inc., is a major retailer with department stores in all 50 states. The dominant portion of the company's business consists of providing merchandise and services to consumers through department stores that include catalog departments. In a recent annual report, JCPenney reported cost of goods sold of $10,969 million, ending inventory for the current year of $3,062 million, and ending inventory for the previous year of $2,969 million.

Required:
Is it possible to develop a reasonable estimate of the merchandise purchases for the year? If so, prepare the estimate; if not, explain why.

Matching Financial Statement Effects to Inventory Costing Methods

M7-5
LO2

Indicate whether the FIFO or LIFO inventory costing method normally produces each of the following effects under the listed circumstances.

a. Rising costs
    Highest net income _____
    Highest inventory _____
b. Declining costs
    Highest net income _____
    Highest inventory _____

Matching Inventory Costing Method Choices to Company Circumstances

M7-6
LO3

Indicate whether the FIFO or LIFO inventory costing method would normally be selected under each of the listed circumstances.

a. Rising costs _____
b. Declining costs _____

Reporting Inventory Under Lower of Cost or Market

M7-7
LO4

Kinney Company had the following inventory items on hand at the end of the year.

	Quantity	Cost per Item	Replacement Cost per Item
Item A	50	$75	$100
Item B	25	60	50

Computing the lower of cost or market on an item-by-item basis, determine what amount would be reported on the balance sheet for inventory.

Determining the Effects of Inventory Management Changes on Inventory Turnover Ratio

M7-8
LO5

Indicate the most likely effect of the following changes in inventory management on the inventory turnover ratio (+ for increase, − for decrease, and NE for no effect).

_____ *a.* Parts inventory delivered daily by suppliers instead of weekly.
_____ *b.* Shorten production process from 10 days to 8 days.
_____ *c.* Extend payments for inventory purchases from 15 days to 30 days.

M7-9 **Determining the Financial Statement Effects of Inventory Errors**

LO7

Assume the 2006 ending inventory was understated by $100,000. Explain how this error would affect the 2006 and 2007 pretax income amounts. What would be the effects if the 2006 ending inventory were overstated by $100,000 instead of understated?

EXERCISES **Available with McGraw-Hill's Homework Manager**

E7-1 **Analyzing Items to Be Included in Inventory**

LO1

Based on its physical count of inventory in its warehouse at year-end, December 31, 2007, Austin Company planned to report inventory of $50,000. During the audit, the independent CPA developed the following additional information:

a. Goods from a supplier costing $300 are in transit with UPS on December 31, 2007. The terms are FOB shipping point (explained in the "Required" section). Because these goods had not arrived, they were excluded from the physical inventory count.

b. Austin delivered samples costing $400 to a customer on December 27, 2007, with the understanding that they would be returned to Austin on January 15, 2008. Because these goods were not on hand, they were excluded from the inventory count.

c. On December 31, 2007, goods in transit to customers, with terms FOB shipping point, amounted to $2,000 (expected delivery date January 10, 2008). Because the goods had been shipped, they were excluded from the physical inventory count.

d. On December 31, 2007, goods in transit to customers, with terms FOB destination, amounted to $1,000 (expected delivery date January 10, 2008). Because the goods had been shipped, they were excluded from the physical inventory count.

Required:

Austin's accounting policy requires including in inventory all goods for which it has title. Note that the point where title (ownership) changes hands is determined by the shipping terms in the sales contract. When goods are shipped "F.O.B. shipping point," title changes hands at shipment and the buyer normally pays for shipping. When they are shipped "F.O.B. destination," title changes hands on delivery, and the seller normally pays for shipping. Begin with the $50,000 inventory amount and compute the correct amount for the ending inventory. Explain the basis for your treatment of each of the preceding items. (*Hint:* Set up three columns: Item, Amount, and Explanation.)

E7-2 **Inferring Missing Amounts Based on Income Statement Relationships**

LO1

Supply the missing dollar amounts for the 2006 income statement of Travis Company for each of the following independent cases (*Hint:* In case B, work from the bottom up.):

	Case A		Case B		Case C	
Net sales revenue		7,950		?		5,920
Beginning inventory	11,000		6,500		4,000	
Purchases	5,000		?		9,420	
Goods available for sale	?		15,270		13,420	
Ending inventory	10,250		11,220		?	
Cost of goods sold		?		?		5,400
Gross profit		?		1,450		?
Expenses		1,300		?		520
Pretax income		$ 900		$(500)		$ 0

E7-3 **Inferring Missing Amounts Based on Income Statement Relationships**

LO1

Supply the missing dollar amounts for the 2004 income statement of Lewis Retailers for each of the following independent cases:

Cases	Sales Revenue	Beginning Inventory	Purchases	Total Available	Ending Inventory	Cost of Goods Sold	Gross Profit	Expenses	Pretax Income or (Loss)
A	$ 650	$100	$700	$?	$500	$?	$?	$200	$?
B	900	200	800	?	?	?	?	150	0
C	?	150	?	?	300	200	400	100	?
D	800	?	600	?	250	?	?	250	100
E	1,000	?	900	1,100	?	?	500	?	(50)

Inferring Merchandise Purchases

American Eagle Outfitters is a leading lifestyle retailer that designs, markets, and sells its own brand of casual clothing for 15- to 25-year-olds. Assume that you are employed as a stock analyst and your boss has just completed a review of the new American Eagle annual report. She provided you with her notes, but they are missing some information that you need. Her notes show that the ending inventory for American Eagle in the current year was $120,586,000 and in the previous year was $124,708,000. Net sales for the current year were $1,519,968,000. Cost of goods sold was $965,716,000. Net income was $60,000,000. For your analysis, you determine that you need to know the amount of purchases for the year.

E7-4
LO1
AMERICAN EAGLE
OUTFITTERS
ae.com

Required:
Can you develop the information from her notes? Explain and show calculations. (*Hint:* Use the cost of goods sold equation or the inventory T-account to solve for the needed value.)

Calculating Ending Inventory and Cost of Goods Sold Under FIFO, LIFO, and Weighted Average

E7-5
LO2

Solar Company uses a periodic inventory system. At the end of the annual accounting period, December 31, 2007, the accounting records provided the following information for product 1:

	Units	Unit Cost
Inventory, December 31, 2006	2,000	$ 6
For the year 2007:		
Purchase, March 21	5,000	9
Purchase, August 1	3,000	10
Inventory, December 31, 2007	4,000	

Required:
Compute ending inventory and cost of goods sold under FIFO, LIFO, and weighted average costing methods. (*Hint:* Set up adjacent columns for each case.)

Calculating Ending Inventory and Cost of Goods Sold Under FIFO, LIFO, and Weighted Average

E7-6
LO2

Clor Company uses a periodic inventory system. At the end of the annual accounting period, December 31, 2007, the accounting records provided the following information for product 1:

	Units	Unit Cost
Inventory, December 31, 2006	3,000	$8
For the year 2007:		
Purchase, March 21	5,000	9
Purchase, August 1	2,000	7
Inventory, December 31, 2007	4,000	

Required:
Compute ending inventory and cost of goods sold under FIFO, LIFO, and weighted average costing methods. (*Hint:* Set up adjacent columns for each case.)

E7-7

LO2, 3

Analyzing and Interpreting the Financial Statement Effects of LIFO and FIFO

Lunar company uses a periodic inventory system. At the end of the annual accounting period, December 31, 2007, the accounting records provided the following information for product 2:

	Units	Unit Cost
Inventory, December 31, 2006	3,000	$12
For the year 2007:		
Purchase, April 11	9,000	10
Purchase, June 1	8,000	13
Sales ($40 each)	11,000	
Operating expenses (excluding income tax expense), $195,000		

Required:

1. Prepare a separate income statement through pretax income that details cost of goods sold for
   a. Case A: FIFO.
   b. Case B: LIFO.
   For each case, show the computation of the ending inventory. (*Hint:* Set up adjacent columns for each case.)
2. Compare the pretax income and the ending inventory amounts between the two cases. Explain the similarities and differences.
3. Which inventory costing method may be preferred for income tax purposes? Explain.

E7-8

LO2, 3

Analyzing and Interpreting the Financial Statement Effects of LIFO and FIFO

Scoresby Inc. uses a periodic inventory system. At the end of the annual accounting period, December 31, 2009, the accounting records provided the following information for product 2:

	Units	Unit Cost
Inventory, December 31, 2008	7,000	$ 8
For the year 2009:		
Purchase, March 5	19,000	9
Purchase, September 19	10,000	11
Sale ($29 each)	8,000	
Sale ($31 each)	16,000	
Operating expenses (excluding income tax expense), $500,000		

Required:

1. Prepare a separate income statement through pretax income that details cost of goods sold for Cases A and B. For each case, show the computation of the ending inventory. (*Hint:* Set up adjacent columns for each case.)
   a. Case A: FIFO.
   b. Case B: LIFO.
2. Compare the pretax income and the ending inventory amounts between the two cases. Explain the similarities and differences.
3. Which inventory costing method may be preferred for income tax purposes? Explain.

E7-9

LO2, 3

Evaluating the Choice among Three Alternative Inventory Methods Based on Income and Cash Flow Effects

Courtney Company uses a periodic inventory system. Data for 2007: beginning merchandise inventory (December 31, 2006), 2,000 units at $35; purchases, 8,000 units at $38; expenses (excluding income taxes), $142,000; ending inventory per physical count at December 31, 2007, 1,800 units; sales 8,200 units; sales price per unit, $70; and average income tax rate, 30 percent.

Required:

1. Prepare income statements under the FIFO, LIFO, and weighted average costing methods. Use a format similar to the following:

Income Statement	Units	FIFO	LIFO	Weighted Average
		INVENTORY COSTING METHOD		
Sales revenue	_____	$_____	$_____	$_____
Cost of goods sold				
Beginning inventory	_____	_____	_____	_____
Purchases	_____	_____	_____	_____
Goods available for sale	_____	_____	_____	_____
Ending inventory	_____	_____	_____	_____
Cost of goods sold	_____	_____	_____	_____
Gross profit		_____	_____	_____
Expenses		_____	_____	_____
Pretax income		_____	_____	_____
Income tax expense		_____	_____	_____
Net income		_____	_____	_____

2. Between FIFO and LIFO, which method is preferable in terms of (a) net income and (b) income taxes paid (cash flow)? Explain.
3. What would your answer to requirement 2 be, assuming that prices were falling? Explain.

Evaluating the Choice Among Three Alternative Inventory Methods Based on Cash Flow Effects

E7-10
LO2, 3

Following is partial information for the income statement of Timber Company under three different inventory costing methods, assuming the use of a periodic inventory system:

	FIFO	LIFO	Weighted Average
Cost of goods sold			
Beginning inventory (340 units)	$11,220	$11,220	$11,220
Purchases (475 units)	17,100	17,100	17,100
Goods available for sale			
Ending inventory (510 units)	_____	_____	_____
Cost of goods sold	_____	_____	_____
Sales, 305 units; unit sales price, $50			
Expenses, $1,600			

Required:

1. Compute cost of goods sold under the FIFO, LIFO, and weighted average inventory costing methods.
2. Prepare an income statement through pretax income for each method.
3. Rank the three methods in order of income taxes paid (favorable cash flow) and explain the basis for your ranking.

Reporting Inventory at Lower of Cost or Market

E7-11
LO4

Peterson Company is preparing the annual financial statements dated December 31, 2007. Ending inventory information about the five major items stocked for regular sale follows:

		ENDING INVENTORY, 2007	
Item	Quantity on Hand	Unit Cost When Acquired (FIFO)	Replacement Cost (Market) at Year-End
A	50	$15	$12
B	75	40	40
C	10	50	52
D	30	30	30
E	400	8	6

Required:

Compute the valuation that should be used for the 2007 ending inventory using the LCM rule applied on an item-by-item basis. (*Hint:* Set up columns for Item, Quantity, Total Cost, Total Market, and LCM Valuation.)

E7-12
LO4

Reporting Inventory at Lower of Cost or Market

Demski Company was formed on January 1, 2007 and is preparing the annual financial statements dated December 31, 2007. Ending inventory information about the four major items stocked for regular sale follows:

		ENDING INVENTORY, 2007	
Item	Quantity on Hand	Unit Cost When Acquired (FIFO)	Replacement Cost (Market) at Year-End
A	20	$12	$13
B	75	40	38
C	35	55	52
D	10	30	35

Required:

1. Compute the valuation that should be used for the 2007 ending inventory using the LCM rule applied on an item-by-item basis. (*Hint:* Set up columns for Item, Quantity, Total Cost, Total Market, and LCM Valuation.)
2. What will be the effect of the write-down of inventory to lower of cost or market on cost of goods sold for the year ended December 31, 2007?

E7-13
LO5

Dell Computer

Analyzing and Interpreting the Inventory Turnover Ratio

Dell Computer is the leading manufacturer of personal computers. In a recent year, it reported the following in dollars in millions:

Net sales revenue	$41,444
Cost of sales	33,892
Beginning inventory	306
Ending inventory	327

Required:

1. Determine the inventory turnover ratio and average days to sell inventory for the current year.
2. Explain the meaning of each number.

E7-14
LO5, 6

Analyzing and Interpreting the Effects of the LIFO/FIFO Choice on Inventory Turnover Ratio

The records at the end of January 2007 for All Star Company showed the following for a particular kind of merchandise:

Inventory, December 31, 2006 at FIFO 19 Units @ $14 = $266
Inventory, December 31, 2006 at LIFO 19 Units @ $10 = $190

Transactions	Units	Unit Cost	Total Cost
Purchase, January 9, 2007	25	$15	$375
Purchase, January 20, 2007	50	16	800
Sale, January 11, 2007 (at $38 per unit)	40		
Sale, January 27, 2007 (at $39 per unit)	28		

Required:
Compute the inventory turnover ratio under the FIFO and LIFO inventory costing methods (show computations and round to the nearest dollar). Explain which you believe is the more accurate indicator of the efficiency of inventory management.

Interpreting the Effect of Changes in Inventories and Accounts Payable on Cash Flow from Operations

First Team Sports, Inc., is engaged in the manufacture (through independent contractors) and distribution of in-line roller skates, ice skates, street hockey equipment, and related accessory products. Its recent annual report included the following on its balance sheet:

E7-15
LO5
First Team Sports, Inc.

CONSOLIDATED BALANCE SHEETS

	Current Year	Previous Year
. . .		
Inventory (Note 3)	22,813,850	20,838,171
. . .		
Trade accounts payable	9,462,883	9,015,376

Required:
Explain the effects of the changes in inventory and trade accounts payable on cash flow from operating activities for the current year.

Analyzing Notes to Adjust Inventory from LIFO to FIFO

The following note was contained in a recent Ford Motor Company annual report:

E7-16
LO6
Ford Motor Company

NOTE 5. INVENTORIES—AUTOMOTIVE SECTOR
Inventories at December 31 were as follows (dollars in millions)

	Current Year	Previous Year
Raw material, work in process, & supplies	$ 3,842	$3,174
Finished products	6,335	4,760
Total inventories at FIFO	10,177	7,934
Less LIFO Adjustment	(996)	(957)
Total	$ 9,181	$6,977

About one-third of inventories were determined under the last-in, first-out method.

Required:

1. What amount of ending inventory would have been reported in the current year if Ford had used only FIFO?
2. The cost of goods sold reported by Ford for the current year was $129,821 million. Determine the cost of goods sold that would have been reported if Ford had used only FIFO for both years.
3. Explain why Ford management chose to use LIFO for certain of its inventories.

E7-17
LO7

Analyzing the Effects of an Error in Recording Purchases

Garraway Ski Company mistakenly recorded purchases of inventory on account received during the last week of December 2006 as purchases during January of 2007 (this is called a *purchases cutoff error*). Garraway uses a periodic inventory system, and ending inventory was correctly counted and reported each year. Assuming that no correction was made in 2006 or 2007, indicate whether each of the following financial statement amounts will be understated, overstated, or correct.

1. Net Income for 2006.
2. Net Income for 2007.
3. Retained Earnings for December 31, 2006.
4. Retained Earnings for December 31, 2007.

E7-18
LO7

Gibson Greeting
Cards

Analyzing the Effect of an Inventory Error Disclosed in an Actual Note to a Financial Statement

Several years ago, the financial statements of Gibson Greeting Cards contained the following note:

> On July 1, the Company announced that it had determined that the inventory . . . had been overstated. . . . The overstatement of inventory . . . was $8,806,000.

Gibson reported an incorrect net income amount of $25,852,000 for the year in which the error occurred and the income tax rate was 39.3 percent.

Required:

1. Compute the amount of net income that Gibson reported after correcting the inventory error. Show computations.
2. Assume that the inventory error was not discovered. Identify the financial statement accounts that would have been incorrect for the year the error occurred and for the subsequent year. State whether each account was understated or overstated.

E7-19
LO7

Analyzing and Interpreting the Impact of an Inventory Error

Dallas Corporation prepared the following two income statements (simplified for illustrative purposes):

	First Quarter 2007		Second Quarter 2007	
Sales revenue		$15,000		$18,000
Cost of goods sold				
Beginning inventory	$ 3,000		$ 4,000	
Purchases	7,000		12,000	
Goods available for sale	10,000		16,000	
Ending inventory	4,000		9,000	
Cost of goods sold		6,000		7,000
Gross profit		9,000		11,000
Expenses		5,000		6,000
Pretax income		$ 4,000		$ 5,000

During the third quarter, it was discovered that the ending inventory for the first quarter should have been $4,400.

Required:

1. What effect did this error have on the combined pretax income of the two quarters? Explain.
2. Did this error affect the EPS amounts for each quarter? (See Chapter 5 discussion of EPS.) Explain.
3. Prepare corrected income statements for each quarter.
4. Set up a schedule with the following headings to reflect the comparative effects of the correct and incorrect amounts on the income statement:

	1st Quarter			2nd Quarter		
Income Statement Item	Incorrect	Correct	Error	Incorrect	Correct	Error

(Supplement A) Analyzing the Effects of a Reduction in the Amount of LIFO Inventory

E7-20
Eastman Kodak

An annual report of Eastman Kodak Company contained the following note:

> During this year and last year, inventory usage resulted in liquidations of LIFO inventory quantities. In the aggregate, these inventories were carried at the lower costs prevailing in prior years as compared with the costs of current purchases. The effect of these LIFO liquidations was to reduce cost of goods sold by $53 million in the current year and $31 million in the previous year.

Required:

1. Explain why the reduction in inventory quantity increased net income for Eastman Kodak.
2. If Eastman Kodak had used FIFO, would the reductions in inventory quantity during the two years have increased net income? Explain.

(Supplement B) Recording Sales and Purchases with Cash Discounts

E7-21

The Cycle Shop sells merchandise on credit terms of 2/10, n/30. A sale invoiced at $800 (cost of sales $500) was made to Missy Clemons on February 1, 2007. The company uses the gross method of recording sales discounts.

Required:

1. Give the journal entry to record the credit sale. Assume use of the perpetual inventory system.
2. Give the journal entry, assuming that the account was collected in full on February 9, 2007.
3. Give the journal entry, assuming, instead, that the account was collected in full on March 2, 2007.

On March 4, 2007, the company purchased bicycles and accessories from a supplier on credit, invoiced at $8,000; the terms were 1/15, n/30. The company uses the gross method to record purchases.

Required:

4. Give the journal entry to record the purchase on credit. Assume the use of the perpetual inventory system.
5. Give the journal entry, assuming that the account was paid in full on March 12, 2007.
6. Give the journal entry, assuming, instead, that the account was paid in full on March 28, 2007.

(Supplement C) Recording Purchases and Sales Using a Perpetual and Periodic Inventory System

E7-22

Snowball Company reported beginning inventory of 100 units at a unit cost of $25. It engaged in the following purchase and sale transactions during 2006:

Jan. 14 Sold 25 units at unit sales price of $45 on open account.
April 9 Purchased 15 additional units at unit cost of $25 on open account.
Sept. 2 Sold 50 units at sales price of $50 on open account.

At the end of 2006, a physical count showed that Snowball Company had 40 units of inventory still on hand.

Required:

Record each transaction, assuming that Snowball Company uses (a) a perpetual inventory system and (b) a periodic inventory system (including any necessary entries at the end of the accounting period on December 31).

PROBLEMS

 Available with McGraw-Hill's Homework Manager

P7-1   **Analyzing Items to Be Included in Inventory**
LO1

Reggie Company has just completed a physical inventory count at year-end, December 31, 2007. Only the items on the shelves, in storage, and in the receiving area were counted and costed on a FIFO basis. The inventory amounted to $70,000. During the audit, the independent CPA developed the following additional information:

a. Goods costing $500 were being used by a customer on a trial basis and were excluded from the inventory count at December 31, 2007.

b. Goods in transit on December 31, 2007, from a supplier, with terms FOB destination (explained in the "Required" section), cost $600. Because these goods had not arrived, they were excluded from the physical inventory count.

c. On December 31, 2007, goods in transit to customers, with terms FOB shipping point, amounted to $1,000 (expected delivery date January 10, 2008). Because the goods had been shipped, they were excluded from the physical inventory count.

d. On December 28, 2007, a customer purchased goods for cash amounting to $2,000 and left them "for pickup on January 3, 2008." Reggie Company had paid $1,200 for the goods and, because they were on hand, included the latter amount in the physical inventory count.

e. On the date of the inventory count, the company received notice from a supplier that goods ordered earlier at a cost of $2,200 had been delivered to the transportation company on December 27, 2007; the terms were FOB shipping point. Because the shipment had not arrived by December 31, 2007, it was excluded from the physical inventory.

f. On December 31, 2007, the company shipped $950 worth of goods to a customer, FOB destination. The goods are expected to arrive at their destination no earlier than January 8, 2008. Because the goods were not on hand, they were not included in the physical inventory count.

g. One of the items sold by the company has such a low volume that the management planned to drop it last year. To induce Reggie Company to continue carrying the item, the manufacturer-supplier provided the item on a "consignment basis." This means that the manufacturer-supplier retains ownership of the item, and Reggie Company (the consignee) has no responsibility to pay for the items until they are sold to a customer. Each month, Reggie Company sends a report to the manufacturer on the number sold and remits cash for the cost. At the end of December 2007, Reggie Company had five of these items on hand; therefore, they were included in the physical inventory count at $1,000 each.

Required:

Assume that Reggie's accounting policy requires including in inventory all goods for which it has title. Note that the point where title (ownership) changes hands is determined by the shipping terms in the sales contract. When goods are shipped "F.O.B. shipping point," title changes hands at shipment and the buyer normally pays for shipping. When they are shipped "F.O.B. destination," title changes hands on delivery, and the seller normally pays for shipping. Begin with the $70,000 inventory amount and compute the correct amount for the ending inventory. Explain the basis for your treatment of each of the preceding items. (*Hint:* Set up three columns: Item, Amount, and Explanation.)

P7-2   **Analyzing the Effects of Four Alternative Inventory Methods** (AP7-1)
LO2

Yalestone Company uses a periodic inventory system. At the end of the annual accounting period, December 31, 2008, the accounting records for the most popular item in inventory showed the following:

Transactions	Units	Unit Cost
Beginning inventory, January 1, 2008	1,800	$2.50
Transactions during 2008:		
a. Purchase, January 30	2,500	3.10
b. Purchase, May 1	1,200	4.00
c. Sale ($5 each)	(1,450)	
d. Sale ($5 each)	(1,900)	

Required:
Compute the amount of (a) goods available for sale, (b) ending inventory, and (c) cost of goods sold at December 31, 2008, under each of the following inventory costing methods (show computations and round to the nearest dollar):

1. Weighted average cost.
2. First-in, first-out.
3. Last-in, first-out.
4. Specific identification, assuming that the first sale was selected two-fifths from the beginning inventory and three-fifths from the purchase of January 30, 2008. Assume that the second sale was selected from the remainder of the beginning inventory, with the balance from the purchase of May 1, 2008.

Evaluating Four Alternative Inventory Methods Based on Income and Cash Flow (AP-2)

P7-3
LO2, 3

At the end of January 2007, the records of Atlanta Company showed the following for a particular item that sold at $18 per unit:

Transactions	Units	Amount
Inventory, January 1, 2007	500	$2,500
Purchase, January 12	600	3,600
Purchase, January 26	160	1,280
Sale	(400)	
Sale	(300)	

Required:
1. Assuming the use of a periodic inventory system, prepare a summarized income statement through gross profit on sales under each method of inventory: (a) weighted average cost, (b) FIFO, (c) LIFO, and (d) specific identification. For specific identification, assume that the first sale was out of the beginning inventory and the second sale was out of the January 12 purchase. Show the inventory computations in detail.
2. Of FIFO and LIFO, which method would result in the higher pretax income? Which would result in the higher EPS?
3. Of FIFO and LIFO, which method would result in the lower income tax expense? Explain, assuming a 30 percent average tax rate.
4. Of FIFO and LIFO, which method would produce the more favorable cash flow? Explain.

Analyzing and Interpreting Income Manipulation under the LIFO Inventory Method

P7-4
LO2, 3

Pacific Company sells electronic test equipment that it acquires from a foreign source. During the year 2011, the inventory records reflected the following:

	Units	Unit Cost	Total Cost
Beginning inventory	15	$12,000	$180,000
Purchases	40	10,000	400,000
Sales (45 units at $25,000 each)			

Inventory is valued at cost using the LIFO inventory method.

Required:
1. Complete the following income statement summary using the LIFO method and the periodic inventory system (show computations):

Sales revenue	$ ____
Cost of goods sold	____
Gross profit	____
Expenses	300,000
Pretax income	$ ____
Ending inventory	$ ____

2. The management, for various reasons, is considering buying 20 additional units before December 31, 2011, at $8,000 each. Restate the income statement (and ending inventory), assuming that this purchase is made on December 31, 2011.

3. How much did pretax income change because of the decision on December 31, 2011? Asuming that the unit cost of test equipment is expected to continue to decline in 2012, is there any evidence of income manipulation? Explain.

P7-5
LO2, 3

Evaluating the LIFO and FIFO Choice When Costs Are Rising and Falling

Income is to be evaluated under four different situations as follows:

a. Prices are rising:
  1. Situation A: FIFO is used.
  2. Situation B: LIFO is used.
b. Prices are falling:
  1. Situation C: FIFO is used.
  2. Situation D: LIFO is used.

The basic data common to all four situations are sales, 500 units for $12,500; beginning inventory, 300 units; purchases, 400 units; ending inventory, 200 units; and operating expenses, $4,000. The following tabulated income statements for each situation have been set up for analytical purposes:

	PRICES RISING		PRICES FALLING	
	Situation A FIFO	Situation B LIFO	Situation C FIFO	Situation D LIFO
Sales revenue	$12,500	$12,500	$12,500	$12,500
Cost of goods sold:				
Beginning inventory	3,600	?	?	?
Purchases	5,200	?	?	?
Goods available for sale	8,800	?	?	?
Ending inventory	2,600	?	?	?
Cost of goods sold	6,200	?	?	?
Gross profit	6,300	?	?	?
Expenses	4,000	4,000	4,000	4,000
Pretax income	2,300	?	?	?
Income tax expense (30%)	690	?	?	?
Net income	$ 1,610			

Required:

1. Complete the preceding tabulation for each situation. In Situations A and B (prices rising), assume the following: beginning inventory, 300 units at $12 = $3,600; purchases, 400 units at $13 = $5,200. In Situations C and D (prices falling), assume the opposite; that is, beginning inventory, 300 units at $13 = $3,900; purchases, 400 units at $12 = $4,800. Use periodic inventory procedures.

2. Analyze the relative effects on pretax income and on net income as demonstrated by requirement 1 when prices are rising and when prices are falling.

3. Analyze the relative effects on the cash position for each situation.

4. Would you recommend FIFO or LIFO? Explain.

P7-6
LO4

Evaluating the Income Statement and Cash Flow Effects of Lower of Cost or Market

Smart Company prepared its annual financial statements dated December 31, 2007. The company applies the FIFO inventory costing method; however, the company neglected to apply LCM to the ending inventory. The preliminary 2007 income statement follows:

Sales revenue		$280,000
Cost of goods sold		
Beginning inventory	$ 30,000	
Purchases	182,000	
Goods available for sale	212,000	
Ending inventory (FIFO cost)	44,000	
Cost of goods sold		168,000
Gross profit		112,000
Operating expenses		61,000
Pretax income		51,000
Income tax expense (30%)		15,300
Net income		$ 35,700

Assume that you have been asked to restate the 2007 financial statements to incorporate LCM. You have developed the following data relating to the 2007 ending inventory:

		Acquisition Cost		Current Replacement Unit Cost
Item	Quantity	Unit	Total	(Market)
A	3,000	$3	$ 9,000	$4
B	1,500	4	6,000	2
C	7,000	2	14,000	4
D	3,000	5	15,000	3
			$44,000	

Required:
1. Restate this income statement to reflect LCM valuation of the 2007 ending inventory. Apply LCM on an item-by-item basis and show computations.
2. Compare and explain the LCM effect on each amount that was changed on the income statement in requirement 1.
3. What is the conceptual basis for applying LCM to merchandise inventories?
4. Thought question: What effect did LCM have on the 2007 cash flow? What will be the long-term effect on cash flow?

Evaluating the Effects of Manufacturing Changes on Inventory Turnover Ratio and Cash Flows from Operating Activities

P7-7
LO5

H.–T. Tan and Company has been operating for five years as an electronics component manufacturer specializing in cellular phone components. During this period, it has experienced rapid growth in sales revenue and in inventory. Mr. Tan and his associates have hired you as its first corporate controller. You have put into place new purchasing and manufacturing procedures that are expected to reduce inventories by approximately one-third by year-end. You have gathered the following data related to the changes:

	(dollars in thousands)	
	Beginning of Year	End of Year (projected)
Inventory	$463,808	$310,270
		Current Year (projected)
Cost of goods sold		$7,015,069

Required:

1. Compute the inventory turnover ratio based on two different assumptions:
   a. Those presented in the preceding table (a decrease in the balance in inventory).
   b. No change from the beginning of the year in the inventory balance.
2. Compute the effect of the projected change in the balance in inventory on cash flow from operating activities for the year (the sign and amount of effect).
3. On the basis of the preceding analysis, write a brief memo explaining how an increase in inventory turnover can result in an increase in cash flow from operating activities. Also explain how this increase can benefit the company.

P7-8 Evaluating the Choice between LIFO and FIFO Based on an Inventory Note
LO6
General Motors

An annual report for General Motors Corporation included the following note:

> Inventories are stated generally at cost, which is not in excess of market. The cost of substantially all domestic inventories was determined by the last-in, first-out (LIFO) method. If the first-in, first-out (FIFO) method of inventory valuation had been used by the corporation for U.S. inventories, it is estimated that they would be $2,077.1 million higher at the end of this year, compared with $1,784.5 million higher at the end of last year.

For the year, GM reported net income (after taxes) of $320.5 million. At year-end, the balance of the GM retained earnings account was $15,340 million.

Required:

1. Determine the amount of net income that GM would have reported for the year if it had used the FIFO method (assume a 30 percent tax rate).
2. Determine the amount of retained earnings that GM would have reported at year-end if it always had used the FIFO method (assume a 30 percent tax rate).
3. Use of the LIFO method reduced the amount of taxes that GM had to pay for the year compared with the amount that would have been paid if it had used FIFO. Calculate the amount of this reduction (assume a 30 percent tax rate).

P7-9 Analyzing and Interpreting the Effects of Inventory Errors (AP7-3)
LO7
eXcel

The income statement for Sherwood Company summarized for a four-year period shows the following:

	2006	2007	2008	2009
Sales revenue	$2,000,000	$2,400,000	$2,500,000	$3,000,000
Cost of goods sold	1,400,000	1,630,000	1,780,000	2,100,000
Gross profit	600,000	770,000	720,000	900,000
Expenses	450,000	500,000	520,000	550,000
Pretax income	150,000	270,000	200,000	350,000
Income tax expense (30%)	45,000	81,000	60,000	105,000
Net income	$ 105,000	$ 189,000	$ 140,000	$ 245,000

An audit revealed that in determining these amounts, the ending inventory for 2007 was overstated by $20,000. The company uses a periodic inventory system.

Required:

1. Recast the income statements to reflect the correct amounts, taking into consideration the inventory error.
2. Compute the gross profit percentage for each year (a) before the correction and (b) after the correction. Do the results lend confidence to your corrected amounts? Explain.
3. What effect would the error have had on the income tax expense assuming a 30 percent average rate?

P7-10 (Supplement A) Analyzing LIFO and FIFO When Inventory Quantities Decline Based on an Actual Note
General Electric

In a recent annual report, General Electric reported the following in its inventory note:

December 31 (dollars in millions)	Current Year	Prior Year
Raw materials and work in progress	$5,603	$5,515
Finished goods	2,863	2,546
Unbilled shipments	246	280
	8,712	8,341
Less revaluation to LIFO	(2,226)	(2,076)
LIFO value of inventories	$6,486	$6,265

It also reported a $23 million change in cost of goods sold due to "lower inventory levels."

Required:

1. Compute the increase or decrease in the pretax operating profit (loss) that would have been reported for the current year had GE employed FIFO accounting for all inventory for both years.
2. Compute the increase or decrease in pretax operating profit that would have been reported had GE employed LIFO but not reduced inventory quantities during the current year.

(Supplement B) Recording Sales and Purchases with Cash Discounts and Returns

P7-11

Campus Stop, Incorporated, is a student co-op. On January 1, 2012, the beginning inventory was $150,000, the Accounts Receivable balance was $4,000, and the Allowance for Doubtful Accounts had a credit balance of $800. Campus Stop uses a perpetual inventory system and records inventory purchases using the gross method.

The following transactions (summarized) have been selected from 2012 for case purposes:

a. Sold merchandise for cash (cost of sales $137,500)	$275,000
b. Received merchandise returned by customers as unsatisfactory, for cash refund (cost of sales $800)	1,600

Purchased merchandise from vendors on credit; terms 3/10, n/30 as follows:

c. August Supply Company invoice price before deduction of cash discount	5,000
d. Other vendors, invoice price before deduction of cash discount	120,000
e. Purchased equipment for use in store; paid cash	2,200
f. Purchased office supplies for future use in the store; paid cash	700
g. Freight on merchandise purchased; paid cash	400

Paid accounts payable in full during the period as follows:

h. Paid August Supply Company after the discount period	5,000
i. Paid other vendors within the 3% discount period	116,400

Required:
Prepare journal entries for each of the preceding transactions.

ALTERNATE PROBLEMS

Analyzing the Effects of Four Alternative Inventory Methods (P7-2)

AP7-1
LO2

Allsigns Company uses a periodic inventory system. At the end of the annual accounting period, December 31, 2010, the accounting records for the most popular item in inventory showed the following:

Transactions	Units	Unit Cost
Beginning inventory, January 1, 2010	400	$30
Transactions during 2010:		
a. Purchase, February 20	600	32
b. Purchase, June 30	500	36
c. Sale ($46 each)	(700)	
d. Sale ($46 each)	(100)	

Required:

Compute the cost of (a) goods available for sale, (b) ending inventory, and (c) goods sold at December 31, 2010, under each of the following inventory costing methods (show computations and round to the nearest dollar):

1. Weighted average cost.
2. First-in, first-out.
3. Last-in, first-out.
4. Specific identification, assuming that the first sale was selected one-fifth from the beginning inventory and four-fifths from the purchase of February 20, 2010. Assume that the second sale was selected from the purchase of June 30, 2010.

AP7-2
LO2, 3

Evaluating Four Alternative Inventory Methods Based on Income and Cash Flow (P7-3)

At the end of January 2007, the records of George Company showed the following for a particular item that sold at $20 per unit:

Transactions	Units	Amount
Inventory, January 1, 2007	600	$2,400
Purchase, January 12	800	4,000
Purchase, January 26	100	600
Sale	(400)	
Sale	(300)	

Required:

1. Assuming the use of a periodic inventory system, prepare a summarized income statement through gross profit on sales under each method of inventory: (a) weighted average cost, (b) FIFO, (c) LIFO, and (d) specific identification. For specific identification, assume that the first sale was out of the beginning inventory and the second sale was out of the January 12 purchase. Show the inventory computations in detail.
2. Of FIFO and LIFO, which method would result in the higher pretax income? Which would result in the higher EPS?
3. Of FIFO and LIFO, which method would result in the lower income tax expense? Explain, assuming a 30 percent average tax rate.
4. Of FIFO and LIFO, which method would produce the more favorable cash flow? Explain.

AP7-3
LO7

Analyzing and Interpreting the Effects of Inventory Errors (P7-9)

The income statements for four consecutive years for Clement Company reflected the following summarized amounts:

	2006	2007	2008	2009
Sales revenue	$50,000	$51,000	$62,000	$58,000
Cost of goods sold	32,500	35,000	43,000	37,000
Gross profit	17,500	16,000	19,000	21,000
Expenses	10,000	12,000	14,000	12,000
Pretax income	$ 7,500	$ 4,000	$ 5,000	$ 9,000

Subsequent to development of these amounts, it has been determined that the physical inventory taken on December 31, 2007, was understated by $3,000.

Required:

1. Recast the income statements to reflect the correct amounts, taking into consideration the inventory error.
2. Compute the gross profit percentage for each year (a) before the correction and (b) after the correction. Do the results lend confidence to your corrected amounts? Explain.
3. What effect would the error have had on the income tax expense assuming a 30 percent average rate?

Annual Report Cases

Finding Financial Information

CP7-1
LO4, 5, 7

PACIFIC SUNWEAR
OF CALIFORNIA, INC.

Refer to the financial statements of Pacific Sunwear of California given in Appendix B at the end of this book or open file PSUN.pdf in the Annual Report Cases directory on the student DVD.

Required:
1. The company uses lower of cost or market to account for its inventory. At the end of the year, do you expect the company to write its inventory down to replacement cost or net realizable value? Explain your answer.
2. If the company overstated ending inventory by $10 million for the year ended January 29, 2005, what would be the corrected value for Income before Income Taxes?
3. Compute Pacific Sunwear of California's inventory turnover ratio for the year ended January 29, 2005. What does an inventory turnover ratio tell you?

Finding Financial Information

CP7-2
LO1, 2, 5

AMERICAN EAGLE
OUTFITTERS
ae.com

Refer to the financial statements of American Eagle Outfitters given in Appendix C at the end of this book or open file AEOS.pdf in the Annual Report Cases directory on the student DVD.

Required:
1. How much inventory does the company hold at the end of the most recent year?
2. Estimate the amount of merchandise that the company purchased during the current year. (*Hint:* Use the cost of goods sold equation and ignore "certain buying, occupancy, and warehousing expenses.")
3. What method does the company use to determine the cost of its inventory?
4. By what amount did inventory change over the most recent reporting year? Would net cash provided by operating activities increase or decrease as a result of the change in inventory for the most recent reporting year?

Comparing Companies within an Industry

CP7-3
LO5

AMERICAN EAGLE
OUTFITTERS
ae.com

PACIFIC SUNWEAR
OF CALIFORNIA, INC.

Refer to the financial statements of Pacific Sunwear of California given in Appendix B, American Eagle Outfitters given in Appendix C, and the Industry Ratio Report given in Appendix D at the end of this book or open file CP7-3.xls in the Annual Report Cases directory on the student DVD.

Required:
1. Compute the inventory turnover ratio for both companies for the current year. What would you infer from the difference?
2. Compare the inventory turnover ratio for both companies to the industry average. Are these two companies doing better or worse than the industry average in turning over their inventory?

Financial Reporting and Analysis Cases

Using Financial Reports: Interpreting Effect of a Change in Accounting for Production-Related Costs

CP7-4
LO1
Dana Corporation

Dana Corporation designs and manufactures component parts for the vehicular, industrial, and mobile off-highway original equipment markets. In a recent annual report, Dana's inventory note indicated the following:.

> Dana changed its method of accounting for inventories effective January 1 . . . to include in inventory certain production-related costs previously charged to expense. This change in accounting principle resulted in a better matching of costs against related revenues. The effect of this change in accounting increased inventories by $23.0 and net income by $12.9.

Required:

1. Under Dana's previous accounting method, certain production costs were recognized as expenses on the income statement in the period they were incurred. When will they be recognized under the new accounting method?

2. Explain how including these costs in inventory increased both inventories and net income for the year.

CP7-5
L05, 6
Caterpillar

Using Financial Reports: Interpreting Effects of the LIFO/FIFO Choice on Inventory Turnover

In its annual report, Caterpillar, Inc., a major manufacturer of farm and construction equipment, reported the following information concerning its inventories:

> The cost of inventories is determined principally by the LIFO (last-in, first-out) method of inventory valuation. This method was first adopted for the major portion of inventories in 1950. The value of inventories on the LIFO basis represented approximately 90% of total inventories at current cost value on December 31, 1995, 1994, and 1993. If the FIFO (first-in, first-out) method had been in use, inventories would have been $2,103, $2,035, and $1,818 higher than reported at December 31, 1995, 1994, and 1993, respectively.

On its balance sheet, it reported:

	1995	1994	1993
Inventories	$1,921	$1,835	$1,525

On its income statement, it reported:

	1995	1994	1993
Cost of goods sold	$12,000	$10,834	$9,075

Required:

As a recently hired financial analyst, you have been asked to analyze the efficiency with which Caterpillar has been managing its inventory and to write a short report. Specifically, you have been asked to compute inventory turnover for 1995 based on FIFO and on LIFO and compare the two ratios with two standards: (1) Caterpillar for the prior year 1994 and (2) its chief competitor, John Deere. For 1995, John Deere's inventory turnover was 4.2 based on FIFO and 9.8 based on LIFO. In your report, include:

1. The appropriate ratios computed based on FIFO and LIFO.
2. An explanation for the differences in the ratios across the FIFO and LIFO methods.
3. An explanation of whether the FIFO or LIFO ratios provide a more accurate representation of the companies' efficiency in use of inventory.

CP7-6
General Motors

(Supplement A) Using Financial Reports: Analysis of the Effects of LIFO Liquidations

Several years ago, General Motors reported the following in its inventory note:

> The cost of substantially all domestic inventories was determined by the last-in, first-out (LIFO) method. If the first-in, first-out (FIFO) method of inventory valuation had been used by the Corporation for U.S. inventories, it is estimated they would be $1,886.0 million higher at December 31 [current year] compared with $2,077.1 million at December 31 [prior year]. As a result of decreases in unit sales and actions taken to reduce inventories, certain LIFO inventory quantities carried at lower costs prevailing in prior years, as compared with the costs of current purchases, were liquidated. . . . These inventory adjustments favorably affected income (loss) before income taxes by approximately $305.0 million [current year].

In the current year, GM recorded a small pretax operating profit of $22.8 million.

Required:

1. Compute the amount of pretax operating profit (loss) that GM would have reported had it not reduced inventory quantities during the current year.
2. Compute the amount of pretax operating profit (loss) for the current year that GM would have reported had it employed FIFO accounting in both years.
3. What is the normal relationship between pretax operating profit computed using LIFO and FIFO when costs are rising? Why is this relationship not in evidence in this case?

Critical Thinking Cases

Making a Decision as a Financial Analyst: Analysis of the Effect of a Change to LIFO

CP7-7
LO6
Quaker Oats

A recent annual report for Quaker Oats included the following information:

> The company adopted the LIFO cost flow assumption for valuing the majority of remaining U.S. Grocery Products inventories. The company believes that the use of the LIFO method better matches current costs with current revenues. The cumulative effect of this change on retained earnings at the beginning of the year is not determinable, nor are the pro forma effects of retroactive application of LIFO to prior years. The effect of this change on the current year was to decrease net income by $16.0 million, or $0.20 per share.

Required:

As a new financial analyst at a leading Wall Street investment banking firm, you are assigned to write a memo outlining the effects of the accounting change on Quaker's financial statements. Assume a 34 percent tax rate. In your report, be sure to include the following:

1. In addition to the reason that was cited, why did management adopt LIFO?
2. As an analyst, how would you react to the $0.20 per share decrease in income caused by the adoption of LIFO?

Evaluating an Ethical Dilemma: Earnings, Inventory Purchases, and Management Bonuses

CP7-8
LO7
Micro Warehouse

Micro Warehouse is a computer software and hardware online and catalogue sales company. A *Wall Street Journal* article disclosed the following:

> **MICRO WAREHOUSE IS REORGANIZING TOP MANAGEMENT**
>
> Micro Warehouse Inc. announced a "significant reorganization" of its management, including the resignation of three senior executives. The move comes just a few weeks after the Norwalk, Conn., computer catalogue sales company said it overstated earnings by $28 million since 1992 as a result of accounting irregularities. That previous disclosure prompted a flurry of shareholder lawsuits against the company. In addition, Micro Warehouse said it is cooperating with an "informal inquiry" by the Securities and Exchange Commission.
>
> Source: Stephan E. Frank, *The Wall Street Journal,* November 21, 1996, p. B2.

Its Form 10–Q quarterly report filed with the Securities and Exchange Commission two days before indicated that inaccuracies involving understatement of purchases and accounts payable in current and prior periods amounted to $47.3 million. It also indicated that, as a result, $2.2 million of executive bonuses for 1995 would be rescinded. Micro Warehouse's total tax rate is approximately 40.4 percent. Both cost of goods sold and executive bonuses are fully deductible for tax purposes.

Required:

As a new staff member at Micro Warehouse's auditing firm, you are assigned to write a memo outlining the effects of the understatement of purchases and the rescinding of the bonuses. In your report, be sure to include the following:

1. The total effect on pretax and after-tax earnings of the understatement of purchases.
2. The total effect on pretax and after-tax earnings of the rescinding of the bonuses.
3. An estimate of the percentage of after-tax earnings management is receiving in bonuses.
4. A discussion of why Micro Warehouse's board of directors may have decided to tie managers' compensation to reported earnings and the possible relation between this type of bonus scheme and the accounting errors.

Financial Reporting and Analysis Team Project

CP7-9
LO2, 3, 5

Team Project: Analyzing Inventories

As a team, select an industry to analyze. Reuters provides a list of industries and their makeup at www.investor.reuters.com/Industries.aspx. Each team member should acquire the annual report or 10-K for one publicly traded company in the industry, with each member selecting a different company. (Library files, the SEC EDGAR service at www.sec.gov, Compustat CD, and the company itself are good sources.)

Required:

On an individual basis, each team member should write a short report answering the following questions about the selected company. Discuss any patterns across the companies that you as a team observe. Then, as a team, write a short report comparing and contrasting your companies.

1. If your company lists inventories in its balance sheet, what percentage is it to total assets for each of the last three years? If your company does not list inventories, discuss why this is so.
2. If your company lists inventories, what inventory costing method is applied to U.S. inventories?
   a. What do you think motivated this choice?
   b. If the company used LIFO, how much higher or lower would net income before taxes be if it had used FIFO or a similar method instead?
3. Ratio Analysis:
   a. What does the inventory turnover ratio measure in general?
   b. If your company reports inventories, compute the ratio for the last three years.
   c. What do your results suggest about the company?
   d. If available, find the industry ratio for the most recent year, compare it to your results, and discuss why you believe your company differs or is similar to the industry ratio.
4. What is the effect of the change in inventories on cash flows from operating activities for the most recent year (that is, did the change increase or decrease operating cash flows)? Explain your answer.

After studying this chapter, you should be able to:

1. Define, classify, and explain the nature of long-lived productive assets and interpret the fixed asset turnover ratio. p. 399

2. Apply the cost principle to measure the acquisition and maintenance of property, plant, and equipment. p. 401

3. Apply various cost allocation methods as assets are held and used over time. p. 406

4. Explain the effect of asset impairment on the financial statements. p. 416

5. Analyze the disposal of property, plant, and equipment. p. 417

6. Apply measurement and reporting concepts for natural resources and intangible assets. p. 419

7. Explain the impact on cash flows of acquiring, using, and disposing of long-lived assets. p. 424

Reporting and Interpreting Property, Plant, and Equipment; Natural Resources; and Intangibles

As of July 2004, Delta Air Lines provided service to 204 domestic cities in 46 states and 52 international cities in 34 foreign countries. Delta is a capital-intensive company with more than $16.0 billion in property, plant, and equipment reported on its balance sheet. In fiscal year 2003, Delta spent $382 million on aircraft and other flight equipment. Since the demand for air travel is seasonal, with peak demand occurring during the summer months, planning for optimal productive capacity in the airline industry is very difficult. Delta's managers must determine how many aircraft are needed in which cities at what points in time to fill all seats demanded. Otherwise, the company loses revenue (not enough seats) or has higher costs (too many seats).

Demand is also highly sensitive to general economic conditions and other events beyond the control of the company. Even the best corporate planners could not have predicted the September 11, 2001, terrorist attacks against the United States that rocked the airline industry. In response to the precipitous drop in the demand for air travel, Delta accelerated retirement of various aircraft, temporarily grounded aircraft, and considered delaying the purchase of new aircraft.

FOCUS COMPANY:

Delta Air Lines

MANAGING PROFITS THROUGH CONTROL OF PRODUCTIVE CAPACITY

www.delta.com

UNDERSTANDING THE BUSINESS

One of the major challenges managers of most businesses face is forecasting the company's long-term productive capacity (that is, the amount of plant and equipment) it will need. If managers underestimate the need, the company will not be able to produce enough goods or services to meet demand and will miss an opportunity to earn revenue. On the other hand, if they overestimate the need, the company will incur excessive costs that will reduce its profitability.

The airline industry provides an outstanding example of the difficulty of planning for and analyzing productive capacity. If an airplane takes off from Kansas City, Missouri, en route to New York City with empty seats, the economic value associated with those seats is lost for that flight. There is obviously no way to sell the seat to a customer after the airplane has left the gate. Unlike a manufacturer, an airline cannot "inventory" seats for the future.

Likewise, if an unexpectedly large number of people want to board a flight, the airline must turn away some customers. You might be willing to buy a television set from Sears even if you had to wait one week for delivery, but you probably wouldn't book a flight home on Thanksgiving weekend on an airline that told you no seats were available. You would simply pick another airline or use a different mode of transportation.

Delta has a number of large competitors with familiar names such as U•S Airways, American, United, and Southwest. Delta's 10-K report mentions that all domestic routes served by Delta "are subject to competition from both new and existing carriers, some of which have substantially lower costs." Service over most of Delta's international routes is also highly competitive.

Much of the battle for passengers in the airline industry is fought in terms of property, plant, and equipment. Passengers want convenient schedules (that requires a large number of aircraft), and they want to fly on new, modern airplanes. Because airlines have such a large investment in equipment but no opportunity to inventory unused seats, they work very hard to fill their aircraft to capacity for each flight. The frequent fare wars you read about in newspaper advertisements occur when airlines try to build customer demand for their productive capacity. Delta's 10-K report for 2003 contains a note addressing this issue.

REAL WORLD EXCERPT

2003 10-K REPORT

Our unit costs are significantly higher than those of Southwest, AirTran and JetBlue and have gone from being among the lowest of the hub-and-spoke carriers to among the highest for the full year 2003. If we are not able to realign our cost structure to compete with that of other carriers, or if fare reductions are not offset by higher yields, our business, financial condition and operating results may be materially adversely affected.

Source: Courtesy of Delta Air Lines, Inc.

As you can see from this discussion, issues surrounding property, plant, and equipment have a pervasive impact on a company in terms of strategy, pricing decisions, and profitability. Managers devote considerable time to planning optimal levels of productive capacity, and financial analysts closely review a company's statements to determine the impact of management's decisions.

This chapter is organized according to the life cycle of long-lived assets—acquisition, use, and disposal. First we will discuss the measuring and reporting issues related to land, buildings, and equipment. Then we will discuss the measurement and reporting issues for natural resources and intangible assets. Among the issues we will discuss are maintaining, using, and disposing of property and equipment over time and measuring and reporting assets considered impaired in their ability to generate future cash flows.

ORGANIZATION of the Chapter

Acquisition and Maintenance of Plant and Equipment	Use, Impairment, and Disposal of Plant and Equipment	Natural Resources and Intangible Assets
■ Classifying Long-Lived Assets ■ Fixed Asset Turnover Ratio ■ Measuring and Recording Acquisition Cost ■ Repairs, Maintenance, and Additions	■ Depreciation Concepts ■ Alternative Depreciation Methods ■ How Managers Choose ■ Measuring Asset Impairment ■ Disposal of Property, Plant, and Equipment	■ Acquisition and Depletion of Natural Resources ■ Acquisition and Amortization of Intangible Assets

Plant and Equipment as a Percent of Total Assets for Selected Focus Companies

Boston Beer	19.5%
Papa John's	58.7%
Harley-Davidson	13.7%

ACQUISITION AND MAINTENANCE OF PLANT AND EQUIPMENT

Exhibit 8.1 shows the asset section of the balance sheet from Delta's annual report for the fiscal year ended December 31, 2003. Nearly 64 percent of Delta's total assets is flight and ground equipment. Delta also reports other assets with probable long-term benefits. Let's begin by classifying these assets.

Classifying Long-Lived Assets

The resources that determine a company's productive capacity are often called long-lived assets. These assets that are listed as noncurrent assets on the balance sheet may be either tangible or intangible, and have the following characteristics:

1. Tangible assets have physical substance; that is, they can be touched. This classification is called **property, plant, and equipment** or **fixed assets.** The three kinds of long-lived tangible assets are

    a. **Land** used in operations. As is the case with Delta, land often is not shown as a separate item on the balance sheet.

    b. **Buildings, fixtures, and equipment** used in operations. For Delta, this category includes aircraft, ground equipment to service the aircraft, and office space.

    c. **Natural resources** used in operations. Delta does not report any natural resources on its balance sheet. However, companies in other industries report natural resources such as timber tracts and silver mines.

2. Intangible assets are long-lived assets without physical substance that confer specific rights on their owner. Examples are patents, copyrights, franchises, licenses, and trademarks. Operating rights and other intangibles are shown on Delta's balance sheet.

Learning Objective 1
Define, classify, and explain the nature of long-lived productive assets and interpret the fixed asset turnover ratio.

LONG-LIVED ASSETS are tangible and intangible resources owned by a business and used in its operations over several years.

TANGIBLE ASSETS (or fixed assets) have physical substance.

INTANGIBLE ASSETS have special rights but not physical substance.

DELTA AIR LINES, INC.
CONSOLIDATED BALANCE SHEETS (partial)
December 31, 2003 and 2002

Assets (dollars in millions)	2003	2002
Current Assets: (summarized)	$ 4,967	$ 3,902
Property and Equipment:		
Flight equipment (owned and leased)	21,008	20,295
Less: Accumulated depreciation and amortization	6,497	6,109
	14,511	14,186
Flight and ground equipment under capital leases	463	439
Less: Accumulated amortization	353	297
	110	142
Ground property and equipment	4,477	4,270
Less: Accumulated depreciation	2,408	2,206
	2,069	2,064
Advance payments for equipment	62	132
Total property and equipment	16,752	16,524
Other Assets:		
Investments in associated companies	21	174
Goodwill	2,092	2,092
Operating rights and other intangibles, net of accumulated amortization of $179 at December 31, 2003 and $172 at December 31, 2002	95	102
Other noncurrent assets and investments (summarized)	2,429	1,926
Total other assets	4,637	4,294
Total assets	$26,356	$24,720

Intangible assets

Fixed Asset Turnover

❓ ANALYTICAL QUESTION:

How effectively is management utilizing fixed assets to generate revenues?

% RATIO AND COMPARISONS:

$$\text{Fixed Asset Turnover} = \frac{\text{Net Sales (or operating revenues)}}{\text{Average Net Fixed Assets*}}$$

[Beginning + Ending Fixed Asset Balance (net of accumulated depreciation)] ÷ 2

The 2003 ratio for Delta is:

$$\$13,303 \text{ operating revenues} \div [(\$16,524 + \$16,752) \div 2] = .80 \text{ times}$$

COMPARISONS OVER TIME			COMPARISONS WITH COMPETITORS	
Delta Air Lines			Southwest	United
2001	2002	2003	2003	2003
0.90	0.82	0.80	0.84	0.85

**Selected Focus
Companies' Fixed Asset
Turnover Ratios for 2003**

Papa John's	4.29
Timberland	17.93
Callaway Golf	4.90

💡 INTERPRETATIONS:

In General → The fixed asset turnover ratio measures the sales dollars generated by each dollar of fixed asset used. A high rate normally suggests effective management. An increasing rate over time signals more efficient fixed asset use. Creditors and security analysts use this ratio to assess a company's effectiveness in generating sales from its long-lived assets.

Focus Company Analysis → Delta's fixed asset turnover ratio decreased considerably over the past few years (from a recent high of 1.83 in 1997). Delta also has a lower fixed asset turnover than Southwest and United, implying that the latter two airlines have maintained slightly higher efficiency in recent years.

One reason for the reduced turnover ratio is the growth in Delta's fleet, from 569 aircraft in 1998 to 833 aircraft in 2003. Future turnover rates will remain low unless Delta can either (1) dispose of older aircraft at a faster rate than it has in the past or (2) increase its revenues from flights, either by adding more flights or increasing the revenues it generates per passenger (which is unlikely given the level of competition in the industry at this time).

A Few Cautions: A lower or declining fixed asset turnover rate may indicate that a company is expanding (by acquiring additional productive assets) in anticipation of higher future sales. An increasing ratio could also signal that a firm has cut back on capital expenditures due to a downturn in business. As a consequence, appropriate interpretation of the fixed asset turnover ratio requires an investigation of related activities.

Measuring and Recording Acquisition Cost

Under the **cost principle,** all reasonable and necessary expenditures made in acquiring and preparing an asset for use (or sale as in the case of inventory) should be recorded as the cost of the asset. We say that the expenditures are **capitalized** when they are recorded as part of the cost of an asset instead of as expenses in the current period. Any sales taxes, legal fees, transportation costs, and installation costs are then added to the purchase price of the asset. However, special discounts are subtracted and any interest charges associated with the purchase are expensed as incurred.

In addition to purchasing buildings and equipment, a company may acquire undeveloped land, typically with the intent to build a new factory or office building. When a company purchases land, all of the incidental costs of the purchase, such as title fees, sales commissions, legal fees, title insurance, delinquent taxes, and surveying fees, should be included in its cost.

Sometimes a company purchases an old building or used machinery for the business operations. Renovation and repair costs incurred by the company prior to the asset's use should be included as a part of its cost. Also, when purchasing land, building, and equipment as a group, the total cost is allocated to each asset in proportion to the asset's market value relative to the total market value of the assets as a whole.

For the sake of illustration, let's assume that Delta purchased a new 737 aircraft from Boeing on January 1, 2007 (the beginning of Delta's fiscal year), for a list price of $73 million. Let's also assume that Boeing offered Delta a discount of $4 million for signing the purchase agreement. That means the price of the new plane to Delta would actually be $69 million. In addition, Delta paid $200,000 to have the plane delivered and $800,000 to prepare the new plane for use. The amount recorded for the purchase, called the acquisition cost, is the net cash amount paid for the asset or, when noncash assets are used as payment, the fair market value of the asset given or asset received,

Learning Objective 2
Apply the cost principle to measure the acquisition and maintenance of property, plant, and equipment.

Topic Tackler 8–1

The ACQUISITION COST is the net cash equivalent amount paid or to be paid for the asset.

whichever can be more clearly determined (called the **cash equivalent price**). Delta would calculate the acquisition cost of the new aircraft as follows:

Invoice price	$73,000,000
Less: Discount from Boeing	4,000,000
Net cash invoice price	69,000,000
Add: Transportation charges paid by Delta	200,000
Preparation costs paid by Delta	800,000
Cost of the aircraft (added to the asset account)	$70,000,000

For Cash

Assuming that Delta paid cash for the aircraft and related transportation and preparation costs, the transaction is recorded as follows:

Flight equipment (+A)	70,000,000	
Cash (−A)		70,000,000

Assets		=	Liabilities	+	Stockholders' Equity
Cash	− 70,000,000				
Flight equipment	+ 70,000,000				

It might seem unusual for Delta to pay cash to purchase new assets that cost $70 million, but this is often the case. When it acquires productive assets, a company may pay with cash that was generated from operations or cash recently borrowed. It also is possible for the seller to finance the purchase on credit.

For Debt

Now let's assume that Delta signed a note payable for the new aircraft and paid cash for the transportation and preparation costs. In that case, Delta would record the following journal entry:

Flight equipment (+A)	70,000,000	
Cash (−A)		1,000,000
Note payable (+L)		69,000,000

Assets		=	Liabilities		+	Stockholders' Equity
Cash	− 1,000,000		Note payable	+69,000,000		
Flight equipment	+ 70,000,000					

For Equity (or Other Noncash Considerations)

A noncash consideration, such as the company's common stock or a right given by the company to the seller to purchase the company's goods or services at a special price, might also be part of the transaction. When a noncash consideration is included in the purchase of an asset, the cash-equivalent cost (fair market value of the asset given or received) is determined.

Assume that Delta gave Boeing 6,000,000 shares of its $1.50 par value common stock with a market value of $7 per share and paid the balance in cash. The journal entry and transaction effects follow:

Flight equipment (+A)	70,000,000	
Common stock (+SE) ($1.50 par value × 6,000,000 shares)		9,000,000
Additional paid-in capital (+SE) ($5.50 × 6,000,000 shares)		33,000,000
Cash (−A)		28,000,000

Assets	=	Liabilities	+	Stockholders' Equity	
Cash	− 28,000,000			Common stock	+ 9,000,000
Flight equipment	+ 70,000,000			Additional paid-in capital	+ 33,000,000

By Construction

In some cases, a company may construct an asset for its own use instead of buying it from a manufacturer. When a company does so, the cost of the asset includes all the necessary costs associated with construction, such as labor, materials, and in most situations, a portion of the interest incurred during the construction period, called **capitalized interest.** The amount of interest expense that is capitalized is recorded by debiting the asset and crediting cash when the interest is paid. The amount of interest to be capitalized is a complex computation discussed in detail in other accounting courses.

CAPITALIZED INTEREST represents interest expenditures included in the cost of a self-constructed asset.

Capitalizing labor, materials, and a portion of interest expense has the effect of increasing assets, decreasing expenses, and increasing net income. Let's assume Delta constructed a new hangar, paying $600,000 in labor costs and $1,300,000 in supplies and materials. Delta also paid $100,000 in interest expense during the year related to the construction project:

Building (+A) 2,000,000	
Cash (−A)	2,000,000

Capitalized Expenditures:

Wages paid	*600,000*
Supplies used	*1,300,000*
Interest paid	*100,000*

Assets	=	Liabilities	+	Stockholders' Equity
Cash	− 2,000,000			
Building	+ 2,000,000			

Delta Air Lines includes a note on capitalized interest in a recent annual report:

NOTES TO CONSOLIDATED FINANCIAL STATEMENTS

1. Summary of Significant Accounting Policies:

. . .

Interest Capitalized—We capitalize interest paid on advance payments used to acquire new aircraft and on construction of ground facilities as an additional cost of the related assets.

Source: Courtesy of Delta Air Lines, Inc.

SELF-STUDY **QUIZ**

In a recent year, McDonald's Corporation purchased property, plant, and equipment priced at $1.8 billion. Assume that the company also paid $70 million for sales tax; $8 million for transportation costs; $1.3 million for installation and preparation of the property, plant, and equipment before use; and $100,000 in maintenance contracts to cover repairs to the property, plant, and equipment during use.

1. Compute the acquisition cost for the property, plant, and equipment:

2. How did you account for the sales tax, transportation costs, and installation costs? Explain why.

3. Under the following assumptions, indicate the effects of the acquisition on the accounting equation. Use + for increase and − for decrease and indicate the accounts and amounts:

	ASSETS	LIABILITIES	STOCKHOLDERS' EQUITY
a. Paid 30 percent in cash and the rest by signing a note payable.			
b. Issued 10 million shares of common stock ($0.10 per share stated value) at a market price of $45 per share and paid the balance in cash.			

After you have completed your answers, check them with the solutions at the bottom of the page.

Repairs, Maintenance, and Additions

Most assets require substantial expenditures during their lives to maintain or enhance their productive capacity. These expenditures include cash outlays for ordinary repairs and maintenance, major repairs, replacements, and additions. Expenditures that are made after an asset has been acquired are classified as follows:

Self-Study Quiz
Solutions

1. **Property, Plant, and Equipment (PPE)**

Acquisition cost	$1,800,000,000
Sales tax	70,000,000
Transportation	8,000,000
Installation	1,300,000
Total	$1,879,300,000

Because the maintenance contracts are not necessary to readying the assets for use, they are not included in the acquisition cost.

2. Sales tax, transportation, and installation costs were capitalized because they are reasonable and necessary for getting the asset ready for its intended use.

3.

	Assets	Liabilities	Stockholders' Equity
a. PPE	+ 1,879,300,000	Note payable +1,315,510,000	
Cash	− 563,790,000		
b. PPE	+ 1,879,300,000		Common stock + 1,000,000
Cash	− 1,429,300,000		Additional Paid-in
			capital +449,000,000

1. **Ordinary repairs and maintenance**—expenditures that maintain the productive capacity of the asset during the current accounting period only. These cash outlays are recorded as **expenses** in the current period. Ordinary repairs and maintenance, also called **revenue expenditures,** are expenditures for the normal maintenance and upkeep of long-lived assets. These expenditures are recurring in nature, involve relatively small amounts at each occurrence, and do not directly lengthen the useful life of the asset.

   In the case of Delta Air Lines, examples of ordinary repairs would include changing the oil in the aircraft engines, replacing the lights in the control panels, and fixing torn fabric on passenger seats. Although the cost of individual ordinary repairs is relatively small, in the aggregate these expenditures can be substantial. In a recent year, Delta paid $711 million for aircraft maintenance and repairs. This amount was reported as an expense on its income statement.

2. **Additions and improvements**—expenditures that increase the productive life, operating efficiency, or capacity of the asset. These **capital expenditures** are added to the appropriate asset accounts. They occur infrequently, involve large amounts of money, and increase an asset's economic usefulness in the future through either increased efficiency or longer life. Examples include additions, major overhauls, complete reconditioning, and major replacements and improvements, such as the complete replacement of an engine on an aircraft.

   In many cases, no clear line distinguishes improvements (assets) from ordinary repairs and maintenance (expenses). In these situations, managers must exercise professional judgment and make a subjective decision. Capitalizing expenses will increase assets and net income in the current year, with future years' income lower by the amount of the annual depreciation. On the other hand, for tax purposes, expensing the amount in the current period will lower taxes immediately. Because the decision to capitalize or expense is subjective, auditors review the items reported as capital and revenue expenditures closely.

   To avoid spending too much time classifying additions and improvements (capital expenditures) and repair expenses (revenue expenditures), some companies develop simple policies to govern the accounting for these expenditures. For example, one large computer company expenses all individual items that cost less than $1,000. Such policies are acceptable because immaterial (relatively small dollar) amounts will not affect users' decisions when analyzing financial statements.

ORDINARY REPAIRS AND MAINTENANCE are expenditures for normal operating upkeep of long-lived assets.

REVENUE EXPENDITURES maintain the productive capacity of the asset during the current accounting period only and are recorded as expenses.

ADDITIONS AND IMPROVEMENTS are infrequent expenditures that increase an asset's economic usefulness in the future.

CAPITAL EXPENDITURES increase the productive life, operating efficiency, or capacity of the asset and are recorded as increases in asset accounts, not as expenses.

WorldCom: Hiding Billions in Expenses through Capitalization

FINANCIAL ANALYSIS

WorldCom

When expenditures that should be recorded as current period expenses are improperly capitalized as part of the cost of an asset, the effects on the financial statements can be enormous. In one of the largest accounting frauds in history, WorldCom (now known as MCI) inflated its income and cash flows from operations by billions of dollars in just such a scheme. This fraud turned WorldCom's actual losses into large profits.

Over five quarters in 2001 and 2002, the company initially announced that it had capitalized $3.8 billion that should have been recorded as operating expenses. By early 2004, auditors discovered $74.4 billion in necessary restatements (reductions to previously reported pretax income) for 2000 and 2001.

Accounting for expenses as capital expenditures increases current income because it spreads a single period's operating expenses over many future periods as depreciation expense. It increases cash flows from operations by moving cash outflows from the operating section to the investing section of the cash flow statement. Go to MCI's website at www.mci.com to read the archived press releases about this accounting scandal.

SELF-STUDY **QUIZ**

A building that originally cost $400,000 has been used over the past 10 years and needs continuous maintenance and repairs. For each of the following expenditures, indicate whether it should be expensed in the current period or capitalized as part of **the cost of the asset.**

EXPENSE OR CAPITALIZE?

1. Replacing electrical wiring throughout the building. _____
2. Repairs to the front door of the building. _____
3. Annual cleaning of the filters on the building's air conditioning system. _____
4. Significant repairs due to damage from an unusual and infrequent flood. _____

After you have completed your answers, check them with the solutions at the bottom of the page.

USE, IMPAIRMENT, AND DISPOSAL OF PLANT AND EQUIPMENT

Depreciation Concepts

Learning Objective 3
Apply various cost allocation methods as assets are held and used over time.

Except for land that is considered to have an unlimited life, a long-lived asset with a limited useful life, such as an airplane, represents the prepaid cost of a bundle of future services or benefits. The **matching principle** requires that a portion of an asset's cost be allocated as an expense in the same period that revenues were generated by its use. Delta Air Lines earns revenue when it provides air travel service and incurs an expense when using its aircraft to generate the revenue.

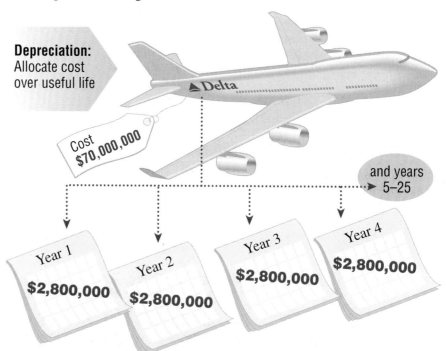

Depreciation: Allocate cost over useful life

Cost $70,000,000

and years 5–25

Year 1 $2,800,000   Year 2 $2,800,000   Year 3 $2,800,000   Year 4 $2,800,000

Using the asset→depreciation expense each year

The term used to identify the matching of the cost of using buildings and equipment with the revenues they generated is depreciation. Thus, depreciation is **the process of allocating the cost of buildings and equipment over their productive lives using a systematic and rational method.**

Students often are confused by the concept of depreciation as accountants use it. In accounting, depreciation is a process of **cost allocation,** not a process of determining an asset's current market value or worth. When an asset is depreciated, the remaining balance sheet amount **probably does not represent its current market value.** On balance sheets subsequent to acquisition, the undepreciated cost is not measured on a market value basis.

An adjusting journal entry is needed at the end of each period to reflect the use of buildings and equipment for the period:

Depreciation expense (+E, −SE) xxx
    Accumulated depreciation (+XA, −A) xxx

Assets	=	Liabilities	+	Stockholders' Equity
Accumulated depreciation (+XA) − xxx				Depreciation expense (+E) − xxx

The amount of depreciation recorded during each period is reported on the income statement as **Depreciation Expense.** The amount of depreciation expense accumulated since the acquisition date is reported on the balance sheet as a contra-account, **Accumulated Depreciation,** and deducted from the related asset's cost. The net amounts on the balance sheet are called **net book values or carrying values.** The net book (or carrying) value of a long-lived asset is its acquisition cost less the accumulated depreciation from acquisition date to the balance sheet date.

From Exhibit 8.1, we see that Delta's acquisition cost for flight equipment is $21,008,000,000 at the end of 2003. The accumulated depreciation on the equipment is $6,497,000,000. Thus, the book value is reported at $14,511,000,000. Delta also reported depreciation and amortization expense of $1,202,000,000 on its income statement for 2003.

DEPRECIATION is the process of allocating the cost of buildings and equipment over their productive lives using a systematic and rational method.

Topic Tackler 8–2

NET BOOK (OR CARRYING) VALUE is the acquisition cost of an asset less accumulated depreciation.

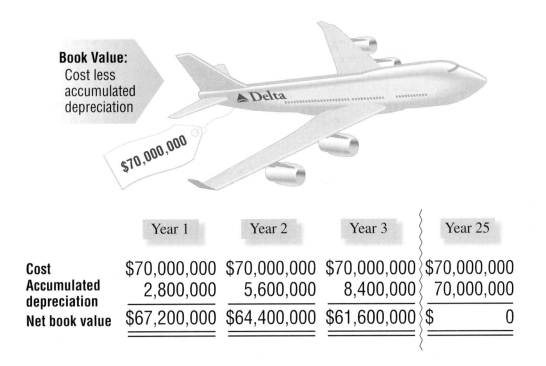

Book Value: Cost less accumulated depreciation

$70,000,000

	Year 1	Year 2	Year 3	Year 25
Cost	$70,000,000	$70,000,000	$70,000,000	$70,000,000
Accumulated depreciation	2,800,000	5,600,000	8,400,000	70,000,000
Net book value	$67,200,000	$64,400,000	$61,600,000	$ 0

FINANCIAL
ANALYSIS

Book Value as an Approximation of Remaining Life

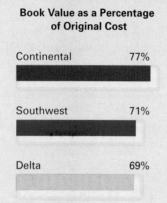

Book Value as a Percentage of Original Cost

Continental   77%

Southwest   71%

Delta   69%

Some analysts compare the book value of assets to their original cost as an approximation of their remaining life. If the book value of an asset is 100 percent of its cost, it is a new asset; if the book value is 25 percent of its cost, the asset has about 25 percent of its estimated life remaining. In Delta's case, the book value of its flight equipment is 69 percent of its original cost, compared to 77 percent for Continental Airlines and 71 percent for Southwest Airlines. This comparison suggests that Delta's flight equipment may have less estimated life remaining than that of Continental. This comparison is only a rough approximation and is influenced by some of the accounting issues discussed in the next section.

To calculate depreciation expense, three amounts are required for each asset:

1. Acquisition cost.
2. **Estimated** useful life to the company.
3. **Estimated** residual (or salvage) value at the end of the asset's useful life to the company.

Of these three amounts, two, the asset's useful life and residual value, are estimates. Therefore, **depreciation expense is an estimate.**

ESTIMATED USEFUL LIFE is the expected service life of an asset to the present owner.

Estimated useful life represents management's estimate of the asset's useful *economic life* to the company rather than its total economic life to all potential users. The asset's expected physical life is often longer than the company intends to use the asset. Economic life may be expressed in terms of years or units of capacity, such as the number of hours a machine is expected to operate or units it can produce. Delta's aircraft fleet is expected to fly for more than 25 years, but Delta wants to offer its customers a high level of service by replacing its older aircraft with modern equipment. For accounting purposes, Delta uses a 25-year estimated useful life. The subsequent owner of the aircraft (a regional airline) would use an estimated useful life based on its own policies.

RESIDUAL (OR SALVAGE) VALUE is the estimated amount to be recovered at the end of the company's estimated useful life of an asset.

Residual (or salvage) value represents management's estimate of the amount the company expects to recover upon disposal of the asset at the end of its estimated useful life. The residual value may be the estimated value of the asset as salvage or scrap or its expected value if sold to another user. In the case of Delta's aircraft, residual value may be the amount it expects to receive when it sells the asset to a small regional airline that operates older equipment. The notes to Delta's financial statements indicate that the company estimates residual value to be between 5 and 40 percent of the cost of the asset, depending on the asset.

FINANCIAL
ANALYSIS

Differences in Estimated Lives within a Single Industry

Notes to recent actual financial statements of various companies in the airline industry reveal the following estimates for the useful lives of flight equipment:

Company	Estimated Life (in years)
Delta	15 to 25
Continental	25 to 30
U•S Airways	11 to 30
Singapore Airlines	5 to 15
Southwest	20 to 25

The differences in the estimated lives may be attributed to a number of factors such as the type of aircraft used by each company, equipment replacement plans, operational differences, and the degree of management's conservatism. In addition, given the same type of aircraft, companies that plan to use the equipment over fewer years may estimate higher residual values than companies that plan to use the equipment longer. For example, Singapore Airlines uses a residual value of 20 percent over a relatively short useful life, compared to 5 percent for Delta Air Lines over a 25-year useful life.

Differences in estimated lives and residual values of assets can have a significant impact on a comparison of the profitability of the competing companies. Analysts must be certain to identify the causes of differences in depreciable lives.

Alternative Depreciation Methods

Because of significant differences among companies and the assets they own, accountants have not been able to agree on a single best method of depreciation. As a result, managers may choose from several acceptable depreciation methods that match depreciation expense with the revenues generated in a period. Once selected, the method should be applied consistently over time to enhance comparability of financial information to users. We will discuss the three most common depreciation methods:

- Straight-line (the most common, used by more than 95 percent of companies surveyed).
- Units-of-production.
- Declining-balance.

To illustrate each method, let's assume that Delta Air Lines acquired a new service vehicle (ground equipment) on January 1, 2007. The relevant information is shown in Exhibit 8.2.

Number of Companies Using Alternative Depreciation Methods*

Straight-line	579
Units-of-production	32
Declining-balance	22
Other	56

* Methods reported by 600 companies sampled in *Accounting Trends & Techniques* (AICPA), 2003.

DELTA AIR LINES
Acquisition of a New Service Vehicle

Cost, purchased on January 1, 2007	$62,500	
Estimated residual value	$2,500	
Estimated useful life	3 years **OR**	100,000 miles
Actual miles driven in:	Year 2007	30,000 miles
	Year 2008	50,000 miles
	Year 2009	20,000 miles

EXHIBIT 8.2

Data for Illustrating the Computation of Depreciation Under Alternative Methods

Straight-Line Method

More companies, including Delta, use straight-line depreciation in their financial statements than all other methods combined. Under the straight-line method, an equal portion of an asset's depreciable cost is allocated to each accounting period over its estimated useful life. The formula to estimate annual depreciation expense follows:

STRAIGHT-LINE DEPRECIATION is the method that allocates the cost of an asset in equal periodic amounts over its useful life.

Straight-Line Formula:

$$(\text{Cost} - \text{Residual Value}) \times \frac{1}{\text{Useful Life}} = \text{Depreciation Expense}$$

$$(\$62,500 - \$2,500) \times \frac{1}{3 \text{ years}} = \$20,000$$

In this formula, "Cost minus Residual Value" is the amount to be depreciated, also called the **depreciable cost.** "1 ÷ Useful Life" is the **straight-line rate.** Using the data provided in Exhibit 8.2, the depreciation expense for Delta's new truck would be $20,000 per year.

Companies often create a **depreciation schedule** that shows the computed amount of depreciation expense each year over the entire useful life of the machine. You can use computerized spreadsheet programs, such as Excel®, to create the depreciation schedule. Using the data in Exhibit 8.2, the depreciation schedule using the straight-line method follows:

Straight-Line Expense

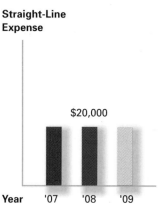

$20,000

Year   '07   '08   '09

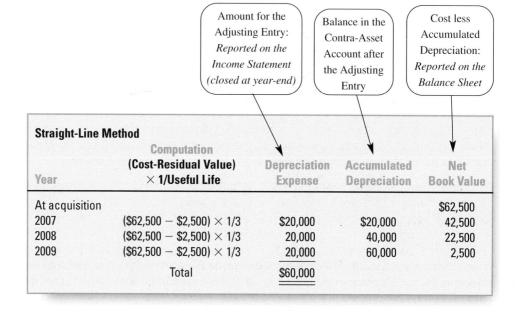

Straight-Line Method				
Year	Computation (Cost-Residual Value) × 1/Useful Life	Depreciation Expense	Accumulated Depreciation	Net Book Value
At acquisition				$62,500
2007	($62,500 − $2,500) × 1/3	$20,000	$20,000	42,500
2008	($62,500 − $2,500) × 1/3	20,000	40,000	22,500
2009	($62,500 − $2,500) × 1/3	20,000	60,000	2,500
	Total	$60,000		

Amount for the Adjusting Entry: Reported on the Income Statement (closed at year-end)

Balance in the Contra-Asset Account after the Adjusting Entry

Cost less Accumulated Depreciation: Reported on the Balance Sheet

Notice that

- Depreciation expense is a constant amount each year.
- Accumulated depreciation increases by an equal amount each year.
- Net book value decreases by the same amount each year until it equals the estimated residual value.

This is the reason for the name **straight-line method.** Notice, too, that the adjusting entry can be prepared from this schedule, and the effect on the income statement and balance sheet are known. Delta Air Lines uses the straight-line method for all its assets. The company reported depreciation expense in the amount of $1,202,000,000 for 2003, equal to 9 percent of the airline's revenues for the year. Most companies in the airline industry use the straight-line method.

Units-of-Production Method

UNITS-OF-PRODUCTION DEPRECIATION is a method to allocate the cost of an asset over its useful life based on the relation of its periodic output to its total estimated output.

The **units-of-production depreciation method** relates depreciable cost to total estimated productive output. The formula to estimate annual depreciation expense under this method is as follows:

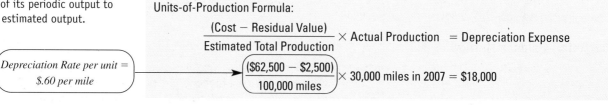

Units-of-Production Formula:

$$\frac{(\text{Cost} - \text{Residual Value})}{\text{Estimated Total Production}} \times \text{Actual Production} = \text{Depreciation Expense}$$

Depreciation Rate per unit = $.60 per mile

$$\frac{(\$62,500 - \$2,500)}{100,000 \text{ miles}} \times 30,000 \text{ miles in 2007} = \$18,000$$

Dividing the depreciable cost by the estimated total production yields the depreciation rate per unit of production, which is then multiplied by the actual production for the period to determine depreciation expense. In our illustration, for every mile that the new vehicle is driven, Delta would record depreciation expense of $.60. The depreciation schedule for the truck under the units-of-production method would appear as follows:

Units-of-Production Method

Year	Computation [(Cost − Residual Value)/ Total Estimated Production] × Actual Production	Depreciation Expense	Accumulated Depreciation	Net Book Value
At acquisition	Rate			$62,500
2007	$.60 per mile × 30,000 miles	$18,000	$18,000	44,500
2008	$.60 per mile × 50,000 miles	30,000	48,000	14,500
2009	$.60 per mile × 20,000 miles	12,000	60,000	2,500
	Total	$60,000		

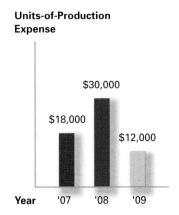

Units-of-Production Expense

$18,000 ('07) $30,000 ('08) $12,000 ('09)

Year   '07   '08   '09

Notice that, from period to period, depreciation expense, accumulated depreciation, and book value vary directly with the units produced. In the units-of-production method, depreciation expense is a **variable expense** because it varies directly with production or use.

You might wonder what happens if the total estimated productive output differs from actual total output. Remember that the estimate is management's best guess of total output. If any difference occurs at the end of the asset's life, the final adjusting entry to depreciation expense should be for the amount needed to bring the asset's net book value equal to the asset's estimated residual value. For example, if, in 2009, Delta's truck ran 25,000 actual miles, the same amount of depreciation expense, $12,000, would be recorded.

Although Delta does not use the units-of-production method, the ExxonMobil Corporation, a major energy company that explores, produces, transports, and sells crude oil and natural gas worldwide, does, as notes to the company's annual report explain.

1. Summary of Accounting Policies

Property, Plant and Equipment. Depreciation, depletion, and amortization, based on cost less estimated salvage value of the asset, are primarily determined under either the unit-of-production method or the straight-line method, which are based on estimated asset service life taking obsolescence into consideration. . . . Unit-of-production rates are based on proved developed reserves, which are oil, gas and other mineral reserves estimated to be recoverable from existing facilities using current operating methods.

REAL WORLD EXCERPT

ExxonMobil Corporation

2004 ANNUAL REPORT

The units-of-production method is based on an estimate of an asset's total future productive capacity or output that is difficult to determine. This is another example of the degree of subjectivity inherent in accounting.

Declining-Balance Method

If an asset is considered to be more efficient or productive when it is newer, managers might choose the declining-balance depreciation method to match a higher depreciation expense with higher revenues in the early years of an asset's life and lower in the

DECLINING-BALANCE DEPRECIATION is the method that allocates the cost of an asset over its useful life based on a multiple of the straight-line rate (often two times).

later years. We say, then, that this is an **accelerated depreciation** method. Although accelerated methods are seldom used for financial reporting purposes, the method that is used more frequently than others is the declining-balance method.

Declining-balance depreciation is based on applying a rate exceeding the straight-line rate to the asset's net book value over time. The rate is often double (two times) the straight-line rate and is termed the **double-declining-balance rate.** For example, if the straight-line rate is 10 percent (1 ÷ 10 years) for a 10-year estimated useful life, then the declining-balance rate is 20 percent (2 × the straight-line rate). Other typical acceleration rates are 1.5 times and 1.75 times. The double-declining-balance rate is adopted most frequently by companies employing an accelerated method, so we will use it in our illustration.

Double-Declining-Balance Formula:

$$(\text{Cost} - \text{Accumulated Depreciation}) \times \frac{2}{\text{Useful Life}} = \text{Depreciation Expense}$$

Accumulated Depreciation increases over time

$$(\$62,500 - \$0 \text{ in } 2007) \times \frac{2}{3 \text{ years}} = \$41,667$$

There are two important differences between this method and the others described previously:

- Notice that accumulated depreciation, not residual value, is included in the formula. Since accumulated depreciation increases each year, net book value (cost minus accumulated depreciation) decreases. The double-declining rate is applied to a lower net book value each year, resulting in a decline in depreciation expense over time.

- An asset's book value cannot be depreciated below residual value. Therefore, if the annual computation reduces net book value below residual value, a lower amount of depreciation expense must be recorded so that net book value equals residual value. No additional depreciation expense is computed in subsequent years.

Computation of double-declining-balance depreciation expense is illustrated in the depreciation schedule:

Double-Declining-Balance Expense

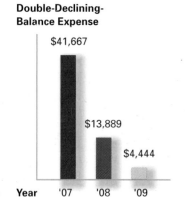

Double-Declining-Balance Method				
	Computation			
	(Cost − Accumulated Depreciation)	**Depreciation**	**Accumulated**	**Net**
Year	**× 2/Useful Life**	**Expense**	**Depreciation**	**Book Value**
At acquisition				$62,500
2007	($62,500 − $0) × 2/3	$41,667	$41,667	20,833
2008	($62,500 − $41,667) × 2/3	13,889	55,556	6,944
2009	($62,500 − $55,556) × 2/3	~~4,629~~	~~60,185~~	~~2,315~~
		4,444	60,000	2,500
	Total	$60,000		

Computed amount is too large.

The calculated depreciation expense for 2009 ($4,629) is not the same as the amount actually reported on the income statement ($4,444). An asset should never be depreciated below the point at which net book value equals its residual value. The asset owned by Delta has an estimated residual value of $2,500. If depreciation expense were recorded in the amount of $4,629, the book value of the asset would be less than $2,500. The correct depreciation expense for year 2009 is therefore $4,444, the amount that will reduce the book value to exactly $2,500.

Companies in industries that expect fairly rapid obsolescence of their equipment use the declining-balance method. Sony is one of the companies that uses this method, as a note to its annual report shows.

2. Summary of significant accounting policies:

Property, plant and equipment and depreciation

Property, plant and equipment are stated at cost. Depreciation of property, plant and equipment is primarily computed on the declining-balance method for Sony Corporation and Japanese subsidiaries . . . and on the straight-line method for foreign subsidiaries at rates based on estimated useful lives of the assets, principally, ranging from 15 up to 50 years for buildings and from 2 years up to 10 years for machinery and equipment.

As this note indicates, companies may use different depreciation methods for different classes of assets. Under the consistency principle, they are expected to apply the same methods to those assets over time.

In Summary

The following table summarizes the three depreciation methods, computations, and the differences in depreciation expense over time for each method.

Method	Computation	Depreciation Expense
Straight-line	(Cost − Residual Value) × 1/Useful Life	Equal amounts each year
Units-of-production	[(Cost − Residual Value)/Estimated Total Production] × Annual Production	Varying amounts based on production level
Double-declining-balance	(Cost − Accumulated Depreciation) × 2/Useful Life	Declining amounts over time

Impact of Alternative Depreciation Methods

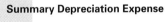

FINANCIAL
ANALYSIS

Assume that you are comparing two companies that are exactly the same, except that one uses accelerated depreciation and the other uses the straight-line method. Which company would you expect to report a higher net income? Actually, this question is a bit tricky. The answer is that you cannot say for certain which company's income would be higher.

The accelerated methods report higher depreciation and therefore lower net income during the early years of an asset's life. As the age of the asset increases, this effect reverses. Therefore, companies that use accelerated depreciation report lower depreciation expense and higher net income during the later years of an asset's life. The graph in the margin shows the pattern of depreciation over the life of an asset for the straight-line and declining-balance methods discussed in this chapter. When the curve for the accelerated method falls below the curve for the straight-line method, the accelerated method produces a higher net income than the straight-line method. However, total depreciation expense by the end of the asset's life is the same for each method.

Users of financial statements must understand the impact of alternative depreciation methods used over time. Differences in depreciation methods rather than real economic differences can cause significant variation in reported net incomes.

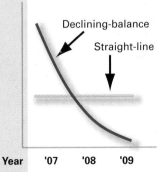

Summary Depreciation Expense

Declining-balance

Straight-line

Year   '07   '08   '09

SELF-STUDY QUIZ

Assume that Delta has acquired new computer equipment at a cost of $240,000. The equipment has an estimated life of six years, an estimated operating life of 50,000 hours, and an estimated residual value of $30,000. Determine depreciation expense for the first full year under each of the following methods:

1. Straight-line depreciation
2. Units-of-production method (assume the equipment ran for 8,000 hours in the first year)
3. Double-declining-balance method

After you have completed your answers, check them with the solutions at the bottom of the page.

FINANCIAL ANALYSIS

Increased Profitability Due to an Accounting Adjustment? Reading the Notes

Financial analysts are particularly interested in changes in accounting estimates because they can have a large impact on a company's before-tax operating income. In 1999, Delta increased the estimated useful life of its aircraft from 20 to 25 years. The change added $92 million in pretax income because of reduced depreciation expense, and would add a similar amount each year over the remaining life of the aircraft. Analysts pay close attention to this number because it represents increased profitability due merely to an accounting adjustment.

To give another example, in its news release, TransAlta Power, a power transmission limited partnership headquartered in Calgary, Alberta, Canada, announced first quarter earnings for 2001 of $4.9 million, up from $3.6 million in the first quarter of 2000. Naturally, the president and director of TransAlta is "very pleased with the first quarter results…" and notes that "our operating performance continues at industry leading levels…."

However, in examining the information presented in the notes to the financial statements, the following disclosure is found: "Effective January 1, 2001, the estimated useful life of the power plant has increased to 27 years from 17 years." This change in estimate—a 59 percent increase in the estimated useful life of the plant—had the effect of increasing TransAlta's net income by $1.35 million.

Therefore, if the change in estimate had not been made, TransAlta's results for the first quarter of 2001 would be $3.55 million, a slight decrease from the first quarter of 2000. TransAlta may still be operating at industry-leading levels, but without a convenient change in estimates, its bottom line would not have improved from the prior year.

Source: "TransAlta Power, L.P. announces first quarter results," CNN Newswire, April 19, 2001.

How Managers Choose

Financial Reporting

For financial reporting purposes, corporate managers must determine which depreciation method provides the best matching of revenues and expenses for any given asset. If the asset is expected to provide benefits evenly over time, then the straight-line method is preferred. Managers also find this method to be easy to use and to explain. If no other method is more systematic or rational, then the straight-line method is selected. Also, during the early years of an asset's life, the straight-line method reports higher income

---

Self-Study Quiz
Solutions

1. ($240,000 − $30,000) × 1/6 = $35,000
2. [($240,000 − $30,000) ÷ 50,000] × 8,000 = $33,600
3. ($240,000 − $0) × 2/6 = $80,000

than the accelerated methods do. For these reasons, the straight-line method is, by far and away, the most common.

On the other hand, certain assets produce more revenue in their early lives because they are more efficient than in later years. In this case, managers select an accelerated method to allocate cost.

Tax Reporting

Delta Air Lines, like most public companies, maintains two sets of accounting records. One set is prepared under GAAP for reporting to stockholders. The other set is prepared to determine the company's tax obligation under the Internal Revenue Code. When they first learn that companies maintain two sets of books, some people question the ethics or legality of the practice. In reality, **it is both legal and ethical to maintain separate records for tax and financial reporting purposes.**

The reason that it is legal to maintain two sets of books is simple: The objectives of GAAP and the Internal Revenue Code differ.

Financial Reporting (GAAP)	Tax Reporting (IRS)
The objective of financial reporting is to provide economic information about a business that is useful in projecting future cash flows of the business. Financial reporting rules follow generally accepted accounting principles.	The objective of the Internal Revenue Code is to raise sufficient revenues to pay for the expenditures of the federal government. Many of the Code's provisions are designed to encourage certain behaviors that are thought to benefit society (e.g., contributions to charities are made tax deductible to encourage people to support worthy programs).

While it is easy to understand why two sets of accounting records are permitted, perhaps the more interesting question is why managers elect to pay the extra cost of maintaining two sets of books. In some cases, differences between the Internal Revenue Code and GAAP leave the manager no choice but to maintain separate records. In other cases, the explanation is an economic one, called the **least and the latest rule.** All taxpayers want to pay the lowest amount of tax that is legally permitted and at the latest possible date. If you had the choice of paying $100,000 to the federal government at the end of this year or at the end of next year, you would choose the end of next year. By doing so, you could invest the money for an extra year and earn a significant return on the investment.

Similarly, by maintaining two sets of books, corporations can defer (delay) paying millions and sometimes billions of dollars in taxes. The following companies reported significant gross deferred tax obligations in a recent year. Much of these deferrals was due to differences in asset cost allocation methods:

Company	Deferred Tax Liabilities	Percentage Due to Applying Different Cost Allocation Methods
Delta Air Lines	$4,432 million	91%
PepsiCo	2,541 million	32
AT&T Corp.	5,939 million	65
Marriott International	148 million	84

Most corporations use the IRS-approved Modified Accelerated Cost Recovery System (MACRS) to calculate depreciation expense for their tax returns. MACRS is similar to the declining-balance method and is applied over relatively short asset lives to yield high depreciation expense in the early years. The high depreciation expense reported under MACRS reduces a corporation's taxable income and therefore the amount it must pay in taxes. MACRS provides an incentive for corporations to invest in modern property, plant, and equipment in order to be competitive in world markets. **It is not acceptable for financial reporting purposes.**

Depreciation Methods in Other Countries

The various depreciation methods discussed in this chapter are used widely by corporations in most countries. Some methods used in other countries are not generally used in the United States. German companies may depreciate an asset's cost based on the number of hours it is used, and British companies may use the annuity method, which results in lower depreciation during the early years of an asset's life (contrasted with accelerated depreciation, which results in higher depreciation during the early years).

Many countries, including Australia, Brazil, England, Hong Kong, Mexico, and Singapore, also permit the revaluation of property, plant, and equipment to their current cost as of the balance sheet date. The primary argument in favor of revaluation is that the historical cost of an asset purchased 15 or 20 years ago is not meaningful because of the impact of inflation. For example, most people would not compare the original price of a 1974 Ford to the original price of a 2004 Ford because the purchasing power of the dollar changed dramatically between those years. However, revaluation to current cost is prohibited in the United States (under GAAP) and in Canada, Germany, and Japan. A primary argument against revaluation is the lack of objectivity involved in estimating an asset's current cost.

Measuring Asset Impairment

Learning Objective 4
Explain the effect of asset impairment on the financial statements.

Corporations must review long-lived tangible and intangible assets for possible impairment. Two steps are necessary:

1. **Impairment** occurs when events or changed circumstances cause the estimated future cash flows (future benefits) of these assets to fall below their book value.

   If net book value > Estimated future cash flows, then the asset is impaired.

2. For any asset considered to be impaired, companies recognize a loss for the difference between the asset's book value and its fair value (a market concept).

   Impairment Loss = Net Book Value − Fair Value

   That is, the asset is **written down** to fair value.

Delta Air Lines reported the following write-down in its 2004 annual report:

REAL WORLD EXCERPT

2004 ANNUAL REPORT

During the December 2002 quarter, we decided to accelerate the retirement of 37 owned EMB-120 aircraft to achieve costs savings and operating efficiencies. We removed these aircraft from service during 2003. The accelerated retirement of these aircraft as well as a reduction in their estimated future cash flows and fair values resulted in an impairment charge.

During 2002, we recorded the following impairment charges for our owned B-727, MD-11 and EMB-120 aircraft:

	Used in Operations		Held for Sale				
	Writedown	No. of Aircraft	Writedown	No. of Aircraft	Subtotal	Spare Parts	Total
B-727	$ 24	23	$ 37	36	$ 61	$—	$ 61
MD-11	141	8			141	18	159
EMB-120	27	37			27	4	31
	$192		$ 37		$229	$22	$251

Source: Courtesy of Delta Air Lines, Inc.

Let's assume that the net book value of Delta's impaired aircraft was $8,320 million. If the future cash flows were estimated to be $8,000 million, then the asset was impaired because it was not expected to generate future benefits equal to its net book value. To compute the amount of the impairment loss, **fair value** is determined. For Delta, that process includes using published sources and third-party bids to obtain the value of the asset. If the asset's fair value was $7,500 million, then the loss is calculated as $820 million ($8,320 million net book value less $7,500 million fair value). The following journal entry would be recorded:

> **An asset is impaired if:**
> Book value > Future cash flows
>
> **Then the impairment loss is =**
> Book value − Fair value

Loss due to impairment of assets (+Loss, −SE) 820,000,000
   Flight equipment (−A) 820,000,000

Assets	=	Liabilities	+	Stockholders' Equity
Flight equipment − 820,000,000				Loss due to impairment − 820,000,000

Disposal of Property, Plant, and Equipment

In some cases, a business may **voluntarily** decide not to hold a long-term asset for its entire life. The company may drop a product from its line and no longer need the equipment that was used to produce its product, or managers may want to replace a machine with a more efficient one. These disposals include sales, trade-ins, or retirements. When Delta disposes of an old aircraft, the company may sell it to a cargo airline or regional airline. A business may also dispose of an asset **involuntarily,** as the result of a casualty such as a storm, fire, or accident.

> **Learning Objective 5**
> Analyze the disposal of property, plant, and equipment.

Disposals of long-term assets seldom occur on the last day of the accounting period. Therefore, depreciation must be recorded to the date of disposal. The disposal of a depreciable asset usually requires two journal entries:

1. An adjusting entry to update the depreciation expense and accumulated depreciation accounts.

2. An entry to record the disposal. The cost of the asset **and** any accumulated depreciation at the date of disposal must be removed from the accounts. The difference between any resources received on disposal of an asset and its book value at the date of disposal is treated as a gain or loss on the disposal of the asset. This gain (or loss) is reported on the income statement. It is not an operating revenue (or expense), however, because it arises from peripheral or incidental activities rather than from central operations. Gains and losses from disposals are usually shown as a separate item on the income statement.

Assume that at the end of year 17, Delta sold an aircraft that was no longer needed because of the elimination of service to a small city. The aircraft was sold for $5 million cash. The original cost of the flight equipment of $20 million was depreciated using the straight-line method over 20 years with no residual value ($1 million depreciation expense per year). The last accounting for depreciation was at the end of year 16; thus, depreciation expense must be recorded for year 17. The computations are as follows:

Cash received		$5,000,000
Original cost of flight equipment	$20,000,000	
Less: Accumulated depreciation ($1,000,000 × 17 years)	17,000,000	
Book value at date of sale		3,000,000
Gain on sale of flight equipment		$2,000,000

The entries and effects of the transaction on the date of the sale are as follows:

(1) Update depreciation expense for year 17:

Depreciation expense (+E, −SE) 1,000,000

    Accumulated depreciation (+XA, −A) 1,000,000

(2) Record the sale:

Cash (+A) 5,000,000

Accumulated depreciation (−XA, +A) 17,000,000

    Flight equipment (−A) 20,000,000

    Gain on sale of flight equipment (+Gain, +SE) 2,000,000

Assets		=	Liabilities	+	Stockholders' Equity	
(1) Accumulated					Depreciation	
depreciation	− 1,000,000				expense (+E)	− 1,000,000
(2) Flight equipment	− 20,000,000				Gain on sale	
Accumulated					of asset	+ 2,000,000
depreciation (+XA)	+17,000,000					
Cash	+ 5,000,000					

SELF-STUDY **QUIZ**

Now let's assume the same facts as above except that the asset was sold for $2,000,000 cash. Prepare the two entries on the date of the sale.

1. Update depreciation expense for year 17:

2. Record the sale:

Assets	=	Liabilities	=	Stockholders' Equity

After you have completed your answers, check them with the solutions at the bottom of the page.

Self-Study Quiz
Solutions

(1) Depreciation expense (+E, −SE) 1,000,000

    Accumulated depreciation (+XA, −A) 1,000,000

(2) Cash (+A) 2,000,000

Accumulated depreciation (−XA, +A) 17,000,000

Loss on sale of flight equipment (+Loss, −SE) 1,000,000

    Flight equipment (−A) 20,000,000

Assets		=	Liabilities	+	Stockholders' Equity	
(1) Accumulated					Depreciation	
depreciation	− 1,000,000				expense	−1,000,000
(2) Flight equipment	− 20,000,000				Loss on sale	
Accumulated					of asset	−1,000,000
depreciation	+17,000,000					
Cash	+ 2,000,000					

Taking a Different Strategy

Singapore Airlines, SIA, formed in 1972, has shown continued profitability as one of the world's largest operators of the most technologically advanced "jumbo jet," the Boeing 747-400. Unlike other airlines whose average fleet age is more than 12 years, Singapore Airlines uses its aircraft for an average of just under six years. This strategy has a dual effect. First, depreciation expense is significantly higher due to the aircraft's shorter estimated useful life and thus reduces net income. Singapore Airlines sells its used aircraft, however—an activity that has resulted in gains reported on the income statement. The choice of estimated useful lives and the timing of asset sales provide management with the flexibility to **manage earnings.**

For example, Singapore Airlines' 2001 annual report shows a gain on disposal of aircraft of $165.6 million representing 14.2 percent of pretax income. This is compared to only $85.8 million in 2000, or 7.8 percent of pretax income. Because the gains on disposals almost doubled, SIA enjoyed an increase in operating profit. Ignoring the effect of the gains, however, reveals that, in both 2000 and 2001, Singapore Airlines' operating profits would have **decreased** by 1.7 percent.

How is this accomplished? SIA depreciates its aircraft faster than most other airlines. Therefore, when it sells its aircraft, the book value used to record the sale is quite low relative to the actual proceeds from the sale, resulting in a gain. When earnings are low, management can retire more aircraft, recognizing the gains and increasing net income.

In general, the practice of using conservative accounting policies (in this case, high depreciation from short useful lives) to increase subsequent net income is called creating a "cookie jar." These "cookies" (aircraft whose sale will result in a large gain) are available as needed to boost net income. However, use of cookie jar reserves to manage earnings is under increasing scrutiny from auditors and regulators and is not desirable.

NATURAL RESOURCES AND INTANGIBLE ASSETS

Acquisition and Depletion of Natural Resources

You are probably most familiar with large companies that are involved in manufacturing (Ford, Black & Decker), distribution (Sears, Home Depot), or services (Federal Express, Holiday Inn). A number of large companies, some of which are less well known, develop raw materials and products from natural resources, including mineral deposits such as gold or iron ore, oil wells, and timber tracts. These resources are often called **wasting assets** because they are depleted (i.e., physically used up). Companies that develop natural resources are critical to the economy because they produce essential items such as lumber for construction, fuel for heating and transportation, and food for consumption. Because of the significant effect they can have on the environment, these companies attract considerable public attention. Concerned citizens often read the financial statements of companies involved in exploration for oil, coal, and various ores to determine the amount of money they spend to protect the environment.

When natural resources are acquired or developed, they are recorded in conformity with the **cost principle.** As a natural resource is used up, its acquisition cost must be apportioned among the periods in which revenues are earned in conformity with the **matching principle.** The term depletion describes the process of allocating a natural resource's cost over the period of its exploitation.[1] The units-of-production method is often applied to compute depletion.

Learning Objective 6
Apply measurement and reporting concepts for natural resources and intangible assets.

NATURAL RESOURCES are assets that occur in nature, such as mineral deposits, timber tracts, oil, and gas.

DEPLETION is the systematic and rational allocation of the cost of a natural resource over the period of exploitation.

[1]Consistent with the procedure for recording depreciation, an accumulated depletion account may be used. In practice, however, most companies credit the asset account directly for periodic depletion. This procedure is also typically used for intangible assets, which are discussed in the next section.

When a natural resource such as an oil well is depleted, the company obtains inventory (oil). Since depleting the natural resource is necessary to obtain the inventory, the depletion computed during a period is added to the cost of the inventory, not expensed in the period. Consider the following illustration:

A timber tract costing $530,000 is depleted over its estimated cutting period based on a "cutting" rate of approximately 20 percent per year:

> Note that the amount of the natural resource that is depleted is capitalized as inventory, not expensed. When the inventory is sold, the cost of goods sold will be included as an expense on the income statement.

Timber inventory (+A) 106,000
   Timber tract (−A) (or Accumulated depletion +XA)   106,000

Assets		=	Liabilities	+	Stockholders' Equity
Timber inventory	+ 106,000				
Timber tract	− 106,000				

Following is an excerpt from the asset section of International Paper's 2003 balance sheet along with the related footnote describing the accounting policies for the company's natural resource, forestland:

CONSOLIDATED BALANCE SHEET (DOLLARS IN MILLIONS)

	2003	2002
Assets		
Cash	$2,363	$1,074
. . .		
Forestlands	4,069	3,846

Note:

Forestlands

At December 31, 2003, International Paper and its subsidiaries controlled about 8.3 million acres of forestlands in the U.S., 1.5 million acres in Brazil, 795,000 acres in New Zealand, and had, through licenses and forest management agreements, harvesting rights on government-owned forestlands in Canada and Russia. Forestlands include owned property as well as certain timber harvesting rights with terms of one or more years, and are stated at cost, less cost of timber harvested. Costs attributable to timber are charged against income as trees are cut. The rate charged is determined annually based on the relationship of incurred costs to estimated current merchantable volume.

Acquisition and Amortization of Intangible Assets

Intangible assets are increasingly important resources for organizations. An intangible asset, like any other asset, has value because of certain rights and privileges often conferred by law on its owner. Unlike tangible assets such as land and buildings, however, an intangible asset has no material or physical substance. Examples of intangible assets include patents, trademarks, and licenses. Most intangible assets usually are evidenced by a legal document. Yet the growth in the importance of intangible assets has been the tremendous expansion in computer information systems and Web technologies and the frenzy in companies purchasing other companies at high prices, with the expectation that these intangible resources will provide significant future benefits to the company.

Intangible assets are recorded **at historical cost only if they have been purchased.** If these assets are developed internally by the company, they are expensed when incurred. Upon acquisition of intangible assets, managers determine whether the separate intangibles have definite or indefinite lives:

Definite Life   The cost of an intangible with a definite life is allocated on a straight-line basis each period over its useful life in a process called amortization that is similar to depreciation and depletion. Most companies do not estimate a residual value for their intangible assets. Amortization expense is included on the income statement each period and the intangible assets are reported at cost less accumulated amortization on the balance sheet.

> AMORTIZATION is the systematic and rational allocation of the acquisition cost of an intangible asset over its useful life.

Let's assume a company purchases a patent for $800,000 and intends to use it for 20 years. The adjusting entry to record $40,000 in patent amortization expense ($800,000 ÷ 20 years) is as follows:

Patent amortization expense (+E, −SE)	40,000	
Patents (−A) (or Accumulated amortization +XA)		40,000

Assets	=	Liabilities	+	Stockholders' Equity	
Patents − 40,000				Patent amortization expense (+E)	− 40,000

Indefinite Life   Intangible assets with indefinite lives are **not amortized.** Instead, these assets are to be tested at least annually for possible impairment, and the asset's book value is written down (decreased) to its fair value if impaired. The two-step process is similar to that used for assets discussed previously and summarized in the margin.

The AICPA's 2003 *Accounting Trends & Techniques* summarizes intangible assets most frequently disclosed by the 600 companies surveyed:

> **An asset is impaired if:**
> Book value > Future cash flows
>
> **Then the impairment loss is =**
> Book value − Fair value

	Number of Companies	Percentage of 600
Goodwill recognized in a business combination	505	84%
Trademarks, brand names, copyrights	165	28
Patents, patent rights	130	22
Customer lists	121	20
Technology	95	16
Noncompete covenants	76	13
Licenses, franchises, memberships	60	10
Other—described in the annual report	127	21

> For accounting purposes, GOODWILL (COST IN EXCESS OF NET ASSETS ACQUIRED) is the excess of the purchase price of a business over the fair market value of the business's assets and liabilities.

Goodwill

By far the most frequently reported intangible asset is goodwill (cost in excess of net assets acquired). The term goodwill, as used by most businesspeople, means the favorable reputation that a company has with its customers. Goodwill arises from factors such as customer confidence, reputation for good service or quality goods, location, outstanding management team, and financial standing. From its first day of operations, a successful business continually builds goodwill. In this context, the goodwill is said to be **internally generated** and is not reported as an asset (i.e., it was not purchased).

The only way to report goodwill as an asset is to purchase another business. Often the purchase price of the business exceeds the fair market value of all of its net assets (assets minus liabilities). Why would a company pay more for a business as a whole than it would pay if it bought the assets individually? The answer is to obtain its goodwill. You could easily buy modern bottling equipment to produce and sell a new cola drink, but you would not make as much money as you would if you acquired the goodwill associated with Coke or Pepsi brand names.

For accounting purposes, goodwill is defined as the difference between the purchase price of a company as a whole and the fair market value of its net assets:

Purchase price
— Fair market value of identifiable assets and liabilities
Goodwill to be reported

Delta Air Lines recently acquired two companies: Comair Holdings for $1.8 billion and ASA Holdings for $700 million. Delta's balance sheet presented in Exhibit 8.1 includes the individual assets from these companies plus an item valued at $2.1 billion called Goodwill. The notes to the statements include the following:

REAL WORLD EXCERPT

2003 ANNUAL REPORT

Note 1.

Basis of Presentation

. . .

Our Consolidated Financial Statements include the accounts of Delta Air Lines, Inc. and our wholly owned subsidiaries, including ASA Holdings, Inc. (ASA Holdings) and Comair Holdings, Inc. (Comair Holdings), collectively referred to as Delta. ASA Holdings is the parent company of Atlantic Southeast Airlines, Inc. (ASA), and Comair Holdings is the parent company of Comair, Inc. (Comair).

Source: Courtesy of Delta Air Lines, Inc.

Goodwill is considered to have an indefinite life and must be reviewed at least annually for possible impairment of value. Delta reported the following

REAL WORLD EXCERPT

2003 ANNUAL REPORT

At December 31, 2003, we performed the required annual impairment test of our goodwill and indefinite-lived intangible assets; that test indicated no impairment.

Trademarks

A **TRADEMARK** is an exclusive legal right to use a special name, image, or slogan.

A trademark is a special name, image, or slogan identified with a product or a company; it is protected by law. Trademarks are among the most valuable assets a company can own. For example, most of us cannot imagine the Walt Disney Company without Mickey Mouse. Similarly, you probably enjoy your favorite soft drink more because of the image that has been built up around its name than because of its taste. Many people can identify the shape of a corporate logo as quickly as they can recognize the shape of a stop sign. Although trademarks are valuable assets, they are rarely seen on balance sheets. The reason is simple; intangible assets are not recorded unless they are purchased. Companies often spend millions of dollars developing trademarks, but most of those expenditures are recorded as expenses rather than being capitalized as an intangible asset.

Copyrights

A **COPYRIGHT** is the exclusive right to publish, use, and sell a literary, musical, or artistic work.

A copyright gives the owner the exclusive right to publish, use, and sell a literary, musical, or artistic piece for a period not exceeding 70 years after the author's death.[2] The book you are reading has a copyright to protect the publisher and authors. It is against the law, for example, for an instructor to copy several chapters from this book and hand them out in class. A copyright that is purchased is recorded at cost.

---

[2]In general, the limit is 70 years beyond the death of an author. For anonymous authors, the limit is 95 years from the first publication date. For more detail, go to lcweb.loc.gov/copyright.

Patents

A patent is an exclusive right granted by the federal government for a period of 20 years, typically granted to a person who invents a new product or discovers a new process.[3] The patent enables the owner to use, manufacture, and sell both the subject of the patent and the patent itself. It prevents a competitor from simply copying a new invention or discovery until the inventor has had time to earn an economic return on the new product. Without the protection of a patent, inventors likely would be unwilling to search for new products. Patents are recorded at their purchase price or, if **developed internally,** at only their registration and legal costs because GAAP require the immediate expensing of research and development costs.

A PATENT is granted by the federal government for an invention; it is an exclusive right given to the owner to use, manufacture, and sell the subject of the patent.

Technology

The number of companies reporting a technology intangible asset jumped by nearly 55 percent between 2001 and 2002. Computer software and Web development costs are becoming increasingly significant. In 2003, IBM Corporation reported $814 million in software on its balance sheet and disclosed the following in the notes to the financial statements:

TECHNOLOGY includes costs for computer software and Web development.

> The company capitalizes certain costs that are incurred to purchase or to create and implement internal use computer software, which includes software coding, installation, testing and data conversion. Capitalized costs are amortized on a straight-line basis over two years.

Franchises

Franchises may be granted by the government or a business for a specified period and purpose. A city may grant one company a franchise to distribute gas to homes for heating purposes, or a company may sell franchises, such as the right to operate a KFC restaurant. Franchise agreements are contracts that can have a variety of provisions. They usually require an investment by the franchisee; therefore, they should be accounted for as intangible assets. The life of the franchise agreement depends on the contract. It may be a single year or an indefinite period. Blockbuster Video's franchise agreement covers a period of 20 years. Blockbuster has more than 900 stores under franchise agreements.

Licenses and Operating Rights

The Delta balance sheet presented in Exhibit 8.1 shows an asset operating rights and other intangibles for $95 million. The operating rights are authorized landing slots that are regulated by the government and are in limited supply at many airports. They are intangible assets that can be bought and sold by the airlines. Other types of licenses that grant permission to companies include using airwaves for radio and television broadcasts and land for cable and telephone lines.

A FRANCHISE is a contractual right to sell certain products or services, use certain trademarks, or perform activities in a geographical region.

Research and Development Expense—*Not an Intangible Asset*

If an intangible asset is developed internally, the cost of development normally is recorded as **research and development expense.** For example, Abbott Laboratories (a manufacturer of pharmaceutical and nutritional products) recently spent more than $1,351 million on research to discover new products. This amount was reported as an

LICENSES AND OPERATING RIGHTS, obtained through agreements with governmental units or agencies, permit owners to use public property in performing their services.

---

[3]For more details, go to www.uspto.gov.web/pac/general/#patent.

expense, not an asset, because research and development expenditures typically do not possess sufficient probability of resulting in measurable future cash flows. If Abbott Labs had spent an equivalent amount to purchase patents for new products from other drug companies, it would have recorded the expenditure as an asset.

FOCUS ON
CASH FLOWS

Productive Assets and Depreciation

Learning Objective 7
Explain the impact on cash flows of acquiring, using, and disposing of long-lived assets.

EFFECT ON STATEMENT OF CASH FLOWS

The indirect method for preparing the operating activities section of the statement of cash flows involves reconciling net income on the accrual basis (reported on the income statement) to cash flows from operations. This means that, among other adjustments, (1) revenues and expenses that do not involve cash and (2) gains and losses that relate to investing or financing activities (not operations) should be eliminated. When depreciation is recorded, no cash payment is made (i.e., there is no credit to Cash). Since depreciation expense (a noncash expense) is subtracted in calculating net income on the income statement, it must be added back to net income to eliminate its effect. Likewise, since any gain (or loss) on sale of long-term assets (an investing activity) is added (or subtracted) to determine net income, it must be subtracted (or added) from net income to eliminate its effect.

In General → Acquiring, selling, and depreciating long-term assets are reflected on a company's cash flow statement as indicated in the following table:

	Effect on Cash Flows
Operating activities (indirect method)	
Net income	$xxx
Adjusted for: Depreciation and amortization expense	+
Gains on sale of long-term assets	−
Losses on sale of long-term assets	+
Losses due to asset impairment write-downs	+
Investing activities	
Purchase of long-term assets	−
Sale of long-term assets	+

Selected Focus Companies: Percentage of Depreciation to Cash Flows from Operations

Timberland   12%

Harley-Davidson   21%

Delta Air Lines   272%

Focus Company Analysis → The following is a condensed version of Delta's statement of cash flows for 2003. Buying and selling long-term assets are investing activities. In 2003, Delta used $744 million in cash to purchase flight equipment and ground property and equipment. Delta also sold flight equipment for $15 million in cash. Since selling long-term assets is not an operating activity, any gains (losses) on sales of long-term assets that were included in net income must be deducted from (added to) net income in the operating activities section to eliminate the effect of the sale. Unless they are large, these gain and loss adjustments normally are not specifically highlighted on the statement of cash flows. Delta did not list any gains or losses in 2003.

Finally, in capital-intensive industries such as airlines, depreciation is a significant noncash expense. In Delta's case, depreciation and amortization expense was the single largest adjustment to net income in determining cash flows from operations. It was 272 percent of operating cash flows in 2003, following two years in which it was even higher. This extreme situation can primarily be explained by net losses over the last several years. Other focus companies that are less capital intensive, such as Timberland and Harley-Davidson, have significantly lower depreciation adjustments as a percentage of cash flows from operations.

DELTA AIR LINES, INC.
CONSOLIDATED STATEMENTS OF CASH FLOWS
For the Years Ended December 31, 2003, 2002, and 2001

(in millions)	2003	2002	2001
Cash Flows from Operating Activities			
Net loss	(773)	(1,272)	(1,216)
Adjustment to reconcile net income to cash provided by operating activities:			
Asset write-downs *(due to impairment)*	47	287	339
Depreciation and amortization	1,230	1,181	1,283
Other *(summarized)*	(51)	89	(170)
Net cash provided by operating activities	453	285	236
Cash Flows from Investing Activities			
Property and equipment additions:			
Flight equipment	(382)	(922)	(2,321)
Ground property and equipment	(362)	(364)	(472)
Proceeds from sale of flight equipment	15	100	66
Other *(summarized)*	469	77	31
Net cash used in investing activities	(260)	(1,109)	(2,696)

A Misinterpretation

FINANCIAL
ANALYSIS

Some analysts misinterpret the meaning of a noncash expense, saying that "cash is provided by depreciation." Although depreciation is added in the operating section of the statement of cash flows, **depreciation is not a source of cash.** Cash from operations can be provided only by selling goods and services. A company with a large amount of depreciation expense does not generate more cash compared with a company that reports a small amount of depreciation expense, assuming that they are exactly the same in every other respect. While depreciation expense reduces the amount of reported net income for a company, it does not reduce the amount of cash generated by the company because it is a noncash expense. Remember that the effects of recording depreciation are a reduction in stockholders' equity and in fixed assets, not in cash. That is why, on the statement of cash flows, depreciation expense is added back to net income on an accrual basis to compute cash flows from operations (on a cash basis).

Although depreciation is a noncash expense, the **depreciation method used for tax purposes can affect a company's cash flows.** Depreciation is a deductible expense for income tax purposes. The higher the amount of depreciation recorded by a company for tax purposes, the lower the company's taxable income and the taxes it must pay. Because taxes must be paid in cash, a reduction in a company's results reduces the company's cash outflows (that is, lower net income leads to lower tax payments).

DEMONSTRATION **CASE**

(Resolve the requirements before proceeding to the suggested solution that follows.) Diversified Industries started as a residential construction company. In recent years, it has expanded into heavy construction, ready-mix concrete, sand and gravel, construction supplies, and earth-moving services. The company completed the following transactions during 2008. Amounts have been simplified.

2008

Jan. 1   The management decided to buy a 10-year-old building for $175,000 and the land on which it was situated for $130,000. It paid $100,000 in cash and signed a mortgage note payable for the rest.

Jan. 12   Paid $38,000 in renovation costs on the building prior to use.

June 19   Bought a third location for a gravel pit (designated Gravel Pit No. 3) for $50,000 cash. It was estimated that 100,000 cubic yards of gravel could be removed.

July 10   Paid $1,200 for ordinary repairs on the building.

Aug. 1   Paid $10,000 for costs of preparing the new gravel pit for exploitation.

Dec. 31   Year-end adjustments:

a. The building will be depreciated on a straight-line basis over an estimated useful life of 30 years. The estimated residual value is $33,000.

b. During 2008, 12,000 cubic yards of gravel were removed from Gravel Pit No. 3.

c. Diversified purchased another company several years ago at $100,000 over the fair value of the net assets acquired. The goodwill has an indefinite life.

d. At the beginning of the year, the company owned equipment with a cost of $650,000 and accumulated depreciation of $150,000. The equipment is being depreciated using the double-declining-balance method, with a useful life of 20 years and no residual value.

e. At year-end, the company tested its long-lived assets for possible impairment of their value. It identified a piece of old excavation equipment with a cost of $156,000 and remaining book value of $120,000. Due to its smaller size and lack of safety features, the old equipment has limited use. The future cash flows are expected to be $40,000 and the fair value is determined to be $35,000. Goodwill was found not to be impaired.

December 31, 2008, is the end of the annual accounting period.

Required:

1. Indicate the accounts affected and the amount and direction (+ for increase and − for decrease) of the effect of each of the preceding events on the financial statement categories at the end of the year. Use the following headings:

Date	Assets	=	Liabilities	+	Stockholders' Equity

2. Record the adjusting journal entries for December 31(a) and (b) only.

3. Show the December 31, 2008, balance sheet classification and amount for each of the following items:

> Fixed assets—land, building, equipment, and gravel pit
> Intangible asset—goodwill

4. Assuming that the company had sales of $1,000,000 for the year and a net book value of $500,000 for fixed assets at the beginning of the year, compute the fixed asset turnover ratio. Explain its meaning.

SUGGESTED SOLUTION

1. Effects of events (with computations):

Date	Assets		=	Liabilities		+	Stockholders' Equity	
Jan. 1	Cash Land Building	− 100,000 + 130,000 + 175,000		Note payable	+205,000			
Jan. 12 (1)	Cash Building	− 38,000 + 38,000						
June 19 (2)	Cash Gravel Pit No. 3	− 50,000 + 50,000						
July 10 (3)	Cash	− 1,200					Repairs expense	− 1,200
Aug. 1 (4)	Cash Gravel Pit No. 3	− 10,000 + 10,000						

Dec. 31 *a*
(5)
	Accumulated
	   depreciation
		− 6,000					Depreciation
							   expense
								− 6,000

Dec. 31 *b* (6)	Gravel Pit No. 3 Gravel inventory	− 7,200 + 7,200						
Dec. 31 *c* (7)	No entry							

Dec. 31 *d*
(8)
	Accumulated
	   depreciation
		− 50,000					Depreciation
							   expense
								− 50,000

Dec. 31 *e* (9)	Equipment	− 85,000					Loss due to asset impairment	− 85,000

(1) Capitalize the $38,000 expenditure because it is necessary to prepare the asset for use.

(2) This is a natural resource.

(3) This is an ordinary repair (revenue expenditure) and should be expensed.

(4) Capitalize the $10,000 expenditure because it is necessary to prepare the asset for use.

(5)

Cost of Building		**Straight-Line Depreciation**
Initial purchase price	$175,000	($213,000 cost − $33,000 residual value) ×
Repairs prior to use	38,000	1/30 years = **$6,000** annual depreciation
Acquisition cost	$213,000	

(6)

Cost of Gravel Pit		**Units-of-Production Depletion**
Initial payment	$50,000	($60,000 cost ÷ 100,000 estimated production) ×
Preparation costs	10,000	12,000 actual cubic yards = **$7,200** annual depletion
Acquisition cost	$60,000	Capitalize the depletion to gravel inventory.

(7) Goodwill has indefinite life and is therefore not amortized. We will test for impairment later.

(8) **Double-declining-balance depreciation**

$$($650,000 \text{ cost} − $150,000 \text{ accumulated depreciation}) × 2/20 \text{ years} =$$
$$$50,000 \text{ depreciation for 2008}$$

(9) **Asset impairment**

Impairment Test: The book value of old equipment, $120,000, exceeds expected future cash flows, $40,000. The asset is impaired.

Impairment Loss	
Book value	$120,000
Less: Fair value	− 35,000
Loss due to impairment	$ 85,000

2. Adjusting entries at December 31, 2008:

     a. Depreciation expense, building (+E, −SE) 6,000
        Accumulated depreciation (+XA, −A) 6,000
     b. Gravel inventory (+A) 7,200
        Gravel pit No. 3 (−A) 7,200

3. Partial balance sheet, December 31, 2008:

Assets		
Fixed assets		
Land		$130,000
Building	$213,000	
Less: Accumulated depreciation	6,000	207,000
Equipment ($650,000 − 85,000)	565,000	
Less: Accumulated depreciation		
($150,000 + 50,000)	200,000	365,000
Gravel pit		52,800
Total fixed assets		$754,800
Intangible asset		
Goodwill		$100,000

4. Fixed asset turnover ratio:

$$\frac{\text{Sales}}{(\text{Beginning Net Fixed Asset Balance} + \text{Ending Net Fixed Asset Balance}) \div 2} = \frac{\$1,000,000}{(\$500,000 + \$754,800) \div 2} = 1.59$$

This construction company is capital intensive. The fixed asset turnover ratio measures the company's efficiency at using its investment in property, plant, and equipment to generate sales.

Chapter Supplement A

Changes in Depreciation Estimates

Depreciation is based on two estimates, useful life and residual value. These estimates are made at the time a depreciable asset is acquired. As experience with the asset accumulates, one or both of these initial estimates may need to be revised. In addition, extraordinary repairs and additions may be added to the original acquisition cost at some time during the asset's use. When it is clear that either estimate should be revised to a material degree or that the asset's cost has changed, the undepreciated asset balance (less any residual value at that date) should be apportioned over the remaining estimated life from the current year into the future. This is called a prospective **change in estimate.**

    To compute the new depreciation expense due to a change in estimate for any of the depreciation methods described here, substitute the net book value for the original acquisition cost, the new residual value for the original amount, and the estimated remaining life in place of the original estimated life. As an illustration, the formula using the straight-line method follows.

Original Straight-Line Formula Modified for a Change in Estimate:

$$(\text{Cost} - \text{Residual Value}) \times \frac{1}{\text{Useful Life}} = \text{Original Depreciation Expense}$$

$$(\text{Net Book Value} - \text{New Residual Value}) \times \frac{1}{\text{Remaining Life}} = \text{Revised Depreciation Expense}$$

Assume Delta purchased an aircraft for $60,000,000 with an estimated useful life of 20 years and estimated residual value of $3,000,000. Shortly after the start of year 5, Delta changed the initial estimated life to 25 years and lowered the estimated residual value to $2,400,000. At the end of year 5, the computation of the new amount for depreciation expense is as follows:

Original depreciation expense

$$(\$60,000,000 - \$3,000,000) \times 1/20 = \$\ 2,850,000 \text{ per year}$$
$$\times\ 4 \text{ years}$$

Accumulated depreciation at the end of year 4 $11,400,000

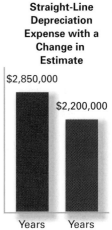

Straight-Line
Depreciation
Expense with a
Change in
Estimate

Net book value at the end of year 4

Acquisition cost	$60,000,000
Less: Accumulated depreciation	11,400,000
Net book value	$48,600,000

Depreciation in years 5 through 25 based on changes in estimates

$$(\text{Net book value} - \text{New residual value}) \times 1/\text{remaining years} = \text{New depreciation expense}$$

$$(\$48,600,000 - \$2,400,000) \times 1/21\ (25 - 4 \text{ years}) = \$2,200,000 \text{ per year}$$

Companies may also change depreciation methods (for example, from declining-balance to straight-line). Such a change requires significantly more disclosure since it violates the consistency principle that requires that accounting information reported in the financial statements be comparable across accounting periods. Under GAAP, changes in accounting estimates and depreciation methods should be made only when a new estimate or accounting method "better measures" the periodic income of the business.

Delta Air Lines changed depreciation estimates in the 1990s. The company's financial statements contained the following note:

As of July 1, 1998, we increased the depreciable lives of certain aircraft types from 20 to 25 years. The change in estimate reduced depreciation expense by $92 million ($.064 basic and $.060 diluted earnings per share) for fiscal 1999.

Source: Courtesy of Delta Air Lines, Inc.

1999 ANNUAL REPORT

Notice that Delta changed the estimated life of its flight equipment. Why would Delta's management revise the estimates of useful life? The notes to the financial statements in 1999 indicate that Delta received delivery of several new aircraft from Boeing, including the Boeing 777. This popular and efficient jet is a type of "new generation aircraft." Delta suggests by the increase in estimated useful life to 25 years that such aircraft will be flown longer than prior jet purchases.

SELF-STUDY **QUIZ**

Assume that Delta Air Lines owned a service truck that originally cost $100,000. When purchased, the truck had an estimated useful life of 10 years with no residual value. After operating the truck for 5 years, Delta determined that the remaining life was only two more years. Based on this change in estimate, what amount of depreciation should be recorded over the remaining life of the asset? Delta uses the straight-line method.

After you have completed your answer, compare it with the solution at the bottom of the page.

CHAPTER **TAKE-AWAYS**

1. **Define, classify, and explain the nature of long-lived productive assets and interpret the fixed asset turnover ratio.**   p. 399

   a. Noncurrent assets are those that a business retains for long periods of time for use in the course of normal operations rather than for sale. They may be divided into tangible assets (land, buildings, equipment, natural resources) and intangible assets (including goodwill, patents, and franchises).

   b. The cost allocation method utilized affects the amount of net property, plant, and equipment that is used in the computation of the fixed asset turnover ratio. Accelerated methods reduce book value and increase the turnover ratio.

2. **Apply the cost principle to measure the acquisition and maintenance of property, plant, and equipment.**   p. 401

   Acquisition cost of property, plant, and equipment is the cash-equivalent purchase price plus all reasonable and necessary expenditures made to acquire and prepare the asset for its intended use. These assets may be acquired using cash, debt, stock, or through self-construction. Expenditures made after the asset is in use are either additions and improvements (capital expenditures) or ordinary repairs (revenue expenditures):

   a. *Revenue expenditures* (ordinary repairs and maintenance) provide benefits during the current accounting period only. Amounts are debited to appropriate current expense accounts when the expenses are incurred.

   b. *Capital expenditures* (additions and improvements) provide benefits for one or more accounting periods beyond the current period. Amounts are debited to the appropriate asset accounts and depreciated, depleted, or amortized over their useful lives.

3. **Apply various cost allocation methods as assets are held and used over time.**   p. 406

   Cost allocation methods: In conformity with the matching principle, cost (less any estimated residual value) is allocated to periodic expense over the periods benefited. Because of depreciation, the net book value of an asset declines over time and net income is reduced by the amount of the expense. Common depreciation methods include straight-line (a constant amount over time), units-of-production (a variable amount over time), and double-declining-balance (a decreasing amount over time).

   • Depreciation—buildings and equipment.

   • Depletion—natural resources.

   • Amortization—intangibles.

4. **Explain the effect of asset impairment on the financial statements.**   p. 416

   When events or changes in circumstances reduce the estimated future cash flows of long-lived assets below their book value, the book values should be written down (by recording a loss) to the fair value of the assets.

Self-Study Quiz
   Solution

$50,000 (book value after 5 years) ÷ 2 years (remaining life) = $25,000 depreciation expense per year.

5. **Analyze the disposal of property, plant, and equipment.** p. 417

   When assets are disposed of through sale or abandonment,

   • Record additional depreciation since the last adjustment was made.

   • Remove the cost of the old asset and its related accumulated depreciation, depletion, or amortization.

   • Recognize the cash proceeds.

   • Recognize any gain or loss when the asset's net book value is not equal to the cash received.

6. **Apply measurement and reporting concepts for natural resources and intangible assets.** p. 419

   The cost principle should be applied in recording the acquisition of natural resources and intangible assets. Natural resources should be depleted (usually by the units-of-production method) usually with the amount of the depletion expense capitalized to an inventory account. Intangibles with definite useful lives are amortized using the straight-line method. Intangibles with indefinite useful lives, including goodwill, are not amortized, but are reviewed at least annually for impairment. Report intangibles at net book value on the balance sheet.

7. **Explain the impact on cash flows of acquiring, using, and disposing of long-lived assets.** p. 424

   Depreciation expense is a noncash expense that has no effect on cash. It is added back to net income on the statement of cash flows to determine cash from operations. Acquiring and disposing of long-lived assets are investing activities.

   In previous chapters, we discussed business and accounting issues related to the assets a company holds. In Chapters 9, 10, and 11, we shift our focus to the other side of the balance sheet to see how managers finance business operations and the acquisition of productive assets. We discuss various types of liabilities in Chapters 9 and 10 and examine stockholders' equity in Chapter 11.

KEY **RATIO**

The **fixed asset turnover ratio** measures how efficiently a company utilizes its investment in property, plant, and equipment over time. Its ratio can then be compared to competitors' ratios. The fixed asset turnover ratio is computed as follows (p. 400):

$$\text{Fixed Asset Turnover} = \frac{\text{Net Sales (or operating revenues)}}{\text{Average Net Fixed Assets}}$$

FINDING **FINANCIAL INFORMATION**

Balance Sheet

Under Noncurrent Assets

Property, plant, and equipment (net of accumulated depreciation)

Natural resources (net of accumulated depletion)

Intangibles (net of accumulated amortization, if any)

Income Statement

Under Operating Expenses

Depreciation, depletion, and amortization expense **or** included in

Selling, general, and administrative expenses and

Cost of goods sold (with the amount for depreciation expense disclosed in a note)

Statement of Cash Flows

Under Operating Activities (indirect method)
Net income
+ Depreciation and amortization expense
− Gains on sales of assets
+ Losses on sales of assets

Under Investing Activities
+ Sales of assets for cash
− Purchases of assets for cash

Notes

Under Summary of Significant Accounting Policies
Description of management's choice for depreciation and amortization methods, including useful lives, and the amount of annual depreciation expense, if not listed on the income statement.

Under a Separate Footnote
If not specified on the balance sheet, a listing of the major classifications of long-lived assets at cost and the balance in accumulated depreciation, depletion, and amortization.

KEY TERMS

QUESTIONS

1. Define *long-lived assets*. Why are they considered to be a "bundle of future services"?
2. How is the fixed asset turnover ratio computed? Explain its meaning.
3. What are the classifications of long-lived assets? Explain each.
4. Relate the cost principle to the accounting for long-lived assets. Under the cost principle, what amounts should be included in the acquisition cost of a long-lived asset?
5. Describe the relationship between the matching principle and accounting for long-lived assets.
6. Distinguish between
   a. Capital expenditures and revenue expenditures. How is each accounted for?
   b. Ordinary repairs and improvements. How is each accounted for?
7. Distinguish among depreciation, depletion, and amortization.
8. In computing depreciation, three values must be known or estimated; identify and explain the nature of each.
9. The estimated useful life and residual value of a long-lived asset relate to the current owner or user rather than all potential users. Explain this statement.
10. What type of depreciation expense pattern is used under each of the following methods and when is its use appropriate?
    a. The straight-line method.
    b. The units-of-production method.
    c. The double-declining-balance method.
11. Over what period should an addition to an existing long-lived asset be depreciated? Explain.

12. What is an *asset impairment?* How is it accounted for?
13. When equipment is sold for more than net book value, how is the transaction recorded? For less than net book value? What is net book value?
14. Define *intangible asset.* What period should be used to amortize an intangible asset with a definite life?
15. Define *goodwill.* When is it appropriate to record goodwill as an intangible asset?
16. Why is depreciation expense added to net income on the statement of cash flows?

MULTIPLE-**CHOICE QUESTIONS**

1. Simon Company and Allen Company both bought a new delivery truck on January 1, 2005. Both companies paid exactly the same cost, $30,000 for their respective vehicles. As of December 31, 2008, the net book value of Simon's truck was less than Allen Company's net book value for the same vehicle. Which of the following is an acceptable explanation for the difference in net book value?
   a. Both companies elected straight-line depreciation, but Simon Company used a longer estimated life.
   b. Simon Company estimated a lower residual value, but both estimated the same useful life and both elected straight-line depreciation.
   c. Because GAAP specifies rigid guidelines regarding the calculation of depreciation, this situation is not possible.
   d. Simon Company is using the straight-line method of depreciation, and Allen Company is using the double-declining-balance method of depreciation.

2. Barber, Inc., followed the practice of depreciating its building on a straight-line basis. A building was purchased in 2007 and had an estimated useful life of 20 years and a residual value of $20,000. The company's depreciation expense for 2007 was $20,000 on the building. What was the original cost of the building?
   a. $360,000   c. $400,000
   b. $380,000   d. $420,000

3. ACME, Inc., uses straight-line depreciation for all of its depreciable assets. ACME sold a used piece of machinery on December 31, 2008, that it purchased on January 1, 2007, for $10,000. The asset had a five-year life, zero residual value, and $2,000 accumulated depreciation as of December 31, 2007. If the sales price of the used machine was $7,500, the resulting gain or loss upon the sale was which of the following amounts?
   a. loss of $500   d. gain of $1,500
   b. gain of $500   e. No gain or loss upon the sale
   c. loss of $1,500

4. Under what method(s) of depreciation is an asset's *net book value* the depreciable base (the amount to be depreciated)?
   a. Straight-line method   c. Declining-balance method
   b. Units-of-production method   d. All of the above

5. What assets should be amortized using the straight-line method?
   a. Natural resources   c. Intangible assets with indefinite lives
   b. Intangible assets with definite lives   d. All of the above

6. A company wishes to report the highest earnings possible for financial reporting purposes. Therefore, when calculating depreciation,
   a. it will follow the MACRS depreciation tables prescribed by the IRS.
   b. it will select the shortest lives possible for its assets.
   c. it will estimate higher residual values for its assets.
   d. it will select the lowest residual values for its assets.

7. How many of the following statements regarding goodwill are true?
   ■ Goodwill is not reported unless purchased in an exchange.
   ■ Goodwill must be reviewed annually for possible impairment.
   ■ Impairment of goodwill results in a decrease in net income.
   a. none   c. two
   b. one   d. three

8. Company X is going to retire equipment that is fully depreciated with no residual value. The equipment will simply be disposed of, not sold. Which of the following statements is false?
   a. Total assets will not change as a result of this transaction.
   b. Net income will not be impacted as a result of this transaction.
   c. This transaction will not impact cash flow.
   d. All of the above statements are true.

9. When recording depreciation, which of the following statements is true?
   a. Total assets increase and stockholders' equity increases.
   b. Total assets decrease and total liabilities increase.
   c. Total assets decrease and stockholders' equity increases.
   d. None of the above are true.

10. (Supplement) Thornton Industries purchased a machine for $45,000 and is depreciating it with the straight-line method over a life of 10 years, using a residual value of $3,000. At the beginning of the sixth year, a major overhaul was made costing $5,000, and the total estimated useful life was extended to 13 years. Depreciation expense for year 6 is:
   a. $1,885.   d. $3,625.
   b. $2,000.   e. $4,200.
   c. $3,250.

For more practice on more multiple-choice questions, go to the text website www.mhhe.com/libby5e or the Topic Tackler DVD for use with this text.

MINI-EXERCISES

 Available with McGraw-Hill's Homework Manager

M8-1
LO1, 3, 6

Classifying Long-Lived Assets and Related Cost Allocation Concepts

For each of the following long-lived assets, indicate its nature and related cost allocation concept. Use the following symbols:

	Nature			Cost Allocation Concept	
L	Land		DR	Depreciation	
B	Building		DP	Depletion	
E	Equipment		A	Amortization	
NR	Natural resource		NO	No cost allocation	
I	Intangible		O	Other	
O	Other				

Asset	Nature	Cost Allocation	Asset	Nature	Cost Allocation
(1) Copyright	___	___	(6) Operating license	___	___
(2) Land held for use	___	___	(7) Land held for sale	___	___
(3) Warehouse	___	___	(8) Delivery vans	___	___
(4) Oil well	___	___	(9) Timber tract	___	___
(5) New engine for old machine	___	___	(10) Production plant	___	___

M8-2
LO1

Computing and Evaluating the Fixed Asset Turnover Ratio

The following information was reported by Cutter's Air Cargo Service for 2003:

Net fixed assets (beginning of year)	$1,450,000
Net fixed assets (end of year)	2,250,000
Net sales for the year	3,250,000
Net income for the year	1,700,000

Compute the company's fixed asset turnover ratio for the year. What can you say about Cutter's ratio when compared to Delta's 2003 ratio?

Identifying Capital and Revenue Expenditures

M8-3
LO2

For each of the following items, enter the correct letter to the left to show the type of expenditure. Use the following:

Type of Expenditure		Transactions
C	Capital expenditure	____ (1) Paid $400 for ordinary repairs.
R	Revenue expenditure	____ (2) Paid $6,000 for extraordinary repairs.
N	Neither	____ (3) Paid cash, $20,000, for addition to old building.
		____ (4) Paid for routine maintenance, $200, on credit.
		____ (5) Purchased a machine, $7,000; gave long-term note.
		____ (6) Paid three-year insurance premium, $900.
		____ (7) Purchased a patent, $4,300 cash.
		____ (8) Paid $10,000 for monthly salaries.
		____ (9) Paid cash dividends, $20,000.

Computing Book Value (Straight-Line Depreciation)

M8-4
LO3

Calculate the book value of a three-year-old machine that cost $21,500, has an estimated residual value of $1,500, and has an estimated useful life of four years. The company uses straight-line depreciation.

Computing Book Value (Double-Declining-Balance Depreciation)

M8-5
LO3

Calculate the book value of a three-year-old machine that cost $21,500, has an estimated residual value of $1,500, and has an estimated useful life of four years. The company uses double-declining-balance depreciation. Round to the nearest dollar.

Computing Book Value (Units-of-Production Depreciation)

M8-6
LO3

Calculate the book value of a three-year-old machine that cost $21,500, has an estimated residual value of $1,500, and has an estimated useful life of 20,000 machine hours. The company uses units-of-production depreciation and ran the machine 3,000 hours in year 1, 8,000 hours in year 2, 7,000 hours in year 3, and 2,000 hours in year 4.

Identifying Asset Impairment

M8-7
LO4

For each of the following scenarios, indicate whether an asset has been impaired (Y for yes and N for no) and, if so, the amount of loss that should be recorded.

	Book Value	Estimated Future Cash Flows	Fair Value	Is Asset Impaired?	If so, Amount of Loss?
a. Machine	$ 16,000	$ 10,000	$ 9,000		
b. Copyright	40,000	41,000	39,000		
c. Factory building	50,000	35,000	30,000		
d. Building	230,000	230,000	210,000		

Recording the Disposal of a Long-Lived Asset (Straight-Line Depreciation)

M8-8
LO5

As part of a major renovation at the beginning of the year, Mullins' Pharmacy, Inc., sold shelving units (store fixtures) that were 10 years old for $1,400 cash. The original cost of the shelves was $6,200 and had been depreciated on a straight-line basis over an estimated useful life of 12 years with an estimated residual value of $200. Record the sale of the shelving units.

Computing Goodwill and Patents

M8-9
LO6

Elizabeth Pie Company has been in business for 30 years and has developed a large group of loyal restaurant customers. Bonanza Foods made an offer to buy Elizabeth Pie Company for $5,000,000. The book value of Elizabeth Pie's recorded assets and liabilities on the date of the offer is $4,400,000 with a market value of $4,600,000. Elizabeth Pie also (1) holds a patent for a pie crust fluting machine that the company invented (the patent with a market value of $200,000 was never recorded by Elizabeth Pie because it was developed internally) and (2) estimates goodwill from loyal customers to be $300,000 (also never recorded by the company). Should Elizabeth Pie Company management accept Bonanza Foods' offer of $5,000,000? If so, compute the amount of goodwill that Bonanza Foods should record on the date of the purchase.

M8-10
LO7

Preparing the Statement of Cash Flows

Wagner Company had the following activities for the year ended December 31, 2008: Sold land for cash at a cost of $15,000. Purchased $80,000 of equipment, paying $75,000 in cash and the rest on a note payable. Recorded $3,000 in depreciation expense for the year. Net income for the year was $10,000. Prepare the operating and investing sections of a statement of cash flows for the year based on the data provided.

EXERCISES

 Available with McGraw-Hill's Homework Manager

E8-1
LO1
Hasbro, Inc.

Preparing a Classified Balance Sheet

The following is a list of account titles and amounts (dollars in millions) reported by Hasbro, Inc., a leading manufacturer of games, toys, and interactive entertainment software for children and families:

Buildings and improvements	$206	Goodwill	$ 464
Prepaid expenses and other		Machinery and equipment	304
current assets	212	Accumulated depreciation	358
Allowance for doubtful accounts	39	Inventories	169
Other noncurrent assets	280	Other intangibles	1,146
Accumulated amortization		Land and improvements	18
(other intangibles)	435	Accounts receivable	646
Cash and cash equivalents	521	Tools, dies, and molds	30

Required:
Prepare the asset section of the balance sheet for Hasbro, Inc., classifying the assets into Current Assets, Property, Plant, and Equipment (net), and Other Assets.

E8-2
LO1
Apple Computer

Computing and Interpreting the Fixed Asset Turnover Ratio from a Financial Analyst's Perspective

The following data were included in a recent Apple Computer annual report:

In millions	2003	2002	2001	2000	1999	1998	1997	1996
Net sales	$6,207	$5,742	$5,363	$7,983	$6,134	$5,941	$7,081	$9,833
Net property, plant, and equipment	669	621	564	313	318	348	486	598

Required:
1. Compute Apple's fixed asset turnover ratio for 1997, 1999, 2001, and 2003 (the odd years).
2. How might a financial analyst interpret the results?

E8-3
LO2, 3

Computing and Recording Cost and Depreciation of Assets (Straight-Line Depreciation)

KD Company bought a building for $71,200 cash and the land on which it is located for $106,800 cash. The company paid transfer costs of $2,000 ($800 for the building and $1,200 for the land). Renovation costs on the building were $21,200.

Required:
1. Give the journal entry to record the purchase of the property, including all expenditures. Assume that all transactions were for cash and that all purchases occurred at the start of the year.

2. Compute straight-line depreciation at the end of one year, assuming an estimated 12-year useful life and a $14,000 estimated residual value.
3. What would be the net book value of the property (land and building) at the end of year 2?

Determining Financial Statement Effects of an Asset Acquisition and Depreciation (Straight-Line Depreciation)

E8-4
LO2, 3

Kalriess Company ordered a machine on January 1, 2008, at an invoice price of $20,000. On date of delivery, January 2, 2008, the company paid $8,000 on the machine, and the balance was on credit at 12 percent interest. On January 3, 2008, it paid $250 for freight on the machine. On January 5, Kalreiss paid installation costs relating to the machine amounting to $1,200. On July 1, 2008, the company paid the balance due on the machine plus the interest. On December 31, 2008 (the end of the accounting period), Kalreiss recorded depreciation on the machine using the straight-line method with an estimated useful life of 10 years and an estimated residual value of $3,450.

Required (round all amounts to the nearest dollar):
1. Indicate the effects (accounts, amounts, and + or −) of each transaction (on January 1, 2, 3, 5, and July 1) on the accounting equation. Use the following schedule:

Date	Assets	=	Liabilities	+	Stockholders' Equity

2. Compute the acquisition cost of the machine.
3. Compute the depreciation expense to be reported for 2008.
4. What is the impact on the cost of the machine of the interest paid on the 12 percent note? Under what circumstances can interest expense be included in acquisition cost?
5. What would be the net book value of the machine at the end of 2009?

Recording Depreciation and Repairs (Straight-Line Depreciation)

E8-5
LO2, 3

Stacey Company operates a small manufacturing facility as a supplement to its regular service activities. At the beginning of 2007, an asset account for the company showed the following balances:

Manufacturing equipment	$80,000
Accumulated depreciation through 2006	55,000

During 2007, the following expenditures were incurred for the equipment:

Routine maintenance and repairs on the equipment	$ 850
Major overhaul of the equipment that improved efficiency	10,500

The equipment is being depreciated on a straight-line basis over an estimated life of 15 years with a $5,000 estimated residual value. The annual accounting period ends on December 31.

Required:
1. Give the adjusting entry that was made at the end of 2006 for depreciation on the manufacturing equipment.
2. Starting at the beginning of 2007, what is the remaining estimated life?
3. Give the journal entries to record the two expenditures during 2007.

Determining Financial Statement Effects of Depreciation and Repairs (Straight-Line Depreciation)

E8-6
LO2, 3

Refer to the information in E8-5.

Required:
Indicate the effects (accounts, amounts, and + or −) of the following on the accounting equation.

Date	Assets	=	Liabilities	+	Stockholders' Equity

1. The adjustment for depreciation at the end of 2006.
2. The two expenditures during 2007.

E8-7 **Computing Depreciation under Alternative Methods**

LO3

Rita's Pita Company bought a new dough machine at the beginning of the year at a cost of $7,600. The estimated useful life was four years, and the residual value was $800. Assume that the estimated productive life of the machine was 10,000 hours. Actual annual usage was 3,500 hours in year 1; 3,200 hours in year 2; 2,200 hours in year 3; and 1,100 hours in year 4.

Required:

1. Complete a separate depreciation schedule for each of the alternative methods. You can round your answers to the nearest dollar.
   a. Straight-line.
   b. Units-of-production.
   c. Double-declining-balance.

Method: _____				
Year	Computation	Depreciation Expense	Accumulated Depreciation	Net Book Value
At acquisition				
1				
2				
etc.				

2. Assuming that the machine was used directly in the production of one of the products that the company manufactures and sells, what factors might management consider in selecting a preferable depreciation method in conformity with the matching principle?

E8-8 **Computing Depreciation under Alternative Methods**

LO3

Alexa Plastics Company purchased a new stamping machine at the beginning of the year at a cost of $125,000. The estimated residual value was $15,000. Assume that the estimated useful life was five years, and the estimated productive life of the machine was 250,000 units. Actual annual production was as follows:

Year	Units
1	75,000
2	60,000
3	30,000
4	45,000
5	40,000

Required:

1. Complete a separate depreciation schedule for each of the alternative methods. You can round your answers to the nearest dollar.
   a. Straight-line.
   b. Units-of-production.
   c. Double-declining-balance.

Method: _____				
Year	Computation	Depreciation Expense	Accumulated Depreciation	Net Book Value
At acquisition				
1				
2				
etc.				

2. Assuming that the machine was used directly in the production of one of the products that the company manufactures and sells, what factors might management consider in selecting a preferable depreciation method in conformity with the matching principle?

Explaining Depreciation Policy

A recent annual report for Ford Motor Company contained the following note:

> **Significant Accounting Policies**
>
> **Depreciation and Amortization of Property, Plant, and Equipment.** Property and equipment are stated at cost and depreciated primarily using the straight-line method over the estimated useful life of the asset. Special tools placed in service before January 1, 1999 are amortized using an accelerated method over the estimated life of those tools. Special tools placed in service beginning in 1999 are amortized using the units-of-production method. Maintenance, repairs, and rearrangement costs are expensed as incurred.

E8-9
LO3
Ford Motor
Company

**REAL WORLD
EXCERPT**

Required:

Why do you think the company changed its depreciation method for special tools acquired in 1999 and subsequent years?

Interpreting Management's Choice of Different Depreciation Methods for Tax and Financial Reporting

A recent annual report for Federal Express Corporation includes the following information:

> For financial reporting purposes, depreciation and amortization of property and equipment is provided on a straight-line basis over the asset's service life. For income tax purposes, depreciation is generally computed using accelerated methods.

E8-10
LO3
Federal Express

Required:

Explain why Federal Express uses different methods of depreciation for financial reporting and tax purposes.

Computing Depreciation and Book Value for Two Years Using Alternative Depreciation Methods and Interpreting the Impact on Cash Flows

E8-11
LO3, 7

Daisey Company bought a machine for $65,000 cash. The estimated useful life was four years, and the estimated residual value was $5,000. Assume that the estimated useful life in productive units is 150,000. Units actually produced were 40,000 in year 1 and 45,000 in year 2.

Required:

1. Determine the appropriate amounts to complete the following schedule. Show computations, and round to the nearest dollar.

Method of Depreciation	Depreciation Expense for		Net Book Value at the End of	
	Year 1	Year 2	Year 1	Year 2
Straight-line				
Units-of-production				
Double-declining-balance				

2. Which method would result in the lowest EPS for year 1? For year 2?
3. Which method would result in the highest amount of cash outflows in year 1? Why?
4. Indicate the effects of (a) acquiring the machine and (b) recording annual depreciation on the operating and investing activities on the statement of cash flows (indirect method) for year 1 (assume the straight-line method).

E8-12

LO4

United Parcel
Service Inc.

**REAL WORLD
EXCERPT**

Inferring Asset Impairment and Recording Disposal of an Asset

United Parcel Service states in a recent 10-K report, "We are the world's largest package delivery company and a leading global provider of specialized transportation and logistics services." The following note and data were reported:

> **NOTE 1—SUMMARY OF ACCOUNTING POLICIES**
>
> **Impairment of Long-Lived Assets**
>
> We review long-lived assets for impairment when circumstances indicate the carrying amount of an asset may not be recoverable based on the undiscounted future cash flows of the asset....In December (of a recent year), we permanently removed from service a number of Boeing 727 and DC-8 aircraft. As a result, we conducted an impairment evaluation, which resulted in....

	Dollars in millions
Cost of property and equipment (beginning of year)	$25,361
Cost of property and equipment (end of year)	26,915
Capital expenditures during the year	1,947
Accumulated depreciation (beginning of year)	11,749
Accumulated depreciation (end of year)	13,007
Depreciation expense during the year	1,549
Cost of property and equipment sold during the year	318
Accumulated depreciation on property sold	291
Cash received on property sold	118

Required:
1. Reconstruct the journal entry for the disposal of property and equipment during the year.
2. Compute the amount of property and equipment that United Parcel wrote off as impaired during the year. (*Hint:* Set up T-accounts.)

E8-13

LO5

Federal Express

Recording the Disposal of an Asset at Three Different Sale Prices

Federal Express is the world's leading express-distribution company. In addition to the world's largest fleet of all-cargo aircraft, the company has more than 645 aircraft and 47,000 vehicles and trailers that pick up and deliver packages. Assume that Federal Express sold a small delivery truck that had been used in the business for three years. The records of the company reflected the following:

Delivery truck cost	$28,000
Accumulated depreciation	23,000

Required:
1. Give the journal entry for the disposal of the truck, assuming that the truck sold for
   a. $5,000 cash.
   b. $5,600 cash.
   c. $4,600 cash.
2. Based on the three preceding situations, explain the effects of the disposal of an asset.

E8-14

LO5

Trump Hotels &
Casino Resorts
Holdings, L.P.

Recording the Disposal of an Asset at Three Different Sale Prices

Trump Hotels & Casino Resorts Holdings, L.P. (THCR Holdings) owns and manages five casino hotel properties, Trump Plaza Hotel and Casino, Trump Taj Mahal Casino Resort, Trump Marina Hotel

Casino, Trump Indiana Casino Hotel, and Trump 29 Casino, totaling over $2.4 billion in property and equipment. Assume that THCR Holdings replaced furniture in one of the hotels that had been used in the business for five years. The records of the company reflected the following regarding the sale of the existing furniture:

Furniture (cost)	$8,000,000
Accumulated depreciation	6,500,000

Required:
1. Give the journal entry for the disposal of the furniture, assuming that it was sold for
   a. $1,500,000 cash.
   b. $2,600,000 cash.
   c. $900,000 cash.
2. Based on the three preceding situations, explain the effects of the disposal of an asset.

Inferring Asset Age and Recording Accidental Loss on a Long-Lived Asset (Straight-Line Depreciation)

E8-15
LO5

On January 1, 2007, the records of Pastuf Corporation showed the following regarding a truck:

Equipment (estimated residual value, $2,000)	$12,000
Accumulated depreciation (straight-line, three years)	6,000

On December 31, 2007, the delivery truck was a total loss as the result of an accident.

Required:
1. Based on the data given, compute the estimated useful life of the truck.
2. Give all journal entries with respect to the truck on December 31, 2007. Show computations.

Computing the Acquisition and Depletion of a Natural Resource

E8-16
LO6
Freeport-McMoRan
Copper & Gold Inc.

Freeport-McMoRan Copper & Gold Inc. is one of the world's largest copper and gold mining and production companies with the majority of its natural resources in Indonesia. Annual revenues exceed $2.2 billion. Assume that in February 2008, Freeport-McMoRan paid $700,000 for a mineral deposit in Bali. During March, it spent $65,000 in preparing the deposit for exploitation. It was estimated that 900,000 total cubic yards could be extracted economically. During 2008, 60,000 cubic yards were extracted. During January 2009, the company spent another $6,000 for additional developmental work that increased the estimated productive capacity of the mineral deposit.

Required:
1. Compute the acquisition cost of the deposit in 2008.
2. Compute depletion for 2008.
3. Compute the net book value of the deposit after payment of the January 2009 developmental costs.

Computing and Reporting the Acquisition and Amortization of Three Different Intangible Assets

E8-17
LO6

Katie Company had three intangible assets at the end of 2007 (end of the accounting year):

a. A patent purchased from J. Miller on January 1, 2007, for a cash cost of $7,650. Miller had registered the patent with the U.S. Patent Office five years ago.
b. An internally developed trademark registered with the federal government for $16,000 on November 1, 2007. Management decided the trademark has an indefinite life.
c. Computer software and Web development technology purchased on January 1, 2006, for $110,000. The technology is expected to have a four-year useful life to the company.

Required:
1. Compute the acquisition cost of each intangible asset.
2. Compute the amortization of each intangible at December 31, 2007. The company does not use contra-accounts.
3. Show how these assets and any related expenses should be reported on the balance sheet and income statement for 2007.

E8-18
LO6

Computing and Reporting the Acquisition and Amortization of Three Different Intangible Assets

Cambridge Company had three intangible assets at the end of 2008 (end of the accounting year):
a. A copyright purchased on January 1, 2007, for a cash cost of $12,300. The copyright is expected to have a 10-year useful life to Cambridge.
b. Goodwill of $65,000 from the purchase of the Hartford Company on July 1, 2006.
c. A patent purchased on January 1, 2008 for $39,200 from the inventor who had registered the patent with the U.S. Patent Office on January 1, 2002.

Required:
1. Compute the acquisition cost of each intangible asset.
2. Compute the amortization of each intangible at December 31, 2008. The company does not use contra-accounts.
3. Show how these assets and any related expenses should be reported on the balance sheet and income statement for 2008.

E8-19
LO6
Starbucks
Corporation

Recording Leasehold Improvements and Related Amortization

Starbucks Corporation is a rapidly expanding retailer of specialty coffee with more than 2,600 company-operated stores worldwide. Assume that Starbucks planned to open a new store on Commonwealth Avenue near Boston University and obtained a 20-year lease starting January 1, 2008. The company had to renovate the facility by installing an elevator costing $275,000. Amounts spent to enhance leased property are capitalized as intangible assets called Leasehold Improvements. The elevator will be amortized over the useful life of the lease.

Required:
1. Give the journal entry to record the installation of the new elevator.
2. Give any adjusting entries required at the end of the annual accounting period on December 31, 2008, related to the new elevator. Show computations.

E8-20
**LO1, 2, 3,
4, 5, 6, 7**

Finding Financial Information as a Potential Investor

You are considering investing the cash gifts you received for graduation in various stocks. You have received several annual reports of major companies.

Required:
For each of the following, indicate where you would locate the information in an annual report. (*Hint:* The information may be in more than one location.):
1. The detail on major classifications of long-lived assets.
2. The accounting method(s) used for financial reporting purposes.
3. Whether the company has had any capital expenditures for the year.
4. Net amount of property, plant, and equipment.
5. Policies on amortizing intangibles.
6. Depreciation expense.
7. Any significant gains or losses on disposals of fixed assets.
8. Prior year's accumulated depreciation.
9. The amount of assets written off as impaired during the year.

E8-21

(Supplement) Recording a Change in Estimate

Refer to E8-5.

Required:
Give the adjusting entry that should be made at the end of 2007 for depreciation of the manufacturing equipment, assuming no change in the original estimated life or residual value. Show computations.

E8-22
LO2, 3

(Supplement) Recording and Explaining Depreciation, Extraordinary Repairs, and Changes in Estimated Useful Life and Residual Value (Straight-Line Depreciation)

At the end of the annual accounting period, December 31, 2007, Shafer Company's records reflected the following for Machine A:

Cost when acquired	$28,000
Accumulated depreciation	10,000

During January 2008, the machine was renovated at a cost of $11,000. As a result, the estimated life increased from five years to eight years, and the residual value increased from $3,000 to $5,000. The company uses straight-line depreciation.

Required:

1. Give the journal entry to record the renovation.
2. How old was the machine at the end of 2007?
3. Give the adjusting entry at the end of 2008 to record straight-line depreciation for the year.
4. Explain the rationale for your entries in requirements 1 and 3.

(Supplement) Computing the Effect of a Change in Useful Life and Residual Value on Financial Statements and Cash Flows (Straight-Line Depreciation)

E8-23
LO3, 7

Todd Company owns the building occupied by its administrative office. The office building was reflected in the accounts at the end of last year as follows:

Cost when acquired	$450,000
Accumulated depreciation (based on straight-line depreciation, an estimated life of 30 years, and a $30,000 residual value)	196,000

During January of this year, on the basis of a careful study, management decided that the total estimated useful life should be changed to 25 years (instead of 30) and the residual value reduced to $23,000 (from $30,000). The depreciation method will not change.

Required:

1. Compute the annual depreciation expense prior to the change in estimates.
2. Compute the annual depreciation expense after the change in estimates.
3. What will be the net effect of changing estimates on the balance sheet, net income, and cash flows for the year?

Available with McGraw-Hill's Homework Manager   **PROBLEMS**

Explaining the Nature of a Long-Lived Asset and Determining and Recording the Financial Statement Effects of Its Purchase (AP8-1)

P8-1
LO1, 2

On January 2, 2007, Shallish Company bought a machine for use in operations. The machine has an estimated useful life of eight years and an estimated residual value of $1,500. The company provided the following expenditures:

a. Invoice price of the machine, $80,000.
b. Freight paid by the vendor per sales agreement, $800.
c. Installation costs, $2,000 paid in cash.
d. Payment of the $80,000 was made as follows:

On January 2:

- Shallish Company common stock, par $1; 2,000 shares (market value, $3 per share).
- Note payable, $40,000, 12 percent due April 16, 2007 (principal plus interest).
- Balance of the invoice price to be paid in cash. The invoice allows for a 2 percent discount for cash paid by January 12.

On January 15:

- Shallish Company paid the balance due.

Required:

1. What are the classifications of long-lived assets? Explain their differences.

2. Record the purchase on January 2 and the subsequent payment on January 15. Show computations.

3. Indicate the accounts, amounts, and effects (+ for increase and − for decrease) of the purchase and subsequent cash payment on the accounting equation. Use the following structure:

Date	Assets	=	Liabilities	+	Stockholders' Equity

4. Explain the basis you used for any questionable items.

P8-2
LO2, 3
Federal Express

Analyzing the Effects of Repairs, an Addition, and Depreciation (AP8-2)

A recent annual report for Federal Express included the following note:

> **Property and Equipment**
>
> Expenditures for major additions, improvements, flight equipment modifications and certain equipment overhaul costs are capitalized when such costs are determined to extend the useful life of the asset. Maintenance and repairs are charged to expense as incurred.

Assume that Federal Express made extensive repairs on an existing building and added a new wing. The building is a garage and repair facility for delivery trucks that serve the Denver area. The existing building originally cost $720,000, and by the end of 2007 (10 years), it was half depreciated on the basis of a 20-year estimated useful life and no residual value. Assume straight-line depreciation was used. During 2008, the following expenditures related to the building were made:

a. Ordinary repairs and maintenance expenditures for the year, $7,000 cash.
b. Extensive and major repairs to the roof of the building, $122,000 cash. These repairs were completed on December 31, 2008.
c. The new wing was completed on December 31, 2008, at a cash cost of $230,000.

Required:

1. Applying the policies of Federal Express, complete the following, indicating the effects for the preceding expenditures. If there is no effect on an account, write NE on the line:

	Building	Accumulated Depreciation	Depreciation Expense	Repairs Expense	Cash
Balance January 1, 2008	$720,000	$360,000			
Depreciation for 2008		_____	_____		_____
Balance prior to expenditures	720,000	_____	_____		
Expenditure (a)	_____	_____	_____	_____	_____
Expenditure (b)	_____	_____	_____	_____	_____
Expenditure (c)	_____	_____	_____	_____	_____
Balance December 31, 2008	_____	_____	_____	_____	_____

2. What was the book value of the building on December 31, 2008?
3. Explain the effect of depreciation on cash flows.

P8-3
LO2, 3

Computing the Acquisition Cost and Recording Depreciation under Three Alternative Methods (AP8-3)

At the beginning of the year, Rattner's Martial Arts Center bought three used fitness machines from Advantage, Inc. The machines immediately were overhauled, installed, and started operating. The machines were different; therefore, each had to be recorded separately in the accounts.

	Machine A	Machine B	Machine C
Amount paid for asset	$7,600	$25,600	$6,800
Installation costs	300	500	200
Renovation costs prior to use	2,000	400	600

By the end of the first year, each machine had been operating 2,000 hours.

Required:
1. Compute the cost of each machine.
2. Give the entry to record depreciation expense at the end of year 1, assuming the following:

Machine	Estimates		Depreciation Method
	Life	Residual Value	
A	5 years	$1,500	Straight-line
B	20,000 hours	900	Units-of-production
C	4 years	2,000	Double-declining-balance

Inferring Depreciation Amounts and Determining the Effects of a Depreciation Error on Key Ratios (AP8-4)

P8-4
LO1, 3
REX Stores
Corporation

REX Stores Corporation, headquartered in Dayton, Ohio, is one of the nation's leading consumer electronics retailers operating more than 240 stores in 37 states. The following is a note from a recent annual report:

(1) SUMMARY OF SIGNIFICANT ACCOUNTING POLICIES—

Property and Equipment—Property and equipment is recorded at cost. Depreciation is computed using the straight-line method. Estimated useful lives are 15 to 40 years for buildings and improvements, and 3 to 12 years for fixtures and equipment. Leasehold improvements are depreciated over 10 to 12 years. The components of cost at January 31, 2004 and 2003 are as follows (amounts in dollars in thousands):

	2004	2003
	(dollars in thousands)	
Land	$ 38,519	$ 38,567
Buildings and improvements	101,448	99,448
Fixtures and equipment	18,567	18,471
Leasehold improvements	9,797	9,882
Construction in progress		1,251
	168,331	167,619
Less: Accumulated depreciation	(36,922)	(33,056)
	$131,409	$134,563

Required:
1. Assuming that REX Stores did not sell any property, plant, and equipment in 2004, what was the amount of depreciation expense recorded in 2004?
2. Assume that REX Stores failed to record depreciation in 2004. Indicate the effect of the error (i.e., overstated or understated) on the following ratios:
   a. Earnings per share.
   b. Fixed asset turnover.
   c. Financial leverage.
   d. Return on equity.

P8-5
LO1, 3

Evaluating the Effect of Alternative Depreciation Methods on Key Ratios from an Analyst's Perspective

You are a financial analyst for General Motors Corporation and have been asked to determine the impact of alternative depreciation methods. For your analysis, you have been asked to compare methods based on a machine that cost $90,225. The estimated useful life is 10 years, and the estimated residual value is $2,225. The machine has an estimated useful life in productive output of 88,000 units. Actual output was 10,000 in year 1 and 8,000 in year 2.

Required:

1. For years 1 and 2 only, prepare separate depreciation schedules assuming:
   a. Straight-line method.
   b. Units-of-production method.
   c. Double-declining-balance method.

Method: _____				
Year	Computation	Depreciation Expense	Accumulated Depreciation	Net Book Value
At acquisition				
1				
2				

2. Evaluate each method in terms of its effect on cash flow, fixed asset turnover, and EPS. Assuming that General Motors is most interested in reducing taxes and maintaining a high EPS for year 1, what would you recommend to management? Would your recommendation change for year 2? Why or why not?

P8-6
LO5

Recording and Interpreting the Disposal of Three Long-Lived Assets (AP8-5)

During 2008, Jensen Company disposed of three different assets. On January 1, 2008, prior to their disposal, the accounts reflected the following:

Asset	Original Cost	Residual Value	Estimated Life	Accumulated Depreciation (straight line)
Machine A	$20,000	$3,000	8 years	$12,750 (6 years)
Machine B	42,600	4,000	20 years	15,440 (8 years)
Machine C	76,200	4,200	15 years	57,600 (12 years)

The machines were disposed of in the following ways:
a. Machine A: Sold on January 1, 2008, for $8,200 cash.
b. Machine B: Sold on December 31, 2008, for $27,000; received cash, $23,000, and a $4,000 interest-bearing (12%) note receivable due at the end of 12 months.
c. Machine C: On January 1, 2008, this machine suffered irreparable damage from an accident. On January 10, 2008, a salvage company removed the machine at no cost.

Required:
1. Give all journal entries related to the disposal of each machine in 2008.
2. Explain the accounting rationale for the way that you recorded each disposal.

P8-7
LO5, 7

Inferring Activities Affecting Fixed Assets from Notes to the Financial Statements and Analyzing the Impact of Depreciation on Cash Flows

Singapore Airlines

Singapore Airlines reported the following information in the notes to a recent annual report (in Singapore dollars):

SINGAPORE AIRLINES

Notes to the Accounts

13. **Fixed Assets** (dollars in millions)
The Company

	Beginning of Year	Additions	Disposals/ Transfers	End of Year
Cost				
Aircraft	10,293.1	954.4	296.4	10,951.1
Other fixed assets (summarized)	3,580.9	1,499.1	1,156.7	3,923.3
	13,874.0	2,453.5	1,453.1	14,874.4
Accumulated depreciation				
Aircraft	4,024.8	683.7	290.1	4,418.4
Other fixed assets (summarized)	1,433.4	158.5	73.8	1,518.1
	5,458.2	842.2	363.9	5,936.5

Singapore Airlines also reported the following cash flow details:

Cash Flow from Operating Activities (dollars in millions)

	The Company	
	Current Year	Prior Year
Operating Profit	755.9	816.5
Adjustments for		
Depreciation of fixed assets	842.2	837.5
Loss/(surplus) on sale of fixed assets	(1.3)	(0.3)
Other adjustments (summarized)	82.3	39.4
Net Cash Provided by Operating Activities	1,679.1	1,693.1

Required:
1. Reconstruct the information in Note 13 into T-accounts for Fixed Assets and Accumulated Depreciation:

Fixed Assets				Accumulated Depreciation	
Beg. balance					Beg. balance
Acquisitions	Disposals/transfers		Disposals/transfers		Depreciation expense
End. balance					End. balance

2. Compute the amount of cash the company received for disposals and transfers for the current year. Show computations.
3. Compute the percentage of depreciation expense to cash flows from operations for the current year. What do you interpret from the result?

P8-8 **Determining Financial Statement Effects of Activities Related to Various Long-Lived**
LO2, 3, 6 **Assets** (AP8-6)

During the 2008 annual accounting period, Terwilliger Company completed the following transactions:

a. On January 1, 2008, purchased a patent for $19,600 cash (estimated useful life, seven years).
b. On January 1, 2008, purchased the assets (not detailed) of another business for cash $160,000, including $46,000 for goodwill. The company assumed no liabilities. Goodwill has an indefinite life.
c. On December 31, 2008, constructed a storage shed on land leased from S. Rhoades. The cost was $10,800. The company uses straight-line depreciation. The lease will expire in three years.
d. Total expenditures during 2008 for ordinary repairs and maintenance were $6,800.
e. On December 31, 2008, sold Machine A for $6,000 cash. Original cost on January 1, 2004, was $26,000; accumulated depreciation (straight line) to December 31, 2007, $18,400 ($3,000 residual value and five-year useful life).
f. On December 31, 2008, paid $7,000 for a complete reconditioning of Machine B acquired on January 1, 2001. Original cost, $32,000; accumulated depreciation (straight line) to December 31, 2007, $18,200 ($6,000 residual value and 10-year useful life).

Required:

1. For each of these transactions, indicate the accounts, amounts, and effects (+ for increase and – for decrease) on the accounting equation. Use the following structure:

Date	Assets	=	Liabilities	+	Stockholders' Equity

2. For each of these assets except the assets not detailed in *b.*, compute depreciation and amortization to be recorded at the end of the year on December 31, 2008.

P8-9 **Computing Goodwill from the Purchase of a Business and Related Depreciation and**
LO6 **Amortization**

The notes to a recent annual report from Weebok Corporation included the following:

Business Acquisitions
During the current year, the Company acquired the assets of Sport Shoes, Inc.

Assume that Weebok acquired Sport Shoes on January 5, 2007. Weebok acquired the name of the company and all of its assets, except cash, for $450,000 cash. Weebok did not assume the liabilities. The transaction was closed on January 5, 2007, at which time the balance sheet of Sport Shoes reflected the following book values and an independent appraiser estimated the following market values for the assets:

SPORT SHOES, INC.

January 5, 2007	Book Value	Market Value*
Accounts receivable (net)	$ 45,000	$ 45,000
Inventory	220,000	210,000
Fixed assets (net)	32,000	60,000
Other assets	3,000	10,000
Total assets	$300,000	
Liabilities	$ 60,000	
Stockholders' equity	240,000	
Total liabilities and stockholders' equity	$300,000	

These values for the purchased assets were provided to Weebok by an independent appraiser.

Required:

1. Compute the amount of goodwill resulting from the purchase. (*Hint:* Assets are purchased at market value in conformity with the cost principle.)
2. Compute the adjustments that Weebok would make at the end of the annual accounting period, December 31, 2007, for the following:
    a. Depreciation of the fixed assets (straight line), assuming an estimated remaining useful life of 15 years and no residual value.
    b. Goodwill (an intangible asset with an indefinite life).

Computing Amortization, Book Value, and Asset Impairment Related to Different Intangible Assets (AP8-7)

P8-10
LO4, 6

Fearn Company has five different intangible assets to be accounted for and reported on the financial statements. The management is concerned about the amortization of the cost of each of these intangibles. Facts about each intangible follow:

a. *Patent.* The company purchased a patent at a cash cost of $54,600 on January 1, 2007. The patent has an estimated useful life of 13 years.
b. *Copyright.* On January 1, 2007, the company purchased a copyright for $22,500 cash. It is estimated that the copyrighted item will have no value by the end of 20 years.
c. *Franchise.* The company obtained a franchise from McKenna Company to make and distribute a special item. It obtained the franchise on January 1, 2007, at a cash cost of $14,400 for a 12-year period.
d. *License.* On January 1, 2006, the company secured a license from the city to operate a special service for a period of five years. Total cash expended to obtain the license was $14,000.
e. *Goodwill.* The company started business in January 2001 by purchasing another business for a cash lump sum of $400,000. Included in the purchase price was "Goodwill, $60,000." Company executives stated that "the goodwill is an important long-term asset to us." It has an indefinite life.

Required:

1. Compute the amount of amortization that should be recorded for each intangible asset at the end of the annual accounting period, December 31, 2007.
2. Give the book value of each intangible asset on December 31, 2008.
3. Assume that on January 2, 2009, the copyrighted item was impaired in its ability to continue to produce strong revenues. The other intangible assets were not affected. Fearn estimated that the copyright will be able to produce future cash flows of $18,000. The fair value of the copyright is determined to be $16,000. Compute the amount, if any, of the impairment loss to be recorded.

(Supplement) Analyzing and Recording Entries Related to a Change in Estimated Life and Residual Value

P8-11

Rungano Corporation is a global publisher of magazines, books, and music and video collections, and is a leading direct mail marketer. Many direct mail marketers use high-speed Didde press equipment to print their advertisements. These presses can cost more than $1 million. Assume that Rungano owns a Didde press acquired at an original cost of $400,000. It is being depreciated on a straight-line basis over a 20-year estimated useful life and has a $50,000 estimated residual value. At the end of 2007, the press had been depreciated for a full eight years. In January 2008, a decision was made, on the basis of improved maintenance procedures, that a total estimated useful life of 25 years and a residual value of $73,000 would be more realistic. The accounting period ends December 31.

Required:

1. Compute (a) the amount of depreciation expense recorded in 2007 and (b) the book value of the printing press at the end of 2007.
2. Compute the amount of depreciation that should be recorded in 2008. Show computations.
3. Give the adjusting entry for depreciation at December 31, 2008.

ALTERNATE **PROBLEMS**

AP8-1
L01, 2

Explaining the Nature of a Long-Lived Asset and Determining and Recording the Financial Statement Effects of Its Purchase (P8-1)

On June 1, 2008, the Wilbur Corp. bought a machine for use in operations. The machine has an estimated useful life of six years and an estimated residual value of $2,000. The company provided the following expenditures:

   a. Invoice price of the machine, $60,000.
   b. Freight paid by the vendor per sales agreement, $650.
   c. Installation costs, $1,500.
   d. Payment of the $60,000 was made as follows:

On June 1:

   • Wilbur Corp. common stock, par $2; 2,000 shares (market value, $5 per share).
   • Balance of the invoice price on a note payable, 12 percent due September 2, 2008 (principal plus interest).

On September 2:

   • Wilbur Corp. paid the balance and interest due on the note payable.

Required:
   1. What are the classifications of long-lived assets? Explain their differences.
   2. Record the purchase on June 1 and the subsequent payment on September 2. Show computations.
   3. Indicate the accounts, amounts, and effects (+ for increase and − for decrease) of the purchase and subsequent cash payment on the accounting equation. Use the following structure:

Date	Assets	=	Liabilities	+	Stockholders' Equity

   4. Explain the basis you used for any questionable items.

AP8-2
L02, 3
AMERCO

REAL WORLD EXCERPT

Analyzing the Effects of Repairs, an Addition, and Depreciation (P8-2)

A recent annual report for AMERCO, the holding company for U-Haul International, Inc., included the following note:

> **PROPERTY, PLANT AND EQUIPMENT**
>
> Property, plant and equipment are stated at cost. Interest costs incurred during the initial construction of buildings or rental equipment are considered part of cost. Depreciation is computed for financial reporting purposes principally using the straight-line method over the following estimated useful lives: rental equipment 2–20 years; buildings and non-rental equipment 3–55 years. Major overhauls to rental equipment are capitalized and are amortized over the estimated period benefited. Routine maintenance costs are charged to operating expense as they are incurred.

AMERCO subsidiaries own property, plant, and equipment that are utilized in the manufacture, repair, and rental of U-Haul equipment and that provide offices for U-Haul. Assume that AMERCO made extensive repairs on an existing building and added a new wing. The building is a garage and repair facility for rental trucks that serve the Seattle area. The existing building originally cost $230,000, and by the end of 2007 (its fifth year), the building was one-quarter depreciated on the basis of a 20-year estimated useful life and no residual value. Assume straight-line depreciation. During 2008, the following expenditures related to the building were made:

   a. Ordinary repairs and maintenance expenditures for the year, $5,000 cash.

b. Extensive and major repairs to the roof of the building, $17,000 cash. These repairs were completed on December 31, 2008.

c. The new wing was completed on December 31, 2008, at a cash cost of $70,000.

Required:

1. Applying the policies of AMERCO, complete the following, indicating the effects for the preceding expenditures. If there is no effect on an account, write NE on the line:

	Building	Accumulated Depreciation	Depreciation Expense	Repairs Expense	Cash
Balance January 1, 2008	$230,000	$57,500			
Depreciation for 2008		___	___		___
Balance prior to expenditures	230,000	___	___		
Expenditure (a)	___	___	___	___	___
Expenditure (b)	___	___	___	___	___
Expenditure (c)	___	___	___	___	___
Balance December 31, 2008	___	___	___	___	

2. What was the book value of the building on December 31, 2008?
3. Explain the effect of depreciation on cash flows.

Computing the Acquisition Cost and Recording Depreciation under Three Alternative Methods (P8-3)

AP8-3
LO2, 3

At the beginning of the year, Labenski Inc. bought three used machines from Moore Corporation. The machines immediately were overhauled, installed, and started operating. The machines were different; therefore, each had to be recorded separately in the accounts.

	Machine A	Machine B	Machine C
Cost of the asset	$10,800	$32,500	$21,700
Installation costs	800	1,100	1,100
Renovation costs prior to use	600	1,400	1,600

By the end of the first year, each machine had been operating 7,000 hours.

Required:

1. Compute the cost of each machine.
2. Give the entry to record depreciation expense at the end of year 1, assuming the following:

Machine	Estimates Life	Residual Value	Depreciation Method
A	8 years	$1,000	Straight-line
B	33,000 hours	2,000	Units-of-production
C	5 years	1,400	Double-declining-balance

Inferring Depreciation Amounts and Determining the Effects of a Depreciation Error on Key Ratios (P8-4)

AP8-4
LO1, 3
The Gap, Inc.

REAL WORLD
EXCERPT

The Gap, Inc., is a global specialty retailer of casual wear products for women, men, and children under the Gap, Banana Republic, and Old Navy brands operating in over 3,000 store locations. As of January 29, 2005, the Company operated 2,994 stores in the U.S., Canada, the U.K., France, and Japan, as well as online. The following is a note from a recent annual report:

(1) SUMMARY OF SIGNIFICANT ACCOUNTING POLICIES—

Property and Equipment

Property and equipment are stated at cost. Depreciation and amortization are computed using the straight-line method over the estimated lives of the related assets.

The components of cost at the end of the current and prior years are as follows (dollars in thousands):

	Current Year	Prior Year
Property and Equipment		
Leasehold improvements	$2,224	$2,242
Furniture and equipment	3,591	3,439
Land and buildings	1,033	943
Construction-in-progress	131	202
	6,979	6,826
Less accumulated depreciation and amortization	3,611	3,049
Net property and equipment	$3,368	$3,777

Required:

1. Assuming that The Gap, Inc., did not have any asset impairment write-offs and did not sell any property, plant, and equipment in the current year, what was the amount of depreciation expense recorded in the current year?
2. Assume that The Gap, Inc., failed to record depreciation in the current year. Indicate the effect of the error (i.e., overstated or understated) on the following ratios:
   a. Earnings per share.
   b. Fixed asset turnover.
   c. Financial leverage.
   d. Return on equity.

AP8-5
LO5

Recording and Interpreting the Disposal of Three Long-Lived Assets (P8-6)

During 2007, Kosik Company disposed of three different assets. On January 1, 2007, prior to their disposal, the accounts reflected the following:

Asset	Original Cost	Residual Value	Estimated Life	Accumulated Depreciation (straight line)
Machine A	$24,000	$2,000	5 years	$17,600 (4 years)
Machine B	16,500	5,000	10 years	8,050 (7 years)
Machine C	59,200	3,200	14 years	48,000 (12 years)

The machines were disposed of in the following ways:

a. Machine A: Sold on January 1, 2007, for $5,750 cash.
b. Machine B: Sold on December 31, 2007, for $9,000; received cash, $4,000, and a $5,000 interest-bearing (10 percent) note receivable due at the end of 12 months.
c. Machine C: On January 1, 2007, this machine suffered irreparable damage from an accident.

Required:

1. Give all journal entries related to the disposal of each machine.
2. Explain the accounting rationale for the way that you recorded each disposal.

AP8-6
LO2, 3, 6

Determining Financial Statement Effects of Activities Related to Various Long-Lived Assets (P8-8)

During the 2008 annual accounting period, Chu Corporation completed the following transactions:

a. On January 1, 2008, purchased a license for $7,200 cash (estimated useful life, three years).
b. On January 1, 2008, repaved the parking lot of the building leased from I. Kumara. The cost was $7,800; the estimated useful life was five years with no residual value. The company uses straight-line depreciation. The lease will expire in 10 years.
c. On July 1, 2008, purchased another business for $120,000 cash. The transaction included $115,000 for assets and $24,000 for the liabilities assumed by Chu. The remainder was goodwill with an indefinite life.
d. On December 31, 2008, sold Machine A for $5,000 cash. Original cost, $21,500; accumulated depreciation (straight line) to December 31, 2007, $13,500 ($3,500 residual value and four-year life).

e. Total expenditures during 2008 for ordinary repairs and maintenance were $6,700.

f. On December 31, 2008, paid $8,000 for a complete reconditioning of Machine B acquired on January 1, 2005. Original cost, $18,000; accumulated depreciation (straight line) to December 31, 2007, $12,000 ($2,000 residual value and four-year life).

Required:

1. For each of these transactions, indicate the accounts, amounts, and effects (+ for increase and − for decrease) on the accounting equation. Use the following structure:

Date	Assets	=	Liabilities	+	Stockholders' Equity

2. For each of these assets, compute depreciation and amortization to be recorded at the end of the year on December 31, 2008.

Computing Amortization, Book Value, and Asset Impairment Related to Different Intangible Assets (P8-10)

AP8-7
LO4, 6

Evans Corporation has five different intangible assets to be accounted for and reported on the financial statements. The management is concerned about the amortization of the cost of each of these intangibles. Facts about each intangible follow:

a. *Patent.* The company purchased a patent at a cash cost of $18,600 on January 1, 2007. It is amortized over its expected useful life of 15 years.

b. *Copyright.* On January 1, 2007, the company purchased a copyright for $24,750 cash. It is estimated that the copyrighted item will have no value by the end of 30 years.

c. *Franchise.* The company obtained a franchise from Farrell Company to make and distribute a special item. It obtained the franchise on January 1, 2007, at a cash cost of $19,200 for a 12-year period.

d. *License.* On January 1, 2006, the company secured a license from the city to operate a special service for a period of seven years. Total cash expended to obtain the license was $21,000.

e. *Goodwill.* The company started business in January 2005 by purchasing another business for a cash lump sum of $650,000. Included in the purchase price was "Goodwill, $75,000." Company executives stated that "the goodwill is an important long-term asset to us." It has an indefinite life.

Required:

1. Compute the amount of amortization that should be recorded for each intangible asset at the end of the annual accounting period, December 31, 2007.

2. Give the book value of each intangible asset on January 1, 2010.

3. Assume that on January 2, 2010, the franchise was impaired in its ability to continue to produce strong revenues. The other intangible assets were not affected. Evans estimated that the franchise will be able to produce future cash flows of $14,500, and the fair value is $13,000. Compute the amount, if any, of the impairment loss to be recorded.

CASES **AND PROJECTS**

Annual Report CASES

Finding Financial Information

Refer to the financial statements and accompanying notes of Pacific Sunwear of California given in Appendix B at the end of this book, or open file PSUN.pdf in the Annual Report Cases directory on the student DVD.

CP8-1
LO1, 2, 3, 4, 6

PACIFIC SUNWEAR
OF CALIFORNIA, INC.

Required:

For each question, answer it and indicate where you located the information to answer the question. (*Hint:* Use the notes to the financial statements for some of these questions.)

1. How much did the company spend on property and equipment (capital expenditures) in fiscal 2004 (the year ended January 29, 2005)?

2. What is the typical estimated useful life of leasehold improvements for amortization purposes?

3. What was the original cost of furniture, fixtures, and equipment held by the company at the end of the most recent reporting year?

4. What was the amount of depreciation and amortization reported as an expense for the current year? Compare this amount to the change in accumulated amortization and depreciation from fiscal 2003 to fiscal 2004. Why would these numbers be different?

5. What is the company's fixed asset turnover ratio for fiscal 2004?

CP8-2 Finding Financial Information

L01, 2, 3, 4, 6

AMERICAN EAGLE
OUTFITTERS
ae.com

Refer to the financial statements and accompanying notes of American Eagle Outfitters given in Appendix C at the end of this book, or open file AEOS.pdf in the Annual Report Cases directory on the student DVD.

Required:

For each question, answer it and indicate where you located the information to answer the question. (*Hint:* Use the notes to the financial statements for many of these questions.)

1. What method of depreciation does the company use?
2. What is the amount of accumulated depreciation and amortization at the end of the most recent reporting year?
3. For depreciation purposes, what is the estimated useful life of fixtures and equipment?
4. What was the original cost of leasehold improvements owned by the company at the end of the most recent reporting year?
5. What amount of depreciation and amortization was reported as expense for the most recent reporting year?
6. What is the company's fixed asset turnover ratio for the most recent year? What does it suggest?

CP8-3 Comparing Companies within an Industry

L01, 3

PACIFIC SUNWEAR
OF CALIFORNIA, INC.

AMERICAN EAGLE
OUTFITTERS
ae.com

Refer to the financial statements of Pacific Sunwear of California given in Appendix B, American Eagle Outfitters given in Appendix C, and the Industry Ratio Report given in Appendix D at the end of this book or open file CP8-3.xls in the Annual Report Cases directory on the student DVD.

Required:

1. Compute the percentage of net fixed assets to total assets for both companies for the most recent year. Why do the companies differ?
2. Compute the percentage of gross fixed assets that has been depreciated for both companies for the most recent year. Why do you think the percentages differ?
3. Compute the fixed asset turnover ratio for the most recent year presented for both companies. Which has higher asset efficiency? Why?
4. Compare the fixed asset turnover ratio for both companies to the industry average. Are these companies doing better or worse than the industry average in asset efficiency?

Financial Reporting and Analysis Cases

CP8-4 Broadening Financial Research Skills: Identifying Competitors in an Industry

Reuters provides lists of industries and the competitors in each at **www.investor.reuters.com**. Click on "Industries," then "Company Ranks," then "By Industry." This will take you to an alphabetical listing of industries.

Required:

Using your Web browser, contact Reuters and identify three competitors for the following industries:

1. Airline.
2. Hotels and motels.
3. Footwear.
4. Computer hardware.

Interpreting the Financial Press

The October 5, 1998, edition of *BusinessWeek* includes the article, "Earnings Hocus-Pocus."* You can access the article on the Libby/Libby/Short website at **www.mhhe.com/libby5e**.

CP8-5
L04

Required:
Read pages 1 through 9 of the article (stopping at the paragraph beginning with "Meanwhile, the SEC. . . ." Then answer the following questions:
1. What is meant by the concept that many companies take a "big bath"?
2. List several companies mentioned in the article that have taken a big bath by writing down fixed assets or intangibles. Indicate for each the nature of the earnings manipulation.

Using Financial Reports: Analyzing the Age of Assets

A note to a recent annual report for Black & Decker contained the following information (dollars in thousands):

CP8-6
L03
Black & Decker

	Current Year
Land and improvements	$ 69,091
Buildings	298,450
Machinery and equipment	928,151
	1,295,692
Less accumulated depreciation	468,511
	$ 827,181

Depreciation expense (in thousands of dollars) charged to operations was $99,234 in the current year. Depreciation generally is computed using the straight-line method for financial reporting purposes.

Required:
1. What is your best estimate of the average expected life for Black & Decker's depreciable assets?
2. What is your best estimate of the average age of Black & Decker's depreciable assets?

Using Financial Reports: Analyzing a Note Concerning Depreciation

A recent annual report for Depp Company contained the following note:

CP8-7
L03

> Property, plant, and equipment is stated at cost, less allowance for depreciation. Depreciation expense is determined principally by the straight-line method. The annual rates of depreciation are 4 percent to 10 percent for buildings and improvements and 10 percent to 40 percent for machinery, equipment, and containers.

Required:
1. What is the range of expected lives for buildings and improvements?
2. Explain why Depp Company depreciates the cost of its containers instead of including the total in cost of goods sold in the year the product is sold.

---

*Reprinted from October 5, 1998 issue of *BusinessWeek* by special permission, copyright © 1998 by The McGraw-Hill Companies, Inc.

CP8-8
LO1, 6, 7

Using Financial Reports: Analyzing Fixed Asset Turnover Ratio and Cash Flows

The Little Company operates in both the beverage and entertainment industries. In June 2001, Little purchased Good Time, Inc., that produces and distributes motion picture, television, and home video products and recorded music; publishes books; and operates theme parks and retail stores. The purchase resulted in $2.7 billion in goodwill. Since 2001, Little has undertaken a number of business acquisitions and divestitures (sales of businesses) as the company expands into the entertainment industry. Selected data from a recent annual report are as follows (amounts are in U.S. dollars in millions):

PROPERTY, PLANT, EQUIPMENT, AND INTANGIBLES		
FROM THE CONSOLIDATED BALANCE SHEET	**Current Year**	**Prior Year**
Film costs, net of amortization	$1,272	$ 991
Artists' contracts, advances, and other entertainment assets	761	645
Property, plant, and equipment, net	2,733	2,559
Excess of cost over fair value of assets acquired	3,076	3,355
FROM THE CONSOLIDATED STATEMENT OF INCOME		
Total revenues	$9,714	$10,644
FROM THE CONSOLIDATED STATEMENT OF CASH FLOWS		
Income from continuing operations	$ 880	$ 445
Adjustments		
Depreciation	289	265
Amortization	208	190
Other adjustments (summarized)	(1,618)	(256)
Net cash provided by continuing operations	(241)	644
FROM THE NOTES TO THE FINANCIAL STATEMENTS		
Accumulated depreciation on property, plant, and equipment	$1,178	$1,023

Required:
1. Compute the cost of the property, plant, and equipment at the end of the current year. Explain your answer.
2. What was the approximate age of the property, plant, and equipment at the end of the current year?
3. Compute the fixed asset turnover ratio for the current year. Explain your results.
4. What is Excess of Cost Over Fair Value of Assets Acquired?
5. On the consolidated statement of cash flows, why are the depreciation and amortization amounts added to income from continuing operations?

CP8-9
LO1, 5, 7
Eastman Kodak

Using Financial Reports: Inferring the Sale of Assets

A recent annual report for Eastman Kodak reported that the balance of property, plant, and equipment at the end of the current year was $16,774 million. At the end of the previous year, it had been $15,667 million. During the current year, the company bought $2,118 million worth of new equipment. The balance of accumulated depreciation at the end of the current year was $8,146 million and at the end of the previous year was $7,654 million. Depreciation expense for the current year was $1,181 million. The annual report does not disclose any gain or loss on the disposition of property, plant, and equipment, so you may assume that the amount was zero.

Required:
What amount of proceeds did Eastman Kodak receive when it sold property, plant, and equipment during the current year? (*Hint:* Set up T-accounts.)

CP8-10
LO3
Diageo

Using Financial Reports: Comparing Depreciation Methods in Different Countries

Diageo is a major international company located in London. A recent annual report contained the following information concerning its accounting policies.

Fixed assets and depreciation

Fixed assets are stated at cost or at professional valuation. Cost includes interest, net of any tax relief, on capital employed in major developments.

No depreciation is provided on freehold land. Other leaseholds are depreciated over the unexpired period of the lease. All other buildings, plant, equipment, and vehicles are depreciated to residual values over their estimated useful lives within the following ranges:

Industrial buildings	25 to 100 years
Plant and machinery	3 to 25 years
Fixtures and fittings	3 to 17 years

Required:
Compare accounting for fixed assets and depreciation in England with procedures used in this country.

Critical Thinking Cases

Making a Decision as a Financial Analyst: Interpreting the Impact of the Capitalization of Interest on an Accounting Ratio

CP8-11
LO2
Amerada Hess
Corporation

The capitalization of interest associated with self-constructed assets was discussed in this chapter. A recent annual report for Amerada Hess Corporation disclosed the following information concerning capitalization of interest:

> Interest costs related to certain long-term construction projects are capitalized to comply with FAS No. 34, "Capitalization of Interest Cost." Capitalized interest in the current year amounted to $34,897,000.

The income statement for that year disclosed that interest expense was $224,200,000. A popular accounting ratio used by some analysts is the interest coverage ratio (Income ÷ Interest Expense).

Required:
1. Explain why an analyst would calculate this ratio.
2. Did Amerada Hess include the $34,897,000 in the reported interest expense of $224,200,000? If not, should an analyst include it when calculating the interest coverage ratio? Explain.

Evaluating an Ethical Dilemma: Analyzing an Accounting Change

CP8-12
LO3, 7
Ford Motor
Corporation

An annual report for Ford Motor Company included the following information:

> **Note 6. Net Property, Depreciation and Amortization—Automotive**
>
> Assets placed in service before January 1, 1993, are depreciated using an accelerated method. Assets placed in service beginning in 1993 will be depreciated using the straight-line method of depreciation. This change in accounting principle is being made to reflect improvements in the design and flexibility of manufacturing machinery and equipment and improvements in maintenance practices. These improvements have resulted in more uniform productive capacities and maintenance costs over the useful life of an asset. Straight-line is preferable in these circumstances. The change is expected to improve 1993 after-tax results by $80 to $100 million.

Required:

1. What was the stated reason for the change in method? What other factors do you think management considered when it decided to make this accounting change?
2. Do you think this is an ethical decision?
3. Who were affected by the change and how were they benefited or harmed?
4. What impact did this change have on cash flows for Ford?
5. As an investor, how would you react to the fact that Ford's net income will increase by $80 to $100 million as the result of this change?

CP8-13
L01, 2, 7
Hilton Hotels

Evaluating the Impact of Capitalized Interest on Cash Flows and Fixed Asset Turnover from an Analyst's Perspective

You are a financial analyst charged with evaluating the asset efficiency of companies in the hotel industry. Recent financial statements for Hilton Hotels include the following note:

REAL WORLD
EXCERPT

> **Summary of Significant Accounting Policies**
>
> *Property and Equipment*
>
> Property and equipment are stated at cost less accumulated depreciation. Interest incurred during construction of facilities is capitalized and depreciated over the life of the asset. Costs of improvements are capitalized.

Required:

1. Assume that Hilton followed this policy for a major construction project this year. How does Hilton's policy affect the following: + for increase, − for decrease, and NE for no effect?
   a. Cash flows.
   b. Fixed asset turnover ratio.
2. Normally, how would your answer to requirement (1*b*) affect your evaluation of Hilton's effectiveness in utilizing fixed assets?
3. If the fixed asset turnover ratio decreases due to interest capitalization, does this change indicate a real decrease in efficiency? Why or why not?

Financial Reporting and Analysis Team Project

CP8-14

Team Project: Analysis of Long-Lived Assets

As a team, select an industry to analyze. *Reuters* provides lists of industries and their makeup at **www.investor.reuters.com/Industries.aspx**. Each team member should acquire the annual report or 10-K for one publicly traded company in the industry, with each member selecting a different company. (Library files, the SEC EDGAR service at **www.sec.gov**, or the company itself are good sources.)

Required:

1. List the accounts and amounts of the company's long-lived assets (land, buildings, equipment, intangible assets, natural resources, and/or other) for the last three years.
   a. What is the percentage of each to total assets?
   b. What do the results of your analysis suggest about the strategy your company has followed with respect to investing in long-lived assets?
2. What cost allocation method(s) and estimates does the company use for each type of long-lived asset?
3. Compute the approximate average life of property, plant, and equipment overall.

4. Ratio Analysis:
   a. What does the fixed asset turnover ratio measure in general?
   b. Compute the ratio for the last three years.
   c. What do your results suggest about the company?
   d. If available, find the industry ratio for the most recent year, compare it to your results, and discuss why you believe your company differs or is similar to the industry ratio.
5. What was the effect of depreciation expense on cash flows from operating activities? Compute the percentage of depreciation expense to cash flows from operating activities for each of the past three years.
6. From the statement of cash flows, what were capital expenditures over the last three years? Did the company sell any long-lived assets?

LEARNING OBJECTIVES

Reporting and Interpreting Liabilities

Each week, more than 28 million people visit a Starbucks coffeehouse. The company, founded in 1971, has 5,784 coffeehouses in the United States and is located in 37 international markets. The mission statement for the company is "to establish Starbucks as the premier purveyor of the finest coffees in the world." The company's goal is to have approximately 25,000 locations worldwide. It is aggressively pursuing this goal, having opened 894 new stores last year.

To achieve its goals, Starbucks must focus on a number of activities. The annual report identifies several of them:

FOCUS COMPANY:

Starbucks

MANAGING FINANCING ACTIVITIES

www.starbucks.com

- Serve the finest cup of coffee in the world.
- Grow the company one customer at a time based on exceptional customer service.
- Make someone's day with a relaxing in-store experience including music, art, and high-speed wireless Internet access.

In addition to these operating activities, management must focus on a number of critical financing activities to ensure that the company remains profitable and is able to generate sufficient resources to eventually meet its goal of opening 25,000 coffeehouses. The financing activities for Starbucks serve two important purposes. They generate funds (1) to finance the current operating activities of the business and (2) to acquire long-term assets that permit the company to grow in the future.

UNDERSTANDING THE BUSINESS

Businesses finance the acquisition of their assets from two sources: funds supplied by creditors (debt) and funds provided by owners (equity). The mixture of debt and equity a business uses is called its *capital structure*. In addition to selecting a capital structure, management can select from a variety of sources from which to borrow money, as illustrated by the liability section of the balance sheet from Starbucks shown in Exhibit 9.1.

STARBUCKS CORPORATION
Consolidated Balance Sheets
(dollars in thousands)

	Sept. 28, 2003	Sept. 29, 2002
LIABILITIES AND SHAREHOLDERS' EQUITY		
Current liabilities:		
Accounts payable	$168,984	$135,994
Accrued compensation and related costs	152,608	105,899
Accrued occupancy costs	56,179	51,195
Accrued taxes	54,934	54,244
Other accrued expenses	101,800	72,289
Deferred revenue	73,476	42,264
Current portion of long-term debt	722	710
Total current liabilities	608,703	462,595
Deferred income taxes, net	33,217	22,496
Long-term debt	4,354	5,076
Other long-term liabilities	1,045	1,036

What factors do managers consider when they borrow money? Two key factors are risk and cost. From the firm's perspective, debt capital is more risky than equity because payments associated with debt are a company's legal obligation. If a company cannot meet a required debt payment (either principal or interest) because of a temporary cash shortage, creditors may force the company into bankruptcy and require the sale of assets to satisfy the debt. As with any business transaction, borrowers and lenders attempt to negotiate the most favorable terms possible. Managers devote considerable effort to analyzing alternative borrowing arrangements.

Companies that include debt in their capital structure must also make strategic decisions concerning the balance between short-term and long-term debt. To evaluate a company's capital structure, financial analysts calculate a number of accounting ratios. In this chapter, we will discuss both short-term and long-term debt, as well as some important accounting ratios. We will also introduce you to present value concepts. In the next chapter, we discuss a special category of long-term debt, bonds payable.

ORGANIZATION of the Chapter

Liabilities Defined and Classified	**Current Liabilities**	**Long-Term Liabilities**	**Present Value Concepts**
■ Current Ratio	■ Accounts Payable ■ Accounts Payable Turnover Ratio ■ Accrued Liabilities ■ Notes Payable ■ Current Portion of Long-Term Debt ■ Deferred Revenues ■ Estimated Liabilities Reported on the Balance Sheet ■ Estimated Liabilities Reported in the Notes ■ Working Capital Management	■ Long-Term Notes Payable and Bonds ■ Lease Liabilities	■ Present Value of a Single Amount ■ Present Value of an Annuity ■ Accounting Applications of Present Value

LIABILITIES DEFINED AND CLASSIFIED

Most people have a reasonable understanding of the definition of the word *liability*. Accountants formally define liabilities as probable debts or obligations of the entity that result from past transactions, which will be paid with assets or services. As Exhibit 9.1 shows, as of September 28, 2003, Starbucks had borrowed long-term debt of $4,354 thousand. The company has a current obligation to pay cash to its creditors at some time in the future based on the borrowing agreements. Because of this obligation, Starbucks must record long-term debt.

When a liability is first recorded, it is measured in terms of its current cash equivalent, which is the cash amount a creditor would accept to settle the liability immediately. Although Starbucks borrowed $4,354 thousand, it will repay much more than that because the company must also pay interest on the debt. Interest that will be paid in the future is not included in the reported amount of the liability because it accrues and becomes a liability with the passage of time.

Like most businesses, Starbucks has several kinds of liabilities as well as a wide range of creditors. The list of liabilities on the balance sheet differs from one company to the next because different operating activities result in different types of liabilities. The liability section of the Starbucks report begins with the caption Current Liabilities. Current liabilities are defined as short-term obligations that will be paid within the current operating cycle of the business or within one year of the balance sheet date, whichever is longer. Because most companies have an operating cycle that is shorter than one year, normally, current liabilities can be defined simply as liabilities that are due within one year. Noncurrent liabilities include all other liabilities.

Information about current liabilities is very important to managers and analysts because these obligations must be paid in the near future. Analysts say that a company has liquidity if it has the ability to meet its current obligations. A number of financial ratios are useful in evaluating liquidity, including the current ratio.

Learning Objective 1
Define, measure, and report current liabilities.

LIABILITIES Probable debts or obligations that result from past transactions, which will be paid with assets or services.

CURRENT LIABILITIES are short-term obligations that will be paid within the current operating cycle or one year, whichever is longer.

LIQUIDITY is the ability to pay current obligations.

KEY RATIO
ANALYSIS

Current Ratio

❓ ANALYTICAL QUESTION:

Does a company currently have the resources to pay its short-term debt?

% RATIO AND COMPARISONS:

The current ratio is computed as follows:

$$\text{Current Ratio} = \text{Current Assets} \div \text{Current Liabilities}$$

The 2003 current ratio for Starbucks:

$$\$924.0 \div \$608.7 = 1.52$$

COMPARISONS OVER TIME		
Starbucks		
2001	**2002**	**2003**
1.74	1.67	1.52

COMPARISONS WITH COMPETITORS	
Panera Bread	**Krispy Kreme**
2003	**2003**
1.53	1.94

💡 INTERPRETATIONS:

Learning Objective 2
Use the current ratio.

In General → While a high ratio normally suggests good liquidity, too high a ratio suggests inefficient use of resources. An old rule of thumb was that companies should have a current ratio between 1.0 and 2.0. Today, many strong companies use sophisticated management techniques to minimize funds invested in current assets and, as a result, have current ratios below 1.0.

Focus Company Analysis → The current ratio for Starbucks is very strong and shows a high level of liquidity. While the ratio has been decreasing in recent years, this trend is not a problem. The ratio is strong, and the balance sheet reports more than $350 million in cash. The ratio for Starbucks is comparable to that of Panera Bread but somewhat lower than the one for Krispy Kreme. Rather than being concerned about Starbucks, most analysts would probably question whether the ratio for Krispy Kreme was an indication that its use of its current assets is inefficient.

A Few Cautions: The current ratio may be a misleading measure of liquidity if significant funds are tied up in assets that cannot easily be converted into cash. A company with a high current ratio might still have liquidity problems if the majority of its current assets is made up of slow-moving inventory. Analysts recognize that managers can manipulate the current ratio by engaging in certain transactions just before the close of the fiscal year. In most cases, for example, the current ratio can be improved by paying creditors immediately prior to preparation of financial statements.

CURRENT LIABILITIES

Many current liabilities have a direct relationship to the operating activities of a business. In other words, specific operating activities are financed, in part, by a related current liability.

Early in this chapter, we mentioned that Starbucks opened 894 new stores last year. As a result, it had to buy more inventory, rent more store space, and hire more employees. By understanding the relationship between operating activities and current liabilities, an analyst can easily explain changes in the various current liability accounts.

Some examples from the Starbucks annual report (Exhibit 9.1) are:

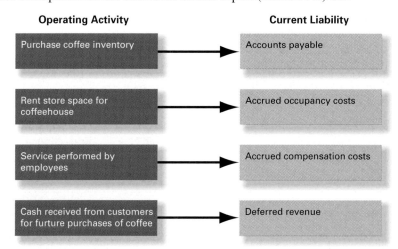

We will now discuss the current liability accounts that are found on most balance sheets.

Accounts Payable

Most companies do not produce all the goods and services that they use in their basic operating activities. Instead, they purchase some goods and services from other businesses. Typically, these transactions are made on credit with cash payments made after the goods and services have been provided. As a result, these transactions create accounts payable, also called **trade accounts payable.** *Accounting Trends & Techniques* (published by the AICPA) examined the reporting practices of 600 companies and found that most companies use the term **accounts payable.**[1]

For many companies, trade credit is a relatively inexpensive way to finance the purchase of inventory because interest does not normally accrue on accounts payable. As an incentive to encourage more sales, some vendors offer generous credit terms that may allow the buyer to resell merchandise and collect cash before payment must be made to the original vendor.

Some managers may be tempted to delay payment to suppliers as long as possible to conserve cash. This strategy normally is not advisable. Most successful companies develop positive working relationships with suppliers to ensure that they receive quality goods and services. A positive relationship can be destroyed by slow payment of debt. In addition, financial analysts become concerned if a business does not meet its obligations to trade creditors on a timely basis because such slowness often indicates that a company is experiencing financial difficulties. Both managers and analysts use the accounts payable turnover ratio to evaluate effectiveness in managing payables.

Accounts Payable Titles
(sample of 600 companies)

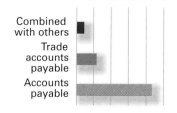

 Accounts Payable Turnover

KEY RATIO
ANALYSIS

? ANALYTICAL QUESTION:
How efficient is management in meeting obligations to suppliers?

% RATIO AND COMPARISONS:
The accounts payable turnover ratio is computed as follows:

Learning Objective 3
Analyze the accounts payable turnover ratio.

---

[1]Reprinted with permission from *Accounting Trends & Techniques.* Copyright © 2003 by the American Institute of Certified Public Accountants, Inc.

Accounts Payable Turnover = Cost of Goods Sold ÷ Average Accounts Payable

The 2003 accounts payable turnover ratio for Starbucks was:

$$\$1,685.9 \div \$152.5^* = 11.0$$

$$^*(\$168.9 + \$136.0) \div 2 = \$152.5$$

COMPARISONS OVER TIME			COMPARISONS WITH COMPETITORS	
Starbucks			**Panera Bread**	**Krispy Kreme**
2001	**2002**	**2003**	**2003**	**2003**
9.9	10.2	11.0	9.29	N/A

💡 INTERPRETATIONS:

In General → The accounts payable turnover ratio measures how quickly management is paying trade accounts. A high accounts payable ratio normally suggests that a company is paying its suppliers in a timely manner. The ratio can be stated more intuitively by dividing it into the number of days in a year:

Average Age of Payables = 365 Days ÷ Turnover Ratio

The 2003 average age of payables for Starbucks was:

365 Days ÷ 11.0 = 33.2 Days

Focus Company Analysis → The accounts payable turnover for Starbucks is better than the one for Panera Bread and is fairly stable over time. Usually, a low ratio would raise questions concerning a company's liquidity. Starbucks, on average, pays its creditors within approximately 30 days, which represents normal credit terms. Analysts would consider this ratio to be strong. We were unable to compute the ratio for Krispy Kreme because the company did not report its cost of goods sold. This problem illustrates that it is not always possible to compare companies in all areas of their operations.

A Few Cautions: The accounts payable turnover ratio is an average based on all accounts payable. The ratio might not reflect reality if a company pays some creditors on time but is late with others. The ratio is also subject to manipulation. Managers could be late in paying creditors during the entire year but catch up at year-end so that the ratio is at an acceptable level. As our focus company analysis indicates, a low ratio can indicate either liquidity problems (i.e., the company is not able to generate sufficient cash to meet its obligations) or aggressive cash management (i.e., the company maintains only the minimum amount of cash necessary to support its operating activities). The first is a problem; the second is a strength. Analysts need to study other factors (such as the current ratio and the amount of cash generated from operating activities) to determine which is the case.

Accrued Liabilities

ACCRUED LIABILITIES are expenses that have been incurred but have not been paid at the end of the accounting period.

In many situations, a business incurs an expense in one accounting period and makes cash payment in another period. Accrued liabilities are expenses that have been incurred before the end of an accounting period but have not been paid. These expenses include items such as property taxes, electricity, and salaries. The balance sheet for Starbucks lists three of these items: accrued compensation and related costs, accrued occupancy costs (rent), and accrued taxes. Accrued liabilities are recorded as adjusting entries at year-end.

Accrued Taxes Payable

Like individuals, corporations must pay taxes on the income they earn. Corporate tax rates are graduated with large corporations paying a top federal tax rate of 35 percent. Corporations may also pay state and local income taxes and, in some cases, foreign income taxes. The notes to the Starbucks annual report include the following information pertaining to taxes:

NOTE 14: INCOME TAXES

The provision for income taxes consists of the following (dollars in thousands):

Fiscal year ended	Sept. 28, 2003	Sept. 29, 2002	Sept. 30, 2001
Currently payable:			
Federal	$140,138	$109,154	$ 91,750
State	25,448	16,820	17,656
Foreign	8,523	5,807	3,198
Deferred tax asset, net	(6,120)	(5,468)	(4,892)
Total	$167,989	$126,313	$107,712

The 2003 federal income tax for Starbucks ($140.1 million) was approximately 52 percent of its U.S. earnings ($268.3 million). For most corporations, federal income taxes represent a major cost.

Accrued Compensation and Related Costs

At the end of each accounting period, employees usually have earned salaries that have not yet been paid. Unpaid salaries may be reported as part of accrued liabilities or as a separate item, as is the case with Starbucks (the amount shown on the balance sheet is $152.6 million). In addition to reporting salaries that have been earned but not paid, companies must report the cost of unpaid benefits, including retirement programs, vacation time, and health insurance.

Let's look at vacation time as an example. Typically, a business grants employees paid vacation time based on the number of months they have worked. Under the matching concept, the cost of vacation time must be recorded in the year employees perform a service rather than the year they actually take vacation. If Starbucks estimates the cost of accrued vacation time to be $125,000, accountants make the following adjusting entry at the end of the fiscal year:

Compensation expense (+E, −SE)	125,000	
Accrued vacation liability (+L)		125,000

Assets	=	Liabilities	+	Stockholders' Equity
		Accrued Vacation Liability +125,000		Compensation expense −125,000

When the vacations are taken (during the next summer), the accountants record the following:

Accrued vacation liability (−L)	125,000	
Cash (−A)		125,000

Assets	=	Liabilities	+	Stockholders' Equity
Cash − 125,000		Accrued Vacation Liability − 125,000		

Starbucks does not separately disclose the amount of accrued vacation liability. Instead, the company reports this liability as part of accrued compensation. Apparently, the amount of accrued vacation liability is not material in management's opinion. Most analysts would probably agree.

Payroll Taxes

All payrolls are subject to a variety of taxes including federal, state, and local income taxes, Social Security taxes, and federal and state unemployment taxes. Employees pay some of these taxes and employers pay others. While we will look at only the two largest deductions for most people, reporting is similar for each type of payroll tax:

Employee Income Taxes   Employers are required to withhold income taxes for each employee. The amount of income tax withheld is recorded by the employer as a current liability between the date of the deduction and the date the amount is remitted to the government. Federal Income Tax Withheld is often referred to as **FITW.**

Employee FICA Taxes   The Social Security taxes paid by employees are called *FICA taxes* because they are required by the Federal Insurance Contributions Act. These taxes are imposed in equal amounts on both the employee and the employer. Effective January 1, 2005, the Social Security tax rate was 6.2 percent on the first $90,000 paid to each employee during the year. In addition, a separate 1.45 percent Medicare tax applies to all income. Therefore, the FICA tax rate is 7.65 percent on income up to $90,000 and 1.45 percent on all income above $90,000.

Employee compensation expense includes all funds earned by employees as well as funds paid to others on behalf of employees. As a result, the cost of hiring employees is much more than the amount that those employees actually receive in cash.

To illustrate a payroll, let's assume that Starbucks accumulated the following information in its records for the first two weeks of June 2006:

Salaries and wages earned	$1,800,000
Income taxes withheld	275,000
FICA taxes (employees' share)	105,000

The entry to record the payroll is normally made with two entries. The first entry records amounts paid to employees or withheld from amounts they have earned:

Compensation expense (+E, −SE)	1,800,000
Liability for income taxes withheld (+L)	275,000
FICA payable (+L)	105,000
Cash (−A)	1,420,000

Assets	=	Liabilities	+	Stockholders' Equity
Cash − 1,420,000		FICA payable + 105,000		Compensation
		Liability for income		expense −1,800,000
		taxes withheld + 275,000		

The second entry records the FICA tax that employers must pay from their own funds. This additional tax payment is required by federal law. The amount is equal to the amount that is withheld from the employees earnings:

Compensation expense (+E, −SE)	105,000
FICA payable (+L)	105,000

Assets	=	Liabilities	+	Stockholders' Equity
		FICA payable + 105,000		Compensation expense −105,000

Accounting Trends & Techniques found that most companies in its sample of 600 companies report employee-related liabilities.[2]

Types of Employee-Related Liabilities (sample of 600 companies)

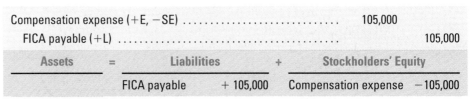

	0 100 200 300 400
Vacations	
Benefits	
Pensions	
Compensation	
Salaries and wages	

---

[2]Reprinted with permission from *Accounting Trends & Techniques.* Copyright © 2003 by the American Institute of Certified Public Accountants, Inc.

Notes Payable

When a company borrows money, a formal written contract is usually prepared. Obligations supported by these contracts are called *notes payable*. A note payable specifies the amount borrowed, the date by which it must be repaid, and the interest rate associated with the borrowing.

Creditors are willing to lend cash because they will earn interest in return for giving up the use of their money for a period. This simple concept is called the time value of money. The longer borrowed money is held, the larger is the total dollar amount of interest expense. Interest at a given interest rate on a two-year loan is more than interest on a one-year loan. To the borrower, interest is an expense; to the creditor, it is revenue.

To calculate interest, three variables must be considered: (1) the principal (i.e., the cash that was borrowed), (2) the annual interest rate, and (3) the time period for the loan. The interest formula is

$$\text{Interest} = \text{Principal} \times \text{Interest Rate} \times \text{Time}$$

To illustrate, assume that on November 1, 2006, Starbucks borrows $100,000 cash on a one-year, 12 percent note payable. The interest is payable on March 31, 2007, and October 31, 2007. The principal is payable at the maturity date, October 31, 2007. The note is recorded in the accounts as follows:

Cash (+A) 100,000
    Notes payable, short-term (+L) 100,000

Assets	=	Liabilities	+	Stockholders' Equity
Cash + 100,000		Notes payable + 100,000		

Interest is an expense of the period in which the money is used. Under the matching concept, interest expense is recorded when it is incurred rather than when the cash actually is paid. Because Starbucks uses the money for two months during 2006, it records interest expense in 2006 for two months, even though cash is not paid until March 31.

The computation of interest expense for 2006 is as follows:

$$\text{Interest} = \text{Principal} \times \text{Interest Rate} \times \text{Time}$$
$$\$2,000 = \$100,000 \times 12\% \times 2/12$$

The entry to record interest expense on December 31, 2006, is

Interest expense (+E, −SE) 2,000
    Interest payable (+L) 2,000

Assets	=	Liabilities	+	Stockholders' Equity
		Interest payable + 2,000		Interest expense − 2,000

On March 31, 2007, Starbucks would pay $5,000 in interest, which includes the $2,000 accrued and reported in 2006 plus the $3,000 interest accrued in the first three months of 2007. The following journal entry would be made:

Interest expense (+E, −SE) 3,000
Interest payable (−L) 2,000
    Cash (−A) 5,000

Assets	=	Liabilities	+	Stockholders' Equity
Cash −5,000		Interest payable − 2,000		Interest expense − 3,000

Learning Objective 4
Report notes payable and explain the time value of money.

The TIME VALUE OF MONEY is interest that is associated with the use of money over time.

Current Portion of Long-Term Debt

The distinction between current and long-term debt is important for both managers and analysts. Because current debt must be paid within the next year, companies must have sufficient cash to repay it. To provide accurate information on its current liabilities, a company must reclassify its long-term debt as a current liability within a year of its maturity date. Assume that Starbucks signed a note payable of $5 million on January 1, 2006. Repayment is required on December 1, 2009. The December 31, 2007 and 2008, balance sheets would report the following:

December 31, 2007

Long-term liabilities:	
Note payable	$5,000,000

December 31, 2008

Current liabilities:	
Current portion of long-term note	$5,000,000

An example of this type of disclosure can be seen in Exhibit 9.1. Notice that in 2003, Starbucks reported $722 thousand as the current portion of long-term debt to be paid in full during the following accounting period. In some cases, companies will refinance debt when it comes due rather than pay out cash currently on hand.

Refinanced Debt: Current or Noncurrent?

Instead of repaying a debt from current cash, a company may refinance it either by negotiating a new loan agreement with a new maturity date or by borrowing money from a new creditor and repaying the original creditor. If a company intends to refinance a currently maturing debt and has the ability to do so, should the debt be classified as a current or a long-term liability? Remember that analysts are interested in a company's current liabilities because those liabilities will generate cash outflows in the next accounting period. If a liability will not generate a cash outflow in the next accounting period, GAAP require that it not be classified as current. This rule is illustrated by a note from the General Mills annual report.

REAL WORLD EXCERPT

General Mills

ANNUAL REPORT

> We have a revolving credit agreement expiring in January 2006 that provides us with the ability to refinance short-term borrowing on a long-term basis. Therefore we have reclassified a portion of our notes payable to long-term debt.

Deferred Revenues

Most business transactions pay cash after the product or service has been delivered. In some cases, cash is paid before delivery. You have probably paid for magazines that you will receive at some time in the future. The publisher collects money for your subscription in advance, before the magazine is published. When a company collects cash before the related revenue has been earned, the cash is called deferred revenues. Starbucks has achieved a goal that is unique in the food industry. The company has introduced the popular Starbucks card that permits customers to pay in advance for their coffee. The advantage for the customer is convenience at the point of sale. The advantage for the company is that Starbucks is able to collect and use cash before customers

DEFERRED REVENUES are revenues that have been collected but not earned; they are liabilities until the goods or services are provided.

actually buy the product. The Starbucks report shows that the company has collected $73.5 million from customers prior to providing them with coffee and explains the amount with the following note

> Revenues from stored value cards are recognized upon redemption. Until the redemption of stored value cards, outstanding customer balances on such cards are included in "Deferred revenue."

Topic Tackler 9–1

Under the revenue principle, revenue cannot be recorded until it has been earned. Deferred revenues are reported as a liability because cash has been collected but the related revenue has not been earned by the end of the accounting period. The obligation to provide services or goods in the future still exists. These obligations are classified as current or long-term, depending on when they must be satisfied.

Estimated Liabilities Reported on the Balance Sheet

Some recorded liabilities are based on estimates because the exact amount will not be known until a future date. For example, an estimated liability is created when a company offers a warranty with the products it sells. The cost of providing future repair work must be estimated and recorded as a liability (and expense) in the period in which the product is sold.

Starbucks offers a warranty on coffee brewing and espresso equipment sold in its stores. The company records an estimated warranty liability at the time of sale. The estimate is based on historical experience. The amount of this liability is not separately reported on the Starbucks balance sheet but is included in the category Other Accrued Expenses. The amount is disclosed in the notes to the statements. The warranty liability recorded by Starbucks is $2.2 million.

Estimated Liabilities Reported in the Notes

Each of the liabilities that we have discussed is reported on the balance sheet at a specific dollar amount because they involve the probable future sacrifice of economic benefits. Some transactions or events create only a reasonably possible (but not probable) future sacrifice of economic benefits. These situations create contingent liabilities, which are potential liabilities that are created as a result of a past event. A contingent liability may or may not become a recorded liability, depending on future events. A situation that produces a contingent liability also causes a contingent loss.

Learning Objective 5
Report contingent liabilities.

A **CONTINGENT LIABILITY** is a potential liability that has arisen as the result of a past event; not an effective liability until some future event occurs.

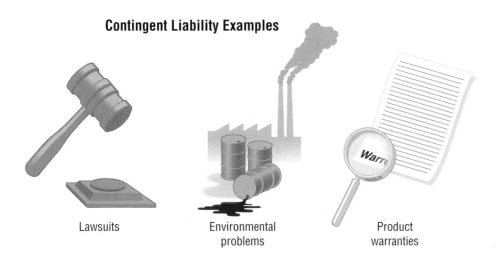

Contingent Liability Examples

Lawsuits   Environmental   Product
                  problems   warranties

Whether a situation produces a recorded or a contingent liability depends on two factors: the probability of a future economic sacrifice and the ability of management to estimate the amount of the liability. The following table illustrates the possibilities:

	Probable	Reasonably Possible	Remote
Subject to estimate	Record as liability	Disclose in note	Disclosure not required
Not subject to estimate	Disclose in note	Disclose in note	Disclosure not required

The probabilities of occurrence are defined in the following manner:

1. Probable—the chance that the future event or events will occur is high.
2. Reasonably possible—the chance that the future event or events will occur is more than remote but less than likely.
3. Remote—the chance that the future event or events will occur is slight.

In summary, (1) a liability that is both probable and capable of being reasonably estimated must be recorded and reported on the balance sheet, (2) a liability that is reasonably possible must be disclosed in a note in the financial statements whether it can be estimated or not, and (3) remote contingencies are not disclosed.

The notes to Starbucks annual report include the following:

REAL WORLD EXCERPT

STARBUCKS

ANNUAL REPORT

NOTE 17: COMMITMENTS AND CONTINGENCIES

The Company is party to various legal proceedings arising in the ordinary course of its business, but it is not currently a party to any legal proceeding that management believes would have a material adverse effect on the consolidated financial position or results of operations of the Company.

Starbucks did not need to record a liability on the balance sheet because a loss was not probable. Harley-Davidson disclosed a common contingency in its notes:

REAL WORLD EXCERPT

Harley-Davidson

ANNUAL REPORT

Note 7

Commitments and Contingencies

A state court jury in California found the Company liable for compensatory and punitive damages of $7.2 million, including interest, in a lawsuit brought by a supplier of aftermarket exhaust systems. The Company immediately appealed the verdict.

In this case, the existence of a liability was a reasonable possibility. As a result, GAAP required Harley-Davidson to disclose the lawsuit in its notes. The company subsequently reached an out-of-court settlement for $5 million. At that point, the loss was probable, which required recording the loss and the related liability on the balance sheet.

Accounting Trends & Techniques studied the financial statements of 600 companies and found that litigation was the most common type of contingent liability.[3]

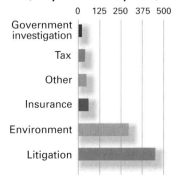

Contingent Liabilities
(sample of 600 companies)

---

[3]Reprinted with permission form *Accounting Trends & Techniques.* Copyright © 2003 by the American Institute of Certified Public Accountants, Inc.

Working Capital Management

Working capital is defined as the dollar difference between current assets and current liabilities. Working capital is important to both managers and financial analysts because it has a significant impact on the health and profitability of a company.

The working capital accounts are actively managed to achieve a balance between costs and benefits. If a business has too little working capital, it runs the risk of not being able to meet its obligations to creditors. On the other hand, too much working capital may tie up resources in unproductive assets and incur additional costs. Excess inventory, for example, ties up dollars that could be invested more profitably elsewhere in the business and incurs additional costs associated with storage and deterioration.

Changes in working capital accounts are also important to managers and analysts because they have a direct impact on cash flows from operating activities reported on the statement of cash flows.

> **Learning Objective 6**
> Explain the importance of working capital and its impact on cash flows.

WORKING CAPITAL is the dollar difference between total current assets and total current liabilities.

Working Capital and Cash Flows

Many working capital accounts have a direct relationship to income-producing activities. Accounts receivable, for example, are related to sales revenue: Accounts receivable increase when sales are made on credit. Cash is collected when the customer pays the bill. Similarly, accounts payable increase when an expense is incurred without a cash payment. A cash outflow occurs when the account is paid. Changes in working capital accounts that are related to income-producing activities must be considered when computing cash flows from operating activities.

EFFECT ON STATEMENT OF CASH FLOWS

In General → Changes in working capital accounts will affect a company's cash flows as indicated in the following table:

	Effect on Cash Flows
Operating activities (indirect method)	
Net income	$xxx
Adjusted for: Decreases in current assets* or increases in current liabilities	+
Adjusted for: Increases in current assets* or decreases in current liabilities	−

*Other than cash

Focus Company Analysis → A segment of the Starbucks consolidated statements of cash flows, prepared using the indirect method, follows. Notice the steady improvement in cash flows from operations from 2001 to 2003. These substantial cash flows are important for a company with the growth strategy that Starbucks is following.

REAL WORLD EXCERPT

STARBUCKS

ANNUAL REPORT

CONSOLIDATED STATEMENTS OF CASH FLOWS

Dollars in thousands

Fiscal year ended	Sept. 28, 2003	Sept. 29, 2002	Sept. 30, 2001
OPERATING ACTIVITIES:			
Net earnings	$268,346	$212,686	$180,335
Adjustments to reconcile net earnings to net cash provided by operating activities:			

Depreciation and amortization	259,271	221,141	177,087
Gain on sale of investment	—	(13,361)	—
Internet-related investment losses	—	—	2,940
Provision for impairments and asset disposals	7,784	26,852	11,044
Deferred income taxes, net	(5,932)	(6,088)	(6,068)
Equity in income of investees	(22,813)	(19,584)	(14,838)
Tax benefit from exercise of nonqualified stock options	36,590	44,199	30,899
Amortization of discount and premium on marketable securities	5,996	—	—
Cash provided/(used) by changes in operating assets and liabilities:			
Inventories	(64,768)	(41,379)	(19,704)
Prepaid expenses and other current assets	(12,861)	(12,460)	(10,919)
Accounts payable	24,990	5,463	54,117
Accrued compensation and related costs	42,132	24,087	12,098
Accrued occupancy costs	4,293	15,343	6,797
Deferred revenue	30,732	15,321	19,594
Other operating assets and liabilities	(7,313)	5,465	12,923
Net cash provided by operating activities	566,447	477,685	456,305

SELF-STUDY QUIZ

Assume that the current ratio for Starbucks is 2.0. For each of the following events, state whether the current ratio and working capital will increase or decrease:

1. Starbucks incurs an account payable of $250,000 with no change in current assets.
2. The company borrows $1,000,000 in long-term debt.
3. The company pays taxes payable in the amount of $750,000.
4. The company finances a new building with long-term debt.

After you have completed your answers, check them with the solutions at the bottom of the page.

Self-Study Quiz
Solutions

Current ratio	Working capital
1. Decrease	Decrease
2. Increase	Increase
3. Increase	No change
4. No change	No change

LONG-TERM LIABILITIES

Long-term liabilities include all obligations that are not classified as current liabilities, such as long-term notes payable and bonds payable. Typically, a long-term liability will require payment more than one year in the future. These obligations may be created by borrowing money, or they may result from other activities.

Most companies borrow money on a long-term basis to purchase operational assets. To reduce risk for creditors, some companies agree to use specific assets as security. If the liability is not satisfied, the creditor may take ownership of the asset. A liability supported by this type of agreement is called a **secured debt.** An unsecured debt is one for which the creditor relies primarily on the borrower's integrity and general earning power.

Long-Term Notes Payable and Bonds

Companies can raise long-term debt capital directly from a number of financial service organizations including banks, insurance companies, and pension plans. Raising debt from one of these organizations is known as **private placement.** This type of debt is often called a **note payable,** which is a written promise to pay a stated sum at one or more specified future dates called the **maturity date(s).**

In many cases, a company's need for debt capital exceeds the financial ability of any single creditor. In these situations, the company may issue publicly traded debt called **bonds.** The opportunity to sell a bond in established markets provides bondholders an important benefit. They can sell their bonds to other investors prior to maturity if they have an immediate need for cash. Because bonds provide liquidity to investors, they are more likely to lend money to a company. Bonds will be discussed in detail in the next chapter.

Accounting for long-term debt is based on the same concepts used in accounting for short-term notes payable. A liability is recorded when the debt is incurred and interest expense is recorded with the passage of time.

Over the past years, business operations have become more global. Successful corporations market their products in many countries and locate manufacturing facilities around the world based on cost and productivity. The financing of corporations also has become international, even for companies that do not have international operations. Borrowing money in a foreign currency raises some interesting accounting and management issues.

> **Learning Objective 7**
> Report long-term liabilities.

> **LONG-TERM LIABILITIES** are all of the entity's obligations not classified as current liabilities.

Borrowing in Foreign Currencies

INTERNATIONAL PERSPECTIVE

Many corporations with foreign operations elect to finance those operations with foreign debt to lessen exchange rate risk. This type of risk exists because the relative value of each nation's currency varies on virtually a daily basis. As this book was being written, the British pound was worth approximately $1.80; a year earlier it was worth $1.65.

A U.S. corporation that conducts business operations in England might decide to borrow pounds to finance its operations there. The profits from the business, which will be in pounds, can be used to pay off the debt, which is in pounds. If this business earned profits in pounds but paid off debt in dollars, it would be exposed to exchange rate risk because the relative value of the dollar and the pound fluctuates.

Foreign corporations face this same problem. A note to a recent annual report from Toyota, a Japanese company that does significant business in the United States, stated:

Earnings declined in the current year ended, as the appreciation of the yen aggravated the adverse effects of sluggish demand. . . . The movement in exchange rates reduced operating income of the company. Losses on currency exchange thus offset most of the cost savings we achieved.

Toyota has borrowed a large amount of money in the United States to lessen the exchange rate risk it faces. The company also owns and operates many factories in the United States.

Even if a company does not have international operations, it may elect to borrow in foreign markets. Interest rates often are low in countries experiencing a recession. These situations give corporations the opportunity to borrow at a lower cost.

For reporting purposes, accountants must convert, or translate, foreign debt into U.S. dollars. Conversion rates for all major currencies are published in most newspapers. To illustrate foreign currency translation, assume that Starbucks borrowed 1 million pounds (£). For the Starbucks annual report, the accountant must use the conversion rate as of the balance sheet date, which we assume was £1.00 to $1.80. The dollar equivalent of the debt is $1,800,000 (£1,000,000 × 1.80). The dollar equivalent of foreign debt may change if the conversion rate changes even without any additional borrowings or repayments.

The notes to the balance sheet for Starbucks indicate that the company has borrowed money only in the United States. In contrast, consider the following note from Toys "R" Us (amounts are stated in dollars in millions). Toys "R" Us is an international company with more than 40 percent of its sales and assets located outside the United States. As a result, the company borrows heavily in international markets to minimize the risks associated with variations in exchange rates. This arrangement is typical for most large corporations.

LONG-TERM DEBT

	February 1, 2003	February 2, 2002
7.625% notes, due fiscal 2011	$ 554	$ 505
6.875% notes, due fiscal 2006	267	254
500 Euro bond, due February 13, 2004	538	431
475 Swiss Franc note, due January 28, 2004	348	277
Equity Security Units	408	—
8¼% debentures, due fiscal 2021, net of expense	198	198
Note at an effective cost of 2.32% due in semi-annual installments through fiscal 2008	158	126
Industrial revenue bonds, net of expenses	21	34
Obligation under capital leases	18	21
Mortgage notes at annual interest rates from 10.16% to 11.00%	8	9
	2,518	1,855
Less current portion	379	39
	$2,139	$1,816

Lease Liabilities

Companies often lease assets rather than purchase them. For example, renting extra delivery trucks during a busy period is more economical than owning them if they are not needed during the rest of the year. When a company leases an asset on a short-term basis, the agreement is called an operating lease. No liability is recorded when an operating lease is created. Instead, a company records rent expense as it uses the asset. Assume that on December 15, 2006, Starbucks signed an operating lease contract to rent five large trucks during January 2007. No liability is recorded in 2006. Rent expense is recorded during January 2007 as the trucks are actually used.

For a number of reasons, a company may prefer to lease an asset on a long-term basis rather than purchase it. This type of lease is called a capital lease. In essence, a capital lease contract represents the purchase and financing of an asset even though it is legally a lease agreement. Unlike an operating lease, capital leases are accounted for as if an asset had been purchased by recording an asset and a liability. Because of the significant differences between operating and capital leases, GAAP have specified criteria to distinguish between them. If a lease meets any of the following criteria, it is considered a capital lease:

- The lease term is 75 percent or more of the asset's expected economic life.

- Ownership of the asset is transferred to the lessee at the end of the lease term.

- The lease contract permits the lessee to purchase the asset at a price that is lower than its fair market value.

- The present value of the lease payments is 90 percent or more of the fair market value of the asset when the lease is signed.

If managers have a choice of recording a lease as either operating or capital, most would prefer to record it as an operating lease. By doing so, the company is able to report less debt on its balance sheet. Walgreen Drugstores reports no long-term debt on its balance sheet but notes to the statements indicate that the company is obligated to pay $19.3 billion over the next 25 years as the result of long-term leases on buildings. Many financial analysts are concerned that companies can avoid reporting debt associated with capital leases by structuring the lease agreement in a manner that meets the requirements for recording it as an operating lease.

To record a capital lease, it is necessary to determine the current cash equivalent of the required lease payments. The next section, on present value concepts, shows how this amount is actually computed.

An **OPERATING LEASE** does not meet any of the four criteria established by GAAP and does not cause the recording of an asset and liability.

A **CAPITAL LEASE** meets at least one of the four criteria established by GAAP and results in the recording of an asset and liability.

Topic Tackler 9–2

PRESENT VALUE CONCEPTS

Our discussion of capital leases raised an interesting question about liabilities: Is the recorded amount of the liability the actual amount of cash that will be paid in the future? For example, if I agree to pay you $10,000 five years from now, should I report a liability of $10,000 on my personal balance sheet? To answer such questions, we will now introduce some relatively simple mathematics called **present value concepts.** These concepts will provide a foundation for our discussion of bond liabilities in the next chapter.

The concept of present value (PV) is based on the time value of money. Quite simply, money received today is worth more than money to be received one year from today (or at any other future date) because it can be used to earn interest. If you invest $1,000 today at 10 percent, you will have $1,100 in one year. In contrast, if you receive $1,000 one year from today, you will lose the opportunity to earn the $100 in interest revenue. The difference between the $1,000 and the $1,100 is the interest that can be earned during the year.

Learning Objective 8
Compute present values.

PRESENT VALUE is the current value of an amount to be received in the future; a future amount discounted for compound interest.

In one of your math classes, you have probably already solved some problems involving the time value of money. In the typical problem, you were told a certain dollar amount had been deposited in a savings account earning a specified rate of interest. You were asked to determine the dollar amount that would be in the savings account after a certain number of years. In this chapter, we will show you how to solve problems that are the opposite of the ones you have worked with. In present value problems, you will be told a dollar amount to be received in the future (such as the balance of a savings account after five years) and will be asked to determine the present value of the amount (which is the amount that must be deposited in the savings account today).

The value of money changes over time because money can earn interest. A present value problem is one when you know the dollar amount of a cash flow that occurs in the future and need to determine its value now. The opposite situation occurs when you know the dollar amount of a cash flow that occurs today and need to determine its value at some point in the future. These problems are called **future value problems.** Future value concepts are discussed in a supplement to this chapter.

Present Value of a Single Amount

Present Value of a Single Amount

The present value of a single amount is the worth to you today of receiving that amount some time in the future. For instance, you might be offered an opportunity to invest in a debt instrument that would pay you $10,000 in 10 years. Before you decided whether to invest, you would want to determine the present value of the instrument. Graphically, the present value of $1 due at the end of the third period with an interest rate of 10 percent can be represented as follows:

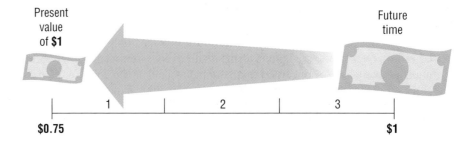

To compute the present value of an amount to be received in the future, we will subtract interest that is earned over time from the amount to be received in the future. For example, if you place $100 in a savings account that earns 5 percent, you will have $105 at the end of a year. In a present value problem, you will be told that you have $105 at the end of the year and must compute the amount to be deposited at the beginning of the year. To solve this type of problem, you must discount the amount to be received in the future at i interest rate for n periods. The formula to compute the present value of a single amount is

$$\text{Present Value} = \frac{1}{(1 + i)^n} \times \text{Amount}$$

The formula is not difficult to use, but most analysts use present value tables, calculators, or Excel for computations. We will illustrate how to use present value tables (an explanation of how to use Excel to compute present values is presented in a supplement to this chapter). Assume that today is January 1, 2006, and you have the opportunity to receive $1,000 cash on December 31, 2008. At an interest rate of 10 percent per year, how much is the $1,000 payment worth to you on January 1, 2006? You could discount the amount year by year,[4] but it is easier to use Table A.1, Appendix A, Present Value of $1. For $i = 10\%$, $n = 3$, we find that the present value of $1 is 0.7513. The present value of $1,000 to be received at the end of three years can be computed as follows:

$$\$1{,}000 \times 0.7513 = \$751.30$$

> *From Table A.1*
> *Interest rate = 10%*
> *n = 3*

Learning how to compute a present value amount is not difficult, but it is more important that you understand what it means. The $751.30 is the amount you would pay now to have the right to receive $1,000 at the end of three years, assuming an interest rate of 10 percent. Conceptually, you should be indifferent between having $751.30 today and receiving $1,000 in three years because you can use financial institutions to convert dollars from the present to the future and vice versa. If you had $751.30 today but preferred $1,000 in three years, you could simply deposit the money in a savings account and it would grow to $1,000 in three years. Alternatively, if you had a contract that promised you $1,000 in three years, you could sell it to an investor for $751.30 in cash today because it would permit the investor to earn the difference in interest.

> To compute the present value using Excel, enter:
> = 1000/(1.10)^3

SELF-STUDY QUIZ

1. If the interest rate in a present value problem increases from 8 percent to 10 percent, will the present value increase or decrease?

2. What is the present value of $10,000 to be received 10 years from now if the interest rate is 5 percent, compounded annually?

After you have completed your answers, check them with the solutions at the bottom of the page.

Present Values of an Annuity

Instead of a single payment, many business problems involve multiple cash payments over a number of periods. An **annuity** is a series of consecutive payments characterized by

1. An equal dollar amount each interest period.

2. Interest periods of equal length (year, half a year, quarter, or month).

3. An equal interest rate each interest period.

Examples of annuities include monthly payments on an automobile or home, yearly contributions to a savings account, and monthly pension benefits.

> An **ANNUITY** is a series of periodic cash receipts or payments that are equal in amount each interest period.

---

[4]The detailed discounting is as follows:

Periods	Interest for the Year	Present Value*
1	$1,000 − ($1,000 × 1/1.10) = $90.91	$1,000 − $90.91 = $909.09
2	$909.09 − ($909.09 × 1/1.10) = $82.65	$909.09 − $82.65 = $826.44
3	$826.44 − ($826.44 × 1/1.10) = $75.14†	$826.44 − $75.14 = $751.30

*Verifiable in Table A.1.   †Adjusted for rounding.

---

1. The present value will be less.
2. $10,000 × 0.6139 = $6,139

Present Value of an Annuity

The present value of an annuity is the value now of a series of equal amounts to be received (or paid out) for some specified number of periods in the future. It is computed by discounting each of the equal periodic amounts. A good example of this type of problem is a retirement program that offers employees a monthly income after retirement. The present value of an annuity of $1 for three periods at 10 percent may be represented graphically as follows:

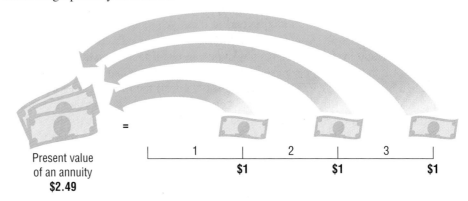

Present value
of an annuity
$2.49

Assume that you are to receive $1,000 cash on each December 31, 2006, 2007, and 2008. How much would the sum of these three $1,000 future amounts be worth on January 1, 2006, assuming an interest rate of 10 percent per year? We could use Table A.1, Appendix A to calculate the present value as follows:

Year	Amount		Factor from Table A.1, Appendix A, $i = 10\%$		Present Value
1	$1,000	×	0.9091 ($n = 1$)	=	$ 909.10
2	$1,000	×	0.8264 ($n = 2$)	=	826.40
3	$1,000	×	0.7513 ($n = 3$)	=	751.30
			Total present value	=	$2,486.80

We can compute the present value of this annuity more easily however, by using Table A.2, Appendix A as follows:

From Table A.2,
Interest rate = 10%
n = 3

$$\$1,000 \times 2.4869 = \$2,487 \text{ (rounded)}$$

To compute the present value using Excel, enter:
$f_x = PV(0.10, 3, -1000)$

Interest Rates and Interest Periods

The preceding illustrations assumed annual periods for compounding and discounting. Although interest rates are almost always quoted on an annual basis, most compounding periods encountered in business are less than one year. When interest periods are less than a year, the values of n and i must be restated to be consistent with the length of the interest period.

To illustrate, 12 percent interest compounded annually for five years requires the use of $n = 5$ and $i = 12\%$. If compounding is quarterly, however, the interest period is one-quarter of a year (i.e., four periods per year), and the quarterly interest rate is one-quarter of the annual rate (i.e., 3 percent per quarter). Therefore, 12 percent interest compounded quarterly for five years requires use of $n = 20$ and $i = 3\%$.

A QUESTION
OF ETHICS

Truth in Advertising

Newspaper, magazine, and television advertisements are easy to misinterpret if the consumer does not understand present value concepts. For example, most car companies offer seasonal promotions with special financing incentives. A car dealer may advertise 4 percent interest on car loans when banks are charging 10 percent. Typically, the lower interest rate is not really an incentive because the dealer simply charges a higher price for cars the dealership finances. Borrowing from the bank and paying cash at the dealership may help the buyer to negotiate a lower price. Customers should use the present value concepts illustrated in this chapter to compare financing alternatives.

Another misleading advertisement, seen every January, promises magazine subscribers a chance to become an instant millionaire. The fine print discloses that the winner will receive $25,000 for 40 years, which amounts to $1,000,000 (40 × $25,000), but the present value of this annuity at 8 percent is only $298,000. Most winners are happy to get the money, but they are not really millionaires.

Some consumer advocates argue that consumers should not have to study present value concepts to understand such advertisements. Some of these criticisms may be valid, but the quality of information in advertisements that include interest rates has improved over the past few years.

Accounting Applications of Present Value

Many business transactions require the use of future and present value concepts. So that you can test your understanding of these concepts, we illustrate two cases.

> **CASE A** On January 1, 2006, Starbucks bought some new delivery trucks. The company signed a note and agreed to pay $200,000 on December 31, 2007, an amount representing the cash equivalent price of the trucks plus interest for two years. The market interest rate for this note was 12 percent.

Learning Objective 9
Apply present value concepts to liabilities.

1. How should the accountant record the purchase?

Answer: This case requires the computation of the present value of a single amount. In conformity with the cost principle, the cost of the trucks is their current cash equivalent price, which is the present value of the future payment. The problem can be shown graphically as follows:

January 1, 2006	December 31, 2006	December 31, 2007
?		$200,000

The present value of the $200,000 is computed as follows:

$$\$200,000 \times 0.7972 = \$159,440$$

> *From Table A.1,*
> *interest rate = 12%*
> *n = 2*

Therefore, the journal entry is as follows:

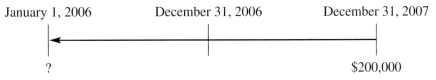

| Delivery trucks (+A) | 159,440 | |
| Note payable (+L) | | 159,440 |

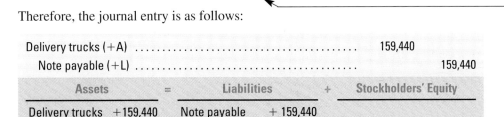

Assets	=	Liabilities	+	Stockholders' Equity
Delivery trucks +159,440		Note payable +159,440		

To compute the present value using Excel, enter:
= 200000 /(1.12)^2

2. What journal entry should be made at the end of the first and second years to record interest expense?

Answer: Each year's interest expense is recorded in an adjusting entry as follows:

| **December 31, 2006** | Interest expense (+E, −SE) | 19,133* | |
| | Note payable (+L) | | 19,133 |

*$159,440 × 12% = $19,133

Assets	=	Liabilities		+	Stockholders' Equity	
		Note payable	+ 19,133		Interest Expense	− 19,133

December 31, 2007   Interest expense (+E, −SE) 21,429*

                  Note payable (+L) 21,429

*($159,440 + $19,133) × 12% = 21,429.

Assets	=	Liabilities		+	Stockholders' Equity	
		Note payable	+ 21,429		Interest Expense	− 21,429

3. What journal entry should be made on December 31, 2007, to record payment of the debt?

Answer: At this date the amount to be paid is the balance of Note Payable, which is the same as the maturity amount on the due date. The journal entry to record full payment of the debt follows:

Note payable (−L) 200,000

    Cash (−A) 200,000

Assets		=	Liabilities		+	Stockholders' Equity
Cash	− 200,000		Note payable	− 200,000		

CASE B On January 1, 2006, Starbucks bought new printing equipment. The company elected to finance the purchase with a note payable to be paid off in three years in annual installments of $163,686. Each installment includes principal plus interest on the unpaid balance at 11 percent per year. The annual installments are due on December 31, 2006, 2007, and 2008. This problem can be shown graphically as follows:

January 1, 2006   December 31, 2006   December 31, 2007   December 31, 2008

? $163,686 $163,686 $163,686

1. What is the amount of the note?

Answer: The note is the present value of each installment payment, $i = 11\%$ and $n = 3$. This is an annuity because payment is made in three equal installments. The amount of the note is computed as follows:

From Table A.2, interest rate = 11% n = 3

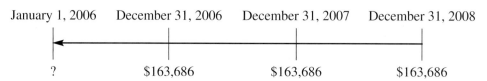

$163,686 × 2.4437 = $400,000

The acquisition on January 1, 2006 is recorded as follows:

To compute the present value using Excel, enter: $f_x = PV(0.11, 3, -163686)$

Printing equipment (+A) 400,000

    Note payable (+L) 400,000

Assets		=	Liabilities		+	Stockholders' Equity
Printing equipment	+ 400,000		Note payable	+ 400,000		

2. What journal entries should be made at the end of each year to record the payments on this note?

Answer:

December 31, 2006	Note payable (−L)	119,686	
	Interest expense (+E, −SE)		
	($400,000 ×11%)	44,000	
	Cash (−A)		163,686

Assets	=	Liabilities	+	Stockholders' Equity	
Cash	− 163,686	Note payable	−119,686	Interest Expense	− 44,000

December 31, 2007	Note payable (−L)	132,851	
	Interest expense (+E, −SE)		
	[($400,000 − $119,686) × 11%]	30,835	
	Cash (−A)		163,686

Assets	=	Liabilities	+	Stockholders' Equity	
Cash	− 163,686	Note payable	− 132,851	Interest expense	− 30,835

December 31, 2008	Note payable (−L)	147,463	
	Interest expense (+E, −SE)	16,223*	
	Cash (−A)		163,686

*Interest: ($400,000 − $119,686 − $132,851) × 11% = $16,223 (rounded to accommodate rounding errors).

Assets	=	Liabilities	+	Stockholders' Equity	
Cash	− 163,686	Note payable	− 147,463	Interest expense	− 16,223

In the next chapter, we will use the present value techniques you have just learned to understand how to account for bonds.

Chapter Supplement A

Income Taxes and Retirement Benefits

Two aspects of business operations, income taxes and employee retirement benefits, may result in the creation of either an asset or a liability. On most financial statements, you will see these items as liabilities, so we will discuss them along with other liabilities.

Deferred Taxes

Because separate rules govern the preparation of financial statements (GAAP) and tax returns (Internal Revenue Code), income tax expense and current taxes payable often differ in amount. To reflect this difference, companies establish a separate account called **Deferred Taxes.** In practice, deferred taxes can be either assets (such as taxes related to cash collected from a customer, which is taxable before it is reported as a revenue on the income statement) or liabilities (such as taxes related to depreciation, which is reported on the tax return before it is reported on the income statement). Starbucks has deferred tax amounts reported as both assets and liabilities.

Deferred tax items exist because of timing differences in the reporting of revenues and expenses on the income statement and tax return. These temporary differences are caused by differences between GAAP, which govern financial statement preparation, and the Internal Revenue Code, which governs the preparation of tax returns.

Deferred tax amounts always reverse themselves. For example, at some point in the future the accelerated depreciation recorded on the tax return will be less than the straight-line depreciation reported on the income statement (recall from Chapter 8 that accelerated depreciation causes higher depreciation expense compared to straight line in the early years of an asset's life and lower depreciation in the later years). When a deferred tax liability reverses, the deferred tax amount is reduced, and the company pays more taxes to the IRS than the amount of income tax expense reported on the income statement.

DEFERRED TAX ITEMS exist because of timing differences caused by reporting revenues and expenses according to GAAP on a company's income statement and according to the Internal Revenue Code on the tax return.

TEMPORARY DIFFERENCES are timing differences that cause deferred income taxes and will reverse, or turn around, in the future.

The computation of deferred taxes involves some complexities that are discussed in advanced accounting courses. At this point, you need to understand only that deferred tax assets and liabilities are caused by temporary differences between the income statement and tax return. Each temporary difference has an impact on the income statement in one accounting period and on the tax return in another.

Accrued Retirement Benefits

Most employers provide retirement programs for their employees. In a **defined contribution program,** the employer makes cash payments to an investment fund. When employees retire, they are entitled to a portion of the fund. If the investment strategy of the fund is successful, the retirement income for the employees will be larger. If the strategy is not successful, it will be lower. The employer's only obligation is to make the required annual payments to the fund that are recorded as pension expense. Starbucks offers a defined contribution program to its employees and, therefore, does not have any pension liabilities.

Other employers offer **defined benefit programs.** Under these programs, employees' retirement benefits are based on a percentage of their pay at retirement or a certain number of dollars for each year of employment. In these cases, the pension expense that must be accrued each year is the change in the current cash value of employees' retirement packages. The current cash value changes each year for a variety of reasons. For example, it will change (1) as employees draw closer to receiving benefits, (2) as employees' retirement benefits increase as a result of higher pay or longer service, and (3) if the employees' life expectancies change. The company must report a pension liability based on any portion of the current cash value of the retirement program that has not actually been funded. For example, if the company were to transfer $8 million to the pension fund while the current cash value of the pension obligation was $10 million, the company would report a $2 million pension liability on its balance sheet.

For many corporations, especially those with unionized work forces, the financial obligation associated with defined benefit retirement programs can be huge. A recent financial statement for Ford Motor Company disclosed the following information:

NOTE 2

Employee Retirement Benefits
(dollars in millions)

Accumulated Postretirement Benefit Obligation	
Retirees	$ 7,035.0
Active employees eligible to retire	2,269.6
Other active employees	5,090.6
Total accumulated obligation	$14,395.2

To put the size of this obligation in perspective, it represents an amount nearly equal to Ford's total stockholders' equity. The retirement benefit expense for the year was $1.3 billion, which exceeded the income Ford earned for the previous three years. This type of information is important to analysts who are interested in forecasting a company's future cash flows. Ford has a very large obligation to transfer cash to its retirement fund.

In recent years, employer-provided health care benefits have been the subject of a great deal of discussion. Many large companies pay for a portion of their employees' health insurance costs. These payments are recorded as an expense in the current accounting period. In addition, some employers continue to pay for health care costs after their employees retire. The cost of these future benefits must be estimated and recorded as an expense for the periods in which the employees perform services. The recording of future health care costs for retired employees is an excellent example of the use of estimates in accounting. Imagine the difficulty of estimating future health care costs when you do not know how long employees will live, how healthy they will be during their retirements, and how much money doctors and hospitals will charge for their services in the future.

Accounting for retirement benefits is a complex topic that is discussed in detail in subsequent accounting courses. We introduce the topic at this point as another example of the application of the matching concept, which requires that expenses be recorded in the year in which benefits are received.

This accounting procedure also avoids creating improper incentives for managers. If the future cost of retirement benefits were not included in the period in which work is performed, managers might have the incentive to offer employees increases in their retirement benefits instead of increases in their salaries. In this manner, managers could understate the true cost of employees' services and make their companies appear more profitable.

Chapter Supplement B

Federal Income Tax Concepts

Unlike sole proprietorships and partnerships, corporations are separate legal entities, so they are required to pay income taxes. Corporations must prepare a U.S. Corporate Tax Return (Form 1120), which lists their revenue and expenses for the year. The amount of the tax payable is based on the taxable income reported on their tax return. As was mentioned earlier, taxable income usually differs from the income reported on the income statement because the income statement is prepared in conformity with GAAP, but the tax return is prepared in conformity with the Internal Revenue Code.

Calculation of Taxes Payable

In most cases, a large corporation's tax obligation is determined by multiplying its taxable income by 35 percent. Rates are graduated, however, so that very small corporations pay lower rates than large corporations do.

Exhibit 9.2 illustrates the calculation of taxes payable at various income levels. Notice in Cases B and C that a portion of the income is taxed at a rate that is higher than the maximum of 35 percent. The purpose of the 39 percent rate is to phase out the benefits of the lower rates that were intended to benefit only smaller corporations. The $136,000 total taxes payable on taxable income of $400,000 is an effective tax rate of exactly 34 percent.

Case A: Taxable Income		**$90,000**
Computation		
0.15 of first $50,000		$ 7,500
0.25 of next $25,000		6,250
0.34 of $15,000 ($90,000 − $75,000)		5,100
Taxes payable		$ 18,850
Case B: Taxable Income		**$150,000**
Computation		
0.15 of first $50,000		$ 7,500
0.25 of next $25,000		6,250
0.34 of next $25,000		8,500
0.39 of $50,000 ($150,000 − $100,000)		19,500
Taxes payable		$ 41,750
Case C: Taxable Income		**$400,000**
Computation		
0.15 of first $50,000		$ 7,500
0.25 of next $25,000		6,250
0.34 of next $25,000		8,500
0.39 of next $235,000		91,650
0.34 of $65,000 ($400,000 − $335,000)		22,100
Taxes payable		$136,000

EXHIBIT 9.2

Calculation of
Taxes Payable

A 35 percent tax rate applies to taxable incomes higher than $10 million. A provision phases out the 34 percent tax rate for very large corporations. The tax rate from $15,000,000 to $18,333,333 is 38 percent. At higher incomes, the rate reverts to 35 percent. This provision results in an effective tax rate of 35 percent once a corporation has taxable income greater than $18,333,333.

Revenue and Expense Recognition for Income Tax Purposes

Several differences exist between GAAP and the rules that govern the preparation of the federal income tax return. The following are common examples:

1. Interest revenue on state and municipal bonds is generally excluded from taxable income, although it is included in accounting income.

2. Revenue collected in advance (e.g., rent revenue) is included in taxable income when it is collected and in accounting income when it is earned.

3. Proceeds from life insurance policies (e.g., key executive insurance) are excluded from taxable income but included in accounting income.

4. Corporations that own less than 20 percent of another corporation's stock may exclude 70 percent of the dividends received from taxable income, although all dividends are included in accounting income. The exclusion is 80 percent if the corporation owns more than 20 percent of the other corporation's stock. A 100 percent exclusion is permitted if 80 percent or more of the stock is owned.

5. For tax purposes, depreciation expense is generally based on the Accelerated Cost Recovery System (ACRS) for assets placed in service after 1980 but before 1987, or on the Modified Accelerated Cost Recovery System (MACRS) for assets placed in service after 1986. These methods were discussed in Chapter 8.

Tax Minimization Versus Tax Evasion

Most large corporations spend considerable time and money developing strategies that **minimize** the amount of federal income taxes they must pay. Nothing is wrong with this approach because courts have stated there is no legal obligation to pay more taxes than the law demands. Even if you do not major in accounting, you will probably want to take a course in federal income taxation because knowledge of the Internal Revenue Code is important for most executives. This knowledge offers opportunities to save significant amounts of money.

In contrast, tax evasion involves the use of illegal means to avoid paying taxes. Use of accelerated depreciation is an example of **tax minimization;** failure to report revenue that was collected in cash is an example of **tax evasion.** While efforts at tax minimization represent good business practice, tax evasion is morally and legally wrong. Individuals who evade taxes run the risk of severe financial penalties as well as the possibility of being sent to jail.

Chapter Supplement C

Present Value Computations Using Excel

The present value tables at the end of this book are useful for educational purposes, but most present value problems in business are solved with calculators or Excel spreadsheets. Because of the widespread availability of Excel, we will show you how to solve present value problems using Excel. There are slightly different versions of Excel available, depending on the age of the computer. The illustrations in this text are based on Microsoft Office 2003.

Present Value of a Single Payment

The calculation of a present value amount is based on a fairly simple mathematical formula:

$$PV = Payment / (1 + i)^n$$

In this formula, *payment* is the cash payment made at some point in the future, *i* is the interest rate each period, and *n* is the number of periods in the problem. We could use this formula to solve all problems involving the present value of a single payment. It is, of course, easier to use a present value table (like the one at the end of this book) that is derived by solving the present value formula for various interest rates and numbers of periods. Unfortunately, a table that includes all interest rates and numbers of periods actually encountered in business would be too large to work with. As a result, most accountants and analysts use Excel to compute a present value.

To compute the present value of a single payment in Excel, you enter the present value formula in a cell, using the format required by Excel. You should select a cell and enter the following formula:

$$= \text{Payment} / (1 + i)^{\wedge}n$$

To illustrate, if you want to solve for the present value of a $100,000 payment to be made in five years with an interest rate of 10 percent, you would enter the following in the function field:

$$= 100000 / (1.10)^{\wedge}5$$

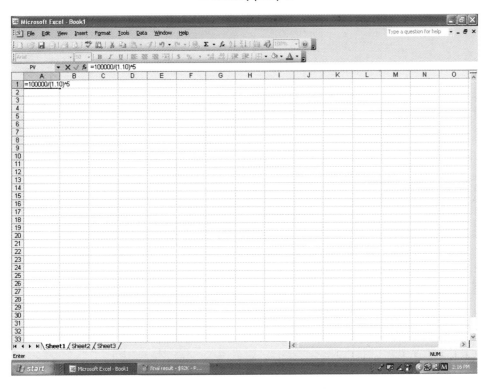

Based on this entry, Excel would compute the present value of $62,092.13. This answer is slightly different than the answer you would have if you used the present value tables at the end of the book. The tables in the book are rounded based on four digits. Excel does not round and, therefore, provides a more accurate computation.

Present Value of an Annuity

The formula for computing the present value of an annuity is a little more complicated than the present value of a single payment. As a result, Excel has been programmed to include the formula so that you do not have to enter it yourself.

To compute the present value of an annuity in Excel, select a cell and click on the insert function button (f_x). The following dropdown box will appear:

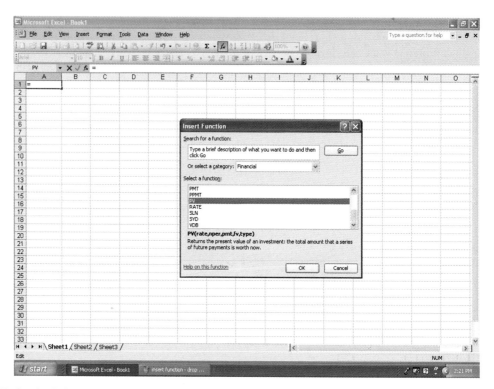

Under the Select Category heading, you should pick "Financial," scroll down under "Select a Function," and click on PV. Click on OK and a new dropdown box will appear:

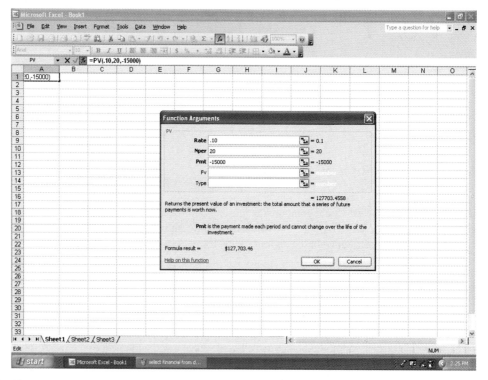

In this box, you should enter the interest rate, 10 percent in this example, under Rate. Notice that the rate must be entered as a decimal (i.e., 0.10). Enter the number of periods (20) under Nper. Excel has an unusual convention associated with the payment. It must be entered as a negative amount (-15000) under Pmt. Notice also that a comma should not be included in the amount you enter. When you click on OK, Excel will enter the present value in the cell you selected. In this example, the value determined by Excel is $127,703.46.

Chapter Supplement D

Future Value Concepts

Future value problems are similar to present value problems in the sense that they are both based on the time value of money. As we saw earlier, a present value problem determines the current cash equivalent of an amount to be received in the future. In comparison, a *future value* is the sum to which an amount will increase as the result of compound interest. The following table illustrates the basic difference between present value and future value problems:

	Now	**Future**
Present value	?	$1,000
Future value	$1,000	?

FUTURE VALUE is the sum to which an amount will increase as the result of compound interest.

Future Value of a Single Amount

In future value of a single amount problems, you will be asked to calculate how much money you will have in the future as the result of investing a certain amount in the present. If you were to receive a gift of $10,000, for instance, you might decide to put it in a savings account and use the money as a down payment on a house after you graduate. The future value computation would tell you how much money will be available when you graduate.

To solve a future value problem, you need to know three items:

1. Amount to be invested.

2. Interest rate (i) the amount will earn.

3. Number of periods (n) in which the amount will earn interest.

Since, the future value concept is based on compound interest, the amount of interest for each period is calculated by multiplying the principal plus any interest not paid out in prior periods. Graphically, the calculation of the future value of $1 for three periods and an interest rate of 10 percent may be represented as follows:

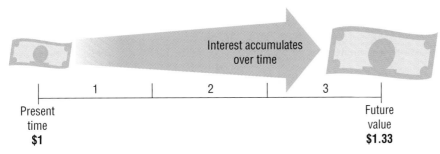

Assume that on January 1, 2006, you deposit $1,000 in a savings account at 10 percent annual interest, compounded annually. At the end of three years, the $1,000 will have increased to $1,331 as follows:

Year	Amount at Start of Year	+	Interest during the Year	=	Amount at End of Year
1	$1,000	+	$1,000 × 10% = $100	=	$1,100
2	1,100	+	1,100 × 10% = $110	=	1,210
3	1,210	+	1,210 × 10% = $121	=	1,331

We can avoid the detailed arithmetic by referring to Table A.3, Future Value of $1. For $i = 10\%$, $n = 3$, we find the value 1.331. We then compute the balance at the end of year 3 as follows:

$$\$1,000 \times 1.3310 = \$1,331$$

From Table A.3, interest rate = 10% n = 3

Note that the increase of $331 is due to the time value of money. It is interest revenue to the owner of the savings account and interest expense to the savings institution.

Future Value of an Annuity

If you are saving money for some purpose, such as a new car or a trip to Europe, you might decide to deposit a fixed amount of money in a savings account each month. The future value of an annuity computation will tell you how much money will be in your savings account at some point in the future.

The future value of an annuity includes compound interest on each payment from the date of payment to the end of the term of the annuity. Each new payment accumulates less interest than prior payments, only because the number of periods remaining in which to accumulate interest decreases. The future value of an annuity of $1 for three periods at 10 percent may be represented graphically as:

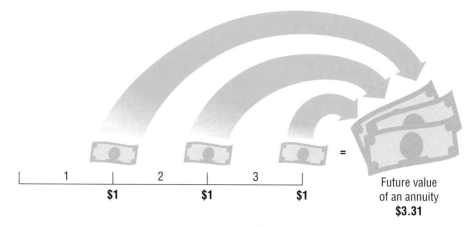

Future value
of an annuity
$3.31

Assume that each year for three years, you deposit $1,000 cash in a savings account at 10 percent interest per year. You make the first $1,000 deposit on December 31, 2006, the second one on December 31, 2007, and the third and last one on December 31, 2008. The first $1,000 deposit earns compound interest for two years (for a total principal and interest of $1,210); the second deposit earns interest for one year (for a total principal and interest of $1,100). The third deposit earns no interest because it was made on the day that the balance is computed. Thus, the total amount in the savings account at the end of three years is $3,310 ($1,210 + $1,100 + $1,000).

To derive the future value of this annuity, we could compute the interest on each deposit. However, we can refer to Table A.4, Appendix A, Future Value of an Annuity of $1 for $i = 10\%$, $n = 3$ to find the value 3.3100. The future value of your three deposits of $1,000 each can be computed as follows:

> *From Table A.4,*
> *interest rate = 10%*
> *n = 3*

$$\$1,000 \times 3.3100 = \$3,310$$

The Power of Compounding

Compound interest is a remarkably powerful economic force. Indeed, the ability to earn interest on interest is the key to building economic wealth. If you save $1,000 per year for the first 10 years of your career, you will have more money when you retire than you would if you had saved $15,000 per year for the last 10 years of your career. This surprising outcome occurs because the money you save early in your career will earn more interest than the money you save at the end of your career. If you start saving money now, the majority of your wealth will not be the money you saved but the interest your money was able to earn.

**Effects of
Compound Interest**

$20
$15
$10
$5
$0

━Deposits
━Deposits with interest

The chart in the margin illustrates the power of compounding over a brief 10-year period. If you deposit $1 each year in an account earning 10 percent interest, at the end of just 10 years, only 64 percent of your balance will be made up of money you have saved; the rest will be interest you have earned. After 20 years, only 35 percent of your balance will be from saved money. The lesson associated with compound interest is clear: Even though saving money is difficult, you should start now.

1. **Define, measure, and report current liabilities.** p. 463

   Strictly speaking, accountants define *liabilities* as probable future sacrifices of economic benefits that arise from past transactions. They are classified on the balance sheet as either current or long term. Current liabilities are short-term obligations that will be paid within the current operating cycle of the business or within one year of the balance sheet date, whichever is longer. Long-term liabilities are all obligations not classified as current.

2. **Use the current ratio.** p. 464

   The current ratio is a comparison of current assets and current liabilities. Analysts use this ratio to assess the liquidity of a company.

3. **Analyze the accounts payable turnover ratio.** p. 465

   This ratio is computed by dividing cost of goods sold by accounts payable. It shows how quickly management is paying its trade creditors and is considered to be a measure of liquidity.

4. **Report notes payable and explain the time value of money.** p. 469

   A note payable specifies the amount borrowed, when it must be repaid, and the interest rate associated with the debt. Accountants must report the debt and the interest as it accrues. The time value of money refers to the fact that interest accrues on borrowed money with the passage of time.

5. **Report contingent liabilities.** p. 471

   A contingent liability is a potential liability that has arisen as the result of a past event. Such liabilities are disclosed in a note if the obligation is reasonably possible.

6. **Explain the importance of working capital and its impact on cash flows.** p. 473

   Working capital is used to fund the operating activities of a business. Changes in working capital accounts affect the statement of cash flows. Cash flows from operating activities are increased by decreases in current assets (other than cash) or increases in current liabilities. Cash flows from operating activities are decreased by increases in current assets (other than cash) or decreases in current liabilities.

7. **Report long-term liabilities.** p. 475

   Usually, long-term liabilities will be paid in more than one year in the future. Accounting for long-term debt is based on the same concepts used in accounting for short-term debt.

8. **Compute present values.** p. 477

   The present value concept is based on the time value of money. Simply stated, a dollar to be received in the future is worth less than a dollar available today (present value). This concept can be applied either to a single payment or multiple payments called *annuities*. Either tables or Excel can be used to determine present values.

9. **Apply present value concepts to liabilities.** p. 481

   Accountants use present value concepts to determine the reported amounts of liabilities. A liability involves the payment of some amount at a future date. The reported liability is not the amount of the future payment. Instead, the liability is reported at the amount of the present value of the future payment.

   In this chapter, we focused on current liabilities and introduced you to present value concepts. In the next chapter, we will use present value concepts to measure long-term liabilities. We will also discuss long-term liabilities in the context of the capital structure of the company.

KEY RATIOS

Current ratio measures the ability of a company to pay its current obligations. It is computed as follows (p. 464):

$$\text{Current Ratio} = \frac{\text{Current Assets}}{\text{Current Liabilities}}$$

Accounts payable turnover is a measure of how quickly a company pays its creditors. It is computed as follows (p. 466):

$$\text{Accounts Payable Turnover} = \frac{\text{Costs of Goods Sold}}{\text{Average Accounts Payable}}$$

FINDING FINANCIAL INFORMATION

Balance Sheet

Under Current Liabilities
Liabilities listed by account title, such as
Accounts payable
Accrued liabilities
Notes payable
Current portion of long-term debt

Under Noncurrent Liabilities
Liabilities listed by account title, such as
Long-term debt
Deferred taxes
Bonds

Income Statement

Liabilities are shown only on the balance sheet, never on the income statement. Transactions affecting liabilities often affect an income statement account. For example, accrued salary compensation affects an income statement account (compensation expense) and a balance sheet account (salaries payable).

Statement of Cash Flows

Under Operating Activities (indirect method)
Net income
 + Increases in most current liabilities
 − Decreases in most current liabilities

Under Financing Activities
 + Increases in long-term liabilities
 − Decreases in long-term liabilities

Notes

Under Summary of Significant Accounting Policies
Description of pertinent information concerning accounting treatment of liabilities. Normally, there is minimal information.

Under a Separate Note
If not listed on the balance sheet, a listing of the major classifications of liabilities with information about maturities and interest rates. Information about contingent liabilities is reported in the notes.

KEY TERMS

Accrued Liabilities p. 466
Annuity p. 479
Capital Lease p. 477
Contingent Liability p. 471
Current Liabilities p. 463
Deferred Revenues p. 470

Deferred Tax Items p. 483
Future Value p. 489
Liabilities p. 463
Liquidity p. 463
Long-Term Liabilities p. 475
Operating Lease p. 477

Present Value p. 477
Temporary Differences p. 483
Time Value of Money p. 469
Working Capital p. 473

QUESTIONS

1. Define *liability*. Differentiate between a current liability and a long-term liability.
2. How can external parties be informed about the liabilities of a business?
3. Liabilities are measured and reported at their current cash equivalent amount. Explain.
4. A *liability* is a known obligation of either a definite or an estimated amount. Explain.
5. Define *working capital*. How is it computed?
6. What is the current ratio? How is it related to the classification of liabilities?
7. Define *accrued liability*. What type of entry usually reflects an accrued liability?
8. Define *deferred revenue*. Why is it a liability?
9. Define *note payable*. Differentiate between a secured and an unsecured note.
10. What is a contingent liability? How is a contingent liability reported?
11. Compute 2006 interest expense for the following note: face, $4,000; 12 percent interest; date of note, April 1, 2006.
12. Explain the concept of the *time value of money*.
13. Explain the basic difference between future value and present value.
14. If you hold a valid contract that will pay you $8,000 cash 10 years hence and the going rate of interest is 10 percent, what is its present value? Show your computations.
15. What is an annuity?
16. Complete the following schedule:

Concept	Table Values $i = 5\%, n = 4; i = 10\%, n = 7; i = 14\%, n = 10$
PV of $1	
PV of annuity of $1	

17. You purchased an XIT auto for $18,000 by making a $3,000 cash payment and six semiannual installment payments for the balance at 12 percent interest. Use a convenient format to display computation of the amount of each payment.

MULTIPLE-**CHOICE QUESTIONS**

1. What is the present value factor for an annuity of five periods and an interest rate of 10 percent?
   a. 1.6105
   b. 6.1051
   c. 3.7908
   d. 7.7217
2. The university spirit organization needs to buy a car to travel to football games. A dealership in Lockhart has agreed to the following terms: $4,000 down plus 20 monthly payments of $750. A dealership in Leander will agree to a $1,000 down payment plus 20 monthly payments of $850. The local bank is currently charging an annual interest rate of 12 percent for car loans. Which is the better deal, *and why?*
   a. The Leander offer is better because the total payments of $18,000 are less than the total payments of $19,000 to be made to the Lockhart dealership.
   b. The Lockhart offer is better because the cost in terms of present value is less than the present value cost of the Leander offer.
   c. The Lockhart offer is better because the monthly payments are less.
   d. The Leander offer is better because the cash down payment is less.
   e. The Leander offer is better because the cost in terms of present value is less than the present value cost of the Lockhart offer.
3. Which of the following best describes *accrued liabilities?*
   a. Long-term liabilities.
   b. Current amounts owed to suppliers of inventory.
   c. Current liabilities to be recognized as revenue in a future period.
   d. Current amounts owed to various parties excluding suppliers of inventory.

4. Company X has borrowed $100,000 from the bank to be repaid over the next five years, with payments beginning next month. Which of the following best describes the presentation of this debt in the balance sheet as of today (the date of borrowing)?
   a. $100,000 in the Long-Term Liability section.
   b. $100,000 plus the interest to be paid over the five-year period in the Long-Term Liability section.
   c. A portion of the $100,000 in the Current Liability section and the remainder of the principal in the Long-Term Liability section.
   d. A portion of the $100,000 plus interest in the Current Liability section and the remainder of the principal plus interest in the Long-Term Liability section.

5. A company is facing a class-action lawsuit in the upcoming year. It is possible, but not probable, that the company will have to pay a settlement of approximately $2,000,000. How would this fact be reported in the financial statements to be issued at the end of the current month?
   a. $2,000,000 in the Current Liability section.
   b. $2,000,000 in the Long-Term Liability section.
   c. In a descriptive narrative in the footnote section.
   d. None because disclosure is not required.

6. Which of the following transactions would usually cause accounts payable turnover to increase?
   a. Payment of cash to a supplier.   c. Purchase of merchandise on credit.
   b. Collection of cash from a customer.   d. None of the above.

7. How is working capital calculated?
   a. Current assets multiplied by current liabilities.
   b. Current assets plus current liabilities.
   c. Current assets minus current liabilities.
   d. Current assets divided by current liabilities.

8. Which of the following is least likely to be an annuity?
   a. Monthly payments to a savings account.   c. Monthly payments on a home mortgage.
   b. Monthly receipts from a pension plan.   d. Monthly utility bill payments.

9. At what value are liabilities presented in the financial statements?
   a. Net book value.   c. Future value.
   b. Present value.   d. Cash flow value.

10. Fred wants to save enough money each year so that he can purchase a sports car in January 2011. Fred receives a large bonus from his employer every December 31. He anticipates that the car will cost $54,000 on January 1, 2011. Which of the following will Fred need to calculate how much he must save each December 31?
    a. The anticipated interest rate and the present value of $1 table.
    b. The anticipated interest rate and the future value of $1 table.
    c. The anticipated interest rate and the present value table for annuities.
    d. The anticipated interest rate and the future value table for annuities.

For more practice with multiple-choice questions, go to the text website at www.mhhe.com/libby5e or the Topic Tackler DVD for use with this text.

MINI-EXERCISES

 Available with McGraw-Hill's Homework Manager

M9-1   Computing Interest Expense
L04

Jacobs Company borrowed $500,000 on a 90-day note at 9 percent interest. The money was borrowed for 30 days in 2006 and 60 days in 2007; the note and interest were to be paid upon maturity in 2007. How much interest expense, if any, would be reported in 2006 and in 2007?

M9-2   Recording a Note Payable
L04

Farmer Corporation borrowed $100,000 on November 1, 2006. The note carried a 12 percent interest rate with the principal and interest payable on June 1, 2007. Prepare the journal entry to record the note on November 1. Prepare the adjusting entry to record accrued interest on December 31.

Finding Financial Information

M9-3
LO1, 3, 6

For each of the following items, specify whether the information would be found in the balance sheet, the income statement, the statement of cash flows, the notes to the statements, or not at all.
a. The amount of working capital.
b. The total amount of current liabilities.
c. Information concerning company pension plans.
d. The accounts payable turnover ratio.
e. Information concerning the impact of changes in working capital on cash flows for the period.

Computing Measures of Liquidity

M9-4
LO2

The balance sheet for Shaver Corporation reported the following: total assets, $250,000; noncurrent assets, $150,000; current liabilities, $40,000; total stockholders' equity, $90,000. Compute Shaver's current ratio and working capital.

Analyzing the Impact of Transactions on Liquidity

M9-5
LO2

BSO, Inc., has a current ratio of 2.0 and working capital in the amount of $1,240,000. For each of the following transactions, determine whether the current ratio and working capital will increase, decrease, or remain the same.

a. Paid accounts payable in the amount of $50,000.
b. Recorded accrued salaries in the amount of $100,000.
c. Borrowed $250,000 from a local bank, to be repaid in 90 days.
d. Purchased $20,000 of new inventory on credit.

Reporting Contingent Liabilities

M9-6
LO5

Buzz Coffee Shops is famous for its large servings of hot coffee. After a famous case involving McDonald's, the lawyer for Buzz warned management (during 2006) that it could be sued if someone were to spill hot coffee and be burned: "With the temperature of your coffee, I can guarantee it's just a matter of time before you're sued for $1,000,000." Unfortunately, in 2008 the prediction came true when a customer filed suit. The case went to trial in 2009, and the jury awarded the customer $400,000 in damages, which the company immediately appealed. During 2010, the customer and the company settled their dispute for $150,000. What is the proper reporting of this liability each year?

Computing the Present Value of a Single Payment

M9-7
LO8

What is the present value of $500,000 to be paid in 10 years with an interest rate of 8 percent?

Computing the Present Value of an Annuity

M9-8
LO8

What is the present value of 10 equal payments of $15,000 with an interest rate of 10 percent?

Computing the Present Value of a Complex Contract

M9-9
LO8

As a result of a slowdown in operations, Mercantile Stores is offering employees who have been terminated a severance package of $100,000 cash, another $100,000 to be paid in one year, and an annuity of $30,000 to be paid each year for 20 years beginning in one year. What is the present value of the package, assuming an interest rate of 8 percent?

Computing the Future Value of an Annuity (Supplement D)

M9-10

You plan to retire in 20 years. Is it better for you to save $25,000 a year for the last 10 years before retirement or $15,000 for each of the 20 years? You are able to earn 10 percent interest on your investments.

Making a Complex Computation of a Future Value (Supplement D)

M9-11

You want a retirement fund of $500,000 when you retire in 20 years. You are able to earn 10 percent on your investments. How much should you deposit each year to build the retirement fund that you want?

EXERCISES

™ **Available with McGraw-Hill's Homework Manager**

E9-1
LO1, 2, 5, 6

Computing Working Capital; Explaining the Current Ratio and Working Capital

Wilemon Corporation is preparing its 2007 balance sheet. The company records show the following selected amounts at the end of the accounting period, December 31, 2007:

Total assets	$695,100
Total noncurrent assets	525,000
Liabilities:	
Notes payable (8%, due in 5 years)	78,000
Accounts payable	60,000
Income taxes payable	12,000
Liability for withholding taxes	3,000
Rent revenue collected in advance	14,000
Bonds payable (due in 15 years)	100,000
Wages payable	7,800
Property taxes payable	2,000
Note payable (10%, due in 6 months)	10,000
Interest payable	400
Common stock	100,000

Required:

1. Compute (a) working capital and (b) the current ratio (show computations). Why is working capital important to management? How do financial analysts use the current ratio?
2. Would your computations be different if the company reported $250,000 worth of contingent liabilities in the notes to the statements? Explain.

E9-2
LO1

Recording Payroll Costs

Warner Company completed the salary and wage payroll for March 2006. The payroll provided the following details:

Salaries and wages earned	$230,000
Employee income taxes withheld	46,000
Insurance premiums withheld	1,200
FICA payroll taxes*	16,445
*$16,445 each for employer and employees.	

Required:

1. Give the journal entry to record the payroll for March, including employee deductions.
2. Give the journal entry to record the employer's payroll taxes.
3. Give a combined journal entry to show the payment of amounts owed to governmental agencies.

E9-3
LO1

Computing Payroll Costs; Discussion of Labor Costs

Colonial Company has completed the payroll for January 2007, reflecting the following data:

Salaries and wages earned	$78,000
Employee income taxes withheld	9,500
FICA payroll taxes*	6,013
*Assessed on both employer and employee (i.e., $6,013 each).	

Required:

1. What amount of additional labor expense to the company was due to tax laws? What was the amount of the employees' take-home pay?
2. List the liabilities and their amounts that are reported on the company's January 31, 2007, balance sheet, assuming the employees have been paid.
3. Would employers react differently to a 10 percent increase in the employer's share of FICA than to a 10 percent increase in the basic level of salaries? Would financial analysts react differently?

Recording a Note Payable through Its Time to Maturity with Discussion of Management Strategy

E9-4
LO1, 4

Many businesses borrow money during periods of increased business activity to finance inventory and accounts receivable. Neiman Marcus is one of America's most prestigious retailers. Each Christmas season, Neiman Marcus builds up its inventory to meet the needs of Christmas shoppers. A large portion of these Christmas sales are on credit. As a result, Neiman Marcus often collects cash from the sales several months after Christmas. Assume that on November 1, 2006, Neiman Marcus borrowed $8 million cash from Texas Capital Bank for working capital purposes and signed an interest-bearing note due in six months. The interest rate was 8 percent per annum payable at maturity. The accounting period ends December 31.

Required:
1. Give the journal entry to record the note on November 1.
2. Give any adjusting entry required at the end of the annual accounting period.
3. Give the journal entry to record payment of the note and interest on the maturity date, April 30, 2007.
4. If Neiman Marcus needs extra cash during every Christmas season, should management borrow money on a long-term basis to avoid the necessity of negotiating a new short-term loan each year?

Determining Financial Statement Effects of Transactions Involving Notes Payable

E9-5
LO1, 4

Using the data from E9-4, complete the following requirements.

Required:
1. Determine the financial statement effects for each of the following: (a) issuance of the note on November 1, (b) impact of the adjusting entry at the end of the accounting period, and (c) payment of the note and interest on April 30, 2007. Indicate the effects (e.g., cash + or −), using the following schedule:

Date	Assets	=	Liabilities	+	Stockholders' Equity

2. If Neiman Marcus needs extra cash every Christmas season, should management borrow money on a long-term basis to avoid negotiating a new short-term loan each year?

Reporting Short-Term Borrowings

E9-6
LO1
PepsiCo. Inc.

PepsiCo, Inc., manufactures a number of products that are part of our daily lives. Its businesses include Pepsi-Cola, Slice, Mountain Dew, and Fritos. The company's annual revenues exceed $22 billion. A recent PepsiCo annual report contained the following information:

> At the end of the current year, $3.6 billion of short-term borrowings were classified as long-term, reflecting PepsiCo's intent and ability to refinance these borrowings on a long-term basis, through either long-term debt issuances or rollover of existing short-term borrowings. The significant amount of short-term borrowings classified as long-term, as compared to the end of the previous year when no such amounts were reclassified, primarily reflects the large commercial paper issuances in the current year but also resulted from a refined analysis of amounts expected to be refinanced beyond one year.

Required:
As an analyst, comment on the company's classification of short-term borrowings as long-term liabilities. What conditions should exist to permit a company to make this type of classification?

Determining the Impact of Transactions, Including Analysis of Cash Flows

E9-7
LO1, 2, 4, 6

Bryant Company sells a wide range of goods through two retail stores operated in adjoining cities. Most purchases of goods for resale are on invoices. Occasionally, a short-term note payable is used to obtain cash for current use. The following transactions were selected from those occurring during 2007:

a. Purchased merchandise on credit, $18,000 on January 10, 2007; the company uses a periodic inventory system.

b. Borrowed $40,000 cash on March 1, 2007 from City Bank and gave an interest-bearing note payable: face amount, $40,000, due at the end of six months, with an annual interest rate of 8 percent payable at maturity.

Required:

1. Describe the impact of each transaction on the balance sheet equation. Indicate the effects (e.g., cash + or −), using the following schedule:

Date	Assets	=	Liabilities	+	Stockholders' Equity

2. What amount of cash is paid on the maturity date of the note?
3. Discuss the impact of each transaction on Bryant's cash flows.
4. Discuss the impact of each transaction on the current ratio.

E9-8   Reporting a Liability

L07

Carnival Cruise Lines

Carnival Cruise Lines provides exotic vacations on board luxurious passenger ships. The company moved its offices and included the following note in its current annual report:

> **Leases**
>
> The Company entered into a 10-year lease for 230,000 square feet of office space located in Miami, Florida. The Company moved its operation to this location in October. The total rent payable over the 10-year term of the lease is approximately $24 million.

Required:

Based on these facts, do you think the company should report this obligation on its balance sheet? Explain. If the obligation should be reported as a liability, how should the amount be measured?

E9-9   Evaluating Lease Alternatives

L07

As the new vice president for consumer products at Acme Manufacturing, you are attending a meeting to discuss a serious problem associated with delivering merchandise to customers. Bob Smith, director of logistics, summarized the problem: "It's easy to understand. We just don't have enough delivery trucks given our recent growth." Barb Bader from the accounting department responded: "Maybe it's easy to understand but it's impossible to do anything. Because of Wall Street's concern about the amount of debt on our balance sheet, we're under a freeze and can't borrow money to acquire new assets. There's nothing we can do."

On the way back to your office after the meeting, your assistant offers a suggestion: "Why don't we just lease the trucks we need? That way we can get the assets we want without having to record a liability on the balance sheet."

How would you respond to this suggestion?

E9-10   Reporting a Liability, with Discussion (Supplement A)

Ford Motor Company

The annual report for Ford Motor Company contained the following information:

> **Postretirement Health Care and Life Insurance Benefits**
>
> The company and certain of its subsidiaries sponsor unfunded plans to provide selected health care and life insurance benefits for retired employees. The company's employees may become eligible for those benefits if they retire while working for the company. However, benefits and eligibility rules may be modified from time to time.

Required:

Should Ford report a liability for these benefits on its balance sheet? Explain.

Computing Deferred Income Tax: One Temporary Difference, with Discussion (Supplements A and B)

E9-11

The comparative income statements of Martin Corporation at December 31, 2007, showed the following summarized pretax data:

	Year 2006	Year 2007
Sales revenue	$65,000	$72,000
Expenses (excluding income tax)	50,000	54,000
Pretax income	$15,000	$18,000

Included in the 2007 data is a $2,800 expense that was deductible only in the 2006 income tax return (rather than in 2007). The average income tax rate was 30 percent. Taxable income from the income tax returns was 2006, $14,000, and 2007, $17,400.

Required:

1. For each year, compute (a) income taxes payable and (b) deferred income tax. Is the deferred income tax a liability or an asset? Explain.
2. Show what amounts related to income taxes should be reported each year on the income statement and balance sheet. Assume that income tax is paid on April 15 of the next year.
3. Explain why tax expense is not simply the amount of cash paid during the year.

Recording Deferred Income Tax: One Temporary Difference; Discussion of Management Strategy (Supplements A and B)

E9-12

The comparative income statement for Chung Corporation at the end of December 31, 2007, provided the following summarized pretax data:

	Year 2006	Year 2007
Revenue	$80,000	$88,000
Expenses (excluding income tax)	65,000	69,000
Pretax income	$15,000	$19,000

Included in the 2007 data is a $5,000 revenue that was taxable only in the 2006 income tax return. The average income tax rate was 32 percent. Taxable income shown in the tax returns was 2006, $13,000, and 2007, $18,500.

Required:

1. For each year, compute (a) income taxes payable and (b) deferred income tax. Is the deferred income tax a liability or an asset? Explain.
2. Give the journal entry for each year to record income taxes payable, deferred income tax, and income tax expense.
3. Show what amounts related to income taxes should be reported each year on the income statement and balance sheet. Assume that income tax is paid on April 15 of the next year.
4. Why would management want to incur the cost of maintaining separate tax and financial accounting records?

Reporting Deferred Taxes (Supplement A)

E9-13

Colgate-Palmolive

The annual report for Colgate-Palmolive contains the following information (dollars in millions):

Income Taxes

Differences between accounting for financial statement purposes and accounting for tax purposes result in taxes currently payable (lower) higher than the total provision for income taxes as follows:

	1999	1998	1997
Excess tax over book depreciation	$(18.0)	$(19.8)	$(18.9)
Other	(31.4)	76.6	(25.5)
Total	$(49.4)	$ 56.8	$(44.4)

Required:
1. Determine whether tax expense is higher or lower than taxes payable for each year.
2. Explain the most likely reason for tax depreciation to be higher than book depreciation.
3. Is the deferred tax liability reported on the 1999 balance sheet $49.4 million? Explain.

E9-14
LO8

Computing Four Present Value Problems

On January 1, 2006, Vigeland Company completed the following transactions (assume a 10 percent annual interest rate):

a. Bought a delivery truck and agreed to pay $50,000 at the end of three years.
b. Rented an office building and was given the option of paying $10,000 at the end of each of the next three years or paying $28,000 immediately.
c. Established a savings account by depositing a single amount that will increase to $40,000 at the end of seven years.
d. Decided to deposit a single sum in the bank that will provide 10 equal annual year-end payments of $15,000 to a retired employee (payments starting December 31, 2006).

Required (show computations and round to the nearest dollar):
1. What is the cost of the truck that should be recorded at the time of purchase?
2. Which option for the office building should the company select?
3. What single amount must be deposited in this account on January 1, 2006?
4. What single sum must be deposited in the bank on January 1, 2006?

E9-15
LO8

Using Present Value Concepts for Decision Making

You have just won the state lottery and have two choices for collecting your winnings. You can collect $100,000 today or receive $11,000 per year for the next 10 years. A financial analyst has told you that you can earn 8 percent on your investments. Which alternative should you select?

E9-16
LO8

Calculating a Retirement Fund

You are a financial adviser who is working with a client who wants to retire in 10 years. The client has a savings account with a local bank that pays 6 percent and she wants to deposit an amount that will provide her with $500,000 when she retires. Currently, she has $200,000 in the account. How much additional money should she deposit now to provide her with $500,000 when she retires?

E9-17
LO8

Determining an Educational Fund

Judge Drago has decided to set up an educational fund for his favorite granddaughter, Emma, who will start college in one year. The Judge plans to deposit an amount in a savings account that pays 8 percent interest. He wants to deposit an amount that is sufficient to permit Emma to withdraw $12,000 starting in one year and continuing each year for a total of four years. How much should he deposit today to provide Emma with a fund to pay for her college tuition?

E9-18
LO8

Computing a Present Value

An investment will pay $10,000 at the end of the first year, $25,000 at the end of the second year, and $50,000 at the end of the third year. Determine the present value of this investment using a 10 percent interest rate.

E9-19
LO8

Computing a Present Value

An investment will pay $10,000 at the end of each year for 10 years and a one-time payment of $100,000 at the end of the tenth year. Determine the present value of this investment using a 6 percent interest rate.

E9-20
LO8

Determining the Value of an Asset

Dan Roger Company has purchased a new office building. The company has agreed to pay the developer $50,000 per year for 10 years. Using present value techniques, determine the value that should be recorded when the building is purchased. Assume a 6 percent interest rate.

Computing Value of an Asset Based on Present Value

You have the chance to purchase the royalty interest in an oil well. Your best estimate is that the net royalty income will average $25,000 per year for five years. There will be no residual value at that time. Assume that the cash inflow occurs at each year-end and that considering the uncertainty in your estimates, you expect to earn 15 percent per year on the investment. What should you be willing to pay for this investment now?

E9-21
LO8

Computing Growth in a Savings Account: A Single Amount (Supplement D)

On January 1, 2006, you deposited $6,000 in a savings account. The account will earn 10 percent annual compound interest, which will be added to the fund balance at the end of each year.

Required (round to the nearest dollar):
1. What will be the balance in the savings account at the end of 10 years?
2. What is the amount of interest earned during the 10 years?
3. How much interest revenue did the fund earn in 2006? 2007?

E9-22

Computing Deposit Required and Accounting for a Single-Sum Savings Account (Supplement D)

On January 1, 2006, Alan King decided to deposit $58,800 in a savings account that will provide funds four years later to send his son to college. The savings account will earn 8 percent, which will be added to the fund each year-end.

Required (show computations and round to the nearest dollar):
1. How much will be available in four years?
2. Give the journal entry that Alan should make on January 1, 2006.
3. What is the interest for the four years?
4. Give the journal entry that Alan should make on (a) December 31, 2006, and (b) December 31, 2007.

E9-23

Recording Growth in a Savings Account with Equal Periodic Payments (Supplement D)

On each December 31, you plan to deposit $2,000 in a savings account. The account will earn 9 percent annual interest, which will be added to the fund balance at year-end. The first deposit will be made December 31, 2006 (end of period).

Required (show computations and round to the nearest dollar):
1. Give the required journal entry on December 31, 2006.
2. What will be the balance in the savings account at the end of the 10th year (i.e., after 10 deposits)?
3. What is the interest earned on the 10 deposits?
4. How much interest revenue did the fund earn in 2007? 2008?
5. Give all required journal entries at the end of 2007 and 2008.

E9-24

Computing Growth for a Savings Fund with Periodic Deposits (Supplement D)

On January 1, 2006, you plan to take a trip around the world upon graduation four years from now. Your grandmother wants to deposit sufficient funds for this trip in a savings account for you. On the basis of a budget, you estimate that the trip currently would cost $15,000. To be generous, your grandmother decided to deposit $3,500 in the fund at the end of each of the next four years, starting on December 31, 2006. The savings account will earn 6 percent annual interest, which will be added to the savings account at each year-end.

Required (show computations and round to the nearest dollar):
1. How much money will you have for the trip at the end of year 4 (i.e., after four deposits)?
2. What is the interest for the four years?
3. How much interest revenue did the fund earn in 2006, 2007, 2008, and 2009?

E9-25

PROBLEMS   Available with McGraw-Hill's Homework Manager

P9-1   Recording and Reporting Current Liabilities
LO1

Curb Company completed the following transactions during 2006. The annual accounting period ends December 31, 2006.

Jan.   15   Purchased and paid for merchandise for resale at an invoice cost of $13,580; assume a periodic inventory system.

Apr.   1   Borrowed $500,000 from Summit Bank for general use; executed an 11-month, 8 percent interest-bearing note payable.

June   14   Received a $10,000 customer deposit from Mark Muller for services to be performed in the future.

July   15   Performed $2,500 of the services paid for by Mr. Muller.

Dec.   12   Received electric bill for $540. The company will pay it in early January.

       31   Determined wages of $12,000 earned but not yet paid on December 31 (disregard payroll taxes).

Required:
1. Prepare journal entries for each of these transactions.
2. Prepare all adjusting entries required on December 31, 2006.

P9-2   Recording and Reporting Current Liabilities with Discussion of Cash Flow Effects (AP9-1)
LO1, 2, 6

Smith Company completed the following transactions during 2006. The annual accounting period ends December 31, 2006.

Jan.   8   Purchased merchandise for resale on account at an invoice cost of $25,000; assume a periodic inventory system.

       17   Paid January 8 invoice.

Apr.   1   Borrowed $40,000 from National Bank for general use; executed a 12-month, 12 percent interest-bearing note payable.

June   3   Purchased merchandise for resale on account at an invoice cost of $18,000.

July   5   Paid June 3 invoice.

Aug.   1   Rented a small office in a building owned by the company and collected six months' rent in advance amounting to $5,100. (Record the collection in a way that will not require an adjusting entry at year-end.)

Dec.   20   Received a $500 deposit from a customer as a guarantee to return a large trailer "borrowed" for 30 days.

       31   Determined wages of $10,000 earned but not yet paid on December 31 (disregard payroll taxes).

Required:
1. Prepare journal entries for each of these transactions.
2. Prepare all adjusting entries required on December 31, 2006.
3. Show how all of the liabilities arising from these transactions are reported on the balance sheet at December 31, 2006.
4. For each transaction, state whether the current ratio is increased, decreased, or remains the same.
5. For each transaction, state whether cash flow from operating activities is increased, decreased, or there is no effect.

P9-3   Determining Financial Effects of Transactions Affecting Current Liabilities with
LO1, 2, 6   Discussion of Cash Flow Effects (AP9-2)

Using data from P9-2, complete the following requirements.

Required:

1. For each transaction (including adjusting entries) listed in P9-2, indicate the effects (e.g., cash + or −), using the following schedule:

Date	Assets	=	Liabilities	+	Stockholders' Equity

2. For each transaction, state whether cash flow from operating activities is increased, decreased, or remains the same.
3. For each transaction, state whether the current ratio is increased, decreased, or remains the same.

Recording and Reporting Accrued Liabilities and Deferred Revenue with Discussion

P9-4
L01

During 2007, Riverside Company completed the following two transactions. The annual accounting period ends December 31.

a. Paid and recorded wages of $130,000 during 2007; however, at the end of December 2007, three days' wages are unpaid and unrecorded because the weekly payroll will not be paid until January 6, 2008. Wages for the three days are $3,600.
b. Collected rent revenue on December 10, 2007, of $2,400 for office space that Riverside rented to another party. The rent collected was for 30 days from December 10, 2007, to January 10, 2008, and was credited in full to Rent Revenue.

Required:

1. Give (a) the adjusting entry required on December 31, 2007, and (b) the January 6, 2008, journal entry for payment of any unpaid wages from December 2007.
2. Give (a) the journal entry for the collection of rent on December 10, 2007, and (b) the adjusting entry on December 31, 2007.
3. Show how any liabilities related to these transactions should be reported on the company's balance sheet at December 31, 2007.
4. Explain why the accrual method of accounting provides more relevant information to financial analysts than the cash method.

Determining Financial Statement Effects of Transactions Involving Accrued Liabilities and Deferred Revenue

P9-5
L01

Using the data from the previous exercise, complete the following requirements.

Required:

1. Determine the financial statement effects for each of the following: (a) the adjusting entry required on December 31, 2007, (b) the January 6, 2008, journal entry for payment of any unpaid wages from December 2007, (c) the journal entry for the collection of rent on December 10, 2007, and (d) the adjusting entry on December 31, 2007. Indicate the effects (e.g., cash + or −), using the following schedule:

Date	Assets	=	Liabilities	+	Stockholders' Equity

2. Explain why the accrual method of accounting provides more relevant information to financial analysts than the cash method.

Determining Financial Statement Effects of Various Liabilities (AP9-3)

P9-6
L01, 5
Polaroid

Polaroid designs, manufactures, and markets products primarily in instant image recording. Its annual report contained the following note:

Product Warranty

Estimated product warranty costs are accrued at the time products are sold.

1. Assume that estimated warranty costs for 2006 were $2 million and that the warranty work was performed during 2007. Describe the financial statement effects for each year.

Reader's Digest Association is a publisher of magazines, books, and music collections. The following note is from its annual report:

Reader's Digest
Association

> **Revenues**
>
> Sales of subscriptions to magazines are recorded as unearned revenue at the time the order is received. Proportional shares of the subscription price are recognized as revenues when the subscription is fulfilled.

2. Assume that Reader's Digest collected $10 million in 2006 for magazines that will be delivered in future years. During 2007, the company delivered $8 million worth of magazines on those subscriptions. Describe the financial statement effects for each year.

Brunswick Corporation is a multinational company that manufactures and sells marine and recreational products. Its annual report contained the following information:

Brunswick
Corporation

> **Litigation**
>
> A jury awarded $44.4 million in damages in a suit brought by Independent Boat Builders, Inc., a buying group of boat manufacturers and its 22 members. Under the antitrust laws, the damage award has been trebled, and the plaintiffs will be entitled to their attorney's fees and interest.
>
> The Company has filed an appeal contending the verdict was erroneous as a matter of law, both as to liability and damages.

3. How should Brunswick account for this litigation?
4. A recent annual report for The Coca-Cola Company reported current assets of $4,247,677 and current liabilities of $5,303,222. Based on the current ratio, do you think that Coca-Cola is experiencing financial difficulty?

Alcoa is involved in the mining and manufacturing of aluminum. Its products can become an advanced alloy for the wing of a Boeing 777 or a common recyclable Coca-Cola can. The annual report for Alcoa stated the following:

Alcoa

> **Environmental Expenditures**
>
> Liabilities are recorded when remedial efforts are probable and the costs can be reasonably estimated.

5. In your own words, explain Alcoa's accounting policy for environmental expenditures. What is the justification for this policy?

P9-7
L05

Making a Decision as an Auditor: Contingent Liabilities

For each of the following situations, determine whether the company should (a) report a liability on the balance sheet, (b) disclose a contingent liability, or (c) not report the situation. Justify and explain your conclusions.

1. An automobile company introduces a new car. Past experience demonstrates that lawsuits will be filed as soon as the new model is involved in any accidents. The company can be certain that at least one jury will award damages to people injured in an accident.

2. A research scientist determines that the company's best-selling product may infringe on another company's patent. If the other company discovers the infringement and files suit, your company could lose millions.

3. As part of land development for a new housing project, your company has polluted a natural lake. Under state law, you must clean up the lake once you complete development. The development project will take five to eight years to complete. Current estimates indicate that it will cost $2 to $3 million to clean up the lake.

4. Your company has just been notified that it lost a product liability lawsuit for $1 million that it plans to appeal. Management is confident that the company will win on appeal, but the lawyers believe that it will lose.

5. A key customer is unhappy with the quality of a major construction project. The company believes that the customer is being unreasonable but, to maintain goodwill, has decided to do $250,000 in repairs next year.

Determining Cash Flow Effects (AP9-4)

P9-8
LO6

For each of the following transactions, determine whether cash flows from operating activities will increase, decrease, or remain the same:

a. Purchased merchandise on credit.
b. Paid an account payable in cash.
c. Accrued payroll for the month but did not pay it.
d. Borrowed money from the bank. The term of the note is 90 days.
e. Reclassified a long-term note as a current liability.
f. Paid accrued interest expense.
g. Recorded a contingent liability based on a pending lawsuit.
h. Paid back the bank for money borrowed in d. (Ignore interest)
i. Collected cash from a customer for services that will be performed in the next accounting period (i.e., deferred revenues are recorded).

Analyzing the Reclassification of Debt (AP9-5)

P9-9
LO7
PepsiCo

PepsiCo, Inc., is a $25 billion company in the beverage, snack food, and restaurant businesses. PepsiCo's annual report included the following note:

> At year-end, $3.5 billion of short-term borrowings were reclassified as long-term, reflecting PepsiCo's intent and ability to refinance these borrowings on a long-term basis, through either long-term debt issuances or rollover of existing short-term borrowings.

As a result of this reclassification, PepsiCo's current ratio improved from 0.51 to 0.79. Do you think the reclassification was appropriate? Why do you think management made the reclassification? As a financial analyst, would you use the current ratio before the reclassification or after the reclassification to evaluate PepsiCo's liquidity?

Recording and Reporting Deferred Income Tax: Depreciation (Supplements A and B) (AP9-6)

P9-10

At December 31, 2006, the records of Pearson Corporation provided the following information:

Income statement	
Revenues	$140,000
Depreciation expense (straight line)	(11,000)†
Remaining expenses (excluding income tax)	(90,000)
Pretax income	$ 39,000

†Equipment depreciated—acquired January 1, 2006, cost $44,000; estimated useful life, four years and no residual value. Accelerated depreciation is used on the tax return as follows: 2006, $17,600; 2007, $13,200; 2008, $8,800; and 2009, $4,400.

  a. Income tax rate, 30 percent. Assume that 85 percent is paid in the year incurred.

  b. Taxable income from the 2006 income tax return, $32,400.

> ***Required:***
>   1. Compute income taxes payable and deferred income tax for 2006. Is the deferred income tax a liability or an asset? Explain.
>   2. Show what amounts related to 2006 income taxes should be reported on the income statement and balance sheet.

P9-11
LO8, 9

Computing Present Values (AP9-7)

On January 1, 2006, Plymouth Company completed the following transactions (use an 8 percent annual interest rate for all transactions):

  a. Borrowed $100,000 for 10 years. Will pay $8,000 interest at the end of each year and repay the $100,000 at the end of the 10th year.

  b. Established a plant addition fund of $400,000 to be available at the end of year 5. A single sum that will grow to $400,000 will be deposited on January 1, 2006.

  c. Agreed to pay a severance package to a discharged employee. The company will pay $50,000 at the end of the first year, $75,000 at the end of the second year and $100,000 at the end of the third year.

  d. Purchased a $180,000 machine on January 1, 2006, and paid cash, $60,000. A four-year note payable is signed for the balance. The note will be paid in four equal year-end payments starting on December 31, 2006.

> ***Required (show computations and round to the nearest dollar):***
>   1. In transaction *a*, determine the present value of the debt.
>   2. In transaction *b*, what single sum amount must the company deposit on January 1, 2006? What is the total amount of interest revenue that will be earned?
>   3. In transaction *c*, determine the present value of this obligation.
>   4. In transaction *d*, what is the amount of each of the equal annual payments that will be paid on the note? What is the total amount of interest expense that will be incurred?

P9-12
LO8

Comparing Options Using Present Value Concepts (AP9-8)

After hearing a knock at your front door, you are surprised to see the Prize Patrol from a large, well-known magazine subscription company. It has arrived with the good news that you are the big winner, having won $20 million. You discover that you have three options: (1) you can receive $1 million per year for the next 20 years, (2) you can have $8 million today, or (3) you can have $2 million today and receive $700,000 for each of the next 20 years. Your lawyer tells you that it is reasonable to expect to earn 10 percent on investments. Which option do you prefer? What factors influence your decision?

P9-13

Computing Future Values (Supplement D) (AP9-9)

On December 31, 2006, Post Company created a fund that will be used to pay the principal amount of a $140,000 debt due on December 31, 2009. The company will make four equal annual deposits on each December 31 in 2006, 2007, 2008, and 2009. The fund will earn 7 percent annual interest, which will be added to the balance at each year-end. The fund trustee will pay the loan principal (to the creditor) on receipt of the last fund deposit. The company's accounting period ends December 31.

> ***Required (show computations and round to the nearest dollar):***
>   1. How much must be deposited each December 31?
>   2. What amount of interest will be earned?
>   3. How much interest revenue will the fund earn in 2006, 2007, 2008, and 2009?

P9-14

Computing Future Values (Supplement D)

On January 1, 2006, Plymouth Company completed the following transactions (use an 8 percent annual interest rate for all transactions):

  a. Deposited $50,000 in a debt retirement fund. Interest will be computed at six-month intervals and added to the fund at those times (i.e., semiannual compounding). (*Hint:* Think carefully about *n* and *i.*)

b. Established a pension retirement fund to be available by the end of year 6 by making six annual deposits of $100,000 at year-end, starting on December 31, 2006.

c. Deposited $200,000 in a debt retirement fund. Interest will be computed annually and added to the fund at those times.

Required:

1. In transaction *a*, what will be the balance in the fund at the end of year 4? What is the total amount of interest revenue that will be earned?

2. In transaction *b*, what is the amount of the retirement fund at the end of year 6? What is the total amount of interest revenue that will be earned?

3. In transaction *c*, what will be the balance in the fund at the end of year 5? What is the total amount of interest revenue that will be earned?

ALTERNATE **PROBLEMS**

Recording and Reporting Current Liabilities with Discussion of Cash Flow Effects (P9-2)

AP9-1
LO1, 6

Curb Company completed the following transactions during 2007. The annual accounting period ends December 31, 2007.

Jan. 15 Recorded tax expense for the year in the amount of $125,000. Current taxes payable were $93,000.

   31 Paid accrued interest expense in the amount of $52,000.

Apr. 30 Borrowed $550,000 from Commerce Bank; executed a 12-month, 12 percent interest-bearing note payable.

June 3 Purchased merchandise for resale at an invoice cost of $75,820, on account.

July 5 Paid June 3 invoice.

Aug. 31 Signed contract to provide security service to a small apartment complex and collected six months' fees in advance amounting to $12,000. (Record the collection in a way that will not require an adjusting entry at year-end.)

Dec. 31 Reclassified a long-term liability in the amount of $100,000 to a current liability classification.

   31 Determined salary and wages of $85,000 earned but not yet paid December 31 (disregard payroll taxes).

Required:

1. Prepare journal entries for each of these transactions.
2. Prepare all adjusting entries required on December 31, 2007.
3. Show how all of the liabilities arising from these transactions are reported on the balance sheet at December 31, 2007.
4. For each transaction, state whether cash flow from operating activities is increased, decreased, or there is no effect.

Determining Financial Effects of Transactions Affecting Current Liabilities with Discussion of Cash Flow Effects (P9-3)

AP9-2
LO1, 6

Using data from AP9-1, complete the following requirements.

Required:

1. For each transaction (including adjusting entries) listed in the previous problem, indicate the effects (e.g., cash + or −), using the following schedule:

Date	Assets	=	Liabilities	+	Stockholders' Equity

2. For each transaction, state whether cash flow from operating activities is increased, decreased, or there is no effect.

AP9-3
L01, 5

Pulte

Determining Financial Statement Effects of Various Liabilities (P9-6)

Pulte Corporation is a national builder of homes that does more than $2 billion in business each year. Its annual report contained the following note:

> **Allowance for Warranties**
>
> Home purchasers are provided with warranties against certain building defects. Estimated warranty cost is provided in the period in which the sale is recorded.

1. Assume that estimated warranty costs for 2006 were $8.5 million and that the warranty work was performed during 2007. Describe the financial statement effects for each year.

Carnival Cruise Lines operates cruise ships in Alaska, the Caribbean, the South Pacific, and the Mediterranean. Some cruises are brief; others can last for several weeks. The company does more than $1 billion in cruise business each year. The following note is from its annual report:

Carnival
Cruise Lines

> **Revenues**
>
> Customer cruise deposits, which represent unearned revenue, are included in the balance sheet when received and are recognized as cruise revenue upon completion of voyages of duration of 10 days or less and on a pro rata basis computed using the number of days completed for voyages in excess of 10 days.

2. In your own words, explain how unearned revenue is reported in the balance sheet for Carnival. Assume that Carnival collected $19 million in 2006 for cruises that will be completed in the following year. Of that amount, $4 million was related to cruises of 10 or fewer days that were not complete; $8 million to cruises more than 10 days that, on average, were 60 percent complete; and $7 million was related to cruises that had not yet begun. What amount of unearned revenue should be reported on the 2006 balance sheet?

Sunbeam Corporation is a consumer products company that manufactures and markets a number of familiar brands including Mr. Coffee, Osterizer, First Alert, and Coleman. Annual revenues for the company exceed $2 billion. Its annual report contained the following information:

Sunbeam

> **Litigation**
>
> The Company and its subsidiaries are involved in various lawsuits arising from time to time that the Company considers to be ordinary routine litigation incidental to its business. In the opinion of the Company, the resolution of these routine matters will not have a material adverse effect upon the financial position, results of operations, or cash flows of the Company. At the end of the current year, the Company had established accruals for litigation matters of $31.2 million.
>
> The Company recorded a $12.0 million charge related to a case for which an adverse development arose. In the fourth quarter of this year, the case was favorably resolved and, as a result, $8.1 million of the charge was reversed into income.

3. Explain the meaning of this note in your own words. Describe how litigation has affected the financial statements for Sunbeam.

ExxonMobil

4. A recent annual report for ExxonMobil reported a current ratio of 0.90. For the previous year, the ratio was 1.08. Based on this information, do you think that Exxon is experiencing financial difficulty? What other information would you want to consider in making this evaluation?

Brunswick Corporation is a multinational company that manufactures and sells marine and recreational products. Its annual report contained the following information:

Legal and Environmental

The company is involved in numerous environmental remediation and clean-up projects with an aggregate estimated exposure of approximately $21 million to $42 million. The Company accrues for environmental remediation-related activities for which commitments or clean-up plans have been developed and for which costs can be reasonably estimated.

Brunswick

5. In your own words, explain Brunswick's accounting policy for environmental expenditures. What is the justification for this policy?

Determining Cash Flow Effects (P9-8)

For each of the following transactions, determine whether cash flows from operating activities will increase, decrease, or remain the same:

a. Purchased merchandise for cash.
b. Paid salaries and wages for the last month of the previous accounting period.
c. Paid taxes to the federal government.
d. Borrowed money from the bank. The term of the note is two years.
e. Withheld FICA taxes from employees' paychecks and immediately paid to the government.
f. Recorded accrued interest expense.
g. Paid cash as the result of losing a lawsuit. A contingent liability associated with the liability had been recorded.
h. Paid salaries and wages for the current month in cash.
i. Performed services for a customer who had paid for them in the previous accounting period (i.e., deferred revenue is earned).

AP9-4
LO6

Analyzing the Reclassification of Debt (P9-9)

General Mills is a multibillion-dollar company that makes and sells products used in the kitchens of most U.S. homes. The company's annual report included the following note:

We have a revolving credit agreement expiring in two years that provides for a credit line (which permits us to borrow money when needed). This agreement provides us with the opportunity to refinance short-term borrowings on a long-term basis.

AP9-5
LO7
General Mills

Should General Mills classify the short-term borrowing as current or noncurrent debt based on this ability to borrow money to refinance the debt if needed? If you were a member of the management team, explain what you would want to do and why. If you were a financial analyst, would your answer be different?

Recording and Reporting Deferred Income Tax: Two Temporary Differences
(Supplements A and B) (P9-10)

AP9-6

The records of Calib Corporation provided the following summarized data for 2006 and 2007:

Year-End December 31		
	2006	2007
Income statement		
Revenues	$210,000	$218,000
Expenses (excluding income tax)	130,000	133,000
Pretax income	$ 80,000	$ 85,000

a. Income tax rate, 32 percent. Assume that income taxes payable are paid 80 percent in the current year and 20 percent on April 15 of the next year.

b. Temporary differences:
  (1) The 2007 expenses include an $8,000 expense that must be deducted only in the 2006 tax return.
  (2) 2007 revenues include a $6,000 revenue that was taxable only in 2008.
c. Taxable income shown in the tax returns was 2006, $82,000, and 2007, $85,000.

Required:
1. For each year compute (a) income taxes payable and (b) deferred income tax. Is each deferred income tax a liability or an asset? Explain.
2. Give the journal entry for each year to record income taxes payable, deferred income tax, and income tax expense.
3. Show what amounts related to income taxes should be reported each year on the income statement and balance sheet.
4. As a financial analyst, would you evaluate a deferred tax liability and taxes currently payable differently?

AP9-7   **Computing Present Values** (P9-11)
LO8, 9

On January 1, 2006, Dodge Company completed the following transactions (use a 10 percent annual interest rate for all transactions):

a. Borrowed $2,000,000 to be repaid in five years. Agreed to pay $150,000 interest each year for the five years.
b. Established a plant addition fund of $1,000,000 to be available at the end of year 10. A single sum that will grow to $1,000,000 will be deposited on January 1, 2006.
c. Purchased a $750,000 machine on January 1, 2006, and paid cash, $400,000. A four-year note payable is signed for the balance. The note will be paid in four equal year-end payments starting on December 31, 2006.

Required (show computations and round to the nearest dollar):
1. In transaction *a,* determine the present value of the obligation.
2. In transaction *b,* what single sum must the company deposit on January 1, 2006? What is the total amount of interest revenue that will be earned?
3. In transaction *c,* what is the amount of each of the equal annual payments that will be paid on the note? What is the total amount of interest expense that will be incurred?

AP9-8   **Comparing Options Using Present Value Concepts** (P9-12)
LO8

After completing a long and successful career as senior vice president for a large bank, you are preparing for retirement. After visiting the human resources office, you have found that you have several retirement options: (1) you can receive an immediate cash payment of $1 million, (2) you can receive $60,000 per year for life (you have a life expectancy of 20 years), or (3) you can receive $50,000 per year for 10 years and then $70,000 per year for life (this option is intended to give you some protection against inflation). You have determined that you can earn 8 percent on your investments. Which option do you prefer and why?

AP9-9   **Computing Future Values (Supplement D)** (P9-13)

On January 1, 2006, Jalopy Company decided to accumulate a fund to build an addition to its plant. The company will deposit $320,000 in the fund at each year-end, starting on December 31, 2006. The fund will earn 9 percent interest, which will be added to balance at each year-end. The accounting period ends December 31.

Required:
1. What will be the balance in the fund immediately after the December 31, 2008, deposit?
2. Complete the following fund accumulation schedule:

Date	Cash Payment	Interest Revenue	Fund Increase	Fund Balance
12/31/2006				
12/31/2007				
12/31/2008				
Total				

Annual Report Cases

Finding Financial Information

Refer to the financial statements of PacSun given in Appendix B at the end of this book, or open file PSUN.pdf in the Annual Report Cases directory on the student DVD.

Required:
1. What is the amount of accrued compensation and benefits at the end of the most recent reporting year?
2. By what amount did accounts payable change over the most recent reporting year? How did this change in accounts payable affect cash flows from operating activities during the most recent reporting year?
3. What is the amount of long-term liabilities at the end of the most recent reporting year?
4. What amount of sold gift cards and store merchandise credits have customers not redeemed at the end of the most recent reporting year?
5. What amount of federal income taxes was deferred during the most recent reporting year?

CP9-1
LO1, 5, 7

PACIFIC SUNWEAR
OF CALIFORNIA, INC.

Finding Financial Information

Refer to the financial statements of American Eagle Outfitters given in Appendix C at the end of this book, or open file AEOS.pdf in the Annual Report Cases directory on the student DVD.

Required:
1. What is the amount of accrued compensation and payroll taxes liability at the end of the most recent reporting year?
2. By what amount did accounts payable change over the most recent reporting year? How did this change in accounts payable affect cash flows from operating activities during the most recent reporting year?
3. What is the amount of long-term liabilities at the end of the most recent reporting year?
4. Does the company have any contingent liabilities?
5. What is the amount of the future minimum lease obligations under operating leases in effect at January 29, 2005?

CP9-2
LO1, 4, 5, 7
AMERICAN EAGLE
OUTFITTERS
ae.com

Comparing Companies within an Industry

Refer to the financial statements of PacSun given in Appendix B, American Eagle Outfitters given in Appendix C, and the Standard and Poor's Industry Ratio Report given in Appendix D at the end of this book, or open file CP9-3.xls in the Annual Report Cases directory on the student DVD.

Required:
1. Compute the current ratio for each company for fiscal 2004 and 2003.
2. Compare the most recent current ratio for each company to the industry average from the Industry Ratio report. Based solely on the current ratio, are these companies more or less liquid than the average company in their industry?
3. Compute the payable turnover ratio for each company for the most recent reporting year. What is the amount of long-term liabilities at the end of the most recent reporting year?
4. Compare the latest year payable turnover ratio for each company to the industry average from the Industry Ratio report. Are these companies doing better or worse than the average company in their industry at paying trade creditors?
5. Using this information and any other data from the annual report, write a brief assessment of the liquidity for the two companies.

CP9-3
LO2, 3

PACIFIC SUNWEAR
OF CALIFORNIA, INC.

AMERICAN EAGLE
OUTFITTERS
ae.com

Financial Reporting and Analysis Cases

CP9-4
L07

Interpreting the Financial Press

Increasingly, companies are becoming sensitive to environmental issues surrounding their business operations. They recognize that some of their actions can have detrimental impacts on the environment in ways that may not be fully understood for years or even decades. Environmental issues present complex problems for companies that must report contingent liabilities. A related article by Munter, Sacasas, and Garcia, "Accounting and Disclosure of Environmental Contingencies,"* is available on the Libby/Libby/Short website at **www.mhhe.com/libby5e**. Read the article and prepare a brief memo concerning how companies should report environmental issues in their financial statements.

CP9-5
L08

Analyzing Hidden Interest in a Real Estate Deal: Present Value

Many advertisements contain offers that seem too good to be true. A few years ago, an actual newspaper ad offered "a $150,000 house with a zero interest rate mortgage" for sale. If the purchaser made monthly payments of $3,125 for four years ($150,000 ÷ 48 months), no interest would be charged. When the offer was made, mortgage interest rates were 12 percent. Present value for $n = 48$, and $i = 1\%$ is 37.9740.

Required:
1. Did the builder actually provide a mortgage at zero interest?
2. Estimate the true price of the home that was advertised. Assume that the monthly payment was based on an implicit interest rate of 12 percent.

Critical Thinking Cases

CP9-6
L01, 2

Making Decisions as a Manager: Liquidity

In some cases, a manager can engage in transactions that improve the appearance of financial reports without affecting the underlying economic reality. In this chapter, we discussed the importance of liquidity as measured by the current ratio and working capital. For each of the following transactions, (a) determine whether reported liquidity is improved and (b) state whether you believe that the fundamental liquidity of the company has been improved. Assume that the company has positive working capital and a current ratio of 2.0.

a. Borrowed $1 million from the bank, payable in 90 days.
b. Borrowed $10 million with a long-term note, payable in five years.
c. Reclassified current portion of long-term debt as long term as the result of a new agreement with the bank that guarantees the company's ability to refinance the debt when it matures.
d. Paid $100,000 of the company's accounts payable.
e. Entered a borrowing agreement that guarantees the company's ability to borrow up to $10 million when needed.
f. Required all employees to take accrued vacation to reduce its liability for vacation compensation.

CP9-7
L02

Evaluating an Ethical Dilemma: Managing Reported Results

The president of a regional wholesale distribution company planned to borrow a significant amount of money from a local bank at the beginning of the next fiscal year. He knew that the bank placed a heavy emphasis on the liquidity of potential borrowers. To improve the company's current ratio, the president told his employees to stop shipping new merchandise to customers and to stop accepting merchandise from suppliers for the last three weeks of the fiscal year. Is this behavior ethical? Would your answer be different if the president had been concerned about reported profits and asked all of the employees to work overtime to ship out merchandise that had been ordered at the end of the year?

---

*Munter, Sacasas, and Garcia, "Accounting Disclosure of Environmental Contingencies," *CPA Journal*, January 1996, pp. 36–37, 50–52. Reprinted with permission.

Evaluating an Ethical Dilemma: Fair Advertising

The New York State Lottery Commission ran the following advertisement in a number of New York newspapers:

> The Lotto jackpot for Wednesday, August 25, will be $3 million including interest earned over a 20-year payment period. Constant payments will be made each year.

Explain the meaning of this advertisement in your own words. Evaluate the "fairness" of this advertisement. Could anyone be misled? Do you agree that the lottery winner has won $3 million? If not, what amount is more accurate? State any assumptions you make.

CP9-8
LO8

Financial Reporting and Analysis Project

Team Project: Examining an Annual Report

As a team, select an industry to analyze. Reuters provides lists of industries and their makeup at **www.investor.reuters.com/Industries.aspx**. Each team member should acquire the annual report or 10-K for one publicly traded company in the industry, with each member selecting a different company. (Library files, the SEC EDGAR service at **www.sec.gov**, Compustat CD, and the company itself are good sources.)

CP9-9
LO1, 2, 3, 4, 6, 7

Required:
On an individual basis, each team member should write a short report answering the following questions about the selected company. Discuss any patterns across the companies that you as a team observe. Then, as a team, write a short report comparing and contrasting your companies.

1. List the accounts and amounts of the company's liabilities for the last three years.
   a. What is the percentage of each to the respective year's total liabilities?
   b. What do the results of your analysis suggest about the strategy your company has followed with respect to borrowed funds overall and over time?
   c. Does the company disclose any lease liabilities in the footnotes? If so, compute the percentage of lease commitments to total liabilities.
2. What, if any, contingent liabilities are reported by the company for the most recent year and what is your assessment of the risk of each after reading the footnote(s)?
3. Ratio analysis:
   a. What does the current ratio measure in general?
   b. Compute the ratio for the last three years.
   c. What do your results suggest about the company?
   d. If available, find the industry ratio for the most recent year, compare it to your results, and discuss why you believe your company differs from or is similar to the industry ratio.
4. Ratio analysis:
   a. What does the accounts payable turnover ratio measure in general?
   b. Compute the ratio for the last three years.
   c. What do your results suggest about the company?
   d. If available, find the industry ratio for the most recent year, compare it to your results, and discuss why you believe your company differs from or is similar to the industry ratio.
5. What is the effect of the change in accounts payable on cash flows from operating activities for the most recent year (that is, did the change increase or decrease operating cash flows)? Explain your answer.

LEARNING OBJECTIVES

Reporting and Interpreting Bonds

aming (gambling) has become big business in this country. Casinos are now just a short drive from most major cities. Many of the most popular ones are owned and operated by major corporations whose stock is traded on the New York Stock Exchange. One of the most successful gaming companies is Harrah's Entertainment, Inc., which operates casinos under the names Harrah's, Horseshoe, Harveys, Showboat, and Rio. Harrah's annual report states the following:

> Harrah's Entertainment's strategy is different from that of our competitors. With casinos in more locations, Harrah's Entertainment has more opportunities to develop valuable relationships with more customers than any other company. Harrah's Entertainment's distribution allows us to serve customers both in their home casino markets and as they travel.

FOCUS COMPANY:

Harrah's Entertainment, Inc.

FINANCING GROWTH WITH BONDS PAYABLE

www.harrahs.com

As the gaming industry has grown and become more competitive, companies such as Harrah's have had to invest large amounts of money to create unique gaming environments. As Harrah's annual report states, "Nothing else matters if customers aren't dazzled with every encounter at every property." To illustrate the magnitude of the investment that is needed, consider the Harrah's casino in Tunica, Mississippi, 30 miles south of Memphis. The facility includes 35,000 square feet of gaming space, 1,180 slot machines, and 22 table games. To support the casino, Harrah's built a hotel with 182 rooms and 18 suites, three restaurants and a snack bar, a 250-seat showroom, a retail shop, 13,464 square feet of convention space, a golf course, and parking for 2,708 cars.

Because of the company's strategy of investing in large and unique casinos, Harrah's has had to raise large amounts of new capital in addition to retaining much of its income. In this chapter, we will study Harrah's sale of $500 million in new bonds. Harrah's has disclosed information concerning its long-term debt shown in Exhibit 10.1. Much of the terminology in this note is new to you. After studying this chapter, you will understand each of the terms used in the note.

UNDERSTANDING THE BUSINESS

Capital structure is the mixture of debt and equity a company uses to finance its operations. Almost all companies employ some debt in their capital structure. Indeed, large

NOTE 6—DEBT

Long-term debt consisted of the following as of December 31:

	2003	2002
Credit facilities		
2.3%–3.0% at December 31, 2003, maturities to 2008	$ 947,800	$1,285,500
Secured Debt		
7.1%, maturity 2028	93,622	94,900
5.5%–7.3%, maturities to 2033	607	785
Unsecured Senior Notes		
5.375%, maturity 2013	496,504	—
7.125%, maturity 2007	498,780	498,425
7.5%, maturity 2009	498,926	498,713
8.0%, maturity 2011	496,079	495,525
Unsecured Senior Subordinated Notes		
7.875%, maturity 2005	590,524	750,000
Other Unsecured Borrowings		
Commercial Paper, maturities to 2004	50,000	139,700
Capitalized Lease Obligations		
7.6%–10.0%, maturities to 2006	679	984
	3,673,521	3,764,532
Current portion of long-term debt	(1,632)	(1,466)
	$3,671,889	$3,763,066

As of December 31, 2003, aggregate annual principal maturities for the four years subsequent to 2004 were as follows: 2005, $614.6 million; 2006, $54.2 million; 2007, $605.5 million; and 2008, $819.6 million.

corporations need to borrow billions of dollars, which makes borrowing from individual creditors impractical. Instead, these corporations issue bonds to raise debt capital.

Bonds are securities that corporations and governmental units issue when they borrow large amounts of money. After bonds have been issued, they can be traded on established exchanges such as the New York Bond Exchange. The ability to sell a bond on the bond exchange is a significant advantage for creditors because it provides them with liquidity, or the ability to convert their investments into cash. If you lend money directly to a corporation for 20 years, you must wait that long before your cash investment is repaid. If you lend money by purchasing a bond, you can always sell it to another creditor if you need cash before it matures.

The liquidity of publicly traded bonds offers an important advantage to corporations. Because most creditors are reluctant to lend money for long periods with no opportunity to receive cash prior to maturity, they demand a higher interest rate for long-term loans. By issuing more liquid debt, corporations can reduce the cost of long-term borrowing.

This chapter provides a basic understanding of the management, accounting, and financial issues associated with bonds. We begin with a description of bonds payable. Then we see how bond transactions are analyzed and recorded. The chapter closes with a discussion of the early retirement of debt.

ORGANIZATION of the Chapter

Characteristics of Bonds Payable	Reporting Bond Transactions	Early Retirement of Debt
■ Bonds Issued at Par ■ Times Interest Earned Ratio	■ Bonds Issued at a Discount ■ Straight-Line Amortization ■ Effective-Interest Amortization	■ Bonds Issued at a Premium ■ Straight-Line Amortization ■ Effective-Interest Amortization ■ Debt-to-Equity Ratio

CHARACTERISTICS OF BONDS PAYABLE

Both stock and bonds are issued by corporations to raise money for long-term purposes. Several reasons that a corporation would want to issue bonds instead of stock are:

Learning Objective 1
Describe the characteristics of bonds.

1. **Stockholders maintain control.** Bondholders do not vote or share in the company's earnings.

2. **Interest expense is tax deductible.** The tax deductibility of interest expense reduces the net cost of borrowing.

3. **The impact on earnings is positive.** Money can often be borrowed at a low interest rate and invested at a higher rate. Assume that Home Video, Inc., owns a video rental store. The company has stockholders' equity of $100,000 invested in the store and earns net income of $20,000 per year. Management plans to open a new store that will also cost $100,000 and earn $20,000 per year. Should management issue new stock or borrow the money at an interest rate of 8 percent? The following analysis shows that the use of debt will increase the return to the owners:

	Option 1 Stock	Option 2 Debt
Income before interest and taxes	$ 40,000	$ 40,000
Interest (8% × $100,000)	—	8,000
Income before taxes	40,000	32,000
Income taxes (35%)	14,000	11,200
Net income	26,000	20,800
Stockholders' equity	200,000	100,000
Return on equity	13%	20.8%

Unfortunately, bonds carry higher risk than equity. The following are the major disadvantages associated with issuing bonds:

1. **Risk of bankruptcy.** Interest payments to bondholders are fixed charges that must be paid each period whether the corporation earns income or incurs a loss.

2. **Negative impact on cash flows.** Debt must be repaid at a specified time in the future. Management must be able to generate sufficient cash to repay the debt or the ability to refinance it.

A bond usually requires the payment of interest over its life with repayment of principal on the maturity date. The bond principal is the amount (1) that is payable at the maturity date and (2) on which the periodic cash interest payments are computed. The principal is also called the par value, face amount, and **maturity value**. All bonds

The BOND PRINCIPAL is the amount (a) payable at the maturity of the bond and (b) on which the periodic cash interest payments are computed.

PAR VALUE is another name for bond principal, or the maturity value of a bond.

FACE AMOUNT is another name for principal, or the maturity value of the bond.

have a par value, which is the amount that will be paid when the bond matures. For most individual bonds, the par value is $1,000, but it can be any amount.

The **STATED RATE** is the rate of cash interest per period stated in the bond contract.

A bond always specifies a stated rate of interest and the timing of periodic cash interest payments, usually annually or semiannually. Each periodic interest payment is computed as principal times the stated interest rate. The selling price of a bond does not affect the periodic cash payment of interest. For example, a $1,000, 8 percent bond always pays cash interest of (1) $80 on an annual basis or (2) $40 on a semiannual basis.

Different types of bonds have different characteristics for good economic reasons. Individual creditors have different risk and return preferences. A retired person may be willing to receive a lower interest rate in return for greater security. This type of creditor might want a mortgage bond that pledges a specific asset as security in case the company cannot repay the bond. Another type of creditor might be willing to accept a low interest rate and an unsecured status in return for the opportunity to convert the bond into common stock at some point in the future. Companies try to design bond features that are attractive to different groups of creditors just as automobile manufacturers try to design cars that appeal to different groups of consumers. Some key types of bonds are shown here:

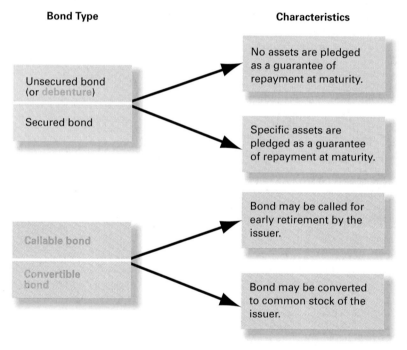

Bond Type	Characteristics
Unsecured bond (or debenture)	No assets are pledged as a guarantee of repayment at maturity.
Secured bond	Specific assets are pledged as a guarantee of repayment at maturity.
Callable bond	Bond may be called for early retirement by the issuer.
Convertible bond	Bond may be converted to common stock of the issuer.

A **DEBENTURE** is an unsecured bond; no assets are specifically pledged to guarantee repayment.

CALLABLE BONDS may be called for early retirement at the option of the issuer.

CONVERTIBLE BONDS may be converted to other securities of the issuer (usually common stock).

An **INDENTURE** is a bond contract that specifies the legal provisions of a bond issue.

When Harrah's decided to issue new bonds, it prepared a bond indenture (bond contract) that specified the legal provisions of the bonds. These provisions include the maturity date, rate of interest to be paid, date of each interest payment, and any conversion privileges. The indenture also contains covenants designed to protect the creditors. Harrah's indenture included limitations on new debt that the company might issue in the future. Other typical covenants include limitations on the payment of dividends and required minimums of certain accounting ratios, such as the current ratio. Because covenants may limit the company's future actions, management prefers those that are least restrictive. Creditors, however, prefer more restrictive covenants, which lessen the risk of the investment. As with any business transaction, the final result is achieved through negotiation.

Bond covenants are typically reported in the notes to the financial statements. *Accounting Trends & Techniques* (published by the AICPA) reviewed the reporting practices of 600 companies.[1] The graph in the margin shows the percentage of companies

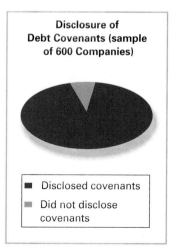

Disclosure of Debt Covenants (sample of 600 Companies)

- ■ Disclosed covenants
- ▪ Did not disclose covenants

---

[1]Reprinted with permission from *Accounting Trends & Techniques.* Copyright © 2003 by the American Institute of Certified Public Accountants, Inc.

that disclosed debt covenants. Harrah's reported the following information about its debt covenants.

REAL WORLD EXCERPT

> **Long-Term Debt**
>
> Our debt agreements contain financial covenants requiring us to maintain a specific tangible net worth and to meet other financial ratios. Covenants limit our ability to pay dividends and to repurchase our outstanding shares.

ANNUAL REPORT

The bond issuer also prepares a prospectus, which is a legal document that is given to potential bond investors. The prospectus describes the company, the bonds, and how the proceeds of the bonds will be used. In the prospectus for the Harrah's bonds, we learn that the company plans to use the proceeds to repay some of its outstanding debt. This debt reduction was required as part of an agreement to purchase another company (Showboat) a few months earlier.

When a bond is issued to an investor, the person receives a bond certificate. All bond certificates for a single bond issue are identical. The face of each certificate shows the same maturity date, interest rate, interest dates, and other provisions. An independent party, called the trustee, is usually appointed to represent the bondholders. A trustee's duties are to ascertain whether the issuing company fulfills all provisions of the bond indenture. Harrah's appointed IBJ Whitehall Bank & Trust Company to act as trustee.

A **BOND CERTIFICATE** is the bond document that each bondholder receives.

A **TRUSTEE** is an independent party appointed to represent the bondholders.

Because of the complexities associated with bonds, several agencies exist to evaluate the probability that a bond issuer will not be able to meet the requirements specified in the indenture. This risk is called **default risk.** Moody's and Standard and Poor's use letter ratings to specify the quality of a bond. Bonds with ratings above Baa/BBB are investment grade; bonds with ratings below that level are speculative and are often called **junk bonds.** Many banks, mutual funds, and trusts are permitted to invest only in investment-grade bonds. In addition to evaluating the risk of a specific bond, analysts also assess the overall risk of the issuer.

 Bond Information from the Business Press

FINANCIAL
ANALYSIS

Bond prices are reported each day in the business press based on transactions that occurred on the bond exchange. The following is typical of the information you will find:

Bond	Yield	Volume	Close	Change
Safeway 6.0 13	6.80	58	97.2	$-\frac{1}{4}$
Sears 7.0 07	6.77	25	101.4	$-\frac{3}{8}$
Harrah's 7.5 09	6.90	580	104.1	$-\frac{1}{8}$

This listing states that the Harrah's bond has a coupon interest rate of 7.5 percent and will mature in the year 2009. The bond currently provides a cash yield of 6.90 percent and has a selling price of 104.10 percent of par, or $1,040.10. On this date, 580 bonds were sold, and the price fell 7/8 point from the closing price on the previous trading day (a point is 1 percent).

It is important to remember that these changes do not affect the company's financial statements. For financial reporting purposes, the company uses the interest rates that existed when the bonds were first sold to the public.

REPORTING BOND TRANSACTIONS

When Harrah's issued its bonds, it specified two types of cash payment in the bond contract:

1. **Principal.** This amount is usually a single payment that is made when the bond matures. It is also called the **par,** or **face, value.**

2. **Cash interest payments.** These payments, which represent an annuity, are computed by multiplying the principal amount times the interest rate stated in the bond contract. This interest is called the **contract, stated,** or coupon rate of interest. The bond contract specifies whether the interest payments are made quarterly, semiannually, or annually.

Neither the issuing company nor the underwriter determines the price at which the bonds sell. Instead, the market determines the price using the present value concepts introduced in the last chapter. To determine the present value of the bond, you compute the present value of the principal (a single payment) and the present value of the interest payments (an annuity) and add the two amounts.

Creditors demand a certain rate of interest to compensate them for the risks related to bonds, called the market interest rate (also known as the yield or effective-interest rate). Because the market rate is the interest rate on a debt when it is incurred, it is the rate that should be used in computing the present value of a bond.

The present value of a bond may be the same as par, above par (bond premium), or below par (bond discount). If the stated and the market interest rates are the same, a bond sells at par; if the market rate is higher than the stated rate, a bond sells at a discount; and if the market rate is lower than the stated rate, the bond sells at a premium. This relationship can be shown graphically as follows:

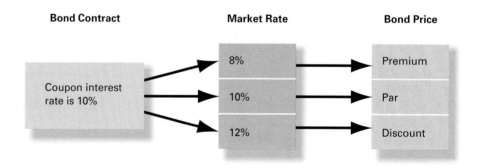

In commonsense terms, when a bond pays an interest rate that is less than the rate creditors demand, they will not buy it unless its price is reduced (i.e., a discount must be provided). When a bond pays more than creditors demand, they will be willing to pay a premium to buy it.

When a bond is issued at par, the issuer receives cash equal to its par value. When a bond is issued at a discount, the issuer receives less cash than the par value. When a bond is issued at a premium, the issuer receives more cash than the par value. Corporations and creditors do not care whether a bond is issued at par, at a discount, or at a premium because bonds are always priced to provide the market rate of interest. To illustrate, consider a corporation that issues three separate bonds on the same day. The bonds are the same except that one has a stated interest rate of 8 percent, another a rate of 10 percent, and a third a rate of 12 percent. If the market rate of interest were 10 percent, the first would be issued at a discount, the second at par, and the third at a premium. As a result, a creditor who bought any one of the bonds would earn the market interest rate of 10 percent.

Learning Objective 2
Report bonds payable and interest expense for bonds sold at par and analyze the times interest earned ratio.

The COUPON RATE is the stated rate of interest on bonds.

MARKET INTEREST RATE is the current rate of interest on a debt when incurred; also called the YIELD or EFFECTIVE-INTEREST RATE.

BOND PREMIUM is the difference between the selling price and par when the bond is sold for more than par.

BOND DISCOUNT is the difference between the selling price and par when the bond is sold for less than par.

Topic Tackler 10–1

During the life of the bond, its market price will change as market interest rates change. While this information is reported in the financial press, it does not affect the company's financial statements and the way its interest payments are accounted for from one period to the next.

In the following sections of this chapter, we will see how to account for bonds issued at par, bonds issued at a discount, and bonds issued at a premium.

SELF-STUDY QUIZ

Your study of bonds will be easier if you understand the new terminology that has been introduced in this chapter. Let's review some of those terms. Define the following:

1. Market interest rate.
2. Coupon interest rate.
3. Synonyms for coupon interest rate.
4. Bond discount.
5. Bond premium.
6. Synonyms for market interest rate.

After you have completed your answers, check them with the solutions at the bottom of the page.

---

1. The market rate is the interest rate demanded by creditors. It is the rate used in the present value computations to discount future cash flows.
2. Coupon interest rate is the stated rate on the bonds.
3. Coupon rate is also called **stated rate** and **contract rate.**
4. A bond that sells for less than par is sold at a discount. This occurs when the coupon rate is lower than the market rate.
5. A bond that sells for more than par is sold at a premium. This occurs when the coupon rate is higher than the market rate.
6. Market interest rate is also called **yield** or **effective-interest rate.**

Self-Study Quiz
Solutions

Bonds Issued at Par

Bonds sell at their par value when buyers are willing to invest in them at the interest rate stated in the bond contract. To illustrate, let's assume that on January 1, 2006, Harrah's issued 10 percent bonds with a par value of $100,000 and received $100,000 in cash (which means that the bonds sold at par). The bonds were dated to start earning interest on January 1, 2006, and will pay interest each December 31. The bonds mature in five years on December 31, 2010.

The amount of money a corporation receives when it sells bonds is the present value of the future cash flows associated with them. When Harrah's issued its bonds, it agreed to make two types of payments in the future: a single payment of $100,000 when the bond matures in five years and an annuity of $10,000 payable once each year for five years. The bond payments can be shown graphically as follows:

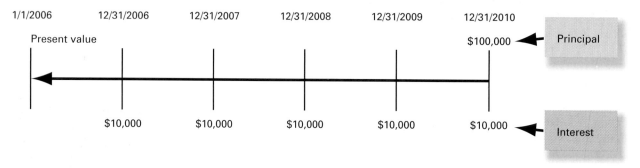

The present value of the bond payments can be computed with the tables contained in Appendix A using the factor for 5 periods and an interest rate of 10 percent:

To compute the present value using Excel, enter:
a. =100000/(1.10)^5
b. f_x =PV(0.10,5,-10000)

	Present Value
a. Single payment: $100,000 × 0.6209	$ 62,090
b. Annuity: $10,000 × 3.7908	37,908
Issue price of Harrah's bonds	$100,000*

Rounded.

When the effective rate of interest equals the stated rate of interest, the present value of the future cash flows associated with a bond always equals the bond's par amount. Remember that a bond's selling price is determined by the present value of its future cash flows, not the par value. On date of issue, bond liabilities are recorded at the present value of future cash flows on date of issue, not the par value, as follows:

| Cash (+A) .... | 100,000 | |
| Bonds payable (+L) .... | | 100,000 |

Assets	=	Liabilities	+	Stockholders' Equity
Cash +100,000		Bonds payable +100,000		

Bonds may pay interest each month, each quarter, each half-year, or each year. In all cases, the present value of the bond is determined using the interest rate factor for the number of interest periods and the interest rate for each period. If the Harrah's bonds had paid interest each six months, there would be 10 interest periods (5 years × 2) and the interest rate per six-month period would be 5% (10% ÷ 2).

Reporting Interest Expense on Bonds Issued at Par

The creditors who bought the bonds did so with the expectation that they would earn interest over the life of the bond. Harrah's will pay interest at 10 percent per year on the par value of the bonds each December 31 until the bond's maturity date. The amount of interest each period will be $10,000 (10% × $100,000). The entry to record the interest payments is as follows:

Bond interest expense (+E, −SE) 10,000
   Cash (−A)   10,000

Assets		=	Liabilities	+	Stockholders' Equity	
Cash	−10,000				Bond interest expense	−10,000

Interest expense is reported on the income statement. Because interest is related to financing activities rather than operating activities, it is normally not included in operating expenses on the income statement. Instead, interest expense is reported as a deduction from "income from operations." The income statement for Harrah's shows how interest expense is usually reported.

HARRAH'S ENTERTAINMENT, INC.
Consolidated Statement of Income
(dollars in thousands)

	2003
Income from operations	726,298
Interest expense	(234,419)
Loss on early extinguishment of debt	(19,074)
Other income	2,913
Income from continuing operations before taxes	475,718
Income taxes	(183,764)
Income from continuing operations	291,954
Discontinued operations	669
Net income	292,623

REAL WORLD EXCERPT

Harrah's
ENTERTAINMENT, INC.
INCOME STATEMENT

Bond interest payment dates rarely coincide with the last day of a company's fiscal year. Under the matching concept, interest expense that has been incurred but not paid must be accrued with an adjusting entry. If Harrah's fiscal year ended on May 31, the company would accrue interest for five months and record interest expense and interest payable.

Because interest payments are legal obligations for the borrower, financial analysts want to be certain that a business is generating sufficient resources to meet its obligations. The times interest earned ratio is useful when making this assessment.

Assume that Harrah's issued $500,000 bonds that will mature in five years. The bonds pay interest at the end of each year at an annual rate of 8 percent. They were sold when the market rate was 8 percent. Compute the selling price of the bonds.

After you have completed your answer, check it with the solution at the bottom of the page.

KEY RATIO
ANALYSIS

Times Interest Earned

⑦ ANALYTICAL QUESTION:

Is the company generating sufficient resources from its profit-making activities to meet its current interest obligations?

% RATIO AND COMPARISONS:

The times interest earned ratio is computed as follows:

$$\text{Times Interest Earned} = \frac{\text{Net Income} + \text{Interest Expense} + \text{Income Tax Expense}}{\text{Interest Expense}}$$

The 2003 ratio for Harrah's:

$$(\$292,623 + \$234,419 + \$183,764) \div \$234,419 = 3.03$$

COMPARISONS OVER TIME			COMPARISONS WITH COMPETITORS	
Harrah's			Mirage Resorts	Trump Casinos
2001	2002	2003	2003	2003
2.31	2.79	3.03	2.51	0.38

💡 INTERPRETATIONS:

In General → A high times interest earned ratio is viewed more favorably than a low one. The ratio shows the amount of resources generated for each dollar of interest expense. A high ratio indicates an extra margin of protection in case profitability deteriorates. Analysts are particularly interested in a company's ability to meet its required interest payments because failure to do so could result in bankruptcy.

Focus Company Analysis → In 2003, profit-making activities for Harrah's generated $3.03 for each dollar of interest, a very comfortable safety margin. In addition, there has been steady improvement over recent years. Harrah's is able to generate significant cash flows from its operating activities. As a result, required interest payments are not at risk. Notice the ratio for Trump Casinos. It is extremely low and represents an early warning of serious danger. Less than a year after this information was reported, Trump Casinos filed for bankruptcy because of its inability to meet its interest obligations.

A Few Cautions: The times interest earned ratio is often misleading for new or rapidly growing companies, which tend to invest considerable resources to build their capacity for future operations. In such cases, the times interest earned ratio will reflect significant amounts of interest expense associated with the new capacity but not the income that will be earned with the new capacity. Analysts should consider the company's long-term strategy when using this ratio. Some analysts prefer to compare interest expense to the amount of cash a company can generate, because creditors cannot be paid with "income" that is generated.

Self-Study Quiz
Solution

$$
\begin{array}{rl}
\$500,000 \times 0.6806 = & \$340,300 \\
(\$500,000 \times 8\%) \times 3.9927 = & \underline{159,708} \\
& \$500,000 \text{ (rounded)}
\end{array}
$$

Bonds Issued at a Discount

Learning Objective 3
Report bonds payable and interest expense for bonds sold at a discount.

Bonds sell at a discount when the market rate of interest is higher than the stated interest rate on them. Let's assume that the market rate of interest was 12 percent when Harrah's sold its bonds (which have a par value of $100,000). The bonds have a stated rate of 10 percent, payable annually, which is less than the market rate on the date of issue. Therefore, the bonds sold at a **discount.**

To compute the cash issue price of the bonds, we can use the tables in Appendix A. As in the previous example, the number of periods is five and we use an interest rate of 12 percent, which is the market rate of interest. The cash issue price of the Harrah's bonds is computed as follows:

	Present Value
a. Single payment: $100,000 × 0.5674	$56,740
b. Annuity: $10,000 × 3.6048	36,048
Issue (sale) price of Harrah's bonds	$92,788*

The amount of the discount: $100,000 − $92,788 = 7,212.

To compute the present value using Excel, enter:
a. =100000/(1.12)^5
b. f_x =PV(0.12,5,-10000)
Result: $92,790.45

The cash price of the bonds issued by Harrah's is $92,788. Some people refer to this price as *92.8*, which means that the bonds were sold at 92.8 percent of their par value ($92,788 ÷ $100,000).

When a bond is sold at a discount, the Bonds Payable account is credited for the par amount, and the discount is recorded as a debit to Discount on Bonds Payable. The issuance of the Harrah's bonds at a discount is recorded as follows:

Topic Tackler
PLUS

Topic Tackler 10–2

Cash (+A)	92,788	
Discount on bonds payable (+XL, −L)	7,212	
Bonds payable (+L)		100,000

Assets	=	Liabilities	+	Stockholders' Equity
Cash	+92,788	Bonds payable	+100,000	
		Discount on bonds	−7,212	

Note that the discount is recorded in a separate contra-liability account (Discount on Bonds Payable) as a debit. The balance sheet reports the bonds payable at their book value, which is their maturity amount less any unamortized discount. Harrah's, like most companies, does not separately disclose the amount of unamortized discount or premium when the amount is small relative to other balance sheet amounts.

Although Harrah's received only $92,788 when it sold the bonds, it must repay $100,000 when the bonds mature. The extra cash that must be paid is an adjustment of interest expense to ensure that creditors earn the market rate of interest. To adjust interest expense, the borrower apportions or amortizes the bond discount to each interest period as an increase in interest expense. Therefore, the amortization of bond discount results in an increase in bond interest expense. Two amortization methods are often used by companies: (1) straight line and (2) effective interest. Many companies use the straight-line amortization because it is easy to compute the required numbers. However, the effective-interest method is theoretically correct. You may wonder why companies are permitted to use a method that is not theoretically correct. The answer is **materiality.** Companies are permitted to use the straight-line method because the results are normally not materially different than the effective-interest method. We will first discuss the straight-line method and then the effective-interest method.

Part A: Reporting Interest Expense on Bonds Issued at a Discount Using Straight-Line Amortization   To amortize the $7,212 bond discount over the life of Harrah's bonds using straight-line amortization, we allocate an equal dollar amount to each interest period. Harrah's bonds have five interest periods. The amortization of discount each period is computed as $7,212 ÷ 5 periods = $1,442 (rounded). We add this amount to the cash payment of interest ($10,000) to compute interest expense for the period ($11,442). The interest payments on Harrah's bonds each period are as follows:

STRAIGHT-LINE AMORTIZATION of a bond discount or premium is a simplified method that allocates an equal dollar amount to each interest period.

Bond interest expense (+E, −SE)	11,442	
Discount on bonds payable (−XL, +L)		1,442
Cash (−A)		10,000

Assets	=	Liabilities	+	Stockholders' Equity
Cash −10,000		Discount on bonds +1,442		Bond interest expense −11,442

Bonds payable are reported on the balance sheet at their book value. At the end of the first year (December 31, 2006), the book value of Harrah's bonds is more than the original issue price. The book value increases to $94,230 ($92,788 + $1,442) because of the amortization of the discount. In each interest period, the book value of the bonds increases by $1,442 because the unamortized discount decreases by $1,442. At the maturity date of the bonds, the unamortized discount (i.e., the balance in the Discount on Bonds Payable account) is zero. At that time, the maturity amount of the bonds and the book value are the same (i.e., $100,000). This process can be seen in the following amortization schedule:

	Amortization Schedule: Bond Discount (straight line)			
Date	(a) Interest to Be Paid (10% × $100,000)	(b) Interest Expense (a + c)	(c) Amortization ($7,212 ÷ 5 periods)	(d) Book Value Beginning Book Value + (c)
1/1/2006				$92,788
12/31/2006	$10,000	$11,442	$1,442	94,230
12/31/2007	10,000	11,442	1,442	95,672
12/31/2008	10,000	11,442	1,442	97,114
12/31/2009	10,000	11,442	1,442	98,556
12/31/2010	10,000	11,442	1,442	99,998*

*This amount should be exactly $100,000. The $2 error is due to rounding.

SELF-STUDY QUIZ

Assume that Harrah's issued $100,000 bonds that will mature in five years. The bonds pay interest at the end of each year at an annual rate of 5 percent. They were sold when the market rate was 6 percent. The bonds were sold at a price of $95,792.

1. What amount of interest was paid at the end of the first year?

2. What amount of interest expense would be reported at the end of the first year using straight-line amortization?

After you have completed your answers, check them with the solution below.

Self-Study Quiz Solutions   1. $5,000 (5% × $100,000)   2. $5,842 [$5,000 + ($4,208 ÷ 5)]

Part B: Reporting Interest Expense on Bonds Issued at a Discount Using Effective-Interest Amortization   Under the effective-interest method, interest expense for a bond is computed by multiplying the current unpaid balance times the market rate of interest that existed on the date the bonds were sold. The periodic amortization of a bond premium or discount is then calculated as the difference between interest expense and the amount of interest paid or accrued. This process can be summarized as follows:

> The EFFECTIVE-INTEREST METHOD amortizes a bond discount or premium on the basis of the effective-interest rate; it is the theoretically preferred method.

Step 1:   Compute interest expense.

Unpaid Balance × Effective Interest Rate × n/12

n = Number of Months in Each Interest Period

Step 2:   Compute amortization amount.

Interest Expense − Cash Interest

The first interest payment on Harrah's bonds is made on December 31, 2006. Interest expense at the end of the first year is calculated by multiplying the unpaid balance of the debt by the market rate of interest ($92,788 × 12% = $11,135). The amount of cash paid is calculated by multiplying the principal by the stated rate of interest ($100,000 × 10% = $10,000). The difference between the interest expense and the interest paid (or accrued) is the amount of discount that has been amortized ($11,135 − $10,000 = $1,135).

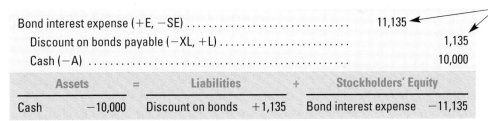

Bond interest expense (+E, −SE)	11,135	
Discount on bonds payable (−XL, +L)		1,135
Cash (−A)		10,000

Assets	=	Liabilities	+	Stockholders' Equity
Cash −10,000		Discount on bonds +1,135		Bond interest expense −11,135

Effective-interest amortization causes these amounts to change each period.

Each period, the amortization of the bond discount increases the bond's book value (or unpaid balance). The amortization of bond discount can be thought of as interest earned by the bondholders but not paid to them. During 2006, the bondholders earned interest of $11,135 but received only $10,000 in cash. The additional $1,135 was added to the principal of the bond and will be paid to bondholders when the bond matures.

Interest expense for 2007 must reflect the change in the unpaid balance of bonds payable that occurred with amortization of the bond discount. The interest expense for 2007 is calculated by multiplying the unpaid balance on December 31, 2006, by the market rate of interest ($93,923 × 12% = $11,271). Thus amortization of the bond discount in 2007 is $1,271.

Bond interest expense (+E, −SE)	11,271	
Discount on bonds payable (−XL, +L)		1,271
Cash (−A)		10,000

Assets	=	Liabilities	+	Stockholders' Equity
Cash −10,000		Discount on bonds +1,271		Bond interest expense −11,271

Notice that interest expense for 2007 is more than interest expense for 2006. Harrah's effectively borrowed more money during the second year because of the unpaid interest. Because of the amortization of the bond discount, interest expense increases each year during the life of the bond. This process can be illustrated with the following amortization schedule:

Date	Amortization Schedule: Bond Discount (effective interest)			
	(a) Interest to Be Paid (10% × $100,000)	(b) Interest Expense (12% × Beginning of Period Book Value)(d)	(c) Amortization (b) − (a)	(d) Book Value Beginning Book Value + (c)
1/1/2006				$92,788
12/31/2006	$10,000	$11,135	$1,135	93,923
12/31/2007	10,000	11,271	1,271	95,194
12/31/2008	10,000	11,423	1,423	96,617
12/31/2009	10,000	11,594	1,594	98,211
12/31/2010	10,000	11,785	1,785	99,996*

This amount should be exactly $100,000. The $4 error is due to rounding.

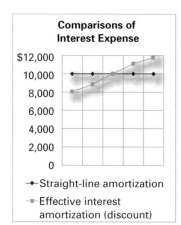

Comparisons of Interest Expense

- Straight-line amortization
- Effective interest amortization (discount)

Interest expense (column b) is computed by multiplying the market rate of interest by the book value of the bonds at the beginning of the period (column d). Amortization is computed by subtracting cash interest (column a) from interest expense (column b). The book value of the bonds (column d) is computed by adding amortization (column c) to the book value at the beginning of the period.

In summary, under the effective-interest method, interest expense changes each accounting period as the effective amount of the liability changes. Under the straight-line method, interest expense remains constant over the life of the bond. The chart in the margin illustrates these differences.

SELF-STUDY **QUIZ**

Assume that Harrah's issued $100,000 bonds that will mature in five years. The bonds pay interest at the end of each year at an annual rate of 5 percent. They were sold when the market rate was 6 percent. The bonds were sold at a price of $95,792.

1. What amount of interest was paid at the end of the first year?

2. What amount of interest expense would be reported at the end of the first year using effective-interest amortization?

After you have completed your answers, check them with the solution at the bottom of the page.

Self-Study Quiz Solutions
1. $5,000 (5% × $100,000)
2. $5,748 (6% × $95,792)

Zero Coupon Bonds

So far, we have discussed common bonds that are issued by many corporations. For a number of reasons, corporations may issue bonds with unusual features. The concepts you have learned will help you understand these bonds. For example, a corporation might issue a bond that does not pay periodic cash interest. These bonds are often called **zero coupon bonds.** Why would an investor buy a bond that did not pay interest? Our discussion of bond discounts has probably given you a good idea of the answer. The coupon interest rate on a bond can be virtually any amount, and the price of the bond will be adjusted so that investors earn the market rate of interest. A bond with a zero coupon interest rate is simply a deeply discounted bond that will sell for substantially less than its maturity value.

Let's use the $100,000 Harrah's bond to illustrate a zero coupon rate. Assume that the market rate is 10 percent and the bond pays no cash interest. The bond matures in five years. The selling price of the bond is the present value of the maturity amount because no other cash payments will be made over the life of the bond. We can compute the present value with the tables in Appendix A, using the factor for five periods and an interest rate of 10 percent:

	Present Value
Single payment: $100,000 × 0.6209	$62,090

To compute the present value using Excel, enter:
= 100000/(1.10)^5
Result: $62,092.13

Accounting for a zero coupon bond is no different from accounting for other bonds sold at a discount. However, the amount of the discount is much larger. The annual report for General Mills contained the following information concerning the company's zero coupon bonds:

Note 9. Long-Term Debt

(dollars in millions)	2003	2002
Zero Coupon notes, yield 11.1% $261 due 2013	$87	$78

These bonds do not pay cash interest, but they have been priced to provide the investor an effective interest rate of 11.1 percent. Notice that the amount of the obligation increases from 2002 to 2003. This increase is the result of the amortization of the bond discount.

Bonds Issued at a Premium

Bonds sell at a premium when the market rate of interest is lower than their stated interest rate. Let's assume that the market rate of interest is 8 percent while the Harrah's bonds pay cash interest of 10 percent. The bonds pay interest annually and mature in five years. The bonds are issued on January 1, 2006.

The present value of Harrah's bonds can be computed from the tables in Appendix A using the factor for five periods and an interest rate of 8 percent:

Learning Objective 4
Report bonds payable and interest expense for bonds sold at a premium.

	Present Value
a. Single payment: $100,000 × 0.6806	$ 68,060
b. Annuity: $10,000 × 3.9927	39,927
Issue (sale) price of Harrah's bonds	$107,987

To compute the present value using Excel, enter:
a. = 100000/(1.08)^5
b. f_x = PV(0.08,5,-10000)
Result: $107,985.42

When a bond is sold at a premium, the Bonds Payable account is credited for the par amount, and the premium is recorded as a credit to Premium on Bonds Payable. The January 1, 2006, issuance of Harrah's bonds at a premium would be recorded as follows:

Cash (+A) 107,987
    Premium on bonds payable (+L) 7,987
    Bonds payable (+L) 100,000

Assets	=	Liabilities	+	Stockholders' Equity
Cash +107,987		Premium on bonds +7,987 Bonds payable +100,000		

The book value of the bond is the sum of the two accounts, Premium on Bonds Payable and Bonds Payable, or $107,987.

Part A: Reporting Interest Expense on Bonds Issued at a Premium Using Straight-Line Amortization   As with a discount, the recorded premium of $7,987 must be apportioned to each interest period. Using the straight-line method, the amortization of premium each annual interest period is $1,597 ($7,987 ÷ 5 periods). This amount is subtracted from the cash interest payment ($10,000) to calculate interest expense ($8,403). Thus, amortization of a bond premium decreases interest expense.

The payment of interest on the bonds is recorded as follows:

Bond interest expense (+E, −SE) 8,403
Premium on bonds payable (−L) 1,597
    Cash (−A) 10,000

Assets	=	Liabilities	+	Stockholders' Equity
Cash −10,000		Premium on bonds −1,597		Bond interest expense −8,403

Notice that the $10,000 cash paid each period includes $8,403 interest expense and $1,597 premium amortization. Thus, the cash payment to investors includes the current interest they have earned plus a return of part of the premium they paid when they bought the bonds.

The book value of the bonds is the amount in the Bonds Payable account plus any unamortized premium. On December 31, 2006, the book value of the bonds is $106,390 ($100,000 + $7,987 − $1,597). A complete amortization schedule follows:

	Amortization Schedule: Bond Premium (straight line)			
Date	**(a)** **Interest to Be Paid** **(10% × $100,000)**	**(b)** **Interest Expense** **(a − c)**	**(c)** **Amortization** **($7,987 ÷ 5 periods)**	**(d)** **Book Value** **Beginning Book Value − (c)**
1/1/2006				$107,987
12/31/2006	$10,000	$8,403	$1,597	106,390
12/31/2007	10,000	8,403	1,597	104,793
12/31/2008	10,000	8,403	1,597	103,196
12/31/2009	10,000	8,403	1,597	101,599
12/31/2010	10,000	8,403	1,597	100,002*

This amount should be exactly $100,000. The $2 error is due to rounding.

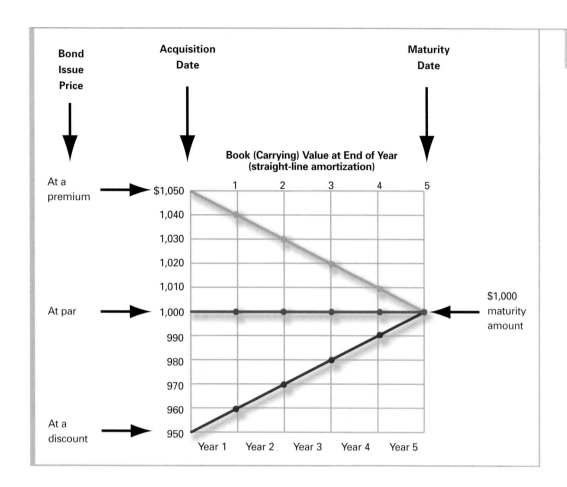

EXHIBIT 10.2

Amortization of
Bond Discount and
Premium Compared

At maturity, after the last interest payment, the bond premium is fully amortized, and the maturity amount equals the book value of the bonds. When the bonds are paid off in full, the same entry will be made whether the bond was originally sold at par, at a discount, or at a premium. Exhibit 10.2 compares the effects of the amortization of bond discount and bond premium on a $1,000 bond.

SELF-STUDY QUIZ

Assume that Harrah's issued $100,000 bonds that will mature in 10 years. The bonds pay interest at the end of each year at an annual rate of 9 percent. They were sold when the market rate was 8 percent. The bonds were sold at a price of $106,711.

1. What amount of interest was paid at the end of the first year?

2. What amount of interest expense would be reported at the end of the first year using straight-line amortization?

After you have completed your answers, check them with the solution at the bottom of the page.

---

1. $9,000 (9% × $100,000)
2. $8,329 [$9,000 − ($6,711 ÷ 10)]

Self-Study Quiz Solutions

Part B: Reporting Interest Expense on Bonds Issued at a Premium Using Effective-Interest Amortization The effective-interest method is basically the same for a discount or a premium. In either case, interest expense for a bond is computed by multiplying the current unpaid balance by the market rate of interest on the date the bonds were sold. The periodic amortization of a bond premium or discount is then calculated as the difference between interest expense and the amount of cash paid or accrued.

The first interest payment on Harrah's bonds is made on December 31, 2006. The interest expense on that date is calculated by multiplying the unpaid balance of the debt by the market rate of interest ($107,987 × 8% = $8,639). The amount of cash paid is calculated by multiplying the principal by the stated rate of interest ($100,000 × 10% = $10,000). The difference between the interest expense and the interest paid (or accrued) is the amount of premium that has been amortized ($10,000 − $8,639 = $1,361).

Bond interest expense (+E, −SE)	8,639	
Bond premium (−L)	1,361	
Cash (−A)		10,000

Assets	=	Liabilities	+	Stockholders' Equity
Cash −10,000		Bond premium −1,361		Bond interest expense −8,639

The basic difference between effective-interest amortization of a bond discount and a bond premium is that the amortization of a discount **increases** the book value of the liability and the amortization of a premium **reduces** it. The following schedule illustrates the amortization of a premium over the life of a bond.

	Amortization Schedule: Bond Premium (effective interest)			
Date	(a) Interest to Be Paid (10% × $100,000)	(b) Interest Expense (8% × Beginning Book Value) (d)	(c) Amortization (b) − (a)	(d) Book Value Beginning Book Value − (c)
1/1/2006				$107,987
12/31/2006	$10,000	$8,639	$1,361	106,626
12/31/2007	10,000	8,530	1,470	105,156
12/31/2008	10,000	8,412	1,588	103,568
12/31/2009	10,000	8,285	1,715	101,853
12/31/2010	10,000	8,148	1,852	101,001*

*This amount should be exactly $100,000. The $1 error is due to rounding.

SELF-STUDY QUIZ

Assume that Harrah's issued $100,000 bonds that will mature in 10 years. The bonds pay interest at the end of each year at an annual rate of 9 percent. They were sold when the market rate was 8 percent. The bonds were sold at a price of $106,711.

1. What amount of interest was paid at the end of the first year?
2. What amount of interest expense would be reported at the end of the first year using effective-interest amortization?

After you have completed your answers, check them with the solution at the bottom of the page.

Self-Study Quiz Solutions   1. $9,000 (9% × $100,000)   2. $8,537 (8% × $106,711)

Debt-to-Equity Ratio

❓ ANALYTICAL QUESTION:

What is the relationship between the amount of capital provided by owners and the amount provided by creditors?

> **Learning Objective 5**
> Analyze the debt-to-equity ratio.

% RATIO AND COMPARISONS:

The debt-to-equity ratio is computed as follows:

$$\text{Debt-to-Equity Ratio} = \text{Total Liabilities} \div \text{Owners' Equity}$$

The 2003 ratio for Harrah's is:

$$\$4,790,415 \div \$1,738,440 = 2.76$$

COMPARISONS OVER TIME		
Harrah's		
2001	**2002**	**2003**
3.55	3.28	2.76

COMPARISONS WITH COMPETITORS	
Mirage Resorts	**Trump Casinos**
2003	**2003**
2.94	27.5

💡 INTERPRETATIONS:

In General → A high ratio suggests that a company relies heavily on funds provided by creditors. Heavy reliance on creditors increases the risk that a company may not be able to meet its contractual financial obligations during a business downturn.

Focus Company Analysis → The debt-to-equity ratio for Harrah's has decreased over the past few years. While the company has invested heavily in the acquisition of other companies and the expansion of facilities, it has been able to do so with cash generated by its operating activities. The company's strong operating results have permitted it to expand and reduce debt in comparison to equity. Most analysts would see this as a very positive situation. As was the case with the times interest earned ratio, the Trump debt-to-equity ratio is a cause for concern. A ratio this high is both unusual and an early warning. Indeed, Trump filed for bankruptcy within a year of reporting this information.

A Few Cautions: The debt-to-equity ratio tells only part of the story with respect to the risks associated with debt. It does not help the analyst understand whether the company's operations can support its debt. Remember that debt carries an obligation to make cash payments for interest and principal. As a result, most analysts would evaluate the debt-to-equity ratio within the context of the amount of cash the company can generate from operating activities.

EARLY RETIREMENT OF DEBT

Bonds are normally issued for long periods, such as 20 or 30 years. As mentioned earlier, bondholders who need cash prior to the maturity date can simply sell the bonds to another investor. This transaction does not affect the books of the company that issued the bonds.

> **Learning Objective 6**
> Report the early retirement of bonds.

In several situations, a corporation may decide to retire bonds before their maturity date. A bond with a **call feature** may be called in for early retirement at the issuer's option. Typically, the bond indenture includes a call premium for bonds retired before the maturity date, which often is stated as a percentage of par value. The prospectus for Harrah's bonds included the following:

BOND PROSPECTUS

The Notes are redeemable, in whole or in part, at any time, at our option at a redemption price equal to the greater of (a) 100% of the principal amount of the Notes then outstanding or (b) the sum of the present values of the remaining scheduled payments of principal and interest thereon discounted at the Treasury Rate, plus .30% interest.

Assume that several years ago, Harrah's issued bonds in the amount of $1 million and that the bonds sold at par. If Harrah's called the bonds in 2006 at 102 percent of par, the company's accountants would make the following journal entry:

Bonds payable (−L) 1,000,000
Loss on bond call (+Loss, −SE) 20,000
   Cash (−A) 1,020,000

Assets	=	Liabilities	+	Stockholders' Equity
Cash −1,020,000		Bonds payable −1,000,000	Loss	−20,000

The loss on the bond call is the amount over par that must be paid according to the bond indenture. This loss on the bond call would be reported on the income statement. The notes to Harrah's statements include the following:

ANNUAL REPORT

Funds from new debt were used to retire certain of our outstanding debt to reduce our effective interest rate and/or lengthen maturities. Charges of $19.1 million are included in income from continuing operations on our Consolidated Statements of Income.

In some cases, a company may elect to retire debt early by purchasing it on the open market, just as an investor would. This approach is necessary when the bonds do not have a call feature. It might also be an attractive approach if the price of the bonds fell after the date of issue. What could cause the price of a bond to fall? The most common cause is a rise in interest rates. As you may have noticed during our discussion of present value concepts, bond prices move in the opposite direction of interest rates. If interest rates go up, bond prices fall, and vice versa. When interest rates have gone up, a company that wants to retire a bond before maturity may find buying the bond on the open market is less expensive than paying a call premium.

SELF-STUDY QUIZ

Which company has a higher level of risk, a company with a high debt-to-equity ratio and a high interest coverage ratio or a company with a low debt-to-equity ratio and a low interest coverage ratio?

After you have completed your answer, check it with the solution at the bottom of the page.

Self-Study Quiz
Solution

A company can be forced into bankruptcy if it does not meet its interest obligations to creditors. Many successful companies borrow very large amounts of money without creating unreasonable risk because they generate sufficient funds from normal operations to meet their obligations. Even a small amount of debt can be a problem if a company does not generate funds to meet current interest obligations. Usually, the company with a high debt-to-equity ratio and a high interest coverage ratio is viewed as being less risky.

Bonds Payable

The issuance of a bond payable is reported as a cash inflow from financing activities on the statement of cash flows. The repayment of principal is reported as a cash outflow from financing activities. Many students are surprised to learn that the payment of bond interest is not reported in the Financing Activities section of the statement of cash flows. Interest payments are related directly to the earning of income and are therefore reported in the Cash Flows from Operating Activities section of the statement. Companies are also required to report the amount of cash paid for interest expense each accounting period. *Accounting Trends & Techniques* reports that companies disclose this information in a variety of locations.

EFFECT ON STATEMENT OF CASH FLOWS

In General → As we saw in Chapter 9, transactions involving short-term creditors (e.g., accounts payable) affect working capital and are therefore reported in the operating activities section of the statement of cash flows. Cash received from long-term creditors is reported as an inflow from financing activities. Cash payments made to long-term creditors (with the exception of interest expense) are reported as outflows from financing activities. Examples are shown in the following table:

	Effect on Cash Flows
Financing activities	
Issuance of bonds	+
Debt retirement	−
Repayment of bond principal upon maturity	−

Focus Company Analysis → A segment of Harrah's statement of cash flows follows. Several items pertain to issues discussed in this chapter. The remaining items will be discussed in other chapters. Notice that Harrah's reports both the early extinguishments (retirement) of debt and new borrowings. Although businesses normally borrow money to finance the acquisition of long-lived assets, they also borrow to rearrange their capital structure. In the case of Harrah's, the company had outstanding debt with an interest rate of 9.25 percent. The company was able to retire this debt by borrowing at an interest rate of 7.875 percent, saving the company nearly $8 million in annual interest cost.

Analysts are particularly interested in the Financing Activities section of the statement of cash flows because it provides important insights about the future capital structure for a company. Rapidly growing companies typically report significant amounts of funds in this section of the statement.

Learning Objective 7
Explain how financing activities are reported on the statement of cash flows.

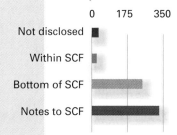
Disclosure of Cash Interest Payments (sample of 600 Companies)

Selected Focus Company Comparisons: Cash Flows from Financing Activities (dollars in millions)

General Mills ($102.3)
Outback (54.7)
Home Depot 737.0

REAL WORLD EXCERPT

ANNUAL REPORT

CONSOLIDATED STATEMENTS OF CASH FLOWS (DOLLARS IN THOUSANDS)

Cash flows from financing activities			
Proceeds from issuance of senior notes, net of discount and issue costs of $6,919 in 2003 and $15,328 in 2001	493,081	—	984,672
Borrowings under lending agreements, net of financing costs of $15,342, $655 and $529	3,368,947	2,772,671	2,732,416
Repayments under lending agreements	(2,526,189)	(2,728,126)	(2,967,814)
Borrowings under retired bank facility	161,125	—	—
Repayments under retired bank facility	(1,446,625)	—	—
Other short-term repayments	(60,250)	—	(184,000)

Early extinguishments of debt	(159,476)	(28,210)	(344,811)
Premiums paid on early extinguishments of debt	(16,125)	—	(7,970)
Scheduled debt retirements	(1,583)	(1,659)	(2,707)
Dividends paid	(66,219)	—	—
Proceeds from exercises of stock options	34,085	48,695	55,303
Purchases of treasury stock	(17,937)	(223,357)	(185,782)
Minority interests' distributions, net of contributions	(10,639)	(12,153)	(8)
Other	(178)	(1,135)	126
Cash flows (used in)/provided by financing activities	(247,983)	(173,274)	79,425

DEMONSTRATION CASE

(Try to answer the questions before proceeding to the suggested solution that follows.) To raise funds to build a new plant, Reed Company's management issued bonds. The bond indenture specified the following:

Par value of the bonds: $100,000.

Date of issue: January 1, 2006; due in 10 years.

Interest rate: 12 percent per annum, payable December 31.

All the bonds were sold on January 1, 2006, at 106. The market rate of interest on the date of issue was 11 percent.

Required:

1. How much cash did Reed Company receive from the sale of the bonds payable? Show computations.

2. What was the amount of premium on the bonds payable?

3. Give the journal entry to record the sale and issuance of the bonds payable.

4. Give the journal entry for payment of interest and amortization of premium for the first interest payment.

SUGGESTED SOLUTION

1. Sale price of the bonds: $100,000 × 106% = $106,000.

2. Premium on the bonds payable: $106,000 − $100,000 = $6,000.

3. January 1, 2006 (issuance date):

Cash (+A)	106,000	
Premium on bonds payable (+L)		6,000
Bonds payable (+L)		100,000
To record sale of bonds payable at 106.		

4. **Part A: Straight-Line Amortization**

December 31, 2006		
Bond interest expense (+E, −SE) ($12,000 − $600)	11,400	
Premium on bonds payable* (−L)	600	
Cash (−A) ($100,000 × 12%)		12,000
To record payment of interest.		

*$6,000 ÷ 10 years = $600

Part B: Effective-Interest Amortization

December 31, 2006		
Bond interest expense* (+E, −SE)	11,660	
Premium on bonds payable (−L)	340	
Cash (−A) ($100,000 × 12%)		12,000
To record payment of interest.		

*$106,000 × 11% = 11,660

Chapter Supplement A

Bond Calculations Using Excel

Instead of using the present value tables in Appendix A, most accountants and analysts use Excel to do the financial computations that are necessary when working with bonds. We can illustrate the Excel process by using the bond example from this chapter. Assume that Harrah's issued a $100,000 bond that matured in five years and paid $10,000 interest per year. When the bond was issued, the market rate of interest was 12 percent. The present value of this bond can be computed with the following steps:*

- **Determine the present value of the maturity payment.** In cell A1, enter the formula for calculating the present value of a single payment. In the format used by Excel, the formula is *=100000/(1.12)^5* where 100000 is the maturity value, 1.12 is 1 plus the market rate of interest per period, and ^5 is the number of periods. Excel will compute this value as $56,742.69.

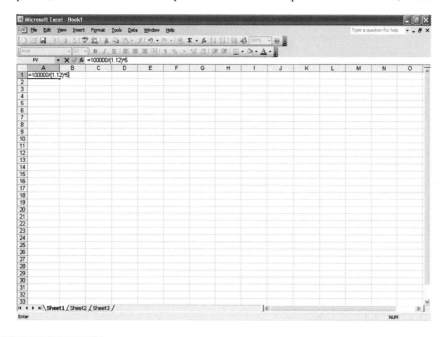

---

*This illustration is based on Microsoft Office 2003. Procedures will be slightly different if you have another version of Office.

■ **Determine the present value of the interest payments.** The present value of an annuity can be computed using an Excel function (you don't have to enter the formula yourself). On the toolbar, click on the insert function button (*fₓ*). A dropdown box will appear. Under select a category, pick "Financial" and under select a function, pick "PV", which is the abbreviation for present value function. Click on "OK" at the bottom and a second dropdown box will appear. You should enter the amounts from the problem in this box: "Rate" is the market rate of interest per period. For this problem, you should enter 0.12. "NPER" is the number of periods. You should enter 5. "PMT" is the cash interest payment per period, which is −10000 for this problem. Notice that when using Excel, this amount must be entered as a negative number because it represents a payment, and you should not enter a comma between the numbers. Excel will compute this value as $36,047.76.

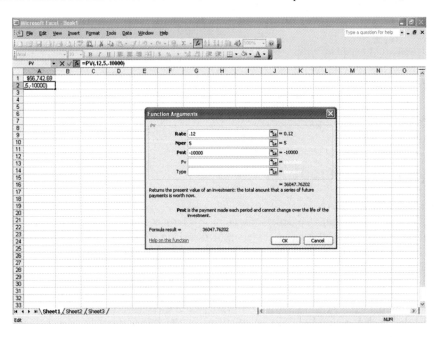

■ **Add the two present value amounts.** In cell A3, add the values from cells A1 and A2 using the AutoSum function (∑) from the tool bar. Excel will compute this amount as $92,790.45. Earlier in the chapter, we computed the present value of this bond as $92,788. The small difference is the result of rounding errors that occur when using the values from the tables. The answer provided by the Excel spreadsheet is more precise, which is why spreadsheets and calculators are used in business instead of the present value tables that are used for educational purposes.

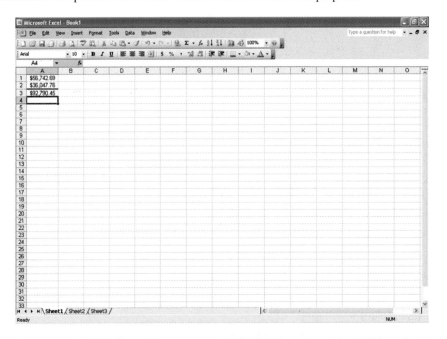

CHAPTER **TAKE-AWAYS**

1. **Describe the characteristics of bonds. p. 517**

   Bonds have a number of characteristics designed to meet the needs of both the issuing corporation and the creditor. A complete listing of bond characteristics is discussed in the chapter.

   Corporations use bonds to raise long-term capital. Bonds offer a number of advantages compared to stock, including the ability to earn a higher return for stockholders, the tax deductibility of interest, and the fact that control of the company is not diluted. Bonds do carry additional risk, however, because interest and principal payments are not discretionary.

2. **Report bonds payable and interest expense for bonds sold at par and analyze the times interest earned ratio. p. 520**

   Three types of events must be recorded over the life of a typical bond: (1) the receipt of cash when the bond is first sold, (2) the periodic payment of cash interest, and (3) the repayment of principal at the maturity of the bond. Bonds are reported at the present value of the future cash flows specified in the bond contract. When the market interest rate and the coupon interest rate are the same, the bond will sell at par, which is the same as the maturity value of the bond.

   The times interest earned ratio measures a company's ability to meet its interest obligations with resources from its profit-making activities. It is computed by comparing interest expense to earnings (including net income, interest expense, and income tax expense).

3. **Report bonds payable and interest expense for bonds sold at a discount. p. 525**

   Bonds are sold at a discount whenever the coupon interest rate is less than the market rate of interest. A discount is the dollar amount of the difference between the par value of the bond and its selling price. The discount is recorded as a contra-liability when the bond is sold and is amortized over the life of the bond as an adjustment to interest expense.

4. **Report bonds payable and interest expense for bonds sold at a premium. p. 529**

   Bonds are sold at a premium whenever the coupon interest rate is more than the market rate of interest. A premium is the dollar amount of the difference between the selling price of the bond and its par value. The premium is recorded as a liability when the bond is sold and is amortized over the life of the bond as an adjustment to interest expense.

5. **Analyze the debt-to-equity ratio. p. 533**

   The debt-to-equity ratio compares the amount of capital supplied by creditors to the amount supplied by owners. It is a measure of a company's debt capacity. It is an important ratio because of the high risk associated with debt capital that requires interest and principal payments.

6. **Report the early retirement of bonds. p. 533**

   A corporation may retire bonds before their maturity date. The difference between the book value and the amount paid to retire the bonds is reported as a gain or loss, depending on the circumstances.

7. **Explain how financing activities are reported on the statement of cash flows. p. 535**

   Cash flows associated with transactions involving long-term creditors are reported in the Financing Activities section of the statement of cash flows. Interest expense is reported in the Operating Activities section.

KEY **RATIOS**

Times interest earned ratio measures a company's ability to generate resources from current operations to meet its interest obligations. The ratio is computed as follows (p. 524):

$$\text{Times Interest Earned} = \frac{\text{Net Income} + \text{Interest Expense} + \text{Income Tax Expense}}{\text{Interest Expense}}$$

Debt-to-equity ratio measures the balance between debt and equity. Debt funds are viewed as being riskier than equity funds. The ratio is computed as follows (p. 533):

$$\text{Debt-to-Equity} = \frac{\text{Total Liabilities}}{\text{Owners' Equity}}$$

FINDING **FINANCIAL INFORMATION**

Balance Sheet

Under Current Liabilities

Bonds are normally listed as long-term liabilities. An exception occurs when the bonds are within one year of maturity. Such bonds are reported as current liabilities with the following title:

Current Portion of Long-Term Debt

Under Noncurrent Liabilities

Bonds are listed under a variety of titles, depending on the characteristics of the bond. Titles include

Bonds Payable

Debentures

Convertible Bonds

Income Statement

Bonds are shown only on the balance sheet, never on the income statement. Interest expense associated with bonds is reported on the income statement. Most companies report interest expense in a separate category on the income statement.

Statement of Cash Flows

Under Financing Activities

+ Cash inflows from long-term creditors

− Cash outflows to long-term creditors

Under Operating Activities

The cash outflow associated with interest expense is reported as an operating activity.

Notes

Under Summary of Significant Accounting Policies

Description of pertinent information concerning accounting treatment of liabilities. Normally, there is minimal information. Some companies report the method used to amortize bond discounts and premiums.

Under a Separate Note

Most companies include a separate note, "Long-Term Debt," that reports information about each major debt issue, including amount and interest rate. The note also provides detail concerning debt covenants.

KEY **TERMS**

Bond Certificate p. 519
Bond Discount p. 520
Bond Premium p. 520
Bond Principal p. 517
Callable Bonds p. 518
Convertible Bonds p. 518
Coupon Rate p. 520

Debenture p. 518
Effective-Interest Method p. 527
Effective-Interest Rate p. 520
Face Amount p. 517
Indenture p. 518
Market Interest Rate p. 520
Par Value p. 517

Stated Rate p. 518
Straight-Line Amortization
  p. 526
Trustee p. 519
Yield p. 520

QUESTIONS

1. What are the primary characteristics of a bond? For what purposes are bonds usually issued?
2. What is the difference between a bond indenture and a bond certificate?
3. Differentiate secured bonds from unsecured bonds.
4. Differentiate between callable and convertible bonds.
5. From the perspective of the issuer, what are some advantages of issuing bonds instead of capital stock?
6. As the tax rate increases, the net cost of borrowing money decreases. Explain.
7. At the date of issuance, bonds are recorded at their current cash equivalent amount. Explain.
8. Explain the nature of the discount and premium on bonds payable.
9. What is the difference between the stated interest rate and the effective-interest rate on a bond?
10. Differentiate among the stated and effective rates of interest on a bond (a) sold at par, (b) sold at a discount, and (c) sold at a premium.
11. What is the book value of a bond payable?
12. Explain the basic difference between the straight-line and effective-interest methods of amortizing bond discount or premium. Explain when each method should or may be used.

MULTIPLE-**CHOICE QUESTIONS**

1. Annual interest expense for a single bond issue continues to increase over the life of the bonds. Which of the following explains this?
   a. The market rate of interest has increased since the bonds were sold.
   b. The coupon rate of interest has increased since the bonds were sold.
   c. The bonds were sold at a discount.
   d. The bonds were sold at a premium.
2. Which of the following is not an advantage of issuing bonds when compared to issuing additional shares of stock in order to obtain additional capital?
   a. Stockholders maintain proportionate ownership percentages.
   b. Interest expense reduces taxable income.
   c. Timing flexibility associated with the payment of interest.
   d. All of the above are advantages associated with bonds.
3. Which of the following does not impact the calculation of the cash interest payments to be made to bondholders?
   a. par value of the bond
   b. coupon rate of interest
   c. market rate of interest
   d. the frequency of the payments
4. Which account would not be included in the debt to equity ratio calculation?
   a. Unearned Revenue
   b. Retained Earnings
   c. Income Taxes Payable
   d. All of the above are included.
5. Which of the following is false when a bond is issued at a premium?
   a. The bond will issue for an amount above its par value.
   b. Bonds Payable will be credited for the par value of the bond.
   c. Interest expense will exceed the cash interest payments.
   d. All of the above are false.
6. When the issuing corporation has the right to terminate the relationship with the bondholder early and repay the amount borrowed ahead of schedule, we say that the bond is
   a. convertible.
   b. secured.
   c. amortizable.
   d. callable.
7. To determine whether a bond will be sold at a premium, discount, or at face value, one must know which of the following pairs of information?
   a. the par value and the coupon rate on the date the bonds were issued
   b. the par value and the market rate on the date the bonds were issued
   c. the coupon rate and the market rate on the date the bonds were issued
   d. the coupon rate and the stated rate on the date the bonds were issued

8. When using the effective-interest method of amortization, interest expense reported in the income statement is impacted by the
   a. par value of the bonds.
   b. coupon rate of interest stated in the bond certificate.
   c. market rate of interest on the date the bonds were issued.
   d. both (a) and (b).

9. Which of the following would not appear in the financing section of the statement of cash flows?
   a. cash interest payments to bondholders
   b. principal repayments to bondholders
   c. amounts borrowed from bondholders
   d. All of the above appear in the financing section.

10. When using the effective-interest method of amortization, the book value of the bonds changes by what amount on each interest payment date?
   a. interest expense   c. amortization
   b. cash interest payment   d. none of the above

For more practice with multiple-choice questions, go to the text website www.mhhe.com/ libby5e or the Topic Tackler DVD for use with this text.

MINI-**EXERCISES**   Available with McGraw-Hill's Homework Manager

M10-1
LO1, 2

Finding Financial Information

For each of the following items, specify whether the information would be found in the balance sheet, the income statement, the statement of cash flows, the notes to the statements, or not at all.

1. The amount of a bond liability.
2. Interest expense for the period.
3. Cash interest paid for the period.
4. Interest rates for specific bond issues.
5. The names of major holders of bonds.
6. The maturity date of specific bond issues.

M10-2
LO2

Computing Bond Issuance Price

Price Company plans to issue $800,000, five-year bonds that pay 8 percent annually on December 31. All of the bonds will be sold on January 1, 2006. Determine the issuance price of the bonds assuming a market yield of 8 percent.

M10-3
LO3

Computing Bond Issuance Price

Waterhouse Company plans to issue $300,000, 10-year, 10 percent bonds. Interest is payable annually on December 31. All of the bonds will be sold on January 1, 2006. Determine the issuance price of the bonds assuming a market yield of 12 percent.

M10-4
LO3

Recording the Issuance of a New Bond and the Payment of Interest (Effective-Interest Amortization)

Hopkins Company issued $800,000, 10-year, 10 percent bonds on January 1, 2006. The bonds sold for $753,000. Interest is payable annually each December 31. Record the sale of the bonds on January 1, 2006, and the payment of interest on December 31, 2006, using effective-interest amortization. The yield on the bonds is 11 percent.

M10-5
LO3

Recording the Issuance of a New Bond and the Payment of Interest (Straight-Line Amortization)

Garland Company issued $600,000, 10-year, 10 percent bonds on January 1, 2006. The bonds sold for $580,000. Interest is payable annually each December 31. Record the sale of the bonds on January 1, 2006, and the payment of interest on December 31, 2006, using straight-line amortization.

Computing Bond Issuance Price

Coopers Company plans to issue $500,000, 10-year, 10 percent bonds. Interest is payable annually each December 31. All of the bonds will be sold on January 1, 2006. Determine the issuance price of the bonds, assuming a market yield of 8 percent.

M10-6
L04

Recording the Issuance of a New Bond and the Payment of Interest (Straight-Line Amortization)

Price Company issued $500,000, 10-year, 8 percent bonds on January 1, 2006. The bonds sold for $545,000. Interest is payable annually each December 31. Record the sale of the bonds on January 1, 2006, and the payment of interest on December 31, 2006, using straight-line amortization.

M10-7
L04

Recording the Issuance of a New Bond and the Payment of Interest (Effective-Interest Amortization)

IDS Company issued $1,000,000, 10-year, 8 percent bonds on January 1, 2006. The bonds sold for $1,070,000. Interest is payable annually each December 31. Record the sale of the bonds on January 1, 2006, and the payment of interest on December 31, 2006, using the effective-interest method of amortization. The yield on the bonds is 7 percent.

M10-8
L04

Understanding Financial Ratios

The debt-to-equity and times interest earned ratios were discussed in this chapter. Which is a better indicator of a company's ability to meet its required interest payments? Explain.

M10-9
L02, 5

Determining Financial Statement Effects of an Early Retirement of Debt

If interest rates fell after the issuance of a bond and the company decided to retire the debt, would you expect the company to report a gain or loss on debt retirement? Describe the financial statement effects of a debt retirement under these circumstances.

M10-10
L06

Determining Cash Flow Effects

If a company issues a bond at a discount, will interest expense each period be more or less than the cash payment for interest? If another company issues a bond at a premium, will interest expense be more or less than the cash payment for interest? Is your answer to either question affected by the method used to amortize the discount or premium?

M10-11
L07

Reporting Cash Flow Effects

In what section of the statement of cash flows would you find cash paid to retire bonds? In what section would you find cash paid for interest?

M10-12
L07

 Available with McGraw-Hill's Homework Manager

EXERCISES

Bond Terminology: Fill in the Missing Blanks

1. The _____ is the amount (a) payable at the maturity of the bond and (b) on which the periodic cash interest payments are computed.
2. _____ is another name for bond principal, or the maturity amount of a bond.
3. _____ is another name for principal, or the principal amount of the bond.
4. The _____ is the rate of cash interest per period stated in the bond contract.
5. A _____ is an unsecured bond; no assets are specifically pledged to guarantee repayment.
6. _____ bonds may be called for early retirement at the option of the issuer.
7. _____ bonds may be converted to other securities of the issuer (usually common stock).

E10-1
L01

E10-2

LO1

AT&T

Interpreting Information Reported in the Business Press

As this book was being written, the business press reported the following information concerning bonds issued by AT&T:

Bonds	Yield	Close
AT&T 6.5	7.3	89.5

Explain the meaning of the reported information. If you bought AT&T bonds with $10,000 face value, how much would you pay (based on the preceding information reported)? Assume that the bonds were originally sold at par. What impact would the decline in value have on the financial statements for AT&T?

E10-3

LO2

Computing the Issue Price of a Bond

Kaizen Corporation issued a $500,000 bond that matures in 10 years. The bond has a stated interest rate of 10 percent. When the bond was issued, the market rate was 10 percent. The bond pays interest once per year. At what price was the bond issued?

E10-4

LO2, 3, 4

Computing Issue Prices of Bonds for Three Cases

Thompson Corporation is planning to issue $100,000, five-year, 8 percent bonds. Interest is payable each December 31. All of the bonds will be sold on January 1, 2006.

Required:

Compute the issue (sale) price on January 1, 2006, for each of the following independent cases (show computations):

  a. **Case A:** Market (yield) rate, 8 percent.
  b. **Case B:** Market (yield) rate, 6 percent.
  c. **Case C:** Market (yield) rate, 10 percent.

E10-5

LO2, 3, 4

Computing Issue Prices of Bonds for Three Cases

Oxxford Corporation is planning to issue $500,000 in bonds that mature in 10 years and pay 7 percent interest each December 31. All of the bonds will be sold on January 1, 2006.

Required:

Compute the issue (sale) price on January 1, 2006, for each of the following independent cases (show computations):

  1. Case A: Market (yield) rate, 6 percent.
  2. Case B: Market (yield) rate, 7 percent.
  3. Case C: Market (yield) rate, 8 percent.

E10-6

LO2, 5

Analyzing Financial Ratios

You have just started your first job as a financial analyst for a large stock brokerage company. Your boss, a senior analyst, has finished a detailed report evaluating bonds issued by two different companies. She stopped by your desk and asked for help: "I have compared two ratios for the companies and found something interesting." She went on to explain that the debt-to-equity ratio for Applied Technologies, Inc., is much lower than the industry average and that the one for Innovative Solutions, Inc., is much higher. On the other hand, the times interest earned ratio for Applied Technologies is much higher than the industry average, and the ratio for Innovative Solutions is much lower. Your boss then asked you to think about what the ratios indicate about the two companies so that she could include the explanation in her report. How would you respond to your boss?

E10-7

LO3

Computing the Issue Price of a Bond

Jacobs Corporation issued a $100,000 bond that matures in five years. The bond has a stated interest rate of 6 percent. When the bond was issued, the market rate was 7 percent. The bond pays interest once per year. At what price was the bond issued?

Recording Bond Issue and First Interest Payment with Discount (Straight-Line Amortization)

E10-8
LO3

On January 1, 2006, Seton Corporation sold a $200,000, 8 percent bond issue (9 percent market rate). The bonds were dated January 1, 2006, pay interest each December 31, and mature in 10 years.

Required:
1. Give the journal entry to record the issuance of the bonds.
2. Give the journal entry to record the interest payment on December 31, 2006. Use straight-line amortization.
3. Show how the bond interest expense and the bonds payable should be reported on the December 31, 2006, annual financial statements.

Recording Bond Issue and First Interest Payment with Discount (Effective-Interest Amortization)

E10-9
LO3

On January 1, 2006, Hyde Corporation sold an $800,000, 8 percent bond issue (9 percent market rate). The bonds were dated January 1, 2006, pay interest each December 31, and mature in 10 years.

Required:
1. Give the journal entry to record the issuance of the bonds.
2. Give the journal entry to record the interest payment on December 31, 2006. Use effective-interest amortization.
3. Show how the bond interest expense and the bonds payable should be reported on the December 31, 2006, annual financial statements.

Recording Bond Issue: Entries for Issuance and Interest (Straight-Line Amortization)

E10-10
LO3

Northland Corporation had $400,000, 10-year coupon bonds outstanding on December 31, 2006 (end of the accounting period). Interest is payable each December 31. The bonds were issued (sold) on January 1, 2006. Use the straight-line method to amortize any premium or discount. The 2006 annual financial statements showed the following:

Income statement	
Bond interest expense	$ 33,200
Balance sheet	
Bonds payable (net liability)	389,200

Required (show computations):
1. What was the issue price of the bonds? Give the journal entry to record this issuance.
2. Give the entry to record 2006 interest.

Analyzing a Bond Amortization Schedule: Reporting Bonds Payable

E10-11
LO3

Stein Corporation sold a $1,000 bond on January 1, 2006. The bond specified an interest rate of 9 percent payable at the end of each year. The bond matures at the end of 2008. It was sold at a market rate of 11 percent per year. The following spreadsheet was completed:

	Cash Paid	Interest Expense	Amortization	Balance
January 1, 2006				$ 951
End of year 2006	$90	$105	$15	966
End of year 2007	90	106	16	982
End of year 2008	90	108	18	1,000

Required:
1. What was the bond's issue price?
2. Did the bond sell at a discount or a premium? How much was the premium or discount?
3. What amount of cash was paid each year for bond interest?
4. What amount of interest expense should be shown each year on the income statement?
5. What amount(s) should be shown on the balance sheet for bonds payable at each year-end? (For year 2008, show the balance just before retirement of the bond.)

6. What method of amortization was used?

7. Show how the following amounts were computed for year 2007: (a) $90, (b) $106, (c) $16, and (d) $982.

8. Is the method of amortization that was used preferable? Explain why.

E10-12

LO3

Apple Computer

Explaining Why Debt Is Sold at a Discount

The annual report of Apple Computer, Inc., contained the following note:

> **Long-Term Debt**
>
> On February 10, 1994, the Company issued $300 million aggregate principal amount of its 6.5% unsecured notes. The notes were sold at 99.925% of par, for an effective yield of 6.51%. The notes pay interest semiannually and mature on February 15, 2007.

After reading this note, one student asked why Apple didn't simply sell the notes for an effective yield of 6.5 percent and avoid having to account for a very small discount over the next 10 years. Prepare a written response to this question.

E10-13

LO3

Carnival Cruise Lines

Explaining Bond Terminology

The balance sheet for Carnival Cruise Lines includes "zero coupon convertible subordinated notes." In your own words, explain the features of this debt. The balance sheet does not report a premium or a discount associated with this debt. Do you think it is recorded at par?

E10-14

LO3

PepsiCo, Inc.

The Walt Disney Company

Evaluating Bond Features

You are a personal financial planner working with a married couple in their early 40s who have decided to invest $100,000 in corporate bonds. You have found two bonds that you think will interest your clients. One is a zero coupon bond issued by PepsiCo with an effective interest rate of 9 percent and a maturity date of 2015. It is callable at par. The other is a Walt Disney bond that matures in 2093. It has an effective interest rate of 9.5 percent and is callable at 105 percent of par. Which bond would you recommend and why? Would your answer be different if you expected interest rates to fall significantly over the next few years? Would you prefer a different bond if the couple were in their late 60s and retired?

E10-15

LO4

Recording Bond Issue and First Interest Payment with Premium (Straight-Line Amortization)

On January 1, 2006, Bochini Corporation sold a $1,000,000, 10 percent bond issue (9 percent market rate). The bonds were dated January 1, 2006, pay interest each December 31, and mature in 10 years.

Required:

1. Give the journal entry to record the issuance of the bonds.

2. Give the journal entry to record the interest payment on December 31, 2006. Use straight-line amortization.

3. Show how the bond interest expense and the bonds payable should be reported on the December 31, 2006, annual financial statements.

E10-16

LO4

Recording Bond Issue and First Interest Payment with Premium (Effective-Interest Amortization)

On January 1, 2006, Frog Corporation sold a $2,000,000, 10 percent bond issue (9 percent market rate). The bonds were dated January 1, 2006, pay interest each December 31, and mature in 10 years.

Required:

1. Give the journal entry to record the issuance of the bonds.

2. Give the journal entry to record the interest payment on December 31, 2006. Use effective-interest amortization.

3. Show how the bond interest expense and the bonds payable should be reported on the December 31, 2006, annual financial statements.

Preparing a Debt Payment Schedule with Effective-Interest Method of Amortization and Determining Reported Amounts

E10–17
LO4

Shuttle Company issued a $10,000, three-year, 10 percent bond on January 1, 2006. The bond interest is paid each December 31. The bond was sold to yield 9 percent.

Required:
1. Complete a bond amortization schedule. Use the effective-interest method.
2. What amounts will be reported on the income statement and balance sheet at the end of 2006, 2007, and 2008?

Determining Financial Statement Effects for Bond Issue and First Interest Payment with Premium (Straight-Line Amortization)

E10–18
LO2, 4, 5

Grocery Corporation sold a $250,000, 11 percent bond issue on January 1, 2006, at a market rate of 8 percent. The bonds were dated January 1, 2006, with interest to be paid each December 31; they mature in 10 years.

Required:
1. How are the financial statements affected by the issuance of the bonds? Describe the impact on the debt-to-equity and times interest earned ratios, if any.
2. How are the financial statements affected by the payment of interest on December 31? Describe the impact on the debt-to-equity and times interest earned ratios, if any.
3. Show how the bond interest expense and the bonds payable should be reported on the December 31, 2006, annual financial statements. Use the straight-line method to amortize any discount or premium.

Computing the Issue Price of a Bond with Analysis of Income and Cash Flow Effects

E10–19
LO4, 7

Imai Company issued a $1 million bond that matures in five years. The bond has a 10 percent stated rate of interest. When the bond was issued, the market rate was 8 percent. The bond pays interest once per year on December 31.

Required:
1. Record the issuance of the bond on January 1. Notice that the company received more than $1 million when it issued the bond.
2. How will this premium affect future income and future cash flows?

Reporting the Early Retirement of a Bond

E10–20
LO6

Several years ago, Walters Company issued a $1,000,000 bond at par value. As a result of declining interest rates, the company has decided to call the bond at a call premium of 5 percent.

Required:
Record the retirement of the bonds.

Reporting the Early Retirement of a Bond with a Discount

E10–21
LO6

The Nair Company issued $500,000 in bonds at a discount five years ago. The current book value of the bonds is $475,000. The company now has excess cash on hand and plans to retire the bonds. The company must pay a 2 percent (of par) call premium to retire the bonds.

Required:
Record the retirement of the bonds.

Determining Effects on the Statement of Cash Flows

E10–22
LO7

A number of events over the life of a bond have effects that are reported on the statement of cash flows. For each of the following events, determine whether the event affects the statement of cash flows. If so, describe the impact and specify where on the statement the effect is reported.

Required:

1. A $1,000,000 bond is issued at a discount. The reported amount of the bond on the balance sheet is $945,000.
2. At year-end, $50,000 accrued interest is reported and $1,000 of the bond discount is amortized using the straight-line method.
3. Early in the second year, accrued interest is paid. At the same time, $8,000 interest that accrued in the second year is paid.
4. The company elects to retire the debt in the fifth year. At that time, the reported carrying value of the bonds is $960,000 and the company reports a $25,000 gain on the early retirement of debt.

PROBLEMS

 **Available with McGraw-Hill's Homework Manager**

P10-1 Analyzing the Use of Debt

L01

Cricket Corporation's financial statements for 2006 showed the following:

Income Statement	
Revenues	$300,000
Expenses	(198,000)
Interest expense	(2,000)
Pretax income	100,000
Income tax (30%)	(30,000)
Net income	$ 70,000

Balance Sheet	
Assets	$300,000
Liabilities (average interest rate, 10%)	$ 20,000
Common stock, par $10	200,000
Retained earnings	80,000
	$300,000

Notice in these data that the company had a debt of only $20,000 compared with common stock outstanding of $200,000. A consultant recommended the following: debt, $100,000 (at 10 percent) instead of $20,000 and common stock outstanding of $120,000 (12,000 shares) instead of $200,000 (20,000 shares). That is, the company should finance the business with more debt and less owner contribution.

Required (round to nearest percent):

1. You have been asked to develop a comparison between (a) the actual results and (b) the results had the consultant's recommendation been followed. To do this, you decided to develop the following schedule:

Item	Actual Results for 2006	Results with an $80,000 Increase in Debt
a. Total debt		
b. Total assets		
c. Total stockholders' equity		
d. Interest expense (total at 10 percent)		
e. Net income		
f. Return on total assets		
g. Earnings available to stockholders:		
(1) Amount		
(2) Per share		
(3) Return on stockholders' equity		

2. Based on the completed schedule in requirement (1), provide a comparative analysis and interpretation of the actual results and the recommendation.

Reporting Bonds Issued at Par (AP10-1)

On January 1, 2006, Donovan Company issued $300,000 in bonds that mature in five years. The bonds have a stated interest rate of 8 percent and pay interest on December 31 each year. When the bonds were sold, the market rate of interest was 8 percent.

Required:
1. What was the issue price on January 1, 2006?
2. What amount of interest should be recorded on December 31, 2006? How much on December 31, 2007?
3. What amount of cash interest should be paid on December 31, 2006? How much on December 31, 2007?
4. What is the book value of the bonds on December 31, 2006? What is the amount on December 31, 2007?

P10-2
LO2

Completing Schedule Comparing Bonds Issued at Par, Discount, and Premium (Straight-Line Amortization) (AP10-2)

Quartz Corporation sold a $500,000, 7 percent bond issue on January 1, 2006. The bonds pay interest each December 31 and mature 10 years from January 1, 2006. For comparative study and analysis, assume three separate cases. Use straight-line amortization and disregard income tax unless specifically required. Assume three independent selling scenarios: Case A, bonds sold at par; Case B, bonds sold at 98; Case C, bonds sold at 102.

Required:
Complete the following schedule as of December 31, 2006, to analyze the differences among the three cases.

P10-3
LO2, 3, 4

	Case A (Par)	Case B (at 98)	Case C (at 102)
a. Cash received at issue.			
b. Bond interest expense, pretax for 2006.			
c. Bonds payable, 7 percent.			
d. Unamortized discount.			
e. Unamortized premium.			
f. Net liability.			
g. Stated interest rate.			

Comparing Bonds Issued at Par, Discount, and Premium (Straight-Line Amortization)

Sikes Corporation, whose annual accounting period ends on December 31, issued the following bonds:

Date of bonds: January 1, 2006.
Maturity amount and date: $100,000 due in 10 years.
Interest: 10 percent per annum payable each December 31.
Date sold: January 1, 2006.
Straight-line amortization was used.

P10-4
LO2, 3, 4

Required:
1. Provide the following amounts to be reported on the December 31, 2006 financial statements:

	Issued at Par Case A	at 96 Case B	at 102 Case C
a. Interest expense.	$	$	$
b. Bonds payable.			
c. Unamortized premium or discount.			
d. Net liability.			
e. Stated rate of interest.			
f. Cash interest paid.			

2. Explain why items *a* and *f* in requirement (1) are different.
3. Assume that you are an investment adviser and a retired person has written to you asking, "Why should I buy a bond at a premium when I can find one at a discount? Isn't that stupid? It's like paying list price for a car instead of negotiating a discount." Write a brief letter in response to the question.

P10-5
LO2, 3, 5

Determining Reported Amounts with Discussion of Management Strategy (Effective-Interest Amortization)

On January 1, 2006, Carter Corporation issued $400,000 in bonds that mature in 10 years. The bonds have a stated interest rate of 6 percent and pay interest on December 31. When the bonds were sold, the market rate of interest was 8 percent. Carter uses the effective-interest method. By December 31, 2006, the market rate of interest had increased to 10 percent.

Required:
1. What amount of bond liability is recorded on January 1, 2006?
2. What amount of interest is recorded on December 31, 2006?
3. As a manager of a company, would you prefer the straight-line or effective-interest method?
4. Determine the impact of these transactions at year-end on the debt-to-equity ratio and times interest earned ratio.

P10-6
LO3

Reporting Bonds Issued at a Discount (Straight-Line Amortization) (AP10-3)

On January 1, 2006, Neeley Company issued $700,000 in bonds that mature in five years. The bonds have a stated interest rate of 8 percent and pay interest on December 31 each year. When the bonds were sold, the market rate of interest was 10 percent. Neeley uses the straight-line amortization method.

Required:
1. What was the issue price on January 1, 2006?
2. What amount of interest should be recorded on December 31, 2006? How much on December 31, 2007?
3. What amount of cash interest should be paid on December 31, 2006? How much on December 31, 2007?
4. What is the book value of the bonds on December 31, 2006? What is the amount on December 31, 2007?

P10-7
LO3

Reporting Bonds Issued at a Discount (Effective-Interest Amortization) (AP10-4)

On January 1, 2006, TCU Utilities issued $1,000,000 in bonds that mature in five years. The bonds have a stated interest rate of 10 percent and pay interest on December 31 each year. When the bonds were sold, the market rate of interest was 12 percent. TCU uses the effective-interest amortization method.

Required:
1. What was the issue price on January 1, 2006?
2. What amount of interest should be recorded on December 31, 2006? How much on December 31, 2007?
3. What amount of cash interest should be paid on December 31, 2006? How much on December 31, 2007?
4. What is the book value of the bonds on December 31, 2006? What is the amount on December 31, 2007?

P10-8
LO3

Computing Amounts for Bond Issue and Comparing Amortization Methods

Dektronik Corporation manufactures electrical test equipment. The company's board of directors authorized a bond issue on January 1, 2006, with the following terms:

Maturity (par) value: $800,000
Interest: 8 percent per annum payable each December 31.
Maturity date: December 31, 2010.
Effective-interest rate when sold: 12 percent.

Required:
1. Compute the bond issue price. Explain why both the stated and effective-interest rates are used in this computation.
2. Assume that the company used the straight-line method to amortize the discount on the bond issue. Compute the following amounts for each year (2006–2010):
   a. Cash payment for bond interest.
   b. Amortization of bond discount or premium.
   c. Bond interest expense.
   d. Interest rate indicated (Item *c* ÷ $800,000).
   e. The straight-line rate is theoretically deficient when interest expense, *d,* is related to the net liability (i.e., book value of the debt). Explain.
3. Assume instead that the company used the effective-interest method to amortize the discount. Prepare an effective-interest bond amortization schedule similar to the one in the text. The effective-interest method provides a constant interest rate when interest expense is related to the net liability. Explain by referring to the bond amortization schedule.
4. Which method should the company use to amortize the bond discount? As a financial analyst, would you prefer one method over the other? If so, why?

Reporting Bonds Issued at a Premium (Straight-Line Amortization) (AP10-5)

P10-9
LO4
e**X**cel

On January 1, 2006, Vigeland Corporation issued $2,000,000 in bonds that mature in five years. The bonds have a stated interest rate of 10 percent and pay interest on December 31 each year. When the bonds were sold, the market rate of interest was 8 percent. Vigeland uses the straight-line amortization method.

Required:
1. What was the issue price on January 1, 2006?
2. What amount of interest should be recorded on December 31, 2006? How much on December 31, 2007?
3. What amount of cash interest should be paid on December 31, 2006? How much on December 31, 2007?
4. What is the book value of the bonds on December 31, 2006? What is the amount on December 31, 2007?

Reporting Bonds Issued at a Premium (Effective-Interest Amortization) (AP10-6)

P10-10
LO4

On January 1, 2006, Moncrief Corporation issued $500,000 in bonds that mature in five years. The bonds have a stated interest rate of 8 percent and pay interest on December 31 each year. When the bonds were sold, the market rate of interest was 6 percent. Moncrief uses the effective-interest amortization method.

Required:
1. What was the issue price on January 1, 2006?
2. What amount of interest should be recorded on December 31, 2006? How much on December 31, 2007?
3. What amount of cash interest should be paid on December 31, 2006? How much on December 31, 2007?
4. What is the book value of the bonds on December 31, 2006? What is the amount on December 31, 2007?

Recording Bond Issuance and Interest Payments (Straight-Line Amortization)

P10-11
LO4

West Company issued bonds with the following provisions:

Maturity value: $600,000.
Interest: 9 percent per annum payable annually each December 31.
Terms: Bonds dated January 1, 2006, due five years from that date.

The annual accounting period ends December 31. The bonds were sold on January 1, 2006, at an 8 percent market rate.

Required:

1. Compute the issue (sale) price of the bonds (show computations).
2. Give the journal entry to record the issuance of the bonds.
3. Give the journal entry at the following date (use straight-line amortization): December 31, 2006.
4. How much interest expense would be reported on the income statement for 2006? Show how the liability related to the bonds should be reported on the December 31, 2006, balance sheet.

P10-12
LO4

eXcel

Completing an Amortization Schedule (Effective-Interest Amortization)

Berkley Corporation issued bonds and received cash in full for the issue price. The bonds were dated and issued on January 1, 2006. The stated interest rate was payable at the end of each year. The bonds mature at the end of four years. The following schedule has been completed (amounts in dollars in thousands):

Date	Cash	Interest	Amortization	Balance
January 1, 2006				$6,101
End of year 2006	$450	$427	$23	6,078
End of year 2007	450	?	?	6,053
End of year 2008	450	?	?	?
End of year 2009	450	?	?	6,000

Required:

1. Complete the amortization schedule.
2. What was the maturity amount of the bonds?
3. How much cash was received at the date of the issuance (sale) of the bonds?
4. Was there a premium or a discount? If so, which and how much?
5. How much cash will be disbursed for interest each period and in total for the full life of the bond issue?
6. What method of amortization is being used? Explain.
7. What is the stated rate of interest?
8. What is the effective rate of interest?
9. What amount of interest expense should be reported on the income statement each year?
10. Show how the bonds should be reported on the balance sheet at the end of each year (show the last year immediately before retirement of the bonds).

P10-13
LO6

Comparing Carrying Value and Market Value

The name Hilton is well known in the hotel industry. The Hilton annual report contained the following information concerning long-term debt:

REAL WORLD EXCERPT
Hilton Hotels, Inc.
ANNUAL REPORT

> **Long-Term Debt**
>
> The estimated current market value of long-term debt is based on the quoted market price for the same or similar issues. The current carrying value for long-term debt is $1,132.5 (million) and the current market value is $1,173.5 (million).

Required:

Explain why there is a difference between the carrying value and the current market value of the long-term debt for Hilton. Assume that Hilton decided to retire all of its long-term debt for cash (a very unlikely event). Prepare the journal entry to record the transaction.

P10-14
LO6

Explaining Note to a Financial Statement (AP10-7)

Federal Express is a name synonymous with overnight delivery of important packages. The annual report for FedEx contains the following note:

An agreement was executed to issue $45,000,000 of City of Indianapolis Airport Facility Refunding Bonds. The refunding will be used to retire 11.25% Indianapolis Special Facilities Bonds, Series 1984, which were originally issued in November 1984 to finance the acquisition, construction and equipping of an express sorting hub at the Indianapolis International Airport. The refunding bonds have a maturity date of 2017 and a coupon rate of 6.85%.

Required:
1. In your own words, explain the meaning of this note.
2. Why did management decide to make an early retirement of this debt?

Reporting Bond Transactions on the SCF

P10-15
LO7

Required:
Determine whether each of the following would be reported in the financing activities section of the statement of cash flows and, if so, specify whether it is a cash inflow or outflow.

1. Sale of bonds at a discount.
2. Payment of interest on a bond.
3. Early retirement of a bond with a 5 percent call premium.
4. Amortization of a bond discount.
5. Payment of bond principal upon maturity.
6. Sale of bond from one investor to another. Transaction was in cash.

ALTERNATE **PROBLEMS**

Reporting Bonds Issued at Par (P10-2)

AP10-1
LO2

On January 1, 2006, Trucks R Us Corporation issued $2,000,000 in bonds that mature in five years. The bonds have a stated interest rate of 10 percent and pay interest on December 31 each year. When the bonds were sold, the market rate of interest was 10 percent.

Required:
1. What was the issue price on January 1, 2006?
2. What amount of interest should be recorded on December 31, 2006? How much on December 31, 2007?
3. What amount of cash interest should be paid on December 31, 2006? How much on December 31, 2007?
4. What is the book value of the bonds on December 31, 2006? What is the amount on December 31, 2007?

Completing a Schedule That Involves a Comprehensive Review of the Issuance of Bonds at Par, Discount, and Premium (Straight-Line Amortization) (P10-3)

AP10-2
LO2, 3, 4

On January 1, 2006, Delaware Corporation sold and issued $100,000, five-year, 10 percent bonds. The bond interest is payable annually each December 31. Assume three separate and independent selling scenarios: Case A, at par; Case B, at 90; and Case C, at 110.

Required:
Complete a schedule similar to the following for each separate case assuming straight-line amortization of discount and premium. Disregard income tax. Give all dollar amounts in thousands.

	At End of 2006	At End of 2007	At End of 2008	At End of 2009
Case A: sold at par (100)	$	$	$	$
Interest expense on income statement				
Net liability on balance sheet				
Case B: sold at a discount (90)				
Interest expense on income statement				
Net liability on balance sheet				
Case C: sold at a premium (110)				
Interest expense on income statement				
Net liability on balance sheet				

AP10-3
LO3

Reporting Bonds Issued at a Discount (Straight-Line Amortization) (P10-6)

On January 1, 2006, Williams Corporation issued $1,000,000 in bonds that mature in five years. The bonds have a stated interest rate of 7 percent and pay interest on December 31 each year. When the bonds were sold, the market rate of interest was 9 percent. Williams uses the straight-line amortization method.

Required:
1. What was the issue price on January 1, 2006?
2. What amount of interest should be recorded on December 31, 2006? How much on December 31, 2007?
3. What amount of cash interest should be paid on December 31, 2006? How much on December 31, 2007?
4. What is the book value of the bonds on December 31, 2006? What is the amount on December 31, 2007?

AP10-4
LO3

Reporting Bonds Issued at a Discount (Effective-Interest Amortization) (P10-7)

On January 1, 2006, Colonial Life Corporation issued $2,000,000 in bonds that mature in five years. The bonds have a stated interest rate of 6 percent and pay interest on December 31 each year. When the bonds were sold, the market rate of interest was 7 percent. Colonial uses the effective-interest amortization method.

Required:
1. What was the issue price on January 1, 2006?
2. What amount of interest should be recorded on December 31, 2006? How much on December 31, 2007?
3. What amount of cash interest should be paid on December 31, 2006? How much on December 31, 2007?
4. What is the book value of the bonds on December 31, 2006? What is the amount on December 31, 2007?

AP10-5
LO4

Reporting Bonds Issued at a Premium (Straight-Line Amortization) (P10-9)

On January 1, 2006, Wellington Corporation issued $900,000 in bonds that mature in five years. The bonds have a stated interest rate of 10 percent and pay interest on December 31 each year. When the bonds were sold, the market rate of interest was 9 percent. Wellington uses the straight-line amortization method.

Required:
1. What was the issue price on January 1, 2006?
2. What amount of interest should be recorded on December 31, 2006? How much on December 31, 2007?
3. What amount of cash interest should be paid on December 31, 2006? How much on December 31, 2007?
4. What is the book value of the bonds on December 31, 2006? What is the amount on December 31, 2007?

Reporting Bonds Issued at a Premium (Effective-Interest Amortization) (P10-10)

On January 1, 2006, Fey Insurance Corporation issued $4,000,000 in bonds that mature in five years. The bonds have a stated interest rate of 9 percent and pay interest on December 31 each year. When the bonds were sold, the market rate of interest was 6 percent. Fey uses the effective-interest amortization method.

Required:
1. What was the issue price on January 1, 2006?
2. What amount of interest should be recorded on December 31, 2006? How much on December 31, 2007?
3. What amount of cash interest should be paid on December 31, 2006? How much on December 31, 2007?
4. What is the book value of the bonds on December 31, 2006? What is the amount on December 31, 2007?

AP10-6
LO4

Understanding the Early Retirement of Debt (P10-14)

AMC Entertainment, Inc., owns and operates 243 movie theaters with 1,617 screens in 22 states. The company sold 11 7/8 percent bonds in the amount of $52,720,000 and used the cash proceeds to retire bonds with a coupon rate of 13.6 percent. At that time, the 13.6 percent bonds had a book value of $50,000,000.

Required:
1. Prepare the journal entry to record the early retirement of the 13.6 percent bonds.
2. How should AMC report any gain or loss on this transaction?
3. Why did the company issue new bonds to retire the old bonds?

AP10-7
LO6
AMC Entertainment, Inc.

CASES **AND PROJECTS**

Annual Reporting Cases

Finding Financial Information

Refer to the financial statements of PacSun given in Appendix B at the end of this book or open file PSUN.pdf in the Annual Report Cases directory on the student DVD.

Required:
1. How much interest was paid in cash during the most recent reporting year?
2. Explain why the company does not report bonds payable on its balance sheet.
3. Describe the company's established arrangements, if any, that permit it to borrow money if needed.

CP10-1
LO1, 2

PACIFIC SUNWEAR
OF CALIFORNIA, INC.

Finding Financial Information

Refer to the financial statements of American Eagle Outfitters given in Appendix C at the end of this book or open file AEOS.pdf in the Annual Report Cases directory on the student DVD.

Required:
1. How much interest was paid during the most recent reporting year? (You may need to use the notes to the financial statements to answer this question.)
2. Explain why the company does not report bonds payable on its balance sheet.
3. Describe the company's established arrangements, if any, that permit it to borrow money if needed.

CP10-2
LO1, 2
AMERICAN EAGLE
OUTFITTERS
ae.com

CP10-3

LO2, 5, 7

AMERICAN EAGLE
OUTFITTERS
ae.com

Comparing Companies within an Industry

Refer to the financial statements of PacSun given in Appendix B, American Eagle Outfitters given in Appendix C, and the Industry Ratio Report given in Appendix D at the end of this book or open file CP10-3.xls in the Annual Report Cases directory on the student DVD. Most companies report some amounts of bonds payable on their balance sheets. It is somewhat surprising, therefore, that neither American Eagle or PacSun reports any bond liabilities.

Required:

1. Examine the statements of cash flow for both companies. What is the primary source for cash flow for both companies?
2. Two financial ratios (the debt-to-equity ratio and times interest earned) are discussed in this chapter. Are they relevant for these companies? Explain.

CP10-4

LO3

JCPenney

Analyzing Zero Coupon Bonds from an Actual Company

JCPenney Company was one of the first companies to issue zero coupon bonds. It issued bonds with a face (maturity) value of $400 million due eight years after issuance. When the bonds were sold to the public, similar bonds paid 15 percent effective interest. An article in *Forbes* magazine discussed the JCPenney bonds and stated: "It's easy to see why corporations like to sell bonds that don't pay interest. But why would anybody want to buy that kind of paper [bond]?"

Required:

1. Explain why an investor would buy a JCPenney bond with a zero interest rate.
2. If investors could earn 15 percent on similar investments, how much did JCPenney receive when it issued the bonds with a face value of $400 million?

CP10-5

LO1

Interpreting the Financial Press

In this chapter, we talked about bonds primarily from the perspective of the issuing corporation. To understand bonds, it is also necessary to develop an understanding of why investors buy bonds. An article on this topic is available on the Libby/Libby/Short website at **www.mhhe.com/libby5e**. You should read the article, "It's Time for Bonds to Get Some Respect,"* and then write a short memo summarizing the article in your own words. What type of investors are interested in buying bonds? Describe the impact of inflation on bonds.

Critical Thinking Cases

CP10-6

LO1

Evaluating an Ethical Dilemma

You work for a small company considering investing in a new Internet business. Financial projections suggest that the company will be able to earn in excess of $40 million per year on an investment of $100 million. The company president suggests borrowing the money by issuing bonds that will carry a 7 percent interest rate. He says, "This is better than printing money! We won't have to invest a penny of our own money, and we get to keep $33 million per year after we pay interest to the bondholders." As you think about the proposed transaction, you feel a little uncomfortable about taking advantage of the creditors in this fashion. You feel that it must be wrong to earn such a high return by using money that belongs to other people. Is this an ethical business transaction?

CP10-7

LO1

Evaluating an Ethical Dilemma

Assume that you are a portfolio manager for a large insurance company. The majority of the money you manage is from retired school teachers who depend on the income you earn on their investments. You have invested a significant amount of money in the bonds of a large corporation and have just received a call from the company's president explaining that it is unable to meet its current interest obligations because of deteriorating business operations related to increased international competition.

---

*"It's Time for Bonds to Get Some Respect," Reprinted from January 19, 1998 issue of *BusinessWeek* by special permission, copyright © 1998 by The McGraw-Hill Companies, Inc.

The president has a recovery plan that will take at least two years. During that time, the company will not be able to pay interest on the bonds and, she admits, if the plan does not work, bondholders will probably lose more than half of their money. As a creditor, you can force the company into immediate bankruptcy and probably get back at least 90 percent of the bondholders' money. You also know that your decision will cause at least 10,000 people to lose their jobs if the company ceases operations. Given only these two options, what should you do?

Financial Reporting and Analysis Team Project

Team Project: Examining an Annual Report

CP10-8
LO1, 2, 3, 4, 5, 7

As a team, select an industry to analyze. Reuters provides lists of industries and their makeup at www.investor.reuters.com/Industries.aspx. Each team member should acquire the annual report or 10-K for one publicly traded company in the industry, with each member selecting a different company. (Library files, the SEC EDGAR service at www.sec.gov, Compustat CD, and the company itself are good sources.)

Required:

On an individual basis, each team member should write a short report answering the following questions about the selected company. Discuss any patterns across the companies that you as a team observe. Then, as a team, write a short report comparing and contrasting your companies.

1. Has your company issued any long-term bonds or notes? If so, read the footnote and list any unusual features (e.g., callable, convertible, secured by specific collateral).
2. If your company issued any bonds, were they issued at either a premium or a discount? If so, does the company use the straight-line or effective-interest amortization method?
3. Ratio analysis:
   a. What does the debt-to-equity ratio measure in general?
   b. Compute the ratio for the last three years.
   c. What do your results suggest about the company?
   d. If available, find the industry ratio for the most recent year, compare it to your results, and discuss why you believe your company differs from or is similar to the industry ratio.
4. Ratio analysis:
   a. What does the times interest earned ratio measure in general?
   b. Compute the ratio for the last three years. If interest expense is not separately disclosed, you will not be able to compute the ratio, but state why you think it is not separately disclosed.
   c. What do your results suggest about the company?
   d. If available, find the industry ratio for the most recent year, compare it to your results, and discuss why you believe your company differs from or is similar to the industry ratio.
5. During the recent year, how much cash did the company receive on issuing debt? How much did it pay on debt principal? What does management suggest were the reasons for issuing and/or repaying debt during the year?

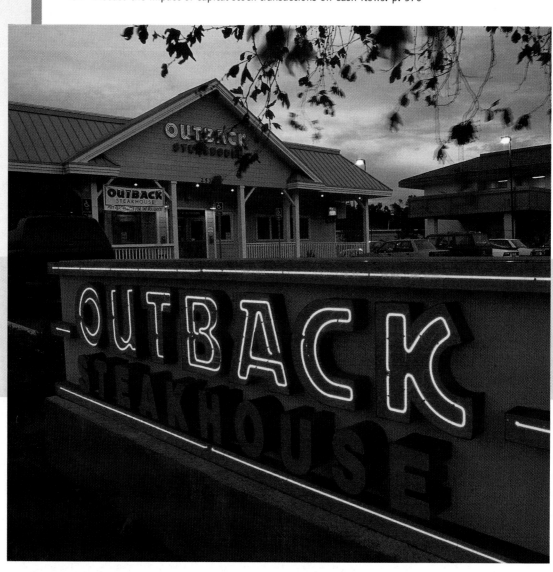

Reporting and Interpreting Owners' Equity

In the early 1990s, Outback Steakhouse was a privately owned company with bold growth plans. To finance the company's growth, management recognized the need to raise large amounts of new capital. Outback would have to "go public," allowing the company's stock to be traded on a major stock exchange. In June 1991, Outback's stock was first sold to the public.

Outback's initial growth strategy has since become a reality. Today, there are more than 825 Outback restaurants as well as more than 200 others operated under different names. Company revenues have grown to nearly $3 billion in food and beverage sales. Still growing at a pace of 100 new restaurants a year, Outback plans to expand internationally in countries such as Japan, Portugal, China, Australia, Malaysia, Bahrain, and Korea.

FOCUS COMPANY:

Outback Steakhouse

FINANCING CORPORATE GROWTH WITH

CAPITAL SUPPLIED BY OWNERS

www.outback.com

Investors who bought Outback's stock when it first went public have benefited from its rapid growth. If you had invested $10,000 in the company in 1991, your stock would be worth $135,000 today. To achieve this level of success, Outback's management needed to develop and execute a sound business strategy. Equally important, however, was management's ability to develop a solid capital structure with which to finance the company's growth. In this chapter, we study the role that stockholders' equity plays in building a successful business.

UNDERSTANDING THE BUSINESS

To some people, the words **corporation** and **business** are almost synonymous. You've probably heard friends refer to a career in business as "the corporate world." Equating business with corporations is understandable because corporations are the dominant form of business organization in terms of volume of operations. If you were to write the names of 50 familiar companies on a piece of paper, all of them probably would be corporations.

The popularity of the corporate form can be attributed to a critical advantage that corporations have over sole proprietorships and partnerships: They can raise large amounts of capital because both large and small investors can easily participate in their ownership. This ease of participation is related to several factors.

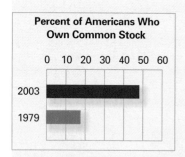

Percent of Americans Who Own Common Stock

- Shares of stock can be purchased in small amounts. You could buy a single share of Outback stock for approximately $40 and become one of the owners of this successful company.
- Ownership interests can easily be transferred through the sale of shares on established markets such as the New York Stock Exchange.
- Stock ownership provides investors with limited liability.*

Many Americans own stock either directly or indirectly through a mutual fund or pension program. Stock ownership offers them the opportunity to earn higher returns than they could on deposits to bank accounts or investments in corporate bonds. Unfortunately, stock ownership also involves higher risk. The proper balance between risk and the expected return on an investment depends on individual preferences.

Exhibit 11.1 presents financial information from Outback's annual report. Notice that the stockholders' equity section of the balance sheet lists two primary sources of stockholders' equity:

1. **Contributed capital** from the sale of stock. This is the amount of money stockholders invested through the purchase of shares.
2. **Retained earnings** generated by the company's profit-making activities. This is the cumulative amount of net income the corporation has earned since its organization less the cumulative amount of dividends paid since organization.

Most companies generate a significant portion of their stockholders' equity from retained earnings. In the case of Outback, retained earnings represents over 90% percent of the company's total stockholders' equity.

ORGANIZATION of the Chapter

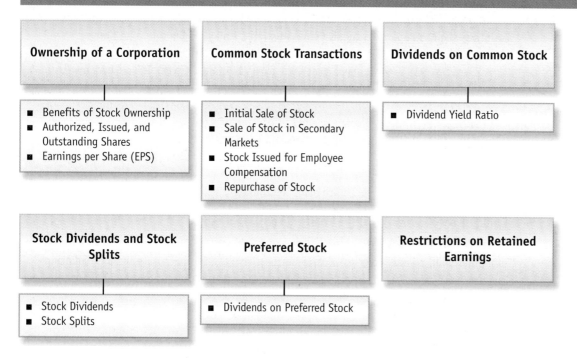

Ownership of a Corporation

- Benefits of Stock Ownership
- Authorized, Issued, and Outstanding Shares
- Earnings per Share (EPS)

Common Stock Transactions

- Initial Sale of Stock
- Sale of Stock in Secondary Markets
- Stock Issued for Employee Compensation
- Repurchase of Stock

Dividends on Common Stock

- Dividend Yield Ratio

Stock Dividends and Stock Splits

- Stock Dividends
- Stock Splits

Preferred Stock

- Dividends on Preferred Stock

Restrictions on Retained Earnings

*If a corporation becomes insolvent, creditors have recourse for their claims only to the corporation's assets. Thus, stockholders stand to lose only their equity in the corporation. In the case of a partnership or sole proprietorship, creditors have recourse to the owners' personal assets if the assets of the business are insufficient to meet its debts.

Stockholders' Equity

	2003	2002
Common stock, $0.01 par value, 200,000 shares authorized; 78,750 and 78,750 shares issued; 74,279 and 75,880 shares outstanding as of December 31, 2003 and 2002, respectively	788	788
Additional paid-in capital	254,852	240,083
Retained earnings	934,516	820,360
Accumulated other comprehensive loss	(2,078)	—
	1,188,078	1,061,231
Less treasury stock, 4,471 and 2,870 shares at December 31, 2003 and 2002, respectively, at cost	(161,808)	(86,948)
Total stockholders' equity	1,026,270	974,283
	$1,474,787	$1,352,832

The accompanying notes are an integral part of these Consolidated Financial Statements.

EXHIBIT 11.1

Excerpt from
Consolidated Balance
Sheets and Statements
of Stockholders'
Equity for Outback
Steakhouse

REAL WORLD EXCERPT

NO RULES. JUST RIGHT.®

ANNUAL REPORT

OUTBACK STEAKHOUSE, INC. AND AFFILIATES
CONSOLIDATED STATEMENTS OF STOCKHOLDERS' EQUITY
(DOLLARS IN THOUSANDS)

	Common Stock Shares	Common Stock Amount	Additional Paid-In Capital	Retained Earnings	Accumulated Other Comprehensive Loss	Treasury Stock	Total
Balance, December 31, 2000	76,632	$785	$216,056	$570,746	$—	$(46,119)	$ 741,468
Issuance of common stock	40	1	272	—	—	—	273
Purchase of treasury stock	(1,210)	—	—	—	—	(31,250)	(31,250)
Reissuance of treasury stock	1,451	—	—	(9,346)	—	35,365	26,019
Stock option income tax benefit	—	—	5,835	—	—	—	5,835
Stock option compensation expense	—	—	1,004	—	—	—	1,004
Net income	—	—	—	124,738	—	—	124,738
Balance, December 31, 2001	76,913	786	223,167	686,138	—	(42,004)	868,087
Issuance of common stock	196	2	6,998	—	—	—	7,000
Purchase of treasury stock	(2,691)	—	—	—	—	(81,650)	(81,650)
Reissuance of treasury stock	1,462	—	—	(6,767)	—	36,706	29,939
Dividends ($0.12 per share)	—	—	—	(9,101)	—	—	(9,101)
Stock option income tax benefit	—	—	8,580	—	—	—	8,580
Stock option compensation expense	—	—	1,338	—	—	—	1,338
Net income	—	—	—	150,090	—	—	150,090
Balance, December 31, 2002	75,880	788	240,083	820,360	—	(86,948)	974,283
Purchase of treasury stock	(3,784)	—	—	—	—	(143,191)	(143,191)
Reissuance of treasury stock	2,183	—	—	(19,133)	—	68,331	49,198
Dividends ($0.49 per share)	—	—	—	(36,917)	—	—	(36,917)
Stock option income tax benefit	—	—	13,189	—	—	—	13,189
Stock option compensation expense	—	—	1,580	—	—	—	1,580
Net income	—	—	—	170,206	—	—	170,206
Foreign currency translation adjustment	—	—	—	—	(2,078)	—	(2,078)
Balance, December 31, 2003	74,279	$788	$254,852	$934,516	$(2,078)	$(161,808)	$1,026,270

OWNERSHIP OF A CORPORATION

The corporation is the only business form the law recognizes as a separate entity. As a distinct entity, the corporation enjoys a continuous existence separate and apart from its owners. It may own assets, incur liabilities, expand and contract in size, sue others, be sued, and enter into contracts independently of its stockholder owners.

To protect everyone's rights, the creation and governance of corporations are tightly regulated by law. Corporations are created by application to a state government (not the federal government). On approval of the application, the state issues a charter, sometimes called the **articles of incorporation.** Corporations are governed by a board of directors elected by the stockholders.

Each state has different laws governing the organization of corporations created within its boundaries. Although Outback has its headquarters in Florida, it elected to incorporate in the state of Delaware. You will find that an unusually large number of corporations were incorporated in Delaware. The reason is simple: That state has some of the most favorable laws for establishing corporations.

Benefits of Stock Ownership

Learning Objective 1

Explain the role of stock in the capital structure of a corporation.

When you invest in a corporation, you are known as a **stockholder** or **shareholder.** As a stockholder, you receive shares of stock that you subsequently can sell on established stock exchanges. Owners of common stock receive a number of benefits:

- **A voice in management.** You may vote in the stockholders' meeting on major issues concerning management of the corporation.
- **Dividends.** You receive a proportional share of the distribution of profits.
- **Residual claim.** You will receive a proportional share of the distribution of remaining assets upon the liquidation of the company.

Owners, unlike creditors, are able to vote at the annual stockholders' meeting, with a number of votes equal to the number of shares owned. The following Notice of Annual Meeting of Shareholders was recently sent to all owners of Outback stock:

REAL WORLD EXCERPT

NO RULES. JUST RIGHT.®

NOTICE OF
SHAREHOLDERS' MEETING

TO BE HELD ON APRIL 21, 2004

Notice is hereby given that the Annual Meeting of Stockholders of OUTBACK STEAKHOUSE, INC. (the "Company") will be held at the A la Carte Event Pavilion, 4050-B Dana Shores Drive, Tampa, Florida 33634, on Wednesday, April 21, 2004 at 10:00 A.M., Tampa time, for the following purposes:

1. To elect two directors, each to serve for a term of three years and until his or her successor is duly elected and qualified;
2. To approve an amendment and restatement of the Company's Amended and Restated Stock Option Plan ("Plan"). The amendments primarily allow for the grant of shares of restricted Common Stock under the Plan and increase the number of shares of Common Stock for which options and shares of restricted Common Stock may be granted from 22,500,000 to 23,500,000; and
3. To transact such other business as may properly come before the meeting.

Only stockholders of record at the close of business on February 27, 2004 are entitled to notice of and to vote at the meeting or any adjournment or postponement of the meeting.

This notice also contained several pages of information concerning the people who were nominated to be members of the board of directors as well as a variety of financial

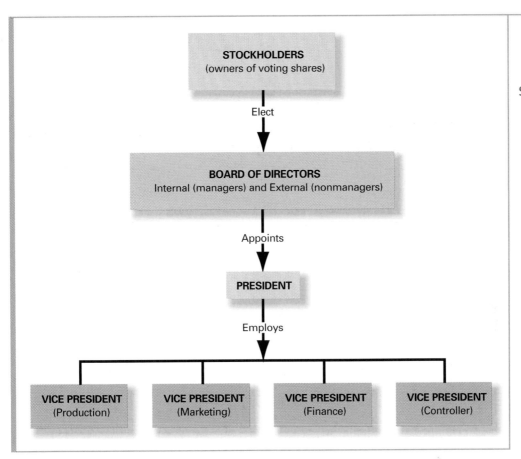

Typical Organizational
Structure of a Corporation

information. Since most owners do not actually attend the annual meeting, the notice included a proxy card, similar to an absentee ballot. Owners may complete the proxy and
mail it to the company, which will include it in the votes at the annual meeting.

As shown in Exhibit 11.2, stockholders have ultimate authority in a corporation.
The board of directors and, indirectly, all employees are accountable to the stockholders. The organizational structure shown is typical of most corporations, but the specific
structure depends on the nature of the company's business.

Authorized, Issued, and Outstanding Shares

The corporate charter specifies the maximum number of shares that can be sold to the
public. The financial statements must report information concerning the number of
shares that have been sold to date. Let's look at the share information reported by Outback as of December 31, 2003, shown in Exhibit 11.1. For Outback, the maximum
number of shares that can be sold, called the authorized number of shares, is 200,000
(thousand). As of December 31, 2003, the company had sold 78,750 (thousand) shares.
Stock that has been sold to the public is called issued shares.

For a number of reasons, a company might want to buy back stock that has already
been sold to the public. Stock that has been bought back is called **treasury stock.**
When a company buys back its stock, a difference is created between the number of issued shares and the number of outstanding shares, or shares currently held by individual stockholders. We can compute outstanding shares for Outback using data from
the December 31, 2003, balance sheet shown in Exhibit 11.1 (in thousands):

Issued shares	78,750
Less: Treasury stock	(4,471)
Outstanding shares	74,279

The **AUTHORIZED NUMBER OF
SHARES** is the maximum number
of shares of a corporation's capital
stock that can be issued as
specified in the charter.

ISSUED SHARES represent the
total number of shares of stock
that have been sold.

OUTSTANDING SHARES refer to
the total number of shares of
stock that are owned by
stockholders on any particular
date.

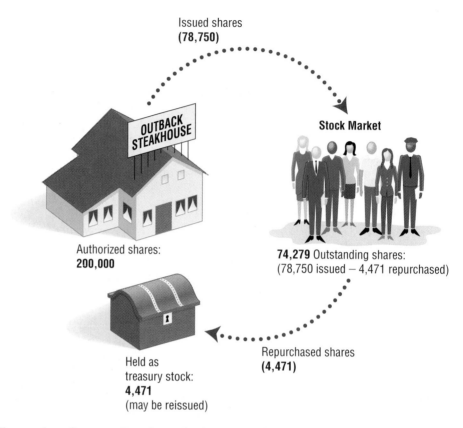

Issued shares
(78,750)

Stock Market

Authorized shares:
200,000

74,279 Outstanding shares:
(78,750 issued − 4,471 repurchased)

Repurchased shares
(4,471)

Held as
treasury stock:
4,471
(may be reissued)

The number of outstanding shares is also reported on the balance sheet shown in Exhibit 11.1. Notice that when treasury stock is held, the number of shares issued and the number of shares outstanding differ by the number of shares of treasury stock held (treasury stock is included in "issued" but not in "outstanding"). The number of shares outstanding is important to financial analysts who need to express certain dollar amounts on a per share basis. One example is the earnings per share ratio.

KEY RATIO
ANALYSIS

Earnings per Share (EPS)

Learning Objective 2
Analyze the earnings per share ratio.

? ANALYTICAL QUESTION:
How profitable is a company?

% RATIO AND COMPARISONS:
Earnings per share is computed as follows:

Earnings per Share = Net Income ÷ Average Number of Shares of Common Stock Outstanding

The 2003 ratio for Outback Steakhouse:

$170 million ÷ 75.26 million shares* = $2.26

COMPARISONS OVER TIME			COMPARISONS WITH COMPETITORS	
Outback			**Ruby Tuesday**	**Wendy's**
2001	**2002**	**2003**	**2003**	**2003**
$1.63	$1.96	$2.26	$1.68	$2.07

As reported in the notes to the financial statements

🔆 INTERPRETATIONS:

In General → All analysts and investors are interested in a company's earnings. You have probably seen newspaper headlines announcing a company's earnings. Notice that those news stories normally report earnings on an earnings per share (EPS) basis. The reason is simple: Numbers are much easier to compare on a per share basis. For example, in 2003, Outback earned income of $170,206,000 compared to $150,090,000 in the previous year. If we make that comparison on a per share basis, we can say that EPS increased from $1.96 to $2.26. EPS is also useful in comparing companies of different sizes. Ruby Tuesday, a smaller company than Outback, earned $110,009,000 in 2003. While net income for Ruby Tuesday is only 65 percent of the net income earned by Outback, EPS for Ruby Tuesday is 74 percent of the EPS for Outback because Ruby Tuesday has fewer stockholders.

Focus Company Analysis → Outback has a strategy of rapid growth and reinvestment of earnings. Analysts are watching EPS to be sure the company will achieve its strategy. Outback's EPS increased by more than 38 percent between 2001 and 2003, a strong level of growth. In comparison, Wendy's EPS increased by a greater percentage during the same period, and its stock price rose more rapidly than did Outback's.

A Few Cautions: While EPS is an effective and widely used measure of profitability, it can be misleading if there are significant differences in the market values of the shares being compared. Two companies earning $1.50 per share might appear to be comparable, but if shares in one company cost $10 while shares of the other cost $175, they are not comparable.

Topic Tackler 11–1

COMMON STOCK TRANSACTIONS

Most corporations issue two types of stock, common stock and preferred stock. All corporations must issue common stock, but only some issue preferred stock. In this section, we discuss common stock and in a subsequent section, we discuss preferred stock.

Common stock is held by individuals who are often thought of as the "owners" of the corporation because they have the right to vote and share in the profitability of the business through dividends. The dividend rate for common stock is determined by the board of directors based on the company's profitability.

The fact that common stock dividends may increase with increases in the company's profitability helps to explain why investors can make money in the stock market. Basically, you can think of the price of a share of stock as the present value of all its future dividends. If a company's profitability improves so that it can pay higher dividends, the present value of its common stock will increase.

Common stock normally has a par value, a nominal value per share established in the corporate charter. Par value has no relationship to the market value of a stock. The notes to Outback's annual report state that their common stock has a par value of $0.01 while its market value is more than $40 per share.

Most states require stock to have a par value. The original purpose of this requirement was to protect creditors by specifying a permanent amount of capital that owners could not withdraw before a bankruptcy, which would leave creditors with an empty corporate shell. This permanent amount of capital is called legal capital. Today, this requirement has little importance because of other contractual protections for creditors.

Some states require the issuance of no-par value stock, which does not have a specified amount per share. When a corporation issues no-par stock, legal capital is as defined by the state law.

Learning Objective 3
Describe the characteristics of common stock and analyze transactions affecting common stock.

COMMON STOCK is the basic voting stock issued by a corporation.

PAR VALUE is the nominal value per share of capital stock specified in the charter; it serves as the basis for legal capital.

LEGAL CAPITAL is the permanent amount of capital defined by state law that must remain invested in the business; it serves as a cushion for creditors.

NO-PAR VALUE STOCK is capital stock that has no par value specified in the corporate charter.

Initial Sale of Stock

Two names are applied to transactions involving the initial sale of a company's stock to the public. An **initial public offering,** or **IPO,** involves the very first sale of a company's stock to the public (i.e., when the company first "goes public"). You have probably heard stories of Internet stocks that have increased dramatically in value the day of the IPO. While investors sometimes earn significant returns on IPOs, they also take significant risks. Once a company's stock has been traded on established markets, additional sales of new stock to the public are called **seasoned new issues.**

Most sales of stock to the public are cash transactions. To illustrate the accounting for an initial sale of stock, assume that Outback sold 100,000 shares of its $0.01 par value stock for $40 per share. The company would record the following journal entry:

Cash (+A) (100,000 × $40)	4,000,000	
Common stock (+SE) (100,000 × $0.01)		1,000
Capital in excess of par value (+SE)		3,999,000

Assets	=	Liabilities	+	Stockholders' Equity	
Cash +4,000,000				Common stock	+1,000
				Capital in excess of par	+3,999,000

Notice that the common stock account is credited for the number of shares sold times the par value per share, and the capital in excess of par value account is credited for the remainder. If the corporate charter does not specify a par value for the stock, the stated value is used in the same manner that par value is used. If there is no par or stated value, the amount of the entire proceeds from the sale will be entered in the common stock account.

Sale of Stock in Secondary Markets

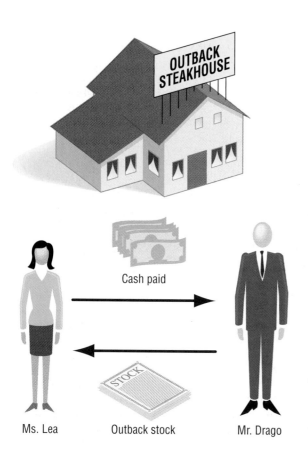

Cash paid

Ms. Lea   Outback stock   Mr. Drago

When a company sells stock to the public, the transaction is between the issuing corporation and the buyer. Subsequent to the initial sale, investors can sell shares to other investors without directly affecting the corporation. For example, if investor Jon Drago sold 1,000 shares of Outback stock to Jennifer Lea, Outback would not record a journal entry on its books. Mr. Drago received cash for the shares he sold, and Ms. Lea received stock for the cash she paid. Outback did not receive or pay anything.

Each business day, *The Wall Street Journal* reports the results of thousands of transactions between investors in secondary markets, such as the New York Stock Exchange (NYSE), the American Stock Exchange (AMEX), and the NASDAQ market. Managers of corporations closely follow the price movements of their company's stock. Stockholders expect to earn money on their investments through both dividends and increases in the stock price. In many instances, senior management has been replaced because of a stock's poor performance in the stock market. While managers watch the stock price on a daily basis, transactions between investors do not directly affect the company's financial statements.

Stock Issued for Employee Compensation

One of the advantages of the corporate form is the ability to separate the management of a business from its ownership. Separation can also be a disadvantage because some managers may not act in the owners' best interests. This problem can be overcome in a number of ways. Compensation packages can be developed to reward managers for meeting goals that are important to stockholders. Another strategy is to offer managers stock options, which permit them to buy stock at a fixed price.

The holder of a stock option has an interest in a company's performance just as an owner does. Stock option plans have become an increasingly common form of compensation over the past few years. Indeed, 98 percent of the companies surveyed by *Accounting Trends & Techniques* now offer stock option plans to their employees.

Outback's annual report contains the following note:

REAL WORLD EXCERPT

ANNUAL REPORT

> **11. Stock Option and Other Benefit Plans**
>
> The purpose of the Stock Option Plan is to attract competent personnel, to provide long-term incentives to Directors and key employees, and to discourage employees from competing with the Company.
>
> As of December 31, 2003 the Company had granted to employees of the Company a cumulative total of approximately 22,081,000 options to purchase the Company's Common Stock at prices ranging from $0.19 to $38.42 per share which was the estimated fair market value at the time of each grant.

The options Outback issued specified that shares could be bought at the then current market price. Granting a stock option is a form of compensation, even if the grant price and the current stock price are the same. You can think of a stock option as a risk-free investment. If you hold a stock option and the stock price declines, you have lost nothing. If the stock price increases, you can exercise your option at the low grant price and sell the stock at the higher price for a profit.

Companies must estimate and report compensation expense associated with stock options. The specific procedures will be discussed in the intermediate accounting course.

Repurchase of Stock

A corporation may want to repurchase its stock from existing stockholders for a number of reasons. One common reason is the existence of an employee bonus plan that provides workers with shares of the company's stock as part of their compensation. Because of Securities and Exchange Commission regulations concerning newly issued shares, most companies find it less costly to give employees repurchased shares than to issue new ones. Stock that has been reacquired and held by the issuing corporation is called treasury stock. These shares have no voting, dividend, or other stockholder rights while held as treasury stock.

Most companies record the purchase of treasury stock based on the cost of the shares that were purchased. Assume that Outback bought 100,000 shares of its stock in the open market when it was selling for $20 per share. Using the cost method, the company would record the following journal entry:

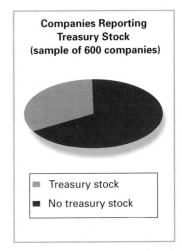

Companies Reporting Treasury Stock (sample of 600 companies)

■ Treasury stock
■ No treasury stock

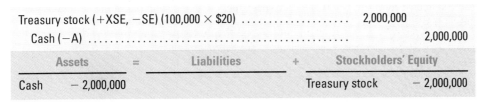

Treasury stock (+XSE, −SE) (100,000 × $20)	2,000,000	
Cash (−A)		2,000,000

Assets	=	Liabilities	+	Stockholders' Equity	
Cash −2,000,000				Treasury stock	−2,000,000

Intuitively, many students expect the Treasury Stock account to be reported as an asset. Such is not the case because a company cannot create an asset by investing in itself. The Treasury Stock account is actually a contra-equity account, which means that

TREASURY STOCK is a corporation's own stock that had been issued but was subsequently reacquired and is still being held by that corporation.

it is subtracted from total stockholders' equity. This practice makes sense because treasury stock is stock that is no longer outstanding and therefore should not be included in stockholders' equity.

As the information in Exhibit 11.1 indicates, Outback reported treasury stock in the amount of $161,808 (thousand) on its balance sheet as of December 31, 2003. The statement of stockholders' equity reports the same amount plus additional information.

When a company sells its treasury stock, it does not report an accounting profit or loss on the transaction, even if it sells the stock for more or less than it paid. GAAP do not permit a corporation to report income or losses from investments in its own stock because transactions with the owners are not considered normal profit-making activities. Based on the previous example, assume that Outback resold 10,000 shares of treasury stock for $30 per share. Remember that the company had purchased the stock for $20 per share. Outback would record the following journal entry:

Cash (+A) (10,000 × $30)	300,000	
Treasury stock (−XSE, +SE) (10,000 × $20)		200,000
Capital in excess of par (+SE)		100,000

Assets	=	Liabilities	+	Stockholders' Equity	
Cash + 300,000				Treasury stock	+ 200,000
				Capital in excess of par	+ 100,000

If treasury stock were sold at a price below its purchase price (i.e., at an economic loss), stockholders' equity would be reduced by the amount of the difference between purchase price and the sale price. Assume that Outback had sold the stock in the previous illustration for only $15 per share:

Cash (+A) (10,000 × $15)	150,000	
Capital in excess of par (−SE) (10,000 × $5)	50,000	
Treasury stock (−XSE, +SE) (10,000 × $20)		200,000

Assets	=	Liabilities	+	Stockholders' Equity	
Cash + 150,000				Treasury stock	+ 200,000
				Capital in excess of par	− 50,000

SELF-STUDY QUIZ

1. Assume that Applied Technology Corporation issued 10,000 shares of its common stock, par value $2, for $150,000 cash. Prepare the journal entry to record this transaction.

2. Assume that Applied Technology repurchased 5,000 shares of its stock in the open market when the stock was selling for $12 per share. Record this transaction.

After you have completed your answers, check them with the solutions at the bottom of the page.

Self-Study Quiz
Solutions

1. Cash	150,000	
Common stock		20,000
Capital in excess of par		130,000
2. Treasury stock	60,000	
Cash		60,000

DIVIDENDS ON COMMON STOCK

Investors buy common stock because they expect a return on their investment. This return can come in two forms: stock price appreciation and dividends. Some investors prefer to buy stocks that pay little or no dividends because companies that reinvest the majority of their earnings tend to increase their future earnings potential, along with their stock price. Wealthy investors in high tax brackets prefer to receive their return in the form of higher stock prices because capital gains may be taxed at a lower rate than dividend income. Other investors, such as retired people who need a steady income, prefer to receive their return in the form of dividends. These people often seek stocks that will pay very high dividends, such as utility stocks. Because of the importance of dividends to many investors, analysts often compute the dividend yield ratio to evaluate a corporation's dividend policy.

Learning Objective 4
Discuss dividends and analyze transactions.

Topic Tackler

PLUS

Topic Tackler 11–2

KEY RATIO
ANALYSIS

 Dividend Yield

? ANALYTICAL QUESTION:
What is return on investment based on dividends?

% RATIO AND COMPARISONS:
The dividend yield ratio is computed as follows:

$$\text{Dividend Yield} = \text{Dividends per Share} \div \text{Market Price per Share}$$

The 2003 ratio for Outback Steakhouse:

$$\$0.49 \div \$40 = 1.23\%$$

Learning Objective 5
Analyze the dividend yield ratio.

COMPARISONS OVER TIME		
Outback		
2001	**2002**	**2003**
0%	0.1%	1.23%

COMPARISONS WITH COMPETITORS	
Ruby Tuesday	**Wendy's**
2003	**2003**
0.1%	0.2%

💡 INTERPRETATIONS:

In General → Investors in common stock earn a return from both dividends and capital appreciation (increases in the market price of the stock). Growth-oriented companies often rely mainly on increases in their market price to provide a return to investors. Others pay large dividends but have more stable market prices. Each type of stock appeals to different types of investors with different risk and return preferences.

Focus Company Analysis → As a growth-oriented company, historically Outback established a policy not to pay dividends. Because of strong cash flows, the company began paying dividends in 2002. Notice that while both the comparison companies are paying dividends, the yields are virtually immaterial in amount. None of these stocks would appeal to investors who need a steady income from dividends.

A Few Cautions: Remember that the dividend yield ratio tells only part of the return on investment story. Often potential capital appreciation is a much more important consideration. Outback is currently reinvesting a large portion of its earnings. As a result, the company is growing rapidly, and its stock price has increased significantly. Investors in Outback have bought the stock with the expectation of earning a return from increases in its market value, not from dividends.

The notes to the Outback annual report contain the following information

DIVIDENDS

Our Board of Directors authorized the following dividends in the year ended December 31, 2003:

Declaration Date	Record Date	Payable Date	Amount per Share of Common Stock
January 22, 2003	February 21, 2003	March 7, 2003	$0.12
April 23, 2003	May 23, 2003	June 6, 2003	0.12
July 23, 2003	August 22, 2003	September 5, 2003	0.12
October 22, 2003	November 21, 2003	December 5, 2003	0.13

On January 28, 2004, our Board of Directors declared a quarterly dividend of $0.13 for each share of our common stock. The dividend was paid March 5, 2004 to shareholders of record as of February 20, 2004. At the current dividend rate, the annual dividend payment is expected to be between $38,000,000 and $40,000,000 depending on the shares outstanding during the respective quarters. We intend to pay the dividend with cash flow from operations.

This note contains three important dates:

The **DECLARATION DATE** is the date on which the board of directors officially approves a dividend.

1. **Declaration date—January 28, 2004.** The declaration date is the date on which the board of directors officially approves the dividend. As soon as it makes the declaration, it creates a dividend liability.

The **RECORD DATE** is the date on which the corporation prepares the list of current stockholders as shown on its records; dividends can be paid only to the stockholders who own stock on that date.

2. **Date of record—February 20, 2004.** The record date follows the declaration; it is the date on which the corporation prepares the list of current stockholders based on its records. The dividend is payable only to those names listed on the record date. No journal entry is made on this date.

3. **Date of payment—March 5, 2004.** The payment date is the date on which the cash is disbursed to pay the dividend liability. It follows the date of record, as specified in the dividend announcement.

The **PAYMENT DATE** is the date on which a cash dividend is paid to the stockholders of record.

These three dates apply for all cash dividends and can be shown graphically as follows:

Declaration Date	Date of Record	Date of Payment

On the declaration date, a company records a liability related to the dividend. To illustrate, on January 28, Outback records the following journal entry. Assuming 75 million shares are outstanding, the dividend amounts to $9,750,000 ($0.13 × 75,000,000):

Retained earnings (−SE)	9,750,000	
Dividends payable (+L)		9,750,000

Assets	=	Liabilities	+	Stockholders' Equity
		Dividends payable + 9,750,000		Retained earnings − 9,750,000

The payment of the liability on March 5 is recorded as follows:

Dividends payable (−L)	9,750,000	
Cash (−A)		9,750,000

Assets	=	Liabilities	+	Stockholders' Equity
Cash − 9,750,000		Dividends payable − 9,750,000		

Notice that the declaration and payment of a cash dividend reduce assets (cash) and stockholders' equity (retained earnings) by the same amount. This observation explains the two fundamental requirements for payment of a cash dividend:

1. **Sufficient retained earnings.** The corporation must have accumulated a sufficient amount of retained earnings to cover the amount of the dividend. State incorporation laws often limit cash dividends to the balance in the Retained Earnings account.

2. **Sufficient cash.** The corporation must have sufficient cash to pay the dividend and meet the operating needs of the business. The mere fact that the Retained Earnings account has a large credit balance does not mean that the board of directors can declare and pay a cash dividend. The cash generated in the past by earnings represented in the Retained Earnings account may have been expended to acquire inventory, buy operational assets, and pay liabilities. Consequently, no necessary relationship exists between the balance of retained earnings and the balance of cash on any particular date. Quite simply, retained earnings is not cash.

 Impact of Dividends on Stock Price

FINANCIAL ANALYSIS

Another date that is important in understanding dividends has no accounting implications. The date two business days before the date of record is known as the **ex-dividend date.** This date is established by the stock exchanges to make certain that dividend checks are sent to the right people. If you buy stock before the ex-dividend date, you will receive the dividend. If you buy stock on the ex-dividend date or later, the previous owner will receive the dividend.

If you follow stock prices, you will notice that they often fall on the ex-dividend date. The reason is simple: On that date, the stock is worth less because it no longer includes the right to receive the next dividend.

SELF-STUDY QUIZ

Answer the following questions concerning dividends:

1. On which dividend date is a liability created?

2. A cash outflow occurs on which dividend date?

3. What are the two fundamental requirements for the payment of a dividend?

After you have completed your answers, check them with the solutions at the bottom of the page.

---

1. Declaration date.
2. Date of payment.
3. Dividends can be paid only if sufficient retained earnings and sufficient cash are both available.

Self-Study Quiz
Solutions

STOCK DIVIDENDS AND STOCK SPLITS

Stock Dividends

Without a qualifier, the term **dividend** means a cash dividend, but dividends can also be paid with additional shares of stock. A stock dividend is a distribution of additional shares of a corporation's stock to its stockholders on a pro rata basis at no cost to the stockholder. The phrase **pro rata basis** means that each stockholder receives additional shares equal to the percentage of shares held. A stockholder with 10 percent of the outstanding shares would receive 10 percent of any additional shares issued as a stock dividend.

The term **stock dividend** is sometimes misused in annual reports and news articles. A recent *Wall Street Journal* headline announced that a particular company had just declared a "stock dividend." A close reading of the article revealed that the company had actually declared a cash dividend on the stock.

The value of a stock dividend is the subject of much debate. In reality, a stock dividend by itself has no economic value. All stockholders receive a pro rata distribution of shares, which means that each stockholder owns exactly the same portion of the company as before. The value of an investment is determined by the percentage of the company that is owned, not the number of shares held. If you get change for a dollar, you do not have more wealth because you hold four quarters instead of only one dollar. Similarly, if you own 10 percent of a company, you are not wealthier simply because the company declares a stock dividend and gives you (and all other stockholders) more shares of stock.

The stock market reacts immediately when a stock dividend is issued, and the stock price falls proportionally. Theoretically, if the stock price was $60 before a stock dividend and the number of shares is doubled, in the absence of events affecting the company, the price would fall to $30. Thus, an investor would own 100 shares worth $6,000 before the stock dividend (100 × $60) and 200 shares worth $6,000 after the stock dividend (200 × $30).

In reality, the fall in price is not exactly proportional to the number of new shares issued. In some cases, the stock dividend makes the stock more attractive to new investors. Many investors prefer to buy stock in round lots, which are multiples of 100 shares. An investor with $10,000 might not buy a stock selling for $150, for instance, because she cannot afford to buy 100 shares. She might buy the stock if the price were less than $100 as the result of a stock dividend. In other cases, stock dividends are associated with increases in cash dividends, which are attractive to some investors.

When a stock dividend occurs, the company must transfer an additional amount from either Retained Earnings or Capital in Excess of Par into the Common Stock account to reflect the additional shares issued. The amount transferred depends on whether the stock dividend is classified as large or small. Most stock dividends are classified as large. A large stock dividend involves the distribution of additional shares that amount to more than 20–25 percent of currently outstanding shares. A small stock dividend involves the distribution of shares that amount to less than 20–25 percent of the outstanding shares. If the stock dividend is classified as large, the amount transferred to the Common Stock account is based on the par value of the additional shares issued. If the stock dividend is small (i.e., less than 20–25 percent), the amount transferred should be the total market value of the shares issued, with the par value of the

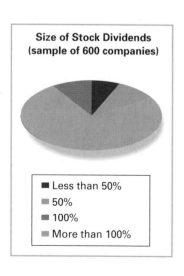

Size of Stock Dividends (sample of 600 companies)

- Less than 50%
- 50%
- 100%
- More than 100%

stock transferred to the Common Stock account and the excess transferred to the Capital in Excess of Par Value account.

Outback Steakhouse issued its last stock dividend in 1999. If we assume that Outback issued 1,000,000 shares as a large stock dividend, the company would make the following journal entry:

Retained earnings (−SE) ($0.01 × 1,000,000)	10,000	
Common stock (+SE)		10,000

Assets	=	Liabilities	+	Stockholders' Equity	
				Retained earnings	− 10,000
				Common stock	+ 10,000

This journal entry moves an amount from Retained Earnings to the company's Common Stock account. Notice that the stock dividend did not change total stockholders' equity. It changed only the balances of some of the accounts that constitute stockholders' equity.

Stock Splits

Stock splits are not dividends. While they are similar to a stock dividend, they are quite different in terms of their impact on the stockholders' equity accounts. In a stock split, the total number of authorized shares is increased by a specified amount, such as 2-for-1. In this instance, each share held is called in and two new shares are issued in its place. Typically, a stock split is accomplished by reducing the par or stated value per share of all authorized shares, so that their total par value is unchanged. For instance, if Outback executes a 2-for-1 stock split, it reduces the par value of its stock from $0.01 to $0.005 and doubles the number of shares outstanding. In contrast to a stock dividend, a stock split does not result in the transfer of a dollar amount to the Common Stock account. The reduction in the par value per share compensates for the increase in the number of shares, so that no transfer is needed.

In both a stock dividend and a stock split, the stockholder receives more shares of stock without having to invest additional resources to acquire the shares. A stock dividend requires a journal entry; a stock split does not but is disclosed in the notes to the financial statements. The comparative effects of a large stock dividend versus a stock split may be summarized as follows:

A STOCK SPLIT is an increase in the total number of authorized shares by a specified ratio; it does not decrease retained earnings.

	Stockholders' Equity		
	Before	After a 100% Stock Dividend	After a Two-for-One Stock Split
Number of shares outstanding	30,000	60,000	60,000
Par value per share	$ 10	$ 10	$ 5
Total par value outstanding	300,000	600,000	300,000
Retained earnings	650,000	350,000	650,000
Total stockholders' equity	950,000	950,000	950,000

SELF-STUDY QUIZ

Barton Corporation issued 100,000 new shares of common stock (par value $10) in a stock dividend when the market value was $30 per share.

1. Record this transaction, assuming that it was a small stock dividend.
2. Record this transaction, assuming that it was a large stock dividend.
3. What journal entry would be required if the transaction were a stock split?

After you have completed your answers, check them with the solutions at the bottom of the page.

PREFERRED STOCK

Learning Objective 7
Describe the characteristics of preferred stock and analyze transactions affecting preferred stock.

PREFERRED STOCK is stock that has specified rights over common stock.

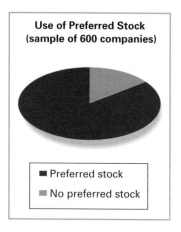

Use of Preferred Stock (sample of 600 companies)

- Preferred stock
- No preferred stock

CURRENT DIVIDEND PREFERENCE is the feature of preferred stock that grants priority on preferred dividends over common dividends.

In addition to common stock, some corporations issue preferred stock. Preferred stock differs from common stock based on a number of rights granted to the stockholders. The most significant differences are:

- **Preferred stock does not grant voting rights.** As a result, preferred stock does not appeal to investors who want some control over the operations of a corporation. Indeed, this is one of the main reasons some corporations issue preferred stock to raise their equity capital: Preferred stock permits them to raise funds without diluting common stockholders' control. The chart in the margin shows the percentage of companies surveyed by *Accounting Trends & Techniques* that include preferred stock in their capital structure.

- **Lower risk for preferred stock.** Generally, preferred stock is less risky than common stock because holders receive priority payment of dividends and distribution of assets if the corporation goes out of business. Usually a specified amount per share must be paid to preferred stockholders upon dissolution, before any remaining assets can be distributed to the common stockholders.

- **Preferred stock typically has a fixed dividend rate.** For example, "6 percent preferred stock, par value $10 per share" pays an annual dividend of 6 percent of par, or $0.60 per share. If preferred stock has no par value, the preferred dividend would be specified as $0.60 per share. The fixed dividend is attractive to certain investors who want a stable income from their investments.

Dividends on Preferred Stock

Because investors who purchase preferred stock give up certain advantages that are available to investors in common stock, preferred stock offers a dividend preference. The two most common dividend preferences are current and cumulative.

Current Dividend Preference

The current dividend preference requires the current preferred dividend to be paid before any dividends are paid on the common stock. This preference is always a fea-

---

Self-Study Quiz
Solutions

1.	Retained earnings	3,000,000	
	Common stock		1,000,000
	Capital in excess of par		2,000,000
2.	Retained earnings	1,000,000	
	Common stock		1,000,000

3. No journal entry is required in the case of a stock split.

ture of preferred stock. After the current dividend preference has been met and if no other preference is operative, dividends can be paid to the common stockholders.

Declared dividends must be allocated between preferred stock and common stock. First, the preferred stock preference must be met; then the remainder of the total dividend can be allocated to the common stock. To illustrate, assume the Sophia company has the following stock outstanding:

Sophia Company
Preferred stock outstanding, 6%, par $20; 2,000 shares = $40,000 par
Common stock outstanding, par $10; 5,000 shares = $50,000 par

Assuming a current dividend preference only, dividends would be allocated as follows:

Example	Total Dividends	6% Preferred Stock*	Common Stock
No. 1	$ 3,000	$2,400	$ 600
No. 2	18,000	2,400	15,600

*Preferred dividend preference, $40,000 × 6% = $2,400.

Cumulative Dividend Preference

The cumulative dividend preference states that if all or a part of the current dividend is not paid in full, the cumulative unpaid amount, known as dividends in arrears, must be paid before any common dividends can be paid. Of course, if the preferred stock is noncumulative, dividends can never be in arrears; any preferred dividends that are not declared are permanently lost. Because preferred stockholders are unwilling to accept this unfavorable feature, preferred stock is usually cumulative.

To illustrate the cumulative preference, assume that Sophia Company has the same amount of stock outstanding as in the last example. In this case, dividends have been in arrears for two years.

Example	Total Dividends	6% Preferred Stock*	Common Stock
No. 1	$ 8,000	$7,200	$ 800
No. 2	30,000	7,200	22,800

*Current dividend preference, $40,000 × 6% = $2,400; dividends in arrears preference, $2,400 × 2 years = $4,800; current dividend preference plus dividends in arrears = $7,200.

CUMULATIVE DIVIDEND PREFERENCE is the preferred stock feature that requires specified current dividends not paid in full to accumulate for every year in which they are not paid. These cumulative preferred dividends must be paid before any common dividends can be paid.

DIVIDENDS IN ARREARS are dividends on cumulative preferred stock that have not been declared in prior years.

Impact of Dividends in Arrears

FINANCIAL
ANALYSIS

The existence of dividends in arrears is important information because it limits a company's ability to pay dividends to common stockholders and can affect a company's future cash flows. Because dividends are never an actual liability until the board of directors declares them, dividends in arrears are not reported on the balance sheet. Instead, they are disclosed in the notes to the statements. The following note from Lone Star Industries is typical:

> The total of dividends in arrears on the $13.50 preferred stock at the end of the year was $11,670,000. The aggregate amount of such dividends must be paid before any dividends are paid on common stock.

REAL WORLD EXCERPT
Lone Star Industries
ANNUAL REPORT

RESTRICTIONS ON RETAINED EARNINGS

Several types of business transactions may cause restrictions to be placed on retained earnings that limit a company's ability to pay dividends. The most typical example is borrowing money from a bank. For additional security, some banks include a loan covenant that limits the amount of dividends a corporation can pay. In addition, debt covenants often include a limit on borrowing and require a minimum balance of cash or working capital. If debt covenants are violated, the creditor can demand immediate repayment of the debt.

The full-disclosure principle requires restrictions on retained earnings be reported in the financial statements or in a separate note to the financial statements. Most companies report these restrictions in the notes, as illustrated in the following note from the annual report of May Department Store:

REAL WORLD EXCERPT

May Department Store

ANNUAL REPORT

> Under the most restrictive covenants of long-term debt agreements, $1.2 billion of retained earnings was restricted as to the payment of dividends and/or common share repurchase.

Analysts are particularly interested in information concerning these restrictions because of the impact they have on the company's dividend policy.

FOCUS ON
CASH FLOWS

Financing Activities

Learning Objective 8
Discuss the impact of capital stock transactions on cash flows.

Transactions involving capital stock have a direct impact on the capital structure of a business. Because of the importance of these transactions, they are reported in the section of the statement called **Cash Flows from Financing Activities.** Examples of cash flows associated with capital stock are included in the statement of cash flows for Outback Steakhouse, shown in Exhibit 11.3.

EFFECT ON STATEMENT OF CASH FLOWS

In General → Cash received from owners is reported as an inflow; cash payments made to owners are reported as outflows. See the following example:

	Effect on Cash Flows
Financing activities	
Issuance of capital stock	+
Purchase of treasury stock	−
Sale of treasury stock	+
Payment of cash dividends	−

Selected Focus Company Comparisons: Dividends paid (dollars in millions)

General Mills	$406.0
Outback	36.9
Home Depot	595.0

Focus Company Analysis → Notice that for each of the last three years, Outback has paid out an increasing amount of cash for dividends (Exhibit 11.3). While the payment of dividends is always optional until declared by the board of directors, most companies are reluctant to reduce dividends. Many analysts view dividend reductions as an early indication of financial difficulties. As a result, analysts pay close attention to the cash flow obligations associated with dividends.

CONSOLIDATED STATEMENTS OF CASH FLOWS (dollars in thousands)			
Cash flows from financing activities:			
Proceeds from issuance of long-term debt	$ 29,497	$ 6,511	$20,329
Proceeds from minority partners' contributions	13,825	5,727	22,819
Distributions to minority partners	(4,841)	(3,289)	(2,539)
Repayments of long-term debt	(23,663)	(1,204)	(10,372)
Dividends paid	(36,917)	(9,101)	—
Payments for purchase of treasury stock	(143,191)	(81,650)	(31,250)
Proceeds from reissuance of treasury stock	41,583	28,722	26,019
Net cash (used in) provided by financing activities	$(123,707)	$(54,284)	$25,006

EXHIBIT 11.3

Excerpt from Statement of Cash Flows for Outback Steakhouse

REAL WORLD EXCERPT

NO RULES. JUST RIGHT.®

ANNUAL REPORT

Notice that Outback has purchased an increasing amount of treasury stock each year. Companies that generate significant cash flows often buy back stock from their owners.

DEMONSTRATION CASE

(Try to resolve the requirements before proceeding to the suggested solution that follows.)

This case focuses on the organization and operations for the first year of Shelly Corporation, which was organized by 10 local entrepreneurs on January 1, 2006, for the purpose of operating a business to sell various supplies to hotels. The charter authorized the following capital stock:

Common stock, no-par value, 20,000 shares

Preferred stock, 5 percent, $100 par value, 5,000 shares

The laws of the state specify that the legal capital for no-par stock is the full sale amount.

The following summarized transactions, selected from 2006, were completed on the dates indicated:

a. Jan. Sold a total of 8,000 shares of common stock to the 10 entrepreneurs for cash at $50 per share. Credit the Common Stock account for the total issue amount.

b. Feb. Sold 2,000 shares of preferred stock at $102 per share; cash collected in full.

c. Mar. Declared cash dividend of $1 on common stock.

d. July Purchased 100 shares of preferred stock that had been sold and issued earlier. Shelly Corporation paid the stockholder $104 per share.

e. Aug. Sold 20 shares of the preferred treasury stock at $105 per share.

Required:

1. Give the appropriate journal entries with a brief explanation for each transaction.

2. Prepare the Stockholders' Equity section of the balance sheet for Shelly Corporation at December 31, 2006. Assume retained earnings is $23,000.

SUGGESTED SOLUTION

1. Journal entries:

a. Jan. 2006   Cash (+A) 400,000

               Common stock (+SE)   400,000

      Sale of no-par common stock ($50 × 8,000 shares = $400,000).

b. Feb. 2006   Cash (+A) 204,000

               Preferred stock (+SE)   200,000

               Capital in excess of par, preferred stock (+SE) ...   4,000

      Sale of preferred stock ($102 × 2,000 shares = $204,000).

c. March 2006   Retained earnings 8,000

               Dividend payable   8,000

               Declared cash dividends.

d. July 2006   Treasury stock (+XSE, −SE) 10,400

               Cash (−A)   10,400

      Purchased 100 shares of preferred stock
      ($104 × 100 shares = $10,400).

e. Aug. 2006   Cash (+A) 2,100

               Treasury stock (−XSE, +SE)   2,080

               Capital in excess of par, preferred stock (+SE) ...   20

      Sold 20 shares of the preferred treasury stock at $105.

2. Stockholders' equity section of the balance sheet:

SHELLY CORPORATION
Balance Sheet
At December 31, 2006

Stockholders' Equity

Contributed capital

   Preferred stock, 5% (par value $100; authorized
     5,000 shares, issued 2,000 shares of which
     80 shares are held as treasury stock) $200,000

   Capital in excess of par, preferred stock   4,020

   Common stock (no-par value; authorized 20,000 shares,
     issued and outstanding 8,000 shares)   400,000

     Total contributed capital   604,020

Retained earnings   23,000

   Total contributed capital and retained earnings   627,020

Less cost of preferred treasury stock held (80 shares)   (8,320)

   Total stockholders' equity $618,700

Chapter Supplement A

Accounting for Owners' Equity for Sole Proprietorships and Partnerships

Owner's Equity for a Sole Proprietorship

A **sole proprietorship** is an unincorporated business owned by one person. Only two owner's equity accounts are needed: (1) a capital account for the proprietor (J. Doe, Capital) and (2) a drawing (or withdrawal) account for the proprietor (J. Doe, Drawings).

The capital account of a sole proprietorship serves two purposes: to record investments by the owner and to accumulate periodic income or loss. The drawing account is used to record the owner's withdrawals of cash or other assets from the business. The drawing account is closed to the capital account at the end of each accounting period. Thus, the capital account reflects the cumulative total of all investments by the owner and all earnings of the entity less all withdrawals from the entity by the owner.

In most respects, the accounting for a sole proprietorship is the same as for a corporation. Exhibit 11.4 presents the recording of selected transactions of Doe Retail Store and the statement of owner's equity.

Selected Entries during 2006

January 1, 2006
J. Doe started a retail store by investing $150,000 of personal savings. The journal entry follows:

Cash (+A) 150,000
   J. Doe, capital (+OE) 150,000

Assets	=	Liabilities	+	Owners' Equity	
Cash + 150,000				J. Doe, capital	+ 150,000

During 2006
Each month during the year, Doe withdrew $1,000 cash from the business for personal living costs. Accordingly, each month the following journal entry was made:

J. Doe, drawings (−OE) 1,000
   Cash (−A) 1,000

Assets	=	Liabilities	+	Owners' Equity	
Cash − 1,000				J. Doe, drawing	− 1,000

Note: At December 31, 2006, after the last withdrawal, the drawings account reflected a debit balance of $12,000.

December 31, 2006
The usual journal entries for the year, including adjusting and closing entries for the revenue and expense accounts, resulted in an $18,000 net income, which were closed to the capital account as follows:

Individual revenue and expense accounts (−R&E) 18,000
   J. Doe, capital (+OE) 18,000

Assets	=	Liabilities	+	Owners' Equity	
				Revenues and expenses	− 18,000
				J. Doe, capital	+ 18,000

EXHIBIT 11.4

Accounting for Owner's Equity for a Sole Proprietorship

EXHIBIT 11.4

concluded

December 31, 2006
The drawings account was closed as follows:

J. Doe, capital (−OE)	12,000
J. Doe, drawings (+OE)	12,000

Assets	=	Liabilities	+	Owners' Equity	
				J. Doe, capital	− 12,000
				J. Doe, drawings	+ 12,000

Balance Sheet December 31, 2006 (partial)

Owner's equity	
J. Doe, capital, January 1, 2006	$150,000
Add: Net income for 2006	18,000
Total	168,000
Less: Withdrawals for 2006	(12,000)
J. Doe, capital, December 31, 2006	$156,000

Because a sole proprietorship does not pay income taxes, its financial statements do not reflect income tax expense or income taxes payable. Instead, the net income of a sole proprietorship is taxed when it is included on the owner's personal income tax return. Likewise, the owner's salary is not recognized as an expense in a sole proprietorship because an employer/employee contractual relationship cannot exist with only one party involved. The owner's salary is therefore accounted for as a distribution of profits (i.e., a withdrawal).

Owners' Equity for a Partnership

The Uniform Partnership Act, which most states have adopted, defines partnership as "an association of two or more persons to carry on as co-owners of a business for profit." Small businesses and professionals such as accountants, doctors, and lawyers often use the partnership form of business.

A partnership is formed by two or more persons reaching mutual agreement about the terms of the relationship. The law does not require an application for a charter as in the case of a corporation. Instead, the agreement between the partners constitutes a partnership contract. This agreement should specify matters such as division of periodic income, management responsibilities, transfer or sale of partnership interests, disposition of assets upon liquidation, and procedures to be followed in case of the death of a partner. If the partnership agreement does not specify these matters, the laws of the resident state are binding.

The primary advantages of a partnership are (1) ease of formation, (2) complete control by the partners, and (3) lack of income taxes on the business itself. The primary disadvantage is the unlimited liability of each partner for the partnership's debts. If the partnership does not have sufficient assets to satisfy outstanding debt, creditors of the partnership can seize the partners' personal assets.

As with a sole proprietorship, accounting for a partnership follows the same underlying principles as any other form of business organization, except for those entries that directly affect owners' equity. Accounting for partners' equity follows the same pattern as for a sole proprietorship, except that separate capital and drawings accounts must be established for each partner. Investments by each partner are credited to that partner's capital account; withdrawals are debited to the respective drawings account. The net income of a partnership is divided among the partners in accordance with the partnership agreement and credited to each account. The respective drawings accounts are closed to the partner capital accounts. After the closing process, each partner's capital account reflects the cumulative total of all of that partner's investments plus that partner's share of the partnership earnings less all that partner's withdrawals.

Exhibit 11.5 presents selected journal entries and partial financial statements for AB Partnership to illustrate the accounting for the distribution of income and partners' equity.

EXHIBIT 11.5

Accounting for
Partners' Equity

Selected Entries during 2006

January 1, 2006

A. Able and B. Baker organized AB Partnership on this date. Able contributed $60,000 and Baker $40,000 cash to the partnership and agreed to divide net income (and net loss) 60% and 40%, respectively. The journal entry for the business to record the investment was as follows:

Cash (+A) 100,000
    A. Able, capital (+OE) 60,000
    B. Baker, capital (+OE) 40,000

Assets	=	Liabilities	+	Owners' Equity	
Cash +100,000				A. Able, capital	+ 60,000
				B. Baker, capital	+ 40,000

During 2006

The partners agreed that Able would withdraw $1,000 and Baker $650 per month in cash. Accordingly, each month the following journal entry was made:

A. Able, drawings (−OE) 1,000
B. Baker, drawings (−OE) 650
    Cash (−A) 1,650

Assets	=	Liabilities	+	Owners' Equity	
Cash −1,650				A. Able, drawings	− 1,000
				B. Baker, drawings	− 650

December 31, 2006

Assume that the normal closing entries for the revenue and expense accounts resulted in a net income of $30,000. The partnership agreement specified Able would receive 60% of earnings and Baker would get 40%. The closing entry was as follows:

Individual revenue and expense accounts (−R&E) 30,000
    A. Able, capital (+OE) 18,000
    B. Baker, capital (+OE) 12,000

Assets	=	Liabilities	+	Owners' Equity	
				Revenues and expenses	− 30,000
				A. Able, capital	+ 18,000
				B. Baker, capital	+ 12,000

December 31, 2006

The journal entry required to close the drawings accounts follows:

A. Able, capital (−OE) 12,000
B. Baker, capital (−OE) 7,800
    A. Able, drawings (+OE) 12,000
    B. Baker, drawings (+OE) 7,800

EXHIBIT 11.5

concluded

Assets	=	Liabilities	+	Owners' Equity	
				A. Able, capital	−12,000
				B. Baker, capital	− 7,800
				A. Able, drawings	+12,000
				B. Baker, drawings	+ 7,800

A separate statement of partners' capital, similar to the following, is customarily prepared to supplement the balance sheet:

AB PARTNERSHIP
Statement of Partners' Capital
For the Year Ended December 31, 2006

	A. Able	B. Baker	Total
Investment, January 1, 2006	$60,000	$40,000	$100,000
Add: Additional investments during the year	0	0	0
Net income for the year	18,000	12,000	30,000
Totals	78,000	52,000	130,000
Less: Drawings during the year	(12,000)	(7,800)	(19,800)
Partners' equity, December 31, 2006	$66,000	$44,200	$110,200

The financial statements of a partnership follow the same format as those for a corporation except that (1) the income statement includes an additional section entitled *Distribution of Net Income,* (2) the partners' equity section of the balance sheet is detailed for each partner, (3) the partnership has no income tax expense because partnerships do not pay income tax (partners must report their share of the partnership profits on their individual tax returns), and (4) salaries paid to the partners are not recorded as expenses but are treated as distributions of earnings.

CHAPTER TAKE-AWAYS

1. **Explain the role of stock in the capital structure of a corporation.** p. 562

   The law recognizes corporations as separate legal entities. Owners invest in a corporation and receive capital stock that can be traded on established stock exchanges. Stock provides a number of rights, including the right to receive dividends.

2. **Analyze the earnings per share ratio.** p. 564

   The earnings per share ratio facilitates the comparison of a company's earnings over time or with other companies' at a single point in time. By expressing earnings on a per share basis, differences in the size of companies becomes less important.

3. **Describe the characteristics of common stock and analyze transactions affecting common stock.** p. 565

   Common stock is the basic voting stock issued by a corporation. Usually it has a par value, but no-par stock can be issued. Common stock offers some special rights that appeal to certain investors.

   A number of key transactions involve capital stock: (1) initial sale of stock, (2) treasury stock transactions, (3) cash dividends, and (4) stock dividends and stock splits. Each is illustrated in this chapter.

4. **Discuss dividends and analyze transactions.** p. 569

The return associated with an investment in capital stock comes from two sources: appreciation and dividends. Dividends are recorded as a liability when they are declared by the board of directors (i.e., on the date of declaration). The liability is satisfied when the dividends are paid (i.e., on the date of payment).

5. **Analyze the dividend yield ratio.** p. 569

The dividend yield ratio measures the percentage of return on an investment from dividends. For most companies, the return associated with dividends is very small.

6. **Discuss the purpose of stock dividends, stock splits, and report transactions.** p. 572

Stock dividends are pro rata distributions of a company's stock to existing owners. The transaction involves transferring an additional amount into the common stock account. A stock split also involves the distribution of additional shares to owners but no additional amount is transferred into the common stock account. Instead, the par value of the stock is reduced.

7. **Describe the characteristics of preferred stock and analyze transactions affecting preferred stock.** p. 574

Preferred stock provides investors certain advantages including dividend preferences and a preference on asset distributions in the event the corporation is liquidated.

8. **Discuss the impact of capital stock transactions on cash flows.** p. 576

Both inflows (e.g., the issuance of capital stock) and outflows (e.g., the purchase of treasury stock) are reported in the Financing Activities section of the statement of cash flows. The payment of dividends is reported as an outflow in this section.

This chapter concludes a major section of the book. In the previous several chapters, we have discussed individual sections of the balance sheet. We will now shift our focus to a common business transaction that affects many accounts on each of the financial statements. For a number of strategic reasons, businesses often invest in other businesses. In the next chapter, you will see why companies invest in other companies and how those investments affect their financial statements.

KEY **RATIOS**

The **earnings per share** ratio states the net income of a corporation on a per share of common stock basis. The ratio is computed as follows (p. 564):

$$\text{Earnings per Share} = \frac{\text{Net Income}}{\text{Average Number of Shares of Common Stock Outstanding}}$$

The **dividend yield ratio** measures the dividend return on the current price of the stock. The ratio is computed as follows (p. 569):

$$\text{Dividend Yield Ratio} = \frac{\text{Dividends per Share}}{\text{Market Price per Share}}$$

FINDING **FINANCIAL INFORMATION**

Balance Sheet

Under Current Liabilities

Dividends, once declared by the board of directors, are reported as a liability (usually current).

Under Noncurrent Liabilities

Transactions involving capital stock do not generate noncurrent liabilities.

Under Stockholders' Equity

Typical accounts include
  Preferred stock
  Common stock
  Capital in excess of par
  Retained earnings
  Treasury stock

Income Statement

Capital stock is never shown on the income statement. Dividends paid are not an expense. They are a distribution of income and are, therefore, not reported on the income statement.

Statement of Cash Flows

Under Financing Activities

+ Cash inflows from initial sale of stock
+ Cash inflows from sale of treasury stock
− Cash outflows for dividends
− Cash outflows for purchase of treasury stock

Statement of Stockholders' Equity

This statement reports detailed information concerning stockholders' equity, including
  (1) amounts in each equity account,
  (2) number of shares outstanding,
  (3) impact of transactions such as earning income, payment of dividends, and purchase of treasury stock.

Notes

Under Summary of Significant Accounting Policies

Usually, very little information concerning capital stock is provided in this summary.

Under a Separate Note

Most companies report information about their stock option plans and information about major transactions such as stock dividends or significant treasury stock transactions. An historical summary of dividends paid per share is typically provided. Any dividends in arrears would also be disclosed.

KEY **TERMS**

QUESTIONS

1. Define the term *corporation* and identify the primary advantages of this form of business organization.
2. What is the charter of a corporation?
3. Explain each of the following terms: (a) authorized capital stock, (b) issued capital stock, and (c) outstanding capital stock.

4. Differentiate between common stock and preferred stock.
5. Explain the distinction between par value and no-par value capital stock.
6. What are the usual characteristics of preferred stock?
7. What are the two basic sources of stockholders' equity? Explain each.
8. Owners' equity is accounted for by source. What does *source* mean?
9. Define *treasury stock*. Why do corporations acquire treasury stock?
10. How is treasury stock reported on the balance sheet? How is the "gain or loss" on treasury stock that has been sold reported on the financial statements?
11. What are the two basic requirements to support the declaration of a cash dividend? What are the effects of a cash dividend on assets and stockholders' equity?
12. Differentiate between cumulative and noncumulative preferred stock.
13. Define *stock dividend*. How does a stock dividend differ from a cash dividend?
14. What are the primary reasons for issuing a stock dividend?
15. Identify and explain the three important dates with respect to dividends.
16. Define *retained earnings*. What are the primary components of retained earnings at the end of each period?
17. What does restrictions on retained earnings mean?

MULTIPLE-CHOICE QUESTIONS

1. Which feature is not applicable to common stock ownership?
   a. right to receive dividends before preferred stock shareholders
   b. right to participate in management through voting
   c. right to receive residual assets upon liquidation of the company
   d. All of the above are features of common stock ownership.
2. Which statement regarding treasury stock is false?
   a. Treasury stock is considered to be issued but not outstanding.
   b. Treasury stock has no voting, dividend, or liquidation rights.
   c. Treasury stock reduces total equity on the balance sheet.
   d. None of the above are false.
3. Which of the following statements about stock dividends is true?
   a. Stock dividends are reported on the statement of cash flow.
   b. Stock dividends are reported on the statement of retained earnings.
   c. Stock dividends increase total equity.
   d. Stock dividends decrease total equity.
4. Which order best describes the largest number of shares to the smallest number of shares?
   a. shares authorized, shares issued, shares outstanding
   b. shares issued, shares outstanding, shares authorized
   c. shares outstanding, shares issued, shares authorized
   d. shares in the treasury, shares outstanding, shares issued
5. Which combination would be the best for an investor when shopping for a new stock?
   a. high dividend yield ratio, high earnings per share
   b. low dividend yield ratio, high earnings per share
   c. high dividend yield ratio, low earnings per share
   d. low dividend yield ratio, low earnings per share
6. A journal entry is not recorded on what date?
   a. date of declaration
   b. date of record
   c. date of payment
   d. A journal entry is recorded on all of these dates.
7. Which section of the statement of cash flows would include cash payments for the purchase of treasury stock?
   a. Operating
   b. Investing
   c. Financing
   d. This transaction would be reported only in the footnotes.

8. Which statement regarding dividends is false?
    a. Dividends represent a sharing of corporate profits with owners.
    b. Both stock and cash dividends reduce retained earnings.
    c. Cash dividends paid to stockholders reduce net income.
    d. None of the above statements are false.
9. When treasury stock is purchased with cash, what is the impact on the balance sheet equation?
    a. No change: the reduction of the asset Cash is offset with the addition of the asset Treasury Stock.
    b. Assets decrease and Stockholders' Equity increases.
    c. Assets increase and Stockholders' Equity decreases.
    d. Assets decrease and Stockholders' Equity decreases.
10. Does a stock dividend increase an investor's personal wealth immediately?
    a. no, because the stock price falls when a stock dividend is issued
    b. yes, because the investor has more shares
    c. yes, because the investor acquired additional shares without paying a brokerage fee
    d. yes, because the investor will receive more in cash dividends by owning more shares

For more practice with multiple-choice questions, go to the text website www.mhhe.com/libby5e or the Topic Tackler DVD for use with this text.

MINI-EXERCISES

 Available with McGraw-Hill's Homework Manager

M11-1
LO1

Evaluating Stockholders' Right

Name three rights of stockholders. Which of these is most important in your opinion? Why?

M11-2
LO1

Computing the Number of Unissued Shares

The balance sheet for Crutcher Corporation reported 147,000 shares outstanding, 200,000 shares authorized, and 10,000 shares in treasury stock. Compute the maximum number of new shares that Crutcher could issue.

M11-3
LO3

Recording the Sale of Common Stock

To expand operations, Aragon Consulting issued 100,000 shares of previously unissued stock with a par value of $1. The selling price for the stock was $75 per share. Record the sale of this stock. Would your answer be different if the par value was $2 per share? If so, record the sale of stock with a par value of $2.

M11-4
LO1, 3, 7

Comparing Common Stock and Preferred Stock

Your parents have just retired and have asked you for some financial advice. They have decided to invest $100,000 in a company very similar to Outback Steakhouse. The company has issued both common and preferred stock. What factors would you consider in giving them advice? Which type of stock would you recommend?

M11-5
LO3

Determining the Effects of Treasury Stock Transactions

Trans Union Corporation purchased 20,000 shares of its own stock for $45 per share. The next year, the company sold 5,000 shares for $50 per share and the following year, it sold 10,000 shares for $37 per share. Determine the impact (increase, decrease, or no change) of each of these transactions on the following classifications:

1. Total assets.
2. Total liabilities.
3. Total stockholders' equity.
4. Net income.

Determining the Amount of a Dividend

Jacobs Company has 300,000 shares of common stock authorized, 270,000 shares issued, and 50,000 shares of treasury stock. The company's board of directors declares a dividend of 50 cents per share. What is the total amount of the dividend that will be paid?

M11-6
LO4

Recording Dividends

On April 15, 2006, the board of directors for Auction.com declared a cash dividend of 20 cents per share payable to stockholders of record on May 20. The dividends will be paid on June 14. The company has 500,000 shares of stock outstanding. Prepare any necessary journal entries for each date.

M11-7
LO4

Determining the Amount of a Preferred Dividend

Colliers, Inc., has 200,000 shares of cumulative preferred stock outstanding. The preferred stock pays dividends in the amount of $2 per share but because of cash flow problems, the company did not pay any dividends last year. The board of directors plans to pay dividends in the amount of $1 million this year. What amount will go to preferred stockholders?

M11-8
LO7

Determining the Impact of Stock Dividends and Stock Splits

Armstrong Tools, Inc., announced a 100 percent stock dividend. Determine the impact (increase, decrease, no change) of this dividend on the following:

M11-9
LO6

1. Total assets.
2. Total liabilities.
3. Common stock.
4. Total stockholders' equity.
5. Market value per share of common stock.
6. Assume that the company announced a 2-for-1 stock split. Determine the impact of the stock split.

Recording a Stock Dividend

Shriver Food Systems, Inc., has issued a 50 percent stock dividend. The company has 800,000 shares authorized and 200,000 shares outstanding. The par value of the stock is $5 per share, and the market value is $100 per share. Record the payment of this stock dividend.

M11-10
LO6

 Available with McGraw-Hill's Homework Manager

EXERCISES

Computing Shares Outstanding

The annual report for Altria Group, Inc., disclosed that 4 billion shares of common stock have been authorized. At the end of last year, 2,805,961,317 shares had been issued and the number of shares in treasury stock was 380,474,028. During the current year, no additional shares were issued, but additional shares were purchased for treasury stock and shares were sold from treasury stock. The net change was a decrease of 5,047,286 shares of treasury stock. Determine the number of shares outstanding at the end of the current year.

E11-1
LO1
Altria Group, Inc.

Computing Number of Shares

The charter of Mansfield Corporation specifies that it may issue 250,000 shares of common stock. Since the company was incorporated, it has sold a total of 200,000 shares to the public but bought back a total of 20,000. The par value of the stock is $1 and the stock was sold at an average price of $20. When the stock was bought back from the public, the market price was $22.

E11-2
LO1

Required:
1. Determine the authorized shares.
2. Determine the issued shares.
3. Determine the outstanding shares.

E11-3
LO1, 3, 7

Determining the Effects of the Issuance of Common and Preferred Stock

Kelly, Incorporated, was issued a charter on January 15, 2006, that authorized the following capital stock:

Common stock, no-par, 100,000 shares.

Preferred stock, 7 percent, par value $10 per share, 5,000 shares.

The board of directors established a stated value on the no-par common stock of $6 per share. During 2006, the following selected transactions were completed in the order given:

a. Sold and issued 20,000 shares of the no-par common stock at $18 cash per share.
b. Sold and issued 3,000 shares of preferred stock at $22 cash per share.
c. At the end of 2006, the accounts showed net income of $38,000.

Required:
1. Prepare the stockholders' equity section of the balance sheet at December 31, 2006.
2. Assume that you are a common stockholder. If Kelly needed additional capital, would you prefer to have it issue additional common stock or additional preferred stock? Explain.

E11-4
LO1, 3

Reporting Stockholders' Equity

The financial statements for Texas Media Corporation included the following selected information:

Common Stock	$1,500,000
Retained earnings	850,000
Net income	1,200,000
Shares issued	100,000
Shares outstanding	90,000
Dividends declared and paid	800,000

The common stock was sold at a price of $20 per share.

Required:
1. What is the amount of capital in excess of par?
2. What was the amount of retained earnings at the beginning of the year?
3. How many shares are in treasury stock?
4. Compute earnings per share.

E11-5
LO1, 3, 4

Reporting Stockholders' Equity and Determining Dividend Policy

Butler Corporation was organized in 2006 to operate a financial consulting business. The charter authorized the following capital stock: common stock, par value $8 per share, 12,000 shares. During the first year, the following selected transactions were completed:

a. Sold and issued 6,000 shares of common stock for cash at $20 per share.
b. Sold and issued 2,000 shares of common stock for cash at $23 per share.
c. At year-end, the accounts reflected a $7,000 loss. Because a loss was incurred, no income tax expense was recorded.

Required:
1. Give the journal entry required for each of these transactions.
2. Prepare the stockholders' equity section as it should be reported on the year-end balance sheet.
3. Can the company pay dividends at this time? Explain.

E11-6
LO1, 3

Finding Amounts Missing from the Stockholders' Equity Section

The stockholders' equity section on the December 31, 2006, balance sheet of Garland Turkey Processors Corporation follows:

Stockholders' Equity

Contributed capital	
Common stock ($1 par; authorized 200,000 shares, issued ? shares)	150,000
Capital in excess of par	200,000
Retained earnings	250,000
Cost of treasury stock (1,000 shares)	(50,000)

Required:
Complete the following statements and show your computations.
1. The number of shares of common stock issued was _____ .
2. The number of shares of common stock outstanding was _____ .
3. The average sales price of the common stock outstanding is $_____ per share.
4. Have the treasury stock transactions (a) increased corporate resources or (b) decreased resources? _____ By how much? _____ .
5. The treasury stock transactions increased (decreased) stockholders' equity by _____ .
6. How much did the treasury stock held cost per share? $_____ .
7. Total stockholders' equity is $_____ .

Reporting Stockholders' Equity

E11-7
LO1, 3

Travis Corporation was organized in 2006 to operate a tax preparation business. The charter authorized the following capital stock: common stock, par value $1 per share, 50,000 shares. During the first year, the following selected transactions were completed:

a. Sold and issued 10,000 shares of common stock for cash at $50 per share.
b. Bought 1,000 shares from a stockholder for cash at $52 per share.

Required:
1. Give the journal entry required for each of these transactions.
2. Prepare the stockholders' equity section as it should be reported on the year-end balance sheet.

Determining the Effects of Transactions on Stockholders' Equity

E11-8
LO1, 3, 7

Shelby Corporation was organized in January 2006 by 10 stockholders to operate an air conditioning sales and service business. The charter issued by the state authorized the following capital stock:

Common stock, $1 par value, 200,000 shares.

Preferred stock, $10 par value, 6 percent, 50,000 shares.

During January and February 2006, the following stock transactions were completed:

a. Collected $40,000 cash from each of the 10 organizers and issued 2,000 shares of common stock to each of them.
b. Sold 15,000 shares of preferred stock at $25 per share; collected the cash and immediately issued the stock.

Required:
Net income for 2006 was $40,000; cash dividends declared and paid at year-end were $10,000. Prepare the stockholders' equity section of the balance sheet at December 31, 2006.

Determining the Effects of Transactions on Stockholders' Equity

E11-9
LO1, 3, 7

Carter Corporation was organized in January 2006 to operate several car repair businesses in a large metropolitan area. The charter issued by the state authorized the following capital stock:

Common stock, $10 par value, 100,000 shares.

Preferred stock, $50 par value, 8 percent, 50,000 shares.

During January and February 2006, the following stock transactions were completed:

a. Sold 80,000 shares of common stock at $25 per share and collected cash.
b. Sold 15,000 shares of preferred stock at $75 per share; collected the cash and immediately issued the stock.
c. Bought 5,000 shares of common stock from a current stockholder for $30 per share.

Required:
Net income for 2006 was $80,000; cash dividends declared and paid at year-end were $30,000. Prepare the stockholders' equity section of the balance sheet at December 31, 2006.

Recording Stockholders' Equity Transactions

E11-10
LO3, 7

Electronic Teacher Corporation obtained a charter at the start of 2006 that authorized 50,000 shares of no-par common stock and 20,000 shares of preferred stock, par value $10. The corporation was organized by four individuals who received shares of the common stock. The remaining shares were to be sold to other individuals at $40 per share on a cash basis. During 2006, the following selected transactions occurred:

a. Collected $15 per share cash from the four organizers and issued 4,000 shares of common stock to each of them.

b. Sold and issued 6,000 shares of common stock to an outsider at $40 cash per share.

c. Sold and issued 8,000 shares of preferred stock at $20 cash per share.

Required:
1. Give the journal entries indicated for each of these transactions.
2. Is it ethical to sell stock to outsiders at a higher price than the amount paid by the organizers?

E11-11
LO1, 3, 7

Finding Amounts Missing from the Stockholders' Equity Section

The stockholders' equity section on the December 31, 2006, balance sheet of Chemfast Corporation follows:

Stockholders' Equity	
Contributed capital	
Preferred stock (par $20; authorized 10,000 shares,	
? issued, of which 500 shares are held as treasury stock)	$104,000
Common stock (no-par; authorized 20,000 shares,	
issued and outstanding 8,000 shares)	600,000
Capital in excess of par, preferred	14,300
Contributed capital, treasury stock transactions	1,500
Retained earnings	30,000
Cost of treasury stock, preferred	(9,500)

Required:
Complete the following statements and show your computations.
1. The number of shares of preferred stock issued was _____ .
2. The number of shares of preferred stock outstanding was _____ .
3. The average sales price of the preferred stock when issued was $_____ per share.
4. Have the treasury stock transactions (a) increased corporate resources or (b) decreased resources? _____ By how much? _____ .
5. The treasury stock transactions increased (decreased) stockholders' equity by _____ .
6. How much did the treasury stock held cost per share? $_____ .
7. Total stockholders' equity is $_____ .
8. The average issue price of the common stock was $_____ .

E11-12
LO1, 3, 4
Procter & Gamble

Finding Information Missing from an Annual Report

Procter & Gamble is a $38 billion company that sells products that are part of most of our daily lives, including Mr. Clean, Cheer, Crest, Vicks, Scope, Pringles, Folgers, Vidal Sassoon, Zest, and Charmin. The annual report for P&G contained the following information:

a. Retained earnings at the end of 2003 totaled $13,611 million.
b. Net income for 2004 was $6,481 million.
c. Par value of the stock is $1 per share.
d. Cash dividends declared in 2004 were $0.934 per share.
e. The Common Stock, Par Value account totaled $2,544 million at the end of 2004 and $2,594 at the end of 2003.

Required: (Assume that no other information concerning stockholders' equity is relevant.)
1. Estimate the number of shares issued at the end of 2004.
2. Estimate the amount of retained earnings at the end of 2003.

E11-13
LO3, 4
Winnebago

Analyzing the Repurchase of Stock

Winnebago is a familiar name on vehicles traveling U.S. highways. The company manufactures and sells large motor homes for vacation travel. These motor homes can be quickly recognized because of the company's "flying W" trademark. A recent news article contained the following information:

The Company's profits have been running double a year ago, revenues were up 27 percent in the May quarter and order backlog stands at 2,229 units. Those are the kind of growth statistics that build confidence in the boardroom. The Company has announced plans to spend $3.6 million to expand its manufacturing facilities and it recently authorized repurchase of $15 million worth of its own shares, the third buyback in two years. The Company's stock is now selling for $25 per share.

Required:
1. Determine the impact of the stock repurchase on the financial statements.
2. Why do you think the board decided to repurchase the stock?
3. What impact will this purchase have on Winnebago's future dividend obligations?

Preparing a Statement of Stockholders' Equity and Evaluating Dividend Policy

E11-14
LO1, 3, 4, 5

The following account balances were selected from the records of Blake Corporation at December 31, 2006, after all adjusting entries were completed:

Common stock (par $15; authorized 100,000 shares, issued 35,000 shares, of which 1,000 shares are held as treasury stock)	$525,000
Capital in excess of par	180,000
Dividends declared and paid in 2006	18,000
Retained earnings, January 1, 2006	76,000
Treasury stock at cost (1,000 shares)	20,000

Net income for the year was $28,000. Restriction on retained earnings equal to the cost of treasury stock held is required by law in this state. The stock price is currently $22.43 per share.

Required:
1. Prepare the stockholders' equity section of the balance sheet at December 31, 2006.
2. Compute and evaluate the dividend yield ratio. Determine the number of shares of stock that received dividends.

Recording Treasury Stock Transactions and Analyzing Their Impact

E11-15
LO3

During 2006 the following selected transactions affecting stockholders' equity occurred for Jacobs Corporation:

a. Apr. 1   Purchased in the market 1,000 shares of the company's own common stock at $50 per share.
b. Jun. 14   Sold 500 shares of treasury stock for $60 cash per share.
c. Sept. 1   Sold 100 shares of treasury stock for $40 cash per share.

Required:
1. Give the journal entries for each of the three transactions.
2. Describe the impact, if any, that these transactions have on the income statement.

Recording Treasury Stock Transactions and Analyzing Their Impact

E11-16
LO3, 4, 8

During 2006 the following selected transactions affecting stockholders' equity occurred for Italy Corporation:

a. Feb. 1   Purchased in the open market 200 shares of the company's own common stock at $22 cash per share.
b. Jul. 15   Sold 100 of the shares purchased on February 1 for $24 cash per share.
c. Sept. 1   Sold 60 more of the shares purchased on February 1 for $20 cash per share.

Required:
1. Give the indicated journal entries for each of the three transactions.
2. What impact does the purchase of treasury stock have on dividends paid?
3. What impact does the sale of treasury stock for an amount higher than the purchase price have on net income and the statement of cash flows?

Analyzing the Impact of Dividend Policy

E11-17
LO4, 6

McDonald and Associates is a small manufacturer of electronic connections for local area networks. Consider three independent situations.

Case 1: McDonald increases its cash dividends by 50 percent, but no other changes occur in the company's operations.

Case 2: The company's income and cash flows increase by 50 percent, but this does not change its dividends.

Case 3: McDonald issues a 50 percent stock dividend, but no other changes occur.

Required:
1. How do you think each situation would affect the company's stock price?
2. If the company changed its accounting policies and reported higher net income, would the change have an impact on the stock price?

E11-18
LO4, 7

Computing Dividends on Preferred Stock and Analyzing Differences

The records of Hoffman Company reflected the following balances in the stockholders' equity accounts at December 31, 2005:

Common stock, par $12 per share, 40,000 shares outstanding.

Preferred stock, 8 percent, par $10 per share, 6,000 shares outstanding.

Retained earnings, $220,000.

On September 1, 2006, the board of directors was considering the distribution of a $62,000 cash dividend. No dividends were paid during the previous two years. You have been asked to determine dividend amounts under two independent assumptions (show computations):

a. The preferred stock is noncumulative.
b. The preferred stock is cumulative.

Required:
1. Determine the total and per share amounts that would be paid to the common stockholders and to the preferred stockholders under the two independent assumptions.
2. Write a brief memo to explain why the dividends per share of common stock were less for the second assumption.
3. What factor would cause a more favorable per share result to the common stockholders?

E11-19
LO4, 7

Determining the Impact of Dividends

Average Corporation has the following capital stock outstanding at the end of 2006:

Preferred stock, 6 percent, par $15, outstanding shares, 8,000.

Common stock, par $8, outstanding shares, 30,000.

On October 1, 2006, the board of directors declared dividends as follows:

Preferred stock: Full cash preference amount, payable December 20, 2006.

Common stock: 50 percent common stock dividend issuable December 20, 2006.

On December 20, 2006, the market prices were preferred stock, $40, and common stock, $32.

Required:
Explain the overall effect of each of the dividends on the assets, liabilities, and stockholders' equity of the company.

E11-20
LO4, 7
Sears, Roebuck
and Company

Recording the Payment of Dividends

A recent annual report for Sears, Roebuck and Co. disclosed that the company paid preferred dividends in the amount of $119.9 million. It declared and paid dividends on common stock in the amount of $2 per share. During the year, Sears had 1,000,000,000 shares of common authorized; 387,514,300 shares had been issued; 41,670,000 shares were in treasury stock. Assume that the transaction occurred on July 15.

Required:
Prepare a journal entry to record the declaration and payment of dividends.

Evaluating the Dividend Yield Ratio

Cinergy is a utility company that provides gas and electric service in Ohio, Kentucky, and Indiana. The company's dividend yield is 6.6 percent. Starbucks, a well-known retailer of coffee products, does not pay dividends, resulting in a dividend yield of 0.0 percent. Both companies are approximately the same size with market values of $5 billion.

E11-21
L05
Cinergy

Required:
1. Based on this limited information, why do you think the dividend policies of the two companies are so different?
2. Will the two companies attract different types of investors? Explain.

Analyzing Stock Dividends

At the beginning of the year, the stockholders' equity section of the balance sheet of R & B Corporation reflected the following:

E11-22
L01, 6

Common stock (par $10; authorized 60,000 shares, outstanding 25,000 shares)	$250,000
Capital in excess of par	120,000
Retained earnings	750,000

On February 1, 2006, the board of directors declared a 100 percent stock dividend to be issued April 30, 2006. The market value of the stock on February 1, 2006, was $18 per share.

Required:
1. For comparative purposes, prepare the Stockholders' Equity section of the balance sheet (a) immediately before the stock dividend and (b) immediately after the stock dividend. (*Hint:* Use two amount columns for this requirement.)
2. Explain the effects of this stock dividend on assets, liabilities, and stockholders' equity.

Recording Dividends

Two billion times a day, Procter & Gamble (P&G) brands touch the lives of people around the world. The company has one of the largest and strongest portfolios of trusted, quality brands, including Pampers, Tide, Bounty, Pringles, Folgers, Charmin, Downy, Crest, and Clairol Nice 'n Easy. The P&G community consists of nearly 98,000 employees working in almost 80 countries worldwide. The company has 5,000 million shares of common stock authorized and 2,500 million shares issued and outstanding. Par value is $1 per share. The company issued the following press release:

E11-23
L03
Procter & Gamble

> CINCINNATI, July 13, 2004—The Procter & Gamble Company (NYSE: PG) declared a quarterly dividend of twenty-five cents ($.25) per share on the Common Stock payable on August 16, 2004 to shareholders of record at the close of business on July 23, 2004. P&G has been paying dividends without interruption since incorporation in 1890.

Required:
Prepare journal entries as appropriate for each date mentioned in the press release.

Comparing Stock Dividends and Splits

On July 1, 2006, Jones Corporation had the following capital structure:

E11-24
L06

Common stock (par $1)	$200,000
Capital in excess of par	880,000
Retained earnings	720,000
Treasury stock, none	

Required:
Complete the following comparative tabulation based on two independent cases:

Case 1: The board of directors declared and issued a 50 percent stock dividend when the stock was selling at $4 per share.

Case 2: The board of directors voted a 6-to-5 stock split (i.e., a 20 percent increase in the number of shares). The market price prior to the split was $4 per share.

Items	Before Dividend and Split	After Stock Dividend	After Stock Split
Common stock account	$	$	$
Par per share	$1	$	$
Shares outstanding	#	#	#
Capital in excess of par	$880,000	$	$
Retained earnings	$720,000	$	$
Total stockholders' equity	$	$	$

E11-25   Comparing Stock Dividends and Splits
LO6

Sally Corporation has 50,000 shares of common stock (par value $5) outstanding.

Required:

Complete the following comparative tabulation based on two independent cases:

Case 1: The board of directors declared and issued a 25 percent stock dividend when the stock was selling at $20 per share. The dividend will be accounted for as a large stock dividend.

Case 2: The board of directors voted a 5-to-4 stock split (i.e., a 25 percent increase in the number of shares). The market price prior to the split was $20 per share.

Items	Before Dividend and Split	After Stock Dividend	After Stock Split
Common stock account	$	$	$
Par per share	$5	$	$
Shares outstanding	#	#	#
Capital in excess of par	$300,000	$	$
Retained earnings	$450,000	$	$
Total stockholders' equity	$	$	$

E11-26   Evaluating Dividend Policy
LO4

H&R Block

H&R Block is a well-known name especially during income tax time each year. The company serves more than 18 million taxpayers in more than 10,000 offices in the United States, Canada, Australia, and England. A recent press release contained the following information:

> H&R Block today reported that revenues for the first quarter ended July 31, 1999, climbed 72 percent to $121 million. The company reported a first quarter net loss of $37 million, or 38 cents per share. The Board of Directors declared a quarterly dividend of 27 cents per share payable October 1, 1999, to shareholders of record on September 10, 1999.

Required:
1. Explain why H&R Block can pay dividends despite its loss.
2. What factors did the board of directors consider when it declared the dividends?

E11-27   Analyzing Dividends in Arrears
LO7

Mission Critical Software

Mission Critical Software, Inc., is listed on the NASDAQ and is a leading provider of systems management software for Windows NT network and Internet infrastructure. Like many start-up companies, Mission Critical struggled with cash flows as it developed new business opportunities. A student found a financial statement for Mission Critical that included the following:

The increase in dividends in arrears on preferred stock was $264,000.

The student who read the note suggested that the Mission Critical preferred stock would be a good investment because of the large amount of dividend income that would be earned when the company started paying dividends again: "As the owner of the stock, I'll get dividends for the period I hold the stock plus some previous periods when I didn't even own the stock." Do you agree? Explain.

 Available with McGraw-Hill's Homework Manager

PROBLEMS

Finding Missing Amounts (AP11-1)

P11-1
LO1, 2, 3, 4, 6

At December 31, 2006, the records of Nortech Corporation provided the following selected and incomplete data:

Common stock (par $10; no changes during the year)

Shares authorized, 200,000.

Shares issued, _____ ? _____; issue price $17 per share; cash collected in full, $2,125,000.

Shares held as treasury stock, 3,000 shares, cost $20 per share.

Net income, $118,000.

Dividends declared and paid, $73,200.

Retained earnings balance, January 1, 2006, $155,000.

The treasury stock was acquired after a stock split was issued.

Required:
1. Complete the following tabulation:
   Shares authorized _____ .
   Shares issued _____ .
   Shares outstanding _____ .
2. The balance in the Capital in Excess of Par account appears to be $_____ .
3. Earnings per Share is $_____ .
4. Dividend paid per share of common stock is $_____ .
5. Treasury stock should be reported on the balance sheet under the major caption _____ in the amount of $_____ .
6. Assume that the board of directors voted a 100 percent stock split (the number of shares will double). After the stock split, the par value per share will be $_____ , and the number of outstanding shares will be _____ .
7. Assuming the stock split mentioned above, give any journal entry that should be made. If none, explain why.
8. Disregard the stock split (assumed above). Assume instead that a 10 percent stock dividend was declared and issued when the market price of the common stock was $21. Give any journal entry that should be made.

Preparing the Stockholders' Equity Section of the Balance Sheet

P11-2
LO1, 3, 7
eXcel

Skyhawk Corporation received its charter during January 2006. The charter authorized the following capital stock:

Preferred stock: 8 percent, par $10, authorized 20,000 shares.

Common stock: par $8, authorized 50,000 shares.

During 2006, the following transactions occurred in the order given:

a. Issued a total of 40,000 shares of the common stock to the four organizers at $11 per share.
b. Sold 5,000 shares of the preferred stock at $18 per share.

c. Sold 3,000 shares of the common stock at $14 per share and 1,000 shares of the preferred stock at $28.

d. Net income for the year was $48,000.

Required:

Prepare the stockholders' equity section of the balance sheet at December 31, 2006.

P11-3
LO3, 7

Recording Transactions Affecting Stockholders' Equity (AP11-2)

McGee Corporation began operations in January 2006. The charter authorized the following capital stock:

Preferred stock: 9 percent, $10 par, authorized 40,000 shares.

Common stock: $5 par, authorized 80,000 shares.

During 2006, the following transactions occurred in the order given:

a. Issued 20,000 shares of common stock to each of the three organizers and collected $9 cash per share from each of them.

b. Sold 6,000 shares of the preferred stock at $18 per share.

c. Sold 500 shares of the preferred stock at $20 and 1,000 shares of common stock at $12 per share.

Required:

Give the journal entries indicated for each of these transactions.

P11-4
LO1, 3

Recording Transactions and Comparing Par and No-Par Stock

McNally Company was issued a charter in January 2006, which authorized 100,000 shares of common stock with a par value of $25. During 2006, the following selected transactions occurred in the order given:

a. Issued 9,000 shares of the stock for cash at $60 per share. Collected the cash and issued the stock immediately.

b. Issued 600 shares of stock. Assume a market value per share of $54.

Required:

1. Record the issuance of stock.

2. Should a stockholder care whether a company issues par or no-par value stock? Explain.

P11-5
LO1, 3

Preparing the Stockholders' Equity Section after Selected Transactions (AP11-3)

Worldwide Company obtained a charter from the state in January 2006, which authorized 200,000 shares of common stock, $10 par value. The stockholders were 30 local citizens. During the first year, the company earned $38,200 and the following selected transactions occurred in the order given:

a. Sold 60,000 shares of the common stock to the 30 stockholders at $12 per share.

b. Purchased 2,000 shares at $15 cash per share from one of the 30 stockholders who needed cash and wanted to sell the stock back to the company.

c. Resold 1,000 of the shares of the treasury stock purchased in transaction *b* two months later to another individual at $18 cash per share.

Required:

Prepare the stockholders' equity section of the balance sheet at December 31, 2006.

P11-6
LO3, 4, 6
Halliburton

Recording Stockholders' Equity Transactions (AP11-4)

Halliburton is a large multinational corporation with extensive operations in energy-related areas. The annual report for Halliburton reported the following transactions affecting stockholders' equity:

a. Purchased $3.5 million in treasury stock.

b. Declared and paid cash dividends in the amount of $254.2 million.

c. Issued 2-for-1 common stock dividend. 222.5 million additional shares were issued with a total par value of $556.3 million.

Required:

Prepare journal entries to record each of these transactions.

Analyzing Stockholders' Equity Transactions, Including Treasury Stock

P11-7
LO3, 4, 6

1. Compare a stock dividend with a cash dividend.
2. Compare a large stock dividend with a small stock dividend.
3. Describe the impact of the sale of treasury stock for more than cost on the income statement and the statement of cash flows.
4. Explain why a company might purchase treasury stock.

Comparing Stock and Cash Dividends (AP11-5)

P11-8
LO4, 6, 7

e**X**cel

Water Tower Company had the following stock outstanding and retained earnings at December 31, 2006:

Common stock (par $8; outstanding, 30,000 shares)	$240,000
Preferred stock, 7% (par $10; outstanding, 6,000 shares)	60,000
Retained earnings	280,000

The board of directors is considering the distribution of a cash dividend to the two groups of stockholders. No dividends were declared during the previous two years. Three independent cases are assumed:

Case A: The preferred stock is noncumulative; the total amount of dividends is $30,000.

Case B: The preferred stock is cumulative; the total amount of dividends is $12,600.

Case C: Same as Case B, except the amount is $66,000.

Required:
1. Compute the amount of dividends, in total and per share, that would be payable to each class of stockholders for each case. Show computations.
2. Assume the company issued a 30 percent common stock dividend on the outstanding shares when the market value per share was $24. Complete the following comparative schedule including explanation of the comparative differences.

	AMOUNT OF DOLLAR INCREASE (DECREASE)	
Item	Cash Dividend—Case C	Stock Dividend
Assets	$	$
Liabilities	$	$
Stockholders' equity	$	$

Analyzing Dividend Policy

P11-9
LO4
Compaq

Dana and David, two young financial analysts, were reviewing financial statements for Compaq, one of the world's largest manufacturers of personal computers. Dana noted that the company did not report any dividends in the Financing Activity section of the statement of cash flows and said, "Just a few years ago, *Forbes* magazine named Compaq as one of the best performing companies. If it's so good, I wonder why it isn't paying any dividends." David wasn't convinced that Dana was looking in the right place for dividends but didn't say anything.

Dana continued the discussion by noting, "When *Forbes* selected it as a best performing company, Compaq's sales doubled over the previous two years just as they doubled over the prior two years. Its income was only $789 million that year compared with $867 million the previous year, but cash flow from operating activities was $943 million compared to an outflow of $101 million the prior year."

At that point, David noted that the statement of cash flows reported that Compaq had invested $703 million in new property this year compared with $408 million the prior year. He also was surprised to see that inventory and accounts receivable had increased by $1 billion and nearly $2 billion, respectively, from the previous year. "No wonder it can't pay dividends; it generated less than $1 billion from operating activities and had to put it all back in accounts receivable and inventory."

Required:
1. Correct any misstatements that either Dana or David made. Explain.
2. Which of the factors presented in the case help you understand Compaq's dividend policy?

P11-10
LO4, 6, 7

Determining the Financial Statement Effects of Dividends

Lynn Company has outstanding 60,000 shares of $10 par value common stock and 25,000 shares of $20 par value preferred stock (8 percent). On December 1, 2006, the board of directors voted an 8 percent cash dividend on the preferred stock and a 40 percent stock dividend on the common stock. At the date of declaration, the common stock was selling at $35 and the preferred at $20 per share. The dividends are to be paid, or issued, on February 15, 2007. The annual accounting period ends December 31.

Required:

Explain the comparative effects of the two dividends on the assets, liabilities, and stockholders' equity (a) through December 31, 2006, (b) on February 15, 2007, and (c) the overall effects from December 1, 2006, through February 15, 2007. A schedule similar to the following might be helpful:

	COMPARATIVE EFFECTS EXPLAINED	
Item	Cash Dividend on Preferred	Stock Dividend on Common
1. Through December 31, 2006: Assets, etc.		

P11-11
LO4, 6
Procter & Gamble

Recording Dividends

Proctor & Gamble is a well-known consumer products company that owns a variety of popular brands. A recent news article contained the following information:

> CINCINNATI, March 9, 2004 /PRNewswire-FirstCall/—The Procter & Gamble Company (NYSE: PG) today said that earnings per share for the January through March 2004 quarter as well as the fiscal year are expected to exceed current consensus estimates by $0.01 to $0.02. The increased earnings are being driven by continued strong organic volume growth.
>
> **STOCK DIVIDEND**
>
> The company also announced today that its board of directors approved a 10% stock dividend to shareholders of record on May 21, 2004. This move does not change the proportionate interest a shareholder maintains in the company. The additional shares will be distributed on June 18, 2004. In a separate action, the board declared an increase in the annual rate of its common stock dividend from $1.82 to $2.00 per share.

Required:

1. Prepare any journal entries that P&G should make as the result of information in the preceding report. Assume that the company has 2,500 million shares outstanding, the par value is $1.00 per share, and the market value is $50 per share.
2. What do you think happened to the company's stock price after the announcement?
3. What factors did the board of directors consider in making this decision?

P11-12
eXcel

(Chapter Supplement A) Comparing Stockholders' Equity Sections for Alternative Forms of Organization

Assume for each of the following independent cases that the annual accounting period ends on December 31, 2006, and that the Income Summary account at that date reflected a debit balance (loss) of $20,000.

Case A: Assume that the company is a *sole proprietorship* owned by Proprietor A. Prior to the closing entries, the capital account reflected a credit balance of $50,000 and the drawings account a balance of $8,000.

Case B: Assume that the company is a *partnership* owned by Partner A and Partner B. Prior to the closing entries, the owners' equity accounts reflected the following balances: A, Capital, $40,000; B, Capital, $38,000; A, Drawings, $5,000; and B, Drawings, $9,000. Profits and losses are divided equally.

Case C: Assume that the company is a *corporation*. Prior to the closing entries, the stockholders' equity accounts showed the following: Capital Stock, par $10, authorized 30,000 shares, outstanding 15,000 shares; Capital in excess of Par, $5,000; Retained Earnings, $65,000.

Required:
1. Give all closing entries indicated at December 31, 2006, for each of the separate cases.
2. Show how the owners' equity section of the balance sheet would appear at December 31, 2006, for each case.

ALTERNATE **PROBLEMS**

Finding Missing Amounts (P11-1)

AP11-1
LO1, 2, 3, 4, 6

At December 31, 2006, the records of Kozmetsky Corporation provided the following selected and incomplete data:

Common stock (par $1; no changes during the year)

Shares authorized, 5,000,000.

Shares issued, _____ ? _____ ; issue price $80 per share.

Shares held as treasury stock, 100,000 shares, cost $60 per share.

Net income $4,800,000.

Common stock account $1,500,000.

Dividends declared and paid $2 per share.

Retained earnings balance, January 1, 2006, $82,900,000.

The treasury stock was acquired after a stock split was issued.

Required:
1. Complete the following tabulation:
   Shares issued _____ .
   Shares outstanding _____ .
2. The balance in the Capital in Excess of Par account appears to be $_____ .
3. EPS on net income is $_____ .
4. Total dividends paid on common stock during 2006 is $_____ .
5. Treasury stock should be reported on the balance sheet under the major caption _____ in the amount of $_____ .
6. Assume that the board of directors voted a 100 percent stock split (the number of shares will double). After the stock split, the par value per share will be $_____ , and the number of outstanding shares will be _____ .

Recording Transactions Affecting Stockholders' Equity (P11-3)

AP11-2
LO3, 7

Gerald Company was granted a charter that authorized the following capital stock:

Common stock: 100,000 shares, par value per share is $40.

Preferred stock: 8 percent, par $5, 20,000 shares.

During the first year, 2006, the following selected transactions occurred in the order given:

a. Sold 30,000 shares of the common stock at $40 cash per share and 5,000 shares of the preferred stock at $26 cash per share.
b. Issued 2,000 shares of preferred stock when the stock was selling at $32.
c. Repurchased 3,000 shares of the common stock sold earlier; paid cash, $38 per share.

Required:

Give the journal entries for each of these transactions.

AP11-3
LO1, 3

Preparing the Stockholders' Equity Section After Selected Transactions (P11-5)

Global Marine obtained a charter from the state in January 2006, which authorized 1,000,000 shares of common stock, $5 par value. During the first year, the company earned $429,000, and the following selected transactions occurred in the order given:

a. Sold 700,000 shares of the common stock at $54 per share. Collected the cash and issued the stock.

b. Purchased 25,000 shares at $50 cash per share to use as stock incentives for senior management.

Required:

Prepare the stockholders' equity section of the balance sheet at December 31, 2006.

AP11-4
LO3, 4, 6, 7
Kmart

Recording Stockholders' Equity Transactions (P11-6)

The annual report for Kmart described the following transactions that affected stockholders' equity:

a. Declared cash dividends of $0.92 per share; total dividends were $374 million.
b. Sold series B preferred stock (no par) in the amount of $157 million.
c. Sold treasury stock for $10 million; original cost was $8 million.
d. Issued a 100 percent stock dividend on common stock; its par value was $206 million, and the market value was $784 million.

Required:

Prepare journal entries to record each of these transactions.

AP11-5
LO4, 6, 7

Comparing Stock and Cash Dividends (P11-8)

Ritz Company had the following stock outstanding and retained earnings at December 31, 2006:

Common stock (par $1; outstanding, 500,000 shares)	$500,000
Preferred stock, 8% (par $10; outstanding, 21,000 shares)	210,000
Retained earnings	900,000

The board of directors is considering the distribution of a cash dividend to the two groups of stockholders. No dividends were declared during the previous two years. Three independent cases are assumed:

Case A: The preferred stock is noncumulative; the total amount of dividends is $25,000.

Case B: The preferred stock is cumulative; the total amount of dividends is $25,000.

Case C: Same as Case B, except the amount is $75,000.

Required:

1. Compute the amount of dividends, in total and per share, payable to each class of stockholders for each case. Show computations.
2. Assume that the company issued a 40 percent common stock dividend on the outstanding shares when the market value per share was $50. Complete the following comparative schedule, including explanation of the comparative differences.

	AMOUNT OF DOLLAR INCREASE (DECREASE)	
Item	Cash Dividend—Case C	Stock Dividend
Assets	$	$
Liabilities	$	$
Stockholders' equity	$	$

Annual Report Cases

Finding Financial Information

Refer to the financial statements of PacSun given in Appendix B at the end of this book, or open file PSUN.pdf in the Annual Report Cases directory on the student DVD.

Required:
1. Does the company have any treasury stock? If so, how much?
2. What was the highest price for company stock during the fourth quarter of fiscal year 2004?
3. Does the company pay dividends?
4. Refer to Item 5 from the 10-K. Provide one reason for why the company pays or does not pay dividends.
5. Over the most recent two years, was there a stock dividend or a stock split? If so, describe. (Item 5 from the 10-K may be useful for this question.)
6. What is the par value of the common stock?

CP11-1

LO1, 3, 4, 6

PACIFIC SUNWEAR
OF CALIFORNIA, INC.

Finding Financial Information

Refer to the financial statements of American Eagle Outfitters given in Appendix C at the end of this book, or open file AEOS.pdf in the Annual Report Cases directory on the student DVD.

Required:
(*Hint:* The Statement of Stockholders' Equity may be useful in answering some of the questions.)
1. How many shares of common stock are authorized as of January 29, 2005? How many shares are issued as of January 29, 2005? How many shares are outstanding as of January 29, 2005?
2. Did the company pay dividends during the most recent reporting year? If so, what was the total amount of dividends paid and how much were they per share?
3. Does the company have any treasury stock as of January 29, 2005? If so, how much?
4. Has the company ever issued a stock dividend or a stock split over the past three reporting years? If so, describe.
5. Does the company's common stock have a par value? If it does, what is the par value?

CP11-2

LO1, 3, 4, 6

AMERICAN EAGLE
OUTFITTERS
ae.com

Comparing Companies within an Industry

Refer to the financial statements of PacSun given in Appendix B and American Eagle Outfitters given in Appendix C at the end of this book or open file CP11-3.xls in the Annual Report Cases directory on the student DVD.

Required:
1. Notice that both American Eagle Outfitters and PacSun have split their stock. What was the highest stock price for each company during the last quarter of fiscal 2004? If the companies had not split their stock, what would have been the highest stock prices in the last quarter of fiscal 2004? Why do some companies elect to split their stock?
2. Calculate the dividend yield ratios for PacSun and American Eagle Outfitters for the most recent reporting year. (Use the highest stock price in the last quarter of the most recent reporting year for the market price.)
3. Why would an investor choose to invest in a stock that does not pay dividends?
4. Using the information from the following table, compare the dividend-related industry average ratios for the retail apparel industry to the pharmaceutical industry and the electric utility industry. What type of investor would be interested in buying stock in a utility instead of a retail store? Why?

CP11-3

LO3, 4

PACIFIC SUNWEAR
OF CALIFORNIA, INC.

AMERICAN EAGLE
OUTFITTERS
ae.com

DIVIDEND RATIOS FOR VARIOUS INDUSTRIES

	Retail Apparel	Pharmaceuticals	Electric Utilities
Dividend yield	1.1%	2.6%	3.8%
Example company	The GAP	Eli Lilly	American Electric Power

Financial Reporting and Analysis Cases

CP11-4
LO1, 4
Halliburton

Computing Dividends for an Actual Company

A recent annual report for Halliburton Company contained the following information (dollars in millions):

Stockholders' Equity	Current Year	Previous Year
Common stock, par value $2.50, authorized 2,000 shares	$ 298.3	$ 298.4
Paid-in capital in excess of par	130.5	129.9
Retained earnings	2,080.8	2,052.3
Less 12.8 and 13.0 treasury stock, at cost	382.2	384.7

In the current year, Halliburton declared and paid cash dividends of $1 per share. What would be the total amount of dividends declared and paid if they had been based on the amount of stock outstanding at the end of the year?

CP11-5
LO2, 3

Interpreting the Financial Press

As discussed in the chapter, companies buy back their own stock for a number of reasons. An article on this topic is available on the Libby/Libby/Short website at **www.mhhe.com/libby5e**. You should read the article, "Stock Market Time Bomb,"* and then write a short memo summarizing the article. In general, do you think large stock buybacks are good for investors?

Critical Thinking Cases

CP11-6
LO4, 6

Evaluating an Ethical Dilemma

You are a member of the board of directors of a large company that has been in business for more than 100 years. The company is proud of the fact that it has paid dividends every year it has been in business. Because of this stability, many retired people have invested large portions of their savings in your common stock. Unfortunately, the company has struggled for the past few years as it tries to introduce new products and is considering not paying a dividend this year. The president wants to skip the dividend in order to have more cash to invest in product development: "If we don't invest this money now, we won't get these products to market in time to save the company. I don't want to risk thousands of jobs." One of the most senior board members speaks next: "If we don't pay the dividend, thousands of retirees will be thrown into financial distress. Even if you don't care about them, you have to recognize our stock price will crash when they all sell." The company treasurer proposes an alternative: "Let's skip the cash dividend and pay a stock dividend. We can still say we've had a dividend every year." The entire board now turns to you for your opinion. What should the company do?

CP11-7
LO4

Evaluating an Ethical Dilemma

You are the president of a very successful Internet company that has had a remarkably profitable year. You have determined that the company has more than $10 million in cash generated by operating activities not needed in the business. You are thinking about paying it out to stockholders as a special dividend. You discuss the idea with your vice president, who reacts angrily to your suggestion:

"Our stock price has gone up by 200 percent in the last year alone. What more do we have to do for the owners? The people who really earned that money are the employees who have been working 12 hours a day, six or seven days a week to make the company successful. Most of them didn't even take vacations last year. I say we have to pay out bonuses and nothing extra for the stockholders." As president, you know that you are hired by the board of directors, which is elected by the stockholders. What is your responsibility to both groups? To which group would you give the $10 million?

---

*Reprinted from November 15, 1999 issue of *BusinessWeek* by special permission, copyright © 1999 by McGraw-Hill Companies, Inc.

Financial Reporting and Analysis Team Projects

Team Project: Examining an Annual Report

CP11-8
LO1, 3, 4, 7

As a team, select an industry to analyze. *Reuters* provides lists of industries and their makeup at **www.investor.reuters.com/Industries.aspx**. Each team member should acquire the annual report or 10-K for one publicly traded company in the industry, with each member selecting a different company. (Library files, the SEC EDGAR service at **www.sec.gov**, Compustat CD, and the company itself are good sources.)

Required:

On an individual basis, each team member should write a short report answering the following questions about the selected company. Discuss any patterns across companies that you as a team observe. Then, as a team, write a short report comparing and contrasting your companies.

1.   *a.*   List the accounts and amounts of the company's stockholders' equity.
     b.   From the footnotes, identify any unusual features in its contributed capital accounts (e.g., convertible preferred, nonvoting common, no par value), if any.

2.   What amount of stock was issued in the most recent year? (You will need to refer to the statement of cash flows for the cash proceeds and the statement of stockholders' equity for the amounts in the capital accounts.)
     a.   What was the average market value per share of the issuance?
     b.   Recreate the journal entry for the issuance.

3.   What amount of treasury stock, if any, did the company purchase during the year?

4.   What types of dividends, if any, did the company declare during the year? How much was paid in cash?

LEARNING OBJECTIVES

Reporting and Interpreting Investments in Other Corporations

12

D ow Jones & Co. is best known for its index of stock prices, the Dow Jones Industrial Average. However, the company does much more. It is the largest global provider of business news and information through print and electronic publishing.

Dow Jones's flagship publication, *The Wall Street Journal,* is the largest daily newspaper in the United States, with a circulation of more than 1.7 million. In print publishing, Dow Jones also produces *The Wall Street Journal Europe, The Asian Wall Street Journal, The Wall Street Journal Americas* (to Central and South America), *Barron's* (a business and financial weekly), *Far Eastern Economic Review,* and various financial magazines. The company also owns Ottaway Newspapers, Inc., which publishes 15 general-interest community newspapers.

FOCUS COMPANY:

Dow Jones & Co., Inc.

INVESTMENT STRATEGIES

IN THE MEDIA INDUSTRY

www.dowjones.com

Dow Jones recognizes that new technologies bring increased efficiency to its operations while expanding business opportunities. For example, *The Wall Street Journal* transmits page images to various printing plants via satellite, speeding delivery of material to the presses. Dow Jones also sells business news programming to CNBC and MSNBC. Moreover, the company is one of the leading providers of business and financial news over the World Wide Web. Its principal electronic products include Dow Jones Newswires, Dow Jones Indexes, and Dow Jones Financial Information Services.

Dow Jones has achieved its diversity in part by investing in the stock of other companies. For example, Dow Jones owns half of CNBC Europe, CNBC Asia, Factiva, and *SmartMoney* magazine. The announcement in early 2000 of the merger of two media giants, Time Warner and America Online, brought speculation of how other media companies might respond to the changing nature of the media industry and technology. So far to meet new challenges, Dow Jones continues to seek out opportunities to create joint ventures with existing publishers and news services around the globe. In 2004, Dow Jones signed an agreement with Bennett Coleman & Company Ltd. to publish *The Wall Street Journal of India,* purchased vwd-Vereinigte Wirtschaftsdienste GmbH (Germany's leading provider of real-time financial news, information, and technology), and joined with Prime-Tass, Russia's leading business-news agency, to unveil DJ FOREX, the first Russian-language news service to focus on the foreign-exchange markets.

UNDERSTANDING THE BUSINESS

Many strategic factors motivate managers to invest in securities. A company that has extra cash and simply wants to earn a return on the idle funds can invest those funds in the stocks and bonds of other companies, either long- or short-term. We say these investments are passive because the managers are not interested in influencing or controlling the other companies. Dow Jones's 2003 balance sheet, shown in Exhibit 12.1, does not reflect any short-term investments but does report a long-term Other Investments account.

EXHIBIT 12.1 **Dow Jones & Company Balance Sheet**

DOW JONES & COMPANY
Consolidated Balance Sheet
December 31, 2003 and 2002

(dollars in thousands)	2003	2002		2003	2002
Assets:			**Liabilities:**		
Current Assets:			Current Liabilities:		
Cash and cash equivalents	$ 23,514	$ 39,346	Accounts payable—trade	$ 65,732	$ 55,285
Accounts receivable—trade, net of allowance for doubtful accounts of $5,229 in 2003 and $5,220 in 2002	157,750	146,305	Accrued wages, salaries and commissions	63,240	69,967
			Retirement plan contributions payable	24,224	23,850
Accounts receivable—other	17,522	23,779	Other payables	71,287	130,373
Newsprint inventory	12,315	9,698	Contract guarantee obligation	164,642	111,619
Prepaid expenses	20,055	16,704	Income taxes	32,987	40,816
Deferred income taxes	14,723	14,772	Unearned revenue	191,411	190,569
Total current assets	245,879	250,604	Total current liabilities	613,523	622,479
			Long-term debt	153,110	92,937
Investments in associated companies, at equity	89,230	83,619	Deferred compensation, principally postretirement benefit obligation	288,364	294,831
Other investments	14,558	5,587	Contract guarantee obligation	89,083	132,584
			Other noncurrent liabilities	23,834	33,696
Plant and property, at cost			Total liabilities	1,167,914	1,176,527
Land	22,173	21,652	Minority Interests in Subsidiaries	6,579	561
Buildings and improvements	431,365	426,540	**Stockholders' Equity:**		
Equipment	1,243,122	1,222,946	Common stock	81,494	81,405
Construction in progress	35,214	20,399	Common stock, class B	20,687	20,776
	1,731,874	1,691,537	Additional paid-in capital	122,012	120,645
Less accumulated depreciation	1,042,590	970,836	Retained earnings	821,733	732,720
	689,284	720,701	Accumulated other comprehensive income:		
			Unrealized gain on investments	5,683	1,565
Goodwill	153,320	56,251	Unrealized gain on hedging	453	2,059
Other intangible assets, less accumulated amortization of $3,138 in 2003 and $1,297 in 2002	70,124	6,779	Foreign currency translation adjustment	3,817	266
			Minimum pension liability	(223)	(9,979)
				1,055,656	949,457
			Less, treasury stock (at cost)	925,995	918,886
Deferred income taxes	17,394	71,643	Total stockholders' equity	129,661	30,571
Other assets	24,365	12,475			
Total assets	$1,304,154	$1,207,659	Total liabilities and stockholders' equity	$1,304,154	$1,207,659

Sometimes a company decides to invest in another company with the purpose of influencing that company's policies and activities. Dow Jones's balance sheet reports these types of investments as "Investments in Associated Companies." Finally, managers may determine that controlling another company, either by purchasing it directly or becoming the majority shareholder, is desirable. In this case, the two companies' financial reports are combined into consolidated financial statements, as Dow Jones has done (see the title to its "consolidated" balance sheet). In the notes to the annual report, we find that Dow Jones's recent acquisitions include Technologic Partners (with eight online newsletters) and *The Record of Stockton* newspaper in California.

In this chapter, we discuss the accounting for four types of investments. First, we discuss using the amortized cost method to account for passive investments in bonds. Second, we examine the market value method of accounting for passive investments in stocks. Third, we present the equity method used to account for stock held to exert significant influence. The chapter closes with a discussion of accounting for mergers and consolidated statements.

ORGANIZATION of the Chapter

Types of Investments and Accounting Methods	Debt Held to Maturity: Amortized Cost Method	Passive Stock Investments: Market Value Method	Investments for Significant Influence: Equity Method	Controlling Interests: Mergers and Acquisitions
■ Passive Investments in Debt and Equity Securities ■ Investments in Stock for Significant Influence ■ Investments in Stock for Control	■ Bond Purchases ■ Interest Earned ■ Principal at Maturity	■ Classifying Passive Stock Investments ■ Securities Available for Sale ■ Comparing Trade and Available-for-Sale Securities	■ Recording Investments Under the Equity Method ■ Reporting Investments Under the Equity Method	■ What Are Consolidated Statements? ■ Recording a Merger ■ Reporting a Merger ■ Return on Assets

TYPES OF INVESTMENTS AND ACCOUNTING METHODS

The accounting methods used to record investments are directly related to how much is owned and how long management intends to hold the investments.

Passive Investments in Debt and Equity Securities

Passive investments are made to earn a high rate of return on funds that may be needed for future short-term or long-term purposes. This category includes both investments in debt (bonds and notes) and equity securities (stock). Debt securities are always considered passive investments. If the company intends to hold the securities until they reach maturity date, the investments are measured and reported at amortized cost. If they are to be sold before maturity, they are reported using the market value method.

For investments in equity securities, the investment is presumed passive if the investing company owns less than 20 percent of the outstanding voting shares of the other company. The market value method is used to measure and report the investments.

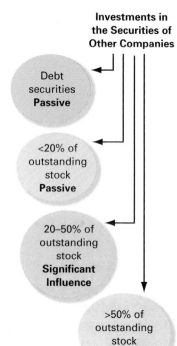

Investments in the Securities of Other Companies

Debt securities
Passive

<20% of outstanding stock
Passive

20–50% of outstanding stock
Significant Influence

>50% of outstanding stock
Control

Investments in Stock for Significant Influence

Significant influence is the ability to have an important impact on the operating and financing policies of another company in which it owns shares of voting stock. Significant influence is presumed if the investing company owns from 20 to 50 percent of the outstanding voting shares of the other company. However, other factors may also indicate that significant influence exists, such as membership on the board of directors of the other company, participation in the policy-making processes, evidence of material transactions between the two companies, an interchange of management personnel, or technological dependency. The equity method is used to measure and report this category of investments.

Investments in Stock for Control

Control is the ability to determine the operating and financing policies of another company through ownership of voting stock. For all practical purposes, control is presumed when the investing company owns more than 50 percent of the outstanding voting stock of the other company. Rules for consolidation are applied to combine the companies.

These categories and the appropriate measuring and reporting methods can be summarized as follows:

	Investment in Debt Securities of Another Entity		Investment in the Voting Common Stock of Another Entity		
Investment Category	Passive		Passive	Significant Influence	Control
Level of Ownership	Held to maturity	Not held to maturity	< 20% of outstanding shares	20–50% of outstanding shares	> 50% of outstanding shares
Measuring and Reporting Method	Amortized cost method	Market value method		Equity method	Consolidation method

DEBT HELD TO MATURITY: AMORTIZED COST METHOD

Learning Objective 1
Analyze and report bond investments held to maturity.

HELD-TO-MATURITY INVESTMENTS are investments in bonds that management has the intent and ability to hold until maturity.

AMORTIZED COST METHOD reports investments in debt securities held to maturity at cost minus any premium or discount.

When management plans to hold a bond (or note) until its maturity date (when the principal is due), it is reported in an account appropriately called held-to-maturity investments. Bonds should be classified as held-to-maturity investments if management has the intent and the ability to hold them until maturity. These investments in debt instruments are listed at cost adjusted for the amortization of any bond discount or premium, not at their fair market value.

Bond Purchases

On the date of purchase, a bond may be acquired at the maturity amount (at **par**), for less than the maturity amount (at a **discount**), or for more than the maturity amount (at a **premium**).[1] The total cost of the bond, including all incidental acquisition costs such as transfer fees and broker commissions, is debited to the Held-to-Maturity Investments account.

---

[1]The determination of the price of the bond is based on the present value techniques discussed in Chapter 9. Many analysts refer to a bond price as a **percentage of par**. For example, *The Wall Street Journal* might report that an Exxon Mobil bond with a par value of $1,000 is selling at 82.97. This means it would cost $829.70 (82.97 percent of $1,000) to buy the bond.

To illustrate accounting for bond investments, assume that on July 1, 2008, Dow Jones paid the par value of $100,000[2] for 8 percent bonds that mature on June 30, 2013. The 8 percent interest is paid each June 30 and December 31. Management plans to hold the bonds for five years, until maturity.

The journal entry to record the purchase of the bonds follows:

| Held-to-maturity investments (+A) | 100,000 | |
| Cash (−A) | | 100,000 |

Assets	=	Liabilities	+	Stockholders' Equity
Cash	−100,000			
Held-to-maturity investments	+100,000			

Interest Earned

The bonds in this illustration were purchased at par, or face value. Since no premium or discount needs to be amortized, the book value remains constant over the life of the investment. In this situation, revenue earned from the investment each period is measured as the amount of interest collected in cash or accrued at year-end. The following journal entry records the receipt of interest on December 31:

| Cash (+A) ($100,000 × 8% × 6/12) | 4,000 | |
| Interest revenue (+R, +SE) | | 4,000 |

Assets	=	Liabilities	+	Stockholders' Equity	
Cash	+4,000			Interest revenue	+4,000

The same entry is made on succeeding interest payment dates.

Principal at Maturity

When the bonds mature on June 30, 2013, the journal entry to record receipt of the principal payment would be:

| Cash (+A) | 100,000 | |
| Held-to-maturity investments (−A) | | 100,000 |

Assets	=	Liabilities	+	Stockholders' Equity
Cash	+100,000			
Held-to-maturity investments	−100,000			

If the bond investment must be sold before maturity, any difference between market value (the proceeds from the sale) and net book value would be reported as a gain or loss on sale. If management **intends** to sell the bonds before the maturity date, they are treated in the same manner as investments in stock classified as available-for-sale securities discussed in the next section.

---

[2]When bond investors accept a rate of interest on a bond investment that is the same as the stated rate of interest on the bonds, the bonds will sell at par (i.e., at 100 or 100% of face value).

PASSIVE STOCK INVESTMENTS: THE MARKET VALUE METHOD

Learning Objective 2
Analyze and report passive investments in securities using the market value method.

When the investing company owns less than 20 percent of the outstanding voting stock of another company, the investment is considered passive. Among the assets and liabilities on the balance sheet, only passive investments in marketable securities are reported using the market value method on the date of the balance sheet.[3] This violates the historical cost principal. Before we discuss the specific accounting for these investments, we should consider the implications of using market value:

MARKET VALUE METHOD reports securities at their current market value.

1. **Why are passive investments reported at fair market value on the balance sheet?** Two primary factors determine the answer to this question:

   ■ **Relevance.** Analysts who study financial statements often attempt to forecast a company's future cash flows. They want to know how a company can generate cash for purposes such as expansion of the business, payment of dividends, or survival during a prolonged economic downturn. One source of cash is the sale of stock from its passive investments portfolio. The best estimate of the cash that could be generated by the sale of these securities is their current market value.

   ■ **Measurability.** Accountants record only items that can be measured in dollar terms with a high degree of reliability (an unbiased and verifiable measurement). Determining the fair market value of most assets is very difficult because they are not actively traded. For example, the John Hancock building is an important part of the Boston skyline. John Hancock's balance sheet reports the building in terms of its original cost less accumulated depreciation in part because of the difficulty in determining an objective market value for it. Contrast the difficulty of determining the value of a building with the ease of determining the value of securities that John Hancock may own. A quick look at *The Wall Street Journal* or an internet financial service is all that is necessary to determine the current price of IBM or Exxon Mobil stock because these securities are traded each day on established stock exchanges.

2. **When the investment account is adjusted to reflect changes in fair market value, what other account is affected when the asset account is increased or decreased?** Under the double-entry method of accounting, every journal entry affects at least two accounts. To report market value, one account is a valuation allowance that is added to or subtracted from the investment account maintained at cost. The other account affected is for unrealized holding gains or losses that are recorded whenever the fair market value of investments changes. These are unrealized because no actual sale has taken place; simply by holding the security, the value has changed. If the value of the investments increased by $100,000 during the year, an adjusting journal entry records the increase in the allowance account and an unrealized holding gain for $100,000. If the value of the investments decreased by $75,000 during the year, an adjusting journal entry records the decrease in the allowance and an unrealized holding loss of $75,000. Recording an unrealized holding gain is a departure from the revenue principle that states that revenues and gains should be recorded when the company has completed the earnings process that generated them. The financial statement treatment of the unrealized holding gains or losses depends on the classification of the passive stock investments.

UNREALIZED HOLDING GAINS AND LOSSES are amounts associated with price changes of securities that are currently held.

Classifying Passive Stock Investments

Depending on management's intent, passive investments may be classified as trading securities or securities available for sale.

Topic Tackler

PLUS

Topic Tackler 12-1

---

[3]All **nonvoting** stock is accounted for under the market value method without regard to the level of ownership.

Trading Securities

Trading securities are actively traded with the objective of generating profits on short-term changes in the price of the securities. This approach is similar to the one taken by many mutual funds. The portfolio manager actively seeks opportunities to buy and sell securities. Trading securities are classified as **current assets** on the balance sheet.

Securities Available for Sale

Most companies do not actively trade the securities of other companies. Instead, they invest to earn a return on funds they may need for future operating purposes. These investments are called securities available for sale. They are classified as current or noncurrent assets on the balance sheet depending on whether management intends to sell the securities during the next year.

Trading securities (TS for short) are most commonly reported by financial institutions that actively buy and sell short-term investments to maximize returns. Most corporations, however, invest in short- and long-term securities available for sale (SAS for short). We will focus on this category in the next section by analyzing Dow Jones's investing activities.

Securities Available for Sale

Dow Jones's Other Investments account is reported for the year 2003 at $14.6 million. The notes to Dow Jones's annual report contain the following information concerning this investment portfolio:

NOTES TO FINANCIAL STATEMENTS

Note 1. Summary of Significant Accounting Policies

INVESTMENTS in marketable equity securities, all of which are classified as available for sale, are carried at their market value in other investments on the consolidated balance sheets. The unrealized gains or losses of these investments are recorded directly to Stockholders' Equity. Any decline in market value below the investment's original cost that is determined to be other than temporary as well as any realized gains or losses would be recognized in income (see Note 15).

TRADING SECURITIES are all investments in stocks or bonds held primarily for the purpose of active trading (buying and selling) in the near future (classified as short term).

SECURITIES AVAILABLE FOR SALE are all passive investments other than trading securities (classified as short or long term).

REAL WORLD EXCERPT

DOW JONES & CO.

ANNUAL REPORT

For simplification, let's assume that Dow Jones had no passive investments at the end of 2007. In the following illustration, we will apply the accounting policy used by Dow Jones.

Purchase of Stock

At the beginning of 2008, Dow Jones purchases 10,000 shares of Internet Financial News[4] (IFNews for short) common stock for $60 per share. There were 100,000 outstanding shares, so Dow Jones owns 10 percent of IFNews ($10,000 \div 100,000$), which is treated as a passive investment. Such investments are recorded initially at cost:

Investment in SAS (+A) 600,000
    Cash (−A) 600,000

Assets	=	Liabilities	+	Stockholders' Equity
Investment in SAS +600,000				
Cash − 600,000				

---

[4]Internet Financial News is a fictitious company.

This entry and those that follow are illustrated in T-accounts in Exhibit 12.2.

Dividends Earned

Investments in equity securities earn a return from two sources: (1) price increases and (2) dividend income. Price increases (or decreases) are analyzed both at year-end and when a security is sold. Dividends earned are reported as investment income on the income statement and are included in the computation of net income for the period. Dow Jones received a $1 per share cash dividend from IFNews, which totals $10,000 ($1 × 10,000 shares).

| Cash (+A) | 10,000 | |
| Investment income (+R, +SE) | | 10,000 |

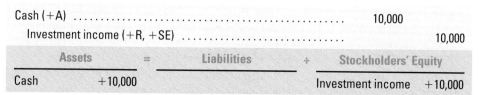

Assets	=	Liabilities	+	Stockholders' Equity
Cash +10,000				Investment income +10,000

This entry is the same for both the trading securities and available-for-sale securities.

Year-End Valuation

At the end of the accounting period, passive investments are reported on the balance sheet at fair market value. Assume that IFNews had a $58 per share market value at the end of the year. That is, the investment had lost value ($60 − $58 = $2 per share) for the year. However, since the investment has not been sold, there is only a holding loss, not a realized loss.

Reporting the SAS investment at market value requires adjusting it to market value at the end of each period using the account Allowance to Value at Market—SAS with an offset to Net Unrealized Gains and Losses in SAS. If the Allowance to Value at Market—SAS account has a **debit balance,** it is **added** to the Investment in SAS account. If it has a **credit balance,** it is **subtracted.** The Net Unrealized Gains and Losses in SAS account is reported in the stockholders' equity section of the balance sheet under Other Comprehensive Income. Thus, the balance sheet remains in balance. Since the SAS investment is expected to be held into the future, the unrealized holding gain or loss is not reported as part of net income. Only when the security is sold are any realized gains or losses included in net income.

The following chart is used to compute any unrealized gain or loss in the SAS portfolio:

Year	Market Value	−	Cost	=	Balance Needed in Valuation Allowance	−	Unadjusted Balance in Valuation Allowance	=	Amount for Adjusting Entry
2008	$580,000 ($58 × 10,000)	−	$600,000 ($60 × 10,000)	=	($20,000)	−	$0 (We assume there were no passive investments at the end of the prior year.)	=	($20,000) An unrealized loss for the period

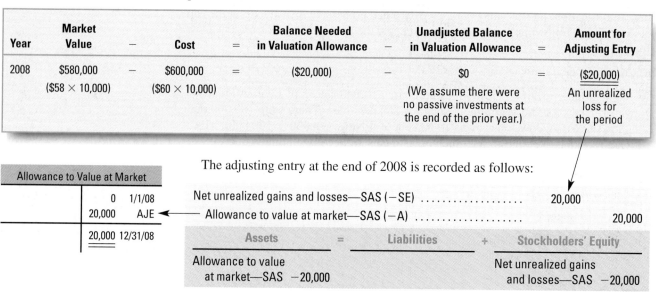

The adjusting entry at the end of 2008 is recorded as follows:

Allowance to Value at Market	
0	1/1/08
20,000	AJE
20,000 12/31/08	

| Net unrealized gains and losses—SAS (−SE) | 20,000 | |
| Allowance to value at market—SAS (−A) | | 20,000 |

Assets	=	Liabilities	+	Stockholders' Equity
Allowance to value at market—SAS −20,000				Net unrealized gains and losses—SAS −20,000

On the 2008 balance sheet under Other Investments, Dow Jones would report an investment in securities available for sale of $580,000 ($600,000 cost less the $20,000 credit balance in the valuation allowance). It would also report under Other Comprehensive Income its net unrealized loss on securities available for sale of $20,000. The only item reported on the income statement for 2008 would be investment income of $10,000 from the dividends earned, classified under other nonoperating items.

Now let's assume that the IFNews securities were held through the year 2009. At the end of 2009, the stock had a $61 per share market value. The adjustment for 2009 would be computed as follows:

On the Balance Sheet:

Assets

Investment in SAS	$600,000
Allowance to value	
at market—SAS	(20,000)
Net investment	$580,000

Stockholders' Equity
  Other Comprehensive Income:
    Net unrealized loss
      in SAS $(20,000)

Year	Market Value	−	Cost	=	Balance Needed in Valuation Allowance	−	Unadjusted Balance in Valuation Allowance	=	Amount for Adjusting Entry
2009	$610,000 ($61 × 10,000)	−	$600,000 ($60 × 10,000)	=	$10,000	−	($20,000)	=	$30,000 An unrealized gain for the period

The adjusting entry at the end of 2009 would be:

Allowance to value at market—SAS (+A)	30,000	
Net unrealized gains and losses—SAS (+SE)		30,000

Assets	=	Liabilities	+	Stockholders' Equity
Allowance to value at market—SAS +30,000				Net unrealized gains and losses—SAS +30,000

Allowance to Value at Market

		0	1/1/08
		20,000	AJE
AJE	30,000	20,000	12/31/08
12/31/09	10,000		

Sale of Stock

When securities available for sale are sold, **three** accounts on the balance sheet (in addition to Cash) are affected:

- Investment in SAS
- Allowance to Value at Market
- Net Unrealized Gains and Losses (equal to the valuation allowance).

Let's assume that in 2010 Dow Jones sold all of its SAS investment in IFNews for $62.50 per share. The company would receive $625,000 in cash ($62.50 × 10,000 shares) for stock it paid $600,000 for in 2008 ($60 × 10,000 shares). In entry (1), a gain on sale of $25,000 ($625,000 − $600,000) would be recorded and the Investment in SAS would be eliminated. In entry (2), the valuation allowance and related net unrealized gains and losses account in stockholders' equity would be eliminated.

(1) Cash (+A)...	625,000	
Investment in SAS (−A)		600,000
Gain on sale of investments (+Gain, +SE)		25,000
(2) Net unrealized gains and losses—SAS (−SE)	10,000	
Allowance to value at market—SAS (−A)		10,000

Assets	=	Liabilities	+	Stockholders' Equity
(1) Cash +625,000				Gain on sale of
Investment in SAS −600,000				investments + 25,000
(2) Allowance to value				Net unrealized gains
at market—SAS −10,000				and losses—SAS − 10,000

EXHIBIT 12.2

T-Accounts for the
Illustrated Transactions

Balance Sheet Accounts

Investment in SAS (at cost) (A)			
1/1/08	0		
Purchase	600,000		
12/31/08	600,000		
12/31/09	600,000		
		600,000	2010 Sale
12/31/10	0		

Allowance to Value at Market—SAS (A)			
		0	1/1/08
		20,000	2008 AJE
		20,000	12/31/08
2009 AJE	30,000		
12/31/09	10,000		
		10,000	2010 Sale
		0	12/31/10

Net Unrealized Gains and Losses—SAS (SE)			
1/1/08	0		
2008 AJE	20,000		
12/31/08	20,000		
		30,000	2009 AJE
		10,000	12/31/09
2010 Sale	10,000		
12/31/10	0		

Income Statement Accounts

Investment Income (R)			
		10,000	Earned
		10,000	12/31/08

Gain on Sale of Investments (Gain)			
		0	1/1/10
		25,000	2010 Sale
		25,000	12/31/10

Comparing Trading and Available-for-Sale Securities

The reporting impact of unrealized holding gains or losses depends on the classification of the investment:

Available-for-sale portfolio. As we learned in the previous section, the balance in net unrealized holding gains and losses is reported as a separate component of stockholders' equity (under **other comprehensive income** as illustrated in Exhibit 12.1 for Dow Jones). It is not reported on the income statement and does not affect net income. At the time of sale, the difference between the proceeds from the sale and the original cost of the investment is recorded as a gain or loss on sale of available-for-sale securities. At the same time, the Net Unrealized Gains and Losses—SAS and Allowance to Value at Market—SAS are eliminated.

Trading securities portfolio. The amount of the adjustment to record net unrealized holding gains and losses is included in each period's income statement. Net holding gains increase and net holding losses decrease net income. This also means that the amount recorded as net unrealized gains and losses on trading securities is closed to Retained Earnings at the end of the period. Thus, when selling a trading security, Cash and only **two** other balance sheet accounts are affected: Investment in TS and the Allowance to Value at Market—TS for the trading securities portfolio. Also, only the difference between the cash proceeds from the sale and Investment in TS **net** of the Allowance to Value at Market is recorded as a gain or loss on sale of trading securities.

Exhibit 12.3 provides comparative journal entries and financial statement balances for the transactions illustrated for Dow Jones from 2008 to 2010. **Note that total income reported for the three years is the same $35,000 for both trading securities and securities available for sale. Only the allocation across the three periods differs.**

Income in	Trading Securities	Securities Available for Sale
2008	$10,000 dividends	$10,000 dividends
	(20,000) unrealized loss	—
2009	30,000 unrealized gain	—
2010	15,000 realized gain	25,000 realized gain
Total	$35,000	$35,000

Comparison of Accounting for Available-for-Sale and Trading Securities Portfolios

EXHIBIT 12.3

Part A: Entries	Trading Securities		Securities Available for Sale	
2008:				
• Purchase (for $600,000 cash)	Investment in TS (+A) 600,000		Investment in SAS (+A) 600,000	
	Cash (−A)	600,000	Cash (−A)	600,000
• Receipt of dividends ($10,000 cash)	Cash (+A) 10,000		Cash (+A) 10,000	
	Investment income (+R, +SE) ...	10,000	Investment income (+R, +SE) ...	10,000
• Year-end adjustment to market (market = $580,000)	Net unrealized gains/losses— TS (+Loss, −SE) 20,000		Net unrealized gains/losses— SAS (+Loss,−SE) 20,000	
	Allowance to value at market—TS (−A)	20,000	Allowance to value at market—SAS (−A)	20,000
2009:				
• Year-end adjustment to market (market = $610,000)	Allowance to value at market— TS (+A) 30,000		Allowance to value at market— SAS (+A) 30,000	
	Net unrealized gains/losses— TS (+Gain, +SE)	30,000	Net unrealized gains/losses— SAS (+Gain,+SE)	30,000
2010:				
• Sale (for $625,000)	*Two balance sheet accounts are eliminated:*		*Three balance sheet accounts are eliminated:*	
	Cash (+A) 625,000		Cash (+A) 625,000	
	Allowance to value at market— TS (−A)	10,000	Investment in SAS (−A)	600,000
	Investment in TS (−A)	600,000	Gain on sale of investment (+Gain, +SE)	25,000
	Gain on sale of investment (+Gain, +SE)	15,000	**Net unrealized gains/ losses—SAS (−SE)**	10,000
			Allowance to value at market—SAS (−A)	10,000

continued

EXHIBIT 12.3   concluded

Part B: Financial Reporting	Trading Securities				Securities Available-for-Sale			
Balance Sheet reporting:	**Assets**	**2010**	**2009**	**2008**	**Assets**	**2010**	**2009**	**2008**
	Investment in TS	—	600,000	600,000	Investment in SAS	—	600,000	600,000
	Allow. to market—TS	—	10,000	(20,000)	Allow. to market—SAS	—	10,000	(20,000)
	Net Investment in TS	—	610,000	580,000	Net Investment in SAS	—	610,000	580,000
					Stockholders' Equity			
					Other comprehensive income:			
					Net unreal. gains/losses—SAS	10,000	(20,000)	
Income Statement reporting:		**2010**	**2009**	**2008**		**2010**	**2009**	**2008**
	Investment income	—	—	10,000	Investment income	—	—	10,000
	Gain on sale	15,000	—	—	Gain on sale	25,000	—	—
	Net unreal. gains/ losses—TS	—	30,000	(20,000)				

FINANCIAL ANALYSIS

Equity Securities and Earnings Management

Most managers prefer to treat their passive investments as securities available for sale. This treatment generally reduces variations in reported earnings by avoiding recognition of unrealized holding gains and losses resulting from quarter-to-quarter stock price changes. It also allows managers to smooth out earnings fluctuations by selling securities with unrealized gains when earnings decline and by selling those with unrealized losses when earnings increase. Diligent analysts can see through this strategy, however, by examining the required note on investments in the financial statements.

SELF-STUDY QUIZ

Now let's reconstruct the activities that Dow Jones undertook in a recent year with a few transactions assumed. Answer the following questions using the T-accounts to help you infer the amounts. The dollars are in thousands.

REAL WORLD EXCERPT

DOW JONES & CO.

ANNUAL REPORT

Balance Sheet Accounts

(In Other Investments)

Investment in SAS			
1/1	4,022		
Purchase	19,000	?	Sale
12/31	8,875		

Allowance to Value at Market—SAS			
1/1	1,565		
AJE	?	1,092	Sale
12/31	5,683		

(In Accumulated Other Comprehensive Income)

Net Unrealized Gains and Losses—SAS			
		1,565	1/1
Sale	?	?	AJE
		5,683	12/31

Income Statement Accounts

Investment Income		
	?	Earned
	7,771	12/31

Gain on Sale of Investments		
	2,384	Sale
	2,384	12/31

a. Purchased securities available for sale for cash. Prepare the journal entry.	
b. Received cash dividends on the investments. Prepare the journal entry.	
c. Sold SAS investments at a gain. Prepare the journal entries.	
d. At year-end, the SAS portfolio had a market value of $14,558. Prepare the adjusting entry.	
e. What would be reported on the balance sheet related to the SAS investments on December 31? On the income statement for the year?	
f. How would year-end reporting change if the investments were categorized as trading securities instead of securities available for sale?	

After you have completed your answers, check them with the solutions at the bottom of the page.

---

a. Investment in SAS (+A) 19,000

    Cash (−A) 19,000

b. Cash (+A) 7,771

    Investment income (+R, +SE) 7,771

c. (1) Cash (+A) 16,531

      Gain on sale of investments (+Gain, +SE) .. 2,384

      Investment in SAS (−A) 14,147

  (2) Net unrealized gains/losses—SAS (−SE) 1,092

      Allowance to value at market—SAS (−A) ... 1,092

d. Allowance to value at market—SAS (+A) 5,210

    Net unrealized gains/losses—SAS (+SE) 5,210

Market Value	−	Cost	=	Balance Needed in Valuation Allowance	−	Unadjusted Balance in Valuation Allowance	=	Adjustment to Valuation Allowance
$14,558	−	$8,875	=	+$5,683	−	$473 ($1,565 beg. bal. − $1,092 sale)	=	+$5,210

e. **Balance Sheet**

  Assets

    Other investments $14,558

  Stockholders' Equity

    Net unrealized gains/losses   5,683

      (in Accumulated Other Comprehensive Income)

Income Statement

  Nonoperating Items

    Gain on sale of investments $2,384

    Investment income   7,771

f. If the securities were categorized as trading securities, no net unrealized gain would appear on the balance sheet. Therefore, when the securities were sold in (c.), no debit would be made to the Net Unrealized Gains/Losses account. Rather, there would be a gain on the sale of $1,292 [$16,531 cash − ($14,147 cost + $1,092 allowance)] reported on the income statement. Then at year-end, the net unrealized gain of $5,210 would be reported on the income statement (not in stockholders' equity).

INVESTMENTS FOR SIGNIFICANT INFLUENCE: EQUITY METHOD

Learning Objective 3
Analyze and report investments involving significant influence using the equity method.

EQUITY METHOD is used when an investor can exert significant influence over an investee; the method permits recording the investor's share of the investee's income.

INVESTMENTS IN ASSOCIATED or affiliated **COMPANIES** are investments in stock held for the purpose of influencing the operating and financing strategies of the entity for the long term.

When Dow Jones invests cash in securities that are reported on its balance sheet as Other Investments, it is a passive investor. However, when the company reports Investments in Associated Companies on its balance sheet, it is taking a more active role as an investor. For a variety of reasons, an investor may want to exert influence (presumed by owning 20 to 50 percent of the outstanding voting stock) without becoming the controlling shareholder (presumed when owning more than 50 percent of the voting stock). Examples follow:

- A retailer may want to influence a manufacturer to be sure that it can obtain certain products designed to its specifications.

- A manufacturer may want to influence a computer consulting firm to ensure that it can incorporate the consulting firm's cutting-edge technology in its manufacturing processes.

- A manufacturer may recognize that a parts supplier lacks experienced management and could prosper with additional managerial support.

The equity method must be used when an investor can exert significant influence over an investee. On the balance sheet, these long-term investments are classified as investments in associated companies (or affiliated companies). Dow Jones reported the following six investments in associated companies in its 2003 annual report:

REAL WORLD EXCERPT

DOW JONES & CO.

ANNUAL REPORT

NOTES TO FINANCIAL STATEMENTS

Note 1. Summary of Significant Accounting Policies

. . . The equity method of accounting is used for investments in other companies in which the Company has significant influence; generally this represents common stock ownership or partnership equity of at least 20% and not more than 50% (see Note 7). . . .

Note 7. Investments in Associated Companies, at Equity

At December 31, 2003, the principal components of Investments in Associated Companies, at Equity were the following:

Investment	Ownership	Description of Business
Business News (Asia) Private	50%	Business and financial news television company broadcasting as CNBC Asia, in partnership with NBC
Business News (Europe) L.P.	50	Business and financial news television company broadcasting as CNBC Europe, in partnership with NBC
Dow Jones Reuters Business Interactive LLC (Factiva)	50	Provides electronic delivery of business news and online research, in partnership with Reuters Group Plc.
F.F. Soucy, Inc. & Partners, L.P.	40	Newsprint mill in Quebec, Canada
HB-Dow Jones S.A.	42	A part-owner of a publishing company in the Czech Republic
SmartMoney	50	Publisher of SmartMoney magazine and SmartMoney.com serving the private-investor market throughout the U.S. and Canada, in partnership with Hearst Corp.

Recording Investments under the Equity Method

Topic Tackler

PLUS

Topic Tackler 12–2

An investing corporation with significant influence over its investee participates in decisions that result in the investee earning income and declaring dividends. This suggests that the investing company should reflect the results of its participation similarly. When the investee reduces its retained earnings when it declares dividends, the investing corporation should reduce its investment account for its percentage share in the dividends to mirror what the investee does (since declared dividends are not an expense to the investee, they should not be treated as a revenue by the investing company). Likewise, when the investee increases (reduces) its retained earnings when it earns income (has a loss) for the period, the investing corporation should increase (decrease) its investment account and report investment income (loss) during the period for its percentage share of the investee's net income (net loss). Specifically:

- **Net income of investee:** If the investee reports positive results of operations for the year, the investor then records investment income equal to its percentage share of the investee's net income and increases its asset account Investments in Associated Companies. If the investee reports a net loss, the investor records the opposite effect.

- **Dividends paid by investee:** If the investee declares and pays dividends during the year (a financing decision), the investor reduces its investment account and increases cash when it receives its share of the dividends.

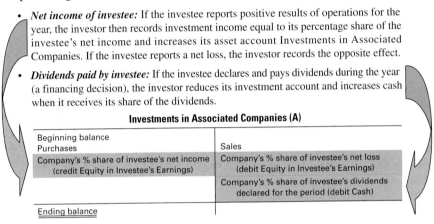

Investments in Associated Companies (A)

Beginning balance	
Purchases	Sales
Company's % share of investee's net income (credit Equity in Investee's Earnings)	Company's % share of investee's net loss (debit Equity in Investee's Earnings)
	Company's % share of investee's dividends declared for the period (debit Cash)
Ending balance	

Purchase of Stock

For simplification, let's assume that, at the beginning of 2008, Dow Jones had no long-term investments in companies over which it exerted significant influence. In 2008, Dow Jones purchased 40,000 shares of the outstanding voting common stock of Internet Financial News (IFNews) for $400,000 in cash. Since IFNews had 100,000 shares of common stock outstanding, Dow Jones acquired 40 percent and was presumed to have significant influence over the investee. Therefore, Dow Jones must use the equity method to account for this investment. The purchase of the asset would be recorded at cost.

| Investments in associated companies (+A) | 400,000 | |
| Cash (−A) | | 400,000 |

Assets	=	Liabilities	+	Stockholders' Equity
Investments in associated companies	+ 400,000			
Cash	− 400,000			

Investee Earnings

Because the investor can influence the process of earning income for the investee, the investor company bases its investment income on the investee's earnings rather than the dividends it pays. During 2008, IFNews reported a net income of $500,000 for the year. Dow Jones's percentage share of IFNews's income was $200,000 (40% × $500,000) and is recorded as follows:

| Investments in associated companies (+A) | 200,000 | |
| Equity in investee earnings (+R, +SE) | | 200,000 |

Assets	=	Liabilities	+	Stockholders' Equity
Investments in associated companies	+200,000		Equity in investee earnings	+200,000

If the investee reports a net loss for the period, the investor records its percentage share of the loss by decreasing the investment account and recording Equity in Investee Loss. The Equity in Investee Earnings (or Loss) is reported in the Other Items section of the income statement, with interest revenue, interest expense, and gains and losses on sales of assets.

Dividends Received

Because Dow Jones can influence the dividend policies of its equity-method investments, any dividends it receives should **not** be recorded as investment income. Instead, dividends received reduce its investment account. During 2008, IFNews declared and paid a cash dividend of $2 per share to stockholders. Dow Jones received $80,000 in cash ($2 × 40,000 shares) from IFNews.

Cash (+A) 80,000
  Investments in associated companies (−A) 80,000

Assets	=	Liabilities	+	Stockholders' Equity
Cash + 80,000				
Investments in associated companies −80,000				

In summary, the effects for 2008 are reflected in the following T-accounts:

Investments in Associated Companies	
1/1/08 0	
Purchase 400,000	
Share of investee net earnings 200,000	80,000 Share of investee dividends
12/31/08 520,000	

Equity in Investee Earnings	
	0 1/1/08
	200,000 Share of investee net earnings
	200,000 12/31/08

Reporting Investments under the Equity Method

The Investments in Associated Companies account is reported on the balance sheet as a long-term asset. However, as these last two entries show, the investment account does not reflect either cost or market value. Instead, the following occurs:

- The investment account is increased by the cost of shares that were purchased and the proportional share of the investee company income.

- The account is reduced by the amount of dividends received from the investee company and the proportional share of any investee company losses.

At the end of the accounting period, accountants **do not adjust the investment account to reflect changes in the fair market value** of the securities that are held. When the securities are sold, the difference between the cash received and the book value of the investment is recorded as a gain or loss on the sale of the asset and is reported on the income statement in the Other Items section.

Improper Influence

A key assumption underlying accounting is that all transactions occur at "arm's length." That is, each party to the transaction is acting in his or her own self-interest. But when one corporation exerts significant influence over another (i.e., it owns 20 to 50 percent of the common stock), it is unreasonable to assume that transactions between the corporations are made at arm's length.

Consider what might happen if an investor corporation could affect the investee's dividend policy. If the investor reported dividends paid by the investee as dividend income, the investor could manipulate its income by influencing the other company's dividend policy. In a bad year, the investor might request large dividend payments to bolster its income. In a good year, it might try to cut dividend payments to build up the investee company's retained earnings to support large dividends in the future.

The equity method prevents this type of manipulation. Instead of recognizing dividends as income, income from the investment is based on a percentage of the affiliated company's reported net income.

SELF-STUDY QUIZ

Now let's reconstruct the activities that Dow Jones actually undertook in 2003 for its investments in associated companies with a few transactions being assumed. Answer the following questions, using the T-accounts to help you infer the amounts. The dollars are in thousands.

REAL WORLD EXCERPT

DOW JONES & CO.

ANNUAL REPORT

Investments in Associated Companies				Equity in Net Earnings/ Losses of Associated Companies		
1/1/2003	83,619			1/1/2003	0	
Purchase	12,844					
Share of		10,102	Share of		2,869	Share of
investee net			investee			investee
income	?		dividends			net income
12/31/2003	89,230				2,869	12/31/2003

a. Purchased additional investments in associated companies for cash. Prepare the journal entry.	
b. Received cash dividends on the investments. Prepare the journal entry.	
c. At year-end, the investments in associated companies had a market value of $62,000; the companies also reported $5,800 in net income for the year. Prepare the adjusting entry.	
d. What would be reported on the December 31, 2003, balance sheet related to the investments in associated companies? What would be reported on the income statement for 2003?	

After you have completed your answers, check them with the solutions at the bottom of the page.

Self-Study Quiz Solutions

a. Investments in associated companies (+A) 12,844
    Cash (−A) 12,844
b. Cash (+A) 10,102
    Investments in associated companies (−A) 10,102
c. Investments in associated companies (+A) 2,869
    Equity in earnings of associated companies (+R, +SE) 2,869
d. **Balance Sheet**   **Income Statement**

Assets   *Other Items*

Investments in associated   Equity in earnings of associated
  companies $89,230   companies $2,869

FINANCIAL
ANALYSIS

Selecting Accounting Methods for Minority Investments

Managers can choose freely between LIFO and FIFO or accelerated depreciation and straight-line depreciation. In the case of minority ($\leq$ 50% owned) investments, they may **not** simply choose between the market value and equity methods. Investments of less than 20 percent of a company's outstanding stock are usually accounted for under the market value method and investments of 20 percent to 50 percent under the equity method.

However, managers may be able to structure the acquisition of stock in a manner that permits them to use the accounting method that they prefer. For example, a company that wants to use the market value method could purchase only 19.9 percent of the outstanding stock of another company and achieve the same investment goals as they would with a 20 percent investment. Why might managers want to avoid using the equity method? Most managers prefer to minimize variations in reported earnings. If a company were planning to buy stock in a firm that reported large earnings in some years and large losses in others, it might want to use the market value method to avoid reporting its share of the investee's earnings and losses.

Analysts who compare several companies must understand management's reporting choices and the way in which differences between the market value and equity methods can affect earnings.

FOCUS ON
CASH FLOWS

Investments

Many of the effects from applying the market value method to passive investments and the equity method to investments held for significant influence affect net income but not cash flow. These items require adjustments under the indirect method when converting net income to cash flows from operating activities.

In General → Sales of securities require a number of adjustments:

1. Any gain on the sale is subtracted from net income in the Operating Activities section.

2. Any loss on the sale is added back in the Operating Activities section.

3. The cash resulting from the sale or purchase is reflected in the Investing Activities section.

Income under the equity method also requires adjustments. Recall that cash dividends received from investees are not recorded as income. In addition, investors record as income their share of investees' earnings even though no cash is involved, resulting in the following:

1. Dividends received are added to net income in the Operating Activities section.

2. Any equity in investee earnings needs to be subtracted in the Operating Activities section.

3. Any equity in investee losses needs to be added in the Operating Activities section.

Effect on Statement of Cash Flows

	Effect on Cash Flows
Operating Activities	
Net income	$xxx
Adjusted for	
Gains/losses on sale of investments	−/+
Equity in net earnings/losses of associated companies	−/+
Dividends received from associated companies	+
Net unrealized holding gains/losses on trading securities	−/+
Investing Activities	
Purchase of investments	−
Sale of investments	+

Focus Company Analysis → A partial statement of cash flows for Dow Jones for 2003 follows. Dow Jones subtracted the equity in earnings of associated companies and added in dividends received from associated companies, showing the net effect on the cash flow statement. If Dow Jones had sold securities during the year; the gain (loss) would be subtracted (added) in the operating section for both investment portfolios (SAS and associated companies).

Dow Jones appropriately adjusted net income for these items. In both the Operating and Investing Activities sections, the effects related to accounting for investments have a significant impact on cash flows for Dow Jones.

DOW JONES & CO. INC.
Consolidated Statement of Cash Flows (partial)
For the year ended December 31, 2003
(dollars in thousands)

Operating Activities	
Consolidated net income	$170,599
Adjustments to reconcile net income to net cash	
provided by operating activities:	
Gain on sale of business and investments	—
Equity in earnings of associated companies, net of distributions	7,233
(other adjustments—not detailed here)	42,068
Net cash provided by operating activities	**219,900**
Investing Activities	
Businesses and investments acquired	(149,135)
Disposition of businesses and investments	—
(other investing activities—not detailed here)	(66,839)
Net cash used in investing activities	**(215,974)**

Equity in earnings	*−2,869*
Dividends	*10,102*
	7,233

CONTROLLING INTERESTS: MERGERS AND ACQUISITIONS

Before we discuss financial reporting issues for situations in which a company owns more than 50 percent of the outstanding common stock of another corporation, we should consider management's reasons for acquiring this level of ownership. The following are some of the reasons for acquiring control of another corporation:

Learning Objective 4
Analyze and report investments in controlling interests.

1. **Vertical integration.** In this type of acquisition, a company acquires another at a different level in the channels of distribution. For example, Dow Jones owns a newsprint company that provides raw materials as well as a national delivery service.

2. **Horizontal growth.** These acquisitions involve companies at the same level in the channels of distribution. For example, Dow Jones has expanded internationally by creating or acquiring newspaper and newswire companies in major international markets.

3. **Synergy.** The operations of two companies together may be more profitable than the combined profitability of the companies as separate entities. Dow Jones has created

or purchased a number of broadcast and Internet news services. Merging these companies and sharing news content may create more profits than operating separate entities could.

Understanding why one company has acquired control over other companies is a key factor in understanding the company's overall business strategy.

What Are Consolidated Statements?

The **PARENT COMPANY** is the entity that gains control over another company.

The **SUBSIDIARY COMPANY** is the entity that is acquired by the parent.

CONSOLIDATED FINANCIAL STATEMENTS combine the operations of two or more companies into a single set of statements

Any corporate acquisition involves two companies. The parent company is the company that gains control over the other company. The subsidiary company is the company that the parent acquires. When a company acquires another, consolidated financial statements must be presented. These statements combine the operations of two or more companies into a single set of statements. Basically, **consolidated statements can be thought of as the adding together of the separate financial statements for two or more companies to make it appear as if a single company exists.** Thus, the cash accounts for each company are added as are the inventory accounts, land accounts, and others.

The notes to Dow Jones's 2003 annual report provide the following information:

REAL WORLD EXCERPT

DOW JONES & CO.

ANNUAL REPORT

NOTES TO FINANCIAL STATEMENTS

Note 1. Summary of Significant Accounting Policies

THE CONSOLIDATED FINANCIAL STATEMENTS include the accounts of the company and its majority-owned subsidiaries. All significant intercompany transactions are eliminated in consolidation. . . .

As the note indicates, eliminating any intercompany items is necessary when consolidated statements are prepared. **Remember that consolidated statements make it appear as though a single company exists when in fact there are two or more separate legal entities.** Intercompany items do not exist for a single corporation. For example, a debt owed by Dow Jones (the parent) to its newsprint subsidiary is not reported on a consolidated statement because a company cannot owe itself money. We discuss the preparation of consolidated statements in more detail in Supplement A at the end of this chapter.

Recording a Merger

A **MERGER** occurs when one company purchases all of the net assets of another and the target company goes out of existence.

We learned that consolidated statements are presented in such a way that two companies appear to have merged into one. In fact, the simplest way to understand the statements that result from the consolidation process is to consider the case of a simple merger where one company purchases all of the net assets of another and the target company goes out of existence. In such a situation, the purchasing company records the net assets of the target according to the cost principle, at the cash equivalent purchase price.

To illustrate, we will use simplified data for Dow Jones (the purchaser) and IFNews (the hypothetical target). Let's assume that, on January 1, 2008, Dow Jones paid $100 (all numbers in millions) in cash to buy all of IFNews's stock.[5] It then merges IFNews

---

[5]Purchasing 100 percent of the outstanding stock results in a wholly owned subsidiary. Purchasing less than 100 percent of the stock results in **minority interest** in the subsidiary, which represents the shares owned by other than the parent.

(dollars in millions)	Dow Jones	IFN Book Value	Market Value
Assets			
Cash and other current assets	$ 123		
Plant and equipment (net)	689	$30	$35
Other assets	492	60	60
Total assets	$1,304	$90	
Liabilities and Stockholders' Equity			
Current liabilities	$ 613	$10	$10
Noncurrent liabilities	561		
Stockholders' equity	130	80	
Total liabilities and stockholders' equity	$1,304	$90	

EXHIBIT 12.4

Balance Sheets Immediately
Before the Merger

into its operations and IFNews goes out of existence as a separate legal entity. Exhibit 12.4 presents Dow Jones and IFNews's balance sheets, and market value data for IFNews's assets and liabilities, immediately **before** the merger.

Note that Dow Jones paid $100 for 100 percent of IFNews even though the total book value of IFNews's net assets was only $80 ($90 assets − $10 liabilities). This is not surprising because **the book value of a company's net assets is not the same as the fair market value.** We will assume that an analysis of IFNews's assets and liabilities on the date of acquisition revealed the following facts:

■ IFNews's Plant and Equipment had a current market value of $35 (net book value of $30).

■ The book values of Other Assets ($60) and Current Liabilities ($10) on IFNews's balance sheet were equal to market values.

■ IFNews had developed a good reputation with an important group of online investors, which increased IFNews's overall value. For these reasons, Dow Jones was willing to pay an additional $15 to acquire IFNews. The $15 difference between the purchase price of the company and the fair market value of its net assets (assets minus liabilities) is called goodwill (or Cost in Excess of Net Assets Acquired). It may be computed as follows:

For accounting purposes, GOODWILL (COST IN EXCESS OF NET ASSETS ACQUIRED) is the excess of the purchase price of a business over the fair market value of the business's assets and liabilities.

Purchase price for IFNews	$100
Less: Net assets purchased, at market ($35 + 60 − 10)	85
Goodwill purchased	$ 15

As noted, the cost principle requires that the assets and liabilities of IFNews be recorded by Dow Jones on its books at the purchase price (fair market value) on the date of the merger. This method of recording mergers and acquisitions, called the purchase method, is the only method allowed by U.S. GAAP. Dow Jones would record the merger as follows:

The PURCHASE METHOD records assets and liabilities acquired in a merger or acquisition at their fair market value.

Plant and equipment (net) (+A)	35	
Other assets (+A)	60	
Goodwill (+A)	15	
Current liabilities (+L)		10
Cash (−A)		100

Assets	=	Liabilities	+	Stockholders' Equity
Plant and equipment (net) + 35		Current liabilities + 10		
Other assets + 60				
Goodwill + 15				
Cash − 100				

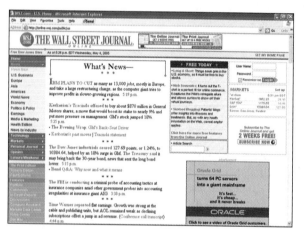

It is important to remember that goodwill can be reported on the balance sheet **only if it is acquired in a purchase transaction.**

Reporting a Merger

Postmerger Balance Sheet

The postmerger balance sheet shown in Exhibit 12.5 was prepared by combining the preceding journal entry with Dow Jones's balance sheet shown in Exhibit 12.4.

Remember the following:

1. IFNews's assets and liabilities are added at their fair market values, not their original book values.

2. Goodwill = Purchase Price − Net Assets Purchased (at their market prices).

3. The cash payment made for the acquisition is subtracted from cash on the balance sheet. If the company is purchased through issuance of additional stock, contributed capital is increased (credited) instead.

4. The balance sheet would be the same if Dow Jones and IFNews continued as separate legal entities after the purchase, and consolidated statements were prepared.

EXHIBIT 12.5
Dow Jones's Balance Sheet Immediately After the Merger

(dollars in millions)	Dow Jones
Assets	
Cash and other current assets ($123 − $100)	$ 23
Plant and equipment (net) ($689 + $35)	724
Other assets ($492 + $60)	552
Goodwill ($100 − $85)	15
Total assets	$1,314
Liabilities and Stockholders' Equity	
Current liabilities ($613 + $10)	$ 623
Noncurrent liabilities	561
Stockholders' equity	130
Total liabilities and stockholders' equity	$1,314

Postmerger Income Statements

After the merger, Dow Jones's accounting system will capture all of the revenues and expenses of the combined company. The resulting income statement is presented in Exhibit 12.6. The combined amounts include the following:

EXHIBIT 12.6

Dow Jones's Income
Statement for the Year
Following the Acquisition

(dollars in millions)	Dow Jones
Revenues ($2,158 + $120)	$2,278
Expenses ($2,150 + $106 + $1)	2,257
Net income	$ 21

1. Revenues that would have been recorded in the separate accounting systems had the combination not taken place (Dow Jones $2,158 + IFNews's $120 = $2,278).

2. Expenses that would have been recorded in the separate accounting systems had the combination not taken place (Dow Jones $2,150 + IFNews's $106 = $2,256).

3. Additional expenses related to the recording of IFNews's assets and liabilities at market value; $1 additional depreciation assuming a five-year useful life ($5 additional plant and equipment over book value ÷ 5 years = $1 per year).[6]

Again, it is important to remember that the income statement would be the same if Dow Jones and IFNews continued as separate legal entities after the purchase and consolidated statements were prepared. These circumstances are illustrated in Chapter Supplement A.

As we noted in Chapter 8, goodwill is considered to have an indefinite life. As a consequence, it is not amortized, but, like all long-lived assets, goodwill is reviewed for possible impairment of value. Recording an impairment loss would increase expenses for the period and reduce the amount of goodwill on the balance sheet. Dow Jones described GAAP for goodwill in its recent 10-K.

REAL WORLD EXCERPT

**DOW JONES
& CO.**

FORM 10-K

NOTE 1. SUMMARY OF SIGNIFICANT ACCOUNTING POLICIES

The Company tests goodwill and other indefinite-lived intangible asset values at least annually for impairment. The balance of goodwill and other intangibles is assigned to a reporting unit, which is defined as an operating segment or one level below the operating segment. To determine whether an impairment exists, the carrying value of the reporting unit is compared with its fair value. An impairment loss would be recognized to the extent that the carrying value of the reporting unit exceeded its fair value. Fair value estimates are based on quoted market values in active markets, if available. If quoted market prices are not available, the estimate of fair value is based on various valuation techniques, including discounted value of estimated future cash flows, market multiples or appraised valuations by experts.

**FINANCIAL
ANALYSIS**

Accounting for Goodwill

Before 2002, GAAP required that goodwill be amortized over no more than 40 years. Beginning in 2002, companies were required to cease amortizing any previously recorded or newly recorded goodwill. For companies with large goodwill balances, this change caused a substantial increase in reported earnings. For example, Dow Jones Corporate Filings Alert reported the following effects for Wal-Mart:

continued

---

[6]Ignoring taxes.

WAL-MART SAYS ACCTG CHANGE TO ADD $223M TO NET IN FY '03

WASHINGTON (Dow Jones)—Wal-Mart Stores Inc. (WMT) Tuesday projected an annual increase of $223 million in reported net income beginning in fiscal 2003 because of a new accounting pronouncement that requires that goodwill and intangible assets with indefinite lives no longer be amortized.

Source: 09/04/2001, Dow Jones Corporate Filings Alert (Copyright © 2001, Dow Jones & Company, Inc.)

In evaluating Wal-Mart's post-2002 performance, analysts needed to adjust for the fact that this change in accounting rules artificially increased net income. Because the amortization of goodwill (like depreciation expense) is a noncash expense, ceasing the amortization had no impact on cash flows from operations.

KEY RATIO ANALYSIS

Return on Assets (ROA)

Learning Objective 5
Analyze and interpret the return on assets ratio.

? ANALYTICAL QUESTION:

During the period, how well has management used the company's total invested capital provided by both debt holders and stockholders?

% RATIO AND COMPARISONS:

$$\text{Return on Assets} = \frac{\text{Net Income*}}{\text{Average Total Assets†}}$$

The 2003 ratio for Dow Jones:

$$\frac{\$170,599}{(\$1,304,154 + \$1,207,659) \div 2} = .136 \,(13.6\%)$$

Selected Focus Companies' Return on Assets Ratio for 2003

Papa John's   9.4%

Harley-Davidson   17.3%

Callaway Golf   6.4%

COMPARISONS OVER TIME		
Dow Jones		
2001	**2002**	**2003**
7.4%	16.1%	13.6%

COMPARISONS WITH COMPETITORS	
New York Times	**Knight-Ridder**
2003	**2003**
8.1%	7.2%

💡 INTERPRETATIONS:

In General → ROA measures how much the firm earned for each dollar of investment. It is the broadest measure of profitability and management effectiveness, independent of financing strategy. ROA allows investors to compare management's investment performance against alternative investment options. Firms with higher ROA are doing a better job of selecting new investments, all other things equal. Company managers often compute the measure on a division-by-division basis and use it to evaluate division managers' relative performance.

Focus Company Analysis → The average ROA for the printing and publishing industry is 9.1 percent.‡ Dow Jones's ROA was well above that amount for the past two years. However, during 2002 and 2003, Dow Jones had large gains from selling businesses and resolving other investing items. Without these nonrecurring gains, Dow Jones's ROA would have been 4.4% in 2002 and 4.7% in 2003, approximately half of the industry average. When analysts use ROA to predict the future, they often remove such nonrecurring items because they will not affect future periods' returns.

A Few Cautions: Like ROE, ROA can be decomposed into its components:

$$\text{ROA} = \text{Net Profit Margin} \times \text{Asset Turnover}$$

$$\frac{\text{Net Income}}{\text{Average Total Assets}} = \frac{\text{Net Income}}{\text{Net Sales}} \times \frac{\text{Net Sales}}{\text{Average Total Assets}}$$

Like ROE, effective analysis of ROA requires understanding why ROA differs from prior levels and that of its competitors. The preceding decomposition, as well as more detailed analyses of components of net profit margin and asset turnover, provides that understanding.

*In more complex return on total asset analyses, interest expense (net of tax) and minority interest are added back to net income in the numerator of the ratio, since the measure assesses return on capital independent of its source.
†Average Total Assets = (Beginning Total Assets + Ending Total Assets) ÷ 2
‡Available from www.investor.reuters.com.

SELF-STUDY QUIZ

Lexis Corporation purchased 100 percent of Nexis Company for $10 million and merged Nexis into Lexis. On the date of the merger, the market value of Nexis's Other Assets was $11 and the book value of Nexis's Liabilities was equal to market value. The two companies' summary balance sheets appeared as follows immediately **before** the merger:

	LEXIS (PARENT)	NEXIS (SUBSIDIARY)
Cash	$10	
Other Assets	90	$10
Liabilities	30	4
Stockholders' Equity	70	6

On the balance sheet after the merger was recorded, what would be the following balances?

1. Goodwill
2. Stockholders' Equity
3. Other Assets (excluding Goodwill)

After you have completed your answers, check them with the solutions at the bottom of the page.

1. Purchase Price ($10) − Market Value of Net Assets ($11 − 4) = Goodwill ($3).
2. Lexis's stockholders' equity is unchanged, leaving $70.
3. Lexis's other assets + Nexis's other assets (at market) = $90 + 11 = $101.

Self-Study Quiz
Solutions

DEMONSTRATION CASE A

(Try to resolve the requirements before proceeding to the suggested solution that follows.) Howell Equipment Corporation sells and services a major line of farm equipment. Both sales and service operations have been profitable. The following transactions affected the company during 2008:

a. Jan. 1   Purchased 2,000 shares of common stock of Dear Company at $40 per share. This purchase represented one percent of the shares outstanding. Management intends to trade these shares actively.

b. Dec. 28   Received $4,000 cash dividend on the Dear Company stock.

c. Dec. 31   Determined that the current market price of the Dear stock was $39.

Required:

1. Prepare the journal entry for each of these transactions.

2. What accounts and amounts will be reported on the balance sheet at the end of 2008? On the income statement for 2008?

SUGGESTED SOLUTION FOR CASE A

1. a. Jan. 1   Investment in TS (+A) 80,000

                 Cash (−A) (2,000 shares × $40) 80,000

    b. Dec. 28   Cash (+A) 4,000

                 Investment income (+R, +SE) 4,000

    c. Dec. 31   Net unrealized gains/losses—TS (+Loss, −SE) ... 2,000

                 Allowance to value at market—TS (−A) 2,000

Year	Market Value	−	Cost	=	Balance Needed in Valuation Allowance	−	Unadjusted Balance in Valuation Allowance	=	Adjustment to Valuation Allowance
2008	$78,000 ($39 × 2000 shares)	−	$80,000	=	$(2,000)	−	$0	=	$(2,000) an unrealized loss for the period

2. *On the Balance Sheet:*

Current Assets

Investment in TS $78,000

    ($80,000 cost − $2,000 allowance)

On the Income Statement:

Other Nonoperating Items

Investment income $4,000

Net unrealized loss on trading securities   2,000

DEMONSTRATION CASE B

Assume the same facts as in Case A except that the securities were purchased as securities available for sale rather than as trading securities.

Required:

1. Prepare the journal entry for each of these transactions.

2. What accounts and amounts will be reported on the balance sheet at the end of 2008? On the income statement for 2008?

SUGGESTED SOLUTION FOR CASE B

1. *a.* Jan. 1   Investment in SAS (+A) 80,000

　　　　　　　Cash (−A) (2,000 shares × $40 per share) ..... 　　　80,000

　　b. Dec. 28   Cash (+A) 4,000

　　　　　　　Investment income (+R, +SE) .... 　　　4,000

　　c. Dec. 31   Net unrealized gains/losses—SAS (−SE) 2,000

　　　　　　　Allowance to value at market—SAS (−A) ..... 　　　2,000

Year	Market Value	−	Cost	=	Balance Needed in Valuation Allowance	−	Unadjusted Balance in Valuation Allowance	=	Adjustment to Valuation Allowance
2008	$78,000 ($39 × 2000 shares)	−	$80,000	=	$(2,000)	−	$0	=	$(2,000) an unrealized loss for the period

2. *On the Balance Sheet:*

Current or Noncurrent Assets
Investment in SAS 　　　　　　　$78,000
　　($80,000 cost − $2,000 allowance)

Stockholders' Equity
Accumulated other comprehensive
　income:
　Net unrealized gains/losses on SAS 　(2,000)

On the Income Statement:

Other Items
Investment income 　　　$4,000

DEMONSTRATION **CASE C**

On January 1, 2007, Connaught Company purchased 40 percent of the outstanding voting shares of London Company on the open market for $85,000 cash. London declared $10,000 in cash dividends and reported net income of $60,000 for the year.

Required:

1. Prepare the journal entries for 2007.

2. What accounts and amounts were reported on Connaught's balance sheet at the end of 2007? On Connaught's income statement for 2007?

SUGGESTED SOLUTION FOR CASE C

1. Jan. 1　　Investments in associated companies (+A) 85,000

　　　　　　Cash (−A) .... 　　　85,000

　　Dividends　Cash (+A) (40% × $10,000) 4,000

　　　　　　Investments in associated companies (−A) ...... 　　　4,000

　　Dec. 31　Investments in associated companies (+A)
　　　　　　(40% × $60,000) 24,000

　　　　　　Equity in investee's net earnings (+R, +SE) ..... 　　　24,000

2. *On the Balance Sheet:*

Noncurrent Assets
Investments in associated
　companies 　　　　　　$105,000
　($85,000 − $4,000 + $24,000)

On the Income Statement:

Other Items
Equity in investee's net earnings 　$24,000

DEMONSTRATION CASE D

On January 1, 2009, Hilton Company purchased 100 percent of the outstanding voting shares of Paris Company in the open market for $85,000 cash and Paris was merged into Hilton. On the date of acquisition, the market value of Paris Company's Plant and Equipment was $79,000 (net book value, $70,000). Hilton had no liabilities or other assets.

Required:

1. Analyze the merger to determine the amount of goodwill purchased.

2. Give the journal entry that Hilton Company should make on the date of the acquisition. If none is required, explain why.

3. Should Paris Company's assets be included on Hilton's balance sheet at book value or market value? Explain.

SUGGESTED SOLUTION FOR CASE D

1.
Purchase price for Paris Company	$85,000
Less: Market value of net assets purchased	79,000
Goodwill	$ 6,000

2.
Jan. 1, 2009	Plant and equipment (+A)	79,000
	Goodwill (+A)	6,000
	Cash (−A)	85,000

3. Paris Company's assets should be included on the postmerger balance sheet at their market values as of the date of acquisition. The cost principle applies as it does with all asset acquisitions.

Chapter Supplement A

Preparing Consolidated Statements

As noted in the chapter, when a company acquires another and **both companies continue their separate legal existence, consolidated financial statements** must be presented. These statements combine the statements of two or more companies into a single set of statements prepared as if they were one company.

Recording Acquisition of a Controlling Interest

By offering cash or shares of its stock or a combination of the two to a target company's shareholders, one company can acquire control of another. When the target company's shareholders accept the offer and the exchange is made, the parent company records the investment in its accounts at the acquisition cost using the purchase method. When both companies maintain their separate legal identities after the acquisition, we say that a **parent-subsidiary relationship** exists. Since both companies continue to exist, both companies' accounting systems continue to record their respective transactions.

Using the same data we used when we discussed the merger of Dow Jones (the parent) and IFNews (the hypothetical subsidiary), let's assume that, on January 1, 2008, Dow Jones paid $100 (all numbers in dollars in millions) cash to buy all of IFNews's stock.[7] Dow Jones would record the acquisition as follows:

Investment in IFNews (+A) 100	
Cash (−A)	100

Assets		=	Liabilities	+	Stockholders' Equity
Investment in IFNews	+ 100				
Cash	− 100				

[7]Purchasing 100 percent of the outstanding stock results in a wholly owned subsidiary. Purchasing less than 100 percent of the stock results in **minority interest** in the subsidiary.

EXHIBIT 12.7

Spreadsheet for
Consolidated
Balance Sheet on the
Date of Acquisition

Immediately After Acquisition

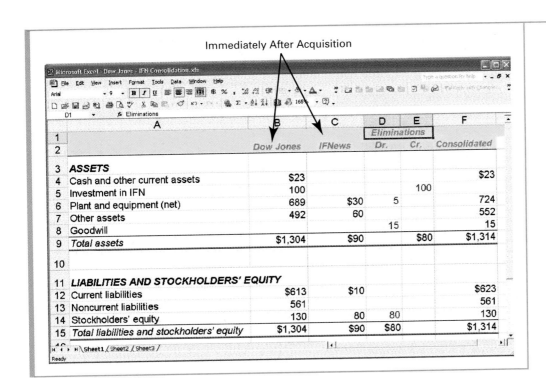

A	Dow Jones	IFNews	Eliminations Dr.	Eliminations Cr.	Consolidated
3 ASSETS					
4 Cash and other current assets	$23				$23
5 Investment in IFN	100			100	
6 Plant and equipment (net)	689	$30	5		724
7 Other assets	492	60			552
8 Goodwill			15		15
9 Total assets	$1,304	$90		$80	$1,314
10					
11 LIABILITIES AND STOCKHOLDERS' EQUITY					
12 Current liabilities	$613	$10			$623
13 Noncurrent liabilities	561				561
14 Stockholders' equity	130	80	80		130
15 Total liabilities and stockholders' equity	$1,304	$90	$80		$1,314

Because the acquisition of IFNews is simply an exchange of shares among owners, no entry is made on IFNews's books. The spreadsheet in Exhibit 12.7 presents Dow Jones's and IFNews's balance sheets immediately **after** the acquisition is recorded by Dow Jones. The Investment in IFNews account is included in Dow Jones's balance sheet.

Preparing Consolidated Financial Statements After Acquisition

Balance Sheet In consolidation, the separate financial statements of the parent (Dow Jones) and the subsidiary (IFNews) are combined into a single consolidated statement. The investment account must be eliminated to avoid double counting the subsidiary's assets and liabilities and the parent company's investment in those assets. Dow Jones paid $100 for all of IFNews's stock even though the total **book value** of IFNews's stockholders' equity was only $80. Thus, the investment account balance of $100 on Dow Jones's books represents the market value of IFNews's net assets (assets minus liabilities) on the date of acquisition. Dow Jones paid $20 in excess of book value for the following reasons:

■ IFNews's plant and equipment had a current market value of $35 and a net book value of $30. (The book values of all other assets and liabilities already on IFNews's balance sheet were equal to their market values.)

■ IFNews had developed a good reputation with an important group of online investors, which increased IFNews's overall value. For these reasons, Dow Jones was willing to pay $15 more than book value to acquire IFNews's stock. The $15 difference between the purchase price of the company and the fair market value of its net assets (assets minus liabilities) is called *goodwill*. It may be analyzed as follows:

Purchase price for 100% interest in IFNews	$100
Less: Net assets purchased, at market ($80 + $5)	85
Goodwill purchased	$ 15

To complete the process of consolidating Dow Jones and IFNews, we must **eliminate** Dow Jones's investment account and replace it with the assets and liabilities of IFNews along with the acquired goodwill. In this process, the goodwill is reported separately, and IFNews's assets and liabilities must be adjusted to market value for items where market value is different than book value, such as the plant and equipment in this illustration. We can accomplish this in the following five steps:

DOW JONES AND SUBSIDIARIES
Consolidated Balance Sheet
January 1, 2008

Assets

Cash and other current assets	$ 23
Plant and equipment (net)	724
Other assets	552
Goodwill	15
Total assets	$1,314

Liabilities and Stockholders' Equity

Current liabilities	$ 623
Noncurrent liabilities	561
Stockholders' equity	130
Total liabilities and stockholders' equity	$1,314

1. Subtract the investment account balance of $100.
2. Add the $15 goodwill purchased as an asset.
3. Add $5 to plant and equipment to adjust the balance to market value.
4. Subtract the IFNews stockholders' equity.
5. Add together what remains of the Dow Jones and IFNews balance sheets.

When these procedures are accomplished, the balance sheet shown in Exhibit 12.8 is produced. Note that this is the same balance sheet presented in Exhibit 12.5 that resulted from the merger of Dow Jones and IFNews into one company. This should not be surprising because consolidated statements present a single set of statements as if the parent and subsidiary companies were one.

Income Statement   When we prepared the consolidated balance sheet, we combined the separate balance sheets to make it appear as if a single company exists. Consolidating the income statements requires a similar process. Prior to preparing consolidated statements for Dow Jones and its subsidiary IFNews, their separate income statements were as follows:

SIMPLIFIED *SEPARATE* INCOME STATEMENTS
Year ended December 31, 2008, One Year After Acquisition

(dollars in millions)	Dow Jones	IFN
Revenues	$2,158	$120
Less: Expenses	2,150	106
Plus: Income from subsidiary	14	
Net income	$ 22	$ 14

The revenues and expenses generated by the parent company's own operations, excluding any investment income from the subsidiary, must now be combined with the subsidiary's revenues and expenses. The revaluation of assets to market value, if any, also has implications for the consolidated income statement. The increase in the assets must be depreciated or amortized in the consolidation process.

In this example, preparing the consolidated income statement requires three steps (ignoring taxes):

1. Add Dow Jones's revenues from its own operations of $2,158 and IFNews's revenues of $120.
2. Add Dow Jones's expenses related to its own operations of $2,150 and IFNews's expenses of $106.

3. Add to the expenses the $1 additional depreciation expense, assuming a five-year useful life ($5 additional plant and equipment over book value ÷ 5 years = $1 per year).

Due to the simplicity of this example, you can directly prepare the simplified consolidated income statement in Exhibit 12.9. Complex adjustments and eliminations would normally be entered into a spreadsheet program.

DOW JONES AND SUBSIDIARIES Consolidated Income Statement Year Ended December 31, 2008 (dollars in millions)	
Revenues ($2,158 + $120)	$2,278
Expenses ($2,150 + $106 + $1)	2,257
Net income	$ 21

EXHIBIT 12.9

Consolidated Income Statement

DEMONSTRATION CASE E

On January 1, 2007, Connaught Company purchased 100 percent of the outstanding voting shares of London Company on the open market for $85,000 cash. On the date of acquisition, the market value of London Company's operational assets was $79,000.

Required:

1. Give the journal entry that Connaught Company should make on the date of acquisition. If none is required, explain why.

2. Give the journal entry that London Company should make on the date of acquisition. If none is required, explain why.

3. Analyze the acquisition to determine the amount of goodwill that was purchased.

4. Should London Company's assets be included on the consolidated balance sheet at book value or market value? Explain.

SUGGESTED SOLUTION FOR CASE E

1. Jan. 1, 2007 Investment in subsidiary (+A) 85,000
          Cash (−A)   85,000

2. London Company does not record a journal entry related to the purchase of its stock by Connaught Company. The transaction was between Connaught and the stockholders of London Company; it did not directly involve London Company.

3.
Purchase price for London Company	$85,000
Market value of net assets purchased	79,000
Goodwill	$ 6,000

4. London Company's assets should be included on the consolidated balance sheet at their market values **as of the date of acquisition.** The cost principle applies as it does with all asset acquisitions.

CHAPTER **TAKE-AWAYS**

1. **Analyze and report bond investments held to maturity.**   p. 608

   When management intends to hold a bond investment until it matures, the held-to-maturity bond is recorded at cost when acquired and reported at amortized cost on the balance sheet. Any interest earned during the period is reported on the income statement.

2. **Analyze and report passive investments in securities using the market value method.**   p. 610

   - Acquiring less than 20 percent of the outstanding voting shares of an investee's common stock is presumed to be a passive stock investment. Passive investments may be classified as
     - Trading securities (actively traded to maximize return) **or**
     - Securities available for sale (earn a return but are not as actively traded), depending on management's intent.
   - The investments are recorded at cost and adjusted to **market value** at year-end. A valuation allowance is increased or decreased to arrive at market value with the resulting unrealized holding gain or loss recorded.
     - For trading securities, the net unrealized gains and losses are reported in net income.
     - For securities available for sale, the net unrealized gains and losses are reported as a component of stockholders' equity in other comprehensive income.
   - Any dividends earned are reported as revenue, and any gains or losses on sales of passive investments are reported on the income statement.

3. **Analyze and report investments involving significant influence using the equity method.**   p. 618

   If between 20 and 50 percent of the outstanding voting shares are owned, significant influence over the investee firm's operating and financing policies is presumed, and the equity method is applied. Under the **equity method,** the investor records the investment at cost on the acquisition date. Each period thereafter, the investment amount is increased (or decreased) by the proportionate interest in the income (or loss) reported by the investee corporation and decreased by the proportionate share of the dividends declared by the investee corporation.

   The investing section of the statement of cash flows discloses purchases and sales of investments. In the operating section, net income is adjusted for any gains or losses on sales of investments and equity in the earnings of associated companies (net of dividends received).

4. **Analyze and report investments in controlling interests.**   p. 623

   Mergers occur when one company purchases all of the net assets of another and the target company ceases to exist as a separate legal entity. Mergers and ownership of a controlling interest of another corporation (more than 50 percent of the outstanding voting shares) must be accounted for using the purchase method. In conformity with the cost principle, the investee's assets and liabilities are measured at their market values. Any amount paid above the market value of the net assets is reported as goodwill by the investor. The concept of consolidation is based on the view that a parent company and its subsidiaries constitute one economic entity. Therefore, the separate income statements, balance sheets, and statements of cash flows should be combined each period on an item-by-item basis as a single set of consolidated financial statements. Consolidated statements are the same as those that result from a merger when all of the assets and liabilities are acquired and the target company ceases to exist.

5. **Analyze and interpret the return on assets ratio.**   p. 628

   The return on assets ratio measures how much the company earned for each dollar of assets. It provides information on profitability and management's effectiveness with an increasing ratio over time suggesting increased efficiency. ROA is computed as net income divided by average total assets.

   Each year, many companies report healthy profits but file for bankruptcy. Some investors consider this situation to be a paradox, but sophisticated analysts understand how this situation can occur. These analysts recognize that the income statement is prepared under the accrual concept (revenue is reported when earned and the related expense is matched with the revenue). The income statement does not report cash collections and cash payments. Troubled companies usually file for bankruptcy because they cannot meet their cash obligations (for example, they cannot pay their suppliers or meet their required interest payments). The income statement does not help analysts assess the cash flows of a company. The statement of cash flows discussed in Chapter 13 is designed to help statement users evaluate a company's cash inflows and outflows.

KEY **RATIO**

Return on assets measures how much the company earned on every dollar of assets during the period. A high or rising ratio suggests that the company is managing its assets efficiently. It is computed as follows (p. 628):

$$\text{Return on Assets (ROA)} = \frac{\text{Net Income}}{\text{Average Total Assets*}}$$

*(Beginning Total Assets + Ending Total Assets) ÷ 2

FINDING **FINANCIAL INFORMATION**

Balance Sheet
Current Assets
 Investment in trading securities (net of valuation allowance)
 Investment in securities available for sale (net of valuation allowance)
Noncurrent Assets
 Investment in securities available for sale (net of valuation allowance)
 Investment in associated companies
 Investments held to maturity
Stockholders' Equity
 Accumulated other comprehensive income:
  Net unrealized gains and losses on securities available for sale

Income Statement
Under "Other Items"
 Investment income
 Loss or gain on sale of investments
 Net unrealized gains and losses on trading securities
 Equity in investee earnings or losses

Notes
In Various Notes
 Accounting policies for investments
 Details on securities held as trading and available-for-sale securities and investments in associated companies

Statement of Cash Flows
Operating Activities
Net income adjusted for:
 Gains/losses on sale of investments
 Equity in earnings/losses of associated companies
 Dividends received from associated companies
 Net unrealized gains/losses on trading securities

KEY TERMS

Amortized Cost Method p. 608
Consolidated Financial Statements p. 624
Equity Method p. 618
Goodwill (Cost in Excess of Net Assets Acquired) p. 625

Held-to-Maturity Investments p. 608
Investments in Associated (or Affiliated) Companies p. 618
Market Value Method p. 610
Merger p. 624
Parent Company p. 624

Purchase Method p. 625
Securities Available for Sale p. 611
Subsidiary Company p. 624
Trading Securities p. 611
Unrealized Holding Gains or Losses p. 610

QUESTIONS

1. Explain the difference between a short-term investment and a long-term investment.
2. Explain the difference in accounting methods used for passive investments, investments in which the investor can exert significant influence, and investments in which the investor has control over another entity.
3. Explain how bonds held to maturity are reported on the balance sheet.
4. Explain the application of the cost principle to the purchase of capital stock in another company.
5. Under the market value method, when and how does the investor company measure revenue?
6. Under the equity method, why does the investor company measure revenue on a proportionate basis when income is reported by the investee company rather than when dividends are declared?
7. Under the equity method, dividends received from the investee company are not recorded as revenue. To record dividends as revenue involves double counting. Explain.
8. What is a business combination by purchase?
9. What is goodwill?
10. What is a parent-subsidiary relationship?
11. Explain the basic concept underlying consolidated statements.
12. What is the basic element that must be present before consolidated statements are appropriate?
13. (Supplement A) What are intercompany eliminations?

MULTIPLE-CHOICE QUESTIONS

1. Company A owns 40 percent of Company B and exercises significant influence over the management of Company B. Therefore, Company A uses what method of accounting for reporting its ownership of stock in Company B?
   a. the amortized cost method
   b. the market-value method
   c. the equity method
   d. consolidation of the financial statements of companies A and B
2. Company A purchases 10 percent of Company X and Company A intends to hold the stock for at least five years. At the end of the current year, how would Company A's investment in Company X be reported on Company A's December 31 (year-end) balance sheet?
   a. at original cost in the current assets section
   b. at the December 31 market value in the current assets section
   c. at original cost in the long-term assets section
   d. at the December 31 market value in the long-term assets section

3. Dividends received from a stock that is reported as a *security available for sale* in the long-term assets section of the balance sheet are reported as which of the following?
    a. an increase to cash and a decrease to the investment in stock account
    b. an increase to cash and an unrealized gain on the balance sheet
    c. an increase to cash and an increase to revenue
    d. an increase to cash and an unrealized gain on the income statement

4. Realized gains and losses are recorded on the income statement for which of the following transactions in *trading securities* and *available-for-sale* securities?
    a. when adjusting a *trading security* to its market value
    b. when adjusting an *available-for-sale security* to its market value
    c. only when recording the sale of a *trading security*
    d. when recording the sale of either a *trading security* or an *available-for-sale security*

5. When recording dividends received from a stock investment accounted for using the equity method, which of the following statements is true?
    a. Total assets are increased and net income is increased.
    b. Total assets are increased and total shareholders' equity is increased.
    c. Total assets are decreased and total shareholders' equity is decreased.
    d. Total assets and total owners' equity do not change.

6. When using the equity method of accounting, when is revenue recorded on the books of the investor company?
    a. when the market value of the investee stock increases
    b. when a dividend is received from the investee
    c. when the investee company reports net income
    d. both (b) and (c)

7. Which of the following items is reported in the investing section of the statement of cash flows when a stock investment is sold?
    a. the subtraction of a resulting gain on the sale
    b. the addition of a resulting loss on the sale
    c. the addition of cash sales proceeds
    d. all of the above

8. Which of the following statements regarding goodwill is false?
    a. Goodwill appears in the noncurrent asset section of the balance sheet.
    b. When the amortization of goodwill was halted in 2002, cash flows for those companies reporting goodwill increased accordingly.
    c. When companies develop goodwill internally rather than acquire the goodwill in an exchange, goodwill is not reported on the balance sheet.
    d. None of the above are false.

9. Which of the following is true regarding the return on assets ratio?
    a. This ratio is used to evaluate the efficiency of a company given the capital contributed by owners.
    b. This ratio is used to evaluate the financing strategy of a company.
    c. Return on assets can be separated into two components, net profit margin and inventory turnover.
    d. This ratio is used to evaluate how efficiently a company manages its total assets.

10. Consolidated financial statements are required in which of the following situations?
    a. only when a company can exert significant influence over another company
    b. only when a company acquires goodwill in the purchase of another company
    c. only when a parent company can exercise control over its subsidiary
    d. only when a company acquires another company for vertical integration

For more practice with multiple-choice questions, go to the text website www.mhhe.com/ libby5e or the Topic Tackler DVD for use with this text.

MINI-**EXERCISES**

 ™ **Available with McGraw-Hill's Homework Manager**

M12-1
LO1, 2, 3, 4

Matching Measurement and Reporting Methods

Match the following. Answers may be used more than once:

Measurement Method

A. Market value method
B. Equity method
C. Consolidation
D. Amortized cost

_____ More than 50 percent ownership
_____ Bonds held to maturity
_____ Less than 20 percent ownership
_____ At least 20 percent but not more than 50 percent ownership
_____ Current market value
_____ Original cost less any amortization of premium or discount associated with the purchase
_____ Original cost plus proportionate part of the income of the investee less proportionate part of the dividends declared by the investee

M12-2
LO1

Recording a Bond Investment

Wall Company purchased $1,000,000, 8 percent bonds issued by Janice Company on January 1, 2007. The purchase price of the bonds was $1,070,000. Interest is payable semiannually each June 30 and December 31. Record the purchase of the bonds on January 1, 2007.

M12-3
LO2

Recording Trading Securities Transactions

During 2008, Princeton Company acquired some of the 50,000 outstanding shares of the common stock, par $10, of Cox Corporation as trading securities. The accounting period for both companies ends December 31. Give the journal entries for each of the following transactions that occurred during 2008:

Dec.   2   Purchased 8,000 shares of Cox common stock at $28 per share.
Dec. 15   Cox Corporation declared and paid a cash dividend of $2 per share.
Dec. 31   Determined the current market price of Cox stock to be $25 per share.

M12-4
LO2

Recording Available-for-Sale Securities Transactions

Using the data in M12-3, assume that Princeton Company purchased the voting stock of Cox Corporation for the available-for-sale portfolio instead of the trading securities portfolio. Give the journal entries for each of the transactions listed.

M12-5
LO2

Determining Financial Statement Effects of Trading Securities Transactions

Using the following categories, indicate the effects of the transactions listed in M12-3 assuming trading securities. Use + for increase and − for decrease and indicate the amounts.

	BALANCE SHEET			INCOME STATEMENT		
Transaction	Assets	Liabilities	Stockholders' Equity	Revenues	Expenses	Net Income

M12-6
LO2

Determining Financial Statement Effects of Available-for-Sale Securities Transactions

Using the following categories, indicate the effects of the transactions listed in M12-3 assuming securities available for sale. Use + for increase and − for decrease and indicate the amounts.

	BALANCE SHEET			INCOME STATEMENT		
Transaction	Assets	Liabilities	Stockholders' Equity	Revenues	Expenses	Net Income

Recording Equity Method Securities Transactions

M12-7
LO3

On January 1, 2008, Ubuy.com acquired 25 percent (10,000 shares) of the common stock of E-Net Corporation. The accounting period for both companies ends December 31. Give the journal entries for each of the following transactions that occurred during 2008:

July 2 E-Net declared and paid a cash dividend of $3 per share.

Dec. 31 E-Net reported net income of $200,000.

Determining Financial Statement Effects of Equity Method Securities

M12-8
LO3

Using the following categories, indicate the effects of the transactions listed in M12-7. Use + for increase and − for decrease and indicate the accounts affected and the amounts.

	BALANCE SHEET			INCOME STATEMENT		
Transaction	Assets	Liabilities	Stockholders' Equity	Revenues	Expenses	Net Income

Recording a Merger

M12-9
LO4

Philadelphia Textile Company acquired Boston Fabric Company for $600,000 cash when Boston's only assets, property and equipment, had a book value of $590,000 and a market value of $630,000. Philadelphia also assumed Boston's bonds payable of $100,000. After the acquisition, Boston would cease to exist as a separate legal entity after merging with Philadelphia. Record the acquisition.

Computing and Interpreting Return on Assets Ratio

M12-10
LO5

M.A.D. Company reported the following information at the end of each year:

Year	Net Income	Total Assets
2006	$152,000	$ 52,000
2007	195,000	68,000
2008	201,000	134,000
2009	212,000	145,000

Compute return on assets for 2007, 2008, and 2009. What do the results suggest about M.A.D. Company?

(Supplement A) Interpreting Goodwill Disclosures

M12-11
The Walt Disney
Company

Disney owns theme parks, movie studios, television and radio stations, newspapers, and television networks, including ABC and ESPN. Its balance sheet recently reported goodwill in the amount of $17 billion, which is more than 33 percent of the company's total assets. This percentage is very large compared to that of most companies. Explain why you think Disney has such a large amount of goodwill reported on its balance sheet.

 **Available with McGraw-Hill's Homework Manager**

EXERCISES

Recording Bonds Held to Maturity

E12-1
LO1
Federated
Department Stores,
Inc.

Federated Department Stores, Inc., operates over 390 department stores and 66 furniture galleries under the names of Macy's, Burdines-Macy's, Bloomingdales, and several others. The company does more than $15 billion in sales each year.

Assume that as part of its cash management strategy, Federated purchased $10 million in bonds at par for cash on July 1, 2007. The bonds pay 10 percent interest each June 30 and December 31 and mature in 10 years. Federated plans to hold the bonds until maturity.

Required:
1. Record the purchase of the bonds on July 1, 2007.
2. Record the receipt of interest on December 31, 2007.

E12-2
LO2, 3

Comparing Market Value and Equity Methods

Company A purchased a certain number of Company B's outstanding voting shares at $19 per share as a long-term investment. Company B had outstanding 20,000 shares of $10 par value stock. Complete the following matrix relating to the measurement and reporting by Company A after acquisition of the shares of Company B stock.

Questions	Market Value Method	Equity Method
a. What is the applicable level of ownership by Company A of Company B to apply the method?	_____%	_____%

For b, e, f, and g, assume the following:		
Number of shares acquired of Company B stock	1,000	5,000
Net income reported by Company B in the first year	$50,000	$50,000
Dividends declared by Company B in the first year	$10,000	$10,000
Market price at end of first year, Company B stock	$ 15	$ 15

	Market Value Method	Equity Method
b. At acquisition, the investment account on the books of Company A should be debited at what amount?	$_____	$_____
c. When should Company A recognize revenue earned on the stock of Company B? Explanation required.	_____	_____
d. After the acquisition date, how should Company A change the balance of the investment account net of the allowance with respect to the stock owned in Company B (other than for disposal of the investment)? Explanation required.	_____	_____
e. What is the net balance in the investment account on the balance sheet of Company A at the end of the first year?	$_____	$_____
f. What amount of revenue from the investment in Company B should Company A report at the end of the first year?	$_____	$_____
g. What amount of unrealized loss should Company A report at the end of the first year?	$_____	$_____

E12-3
LO2

Recording Transactions in the Trading Securities Portfolio

On June 30, 2007, MetroMedia, Inc., purchased 10,000 shares of Mitek stock for $20 per share. Management purchased the stock for speculative purposes and recorded the stock in the trading securities portfolio. The following information pertains to the price per share of Mitek stock:

	Price
12/31/2007	$24
12/31/2008	31
12/31/2009	25

MetroMedia sold all of the Mitek stock on February 14, 2010, at a price of $22 per share. Prepare any journal entries that are required by the facts presented in this case.

E12-4
LO2

Recording Transactions in the Available-for-Sale Portfolio

Using the data in E12-3, assume that MetroMedia management purchased the Mitek stock for the available-for-sale portfolio instead of the trading securities portfolio. Prepare any journal entries that are required by the facts presented in the case.

E12-5
LO2

Reporting Gains and Losses in the Trading Securities Portfolio

On March 10, 2006, General Solutions, Inc., purchased 5,000 shares of MicroTech stock for $50 per share. Management purchased the stock for speculative purposes and recorded it in the trading securities portfolio. The following information pertains to the price per share of MicroTech stock:

	Price
12/31/2006	$55
12/31/2007	40
12/31/2008	42

General Solutions sold all of the MicroTech stock on September 12, 2009, at a price of $39 per share. Prepare any journal entries that are required by the facts presented in this case.

Reporting Gains and Losses in the Available-for-Sale Portfolio

E12-6
LO2

Using the data in E12-5, assume that General Solutions management purchased the MicroTech stock for the available-for-sale portfolio instead of the trading securities portfolio. Prepare any journal entries that are required by the facts presented in the case.

Recording and Reporting an Equity Method Security

E12-7
LO3

Felicia Company acquired some of the 60,000 shares of outstanding common stock (no-par) of Nueces Corporation during 2008 as a long-term investment. The annual accounting period for both companies ends December 31. The following transactions occurred during 2008:

Jan. 10   Purchased 21,000 shares of Nueces common stock at $12 per share.

Dec. 31   a. Received the 2008 financial statements of Nueces Corporation that reported net income of $90,000.

b. Nueces Corporation declared and paid a cash dividend of $0.60 per share.

c. Determined the market price of Nueces stock to be $11 per share.

Required:
1. What accounting method should the company use? Why?
2. Give the journal entries for each of these transactions. If no entry is required, explain why.
3. Show how the long-term investment and the related revenue should be reported on the 2008 financial statements (balance sheet and income statement) of the company.

Interpreting the Effects of Equity Method Investments on Cash Flow from Operations

E12-8
LO3

Using the data in E12-7, answer the following questions.

Required:
1. On the current year cash flow statement, how would the investing section of the statement be affected by the preceding transactions?
2. On the current year cash flow statement (indirect method), how would the equity in the earnings of the associated company and the dividends from the associated company affect the operating section? Explain the reasons for the effects.

Determining the Appropriate Accounting Treatment for an Acquisition

E12-9
LO4

The notes to the financial statements of Colgate-Palmolive contained the following information:

The Colgate-Palmolive Company

2. Acquisitions

On December 18, 2003, the Company agreed to acquire GABA Holding AG (GABA), a privately owned European oral care company headquartered in Switzerland. The transaction is structured as an all-cash acquisition of between 80% and 100% of the outstanding shares of GABA for an aggregate price ranging from 800 million Swiss francs to 1,050 million Swiss francs (approximately $645.0 to $846.5 based on December 31, 2003 exchange rates). . . .

Assume that Colgate-Palmolive acquired 100 percent of the fair value of the net assets of GABA in 2004 for $700 million in cash. GABA's assets at the time of the acquisition had a book value of $510 million and a market value of $550 million. Colgate-Palmolive also assumed GABA's liabilities of $170 million (book value and market value are the same). Prepare the entry on the date of the acquisition assuming it is a merger.

E12-10

LO5

Timberland

Analyzing and Interpreting the Return on Assets Ratio

Timberland is a leading designer of shoes and clothing. In a recent year, it reported the following:

	Current Year	Prior Year
Revenue	$1,342,123	$1,190,896
Net income	117,879	95,113
Total assets	641,716	538,671
Total stockholders' equity	428,463	372,785

Required:
1. Determine the return on assets ratio for the current year.
2. Explain the meaning of the ratio.

E12-11

DaimlerChrysler AG

(Supplement A) Interpreting Consolidation Policy

DaimlerChrysler AG, headquartered in Stuttgart, Germany, produces vehicles including small cars, sports cars, luxury sedans, versatile vans, heavy duty trucks, and coaches. Passenger car brands include Maybach, Mercedes-Benz, Chrysler, Jeep®, and Dodge. A recent annual report for Daimler-Chrysler includes the statement that "all significant intercompany transactions and balances relating to these majority-owned subsidiaries and variable interests have been eliminated." In your own words, explain the meaning of this statement. Why is it necessary to eliminate all intercompany accounts and transactions in consolidation?

E12-12

(Supplement A) Analyzing Goodwill and Reporting the Consolidated Balance Sheet

On January 1, 2007, Company P purchased 100 percent of the outstanding voting shares of Company S in the open market for $80,000 cash. On that date, the separate balance sheets (summarized) of the two companies reported the following book values:

	IMMEDIATELY AFTER THE ACQUISITION JANUARY 1, 2007	
	Company P	Company S
Cash	$ 12,000	$18,000
Investment in Co. S (at cost)	80,000	
Property and Equipment (net)	48,000	42,000
Total assets	$140,000	$60,000
Liabilities	$ 40,000	$ 9,000
Common stock:		
Company P (no-par)	90,000	
Company S (par $10)		40,000
Retained earnings	10,000	11,000
Total liabilities and stockholders' equity	$140,000	$60,000

It was determined on the date of acquisition that the market value of the assets and liabilities of Company S were equal to their book values.

Required:
1. Give the journal entry that Company P made at date of acquisition to record the investment. If none is required, explain why.
2. Analyze the acquisition to determine the amount of goodwill purchased.
3. Prepare a consolidated balance sheet immediately after acquisition.

(Supplement A) Determining Consolidated Net Income

Assume that P Company acquired S Company on January 1, 2008, for $100,000 cash. At the time, the net book value of S Company was $90,000. The market value was $96,000 with property and equipment having a market value of $6,000 over book value. The property and equipment has a three-year remaining life and is depreciated straight-line with no residual value. During 2008, the companies reported the following operating results:

	P Company	S Company
Revenues related to their own operations	$500,000	$75,000
Expenses related to their own operations	350,000	50,000

Compute consolidated net income for the year ended December 31, 2008.

 Available with McGraw-Hill's Homework Manager

PROBLEMS

Determining Financial Statement Effects for Bonds Held to Maturity (AP12-1)

P12-1
LO1
Starbucks
Corporation

Starbucks is a rapidly expanding company that provides high-quality coffee products. Assume that as part of its expansion strategy, Starbucks plans to open numerous new stores in Mexico in five years. The company has $5 million to support the expansion and has decided to invest the funds in corporate bonds until the money is needed. Assume that Starbucks purchased bonds with $5 million face value at par for cash on July 1, 2008. The bonds pay 8 percent interest each June 30 and December 31 and mature in five years. Starbucks plans to hold the bonds until maturity.

Required:
1. What accounts are affected when the bonds are purchased on July 1, 2008?
2. What accounts are affected when interest is received on December 31, 2008?
3. Should Starbucks prepare a journal entry if the market value of the bonds decreased to $4,000,000 on December 31, 2008? Explain.

Recording Passive Investments (AP12-2)

P12-2
LO2
e**X**cel

On March 1, 2006, HiTech Industries purchased 10,000 shares of Integrated Services Company for $20 per share. The following information applies to the stock price of Integrated Services:

	Price
12/31/2006	$17
12/31/2007	24
12/31/2008	31

Required:
1. Prepare journal entries to record the facts in the case, assuming that HiTech purchased the shares for the trading portfolio.
2. Prepare journal entries to record the facts in the case, assuming that HiTech purchased the shares for the available-for-sale portfolio.

Reporting Passive Investments (AP12-3)

P12-3
LO2

During January 2008, Nash Glass Company purchased the following shares as a long-term investment:

Stock	Number of Shares Outstanding	Purchase	Cost per Share
Q Corporation Common (no-par)	90,000	12,600	$ 5
R Corporation Preferred, nonvoting (par $10)	20,000	12,000	30

Subsequent to acquisition, the following data were available:

	2008	2009
Net income reported at December 31		
Q Corporation	$30,000	$36,000
R Corporation	40,000	48,000
Dividends declared and paid per share during the year		
Q Corporation common stock	$0.85	$0.90
R Corporation preferred stock	1.00	1.10
Market value per share at December 31		
Q Corporation common stock	$ 4.00	$ 4.00
R Corporation preferred stock	29.00	30.00

Required:

1. What accounting method should be used for the investment in Q common stock? R preferred stock? Why?
2. Give the journal entries for the company for each year in parallel columns (if none, explain why) for each of the following:
   a. Purchase of the investments.
   b. Income reported by Q and R Corporations.
   c. Dividends received from Q and R Corporations.
   d. Market value effects at year-end.
3. For each year, show how the following amounts should be reported on the financial statements:
   a. Long-term investment.
   b. Stockholders' equity—net unrealized gains and losses.
   c. Revenues.

P12-4
LO2, 3

Recording Passive Investments and Investments for Significant Influence

On August 4, 2007, Coffman Corporation purchased 1,000 shares of Dittman Company for $45,000. The following information applies to the stock price of Dittman Company:

	Price
12/31/2007	$52
12/31/2008	47
12/31/2009	38

Dittman Company declares and pays cash dividends of $2 per share on June 1 of each year.

Required:

1. Prepare journal entries to record the facts in the case, assuming that Coffman purchased the shares for the trading portfolio.
2. Prepare journal entries to record the facts in the case, assuming that Coffman purchased the shares for the available-for-sale portfolio.
3. Prepare journal entries to record the facts in the case, assuming that Coffman used the equity method to account for the investment. Coffman owns 30 percent of Dittman and Dittman reported $50,000 in income each year.

P12-5
LO2, 3

Comparing Methods to Account for Various Levels of Ownership of Voting Stock

Company C had outstanding 30,000 shares of common stock, par value $10 per share. On January 1, 2007, Company D purchased some of these shares as a long-term investment at $25 per share. At the end of 2007, Company C reported the following: income, $50,000, and cash dividends declared and paid during the year, $25,500. The market value of Company C stock at the end of 2007 was $22 per share.

Required:

1. For each of the following cases (in the tabulation), identify the method of accounting that Company D should use. Explain why.

2. Give the journal entries for Company D at the dates indicated for each of the two independent cases, assuming that the investments will be held long term. If no entry is required, explain why. Use the following format:

Tabulation of Items	Case A: 3,600 Shares Purchased	Case B: 10,500 Shares Purchased

1. Accounting method?
2. Journal entries:
   a. To record the acquisition at January 1, 2007.
   b. To recognize the income reported by Company C for 2007.
   c. To recognize the dividends declared and paid by Company C.
   d. Entry to recognize market value effect at end of 2007.
3. Complete the following schedule to show the separate amounts that should be reported on the 2007 financial statements of Company D:

	DOLLAR AMOUNTS	
	Case A	Case B
Balance sheet		
Investments		
Stockholders' equity		
Income statement		
Investment income		
Equity in earnings of investee		

4. Explain why assets, stockholders' equity, and revenues for the two cases are different.

Comparing the Market Value and Equity Methods (AP12-4)

P12-6
LO2, 3
eXcel

Ship Corporation had outstanding 100,000 shares of no-par common stock. On January 10, 2008, Shore Company purchased a block of these shares in the open market at $20 per share for long-term investment purposes. At the end of 2008, Ship reported net income of $300,000 and cash dividends of $.60 per share. At December 31, 2008, Ship stock was selling at $18 per share. This problem involves two separate cases:

Case A Purchase of 10,000 shares of Ship common stock.

Case B Purchase of 40,000 shares of Ship common stock.

Required:
1. For each case, identify the accounting method that the company should use. Explain why.
2. For each case, in parallel columns, give the journal entries for each of the following (if no entry is required, explain why):
   a. Acquisition.
   b. Revenue recognition.
   c. Dividends received.
   d. Market value effects.
3. For each case, show how the following should be reported on the 2008 financial statements:
   a. Long-term investments.
   b. Shareholders' equity.
   c. Revenues.
4. Explain why the amounts reported in requirement (3) are different for the two cases.

Determining Cash Flow Statement Effects of Investments for Significant Influence (AP12-5)

P12-7
LO3

During 2008, Oscar Company purchased some of the 90,000 shares of common stock, par $8, of Selma, Inc., as a long-term investment. The annual accounting period for each company ends December 31. The following transactions occurred during 2008:

Jan. 7   Purchased 40,500 shares of Selma stock at $33 per share.

Dec. 31   a. Received the 2008 financial statement of Selma, which reported net income
             of $220,000.

          b. Selma declared and paid a cash dividend of $2 per share.

          c. Determined that the current market price of Selma stock was $40 per share.

Required:

Indicate how the Operating Activities and Investing Activities sections of the cash flow statement (indirect method) will be affected by each transaction.

P12-8
LO4

Analyzing Goodwill and Reporting a Merger (AP12-6)

On January 4, 2007, Pronti Company acquired all of the net assets of Scott Company for $120,000 cash. The two companies merged with Pronti Company surviving. The balance sheets for each company prior to the merger follow.

Balance Sheets at January 4, 2007	Pronti Company	Scott Company
Cash	$118,000	$23,000
Property and equipment (net)	132,000	65,000*
Total assets	$250,000	$88,000
Liabilities	$ 27,000	$12,000
Common stock (par $5)	120,000	40,000
Retained earnings	103,000	36,000
Total liabilities and stockholders' equity	$250,000	$88,000

Determined by Pronti Company to have a market value of $72,000 at date of acquisition.

Required:

1. How much goodwill was involved in this merger? Show computations.
2. Record the merger by Pronti Company on January 4, 2007.
3. Prepare a consolidated balance sheet immediately after the acquisition.

P12-9
LO5

Verizon
Communications,
Inc.

Interpreting the Return on Assets Ratio (AP12-7)

Verizon Communications Inc. was formed by the merger of Bell Atlantic Corporation and GTE Corporation in 2000. It is the largest provider of wireline and wireless communication services in the United States with presence in over 40 other countries. The following information was reported in the company's 2003 annual report:

	2003	2002	2001	2000
		(dollars in millions)		
Net income	$ 3,077	$ 4,079	$ 389	$ 11,797
Total assets	165,968	167,468	170,795	164,735

Required:

1. Compute the return on assets ratio for 2003, 2002, and 2001.
2. What do the results in requirement (1) suggest about Verizon?

P12-10

(Supplement A) Analyzing Goodwill and Reporting the Consolidated Balance Sheet

On January 4, 2008, Penn Company acquired all 8,000 outstanding shares of Syracuse Company for $12 cash per share. Immediately after the acquisition, the balance sheets reflected the following:

Balance Sheets at January 4, 2008	Penn Company	Syracuse Company
Cash	$ 22,000	$23,000
Investment in Syracuse Company	96,000	
Property and equipment (net)	132,000	65,000*
Total assets	$250,000	$88,000
Liabilities	$ 27,000	$12,000
Common stock (par $5)	120,000	40,000
Retained earnings	103,000	36,000
Total liabilities and stockholders' equity	$250,000	$88,000

Determined by Penn Company to have a market value of $72,000 at date of acquisition.

Required:
1. Give the journal entry that Penn Company made to record the acquisition.
2. Analyze the acquisition to determine the amount of goodwill purchased.
3. Should Syracuse Company's assets be included on the consolidated balance sheet at book value or market value? Explain.
4. Prepare a consolidated balance sheet immediately after acquisition. (*Hint:* Consider your answer to requirement [3].)

ALTERNATE **PROBLEMS**

Determining Financial Statement Effects for Bonds Held to Maturity (P12-1)

AP12-1
LO1
Sonic Corporation

Sonic Corporation operates and franchises a chain of quick-service drive-in restaurants in most of the United States and in Mexico. Customers drive up to a canopied parking space and order food through an intercom speaker system. A carhop then delivers the food to the customer. Assume that Sonic has $10 million in cash to support future expansion and has decided to invest the funds in corporate bonds until the money is needed. Sonic purchases bonds with $10 million face value for $10.3 million cash on January 1, 2008. The bonds pay 8 percent interest each June 30 and December 31 and mature in four years. Sonic plans to hold the bonds until maturity.

Required:
1. What accounts were affected when the bonds were purchased on January 1, 2008?
2. What accounts were affected when interest was received on June 30, 2008?
3. Should Sonic prepare a journal entry if the market value of the bonds decreased to $9,700,000 on December 31, 2008? Explain.

Recording Passive Investments (P12-2)

AP12-2
LO2

On September 15, 2007, James Media Corporation purchased 5,000 shares of Community Broadcasting Company for $32 per share. The following information applies to the stock price of Community Broadcasting:

	Price
12/31/2007	$34
12/31/2008	25
12/31/2009	21

Required:
1. Prepare journal entries to record the facts in the case, assuming that James Media purchased the shares for the trading portfolio.
2. Prepare journal entries to record the facts in the case, assuming that James Media purchased the shares for the available-for-sale portfolio.

AP12-3
LO2

Reporting Passive Investments (P12-3)

During January 2008, Hexagon Company purchased 12,000 shares of the 200,000 outstanding common shares (no-par value) of Seven Corporation at $30 per share. This block of stock was purchased as a long-term investment. Assume that the accounting period for each company ends December 31. Subsequent to acquisition, the following data were available:

	2008	2009
Income reported by Seven Corporation at December 31	$40,000	$60,000
Cash dividends declared and paid by Seven Corporation during the year	60,000	80,000
Market price per share of Seven common stock on December 31	28	29

Required:

1. What accounting method should the company use? Why?
2. Give the journal entries for the company for each year (use parallel columns) for the following (if none, explain why):
   a. Acquisition of Seven Corporation stock.
   b. Net income reported by Seven Corporation.
   c. Dividends received from Seven Corporation.
   d. Market value effects at year-end.
3. Show how the following amounts should be reported on the financial statements for each year:
   a. Long-term investment.
   b. Stockholders' equity—net unrealized gain/loss.
   c. Revenues.

AP12-4
LO2, 3

Comparing the Market Value and Equity Methods (P12-6)

Packer Company purchased, as a long-term investment, some of the 200,000 shares of the outstanding common stock of Boston Corporation. The annual accounting period for each company ends December 31. The following transactions occurred during 2009:

Jan. 10   Purchased shares of common stock of Boston at $15 per share as follows:

        Case A—30,000 shares.

        Case B—80,000 shares.

Dec. 31   a. Received the 2009 financial statements of Boston Corporation; the reported net income was $90,000.

        b. Received a cash dividend of $0.60 per share from Boston Corporation.

        c. Determined that the current market price of Boston stock was $9 per share.

Required:

1. For each case, identify the accounting method that the company should use. Explain why.
2. Give the journal entries for each case for these transactions. If no entry is required, explain why. (*Hint:* Use parallel columns for Case A and Case B.)
3. Give the amounts for each case that should be reported on the 2009 financial statements. Use the following format:

	Case A	Case B
Balance sheet (partial)		
Investments		
Investments in common stock, Boston Corporation		
Stockholders' equity		
Net unrealized gain or loss		
Income statement (partial)		
Investment income		
Equity in earnings of investee		

Determining Cash Flow Statement Effects of Passive Investments and Investments for Significant Influence (P12-7)

For each of the transactions in AP12-4, indicate how the Operating Activities and Investing Activities sections of the cash flow statement (indirect method) will be affected.

AP12-5
LO2, 3

Analyzing Goodwill and Reporting a Merger (P12-8)

On June 1, 2008, Kappa Company acquired all of the net assets of Delta Company for $120,000 cash. The two companies merged with Kappa Company surviving. The balance sheets for each company prior to the merger follow.

AP12-6
LO4

Balance Sheets at June 1, 2008	Kappa Company	Delta Company
Cash	$176,000	$ 13,000
Property and equipment (net)	352,000	165,000*
Total assets	$528,000	$178,000
Liabilities	$ 93,000	$ 82,000
Common stock (par $1)	250,000	65,000
Retained earnings	185,000	31,000
Total liabilities and stockholders' equity	$528,000	$178,000

Determined by Kappa Company to have a market value of $180,000 at date of acquisition.

Required:
1. How much goodwill was involved in this merger? Show computations.
2. Record the merger by Kappa Company on June 1, 2008.
3. Prepare a consolidated balance sheet immediately after the acquisition.

Interpreting the Return on Assets Ratio (P12-9)

Marriott International, Inc., is a global leader in the hospitality industry operating or franchising more than 2,700 lodging units and nearly 3,000 furnished corporate housing units in 68 countries. The following information was reported in the company's 2003 annual report:

AP12-7
LO5
Marriott International

	2003	2002	2001	2000
		(dollars in millions)		
Net income	$ 502	$ 277	$ 236	$ 479
Total assets	8,177	8,296	9,107	8,237

Required:
1. Compute the return on assets ratio for 2003, 2002, and 2001.
2. What do the results in requirement (1) suggest about Marriott?

CASES **AND PROJECTS**

Annual Report Cases

Finding Financial Information

Refer to the financial statements of Pacific Sunwear of California given in Appendix B at the end of this book, or open file PSUN.pdf in the Annual Report Cases directory on the student DVD.

CP12-1
LO1, 2, 5

PACIFIC SUNWEAR
OF CALIFORNIA, INC.

Required:
1. What types of securities were included in the short-term investments reported on the company's balance sheet as of the end of fiscal 2004 (statement dated January 29, 2005)? (*Hint:* The notes to the financial statements may be helpful for this question.)

2. How much cash did the company receive during the most recent reporting year (fiscal 2004) when its available-for-sale short-term investments and its held-to-maturity short-term investments matured?

3. Has the firm increased or decreased its performance as measured by return on assets from fiscal 2003 to 2004? Note that the company's total assets as of February 1, 2003 (the beginning of fiscal 2003) were $463,993,000.

CP12-2
LO1, 2, 5

AMERICAN EAGLE OUTFITTERS
ae.com

Finding Financial Information

Refer to the financial statements of American Eagle Outfitters given in Appendix C at the end of this book, or open file AEOS.pdf in the Annual Report Cases directory on the student DVD.

Required:

1. What was the balance in short-term investments reported by the company on January 29, 2005? What types of securities were included in this account? (*Hint:* The notes to the financial statements may be helpful for this question.)

2. How much cash did the company use to purchase short-term securities during the year ended January 29, 2005?

3. What was the balance of goodwill reported by the company at January 29, 2005? What does the change in goodwill from January 31, 2004, imply about corporate acquisition activities in the 2004 fiscal year? Do the notes to the financial statements indicate any acquisition or disposition activity in either fiscal 2003 or 2004? If so, what were the activities?

4. Has the firm increased or decreased its performance as measured by return on assets from fiscal 2003 to 2004? Note that the company's total assets as of February 1, 2003 (the beginning of fiscal 2003) were $802,854,000.

CP12-3
LO5

PACIFIC SUNWEAR
OF CALIFORNIA, INC.

AMERICAN EAGLE OUTFITTERS
ae.com

Comparing Companies Within an Industry

Refer to the financial statements of Pacific Sunwear of California given in Appendix B, American Eagle Outfitters given in Appendix C, and the Industry Ratio Report given in Appendix D at the end of this book, or open file CP12-3.xls in the Annual Report Cases directory on the student DVD.

Required:

1. Compute the profit margin, asset turnover, and return on assets ratios for both companies for the most recent reporting year. Which company provided the higher return on its total assets during the current year?

2. Was the difference in ROA due primarily to profitability or efficiency differences? How did you know?

3. Was the return on assets for American Eagle Outfitters and Pacific Sunwear of California higher or lower than the industry average?

Financial Reporting and Analysis Cases

CP12-4
LO2, 3

Using Financial Reports: Analyzing the Financial Effects of the Market Value and Equity Methods

On January 1, 2008, Woodrow Company purchased 30 percent of the outstanding common stock of Trevor Corporation at a total cost of $560,000. Management intends to hold the stock for the long term. On the December 31, 2008, balance sheet, the investment in Trevor Corporation was $720,000, but no additional Trevor stock was purchased. The company received $80,000 in cash dividends from Trevor. The dividends were declared and paid during 2008. The company used the equity method to account for its investment in Trevor. The market price of Trevor stock increased during 2008 to a total value of $600,000.

Required:

1. Explain why the investment account balance increased from $560,000 to $720,000 during 2008.

2. What amount of revenue from the investment was reported during 2008?

3. If Woodrow did not have significant influence over Trevor and used the market value method, what amount of revenue from the investment should have been reported in 2008?

4. If Woodrow did not have significant influence over Trevor and used the market value method, what amount should be reported as the investment in Trevor Corporation on the December 31, 2008, balance sheet?

Using Financial Reports: Interpreting International Goodwill Disclosures

Diageo is a major international company located in London. A recent annual report contained the following information concerning its accounting policies.

> **Acquisitions** On the acquisition of a business, including an interest in a related company, fair values are attributed to the group's share of net tangible assets and significant owned brands acquired. Where the cost of acquisition exceeds the values attributable to such net assets, the difference is treated as goodwill and is written off directly to reserves in the year of acquisition.
>
> **Intangible assets** Significant owned brands, acquired after 1st January 1985, the value of which is not expected to diminish in the foreseeable future, are recorded in the balance sheet as fixed intangible assets. No amortisation is provided on these assets but their value is reviewed annually by the directors and the cost written down as an exceptional item where permanent diminution in value has occurred.

Required:
Diageo used the word *reserves* to mean *retained earnings*. Discuss how this accounting treatment compares with procedures used in this country.

Critical Thinking Cases

Evaluating an Ethical Dilemma: Using Inside Information

Assume that you are on the board of directors of a company that has decided to buy 80 percent of the outstanding stock of another company within the next three or four months. The discussions have convinced you that this company is an excellent investment opportunity, so you decide to buy $10,000 worth of the company's stock for your personal portfolio. Is there an ethical problem with your decision? Would your answer be different if you planned to invest $500,000? Are there different ethical considerations if you don't buy the stock but recommend that your brother do so?

Evaluating an Acquisition from the Standpoint of a Financial Analyst

Assume that you are a financial analyst for a large investment banking firm. You are responsible for analyzing companies in the retail sales industry. You have just learned that a large West Coast retailer has acquired a large East Coast retail chain for a price more than the net book value of the acquired company. You have reviewed the separate financial statements for the two companies before the announcement of the acquisition. You have been asked to write a brief report explaining what will happen when the financial results of the companies are consolidated under the purchase method, including the impact on the return on assets ratio.

Financial Reporting and Analysis Team Project

Team Project: Examining an Annual Report

As a team, select an industry to analyze. *Reuters* provides lists of industries and their makeup at www.investor.reuters.com/Industries.aspx. Each team member should acquire the annual report or 10-K for one publicly traded company in the industry, with each member selecting a different company. (Library files, the SEC EDGAR service at www.sec.gov, or the company itself are good sources.)

Required:

On an individual basis, each team member should write a short report answering the following questions about the selected company. Discuss any patterns across the companies that you as a team observe. Then, as a team, write a short report comparing and contrasting your companies.

a. Determine whether the company prepared consolidated financial statements. If so, did it use the purchase method? How do you know?

b. Does the company use the equity method for any of its investments?

c. Does the company hold any investments in securities? If so, what is their market value? Does the company have any unrealized gains or losses?

d. Identify the company's lines of business. Why does management want to engage in these business activities?

e. Compute the return on assets ratio for the two most recent years reported. What do the results suggest about your company?

LEARNING OBJECTIVES

Statement of Cash Flows

I t was no accident when Jim Koch, founder of Boston Beer Company, named his products for Samuel Adams, the American revolutionary who led the Boston Tea Party. When Koch delivered the first 25 cases of Samuel Adams Boston Lager to a Boston bar in 1985, he fired the first shot in a revolution that stunned the brewing industry. At that point, megabrewers such as Anheuser-Busch and Miller dominated beer brewing; annual sales by all small "craft" brewers totaled just over 100,000 barrels. By the year 2003, Boston Beer alone sold more than 1.2 million barrels and reported net income of $10.5 million.

Although it may seem puzzling, growing profitable operations does not always ensure positive cash flow. Also, seasonal fluctuations in sales, purchases of inventory, and advertising expenditures may bring **high profits** and **net cash outflows** in some quarters and **losses** and **net cash inflows** in others. As we have seen in earlier chapters, this occurs because the timing of revenues and expenses does not always match cash inflows and outflows. As a consequence, Boston Beer must carefully manage cash flows as well as profits. For the same reasons, financial analysts must consider the information provided in Boston Beer's cash flow statement in addition to its income statement and balance sheet.

FOCUS COMPANY:

Boston Beer Company

MANAGING PRODUCTION AND CASH FLOWS IN A

SEASONAL BUSINESS

www.bostonbeer.com

UNDERSTANDING THE BUSINESS

Clearly, net income is important, but cash flow is also critical to a company's success. Cash flow permits a company to expand operations, replace worn assets, take advantage of new investment opportunities, and pay dividends to its owners. Some Wall Street analysts go so far as to say "cash flow is king." Both managers and analysts need to understand the various sources and uses of cash that are associated with business activity.

The cash flow statement focuses attention on a firm's ability to generate cash internally, its management of current assets and current liabilities, and the details of its investments and its external financing. It is designed to help both managers and analysts answer important cash-related questions such as these:

■ Will the company have enough cash to pay its short-term debts to suppliers and other creditors without additional borrowing?

- Is the company adequately managing its accounts receivable and inventory?
- Has the company made necessary investments in new productive capacity?
- Did the company generate enough cash flow internally to finance necessary investments, or did it rely on external financing?
- Is the company changing the makeup of its external financing?

Boston Beer is a particularly good example to illustrate the importance of the cash flow statement for two reasons. First, like all companies in its industry, Boston Beer's inventory purchases and sales vary with the seasons. This seasonal variation has surprising effects on cash flows and net income. Second, an important element of Boston Beer's business strategy is the outsourcing of much of its product manufacturing. The decision to outsource dramatically affects investments in plant and equipment and the need for external financing.

We begin our discussion with an overview of the statement of cash flows. Then we examine the information reported in each section of the statement in depth. The chapter ends with a discussion of additional cash flow disclosures.

ORGANIZATION of the Chapter

Classifications of the Statement of Cash Flows	Reporting and Interpreting Cash Flows from Operating Activities	Reporting and Interpreting Cash Flows from Investing Activities	Reporting and Interpreting Cash Flows from Financing Activities	Additional Cash Flow Disclosures
■ Cash Flows from Operating Activities ■ Cash Flows from Investing Activities ■ Cash Flows from Financing Activities ■ Net Increase (Decrease) in Cash ■ Relationships to the Balance Sheet and Income Statement	■ **Part A:** Reporting Cash Flows from Operating Activities—Indirect Method **OR** ■ **Part B:** Reporting Cash Flows from Operating Activities—Direct Method ■ Interpreting Cash Flow from Operating Activities ■ Quality of Income Ratio	■ Reporting Cash Flows from Investing Activities ■ Interpreting Cash Flow from Investing Activities ■ Capital Acquisitions Ratio	■ Reporting Cash Flows from Financing Activities ■ Interpreting Cash Flow from Financing Activities	■ Noncash Investing and Financing Activities ■ Supplemental Cash Flow Information ■ Epilogue

A **CASH EQUIVALENT** is a short-term, highly liquid investment with an original maturity of less than three months.

Learning Objective 1
Classify cash flow statement items as part of net cash flows from operating, investing, and financing activities.

CLASSIFICATIONS OF THE STATEMENT OF CASH FLOWS

Basically, the statement of cash flows explains how the amount of cash on the balance sheet at the beginning of the period became the amount of cash reported at the end of the period. For purposes of this statement, the definition of cash includes cash and cash equivalents. **Cash equivalents** are short-term, highly liquid investments that are both

1. Readily convertible to known amounts of cash.
2. So near to maturity there is little risk that their value will change if interest rates change.

EXHIBIT 13.1

Consolidated Statement
of Cash Flows

THE BOSTON BEER COMPANY, INC.
Consolidated Statement of Cash Flows

(unaudited) Dollars in Thousands*	Three months ended March 27, 2004
Cash flows from operating activities:	
Net income	$ 1,271
Adjustments to reconcile net income to net cash provided by operating activities:	
Depreciation and amortization	2,543
Changes in assets and liabilities:	
Accounts receivable	861
Inventory	(577)
Prepaid expenses	(322)
Accounts payable	(52)
Accrued expenses	(954)
Net cash provided by operating activities	2,770
Cash flows from investing activities:	
Purchases of property, plant, and equipment	(2,373)
Purchase of short-term investments	(4,627)
Net cash used in investing activities	(7,000)
Cash flows from financing activities:	
Purchase of treasury stock	(4,409)
Proceeds from issuance of stock	5,593
Net cash provided by financing activities	1,184
Net decrease in cash and cash equivalents	(3,046)
Cash and cash equivalents at beginning of period	27,792
Cash and cash equivalents at end of period	$24,746

Certain amounts have been adjusted to simplify the presentation.

REAL WORLD EXCERPT

SAMUEL
ADAMS

QUARTERLY REPORT

Topic Tackler 13–1

Generally, only investments with original maturities of three months or less qualify as a cash equivalent under this definition.[1] Examples of cash equivalents are Treasury bills (a form of short-term U.S. government debt), money market funds, and commercial paper (short-term notes payable issued by large corporations).

As you can see in Exhibit 13.1, the statement of cash flows reports cash inflows and outflows in three broad categories: (1) operating activities, (2) investing activities, and (3) financing activities. Together, these three cash flow categories explain the change from the beginning balance to the ending balance in cash on the balance sheet.

Cash Flows from Operating Activities

Cash flows from operating activities (cash flows from operations) are the cash inflows and outflows that relate directly to revenues and expenses reported on the

CASH FLOWS FROM
OPERATING ACTIVITIES (cash
flows from operations) are cash
inflows and outflows directly
related to earnings from normal
operations.

[1]**Original maturity** means original maturity to the entity holding the investment. For example, both a three-month Treasury bill and a three-year Treasury note purchased three months from maturity qualify as cash equivalents. A Treasury note purchased three years ago, however, does not become a cash equivalent when its remaining maturity is three months.

income statement. There are two alternative approaches for presenting the operating activities section of the statement:

The **DIRECT METHOD** of presenting the Operating Activities section of the cash flow statement reports components of cash flows from operating activities as gross receipts and gross payments.

1. The **direct method** reports the components of cash flows from operating activities as gross receipts and gross payments.

Inflows	Outflows
Cash received from	**Cash paid for**
Customers	Purchase of goods for resale and
Dividends and interest on investments	services (electricity, etc.)
	Salaries and wages
	Income taxes
	Interest on liabilities

The difference between the inflows and outflows is called the **net cash inflow (outflow) from operating activities.** Boston Beer experienced a net cash inflow of $2,770 (dollars in thousands) from its operations for the first quarter of 2004. Although the FASB recommends the direct method, it is rarely used in the United States. The direct method is the required format in a number of countries. Many financial executives have reported that they do not use it because it is more expensive to implement than the indirect method.

The **INDIRECT METHOD** of presenting the Operating Activities section of the cash flow statement adjusts net income to compute cash flows from operating activities.

2. The **indirect method** starts with net income from the income statement and then eliminates noncash items to arrive at net cash inflow (outflow) from operating activities.

Net income
+/− Adjustments for noncash items
_____
Net cash inflow (outflow) from operating activities

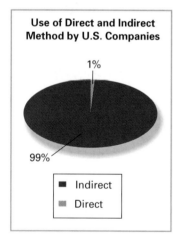

Use of Direct and Indirect Method by U.S. Companies

1%

99%

■ Indirect
■ Direct

Almost 99 percent of large U.S. companies, including Boston Beer, use this method.[2] Notice in Exhibit 13.1 that in the first quarter of 2004, Boston Beer reported positive net income of $1,271 but generated positive cash flows from operating activities of $2,770. Why should income and cash flows from operating activities differ? Remember that on the income statement, revenues are recorded when they are earned, without regard to when the related cash inflows occur. Similarly, expenses are matched with revenues and recorded without regard to when the related cash outflows occur.

For now, the most important thing to remember about the two methods is that they are simply alternative ways to arrive at the same number. The total amount of **cash flows from operating activities is always the same** (an inflow of $2,770 in Boston Beer's case), **regardless of whether it is computed using the direct or indirect method.**

Cash Flows from Investing Activities

CASH FLOWS FROM INVESTING ACTIVITIES are cash inflows and outflows related to the acquisition or sale of productive facilities and investments in the securities of other companies.

Cash flows from investing activities are cash inflows and outflows related to the purchase and disposal of long-lived productive assets and investments in the securities of other companies. Typical cash flows from investing activities include:

Inflows	Outflows
Cash received from	**Cash paid for**
Sale or disposal of property, plant, and equipment	Purchase of property, plant, and equipment
Sale or maturity of investments in securities	Purchase of investments in securities

[2]*Accounting Trends & Techniques* (New York: American Institute of CPAs, 2003).

The difference between these cash inflows and outflows is called **net cash inflow (outflow) from investing activities.**

For Boston Beer, this amount was an outflow of $7,000 for the first quarter of 2004. Most of the activity related to the purchase of short-term securities. Since purchases exceeded sales (sales were zero), there was a net cash outflow.

Cash Flows from Financing Activities

Cash flows from financing activities include exchanges of cash with creditors (debtholders) and owners (stockholders). Usual cash flows from financing activities include the following:

CASH FLOWS FROM FINANCING ACTIVITIES are cash inflows and outflows related to external sources of financing (owners and creditors) for the enterprise.

Inflows	Outflows
Cash received from	**Cash paid for**
Borrowing on notes, mortgages, bonds, etc. from creditors	Repayment of principal to creditors (excluding interest, which is an operating activity)
Issuing stock to owners	Repurchasing stock from owners
	Dividends to owners

The difference between these cash inflows and outflows is called **net cash inflow (outflow) from financing activities.**

Boston Beer experienced a net cash inflow from financing activities of $1,184 for the first quarter of 2004. The Financing Activities section of its statement shows that Boston Beer paid $4,409 to repurchase its stock from owners and received $5,593 for new stock issuances. No dividends were paid and no cash was borrowed or repaid.

Net Increase (Decrease) in Cash

The combination of **the net cash flows from operating activities, investing activities, and financing activities must equal the net increase (decrease) in cash** for the reporting period. For the first quarter of 2004, Boston Beer reported a net decrease in cash of $3,046, which explains the change in cash on the balance sheet from the beginning balance of $27,792 to the ending balance of $24,746.

Net cash provided by operating activities	$ 2,770
Net cash used in investing activities	(7,000)
Net cash provided by financing activities	1,184
Net decrease in cash and cash equivalents	(3,046)
Cash and cash equivalents at beginning of period	27,792
Cash and cash equivalents at end of period	$24,746

To give you a better understanding of the statement of cash flows, we now discuss Boston Beer's statement in more detail including the way that it relates to the balance sheet and income statement. Then we will examine the way each section of the statement describes a set of important decisions that Boston Beer management made and the way financial analysts use each section to evaluate the company's performance.

SELF-STUDY **QUIZ**

Big Rock Brewery Ltd. is one of the larger craft brewers in Canada. A listing of some of its cash flows follows. Indicate whether each item is disclosed in the Operating Activities (O), Investing Activities (I), or Financing Activities (F) section of the statement of cash flows.

Big Rock Brewery

___ 1. Shares repurchased from stockholders

___ 2. Collections from customers

___ 3. Payment of interest on debt

___ 4. Purchase of plant and equipment

___ 5. Acquisition of investment securities

After you have completed your answers, check them with the solutions at the bottom of the page.

Relationships to the Balance Sheet and Income Statement

Preparing and interpreting the cash flow statement requires an analysis of the balance sheet and income statement accounts that relate to the three sections of the cash flow statement. In previous chapters, we emphasized that companies record transactions as journal entries that are posted to T-accounts, which are used to prepare the income statement and the balance sheet. But companies cannot prepare the statement of cash flows using the amounts recorded in the T-accounts because those amounts are based on accrual accounting. Instead, they must analyze the numbers recorded under the accrual method and adjust them to a cash basis. To prepare the statement of cash flows, they need the following data:

1. **Comparative balance sheets** used in calculating the cash flows from all activities (operating, investing, and financing).

2. A **complete income statement** used primarily in calculating cash flows from operating activities.

3. **Additional details** concerning selected accounts where the total change amount in an account balance during the year does not reveal the underlying nature of the cash flows.

Our approach to preparing and understanding the cash flow statement focuses on the changes in the balance sheet accounts. It relies on a simple manipulation of the balance sheet equation:

$$\text{Assets} = \text{Liabilities} + \text{Stockholders' Equity}$$

First, assets can be split into cash and noncash assets:

$$\text{Cash} + \text{Noncash Assets} = \text{Liabilities} + \text{Stockholders' Equity}$$

If we move the noncash assets to the right side of the equation, then:

$$\text{Cash} = \text{Liabilities} + \text{Stockholders' Equity} - \text{Noncash Assets}$$

Given this relationship, the changes (Δ) in cash between the beginning and the end of the period must equal the changes (Δ) in the amounts on the right side of the equation between the beginning and the end of the period:

$$\Delta\text{ Cash} = \Delta\text{ Liabilities} + \Delta\text{ Stockholders' Equity} - \Delta\text{ Noncash Assets}$$

Thus, **any transaction that changes cash must be accompanied by a change in liabilities, stockholders' equity, or noncash assets.** Exhibit 13.2 illustrates this concept for selected cash transactions.

Next, we will compute the change in each balance sheet account (ending balance − beginning balance) and classify each change as relating to operating (O), investing (I), or financing (F) activities by marking them with the corresponding letter. **The balance**

Category	Transaction	Cash Effect	Other Account Affected
Operating	Collect accounts receivable	+Cash	−Accounts Receivable (A)
	Pay accounts payable	−Cash	−Accounts Payable (L)
	Prepay rent	−Cash	+Prepaid Rent (A)
	Pay interest	−Cash	−Retained Earnings (SE)
	Sale for cash	+Cash	+Retained Earnings (SE)
Investing	Purchase equipment for cash	−Cash	+Equipment (A)
	Sell investment securities for cash	+Cash	−Investments (A)
Financing	Pay back debt to bank	−Cash	−Notes Payable—Bank (L)
	Issue stock for cash	+Cash	+Common Stock and Paid-in-Capital (SE)

sheet accounts related to earning income (operating items) should be marked with an O. These accounts include the following:

- most current assets (other than short-term investments, which relate to investing activities, and cash).[3]

- most current liabilities (other than amounts owed to investors and financial institutions,[4] all of which relate to financing activities).

- retained earnings because it increases by the amount of net income, which is the starting point for the Operating section. (Retained earnings also decreases by dividends declared and paid, which is a financing outflow noted by an F.)

In Exhibit 13.3, all of the relevant current assets and liabilities have been marked with an O. These items include:

- Accounts Receivable
- Inventories
- Prepaid Expenses
- Accounts Payable
- Accrued Expenses

As we have noted, retained earnings is also relevant to operations.

The balance sheet accounts related to investing activities should be marked with an I. These include all of the remaining assets on the balance sheet. In Exhibit 13.3:

- Short-term investments
- Equipment, net

The balance sheet accounts related to financing activities should be marked with an F. These include all of the remaining liability and stockholders' equity accounts on the balance sheet. In Exhibit 13.3:

- Contributed Capital
- Retained Earnings (for decreases resulting from dividends declared and paid)

Next, we use this information to prepare each section of the statement.

---

[3]Certain noncurrent assets such as long-term receivables from customers and noncurrent liabilities such as postretirement obligations to employees are considered to be operating items. These items are covered in more advanced accounting classes.

[4]Examples of the accounts excluded are Dividends Payable, Short-Term Debt to Financial Institutions, and Current Maturities of Long-Term Debt. Current maturities of long-term debt are amounts of debt with an original term of more than one year that are due within one year of the statement date.

The Boston Beer Company:
Comparative Balance Sheet
and Current Income
Statement

*Related Cash
Flow Section*

Change in Cash

REAL WORLD EXCERPT

SAMUEL
ADAMS

QUARTERLY REPORT

I
O
O
O

I†

O
O

F
O and F

THE BOSTON BEER COMPANY, INC.
Consolidated Balance Sheet

(unaudited) Dollars in Thousands*	March 27, 2004	December 27, 2003	
Assets			
Current assets:			*Change*
Cash and cash equivalents	24,746	27,792	−3,046
Short-term investments	19,725	15,098	+4,627
Accounts receivable	9,571	10,432	−861
Inventories	10,467	9,890	+577
Prepaid expenses	1,448	1,126	+322
Total current assets	65,957	64,338	
Equipment, net	16,889	17,059	−170
Total assets	$82,846	$81,397	
Liabilities and Stockholders' Equity			
Current liabilities:			
Accounts payable	$ 6,343	$ 6,395	−52
Accrued expenses	14,550	15,504	−954
Total current liabilities	20,893	21,899	
Stockholders' equity:			
Contributed capital	24,107	22,923	+1,184
Retained earnings	37,846	36,575	+1,271
Total stockholders' equity	61,953	59,498	
Total liabilities and stockholders' equity	$82,846	$81,397	

THE BOSTON BEER COMPANY, INC.
Consolidated Statements of Operations

(unaudited) Dollars in Thousands	Three Months Ended March 27, 2004
Net sales	$44,655
Cost of sales	18,073
Gross profit	26,582
Operating expenses:	
Selling, general, and administrative expense	22,188
Depreciation and amortization expense	2,543
Total operating expenses	24,731
Operating income	1,851
Interest income	192
Income before provision for income taxes	2,043
Provision for income taxes	772
Net income	$ 1,271

*Certain balances have been adjusted to simplify the presentation.

†The Accumulated Depreciation account is also related to operations because it relates to depreciation.

REPORTING AND INTERPRETING CASH FLOWS FROM OPERATING ACTIVITIES

Since the operating section can be prepared in one of two formats, we discuss them separately. Part A describes the indirect method and part B the direct method. Your instructor may choose to assign one, the other, or both. After you have completed the part(s) assigned, you should move on to the discussion of interpreting cash flow from operations.

Remember that

1. Cash flow from operating activities is always the same regardless of whether it is computed using the direct or indirect method.

2. The investing and financing sections are always presented in the same manner regardless of the format of the operating section.

Part A: Reporting Cash Flows from Operating Activities— Indirect Method

Exhibit 13.3 shows Boston Beer's comparative balance sheet and income statement. Remember that the indirect method starts with net income and converts it to cash flows from operating activities. This involves adjusting net income for the differences in the timing of accrual basis net income and cash flows. The general structure of the operating activities section is:

Operating Activities:

Net Income
Add/Subtract to convert to cash basis:
+Depreciation and amortization expense
+Decreases in current assets
+Increases in current liabilities
−Increases in current assets
−Decreases in current liabilities

Net Cash Flow from Operating Activities

Learning Objective 2A
Report and interpret cash flows from operating activities using the indirect method.

Topic Tackler 13-2

To keep track of all the additions and subtractions made to convert net income to cash flows from operating activities, it is helpful to set up a schedule to record the computations. We will construct a schedule for Boston Beer in Exhibit 13.4.

We begin our schedule presented in Exhibit 13.4 with net income of $1,271 taken from Boston Beer's income statement (Exhibit 13.3). Completing the operating section using the indirect method involves two steps:

Step 1. Adjust net income for depreciation and amortization expense. Recording depreciation and amortization expense does not affect the cash account (or any other current asset or liability). It affects a noncurrent asset (such as Equipment, net). Since depreciation and amortization expense are **subtracted in computing net income but do not affect cash, we always add each back** to convert net income to cash flow from operating activities. In the case of Boston Beer, we need to remove the effect of depreciation and amortization expense by adding back $2,543 to net income (see Exhibit 13.4).[5]

Step 2. Adjust net income for changes in current assets and current liabilities marked as operating (O). Each **change** in current assets (other than cash and short-term investments) and current liabilities (other than amounts owed to owners and financial institutions)

[5]Gains and losses on sales of equipment and investments are dealt with in a similar manner and are discussed in Chapter Supplement A. Other similar additions and subtractions are discussed in more advanced accounting courses.

EXHIBIT 13.4

Boston Beer Company:
Schedule for Net Cash Flow
from Operating Activities,
Indirect Method (dollars in
thousands)

Conversion of Net Income to Net Cash Flow from Operating Activities

Items	Amount	Explanation
Net income, accrual basis	$1,271	From income statement.
Add (subtract) to convert to cash basis:		
Depreciation and amortization	+2,543	Add back because depreciation and amortization expense does not affect cash.
Accounts receivable decrease	+ 861	Add back because cash collected from customers is more than accrual basis revenues.
Inventory increase	− 577	Subtract because purchases are more than cost of goods sold expense.
Prepaid expense increase	− 322	Subtract because cash prepayments for expenses are more than accrual basis expenses.
Accounts payable decrease	− 52	Subtract because cash payments to suppliers are more than amounts purchased on account (borrowed from suppliers).
Accrued expenses decrease	− 954	Subtract because cash payments for expenses are more than accrual basis expenses.
Net cash inflow from operating activities	$2,770	Reported on the statement of cash flows.

causes a difference between net income and cash flow from operating activities.[6] When converting net income to cash flow from operating activities, apply the following general rules:

■ **Add the change when a current asset decreases or current liability increases.**

■ **Subtract the change when a current asset increases or current liability decreases.**

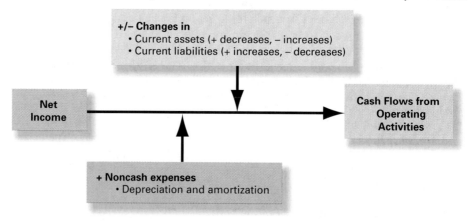

Understanding what makes these current assets and current liabilities increase and decrease is the key to understanding the logic of these additions and subtractions.

---

[6]As noted earlier, certain noncurrent assets such as long-term receivables from customers and noncurrent liabilities such as postretirement obligations to employees are considered to be operating items. These items are covered in more advanced accounting classes.

Change in Accounts Receivable

We illustrate this logic with the first operating item (O) listed on Boston Beer's balance sheet (Exhibit 13.3), accounts receivable. Remember that the income statement reflects sales revenue, but the cash flow statement must reflect cash collections from customers. As the following accounts receivable T-account illustrates, when sales revenues are recorded, accounts receivable increases, and when cash is collected from customers, accounts receivable decrease.

Accounts Receivable (A)			
Beginning balance	10,432		
Sales revenue (on account)	44,655	Collections from customers	45,516
Ending balance	9,571		

Change − $861 { (brace spanning Beginning balance through Ending balance)

In the Boston Beer example, sales revenue reported on the income statement is lower than cash collections from customers by $44,655 − $45,516 = −$861. Since more money was collected from customers, this amount must be added to net income to convert to cash flows from operating activities. Note that this amount is also the same as the **change** in the accounts receivable account:

Ending balance	$ 9,571
− Beginning balance	10,432
Change	$ (861)

This same underlying logic is used to determine adjustments for the other current assets and liabilities.

To summarize, the income statement reflects revenues of the period, but cash flow from operating activities must reflect cash collections from customers. Sales on account increase the balance in accounts receivable, and collections from customers decrease the balance.

Accounts Receivable (A)			
Beg.	10,432		
		Decrease	861
End.	9,571		

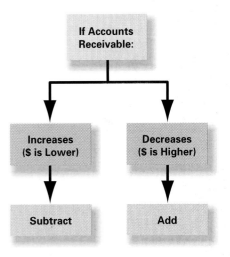

The balance sheet for Boston Beer Company (Exhibit 13.3) indicates a **decrease** in accounts receivable of $861 for the period, which means that cash collected from customers is higher than revenue. To convert to cash flows from operating activities, the amount of the decrease (the extra collections) must be **added** in Exhibit 13.4. (An increase is subtracted.)

Change in Inventory

The income statement reflects merchandise sold for the period, whereas cash flow from operating activities must reflect cash purchases. As shown in the T-account on the left, purchases of goods increase the balance in inventory, and recording merchandise sold decreases the balance in inventory.

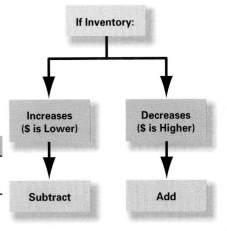

Inventories (A)			
Beg. Bal.		Cost of goods sold	
Purchases			
End. Bal.			

Inventories (A)			
Beg.	9,890		
Increase	577		
End.	10,467		

Boston Beer's balance sheet (Exhibit 13.3) indicates that inventory **increased** by $577, which means that the amount of purchases is more than the amount of merchandise sold. The increase (the extra purchases) must be **subtracted** from net income to convert to cash flow from operating activities in Exhibit 13.4. (A decrease is added.)

Change in Prepaid Expenses

The income statement reflects expenses of the period, but cash flow from operating activities must reflect the cash payments. Cash prepayments increase the balance in prepaid expenses, and recording of expenses decreases the balance in prepaid expenses.

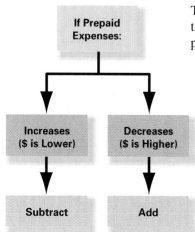

Prepaid Expenses (A)	
Beg. Bal.	Services used
Cash prepayments	(expenses)
End. Bal.	

Prepaid Expenses (A)		
Beg.	1,126	
Increase	322	
End.	1,448	

The Boston Beer balance sheet (Exhibit 13.3) indicates a $322 **increase** in prepaid expenses, which means that new cash prepayments are more than the amount of expenses. The increase (the extra prepayments) must be **subtracted** from net income in Exhibit 13.4. (A decrease is added.)

Change in Accounts Payable

Cash flow from operations must reflect cash purchases, but not all purchases are for cash. Purchases on account increase accounts payable and cash paid to suppliers decreases accounts payable.

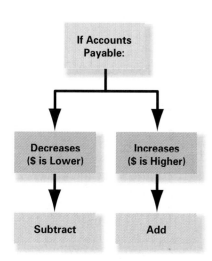

Accounts Payable (L)	
Cash payments	Beg. bal.
	Purchases on account
	End. bal.

Accounts Payable (L)		
	Beg.	6,395
Decrease 52		
	End.	6,343

Boston Beer's accounts payable **decreased** by $52, which means that cash payments were more than purchases on account, and this decrease (the extra payments) must be **subtracted** in Exhibit 13.4. (An increase is added.)

Change in Accrued Expenses

The income statement reflects all accrued expenses, but the cash flow statement must reflect actual payments for those expenses. Recording accrued expenses increases the balance in the liability accrued expenses and cash payments for the expenses decrease accrued expenses.

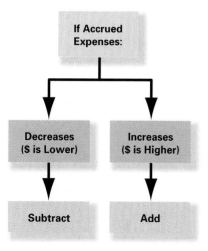

Accrued Expenses (L)	
Pay off accruals	Beg. bal.
	Accrued expenses
	End. bal.

Accrued Expenses (L)		
	Beg.	15,504
Decrease 954		
	End.	14,550

Boston Beer's accrued expenses (Exhibit 13.3) **decreased** by $954, which indicates that cash paid for the expenses is more than accrual basis expenses. The decrease (the extra cash paid) must be **subtracted** in Exhibit 13.4. (An increase is added.)

Summary

We can summarize the typical additions and subtractions that are required to reconcile net income with cash flow from operating activities as follows:

	Additions and Subtractions to Reconcile Net Income to Cash Flow from Operating Activities	
Item	**When Item Increases**	**When Item Decreases**
Depreciation and amortization	+	NA
Accounts receivable	−	+
Inventory	−	+
Prepaid expenses	−	+
Accounts payable	+	−
Accrued expense liabilities	+	−

Notice again in this table that to reconcile net income to cash flows from operating activities, you must:

■ **Add the change when a current asset decreases or current liability increases.**

■ **Subtract the change when a current asset increases or current liability decreases.**

The cash flow statement for Boston Beer (Exhibit 13.1) shows the same additions and subtractions to reconcile net income to cash flows from operating activities described in Exhibit 13.4.

Foreign Currency and the Cash Flow Statement	**INTERNATIONAL PERSPECTIVE**

Consolidated statements may include one or more subsidiaries located in other countries whose statements report in a currency other than the U.S. dollar (for example, the euro or Mexican peso). The process of translating those statements into dollars may cause the changes in the current assets and liabilities on the balance sheet not to match the changes reported on the cash flow statement. Acquisitions and sales of subsidiaries during the period can have a similar effect.[*]

[*]P. R. Bahnson, P. B. W. Miller, and B. P. Budge, "Nonarticulation in Cash Flow Statements and Implications for Education, Research and Practice," *Accounting Horizons,* December 1996, pp. 1–15.

SELF-STUDY **QUIZ**

Big Rock Brewery

Indicate which of the following items taken from Big Rock Brewery's cash flow statement would be added (+), subtracted (−), or not included (0) in the reconciliation of net income to cash flow from operations.

_____ 1. Increase in inventories.

_____ 2. Increase in bank indebtedness.

_____ 3. Amortization expense.

_____ 4. Decrease in accounts receivable.

_____ 5. Increase in accounts payable.

_____ 6. Increase in prepaid expenses.

After you have completed your answers, check them with the solutions at the bottom of the page.

If your instructor has assigned only the indirect method, you should skip the next section and go to the discussion of Interpreting Cash Flow from Operating Activities (page 674).

Part B: Reporting Cash Flows from Operating Activities— Direct Method

Learning Objective 2B
Report and interpret cash flows from operating activities using the direct method.

The direct method presents a summary of all operating transactions that result in either a debit or a credit to cash. It is prepared by adjusting each item on the income statement from an accrual basis to a cash basis. We will complete this process for all of the revenues and expenses reported in Boston Beer's income statement in Exhibit 13.3 and accumulate them in a new schedule in Exhibit 13.5.

Cash Flows from Operating Activities

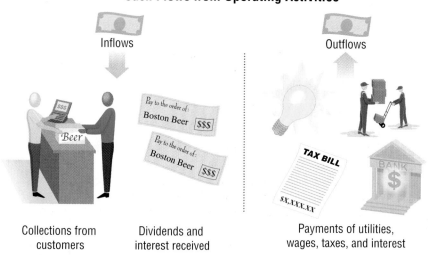

| Collections from customers | Dividends and interest received | Payments of utilities, wages, taxes, and interest |

Converting Revenues to Cash Inflows

When sales are recorded, accounts receivable increases, and when cash is collected, accounts receivable decreases. Thus, the following formula will convert sales revenue amounts from the accrual basis to the cash basis:

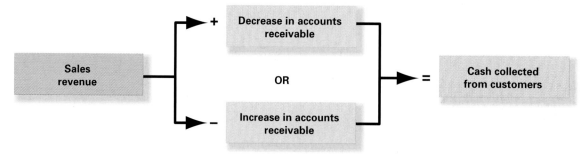

Using information from Boston Beer's income statement and balance sheet presented in Exhibit 13.3, we can compute cash collected from customers as follows:

		Accounts Receivable (A)		
Net sales	$44,655	Beg.	10,432	
+ Decrease in accounts receivable	861 ◄			Decrease 861
Cash collected from customers	$45,516	End.	9,571	

Cash flows from operating activities	
Cash collected from customers	$45,516
Cash collected for interest	192
Cash payments to suppliers	(18,702)
Cash payments for expenses	(23,464)
Cash payments for income taxes	(772)
Net cash provided by operating activities	$ 2,770

EXHIBIT 13.5

Boston Beer Company: Schedule for Net Cash Flow from Operating Activities, Direct Method (dollars in thousands)

Boston Beer's second revenue is interest income. Since there is no interest receivable balance, using the same logic, we can see that interest income must be equal to cash collected for interest.

Interest income	$192
No change in interest receivable	0
Cash collected for interest	$192

Converting Cost of Goods Sold to Cash Paid to Suppliers

Cost of goods sold represents the cost of merchandise sold during the accounting period. It may be more or less than the amount of cash paid to suppliers during the period. In Boston Beer's case, inventory increased during the quarter because the company bought more merchandise from suppliers than it sold to customers. If the company paid cash to suppliers of inventory, it must have paid more cash to suppliers than the amount of cost of goods sold, so the increase in inventory must be added to compute cash paid to suppliers.

Typically, companies owe their suppliers money (an accounts payable balance will appear on the balance sheet). To convert cost of goods sold to cash paid to suppliers, the borrowing and repayments represented by the accounts payable must also be considered. Borrowing increases cash and accounts payable and repayment decreases cash and accounts payable, so Boston Beer's decrease in accounts payable must also be added in the computation. Cost of goods sold can therefore be converted to a cash basis in the following manner:

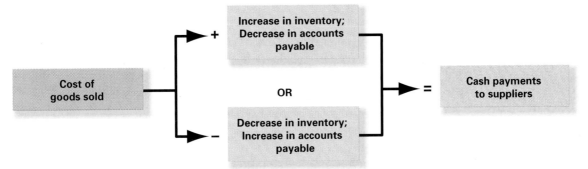

Using information from Exhibit 13.3, we can compute cash paid to suppliers as follows:

Inventories (A)		
Beg.	9,890	
Increase	577	
End.	10,467	

Cost of goods sold	$18,073
+ Increase in inventory	577
+ Decrease in accounts payable	52
Cash payments to suppliers	$18,702

Accounts Payable (L)		
	Beg.	6,395
Decrease 52		
	End.	6,343

Converting Operating Expenses to a Cash Outflow

The total amount of an expense on the income statement may differ from the cash outflow associated with that activity. Some expenses are paid before they are recognized as expenses (e.g., prepaid rent). When prepayments are made, the balance in the asset prepaid expenses increases; when expenses are recorded, prepaid expenses decreases. When Boston Beer's prepaid expenses increased by $322 during the period, it paid more cash than it recorded as operating expenses. The increase must be added in computing cash paid for expenses.

Some other expenses are paid for after they are recognized (e.g., accrued expenses). In this case, when expenses are recorded, the balance in the liability accrued expenses increases; when payments are made, accrued expenses decreases. When Boston Beer's accrued expenses decreased by $954, it paid more cash than it recorded as operating expenses. The decrease must also be subtracted in computing cash paid for expenses.

Generally, other expenses can be converted from the accrual basis to the cash basis in the following manner:

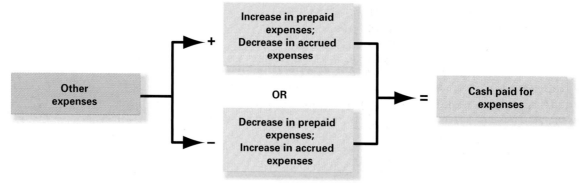

Using information from Exhibit 13.3, we can compute cash paid for expenses as follows:

Prepaid Expenses (A)			Selling, general, and administrative expense	$22,188		Accrued Expenses (L)		
Beg.	1,126		+ Increase in prepaid expenses	322			Beg.	15,504
Increase	322		+ Decrease in accrued expenses	954	← Decrease 954			
End.	1,448		Cash payments for expenses	$23,464			End.	14,550

The same logic can be applied to income taxes. Boston Beer presents income tax expense of $772. Since there is no balance in Income Taxes Payable (or change in Deferred Taxes), income taxes paid must be the same as income tax expense.

Income tax expense	$772
No change in taxes payable	0
Cash payments for income taxes	$772

These amounts of the operating cash inflows and outflows are accumulated in Exhibit 13.5.

To summarize, the following adjustments must commonly be made to convert income statement items to the related operating cash flow amounts:

Income Statement Account	+/− Change in Balance Sheet Account(s)	= Operating Cash Flow
Sales revenue	+Decrease in Accounts Receivable (A) −Increase in Accounts Receivable (A)	= Collections from customers
Interest/Dividend revenue	+Decrease in Interest/Dividends Receivable (A) −Increase in Interest/Dividends Receivable (A)	= Collections of interest/dividends on investments
Cost of goods sold	+Increase in Inventory (A) −Decrease in Inventory (A) −Increase in Accounts Payable (L) +Decrease in Accounts Payable (L)	= Payments to suppliers of inventory
Other expenses	+Increase in Prepaid Expenses (A) −Decrease in Prepaid Expenses (A) −Increase in Accrued Expenses (L) +Decrease in Accrued Expenses (L)	= Payments to suppliers of services (e.g., rent, utilities, wages, interest)
Income tax expense	+Increase in Prepaid Income Taxes (Deferred Taxes) (A) −Decrease in Prepaid Income Taxes (Deferred Taxes) (A) −Increase in Income Taxes Payable (Deferred Taxes) (L) +Decrease in Income Taxes Payable (Deferred Taxes) (L)	= Payments of income taxes

It is important to note again that the net cash inflow or outflow is the same regardless of whether the direct or indirect method of presentation is used (in this case, an inflow of $2,770). The two methods differ only in terms of the details reported on the statement.

Australian Practices

INTERNATIONAL
PERSPECTIVE

Foster's Brewing is the first name in Australian beer and a major player in world beverage markets. Following Australian GAAP, which requires use of the direct method of presentation, Foster's cash flow from operations is presented as follows. Note that Foster's combines payments to suppliers, governments, and employees, but other companies report these items separately. Like U.S. companies that choose the direct method, Foster's reports the indirect presentation in a note to the financial statements.

STATEMENT OF CASH FLOWS
FOR THE YEAR ENDED 30 JUNE 2004
(dollars in millions)

REAL WORLD EXCERPT
Foster's Brewing
ANNUAL REPORT

Cash flows from operating activities

Receipts from customers	7,150.0
Payments to suppliers, governments, and employees	(6,039.7)
Interest received	146.8
Borrowing costs [interest paid]	(303.6)
Income taxes paid	(257.0)
Net cash flows from operating activities	696.5

Indicate which of the following line items taken from the cash flow statement would be added (+), subtracted (−), or not included (0) in the cash flow from operations section when the direct method is used.

_____ 1. Increase in inventories.

_____ 2. Payment of dividends to stockholders.

_____ 3. Cash collections from customers.

_____ 4. Purchase of plant and equipment for cash.

_____ 5. Payments of interest to debtholders.

_____ 6. Payment of taxes to the government.

After you have completed your answers, check them with the solutions at the bottom of the page.

Interpreting Cash Flow from Operating Activities

The Operating Activities section of the cash flow statement focuses attention on the firm's ability to generate cash internally through operations and its management of current assets and current liabilities (also called **working capital**). Most analysts believe that this is the most important section of the statement because, in the long run, operations are the only source of cash. That is, investors will not invest in a company if they do not believe that cash generated from operations will be available to pay them dividends or expand the company. Similarly, creditors will not lend money if they do not believe that cash generated from operations will be available to pay back the loan. For example, many dot.com companies crashed when investors lost faith in their ability to turn business ideas into cash flows from operations.

A common rule of thumb followed by financial and credit analysts is to avoid firms with rising net income but falling cash flow from operations. Rapidly rising inventories or receivables often predict a slump in profits and the need for external financing. A true understanding of the meaning of the difference requires a detailed understanding of its causes.

In the first quarter of 2003, Boston Beer reported that net income was higher than cash flow from operations. However, during the same quarter of 2004, Boston Beer generated over twice as much in cash flow from operations as net income. How was the leader of the craft beer industry able to orchestrate such a turnaround? To answer these questions, we must carefully analyze how Boston Beer's operating activities are reported in its cash flow statement. To properly interpret this information, we also must learn more about the brewing industry.

Analyzing Accounts Receivable Changes

Analysts who cover the beverage industry know that Boston Beer normally sees an increase in receivables from normal seasonal fluctuations in beer sales to distributors. Beer sales to distributors are low in the last month of the fourth quarter (December) because of the onset of winter. As a result, the beginning balance in Accounts Receivable in January is low. However, sales are high at the end of the first quarter (March) in anticipation of spring. The higher March sales cause accounts receivable to increase, but the cash is not collected until April. This was the pattern in 2003. This normal seasonal fluctuation in sales is clearly not a sign of problems for Boston Beer. In 2004, Boston

---

Self-Study Quiz Solutions   1. 0, 2. 0, 3. +, 4. 0, 5. −, 6. −

Beer completed implementing shorter payment terms for its customers, which reversed this effect. We discuss the effects of receivables management on cash flows in more detail in Chapter 6.

Managers sometimes attempt to boost declining sales by extending credit terms (for example, from 30 to 60 days) or by lowering credit standards (that is, lending to riskier customers). The resulting increase in accounts receivable can cause net income to outpace cash flow from operations. As a consequence, many analysts view this pattern as a warning sign.

Analyzing Inventory Changes

An unexpected increase in inventory can also cause net income to outpace cash flow from operations. Such inventory growth can be a sign that planned sales growth did not materialize. Alternatively, a decline in inventory can be a sign that the company is anticipating lower sales in the next quarter. Many analysts compute the quality of income ratio as a general warning sign of these and similar problems.

 Quality of Income Ratio

? ANALYTICAL QUESTION:

How much cash does each dollar of net income generate?

% RATIO AND COMPARISONS:

$$\text{Quality of Income Ratio} = \frac{\text{Cash Flow from Operating Activities}}{\text{Net Income}}$$

Boston Beer ratio for the **year*** 2003 was:

$$\frac{\$19,641}{\$10,558} = 1.86 \ (186\%)$$

COMPARISONS OVER TIME			COMPARISONS WITH COMPETITORS	
Boston Beer (Annual)			Anheuser Busch	Coors
2001	2002	2003	2003	2003
2.46	1.62	1.86	1.43	3.12

Learning Objective 3
Analyze and interpret the quality of income ratio.

Selected Focus Company Comparisons

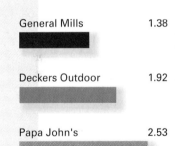

General Mills	1.38
Deckers Outdoor	1.92
Papa John's	2.53

💡 INTERPRETATIONS:

In General → The quality of income ratio measures the portion of income that was generated in cash. All other things equal, a higher quality of income ratio indicates greater ability to finance operating and other cash needs from operating cash inflows.[†] A higher ratio also indicates that it is less likely that the company is using aggressive revenue recognition policies to increase net income, and therefore is less likely to experience a decline in earnings in the future.[‡] When this ratio does not equal 1.0, analysts must establish the sources of the difference to determine the significance of the findings. There are four potential causes of any difference:

1. **The corporate life cycle (growth or decline in sales).** When sales are increasing, receivables and inventory normally increase faster than accounts payable. This often reduces operating cash flows below income, which, in turn, reduces the ratio. When sales are declining, the opposite occurs, and the ratio increases.

2. **Seasonality.** As is the case for Boston Beer, seasonal variations in sales and purchases of inventory can cause the ratio to deviate from 1.0.

continued

3. **Changes in revenue and expense recognition.** Aggressive revenue recognition or failure to accrue appropriate expenses will inflate net income and reduce the ratio.

4. **Changes in management of operating assets and liabilities.** Inefficient management will increase operating assets and decrease liabilities, reducing operating cash flows and the quality of income ratio. More efficient management, such as Boston Beer's shortening of payment terms, will have the opposite effect.

Focus Company Analysis → During the past three years, Boston Beer's quality of income ratio has ranged from 1.62 to 2.46. As we noted earlier, the difference between net income and cash flow from operations in the case of Boston Beer for the first quarter of 2004 was due to a change in customer payment terms. During the last three years, its ratio has remained between those for Anheuser-Busch and Coors. The variation in Boston Beer's ratio would prompt analysts to read the management's discussion and analysis section of the annual report to determine its causes.

A Few Cautions: The quality of income ratio can be interpreted only based on an understanding of the company's business operations and strategy. For example, a low ratio can be due simply to normal seasonal changes. However, it also can indicate obsolete inventory, slowing sales, or failed expansion plans. To test for these possibilities, analysts often analyze this ratio in tandem with the accounts receivable turnover and inventory turnover ratios.

*To eliminate the effects of seasonality, we look at the ratio for the annual period.
†When a net loss is reported, a more negative ratio indicates greater ability to finance the company from operations.
‡See S. Richardson, "Earnings Quality and Short Sellers," *Accounting Horizons,* Supplement 2003, pp. 49–61 for a discussion of related research.

A QUESTION
OF ETHICS   **Fraud and Cash Flows from Operations**

The cash flow statement often gives outsiders the first hint that financial statements may contain errors and irregularities. The importance of this indicator as a predictor is receiving more attention in the United States and internationally. *Investors Chronicle* recently reported on an accounting fraud at a commercial credit company, suggesting that

REAL WORLD EXCERPT
Investors Chronicle

> . . . a look at Versailles's cash flow statement—an invaluable tool in spotting creative accounting—should have triggered misgivings. In the company's last filed accounts in 1999 Versailles reported operating profits of . . . $25 million but a cash outflow from operating activities of $24 million. . . . such figures should . . . have served as a warning. After all, what use is a company to anyone if it reports only accounting profits which are never translated into cash?

As noted in earlier chapters, unethical managers sometimes attempt to reach earnings targets by manipulating accruals and deferrals of revenues and expenses to inflate income. Since these adjusting entries do not affect the cash account, they have no effect on the cash flow statement. A growing difference between net income and cash flow from operations can be a sign of such manipulations. This early warning sign has signaled some famous bankruptcies, such as that of W. T. Grant in 1975. The company had inflated income by failing to make adequate accruals of expenses for uncollectible accounts receivable and obsolete inventory. The more astute analysts noted the growing difference between net income and cash flow from operations and recommended selling the stock long before the bankruptcy.

Source: James Chapman, "Creative Accounting: Exposed!" *Investors Chronicle,* February 3, 2001.

REPORTING AND INTERPRETING CASH FLOWS FROM INVESTING ACTIVITIES

Reporting Cash Flows from Investing Activities

Preparing this section of the cash flow statement requires an analysis of the accounts related to property, plant, and equipment; intangible assets; and investments in the securities of other companies. Normally, the relevant balance sheet accounts include Short-term Investments and long-term asset accounts such as Long-Term Investments and Property, Plant, and Equipment. The following relationships are the ones that you will encounter most frequently:

Learning Objective 4
Report and interpret cash flows from investing activities.

Related Balance Sheet Account(s)	Investing Activity	Cash Flow Effect
Property, plant, and equipment and intangible assets (patents, etc.)	Purchase of property, plant, and equipment or intangible assets for cash	Outflow
	Sale of property, plant, and equipment or intangible assets for cash	Inflow
Short- or long-term investments (stocks and bonds of other companies)	Purchase of investment securities for cash	Outflow
	Sale (maturity) of investment securities for cash	Inflow

Remember this:

- **Only purchases paid for with cash or cash equivalents are included.**
- **The amount of cash that is received from the sale of assets is included, regardless of whether the assets are sold at a gain or loss.**

In Boston Beer's case, the balance sheet (Exhibit 13.3) shows two investing assets (noted with an I) that have changed during the period: Equipment, net (fixed assets) and Short-term investments. To determine the causes of these changes, accountants need to search the related company records.

Cash Flows from Investing Activities

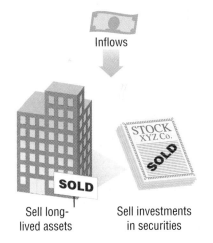

Inflows

Sell long-lived assets   Sell investments in securities

Equipment, Net

They would discover that the company purchased new equipment for $2,373 cash, which is a cash outflow. This investing item is listed in the schedule of investing activities in Exhibit 13.6. This item, less the amount of depreciation expense added back in the Operations section ($2,543), explains the decrease in Equipment, net of $170.

Equipment, Net (A)			
Beg.	17,059	Sold	0
Purch.	2,373	Depr.	2,543
End.	16,889		

Investments

Boston Beer's records also indicate that it purchased $4,627 in short-term investments during the quarter for cash, which is an investing cash outflow. This investing item is listed in the schedule of investing activities in Exhibit 13.6. It explains the $4,627 increase ($19,725 − $15,098 = $4,627) in short-term investments reported on the balance sheet.

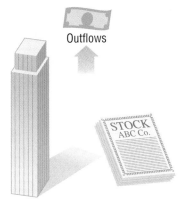

Outflows

Purchase long-lived assets   Purchase investments in securities

EXHIBIT 13.6

Boston Beer Company:
Schedule for Net Cash Flow
from Investing Activities
(dollars in thousands)

Items	Cash Inflows (Outflows)	Explanation
Purchase of equipment	$(2,373)	Payment in cash for equipment
Purchase of short-term investments	(4,627)	Payment in cash for new investments
Net cash inflow (outflow) from investing activities	$(7,000)	Reported on the statement of cash flows

Short-Term Investments (A)			
Beg.	15,098		
Purch.	4,627	Sold	0
End.	19,725		

The resulting net cash flow from investing activities is a $7,000 outflow (see Exhibit 13.6).

Interpreting Cash Flows from Investing Activities

Two common ways to assess a company's ability to internally finance its expansion needs are the capital acquisitions ratio and free cash flow.

KEY RATIO
ANALYSIS

Capital Acquisitions Ratio

Learning Objective 5
Analyze and interpret the capital acquisitions ratio.

? ANALYTICAL QUESTION:

To what degree was the company able to finance purchases of property, plant, and equipment with cash provided by operating activities?

% RATIO AND COMPARISONS:

$$\text{Capital Acquisitions Ratio} = \frac{\text{Cash Flow from Operating Activities}}{\text{Cash Paid for Property, Plant, and Equipment}}$$

Boston Beer's ratio for 2001 through 2003* was

$$\frac{\$52,739}{\$7,046} = 7.49$$

**Selected Focus
Company Comparisons**

Harley-Davidson   2.92

Outback Steakhouse   1.4

General Mills   2.34

Examine the ratio using two techniques:

COMPARISONS OVER TIME		COMPARISONS WITH COMPETITORS	
Boston Beer		Anheuser-Busch	Redhook Ale
1998–2000	2001–2003	2001–2003	2001–2003
3.47	7.49	4.19	2.04

💡 INTERPRETATIONS:

In General → The capital acquisitions ratio reflects the portion of purchases of property, plant, and equipment financed from operating activities (without the need for outside debt or equity financing or the sale of other investments or fixed assets). A high ratio indicates less need for outside financing for current and future expansion. It benefits the company because it provides the company opportunities for strategic acquisitions, avoids the cost of additional debt, and reduces the risk of bankruptcy that comes with additional leverage (see Chapter 10).

Focus Company Analysis → Boston Beer's capital acquisitions ratio has increased from 3.47 to 7.49 in recent years. The high ratio for the 2001–2003 period may be attributable to general slow growth in beer sales and its dampening effects on new investment. When companies in an industry acquire more productive capacity than is necessary to meet customer demand, the costs of maintaining and financing idle plant can drive a company to ruin. Boston Beer minimizes the risks of overcapacity by outsourcing a significant portion of its production to other brewers. This practice lowers Boston Beer's borrowing, depreciation, and transportation costs compared to those of companies with a single large brewery. Redhook's moderate ratio for the 2001–2003 period indicates that it significantly decreased capital investments in recent years compared to 1996–1998 when its ratio was 0.30. Anheuser-Busch falls between Boston Beer and Redhook Ale with respect to capital acquisitions.

A Few Cautions: Since the needs for investment in plant and equipment differ dramatically across industries (for example, airlines versus pizza delivery restaurants), a particular firm's ratio should be compared only with its prior years figures or with other firms in the same industry. Also, a high ratio may indicate a failure to update plant and equipment, which can limit a company's ability to compete in the future.

*Since capital expenditures for plant and equipment often vary greatly from year to year, this ratio is often computed over longer periods of time than one year, such as three years used here.

Free Cash Flow

FINANCIAL
ANALYSIS

Managers and analysts often calculate free cash flow as a measure of a firm's ability to pursue long-term investment opportunities. Free cash flow is normally calculated as follows:

> FREE CASH FLOW = Cash Flows from Operating Activities − Dividends − Capital Expenditures

$$\text{Free Cash Flow} = \text{Cash Flows from Operating Activities} - \text{Dividends} - \text{Capital Expenditures}$$

Any positive free cash flow is available for additional capital expenditures, investments in other companies, and mergers and acquisitions without the need for external financing. While free cash flow is considered a positive sign of financial flexibility, it also can represent a hidden cost to shareholders. Sometimes managers use free cash flow to pursue unprofitable investments just for the sake of growth or to obtain perquisites (such as fancy offices and corporate jets) that do not benefit the shareholders. In these cases, the shareholders would be better off if free cash flow were paid as additional dividends or used to repurchase the company's stock on the open market.

REPORTING AND INTERPRETING CASH FLOWS FROM FINANCING ACTIVITIES

Reporting Cash Flows from Financing Activities

Financing activities are associated with generating capital from creditors and owners. This section of the cash flow statement reflects changes in two current liabilities, Notes Payable to Financial Institutions (often called short-term debt) and Current Maturities of Long-Term Debt, as well as changes in long-term liabilities and stockholders' equity accounts. These balance sheet accounts relate to the issuance and retirement of debt and stock and the payment of dividends. The following relationships are the ones that you will encounter most frequently:

> **Learning Objective 6**
> Report and interpret cash flows from financing activities.

Related Balance Sheet Account(s)	Financing Activity	Cash Flow Effect
Short-term debt (notes payable)	Borrowing cash from bank or other financial institution	Inflow
	Repayment of loan principal	Outflow
Long-term debt	Issuance of bonds for cash	Inflow
	Repayment of bond principal	Outflow
Common stock and additional paid-in capital	Issuance of stock for cash	Inflow
	Repurchase (retirement) of stock with cash	Outflow
Retained earnings	Payment of cash dividends	Outflow

Remember this:

- **If debt or stock is issued for other than cash, it is not included in this section.**
- **Cash repayments of principal are cash flows from financing activities.**
- **Interest payments are cash flows from operating activities.** Since interest expense is reported on the income statement, the related cash flow is shown in the operating section.
- **Dividend payments are cash flows from financing activities.** They are not reported on the income statement because they represent a distribution of income to owners, so they are shown in the financing section.

To compute cash flows from financing activities, you should review changes in debt and stockholders' equity accounts. In the case of Boston Beer Company, the analysis of changes in the balance sheet (Exhibit 13.3) finds that only contributed capital changed during the period (noted with an F).

Contributed Capital

The change in contributed capital resulted from two decisions. First, Boston Beer repurchased outstanding stock for $4,409 cash, which is a cash outflow. The company also issued common stock to employees for $5,593 in cash, which is a cash inflow. Together, these two amounts account for the $1,184 increase in contributed capital. They are listed in the schedule of financing activities in Exhibit 13.7, which shows a net cash inflow of $1,184.

	Contributed Capital (SE)	
	Beg.	22,923
Repurch. 4,409	Issue	5,593
	End.	24,107

EXHIBIT 13.7

Boston Beer Company: Schedule for Net Cash Flow from Financing Activities (dollars in thousands)

Items	Cash Inflows (Outflows)	Explanation
Repurchase of stock (treasury stock)	($4,409)	Cash payments to repurchase outstanding stock
Net proceeds from stock issuance	5,593	Cash proceeds from issue of common stock
Net cash inflow (outflow) from financing activities	$1,184	Reported on the statement of cash flows

Short- and Long-Term Debt

If Boston Beer had borrowed or repaid principal on short- or long-term debt during the period, these also would be listed in this section. The appropriate amounts would be determined by analyzing the short- and long-term debt accounts.

Short- or Long-Term Debt (L)	
Retire (repay)	Beginning Issue (borrow)
	Ending

Retained Earnings

Finally, retained earnings should be analyzed. Retained earnings rise when income is earned and fall when dividends are declared and paid. Boston Beer's retained earnings rose by an amount equal to its net income, so no dividends were declared and paid. Should Boston Beer ever decide to pay dividends, it would also list them as financing cash outflows.

Retained Earnings (SE)			
Dividends	0	Beg. Net Income	36,575 1,271
		End.	37,846

Cash Flows from Financing Activities

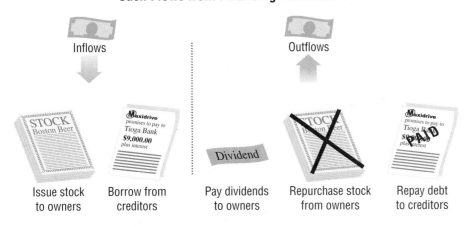

Inflows			Outflows	
Issue stock to owners	Borrow from creditors	Pay dividends to owners	Repurchase stock from owners	Repay debt to creditors

Interpreting Cash Flows from Financing Activities

The long-term growth of a company is normally financed from three sources: internally generated funds (cash from operating activities), the issuance of stock, and money borrowed on a long-term basis. As we discussed in Chapter 10, companies can adopt a number of different capital structures (the balance of debt and equity). The financing sources that management uses to fund growth will have an important impact on the firm's risk and return characteristics. The statement of cash flows shows how management has elected to fund its growth. This information is used by analysts who wish to evaluate the capital structure and growth potential of a business.

SELF-STUDY **QUIZ**

Pyramid Breweries

Indicate which of the following items taken from the cash flow statement of Pyramid Breweries Inc. would be reported in the Investing section (I) or Financing section (F) and whether the amount would be an inflow (+) or an outflow (−).

____ 1. Purchases of short-term investments.

____ 2. Repayment of principal on note payable (to bank).

____ 3. Cash dividends paid.

____ 4. Proceeds from sale of common stock.

____ 5. Proceeds from sale of fixed assets.

After you have completed your answers, check them with the solutions at the bottom of the page.

ADDITIONAL CASH FLOW DISCLOSURES

Learning Objective 7
Explain the impact of additional cash flow disclosures.

Refer to the formal statement of cash flows for Boston Beer Company shown in Exhibit 13.1. As you can see, it is a simple matter to construct the statement after the detailed analysis of the accounts and transactions has been completed (shown in Exhibits 13.4, 13.5, 13.6, and 13.7). If the company uses the direct method for computing cash flow from operations, it must present the reconciliation of net income to cash flow from operations (the indirect method as presented in Exhibit 13.4) as a supplemental schedule. Companies also must provide two other disclosures related to the cash flow statement.

Noncash Investing and Financing Activities

NONCASH INVESTING AND FINANCING ACTIVITIES are transactions that do not have direct cash flow effects; they are reported as a supplement to the statement of cash flows in narrative or schedule form.

Certain transactions are important investing and financing activities but have no cash flow effects. These are called noncash investing and financing activities. For example, the purchase of a $100,000 building with a $100,000 mortgage given by the former owner does not cause either an inflow or an outflow of cash. As a result, these noncash activities are not listed in the three main sections of the cash flow statement. However, supplemental disclosure of these transactions is required, in either narrative or schedule form. Boston Beer's statement of cash flows does not list any noncash investing and financing activities. The following schedule from the annual report of Pacific Aerospace & Electronics illustrates the significance and diversity of noncash transactions.

REAL WORLD EXCERPT
Pacific Aerospace & Electronics
ANNUAL REPORT

PACIFIC AEROSPACE & ELECTRONICS, INC.

Noncash investing and financing activities

Year ended May 31,

	2001	2002	2003
Issuance of common stock on conversion of Series C Preferred Stock	—	—	18,715,000
Short-term obligations refinanced with long-term debt	9,306,000	—	—
Issuance of warrants in connection with debt	1,886,000	—	—
Purchase of patent with a note payable	—	950,000	—

Self-Study Quiz Solutions   a. I−, 2. F−, 3. F−, 4. F+, 5. I+

Supplemental Cash Flow Information

Companies that use the indirect method of presenting cash flows from operations also must provide two other figures: cash paid for interest and cash paid for income taxes. These are normally listed at the bottom of the statement or in the notes.

EPILOGUE

Our more detailed analysis of Boston Beer's first-quarter cash flow indicates the causes of the difference between net income and cash flows in the first quarter. In fact, it was a normal consequence of seasonal variations in sales, purchases of raw materials, and a change in credit policies. Our further analysis of Boston Beer's investing and financing indicates that the cash needed to continue its investment strategy should be more than met by operations.

DEMONSTRATION **CASE**

Complete the following requirements before proceeding to the suggested solution. During a recent year (ended December 31), Redhook Ale Brewery, a Seattle-based craft brewer, reported net income of $3,182 (all numbers in dollars in thousands) and cash and cash equivalents at the beginning of the year of $472. It also engaged in the following activities:

Redhook Ale Brewery

a. Paid $18,752 in principal on debt.

b. Received $46,202 in cash from initial public offering of common stock.

c. Incurred other noncurrent accrued operating expenses of $857.

d. Paid $18,193 in cash for purchase of fixed assets.

e. Accounts receivable increased by $881.

f. Borrowed $16,789 from various lenders.

g. Refundable deposits payable increased by $457.

h. Inventories increased by $574.

i. Made cash deposits on equipment of $5,830.

j. Income tax refund receivable decreased by $326.

k. Sold (issued) stock to employees for $13 in cash.

l. Accounts payable decreased by $391.

m. Received $4 from other investing activities.

n. Accrued expenses increased by $241.

o. Prepaid expenses increased by $565.

p. Recorded depreciation of $1,324.

q. Paid $5 cash in other financing activities.

Required:

Based on this information, prepare the cash flow statement using the indirect method.

SUGGESTED SOLUTION

REDHOOK ALE BREWERY
Statement of Cash Flows
For the Year Ended December 31
(dollars in thousands)

Operating activities

Net income	$ 3,182
Adjustments:	
Depreciation	1,324
Other noncurrent accrued expenses	857
Change in accounts receivable	(881)
Change in inventories	(574)
Change in income taxes receivable	326
Change in prepaid expenses	(565)
Change in accounts payable	(391)
Change in accrued expenses	241
Change in refundable deposits payable	457
Net cash flow from operating activities	3,976
Investing activities	
Expenditures for fixed assets	(18,193)
Deposits on equipment	(5,830)
Other	4
Net cash flow from investing activities	(24,019)
Financing activities	
Proceeds from debt	16,789
Repayment of debt	(18,752)
Proceeds from sale of stock (IPO)	46,202
Proceeds from sale of stock (options)	13
Other	(5)
Net cash flow from financing activities	44,247
Increase in cash and cash equivalents	24,204
Cash and cash equivalents:	
Beginning of year	472
End of year	$24,676

Chapter Supplement A

Adjustment for Gains and Losses: Indirect Method

As noted earlier, the Operating Activities section of the statement of cash flows may include an adjustment for gains and losses reported on the income statement. The transactions that cause gains and losses should be classified on the cash flow statement as operating, investing, or financing activities, depending on their dominant characteristics. For example, if the sale of a productive asset (e.g., a delivery truck) produced a gain, it would be classified as an investing activity.

An adjustment must be made in the Operating Activities section to avoid double counting the gain or loss. To illustrate, consider the following entry for Boston Beer to record the disposal of a delivery truck:

Cash (+A)   8,000
Accumulated depreciation (−XA, +A)   4,000
  Property, plant, and equipment (−A)   10,000
  Gain on disposal (+Gain, +SE)   2,000

Assets		=	Liabilities	+	Stockholders' Equity	
Cash	+8,000				Gain on disposal	+2,000
Accumulated depreciation	+4,000					
Property, plant, and equipment	−10,000					

The $8,000 inflow of cash is an investing cash inflow, but the reported gain of $2,000 was also shown on the income statement. Because the gain was included in the computation of income, it is necessary to remove (subtract) the $2,000 gain from the Operating Activities section of the statement to avoid double counting.

When a loss is reported on the income statement, it also must be removed from cash flows from operating activities. Consider the following entry to record the sale of assets:

Cash (+A)   41,000
Accumulated depreciation (−XA, +A)   15,000
Loss on disposal (+Loss, −SE)   12,000
  Property, plant, and equipment (−A)   68,000

Assets		=	Liabilities	+	Stockholders' Equity	
Cash	+41,000				Loss on disposal	−12,000
Accumulated depreciation	+15,000					
Property, plant, and equipment	−68,000					

On the cash flow statement, the loss of $12,000 must be removed (added back) in the computation of cash from operating activities, and the total cash collected of $41,000 must be shown in the investing activities section of the statement.

Chapter Supplement B

Spreadsheet Approach—Statement of Cash Flows: Indirect Method

As situations become more complex, the analytical approach that we used to prepare the statement of cash flows for Boston Beer Company becomes cumbersome and inefficient. In actual practice, many companies use a spreadsheet approach to prepare the statement of cash flows. The spreadsheet is based on the same logic that we used in our previous illustration. The spreadsheet's primary advantage is that it offers a more systematic way to keep track of data. You may find it useful even in simple situations.

Exhibit 13.8 shows Boston Beer Company's spreadsheet, which is organized as follows:

1. Four columns to record dollar amounts are established. The first column is for the beginning balances for items reported on the balance sheet; the next two columns reflect debit and credit changes to those balances; the final column contains the ending balances for the balance sheet accounts.
2. On the far left of the top half of the spreadsheet, each account name from the balance sheet is entered.
3. On the far left of the bottom half of the spreadsheet, the name of each item that will be reported on the statement of cash flows is entered.

Changes in the various balance sheet accounts are analyzed in terms of debits and credits in the top half of the spreadsheet with the offsetting debits and credits being recorded in the bottom half of the spreadsheet in terms of their impact on cash flows. Each change in the noncash balance sheet accounts

| EXHIBIT 13.8 | Spreadsheet to Prepare Statement of Cash Flows, Indirect Method |

BOSTON BEER COMPANY
Quarter Ended March 27, 2004
(dollars in thousands)

	Beginning Balances, 12/27/2003	Analysis of Change				Ending Balances, 3/27/2004
		Debit		**Credit**		
Items from Balance Sheet						
Cash and cash equivalents	27,792			(n)	3,046	24,746
Short-term investments	15,098	(k)	4,627	(j)	—	19,725
Accounts receivable	10,432			(d)	861	9,571
Inventories	9,890	(e)	577			10,467
Prepaid expenses	1,126	(f)	322			1,448
Equipment, net	17,059	(i)	2,373	(b)	2,543	16,889
				(c)	—	
Accounts payable	6,395	(g)	52			6,343
Accrued expenses	15,504	(h)	954			14,550
Contributed capital	22,923	(l)	4,409	(m)	5,593	24,107
Retained earnings	36,575			(a)	1,271	37,846
		Inflows		**Outflows**		**Subtotals**
Statement of Cash Flows						
Cash flows from operating activities:						
Net income		(a)	1,271			
Adjustments to reconcile net income to cash provided by operating activities						
Depreciation and amortization		(b)	2,543			
Changes in assets and liabilities:						
Accounts receivable		(d)	861			
Inventories				(e)	577	
Prepaid expenses				(f)	322	
Accounts payable				(g)	52	
Accrued expenses				(h)	954	
						2,770
Cash flows from investing activities:						
Proceeds from sale of equipment		(c)	—			
Purchases of equipment				(i)	2,373	
Maturities (sale) of short-term investments		(j)	—			
Purchase of short-term investments				(k)	4,627	
						(7,000)
Cash flows from financing activities:						
Purchase of treasury stock				(l)	4,409	
Net proceeds from stock issuance		(m)	5,593			
						1,184
Net decrease in cash and cash equivalents		(n)	3,046			
			26,628		26,628	(3,046)

explains part of the change in the Cash account. To illustrate, let's examine each of the entries on the spreadsheet for Boston Beer Company shown in Exhibit 13.8. You will note that they follow each of the items presented in the schedule to prepare the cash flow statement shown in Exhibits 13.4, 13.6, and 13.7.

a. This entry is used to start the reconciliation; net income of $1,271 is shown as an inflow in the Operating Activities section to be adjusted by the noncash reconciling entries. The credit to Retained Earnings reflects the effects of the original closing entry. This is the starting point for the reconciliation.

b. Depreciation expense of $2,543 is a noncurrent accrued expense. It is added back to net income because this type of expense does not cause a cash outflow when it is recorded. The credit to Accumulated Depreciation reflects the effects of the original entry to record depreciation.

c. When an asset that was classified as part of fixed assets is sold, the actual cash proceeds appear in the Investing Section of the statement of cash flows. In this case, no sales were made.

d. This entry reconciles the change in accounts receivable during the period with net income. It is added to net income because cash collections from customers totaled more than sales revenue.

e. This entry reconciles the purchases of inventory with cost of goods sold. It is subtracted from net income because more inventory was purchased than was sold.

f. This entry reconciles the prepayment of expenses with their expiration. It is subtracted from net income because cash payments for new prepayments are more than the amounts that expired and were recorded on the income statement during the period.

g. This entry reconciles cash paid to suppliers with purchases on account. It is subtracted because more cash was paid than was borrowed during the period.

h. This entry reconciles the accrual of expenses with payments for these expenses. It is subtracted because cash payments for expenses are more than new accruals.

i. This entry records the purchases of new plant and equipment (fixed assets) for cash.

j. This entry records the receipt of cash on maturity of some short-term investments. In this case, there was no receipt.

k. This entry records the purchases of short-term investments for cash.

l. This entry records cash paid to repurchase some of Boston Beer's own stock from shareholders.

m. This entry records the cash received from the issuance of stock.

n. This entry shows that the net increase or decrease reported on the statement of cash flows is the same as the change in the cash balance on the balance sheet during the period.

The preceding entries complete the spreadsheet analysis because all accounts are reconciled. The accuracy of the analysis can be checked by adding the two analysis columns to verify that Debits = Credits. You should also note that the debits and credits to the balance sheet accounts directly match those recorded in the T-accounts presented in the body of the chapter. The formal statement of cash flows can be prepared directly from the spreadsheet.

The analytical technique that you have learned for preparing the statement of cash flows will help you deal with other significant business problems. For example, this type of analysis is useful for developing cash budgets for a business. Many small businesses that experience rapid sales growth get into serious financial difficulties because they did not forecast the cash flow effects associated with credit sales and large increases in inventory.

CHAPTER **TAKE-AWAYS**

1. Classify cash flow statement items as part of net cash flows from operating, investing, and financing activities. p. 658

The statement has three main sections: Cash Flows from Operating Activities, which are related to earning income from normal operations; Cash Flows from Investing Activities, which are related to the acquisition and sale of productive assets; and Cash Flows from Financing Activities, which are related to external financing of the enterprise. The net cash inflow or outflow for the year is the same amount as the increase or decrease in cash and cash equivalents for the year on the balance sheet. Cash equivalents are highly liquid investments with original maturities of three months or less.

2a. Report and interpret cash flows from operating activities using the indirect method. p. 665

The indirect method for reporting cash flows from operating activities reports a conversion of net income to net cash flow from operating activities. The conversion involves additions and subtractions for (1) noncurrent accruals including expenses (such as depreciation expense) and revenues that do not affect current assets or current liabilities and (2) changes in each of the individual current assets (other than cash and short-term investments) and current liabilities (other than short-term debt to financial institutions and current maturities of long-term debt, which relate to financing), which reflect differences in the timing of accrual basis net income and cash flows.

2b. Report and interpret cash flows from operating activities using the direct method. p. 670

The direct method for reporting cash flows from operating activities accumulates all of the operating transactions that result in either a debit or a credit to cash into categories. The most common inflows are cash received from customers, dividends, and interest on investments. The most common outflows are cash paid for purchase of services and goods for resale, salaries and wages, income taxes, and interest on liabilities. It is prepared by adjusting each item on the income statement from an accrual basis to a cash basis.

3. Analyze and interpret the quality of income ratio. p. 675

Quality of income ratio (Cash Flow from Operating Activities ÷ Net Income) measures the portion of income that was generated in cash. A higher quality of income ratio indicates greater ability to finance operating and other cash needs from operating cash inflows. A higher ratio also indicates that it is less likely that the company is using aggressive revenue recognition policies to increase net income.

4. Report and interpret cash flows from investing activities. p. 677

Investing activities reported on the cash flow statement include cash payments to acquire fixed assets and short- and long-term investments and cash proceeds from the sale of fixed assets and short- and long-term investments.

5. Analyze and interpret the capital acquisitions ratio. p. 678

The capital acquisitions ratio (Cash Flow from Operating Activities ÷ Cash Paid for Property, Plant, and Equipment) reflects the portion of purchases of property, plant, and equipment financed from operating activities without the need for outside debt or equity financing or the sale of other investments or fixed assets. A high ratio benefits the company because it provides the company with opportunities for strategic acquisitions.

6. Report and interpret cash flows from financing activities. p. 679

Cash inflows from financing activities include cash proceeds from issuance of short- and long-term debt and common stock. Cash outflows include cash principal payments on short- and long-term debt, cash paid for the repurchase of the company's stock, and cash dividend payments. Cash payments associated with interest are a cash flow from operating activities.

7. Explain the impact of additional cash flow disclosures. p. 682

Noncash investing and financing activities are investing and financing activities that do not involve cash. They include, for example, purchases of fixed assets with long-term debt or stock, exchanges of fixed assets, and exchanges of debt for stock. These transactions are disclosed only as supplemental disclosures to the cash flow statement along with cash paid for taxes and interest under the indirect method.

Throughout the preceding chapters, we emphasized the conceptual basis of accounting. An understanding of the rationale underlying accounting is important for both preparers and users of financial statements. In Chapter 14, we bring together our discussion of the major users of financial statements and how they analyze and use them. We discuss and illustrate many widely used analytical techniques discussed in earlier chapters, as well as additional techniques. As you study Chapter 14, you will see that an understanding of accounting rules and concepts is essential for effective analysis of financial statements.

KEY RATIOS

Quality of income ratio indicates what portion of income was generated in cash. It is computed as follows (p. 675):

$$\text{Quality of Income Ratio} = \frac{\text{Cash Flow from Operating Activities}}{\text{Net Income}}$$

Capital acquisitions ratio measures the ability to finance purchases of plant and equipment from operations. It is computed as follows (p. 678):

$$\text{Capital Acquisitions Ratio} = \frac{\text{Cash Flow from Operating Activities}}{\text{Cash Paid for Property, Plant, and Equipment}}$$

FINDING FINANCIAL INFORMATION

Balance Sheet

Changes in Assets, Liabilities, and Stockholders' Equity

Income Statement

Net Income and Noncurrent Accruals

Statement of Cash Flows

Cash Flows from Operating Activities
Cash Flows from Investing Activities
Cash Flows from Financing Activities
Separate Schedule (or note)
Noncash investing and financing activities
Interest and taxes paid

Notes

Under Summary of Significant Accounting Policies
Definition of cash equivalents

Under Separate Note
If not listed on cash flow statement:
Noncash investing and financing activities
Interest and taxes paid

KEY TERMS

Cash Equivalent   p. 658
Cash Flows from Financing
   Activities   p. 661
Cash Flows from Investing
   Activities   p. 660

Cash Flows from Operating
   Activities (Cash Flows from
   Operations)   p. 659
Direct Method   p. 660
Free Cash Flow   p. 679

Indirect Method   p. 660
Noncash Investing and Financing
   Activities   p. 682

QUESTIONS

1. Compare the purposes of the income statement, the balance sheet, and the statement of cash flows.
2. What information does the statement of cash flows report that is not reported on the other required financial statements? How do investors and creditors use that information?
3. What are cash equivalents? How are purchases and sales of cash equivalents reported on the statement of cash flows?
4. What are the major categories of business activities reported on the statement of cash flows? Define each of these activities.
5. What are the typical cash inflows from operating activities? What are the typical cash outflows from operating activities?
6. Under the indirect method, depreciation expense is added to net income to report cash flows from operating activities. Does depreciation cause an inflow of cash?
7. Explain why cash paid during the period for purchases and for salaries is not specifically reported on the statement of cash flows, indirect method, as cash outflows.
8. Explain why a $50,000 increase in inventory during the year must be included in developing cash flows for operating activities under both the direct and indirect methods.
9. Compare the two methods of reporting cash flows from operating activities in the statement of cash flows.
10. What are the typical cash inflows from investing activities? What are the typical cash outflows from investing activities?
11. What are the typical cash inflows from financing activities? What are the typical cash outflows from financing activities?
12. What are noncash investing and financing activities? Give two examples. How are they reported on the statement of cash flows?
13. How is the sale of equipment reported on the statement of cash flows using the indirect method?

MULTIPLE-CHOICE QUESTIONS

1. Most companies use the indirect method of computing the change in cash from operating activities for the following reason(s):
   a. The FASB prefers the indirect method.
   b. It is less costly to prepare than the direct method.
   c. The indirect method arrives at a higher cash inflow amount.
   d. Both (a) and (b) are correct.
2. In what order do the three sections of the statement of cash flows appear when reading from top to bottom?
   a. Financing, Investing, Operating
   b. Investing, Operating, Financing
   c. Operating, Financing, Investing
   d. Operating, Investing, Financing
3. Total cash inflow in the operating section of the statement of cash flows should include which of the following?
   a. cash received from customers at the point of sale
   b. cash collections from customer accounts receivable
   c. cash received in advance of revenue recognition (unearned revenue)
   d. all of the above
4. If the balance in prepaid expenses increased during the year, what action should be taken on the statement of cash flows when following the indirect method, *and why?*
   a. The change in the account balance should be subtracted from net income because the net increase in prepaid expenses did not impact net income but did reduce the cash balance.
   b. The change in the account balance should be added to net income because the net increase in prepaid expenses did not impact net income but did increase the cash balance.

    c. The net change in prepaid expenses should be subtracted from net income to reverse the income statement effect that had no impact on cash.

    d. The net change in prepaid expenses should be added to net income to reverse the income statement effect that had no impact on cash.

5. Which of the following would not appear in the investing section of the statement of cash flows?

    a. purchase of inventory

    b. sale of obsolete equipment used in the factory

    c. purchase of land for a new office building

    d. All of the above would appear.

6. Which of the following items would not appear in the financing section of the statement of cash flows?

    a. the repurchase of the company's own stock   c. the repayment of debt

    b. the receipt of dividends   d. the payment of dividends

7. Which of the following is not added to net income when computing cash flows from operations under the indirect method?

    a. the net increase in accounts payable

    b. the net decrease in accounts receivable

    c. depreciation expense reported on the income statement

    d. All of the above are added.

8. If a company engages in a noncash material transaction, which of the following is required?

    a. The company must include an explanatory narrative or schedule along with the statement of cash flows.

    b. No disclosure is necessary.

    c. The company must include an explanatory narrative or schedule along with the balance sheet.

    d. It must be reported in the investing and financing section of the statement of cash flows.

9. The change in cash shown *in the operating section* of the statement of cash flows should equal which of the following?

    a. net income on the income statement   c. the change in accounts payable

    b. the change in accounts receivable   d. none of the above

10. The *total* change in cash as shown near the bottom of the statement of cash flows for the year should agree to which of the following?

    a. the difference in retained earnings when reviewing the comparative balance sheet

    b. net income or net loss as found on the income statement

    c. the difference in cash when reviewing the comparative balance sheet

    d. none of the above

For more practice with multiple-choice questions, go to the text website at www.mhhe.com/libby5e or the Topic Tackler DVD for use with this text.

 Available with McGraw-Hill's Homework Manager

MINI-**EXERCISES**

Matching Items Reported to Cash Flow Statement Categories (Indirect Method)

M13-1
LO1, 2A
Adolph Coors

Adolph Coors Company, founded in 1873, is the third largest U.S. brewer. Its tie to the magical appeal of the Rocky Mountains is one of its most powerful trademarks. Some of the items included in its recent annual consolidated statement of cash flows presented using the *indirect method* are listed here. Indicate whether each item is disclosed in the Operating Activities (O), Investing Activities (I), or Financing Activities (F) section of the statement or (NA) if the item does not appear on the statement. (*Note:* This is the exact wording used on the actual statement.)

    _____ 1. Proceeds from sale of properties.

    _____ 2. Purchase of stock. [This involves repurchase of its own stock.]

    _____ 3. Depreciation, depletion, and amortization.

    _____ 4. Accounts payable (decrease).

    _____ 5. Inventories (decrease).

    _____ 6. Principal payment on long-term debt.

M13-2
LO2A

Determining the Effects of Account Changes on Cash Flow from Operating Activities (Indirect Method)

Indicate whether each item would be added (1) or subtracted (2) in the computation of cash flow from operating activities using the indirect method.

_____ 1. Depreciation, depletion, and amortization.
_____ 2. Inventories (increase).
_____ 3. Accounts payable (decrease).
_____ 4. Accounts receivable (decrease).
_____ 5. Accrued expenses (increase).

M13-3
LO1, 2B

Lion Nathan

Matching Items Reported to Cash Flow Statement Categories (Direct Method)

Lion Nathan, brewer of XXXX, Toohey's, and other well-known Australian brands, has net revenue of more than $1 billion Australian. Some of the items included in its recent annual consolidated statement of cash flows presented using the *direct method* are listed here. Indicate whether each item is disclosed in the Operating Activities (O), Investing Activities (I), or Financing Activities (F) section of the statement or (NA) if the item does not appear on the statement. (*Note:* This is the exact wording used on the actual statement.)

_____ 1. Repayments of borrowings (bank debt).
_____ 2. Dividends paid.
_____ 3. Proceeds from sale of property, plant, and equipment.
_____ 4. Net interest paid.
_____ 5. Receipts from customers.
_____ 6. Payment for share buy-back.

M13-4
LO3

Analyzing the Quality of Income Ratio

Lisa K. Corporation reported net income of $80,000, depreciation expense of $3,000, and cash flow from operations of $60,000. Compute the quality of income ratio. What does the ratio tell you about the company's ability to finance operating and other cash needs from operating cash inflows?

M13-5
LO4

Computing Cash Flows from Investing Activities

Based on the following information, compute cash flows from investing activities.

Cash collections from customers	$800
Sale of used equipment	250
Depreciation expense	100
Purchase of short-term investments	300

M13-6
LO6

Computing Cash Flows from Financing Activities

Based on the following information, compute cash flows from financing activities.

Purchase of short-term investments	$ 250
Dividends paid	800
Interest paid	400
Additional short-term borrowing from bank	1,000

M13-7
LO7

Reporting Noncash Investing and Financing Activities

Which of the following transactions qualify as noncash investing and financing activities?
_____ Purchase of equipment with short-term investments
_____ Dividends paid in cash
_____ Purchase of building with mortgage payable
_____ Additional short-term borrowing from bank

Available with McGraw-Hill's Homework Manager

EXERCISES

Matching Items Reported to Cash Flow Statement Categories (Indirect Method)

Reebok International Ltd. is a global company that designs and markets sports and fitness products, including footwear, apparel, and accessories. Some of the items included in its recent annual consolidated statement of cash flows presented using the *indirect method* are listed here.

Indicate whether each item is disclosed in the Operating Activities (O), Investing Activities (I), or Financing Activities (F) section of the statement or (NA) if the item does not appear on the statement. (*Note:* This is the exact wording used on the actual statement.)

E13-1
LO1, 2A
Reebok

_____ 1. Depreciation and amortization
_____ 2. Cash collections from customers
_____ 3. Dividends paid
_____ 4. [Change in] Inventory
_____ 5. Payments to acquire property and equipment
_____ 6. Repayments of long-term debt
_____ 7. Net income
_____ 8. Proceeds from issuance of common stock to employees
_____ 9. Net repayments of notes payable to banks
_____ 10. [Change in] Accounts payable and accrued expenses

Matching Items Reported to Cash Flow Statement Categories (Direct Method)

The Australian company BHP Billiton is the world's biggest mining company. Some of the items included in its recent annual consolidated statement of cash flows presented using the *direct method* are listed here.

Indicate whether each item is disclosed in the Operating Activities (O), Investing Activities (I), or Financing Activities (F) section of the statement or (NA) if the item does not appear on the statement. (*Note:* This is the exact wording used on the actual statement.)

E13-2
LO1, 2B
BHP Billiton

_____ 1. Dividends paid
_____ 2. Income taxes paid
_____ 3. Interest received
_____ 4. Net income
_____ 5. Payments for property, plant, and equipment
_____ 6. Payments in the course of operations
_____ 7. Proceeds from ordinary share [stock] issues
_____ 8. Proceeds from sale of property, plant, and equipment
_____ 9. Receipts from customers
_____ 10. Repayments of loans

Determining Cash Flow Statement Effects of Transactions

Stanley Furniture Company is a Virginia-based furniture manufacturer. For each of the following first-quarter transactions, indicate whether *net cash inflows (outflows)* from operating activities (NCFO), investing activities (NCFI), or financing activities (NCFF) are affected and whether the effect is an inflow (+) or outflow (−), or (NE) if the transaction has no effect on cash. (*Hint:* Determine the journal entry recorded for the transaction. The transaction affects net cash flows *if and only if* the account Cash is affected.)

E13-3
LO1
Stanley Furniture

_____ 1. Paid cash to purchase new equipment.
_____ 2. Purchased raw materials inventory on account.
_____ 3. Collected payments on account from customers.
_____ 4. Recorded an adjusting entry to record accrued salaries expense.
_____ 5. Recorded and paid interest on debt to creditors.
_____ 6. Repaid principal on revolving credit loan from bank.
_____ 7. Prepaid rent for the following period.

_____ 8. Sold used equipment for cash at book value.
_____ 9. Made payment to suppliers on account.
_____ 10. Declared and paid cash dividends to shareholders.

E13-4

LO1

Hewlett-Packard

Determining Cash Flow Statement Effects of Transactions

Hewlett-Packard is a leading manufacturer of computer equipment for the business and home markets. For each of the following recent transactions, indicate whether *net cash inflows (outflows)* from operating activities (NCFO), investing activities (NCFI), or financing activities (NCFF) are affected and whether the effect is an inflow (+) or outflow (−), or (NE) if the transaction has no effect on cash. (*Hint:* Determine the journal entry recorded for the transaction. The transaction affects net cash flows *if and only if* the account Cash is affected.)

_____ 1. Recorded and paid income taxes to the federal government.
_____ 2. Sold equipment for cash equal to its net book value.
_____ 3. Issued long-term debt for cash.
_____ 4. Collected payments on account from customers.
_____ 5. Purchased raw materials inventory on account.
_____ 6. Purchased investment securities for cash.
_____ 7. Purchased new equipment by signing a three-year note.
_____ 8. Issued common stock for cash.
_____ 9. Prepaid rent for the following period.
_____ 10. Recorded an adjusting entry for expiration of a prepaid expense.

E13-5

LO2A, 2B

Comparing the Direct and Indirect Methods

To compare statement of cash flows reporting under the direct and indirect methods, enter check marks to indicate which items are used with each method.

Cash Flows (and Related Changes)	STATEMENT OF CASH FLOWS METHOD	
	Direct	Indirect
1. Accounts payable increase or decrease		
2. Payments to employees		
3. Cash collections from customers		
4. Accounts receivable increase or decrease		
5. Payments to suppliers		
6. Inventory increase or decrease		
7. Wages payable, increase or decrease		
8. Depreciation expense		
9. Net income		
10. Cash flows from operating activities		
11. Cash flows from investing activities		
12. Cash flows from financing activities		
13. Net increase or decrease in cash during the period		

E13-6

LO2A

Reporting Cash Flows from Operating Activities (Indirect Method)

The following information pertains to Night Company:

Income Statement		
Sales		$80,000
Expenses		
Cost of goods sold	$50,000	
Depreciation expense	7,000	
Salaries expense	11,000	68,000
Net income		$12,000

Partial Balance Sheet	2006	2005
Accounts receivable	$14,000	$10,000
Inventory	7,000	15,000
Salaries payable	1,500	1,000

Required:

Present the Operating Activities section of the statement of cash flows for Night Company using the indirect method.

Reporting and Interpreting Cash Flows from Operating Activities from an Analyst's Perspective (Indirect Method)

E13-7
LO2A

Able Company completed its income statement and balance sheet for 2006 and provided the following information:

Income Statement		
Service revenue		$52,000
Expenses		
Salaries	$42,000	
Depreciation	7,000	
Amortization of copyrights	300	
Other expenses	8,700	58,000
Net loss		($ 6,000)
Partial Balance Sheet	2006	2005
Accounts receivable	$ 8,000	$20,000
Salaries payable	12,000	3,000
Other accrued liabilities	1,000	5,000

In addition, Able bought a small service machine for $5,000.

Required:

1. Present the Operating Activities section of the statement of cash flows for Able Company using the indirect method.
2. What were the major reasons that Able was able to report a net loss but positive cash flow from operations? Why are the reasons for the difference between cash flow from operations and net income important to financial analysts?

Reporting and Interpreting Cash Flows from Operating Activities from an Analyst's Perspective (Indirect Method)

E13-8
LO2A
Sizzler
International, Inc.

Sizzler International, Inc., operates 700 family restaurants around the world. The company's recent annual report contained the following information (dollars in thousands):

Net loss	$ (9,482)
Depreciation and amortization	33,305
Increase in receivables	170
Decrease in inventories	643
Increase in prepaid expenses	664
Decrease in accounts payable	2,282
Decrease in accrued liabilities	719
Increase in income taxes payable	1,861
Reduction of long-term debt	12,691
Additions to equipment	29,073

Required:

1. Based on this information, compute cash flow from operating activities using the indirect method.

2. What were the major reasons that Sizzler was able to report a net loss but positive cash flow from operations? Why are the reasons for the difference between cash flow from operations and net income important to financial analysts?

E13-9
LO2A
Colgate-Palmolive

Inferring Balance Sheet Changes from the Cash Flow Statement (Indirect Method)

A recent statement of cash flows for Colgate-Palmolive reported the following information (dollars in millions):

Operating Activities	
Net income	$477.0
Depreciation	192.5
Cash effect of changes in	
Receivables	(38.0)
Inventories	28.4
Other current assets	10.6
Payables	(10.0)
Other	(117.8)
Net cash provided by operations	$542.7

Required:
Based on the information reported on the statement of cash flows for Colgate-Palmolive, determine whether the following accounts increased or decreased during the period: Receivables, Inventories, Other Current Assets, and Payables.

E13-10
LO2A
Apple Computer, Inc.

Inferring Balance Sheet Changes from the Cash Flow Statement (Indirect Method)

A recent statement of cash flows for Apple Computer contained the following information (dollars in thousands):

Operations	
Net income	$310,178
Depreciation	167,958
Changes in assets and liabilities	
Accounts receivable	(199,401)
Inventories	418,204
Other current assets	33,616
Accounts payable	139,095
Income taxes payable	50,045
Other current liabilities	39,991
Other adjustments	(222,691)
Cash generated by operations	$736,995

Required:
For each of the asset and liability accounts listed on the statement of cash flows, determine whether the account balances increased or decreased during the period.

E13-11
LO2B

Reporting Cash Flows from Operating Activities from an Analyst's Perspective (Direct Method)

Refer to the information for Night Company in Exercise 13-6.

Required:
Present the Operating Activities section of the statement of cash flows for Night Company using the direct method.

Reporting and Interpreting Cash Flows from Operating Activities from an Analyst's Perspective (Direct Method)

E13-12
LO2B

Refer to the information for Able Company in Exercise 13-7.

Required:

1. Present the Operating Activities section of the statement of cash flows for Able Company using the direct method. Assume that other accrued liabilities relate to other expenses on the income statement.
2. What were the major reasons that Able was able to report a net loss but positive cash flow from operations? Why are the reasons for the difference between cash flow from operations and net income important to financial analysts?

Reporting and Interpreting Cash Flows from Operating Activities from an Analyst's Perspective (Direct Method)

E13-13
LO2B
Sizzler
International, Inc.

Refer to the following summarized income statement and additional selected information for Sizzler International, Inc.:

Income Statement		Other Information:	
Revenues	$136,500	Increase in receivables	$ 170
Cost of sales	45,500	Decrease in inventories	643
Gross margin	91,000	Increase in prepaid expenses	664
Salary expense	56,835	Decrease in accounts payable	2,282
Depreciation and amortization	33,305	Decrease in accrued liabilities	719
Other expense	7,781	Increase in income taxes payable	1,861
Net loss before tax	(6,921)		
Income tax expense	2,561		
Net loss	$ (9,482)		

Required:

1. Based on this information, compute cash flow from operating activities using the direct method. Assume that prepaid expenses and accrued liabilities relate to other expense.
2. What were the major reasons that Sizzler was able to report a net loss but positive cash flow from operations? Why are the reasons for the difference between cash flow from operations and net income important to financial analysts?

Analyzing Cash Flows from Operating Activities; Interpreting the Quality of Income Ratio

E13-14
LO2A, 3
PepsiCo

A recent annual report for PepsiCo contained the following information for the period (dollars in millions):

Net income	$1,587.9
Depreciation and amortization	1,444.2
Increase in accounts receivable	161.0
Increase in inventory	89.5
Decrease in prepaid expense	3.3
Increase in accounts payable	143.2
Decrease in taxes payable	125.1
Decrease in other current liabilities	96.7
Cash dividends paid	461.6
Treasury stock purchased	463.5

Required:

1. Compute cash flows from operating activities for PepsiCo using the indirect method.
2. Compute the quality of income ratio.
3. What were the major reasons that Pepsi's quality of income ratio did not equal 1.0?

E13-15

LO4, 6

Rowe Furniture

Reporting Cash Flows from Investing and Financing Activities

Rowe Furniture Corporation is a Virginia-based manufacturer of furniture. In a recent quarter, it reported the following activities:

Net income	$ 4,135
Purchase of property, plant, and equipment	871
Borrowings under line of credit (bank)	1,417
Proceeds from issuance of stock	11
Cash received from customers	29,164
Payments to reduce long-term debt	46
Sale of marketable securities	134
Proceeds from sale of property and equipment	6,594
Dividends paid	277
Interest paid	90
Purchase of treasury stock (stock repurchase)	1,583

Required:

Based on this information, present the Cash Flow from Investing and Financing Activities sections of the cash flow statement.

E13-16

LO4, 5, 6

Gibraltar Industries

Reporting and Interpreting Cash Flows from Investing and Financing Activities with Discussion of Management Strategy

Gibraltar Industries is a Buffalo, New York–based manufacturer of high-value-added steel products. In a recent year, it reported the following activities:

Acquisitions (investments in other companies)	$ (84,243)
Decrease in inventories	11,056
Depreciation and amortization	22,448
Long-term debt reduction	(118,100)
Net cash provided by operating activities	64,663
Net income	26,953
Net proceeds from issuance of common stock	73,558
Net proceeds from sale of property and equipment	436
Payment of dividends	(2,733)
Proceeds from long-term debt	122,144
Purchases of other equity investments	(7,797)
Purchases of property, plant, and equipment	(22,571)

Required:

1. Based on this information, present the Cash Flow from Investing and Financing Activities sections of the cash flow statement.
2. Compute the capital acquisitions ratio. What does the ratio tell you about Gibraltar's ability to finance purchases of property, plant, and equipment with cash provided by operating activities?
3. What do you think was Gibraltar management's plan for the use of the cash generated by the issuance of common stock?

E13-17

LO5, 7

Reporting Noncash Transactions on the Statement of Cash Flows; Interpreting the Effect on the Capital Acquisitions Ratio

An analysis of Martin Corporation's operational asset accounts provided the following information:

a. Acquired a large machine that cost $26,000, paying for it by giving a $15,000, 12 percent interest-bearing note due at the end of two years and 500 shares of its common stock, with a par value of $10 per share and a market value of $22 per share.

b. Acquired a small machine that cost $8,700. Full payment was made by transferring a tract of land that had a book value of $8,700.

Required:
1. Show how this information should be reported on the statement of cash flows.
2. What would be the effect of these transactions on the capital acquisitions ratio? How might these transactions distort interpretation of the ratio?

(Supplement A) Determining Cash Flows from the Sale of Property

E13-18

During three recent years A. Klein, Inc., disposed of the following plant and equipment:

	Year 3	Year 2	Year 1
Plant and equipment (at cost)	$54,000	$ 8,000	$11,000
Accumulated depreciation on equipment disposed of	29,594	3,691	9,203
Cash received	14,768	11,623	1,797

Required:
1. Determine the cash flow from the sale of property for each year that would be reported in the Investing Activities section of the cash flow statement.
2. Klein uses the indirect method for the Operating Activities section of the cash flow statement. What amounts related to the sales would be added or subtracted in the computation of Net Cash Flows from Operating Activities for each year?

(Supplement A) Determining Cash Flows from the Sale of Equipment

E13-19

During the period, English Company sold some excess equipment at a loss. The following information was collected from the company's accounting records:

From the Income Statement	
Depreciation expense	$ 700
Loss on sale of equipment	3,000
From the Balance Sheet	
Beginning equipment	12,500
Ending equipment	8,000
Beginning accumulated depreciation	2,000
Ending accumulated depreciation	2,400

No new equipment was bought during the period.

Required:
For the equipment that was sold, determine its original cost, its accumulated depreciation, and the cash received from the sale.

Preparing a Statement of Cash Flows, Indirect Method: Complete Spreadsheet (Supplement B)

E13-20

An analysis of accounts follows:

a. Purchased equipment, $20,000, and issued capital stock in full payment.
b. Purchased a long-term investment for cash, $15,000.
c. Paid cash dividend, $12,000.
d. Sold operational asset for $6,000 cash (cost, $21,000, accumulated depreciation, $15,000).
e. Sold capital stock, 500 shares at $12 per share cash.

Items from Financial Statements	Beginning Balances, 12/31/2003	ANALYSIS OF CHANGES		Ending Balances, 12/31/2004
		Debit	Credit	
Income statement items				
Sales			$140,000	
Cost of goods sold		$59,000		
Depreciation		3,000		
Wage expense		28,000		
Income tax expense		9,000		
Interest expense		5,000		
Remaining expenses		15,800		
Net income		20,200		
Balance sheet items				
Cash	$ 20,500			$ 19,200
Accounts receivable	22,000			22,000
Merchandise inventory	68,000			75,000
Investments, long-term				15,000
Equipment	114,500			113,500
Total debits	$225,000			$244,700
Accumulated depreciation	$ 32,000			$ 20,000
Accounts payable	17,000			14,000
Wages payable	2,500			1,500
Income taxes payable	3,000			4,500
Bonds payable	54,000			54,000
Common stock, no par	100,000			126,000
Retained earnings	16,500			24,700
Total credits	$225,000			$244,700
		Inflows	Outflows	
Statement of cash flows				
Cash flows from operating activities:				
Cash flows from investing activities:				
Cash flows from financing activities:				
Net increase (decrease) in cash				
Totals				

Required:
Complete the spreadsheet for the statement of cash flows, indirect method.

PROBLEMS

 Available with McGraw-Hill's Homework Manager

P13-1
L01, 2A, 4, 6

Preparing a Statement of Cash Flows (Indirect Method) (AP13-1)

MetroVideo Inc. is developing its annual financial statements at December 31, 2004. The statements are complete except for the statement of cash flows. The completed comparative balance sheets and income statement are summarized:

	2004	2003
Balance sheet at December 31		
Cash	$ 68,000	$ 65,000
Accounts receivable	15,000	22,000
Merchandise inventory	22,000	18,000
Property and equipment	210,000	150,000
Less: Accumulated depreciation	(60,000)	(45,000)
	$255,000	$210,000
Accounts payable	$ 8,000	$ 19,000
Wages payable	2,000	1,000
Note payable, long-term	60,000	70,000
Contributed capital	100,000	75,000
Retained earnings	85,000	45,000
	$255,000	$210,000
Income statement for 2004		
Sales	$195,000	
Cost of goods sold	90,000	
Depreciation expense	15,000	
Other expenses	45,000	
Net income	$ 45,000	

Additional Data:
a. Bought equipment for cash, $60,000.
b. Paid $10,000 on the long-term note payable.
c. Issued new shares of stock for $25,000 cash.
d. Dividends of $5,000 were declared and paid.
e. Other expenses all relate to wages.
f. Accounts payable includes only inventory purchases made on credit.

Required:
1. Prepare the statement of cash flows using the indirect method for the year ended December 31, 2004.
2. Evaluate the statement of cash flows.

Preparing a Statement of Cash Flows (Indirect Method)

Rocky Mountain Chocolate Factory manufactures an extensive line of premium chocolate candies for sale at its franchised and company-owned stores in malls throughout the United States. Its balance sheet for the first quarter of a recent year is presented along with an analysis of selected accounts and transactions:

P13-2
L01, 2A, 4, 6
Rocky Mountain
Chocolate Factory

e**X**cel

ROCKY MOUNTAIN CHOCOLATE FACTORY, INC.
Balance Sheets

Assets	May 31 (Unaudited)	February 29
CURRENT ASSETS		
Cash and cash equivalents	$ 921,505	$ 528,787
Accounts and notes receivable—trade, less allowance for doubtful accounts of $43,196 at May 31 and $28,196 at February 29	1,602,582	1,463,901

Assets	May 31 (Unaudited)	February 29
Inventories	$ 2,748,788	$ 2,504,908
Deferred tax asset	59,219	59,219
Other	581,508	224,001
Total current assets	5,913,602	4,780,816
PROPERTY AND EQUIPMENT—AT COST	14,010,796	12,929,675
Less accumulated depreciation and amortization	−2,744,388	−2,468,084
	11,266,408	10,461,591
OTHER ASSETS		
Notes and accounts receivable due after one year	100,206	111,588
Goodwill, net of accumulated amortization of $259,641 at May 31 and $253,740 at Feb. 29	330,359	336,260
Other	574,130	624,185
	1,004,695	1,072,033
	$18,184,705	$16,314,440
Liabilities and Equity		
CURRENT LIABILITIES		
Short-term debt	$ 0	$ 1,000,000
Current maturities of long-term debt	429,562	134,538
Accounts payable—trade	1,279,455	998,520
Accrued liabilities	714,473	550,386
Income taxes payable	11,198	54,229
Total current liabilities	2,434,688	2,737,673
LONG-TERM DEBT, less current maturities	4,193,290	2,183,877
DEFERRED INCOME TAXES	275,508	275,508
Stockholders' Equity		
Common stock—authorized 7,250,000 shares, $.03 par value; issued 3,034,302 shares at May 31 and at Feb. 29	91,029	91,029
Additional paid-in capital	9,703,985	9,703,985
Retained earnings	2,502,104	2,338,267
	12,297,118	12,133,281
Less common stock held in treasury, at cost— 129,153 shares at May 31 and at February 29	1,015,899	1,015,899
	11,281,219	11,117,382
	$18,184,705	$16,314,440

The accompanying notes are an integral part of these statements.

Analysis of Selected Accounts and Transactions:

a. Net income was $163,837. Notes and accounts receivable due after one year relate to operations.

b. Depreciation and amortization totaled $282,205.

c. No "other" noncurrent assets (which relate to investing activities) were purchased this period.

d. No property, plant, and equipment were sold during the period. No goodwill was acquired or sold.

e. Proceeds from issuance of long-term debt were $4,659,466 and principal payments were $2,355,029. (Combine the current maturities with the long-term debt in your analysis.)

f. No dividends were declared or paid.

g. Ignore the "deferred tax asset" and "deferred income taxes" accounts.

Required:

Prepare a statement of cash flows, indirect method, for the first quarter.

Preparing a Statement of Cash Flows (Direct Method) (AP13-2)

P13-3
LO1, 2B, 4, 6

Use the information concerning MetroVideo Inc. provided in Problem 13-1 to fulfill the following requirements.

Required:

1. Prepare the statement of cash flows using the direct method for the year ended December 31, 2004.
2. Evaluate the statement of cash flows.

Comparing Cash Flows from Operating Activities (Direct and Indirect Methods)

P13-4
LO2A, 2B

Beta Company's accountants just completed the income statement and balance sheet for the year and have provided the following information (dollars in thousands):

Income Statement		
Sales revenue		$20,600
Expenses		
Cost of goods sold	$9,000	
Depreciation expense	2,000	
Salaries expense	5,000	
Rent expense	2,500	
Insurance expense	800	
Utilities expense	700	
Interest expense on bonds	600	
Loss on sale of investments	400	21,000
Net loss		$ (400)

SELECTED BALANCE SHEET ACCOUNTS		
	2003	2004
Merchandise inventory	$ 60	$ 82
Accounts receivable	450	380
Accounts payable	210	240
Salaries payable	20	29
Rent payable	6	2
Prepaid rent	7	2
Prepaid insurance	5	14

Other Data:

The company issued $20,000, 8 percent bonds payable during the year.

Required:

1. Prepare the Cash Flows from Operating Activities section of the statement of cash flows using the direct method.
2. Prepare the Cash Flows from Operating Activities section of the statement of cash flows using the indirect method.

(Supplement B) Preparing Statement of Cash Flows Spreadsheet, Statement of Cash Flows, and Schedules Using Indirect Method

P13-5

*e*X*cel*

Hunter Company is developing its annual financial statements at December 31, 2004. The statements are complete except for the statement of cash flows. The completed comparative balance sheets and income statement are summarized:

	2004	2003
Balance sheet at December 31		
Cash	$ 44,000	$ 18,000
Accounts receivable	27,000	29,000
Merchandise inventory	30,000	36,000
Fixed assets (net)	75,000	72,000
	$176,000	$155,000
Accounts payable	$ 25,000	$ 22,000
Wages payable	800	1,000
Note payable, long-term	38,000	48,000
Common stock, no par	80,000	60,000
Retained earnings	32,200	24,000
	$176,000	$155,000
Income statement for 2004		
Sales	$100,000	
Cost of goods sold	(61,000)	
Expenses	(27,000)	
Net income	$ 12,000	

Additional Data:

a. Bought fixed assets for cash, $9,000.
b. Paid $10,000 on the long-term note payable.
c. Sold unissued common stock for $20,000 cash.
d. Declared and paid a $3,800 cash dividend.
e. Incurred expenses that included depreciation, $6,000; wages, $10,000; taxes, $3,000; other, $8,000.

Required:

1. Prepare a statement of cash flows spreadsheet using the indirect method to report cash flows from operating activities.
2. Prepare the statement of cash flows.
3. Prepare a schedule of noncash investing and financing activities if necessary.

ALTERNATE PROBLEMS

AP13-1
LO1, 2A, 4, 6

Preparing a Statement of Cash Flows (Indirect Method) (P13-1)

McPherson Construction Supply Company is developing its annual financial statements at December 31, 2004. The statements are complete except for the statement of cash flows. The completed comparative balance sheets and income statement are summarized:

	2004	2003
Balance sheet at December 31		
Cash	$ 34,000	$ 29,000
Accounts receivable	45,000	28,000
Merchandise inventory	31,000	38,000
Property and equipment	121,000	100,000
Less: Accumulated depreciation	(30,000)	(25,000)
	$201,000	$170,000

continued

Accounts payable	$ 36,000	$ 27,000
Wages payable	1,200	1,400
Note payable, long-term	38,000	44,000
Contributed capital	88,600	72,600
Retained earnings	37,200	25,000
	$201,000	$170,000
Income statement for 2004		
Sales	$130,000	
Cost of goods sold	70,000	
Other expenses	37,800	
Net income	$ 22,200	

Additional Data:
a. Bought equipment for cash, $21,000.
b. Paid $6,000 on the long-term note payable.
c. Issued new shares of stock for $16,000 cash.
d. Dividends of $10,000 were declared and paid.
e. Other expenses included depreciation, $5,000; wages, $20,000; taxes, $6,000; other, $6,800.
f. Accounts payable includes only inventory purchases made on credit. Because there are no liability accounts relating to taxes or other expenses, assume that these expenses were fully paid in cash.

Required:
1. Prepare the statement of cash flows using the indirect method for the year ended December 31, 2004.
2. Evaluate the statement of cash flows.

Preparing a Statement of Cash Flows (Direct Method) (P13-3)

AP13-2
LO1, 2B, 4, 6

Use the information concerning McPherson Construction Supply provided in Alternate Problem 13-1 to fulfill the following requirements.

Required:
1. Prepare the statement of cash flows using the direct method for the year ended December 31, 2004.
2. Evaluate the statement of cash flows.

CASES AND PROJECTS

Annual Report Cases

Finding Financial Information

CP13-1
LO2A, 4, 6

PACIFIC SUNWEAR
OF CALIFORNIA, INC.

Refer to the financial statements of Pacific Sunwear of California given in Appendix B at the end of this book, or open file PSUN.pdf in the Annual Report Cases directory on the student DVD.

Required:
1. What were the two largest (in absolute value) "Adjustments to reconcile net income to net cash provided by operating activities?" Explain the direction of the effect of each in the reconciliation.
2. Examine Pacific Sunwear of California's investing and financing activities. List Pacific Sunwear of California's three largest uses of cash over the past three years. List two major sources of cash for these activities.
3. What was free cash flow for the year ended January 29, 2005? What does this imply about the company's financial flexibility?

Finding Financial Information

CP13-2
LO2A, 4, 6

AMERICAN EAGLE
OUTFITTERS
ae.com

Refer to the financial statements of American Eagle Outfitters given in Appendix C at the end of this book, or open file AEOS.pdf in the Annual Report Cases directory on the student DVD.

Required:

1. Does American Eagle Outfitters use the direct or indirect method to report cash flows from operating activities?
2. What amount of tax payments did the company make during the most recent reporting year? (*Hint:* The notes to the financial statements may be helpful to answer this question.)
3. Explain why the "stock compensation" and "depreciation and amortization" were added in the reconciliation of net income to net cash provided by operating activities.
4. Has the company paid cash dividends during the last three years? How did you know?
5. What was free cash flow for the year ended January 29, 2005?

CP13-3
LO3, 5

PACIFIC SUNWEAR
OF CALIFORNIA, INC.

AMERICAN EAGLE
OUTFITTERS
ae.com

Comparing Companies within an Industry

Refer to the financial statements of Pacific Sunwear of California given in Appendix B, American Eagle Outfitters given in Appendix C, and the Industry Ratio Report given in Appendix D at the end of this book, or open file CP13-3.xls in the Annual Report Cases directory on the student DVD.

Required:

1. Compute the quality of income ratio for both companies for the most recent reporting year. Which company has a better quality of income ratio?
2. Compare the quality of income ratio for both companies to the industry average. Are these companies producing more or less cash from operating activities relative to net income than the average company in the industry? Does comparing the sales growth rate for these two companies to the industry average help explain why their quality of income ratio is above or below the industry average? Explain. Note that Sales Growth Rate = (Current Net Sales − Prior Net Sales)/Prior Net Sales.
3. Compute the capital acquisitions ratio for both companies for the most recent reporting year. Compare their abilities to finance purchases of property, plant, and equipment with cash provided by operating activities.
4. Compare the capital acquisitions ratio for both companies to the industry average. How do these two companies' abilities to finance the purchase of property, plant, and equipment with cash provided by operating activities compare to those of the industry?

Financial Reporting and Analysis Cases

CP13-4
LO2A
Carlyle Golf, Inc.

Making a Decision as a Financial Analyst: Analyzing Cash Flow for a New Company

Carlyle Golf, Inc., was formed in September of last year. The company designs, contracts for the manufacture of, and markets a line of men's golf apparel. A portion of the statement of cash flows for Carlyle follows:

	Current Year
Cash flows from operating activities	
Net income	$(460,089)
Depreciation	3,554
Noncash compensation (stock)	254,464
Deposits with suppliers	(404,934)
Increase in prepaid assets	(42,260)
Increase in accounts payable	81,765
Increase in accrued liabilities	24,495
Net cash flows	$(543,005)

Management expects a solid increase in sales in the near future. To support the increase in sales, it plans to add $2.2 million to inventory. The company did not disclose a sales forecast. At the end of the current year, Carlyle had less than $1,000 in cash. It is not unusual for a new company to experience a loss and negative cash flows during its start-up phase.

Required:

As a financial analyst recently hired by a major investment bank, you have been asked to write a short memo to your supervisor evaluating the problems facing Carlyle. Emphasize typical sources of financing that may or may not be available to support the expansion.

Critical Thinking Cases

Ethical Decision-Making: A Real-Life Example

CP13-5

In a February 19, 2004, press release, the Securities and Exchange Commission described a number of fraudulent transactions that Enron executives concocted in an effort to meet the company's financial targets. One particularly well-known scheme is called the "Nigerian barge" transaction, which took place in the fourth quarter of 1999. According to court documents, Enron arranged to sell three electricity-generating power barges moored off the coast of Nigeria. The "buyer" was the investment banking firm of Merrill Lynch. Although Enron reported this transaction as a sale in its income statement, it turns out this was no ordinary sale. Merrill Lynch didn't really want the barges and had only agreed to buy them because Enron guaranteed, in a secret side deal, that it would arrange for the barges to be bought back from Merrill Lynch within six months of the initial transaction. In addition, Enron promised to pay Merrill Lynch a hefty fee for doing the deal. In an interview on National Public Radio on August 17, 2002, Michigan Senator Carl Levin declared, "(t)he case of the Nigerian barge transaction was, by any definition, a loan."

Required:

1. Discuss whether the Nigerian barge transaction should have been considered a loan rather than a sale. As part of your discussion, consider the following questions. Doesn't the Merrill Lynch payment to Enron at the time of the initial transaction automatically make it a sale, not a loan? What aspects of the transaction are similar to a loan? Which aspects suggest that the four criteria for revenue recognition (summarized near the end of Chapter 3) are not fulfilled?

2. The income statement effect of recording the transaction as a sale rather than a loan is fairly clear: Enron was able to boost its revenues and net income. What is somewhat less obvious, but nearly as important, are the effects on the statement of cash flows. Describe how recording the transaction as a sale rather than as a loan would change the statement of cash flows.

3. How would the two different statements of cash flows (described in your response to requirement 2) affect financial statement users?

Financial Reporting and Analysis Team Project

Team Project: Analyzing Cash Flows

CP13-6
LO1, 2, 3, 4, 5, 6

As a team, select an industry to analyze. *Reuters* provides lists of industries and their makeup at www.investor.reuters.com/Industries.aspx. Each team member should acquire the annual report or 10-K for one publicly traded company in the industry, with each member selecting a different company. (Library files, the SEC EDGAR service at www.sec.gov, or the company itself are good sources.)

Required:

On an individual basis, each team member should write a short report answering the following questions about the selected company. Discuss any patterns across the companies that you as a team observe. Then, as a team, write a short report comparing and contrasting your companies.

1. Which of the two basic reporting approaches for cash flows from operating activities did the company adopt?

2. What is the quality of earnings ratio for the most current year? What were the major causes of differences between net income and cash flow from operations?

3. What is the capital acquisitions ratio for the three-year period presented in total? How is the company financing its capital acquisitions?

4. What portion of the cash from operations in the current year is being paid to stockholders in the form of dividends?

LEARNING OBJECTIVES

Analyzing Financial Statements

14

FOCUS COMPANY:

Home Depot

FINANCIAL ANALYSIS: BRINGING IT ALL TOGETHER

www.homedepot.com

The history of Home Depot is an unusual success story. Founded in 1978 in Atlanta, Home Depot has grown to be America's largest home improvement retailer, and according to *Fortune* magazine, one of the nation's 30 largest retailers. Financial statements for Home Depot are presented in Exhibit 14.1. As you can see, Home Depot's rapid growth has continued in recent years. Sales revenue for the year ended February 1, 2004, was 21 percent higher than in 2002, and the company's net earnings increased 41 percent.

With this rapid growth, would you want to invest in Home Depot? A number of professional analysts think you should, including those who work for Bear Stearns, a large investment firm. In a report in which they recommended investors buy stock in Home Depot, they wrote: "We continue to believe that the company's stock should be a core retail holding for investors, given the company's industry-leading position in a growing market, superb management, and focus on improving sales and gross margins."

Professional analysts consider a large number of factors in developing the type of recommendation contained in the Bear Stearns report, including information reported in a company's financial statements. In this chapter, we use accounting information and a variety of analytical tools to study Home Depot and its major competitor, Lowe's.

UNDERSTANDING THE BUSINESS

In the United States, companies spend billions of dollars each year preparing, auditing, and publishing their financial statements. These statements are then mailed to current and prospective investors. Most companies also make financial information available to investors on the Internet. Home Depot has a particularly interesting home page (http://www.homedepot.com) that contains current financial statements, recent news articles about the company, and a variety of relevant information.

The reason that Home Depot and other companies spend so much money to provide information to investors is simple: Financial statements help people to make better economic decisions. In fact, published financial statements are designed primarily to meet the needs of external decision makers, including present and potential owners, investment analysts, and creditors.

EXHIBIT 14.1

Home Depot Financial
Statements

CONSOLIDATED STATEMENTS OF EARNINGS
The Home Depot, Inc. and Subsidiaries

	Fiscal Year Ended[1]		
dollars in millions, except per share data	February 1, 2004	February 2, 2003	February 3, 2002
NET SALES	$64,816	$58,247	$53,553
Cost of Merchandise Sold	44,236	40,139	37,406
GROSS PROFIT	20,580	18,108	16,147
Operating Expenses:			
Selling and Store Operating	12,502	11,180	10,163
Pre-Opening	86	96	117
General and Administrative	1,146	1,002	935
Total Operating Expenses	13,734	12,278	11,215
OPERATING INCOME	6,846	5,830	4,932
Interest Income (Expense):			
Interest and Investment Income	59	79	53
Interest Expense	(62)	(37)	(28)
Interest, net	(3)	42	25
EARNINGS BEFORE PROVISION FOR INCOME TAXES	6,843	5,872	4,957
Provision for Income Taxes	2,539	2,208	1,913
NET EARNINGS	$ 4,304	$ 3,664	$ 3,044
Weighted Average Common Shares	2,283	2,336	2,335
BASIC EARNINGS PER SHARE	$1.88	$1.57	$1.30
Diluted Weighted Average Common Shares	2,289	2,344	2,353
DILUTED EARNINGS PER SHARE	$1.88	$1.56	$1.29

[1]Fiscal years ended February 1, 2004 and February 2, 2003 include 52 weeks. Fiscal year ended February 3, 2002 includes 53 weeks.

See accompanying Notes to Consolidated Financial Statements.

CONSOLIDATED BALANCE SHEETS
The Home Depot, Inc. and Subsidiaries

dollars in millions	February 1, 2004	February 2, 2003
ASSETS		
Current Assets:		
Cash and Cash Equivalents	$ 2,826	$ 2,188
Short-Term Investments, including current maturities of long-term investments	26	65
Receivables, net	1,097	1,072

continued

EXHIBIT 14.1

continued

Merchandise Inventories	9,076	8,338
Other Current Asses	303	254
Total Current Assets	13,328	11,917
Property and Equipment, at cost:		
Land	6,397	5,560
Buildings	10,920	9,197
Furniture, Fixtures, and Equipment	5,163	4,074
Leasehold Improvements	942	872
Construction in Progress	820	724
Capital Leases	352	306
	24,594	20,733
Less Accumulated Depreciation and Amortization	4,531	3,565
Net Property and Equipment	20,063	17,168
Notes Receivable	84	107
Cost in Excess of the Fair Value of Net Assets Acquired, net of accumulated amortization of $54 at February 1, 2004 and $50 at February 2, 2003	833	575
Other Assets	129	244
Total Assets	$34,437	$30,011

LIABILITIES AND STOCKHOLDERS' EQUITY

Current Liabilities:		
Accounts Payable	$5,159	$4,560
Accrued Salaries and Related Expenses	801	809
Sales Taxes Payable	419	307
Deferred Revenue	1,281	998
Income Taxes Payable	175	227
Current Installments of Long-Term Debt	509	7
Other Accrued Expenses	1,210	1,127
Total Current Liabilities	9,554	8,035
Long-Term Debt, excluding current installments	856	1,321
Other Long-Term Liabilities	653	491
Deferred Income Taxes	967	362

STOCKHOLDERS' EQUITY

Common Stock, par value $0.05; authorized: 10,000 shares, issued and outstanding 2,373 shares at February 1, 2004 and 2,362 shares at February 2, 2003	119	118
Paid-In Capital	6,184	5,858
Retained Earnings	19,680	15,971
Accumulated Other Comprehensive Income (Loss)	90	(82)
Unearned Compensation	(76)	(63)
Treasury Stock, at cost, 116 shares at February 1, 2004 and 69 shares at February 2, 2003	(3,590)	(2,000)
Total Stockholders' Equity	22,407	19,802
Total Liabilities and Stockholders' Equity	$34,437	$30,011

See accompanying Notes to Consolidated Financial Statements.

EXHIBIT 14.1

continued

CONSOLIDATED STATEMENTS OF CASH FLOWS
The Home Depot, Inc. and Subsidiaries

dollars in millions	Fiscal Year Ended[1]		
	February 1, 2004	February 2, 2003	February 3, 2002
CASH FLOWS FROM OPERATIONS:			
Net Earnings	$4,304	$3,664	$3,044
Reconciliation of Net Earnings to Net Cash Provided by Operations:			
Depreciation and Amortization	1,076	903	764
Decrease (Increase) in Receivables, net	25	(38)	(119)
Increase in Merchandise Inventories	(693)	(1,592)	(166)
Increase in Accounts Payable and Accrued Liabilities	790	1,394	1,878
Increase in Deferred Revenue	279	147	200
(Decrease) Increase in Income Taxes Payable	(27)	83	272
Increase (Decrease) in Deferred Income Taxes	605	173	(6)
Other	186	68	96
Net Cash Provided by Operations	6,545	4,802	5,963
CASH FLOWS FROM INVESTING ACTIVITIES:			
Capital Expenditures, net of $47, $49, and $5 of noncash capital expenditures in fiscal 2003, 2002, and 2001, respectively	(3,508)	(2,749)	(3,393)
Purchase of Assets from Off-Balance Sheet Financing Arrangement	(598)	—	—
Payments for Businesses Acquired, net	(215)	(235)	(190)
Proceeds from Sales of Businesses, net	—	22	64
Proceeds from Sales of Property and Equipment	265	105	126
Purchases of Investments	(159)	(583)	(85)
Proceeds from Maturities of Investments	219	506	25
Other	—	—	(13)
Net Cash Used in Investing Activities	(3,996)	(2,934)	(3,466)
CASH FLOWS FROM FINANCING ACTIVITIES:			
Repayments of Commercial Paper Obligations, net	—	—	(754)
Proceeds from Long-Term Debt	—	1	532
Repayments of Long-Term Debt	(9)	—	—
Repurchase of Common Stock	(1,554)	(2,000)	—
Proceeds from Sale of Common Stock, net	227	326	445
Cash Dividends Paid to Stockholders	(595)	(492)	(396)
Net Cash Used in Financing Activities	(1,931)	(2,165)	(173)
Effect of Exchange Rate Changes on Cash and Cash Equivalents	20	8	(14)
Increase (Decrease) in Cash and Cash Equivalents	638	(289)	2,310
Cash and Cash Equivalents at Beginning of Year	2,188	2,477	167
Cash and Cash Equivalents at End of Year	$2,826	$2,188	$2,477

continued

SUPPLEMENTAL DISCLOSURE OF CASH PAYMENTS MADE FOR:				EXHIBIT 14.1
Interest, net of interest capitalized	$ 70	$ 50	$ 18	concluded
Income Taxes	$2,037	$1,951	$1,685	

[1]*Fiscal years ended February 1, 2004 and February 2, 2003 include 52 weeks. Fiscal year ended February 3, 2002 includes 53 weeks.*

See accompanying Notes to Consolidated Financial Statements.

ORGANIZATION of the Chapter

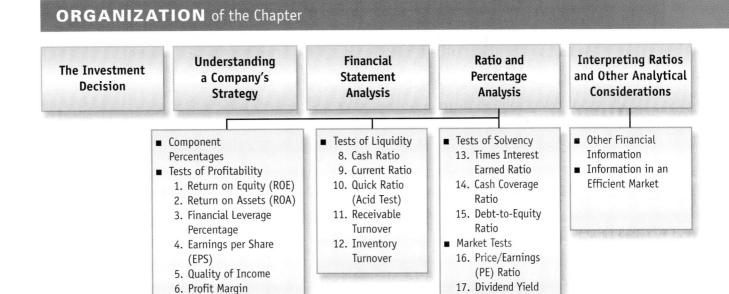

The Investment Decision	Understanding a Company's Strategy	Financial Statement Analysis	Ratio and Percentage Analysis	Interpreting Ratios and Other Analytical Considerations
	■ Component Percentages ■ Tests of Profitability 1. Return on Equity (ROE) 2. Return on Assets (ROA) 3. Financial Leverage Percentage 4. Earnings per Share (EPS) 5. Quality of Income 6. Profit Margin 7. Fixed Asset Turnover	■ Tests of Liquidity 8. Cash Ratio 9. Current Ratio 10. Quick Ratio (Acid Test) 11. Receivable Turnover 12. Inventory Turnover	■ Tests of Solvency 13. Times Interest Earned Ratio 14. Cash Coverage Ratio 15. Debt-to-Equity Ratio ■ Market Tests 16. Price/Earnings (PE) Ratio 17. Dividend Yield	■ Other Financial Information ■ Information in an Efficient Market

THE INVESTMENT DECISION

Of the people who use financial statements, investors are perhaps the single largest group. They often rely on the advice of professional analysts, who develop recommendations on widely held stocks such as Home Depot. Most individual investors use analysts' reports and track their recommendations. As this book was being written, professional analysts issued the following investment recommendations for Home Depot:

	Current	1 Month Ago	2 Months Ago	3 Months Ago
Strong buy	9	9	8	10
Moderate buy	2	2	2	2
Hold	9	9	9	10
Moderate Sell	0	0	0	0
Strong Sell	1	1	1	1

Source: Quicken.com/investments/

Perhaps the most important thing to notice about this summary of investment recommendations is the degree of disagreement. Currently, nine analysts recommend buying more Home Depot stock, but nine others recommend holding Home Depot stock only if one already owns it. One analyst recommends selling any currently held Home Depot stock. This level of disagreement shows that financial analysis is part art and part science.

In considering an investment in stock, investors should evaluate the company's future income and growth potential on the basis of three factors:

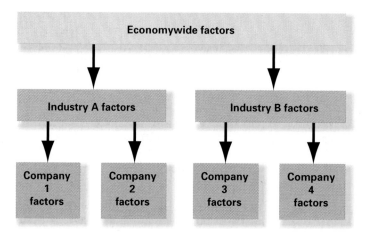

1. **Economywide factors.** Often the overall health of the economy has a direct impact on the performance of an individual business. Investors should consider data such as the unemployment rate, general inflation rate, and changes in interest rates. For example, in a research report issued by Edward Jones, a large brokerage firm, an analyst determined "rising interest rates could negatively impact Home Depot's sales." The reason for a negative impact on sales, according to the analyst, is nearly one-third of the dollars saved on refinancing mortgages are spent on home-improvement projects.

2. **Industry factors.** Certain events have a major impact on each company within an industry, but only a minor impact on other companies outside the industry. For example, the Edward Jones' report predicted increased sales at Home Depot because of "a new consumer trend toward 'nestling,' which refers to spending more time and money transforming one's home into a sanctuary."

3. **Individual company factors.** To properly analyze a company, good analysts do not rely only on the information contained in the financial statements. They visit the company, buy its products, and read about it in the business press. If you evaluate McDonald's, it is equally important to assess the quality of its balance sheet and the quality of its Big Mac. An example of company-specific information is contained in the Edward Jones' report: New managers have been hired because the management skills "that grew Home Depot to 1,000 stores was probably different from the skill set needed to grow to 2,000 stores."

Besides considering these factors, investors should understand a company's business strategy when evaluating its financial statements. Before discussing analytical techniques, we will show you how business strategy affects financial statement analysis.

UNDERSTANDING A COMPANY'S STRATEGY

Financial statement analysis involves more than just "crunching numbers." Before you start looking at numbers, you should know what you are looking for. While financial statements report on transactions, each of those transactions is the result of a company's operating decisions as it implements its business strategy.

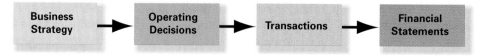

The DuPont model (introduced in Chapter 5) helps us understand that a number of business strategies affect the profitability of a business. The model follows:

$$\text{ROE} = \text{Net Profit Margin} \times \text{Asset Turnover} \times \text{Financial Leverage}$$

$$\frac{\text{Net Income}}{\text{Average Stockholders' Equity}} = \frac{\text{Net Income}}{\text{Net Sales}} \times \frac{\text{Net Sales}}{\text{Average Total Assets}} \times \frac{\text{Average Total Assets}}{\text{Average Stockholders' Equity}}$$

Businesses can earn a high rate of return by following different strategies. These are two fundamental strategies:

1. **Product differentiation.** Under this strategy, companies offer products with unique benefits, such as high quality or unusual style or features. These unique benefits allow a company to charge higher prices. In general, higher prices yield higher profit margins, which lead to higher returns on equity (as shown in the ROE model).

2. **Cost advantage.** Under this strategy, companies attempt to operate more efficiently than their competitors, which permits them to offer lower prices to attract customers. The efficient use of resources is captured in the asset turnover ratio, and as the ROE model illustrates, higher asset turnover ratio leads to higher return on investment.

You can probably think of a number of companies that have followed one of these two basic strategies. Here are some examples:

Differentiation on Quality	Differentiation on Cost
Cars:	**Cars:**
Cadillac	Ford Escort
Mercedes	Dodge Neon
Lincoln	Kia Rio
Retail Stores:	**Retail Stores:**
Nordstrom	Kmart
Tiffany	Wal-Mart
Saks	Dollar General

The best place to start financial analysis is with a solid understanding of a company's business strategy. To evaluate how well a company is doing, you must know what managers are trying to do. You can learn a great deal about a company's business strategy by reading its annual report, especially the letter from the president. It also is useful to read articles about the company in the business press.

Home Depot's business strategy is described in its 10-K report as follows:

REAL WORLD EXCERPT

OPERATING STRATEGY. The operating strategy for Home Depot stores is to offer a broad assortment of high-quality merchandise and services at competitive prices using highly knowledgeable, service-oriented personnel and aggressive advertising. We believe that our associates' knowledge of products and home improvement techniques and applications is very important in our marketing approach and our ability to maintain customer satisfaction. We regularly check our competitors' prices to ensure that our prices are competitive within each market.

10-K REPORT

This strategy has several implications for our analysis of Home Depot:

1. Cost control is critical. Home Depot must be able to purchase merchandise at low prices in order to beat competitors.

2. To cover the cost of operating large stores, Home Depot must be able to generate a high volume of business.

3. To offer a high level of service, Home Depot must incur employee compensation and training costs that are higher than competitors' costs. This puts pressure on Home Depot to control costs in other areas.

With these implications in mind, we can attach more meaning to the information contained in Home Depot's financial statements.

FINANCIAL STATEMENT ANALYSIS

Analyzing financial data without a basis for comparison is impossible. For example, would you be impressed with a company that earned $1 million last year? You are probably thinking, "It depends." A $1 million profit might be very good for a company that lost money the year before but not good for a company that made $500 million the preceding year. It might be good for a small company but not for a very large company. And it might be considered good if all other companies in the industry lost money the same year but not good if they all earned much larger profits.

As you can see from this simple example, financial results cannot be evaluated in isolation. To properly analyze the information reported in financial statements, you must develop appropriate comparisons. The task of finding appropriate benchmarks requires judgment and is not always easy. Financial analysis is a sophisticated skill, not a mechanical process.

There are two methods for making financial comparisons: times series analysis and comparisons with similar companies.

1. **Time series analysis.** Information on a single company is compared over time. For example, a key measure of performance for a retail company is the change in sales volume each year for its existing stores. The following time series chart shows that in 2004, Home Depot was able to achieve sales growth in existing stores for the first time in two years. This turnaround is a critical part of the company's growth strategy and is an indication of management effectiveness. However, the chart shows that additional work remains to be done if Home Depot wants to return to historical levels of growth in sales volume.

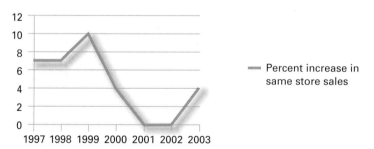

2. **Comparison with similar companies.** We have seen that financial results are often affected by industry and economywide factors. By comparing a company with another one in the same line of business, an analyst can gain better insight into its performance. The comparison of various measures for Home Depot and Lowe's (in the following graph) provides a mixed picture. The gross margin and income as a percentage of sales show that Home Depot is operating a little more efficiently than Lowe's but Lowe's is the clear leader in terms of sales growth.

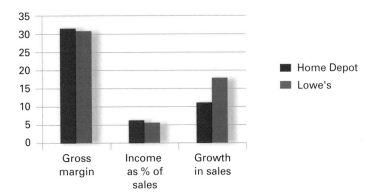

Finding comparable companies is often very difficult. Fortune Brands, for example, is a well-known company that each year sells more than $7 billion worth of distilled spirits, home improvement products, office products, and golf equipment. No other company sells exactly that group of products. Care must be exercised in selecting comparable companies from the same basic industry. Days Inn, La Quinta, Hilton, Four Seasons, Marriott, and Mirage Resorts are all well-known companies in the hotel industry, but not all could be considered comparable companies for purposes of financial analysis. These hotels offer different levels of quality and appeal to different types of customers.

The federal government has developed the North American Industry Classification System for use in reporting economic data. The system assigns a specific industry code to each corporation based on its business operations. Analysts often use these six-digit codes to identify companies that have similar business operations. In addition, financial information services such as Robert Morris Associates provide averages for many common accounting ratios for various industries defined by the industrial classification codes. Because of the diversity of companies included in each industry classification, however, these data should be used with great care. For this reason, some analysts prefer to compare two companies that are very similar instead of using industrywide comparisons.

RATIO AND PERCENTAGE ANALYSIS

All financial analysts use **ratio analysis** or **percentage analysis** when they review companies. A ratio or percentage expresses the proportionate relationship between two different amounts, allowing for easy comparisons. Assessing a company's profitability is difficult if you know only that it earned a net income of $500,000. Comparing income to other numbers, such as stockholders' equity, provides additional insights. If stockholders' equity is $5 million, for example, then the relationship of earnings to investment is $500,000 ÷ $5,000,000 = 10 percent. This measure indicates a different level of performance than would be the case if stockholders' equity were $250 million. Ratio analysis helps decision makers to identify significant relationships and make meaningful comparisons between companies.

Ratios may be computed using amounts in one statement, such as the income statement, or in two different statements, such as the income statement and the balance sheet. In addition, amounts on a single statement may be expressed as a percentage of a base amount.

Component Percentages

Analysts often compute **component percentages,** which express each item on a financial statement as a percentage of a single base amount (the ratio's denominator). To compute component percentages for the income statement, the base amount is net sales revenue. Each expense is expressed as a percentage of net sales revenue. On the

Learning Objective 3
Compute and interpret component percentages.

Topic Tackler

Topic Tackler 14–1

RATIO (PERCENTAGE) ANALYSIS is an analytical tool that measures the proportional relationship between two financial statement amounts.

COMPONENT PERCENTAGES express each item on a particular financial statement as a percentage of a single base amount.

EXHIBIT 14.2

Component Percentages
for Home Depot

	Component Percentages		
Income Statement	**2004**	**2003**	**2002**
Net sales	100.0%	100.0%	100.0%
Cost of merchandise sold	68.2	68.9	69.8
Gross profit	31.8	31.1	30.2
Operating expenses			
Selling and store operating	19.3	19.2	19.0
Pre-opening	0.1	0.2	0.2
General and administrative	1.8	1.7	1.7
Total operating expenses	21.2	21.1	20.9
Operating income	10.6	10.0	9.3
Interest income	0.1	0.1	0.1
Interest expense	0.1	(0.0)	(0.1)
Interest, net	0.0	0.1	0.0
Earnings, before taxes	10.6	10.1	9.3
Income taxes	3.9	3.8	3.6
Net earnings	6.7	6.3	5.7

balance sheet, the base amount is total assets; each balance sheet account is divided by total assets.

Exhibit 14.2 shows a component percentage analysis for Home Depot's income statement (shown in Exhibit 14.1). If you simply reviewed the dollar amounts on the income statement, you might be concerned about several significant differences. For example, cost of merchandise sold increased by more than $4 million between 2003 and 2004. But the component percentage provides an important insight: Cost of merchandise sold actually decreased as a percentage of sales during that period. In other words, cost of merchandise sold increased primarily because of the increase in the company's sales revenue.

The component analysis (in Exhibit 14.2) helps to highlight several additional issues for Home Depot, such as these:

1. Net income increased by $1,260 million between 2002 and 2004. A portion of the increase in income can be attributed to an increase in sales revenue, but a portion is attributable to improvement in the margin between cost and selling price for merchandise sold (gross profit increased from 30.2 percent to 31.8 percent). Unfortunately, this improvement was offset by a small increase in selling and store operating expense as a percentage of sales (19.0 percent to 19.3 percent).

2. Some of the percentage changes may seem immaterial, but they involve significant amounts of money. The increase in the ratio of total operating expense as a percentage of sales from 2002 to 2004 reduced earnings before taxes by nearly $200 million.

3. Cost of merchandise sold as a percentage of sales declined consistently between 2002 and 2004. As we mentioned earlier, a key part of Home Depot's strategy is selling merchandise at low prices. Companies following this strategy must control the margin between the cost of merchandise and its selling price. The improvement in the ratio of cost of goods sold to sales revenue is a positive indication of the successful implementation of the company's strategy.

4. Significant stability in all income statement relationships indicates a well-run company. Note that most of the individual income statement items changed less than one percentage point over the three-year period.

Many analysts use graphics software in their study of financial results. Graphic representation is especially useful when communicating findings during meetings or in printed form. The charts in the margin summarize key 2004 data from Exhibit 14.2 along with comparable data from Lowe's, a key competitor.

In addition to component percentages, analysts use ratios to compare related items from the financial statements. Of the many ratios that can be computed from a single set of financial statements, analysts use only those that can be helpful in a given situation. Comparing cost of goods sold to property, plant, and equipment is never useful because these items have no natural relationship. Instead, an analyst will often compute certain widely used ratios and then decide which additional ratios could be relevant to a particular decision. Research and development costs as a percentage of sales is not a commonly used ratio, for example, but it is useful when analyzing companies that depend on new products, such as drug or computer firms.

When you compute ratios, remember a basic fact about financial statements: Balance sheet amounts relate to an instant in time while income statement amounts relate to an entire period. In comparing an income statement amount to a balance sheet amount, you should express the balance sheet as an average of the beginning and ending balances. In practice, many analysts simply use the ending balance sheet amount, an approach that is appropriate only if no significant changes have occurred in the balance sheet amounts. For consistency, we always use average amounts.

Financial statement analysis is a judgmental process; not all ratios are helpful in a given situation. We will discuss several ratios that are appropriate to most situations. They can be grouped into the categories shown in Exhibit 14.3.

Tests of Profitability

Profitability is a primary measure of the overall success of a company. Indeed, it is necessary for a company's survival. Several tests of profitability focus on measuring the adequacy of income by comparing it to other items reported on the financial statements. Return on equity is a widely used measure of profitability.

1. Return on Equity (ROE)

Return on equity relates income earned to the investment made by the owners. This ratio reflects the simple fact that investors expect to earn more money if they invest more money. Two investments that offer a return of $10,000 are not comparable if one requires a $100,000 investment and the other requires a $250,000 investment. The return on equity ratio is computed as follows:[1]

$$\text{Return on Equity} = \frac{\text{Net Income}}{\text{Average Stockholders' Equity}}$$

$$\text{Home Depot 2004} = \frac{\$4,304}{\$21,105^*} = 20.4\%$$

*($22,407 + $19,802) ÷ 2 = $21,105.

Home Depot earned 20.4 percent on the owners' investment. Was that return good or bad? We can answer this question by comparing Home Depot's return on equity with the ratio for a similar company. Return on equity for Lowe's was 20.2 percent in 2004, not much different compared to Home Depot. Clearly, Home Depot did not produce a much better return than its strongest competitor.

We can gain additional insight by examining Home Depot's ROE over time:

	2004	2003	2002
ROE	20.4%	19.3%	18.4%

[1]The figures for Home Depot used throughout the following examples are taken from the financial statements in Exhibit 14.1.

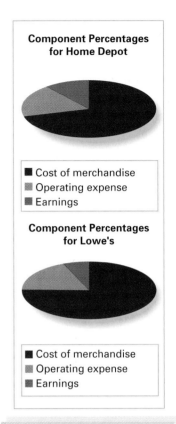

Component Percentages for Home Depot

- ■ Cost of merchandise
- ■ Operating expense
- ■ Earnings

Component Percentages for Lowe's

- ■ Cost of merchandise
- ■ Operating expense
- ■ Earnings

Learning Objective 4
Compute and interpret profitability ratios.

TESTS OF PROFITABILITY
compare income with one or more primary activities.

Topic Tackler

PLUS

Topic Tackler 14–2

EXHIBIT 14.3	Ratio	Basic Computation
Widely Used Accounting Ratios	**Tests of Profitability**	

Tests of Profitability

1. Return on equity (ROE)

$$\frac{\text{Net Income}}{\text{Average Stockholders' Equity}}$$

2. Return on assets (ROA)

$$\frac{\text{Net Income} + \text{Interest Expense (net of tax)}}{\text{Average Total Assets}}$$

3. Financial leverage percentage

Return on Equity − Return on Assets

4. Earnings per share (EPS)

$$\frac{\text{Net Income}}{\text{Average Number of Shares of Common Stock Outstanding}}$$

5. Quality of income

$$\frac{\text{Cash Flows from Operating Activities}}{\text{Net Income}}$$

6. Profit margin

$$\frac{\text{Net Income}}{\text{Net Sales Revenue}}$$

7. Fixed asset turnover

$$\frac{\text{Net Sales Revenue}}{\text{Average Net Fixed Assets}}$$

Tests of Liquidity

8. Cash ratio

$$\frac{\text{Cash} + \text{Cash Equivalents}}{\text{Current Liabilities}}$$

9. Current ratio

$$\frac{\text{Current Assets}}{\text{Current Liabilities}}$$

10. Quick ratio

$$\frac{\text{Quick Assets}}{\text{Current Liabilities}}$$

11. Receivable turnover ratio

$$\frac{\text{Net Credit Sales}}{\text{Average Net Receivables}}$$

12. Inventory turnover ratio

$$\frac{\text{Cost of Goods Sold}}{\text{Average Inventory}}$$

Tests of Solvency

13. Times interest earned ratio

$$\frac{\text{Net Income} + \text{Interest Expense} + \text{Income Tax Expense}}{\text{Interest Expense}}$$

14. Cash coverage ratio

$$\frac{\text{Cash Flows from Operating Activities (before interest and taxes paid)}}{\text{Interest Paid}}$$

15. Debt-to-equity ratio

$$\frac{\text{Total Liabilities}}{\text{Stockholders' Equity}}$$

Market Tests

16. Price/earnings ratio

$$\frac{\text{Current Market Price per Share}}{\text{Earnings per Share}}$$

17. Dividend yield ratio

$$\frac{\text{Dividends per Share}}{\text{Market Price per Share}}$$

This comparison shows that Home Depot's performance in 2004 as measured by its ROE shows consistent improvement over previous years. As mentioned earlier, new management was hired to improve Home Depot's performance. This comparison suggests that they have been effective.

2. Return on Assets (ROA)

Another test of profitability compares income to the total assets (i.e., total investment) used to earn the income. Many analysts consider the return on assets ratio to be a better measure (compared to ROE) of management's ability to utilize assets effectively because it is not affected by the way in which the assets were financed. For example, the return on equity could be very high for a company that has borrowed a large amount of debt compared to a company that earned the same return on the same amount of assets but borrowed less money. Return on assets is computed as follows:

$$\text{Return on Assets} = \frac{\text{Net Income} + \text{Interest Expense (net of tax)}^*}{\text{Average Total Assets}}$$

$$\text{Home Depot 2004} = \frac{\$4,304 + (\$62 \times 66\%)}{\$32,224^\dagger} = 13.5\%$$

*This illustration assumes a corporate tax rate of 34 percent.
†($34,437 + $30,011) ÷ 2 = $32,224.

Note that interest expense has been added to net income in the numerator of the ratio. Because the denominator of the ratio includes resources provided by both owners and creditors, the numerator must include the return that was available to each group. Interest expense is added back because it was previously deducted in the computation of net income. Note, too, that interest expense is measured net of income tax. This amount is used because it represents the net cost to the corporation for the funds provided by creditors.

The return on assets for Lowe's was 11.3 percent, lower than Home Depot's. This comparison indicates that Home Depot utilizes its assets more effectively than Lowe's.

3. Financial Leverage Percentage

Financial leverage percentage measures the advantage or disadvantage that occurs when a company's return on equity differs from its return on assets (i.e., ROE − ROA). In the DuPont model discussed earlier in this chapter, **financial leverage** was defined as the proportion of assets acquired with funds supplied by owners. The ratio **financial leverage percentage** measures a related but different concept. This ratio describes the relationship between the return on equity and the return on assets. Leverage is positive when the rate of return on a company's assets exceeds the average after-tax interest rate on its borrowed funds. Basically, the company borrows at one rate and invests at a higher rate of return. Most companies have positive leverage.

Financial leverage percentage can be measured by comparing the two return ratios as follows:

$$\text{Financial Leverage Percentage} = \text{Return on Equity} - \text{Return on Assets}$$

$$\text{Home Depot 2004} = 20.4\% - 13.5\% = 6.9\% \text{ (positive leverage)}$$

When a company borrows funds at an after-tax interest rate and invests those funds to earn a higher after-tax rate of return, the difference accrues to the benefit of the owners. The notes to Home Depot's annual report indicate that the company borrowed money at rates ranging from 5.375 percent to 6.5 percent and invested it in assets earning 13.5 percent. The difference between the income earned on the money it borrows and the interest it paid to creditors is available for the owners of Home Depot. This benefit of financial leverage is the primary reason most companies obtain a significant amount of their resources from creditors rather than from the sale of capital stock. Note that financial leverage can be enhanced either by investing effectively (i.e., earning a high return on investment) or by borrowing effectively (i.e., paying a low rate of interest).

Lowe's financial leverage ratio (8.5 percent) is higher than Home Depot's. Lowe's has achieved its higher ratio by utilizing comparatively more debt in its capital structure.

4. Earnings per Share (EPS)

The earnings per share ratio is a measure of return on investment that is based on the number of shares outstanding instead of the dollar amounts reported on the balance sheet. In simple situations,[2] EPS is computed as follows:

$$\text{Earnings per Share} = \frac{\text{Net Income}}{\text{Average Number of Shares of Common Stock Outstanding}}$$

$$\text{Home Depot 2004} = \frac{\$4,304}{2,368^*} = \$1.82 \text{ per share}$$

*(2,373 + 2,362) ÷ 2 = 2,368

Earnings per share is probably the single most widely watched ratio. Its importance is illustrated by a news story published in TheStreet.com (February 24, 2004):

REAL WORLD EXCERPT

EPS ANNOUNCEMENT

The home improvement retailer bested earnings expectations with a 40% jump in earnings per share on a 14% sales increase. And with the help of the holiday quarter, the company posted a 3.8% gain in same-store sales, its first year of positive growth since 2000, noted CFO Carol Tome on a conference call with investors and analysts.

Investors reacted positively to the company's report; Home Depot shares went up 61 cents, or 1.7 percent, to $35.99.

5. Quality of Income

Most financial analysts are concerned about the quality of a company's earnings because some accounting procedures can be used to report higher income. For example, a company that uses LIFO and short estimated lives for depreciable assets will report lower earnings than a similar company that uses FIFO and longer estimated lives. One method of evaluating the quality of a company's earnings is to compare its reported earnings to its cash flows from operating activities, as follows:

$$\text{Quality of Income} = \frac{\text{Cash Flows from Operating Activities}}{\text{Net Income}}$$

$$\text{Home Depot 2004} = \frac{\$6,545}{\$4,304} = 1.52$$

A quality of income ratio that is higher than 1 is considered to indicate high-quality earnings because each dollar of income is supported by one dollar or more of cash flow. A ratio that is below 1 represents lower-quality earnings.

---

[2]The computation of EPS is more complex if a company has issued different types of stock; these complexities are discussed in advanced accounting courses. Note, for example, that EPS and the average number of shares shown in Exhibit 14.1 differs from this simple calculation.

A research report from Edward Jones discusses the issue of quality of earnings for Home Depot:

> Net income historically grew in line with cash flows from operating activities. But over the past three years, Home Depot has become much more efficient with its working capital, driving down net income as a percentage of cash flows from operating activities. Also, the company is using more conservative accounting methodology.

6. Profit Margin

The profit margin measures the percentage of each sales dollar, on average, that represents profit. It is computed as follows:

$$\text{Profit Margin} = \frac{\text{Net Income}}{\text{Net Sales Revenue}}$$

$$\text{Home Depot 2004} = \frac{\$4,304}{\$64,816} = 6.6\%$$

For 2004, each dollar of Home Depot's sales generated 6.6 cents of profit. In comparison, Lowe's earned 6.1 cents for each dollar of sales. Although the difference might seem small, it represents a significant advantage for Home Depot.

Profit margin is a good measure of operating efficiency, but care must be used in analyzing it because it does not consider the resources (i.e., total investment) needed to earn income. It is very difficult to compare profit margins for companies in different industries. For example, profit margins are low in the food industry while profit margins in the jewelry business are high. Both types of business can be quite profitable, however, because a high sales volume can compensate for a low profit margin. Grocery stores have low profit margins, but they generate a high sales volume from their relatively inexpensive stores and inventory. Although jewelry stores earn comparatively more profit from each sales dollar, they require a large investment in luxury stores and very expensive inventory.

The trade-off between profit margin and sales volume can be stated in simple terms: Would you prefer to have 5 percent of $1,000,000 or 10 percent of $100,000? As you can see, a larger profit margin is not always better.

7. Fixed Asset Turnover Ratio

Another measure of operating efficiency is the fixed asset turnover ratio, which compares sales volume with a company's investment in fixed assets. The term **fixed assets** is synonymous with property, plant, and equipment. The ratio is computed as follows:

$$\text{Fixed Asset Turnover Ratio} = \frac{\text{Net Sales Revenue}}{\text{Average Net Fixed Assets}}$$

$$\text{Home Depot 2004} = \frac{\$64,816}{\$18,616^*} = 3.5$$

*($20,063 + $17,168) ÷ 2 = $18,616.

In 2004, Home Depot's fixed asset turnover was better than Lowe's (2.8). In simple terms, this means that Home Depot had a competitive advantage over Lowe's in terms of its ability to effectively utilize its fixed assets to generate revenue. For each dollar Home Depot invested in property, plant, and equipment, the company was able to earn $3.50 in sales revenue while Lowe's could earn only $2.80. This comparison is extremely important because it indicates that management of Home Depot was able to operate more efficiently than its main competitor.

The fixed asset turnover ratio is used widely to analyze capital-intensive companies such as airlines and electric utilities. For companies that hold large amounts of inventory and accounts receivable, analysts often prefer to use the asset turnover ratio, which is based on total assets rather than fixed assets:

$$\text{Asset Turnover Ratio} = \frac{\text{Net Sales Revenue}}{\text{Average Total Assets}}$$

$$\text{Home Depot 2004} = \frac{\$64,816}{\$32,224^*} = 2.01$$

*($34,437 + $30,011) ÷ 2 = $32,224.

In 2004, Home Depot was able to generate $2.01 in revenue for each dollar invested in assets. In comparison, Lowe's asset turnover ratio was 1.76. Both turnover ratios show that Home Depot was able to operate more efficiently than Lowe's. This comparison is important because operating efficiency has a significant impact on profitability as shown by the DuPont model (discussed earlier in this chapter).

SELF-STUDY **QUIZ**

Show how to compute the following ratios:

1. Return on equity =

2. Return on assets =

3. Profit margin =

After you have completed your answers, check them with the solutions at the bottom of the page.

Learning Objective 5
Compute and interpret liquidity ratios.

TESTS OF LIQUIDITY are ratios that measure a company's ability to meet its currently maturing obligations.

Tests of Liquidity

Liquidity refers to a company's ability to meet its currently maturing debts. **Tests of liquidity** focus on the relationship between current assets and current liabilities. The ability to pay current liabilities is an important factor in evaluating a company's short-term financial strength. A company that does not have cash available to pay for purchases on a timely basis will lose its cash discounts and run the risk of having its credit discontinued by vendors. We discuss three ratios that are used to measure liquidity: the cash ratio, the current ratio, and the quick ratio.

8. Cash Ratio

Cash is the lifeblood of a business. Without cash, a company cannot pay its employees or meet its obligations to creditors. Even a profitable business will fail without suffi-

---

Self-Study Quiz
Solutions

1. $\dfrac{\text{Net Income}}{\text{Average Stockholders' Equity}}$

2. $\dfrac{\text{Net Income} + \text{Interest Expense (net of tax)}}{\text{Average Total Assets}}$

3. $\dfrac{\text{Net Income}}{\text{Net Sales Revenue}}$

cient cash. One measure of the adequacy of available cash, called the **cash ratio,** is computed as follows:

$$\text{Cash Ratio} = \frac{\text{Cash} + \text{Cash Equivalents}}{\text{Current Liabilities}}$$

$$\text{Home Depot 2004} = \frac{\$2,826}{\$9,554} = 0.30 \text{ to } 1$$

In 2004, Lowe's cash ratio was 0.33, indicating that its cash reserve was larger than Home Depot's. Would analysts be concerned about Home Depot's lower ratio? Probably not, because there were other factors to consider. For example, Home Depot's statement of cash flows showed that the company generated a large amount of cash from its operating activities. As a result, it did not need to keep a large amount of cash on hand to meet unexpected needs. Indeed, most analysts believe the cash ratio should not be too high because holding excess cash is usually uneconomical. It is far better to invest the cash in productive assets or reduce debt.

Home Depot's cash ratio has decreased in recent years. In most cases, deterioration of the cash ratio might be a cause for concern. For instance, it could be an early warning that the company was experiencing financial difficulty. Given Home Depot's strong performance, however, the deterioration of its cash ratio was more likely the result of aggressive efforts by managers to minimize the amount of cash used to operate the business.

Some analysts do not use the cash ratio because it is very sensitive to small events. The collection of a large account receivable, for example, could have a significant impact on a company's cash ratio. The current ratio and the quick ratio are much less sensitive to the timing of such transactions.

9. Current Ratio

The current ratio measures the relationship between total current assets and total current liabilities on a specific date. It is computed as follows:

$$\text{Current Ratio} = \frac{\text{Current Assets}}{\text{Current Liabilities}}$$

$$\text{Home Depot 2004} = \frac{\$13,328}{\$9,554} = 1.39 \text{ to } 1$$

The current ratio measures the cushion of working capital that companies maintain to allow for the inevitable unevenness in the flow of funds through the working capital accounts. At the end of 2004, Home Depot had $1.39 in current assets for each $1 in current liabilities. Most analysts would judge that ratio to be very strong, given Home Depot's ability to generate cash.

To properly use the current ratio, analysts must understand the nature of a company's business. Many manufacturing companies have developed sophisticated systems to minimize the amount of inventory they must hold. These systems, called **just-in-time inventory,** are designed to have an inventory item arrive just when it is needed. While these systems work well in manufacturing processes, they do not work as well in retailing. Customers expect to find merchandise in the store when they want it, and it has proven difficult to precisely forecast consumer behavior. As a result, most retailers have comparatively high current ratios because they must carry large inventories. Home Depot, for example, maintains an inventory of 50,000 different products in each store.

Analysts consider a current ratio of 2 to be financially conservative. Indeed, most companies have current ratios that are below 2. The optimal level of the current ratio depends on the business environment in which a company operates. If cash flows are predictable and stable (as they are for a utility company), the current ratio can be low, even less than 1. For example, Procter & Gamble, a strong and fiscally conservative company, has a current ratio of 0.77. When cash flows are highly variable, a higher current ratio is desirable.

Analysts become concerned if a company's current ratio is high compared to that of other companies. A firm is operating inefficiently when it ties up too much money in inventory or accounts receivable. There is no reason, for instance, for a Home Depot store to hold 1,000 hammers in stock if it sells only 100 hammers a month.

10. Quick Ratio (Acid Test)

The quick ratio is a more stringent test of short-term liquidity than is the current ratio. The quick ratio compares quick assets, defined as **cash and near-cash assets,** to current liabilities. Quick assets include cash, short-term investments, and accounts receivable (net of the allowance for doubtful accounts). Inventory is omitted from quick assets because of the uncertainty of the timing of cash flows from its sale. Prepaid expenses are also excluded from quick assets. The quick ratio is computed as follows:

$$\text{Quick Ratio} = \frac{\text{Quick Assets}}{\text{Current Liabilities}}$$

$$\text{Home Depot 2004} = \frac{\$3,949}{\$9,554} = 0.41 \text{ to } 1$$

The quick ratio is a measure of the safety margin that is available to meet a company's current liabilities. Home Depot has 41 cents in cash and near-cash assets for every $1 in current liabilities. This margin of safety is typical of the retail industry and would be considered a good margin in light of the large amount of cash that Home Depot generates from its operating activities. In comparison, the quick ratio for Lowe's is virtually the same as Home Depot (0.40 to 1).

11. Receivable Turnover Ratio

Accounts receivable are closely related to both short-term liquidity and operating efficiency. A company that can quickly collect cash from its customers has good liquidity and does not needlessly tie up funds in unproductive assets. The receivable turnover ratio is computed as follows:

$$\text{Receivable Turnover Ratio} = \frac{\text{Net Credit Sales*}}{\text{Average Net Receivables}}$$

$$\text{Home Depot 2004} = \frac{\$64,816}{\$1,085†} = 60 \text{ Times}$$

*When the amount of credit sales is not known, total sales may be used as a rough approximation.
†($1,097 + $1,072) ÷ 2 = $1,085

A high receivable turnover ratio suggests that a company is effective in its credit-granting and collection activities. Granting credit to poor credit risks and making ineffective collection efforts will produce a low receivable turnover ratio. While a very low ratio is obviously a problem, a very high ratio also can be troublesome because it suggests an overly stringent credit policy that could cause lost sales and profits.

The receivable turnover ratio is often converted to a time basis known as the **average age of receivables.** The computation is as follows:

$$\text{Average Age of Receivables} = \frac{\text{Days in a Year}}{\text{Receivable Turnover}}$$

$$\text{Home Depot 2004} = \frac{365}{60} = 6.1 \text{ Average Days to Collect}$$

The effectiveness of credit and collection activities is sometimes judged by the rule of thumb that the average days to collect should not exceed 1.5 times the credit terms.

For example, if the credit terms require payment in 30 days, the average days to collect should not exceed 45 days (i.e., not more than 15 days past due). Like all rules of thumb, this one has many exceptions.

Although the receivable turnover ratio normally provides useful insights, the one for Home Depot is not meaningful. It is highly unlikely that Home Depot collects cash from its credit customers in just 6.1 days, on average. Because we did not know the amount of Home Depot's credit sales, we used total sales as an approximation. In this case, the approximation is not reasonable. Think about the last time you watched a customer buying merchandise on credit in a retail store. Most customers use a bank credit card such as MasterCard or Visa. From the seller's perspective, a sales transaction involving a bank credit card is recorded in virtually the same manner as a cash sale. In other words, a sale involving a credit card does not create an account receivable on the seller's books; instead, the account receivable is recorded on the credit card company's books. In practice, the majority of Home Depot's credit sales involve bank credit cards. As a result, Home Depot's accounts receivable turnover ratio is not meaningful.

12. Inventory Turnover Ratio

Like receivable turnover, inventory turnover is a measure of both liquidity and operating efficiency. This ratio reflects the relationship of inventory to the volume of goods sold during the period. It is computed as follows:

$$\text{Inventory Turnover Ratio} = \frac{\text{Cost of Goods Sold}}{\text{Average Inventory}}$$

$$\text{Home Depot 2004} = \frac{\$44,236}{\$8,707^*} = 5.1 \text{ Times}$$

*($9,076 + $8,338) ÷ 2 = $8,707

Because a company normally realizes profit each time inventory is sold, an increase in this ratio is usually favorable. If the ratio is too high, however, it may be an indication that sales were lost because desired items were not in stock. The cost of a lost sale is often much higher than the lost profit. When a business is out of stock on an item desired by a customer, the individual will often go to a competitor to find it. That visit may help the competitor establish a business relationship with the customer. Thus, the cost of being out of stock may be all future profits on sales to a lost customer.

On average, Home Depot's inventory was acquired and sold to customers 5.1 times during the year. The inventory turnover ratio is critical for Home Depot because of its business strategy. It wants to be able to offer customers the right product when they need it at a price that beats the competition. If Home Depot does not effectively manage its inventory levels, it will incur extra costs that must be passed on to the customer.

Inventory turnover for Lowe's was 5.0. Historically, Home Depot has enjoyed a significant advantage over Lowe's in terms of inventory management. The inventory turnover ratio shows that Lowe's has been able to close the gap.

Turnover ratios vary significantly from one industry to the next. Companies in the food industry (grocery stores and restaurants) have high inventory turnover ratios because their inventory is subject to rapid deterioration in quality. Companies that sell expensive merchandise (automobiles and high-fashion clothes) have much lower ratios because although sales of those items are infrequent, customers want to have a selection to choose from when they do buy.

The turnover ratio is often converted to a time basis called the **average days' supply in inventory.** The computation is:

$$\text{Average Days' Supply in Inventory} = \frac{\text{Days in Year}}{\text{Inventory Turnover}}$$

$$\text{Home Depot 2004} = \frac{365}{5.1} = 71.6 \text{ Average Days' Supply in Inventory}$$

Using Ratios to Analyze the Operating Cycle

In Chapter 3, we introduced the concept of the operating cycle, which is the time it takes for a company to pay cash to its suppliers, sell goods to its customers, and collect cash from its customers. Analysts are interested in the operating cycle because it helps them evaluate a company's cash needs and is a good indicator of management efficiency.

The operating cycle for most companies involves three distinct phases; the acquisition of inventory, the sale of the inventory, and the collection of cash from the customer. We have discussed several ratios that are helpful when evaluating a company's operating cycle:

Ratio	Operating Activity
Accounts payable turnover ratio*	Purchase of inventory
Inventory turnover ratio	Sale of inventory
Accounts receivable turnover ratio	Collection of cash from customers
*Discussed in Chapter 9	

Each of the ratios measures the number of days it takes, on average, to complete an operating activity. We have already computed two of the needed ratios for Home Depot, so if we compute the accounts payable turnover ratio, we can analyze the operating cycle:

$$\text{Accounts Payable Turnover Ratio} = \frac{\text{Cost of Goods Sold}}{\text{Average Accounts Payable}}$$

$$\text{Home Depot 2004} = \frac{\$44,236}{\$4,860^*} = 9.1 \text{ Times}$$

*($5,159 + $4,560) ÷ 2 = $4,860

$$\text{Average Age of Payables} = \frac{\text{Days in a Year}}{\text{Accounts Payable Turnover Ratio}}$$

$$\text{Home Depot 2004} = \frac{365}{9.1} = 40.1 \text{ Average Days to Pay Suppliers}$$

The length of the component parts for Home Depot's operating cycle are:

Ratio	Time
Accounts payable turnover ratio	40.1 days
Inventory turnover ratio	71.6 days
Accounts receivable turnover ratio	6.1 days

The component parts of the operating cycle help us understand the cash needs of the company. Home Depot on average pays for its inventory 40.1 days after it receives it. It takes, on average, 77.7 days (71.6 + 6.1) for it to sell and for the company to collect cash from the customer. Therefore, Home Depot must invest cash in its operating activities for nearly 38 days between the time it pays its vendors and the time it collects from its customers. Companies prefer to minimize the time between paying vendors and collecting cash from customers because it frees up cash for other productive purposes. Home Depot could reduce this time by slowing payments to creditors or by increasing the inventory turnover.

Show how to compute the following ratios:

1. Quality of income =

2. Quick ratio =

3. Cash ratio =

After you have completed your answers, check them with the solutions at the bottom of the page.

Tests of Solvency

Solvency refers to a company's ability to meet its long-term obligations. Tests of solvency, which are measures of a company's ability to meet these obligations, include the times interest earned, cash coverage, and debt-to-equity ratios.

13. Times Interest Earned Ratio

Interest payments are a fixed obligation. If a company fails to make required interest payments, creditors may force it into bankruptcy. Because of the importance of meeting interest payments, analysts often compute a ratio called **times interest earned:**

$$\text{Time Interest Earned Ratio} = \frac{\text{Net Income} + \text{Interest Expense} + \text{Income Tax Expense}}{\text{Interest Expense}}$$

$$\text{Home Depot 2004} = \frac{\$4{,}304 + \$62 + \$2{,}539}{\$62} = 111 \text{ Times}$$

The times interest earned ratio compares the income a company generated in a period to its interest obligation for the same period. It represents a margin of protection for creditors. In 2004, Home Depot generated more than $111 in income for each $1 of interest expense, a high ratio that indicates a secure position for creditors.

Some analysts prefer to calculate the times interest earned ratio based on all contractually required payments, including principal and rent payments. Others believe that the ratio is flawed because interest expense and other obligations are paid in cash, not with net income. These analysts prefer to use the cash coverage ratio.

14. Cash Coverage Ratio

Given the importance of cash flows and required interest payments, it is easy to understand why many analysts use the cash coverage ratio. It is computed as follows:

$$\text{Cash Coverage Ratio} = \frac{\text{Cash Flows from Operating Activities before Interest and Taxes Paid}}{\text{Interest Paid (from statement of cash flows)}}$$

$$\text{Home Depot 2004} = \frac{\$6{,}545 + \$70 + \$2{,}037}{\$70} = 124$$

> **Learning Objective 6**
> Compute and interpret solvency ratios.
>
> **TESTS OF SOLVENCY** are ratios that measure a company's ability to meet its long-term obligations.

---

1. $\dfrac{\text{Cash Flows from Operating Activities}}{\text{Net Income}}$

2. $\dfrac{\text{Quick Assets}}{\text{Current Liabilities}}$

3. $\dfrac{\text{Cash} + \text{Cash Equivalents}}{\text{Current Liabilities}}$

Self-Study Quiz
Solutions

The cash coverage ratio compares the cash generated by a company to its cash obligations for the period. Remember that analysts are concerned about a company's ability to make required interest payments. Home Depot's cash coverage ratio shows that the company generated nearly $124 in cash for every $1 of interest paid, which is strong coverage. Note that the numerator and the denominator of the cash coverage ratio use **interest paid** from the statement of cash flows instead of **interest expense** from the income statement. Accrued interest and interest payments are normally similar in amount, but are not always the same.

15. Debt-to-Equity Ratio

The debt-to-equity ratio expresses a company's debt as a proportion of its stockholders' equity. It is computed as follows:

$$\text{Debt-to-Equity Ratio} = \frac{\text{Total Liabilities}}{\text{Stockholders' Equity}}$$

$$\text{Home Depot 2004} = \frac{\$12,030}{\$22,407} = 0.54$$

In 2004 for each $1 of stockholders' equity, Home Depot had 54 cents of liabilities. By comparison, Lowe's debt-to-equity ratio was 0.85.

Debt is risky for a company because specific interest payments must be made even if the company has not earned sufficient income to pay them. In contrast, dividends are always at the company's discretion and are not legally enforceable until they are declared by the board of directors. Thus, equity capital is usually considered much less risky than debt.

Despite the risk associated with debt, however, most companies obtain significant amounts of resources from creditors because of the advantages of financial leverage discussed earlier. In addition, interest expense is a deductible expense on the corporate income tax return. In selecting a capital structure, a company must balance the higher returns available through leverage against the higher risk associated with debt. Because of the importance of the risk-return relationship, most analysts consider the debt-to-equity ratio a key part of any company evaluation.

Market Tests

Learning Objective 7
Compute and interpret market test ratios.

Several ratios, often called market tests, relate the current price per share of stock to the return that accrues to investors. Many analysts prefer these ratios because they are based on the current value of an owner's investment in a company.

MARKET TESTS are ratios that tend to measure the market worth of a share of stock.

16. Price/Earnings (P/E) Ratio

The price/earnings (P/E) ratio measures the relationship between the current market price of a stock and its earnings per share. Recently, when the price of Home Depot stock was $40 per share, EPS for Home Depot was $1.88. The P/E ratio for Home Depot is computed as follows:

$$\text{Price/Earnings Ratio} = \frac{\text{Current Market Price per Share}}{\text{Earnings per Share}}$$

$$\text{Home Depot 2004} = \frac{\$40}{\$1.88} = 21$$

This P/E ratio indicates that Home Depot's stock was selling at a price that was 21 times its earnings per share. The P/E ratio reflects the stock market's assessment of a company's future performance. A high ratio indicates that earnings are expected to grow rapidly. Home Depot's P/E ratio is lower compared to previous years and is lower than Lowe's, which reported a P/E ratio of 23. The P/E ratio for Home Depot suggests that the market believes that Home Depot does not have the same growth potential that it had in recent years.

In economic terms, the value of a stock is related to the present value of the company's future earnings. Thus, a company that expects to increase its earnings in the future is worth more than one that cannot grow its earnings (assuming other factors are the same). But while a high P/E ratio and good growth prospects are considered favorable, there are risks. When a company with a high P/E ratio does not meet the level of earnings expected by the market, the negative impact on its stock can be dramatic.

17. Dividend Yield Ratio

When investors buy stock, they expect two kinds of return: dividend income and price appreciation. The dividend yield ratio measures the relationship between the dividends per share paid to stockholders and the current market price of a stock. Home Depot paid dividends of 27 cents per share when the market price of its stock was $40 per share. Its dividend yield ratio is computed as follows:

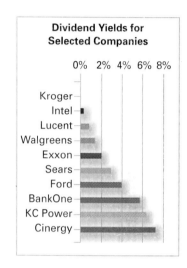

Dividend Yields for Selected Companies

$$\text{Dividend Yield Ratio} = \frac{\text{Dividends per Share}}{\text{Market Price per Share}}$$

$$\text{Home Depot 2004} = \frac{\$0.27}{\$40} = 0.68\%$$

You might be surprised that Home Depot's dividend yield was below 1 percent, when an investor could earn more than 4 percent in a federally insured savings account. In fact, the dividend yield for most stocks is not high compared to alternative investments. Investors are willing to accept low dividend yields if they expect that the price of a stock will increase while they own it. Clearly, investors who bought Home Depot's stock did so with the expectation that its price would increase. In contrast, stocks with low growth potential tend to offer much higher dividend yields than do stocks with high growth potential. These stocks often appeal to retired investors who need current income rather than future growth potential.

Like Home Depot, the dividend yield for Lowe's is very low, 0.2 percent in 2004. The chart in the margin shows dividend yields for some companies in other industries.

SELF-STUDY QUIZ

Show how to compute the following ratios:

1. Current ratio =

2. Inventory turnover =

3. Price/earnings ratio =

After you have completed your answers, check them with the solutions at the bottom of the page.

---

1. $\dfrac{\text{Current Assets}}{\text{Current Liabilities}}$

2. $\dfrac{\text{Cost of Goods Sold}}{\text{Average Inventory}}$

3. $\dfrac{\text{Current Market Price per Share}}{\text{Earnings per Share}}$

*Self-Study Quiz
Solutions*

INTERPRETING RATIOS AND OTHER ANALYTICAL CONSIDERATIONS

Except for earnings per share, the computation of financial ratios has not been standardized by either the accounting profession or security analysts. Thus, users of financial statements should compute the various ratios in accordance with their decision objectives. Before using ratios computed by others, they should determine the computational approach that was used.

As we have seen, ratios can be interpreted only by comparing them to other ratios or to some optimal value. Some ratios, by their very nature, are unfavorable at either very high or very low values. For example, a very low current ratio may indicate an inability to meet maturing debts, and a very high current ratio may indicate an unprofitable use of funds. Furthermore, an optimal ratio for one company may not be optimal for another. Comparisons among the ratios for different companies are appropriate only if the companies are comparable in terms of their industry, operations, size, and accounting policies.

Because ratios are based on the aggregation of information, they may obscure underlying factors that are of interest to the analyst. For example, a current ratio that is considered optimal can obscure a short-term liquidity problem in a company with a large amount of inventory but a minimal amount of cash with which to pay debts as they mature. Careful analysis can uncover this type of problem.

In other cases, analysis cannot uncover obscured problems. For example, consolidated statements include financial information about a parent company and its subsidiaries. The parent company could have a high current ratio and the subsidiary a low one, but when their statements are consolidated, their current ratios are in effect averaged and can fall within an acceptable range. The fact that the subsidiary could have a serious liquidity problem is obscured.

Despite limitations, ratio analysis is a useful analytical tool. For instance, financial ratios are effective for predicting bankruptcy. Exhibit 14.4 presents the current and debt-to-equity ratios for Hechinger, a former competitor of Home Depot, for the five years before its recent bankruptcy. Notice the progressive deterioration of these ratios. Analysts who studied these ratios probably were not surprised when Hechinger filed for bankruptcy.

Financial statements provide information to all investors, both sophisticated and unsophisticated. However, users who understand basic accounting principles and terminology are able to more effectively analyze the information contained in financial statements. For example, some unsophisticated users who do not understand the cost principle believe that assets are reported on the balance sheet at their fair market value. Interpreting accounting numbers correctly without an understanding of the concepts that were used to develop them is impossible.

In analyzing different companies, you will find that they rarely use exactly the same accounting policies. Comparisons among companies are appropriate only if the analyst who is making them understands the impact of different accounting alternatives. For example, one company may use conservative accounting alternatives such as acceler-

---

EXHIBIT 14.4

Selected Financial Ratios for Hechinger

REAL WORLD EXCERPT

Hechinger

	Years before Bankruptcy				
	5	**4**	**3**	**2**	**1**
Current ratio	1.8	1.7	1.7	1.2	1.2
Debt-to-equity ratio	1.6	1.8	2.0	5.0	5.6

ated depreciation and LIFO while another may use income-maximizing alternatives such as straight-line depreciation and FIFO. Analysts who do not understand the different effects of these accounting methods could misinterpret financial results. Perhaps the most important first step in analyzing financial statements is a review of the company's accounting policies, which are disclosed in a note to the statements.

Other Financial Information

The ratios we have discussed are useful for most analytical purposes. Because each company is different, however, you must exercise professional judgment when you conduct each financial analysis. To illustrate, let's look at some special factors that could affect our analysis of Home Depot.

1. **Rapid growth**. Growth in total sales volume does not always indicate that a company is successful. Sales volume from new stores may obscure the fact that existing stores are not meeting customer needs and are experiencing declines in sales. The family pizza chain Chuck-E-Cheese appeared to be a success when it reported rapid growth in total sales revenue by opening new restaurants. Unfortunately, the novelty of the new Chuck-E-Cheese restaurants proved to be short-lived fads, and their sales volume fell quickly. Because its older restaurants were unprofitable, Chuck-E-Cheese was forced to reorganize. In contrast, Home Depot's annual report shows that the company's stores posted sales increases ranging from 3 percent to 15 percent in each of the previous 10 years. Clearly, Home Depot can generate sales increases from both new and existing stores.

2. **Uneconomical expansion**. Some growth-oriented companies will open stores in less desirable locations if good locations cannot be found. These poor locations can cause a company's average productivity to decline. One measure of productivity in the retail industry is sales volume per square foot of selling space. For Home Depot, productivity results are a cause for concern:

Year	Sales per Square Foot
2004	$371
2003	370
2002	388
2001	415
2000	423

Sales per square foot have been in a steady decline for the past several years. Management explains the slowdown in growth is the direct result of its strategy:

> We strategically open stores near market areas served by existing stores ("cannibalize") to gain incremental sales and increase market penetration. New stores cannibalized approximately 17% of our existing stores and reduced sales volume by approximately 2.7%.

As the note indicates, Home Depot is willing to accept lower productivity at certain existing stores in order to achieve high sales levels in a region. An analyst who reviewed only the number reported in the annual report without carefully reading the notes would probably misinterpret the decline in sales per square foot.

3. **Subjective factors**. Remember that vital information about a company is not contained in the annual report. The best way to evaluate Home Depot's strategy of being a price leader, for instance, is to visit its stores and those of competitors. An analyst who studied Home Depot for Smith Barney did exactly that:

On July 15, we surveyed the Boca Raton, Florida market. The Home Depot store is about two years old and was particularly impressive with respect to its in-stock position, customer service and total store presentation. We were able to compare Home Depot's pricing on 20 sample items. Our price analysis revealed that Home Depot is the price leader in the market by an average of 11 percent below the average total price of our 20-item market basket. Given the Home Depot's low cost structure, we believe that it will remain the price leader in this important market.

As these examples illustrate, no single approach can be used to analyze all companies. Furthermore, an effective analyst will look beyond the information contained in an annual report.

A QUESTION OF ETHICS

Insider Information

Financial statements are an important source of information for investors. Announcement of unexpected information can cause a substantial movement in the price of a company's stock.

A company's accountants often are aware of important financial information before it is made available to the public. This type of data is called **insider information.** Some people might be tempted to buy or sell stock based on insider information, but to do so is a serious criminal offense. The Securities and Exchange Commission has brought a number of cases against individuals who traded on insider information. Their convictions resulted in large fines and time served in jail.

In some cases, determining whether something is insider information is difficult. For example, an individual could overhear a comment made in the company elevator by two executives. A well-respected Wall Street investment banker gave good advice on dealing with such situations: "If you are not sure if something is right or wrong, apply the newspaper headline test. Ask yourself how you would feel to have your family and friends read about what you had done in the newspaper." Interestingly, many people who have spent time in jail and lost small fortunes in fines because of insider trading say that the most difficult part of the process was telling their families.

To uphold the highest ethical standard, many public accounting firms have adopted rules that prevent their staff from investing in companies that the firms audit. Such rules are designed to ensure that a company's auditors cannot be tempted to engage in insider trading.

Information in an Efficient Market

Considerable research has been performed on the way in which stock markets react to new information. Much of this evidence supports the view that the markets react very quickly to new information in an unbiased manner (that is, the market does not systematically overreact or underreact to new information). A market that reacts to information in this manner is called an *efficient market.* In an efficient market, the price of a security fully reflects all available information.

EFFICIENT MARKETS are securities markets in which prices fully reflect available information.

It is not surprising that the stock markets react quickly to new information. Many professional investors manage stock portfolios valued in the hundreds of millions of dollars. These investors have a financial incentive to discover new information about a company and to trade quickly based on it.

The research on efficient markets has important implications for financial analysts. It probably is not beneficial to study old information (say an annual report that was released six months earlier) in an effort to identify an undervalued stock. In an efficient market, the price of a stock reflects all information contained in the annual report shortly after its release. In an efficient market, moreover, a company cannot manipulate the price of its stock by manipulating its accounting policy. The market should be able to differentiate between a company whose earnings are increasing due to improved productivity and one whose earnings have increased simply because of changes in accounting policies.

CHAPTER **TAKE-AWAYS**

1. **Explain how a company's business strategy affects financial analysis.   p. 714**
   In simple terms, a business strategy establishes the objectives a business is trying to achieve. Performance is best evaluated by comparing the financial results to the objectives that the business was working to achieve. In other words, an understanding of a company's strategy provides the context for conducting financial statement analysis.

2. **Discuss how analysts use financial statements.   p. 716**
   Analysts use financial statements to understand present conditions and past performance as well as to predict future performance. Financial statements provide important information to help users understand and evaluate corporate strategy. The data reported on statements can be used for either time-series analysis (evaluating a single company over time) or in comparison with similar companies at a single point in time. Most analysts compute component percentages and ratios when using statements.

3. **Compute and interpret component percentages.   p. 717**
   To compute component percentages for the income statement, the base amount is net sales revenue. Each expense is expressed as a percentage of net sales revenue. On the balance sheet, the base amount is total assets; each balance sheet account is divided by total assets. Component percentages are evaluated by comparing them over time for a single company or by comparing them with percentages for similar companies.

4. **Compute and interpret profitability ratios.   p. 719**
   Several tests of profitability focus on measuring the adequacy of income by comparing it to other items reported on the financial statements. Exhibit 14.3 lists these ratios and shows how to compute them. Profitability ratios are evaluated by comparing them over time for a single company or by comparing them with ratios for similar companies.

5. **Compute and interpret liquidity ratios.   p. 724**
   Tests of liquidity measure a company's ability to meet its current maturing debt. Exhibit 14.3 lists these ratios and shows how to compute them. Liquidity ratios are evaluated by comparing them over time for a single company or by comparing them with ratios for similar companies.

6. **Compute and interpret solvency ratios.   p. 729**
   Solvency ratios measure a company's ability to meet its long-term obligations. Exhibit 14.3 lists these ratios and shows how to compute them. Solvency ratios are evaluated by comparing them over time for a single company or by comparing them with ratios for similar companies.

7. **Compute and interpret market test ratios.   p. 730**
   Market test ratios relate the current price of a stock to the return that accrues to investors. Exhibit 14.3 lists these ratios and shows how to compute them. Market test ratios are evaluated by comparing them over time for a single company or by comparing them with ratios for similar companies.

FINDING **FINANCIAL INFORMATION**

Balance Sheet

Ratios are not reported on the balance sheet, but analysts use balance sheet information to compute many ratios. Most analysts use an average of the beginning and ending amounts for balance sheet accounts when comparing the account to an income statement account.

Income Statement

Earnings per share is the only ratio that is required to be reported on the financial statements. It is usually reported at the bottom of the income statement.

Statement of Cash Flows

Ratios are not reported on this statement, but some analysts use amounts from this statement to compute some ratios.

Statement of Stockholders' Equity

Ratios are not reported on this statement, but analysts use amounts from this statement to compute some ratios.

Notes

Under Summary of Significant Accounting Policies

This note has no information pertaining directly to ratios, but it is important to understand accounting differences if you are comparing two companies.

Under a Separate Note

Most companies include a 10-year financial summary as a separate note. These summaries include data for significant accounts, some accounting ratios, and nonaccounting information.

KEY **TERMS**

Component Percentages   p. 717
Efficient Markets   p. 734
Market Tests   p. 730

Ratio (Percentage) Analysis   p. 717
Tests of Liquidity   p. 724

Tests of Profitability   p. 719
Tests of Solvency   p. 729

QUESTIONS

1. What are some of the primary items on financial statements about which creditors usually are concerned?
2. Why are the notes to the financial statements important to decision makers?
3. What is the primary purpose of comparative financial statements?
4. Why are statement users interested in financial summaries covering several years? What is the primary limitation of long-term summaries?
5. What is ratio analysis? Why is it useful?
6. What are component percentages? Why are they useful?
7. Explain the two concepts of return on investment.
8. What is financial leverage? How is it measured as a percentage?
9. Is profit margin a useful measure of profitability? Explain.
10. Compare and contrast the current ratio and the quick ratio.
11. What does the debt-to-equity ratio reflect?
12. What are market tests?
13. Identify two factors that limit the effectiveness of ratio analysis.

MULTIPLE-CHOICE QUESTIONS

1. Which of the following ratios is *not* used to analyze profitability?
   - a. quality of income ratio
   - b. return on assets
   - c. quick ratio
   - d. return on equity

2. Which of the following would *not* change the receivables turnover ratio for a retail company?
   - a. increases in the retail prices of inventory
   - b. a change in credit policy
   - c. increases in the cost incurred to purchase inventory
   - d. none of the above

3. Which of the following ratios is used to analyze liquidity?
   - a. earnings per share
   - b. debt-to-equity ratio
   - c. current ratio
   - d. both (a) and (c)

4. Positive financial leverage indicates
   - a. positive cash flow from financing activities
   - b. a debt-to-equity ratio higher than 1
   - c. a rate of return on assets exceeding the interest rate on debt
   - d. a profit margin in one year exceeding the previous year's profit margin

5. If a potential investor is analyzing three companies in the same industry and wishes to invest in only one, which ratio is least likely to affect the investor's decision?
   - a. quick ratio
   - b. earnings per share
   - c. price to earnings ratio
   - d. dividend yield ratio

6. Analysts use ratios to
   - a. compare different companies in the same industry.
   - b. track a company's performance over time.
   - c. compare a company's performance to industry averages.
   - d. Do all of the above.

7. Which of the following ratios incorporates cash flows from operations?
   - a. inventory turnover
   - b. earnings per share
   - c. quality of income
   - d. all of the above

8. Given the following ratios for four companies, which company is least likely to experience problems paying its current liabilities promptly?

	Quick Ratio	Receivable Turnover
a.	1.2	58
b.	1.2	45
c.	1.0	55
d.	.5	60

9. A decrease in selling and administrative expenses would impact what ratio?
   - a. fixed asset turnover ratio
   - b. times interest earned ratio
   - c. debt-to-equity ratio
   - d. current ratio

10. A creditor is least likely to use what ratio when analyzing a company that has borrowed funds on a long-term basis?
    - a. cash coverage ratio
    - b. debt-to-equity ratio
    - c. times interest earned ratio
    - d. profit margin

For more practice with multiple-choice questions, go to the text website www.mhhe.com/ libby5e or the Topic Tackler DVD for use with this text.

MINI-**EXERCISES**

 Available with McGraw-Hill's Homework Manager

M14-1
LO3

Inferring Financial Information Using Component Percentages

A large retailer reported revenue of $1,680,145,000. The company's gross profit percentage was 55.9 percent. What amount of cost of goods sold did the company report?

M14-2
LO3

Inferring Financial Information Using Component Percentages

A consumer products company reported a 6.8 percent increase in sales from 2006 to 2007. Sales in 2006 were $20,917. In 2007, the company reported cost of goods sold in the amount of $9,330. What was the gross profit percentage in 2007?

M14-3
LO4

Computing the Return on Owners' Investment Ratio

Compute the return on equity ratio for 2007 given the following data:

	2007	2006
Net income	$ 185,000	$ 160,000
Stockholders' equity	1,000,000	1,200,000
Total assets	2,400,000	2,600,000
Interest expense	40,000	30,000

M14-4
LO4

Inferring Financial Information

Compute the financial leverage percentage for 2007 given the following data:

	2007	2006
Return on equity	22%	24%
Return on assets	8	6
Profit margin	12	10

M14-5
LO5

Analyzing the Inventory Turnover Ratio

A manufacturer reported an inventory turnover ratio of 8.6 during 2006. During 2007, management introduced a new inventory control system that was expected to reduce average inventory levels by 25 percent without affecting sales volume. Given these circumstances, would you expect the inventory turnover ratio to increase or decrease during 2007? Explain.

M14-6
LO5

Inferring Financial Information Using a Ratio

Scruggs Company reported total assets of $1,200,000 and noncurrent assets of $480,000. The company also reported a current ratio of 1.5. What amount of current liabilities did the company report?

M14-7
LO4, 5

Analyzing Financial Relationships

Doritos Company has prepared draft financial results now being reviewed by the accountants. You notice that the financial leverage percentage is negative. You also note that the current ratio is 2.4 and the quick ratio is 3.7. You recognize that these financial relationships are unusual. Does either imply that a mistake has been made? Explain.

M14-8
LO7

Inferring Financial Information Using a Ratio

In 2006, Drago Company reported earnings per share of $8.50 when its stock was selling for $212.50. In 2007, its earnings increased by 20 percent. If all other relationships remain constant, what is the price of the stock? Explain.

M14-9
LO7

Inferring Financial Information Using a Ratio

An Internet company earned $5 per share and paid dividends of $2 per share. The company reported a dividend yield of 5 percent. What was the price of the stock?

Analyzing the Impact of Accounting Alternatives

M14-10
LO3, 4, 5

Lexis Corporation is considering changing its inventory method from FIFO to LIFO and wants to determine the impact on selected accounting ratios. In general, what impact would you expect on the following ratios: profit margin, fixed asset turnover, current ratio, and quick ratio?

 Available with McGraw-Hill's Homework Manager

EXERCISES

Using Financial Information to Identify Mystery Companies

E14-1
LO1, 2, 3, 5, 6

The following selected financial data pertain to four unidentified companies:

	Companies			
	1	2	3	4
Balance Sheet Data				
(component percentage)				
Cash	3.5	4.7	8.2	11.7
Accounts receivable	16.9	28.9	16.8	51.9
Inventory	46.8	35.6	57.3	4.8
Property and equipment	18.3	21.7	7.6	18.7
Income Statement Data				
(component percentage)				
Gross profit	22.0	22.5	44.8	N/A*
Profit before taxes	2.1	0.7	1.2	3.2
Selected Ratios				
Current	1.3	1.5	1.6	1.2
Inventory turnover	3.6	9.8	1.5	N/A
Debt to equity	2.6	2.6	3.2	3.2
*N/A = Not applicable				

This financial information pertains to the following companies:

a. Retail fur store
b. Advertising agency
c. Wholesale candy company
d. Car manufacturer

Required:
Match each company with its financial information.

Using Financial Information to Identify Mystery Companies

E14-2
LO1, 2, 3, 5, 6

The following selected financial data pertain to four unidentified companies:

	Companies			
	1	2	3	4
Balance Sheet Data				
(component percentage)				
Cash	7.3	21.6	6.1	11.3
Accounts receivable	28.2	39.7	3.2	22.9
Inventory	21.6	0.6	1.8	27.5
Property and equipment	32.1	18.0	74.6	25.1
Income Statement Data				
(component percentage)				
Gross profit	15.3	N/A*	N/A	43.4
Profit before taxes	1.7	3.2	2.4	6.9
Selected Ratios				
Current	1.5	1.2	0.6	1.9
Inventory turnover	27.4	N/A	N/A	3.3
Debt to equity	1.7	2.2	5.7	1.3
*N/A = Not applicable				

This financial information pertains to the following companies:

a. Travel agency
b. Hotel
c. Meat packer
d. Drug company

Required:
Match each company with its financial information.

E14-3 Using Financial Information to Identify Mystery Companies

LO1, 2, 3, 5, 6

The following selected financial data pertain to four unidentified companies:

	Companies			
	1	2	3	4
Balance Sheet Data				
(component percentage)				
Cash	5.1	8.8	6.3	10.4
Accounts receivable	13.1	41.5	13.8	4.9
Inventory	4.6	3.6	65.1	35.8
Property and equipment	53.1	23.0	8.8	35.7
Income Statement Data				
(component percentage)				
Gross profit	N/A*	N/A	45.2	22.5
Profit before taxes	0.3	16.0	3.9	1.5
Selected Ratios				
Current	0.7	2.2	1.9	1.4
Inventory turnover	N/A	N/A	1.4	15.5
Debt to equity	2.5	0.9	1.7	2.3

*N/A = Not applicable

This financial information pertains to the following companies:

a. Cable TV company
b. Grocery store
c. Accounting firm
d. Retail jewelry store

Required:
Match each company with its financial information.

E14-4 Using Financial Information to Identify Mystery Companies

LO1, 2, 3, 5, 6

The selected financial data on the following page pertain to four unidentified companies:

	Companies			
	1	2	3	4
Balance Sheet Data				
(component percentage)				
Cash	11.6	6.6	5.4	7.1
Accounts receivable	4.6	18.9	8.8	35.6
Inventory	7.0	45.8	65.7	26.0
Property and equipment	56.0	20.3	10.1	21.9
Income Statement Data				
(component percentage)				
Gross profit	56.7	36.4	14.1	15.8
Profit before taxes	2.7	1.4	1.1	0.9
Selected Ratios				
Current	0.7	2.1	1.2	1.3
Inventory turnover	30.0	3.5	5.6	16.7
Debt to equity	3.3	1.8	3.8	3.1

This financial information pertains to the following companies:

a. Full-line department store
b. Wholesale fish company
c. Automobile dealer (both new and used cars)
d. Restaurant

Required:
Match each company with its financial information.

Matching Each Ratio with Its Computational Formula

Match each ratio or percentage with its computation by entering the appropriate letters in the blanks.

E14-5
LO3, 4, 5, 6, 7

Ratios or Percentages	Definitions
_____ 1. Profit margin	A. Net Income (before extraordinary items) ÷ Net Sales
_____ 2. Inventory turnover ratio	B. Days in Year ÷ Receivable Turnover
_____ 3. Average collection period	C. Net Income ÷ Average Stockholders' Equity
_____ 4. Dividend yield ratio	D. Net Income ÷ Average Number of Shares of
_____ 5. Return on equity	Common Stock Outstanding
_____ 6. Current ratio	E. Return on Equity − Return on Assets
_____ 7. Debt-to-equity ratio	F. Quick Assets ÷ Current Liabilities
_____ 8. Price/earnings ratio	G. Current Assets ÷ Current Liabilities
_____ 9. Financial leverage percentage	H. Cost of Goods Sold ÷ Average Inventory
_____ 10. Receivable turnover ratio	I. Net Credit Sales ÷ Average Net Receivables
_____ 11. Average days' supply of	J. Days in Year ÷ Inventory Turnover
inventory	K. Total Liabilities ÷ Stockholders' Equity
_____ 12. Earnings per share	L. Dividends per Share ÷ Market Price per Share
_____ 13. Return on assets	M. Current Market Price per Share ÷ Earnings per
_____ 14. Quick ratio	Share
_____ 15. Times interest earned ratio	N. [Net Income + Interest Expense (net of tax)] ÷
_____ 16. Cash coverage ratio	Average Total Assets
_____ 17. Fixed asset turnover	O. Cash from Operating Activities (before interest and
	taxes) ÷ Interest Paid
	P. Net Sales Revenue ÷ Net Fixed Assets
	Q. (Net Income + Interest Expense + Income Tax
	Expense) ÷ Interest Expense

Preparing a Schedule Using Component Percentages

Lowe's is a leading retailer in the home improvement field. Complete the component percentage analysis on the company's income statement follows. Discuss any insights provided by this analysis.

E14-6
LO3
Lowe's

(dollars in millions, except per share data) Years Ended on	January 30, 2004	% Sales	January 31, 2003	% Sales
Net Sales	$30,838	%	$26,112	%
Cost of Sales	21,231		18,164	
Gross Margin	**9,607**		**7,948**	
Expenses:				
Selling, General and Administrative	5,543		4,676	
Store Opening Costs	128		129	
Depreciation	758		622	
Interest	180		182	
Total Expenses	**6,609**		**5,609**	
Pre-Tax Earnings	2,998		2,339	
Income Tax Provision	1,136		880	
Earnings from Continuing Operations	**1,862**		**1,459**	
Earnings from Discontinued Operations,				
Net of Tax	15		12	
Net Earnings	**$1,877**		**$1,471**	

E14-7

LO5

Analyzing the Impact of Selected Transactions on the Current Ratio

Current assets totaled $54,000, and the current ratio was 1.8. Assume that the following transactions were completed: (1) purchased merchandise for $6,000 on short-term credit and (2) purchased a delivery truck for $10,000, paid $1,000 cash, and signed a two-year interest-bearing note for the balance.

Required:
Compute the cumulative current ratio after each transaction.

E14-8

LO5

Sunbeam

Analyzing the Impact of Selected Transactions on the Current Ratio

Sunbeam was a leading designer, manufacturer, and marketer of branded consumer products, including Mr. Coffee, Osterizer, First Alert, and Coleman camping gear. Recently, the company filed for bankruptcy following significant financial difficulties. The company was also named in a number of lawsuits alleging material misstatements in its financial statements. The company's financial statements acknowledged that actions pending against the company "could have a material adverse impact on the Company's financial position."

In its last financial statement prior to bankruptcy, Sunbeam reported current assets of $1,090,068,000 and current liabilities of $602,246,000. Determine the impact of the following transactions on the current ratio for Sunbeam: (1) sold long-term assets that represented excess capacity, (2) accrued severance pay and fringes for employees who will be terminated, (3) wrote down the carrying value of certain inventory items that were deemed to be obsolete, and (4) acquired new inventory; supplier was not willing to provide normal credit terms, so an 18-month interest-bearing note was signed.

E14-9

LO5

Procter & Gamble

Analyzing the Impact of Selected Transactions on Accounts Receivable and Inventory Turnover

Procter & Gamble is a multinational corporation that manufactures and markets many products that are probably in your home. Last year, sales for the company were $51,407 (all amounts in dollars in millions). The annual report did not disclose the amount of credit sales, so we will assume that 30 percent of sales was on credit. The average gross margin rate was 45 percent on sales. Account balances follow:

	Beginning	Ending
Accounts receivable (net)	$3,038	$4,062
Inventory	3,640	4,400

Required:
Compute the turnover for the accounts receivable and inventory, the average age of receivables, and the average days' supply of inventory.

E14-10

LO4

Motorola

Computing Financial Leverage

Motorola is a global leader in providing integrated communications and electronic solutions for businesses. Its financial statements reported the following at year-end (dollars in millions):

Total assets	$28,728
Total debt (average 8 percent interest)	16,506
Net income (average tax rate 30 percent)	1,180

Required:
Compute the financial leverage percentage. Was it positive or negative?

E14-11

LO5

Analyzing the Impact of Selected Transactions on the Current Ratio

Current assets totaled $100,000, and the current ratio was 1.5. Assume that the following transactions were completed: (1) paid $6,000 for merchandise purchased on short-term credit, (2) purchased a delivery truck for $10,000 cash, (3) wrote off a bad account receivable for $2,000, and (4) paid previously declared dividends in the amount of $25,000.

Required:
Compute the cumulative current ratio after each transaction.

Inferring Financial Information

Dollar General Corporation operates general merchandise stores that feature quality merchandise at low prices to meet the needs of middle-, low-, and fixed-income families. All stores are located in the United States, predominantly in small towns in 24 midwestern and southeastern states. In a recent year, the company reported average inventories of $721,843,000 and an inventory turnover of 3. Average total fixed assets were $283,142,000, and the fixed asset turnover ratio was 11.4. Determine the gross margin for Dollar General.

E14-12
LO3, 5
Dollar General
Corporation

Computing Selected Ratios

Sales for the year were $900,000, of which 80 percent was on credit. The average gross margin rate was 40 percent on sales. Account balances follow:

E14-13
LO5

	Beginning	Ending
Accounts receivable (net)	$80,000	$60,000
Inventory	50,000	90,000

Required:
Compute the turnover for the accounts receivable and inventory, the average age of receivables, and the average days' supply of inventory.

Analyzing the Impact of Selected Transactions on the Current Ratio

Current assets totaled $500,000, the current ratio was 2.0, and the company uses the periodic inventory method. Assume that the following transactions were completed: (1) sold $12,000 in merchandise on short-term credit, (2) declared but did not pay dividends of $50,000, (3) paid prepaid rent in the amount of $12,000, (4) paid previously declared dividends in the amount of $50,000, (5) collected an account receivable in the amount of $12,000, and (6) reclassified $40,000 of long-term debt as a short-term liability.

E14-14
LO5

Required:
Compute the cumulative current ratio after each transaction.

Computing Liquidity Ratios

Cintas designs, manufactures, and implements corporate identity uniform programs that it rents or sells to customers throughout the United States and Canada. The company's stock is traded on the NASDAQ and has provided investors with significant returns over the past few years. Selected information from the company's balance sheet follows. For 2004, the company reported sales revenue of $2,686,585 and cost of goods sold of $1,173,666.

E14-15
LO5
Cintas

CINTAS
Balance Sheet
(Amounts in dollars in thousands)

Cintas	2004	2003
Cash	$ 81,949	$ 54,914
Marketable securities	182,028	37,371
Accounts receivable, net	291,277	271,766
Inventories	492,156	524,571
Prepaid expense	12,041	8,759
Accounts payable	55,326	48,839
Accrued taxes	105,604	97,899
Accrued liabilities	108,562	85,904
Long-term debt due within one year	10,472	26,653

Required:
Compute the current ratio, inventory turnover ratio, and accounts receivable turnover ratio (assuming that 60 percent of sales was on credit) for 2004.

PROBLEMS

    ™ **Available with McGraw-Hill's Homework Manager**

P14-1
LO5, 6, 7

Analyzing an Investment by Comparing Selected Ratios (AP14-1)

You have the opportunity to invest $10,000 in one of two companies from a single industry. The only information you have follows. The word *high* refers to the top third of the industry; *average* is the middle third; *low* is the bottom third. Which company would you select? Write a brief paper justifying your recommendation.

Ratio	Company A	Company B
Current	High	Average
Quick	Low	Average
Debt to equity	High	Average
Inventory turnover	Low	Average
Price/earnings	Low	Average
Dividend yield	High	Average

P14-2
LO5, 6, 7

Analyzing an Investment by Comparing Selected Ratios (AP14-2)

You have the opportunity to invest $10,000 in one of two companies from a single industry. The only information you have is shown here. The word *high* refers to the top third of the industry; *average* is the middle third; *low* is the bottom third. Which company would you select? Write a brief paper justifying your recommendation.

Ratio	Company A	Company B
Current	Low	Average
Quick	Average	Average
Debt to equity	Low	Average
Inventory turnover	High	Average
Price/earnings	High	Average
Dividend yield	Low	Average

P14-3
LO7

Identifying Companies Based on the Price/Earnings Ratio

The price/earnings ratio provides important information concerning the stock market's assessment of the growth potential of a business. The following are price/earnings ratios for selected companies as of the date this book was written. Match the company with its ratio and explain how you made your selections. If you are not familiar with a company, you should contact its website.

Company	Price/Earnings Ratio
1. Commerce Bank	A. 55
2. Cinergy Gas and Electric	B. 12
3. Compaq Computers	C. 26
4. Home Depot	D. not applicable (no earnings)
5. Motorola	E. 10
6. Starbucks	F. 143
7. America Online	G. 108
8. Amazon.com	H. 65
9. Pepsi	I. 82

P14-4
LO1, 2, 3,
4, 5, 6, 7
Sears, Roebuck,
and JCPenney

Analyzing Ratios (AP14-3)

Sears, Roebuck and JCPenney are two giants of the retail industry. Both offer full lines of moderately priced merchandise. Annual sales for Sears total $41 billion. JCPenney is somewhat smaller with $30 billion in revenues. Compare the two companies as a potential investment based on the following ratios:

Ratio	Sears	JCPenney
P/E	8.1	9.7
Gross profit margin	33.5	23.1
Profit margin	3.6	1.7
Quick	0.1	0.6
Current	2.2	1.6
Debt to equity	2.8	1.4
Return on equity	23.5	7.5
Return on assets	4.1	3.2
Dividend yield	3.0%	5.9%
Dividend payout	24.0%	118.0%

Comparing Alternative Investment Opportunities (AP14-4)

P14-5
LO3, 4, 5, 6, 7

The 2007 financial statements for Armstrong and Blair companies are summarized here:

	Armstrong Company	Blair Company
Balance Sheet		
Cash	$ 35,000	$ 22,000
Accounts receivable (net)	40,000	30,000
Inventory	100,000	40,000
Operational assets (net)	140,000	400,000
Other assets	85,000	308,000
Total assets	$400,000	$800,000
Current liabilities	$100,000	$ 50,000
Long-term debt (10% interest)	60,000	70,000
Capital stock (par $10)	150,000	500,000
Contributed capital in excess of par	30,000	110,000
Retained earnings	60,000	70,000
Total liabilities and stockholders' equity	$400,000	$800,000
Income Statement		
Sales revenue (1/3 on credit)	$450,000	$810,000
Cost of goods sold	(245,000)	(405,000)
Expenses (including interest and income tax)	(160,000)	(315,000)
Net income	$ 45,000	$ 90,000
Selected data from the 2006 statements		
Accounts receivable (net)	$ 20,000	$ 38,000
Inventory	92,000	45,000
Long-term debt	60,000	70,000
Other data		
Per share price at end of 2007 (offering price)	$ 18	$ 15
Average income tax rate	30%	30%
Dividends declared and paid in 2007	$ 36,000	$150,000

The companies are in the same line of business and are direct competitors in a large metropolitan area. Both have been in business approximately 10 years, and each has had steady growth. The management of each has a different viewpoint in many respects. Blair is more conservative, and as its president said, "We avoid what we consider to be undue risk." Neither company is publicly held. Armstrong Company has an annual audit by a CPA but Blair Company does not.

Required:
1. Complete a schedule that reflects a ratio analysis of each company. Compute the ratios discussed in the chapter.
2. A client of yours has the opportunity to buy 10 percent of the shares in one or the other company at the per share prices given and has decided to invest in only one of the companies. Based on the data given, prepare a comparative written evaluation of the ratio analyses (and any other available information) and give your recommended choice with the supporting explanation.

P14-6
LO3

eXcel

Analyzing Comparative Financial Statement Using Percentages (AP14-5)

The comparative financial statements prepared at December 31, 2007, for King Company showed the following summarized data:

	2007	2006
Income Statement		
Sales revenue	$180,000*	$165,000
Cost of goods sold	110,000	100,000
Gross margin	70,000	65,000
Operating expenses and interest expense	56,000	53,000
Pretax income	14,000	12,000
Income tax	4,000	3,000
Net income	$ 10,000	$ 9,000
Balance Sheet		
Cash	$ 4,000	$ 8,000
Accounts receivable (net)	14,000	18,000
Inventory	40,000	35,000
Operational assets (net)	45,000	38,000
	$103,000	$ 99,000
Current liabilities (no interest)	$ 16,000	$ 19,000
Long-term liabilities (10% interest)	45,000	45,000
Common stock (par $5)	30,000	30,000
Retained earnings†	12,000	5,000
	$103,000	$ 99,000

*One-third was credit sales.

†During 2007, cash dividends amounting to $3,000 were declared and paid.

Required:

1. Complete the following columns for each item in the preceding comparative financial statements:

Increase (Decrease)
2007 over 2006

Amount	Percent

2. By what amount did working capital change? What was the amount of cash inflow from revenues for 2007?

P14-7
LO3, 4, 6

Analyzing Comparative Financial Statements Using Percentages and Selected Ratios (AP14-6)

Use the data given in P14-6 for King Company.

Required:

1. Present component percentages for 2007 only.
2. Respond to the following for 2007:
   a. What was the average percentage markup on sales?
   b. What was the average income tax rate?
   c. Compute the profit margin. Was it a good or poor indicator of performance? Explain.
   d. What percentage of total resources was invested in operational assets?
   e. Compute the debt-to-equity ratio. Does it look good or bad? Explain.
   f. What was the return on equity?
   g. What was the return on assets?
   h. Compute the financial leverage percentage. Was it positive or negative? Explain.

Analyzing a Financial Statement Using Ratios

Use the 2004 data in P14-6 for King Company. Assume a stock price of $28 per share. Compute appropriate ratios and explain the meaning of each.

P14-8
LO3, 4, 5, 6, 7
e**X**cel

Analyzing a Financial Statement Using Ratios

Summer Corporation has just completed its comparative statements for the year ended December 31, 2007. At this point, certain analytical and interpretive procedures are to be undertaken. The completed statements (summarized) are as follows:

P14-9
LO3, 4, 5, 6, 7

e**X**cel

	2007	2006
Income Statement		
Sales revenue	$450,000*	$420,000*
Cost of goods sold	250,000	230,000
Gross margin	200,000	190,000
Operating expenses		
(including interest on bonds)	167,000	168,000
Pretax income	33,000	22,000
Income tax	10,000	6,000
Net income	$ 23,000	$ 16,000
Balance Sheet		
Cash	$ 6,800	$ 3,900
Accounts receivable (net)	42,000	28,000
Merchandise inventory	25,000	20,000
Prepaid expenses	200	100
Operational assets (net)	130,000	120,000
	$204,000	$172,000
Accounts payable	$ 17,000	$ 18,000
Income taxes payable	1,000	2,000
Bonds payable (10% interest rate)	70,000†	50,000
Common stock (par $5)	100,000‡	100,000
Retained earnings	16,000#	2,000
	$204,000	$172,000

*Credit sales totaled 40 percent.

†$20,000 of bonds were issued on 1/2/2007.

‡The market price of the stock at the end of 2007 was $18 per share.

#During 2007, the company declared and paid a cash dividend of $9,000.

Required:
1. Compute appropriate ratios for 2007 and explain the meaning of each.
2. Respond to the following for 2007:
   a. Evaluate the financial leverage. Explain its meaning using the computed amount(s).
   b. Evaluate the profit margin amount and explain how a stockholder might use it.
   c. Explain to a stockholder why the current ratio and the quick ratio are different. Do you observe any liquidity problems? Explain.
   d. Assuming that credit terms are 1/10, n/30, do you perceive an unfavorable situation for the company related to credit sales? Explain.

Analyzing the Impact of Alternative Inventory Methods on Selected Ratios

Company A uses the FIFO method to cost inventory, and Company B uses the LIFO method. The two companies are exactly alike except for the difference in inventory costing methods. Costs of inventory items for both companies have been rising steadily in recent years, and each company has increased its inventory each year. Each company has paid its tax liability in full for the current year (and all

P14-10
LO4, 5, 6

previous years), and each company uses the same accounting methods for both financial reporting and income tax reporting.

Required:

Identify which company will report the higher amount for each of the following ratios. If it is not possible, explain why.

1. Current ratio.
2. Quick ratio.
3. Debt-to-equity ratio.
4. Return on equity.
5. Earnings per share.

P14-11

LO3, 4, 5, 6, 7

Hershey's

Analyzing a Financial Statement Using Appropriate Ratios (AP14-7)

Hershey's is a familiar name in snacks. There's a good chance you have recently enjoyed one of their products. The company manufactures confectionery products in a variety of packaged forms and markets them under more than 50 brands. Among the principal confectionery products in the United States are: Hershey's chocolates; Hershey's Kisses chocolates; Kit Kat, Krackel, and Mr. Goodbar chocolate bars; Reese's peanut butter cups; Almond Joy candy bars; Bubble Yum bubble gum; Good & Plenty candy; Mounds candy bars; Payday candy bars; and 5th Avenue candy bars.

The following information was reported in a recent annual statement. For the year 2003, compute the ratios discussed in this chapter. If there is not sufficient information, describe what is missing and explain what you would do. Assume a 34% tax rate.

HERSHEY FOODS CORPORATION
Consolidated Statements of Income

For the years ended December 31,	2003	2002	2001
In dollars in thousands, except per share amounts			
Net Sales	$4,172,551	$4,120,317	$4,137,217
Costs and Expenses:			
Cost of sales	2,544,726	2,561,052	2,668,530
Selling, marketing and administrative	816,442	833,426	846,976
Business realignment and asset impairments, net	23,357	27,552	228,314
Gain on sale of business	(8,330)	—	(19,237)
Total costs and expenses	3,376,195	3,422,030	3,724,583
Income before Interest and Income Taxes	796,356	698,287	412,634
Interest expense, net	63,529	60,722	69,093
Income before Income Taxes	732,827	637,565	343,541
Provision for income taxes	267,875	233,987	136,385
Income before Cumulative Effect of Accounting Change	464,952	403,578	207,156
Cumulative effect of accounting change, net of $4,933 tax benefit	7,368	—	—
Net Income	$ 457,584	$ 403,578	$ 207,156
Earnings Per Share—Basic			
Income before Cumulative Effect of Accounting Change	$3.54	$2.96	$1.52
Cumulative Effect of Accounting Change, net of $.04 Tax Benefit	.06	—	—
Net Income	$ 3.48	$ 2.96	$ 1.52

continued

Earnings Per Share—Diluted

Income before Cumulative Effect of Accounting Change	$	3.52	$	2.93	$	1.50
Cumulative Effect of Accounting Change, net of $.04 Tax Benefit		.06		—		—
Net Income	$	3.46	$	2.93	$	1.50

Cash Dividends Paid Per Share:

Common Stock	$	1.445	$	1.260	$	1.165
Class B Common Stock		1.305		1.135		1.050

The notes to consolidated financial statements are an integral part of these statements.

Consolidated Balance Sheets

December 31,	2003	2002
In dollars in thousands		
ASSETS		
Current Assets:		
Cash and cash equivalents	$ 114,793	$ 297,743
Accounts receivable—trade	407,612	370,976
Inventories	492,859	503,291
Deferred income taxes	13,285	—
Prepaid expenses and other	103,020	91,608
Total current assets	1,131,569	1,263,618
Property, Plant and Equipment, Net	1,661,939	1,486,055
Goodwill	388,960	378,453
Other Intangibles	38,511	39,898
Other Assets	361,561	312,527
Total assets	$3,582,540	$3,480,551
LIABILITIES AND STOCKHOLDERS' EQUITY		
Current Liabilities:		
Accounts payable	$ 132,222	$ 124,507
Accrued liabilities	416,181	356,716
Accrued income taxes	24,898	12,731
Deferred income taxes	—	24,768
Short-term debt	12,032	11,135
Current portion of long-term debt	477	16,989
Total current liabilities	585,810	546,846
Long-term Debt	968,499	851,800
Other Long-term Liabilities	370,776	362,162
Deferred Income Taxes	377,589	348,040
Total liabilities	2,302,674	2,108,848
Stockholders' Equity:		
Preferred Stock, shares issued: none in 2003 and 2002	—	—
Common Stock, shares issued: 149,528,776 in 2003 and 149,528,564 in 2002	149,528	149,528

continued

Class B Common Stock, shares issued:		
30,422,096 in 2003 and 30,422,308 in 2002	30,422	30,422
Additional paid-in capital	4,034	593
Unearned ESOP compensation	(9,580)	(12,774)
Retained earnings	3,263,988	2,991,090
Treasury—Common Stock shares, at cost:		
50,421,139 in 2003 and 45,730,735 in 2002	(2,147,441)	(1,808,227)
Accumulated other comprehensive (loss) income	(11,085)	21,071
Total stockholders' equity	1,279,866	1,371,703
Total liabilities and stockholders' equity	$3,582,540	$3,480,551

ALTERNATE PROBLEMS

AP14-1
LO4, 5, 6, 7

Analyzing an Investment by Comparing Selected Ratios (P14-1)

You have the opportunity to invest $10,000 in one of two companies from a single industry. The only information you have is shown here. The word *high* refers to the top third of the industry; *average* is the middle third; *low* is the bottom third. Which company would you select? Write a brief paper justifying your recommendation.

Ratio	Company A	Company B
EPS	High	Low
ROA	Low	High
Debt to equity	High	Average
Current	Low	Average
Price/earnings	Low	High
Dividend yield	High	Average

AP14-2
LO4, 5, 6, 7

Analyzing an Investment by Comparing Selected Ratios (P14-2)

You have the opportunity to invest $10,000 in one of two companies from a single industry. The only information you have is shown here. The word *high* refers to the top third of the industry; *average* is the middle third; *low* is the bottom third. Which company would you select? Write a brief paper justifying your recommendation.

Ratio	Company A	Company B
ROA	High	Average
Profit margin	High	Low
Financial leverage	High	Low
Current	Low	High
Price/earnings	High	Average
Debt to equity	High	Low

AP14-3
LO3, 4, 5, 6, 7

Coca-Cola

PepsiCo

Analyzing Ratios (P14-4)

Coke and Pepsi are well-known international brands. Coca-Cola sells more than $13 billion worth of beverages each year while annual sales of PepsiCo products exceed $22 billion. Compare the two companies as a potential investment based on the following ratios:

Ratio	Coca-Cola	PepsiCo
P/E	65.0	26.5
Gross profit margin	69.3	58.4
Profit margin	12.2	8.8
Quick ratio	0.4	0.7
Current ratio	0.6	1.1
Debt to equity	0.7	0.4
Return on equity	27.4	29.1
Return on assets	28.0	16.6
Dividend yield	1.0%	1.6%
Dividend payout ratio	65.0%	41.0%

Comparing Loan Requests from Two Companies Using Ratios (P14-5)

AP14-4
LO3, 4, 5, 6, 7

The 2007 financial statements for Rand and Tand companies are summarized here:

	Rand Company	Tand Company
Balance Sheet		
Cash	$ 25,000	$ 45,000
Accounts receivable (net)	55,000	5,000
Inventory	110,000	25,000
Operational assets (net)	550,000	160,000
Other assets	140,000	57,000
Total assets	$880,000	$292,000
Current liabilities	$120,000	$ 15,000
Long-term debt (12% interest)	190,000	55,000
Capital stock (par $20)	480,000	210,000
Contributed capital in excess of par	50,000	4,000
Retained earnings	40,000	8,000
Total liabilities and stockholders' equity	$880,000	$292,000
Income Statement		
Sales revenue (on credit)	(1/2) $800,000	(1/4) $280,000
Cost of goods sold	(480,000)	(150,000)
Expenses (including interest and income tax)	(240,000)	(95,000)
Net income	$ 80,000	$ 35,000
Selected Data from the 2006 Statements		
Accounts receivable, net	$ 47,000	$ 11,000
Long-term debt (12%)	190,000	55,000
Inventory	95,000	38,000
Other Data		
Per share price at end of 2007	$ 14.00	$ 11.00
Average income tax rate	30%	30%
Dividends declared and paid in 2007	$ 20,000	$ 9,000

These two companies are in the same line of business and in the same state but in different cities. Each company has been in operation for about 10 years. Rand Company is audited by one of the national accounting firms; Tand Company is audited by a local accounting firm. Both companies received an unqualified opinion (i.e., the independent auditors found nothing wrong) on the financial statements. Rand Company wants to borrow $75,000 cash, and Tand Company needs $30,000. The loans will be for a two-year period and are needed for "working capital purposes."

Required:
1. Complete a schedule that reflects a ratio analysis of each company. Compute the ratios discussed in the chapter.
2. Assume that you work in the loan department of a local bank. You have been asked to analyze the situation and recommend which loan is preferable. Based on the data given, your analysis prepared in requirement 1, and any other information, give your choice and the supported explanation.

AP14-5
LO3, 4, 5, 6, 7

Analyzing a Financial Statement Using Ratios and Percentage Changes (P14-6)

Taber Company has just prepared the following comparative annual financial statements for 2007:

TABER COMPANY
Comparative Income Statement
For the Years Ended December 31, 2007 and 2006

		2007	2006
Sales revenue (one-half on credit)		$110,000	$99,000
Cost of goods sold		52,000	48,000
Gross margin		$ 58,000	$51,000
Expenses (including $4,000 interest expense each year)		40,000	37,000
Pretax income		$ 18,000	$14,000
Income tax on operations (30%)		5,400	4,200
Income before extraordinary items		$ 12,600	$ 9,800
Extraordinary loss	$2,000		
Less income tax saved	600	1,400	
Extraordinary gain		$3,000	
Applicable income tax		900	2,100
Net income		$ 11,200	$11,900

TABER COMPANY
Comparative Balance Sheet
At December 31, 2007, and 2006

	2007	2006
Assets		
Cash	$ 49,500	$ 18,000
Accounts receivable (net; terms 1/10, n/30)	37,000	32,000
Inventory	25,000	38,000
Operational assets (net)	95,000	105,000
Total assets	$206,500	$193,000
Liabilities		
Accounts payable	$ 42,000	$ 35,000
Income taxes payable	1,000	500
Note payable, long-term	40,000	40,000
Stockholders' equity		
Capital stock (par $10)	90,000	90,000
Retained earnings	33,500	27,500
Total liabilities and stockholders' equity	$206,500	$193,000

Required (round percentage and ratios to two decimal places):

1. For 2007, compute the tests of (a) profitability, (b) liquidity, (c) solvency, and (d) market. Assume that the quoted price of the stock was $23 for 2007. Dividends declared and paid during 2007 were $6,750.
2. Respond to the following for 2007:
   a. Compute the percentage changes in sales, income before extraordinary items, net income, cash, inventory, and debt.
   b. What appears to be the pretax interest rate on the note payable?
3. Identify at least two problems facing the company that are suggested by your responses to requirements 1 and 2.

Using Ratios to Analyze Several Years of Financial Data (P14-7)

The following information was contained in the annual financial statements of Pine Company, which started business January 1, 2006 (assume account balances only in Cash and Capital Stock on this date; all amounts are in dollars in thousands).

	2006	2007	2008	2009
Accounts receivable (net; terms n/30)	$11	$12	$18	$24
Merchandise inventory	12	14	20	30
Net sales (3/4 on credit)	44	66	80	100
Cost of goods sold	28	40	55	62
Net income (loss)	(8)	5	12	11

Required (show computations):
1. Complete the following tabulation

Items	2006	2007	2008	2009

 a. Profit margin percentage
 b. Gross margin ratio
 c. Expenses as percentage of sales, excluding cost of goods sold
 d. Inventory turnover
 e. Days' supply in inventory
 f. Receivable turnover
 g. Average days to collect

2. Evaluate the results of the related ratios *a, b,* and *c* to identify the favorable or unfavorable factors. Give your recommendations to improve the company's operations.
3. Evaluate the results of the last four ratios (*d, e, f,* and *g*), and identify any favorable or unfavorable factors. Give your recommendations to improve the company's operations.

Analyzing a Financial Statement Using Appropriate Ratios (P14-11)

Lennar is one of the nation's largest homebuilders and a provider of financial services. Homebuilding operations include the sale and construction of single-family attached and detached homes, as well as the purchase, development, and sale of residential land directly and through its unconsolidated partnerships. Financial services subsidiaries provide mortgage financing, title insurance, closing services, and insurance agency services for both buyers of their homes and others, and sell the loans they originate in the secondary mortgage market. These subsidiaries also provide high-speed Internet access, cable television, and alarm installation and monitoring services to residents of communities they develop and others.

 For 2003, compute each of the ratios discussed in this chapter. If there is not sufficient information, state what is needed. If a ratio is not meaningful for this type of company, explain why.

LENNAR CORPORATION AND SUBSIDIARIES
Consolidated Balance Sheets
November 30, 2003 and 2002

(In dollars in thousands, except per share amounts)	2003	2002
ASSETS		
Homebuilding:		
Cash	$1,201,276	$ 731,163
Receivables, net	60,392	48,432
Inventories:		
Finished homes and construction in progress	2,006,548	2,044,694
Land under development	1,592,978	1,185,473
Consolidated inventory not owned	49,329	—
Land held for development	7,246	7,410
Total inventories	3,656,101	3,237,577

continued

Investments in unconsolidated partnerships	**390,334**	285,594
Other assets	**450,619**	357,738
	5,758,722	4,660,504
Financial services	**1,016,710**	1,095,129
Total assets	**$6,775,432**	$5,755,633

LIABILITIES AND STOCKHOLDERS' EQUITY
Homebuilding:

Accounts payable and other liabilities	**$1,040,961**	$ 969,779
Liabilities related to consolidated inventory not owned	**45,214**	—
Senior notes and other debts payable, net	**1,552,217**	1,585,309
	2,638,392	2,555,088
Financial services	**873,266**	971,388
Total liabilities	**3,511,658**	3,526,476

Stockholders' equity:

Preferred stock	**—**	—
Class A common stock of $0.10 par value per share		
Authorized: 2003—300,000 shares; 2002—100,000,		
Issued: 2003—125,328; 2002—130,122	**12,533**	13,012
Class B common stock of $0.10 par value per share		
Authorized: 2003—90,000 shares; 2002—30,000,		
Issued: 2003—32,508; 2002—19,400	**3,251**	1,940
Additional paid-in capital	**1,358,304**	866,026
Retained earnings	**1,914,963**	1,538,945
Unearned restricted stock	**(4,301)**	(7,337)
Deferred compensation plan—2003—534		
Class A common shares and 53 Class B common shares;		
2002—120 Class A common shares and 12 Class B		
common shares	**(4,919)**	(1,103)
Deferred compensation liability	**4,919**	1,103
Treasury stock, at cost; 2002—9,848 Class A common shares	**—**	(158,992)
Accumulated other comprehensive loss	**(20,976)**	(24,437)
Total stockholders' equity	**3,263,774**	2,229,157
Total liabilities and stockholders' equity	**$6,775,432**	$5,755,633

Consolidated Statements of Earnings
Years Ended November 30, 2003, 2002, and 2001

(In dollars in thousands, except per share amounts)	2003	2002	2001
Revenues:			
Homebuilding	**$8,348,645**	$6,751,301	$5,554,747
Financial services	**558,974**	484,219	425,354
Total revenues	**8,907,619**	7,235,520	5,980,101
Costs and expenses:			
Homebuilding	**7,288,356**	5,993,209	4,934,071
Financial services	**404,521**	356,608	336,223
Corporate general and administrative	**111,488**	85,958	75,831
Total costs and expenses	**7,804,365**	6,435,775	5,346,125
Equity in earnings from unconsolidated partnerships	**81,937**	42,651	27,051
Management fees and other income, net	**21,863**	33,313	18,396
Earnings before provision for income taxes	**1,207,054**	875,709	679,423
Provision for income taxes	**455,663**	330,580	261,578
Net earnings	**$ 751,391**	$ 545,129	$ 417,845

Annual Report Cases

Analyzing Financial Statements

Refer to the financial statements of PacSun given in Appendix B, or open file PSUN.pdf in the Annual Report Cases directory on the student DVD. From the list of ratios displayed in Exhibit 14.3, compute the ratios for the most recent reporting year for which you have available information. (Note: For Return on Assets use cash paid for interest if interest expense is unavailable and assume a corporate tax rate of 35%.)

CP14-1
LO4, 5, 6, 7

PACIFIC SUNWEAR
OF CALIFORNIA, INC.

Analyzing Financial Statements

Refer to the financial statements of American Eagle Outfitters given in Appendix C, or open file AEOS.pdf in the Annual Report Cases directory on the student DVD. From the list of ratios displayed in Exhibit 14.3, compute the ratios for the most recent reporting year for which you have available information. (Note: For Return on Assets use cash paid for interest if interest expense is unavailable and assume a corporate tax rate of 35%.)

CP14-2
LO4, 5, 6, 7

AMERICAN EAGLE
OUTFITTERS
ae.com

Comparing Companies within an Industry

Refer to the financial statements of PacSun given in Appendix B, American Eagle Outfitters given in Appendix C, and the Industry Ratio Report given in Appendix D at the end of this book or open file CP14-3.xls in the Annual Report Cases directory on the student DVD. From the list of ratios displayed in Exhibit 14.3, compute the ratios for the most recent reporting year for which you have available information. (Note: For Return on Assets use cash paid for interest if interest expense is unavailable.) Compare the ratios for each company to the industry average ratios.

CP14-3
LO4, 5, 6, 7

PACIFIC SUNWEAR
OF CALIFORNIA, INC.

AMERICAN EAGLE
OUTFITTERS
ae.com

Financial Reporting and Analysis Cases

Inferring Information from the ROE Model

In this chapter, we discussed the ROE profit driver (or DuPont model). Using that framework, find the missing amount in each case that follows:

CP14-4
LO1

Case 1: ROE is 10 percent; net income is $200,000; asset turnover is 5; and net sales are $1,000,000. What is the amount of average stockholders' equity?

Case 2: Net income is $1,500,000; net sales are $8,000,000; average stockholders' equity is $12,000,000; ROE is 22 percent and asset turnover is 8. What is the amount of average total assets?

Case 3: ROE is 15 percent; net profit margin is 10 percent; asset turnover is 5; and average total assets are $1,000,000. What is the amount of average stockholders' equity?

Case 4: Net income is $500,000; ROE is 15 percent; asset turnover is 5; net sales are $1,000,000; and financial leverage is 2. What is the amount of average total assets?

Interpreting Financial Results Based on Corporate Strategy

In this chapter, we discussed the importance of analyzing financial results based on an understanding of the company's business strategy. Using the ROE model, we illustrated how different strategies could earn high returns for investors. Assume that two companies in the same industry adopt fundamentally different strategies. One manufactures high-quality consumer electronics. Its products employ state-of-the-art technology, and the company offers a high level of customer service both before and after the sale. The other company emphasizes low cost with good performance. Its products utilize well-established technology but are never innovative. Customers buy these products at large, self-service warehouses and are expected to install the products using information contained in printed brochures. Which of the ratios discussed in this chapter would you expect to differ for these companies as a result of their different business strategies?

CP14-5
LO1

CP14-6

LO1, 4, 5, 6, 7

Nordstrom and JCPenney

Interpreting Financial Results Based on Corporate Strategy

In this chapter, we discussed the importance of analyzing financial results based on an understanding of the company's business strategy. Using the ROE model, we illustrated how different strategies could earn high returns for investors. Both Nordstrom and JCPenney are in the retail industry. Nordstrom is a specialty apparel retailer operating in 23 states. Annual revenues exceed $5 billion. The store is well known for high-quality merchandise and a high level of customer service. JCPenney is a full-line retailer appealing to middle income shoppers. Its merchandise is moderately priced, and customers receive a lower level of service. The following are several ratios from each company. Identify which company is Nordstrom and which is JCPenney. Which of these ratios do you think are affected by the different strategies? Explain.

Ratio	Company A	Company B
Gross margin	34.4	23.1
Profit margin	4.0	1.7
Current ratio	1.8	1.6
Debt-to-equity	0.8	1.4
Return on equity	15.9	7.5
Return on assets	6.5	2.3
Dividend payout	22.1	117.0
Price/earnings	15.3	9.3

CP14-7

LO3, 4, 5, 6, 7

Interpreting Financial Publications

An important source of information for most investors is the analyst report published by all large investment firms. A professional analyst report* for Home Depot is available on the Libby/Libby/Short website at www.mhhe.com/libby5e. You should read this report and then write a short memo discussing the use of financial information in the report.

Critical Thinking Cases

CP14-8

LO5

Evaluating an Ethical Dilemma

Barton Company requested a sizable loan from First Federal Bank to acquire a large tract of land for future expansion. Barton reported current assets of $1,900,000 ($430,000 in cash) and current liabilities of $1,075,000. First Federal denied the loan request for a number of reasons, including the fact that the current ratio was below 2:1. When Barton was informed of the loan denial, the comptroller of the company immediately paid $420,000 that was owed to several trade creditors. The comptroller then asked First Federal to reconsider the loan application. Based on these abbreviated facts, would you recommend that First Federal approve the loan request? Why? Are the comptroller's actions ethical?

Financial Reporting and Analysis Team Project

CP14-9

LO3, 4, 5, 6, 7

Team Project: Examining an Annual Report

As a team, select an industry to analyze. *Reuters* provides lists of industries and their makeup at www.investor.reuters.com/Industries.aspx. Each team member should acquire the annual report or 10-K for one publicly traded company in the industry, with each member selecting a different company. (Library files, the SEC EDGAR service at www.sec.gov, CompuStat CD, or the company itself, are good sources.)

Required:

On an individual basis, each team member should write a short report providing the following information about the selected company. Discuss any patterns across the companies that you as a team observe. Then, as a team, write a short report comparing and contrasting your companies.

Compute and interpret each of the ratios discussed in this chapter. The most frequently used sections will be the financial statements. Also, you may want to review footnotes, summary of financial information (usually for the past five years or longer), and management's discussion and analysis.

---

*Linda Bannister, "Home Depot's Analyst's Report," Dec. 31, 1999. Reprinted with permission of Edward Jones.

handwritten: 110,000 × .07 [-7700] × 4.1002 = 31571.54

handwritten: 78430

handwritten: 110,000 × .7130

TABLE A.1
Present Value of $1

Periods	2%	3%	3.75%	4%	4.25%	5%	6%	7%	8%
1	0.9804	0.9709	0.9639	0.9615	0.9592	0.9524	0.9434	0.9346	0.9259
2	0.9612	0.9426	0.9290	0.9246	0.9201	0.9070	0.8900	0.8734	0.8573
3	0.9423	0.9151	0.8954	0.8890	0.8826	0.8638	0.8396	0.8163	0.7938
4	0.9238	0.8885	0.8631	0.8548	0.8466	0.8227	0.7921	0.7629	0.7350
5	0.9057	0.8626	0.8319	0.8219	0.8121	0.7835	0.7473	0.7130	0.6806
6	0.8880	0.8375	0.8018	0.7903	0.7790	0.7462	0.7050	0.6663	0.6302
7	0.8706	0.8131	0.7728	0.7599	0.7473	0.7107	0.6651	0.6227	0.5835
8	0.8535	0.7894	0.7449	0.7307	0.7168	0.6768	0.6274	0.5820	0.5403
9	0.8368	0.7664	0.7180	0.7026	0.6876	0.6446	0.5919	0.5439	0.5002
10	0.8203	0.7441	0.6920	0.6756	0.6595	0.6139	0.5584	0.5083	0.4632
20	0.6730	0.5537	0.4789	0.4564	0.4350	0.3769	0.3118	0.2584	0.2145

Periods	9%	10%	11%	12%	13%	14%	15%	20%	25%
1	0.9174	0.9091	0.9009	0.8929	0.8850	0.8772	0.8696	0.8333	0.8000
2	0.8417	0.8264	0.8116	0.7972	0.7831	0.7695	0.7561	0.6944	0.6400
3	0.7722	0.7513	0.7312	0.7118	0.6931	0.6750	0.6575	0.5787	0.5120
4	0.7084	0.6830	0.6587	0.6355	0.6133	0.5921	0.5718	0.4823	0.4096
5	0.6499	0.6209	0.5935	0.5674	0.5428	0.5194	0.4972	0.4019	0.3277
6	0.5963	0.5645	0.5346	0.5066	0.4803	0.4556	0.4323	0.3349	0.2621
7	0.5470	0.5132	0.4817	0.4523	0.4251	0.3996	0.3759	0.2791	0.2097
8	0.5019	0.4665	0.4339	0.4039	0.3762	0.3506	0.3269	0.2326	0.1678
9	0.4604	0.4241	0.3909	0.3606	0.3329	0.3075	0.2843	0.1938	0.1342
10	0.4224	0.3855	0.3522	0.3220	0.2946	0.2697	0.2472	0.1615	0.1074
20	0.1784	0.1486	0.1240	0.1037	0.0868	0.0728	0.0611	0.0261	0.0115

handwritten: 86185

TABLE A.2
Present Value of Annuity of $1

Periods*	2%	3%	3.75%	4%	4.25%	5%	6%	7%	8%
1	0.9804	0.9709	0.9639	0.9615	0.9592	0.9524	0.9434	0.9346	0.9259
2	1.9416	1.9135	1.8929	1.8861	1.8794	1.8594	1.8334	1.8080	1.7833
3	2.8839	2.8286	2.7883	2.7751	2.7620	2.7232	2.6730	2.6243	2.5771
4	3.8077	3.7171	3.6514	3.6299	3.6086	3.5460	3.4651	3.3872	3.3121
5	4.7135	4.5797	4.4833	4.4518	4.4207	4.3295	4.2124	4.1002	3.9927
6	5.6014	5.4172	5.2851	5.2421	5.1997	5.0757	4.9173	4.7665	4.6229
7	6.4720	6.2303	6.0579	6.0021	5.9470	5.7864	5.5824	5.3893	5.2064
8	7.3255	7.0197	6.8028	6.7327	6.6638	6.4632	6.2098	5.9713	5.7466
9	8.1622	7.7861	7.5208	7.4353	7.3513	7.1078	6.8017	6.5152	6.2469
10	8.9826	8.5302	8.2128	8.1109	8.0109	7.7217 .	7.3601	7.0236	6.7101
20	16.3514	14.8775	13.8962	13.5903	13.2944	12.4622	11.4699	10.5940	9.8181

*There is one payment each period.

TABLE A.2 *(continued)*

Present Value of Annuity of $1

Periods*	9%	10%	11%	12%	13%	14%	15%	20%	25%
1	0.9174	0.9091	0.9009	0.8929	0.8550	0.8772	0.8696	0.8333	0.8000
2	1.7591	1.7355	1.7125	1.6901	1.6681	1.6467	1.6257	1.5278	1.4400
3	2.5313	2.4869	2.4437	2.4018	2.3612	2.3216	2.2832	2.1065	1.9520
4	3.2397	3.1699	3.1024	3.0373	2.9745	2.9137	2.8550	2.5887	2.3616
5	3.8897	3.7908	3.6959	3.6048	3.5172	3.4331	3.3522	2.9906	2.6893
6	4.4859	4.3553	4.2305	4.1114	3.9975	3.8887	3.7845	3.3255	2.9514
7	5.0330	4.8684	4.7122	4.5638	4.4226	4.2883	4.1604	3.6046	3.1611
8	5.5348	5.3349	5.1461	4.9676	4.7988	4.6389	4.4873	3.8372	3.3289
9	5.9952	5.7590	5.5370	5.3282	4.1317	4.9464	4.7716	4.0310	3.4631
10	6.4177	6.1446	5.8892	5.6502	5.4262	5.2161	5.0188	4.1925	3.5705
20	9.1285	8.5136	7.9633	7.4694	7.0248	6.6231	6.2593	4.8696	3.9539

*There is one payment each period.

TABLE A.3

Future Value of $1

Periods	2%	3%	3.75%	4%	4.25%	5%	6%	7%	8%
0	1.	1.	1.	1.	1.	1.	1.	1.	1.
1	1.02	1.03	1.0375	1.04	1.0425	1.05	1.06	1.07	1.08
2	1.0404	1.0609	1.0764	1.0816	1.0868	1.1025	1.1236	1.1449	1.1664
3	1.0612	1.0927	1.1168	1.1249	1.1330	1.1576	1.1910	1.2250	1.2597
4	1.0824	1.1255	1.1587	1.1699	1.1811	1.2155	1.2625	1.3108	1.3605
5	1.1041	1.1593	1.2021	1.2167	1.2313	1.2763	1.3382	1.4026	1.4693
6	1.1262	1.1941	1.2472	1.2653	1.2837	1.3401	1.4185	1.5007	1.5869
7	1.1487	1.2299	1.2939	1.3159	1.3382	1.4071	1.5036	1.6058	1.7138
8	1.1717	1.2668	1.3425	1.3686	1.3951	1.4775	1.5938	1.7182	1.8509
9	1.1951	1.3048	1.3928	1.4233	1.4544	1.5513	1.6895	1.8385	1.9990
10	1.2190	1.3439	1.4450	1.4802	1.5162	1.6289	1.7908	1.9672	2.1589
20	1.4859	1.8061	2.0882	2.1911	2.2989	2.6533	3.2071	3.8697	4.6610

Periods	9%	10%	11%	12%	13%	14%	15%	20%	25%
0	1.	1.	1.	1.	1.	1.	1.	1.	1.
1	1.09	1.10	1.11	1.12	1.13	1.14	1.15	1.20	1.25
2	1.1881	1.2100	1.2321	1.2544	1.2769	1.2996	1.3225	1.4400	1.5625
3	1.2950	1.3310	1.3676	1.4049	1.4429	1.4815	1.5209	1.7280	1.9531
4	1.4116	1.4641	1.5181	1.5735	1.6305	1.6890	1.7490	2.0736	2.4414
5	1.5386	1.6105	1.6851	1.7623	1.8424	1.9254	2.0114	2.4883	3.0518
6	1.6771	1.7716	1.8704	1.9738	2.0820	2.1950	2.3131	2.9860	3.8147
7	1.8280	1.9487	2.0762	2.2107	2.3526	2.5023	2.6600	3.5832	4.7684
8	1.9926	2.1436	2.3045	2.4760	2.6584	2.8526	3.0590	4.2998	5.9605
9	2.1719	2.3579	2.5580	2.7731	3.0040	3.2519	3.5179	5.1598	7.4506
10	2.3674	2.5937	2.8394	3.1058	3.3946	3.7072	4.0456	6.1917	9.3132
20	5.6044	6.7275	8.0623	9.6463	11.5231	13.7435	16.3665	38.3376	86.7362

TABLE A.4

Future Value of Annuity of $1

Periods*	2%	3%	3.75%	4%	4.25%	5%	6%	7%	8%
1	1.	1.	1.	1.	1.	1.	1.	1.	1.
2	2.02	2.03	2.0375	2.04	2.0425	2.05	2.06	2.07	2.08
3	3.0604	3.0909	3.1139	3.1216	3.1293	3.1525	3.1836	3.2149	3.2464
4	4.1216	4.1836	4.2307	4.2465	4.2623	4.3101	4.3746	4.4399	4.5061
5	5.2040	5.3091	5.3893	5.4163	5.4434	5.5256	5.6371	5.7507	5.8666
6	6.3081	6.4684	6.5914	6.6330	6.6748	6.8019	6.9753	7.1533	7.3359
7	7.4343	7.6625	7.8386	7.8983	7.9585	8.1420	8.3938	8.6540	8.9228
8	8.5830	8.8923	9.1326	9.2142	9.2967	9.5491	9.8975	10.2598	10.6366
9	9.7546	10.1591	10.4750	10.5828	10.6918	11.0266	11.4913	11.9780	12.4876
10	10.9497	11.4639	11.8678	12.0061	12.1462	12.5779	13.1808	13.8164	14.4866
20	24.2974	26.8704	29.0174	29.7781	30.5625	33.0660	36.7856	40.9955	45.7620

Periods*	9%	10%	11%	12%	13%	14%	15%	20%	25%
1	1.	1.	1.	1.	1.	1.	1.	1.	1.
2	2.09	2.10	2.11	2.12	2.13	2.14	2.15	2.20	2.25
3	3.2781	3.3100	3.3421	3.3744	3.4069	3.4396	3.4725	3.6400	3.8125
4	4.5731	4.6410	4.7097	4.7793	4.8498	4.9211	4.9934	5.3680	5.7656
5	5.9847	6.1051	6.2278	6.3528	6.4803	6.6101	6.7424	7.4416	8.2070
6	7.5233	7.7156	7.9129	8.1152	8.3227	8.5355	8.7537	9.9299	11.2588
7	9.2004	9.4872	9.7833	10.0890	10.4047	10.7305	11.0668	12.9159	15.0735
8	11.0285	11.4359	11.8594	12.2997	12.7573	13.2328	13.7268	16.4991	19.8419
9	13.0210	13.5975	14.1640	14.7757	15.4157	16.0853	16.7858	20.7989	25.8023
10	15.1929	15.9374	16.7220	17.5487	18.4197	19.3373	20.3037	25.9587	33.2529
20	51.1601	57.2750	64.2028	72.0524	80.9468	91.0249	102.4436	186.6880	342.9447

*There is one payment each period.

pacific sunwear of california, inc. annual report 2004

to our **shareholders**

We are very pleased to report another very strong year of sales and earnings growth at Pacific Sunwear. Sales grew by $188 million to $1.23 billion, an increase of 18 percent. Earnings grew by 33 percent to $106.9 million. Same store sales grew by 7.3 percent, with PacSun up 7.5 percent and d.e.m.o. up 5.7 percent. We opened 113 new stores in 2004 and expanded 35 of our most productive stores. Operating income reached a record 13.8 percent for the year.

Total Company sales per square foot increased for the year to $374 per square foot, with PacSun at $370 per square foot and d.e.m.o. at $402 per square foot. We ended 2004 with 990 stores, which included 828 PacSun stores and 162 d.e.m.o. stores.

We enter 2005 with an enhanced management team and aggressive plans for the future. We will open 120 new stores in 2005 and will again expand 35 of our most productive stores. We will end 2005 with 1,110 stores: 908 PacSun stores and 202 d.e.m.o. stores.

During the year we repurchased 5.2 million of our outstanding shares for $110 million.

In 2004 Seth Johnson joined us as Chief Operating Officer and member of the Board of Directors; he became Chief Executive Officer on April 1, 2005. We were pleased to have Tom Kennedy join us as Division President of PacSun. Gerald Chaney joined us as Chief Financial Officer, replacing Carl Womack, who retired after 18 years with the Company. Greg Weaver will remain as Executive Chairman of the Board and will focus primarily on new business

development. The Company is now working on a new retail concept to be launched in spring 2006.

We feel very good about our company as we enter 2005. Very few companies reach the 1,000–store threshold as

successfully as Pacific Sunwear has. As a company, we have learned a great deal and grown a great deal. We look

forward to continuing to grow our business and our people.

Our thanks to our more than 13,000 employees throughout the United States and Puerto Rico, as well as to our vendors,

who are exceptional business partners. We also thank our shareholders for their interest and support of our Company.

Yours truly,

Seth R. Johnson
Chief Executive Officer, Director

Yours truly,

Greg H. Weaver
Executive Chairman of the Board

United States
Securities and Exchange Commission

Washington, D.C. 20549

FORM 10-K

(Mark One)

[X] Annual Report Pursuant to Section 13 or 15(d) of the Securities Exchange Act of 1934
For the fiscal year ended: January 29, 2005

or

[   ] Transition Report Pursuant to Section 13 or 15(d) of the Securities Exchange Act of 1934
For the transition period from _____ to _____

Commission File Number 0-21296

PACIFIC SUNWEAR OF CALIFORNIA, INC.

(Exact name of Registrant as specified in its charter)

CALIFORNIA	95-3759463
(State or other jurisdiction of incorporation or organization)	(I.R.S. Employer Identification No.)
3450 E. Miraloma Avenue, Anaheim, California	92806
(Address of principal executive offices)	(Zip code)

(714) 414-4000
(Registrant's telephone number, including area code)

Securities Registered Pursuant to Section 12(b) of the Act:
NONE

Securities Registered Pursuant to Section 12(g) of the Act:
COMMON STOCK, $.01 PAR VALUE
PREFERRED STOCK PURCHASE RIGHTS
(Title of Class)

Indicate by check mark whether the registrant (1) has filed all reports required to be filed by Section 13 or 15(d) of the Securities Exchange Act of 1934 during the preceding 12 months (or for such shorter period that the registrant was required to file such reports), and (2) has been subject to such filing requirements for the past 90 days. Yes [X] No [   ]

Indicate by check mark whether the registrant is an accelerated filer (as defined in Rule 12b-2 of the Exchange Act). Yes [X] No [   ]

Indicate by check mark if disclosure of delinquent filers pursuant to Item 405 of Regulation S-K is not contained herein, and will not be contained, to the best of the registrant's knowledge, in definitive proxy or information statements incorporated by reference in Part III of this Form 10-K or any amendment to this Form 10-K. [   ]

The aggregate market value of Common Stock held by non-affiliates of the registrant as of July 31, 2004, the end of the most recently completed second quarter, was approximately $1.5 billion. All outstanding shares of voting stock, except for shares held by executive officers and members of the Board of Directors and their affiliates, are deemed to be held by non-affiliates.

On April 4, 2005, the registrant had 75,498,028 shares of Common Stock outstanding.

DOCUMENTS INCORPORATED BY REFERENCE

Part III incorporates information by reference from the definitive Proxy Statement for the 2005 Annual Meeting of Shareholders, to be filed with the Commission no later than 120 days after the end of the registrant's fiscal year covered by this Form 10-K.

Part I

Item 1. Business

Pacific Sunwear of California, Inc. and its wholly owned subsidiaries (the "Company," "Registrant," "we," "us," or "our") is a leading specialty retailer of everyday casual apparel, accessories and footwear designed to meet the needs of active teens and young adults.

We operate three nationwide, primarily mall-based chains of retail stores under the names "Pacific Sunwear" (also "PacSun"), "Pacific Sunwear (PacSun) Outlet," and "d.e.m.o." PacSun and PacSun Outlet stores specialize in board-sport inspired casual apparel, footwear and related accessories catering to teenagers and young adults. d.e.m.o. specializes in hip-hop inspired casual apparel, footwear and related accessories catering to teenagers and young adults. In addition, we operate a website that sells PacSun merchandise online, provides content and community for our target customers and provides information about us. We plan to begin selling d.e.m.o. merchandise through our new d.e.m.o. website during fiscal 2005.

The Company, a California corporation, was incorporated in August 1982. At the end of fiscal 2004, we operated 744 PacSun stores comprising approximately 2.7 million total square feet, 84 PacSun Outlet stores comprising approximately 0.3 million square feet, and 162 d.e.m.o. stores comprising approximately 0.4 million square feet for a total of 990 stores in 50 states and Puerto Rico comprising approximately 3.4 million square feet. As of April 4, 2005, we operated 751 PacSun stores, 85 PacSun Outlet stores and 169 d.e.m.o. stores for a total of 1,005 stores in 50 states and Puerto Rico.

Our executive offices are located at 3450 East Miraloma Avenue, Anaheim, California, 92806; the telephone number is (714) 414-4000; and our internet address is *www.pacsun.com*. Through our website, we make available free of charge, as soon as reasonably practicable after such information has been filed or furnished to the Securities and Exchange Commission (the "Commission"), our annual reports on Form 10-K, quarterly reports on Form 10-Q, current reports on Form 8-K, and amendments to those reports filed or furnished pursuant to Section 13(a) or 15(d) of the Securities Exchange Act of 1934, as amended (the "Exchange Act").

The Company's fiscal year is the 52- or 53-week period ending on the Saturday closest to January 31. Fiscal 2004 was the 52-week period ended January 29, 2005. Fiscal 2003 was the 52-week period ended January 31, 2004. Fiscal 2002 was the 52-week period ended February 1, 2003. Fiscal 2005 will be the 52-week period ending January 28, 2006.

CAUTIONARY NOTE REGARDING FORWARD-LOOKING STATEMENTS

This report on Form 10-K contains "forward-looking statements" within the meaning of Section 27A of the Securities Act of 1933 and Section 21E of the Exchange Act, and we intend that such forward-looking statements be subject to the safe harbors created thereby. We are hereby providing cautionary statements identifying important factors that could cause our actual results to differ materially from those projected in forward-looking statements of the Company herein. Any statements that express, or involve discussions as to, expectations, beliefs, plans, objectives, assumptions, future events or performance (often, but not always through the use of words or phrases such as "will result," "expects to," "will continue," "anticipates," "plans," "intends," "estimated," "projects" and "outlook") are not historical facts and may be forward-looking and, accordingly, such statements involve estimates, assumptions and uncertainties which could cause actual results to differ materially from those expressed in the forward-looking statements. All forward-looking statements included in this report, including forecasts of fiscal 2005 planned new store openings and capital expenditures, are based on information available to us as of the date hereof, and we assume no obligation to update or revise any such forward-looking statements to reflect events or circumstances that occur after such statements are made. See "Risk Factors" within Item 7, "Management's Discussion and Analysis of Financial Condition and Results of Operations."

OUR MISSION AND STRATEGIES

Our mission is to be the leading lifestyle retailer of casual fashion apparel, footwear and accessories for teens. Our target customers are young men and women between the ages of 12 and 24. We believe our customers want to stay current with, or ahead of, fashion trends and continually seek newness in their everyday wear. We offer a complete wardrobe selection representing fashion trends considered timely by our target customers. We believe the following items are the key strategic elements necessary to achieve our mission:

Offer Popular Name Brands Supplemented by Private Brands. In each of our store formats, we offer a carefully edited selection of popular name brands supplemented by our own proprietary brands, with the goal of being seen by our teenage and young adult customers as the source for wardrobe choices appropriate to their lifestyle. We believe that our merchandising strategy differentiates our stores from competitors who may offer 100% proprietary brands, greater than 80% name brands, or seek to serve a wider customer base and age range. See "Merchandising."

Promote the PacSun and d.e.m.o. Brand Images. We promote the PacSun and d.e.m.o. brands primarily through national print advertising in major magazines that target teens and young adults. We also maintain a proprietary brand credit card through a third party to promote the PacSun brand image and lifestyle.

Actively Manage Merchandise Trends. We do not attempt to dictate fashion, but instead devote considerable effort to identifying emerging fashion trends and brand names. We use focus groups, listen to our customers and store employees, monitor sell-through trends, test small quantities of new merchandise in a limited number of stores, and maintain close domestic and international sourcing relationships. We believe that these practices enhance our ability to identify and respond to emerging fashion trends and brand names as well as develop new proprietary brand styles in order to capitalize on existing fashion trends.

Maintain Strong Vendor Relationships. We view our vendor relationships as important to our success and we promote frequent personal interaction with our vendors. We believe many of our vendors view PacSun, PacSun Outlet and d.e.m.o. stores as important distribution channels due to our nationwide presence and ability to introduce products to a broad audience. We tend to be one of the largest, if not the largest, customers for many of our vendors and we work closely with them to respond to emerging fashion trends and to obtain PacSun and d.e.m.o. "exclusives," which are products that cannot be found at any other retailer.

Provide Attentive Customer Service. We are committed to offering courteous, professional and non-intrusive customer service. We strive to give our young customers the same level of respect that is generally given to adult customers at other retail stores, and to provide friendly and informed customer service for parents. Responding to the expressed preferences of our customers, we train our employees to greet each customer, to give prompt and courteous assistance when asked, and to thank customers after purchases are made, but to refrain from giving extensive unsolicited advice. PacSun and PacSun Outlet stores display large assortments of name brands and proprietary brands, merchandised by category. d.e.m.o. merchandise is displayed by brand accompanied by vendor logo signage. Additionally, the stores provide a friendly and social atmosphere for teens with appropriate background music, while also providing a comfortable environment for parents and other adults. We believe the combination of our attentive customer service and unique store environments is key to our success.

Continue to Expand the Number of Stores. We intend to continue our store growth through the opening of new stores under our three existing formats in the next three years. We may also continue our growth through the launch of a fourth store format or by acquiring an existing retail chain. In each of the last three fiscal years in the period ended January 29, 2005, we opened 113, 86, and 73 net new stores, respectively. See "Store Expansion" within the "Stores" section of this document for further details regarding plans for fiscal 2005.

Offer Merchandise for Sale Over the Internet. We sell merchandise over the internet at *www.pacsun.com.* The website offers a selection of the same merchandise carried in PacSun stores. We maintain a substantial database of e-mail names that we use for marketing purposes. We also advertise our website as a shopping destination on certain internet portals and search engines and market our website in our PacSun stores using in-store signage, merchandise bags and receipts. Our internet strategy benefits from the nationwide retail presence of our stores, the strong brand

04 / Pacific Sunwear of California, Inc.

recognition of PacSun, a loyal and internet-savvy customer base, the participation of PacSun's key brands and the ability to return merchandise to PacSun stores. We plan to begin selling merchandise on our d.e.m.o. website at www.demostores.com during fiscal 2005.

MERCHANDISING

Merchandise. PacSun, PacSun Outlet and d.e.m.o. stores offer a broad selection of casual apparel, related accessories and footwear for young men ("guys") and young women ("girls"), with the goal of being viewed by our customers as the dominant retailer for their lifestyle. The following table sets forth our merchandise assortment as a percentage of net sales for the periods shown:

| | FISCAL YEAR ENDED | | |
	Jan. 29, 2005	Jan. 31, 2004	Feb. 1, 2003
Guys apparel	37%	38%	41%
Girls apparel	30	31	31
Accessories	19	19	18
Footwear	14	12	10
Total	100%	100%	100%

We offer many name brands best known by our target customers. PacSun offers a wide selection of well-known board-sport inspired name brands, such as Quiksilver/Roxy/DC Shoes, Billabong/Element, Hurley and Volcom. d.e.m.o. offers well-known name brands sought by its target customers, such as Ecko, Phat Farm/Baby Phat, Enyce, Rocawear, Sean John, Akademiks and Apple Bottoms. In addition, we continuously add and support up-and-coming new brands in both PacSun and d.e.m.o. During fiscal 2004, Quiksilver (which incorporates the Quiksilver, Roxy, and DC Shoes brands) accounted for 10.9% of total net sales and Billabong (which incorporates both Billabong and Element brands) accounted for 9.4% of total net sales. No other individual branded vendor accounted for more than 4% of total net sales during fiscal 2004.

We supplement our name brand offerings with our own proprietary brands. Proprietary brands provide us an opportunity to broaden our customer base by providing merchandise of comparable quality to brand name merchandise at lower prices, to capitalize on emerging fashion trends when branded merchandise is not available in sufficient quantities, and to exercise a greater degree of control over the flow of our merchandise. Our own product design group, in collaboration with our buying staff, designs our proprietary brand merchandise. We have a sourcing group that oversees the manufacture and delivery of our proprietary brand merchandise, with manufacturing contracted both domestically and internationally. Proprietary brand merchandise sales accounted for approximately 30%, 32% and 33% of total net sales in each of fiscal 2004, 2003 and 2002, respectively.

Vendor and Contract Manufacturer Relationships. We maintain strong and interactive relationships with our vendors, many of whose philosophies of controlled distribution and merchandise development are consistent with our own strategy. We generally purchase merchandise from vendors who prefer distributing through specialty retailers, small boutiques and, in some cases, better department stores, rather than distributing their merchandise through mass-market channels.

To encourage the design and development of new merchandise, we frequently share ideas regarding fashion trends and merchandise sell-through information with our vendors. We also suggest merchandise design and fabrication to certain vendors. We encourage the development of new vendor relationships by attending trade shows and inviting potential new vendors to make presentations of their merchandise to our buying staff.

We have cultivated our proprietary brand sources with a view toward high-quality merchandise, production reliability and consistency of fit. We source our proprietary brand merchandise both domestically and internationally in order to benefit from the lower costs associated with foreign manufacturing and the shorter lead times associated with domestic manufacturing.

Purchasing, Allocation and Distribution. Our merchandising department oversees the purchasing and allocation of our merchandise. Our buyers are responsible for reviewing branded merchandise lines from new and existing vendors, identifying emerging fashion trends, and selecting branded and proprietary brand merchandise styles in quantities, colors and sizes to meet inventory levels established by Company management. Our planning and allocation department is responsible for management of inventory levels by store and by class, allocation of merchandise to stores and inventory replenishment based upon information generated by our merchandise management information systems. These systems provide the planning department with current inventory levels at each store and for the Company as a whole, as well as current selling history within each store by merchandise classification and by style. See "Information Systems."

All merchandise is delivered to our distribution facility in Anaheim, California, where it is inspected, received into our computer system, allocated to stores, ticketed when necessary, and boxed for distribution to our stores or packaged for delivery to our internet customers. Each store is typically shipped merchandise three to five times a week, providing it with a steady flow of new merchandise. We use a national and a regional small package carrier to ship merchandise to our stores and internet customers. We may occasionally use airfreight to ship merchandise to stores during peak selling periods.

STORES

Locations. The Company has expanded from 11 stores in California at the end of fiscal 1986 to 990 stores in 50 states and Puerto Rico at the end of fiscal 2004. The table below sets forth the number of stores located in each state as of the end of fiscal 2004:

State	PacSun	PacSun Outlets	d.e.m.o.	Total	State	PacSun	PacSun Outlets	d.e.m.o.	Total
Alabama	11	2		13	Nebraska	4			4
Alaska	3		3	6	Nevada	5	2	2	9
Arizona	15	2	3	20	New Hampshire	5	1	1	7
Arkansas	2			2	New Jersey	21	3	7	31
California	83	16	35	134	New Mexico	7		1	8
Colorado	15	3	2	20	New York	35	6	9	50
Connecticut	10		4	14	North Carolina	20	2	3	25
Delaware	3	1	1	5	North Dakota	4			4
Florida	55	6	15	76	Ohio	33	2	5	40
Georgia	21	1	6	28	Oklahoma	5			5
Hawaii	7		1	8	Oregon	8	2	2	12
Idaho	4			4	Pennsylvania	42	4	7	53
Illinois	23	2	8	33	Rhode Island	2			2
Indiana	15	2	3	20	South Carolina	12	2	4	18
Iowa	9			9	South Dakota	2			2
Kansas	7			7	Tennessee	10	2	1	13
Kentucky	8		1	9	Texas	50	4	6	60
Louisiana	10		4	14	Utah	10	1		11
Maine	2	2	1	5	Vermont	3	1		4
Maryland	14	2	4	20	Virginia	20	2	5	27
Massachusetts	20	1	4	25	Washington	20	1		21
Michigan	24	3	7	34	West Virginia	7			7
Minnesota	14	1	3	18	Wisconsin	14			14
Mississippi	3			3	Wyoming	2			2
Missouri	11	3	1	15	Puerto Rico	10	2	3	15
Montana	4			4	Total	744	84	162	990

Store Expansion. During fiscal 2004, we opened 113 net new stores, which included 67 PacSun stores, 5 PacSun Outlet stores and 41 d.e.m.o. stores. In addition, we expanded or relocated 35 existing stores during fiscal 2004.

During fiscal 2005, we plan to open approximately 120 net new stores, of which approximately 70 will be PacSun stores, approximately 10 will be PacSun Outlet stores and approximately 40 will be d.e.m.o. stores, resulting in an ending total store count of approximately 1,110 stores. We also plan to expand or relocate approximately 35 existing smaller stores during fiscal 2005. As of the date of this filing, approximately 70% of the leases for the approximately 120 net new stores we expect to open in fiscal 2005 have been executed.

Our store site selection strategy is to locate our stores primarily in high-traffic, regional malls serving markets that meet our demographic criteria, including average household income and population density. We also consider mall sales per square foot, the performance of other retail tenants serving teens and young adult customers, anchor tenants and occupancy costs. We currently seek PacSun and PacSun Outlet store locations of approximately 4,000 square feet and d.e.m.o. store locations of approximately 3,000 square feet. We will begin testing 3 large-format PacSun stores during fiscal 2005 that will encompass approximately 7,500-9,000 square feet. For details concerning average costs to build and stock new and relocated stores in fiscal 2004, see Item 7, Management's Discussion and Analysis of Financial Condition and Results of Operations, "Liquidity and Capital Resources."

Our continued growth depends upon our ability to open and operate stores on a profitable basis. Our ability to expand successfully will be dependent upon a number of factors, including sufficient demand for our merchandise in existing and new markets, our ability to locate and obtain favorable store sites, negotiate acceptable lease terms, obtain adequate merchandise supply, and hire and train qualified management and other employees.

Store Operations. Our stores are open for business during mall shopping hours. Each store has a manager, one or more co-managers or assistant managers, and approximately six to twelve part-time sales associates. District managers supervise approximately seven to twelve stores and approximately six to ten district managers report to a regional director. District and store managers as well as store co-managers participate in a bonus program based on achieving predetermined levels of sales and inventory shrinkage. We have well-established store operating policies and procedures and an extensive in-store training program for new store managers and co-managers. We place great emphasis on loss prevention programs in order to control inventory shrinkage. These programs include the installation of electronic article surveillance systems in all stores, education of store personnel on loss prevention, and monitoring of returns, voids and employee sales. In each fiscal year since fiscal 1991, we have achieved an inventory shrinkage rate of 1.3% or less of net sales at retail, or 0.6% or less of net sales at cost.

INFORMATION SYSTEMS

Our merchandise, financial and store computer systems are fully integrated and operate using primarily IBM equipment. Our software is regularly upgraded or modified as needs arise or change. Our information systems provide Company management, buyers and planners with comprehensive data that helps them identify emerging trends and manage inventories. The systems include purchase order management, electronic data interchange, open order reporting, open-to-buy, receiving, distribution, merchandise allocation, basic stock replenishment, inter-store transfers, inventory and price management. Company management uses weekly best/worst item sales reports to enhance the timeliness and effectiveness of purchasing and markdown decisions. Merchandise purchases are based on planned sales and inventory levels and are frequently revised to reflect changes in demand for a particular item or classification.

All of our stores have a point-of-sale system operating on IBM in-store computer hardware. The system features bar-coded ticket scanning, automatic price look-up, electronic check and credit authorization and automatic nightly transmittal of data between the store and our corporate offices. Each of the regional directors and district managers uses a laptop computer and can instantly access appropriate or relevant Company-wide information, including actual and budgeted sales by store, district and region, transaction information and payroll data. We believe our management information systems are adequate to support our planned expansion at least through fiscal 2005.

COMPETITION

The retail apparel, footwear and accessory business is highly competitive. PacSun stores, PacSun Outlets and d.e.m.o. stores compete on a national level with certain leading department stores and national chains that offer the same or similar brands and styles of merchandise. Our stores compete with Abercrombie and Fitch, American Eagle

Outfitters, The Gap, Aeropostale and Hot Topic as well as a wide variety of regional and local specialty stores. Many of our competitors are larger and have significantly greater resources than us. We believe the principal competitive factors in our industry are fashion, merchandise assortment, quality, price, store location, environment and customer service.

TRADEMARKS AND SERVICE MARKS

We are the owner in the United States of the marks "Pacific Sunwear of California," "PacSun," "Pacific Sunwear," and "d.e.m.o." We also use and have registered, or have a pending registration on, a number of other marks. We have also registered many of our marks outside of the United States. We believe our rights in our marks are important to our business and intend to maintain our marks and the related registrations.

SEASONALITY

For details concerning the seasonality of our business, see Item 7, Management's Discussion and Analysis of Financial Condition and Results of Operations, "Seasonality and Quarterly Results."

WORKING CAPITAL CONCENTRATION

A significant portion of our working capital is related to finished goods inventory available for sale to customers as well as in our distribution center. For details concerning working capital and the merchandising risk associated with our inventories, see "Working Capital" and "Risk Factors" within Item 7, Management's Discussion and Analysis of Financial Condition and Results of Operations.

EMPLOYEES

At the end of fiscal 2004, we had approximately 13,700 employees, of whom approximately 9,800 were part-time. Of the total employees, approximately 500 were employed at our corporate headquarters and distribution center. A significant number of seasonal employees are hired during peak selling periods. None of our employees are represented by a labor union, and we believe that our relationships with our employees are good.

EXECUTIVE OFFICERS OF THE REGISTRANT

Set forth below are the names, ages, titles, and certain background information of persons serving as executive officers of the Company as of April 4, 2005:

Executive Officer	Age	Title
Greg H. Weaver	51	Executive Chairman of the Board
Seth R. Johnson	51	Chief Executive Officer
Timothy M. Harmon	53	President, Chief Merchandising Officer
Gerald M. Chaney	58	Senior Vice President, Chief Financial Officer
Thomas M. Kennedy	43	Division President of PacSun

Greg H. Weaver has served as Chairman of the Board since October 1997, as Chief Executive Officer since October 1996 and as a member of the Board of Directors since February 1996. As previously announced, Mr. Weaver will serve as Executive Chairman of the Board effective April 1, 2005 and will no longer retain the title of Chief Executive Officer. He joined the Company in July 1987 as Vice President of Stores and was promoted many times during his tenure at Pacific Sunwear, holding the titles of Senior Vice President, Executive Vice President, Chief Operating Officer and President until he ascended to his current position. Prior to joining the Company, he was employed for 13 years by Jaeger Sportswear Ltd. in both operational and merchandising capacities for the U.S. and Canadian stores.

Seth R. Johnson joined the Company in November 2004 as Chief Operating Officer and a member of the Board of Directors. He will assume the role of Chief Executive Officer beginning April 1, 2005. Prior to joining the Company, he was employed for 12 years by Abercrombie & Fitch, most recently as Chief Operating Officer and a member of their Board of Directors. Prior retail experience included employment at The Limited, BATUS Retail Group and Dayton Hudson, Inc. during a retail career that has spanned 26 years.

Timothy M. Harmon has served as President and Chief Merchandising Officer since November 1997. He joined the Company in September 1991 as Vice President of Merchandising and was promoted three times during his tenure, holding the titles of Senior Vice President and Executive Vice President of Merchandising. Prior to joining the Company, he was Vice President and General Manager of Wide-World MTV Sportswear from 1990 to 1991 and was Vice President and General Manager, Women's Division, of Chauvin International from 1986 to 1990. Prior to that, he served in various merchandising positions at Anchor Blue and at several department stores during a retail career that has spanned over 20 years.

Gerald M. Chaney joined the Company in December 2004 as Senior Vice President and Chief Financial Officer. Prior to joining the Company, he most recently served as Chief Financial Officer of Polo Ralph Lauren since November 2000. Prior to that, Mr. Chaney served as Chief Financial Officer of Kellwood Company, Senior Vice President of Administration and Chief Financial Officer of Petrie Retail, Senior Vice President of Operations and Chief Financial Officer at Crystal Brands, and held Director of Finance and Vice President of Finance roles at General Mills Fashion Group and Scott Paper.

Thomas M. Kennedy joined the Company in May 2004 as Division President of PacSun. In this position, he has responsibility for all merchandising, design and marketing of the PacSun division. Mr. Kennedy has more than 19 years experience in the retail and apparel industries, most recently as Vice President of Global Lifestyle Apparel at Nike, Inc. Prior to that, Mr. Kennedy served in various merchandising positions in roles of increased responsibility, including Buyer, Merchandise Manager, Divisional Merchandise Manager, and Vice President of Men's Apparel, at The Gap, Inc. from March 1993 to May 2001 at both Gap and Old Navy.

Item 2. Properties

Our corporate office and distribution center are located in Anaheim, California and encompass a total of approximately 550,000 square feet. We believe the current facilities are capable of servicing our operational needs through fiscal 2007. We plan to purchase additional land and begin construction of a new, additional corporate office and a new, additional distribution center before the end of fiscal 2007. We have initiated planning efforts to assess these future needs.

We lease our retail stores under operating lease agreements with initial terms ranging from approximately eight to ten years that expire at various dates through December 2018 (see Note 7 to the consolidated financial statements).

Item 3. Legal Proceedings

During fiscal 2003, we reached an agreement to settle all claims related to two lawsuits concerning overtime pay for a total of $4.0 million. The suits were Auden v. Pacific Sunwear of California, Inc., which was filed September 17, 2001, and Adams v. Pacific Sunwear of California, Inc., which was filed November 1, 2002. The complaints alleged that we improperly classified certain California-based employees as "exempt" from overtime pay. In fiscal 2004, we paid substantially all amounts due pursuant to the terms of the settlement agreement, which had been primarily accrued for during fiscal 2002. Accordingly, the settlement did not have a material impact on our results of operations for fiscal 2004 or 2003.

We are involved from time to time in litigation incidental to our business. We believe that the outcome of current litigation will not likely have a material adverse effect on our results of operations or financial condition.

Item 4. Submission of Matters to a Vote of Security Holders

No matters were submitted to a vote of the Company's shareholders during the fourth quarter of the fiscal year covered by this report.

Part II

Item 5. Market for Registrant's Common Equity and Related Stockholder Matters

Our common stock trades on the NASDAQ National Market under the symbol "PSUN". The following table sets forth for the quarterly periods indicated the high and low bid prices per share of the common stock as reported by NASDAQ (as adjusted to reflect the Company's 3-for-2 stock split in August 2003):

Fiscal 2004	High	Low	Fiscal 2003	High	Low
1st Quarter	$25.78	$21.24	1st Quarter	$15.67	$10.74
2nd Quarter	22.48	17.25	2nd Quarter	20.43	13.07
3rd Quarter	23.63	17.64	3rd Quarter	24.22	19.00
4th Quarter	25.46	21.00	4th Quarter	24.56	19.49

As of April 4, 2005, the number of holders of record of common stock of the Company was approximately 150, and the number of beneficial holders of the common stock was in excess of 32,000.

We have never declared or paid any dividends on our common stock. Our credit facility currently prohibits us from paying cash dividends on our capital stock.

Item 6. Selected Financial Data

The selected consolidated balance sheet and consolidated income statement data as of January 29, 2005, and January 31, 2004, and for each of the three fiscal years in the period ended January 29, 2005, are derived from audited consolidated financial statements of the Company included herein and should be read in conjunction with such financial statements. Such data and the selected consolidated operating data below should also be read in conjunction with "Management's Discussion and Analysis of Financial Condition and Results of Operations" included in this report. The consolidated balance sheet data as of February 1, 2003, February 2, 2002 ("fiscal 2001"), and February 4, 2001 ("fiscal 2000"), and the consolidated income statement data for each of the two fiscal years in the period ended February 2, 2002, are derived from audited consolidated financial statements of the Company, which are not included herein. All balance sheet and income statement data for prior years have been restated to reflect the impact of certain lease accounting corrections and the reclassification of e-commerce shipping and handling revenues and expenses (see Note 2 to the consolidated financial statements).

10 / Pacific Sunwear of California, Inc.

(In thousands, except per share and selected operating data)	Jan. 29, 2005	Jan. 31, 2004 (as restated)	Feb. 1, 2003 (as restated)	Feb. 2, 2002 (as restated)	Feb. 4, 2001 (as restated)
CONSOLIDATED INCOME STATEMENT DATA:					
Net sales	$1,229,762	$1,041,456	$ 847,150	$ 685,352	$ 589,707
Cost of goods sold (including buying, distribution and occupancy costs)	781,828	668,807	554,829	459,364	388,317
Gross margin	447,934	372,649	292,321	225,988	201,390
Selling, general and administrative expenses	277,921	244,422	211,101	181,717	137,767
Operating income	170,013	128,227	81,220	44,271	63,623
Net interest income/(expense)	1,889	732	(594)	470	1,344
Income before income tax expense	171,902	128,959	80,626	44,741	64,967
Income tax expense	64,998	48,759	30,960	17,182	25,213
Net income	$ 106,904	$ 80,200	$ 49,666	$ 27,559	$ 39,754
Net income per share, diluted	$ 1.38	$ 1.02	$ 0.66	$ 0.37	$ 0.54
Weighted average shares outstanding, diluted	77,464	78,850	75,147	74,488	73,234
SELECTED CONSOLIDATED OPERATING DATA:					
Stores open at end of period	990	877	791	718	589
Stores opened during period	118	90	85	135	142
Stores closed during period	5	4	12	6	3
Capital expenditures (000's)	$ 81,992	$ 49,568	$ 53,288	$ 108,065	$ 77,398
Average net sales per gross square foot [2][3]	$ 374	$ 363	$ 330	$ 321	$ 368
Average net sales per store (000's) [2][3]	$ 1,290	$ 1,229	$ 1,102	$ 1,031	$ 1,082
Square footage of gross store space	3,447,850	2,996,635	2,647,343	2,319,149	1,764,123
Comparable store net sales increase/(decrease) [3][4]	7.3%	13.1%	9.7%	(2.5)%	3.5%
CONSOLIDATED BALANCE SHEET DATA:					
Working capital	$ 257,508	$ 242,998	$ 109,305	$ 78,899	$ 79,799
Total assets	677,778	644,487	463,993	413,173	318,629
Long-term debt	–	228	1,102	24,597	–
Shareholders' equity	$ 458,034	$ 428,732	$ 302,373	$ 247,949	$ 213,131

FISCAL YEAR ENDED [1]

(1) Except for the fiscal year ended February 4, 2001, which included 53 weeks, all fiscal years presented included 52 weeks. Effective February 1, 2002, we changed our fiscal year end from the Sunday closest to the end of January to the Saturday closest to the end of January. As a result, the last day of fiscal 2001 was Saturday, February 2, 2002.

(2) For purposes of calculating these amounts, the number of stores and the amount of square footage reflect the number of months during the period that new stores and closed stores were open.

(3) These amounts have been adjusted to exclude the fifty-third week in the fiscal year ended February 4, 2001.

(4) Stores are deemed comparable stores on the first day of the first month following the one-year anniversary of their opening, relocation, expansion or conversion. In conjunction with the expansion or relocation of certain stores to a larger format with a square footage increase of 15% or more or with the conversion of certain PacSun stores to the d.e.m.o. format, we exclude each such store's net sales results from the first day of the month of its expansion, relocation or conversion.

Pacific Sunwear of California, Inc.

Index to Consolidated Financial Statements

YEARS ENDED JANUARY 29, 2005, JANUARY 31, 2004, AND FEBRUARY 1, 2003:

CONSOLIDATED FINANCIAL STATEMENTS:

Report of Independent Registered Public Accounting Firm

To the Board of Directors and Stockholders of
Pacific Sunwear of California, Inc.
Anaheim, California

We have audited the accompanying consolidated balance sheets of Pacific Sunwear of California, Inc. and subsidiaries (the "Company") as of January 29, 2005 and January 31, 2004, and the related consolidated statements of income and comprehensive income, shareholders' equity, and cash flows for each of the three years in the period ended January 29, 2005. These financial statements are the responsibility of the Company's management. Our responsibility is to express an opinion on these financial statements based on our audits.

We conducted our audits in accordance with the standards of the Public Company Accounting Oversight Board (United States). Those standards require that we plan and perform the audit to obtain reasonable assurance about whether the financial statements are free of material misstatement. An audit includes examining, on a test basis, evidence supporting the amounts and disclosures in the financial statements. An audit also includes assessing the accounting principles used and significant estimates made by management, as well as evaluating the overall financial statement presentation. We believe that our audits provide a reasonable basis for our opinion.

In our opinion, such consolidated financial statements present fairly, in all material respects, the financial position of Pacific Sunwear of California, Inc. and subsidiaries as of January 29, 2005 and January 31, 2004, and the results of their operations and their cash flows for each of the three years in the period ended January 29, 2005, in conformity with accounting principles generally accepted in the United States of America.

We have also audited, in accordance with the standards of the Public Company Accounting Oversight Board (United States), the effectiveness of the Company's internal control over financial reporting as of January 29, 2005, based on the criteria established in *Internal Control – Integrated Framework* issued by the Committee of Sponsoring Organizations of the Treadway Commission and our report, dated April 4, 2005, expressed an unqualified opinion on management's assessment of the effectiveness of the Company's internal control over financial reporting and an unqualified opinion on the effectiveness of the Company's internal control over financial reporting.

As discussed in Note 2, the accompanying consolidated financial statements as of January 31, 2004 and for the years ended January 31, 2004 and February 1, 2003 have been restated.

DELOITTE & TOUCHE LLP
Costa Mesa, California
April 4, 2005

Pacific Sunwear of California, Inc.

Consolidated Balance Sheets

(in thousands, except per share amounts)	January 29, 2005	January 31, 2004 (as restated, see Note 2)
ASSETS		
CURRENT ASSETS:		
Cash and cash equivalents	$ 64,308	$ 109,640
Short-term investments	79,223	66,235
Accounts receivable	8,129	5,194
Merchandise inventories	175,081	147,751
Prepaid expenses, includes $12,476 and $10,711 of prepaid rent, respectively	19,943	16,492
Deferred income taxes	6,134	8,225
Total current assets	352,818	353,537
PROPERTY AND EQUIPMENT:		
Land	12,156	12,156
Buildings and building improvements	26,707	26,686
Leasehold improvements	258,739	217,251
Furniture, fixtures and equipment	206,143	173,550
Total property and equipment	503,745	429,643
Less accumulated depreciation and amortization	(199,523)	(156,774)
Net property and equipment	304,222	272,869
OTHER ASSETS:		
Goodwill	6,492	6,492
Deferred compensation and other assets	14,246	11,589
Total other assets	20,738	18,081
TOTAL ASSETS	$ 677,778	$ 644,487
LIABILITIES AND SHAREHOLDERS' EQUITY		
CURRENT LIABILITIES:		
Accounts payable	$ 38,753	$ 38,668
Accrued liabilities	49,028	54,966
Current portion of capital lease obligations	1,308	1,008
Current portion of long-term debt	228	878
Income taxes payable	5,993	15,019
Total current liabilities	95,310	110,539
LONG-TERM LIABILITIES:		
Long-term debt, net of current portion	–	228
Long-term capital lease obligations, net of current portion	403	1,227
Deferred lease incentives	67,683	56,996
Deferred rent	26,826	24,325
Deferred compensation	13,298	10,925
Deferred income taxes	16,132	11,515
Other long-term liabilities	92	–
Total long-term liabilities	124,434	105,216
Commitments and contingencies (Note 7)		
SHAREHOLDERS' EQUITY:		
Preferred stock, $.01 par value; 5,000,000 shares authorized; none issued	–	–
Common stock, $.01 par value; 170,859,375 shares authorized; 74,916,773 and 78,351,302 shares issued and outstanding, respectively	749	784
Additional paid-in capital	61,310	138,877
Retained earnings	395,975	289,071
Total shareholders' equity	458,034	428,732
TOTAL LIABILITIES AND SHAREHOLDERS' EQUITY	$ 677,778	$ 644,487

See notes to consolidated financial statements

Pacific Sunwear of California, Inc.

Consolidated Statements of Income and Comprehensive Income

	FISCAL YEAR ENDED		
(in thousands, except per share amounts)	January 29, 2005	January 31, 2004 (as restated, see Note 2)	February 1, 2003 (as restated, see Note 2)
Net sales	$ 1,229,762	$ 1,041,456	$ 847,150
Cost of goods sold, including buying, distribution and occupancy costs	781,828	668,807	554,829
Gross margin	447,934	372,649	292,321
Selling, general and administrative expenses	277,921	244,422	211,101
Operating income	170,013	128,227	81,220
Interest income/(expense), net	1,889	732	(594)
Income before income tax expense	171,902	128,959	80,626
Income tax expense	64,998	48,759	30,960
Net income	$ 106,904	$ 80,200	$ 49,666
Comprehensive income	$ 106,904	$ 80,200	$ 49,666
Net income per share, basic	$ 1.41	$ 1.05	$ 0.67
Net income per share, diluted	$ 1.38	$ 1.02	$ 0.66
Weighted average shares outstanding, basic	75,825,897	76,595,758	73,931,520
Weighted average shares outstanding, diluted	77,464,115	78,849,651	75,146,991

See notes to consolidated financial statements

Pacific Sunwear of California, Inc.
Consolidated Statements of Shareholders' Equity

(in thousands, except share amounts)	Common Stock Shares	Common Stock Amount	Additional Paid-In Capital	Retained Earnings	Total
BALANCE, February 2, 2002 (as previously reported)	73,733,630	$737	$ 88,007	$159,211	$ 247,955
Prior period adjustment (Note 2)	–	–	–	(6)	(6)
BALANCE, February 2, 2002 (as restated)	73,733,630	737	88,007	159,205	247,949
Exercise of stock options and shares sold under employee stock purchase plan and restricted stock grant	500,704	5	3,439	–	3,444
Cancellation of fractional shares due to 3-for-2 stock split	(1,188)	–	(14)	–	(14)
Restricted stock award, vesting of shares	–	–	291	–	291
Tax benefits related to exercise of stock options	–	–	1,038	–	1,038
Net income (as restated, see Note 2)	–	–	–	49,666	49,666
BALANCE, February 1, 2003 (as restated, see Note 2)	74,233,146	742	92,761	208,871	302,374
Exercise of stock options and shares sold under employee stock purchase plan	4,119,753	42	30,339	–	30,381
Cancellation of fractional shares due to 3-for-2 stock split	(1,597)	–	(33)	–	(33)
Tax benefits related to exercise of stock options	–	–	15,810	–	15,810
Net income (as restated, see Note 2)	–	–	–	80,200	80,200
BALANCE, January 31, 2004 (as restated, see Note 2)	78,351,302	784	138,877	289,071	428,732
Exercise of stock options and shares sold under employee stock purchase plan	1,829,671	18	18,176	–	18,194
Repurchase and retirement of common stock	(5,264,200)	(53)	(109,449)	–	(109,502)
Restricted stock award, vesting of shares	–	–	5,471	–	5,471
Tax benefits related to exercise of stock options	–	–	8,235	–	8,235
Net income	–	–	–	106,904	106,904
BALANCE, January 29, 2005	74,916,773	$749	$ 61,310	$395,975	$ 458,034

See notes to consolidated financial statements

Pacific Sunwear of California, Inc.

Consolidated Statements of Cash Flows

	FISCAL YEAR ENDED		
(in thousands)	January 29, 2005	January 31, 2004 (as restated, see Note 2)	February 1, 2003 (as restated, see Note 2)
CASH FLOWS FROM OPERATING ACTIVITIES:			
Net income	$ 106,904	$ 80,200	$ 49,666
Adjustments to reconcile net income to net cash provided by operating activities:			
Depreciation and amortization	51,685	45,149	40,254
Loss on disposal of equipment	3,692	2,753	5,184
Tax benefits related to exercise of stock options	8,235	15,810	1,038
Change in operating assets and liabilities:			
Accounts receivable	(2,935)	(2,278)	128
Merchandise inventories	(27,330)	(24,318)	(20,921)
Prepaid expenses	(3,451)	(1,621)	(1,949)
Deferred compensation and other assets	(284)	1,344	231
Accounts payable	85	10,212	(9,037)
Accrued liabilities	(851)	17,313	16,773
Income taxes payable and deferred income taxes	(2,318)	12,279	2,191
Deferred lease incentives	10,687	4,273	5,522
Deferred rent	(1,199)	(112)	436
Other liabilities	92	–	(28)
Net cash provided by operating activities	143,012	161,004	89,488
CASH FLOWS FROM INVESTING ACTIVITIES:			
Purchases of property and equipment	(81,992)	(49,568)	(53,288)
Purchases of available-for-sale short-term investments	(1,159,375)	(436,875)	–
Maturities of available-for-sale short-term investments	1,150,125	403,675	–
Purchases of held-to-maturity short-term investments	(40,695)	(33,035)	–
Maturities of held-to-maturity short-term investments	36,957	–	–
Net cash used in investing activities	(94,980)	(115,803)	(53,288)
CASH FLOWS FROM FINANCING ACTIVITIES:			
Repurchase and retirement of common stock	(109,502)	–	–
Proceeds from exercise of stock options	18,194	30,381	3,444
Principal payments under capital lease obligations	(1,178)	(1,522)	(824)
Repayments of long-term debt obligations	(878)	(825)	(25,504)
Cash paid in lieu of fractional shares due to 3-for-2 stock split	–	(33)	(14)
Net cash (used in)/provided by financing activities	(93,364)	28,001	(22,898)
NET (DECREASE)/INCREASE IN CASH AND CASH EQUIVALENTS:	(45,332)	73,202	13,302
CASH AND CASH EQUIVALENTS, beginning of fiscal year	109,640	36,438	23,136
CASH AND CASH EQUIVALENTS, end of fiscal year	$ 64,308	$ 109,640	$ 36,438
SUPPLEMENTAL DISCLOSURES OF CASH FLOW INFORMATION:			
Cash paid for interest	$ 142	$ 226	$ 944
Cash paid for income taxes	$ 59,081	$ 20,670	$ 27,731
SUPPLEMENTAL DISCLOSURES OF NON-CASH TRANSACTIONS:			
Increase to additional paid-in capital related to the issuance of stock to satisfy certain deferred compensation liabilities	$ 5,471	$ –	$ 291
Increase in accrued capital expenditures	$ 4,084	$ 5,440	$ 2,402
Purchases of property pursuant to capital lease obligations	$ 654	$ –	$ 3,016
Purchase of maintenance agreement under long-term debt obligation	$ –	$ –	$ 2,413

See notes to consolidated financial statements

Pacific Sunwear of California, Inc.

Notes to Consolidated Financial Statements

For the Fiscal Years Ended January 29, 2005, January 31, 2004, and February 1, 2003
(all amounts in thousands, except share and per share amounts, unless otherwise indicated)

1. Summary of Significant Accounting Policies and Nature of Business

Nature of Business – Pacific Sunwear of California, Inc. and its subsidiaries (the "Company") is a leading specialty retailer of everyday casual apparel, footwear and accessories designed to meet the needs of active teens and young adults. The Company operates three nationwide, primarily mall-based chains of retail stores, under the names "Pacific Sunwear" (as well as "PacSun"), "Pacific Sunwear (PacSun) Outlet" and "d.e.m.o." Pacific Sunwear and Pacific Sunwear Outlet stores specialize in board-sport inspired casual apparel, footwear and related accessories catering to teens and young adults. d.e.m.o. specializes in hip-hop inspired casual apparel, footwear and related accessories catering to teens and young adults. In addition, the Company operates a website (www.pacsun.com) which sells PacSun merchandise online, provides content and community for its target customers, and provides information about the Company. The Company will begin selling d.e.m.o. merchandise through a new website (www.demostores.com) during fiscal 2005.

The Company's fiscal year is the 52- or 53-week period ending on the Saturday closest to January 31. Fiscal 2004 was the 52-week period ended January 29, 2005. Fiscal 2003 was the 52-week period ended January 31, 2004. Fiscal 2002 was the 52-week period ended February 1, 2003. Fiscal 2005 will be the 52-week period ending January 28, 2006.

Principles of Consolidation – The consolidated financial statements include the accounts of Pacific Sunwear of California, Inc. and its subsidiaries, Pacific Sunwear Stores Corp. and Miraloma Corp. (formerly "ShopPacSun.com Corp."). All intercompany transactions have been eliminated in consolidation.

Basis of Presentation – The consolidated financial statements have been prepared in accordance with accounting principles generally accepted in the United States of America ("GAAP").

Use of Estimates – The preparation of consolidated financial statements in conformity with accounting principles generally accepted in the United States of America necessarily requires management to make estimates and assumptions that affect the reported amounts of assets and liabilities and the disclosure of contingent assets and liabilities at the date of the consolidated financial statements as well as the reported revenues and expenses during the reporting period. Actual results could differ from these estimates.

Fair Value of Financial Instruments – Statement of Financial Accounting Standards No. 107 ("SFAS 107"), "Disclosures About Fair Value of Financial Instruments," requires management to disclose the estimated fair value of certain assets and liabilities defined by SFAS 107 as financial instruments. Financial instruments are generally defined by SFAS 107 as cash, evidence of ownership interest in an entity, or a contractual obligation that both conveys to one entity a right to receive cash or other financial instruments from another entity and imposes on the other entity the obligation to deliver cash or other financial instruments to the first entity. At January 29, 2005, management believes that the carrying amounts of cash, short-term investments, receivables and payables approximate fair value because of the short maturity of these financial instruments.

Cash and Cash Equivalents and Short-Term Investments – The Company considers all highly liquid financial instruments purchased with an original maturity of three months or less to be cash equivalents. Cash and cash equivalents consist primarily of investment grade asset-backed debt obligations, commercial paper and money market funds.

Auction rate securities, which had historically been classified as cash and cash equivalents, have been reclassified to short-term investments at January 29, 2005 and January 31, 2004, thereby reducing cash and cash equivalents by $42.5 million and $33.2 million, respectively, with corresponding increases in short-term investments. The reclassification also resulted in an increase in net cash used in investing activities for the fiscal years ended January 29, 2005 and January 31, 2004 of $9.3 million and $33.2 million, respectively. These investments, classified as available for sale, have long-term stated contractual maturities, but have variable interest rates that reset at each auction period (typically

7 days, or as long as 28 or 35 days in some cases). These securities trade in a broad, highly liquid market and the Company has never had difficulty being able to liquidate any such investment at the end of a given auction period. The Company typically reinvests these securities multiple times during the year at each new auction period. The Company has revised its presentation in the cash flow statement for fiscal 2004 and 2003 to include the gross purchases and sales of these securities as investing activities rather than as a component of cash and cash equivalents. As a result of the resetting variable rates, the Company had no cumulative gross unrealized or realized gains or losses from these investments. All income from these investments was recorded as interest income for each periods presented.

Short-term investments, other than auction rate securities, are classified as held-to-maturity and consist of marketable corporate and U.S. agency debt instruments with original maturities of three months to one year and are carried at amortized cost, less other than temporary impairments in value. At January 29, 2005, the fair value of the Company's held-to-maturity portfolio was $36.7 million, consisting of corporate debentures of $25.3 million, U.S. treasury/agency debentures of $9.9 million, and commercial paper of $1.5 million. Cost is determined by specific identification, which approximates fair value at January 29, 2005 due to the relatively short maturity period of such investments.

Merchandise Inventories – Merchandise inventories are stated at the lower of cost (first-in, first-out method) or market. Cost is determined using the retail inventory method. At any one time, inventories include items that have been marked down to management's best estimate of their fair market value. Management bases the decision to mark down merchandise primarily upon its current rate of sale and the age of the item, among other factors.

Property and Equipment – Leasehold improvements and furniture, fixtures and equipment are stated at cost. Amortization of leasehold improvements is computed on the straight-line method over the lesser of an asset's estimated useful life or the related store's lease term (generally 10 years), excluding any lease renewal options. Depreciation on furniture, fixtures and equipment is computed on the straight-line method over five years. Depreciation on buildings and building improvements is computed on the straight-line method over the estimated useful life of the asset (generally 39 years).

Goodwill and Other Intangible Assets – The Company accounts for goodwill and other intangible assets in accordance with SFAS 142, "Goodwill and Intangible Assets." The Company evaluates the recoverability of goodwill at least annually based on a two-step impairment test. The first step compares the fair value of each reporting unit with its carrying amount, including goodwill. If the carrying amount exceeds fair value, then the second step of the impairment test is performed to measure the amount of any impairment loss. Fair value is determined based on estimated future cash flows, discounted at a rate that approximates the Company's cost of capital. Such estimates are subject to change and the Company may be required to recognize impairment losses in the future.

Other Long-Lived Assets – The Company accounts for other long-lived assets in accordance with SFAS 144, "Accounting for the Impairment or Disposal of Long-Lived Assets." Under SFAS 144, long-lived assets, including amortizing intangible assets, are tested for impairment whenever events or changes in circumstances indicate that the carrying value of such assets may not be recoverable.

Insurance Reserves – The Company is responsible for workers' compensation insurance claims up to a specified aggregate stop loss amount. The Company maintains a reserve for estimated claims, both reported and incurred but not reported, based on historical claims experience and other estimated assumptions.

Income Taxes – Current income tax expense is the amount of income taxes expected to be payable for the current year. The combined federal and state income tax expense was calculated using estimated effective annual tax rates. A deferred income tax asset or liability is established for the expected future consequences of temporary differences in the financial reporting and tax bases of assets and liabilities. The Company considers future taxable income and ongoing prudent and feasible tax planning in assessing the value of its deferred tax assets. Evaluating the value of these assets is necessarily based on the Company's judgment. If the Company determines that it is more likely than not that these assets will not be realized, the Company would reduce the value of these assets to their expected realizable value through a valuation allowance, thereby decreasing net income. If the Company subsequently determined that the deferred tax assets, which had been written down, would be realized in the future, the value of the deferred tax assets would be increased, thereby increasing net income in the period when that determination was made.

Litigation – The Company is involved from time to time in litigation incidental to its business. Management believes that the outcome of current litigation will not likely have a material adverse effect upon the results of operations or financial condition of the Company and, from time to time, may make provisions for probable litigation losses. Depending on the actual outcome of pending litigation, charges in excess of any provisions could be recorded in the future, which may have an adverse affect on the Company's operating results (see Note 7).

Deferred Lease Incentives – The Company accounts for landlord allowances in accordance with SFAS 13, "Accounting for Leases," and FASB Technical Bulletin 88-1, "Issues Relating to Accounting for Leases." Accordingly, all amounts received from landlords to fund tenant improvements are recorded as a deferred liability, which is then amortized over the related store's lease term (see Note 2).

Revenue Recognition – Sales are recognized upon purchase by customers at the Company's retail store locations or upon delivery to and acceptance by the customer for orders placed through the Company's website. The Company records the sale of gift cards as a current liability and recognizes a sale when a customer redeems a gift card. The amount of the gift card liability is determined taking into account our estimate of the portion of gift cards that will not be redeemed or recovered. The Company accrues for estimated sales returns by customers based on historical sales return results. Sales return accrual activity for each of the three fiscal years in the period ended January 29, 2005 is as follows:

	Fiscal 2004	Fiscal 2003	Fiscal 2002
Beginning balance	$ 581	$ 460	$ 113
Provisions	23,812	20,629	17,363
Usage	(23,630)	(20,508)	(17,016)
Ending balance	$ 763	$ 581	$ 460

E-commerce Shipping and Handling Revenues and Expenses – The Company accounts for shipping and handling revenues and expenses in accordance with Emerging Issues Task Force ("EITF") Issue 00-10, "Accounting for Shipping and Handling Fees and Costs." All shipping and handling revenues and expenses relate to sales activity generated from the Company's website. Amounts charged to the Company's internet customers for shipping and handling revenues are included in net sales. Amounts paid by the Company for internet shipping and handling expenses are included in cost of goods sold and encompass payments to third party shippers and costs to store, move and prepare merchandise for shipment.

Customer Loyalty Programs – The Company's primary customer loyalty programs are referred to as "PacBucks" for PacSun and PacSun Outlet stores and "d.e.m.o. Dollars" for d.e.m.o. stores. The Company also has a customer loyalty discount program related to its private label credit card. These programs offer customers dollar-for-dollar discounts on future merchandise purchases within stated redemption periods if they purchase specified levels of merchandise in a current transaction. These programs are recorded as a direct reduction in net sales upon redemption, which is generally within 30 days of the original issuance and always within a given quarterly reporting period.

Cost of Goods Sold, including Buying, Distribution and Occupancy Costs – Cost of goods sold includes the landed cost of merchandise and all expenses incurred by the Company's buying and distribution functions. These costs include inbound freight, purchasing and receiving costs, inspection costs, warehousing costs, internal transfer costs, and any other costs borne by the Company's buying department and distribution center. Occupancy costs include store rents, common area charges, as well as store expenses related to telephone service, supplies, repairs and maintenance, insurance, loss prevention, and taxes and licenses.

Straight-Line Rent – The Company accounts for rent expense in accordance with SFAS 13, "Accounting for Leases," and FASB Technical Bulletin 85-3, "Accounting for Operating Leases with Scheduled Rent Increases." Accordingly, rent expense under the Company's store operating leases is recognized on a straight-line basis over the original term of each store's lease, inclusive of rent holiday periods during store construction and excluding any lease renewal options (see Note 2). The Company capitalizes rent expense attributable to the build-out period of its stores as a component cost of construction and amortizes this amount over the life of the related store's lease term once construction has completed, generally upon the commencement of store operations.

Selling, General and Administrative Expenses – Selling, general and administrative expenses include payroll, depreciation and amortization, advertising, credit authorization charges, expenses associated with the counting of physical inventories, and all other general and administrative expenses not directly related to merchandise or operating the Company's stores.

Advertising Costs – Costs associated with the production of advertising, such as photography, design, creative talent, editing and other costs, are expensed the first time the advertising becomes publicly available. Costs associated with placing advertising that has been produced, such as television and magazine advertising, are expensed when the advertising becomes publicly available. Advertising costs were $11.4 million, $10.4 million, and $8.9 million in fiscal 2004, 2003, and 2002, respectively.

Stock-Based Compensation – The Company accounts for stock-based compensation in accordance with Accounting Principles Board Opinion No. 25 (APB 25) and Financial Accounting Standards Board ("FASB") Interpretation No. 44, "Accounting for Certain Transactions Involving Stock Compensation." The Company follows the disclosure provisions of SFAS 148, "Accounting for Stock-Based Compensation – Transition and Disclosure." SFAS 148 amended SFAS 123, "Accounting for Stock-Based Compensation," to provide alternative methods for voluntary transition to SFAS 123's fair value method of accounting for stock-based employee compensation ("the fair value method"). SFAS 148 also requires disclosure of the effects of an entity's accounting policy with respect to stock-based employee compensation on reported net income (loss) and earnings (loss) per share in annual and interim financial statements. The Company has provided the additional disclosures required by SFAS 148 for fiscal 2004, 2003 and 2002 below. Beginning with the third quarter of fiscal 2005, the Company will begin expensing stock options in accordance with SFAS 123(R) (see "New Accounting Pronouncements").

SFAS 123, "Accounting for Stock-Based Compensation," requires the disclosure of pro forma net income and earnings per share. Under SFAS 123, the fair value of stock-based awards to employees is calculated through the use of option-pricing models, even though such models were developed to estimate the fair value of freely tradable, fully transferable options without vesting restrictions, which significantly differ from the Company's stock option awards. These models also require subjective assumptions, including future stock price volatility and expected time to exercise, which greatly affect the calculated values. The Company's calculations were made using the Black-Scholes option-pricing model with the following ranges of weighted average assumptions: expected life, 5 years from option date; stock volatility, 37.0% to 37.9% in fiscal 2004, 37.1% to 53.7% in fiscal 2003 and 55.1% to 62.7% in fiscal 2002; risk-free interest rates, 3.3% to 3.7% in fiscal 2004, 2.9% to 3.3% in fiscal 2003 and 3.0% to 4.7% in fiscal 2002; and no dividends during the expected term. The Company's calculations are based on a single-option valuation approach and forfeitures are recognized as they occur. If the computed fair values of the fiscal 2004, 2003 and 2002 awards had been amortized to expense over the vesting period of the awards, pro forma net income and earnings per share would have been reduced to the pro forma amounts indicated in the following table:

	Fiscal 2004	Fiscal 2003	Fiscal 2002
NET INCOME			
As reported	$106,904	$80,200	$49,666
Deduct: Total stock-based employee compensation expense determined under fair value based method for all awards, net of related tax effects	(6,330)	(5,785)	(5,589)
Pro forma	$100,574	$74,415	$44,077
NET INCOME PER SHARE, BASIC			
As reported	$ 1.41	$ 1.05	$ 0.67
Deduct: Total stock-based employee compensation expense determined under fair value based method for all awards, net of related tax effects	(0.09)	(0.07)	(0.07)
Pro forma	$ 1.32	$ 0.98	$ 0.60
NET INCOME PER SHARE, DILUTED			
As reported	$ 1.38	$ 1.02	$ 0.66
Deduct: Total stock-based employee compensation expense determined under fair value based method for all awards, net of related tax effects	(0.08)	(0.06)	(0.06)
Pro forma	$ 1.30	$ 0.96	$ 0.60

Earnings per Share – The Company reports earnings per share in accordance with the provisions of SFAS 128, "Earnings Per Share." Basic earnings per common share is computed using the weighted average number of shares outstanding. Diluted earnings per common share is computed using the weighted average number of shares outstanding adjusted for the incremental shares attributed to outstanding options to purchase common stock. Incremental shares of 1,638,218, 2,253,893, and 1,215,471, in fiscal 2004, 2003 and 2002, respectively, were used in the calculation of diluted earnings per common share. Options to purchase 998,985, 31,996, and 2,033,399 shares of common stock in fiscal 2004, 2003 and 2002, respectively, were not included in the computation of diluted earnings per common share because the option exercise price was greater than the average market price of the common stock during the respective period.

Comprehensive Income – The Company reports comprehensive income in accordance with the provisions of SFAS 130, "Reporting Comprehensive Income." SFAS 130 established standards for the reporting and display of comprehensive income. Components of comprehensive income include net earnings (loss), foreign currency translation adjustments and gains/losses associated with investments available for sale. There was no difference between net income and comprehensive income for fiscal 2004, 2003 and 2002.

Vendor and Merchandise Concentrations – During fiscal 2004, Quiksilver (which incorporates the Quiksilver, Roxy, and DC Shoes brands) accounted for 10.9% of total net sales and Billabong (which incorporates both Billabong and Element brands) accounted for 9.4% of total net sales. No other individual branded vendor accounted for more than 4% of total net sales during fiscal 2004. In prior years, no single branded vendor accounted for more than 8% of total net sales. The Company's merchandise assortment as a percentage of net sales for each of fiscal 2004, 2003 and 2002 was as follows:

Merchandise Category	Fiscal 2004	Fiscal 2003	Fiscal 2002
Guys apparel	37%	38%	41%
Girls apparel	30%	31%	31%
Accessories	19%	19%	18%
Footwear	14%	12%	10%
Total	100%	100%	100%

Segment Reporting – The Company operates exclusively in the retail apparel industry in which the Company distributes, designs and produces clothing, accessories and related products catering to the teenage/young adult demographic through primarily mall-based retail stores. The Company has identified four operating segments (PacSun stores, PacSun Outlet stores, d.e.m.o. stores, and e-commerce) as defined by SFAS 131, "Disclosures about Segments of an Enterprise and Related Information." The four operating segments have been aggregated into one reportable segment based on the similar nature of products sold, production, merchandising and distribution processes involved, target customers, and economic characteristics among the four operating segments.

New Accounting Pronouncements – In January 2003, the Financial Accounting Standards Board ("FASB") issued FIN 46, "Consolidation of Variable Interest Entities" and in December 2003, issued FIN 46(R) (revised December 2003) "Consolidation of Variable Interest Entities – An Interpretation of ARB No. 51." FIN 46 requires certain variable interest entities to be consolidated in certain circumstances by the primary beneficiary of the entity even if the investors in the entity do not have the characteristics of a controlling financial interest. The adoption of FIN 46 and FIN 46(R) did not have a material impact on the Company's financial position or results of operations because the Company has no variable interests in variable interest entities.

In March 2004, the Emerging Issues Task Force ("EITF") reached a consensus on EITF Issue No. 03-1 ("EITF 03-1"), "The Meaning of Other-Than-Temporary Impairment and Its Application to Certain Investments," for which the measurement and recognition provisions are effective for reporting periods beginning after June 15, 2004. EITF 03-1 provides a three-step process for determining whether investments, including debt securities, are other than temporarily impaired and requires additional disclosures in annual financial statements. An investment is impaired if the fair value of the investment is less than its cost. The adoption of EITF 03-1 did not have a material impact on the Company's financial position or results of operations because the Company has the ability and intent to hold all of its held-to-maturity marketable securities until maturity.

In December 2004, the FASB issued SFAS 123(R), "Share-Based Payment." SFAS 123(R) requires that companies recognize compensation expense equal to the fair value of stock options or other share-based payments over the requisite service period. The standard is effective for the Company beginning with the third quarter of fiscal 2005. The Company's net income will be reduced as a result of the recognition of the remaining amortization of the fair value of existing options (currently disclosed as pro-forma expense above in this Note 1) as well as the recognition of the fair value of all newly issued stock options, which is contingent upon the number of future options granted and other variables. The adoption of this standard will have no impact on the Company's cash flows.

Reclassifications – Certain prior year amounts have been reclassified to conform to the current year presentation.

2. Restatement of Previously Issued Financial Statements

In December 2004, the Company initiated a review of its lease accounting practices at the suggestion of a member of its Board of Directors. As a result of this review and the clarifications contained in the February 7, 2005 letter from the Office of the Chief Accountant of the Securities and Exchange Commission ("SEC") to the Center for Public Company Audit Firms of the American Institute of Certified Public Accountants regarding specific lease accounting issues, management and the Audit Committee of the Board of Directors of the Company determined that the Company's accounting practices were incorrect with respect to rent holiday periods and the classification of landlord incentives and their related amortization. The Company has made all appropriate adjustments to correct these errors for all periods presented.

In prior periods, the Company recorded straight-line rent expense for store operating leases over the related store's original lease term, beginning with the commencement date of store operations. This practice excluded recognition of rent expense for the build-out period of the Company's stores during which the Company was not required to make any rent payments and the store was not yet in operation. In correcting this practice, the Company adopted a policy wherein the rent expense attributable to the build-out period of a particular store is capitalized as a component cost of construction and amortized over the life of the related store's lease term once construction has completed, generally upon the commencement of store operations. The adoption of this policy and the correction of the lease term used in straight-line rent calculations resulted in immaterial reduction in net income of less than $0.1 million for all periods presented. However, these corrections did result in a reclassification from rent expense (within cost of goods sold) to depreciation expense (within selling, general and administrative expenses) of $1.6 million and $1.4 million for the fiscal years ended January 31, 2004 and February 1, 2003, respectively. Additionally, the cumulative impact of the corrections made to the balance sheet at January 31, 2004 resulted in an increase to each of net property and equipment and deferred rent of $12.3 million.

Also in prior periods, the Company classified landlord incentives received to fund its tenant improvements as a reduction of property and equipment rather than as a deferred lease incentive liability. The amortization of these landlord incentives was recorded as a reduction in depreciation expense rather than as a reduction of rent expense. In addition, the Company's statements of cash flow had reflected these incentives as a reduction of capital expenditures within cash flows from investing activities rather than as cash flows from operating activities. These corrections resulted in an increase to each of net property and equipment and deferred lease incentive liabilities of $56.9 million at January 31, 2004. Additionally, for each of the fiscal years in the two-year period ended January 31, 2004, the reclassification of the amortization of deferred lease incentives resulted in a decrease to rent expense (within cost of goods sold) with a corresponding increase to depreciation expense (within selling, general and administrative expenses) of $8.2 million and $7.4 million, respectively.

A summary of the impact of the restatement on the Company's consolidated balance sheet at January 31, 2004, and the consolidated income statements for the fiscal years ended January 31, 2004 and February 1, 2003, including the restatement of e-commerce shipping and handling revenues and expenses (see Note 1, "E-commerce Shipping and Handling Revenues and Expenses"), is as follows:

	JANUARY 31, 2004		
(all amounts in thousands)	As Previously Reported	Lease Accounting Adjustments	As Restated
CONSOLIDATED BALANCE SHEET			
Gross Property	$ 331,274	$ 98,369	$ 429,643
Accumulated Depreciation	(127,630)	(29,144)	(156,774)
Net Property	203,644	69,225	272,869
Deferred Income Taxes	8,224	1	8,225
Total Assets	575,261	69,226	644,487
Income Taxes Payable	15,024	(5)	15,019
Deferred Lease Incentives	–	56,996	56,996
Deferred Rent	12,046	12,279	24,325
Deferred Income Taxes	11,529	(14)	11,515
Total Long-term Liabilities	146,499	69,256	215,755
Shareholders' Equity	428,762	(30)	428,732

	FISCAL YEAR ENDED JANUARY 31, 2004			
(all amounts in thousands)	As Previously Reported	Lease Accounting Adjustments	E-commerce Adjustments	As Restated
CONSOLIDATED INCOME STATEMENT				
Net Sales	$1,040,294	$ –	$1,162	$1,041,456
Cost of Sales	676,977	(9,801)	1,631	668,807
Gross Margin	363,317	9,801	(469)	372,649
SG&A Expenses	235,068	9,823	(469)	244,422
Operating Income	128,249	(22)	–	128,227
Income Tax Provision	48,768	(9)	–	48,759
Net Income	80,213	(13)	–	80,200
Earnings Per Share, diluted	1.02	(0.00)	(0.00)	1.02

	FISCAL YEAR ENDED FEBRUARY 1, 2003			
(all amounts in thousands)	As Previously Reported	Lease Accounting Adjustments	E-commerce Reclassification	As Restated
CONSOLIDATED INCOME STATEMENT				
Net Sales	$846,393	$ –	$ 757	$847,150
Cost of Sales	562,710	(8,728)	847	554,829
Gross Margin	283,683	8,728	(90)	292,321
SG&A Expenses	202,445	8,746	(90)	211,101
Operating Income	81,238	(18)	–	81,220
Income Tax Provision	30,967	(7)	–	30,960
Net Income	49,677	(11)	–	49,666
Earnings Per Share, diluted	0.66	(0.00)	(0.00)	0.66

The corrections described above also resulted in increases in cash provided by operating activities (primarily due to increases in deferred lease incentives) with corresponding increases in cash used in investing activities (due to increased capital expenditures) for each of the fiscal years in the two-year period ended January 31, 2004 of $9.4 million, and $12.9 million, respectively. The impact of these corrections to the cash flow statements, including the impact of the reclassification of auction rate securities (see Note 1, "Cash and Cash Equivalents and Short-Term Investments"), is as follows:

(all amounts in thousands)	As Previously Reported	Lease Accounting Adjustments	Reclassification of Auction Rate Securities	As Restated
CONSOLIDATED CASH FLOW STATEMENT				
For the fiscal year ended January 31, 2004:				
Net Cash Provided by Operating Activities	$151,647	$ 9,357	$ –	$ 161,004
Net Cash Used in Investing Activities	(73,246)	(9,357)	(33,200)	(115,803)
Net Increase in Cash and Cash Equivalents	106,402	–	(33,200)	73,202
For the fiscal year ended February 1, 2003:				
Net Cash Provided by Operating Activities	76,623	12,865	–	89,488
Net Cash Used in Investing Activities	(40,423)	(12,865)	–	(53,288)
Net Increase in Cash and Cash Equivalents	13,302	–	–	13,302

3. Deferred Compensation and Other Assets

The Company maintains an Executive Deferred Compensation Plan (the "Executive Plan") covering Company officers that is funded by participant contributions and periodic Company discretionary contributions. For fiscal 2004, 2003 and 2002, the Company made contributions of $0.3 million, $0.3 million and $0.2 million, respectively, to the Executive Plan. The deferred compensation asset balance represents the investments held by the Company to cover the vested participant balances in the Executive Plan, which are represented by the deferred compensation liability of $13.3 million and $10.9 million included in long-term liabilities as of January 29, 2005 and January 31, 2004, respectively. These deferred compensation asset investments are classified as trading securities and are stated at fair market value in accordance with SFAS 115, "Accounting for Certain Investments in Debt and Equity Securities." Fair market value is determined by the most recent publicly quoted market price of the securities at the balance sheet date. For a description of other employee compensation arrangements, see Note 8.

As of the dates presented, deferred compensation and other assets consisted of the following:

	January 29, 2005	January 31, 2004
Deferred compensation investments	$13,990	$10,919
Long-term maintenance contracts	124	502
Other assets	132	168
	$14,246	$11,589

4. Credit Facility

The Company has a credit facility with a bank, which expires April 1, 2007. The credit facility provides for a $45.0 million line of credit (the "Credit Line") through March 31, 2005 to be used for cash advances, commercial letters of credit and shipside bonds. The Credit Line increases to $50.0 million from April 1, 2005 through March 31, 2006, and $60.0 million from April 1, 2006 through expiration on April 1, 2007. Interest on the Credit Line is payable monthly at the bank's prime rate (5.25% at January 29, 2005) or at optional interest rates that are primarily dependent upon the London Inter-bank Offered Rates for the time period chosen. The Company did not borrow under the credit facility at any time during fiscal 2004 or fiscal 2003. The Company had $13.1 million outstanding in commercial letters of credit at January 29, 2005. The credit facility subjects the Company to various restrictive covenants, including maintenance of certain financial ratios, and prohibits payment of cash dividends on common stock. At January 29, 2005, the Company was in compliance with all of the covenants.

5. Accrued Liabilities

As of the dates presented, accrued liabilities consisted of the following:

	January 29, 2005	January 31, 2004
Accrued compensation and benefits	$13,284	$17,578
Accrued gift cards and store merchandise credits	10,386	4,618
Accrued sales tax payable	6,647	6,189
Accrued capital expenditures	6,223	5,838
Accrued sublease loss charges (Note 7)	2,441	5,543
Accrued restricted stock compensation (Note 9)	904	5,118
Other	9,143	10,082
	$49,028	$54,966

6. Income Taxes

The components of income tax expense for the periods presented were as follows:

	Fiscal 2004	Fiscal 2003	Fiscal 2002
Current income taxes:			
Federal	$51,252	$38,129	$23,937
State	7,038	5,369	3,397
	58,290	43,498	27,334
Deferred income taxes:			
Federal	6,486	5,315	3,225
State	222	(54)	401
	6,708	5,261	3,626
	$64,998	$48,759	$30,960

A reconciliation of income tax expense to the amount of income tax expense that would result from applying the federal statutory rate to income before income taxes for the periods presented was as follows:

	Fiscal 2004	Fiscal 2003	Fiscal 2002
Provision for income taxes at statutory rate	$60,166	$45,136	$28,219
State income taxes, net of federal income tax benefit	4,719	3,455	2,469
Other	113	168	272
	$64,998	$48,759	$30,960

The major components of the Company's overall net deferred tax liability of $10.0 million and $3.3 million at January 29, 2005 and January 31, 2004, respectively, were as follows:

	January 29, 2005	January 31, 2004
Current net deferred tax asset	$ 6,134	$ 8,225
Long-term net deferred tax liability	(16,132)	(11,515)
Overall net deferred tax liability	$ (9,998)	$ (3,290)
Components:		
Depreciation and amortization	$(53,032)	$(42,964)
Deferred lease incentives	26,543	22,293
State income taxes	1,176	548
Inventory cost capitalization	2,431	1,992
Reserve for store expansion/relocation and closing costs	957	2,866
Deferred rent	4,986	4,707
Deferred compensation	5,571	6,275
Other	1,370	993
	$ (9,998)	$ (3,290)

7. Commitments and Contingencies

Operating Leases – The Company leases its retail stores and certain equipment under operating lease agreements expiring at various dates through December 2018. Substantially all of the Company's retail store leases require the Company to pay common area maintenance charges, insurance, property taxes and percentage rent ranging from 5% to 7% based on sales volumes exceeding certain minimum sales levels. The initial terms of such leases are typically ten years, many of which contain renewal options exercisable at the Company's discretion. Most leases also contain rent escalation clauses that come into effect at various times throughout the lease term. Rent expense is recorded under the straight-line method over the life of the lease (see "Straight-Line Rent" in Note 1). Other rent escalation clauses can take effect based on changes in primary mall tenants throughout the term of a given lease. Most leases also contain cancellation or kick-out clauses in the Company's favor that relieve the Company of any future obligation under a lease if specified sales levels are not achieved by a specified date. None of the Company's retail store leases contain purchase options.

As of January 29, 2005, minimum future rental commitments under non-cancelable operating leases were as follows:

FISCAL YEAR ENDING:	
January 28, 2006	$ 92,935
February 3, 2007	93,827
February 2, 2008	92,226
January 31, 2009	87,852
January 30, 2010	82,586
Thereafter	229,307
	$678,733

The rental commitments table above does not include common area maintenance (CAM) charges, which are also a required contractual obligation under the Company's store operating leases. In many of the Company's leases, CAM charges are not fixed and can fluctuate significantly from year to year for any particular store. Store rental expenses, including CAM, were $141.4 million, $121.6 million, and $111.3 million, of which $6.6 million, $4.6 million, and $2.2 million was paid as percentage rent based on sales volume for fiscal 2004, 2003 and 2002, respectively. The Company expects total CAM expenses to continue to increase as the number of stores increases from year to year.

Capital Leases – The Company acquires computer equipment from time to time pursuant to capital lease obligations. At January 29, 2005, capital leases contained interest rates ranging from 4% to 5%, required monthly principal and interest payments of $0.1 million, and expired at various dates through November 2007. The net book value of capital lease assets was $2.7 million and $3.3 million, respectively, at January 29, 2005 and January 31, 2004. Future commitments under capital lease obligations at January 29, 2005 were as follows:

FISCAL YEAR ENDING:	
January 28, 2006	$1,370
February 3, 2007	355
February 2, 2008	43
Total payments, including interest	1,768
Less interest portion	(57)
Total principal payments remaining at January 29, 2005	$1,711

Other Long-Term Debt Obligations – During fiscal 2002, the Company purchased a three-year computer maintenance agreement under a long-term debt obligation for $2.4 million. The debt obligation bears interest at 6.2% and requires quarterly principal and interest payments of $0.2 million through March 2005. Future commitments under this long-term debt obligation are as follows:

FISCAL YEAR ENDING:	
January 28, 2006	$232
Less interest portion	(4)
Total principal payments remaining at January 29, 2005	$228

Litigation – During fiscal 2003, the Company reached an agreement to settle all claims related to two lawsuits concerning overtime pay for a total of $4.0 million. The suits were Auden v. Pacific Sunwear of California, Inc., which was filed September 17, 2001, and Adams v. Pacific Sunwear of California, Inc., which was filed November 1, 2002. The complaints alleged that the Company improperly classified certain California based employees as "exempt" from overtime pay. In fiscal 2004, the Company paid substantially all amounts due pursuant to the terms of the settlement agreement, which had been primarily accrued for during fiscal 2002. The settlement did not have a material impact on the Company's results of operations for fiscal 2004 or fiscal 2003.

The Company is involved from time to time in litigation incidental to its business. Management believes that the outcome of current litigation will not likely have a material adverse effect upon the results of operations or financial condition of the Company.

Indemnities, Commitments, and Guarantees – During its normal course of business, the Company has made certain indemnities, commitments and guarantees under which it may be required to make payments in relation to certain transactions. These indemnities include those given to various lessors in connection with facility leases for certain claims arising from such facility or lease and indemnities to directors and officers of the Company to the maximum extent permitted under the laws of the State of California. The Company has issued guarantees in the form of commercial letters of credit as security for merchandise shipments from overseas. There were $13.1 million of these letters of credit outstanding at January 29, 2005. The Company has also issued a guarantee within a sublease on one of its store locations under which the Company remains secondarily liable on the sublease should the sublessee default on its lease payments. The term of the sublease ends December 31, 2014. The Company has recorded $0.4 million in accrued liabilities to recognize the estimated fair value of this guarantee, assuming that another sublessee would be found within one year should the original sublessee default. The aggregate rental payments remaining on the master lease agreement at January 29, 2005, were $5.4 million. The duration of these indemnities, commitments and guarantees varies, and in certain cases, is indefinite. The majority of these indemnities, commitments and guarantees do not provide for any limitation of the maximum potential future payments the Company could be obligated to make. The Company has not recorded any liability for these indemnities, commitments and guarantees in the accompanying consolidated balance sheets other than as noted.

The Company maintains a private label credit card through a third party to promote the PacSun brand image and lifestyle. The third party services the customer accounts and retains all risk and financial obligation associated with any outstanding balances on customer accounts. The Company has no financial obligation and does not provide any guarantee related to any outstanding balances resulting from the use of these private label credit cards by its customers.

Sublease Loss Charges – During fiscal 2004, the Company executed a lease termination agreement related to the Company's former corporate offices and distribution center. The Company retains no future obligations regarding these premises.

The Company remains liable under an operating lease covering a former store location. The Company has subleased 4,400 of a total 5,200 square feet of these premises. At January 29, 2005, the Company had $2.0 million recorded in accrued liabilities to account for the Company's net remaining contractual lease obligations for this location, which includes estimated sublease assumptions for the remaining 800 square feet. The Company continues to update its sublease assumptions on a quarterly basis based on its review of current real estate market conditions and any ongoing negotiations. To the extent management's estimates relating to the Company's ability to sublease these facilities at the assumed rates or within the assumed timeframes changes or is incorrect, additional charges or reversals of previous charges may be recorded in the future. At January 29, 2005, the gross remaining obligations under the Company's original lease, exclusive of any sublease income, were approximately $6.1 million.

8. Common Stock

Stock Split – On August 25, 2003, the Company effected a three-for-two stock split. Shareholders' equity was restated to give retroactive recognition to the stock split in prior periods by reclassifying the par value ($0.2 million) of the additional shares arising from the split from additional paid-in capital to common stock. Additionally, all share and per share amounts were restated to give effect to the stock split in prior periods.

Common Stock Purchase and Retirement – The Company's Board of Directors has authorized a common stock repurchase plan in three separate authorizations. The Company's stock repurchase activity under this plan is as follows:

Period	# of Shares Purchased	Average Price Paid Per Share	# of Shares Purchased as Part of Publicly Announced Plan	Value of Shares Purchased	Maximum Value of Shares that May Yet be Purchased Under the Plan
AUTHORIZATION #1(1)					
February 2004	75.0	$23.99	75.0	$ 1,799.3	
April 2004	2,148.7	$22.43	2,148.7	$ 48,195.4	
Total	2,223.7	$22.48	2,223.7	$ 49,994.7	$ 5.3
AUTHORIZATION #2(2)					
June 2004	482.1	$19.70	482.1	$ 9,495.3	
July 2004	812.4	$19.01	812.4	$ 15,440.6	
Total	1,294.5	$19.26	1,294.5	$ 24,935.9	$ 64.1
AUTHORIZATION #3(3)					
August 2004	1,746.0	$19.80	1,746.0	$ 34,570.8	$15,429.2
GRAND TOTAL	5,264.2	$20.80	5,264.2	$109,501.4	$15,498.6

(1) On January 28, 2004, the Company announced that the Board of Directors had authorized the Company to purchase up to $50 million or 2.5 million shares of the Company's common stock in open market transactions. There was no expiration date specified for this authorization. The Company has substantially completed its repurchase and retirement of shares pursuant to this authorization.

(2) On May 10, 2004, the Company announced that the Board of Directors had authorized the Company to purchase up to an additional $25 million of the Company's common stock in open market transactions. There was no expiration date specified for this authorization. The Company has substantially completed its repurchase and retirement of shares pursuant to this authorization.

(3) On August 18, 2004, the Company's Board of Directors authorized the Company to purchase up to an additional $50 million of the Company's common stock in open market transactions. There was no expiration date specified for this authorization.

Shareholder Rights Plan – In December 1998, the Board of Directors approved the adoption of a Shareholder Rights Plan ("the Rights Plan"). The Rights Plan provides for the distribution to the Company's shareholders of one preferred stock purchase "Right" for each outstanding share of the Company's common stock. The Rights have an exercise price of $75 per Right, subject to subsequent adjustment. Initially, the Rights will trade with the Company's common stock, and will not be exercisable until the occurrence of certain takeover-related events, as defined. The Rights Plan provides that if a person or group acquires more than 15% of the Company's stock without prior approval of the Board of Directors, holders of the Rights will be entitled to purchase the Company's stock at half of market value. The Rights Plan also provides that if the Company is acquired in a merger or other business combination after a person or group acquires more than 15% of the Company's stock without prior approval of the Board of Directors, holders of the Rights will be entitled to purchase the acquirer's stock at half of market value. The Rights were distributed to holders of the Company's common stock of record on December 29, 1998, as a dividend, and will expire, unless earlier redeemed, on December 29, 2008.

9. Stock Option and Retirement Plans

Under the Company's stock option plans, incentive and nonqualified options have been granted to employees and directors to purchase common stock at prices equal to the fair value of the Company's shares at the respective grant dates.

At January 29, 2005, outstanding incentive and nonqualified options had exercise prices ranging from $0.68 to $25.50 per share, with an average exercise price of $14.68 per share, and generally begin vesting one year after the grant date. On the initial vesting date, 25% of the options vest and, thereafter, options generally continue to vest at 2.08% each calendar month. The options generally expire ten years from the date of grant or 90 days after employment or services are terminated.

At January 29, 2005, incentive and nonqualified options to purchase 4,891,847 shares were outstanding and 2,851,216 shares were available for future grant under the Company's stock option plans. During fiscal 2004, 2003 and 2002, the Company recognized tax benefits of $8.2 million, $15.8 million, and $1.0 million, respectively, resulting from the exercise of certain nonqualified stock options.

Stock option (incentive and nonqualified) activity for each of the fiscal years in the three-year period ended January 29, 2005, was as follows:

	Fiscal 2004	Fiscal 2003	Fiscal 2002
BEGINNING OPTIONS OUTSTANDING	5,474,092	8,691,197	7,198,026
Options granted	1,613,700	1,101,351	2,289,238
Options canceled	(425,290)	(253,916)	(354,282)
Options exercised	(1,770,655)	(4,064,540)	(441,785)
Ending options outstanding	4,891,847	5,474,092	8,691,197
Ending options exercisable	2,040,723	2,272,058	4,576,850
BEGINNING WEIGHTED AVERAGE EXERCISE PRICE	$ 10.47	$ 8.56	$ 7.98
Options granted	23.69	13.92	10.23
Options canceled	15.51	10.65	9.91
Options exercised	9.69	7.31	6.68
Ending weighted average exercise price	$ 14.68	$ 10.47	$ 8.56
Ending weighted average exercise price of exercisable options	$ 10.40	$ 9.68	$ 7.59
Weighted average fair value of options granted during the fiscal year	$ 9.26	$ 5.27	$ 5.09

Additional information regarding options outstanding as of January 29, 2005, is as follows:

	Options Outstanding			Options Exercisable	
Range of Exercise Prices	Number Outstanding as of Jan. 29, 2005	Weighted Average Remaining Contractual Life	Weighted Average Exercise Price	Number Exercisable as of Jan. 29, 2005	Weighted Average Exercise Price
$ 0.68 – $ 7.55	635,507	5.60	$ 6.89	408,022	$ 6.57
7.60 – 9.36	269,118	3.67	8.87	228,015	8.94
9.44 – 9.49	529,394	7.01	9.49	259,967	9.49
9.51 – 11.47	541,922	5.14	10.84	512,224	10.88
11.67 – 12.11	514,349	7.96	12.10	166,733	12.10
12.13 – 13.36	554,136	7.46	12.65	298,684	12.80
13.56 – 21.22	491,402	8.13	17.03	154,183	15.10
21.30 – 24.61	488,219	9.59	22.64	12,895	22.53
24.75 – 24.75	855,800	9.07	24.75	0	N/A
24.82 – 25.50	12,000	9.07	25.20	0	N/A
$ 0.68 – $25.50	4,891,847	7.32	$14.68	2,040,723	$10.40

During the year ended February 1, 1998, the Company granted a restricted stock award of 427,141 shares with a purchase price of $0.01 per share to its Chief Executive Officer ("CEO"). The award vested 25% on each of March 31, 1999, 2000, 2001 and 2002, as, in each instance, certain cumulative earnings per share growth targets had been satisfied. The Company recorded $40 of compensation expense for this award during fiscal 2002.

During the year ended January 30, 2000, the Company granted a restricted stock award of 112,500 shares with a purchase price of $0.01 per share to its Chief Executive Officer ("CEO"). The award was scheduled to vest 25% on each of September 17, 2001, 2002, 2003 and 2004, if, in each instance, certain cumulative annual earnings per share growth targets had been satisfied. Under the award agreement, shares that did not vest at a given vesting date due to the cumulative annual earnings per share growth targets not being met remained available for future vesting if the cumulative annual earnings per share growth targets were met as of a subsequent vesting date. During fiscal 2004, the Company's Board of Directors verified that the final cumulative annual earnings per share growth target for this award had been met. Accordingly, the CEO became vested in and received the total share award of 112,500 shares during fiscal 2004 and, as a result, the Company reclassified previously recognized accrued compensation of $2.6 million from accrued liabilities to additional paid-in capital.

During the year ended February 4, 2001, the Company granted a restricted stock award of 168,750 shares with a purchase price of $0.01 per share to its CEO. The award was scheduled to vest 25% on each of March 15, 2002, 2003, 2004 and 2005, if, in each instance, certain cumulative annual earnings per share growth targets have been satisfied. Under the award agreement, shares that do not vest at a given vesting date due to the cumulative annual earnings per share growth targets not being met remain available for future vesting if the cumulative annual earnings per share growth targets are met as of a subsequent vesting date. During fiscal 2004, the Company's Board of Directors verified that the third cumulative annual earnings per share growth target for this award had been met. Accordingly, the CEO became vested in and received 75% of the total share award, or 126,563 shares. As a result of the delivery of 126,563 shares to the CEO during fiscal 2004, the Company reclassified previously recognized accrued compensation of $2.9 million from accrued liabilities to additional paid-in capital. At January 29, 2005, the Company had accrued $0.9 million to recognize the cumulative vested fair value of the remaining 42,187 shares. This amount is included in accrued liabilities (see Note 5) on the balance sheet. Subsequent to January 29, 2005, the Company's Board of Directors verified that the final cumulative annual earnings per share growth target for this award had been met. Accordingly, the CEO became vested in and received the remaining 42,187 shares in March 2005. As a result of the delivery of the final 42,187 shares to the CEO in March 2005, the Company reclassified previously recognized accrued compensation of $1.1 million from accrued liabilities to additional paid-in capital.

The Company accounts for its stock-based awards issued to employees using the intrinsic value method in accordance with APB Opinion No. 25, "Accounting for Stock Issued to Employees," and its related interpretations. Accordingly, no compensation expense has been recognized in the financial statements for employee stock arrangements, other than described above. Beginning with the third quarter of fiscal 2005, the Company will begin expensing stock options in accordance with SFAS 123(R) (see "New Accounting Pronouncements" in Note 1).

The Company maintains an Employee Stock Purchase Plan (the "ESPP"), which provides a method for Company employees to voluntarily purchase Company common stock at a 10% discount from fair market value as of the beginning or the end of each six-month purchasing period, whichever is lower. The ESPP covers substantially all employees, except officers, who have three months of service with the Company. The ESPP is intended to constitute an "employee stock purchase plan" within the meaning of Section 423 of the Internal Revenue Code of 1986, as amended, and therefore the Company does not recognize compensation expense related to the ESPP. In fiscal 2004 and 2003, 59,016 and 55,293 shares were issued at an average price of $17.52 and $12.46, respectively, under the ESPP.

The Company also maintains an Employee Savings Plan (the "401(k) Plan"). The 401(k) Plan is a defined contribution plan covering substantially all employees who have reached age 21 and have one year of service with the Company. The 401(k) Plan is funded by employee contributions and periodic Company discretionary contributions, which are subject to approval by the Company's Board of Directors. For fiscal 2004, 2003 and 2002, the Company made contributions, net of forfeitures, of $0.5 million, $0.5 million, and $0.3 million, respectively, to the 401(k) Plan.

10. Quarterly Financial Data (Unaudited)

Summarized quarterly financial information in each of fiscal 2004 and 2003 has been restated for the Company's corrections to properly account for tenant improvement allowances and rent holidays (see Note 2). Restated amounts also include the impact of the reclassification of e-commerce shipping and handling revenues and expenses.

(in thousands, except share and per share amounts)	First Quarter (as restated)	Second Quarter (as restated)	Third Quarter (as restated)	Fourth Quarter (as restated)
FISCAL YEAR ENDED JANUARY 29, 2005:				
Net sales	$ 245,501	$ 275,139	$ 329,447	$ 379,675
Gross margin	86,205	97,614	121,559	142,556
Operating income	23,613	30,749	50,875	64,775
Net income	14,969	19,317	31,889	40,728
Net income per share, basic	$ 0.19	$ 0.25	$ 0.43	$ 0.55
Net income per share, diluted	$ 0.19	$ 0.25	$ 0.42	$ 0.54
Wtd. avg. shares outstanding, basic (Note 1)	78,157,771	76,322,161	74,415,403	74,408,255
Wtd. avg. shares outstanding, diluted (Note 1)	80,146,144	77,911,595	75,919,451	75,856,319
FISCAL YEAR ENDED JANUARY 31, 2004:				
Net sales	$ 198,519	$ 234,612	$ 281,541	$ 326,784
Gross margin	65,975	82,239	103,074	121,362
Operating income	12,889	21,649	39,254	54,435
Net income	7,977	13,377	24,505	34,340
Net income per share, basic	$ 0.11	$ 0.18	$ 0.32	$ 0.44
Net income per share, diluted	$ 0.10	$ 0.17	$ 0.31	$ 0.43
Wtd. avg. shares outstanding, basic (Note 1)	74,524,548	75,885,641	77,685,516	78,287,219
Wtd. avg. shares outstanding, diluted (Note 1)	76,472,511	78,104,037	79,876,426	80,226,072

(in thousands, except share and per share amounts)	First Quarter (as previously reported)	Second Quarter (as previously reported)	Third Quarter (as previously reported)	Fourth Quarter (as previously reported)
FISCAL YEAR ENDED JANUARY 29, 2005:				
Net sales	$ 245,131	$ 274,797	$ 329,447	$ 379,675
Gross margin	83,572	94,820	118,620	142,556
Operating income	23,621	30,759	50,887	64,775
Net income	14,974	19,325	31,897	40,728
Net income per share, basic	$ 0.19	$ 0.25	$ 0.43	$ 0.55
Net income per share, diluted	$ 0.19	$ 0.25	$ 0.42	$ 0.54
Wtd. avg. shares outstanding, basic (Note 1)	78,157,771	76,322,161	74,415,403	74,408,255
Wtd. avg. shares outstanding, diluted (Note 1)	80,146,144	77,911,595	75,919,451	75,856,319
FISCAL YEAR ENDED JANUARY 31, 2004:				
Net sales	$ 198,331	$ 234,392	$ 281,541	$ 326,318
Gross margin	63,855	79,834	100,500	119,011
Operating income	12,893	21,654	39,259	54,442
Net income	7,979	13,380	24,509	34,346
Net income per share, basic	$ 0.11	$ 0.18	$ 0.32	$ 0.44
Net income per share, diluted	$ 0.10	$ 0.17	$ 0.31	$ 0.43
Wtd. avg. shares outstanding, basic (Note 1)	74,524,548	75,885,641	77,685,516	78,287,219
Wtd. avg. shares outstanding, diluted (Note 1)	76,472,511	78,104,037	79,876,426	80,226,072

Earnings per basic and diluted share are computed independently for each of the quarters presented based on diluted shares outstanding per quarter and, therefore, may not sum to the totals for the year. Additionally, the sum of the four quarterly amounts for any line item may not agree to the fiscal year total in the consolidated financial statements due to rounding.

AMERICAN EAGLE
OUTFITTERS
ae.com

2004 ANNUAL REPORT

Dear Shareholders:

During the year, our brand gained momentum and we strengthened our organization throughout. Our customers responded with enthusiasm to compelling merchandise assortments and a renewed AE brand focus.

We ended the year in excellent financial condition. Sales for the year reached a record $1.9 billion, increasing 31%, driven by a comparable store sales increase of 21%. Strong full-priced selling and significantly lower markdowns drove our income from continuing operations to a record $224 million for the year, reflecting a 170% increase. Cash, short and long-term investments increased $312 million to a year-end balance of $674 million.

Fiscal 2004 marked an important turning point for our company. The year was driven by significant changes that were made throughout our organization. We strengthened our talent, retooled our process, upgraded systems and re-connected with our core customers. All of these improvements remain in place today, which I am certain have enhanced our brand's position in the marketplace, and will enable us to sustain earnings growth for years to come.

Today, I believe we have the best, most talented and experienced professionals our company has ever had. Our merchandising and design teams are creating fashion-right collections that are defining the American Eagle brand. As we move forward, delivering trend-right, quality merchandise is our number one priority.

Last year, we strengthened the commitment to our 15 to 25 year-old target customers. Several thousand one-on-one interviews led us to make changes to our fits and styles. Just as importantly, we enhanced our value message, offering great items at great prices, everyday. Our customers have responded with enthusiasm. Strong comparable store sales in 2004 were led by higher transaction counts and increased full-priced selling. We recognize now more than ever, the importance of staying true to our core customers - and that's a key focus at American Eagle Outfitters today.

With that in mind, we've built a powerful, brand-defining denim business. American Eagle has become a true destination store for jeans. In 2004, we nearly doubled our market share in specialty store denim, making AE jeans the 2nd most purchased brand by 15 to 25 year-olds. Now, we're after the number one slot. We have tremendous opportunities in other product categories as well. Driving productivity across key areas of our business is a major initiative going forward.

I believe we have one of the best real estate portfolios in all of specialty retail. Over the past five years, we have vastly upgraded our store base. Since 2000, we have opened 220 "A" center stores, located in the busiest and most productive malls. We completed 257 store renovations, giving new life to some of our older real estate. And for 94 additional stores, we relocated to a better location within the mall, providing greater access and visibility to the American Eagle brand.

Over the next several years, we will continue upgrading stores across the country, penetrating existing markets, expanding important regions including the West Coast and adding new flagship stores to key markets like Manhattan and Seattle. While obtaining the best real estate is important, we clearly recognize that highly productive stores are created by more than brick and mortar. I can say with confidence that we have one of the best teams in the industry operating our store base, with the experience and know-how to drive our business further.

Gaining efficiencies through new systems continues to be a top priority. Last year, we invested in markdown optimization software. We expect this tool to help us more effectively manage and reduce our markdowns. Within stores, we have traffic counters fully installed across the chain. Everyday, we are learning more about store traffic trends and transaction data — knowledge that I believe will lead us to increased store productivity.

With the American Eagle brand refocused and on-track, the time was right to start building the groundwork for our next concept. In late 2004, we hired a seasoned and highly talented team to lead the development and expansion of our next brand. I am confident that we will create an exciting new specialty retailer that is unique in the marketplace and complementary to the AE brand.

We entered the new year with optimism and passion about our future opportunities. Our outlook is bright, and our enthusiasm is high. I am absolutely convinced that we are very well positioned for continued success. We have a lot to look forward to!

Thank you for your loyalty and continued support.

James V. O'Donnell
Chief Executive Officer

1

PART I

ITEM 1. BUSINESS.

Overview

American Eagle Outfitters, Inc., a Delaware corporation, is a leading lifestyle retailer that designs, markets and sells our own brand of relaxed, casual clothing for 15 to 25 year olds, providing high-quality merchandise at affordable prices. We opened our first American Eagle Outfitters store in the United States in 1977 and expanded the brand into Canada in 2001. We also distribute merchandise via our e-commerce operation, ae.com. Our collection offers modern basics like jeans, cargo pants, and graphic T's as well as a stylish assortment of accessories, outerwear and footwear under our American Eagle Outfitters® and AE® brand names.

As of January 29, 2005, we operated 846 American Eagle Outfitters stores in the United States and Canada.

As used in this report, all references to "we," "our," and "the Company" refer to American Eagle Outfitters, Inc. and its wholly-owned subsidiaries. The term "American Eagle" refers to our U.S. and Canadian American Eagle Outfitters stores and the Company's e-commerce operation. "Bluenotes" refers to the Bluenotes/Thriftys specialty apparel chain which we operated in Canada prior to its disposition during Fiscal 2004.

Information concerning the Company's business segments and certain geographic information is contained in Note 2 of the Consolidated Financial Statements included in this Form 10-K and is incorporated herein by reference.

Organization

On April 13, 1994, the Company successfully completed an initial public offering of its common stock. Our stock is traded on the Nasdaq National Market under the symbol "AEOS".

In November 2000, we acquired three businesses in Canada - the Bluenotes chain, a Canadian brand which we disposed of during Fiscal 2004; the Braemar chain, with real estate in prime mall locations, of which 46 were converted to American Eagle stores during Fiscal 2001; and National Logistics Services ("NLS"), a 400,000 square foot distribution center near Toronto, which handles all of the distribution needs for our Canadian stores and provides services to third parties.

In December 2004, we completed the disposition of Bluenotes to 6295215 Canada Inc. (the "Purchaser"), a privately held Canadian company. As a result, the Company's Consolidated Statements of Operations and Consolidated Statements of Cash Flows reflect Bluenotes' results of operations as discontinued operations for all periods presented (note that amounts in the Company's Consolidated Balance Sheets have not been reclassified to reflect Bluenotes as discontinued operations). See Note 10 of the Consolidated Financial Statements for additional information regarding this transaction.

Our financial year is a 52/53 week year that ends on the Saturday nearest to January 31. As used herein, "Fiscal 2004," "Fiscal 2003" and "Fiscal 2002" refer to the fifty-two week periods ended January 29, 2005, January 31, 2004 and February 1, 2003, respectively. "Fiscal 2005" refers to the fifty-two week period ending January 28, 2006.

2

Growth Strategy

Store Growth

Our primary store growth strategy is to continue our expansion throughout the United States and Canada by filling in existing markets. At the end of Fiscal 2004, we operated in 49 states, the District of Columbia and Puerto Rico. We opened 37 net new U.S. stores during Fiscal 2004, increasing our U.S. store base by approximately 5% to 777 stores. Additionally, our U.S. gross square footage increased by approximately 7% during Fiscal 2004 due to the new store openings as well as incremental square footage from 36 U.S. store remodels.

During Fiscal 2004, we continued to grow in the western U.S. with 40% of our store openings in that region. We added seven new stores in California, a market with strong demographics for our target customer. We continue to expand in our newer markets including Puerto Rico, where we opened an additional store during Fiscal 2004. We also opened our second "flagship" store in New York City this year, located on West 34th Street in Herald Square. Our flagship locations utilize a larger store format in which we offer our customers a broader merchandise selection.

In Fiscal 2005, we plan to enter Alaska with two new store locations. These openings will expand our operations into all 50 states. We also plan to open our third "flagship" store in New York City, located in Union Square, and an additional "flagship" store in downtown Seattle next year. Our performance is strong in our new markets and we will continue to explore similar opportunities for new store growth. Our research has shown that there are still attractive retail locations where we can open American Eagle stores in enclosed regional malls, urban areas and lifestyle centers.

During Fiscal 2004, we opened five new stores in Canada, including four locations in the province of Quebec, which increased our total Canadian store base by approximately 6% to 69 stores. We also closed one Canadian store during the year. We remain pleased with the results of our American Eagle expansion into Canada and look to a long-term potential of approximately 80 stores across the country.

The table below shows certain information relating to our historical American Eagle store growth in the U.S. and Canada:

	Fiscal 2004	Fiscal 2003	Fiscal 2002	Fiscal 2001	Fiscal 2000
Stores at beginning of period	805	753	678	554	466
Stores opened during the period	50	59	79	127	90
Stores closed during the period	(9)	(7)	(4)	(3)	(2)
Total stores at end of period	**846**	**805**	**753**	**678**	**554**

Store Remodeling and Refurbishment Opportunities

The Company continues to remodel its older stores into its new store format. In order to maintain a balanced presentation and to accommodate additional product categories, we selectively enlarge our stores during the remodeling process. We select stores for expansion based on market demographics and store volume forecasts. In most cases stores selected for expansion increase from an average of 4,000 gross square feet to an average of 6,000 gross square feet. We believe the larger format can better accommodate our new merchandise categories and support future growth. In certain cases, we also upgrade the store location within the mall. During Fiscal 2004 we remodeled 36 stores in the U.S. to the new store design, of which 9 stores were expanded, 13 stores were relocated within the mall and 14 stores were refurbished as further discussed below. As of January 29, 2005, approximately three-fourths of all American Eagle stores in the U.S. are in our new store format.

3

During Fiscal 2004, the Company initiated a store refurbishment program, targeted towards our lower volume stores, typically located in smaller markets. Stores selected as part of this program maintain their current location and size but are updated with certain aspects of our new store format, including paint and certain new fixtures. This program provides a cost effective update for our lower volume stores. We refurbished 14 stores in the U.S. during Fiscal 2004.

Other Growth Opportunities

American Eagle sells merchandise via its e-commerce site, ae.com, which is an extension of the lifestyle that we convey in our stores. During Fiscal 2004, ae.com began shipping internationally to 24 countries, providing us an opportunity to grow in regions where we do not currently have store locations.

During Fiscal 2004, the Company announced plans to develop a new brand (the "new concept") that will target a different demographic than the American Eagle brand. The Company currently has creative and operational teams in place and we expect to open test stores for the new concept in 2006.

Store Locations

Our stores average approximately 5,400 gross square feet and approximately 4,400 on a selling square foot basis. At January 29, 2005, we operated 846 stores in the United States and Canada as shown below:

United States, including the Commonwealth of Puerto Rico - 777 stores

Alabama	15	Indiana	18	Nebraska	6	Rhode Island	3
Arizona	12	Iowa	14	Nevada	5	South Carolina	12
Arkansas	4	Kansas	7	New Hampshire	5	South Dakota	2
California	62	Kentucky	12	New Jersey	20	Tennessee	20
Colorado	12	Louisiana	13	New Mexico	4	Texas	56
Connecticut	10	Maine	3	New York	37	Utah	11
Delaware	3	Maryland	17	North Carolina	24	Vermont	3
District of Columbia	1	Massachusetts	25	North Dakota	4	Virginia	26
Florida	42	Michigan	30	Ohio	38	Washington	16
Georgia	23	Minnesota	15	Oklahoma	11	West Virginia	7
Hawaii	4	Mississippi	6	Oregon	9	Wisconsin	13
Idaho	3	Missouri	16	Pennsylvania	46	Wyoming	2
Illinois	26	Montana	2	Puerto Rico	2		

Canada - 69 stores

Alberta	7	New Brunswick	3	Ontario	37
British Columbia	10	Newfoundland	2	Quebec	4
Manitoba	2	Nova Scotia	2	Saskatchewan	2

Purchasing

The Company purchases merchandise from suppliers who either manufacture their own merchandise or supply merchandise manufactured by others, or both. During Fiscal 2004, the Company purchased a majority of its merchandise from non-North American suppliers.

All of our merchandise suppliers receive a vendor compliance manual that describes our quality standards and shipping instructions. We maintain a quality control department at our distribution centers to inspect incoming merchandise shipments for uniformity of sizes and colors, and for overall quality of manufacturing. Periodic quality

4

inspections are also made by our employees at manufacturing facilities to identify quality problems prior to shipment of merchandise.

Global Labor Compliance

The Company is firmly committed to the goal of using only the most highly regarded and efficient suppliers throughout the world. We require our suppliers to provide a workplace environment that not only meets basic human rights standards, but also one that complies with all local legal requirements and encourages opportunity for all, with dignity and respect.

For many years, we have had a policy for the inspection of factories throughout the world where goods are produced to our order. This inspection process is important for quality control purposes, as well as customs compliance and human rights standards. During Fiscal 2001, we strengthened and formalized the process by developing and implementing a comprehensive vendor compliance program with the assistance of an internationally recognized consulting firm. This program contractually requires all suppliers to meet our global workplace standards, including human rights standards, as set forth in our Code of Conduct. The Code of Conduct is required to be posted in all factories in the local language. The program utilizes third party inspectors to audit compliance by vendor factories with our workplace standards and Code of Conduct.

Security Compliance

During recent years, there has been an increasing focus within the international trade community on concerns related to global terrorist activity. The security issues posed by 9/11 and other terrorist threats have brought increased demands from the Bureau of Customs and Border Protection ("CBP") and other agencies within the Department of Homeland Security that importers take responsible action to secure their supply chains. In response, the Company became a certified member of the Customs – Trade Partnership Against Terrorism program ("C-TPAT") during 2004. C-TPAT is a voluntary program offered by CBP in which an importer agrees to work with CBP to strengthen overall supply chain security. As a result, the Company's internal security procedures were validated by CBP during February 2005 and a validation of processes with respect to our external partners will be completed in June 2005. Additionally, the Company took significant steps to expand the scope of our security procedures during 2004, including, but not limited to, a significant increase in the number of factory audits performed; a revision of the factory audit format to include a review of all critical security issues as defined by CBP; a review of security procedures of our other international trading partners, including forwarders, consolidators, shippers and brokers; and a requirement that all of our international trading partners be members of C-TPAT.

Trade Compliance

During 2003, the Company was selected by CBP for a Focused Assessment Audit. The purpose of this audit was to review and evaluate our adherence to CBP's rules and regulations regarding trade compliance issues such as merchandise classification, valuation and origin. The Company's audit was completed during May 2004 and resulted in no unacceptable risks of non-compliance being found.

Merchandise Inventory, Replenishment and Distribution

Purchase orders, executed by our buyers, are entered into the merchandise system at the time of order. Merchandise is normally shipped directly from vendors and routed to our two distribution centers, one in Warrendale, PA and the other in Ottawa, KS. Upon receipt, merchandise is entered into the merchandise system, then processed and prepared for shipment to the stores or forwarded to a warehouse holding area to be used as store replenishment goods. The allocation of merchandise among stores varies based upon a number of factors, including geographic location, customer demographics and store size. These factors impact anticipated sales volume and the quantity and mix of merchandise allocated to stores. Merchandise is shipped to the stores two to five times per week depending upon the season and store requirements. Ae.com, the Company's e-commerce operation, uses a third-party vendor for its fulfillment services.

Part I

5

Our stores in Canada receive merchandise from NLS, our Canadian distribution network which consists of a 400,000 square foot central distribution center near Toronto and five smaller sub-centers located in Toronto and across Canada totaling approximately 120,000 square feet. Merchandise is shipped to the stores two to five times per week depending upon the season and store requirements.

To support new store growth, over the past several years, we have improved our primary distribution facilities by installing a new warehouse management system, which makes the distribution process more efficient and productive. Additionally, to support our geographical expansion into the Northwest and Southwest, we purchased an existing distribution center in Ottawa, Kansas, which was opened in June 2001. This facility comprises approximately 400,000 square feet and will support our continuing American Eagle store growth in the western U.S. as well as the store growth of our new concept. This second facility increases our potential capacity to roughly 1,100 stores and gives the Company one or two day shipping times to approximately 85% of our stores. We also operate a facility near Puebla, Mexico, which supports our knit and denim production with warehousing, deconsolidation, product development and testing, quality control, and other value added services.

Customer Credit and Returns

We offer our U.S. customers an American Eagle private label credit card, issued by a third-party bank. We have no liability to the card issuer for bad debt expense, provided that purchases are made in accordance with the issuing banks' procedures. We believe that providing in-store credit through use of our proprietary credit card promotes incremental sales and encourages customer loyalty. Our credit card holders receive special promotional offers and advance notice of all in-store sales events. The names and addresses of these preferred customers are added to our customer database, which is used primarily for direct mail purposes. American Eagle customers in the U.S. and Canada may also pay for their purchases with American Express®, Discover®, MasterCard®, Visa®, bank debit cards, cash or check.

Gift cards can be purchased in our American Eagle stores in the U.S. and Canada, as well as through our e-commerce site, ae.com. When the recipient uses the gift card, the value of the purchase is electronically deducted from the card and any remaining value can be used for future purchases. If a gift card remains inactive for greater than twenty-four months, the Company assesses the recipient a one dollar per month service fee, where allowed by law, which is automatically deducted from the remaining value of the card. This service fee is recorded within selling, general and administrative expenses on the Company's Consolidated Statements of Operations.

We offer our customers a hassle-free return policy. The Company believes that certain of its competitors offer similar credit card and service policies.

Competition

The retail apparel industry is very competitive. We compete primarily on the basis of quality, fashion, service, selection and price. Our stores in the U.S. compete with various divisions of The Limited, The Gap, Abercrombie & Fitch, Pacific Sunwear and Hot Topic as well as with retail chains such as Aeropostale, The Buckle and other national, regional and local retailers catering to a youthful customer. We also compete with the casual apparel and footwear departments of department stores and discount retailers.

Our stores in Canada compete with a variety of national specialty retail chains, a number of independent retailers and casual clothing shops within department stores, as well as various divisions of The Gap.

Trademarks and Service Marks

We have registered American Eagle Outfitters® in the U.S. Patent and Trademark Office ("PTO") as a trademark for clothing and for a variety of non-clothing products, including jewelry, perfume, and personal care products, and as a service mark for retail clothing stores and credit card services. We have also registered AE® for clothing and footwear products and an application is pending to register AE® for a variety of non-clothing items. An application

6

for American Eagle™ is pending for a variety of clothing items and we have also registered a number of other marks used in our business.

We have registered American Eagle Outfitters® in the Canadian Trademark Office for a wide variety of clothing products, as well as for retail clothing store services. In addition, we are exclusively licensed in Canada to use AE® and AEO® in connection with the sale of a wide range of clothing products.

Employees

As of January 29, 2005, we had approximately 20,600 employees in the United States, of whom approximately 16,100 were part-time and seasonal hourly employees. We consider our relationship with our employees to be satisfactory.

Seasonality

Historically, our operations have been seasonal, with a significant amount of net sales and net income occurring in the fourth fiscal quarter, reflecting increased demand during the year-end holiday selling season and, to a lesser extent, the third quarter, reflecting increased demand during the back-to-school selling season. During Fiscal 2004, the third and fourth fiscal quarters accounted for approximately 61% of our sales and approximately 74% of our income from continuing operations. As a result of this seasonality, any factors negatively affecting us during the third and fourth fiscal quarters of any year, including adverse weather or unfavorable economic conditions, could have a material adverse effect on our financial condition and results of operations for the entire year. Our quarterly results of operations also may fluctuate based upon such factors as the timing of certain holiday seasons, the number and timing of new store openings, the amount of net sales contributed by new and existing stores, the timing and level of markdowns, store closings, refurbishments and relocations, competitive factors, weather and general economic conditions.

Available Information

The Company's annual reports on Form 10-K, quarterly reports on Form 10-Q, current reports on Form 8-K and amendments to those reports are available, free of charge, under the "About AE" section of our website at www.ae.com. These reports are available as soon as reasonably practicable after such material is electronically filed with the Securities and Exchange Commission.

The Company's corporate governance materials, including our corporate governance guidelines; the charters of our audit, compensation, and nominating and corporate governance committees; and our code of ethics may also be found under the "About AE section of our website at www.ae.com. A copy of the corporate governance materials are also available upon written request.

Additionally, the Company's investor presentations are available under the "About AE" section of our website at www.ae.com. These presentations are available as soon as reasonably practicable after they are presented at investor conferences.

8

PART II

ITEM 5.   MARKET FOR THE REGISTRANT'S COMMON EQUITY, RELATED STOCKHOLDER MATTERS AND ISSUER PURCHASES OF EQUITY SECURITIES.

Our stock is traded on the Nasdaq National Market under the symbol "AEOS". The following table sets forth the range of high and low sales prices of the common stock as reported on the Nasdaq National Market during the periods indicated. As of April 1, 2005, there were 715 stockholders of record. However, when including associates who own shares through the Company's 401(k) retirement plan and employee stock purchase plan, and others holding shares in broker accounts under street name, the Company estimates the shareholder base at approximately 60,000. The following information reflects the March 2005 two-for-one stock split.

For the Quarters Ended	Market Price	
	High	Low
January 2005	$25.24	$20.08
October 2004	$20.77	$15.27
July 2004	$16.39	$12.83
April 2004	$14.26	$9.55
January 2004	$9.41	$7.44
October 2003	$11.08	$7.40
July 2003	$11.21	$7.30
April 2003	$8.73	$6.76

During the third quarter of Fiscal 2004, our Board of Directors (the "Board") authorized the Company's first-ever quarterly cash dividend of three cents per share, which was paid on October 8, 2004. A second quarterly dividend of three cents per share was paid on January 7, 2005. During the first quarter of Fiscal 2005, the Board voted to raise the Company's cash dividend to an annual rate of twenty cents per share. A quarterly dividend of five cents per share was paid on April 8, 2005. The payment of future dividends is at the discretion of our Board and is based on future earnings, cash flow, financial condition, capital requirements, changes in U.S. taxation and other relevant factors. It is anticipated that any future dividends paid will be declared on a quarterly basis.

The Company did not repurchase any shares of its Common Stock during Fiscal 2004.

ITEM 6. SELECTED CONSOLIDATED FINANCIAL DATA.

The following Selected Consolidated Financial Data should be read in conjunction with "Management's Discussion and Analysis of Financial Condition and Results of Operations," included under Item 7 below and the Consolidated Financial Statements and notes thereto, included in Item 8 below. Most of the selected data presented below is derived from the Company's Consolidated Financial Statements, which are filed in response to Item 8 below. The selected consolidated income statement data for the years ended February 2, 2002 and February 3, 2001 and the selected consolidated balance sheet data as of February 1, 2003, February 2, 2002 and February 3, 2001 are derived from audited consolidated financial statements not included herein.

The five-year selected consolidated financial data presented below has been revised to reflect the Company's restatement related to lease accounting and the two-for-one stock split distributed on March 7, 2005. See Note 2 and Note 16 of the accompanying Consolidated Financial Statements for additional information regarding the restatement and the stock split, respectively.

9

(In thousands, except per share amounts, ratios and other financial information)	January 29, 2005	January 31, 2004 (Restated)	February 1, 2003 (Restated)	February 2, 2002 (Restated)	February 3, 2001 (Restated)
			For the Years Ended (1)		
Summary of Operations (2)					
Net sales	$1,881,241	$1,435,436	$1,382,923	$1,271,248	$1,058,454
Comparable store sales increase (decrease) (3)	21.4%	(6.6%)	(4.3%)	2.3%	5.8%
Gross profit	$877,808	$549,497	$540,955	$520,470	$426,609
Gross profit as a percentage of net sales	46.7%	38.3%	39.1%	40.9%	40.3%
Operating income	$362,706	$133,271	$158,861	$159,681	$140,841
Operating income as a percentage of net sales	19.3%	9.3%	11.5%	12.6%	13.3%
Income from continuing operations	$224,232	$83,108	$99,644	$101,666	$91,152
Income from continuing operations as a percentage of net sales	11.9%	5.8%	7.2%	8.0%	8.6%
Per Share Results (4)					
Income from continuing operations per common share-basic	$1.55	$0.59	$0.69	$0.71	$0.65
Income from continuing operations per common share-diluted	$1.49	$0.57	$0.68	$0.69	$0.63
Weighted average common shares outstanding – basic	145,150	142,226	143,418	143,058	139,304
Weighted average common shares outstanding – diluted	150,244	144,414	145,566	147,594	144,264
Cash dividends per common share (5)	$0.06	-	-	-	-
Balance Sheet Information					
Total assets	$1,293,659	$932,414	$802,854	$723,480	$583,748
Total cash and short-term investments	$589,607	$337,812	$241,573	$225,483	$161,373
Long-term investments	$84,416	$24,357	-	-	-
Working capital	$574,375	$321,721	$272,288	$218,963	$161,986
Stockholders' equity	$963,486	$637,377	$571,590	$496,792	$363,360
Long-term debt	-	$13,874	$16,356	$19,361	$24,889
Current ratio	3.27	2.54	2.72	2.34	2.01
Average return on stockholders' equity	26.7%	9.9%	16.5%	24.3%	29.3%
Other Financial Information (6)					
Total stores at year-end	846	805	753	678	554
Capital expenditures (000's)	$97,288	$77,544	$78,787	$127,622	$102,747
Net sales per average selling square foot (7)	$504	$420	$460	$516	$558
Total selling square feet at end of period	3,709,012	3,466,368	3,108,556	2,705,314	2,092,864
Net sales per average gross square foot (7)	$412	$343	$374	$417	$448
Total gross square feet at end of period	4,540,095	4,239,497	3,817,442	3,334,694	2,596,863
Number of employees at end of period	20,600	15,800	14,100	12,500	11,250

See footnotes on page 10.

(1) Except for the fiscal year ended February 3, 2001, which includes 53 weeks, all fiscal years presented include 52 weeks.

(2) All amounts presented are from continuing operations and exclude Bluenotes' results of operations for all periods. See Note 10 of the accompanying Consolidated Financial Statements for additional information regarding discontinued operations and the disposition of Bluenotes.

(3) The comparable store sales increase for the period ended February 3, 2001 was compared to the corresponding 53-week period in the prior year.

(4) Per share results for all periods presented have been restated to reflect the two-for-one stock split distributed on March 7, 2005. See Note 16 of the accompanying Consolidated Financial Statements for additional information regarding the stock split.

(5) Amount represents cash dividends paid for two quarters only. Note that the Company's first ever cash dividend was initiated during the third quarter of Fiscal 2004.

(6) All amounts have been updated to reflect American Eagle operations only and exclude Bluenotes for all periods presented. See Note 10 of the accompanying Consolidated Financial Statements for additional information regarding the disposition of Bluenotes.

(7) Net sales per average square foot is calculated using retail sales for the year divided by the straight average of the beginning and ending square footage for the year.

27

Report of Independent Registered Public Accounting Firm

The Board of Directors and Stockholders of
American Eagle Outfitters, Inc.

We have audited the accompanying consolidated balance sheets of American Eagle Outfitters, Inc. (the Company) as of January 29, 2005 and January 31, 2004, and the related consolidated statements of operations, comprehensive income, stockholders' equity, and cash flows for each of the three fiscal years in the period ended January 29, 2005. These financial statements are the responsibility of the Company's management. Our responsibility is to express an opinion on these financial statements based on our audits.

We conducted our audits in accordance with the standards of the Public Company Accounting Oversight Board (United States). Those standards require that we plan and perform the audit to obtain reasonable assurance about whether the financial statements are free of material misstatement. An audit includes examining, on a test basis, evidence supporting the amounts and disclosures in the financial statements. An audit also includes assessing the accounting principles used and significant estimates made by management, as well as evaluating the overall financial statement presentation. We believe that our audits provide a reasonable basis for our opinion.

In our opinion, the financial statements referred to above present fairly, in all material respects, the consolidated financial position of American Eagle Outfitters, Inc. at January 29, 2005 and January 31, 2004, and the consolidated results of their operations and their cash flows for each of the three fiscal years in the period ended January 29, 2005, in conformity with U.S. generally accepted accounting principles.

As discussed in Note 2 to the consolidated financial statements, during the period ended January 29, 2005, the Company corrected its policies for accounting for leases and tenant allowances. The prior periods presented have been restated for this correction.

We also have audited, in accordance with the standards of the Public Company Accounting Oversight Board (United States), the effectiveness of the Company's internal control over financial reporting as of January 29, 2005, based on criteria established in Internal Control-Integrated Framework issued by the Committee of Sponsoring Organizations of the Treadway Commission and our report dated April 8, 2005 expressed an unqualified opinion on management's assessment and an adverse opinion on the effectiveness of internal control over financial reporting.

Ernst & Young LLP

Pittsburgh, Pennsylvania
April 8, 2005

28

AMERICAN EAGLE OUTFITTERS, INC.
CONSOLIDATED BALANCE SHEETS

(In thousands)	January 29, 2005	January 31, 2004 (Restated)
Assets		
Current assets:		
Cash and cash equivalents	$275,061	$137,087
Short-term investments	314,546	200,725
Merchandise inventory	137,991	120,586
Accounts and note receivable, including related party	26,432	24,129
Prepaid expenses and other	25,856	27,589
Deferred income taxes	47,754	20,584
Total current assets	827,640	530,700
Property and equipment, at cost, net of accumulated depreciation and amortization	353,213	340,955
Goodwill	10,136	10,136
Long-term investments	84,416	24,357
Other assets, net	18,254	26,266
Total assets	$1,293,659	$932,414
Liabilities and Stockholders' Equity		
Current liabilities:		
Accounts payable	$76,344	$71,330
Current portion of note payable	-	4,832
Accrued compensation and payroll taxes	36,008	14,409
Accrued rent	45,089	40,668
Accrued income and other taxes	33,926	28,669
Unredeemed stored value cards and gift certificates	32,724	25,785
Current portion of deferred lease credits	9,798	10,261
Other liabilities and accrued expenses	19,376	13,025
Total current liabilities	253,265	208,979
Non-current liabilities:		
Note payable	-	13,874
Deferred lease credits	57,758	53,936
Other non-current liabilities	19,150	18,248
Total non-current liabilities	76,908	86,058
Commitments and contingencies	-	-
Stockholders' equity	963,486	637,377
Total liabilities and stockholders' equity	$1,293,659	$932,414

See Notes to Consolidated Financial Statements

29

AMERICAN EAGLE OUTFITTERS, INC.
CONSOLIDATED STATEMENTS OF OPERATIONS

	For the Years Ended		
(In thousands, except per share amounts)	January 29, 2005	January 31, 2004	February 1, 2003
		(Restated)	(Restated)
Net sales	$1,881,241	$1,435,436	$1,382,923
Cost of sales, including certain buying, occupancy and warehousing expenses	1,003,433	885,939	841,968
Gross profit	877,808	549,497	540,955
Selling, general and administrative expenses	446,829	356,261	328,733
Depreciation and amortization expense	68,273	59,965	53,361
Operating income	362,706	133,271	158,861
Other income, net	4,129	2,016	2,418
Income before income taxes	366,835	135,287	161,279
Provision for income taxes	142,603	52,179	61,635
Income from continuing operations	224,232	83,108	99,644
Loss from discontinued operations, net of income tax benefit	(10,889)	(23,486)	(11,536)
Net income	$213,343	$59,622	$88,108
Basic income per common share:			
Income from continuing operations	$1.55	$0.59	$0.69
Loss from discontinued operations	(0.08)	(0.17)	(0.08)
Net income per basic share	$1.47	$0.42	$0.61
Diluted income per common share:			
Income from continuing operations	$1.49	$0.57	$0.68
Loss from discontinued operations	(0.07)	(0.16)	(0.08)
Net income per diluted share	$1.42	$0.41	$0.60
Weighted average common shares outstanding - basic	145,150	142,226	143,418
Weighted average common shares outstanding - diluted	150,244	144,414	145,566

See Notes to Consolidated Financial Statements

30

CONSOLIDATED STATEMENTS OF COMPREHENSIVE INCOME

(In thousands)	For the Years Ended		
	January 29, 2005	January 31, 2004	February 1, 2003
		(Restated)	(Restated)
Net income	$213,343	$59,622	$88,108
Other comprehensive income:			
Unrealized (loss) gain on investments, net of tax	(231)	(84)	58
Foreign currency translation adjustment	7,315	3,958	1,502
Reclassification adjustment for losses realized in net income related to the sale of Bluenotes	2,467	-	-
Unrealized derivative gains (losses) on cash flow hedge, net of tax	71	(148)	299
Reclassification adjustment for losses realized in net income related to termination of the cash flow hedge, net of tax	437	-	-
Other comprehensive income	10,059	3,726	1,859
Comprehensive income	$223,402	$63,348	$89,967

See Notes to Consolidated Financial Statements

31

AMERICAN EAGLE OUTFITTERS, INC.
CONSOLIDATED STATEMENTS OF STOCKHOLDERS' EQUITY

(In thousands)

	Shares (1)	Common Stock	Contributed Capital	Retained Earnings	Treasury Stock	Deferred Compensation Expense	Accumulated Other Comprehensive Income/(Loss)	Stockholders' Equity
Balance at February 2, 2002 (Previously reported)	71,906	$731	$151,227	$379,787	$(24,852)	$(2,946)	$(1,895)	$502,052
Cumulative effect of restatement on prior years (see Note 2)	–	–	–	(5,259)	–	–	(1)	(5,260)
Balance at February 2, 2002 (Restated)	71,906	731	151,227	374,528	(24,852)	(2,946)	(1,896)	496,792
Stock options and restricted stock	339	2	3,613	-	-	693	-	4,308
Repurchase of common stock	(1,198)	-	-	-	(19,477)	-	-	(19,477)
Net income	-	-	-	88,108	-	-	-	88,108
Other comprehensive income, net of tax	–	–	–	–	–	–	1,859	1,859
Balance at February 1, 2003 (Restated)	71,047	733	154,840	462,636	(44,329)	(2,253)	(37)	571,590
Stock options and restricted stock	192	2	1,934	-	-	1,192	-	3,128
Repurchase of common stock	(48)	-	-	-	(689)	-	-	(689)
Net income	-	-	-	59,622	-	-	-	59,622
Other comprehensive income, net of tax	–	–	–	–	–	–	3,726	3,726
Balance at January 31, 2004 (Restated)	71,191	735	156,774	522,258	(45,018)	(1,061)	3,689	637,377
Stock options and restricted stock	3,553	35	112,259	-	-	(746)	-	111,548
Two-for-one stock split – March 7, 2005	74,744	747	(747)	-	-	-	-	-
Net income	-	-	-	213,343	-	-	-	213,343
Other comprehensive income, net of tax	-	-	-	-	-	-	10,059	10,059
Cash dividends ($0.06 per share) (2)	–	–	–	(8,841)	–	–	–	(8,841)
Balance at January 29, 2005	149,488	$1,517	$268,286	$726,760	$(45,018)	$(1,807)	$13,748	$963,486

(1) 250 million authorized, 156 million issued and 149 million outstanding, $.01 par value common stock at January 29, 2005, 250 million authorized, 149 million issued and 142 million outstanding at January 31, 2004 and 250 million authorized, 148 million issued and 142 million outstanding at February 1, 2003. The Company has 5 million authorized, with none issued or outstanding, $.01 par value preferred stock at January 29, 2005, January 31, 2004 and February 1, 2003.

(2) Amount represents cash dividends paid for two quarters only. Note that the Company's first ever cash dividend was initiated during the third quarter of Fiscal 2004.

See Notes to Consolidated Financial Statements

32

AMERICAN EAGLE OUTFITTERS, INC.
CONSOLIDATED STATEMENTS OF CASH FLOWS

(In thousands)	For the Years Ended		
	January 29, 2005	January 31, 2004	February 1, 2003
		(Restated)	(Restated)
Operating activities:			
Net income	$213,343	$59,622	$88,108
Loss from discontinued operations	10,889	23,486	11,536
Income from continuing operations	224,232	83,108	99,644
Adjustments to reconcile income from continuing operations to net cash provided by operating activities:			
Depreciation and amortization	68,273	59,965	53,361
Stock compensation	25,166	1,192	853
Deferred income taxes	(17,087)	13,008	8,012
Tax benefit from exercise of stock options	28,800	674	1,155
Other adjustments	2,796	5,999	3,091
Changes in assets and liabilities:			
Merchandise inventory	(25,840)	6,681	(34,516)
Accounts and note receivable, including related party	3,878	(9,344)	4,941
Prepaid expenses and other	1,918	3,342	(8,495)
Accounts payable	4,466	21,124	12,752
Unredeemed stored value cards and gift certificates	7,373	2,725	5,226
Deferred lease credits	3,359	5,290	9,999
Accrued liabilities	41,349	21,437	(20,967)
Total adjustments	144,451	132,093	35,412
Net cash provided by operating activities from continuing operations	368,683	215,201	135,056
Investing activities:			
Capital expenditures	(97,288)	(77,544)	(78,787)
Purchase of investments	(483,083)	(353,486)	(132,532)
Sale of investments	309,203	203,755	102,265
Other investing activities	(14)	(1,513)	(5,102)
Net cash used for investing activities from continuing operations	(271,182)	(228,788)	(114,156)
Financing activities:			
Payments on note payable and line of credit	(2,655)	(5,434)	(9,555)
Retirement of note payable and termination of swap agreement	(16,915)	-	-
Proceeds from borrowings from line of credit	-	-	4,777
Repurchase of common stock	-	(689)	(19,476)
Net proceeds from stock options exercised	57,533	1,139	1,840
Payment of cash dividend	(8,841)	-	-
Net cash provided by (used for) financing activities from continuing operations	29,122	(4,984)	(22,414)
Effect of exchange rates on cash	1,903	1,055	275
Net cash provided by (used for) discontinued operations	9,448	(11,618)	(12,938)
Net increase (decrease) in cash and cash equivalents	137,974	(29,134)	(14,177)
Cash and cash equivalents - beginning of period	137,087	166,221	180,398
Cash and cash equivalents - end of period	$275,061	$137,087	$166,221

See Notes to Consolidated Financial Statements

Part II

33

AMERICAN EAGLE OUTFITTERS, INC.
NOTES TO CONSOLIDATED FINANCIAL STATEMENTS
FOR THE YEAR ENDED JANUARY 29, 2005

1. Business Operations

The Company designs, markets, and sells its American Eagle brand of relaxed, casual clothing for 15 to 25 year olds in its United States and Canadian retail stores. We also operate via the Internet at ae.com. The American Eagle brand provides high quality merchandise at affordable prices. American Eagle's collection offers modern basics like jeans, cargo pants, and graphic T's as well as a stylish assortment of accessories, outerwear and footwear. The Company operates retail stores located primarily in regional enclosed shopping malls in the United States and Canada.

The following table sets forth the approximate consolidated percentage of net sales attributable to each merchandise group for each of the periods indicated:

	For the Years Ended		
	January 29, 2005	January 31, 2004	February 1, 2003
Men's apparel and accessories	34%	35%	38%
Women's apparel and accessories	61%	60%	57%
Footwear – men's and women's	5%	5%	5%
Total	100%	100%	100%

2. Summary of Significant Accounting Policies

Principles of Consolidation

The Consolidated Financial Statements include the accounts of the Company and its wholly-owned subsidiaries. All intercompany transactions and balances have been eliminated in consolidation. At January 29, 2005, the Company operated in one reportable segment, American Eagle.

In December 2004, the Company completed the disposition of Bluenotes, which refers to the Bluenotes/Thriftys specialty apparel chain which we operated in Canada. As a result, the Company's Consolidated Statements of Operations and Consolidated Statements of Cash Flows reflect Bluenotes' results of operations as discontinued operations for all periods presented (note that amounts in the Company's Consolidated Balance Sheets have not been reclassified to reflect Bluenotes as discontinued operations). Prior to the disposition, Bluenotes was presented as a separate reportable segment. Additional information regarding the disposition is contained in Note 10 of the Consolidated Financial Statements.

Fiscal Year

Our financial year is a 52/53 week year that ends on the Saturday nearest to January 31. As used herein, "Fiscal 2004," "Fiscal 2003" and "Fiscal 2002" refer to the fifty-two week periods ended January 29, 2005, January 31, 2004 and February 1, 2003, respectively. "Fiscal 2005" refers to the fifty-two week period ending January 28, 2006.

34

Estimates

The preparation of financial statements in conformity with accounting principles generally accepted in the United States of America requires management to make estimates and assumptions that affect the reported amounts of assets and liabilities and disclosure of contingent assets and liabilities at the date of the financial statements and the reported amounts of revenues and expenses during the reporting period. Actual results could differ from those estimates. On an ongoing basis, management reviews its estimates based on currently available information. Changes in facts and circumstances may result in revised estimates.

Restatement of Prior Financial Information

On February 7, 2005, the Office of the Chief Accountant of the Securities and Exchange Commission ("SEC") issued a letter to the American Institute of Certified Public Accountants expressing its views regarding certain operating lease accounting issues and their application under generally accepted accounting principles ("GAAP"). In light of this letter, the Company's management initiated a review of its lease-related accounting and determined that its historical method of accounting for rent holidays and tenant allowances, as more fully described below, was not in accordance with GAAP. As a result, the Company restated its previously filed Consolidated Financial Statements for the years ended January 31, 2004 and February 1, 2003. The Company also restated its quarterly financial information for Fiscal 2003 and the first three quarters of Fiscal 2004, as shown in Note 16 of the Consolidated Financial Statements. The restatement also affects periods prior to Fiscal 2002. The impact of the restatement on prior periods has been reflected as a cumulative adjustment of $5.3 million to retained earnings as of February 2, 2002 in the Consolidated Statement of Stockholders' Equity.

Historically, the Company has recognized straight line rent expense for leases beginning on the store opening date. This had the effect of excluding the build-out period of its stores from the calculation of the period over which it expenses rent and recognizes construction allowances. In accordance with Financial Accounting Standards Board Technical Bulletin No. 85-3, *Accounting for Operating Leases with Scheduled Rent Increases*, the Company is now changing this practice to include the build-out period in the calculations of rent expense and construction allowance amortization.

Additionally, in accordance with Financial Accounting Standards Board Technical Bulletin No. 88-1, *Issues Relating to Accounting for Leases*, the Company is changing its classification of construction allowances on its Consolidated Financial Statements to record them as deferred liabilities, which will be amortized as a reduction to rent expense. Furthermore, construction allowances will be presented within operating activities on its Consolidated Statements of Cash Flows. Historically, construction allowances have been classified on the Company's Consolidated Balance Sheets as a reduction of property and equipment and the related amortization had been classified as a reduction to depreciation and amortization expense (over the lesser of the useful life or the life of the lease) on the consolidated statements of operations. The Company's consolidated statements of cash flows have historically reflected construction allowances as a reduction of capital expenditures within investing activities.

The Company did not amend its previously filed Annual Reports on Form 10-K or Quarterly Reports on Form 10-Q for the restatement. Accordingly, the financial statements and related financial information contained in such reports should no longer be relied upon. All referenced amounts for prior periods in this Annual Report on Form 10-K are presented on a restated basis.

35

The following is a summary of the effects of the restatement adjustments on our Consolidated Financial Statements.

Consolidated Statements of Operations

(In thousands, except per share amounts)	As Previously Reported (1)	Adjustments	As Restated
Fiscal year ended January 31, 2004			
Cost of sales	$895,444	$(9,505)	$885,939
Gross profit	539,992	9,505	549,497
Selling, general and administrative expenses	354,749	1,512	356,261
Depreciation and amortization expense	51,355	8,610	59,965
Operating income	133,888	(617)	133,271
Income before income taxes	135,904	(617)	135,287
Provision for income taxes	52,418	(239)	52,179
Income from continuing operations	83,486	(378)	83,108
Net income	60,000	(378)	59,622
Basic income from continuing operations per common share	0.59	-	0.59
Diluted income from continuing operations per common share	0.58	(0.01)	0.57
Basic income per common share	0.42	-	0.42
Diluted income per common share	0.42	(0.01)	0.41
Fiscal year ended February 1, 2003			
Cost of sales	$848,813	$(6,845)	$841,968
Gross profit	534,110	6,845	540,955
Selling, general and administrative expenses	328,185	548	328,733
Depreciation and amortization expense	46,040	7,321	53,361
Operating income	159,885	(1,024)	158,861
Income before income taxes	162,303	(1,024)	161,279
Provision for income taxes	62,032	(397)	61,635
Income from continuing operations	100,271	(627)	99,644
Net income	88,735	(627)	88,108
Basic income from continuing operations per common share	0.70	(0.01)	0.69
Diluted income from continuing operations per common share	0.69	(0.01)	0.68
Basic income per common share	0.62	(0.01)	0.61
Diluted income per common share	0.61	(0.01)	0.60

(1) Amounts have been reclassified to reflect the Bluenotes' results of operations as discontinued operations. See Note 10 of the Consolidated Financial Statements for additional information.

Part II

36

Consolidated Balance Sheets

(In thousands, except per share amounts)	As Previously Reported	Adjustments	As Restated
As of January 31, 2004			
Accounts and note receivable, including related party	$22,820	$1,309	$24,129
Deferred income taxes	16,816	3,768	20,584
Total current assets	525,623	5,077	530,700
Property and equipment, at cost, net of accumulated depreciation and amortization	278,689	62,266	340,955
Total assets	865,071	67,343	932,414
Accrued rent	30,985	9,683	40,668
Current portion of deferred lease credits	-	10,261	10,261
Total current liabilities	189,035	19,944	208,979
Deferred lease credits	-	53,936	53,936
Other non-current liabilities	18,492	(244)	18,248
Total non-current liabilities	32,366	53,692	86,058
Stockholders' equity	643,670	(6,293)	637,377
Total liabilities and stockholders' equity	865,071	67,343	932,414

Recent Financial Accounting Standards Board Pronouncements

FIN No. 46, *Consolidation of Variable Interest Entities*

The FASB issued Interpretation No. 46, *Consolidation of Variable Interest Entities*, *an interpretation of Accounting Research Bulletin No. 51, Consolidated Financial Instruments*, in January 2003 and subsequently issued a revision of the Interpretation in December 2003 ("FIN 46R"). FIN 46R requires certain variable interest entities to be consolidated by the primary beneficiary of the entity if the equity investors in the entity do not have the characteristics of a controlling financial interest or do not have sufficient equity at risk for the entity to finance its activities without additional financial support from other parties. All provisions of FIN 46R were effective for the first reporting period ended after March 15, 2004. The Company fully adopted the provisions of FIN 46R during the three months ended May 1, 2004, which did not have an impact on the Company's consolidated financial position, results of operations or liquidity because the Company has no interest in any variable interest entities.

FSP No. FAS 109-2, *Accounting and Disclosure Guidance for the Foreign Earnings Repatriation Provision within the American Jobs Creation Act of 2004*

In December 2004, the FASB issued Staff Position No. FAS 109-2, *Accounting and Disclosure Guidance for the Foreign Earnings Repatriation Provision within the American Jobs Creation Act of 2004* ("FSP No. 109-2"). FSP No. 109-2 allows additional time for companies to determine how the American Jobs Creation Act of 2004 (the "Act") affects a company's accounting for the deferred tax liabilities on un-remitted foreign earnings. The Act provides for a special one-time deduction of 85% of certain foreign earnings that are repatriated and which meet certain requirements. The Company is currently evaluating whether any of the earnings of our non-U.S. operations will be repatriated in accordance with the terms of the Act. At this time, the Company has not yet identified qualified earnings that would be beneficial to repatriate. The Company will continue to monitor its foreign earnings during Fiscal 2005 to determine whether it is beneficial to repatriate earnings under the Act.

37

SFAS No. 123 (revised 2004), *Share-Based Payment*

In December 2004, the FASB issued Statement of Financial Accounting Standards No. 123 (revised 2004), *Share-Based Payment*, ("SFAS No. 123(R)"). SFAS No. 123(R) is a revision of SFAS No. 123, *Accounting for Stock-Based Compensation*, supersedes APB Opinion No. 25, *Accounting for Stock Issued to Employees*, and amends FASB Statement No. 95, *Statement of Cash Flows*. SFAS No. 123(R) requires that companies recognize all share-based payments to employees, including grants of employee stock options, in the financial statements. The recognized cost will be based on the fair value of the equity or liability instruments issued. Pro forma disclosure of this cost will no longer be an alternative under SFAS No. 123(R).

SFAS No. 123(R) is effective for public companies at the beginning of the first interim or annual period beginning after June 15, 2005. Transition methods available to public companies include either the modified prospective or modified retrospective adoption. The modified prospective transition method requires that compensation cost be recognized beginning on the effective date, or date of adoption if earlier, for all share-based payments granted after the date of adoption and for all unvested awards existing on the date of adoption. The modified retrospective transition method, which includes the requirements of the modified prospective transition method, additionally requires the restatement of prior period financial information based on amounts previously recognized under SFAS No. 123 for purposes of pro forma disclosures. The Company will adopt SFAS No. 123(R) in its third quarter of Fiscal 2005, beginning July 31, 2005, as required. The Company is currently in the process of determining the transition method that it will use to adopt the new standard.

The Company currently accounts for its stock-based compensation plans under Accounting Principles Board Opinion No. 25, *Accounting for Stock Issued to Employees*, using the intrinsic value method. As a result of using this method, the Company generally recognizes no compensation cost for employee stock options. The adoption of SFAS No. 123(R) and the use of the fair value method will have a significant impact on our results of operations. The impact of SFAS No. 123(R) cannot be predicted at this time because it will depend on levels of share-based payments granted in the future. However, had we adopted SFAS No. 123(R) in prior periods, the impact would have approximated the amounts in our pro forma disclosure within the *Stock Option Plan* section of Note 2 of the Consolidated Financial Statements. SFAS No. 123(R) also requires the benefits of tax deductions in excess of recognized compensation cost to be reported as a financing cash flow, rather than as an operating cash flow as required under current standards. This requirement will reduce net operating cash flows and increase net financing cash flows in the periods after adoption. We cannot estimate what those amounts will be in the future because they are dependent on, among other things, when employees exercise stock options. The amount of operating cash flows recognized for such excess tax deductions was $28.8 million, $0.7 million and $1.2 million during Fiscal 2004, Fiscal 2003 and Fiscal 2002, respectively.

Foreign Currency Translation

The Canadian dollar is the functional currency for the Canadian businesses. In accordance with SFAS No. 52, *Foreign Currency Translation*, assets and liabilities denominated in foreign currencies were translated into U.S. dollars (the reporting currency) at the exchange rate prevailing at the balance sheet date. Revenues and expenses denominated in foreign currencies were translated into U.S. dollars at the monthly average exchange rate for the period. Gains or losses resulting from foreign currency transactions are included in the results of operations, whereas, related translation adjustments are reported as an element of other comprehensive income in accordance with SFAS No. 130, *Reporting Comprehensive Income* (see Note 8 of the Consolidated Financial Statements).

Fair Value of Financial Instruments

Statement of Financial Accounting Standards No. 107 ("SFAS No. 107"), *Disclosures about Fair Value of Financial Instruments*, requires management to disclose the estimated fair value of certain assets and liabilities defined by SFAS No. 107 as financial instruments. At January 29, 2005, Management believes that the carrying amounts of cash, short-term investments, receivables and payables approximate fair value because of the short maturity of these financial instruments. The fair value of long-term investments is estimated based on quoted market prices for those or similar investments. The estimated fair value of the Company's long-term investments at January 29, 2005 and January 31, 2004 was $84.2 million and $24.3 million, respectively. Considerable judgment is required when interpreting market information and other data to develop estimates of fair value. Accordingly, the estimates presented are not necessarily indicative of the amounts that could be realized in a current market exchange.

Cash and Cash Equivalents

Cash includes cash equivalents. The Company considers all highly liquid investments purchased with a maturity of three months or less to be cash equivalents.

Short-term Investments

Cash in excess of operating requirements is invested in taxable or tax-exempt fixed income notes or bonds. As of January 29, 2005, short-term investments included investments with an original maturity of greater than three months (averaging approximately six months) and consisted primarily of tax-exempt municipal bonds, taxable agency bonds and corporate notes classified as available for sale. The Company had previously included auction rate securities as a component of cash and cash equivalents on its Consolidated Balance Sheets, but has now determined that categorization as a component of short-term investments is more appropriate. Accordingly, these auction rate securities have been reclassified from cash and cash equivalents to short-term investments for all periods presented. This reclassification also resulted in changes in the Company's Consolidated Statements of Cash Flows. The purchase and sale of auction rate securities previously presented as cash and cash equivalents have been reclassified to investing activities for all periods presented.

The following table summarizes our cash and marketable securities, which are recorded as cash and cash equivalents on the Consolidated Balance Sheets, and our short-term investments:

(In thousands, except per share amounts) Balance at January 29, 2005	Cost	Fair Value	Cash and Cash Equivalents	Short-term Investments
Original maturity less than 91 days				
Cash and money market investments	$90,200	$90,200	$90,200	$ -
Tax exempt investments	148,685	148,685	148,685	-
Taxable investments	36,176	36,176	36,176	-
Original maturity greater than 91 days				
Tax exempt investments	305,726	305,726	-	305,726
Taxable investments	8,820	8,820	-	8,820
Total	$589,607	$589,607	$275,061	$314,546

Merchandise Inventory

Merchandise inventory is valued at the lower of average cost or market, utilizing the retail method. Average cost includes merchandise design and sourcing costs and related expenses. The Company recognizes its inventory at the point when it arrives at one of our deconsolidation centers.

The Company reviews its inventory levels in order to identify slow-moving merchandise and generally uses markdowns to clear merchandise. Markdowns may occur when inventory exceeds customer demand for reasons of

39

style, seasonal adaptation, changes in customer preference, lack of consumer acceptance of fashion items, competition, or if it is determined that the inventory in stock will not sell at its currently ticketed price. Such markdowns may have a material adverse impact on earnings, depending on the extent and amount of inventory affected.

Property and Equipment

Property and equipment is recorded on the basis of cost with depreciation computed utilizing the straight-line method over the estimated useful lives as follows:

Buildings	25 to 40 years
Leasehold improvements	5 to 10 years
Fixtures and equipment	3 to 5 years

In accordance with SFAS No. 144, *Accounting for the Impairment or Disposal of Long-Lived Assets*, management evaluates the ongoing value of leasehold improvements and store fixtures associated with retail stores which have been open longer than one year. Impairment losses are recorded on long-lived assets used in operations when events and circumstances indicate that the assets might be impaired and the undiscounted cash flows estimated to be generated by those assets are less than the carrying amounts of those assets. When events such as these occur, the impaired assets are adjusted to estimated fair value and an impairment loss is recorded in selling, general and administrative expenses. The Company recognized $1.4 million, $1.4 million and $0.5 million in impairment losses during Fiscal 2004, Fiscal 2003 and Fiscal 2002, respectively.

Goodwill

The Company adopted SFAS No. 142, *Goodwill and Other Intangible Assets* ("SFAS No. 142"), on February 3, 2002, the beginning of Fiscal 2002. In accordance with SFAS No. 142, Management evaluates goodwill for impairment by comparing the fair value of the reporting unit to the book value. At the time of adoption, the book value of goodwill was assigned to the Company's American Eagle and Bluenotes reporting units. Approximately $10.3 million and $13.7 million in goodwill was assigned to American Eagle and Bluenotes, respectively. The fair value of the Company's reporting units is estimated using discounted cash flow methodologies and market comparable information. Based on the analysis, if the implied fair value of each reporting unit exceeds the book value of the goodwill, no impairment loss is recognized.

Due to the unanticipated and continued weak performance of the Bluenotes division during Fiscal 2003, the Company believed that certain indicators of impairment were present. At that time, an impairment test was performed in accordance with SFAS No. 142 and the Company determined that the carrying value of the goodwill was impaired. As a result, the Company recorded a $14.1 million impairment loss during Fiscal 2003, which reduced the goodwill carrying value to zero. Due to the disposition of Bluenotes during Fiscal 2004, this impairment loss has been reclassified to discontinued operations in the accompanying Consolidated Financial Statements.

The Company has approximately $10.1 million of goodwill remaining at January 29, 2005, which is attributed to the American Eagle reportable segment.

Long-term Investments

As of January 29, 2005, long-term investments included investments with an original maturity of greater than twelve months, but not exceeding five years (averaging approximately twenty-four months) and consisted primarily of agency bonds and debt securities issued by states and local municipalities classified as available-for-sale.

Other Assets

Other assets consist primarily of deferred taxes, lease buyout costs, trademark costs and acquisition costs. The lease buyout costs are amortized over the remaining life of the leases, generally for no greater than ten years. The trademark costs are amortized over five to fifteen years. Acquisition costs are amortized over five years. These assets, net of amortization, are presented as other assets (long-term) on the Consolidated Balance Sheets.

Deferred Lease Credits

Deferred lease credits represent the unamortized portion of construction allowances received from landlords related to the Company's retail stores. Construction allowances are generally comprised of cash amounts promised to the Company by its landlords as part of the negotiated lease terms. The Company records a receivable and a deferred lease credit liability at the lease commencement date (date of initial possession of the store). The deferred lease credit is amortized as a reduction of rent expense over the term of the lease (including the pre-opening build-out period) and the receivable is reduced as amounts are received from the landlord.

Self Insurance Reserve

The Company is self-insured for certain losses related to employee medical benefits. Costs for self-insurance claims filed and claims incurred but not reported are accrued based on known claims and historical experience. Management believes that it has adequately reserved for its self-insurance liability, which is capped through the use of stop loss contracts with insurance companies. However, any significant variation of future claims from historical trends could cause actual results to differ from the accrued liability.

Interest Rate Swap

During Fiscal 2004, the Company terminated its interest rate swap agreement, which was previously used to manage interest rate risk. The derivative effectively changed the interest rate on the borrowings under the non-revolving term facility from a variable rate to a fixed rate. The Company recognized its derivative on the balance sheet at fair value at the end of each period. Changes in the fair value of the derivative that was designated and met all the required criteria for a cash flow hedge were recorded in accumulated other comprehensive income (loss). During Fiscal 2003, unrealized net losses on derivative instruments of approximately $0.1 million, net of related tax effects, were recorded in other comprehensive income (loss). On October 1, 2004, the interest rate swap was terminated at its fair value, which represented a net loss of $0.7 million, in conjunction with the payoff of the term facility. As a result, the Company reclassified approximately $0.4 million, net of tax, of unrealized net losses into earnings during Fiscal 2004. The Company does not hold or issue derivative financial instruments for trading purposes.

Stock Repurchases

On February 24, 2000, the Company's Board of Directors authorized the repurchase of up to 7,500,000 shares of its stock. The Company did not purchase any shares of common stock on the open market during Fiscal 2004 as part of this stock repurchase program. The Company purchased 80,000 and 2,280,000 shares of common stock for approximately $0.6 million and $17.8 million on the open market during Fiscal 2003 and Fiscal 2002, respectively. Prior to Fiscal 2002, the Company had purchased approximately 3,740,000 shares of common stock on the open market under this stock repurchase program. As of January 29, 2005, approximately 1,400,000 shares remain authorized for repurchase. Additionally, during Fiscal 2003 and Fiscal 2002, the Company purchased 16,000 shares and 116,000 shares, respectively, from certain employees at market prices totaling $0.1 million and $1.6 million, respectively, for the payment of taxes in connection with the vesting of restricted stock as permitted under the 1999 Stock Incentive Plan. These repurchases have been recorded as treasury stock.

41

Income Taxes

The Company calculates income taxes in accordance with SFAS No. 109, *Accounting for Income Taxes*, which requires the use of the asset and liability method. Under this method, deferred tax assets and liabilities are recognized based on the difference between the consolidated financial statement carrying amounts of existing assets and liabilities and their respective tax bases. Deferred tax assets and liabilities are measured using the tax rates in effect in the years when those temporary differences are expected to reverse. A valuation allowance is established against the deferred tax assets when it is more likely than not that some portion or all of the deferred taxes may not be realized.

Stock Option Plan

The Company accounts for its stock-based compensation plans under Accounting Principles Board Opinion No. 25, *Accounting for Stock Issued to Employees* ("APB No. 25"). The pro forma information below is based on provisions of SFAS No. 123, *Accounting for Stock-Based Compensation*, as amended by SFAS No. 148, *Accounting for Stock-Based Compensation-Transition and Disclosure* ("SFAS No. 148"), issued in December 2002. SFAS No. 148 requires that the pro forma information regarding net income and earnings per share be determined as if the Company had accounted for its employee stock options granted beginning in the fiscal year subsequent to December 31, 1994 under the fair value method of that Statement. The fair value for these options was estimated at the date of grant using a Black-Scholes option pricing model with the following weighted-average assumptions:

	For the Years Ended		
	January 29, 2005	January 31, 2004	February 1, 2003
Risk-free interest rates	2.9%	2.6%	4.6%
Dividend yield	0.48%	None	None
Volatility factors of the expected market price of the Company's common stock	31.4%	50.3%	62.9%
Weighted-average expected life	6 years	5 years	5 years
Expected forfeiture rate	13.6%	11.5%	10.2%

The Black-Scholes option valuation model was developed for use in estimating the fair value of traded options which have no vesting restrictions and are fully transferable. In addition, option valuation models require the input of highly subjective assumptions including the expected stock price volatility. Because the Company's employee stock options have characteristics significantly different from those of traded options, and because changes in the subjective input assumptions can materially affect the fair value estimate, in management's opinion, the existing models do not necessarily provide a reliable single measure of the fair value of its employee stock options.

42

For purposes of pro forma disclosures, the estimated fair value of the options is amortized to expense over the options' vesting period. The Company's pro forma information follows:

	For the Years Ended		
(In thousands, except per share amounts)	January 29, 2005	January 31, 2004 (Restated)	February 1, 2003 (Restated)
Net income, as reported	$213,343	$59,622	$88,108
Add: stock-based compensation expense included in reported net income, net of tax	1,301	767	592
Less: total stock-based compensation expense determined under fair value method, net of tax	(10,948)	(14,463)	(8,489)
Pro forma net income	$203,696	$45,926	$80,211
Basic income per common share:			
As reported	$1.47	$0.42	$0.61
Pro forma	$1.40	$0.32	$0.56
Diluted income per common share:			
As reported	$1.42	$0.41	$0.60
Pro forma	$1.36	$0.32	$0.55

Revenue Recognition

The Company records revenue for store sales upon the purchase of merchandise by customers. The Company's e-commerce operation records revenue at the time the goods are shipped. Revenue is not recorded on the purchase of gift cards. A current liability is recorded upon purchase and revenue is recognized when the gift card is redeemed for merchandise. Revenue is recorded net of sales returns.

Revenue is not recorded on the sell-off of end-of-season, overstock and irregular merchandise to off-price retailers. These sell-offs are typically sold below cost and the proceeds are reflected in cost of sales. See Note 3 of the Consolidated Financial Statements for further discussion.

Cost of Sales, Including Certain Buying, Occupancy and Warehousing Expenses

Cost of sales consists of merchandise costs, including design, sourcing, importing and inbound freight costs, as well as markdowns, shrinkage and promotional costs. Buying, occupancy and warehousing costs consists of compensation and travel for our buyers; rent and utilities related to our stores, corporate headquarters, distribution centers and other office space; freight from our distribution centers to the stores; and compensation and supplies for our distribution centers, including purchasing, receiving and inspection costs.

The gross profit impact of a sales returns reserve, which is recorded in cost of sales, is provided on gross sales for projected merchandise returns based on historical average return percentages.

Selling, General and Administrative Expenses

Selling, general and administrative expenses consist of compensation and employee benefit expenses, other than for our design, sourcing and importing teams, our buyers and our distribution centers. Such compensation and employee benefit expenses include salaries, incentives and related benefits associated with our stores and corporate headquarters, except as previously noted. Selling, general and administrative expenses also include advertising costs,

43

supplies for our stores and home office, freight related to inter-store transfers, communication costs, travel and entertainment, leasing costs and services purchased.

Advertising Costs

Certain advertising costs, including direct mail, in-store photographs and other promotional costs are expensed when the marketing campaign commences. Costs associated with the production of television advertising are expensed over the life of the campaign. All other advertising costs are expensed as incurred. The Company recognized $41.4 million, $44.8 million and $44.4 million in advertising expense during Fiscal 2004, Fiscal 2003 and Fiscal 2002, respectively.

Design Costs

The Company has certain design costs, including compensation, rent, travel, supplies and samples, which are included in cost of sales as the respective inventory is sold.

Store Pre-Opening Costs

Store pre-opening costs consist primarily of rent, advertising, supplies and payroll expenses. These costs are expensed as incurred.

Legal Proceedings and Claims

The Company is subject to certain legal proceedings and claims arising out of the conduct of its business. In accordance with SFAS No. 5, *Accounting for Contingencies*, Management records a reserve for estimated losses when the amount is probable and can be reasonably estimated. If a range of possible loss exists, the Company records the accrual at the low end of the range, in accordance with FIN 14, an interpretation of SFAS No. 5. As the Company has provided adequate reserves, it believes that the ultimate outcome of any matter currently pending against the Company will not materially affect the financial position or results of operations of the Company.

Supplemental Disclosures of Cash Flow Information

(In thousands)	For the Years Ended		
	January 29, 2005	January 31, 2004	February 1, 2003
Cash paid during the periods for:		(Restated)	(Restated)
Income taxes	$121,138	$25,496	$64,547
Interest	$1,188	$1,510	$1,964

Earnings Per Share

The following table shows the amounts used in computing earnings per share and the effect on income and the weighted average number of shares of potential dilutive common stock equivalents (stock options and restricted stock).

Part II

44

(In thousands)	For the Years Ended		
	January 29, 2005	January 31, 2004	February 1, 2003
Net income	$213,343	$59,622	$88,108
Weighted average common shares outstanding:			
Basic shares	145,150	142,226	143,418
Dilutive effect of stock options and non-vested restricted stock	5,094	2,188	2,148
Diluted shares	150,244	144,414	145,566

Options to purchase 1,327,000, 10,543,000 and 10,876,000 shares of common stock during Fiscal 2004, Fiscal 2003 and Fiscal 2002, respectively, were outstanding, but were not included in the computation of net income per diluted share because the options' exercise prices were greater than the average market price of the underlying shares.

Segment Information

As a result of the Bluenotes' disposition during Fiscal 2004 (see Note 10 of the Consolidated Financial Statements), the Company's operations are now conducted in one reportable segment. Prior to its disposition, Bluenotes was presented as a separate reportable segment.

The following is geographical information as of and for the years ended January 29, 2005, January 31, 2004 and February 1, 2003:

(In thousands)	January 29, 2005	January 31, 2004 (Restated)	February 1, 2003 (Restated)
Net sales (1):			
United States	$1,751,776	$1,339,636	$1,304,890
Foreign (2)	129,465	95,800	78,033
Total net sales	$1,881,241	$1,435,436	$1,382,923
Long-lived assets, net:			
United States	$320,021	$295,557	$279,692
Foreign	43,328	55,534	68,844
Total long-lived assets, net	$363,349	$351,091	$348,536

(1) Net sales data represents American Eagle operations only. Bluenotes' net sales amounts have been excluded as they are being presented in discontinued operations. See Note 10 of the Consolidated Financial Statements for additional information regarding Bluenotes.

(2) Amounts represent sales from American Eagle's Canadian retail stores, as well as AE Direct sales which are billed to and/or shipped to foreign countries, including Canada.

Reclassification

Certain reclassifications have been made to the Consolidated Financial Statements for prior periods in order to conform to the Fiscal 2004 presentation.

45

3. Related Party Transactions

The Company and its wholly-owned subsidiaries historically had various transactions with related parties. The nature of the Company's relationship with the related parties and a description of the respective transactions is stated below.

As of January 29, 2005, the Schottenstein-Deshe-Diamond families (the "families") owned 17% of the outstanding shares of Common Stock of the Company. The families also own a private company, Schottenstein Stores Corporation ("SSC"), which includes a publicly-traded subsidiary, Retail Ventures, Inc. ("RVI"), formerly Value City Department Stores, Inc., and also owned 99% of Linmar Realty Company II ("Linmar Realty") until June 4, 2004. During Fiscal 2004, the Company implemented a strategic plan to eliminate related party transactions with the families. As a result, we did not have any material transactions remaining with the families as of January 29, 2005. We believe that the terms of the prior transactions were as favorable to the Company as those that could have been obtained from unrelated third parties. The Company had the following transactions with these related parties during Fiscal 2004, Fiscal 2003 and Fiscal 2002.

During Fiscal 2004, the Company, through a subsidiary, Linmar Realty Company II LLC, acquired for $20.0 million Linmar Realty Company II, a general partnership that owned the Company's corporate headquarters and distribution center. The acquisition price, less a straight-line rent accrual adjustment of $2.0 million, was recorded as land and building on the consolidated balance sheet during the three months ended July 31, 2004 and is being depreciated over its anticipated useful life of twenty-five years. Prior to the acquisition, the Company had an operating lease with Linmar Realty for these properties. Rent expense was $0.8 million during Fiscal 2004 and $2.4 million during both Fiscal 2003 and Fiscal 2002 under the lease.

The Company and its subsidiaries sell end-of-season, overstock and irregular merchandise to various parties, including RVI. These sell-offs, which are without recourse, are typically sold below cost and the proceeds are reflected in cost of sales. During April 2004, the Company entered into an agreement with an independent third-party vendor for the sale of merchandise sell-offs, thus reducing sell-offs to related parties. Below is a summary of merchandise sell-offs for Fiscal 2004, Fiscal 2003 and Fiscal 2002:

(In thousands)	Related Party	Non-Related Party	Total
Fiscal 2004			
Marked-down cost of merchandise disposed of via sell-offs	$147	$15,633	$15,780
Proceeds from sell-offs	148	15,273	15,421
Increase (decrease) to cost of sales	$(1)	$360	$359
Fiscal 2003			
Marked-down cost of merchandise disposed of via sell-offs	$12,924	$23,538	$36,462
Proceeds from sell-offs	13,256	18,688	31,944
Increase (decrease) to cost of sales	$(332)	$4,850	$4,518
Fiscal 2002			
Marked-down cost of merchandise disposed of via sell-offs	$7,787	$12,462	$20,249
Proceeds from sell-offs	7,639	11,360	18,999
Increase to cost of sales	$148	$1,102	$1,250

At January 29, 2005, the Company did not have a balance in accounts receivable that pertained to related parties. At January 31, 2004, approximately $4.2 million was included in accounts receivable pertaining to related party merchandise sell-offs as well as a corporate aircraft arrangement, which is further discussed below.

SSC and its affiliates charge the Company for various professional services provided to the Company, including certain legal, real estate, travel and insurance services. For Fiscal 2004, Fiscal 2003 and Fiscal 2002, the Company paid approximately $0.2 million, $0.9 million and $0.5 million, respectively, for these services.

46

During Fiscal 2004, the Company discontinued its cost sharing arrangement with SSC for the acquisition of an interest in several corporate aircraft. The Company paid $0.1 million during Fiscal 2004 and $1.0 million during Fiscal 2003 and Fiscal 2002 to cover its share of operating costs based on usage of the corporate aircraft under the cost sharing arrangement.

See Part III, Item 13 of this Form 10-K for additional information regarding related party transactions.

4. Accounts and Note Receivable

Accounts and note receivable are comprised of the following:

(In thousands)	January 29, 2005	January 31, 2004
		(Restated)
Fabric	$2,871	$5,136
Related party	-	4,219
Construction allowances	6,801	5,188
Sell-offs to non-related parties	6,657	2,479
Taxes	2,584	2,319
Distribution services	2,015	1,040
Sale of Bluenotes	2,707	-
Other	2,797	3,748
Total	$26,432	$24,129

The fabric receivable represents amounts due from a third party vendor for fabric purchased by the Company and sold to the respective vendor. Upon receipt of the finished goods from the vendor, the Company records the full cost of the merchandise in inventory, and reduces the amount of payment due to the third party by the respective fabric receivable.

5. Property and Equipment

Property and equipment consists of the following:

(In thousands)	January 29, 2005	January 31, 2004
		(Restated)
Land	$4,655	$2,355
Buildings	36,301	20,999
Leasehold improvements	358,408	354,406
Fixtures and equipment	218,050	187,304
Construction in progress	2,318	1,693
	619,732	566,757
Less: Accumulated depreciation and amortization	(266,519)	(225,802)
Net property and equipment	$353,213	$340,955

47

Depreciation expense is summarized as follows:

(In thousands)	For the Years Ended		
	January 29, 2005	January 31, 2004	February 1, 2003
		(Restated)	(Restated)
Depreciation expense	$66,326	$59,083	$52,128

6. Note Payable and Other Credit Arrangements

Unsecured Demand Lending Arrangement

The Company has an unsecured demand lending arrangement (the "facility") with a bank to provide a $118.6 million line of credit at either the lender's prime lending rate (5.25% at January 29, 2005) or at LIBOR plus a negotiated margin rate. The facility has a limit of $40.0 million to be used for direct borrowing. Because there were no borrowings during any of the past three years, there were no amounts paid for interest on this facility. At January 29, 2005, letters of credit in the amount of $55.0 million were outstanding on this facility, leaving a remaining available balance on the line of $63.6 million.

Uncommitted Letter of Credit Facility

The Company also has an uncommitted letter of credit facility for $50.0 million with a separate financial institution. At January 29, 2005, letters of credit in the amount of $17.6 million were outstanding on this facility, leaving a remaining available balance on the line of $32.4 million.

Non-revolving Term Facility and Revolving Operating Facility

During Fiscal 2004, the Company retired its $29.1 million non-revolving term facility (the "term facility") for $16.2 million. The term facility required annual payments of $4.8 million, with interest at the one-month Bankers' Acceptance Rate plus 140 basis points, and was originally scheduled to mature in December 2007. Interest paid under the term facility was $1.2 million, $1.5 million and $1.6 million for the years ended January 29, 2005, January 31, 2004 and February 1, 2003, respectively.

The Company also had an $11.2 million revolving operating facility (the "operating facility") that was used to support the working capital and capital expenditures of the acquired Canadian businesses. The operating facility was due in November 2003 and had four additional one-year extensions. During Fiscal 2003, the Company chose not to extend the operating facility for another year.

7. Accounting for Derivative Instruments and Hedging Activities

On November 30, 2000, the Company entered into an interest rate swap agreement totaling $29.2 million in connection with the term facility. The swap amount decreased on a monthly basis beginning January 1, 2001 until the early termination of the agreement during Fiscal 2004. In accordance with SFAS No. 133, *Accounting for Derivative Instruments and Hedging Activities*, the Company recognized its derivative on the balance sheet at fair value at the end of each period. Changes in the fair value of the derivative, which was designated and met all the required criteria for a cash flow hedge, were recorded in accumulated other comprehensive income (loss). Unrealized net gains (losses) on derivative instruments of approximately $(0.1) million and $0.3 million for the years ended January 31, 2004 and February 1, 2003, respectively, net of related tax effects, were recorded in other comprehensive income (loss). During Fiscal 2004, the interest rate swap was terminated at its fair value, which represented a net loss of $0.7

48

million, in conjunction with the payoff of the term facility (see Note 6 to the Consolidated Financial Statements). As a result, the Company reclassified approximately $0.4 million, net of tax, of unrealized net losses from other comprehensive income into earnings during Fiscal 2004. As of January 29, 2005, the Company does not have any remaining derivative instruments.

8. Other Comprehensive Income (Loss)

The accumulated balances of other comprehensive income (loss) included as part of the Consolidated Statements of Stockholders' Equity follow:

(In thousands)	Before Tax Amount	Tax Benefit (Expense)	Other Comprehensive Income (Loss)
Balance at February 2, 2002 (Restated)	**$(3,058)**	**$1,162**	**$(1,896)**
Unrealized gain on investments	94	(36)	58
Foreign currency translation adjustment	2,423	(921)	1,502
Unrealized derivative gain on cash flow hedge	480	(181)	299
Balance at February 1, 2003 (Restated)	**(61)**	**24**	**(37)**
Unrealized (loss) on investments	(135)	51	(84)
Foreign currency translation adjustment	6,521	(2,563)	3,958
Unrealized derivative (loss) on cash flow hedge	(247)	99	(148)
Balance at January 31, 2004 (Restated)	**6,078**	**(2,389)**	**3,689**
Unrealized (loss) on investments	(378)	147	(231)
Foreign currency translation adjustment (1)	4,581	2,734	7,315
Reclassification adjustment for losses realized in net income related to the disposition of Bluenotes	2,467	-	2,467
Unrealized derivative gain on cash flow hedge	116	(45)	71
Reclassification adjustment for loss realized in net income related to termination of the cash flow hedge	714	(277)	437
Balance at January 29, 2005	**$13,578**	**$170**	**$13,748**

(1) During Fiscal 2004, the Company reclassified the income tax provision related to its foreign currency translation gains, as it is the Company's intention to utilize the earnings of its foreign subsidiaries in the foreign operations for an indefinite period of time. See Note 11 of the Consolidated Financial Statements for additional information.

9. Leases

The Company leases all store premises, some of our office and distribution facility space, and certain information technology and office equipment. The store leases generally have initial terms of ten years. Most of these store leases provide for base rentals and the payment of a percentage of sales as additional rent when sales exceed specified levels. Additionally, most leases contain construction allowances and/or rent holidays. In recognizing landlord incentives and minimum rent expense, the Company amortizes the charges on a straight line basis over the lease term (including the pre-opening build-out period). These leases are classified as operating leases.

A summary of fixed minimum and contingent rent expense for all operating leases follows:

(In thousands)	For the Years Ended		
	January 29, 2005	January 31, 2004 (Restated)	February 1, 2003 (Restated)
Store rent:			
Fixed minimum	$124,507	$100,418	$85,285
Contingent	6,788	4,758	5,304
Total store rent, excluding common area maintenance charges, real estate taxes and certain other expenses	131,295	105,176	90,589
Offices, distribution facilities, equipment and other	11,265	16,943	17,525
Total rent expense	$142,560	$122,119	$108,114

In addition, the Company is typically responsible under its store, office and distribution center leases for common area maintenance charges, real estate taxes and certain other expenses.

The table below summarizes future minimum lease obligations, consisting of fixed minimum rent, under operating leases in effect at January 29, 2005:

Fiscal years: *(In thousands)*	Future Minimum Lease Obligations
2005	$135,410
2006	135,810
2007	132,950
2008	129,295
2009	121,059
Thereafter	327,896
Total	$982,420

10. Discontinued Operations

During December 2004, the Company completed its disposition of Bluenotes to 6295215 Canada Inc (the "Purchaser"). The transaction had an effective date of December 5, 2004. In accordance with SFAS No. 144, *Accounting for the Impairment or Disposal of Long-Lived Assets*, the accompanying Consolidated Statements of Operations reflect Bluenotes' results of operations as discontinued operations for all periods presented. Additionally, the accompanying Consolidated Statements of Cash Flows reflect Bluenotes' results of operations as discontinued operations (note that amounts in the Company's Consolidated Balance Sheets have not been reclassified to reflect Bluenotes as discontinued operations).

The Company expects to receive approximately $23 million as consideration for the sale of certain of its Bluenotes assets, including inventory and property and equipment. As of January 29, 2005, the Company had received $20.7 million of the aforementioned consideration. In accordance with the terms of the sale, the remaining cash proceeds will be received as the inventory is sold by the Purchaser in the normal course of business through April 2, 2005. The transaction resulted in an after-tax loss of $4.8 million, or $0.03 per diluted share, which has been recorded in discontinued operations during Fiscal 2004.

50

The operating results of Bluenotes, which are being presented as discontinued operations, were as follows:

(In thousands)	January 29, 2005	January 31, 2004	February 1, 2003
Net sales	$69,825	$84,532	$80,218
Loss from operations, net of income tax benefit (1)	$ (6,070)	$(23,486)	$(11,536)
Loss on disposition, net of income tax benefit	(4,819)	-	-
Loss from discontinued operations, net of income tax benefit (2)	$(10,889)	$(23,486)	$(11,536)

(1) Fiscal 2003 includes a goodwill impairment charge of $14.1 million, for which no tax benefit was realized.

(2) Amounts are net of income tax benefit of $3.9 million, $5.8 million and $7.1 million, respectively.

11. Income Taxes

The components of income from continuing operations before taxes on income were:

(In thousands)	January 29, 2005	January 31, 2004	February 1, 2003
U.S.	$339,328	$131,804	$158,113
Foreign	27,507	3,483	3,166
Total	$366,835	$135,287	$161,279

51

The significant components of the Company's deferred tax assets and liabilities were as follows:

(In thousands)	January 29, 2005	January 31, 2004
Deferred tax assets:		
Current:		
Inventories	$4,192	$4,037
Rent	14,732	13,768
Deferred compensation	26,003	1,432
Capital loss	1,426	1,455
Valuation allowance	(1,426)	(1,455)
Other	2,827	1,347
Total current deferred tax assets	47,754	20,584
Long-term:		
Purchase accounting basis differences	1,194	7,384
Operating losses	9,750	12,073
Other	1,987	1,427
Total long-term deferred tax assets	12,931	20,884
Total deferred tax assets	$60,685	$41,468
Deferred tax liabilities:		
Property and equipment	$18,147	$14,399
Other Comprehensive Income	-	2,755
Total deferred tax liabilities	$18,147	$17,154

Significant components of the provision for income taxes are as follows:

(In thousands)	For the Years Ended		
	January 29, 2005	January 31, 2004	February 1, 2003
Current:			
Federal	$130,988	$33,519	$47,470
State	24,338	5,860	7,054
Total current	155,326	39,379	54,524
Deferred:			
Federal	(18,860)	10,424	6,396
Foreign taxes	9,572	525	(263)
State	(3,435)	1,851	978
Total deferred	(12,723)	12,800	7,111
Provision for income taxes	$142,603	$52,179	$61,635

As a result of additional tax deductions related to vested restricted stock grants and stock option exercises, tax benefits have been recognized as contributed capital for the years ended January 29, 2005, January 31, 2004 and February 1, 2003 in the amounts of $28.8 million, $0.7 million and $1.2 million, respectively.

No provision was made for U.S. income taxes on any undistributed earnings of the Canadian subsidiaries as it is the Company's intention to utilize those earnings in the Canadian operations for an indefinite period of time.

Part II

52

Income tax accruals of $25.4 million and $21.4 million were recorded at January 29, 2005 and January 31 2004, respectively. As of January 29, 2005 contingent tax reserves of approximately $7.4 million were recorded, of which $6.8 million related to potential state and local income tax liabilities.

Of the $9.8 million deferred tax asset related to net operating loss carryforwards, $9.6 million was associated with Canadian tax loss carryforwards, of which $8.0 million expires over the next five tax years and $1.6 million expires over the next six tax years. Assuming a 37% effective tax rate, we will need to recognize pretax net income of approximately $26 million in future periods to recover this deferred tax amount. We anticipate that future Canadian taxable income will be sufficient to utilize the full amount of this deferred tax asset. For the year ended January 31, 2004, the Company recorded a valuation allowance against a capital loss deferred tax asset of $1.4 million. The capital loss carryforward will expire in July 2006.

A reconciliation between statutory federal income tax and the effective tax rate from continuing operations follows:

	For the Years Ended		
	January 29, 2005	January 31, 2004	February 1, 2003
Federal income tax rate	35%	35%	35%
State income taxes, net of federal income tax effect	4	4	3
Change in valuation reserve for capital losses	-	1	-
Change in tax reserves	-	(1)	-
	39%	39%	38%

12. Retirement Plan and Employee Stock Purchase Plan

The Company maintains a profit sharing and 401(k) plan (the "Retirement Plan"). Under the provisions of the Retirement Plan, full-time employees and part-time employees are automatically enrolled to contribute 3% of their salary if they have attained twenty one years of age, have completed sixty days of service, and work at least twenty hours per week. Individuals can decline enrollment or can contribute up to 30% of their salary to the 401(k) plan on a pretax basis, subject to IRS limitations. After one year of service, the Company will match up to 4.5% of participants' eligible compensation. Contributions to the profit sharing plan, as determined by the Board of Directors, are discretionary. The Company recognized $4.8 million, $2.1 million and $3.1 million in expense during Fiscal 2004, Fiscal 2003 and Fiscal 2002, respectively, in connection with the 401(k) retirement plan and profit sharing plan.

The Employee Stock Purchase Plan is a non-qualified plan that covers employees who are at least 18 years old, have completed sixty days of service, and work at least twenty hours a week. Contributions are determined by the employee, with a maximum of $60 per pay period, with the Company matching 15% of the investment. These contributions are used to purchase shares of Company stock in the open market.

13. Stock Incentive Plan, Stock Option Plan, and Restricted Stock Grants

All amounts below have been updated to reflect the Company's two-for-one stock split, unless otherwise indicated.

Stock Option Plan

On February 10, 1994, the Company's Board of Directors adopted the American Eagle Outfitters, Inc. 1994 Stock Option Plan (the "1994 Plan"). The 1994 Plan provided for the grant of 8,100,000 incentive or non-qualified options to purchase common stock. The 1994 Plan was subsequently amended to increase the shares available for grant to 16,200,000 shares. Additionally, the amendment provided that the maximum number of options which may be granted to any individual may not exceed 5,400,000 shares. The options granted under the 1994 Plan are approved

53

by the Compensation and Stock Option Committee of the Board of Directors, primarily vest over five years and expire ten years from the date of grant. The 1994 Plan terminated on January 2, 2004 with all rights of the optionees and all unexpired options continuing in force and operation after the termination.

Stock Incentive Plan

The 1999 Stock Incentive Plan (the "1999 Plan") was approved by the shareholders on June 8, 1999. The 1999 Plan authorized 12,000,000 shares for issuance in the form of stock options, stock appreciation rights, restricted stock awards, performance units, or performance shares. The 1999 Plan was subsequently amended, in June 2001, to increase the shares available for grant to 22,000,000. Additionally, the 1999 Plan provides that the maximum number of shares awarded to any individual may not exceed 6,000,000 shares. The 1999 Plan allows the Compensation and Stock Option Committee to determine which employees and consultants will receive awards and the terms and conditions of these awards. The 1999 Plan provides for a grant of 1,875 stock options quarterly (not to be adjusted for stock split) to each director who is not an officer or employee of the Company. At January 29, 2005, 21,426,790 non-qualified stock options and 3,874,722 shares of restricted stock were granted under the 1999 Plan to employees and certain non-employees. Approximately 35% of the options granted vest eight years after the date of grant but can be accelerated to vest over three years if the Company meets annual performance goals. Approximately 32% of the options granted under the 1999 Plan vest over three years, 24% vest over five years and the remaining grants vest over one year. All options expire after ten years. Restricted stock is earned if the Company meets established performance goals.

A summary of the Company's stock option activity under all plans follows:

	For the Years Ended					
	January 29, 2005 (1)		January 31, 2004 (1)		February 1, 2003 (1)	
	Options	Weighted-Average Exercise Price	Options	Weighted-Average Exercise Price	Options	Weighted-Average Exercise Price
Outstanding - beginning of year	20,050,190	$9.28	16,211,712	$9.92	13,898,678	$9.43
Granted (Exercise price equal to fair value)	1,581,250	$15.63	5,257,560	$7.18	3,055,608	$11.74
Exercised (2)	(7,105,752)	$8.10	(397,656)	$2.86	(393,856)	$4.68
Cancelled	(1,044,440)	$10.74	(1,021,426)	$11.05	(348,718)	$13.16
Outstanding - end of year	13,481,248	$10.53	20,050,190	$9.28	16,211,712	$9.92
Exercisable - end of year	4,699,874	$11.69	9,222,422	$8.73	7,539,650	$7.95
Weighted-average fair value of options granted during the year (Black-Scholes method)		$6.34		$3.74		$6.56

(1) As of January 29, 2005, January 31, 2004 and February 1, 2003, the Company had 1,396,482 shares, 2,939,962 shares and 7,242,532 shares, available for grant, respectively.

(2) Options exercised during Fiscal 2004 ranged in price from $0.46 to $19.32 with an average of $8.10.

The following table summarizes information about stock options outstanding and exercisable at January 29, 2005:

| | Options Outstanding | | | Options Exercisable | |
Range of Exercise Prices	Number Outstanding at January 29, 2005	Weighted-Average Remaining Contractual Life (in years)	Weighted-Average Exercise Price	Number Exercisable at January 29, 2005	Weighted-Average Exercise Price
$0.57 to $7.03	4,041,342	7.47	$5.85	1,107,840	$7.03
$7.17 to $10.83	3,761,118	5.61	$9.78	1,632,946	$9.92
$10.85 to $13.15	3,288,246	6.54	$12.46	1,228,908	$12.04
$13.20 to $24.50	2,390,542	8.05	$16.97	730,180	$17.69
$0.57 to $24.50	13,481,248	7.12	$10.53	4,699,874	$11.69

Restricted Stock Grants

The Company issued restricted stock awards under the 1999 plan to compensate certain employees. Through January 29, 2005 a total of 7,974,612 shares of restricted stock had been granted, of which 2,136,826 shares have been forfeited and 4,884,966 shares have vested. The Fiscal 2004 performance-based restricted stock award of 862,820 shares vested on March 8, 2005 and a time-based restricted stock award of 90,000 shares will vest over 3 years beginning in May 2004.

For Fiscal 2004, Fiscal 2003 and Fiscal 2002, the Company recorded approximately $25.2 million, $1.3 million and $1.4 million, respectively, in compensation expense related to stock options and restricted stock in connection with the above Plans. The compensation expense related to stock options was recorded for non-employee grants in accordance with APB No. 25.

14. Contingencies

Guarantees

In connection with the disposition of Bluenotes, the Company has provided guarantees related to two store leases that were assigned to the Purchaser. These guarantees were provided to the applicable landlords and will remain in effect until the leases expire in 2007 and 2015, respectively. The lease guarantees require the Company to make all required payments under the lease agreements in the event of default by the Purchaser. The maximum potential amount of future payments (undiscounted) that the Company could be required to make under the guarantees is approximately $1.6 million as of January 29, 2005. In the event that the Company would be required to make any such payments, it would pursue full reimbursement from YM, Inc., a related party of the Purchaser, in accordance with the Bluenotes Asset Purchase Agreement.

In accordance with FASB Interpretation 45, *Guarantor's Accounting and Disclosure Requirements for Guarantees, Including Indirect Guarantees of Indebtedness of Others—an interpretation of FASB Statements No. 5, 57, and 107 and rescission of FASB Interpretation No. 34* ("FIN 45"), as the Company issued the guarantees at the time it became secondarily liable under a new lease, no amounts have been accrued in the Company's Consolidated Financial Statements related to these guarantees. Additionally, Management believes that the likelihood of having to perform under the guarantees is remote.

55

15. Quarterly Financial Information - Unaudited

Due to the disposition of Bluenotes during December 2004, Bluenotes' results of operations are presented as discontinued operations for all periods. As a result, the quarterly data presented below will not agree to previously issued quarterly statements. Additionally, due to the restatement related to changes in the Company's accounting practices for leasing transactions, a reconciliation has been provided to illustrate the effect of this change. See Note 2 of the Consolidated Financial Statements for additional information regarding the restatement.

All per share amounts below have been restated to reflect the two-for-one stock split which was distributed on March 7, 2005. Additionally, the sum of the quarterly EPS amounts may not equal the full year amount as the computations of the weighted average shares outstanding for each quarter and the full year are calculated independently.

(In thousands, except per share amounts)	As Previously Reported May 3, 2003	Restatement Due to Change in Lease Accounting Practices	As Restated May 3, 2003
Net sales	$276,069	$ -	$276,069
Gross profit	105,025	2,505	107,530
Income from continuing operations, net of tax	9,894	56	9,950
Loss from discontinued operations, net of income tax benefit	(3,491)	-	(3,491)
Net income	6,403	56	6,459
Basic per common share amounts:			
Income from continuing operations	0.07	-	0.07
Loss from discontinued operations	(0.02)	-	(0.02)
Net income per basic share	0.05	-	0.05
Diluted per common share amounts:			
Income from continuing operations	0.07	-	0.07
Loss from discontinued operations	(0.02)	-	(0.02)
Net income per diluted share	0.05	-	0.05

56

(In thousands, except per share amounts)	As Previously Reported August 2, 2003	Restatement Due to Change in Lease Accounting Practices	As Restated August 2, 2003
Net sales	$317,766	$ -	$317,766
Gross profit	108,762	2,406	111,168
Income from continuing operations, net of tax	10,811	23	10,834
Loss from discontinued operations, net of income tax benefit	(2,707)	-	(2,707)
Net income	8,104	23	8,127
Basic per common share amounts:			
Income from continuing operations	0.08	-	0.08
Loss from discontinued operations	(0.02)	-	(0.02)
Net income per basic share	0.06	-	0.06
Diluted per common share amounts:			
Income from continuing operations	0.08	-	0.08
Loss from discontinued operations	(0.02)	-	(0.02)
Net income per diluted share	0.06	-	0.06

(In thousands, except per share amounts)	As Previously Reported November 1, 2003	Restatement Due to Change in Lease Accounting Practices	As Restated November 1, 2003
Net sales	$351,021	$ -	$351,021
Gross profit	137,475	2,544	140,019
Income from continuing operations, net of tax	19,611	(97)	19,514
Loss from discontinued operations, net of income tax benefit	(9,472)	-	(9,472)
Net income	10,139	(97)	10,042
Basic per common share amounts:			
Income from continuing operations	0.14	-	0.14
Loss from discontinued operations	(0.07)	-	(0.07)
Net income per basic share	0.07	-	0.07
Diluted per common share amounts:			
Income from continuing operations	0.14	-	0.14
Loss from discontinued operations	(0.07)	-	(0.07)
Net income per diluted share	0.07	-	0.07

57

(In thousands, except per share amounts)	As Previously Reported January 31, 2004	Restatement Due to Change in Lease Accounting Practices	As Restated January 31, 2004
Net sales	$490,580	$ -	$490,580
Gross profit	188,730	2,050	190,780
Income from continuing operations, net of tax	43,170	(360)	42,810
Loss from discontinued operations, net of income tax benefit	(7,816)	-	(7,816)
Net income	35,354	(360)	34,994
Basic per common share amounts:			
Income from continuing operations	0.30	-	0.30
Loss from discontinued operations	(0.05)	-	(0.05)
Net income per basic share	0.25	-	0.25
Diluted per common share amounts:			
Income from continuing operations	0.29	-	0.29
Loss from discontinued operations	(0.05)	-	(0.05)
Net income per diluted share	0.24	-	0.24

(In thousands, except per share amounts)	As Previously Reported May 1, 2004	Restatement Due to Change in Lease Accounting Practices	As Restated May 1, 2004
Net sales	$332,230	$ -	$332,230
Gross profit	146,052	2,667	148,719
Income from continuing operations, net of tax	26,834	167	27,001
Loss from discontinued operations, net of income tax benefit	(1,727)	-	(1,727)
Net income	25,107	167	25,274
Basic per common share amounts:			
Income from continuing operations	0.19	-	0.19
Loss from discontinued operations	(0.01)	-	(0.01)
Net income per basic share	0.18	-	0.18
Diluted per common share amounts:			
Income from continuing operations	0.18	-	0.18
Loss from discontinued operations	(0.01)	-	(0.01)
Net income per diluted share	0.17	-	0.17

Part II

58

(In thousands, except per share amounts)	As Previously Reported July 31, 2004	Restatement Due to Change in Lease Accounting Practices	As Restated July 31, 2004
Net sales	$395,402	$ -	$395,402
Gross profit	161,129	1,725	162,854
Income from continuing operations, net of tax	31,952	(370)	31,582
Loss from discontinued operations, net of income tax benefit	(2,328)	-	(2,328)
Net income	29,624	(370)	29,254
Basic per common share amounts:			
Income from continuing operations	0.22	-	0.22
Loss from discontinued operations	(0.02)	-	(0.02)
Net income per basic share	0.20	-	0.20
Diluted per common share amounts:			
Income from continuing operations	0.22	-	0.22
Loss from discontinued operations	(0.02)	-	(0.02)
Net income per diluted share	0.20	-	0.20

(In thousands, except per share amounts)	As Previously Reported October 30, 2004	Restatement Due to Change in Lease Accounting Practices	As Restated October 30, 2004
Net sales	$479,585	$ -	$479,585
Gross profit	231,631	2,227	233,858
Income from continuing operations, net of tax	58,856	(151)	58,705
Loss from discontinued operations, net of income tax benefit	(807)	-	(807)
Net income	58,049	(151)	57,898
Basic per common share amounts:			
Income from continuing operations	0.40	-	0.40
Loss from discontinued operations	-	-	-
Net income per basic share	0.40	-	0.40
Diluted per common share amounts:			
Income from continuing operations	0.39	-	0.39
Loss from discontinued operations	(0.01)	-	(0.01)
Net income per diluted share	0.38	-	0.38

59

(In thousands, except per share amounts)	As Previously Reported January 29, 2005	Restatement Due to Change in Lease Accounting Practices	As Restated January 29, 2005
Net sales	$674,024	$ -	$674,024
Gross profit	330,281	2,096	332,377
Income from continuing operations, net of tax	107,238	(294)	106,944
Loss from discontinued operations, net of income tax benefit	(6,027)	-	(6,027)
Net income	101,211	(294)	100,917
Basic per common share amounts:			
Income from continuing operations	0.73	-	0.73
Loss from discontinued operations	(0.04)	-	(0.04)
Net income per basic share	0.69	-	0.69
Diluted per common share amounts:			
Income from continuing operations	0.70	-	0.70
Loss from discontinued operations	(0.04)	-	(0.04)
Net income per diluted share	0.66	-	0.66

16. Subsequent Event

On February 4, 2005, the Company's Board of Directors approved a two-for-one stock split that was distributed on March 7, 2005, to shareholders of record on February 14, 2005. All share amounts and per share data have been restated to reflect this stock split.

On March 8, 2005, the Company's Board of Directors voted to raise its cash dividend payment by 67% to an annual rate of $0.20 per share, from $0.12 per share. A quarterly cash dividend of $0.05 per share was paid on April 8, 2005 to stockholders of record on March 25, 2005.

68

Exhibit 31.1

CERTIFICATION OF CHIEF EXECUTIVE OFFICER

I, James V. O'Donnell, Chief Executive Officer of American Eagle Outfitters, Inc., certify that:

1. I have reviewed this annual report on Form 10-K of American Eagle Outfitters, Inc.;

2. Based on my knowledge, this annual report does not contain any untrue statement of a material fact or omit to state a material fact necessary to make the statements made, in light of the circumstances under which such statements were made, not misleading with respect to the period covered by this annual report;

3. Based on my knowledge, the financial statements, and other financial information included in this annual report, fairly present in all material respects the financial condition, results of operations and cash flows of the registrant as of, and for, the periods presented in this annual report.

4. The registrant's other certifying officer and I are responsible for establishing and maintaining disclosure controls and procedures (as defined in Exchange Act Rules 13a-14 and 15d-14) and internal control over financial reporting (as defined in Exchange Act Rules 13a-15(f) and 15d-15(f)) for the registrant and we have:

   a) designed such disclosure controls and procedures, or caused such disclosure controls and procedures to be designed under our supervision, to ensure that material information relating to the registrant, including its consolidated subsidiaries, is made known to us by others within those entities, particularly during the period in which this annual report is being prepared;

   b) designed such internal control over financial reporting, or caused such internal control over financial reporting to be designed under our supervision, to provide reasonable assurance regarding the reliability of financial reporting and the preparation of financial statements for external purposes in accordance with generally accepted accounting principles;

   c) evaluated the effectiveness of the registrant's disclosure controls and procedures and presented in this annual report our conclusions about the effectiveness of the disclosure controls and procedures, as of the end of the period covered by this annual report based on such evaluation; and

   d) disclosed in this annual report any change in the registrant's internal control over financial reporting that occurred during the registrants most recent fiscal quarter (the registrant's fourth fiscal quarter in the case of an annual report) that has materially affected, or is reasonably likely to materially effect, the registrant's internal control over financial reporting; and

5. The registrant's other certifying officer and I have disclosed, based on our most recent evaluation of internal controls over financial reporting, to the registrant's auditors and the audit committee of registrant's board of directors (or persons performing the equivalent function):

   a) all significant deficiencies and material weaknesses in the design or operation of internal control over financial reporting which are reasonably likely to adversely affect the registrant's ability to record, process, summarize and report financial information; and

   b) any fraud, whether or not material, that involves management or other employees who have a significant role in the registrant's internal control over financial reporting.

April 14, 2005
/s/ James V. O'Donnell
James V. O'Donnell
Chief Executive Officer

69

Exhibit 31.2

CERTIFICATION OF CHIEF FINANCIAL OFFICER

I, Laura A. Weil, Chief Financial Officer of American Eagle Outfitters, Inc., certify that:

1. I have reviewed this annual report on Form 10-K of American Eagle Outfitters, Inc.;

2. Based on my knowledge, this annual report does not contain any untrue statement of a material fact or omit to state a material fact necessary to make the statements made, in light of the circumstances under which such statements were made, not misleading with respect to the period covered by this annual report;

3. Based on my knowledge, the financial statements, and other financial information included in this annual report, fairly present in all material respects the financial condition, results of operations and cash flows of the registrant as of, and for, the periods presented in this annual report.

4. The registrant's other certifying officer and I are responsible for establishing and maintaining disclosure controls and procedures (as defined in Exchange Act Rules 13a-14 and 15d-14) and internal control over financial reporting (as defined in Exchange Act Rules 13a-15(f) and 15d-15(f)) for the registrant and we have:

   a) designed such disclosure controls and procedures, or caused such disclosure controls and procedures to be designed under our supervision, to ensure that material information relating to the registrant, including its consolidated subsidiaries, is made known to us by others within those entities, particularly during the period in which this annual report is being prepared;

   b) designed such internal control over financial reporting, or caused such internal control over financial reporting to be designed under our supervision, to provide reasonable assurance regarding the reliability of financial reporting and the preparation of financial statements for external purposes in accordance with generally accepted accounting principles;

   c) evaluated the effectiveness of the registrant's disclosure controls and procedures and presented in this annual report our conclusions about the effectiveness of the disclosure controls and procedures, as of the end of the period covered by this annual report based on such evaluation; and

   d) disclosed in this annual report any change in the registrant's internal control over financial reporting that occurred during the registrants most recent fiscal quarter (the registrant's fourth fiscal quarter in the case of an annual report) that has materially affected, or is reasonably likely to materially effect, the registrant's internal control over financial reporting; and

5. The registrant's other certifying officer and I have disclosed, based on our most recent evaluation of internal controls over financial reporting, to the registrant's auditors and the audit committee of registrant's board of directors (or persons performing the equivalent function):

   a) all significant deficiencies and material weaknesses in the design or operation of internal control over financial reporting which are reasonably likely to adversely affect the registrant's ability to record, process, summarize and report financial information; and

   b) any fraud, whether or not material, that involves management or other employees who have a significant role in the registrant's internal control over financial reporting.

April 14, 2005
/s/ Laura A. Weil
Laura A. Weil
Executive Vice President and Chief Financial Officer

Industry Ratio Report
Retail—Family Clothing Stores

Liquidity

Current Ratio	2.32
Quick Ratio	.88

Activity

Inventory Turnover	4.46
Days to Sell Inventory	80.72 days
Receivables Turnover	104.66
Average Collection Period	3.44 days
Fixed Asset Turnover	7.44
Total Asset Turnover	2.03
Accounts Payable Turnover	12.75

Profitability

Gross Profit Margin	36.42%
Operating Profit Margin	7.72%
Net Profit Margin	4.52%
Return on Equity	14.77%
Return on Assets	8.91%
Quality of Income	2.28

Leverage

Times Interest Earned	19.40
Interest Coverage Ratio	31.44
Total Debt/Total Equity	.61
Total Assets/Total Equity	1.61

Dividends

Dividend Payout	6.47%
Dividend Yield	.33%

Other

Advertising-to-Sales	3.03%
Sales Growth	16.32%
Capital Acquisitions Ratio	2.72
Price/Earnings	18.02

COMPANIES USED IN INDUSTRY ANALYSIS

Company Name	Ticker Symbol
Abercrombie & Fitch	ANF
American Eagle Outfitters Inc	AEOS
Big Dog Holdings Inc.	BDOG
Buckle Inc.	BKE
Casual Male Retail Group Inc	CMRG
Childrens Place Retail Stores	PLCE
Gap Inc	GPS
Goodys Family Clothing Inc	GDYS
Guess Inc	GES
Harolds Stores Inc	HLD
Nordstrom Inc	JWN
Pacific Sunwear of California Inc	PSUN
Ross Stores Inc	ROST
Stage Stores Inc	3SGEEQ
Stein Mart Inc	SMRT
Syms Corp	SYM
TJX Companies Inc	TJX
Urban Outfitters Inc	URBN
Wilsons the Leather Experts	WLSN

Industry Return on Equity (ROE) profit driver analysis.

ROE = Net Profit Margin × Asset Turnover × Financial Leverage

14.77% = 4.52% × 2.03 × 1.61

A

Account A standardized format that organizations use to accumulate the dollar effects of transactions on each financial statement item. (56)

Accounting A system that collects and processes (analyzes, measures, and records) financial information about an organization and reports that information to decision makers. (4)

Accounting Cycle The process used by entities to analyze and record transactions, adjust the records at the end of the period, prepare financial statements, and prepare the records for the next cycle. (167)

Accounting Entity The organization for which financial data are to be collected. (7)

Accounting Period The time period covered by the financial statements. (10)

Accounts Receivable (Trade Receivables, Receivables) Open accounts owed to the business by trade customers. (290)

Accrual Basis Accounting Records revenues when earned and expenses when incurred, regardless of the timing of cash receipts or payments. (112)

Accrued Expenses Previously unrecorded expenses that need to be adjusted at the end of the accounting period to reflect the amount incurred and its related payable account. (171)

Accrued Liabilities Expenses that have been incurred but have not been paid at the end of the accounting period. (466)

Accrued Revenues Previously unrecorded revenues that need to be adjusted at the end of the accounting period to reflect the amount earned and its related receivable account. (170)

Acquisition Cost Net cash equivalent amount paid or to be paid for the asset. (401)

Additional Paid-In Capital (Paid-In Capital, Contributed Capital in Excess of Par) The amount of contributed capital less the par value of the stock. (245)

Additions and Improvements Infrequent expenditures that increase an asset's economic usefulness in the future. (405)

Adjusting Entries Entries necessary at the end of the accounting period to measure all revenues and expenses of that period. (169)

Aging of Accounts Receivable Method Estimates uncollectible accounts based on the age of each account receivable. (295)

Allowance for Doubtful Accounts (Allowance for Bad Debts, Allowance for Uncollectible Accounts) Contra-asset account containing the estimated uncollectible accounts receivable. (291)

Allowance Method Bases bad debt expense on an estimate of uncollectible accounts. (291)

Amortization Systematic and rational allocation of the acquisition cost of an intangible asset over its useful life. (421)

Amortized Cost Method Reports investments in debt securities held to maturity at cost minus any premium or discount. (608)

Annuity A series of periodic cash receipts or payments that are equal in amount each interest period. (479)

Assets Probable future economic benefits owned by the entity as a result of past transactions. (51)

Audit An examination of the financial reports to ensure that they represent what they claim and conform with generally accepted accounting principles. (24)

Authorized Number of Shares Maximum number of shares of a corporation's capital stock that can be issued as specified in the charter. (563)

Average Cost Method Uses the weighted average unit cost of the goods available for sale for both cost of goods sold and ending inventory. (348)

B

Bad Debt Expense (Doubtful Accounts Expense, Uncollectible Accounts Expense, Provision for Uncollectible Accounts) Expense associated with estimated uncollectible accounts receivable. (291)

Balance Sheet (Statement of Financial Position) Reports the amount of assets, liabilities, and stockholders' equity of an accounting entity at a point in time. (7)

Bank Reconciliation Process of verifying the accuracy of both the bank statement and the cash accounts of a business. (302)

Bank Statement Monthly report from a bank that shows deposits recorded, checks cleared, other debits and credits, and a running bank balance. (301)

Basic Accounting Equation (Balance Sheet Equation) Assets = Liabilities + Stockholders' Equity. (8)

Board of Directors Elected by the shareholders to represent their interests; is responsible for maintaining the integrity of the company's financial reports. (234)

Bond Certificate The bond document that each bondholder receives. (519)

Bond Discount The difference between selling price and par when a bond is sold for less than par. (520)

Bond Premium The difference between selling price and par when a bond is sold for more than par. (520)

Bond Principal The amount (1) payable at the maturity of the bond and (2) on which the periodic cash interest payments are computed. (517)

C

Callable Bonds Bonds that may be called for early retirement at the option of the issuer. (518)

Capital Expenditures Expenditures that increase the productive life, operating efficiency, or capacity of the asset and are recorded as increases in asset accounts, not as expenses. (405)

Capital Lease meets at least one of the four criteria established by GAAP and results in the recording of an asset and liability. (477)

Capitalized Interest Interest expenditures included in the cost of a self-constructed asset. (403)

Cash Money or any instrument that banks will accept for deposit and immediate credit to the company's account, such as a check, money order, or bank draft. (299)

Cash Basis Accounting Records revenues when cash is received and expenses when cash is paid. (111)

Cash Equivalents Short-term investments with original maturities of three months or less that are readily convertible to cash and whose value is unlikely to change. (299, 658)

Cash Flows from Financing Activities Cash inflows and outflows related to external sources of financing (owners and creditors) for the enterprise. (661)

Cash Flows from Investing Activities Cash inflows and outflows related to the acquisition or sale of productive facilities and investments in the securities of other companies. (660)

Cash Flows from Operating Activities (Cash Flows from Operations) Cash inflows and outflows directly related to earnings from normal operations. (659)

Closing Entries Made at the end of the accounting period to transfer balances in temporary accounts to Retained Earnings and to establish a zero balance in each of the temporary accounts. (184)

Common Stock The basic voting stock issued by a corporation. (565)

Comparable Information Information that can be compared across businesses because similar accounting methods have been applied. (239)

Component Percentage Expresses each item on a particular financial statement as a percentage of a single base amount. (717)

Conservatism Suggests that care should be taken not to overstate assets and revenues or understate liabilities and expenses. (239)

Consistent Information Information that can be compared over time because similar accounting methods have been applied. (239)

Consolidated Financial Statements The financial statements of two or more companies that have been combined into a single set of financial statements as if the companies were one. (624)

Contingent Liability Potential liability that has arisen as the result of a past event; not an effective liability until some future event occurs. (471)

Continuity (Going-Concern) Assumption States that businesses are assumed to continue to operate into the foreseeable future. (51)

Contra-Account An account that is an offset to, or reduction of, the primary account. (168)

Contributed Capital Results from owners providing cash (and sometimes other assets) to business. (55)

Convertible Bonds Bonds that may be converted to other securities of the issuer (usually common stock). (518)

Copyright Exclusive right to publish, use, and sell a literary, musical, or artistic work. (422)

Corporate Governance The procedures designed to ensure that the company is managed in the interests of the shareholders. (232)

Cost-Benefit Constraint Suggests that the benefits of accounting for and reporting of information should outweigh the costs. (239)

Cost of Goods Sold Equation BI + P − EI = CGS. (343)

Cost Principle See *historical cost principle.*

Coupon Rate The stated rate of interest on bonds. (520)

Credit The right side of an account. (63)

Credit Card Discount Fee charged by the credit card company for its services. (285)

Cumulative Dividend Preference Preferred stock feature that requires specified current dividends not paid in full to accumulate for every year in which they are not paid. These cumulative preferred dividends must be paid before any common dividends can be paid. (575)

Cumulative Effects of Changes in Accounting Methods Amounts reflected on the income statement for adjustments made to balance sheet accounts when applying different accounting principles. (259)

Current Assets Assets that will be used or turned into cash within one year. Inventory is always considered a current asset regardless of the time needed to produce and sell it. (52)

Current Dividend Preference The feature of preferred stock that grants priority on preferred dividends over common dividends. (574)

Current Liabilities Short-term obligations that will be paid in cash (or other current assets) within the current operating cycle or one year, whichever is longer. (54, 463)

D

Debenture An unsecured bond; no assets are specifically pledged to guarantee repayment. (518)

Debit The left side of an account. (63)

Declaration Date The date on which the board of directors officially approves a dividend. (570)

Declining-Balance Depreciation The method that allocates the cost of an asset over its useful life based on a multiple of (often two times) the straight-line rate. (411)

Deferred Expenses Previously acquired assets that need to be adjusted at the end of the accounting period to reflect the amount of expense incurred in using the asset to generate revenue. (170)

Deferred Revenues Previously recorded liabilities that need to be adjusted at the end of the period to reflect the amount of revenue earned. (169, 470)

Deferred Tax Items Timing differences caused by reporting revenues and expenses according to GAAP on a company's income statement and according to the Internal Revenue Code on the tax return. (483)

Depletion Systematic and rational allocation of the cost of a natural resource over the period of exploitation. (419)

Depreciation Process of allocating the cost of buildings and equipment over their productive lives using a systematic and rational allocation of the cost of property, plant, and equipment (but not land) over their useful lives. (407)

Direct Labor The earnings of employees who work directly on the products being manufactured. (342)

Direct Method The method of presenting the operating activities section of the statement of cash flows reporting components of cash flows from operating activities as gross receipts and gross payments. (660)

Discontinued Operations Financial results from the disposal of a major component of the business and are reported net of income tax effects. (258)

Dividends in Arrears Dividends on cumulative preferred stock that have not been declared in prior years. (575)

E

Earnings Forecasts Predictions of earnings for future accounting periods. (236)

Effective-Interest Method Amortizes a bond discount or premium on the basis of the effective-interest rate; it is the theoretically preferred method. (527)

Effective-Interest Rate Another name for the market rate of interest on a bond. (520)

Efficient Markets Securities markets in which prices fully reflect available information. (734)

Equity Method Used when an investor can exert significant influence over an investee. It permits recording the investor's share of the investee's income. (618)

Estimated Useful Life Expected service life of an asset to the present owner. (408)

Expenses Decreases in assets or increases in liabilities from ongoing operations incurred to generate revenues during the period. (110)

Extraordinary Items Gains and losses that are both unusual in nature and infrequent in occurrence; they are reported net of tax on the income statement. (259)

F

Face Amount Another name for principal or the principal amount of a bond. (517)

Factory Overhead Manufacturing costs that are not raw material or direct labor costs. (342)

Financial Accounting Standards Board (FASB) The private sector body given the primary responsibility to work out the detailed rules that become generally accepted accounting principles. (21)

Finished Goods Inventory Manufactured goods that are completed and ready for sale. (340)

First-In, First-Out (FIFO) Method Assumes that the first goods purchased (the first in) are the first goods sold. (346)

Form 8-K The report used by publicly traded companies to disclose any material event not previously reported that is important to investors. (243)

Form 10-K The annual report that publicly traded companies must file with the SEC. (243)

Form 10-Q The quarterly report that publicly traded companies must file with the SEC. (243)

Franchise A contractual right to sell certain products or services, use certain trademarks, or perform activities in a geographical region. (423)

Free Cash Flow Cash Flows from Operating Activities — Dividends — Capital Expenditures. (679)

Future Value The sum to which an amount will increase as the result of compound interest. (489)

G

Gains Increases in assets or decreases in liabilities from peripheral transactions. (110)

Generally Accepted Accounting Principles (GAAP) The measurement rules used to develop the information in financial statements. (21)

Goods Available for Sale The sum of beginning inventory and purchases (or transfers to finished goods) for the period. (343)

Goodwill (Cost in Excess of Net Assets Acquired) For accounting purposes, the excess of the purchase price of a business over the market value of the business's assets and liabilities. (421, 625)

Gross Profit (Gross Margin) Net sales less cost of goods sold. (245)

H

Held-to-Maturity Investments A long-term investment in bonds that management has the ability and intent to hold until maturity. (608)

Historical Cost Principle Requires assets to be recorded at the historical cash-equivalent cost, which on the date of the transaction is cash paid plus the current dollar value of all noncash considerations also given in the exchange. (53)

I

Income before Income Taxes (Pretax Earnings) Revenues minus all expenses except income tax expense. (246)

Income from Operations (Operating Income) Equals net sales less cost of goods sold and other operating expenses. (245)

Income Statement (Statement of Income, Statement of Earnings, Statement of Operations) Reports the revenues less the expenses of the accounting period. (10)

Indenture A bond contract that specifies the legal provisions of a bond issue. (518)

Indirect Method The method of presenting the operating activities section of the statement of cash flows that adjusts net income to compute cash flows from operating activities. (660)

Institutional Investors Managers of pension, mutual, endowment, and other funds that invest on the behalf of others. (238)

Intangible Assets Assets that have special rights but not physical substance. (399)

Internal Controls Processes by which a company provides reasonable assurance regarding the reliability of the company's financial reporting, the effectiveness and efficiency of its operations, and its compliance with applicable laws and regulations. (300)

Inventory Tangible property held for sale in the normal course of business or used in producing goods or services for sale. (340)

Investments in Associated (or Affiliated) Companies are investments in stock held for the purpose of influencing the operating and financing strategies for the long term. (618)

Issued Shares Total number of shares of stock that have been sold; shares outstanding plus treasury shares held. (563)

J

Journal Entry An accounting method for expressing the effects of a transaction on accounts in a debits-equal-credits format. (64)

L

Last-In, First-Out (LIFO) Method Assumes that the most recently purchased units (the last in) are sold first. (348)

Legal Capital The permanent amount of capital defined by state law that must remain invested in the business; serves as a cushion for creditors. (565)

Lenders (Creditors) Suppliers and financial institutions that lend money to companies. (238)

Liabilities Probable debts or obligations of the entity that result from past transactions, which will be paid with assets or services. (54, 463)

Licenses and **Operating Rights** Obtained through agreements with governmental units or agencies; permit owners to use public property in performing its services. (423)

LIFO Liquidation A sale of a lower-cost inventory item from beginning LIFO inventory. (365)

LIFO Reserve A contra-asset for the excess of FIFO over LIFO inventory. (358)

Liquidity The ability to pay current obligations. (463)

Long-Lived Assets Tangible and intangible resources owned by a business and used in its operations over several years. (399)

Long-Term Liabilities All of the entity's obligations that are not classified as current liabilities. (475)

Losses Decreases in assets or increases in liabilities from peripheral transactions. (110)

Lower of Cost or Market (LCM) Valuation method departing from the cost principle; it serves to recognize a loss when replacement cost or net realizable value drops below cost. (353)

M

Market Interest Rate Current rate of interest on a debt when incurred; also called *yield* or *effective-interest rate*. (520)

Market Tests Ratios that tend to measure the market worth of a share of stock. (730)

Market Value Method Reports securities at their current market value. (610)

Matching Principle Requires that expenses be recorded when incurred in earning revenue. (115)

Material Amounts Amounts that are large enough to influence a user's decision. (239)

Merchandise Inventory Goods held for resale in the ordinary course of business. (340)

Merger Occurs when one company purchases all of the net assets of another and the target company goes out of existence. (624)

N

Natural Resources Assets occurring in nature, such as mineral deposits, timber tracts, oil, and gas. (419)

Net Book Value (Book Value, Carrying Value) The acquisition cost of an asset less accumulated depreciation, depletion, or amortization. (169, 407)

Net Realizable Value The expected sales price less selling costs (e.g., repair and disposal costs). (353)

Noncash Investing and Financing Activities Transactions that do not have direct cash flow effects; reported as a supplement to the statement of cash flows in narrative or schedule form. (682)

No-Par Value Stock Capital stock that has no par value specified in the corporate charter. (565)

Notes (Footnotes) Provide supplemental information about the financial condition of a company, without which the financial statements cannot be fully understood. (17)

Notes Receivable Written promises that require another party to pay the business under specified conditions (amount, time, interest). (290)

O

Operating Cycle (Cash-to-Cash Cycle) The time it takes for a company to pay cash to suppliers, sell those goods and services to customers, and collect cash from customers. (107)

Operating Lease Does not meet any of the four criteria established by GAAP and does not cause the recording of an asset and liability. (477)

Ordinary Repairs and Maintenance Expenditures for the normal operating upkeep of long-lived assets. (405)

Outstanding Shares Total number of shares of stock that are owned by stockholders on any particular date. (563)

P

Paid-In Capital (Additional Paid-in Capital, Contributed Capital in Excess of Par) The amount of contributed capital less the par value of the stock. (245)

Par Value (1) A legal amount per share of stock established by the board of directors; it establishes the minimum amount a stockholder must contribute and has no relationship to the market price of the stock. (2) Also, another name for bond principal or the maturity amount of a bond. (244, 517, 565)

Parent Company The entity that gains a controlling influence over another company (the subsidiary). (624)

Patent Granted by the federal government for an invention; gives the owner the exclusive right to use, manufacture, and sell the subject of the patent. (423)

Payment Date The date on which a cash dividend is paid to the stockholders of record. (570)

Percentage of Credit Sales Method Bases bad debt expense on the historical percentage of credit sales that result in bad debts. (294)

Periodic Inventory System Ending inventory and cost of goods sold determined at the end of the accounting period based on a physical inventory count. (361)

Permanent (Real) Accounts The balance sheet accounts that carry their ending balances into the next accounting period. (184)

Perpetual Inventory System A detailed inventory record maintained recording each purchase and sale during the accounting period. (361)

Post-Closing Trial Balance Should be prepared as the last step in the accounting cycle to check that debits equal credits and all temporary accounts have been closed. (186)

Preferred Stock Stock that has specified rights over common stock. (574)

Present Value The current value of an amount to be received in the future; a future amount discounted for compound interest. (477)

Press Release A written public news announcement normally distributed to major news services. (240)

Primary Objective of External Financial Reporting Provides useful economic information about a business to help external parties make sound financial decisions. (51)

Private Investors Individuals who purchase shares in companies. (238)

Public Company Accounting Oversight Board (PCAOB) The private sector body given the primary responsibility to work out detailed auditing standards. (24)

Purchase Discount Cash discount received for prompt payment of an account. (368)

Purchase Method Records assets and liabilities acquired in a merger or acquisition at their fair market value. (625)

Purchase Returns and Allowances A reduction in the cost of purchases associated with unsatisfactory goods. (368)

R

Ratio (Percentage) Analysis An analytical tool that measures the proportional relationship between two financial statement amounts. (717)

Raw Materials Inventory Items acquired for the purpose of processing into finished goods. (340)

Record Date The date on which the corporation prepares the list of current stockholders as shown on its records; dividends can be paid only to the stockholders who own stock on that date. (570)

Relevant Information Information that can influence a decision; it is timely and has predictive and/or feedback value. (239)

Reliable Information Information that is accurate, unbiased, and verifiable. (239)

Replacement Cost The current purchase price for identical goods. (353)

Residual (or Salvage) Value Estimated amount to be recovered, less disposal costs, at the end of the company's estimated useful life of an asset. (408)

Retained Earnings Cumulative earnings of a company that are not distributed to the owners and are reinvested in the business. (55)

Revenue Expenditures Expenditures that maintain the productive capacity of an asset during the current accounting period only and are recorded as expenses. (405)

Revenue Principle Revenues are recognized when goods or services are delivered, there is evidence of an arrangement for customer payment, the price is fixed or determinable, and collection is reasonably assured. (112)

Revenues Increases in assets or settlements of liabilities from ongoing operations. (108)

S

Sales (or Cash) Discount Cash discount offered to encourage prompt payment of an account receivable. (286)

Sales Returns and Allowances Reduction of sales revenues for return of or allowances for unsatisfactory goods. (287)

Securities and Exchange Commission (SEC) The U.S. government agency that determines the financial statements that public companies must provide to stockholders and the measurement rules that they must use in producing those statements. (21)

Securities Available for Sale All passive investments other than trading securities (classified as either short-term or long-term). (611)

Separate-Entity Assumption States that business transactions are separate from the transactions of the owners. (51)

Specific Identification Method Identifies the cost of the specific item that was sold. (345)

Stated Rate The rate of cash interest per period specified in the bond contract. (518)

Statement of Cash Flows Reports inflows and outflows of cash during the accounting period in the categories of operating, investing, and financing. (14)

Statement of Retained Earnings Reports the way that net income and the distribution of dividends affected the financial position of the company during the accounting period. (13)

Stock Dividend Distribution of additional shares of a corporation's own stock. (572)

Stock Split An increase in the total number of authorized shares by a specified ratio; does not decrease retained earnings. (573)

Stockholders' Equity (Owners' Equity or Shareholders' Equity) The financing provided by the owners and the operations of the business. (55)

Straight-Line Amortization Simplified method of amortizing a bond discount or premium that allocates an equal dollar amount to each interest period. (526)

Straight-Line Depreciation Method that allocates the cost of an asset in equal periodic amounts over its useful life. (409)

Subsidiary Company The entity that is acquired by the parent company. (624)

T

T-account A tool for summarizing transaction effects for each account, determining balances, and drawing inferences about a company's activities. (65)

Tangible Assets (or fixed assets) Assets that have physical substance. (399)

Technology Includes costs for computer software and Web development. (423)

Temporary (Nominal) Accounts Income statement (and sometimes dividends declared) accounts that are closed to Retained Earnings at the end of the accounting period. (184)

Temporary Differences Timing differences that cause deferred income taxes and will reverse, or turn around, in the future. (483)

Tests of Liquidity Ratios that measure a company's ability to meet its currently maturing obligations. (724)

Tests of Profitability Compare income with one or more primary activities. (719)

Tests of Solvency Ratios that measure a company's ability to meet its long-term obligations. (729)

Time Period Assumption The long life of a company can be reported in shorter time periods. (108)

Time Value of Money Interest that is associated with the use of money over time. (469)

Trademark An exclusive legal right to use a special name, image, or slogan. (422)

Trading Securities All investments in stocks or bonds that are held primarily for the purpose of active trading (buying and selling) in the near future (classified as short-term). (611)

Transaction (1) An exchange between a business and one or more external parties to a business or (2) a measurable internal event such as the use of assets in operations. (56)

Transaction Analysis The process of studying a transaction to determine its economic effect on the business in terms of the accounting equation. (57)

Treasury Stock A corporation's own stock that has been issued but was subsequently reacquired and is still being held by that corporation. (567)

Trial Balance A list of all accounts with their balances to provide a check on the equality of the debits and credits. (167)

Trustee An independent party appointed to represent the bondholders. (519)

U

Unit-of-Measure Assumption States that accounting information should be measured and reported in the national monetary unit. (51)

Units-of-Production Depreciation Method that allocates the cost of an asset over its useful life based on its periodic output related to its total estimated output. (410)

Unqualified (Clean) Audit Opinion Auditors' statement that the financial statements are fair presentations in all material respects in conformity with GAAP. (235)

Unrealized Holding Gains and Losses Amounts associated with price changes of securities that are currently held. (610)

W

Work in Process Inventory Goods in the process of being manufactured. (340)

Working Capital The dollar difference between total current assets and total current liabilities. (473)

Y

Yield (Effective Interest Rate) The current rate of interest on a debt when incurred. (520)